A Companion to English Renaissance Literature and Culture

Blackwell Companions to Literature and Culture

This series offers comprehensive, newly written surveys of key periods and movements and certain major authors, in English literary culture and history. Extensive volumes provide new perspectives and positions on contexts and on canonical and post-canonical texts, orientating the beginning student in new fields of study and providing the experienced undergraduate and new graduate with current and new directions, as pioneered and developed by leading scholars in the field.

A COMPANION TO

ENGLISH RENAISSANCE LITERATURE AND CULTURE

EDITED BY MICHAEL HATTAWAY

BLACKWELL
Publishers

Copyright © Blackwell Publishers Ltd 2000
Editorial matter, selection and arrangement copyright © Michael Hattaway 2000

First published 2000

2 4 6 8 10 9 7 5 3 1

Blackwell Publishers Ltd
108 Cowley Road
Oxford OX4 1JF
UK

Blackwell Publishers Inc.
350 Main Street
Malden, Massachusetts 02148
USA

British Library Cataloguing in Publication Data

A CIP catalogue record for this book is available from the
British Library.

Library of Congress Cataloging-in-Publication Data

A companion to English renaissance literature and culture / edited by Michael Hattaway.
    p.   cm. – (Blackwell companions to literature and culture)
Includes bibliographical references and index.
ISBN 0-631-21668-5 (alk. paper)
1. English literature – Early modern, 1500–1700 – History and criticism – Handbooks, manuals, etc.
2. England – Civilization – 16th century – Handbooks, manuals, etc.   3. England – Civilization –
17th century – Handbooks, manuals, etc.   4. Renaissance – England – Handbooks, manuals, etc.
    I. Title: English renaissance literature and culture.   II. Hattaway, Michael.   III. Series.

PR411 .C66   2000
820.9'003 – dc21

Typeset in 11 on 13 pt Garamond 3
by Best-set Typesetter Ltd, Hong Kong
Printed in Great Britain by Biddles Ltd, Guildford, Surrey
This book is printed on acid-free paper

Contents

PART FOUR Genres and Modes

PART FIVE Issues and Debates

Illustrations

Contributors

Judith H. Anderson is Chancellors' Professor of English in Indiana University and author of *The Growth of A Personal Voice: 'Piers Plowman' and 'The Faerie Queene'* (1976), *Biographical Truth: The Representation of Historical Persons in Tudor–Stuart Writing* (1984), and *Words That Matter: Linguistic Perception in Renaissance English* (1996); she is also a co-editor of Donaldson's translation of *Piers Plowman* (1990) *and Spenser's Life and the Subject of Biography* (1996). She is currently writing a book about Renaissance metaphor called 'Translating Investments'.

N. F. Blake has retired from the Chair of English Language at the University of Sheffield. He has written widely on medieval literature, especially Chaucer, the history of the English language, and Shakespeare's language. He is the author of *Shakespeare's Language An Introduction* (1983; re-issued as *The Language of Shakespeare* and *Essays on Shakespeare's Language 1st Series* (1996). The latter is a collection of some of his essays on Shakespeare's language. He has continued to write articles on Shakespeare's language and he is currently preparing a grammar of Shakespeare's language.

Robyn Bolam is Professor of Literature at St Mary's College, Strawberry Hill: a college of the University of Surrey. She is also published as Marion Lomax and her work includes: *Stage Images and Traditions: Shakespeare to Ford* (1987), editions of *'Tis Pity She's a Whore and Other Plays* (1995) and Aphra Behn's *The Rover* (1995), and essays *in Feminist Linguistics and Literary Criticism*, ed. Katie Wales (1994), *Larkin with Poetry*, ed. M. Baron (1997), and *Contemporary Women's Poetry: Reading, Writing, Practice*, ed. D. Rees-Jones and Alison Marks (2000). She is currently editing an anthology of four centuries of women's poetry.

Roy Booth is a lecturer in the English Department at Royal Holloway College, University of London. Recent publications include essays on *The Merchant of Venice* (1999) and *Venus and Adonis* (1998). He is currently working on a study provisionally entitled 'Married and Marred: the Misogamist in English Renaissance Drama'.

Jean R. Brink is a professor of English and comparative literature at Arizona State University, Tempe, AZ. She is the author of *Michael Drayton Revisited* (1990) and articles on Elizabethan biography and bibliography. She has recently published an article on manuscript culture in *Sidney Journal* (1999) and is currently working on a documentary biography of Edmund Spenser.

Elizabeth Clarke is Research Lecturer at Nottingham Trent University where she leads the Perdita Project for Early Modern Women's Manuscript Compilations. Her book, *Theory and Theology in George Herbert's Poetry: 'Divinitie, and Poesie, Met'* came out with the Clarendon Press in 1997. She has published several articles on the religious lyric and women's manuscript writing and has edited a collection of essays, *'This Double Voice': Gendered Writing in Early Modern England* (2000) with Danielle Clarke.

David Colclough is Lecturer in English at Queen Mary and Westfield College, University of London. He has published on Renaissance rhetoric and the poems of John Hoskyns, and he is writing a book on freedom of speech in early Stuart England.

Patrick Collinson is Regius Professor of Modern History, Emeritus, in the University of Cambridge, and a Fellow of Trinity College. He previously held chairs at the Universities of Sydney, Kent at Canterbury, and Sheffield. He is a Fellow of the British Academy and of the Australian Academy of the Humanities. He is the author of numerous studies of Elizabethan Protestantism and Puritanism, including *The Elizabethan Puritan Movement* (1967, 1990), *The Religion of Protestants* (1982), and *The Birthpangs of Protestant England* (1987). He has co-authored histories of Canterbury Cathedral and Emmanuel College, Cambridge, and is currently at work on a biography of Elizabeth I.

Mary Thomas Crane is Associate Professor of English at Boston College. She is the co-editor, with Amy Boesky, of *Form and Reform in Renaissance England: Essays in Honor of Barbara Kiefer Lewalski* (U of Delaware Press), and author of *Framing Authority: Sayings, Self and Society in Sixteenth-Century England*, and *Shakespeare's Brain: Reading with Cognitive Theory* (forthcoming).

Martin Dzelzainis is Reader in Renaissance Literature and Thought in the English Department at Royal Holloway, University of London. He has edited *John Milton's Political Writings* for Cambridge University Press and, with Warren Chernaik, *Marvell and Liberty*. He is currently working on *The Rehearsal Transpros'd* for the forthcoming Yale University Press edition of The Prose Works of Andrew Marvell.

Rachel Falconer is a lecturer at the University of Sheffield. Her publications include, *Orpheus (Dis)remembered: Milton and the Myth of the Poet-Hero* (1996); co-editor with Carol Adlam, Alastair Renfrew and Vitalii Makhlin, *Face to Face: Bakhtin Studies in Russia and the West* (1997). She is currently working on a monograph about descents into hell in contemporary prose narrative.

Alison Findlay is a Senior Lecturer at Lancaster University where she teaches courses on Shakespeare, Renaissance drama and women's writing. She is author of *Illegitimate Power: Bastards in Renaissance Drama* (1994) and *A Feminist Perspective on Renaissance Drama* (1999). She has published essays on Shakespeare and his contemporaries and reviewed books on Shakespeare's Life, Times and Stage for *Shakespeare Survey*. She is co-director of a practical research project on early modern women's drama and co-author of *Women and Dramatic Production 1550–1700* (2000). She is currently preparing an edition of the works of Richard Brome.

Jonathan Gibson has taught at the universities of Durham and Exeter and is currently a research fellow working at the Perdita Project on Early Modern Women's Manuscript Miscellanies at Nottingham Trent University. He has published articles on early modern topics in *The Review of English Studies* and *The Seventeenth Century* and is co-editor of *A Companion to the Gawain-Poet*.

Germaine Greer is currently Professor of English and Comparative Studies, University of Warwick. She is the author of *The Female Eunuch* (1969), *The Obstacle Race: the Fortunes of Women Painters and their Work* (1975), *Sex and Destiny: the Politics of Human Fertility* (1984), *The Change: Women, Ageing and the Menopause* (1991), *Slip-Shod Sibyls: Recognition, Rejection and the Woman Poet* (1995), *The Whole Woman* (1999), *John Wilmot, Earl of Rochester* (2000). She is also founder-director and proprietor of Stump Cross Books, which publishes scholarly editions of works by early modern women.

Andrew Hadfield is Professor of English at the University of Wales, Aberystwyth. His most recent publications include *Literature, Travel and Colonial Writing in the English Renaissance, 1545–1625* (1998) and *The Blackwell Guide to the English Renaissance, 1500–1620* (2000).

Donna B. Hamilton is Professor of English at the University of Maryland. Her publications include 'Shakespeare and Religion', *Shakespearean International Yearbook* 1 (1999): 187–202; *Shakespeare and the Politics of Protestant England* (1992); *Virgil and 'The Tempest': The Politics of Imitation* (1990); ed., *The Puritan*, in *The Complete Works of Thomas Middleton*, ed. Gary Taylor (forthcoming); *Religion, Literature and Politics in Post-Reformation England, 1580–1680*, ed. with Richard Strier (1996).

Gerald Hammond is the John Edward Taylor Professor of English Literature at the University of Manchester. He is the author of *Fleeting Things: English Poets and Poems 1616–1660*, *The Making of the English Bible*, *The Reader and Shakespeare's Young Man Sonnets*, and the contributor of the piece on English Bible translation to Robert Alter and Frank Kermode's *Literary Guide to the Bible*. He is presently working with Herbert Marks on the Norton Critical Edition of the English Bible.

Richard Harries has been Bishop of Oxford since 1987. Before that he was Dean of Kings College, London. He has written some eighteen books including *Art and the Beauty of God* (1993), selected by Anthony Burgess in *The Observer* as a book of the year. Some of his essays on the interaction of religion and literature appear in *Questioning Belief* (1995). He is a Fellow of the Royal Society of Literature.

Michael Hattaway is Professor of English Literature at the University of Sheffield. He is the author of *Elizabethan Popular Theatre* (1982) and *Hamlet: The Critics Debate* (1987), and is the editor of *As You Like It* (2000), and *1–3 Henry VI* (1990–3) for the New Cambridge Shakespeare, of plays by Jonson and Beaumont, co-editor, with A. R. Braunmuller, of *The Cambridge Companion to English Renaissance Drama* (1990) and, with Derek Roper and Boika Sokolova, of

Shakespeare in the New Europe (1994). He has published articles in *The Journal of the History of Ideas* and *Renaissance Drama*.

Diana E. Henderson, Associate Professor of Literature at MIT, is the author of *Passion Made Public: Elizabethan Lyric, Gender, and Performance* (1995) as well as articles on works by Spenser, Thomas Heywood, Henry King, James Joyce, and Virginia Woolf. Other recent essays have appeared in *Shakespeare: The Movie, A New History of Early English Drama, Dwelling in Possibility: Women Poets and Critics on Poetry*, and Blackwell's *Companion to Shakespeare*. Her current book manuscript is entitled 'Uneasy Collaborations: Transforming Shakespeare across Time and Media'.

Margo Hendricks, Associate Professor in the Department of Literature at the University of California at Santa Cruz, is the co-editor of *Women, Race and Writing in the Early Modern Period* (1994). Her publications include articles on Marlowe, Shakespeare, Behn, and on race and post-colonial identity.

Jean E. Howard is Professor of English at Columbia University. Her most recent books include *The Stage and Social Struggle in Early Modern England* (1994) and, with Phyllis Rackin, *Engendering a Nation: A Feminist Account of Shakespeare's English Histories* (1997). She is one of the co-editors of *The Norton Shakespeare* (1997) and is currently working on a book entitled 'Theater of a City: Social Change and Generic Innovation on the Early Modern Stage'.

Sarah Hutton is Reader in Renaissance and Seventeenth-Century Studies at Middlesex University. Her publications include *New Perspectives on Renaissance Thought* (1990), *Henry More (1614–1687) Tercentenary Studies* (1992) and a revised edition of Marjorie Nicolson's *Conway Letters* (1992). Her edition of Cudworth's *Treatise Concerning Eternal and Immutable Morality* was published by Cambridge University Press in 1996. Most recently she has edited, with Lynette Hunter, *Women, Science and Medicine, 1500–1700* (1997). She is currently working on a book-length study of Anne Conway.

Malcolm Jones is Lecturer in Folklore and Folklife Studies in the Department of English Language and Linguistics at the University of Sheffield. Before entering the university he worked in the British and other museums, as a lexicographer, and as a supply teacher. He is currently working on a book on late medieval and early modern non-religious iconography. Recent publications include 'The Horn of Suretyship' in *Print Quarterly*, 'The parodic sermon in medieval and Early Modern England' in *Medium Aevum*, 'Emblems from Thomas Combe in Wall Paintings at Bury St Edmunds and Emblems and Trencher Decorations: Further Examples' in *Emblematica*.

John N. King is Professor of English at The Ohio State University. His books include *English Reformation Literature: The Tudor Origins of the Protestant Tradition* (1982); *Tudor Royal Iconography: Literature and Art in an Age of Religious Crisis*, Princeton Essays on the Arts (1989); *Spenser's Poetry and the Reformation Tradition* (1990); and *Milton and Religious Controversy: Satire and Polemic in 'Paradise Lost'* (2000). In addition to serving as co-editor of *Literature and History* and literature editor of *Reformation*, he is presently working on a monograph on John Foxe.

Arthur F. Kinney is Thomas W. Copeland Professor of Literary History and Director of the Massachusetts Center for Renaissance Studies, University of Massachusetts, Amherst, and Adjunct Professor of English at New York University. He is the author of *Humanist Poetics* (1986), *John Skelton: Priest as Poet* (1987), and *Continental Humanist Poetics* (1989) among other books, and, most recently, editor of *Renaissance Drama* (1999) and the *Cambridge Companion to English Literature 1500–1600* (2000). He is the founding editor of the journal *English Literary Renaissance* as well as the book series entitled *Massachusetts Studies in Early Modern Culture*.

James Knowles teaches in the Department of English Studies, University of Stirling. He has edited *Shakespeare's Late Plays: New Essays* with Jenny Richards and written extensively on the masque, including Jonson's 'Entertainment at Britain's Burse'. He is currently writing a monograph 'The Theatrical Closet: Space, Sexuality and Selfhoods in Jacobean Culture' and editing Jonson's entertainments and masques for the New Cambridge Ben Jonson.

John Lee is a lecturer at the University of Bristol, England. He is the editor of the Everyman edition of *Spenser's Shorter Poems: A Selection* (1998) and the author of *Shakespeare's Hamlet and the Controversies of Self* (2000).

Stephen Longstaffe teaches English and Drama at Saint Martin's College, Lancaster. His main research interest is in the politics of the English history play. He has published on Shakespeare and Marlowe, and his edition of the anonymous history play *Jack Straw* is forthcoming from Edwin Mellen Press.

John Lyon is a Senior Lecturer in English Literature at Bristol University and Gillespie Visiting Professor at the College of Wooster, Ohio. Author of a study of *The Merchant of Venice* (1988), he also works on elegiac poetry, on the novel and on influence, particularly Shakespearean.

Helen Moore is Fellow and Tutor in English at Corpus Christi College, University of Oxford. She has published articles on medieval romance, Elizabethan fiction and Jacobean drama. She is currently editing Anthony Munday's translation of *Amadis de Gaule* and writing a study of the influence of *Amadis* on English literature.

Clara Mucci, Associate Professor of English Literature at the University of Pescara, Italy. She is the author of *Liminal Personae. Marginalità e sovversione nel teatro elisabettiano e giacomiano* (1995) and *Tempeste. Narrazioni di esilio in Shakespeare e Karen Blixen* (1998). She co-edited with Sergio Rufini '*O Sir you are old*'. *Reflessioni sulla vecchiaia a partire da Shakespeare* (1999).

Michelle O'Callaghan is a lecturer in the Department of English and Drama at Loughborough University. She is author of *The 'shepherds nation': Jacobean Spenserians and Early Stuart Cultural Politics* (2000) and is currently working on early modern textual communities.

Michael O'Connell, Professor of English at the University of California, Santa Barbara, is the author of *The Idolatrous Eye: Iconoclasm and Theater in Early Modern England* (2000), *Robert Burton*

(1986), *Mirror and Veil: the Historical Dimension of Spenser's 'Faerie Queene'* (1977), and of articles on Elizabethan and medieval drama, Shakespeare, Milton, and Spenser.

Curtis Perry, Associate Professor of English at Arizona State University, is the author of *The Making of Jacobean Culture: James I and the Renegotiation of Elizabethan Literary Practice* (1997) and editor of *Material Culture and Cultural Materialisms in the Middle Ages and the Renaissance* (2001). He has also published a number of articles on early modern English literature and culture.

Thomas Pettitt is an Associate Professor in the Institute for Literature, Culture and Media Studies, University of Southern Denmark, Odense. He has published several articles on folk drama, medieval and Elizabethan theatre, ballads and urban legends, and is currently working on the relationship between folk tradition and drama in the late-medieval and early-modern periods.

A. J. Piesse teaches Renaissance prose and drama at Trinity College, Dublin. She has published on allegory, early modern identity and medieval and Renaissance drama. *The Making of Sixteenth Century Identity*, a collection of essays of which she is editor, is about to be published by Manchester University Press.

Nicole Pohl is lecturer in English at University College Northampton. She has co-edited *Female Communities: Literary Visions and Cultural Realities 1600–1800* (2000) and is currently co-editing 'Gender and Utopianism in the Eighteenth Century' with Brenda Tooley.

Robin Robbins is a fellow of Wadham College, Oxford. He produced a critical edition with commentary of Sir Thomas Browne's *Pseudodoxia Epidemica* (1646–1672), 2 vols, (1981) and is currently working on a fully annotated edition of the complete poems of John Donne.

John Roe is a Senior Lecturer at the University of York and editor of *Shakespeare: The Poems* (1992); he is currently writing a monograph on Shakespeare and Machiavelli to be published by Boydell and Brewer.

Nicola Royan has taught at St Andrews and is now a faculty assistant in the Department of Scottish Literature at the University of Glasgow. Publications include articles for the New *DNB*, 'The Relationship between the *Scotorum Historia* of Hector Boece and John Bellenden's *Chronicles of Scotland*' in *The Rose and the Thistle: Essays on the Culture of Late Medieval and Renaissance Scotland*, ed. S. Mapstone and J. Wood, (1998), and '*Scotichronicon* rewritten? – Hector Boece's debt to Bower in the *Scotorum Historia*', in *Church, Chronicle and Learning in Medieval and Early Renaissance Scotland*, ed. B. E. Crawford (1999).

James Sharpe took his BA and DPhil degrees at Oxford, and after holding temporary posts at Durham and Exeter has been employed at the University of York since 1973. He has researched and published extensively on crime and punishment in early modern England, and, more recently, on witchcraft. His publications on witchcraft include *Instruments of Darkness: Witchcraft in England 1550–1750* (1996), and *The Bewitching of Anne Gunter* (1999).

James R. Siemon is Professor of English at Boston University. He is author of *Shakespearean Iconoclasm* and the forthcoming *Word Against Word: Shakespeare and Bakhtinian Utterance*. He has edited Christopher Marlowe's *Jew of Malta* for the New Mermaids series, and is currently editing the Arden *Richard III*.

Peter J. Smith is Senior Lecturer in English at Nottingham Trent University. He has worked professionally in theatre. His publications include *Social Shakespeare: Aspects of Renaissance Dramaturgy and Contemporary Society* (1995) and *Hamlet: Theory in Practice* (1996). He has edited Marlowe's *Jew of Malta* (1994) and *Edward II* (1998). Since 1992 he has been Associate Editor of *Cahiers Élisabéthains* and is currently working on a history of literature and scatology.

Boika Sokolova, for many years Senior Lecturer at the University of Sofia, at present lectures at Royal Holloway, University of London. Author of articles on Renaissance Literature, Shakespeare, and the reception of Shakespeare in Europe, and of *Shakespeare's Romances as Interrogative Texts* (1992), *Painting Shakespeare Red* (2000) with A. Shurbanov; editor, with Michael Hattaway and Derek Roper, of *Shakespeare in the New Europe* (1994).

Marion Trousdale is Professor of English Emeritus at the University of Maryland at College Park and the author of *Shakespeare and the Rhetoricians* (1982). Her articles have appeared in *English Literary Renaissance*, *Shakespeare Quarterly*, *Shakespeare Survey*, and *ELH*. She is currently finishing a book on *Coriolanus*.

John A. Twyning took his PhD from the University of East Anglia and is now Associate Professor and Director of the Literature Program in the English Department at the University of Pittsburgh. He is the author of *London Dispossessed: Literature and Social Space in the Early Modern City* (1998).

Greg Walker is Professor of Early Modern Literature and Culture at the University of Leicester. He has written widely on the literary and political culture of the early modern period, most recently in *The Politics of Performance in Early Renaissance Drama* (1998). He is the editor of *Medieval Drama: An Anthology* (2000).

Judith Weil teaches at the University of Manitoba in Winnipeg. She is the author of *Christopher Marlowe: Merlin's Prophet* (1977) and co-editor, with Herbert Weil, of the New Cambridge *King Henry IV, Part One* (1997). She is currently at work on a book about service and dependency in Shakespeare.

Peter Womack teaches literature at the University of East Anglia. He is the author of *Ben Jonson* (1986), *Improvement and Romance: Constructing the Myth of the Highlands* (1989), and (with Simon Shepherd) *English Drama: A Cultural History* (1996). He is preparing a study of Shakespeare and the meanings of the sea.

Rowland Wymer is a Senior Lecturer in English at the University of Hull. His publications include *Suicide and Despair in the Jacobean Drama* (1986), *Webster and Ford* (1995), and co-edited volumes on *Shakespeare and History* (1996), *The Iconography of Power on the Renaissance Stage*

(2000), and *Neo-Historicism: Studies in English Renaissance Literature, History and Politics* (2000). In addition to his work on Elizabethan and Jacobean drama, he has published articles on contemporary fiction, science fiction, and literary theory. He is currently writing a book on Derek Jarman.

PART ONE
Introduction

1

Introduction

Michael Hattaway

What does it mean to speak of 'the English Renaissance'? Within the parts of this volume, defining historical contexts and perspectives, the next offering readings of particular texts along with accounts of genres and modes, and the last presenting engagements with a number of critical issues and debates, we approach the question in a variety of ways.

The word 'Renaissance' designates 'rebirth', a metaphor applied, from its beginnings, to a cultural vision that originated in Italy. For the nineteenth and twentieth centuries this was projected in a magnificent synthesis by Jacob Burckhardt, *The Civilization of the Renaissance in Italy* (1860). Burckhardt retrospectively laid out a master proposal to revive the art and learning of the classical world, to emulate the grandeur of ancient cities, to stimulate science and geographical discovery, and to produce art and literature that imitated antique models, an undertaking which was dedicated as much to the profane as to the spiritual. Rival city states of Italy required monuments to enhance their fame, and thus ensured patronage for the writers and artists who duly bequeathed to posterity the texts and great architectural and visual exemplars with which we are all familiar. Burckhardt's categories, which rest upon notions of 'genius', 'individuality' and secularization, have percolated into all too many derivative handbooks for the period: they may not, however, fit the English experience.

England did enjoy a phenomenal energizing of literature: this is an age that, traditionally, has at its centre, Spenser and Sidney, Marlowe and Nashe, Shakespeare, and Jonson. Ben Jonson, exceptionally, did publish his 'works' in a manner befitting an author of the Renaissance, although some of the dramatic genres he used have medieval origins. The other writers too are as 'medieval' as they are 'Renaissance' – although any endeavour to categorize them in these terms would be not only equivocal but misguided. However, none would have written the way they did without a typical 'Renaissance' education, in particular a vigorous training in classical rhetoric; none would have written what they did without being concerned with the dissemination and imitation of classical forms.[1] The investigation of republicanism in Shakespeare's *Julius Caesar* (1599) would not have been possible without Plutarch, the political radicalism of Marlowe and Jonson without Tacitus and Livy refracted through Machiavelli, the satires of Nashe without Juvenal and Horace. Ovid's influence is pervasive – as it was in 'the middle ages' – and Platonic ideas of love became familiar through Italian courtesy books. Many writers prefaced their texts in prose or verse with a definition of the role of an author, and many fashioned themselves on classical models. An agenda for a Renaissance author was comprehensive: this was an age of polemic and satire as well as of madrigal verse, of political engagement as well as of lyric grace. Our own age is also inclined to read the personal as the political; we recognise praise for the 'golden' qualities of certain poets at the expense of the 'drab' verse produced by their contemporaries as sign of a past generation's restrained and restrictive 'literary canon'.[2]

This volume ranges from roughly the period of Sir Thomas More (1478–1535) until that of John Milton (1608–74), although there is no attempt to be comprehensive. It moves from the period of Humanism, the age of the revival of *litterae humaniores*, until the time when England had suffered the trauma of its Civil War (to some historians the first significant European revolution) and when Milton had, in *Paradise Lost*, written an epic that magisterially fused classical and Christian traditions in a text that remembers the scars of recent political and cultural upheaval.[3]

It was not until the seventeenth century, the 'age of the baroque' in continental Europe, that there was in England a sense of programmed and collective endeavour in the cognate arts of music, painting or architecture. The Jacobean court masques[4] that epitomize this high combinate art are contemporary with artefacts that are as 'indecorous' as Shakespeare's *Pericles* (1607) or as backward looking as the translations of Iberian chivalric romance that continued to be enjoyed in a manner that suggests that Cervantes' *Don Quixote* (1605) was quite disregarded. Printing may have generated a 'communication revolution', but circulation of texts in manuscript was the preferred practice in some elite coteries.[5] There was no attempt to design great civic churches or to plan cities before the times of Inigo Jones (1573–1652) and Sir Christopher Wren (1632–1732), and country houses and gardens manifest an intriguing union of neo-classical and older romantic styles. While depictions of landscape are almost non-existent in English painting, there are suggestive essays in literary topography.[6] Great examples of English portrait painting abound, but their images are not lifelike but iconic, their subjects explained by allegorical *imprese* or insets rather than fixed by gleams of 'personality'.[7] The fact that diaries were only beginning to be written suggests that 'a new concept of "individuality" is problematic: it certainly did not emerge into the new seventeenth century from Act 1 Scene 2 of *Hamlet*.[8] So any expedition to explore English culture that used as a map, say, Vasari's *Lives of the Artists*, an Italian text of 1550 that in its own time set a cultural agenda, would rapidly lose its way – which is why this *Companion* could not be organized around a series of biographies of authors and their 'works'.

Moreover, an 'English Renaissance' is technically an anachronism. The word 'Renaissance' is not recorded in the *Oxford English Dictionary* until the 1840s, the age of John Ruskin. Any idea of a cultural 'revolution' is certainly misleading: literary and visual artefacts of the period record patterns of evolution from medieval antecedents that are as least as important as their debts to new models of representation and orientation emerging from Italy and later from France. 'Renaissance' also signals points of origin, for capitalist organization of commerce and manufacture, for the reconstitution of political and family institutions, for patterns of identity, status, gender, race and class, for philosophical and political thought. It would be misleading in the extreme to point to specific beginnings for these phenomena, although essays in the 'Issues and Debates' part do approach some of them. A cliché in cultural history is the emergence of 'men of genius' as a sub-species of that epistemological monstrosity 'Renaissance Man'. However, in this sense, 'genius' is another anachronism: the notion derives from the middle of the eighteenth century. Moreover, not only has it occluded the power of material forms and pressures in the production of talent but it is a masculine construction that has excluded the writings of women. Essays in this volume concern themselves with writing by, about and for women.[9] 'Renaissance' is also, conventionally, an aristocratic phenomenon (although it took bourgeois capital to generate the necessary expenditure) and, in the fine arts, traditionally associated with connoisseurship: we redress this with chapters on popular arts of the period.[10] Both endeavours imply varieties of 'counter-canon'.

It has become fashionable to avoid problems of origin by relabelling the era the 'early modern', a term taken from social historians. It reminds us that the period saw the posing of some of the great political and cultural questions that have shaped the forging of modernity, and encourages us to look in texts for scepticism and doubt rather than reconciliation, harmony and 'closure'. But this label also raises difficulties: like 'Renaissance', it suggests a break with a 'medieval' past, implies continuities with what comes later, and, dangerously, invites the importation back into our period of cultural paradigms that we associate with eighteenth-century Enlightenment and even the revolutionary epoch of the early nineteenth century. Essays on allegory, continuities in drama and the longevity of the 'medieval' genre of romance, on witchcraft and on the 'scientific' texts of the period, reveal how distant this foreign country, sixteenth- and seventeenth-century England, lies from the continents of classical decorum in the arts and of rationality and tolerance in politics and philosophy.

Our period may well be better described as 'Reformation England', a hypothesis I endorse by choosing as a cover illustration a painting owned by Henry VIII, the style of which is immediately apparent as deriving from the Italian High Renaissance but the subject of which, the Pope being stoned by the four evangelists, recalls the religious division and the violence which beset England for a century and a half. Among the illustrations we have included a selection of polemical prints, sometimes brutal and not sufficiently known, on which are inscribed religious divisions in the kingdom, divisions that, inevitably for the times, were also political. The fissiparous energies of religious dissent and reform generated political factionalism and the scrutiny of institutions and culture that could, on the other hand, lead to literary analyses of the highest order. Shakespeare's *Measure for Measure* (1603) is not only a massively intelligent probing of the ordeals of Reformation but a paradigm example of the way in which the secular and the religious were inseparable. In such a world Jacob Burckhardt's idea of Renaissance being categorized by the melting into air of 'the veil of illusion' and by the emergence of states that were 'works of art' scarcely fits the realities of early modern England.[11] Sir Thomas More may have produced a blueprint for an ordered society in his *Utopia* but the kind of absolutism needed to sustain his ideals never existed in this period. The reach of the Tudor and Stuart regimes always exceeded their grasp, and essays record as many voices of dissent as consensual choruses. The notion of 'Merry England' can be traced back to the fourteenth century, but the Cade episodes in Shakespeare's *2 Henry VI* remind us that the happiness the phrase conjures is predicated on a myth of social equality. The rest of the play exposes not only aristocratic factionalism but the terror of a regime dominated by war-lords. Having noted that, however, we must not equate early modern dissent with modern radicalism. Most oppositional writing is fired by religious ideology rather than by political principles derived from any concept of rights.

A single volume can offer neither one definitive overview either of the period nor any single account of how it was seen by contemporaries. Describing the course of history by means of narratives with beginnings, middles, and ends or enclosing parts of extensive cultural fields is problematic. Inspection of the map of this book will reveal lacunae, and its organization will complicate parts of what it seeks to clarify. Its very title will have confronted readers with three difficulties. One is acknowledged: only limited attention could be paid to texts associated with three of the four nations that inhabit 'the British Isles'.[12] That designation emerged in the seventeenth century as an instrument of English political and cultural hegemony – the endeavour is registered specifically in Shakespeare's allegory of empire *Cymbeline* (1610) where 'Britain', the designation for a long wished for but never achieved nation state, occurs no fewer than thirty-four times.[13] I have warned of the snares that derive from using 'Renaissance' to designate both a period and a category of artistic styles within the art and culture of sixteenth- and seventeenth-century Britain. The third problematic is the way the title links 'literature' with 'culture'. Few readers will be surprised to find chapters in the 'Contexts and Perspectives' part on history, religion, language, and education cheek by jowl with accounts of 'literature'. (The book also offers readings of prints and engravings among 'Genres and Modes', but there was no space, for example, for a separate chapter on music.[14]) These chapters and those on literary forms stand not as accounts of 'background', a misleading metaphor from theatre and the visual arts, but to kindle awareness of cultural pressures: many essays investigate material and ideological environments as well as particular 'literary' texts. This *Companion* acknowledges lines of cultural force, surveys some of the fault-lines generated by seismic movements in fiscal policy, religion and politics, but does not treat of 'culture' as something analogous to a physical substance with consistent and enduring properties. No historicizing programme is followed, nor are crisis and contestation privileged over consensualism. Cultural generalizations in the period are likely to be invalidated by the way in which at this time, far more than now, that imagined community of 'Britain' was possessed of a plurality of discrete cultures, created by regional and political difference, rank, religion, gender or any combination of these.[15]

Some contributors would read from texts to cultural conditions, fewer would insist that particular material conditions determine rather than enable the texts that are the subjects of their chapters. Theatrical representations of the market, for example, sketched in texts as different as Dekker's *The Shoemaker's Holiday* (1599), Middleton's *A Chaste Maid in Cheapside* (1613) and Jonson's *Bartholomew Fair* (1614), are as implicated in a traditional 'moral economy' as they are patterned by contemporary economies, and are structured around patterns of festivity that reach back to both the Christian calendrical year and classical comedy. Some chapters seek to embed texts within early modern history and culture, others, particularly in the 'Readings' part, indicate how Renaissance texts might be read not only contextually but also from the perspectives of the theories and preconceptions of our own day. This needs no apology: we have long realised that, to tweak a familiar aspiration of Matthew Arnold, the endeavour to see a text as itself, 'as it really was', is impossible. All readings are mediated: by the irrecoverability of the past, by our membership of interpretative communities (is a work canonical or not, 'major' or minor?), as well as by preconceptions moulded by our own race, class and gender. 'Meanings' are created as much by readers as by writers.

Spelling in this volume, of quotations and, usually, titles, has been silently modernized. (Exceptions have been made when, for example, Spenser is cited or when modernization would obscure a semantic point.)

I should like to express my thanks to David Daniell, Richard Dutton, Martin Dzelzainis, Andrew Hatfield, Diana Henderson, Jean Howard, Lorna Hutson, Sally Mapstone and James Siemon, all of whom commented on my proposal for the volume. The selection of illustrations could not have been made without the encyclopaedic knowledge, generosity, and enthusiasm of my friend and colleague Malcolm Jones. From all contributors I have learned as much as I hoped – and more than I care to acknowledge. Judi Shepherd provided a centre for a whirling life that took me to Krakow where, as a guest of the Jagellionian University, I wrote this introduction.

NOTES

1 See Bolgar.
2 See Lewis.
3 See EARLY TUDOR HUMANISM, EPIC, and Hill.
4 See Orgel and Strong and COURT DRAMA AND THE MASQUE.
5 See PUBLICATION: PRINT AND MANUSCRIPT.
6 See THE WRITING OF TRAVEL.
7 See Strong (1969).
8 See DIARIES and IDENTITY.
9 See Lanyer's 'The Description of Cookham'
    and Jonson's 'To Penshurst', Mary Wroth's *Pamphilia to Amphilanthus*, WOMEN AND DRAMA, and WAS THERE A RENAISSANCE FEMINISM?
10 See THE ENGLISH PRINT, THE NEGLECTED GENRES OF POPULAR VERSE and LOCAL AND 'CUSTOMARY' DRAMA.
11 See Burckhardt, p. 81, and SCIENTIFIC WRITING.
12 See, however, Spenser's *Faerie Queene*, Book

V: Poetry, Politics, and Justice and
Writing the Nation.

13   The mere thirteen instances of the word in
the remainder of the Shakespearean canon
often designate 'Brittany'.

14   See, however, Bray and Spink.
15   See, for example, Spufford (1974), Underdown and Trill.

References and Further Reading

Bolgar, R. R. (1954). *The Classical Heritage and its Beneficiaries.* Cambridge: Cambridge University Press.

Bray, Roger (ed.) (1995). *The Blackwell History of Music in Britain Vol. 2: The Sixteenth Century.* Oxford: Blackwell.

Burckhardt, Jacob (1960). *The Civilization of the Renaissance in Italy*, tr. S. G. C. Middlemore. London: Phaidon.

Collinson, Patrick (1982). *The Religion of Protestants: The Church in English Society 1559–1625.* Oxford: Oxford University Press.

Ferguson, Wallace K. (1948). *The Renaissance in Historical Thought: Five Centuries of Interpretation.* Cambridge, MA: Riverside.

Girouard, Mark (1983). *Robert Smythson and the Elizabethan Country House.* New Haven: Yale University Press.

Grazia, M. de., Quilligan, M. and Stallybrass, P. (eds) (1996). *Subject and Object in Renaissance Culture.* Cambridge: Cambridge University Press.

Greenblatt, Stephen (1980). *Renaissance Self-fashioning.* Chicago: University of Chicago Press.

Helgerson, Richard (1992). *Forms of Nationhood: The Elizabethan Writing of England.* Chicago: University of Chicago Press.

Hill, Christopher (1975). *The World Turned Upside Down: Radical Ideas during the English Revolution.* Harmondsworth: Penguin.

Hutton, Ronald (1994). *The Rise and Fall of Merry England: The Ritual Year 1400–1700.* Oxford: Oxford University Press.

Lewis, C. S. (1954). *English Literature in the Sixteenth Century.* Oxford: Clarendon Press.

Manley, L. (1995). *Literature and Culture in Early Modern London.* Cambridge: Cambridge University Press.

Miller, David L., O'Dair, Sharon and Weber, Harold (eds) (1994). *The Production of English Renaissance Culture.* Ithaca: Cornell University Press.

Norbrook, D. (1984). *Poetry and Politics in the English Renaissance.* London: Routledge and Kegan Paul.

Orgel, Stephen and Strong, Roy (eds) (1973). *Inigo Jones: The Theatre of the Stuart Court.* London: Sotheby Parke Bernet.

Parry, G. (1981). *The Golden Age Restor'd: The Culture of the Stuart Court 1603–1642.* Manchester: Manchester University Press.

Pocock, J. G. A. (1987). 'Texts as Events: Reflections on the History of Political Thought'. In S. Zwicker and K. Sharpe (eds), *The Politics of Discourse* (pp. 21–34). Berkeley: University of California Press.

Shuger, Deborah, K. (1990). *Habits of Thought in the English Renaissance.* Berkeley: University of California Press.

Skinner, Quentin (1978). *The Foundations of Modern Political Thought: The Age of Reformation.* Cambridge: Cambridge University Press.

Spink, Ian (1992). *The Blackwell History of Music in Britain, Vol. 3: The Seventeenth Century.* Oxford: Blackwell.

Spufford, Margaret (1974). *Contrasting Communities: English Villagers in the Sixteenth and Seventeenth Centuries.* Cambridge: Cambridge University Press.

——(1981). *Small Books and Pleasant Histories: Popular Fiction and its Readership in Seventeenth Century England.* Cambridge: Cambridge University Press.

Strong, Roy (1969). *The English Icon: Elizabethan and Jacobean Portraiture.* London: Routledge and Kegan Paul.

——(1979). *The Renaissance Garden in England.* London: Thames and Hudson.

Thomas, Keith (1978 edn). *Religion and the Decline of Magic.* Harmondsworth: Penguin.

Trill, Suzanne (1996). 'Religion and the Construction of Femininity'. In H. Wilcox (ed), *Women and Literature in Britain 1500–1700*. Cambridge: Cambridge University Press.

Underdown, David (1985). *Revel, Riot, and Rebellion: Popular Politics and Culture in England 1603–1660*. Oxford: Clarendon Press.

Woodbridge, Linda (1984). *Women and the English Renaissance: Literature and the Nature of Womankind, 1540–1620*. Brighton: Harvester.

PART TWO
Contexts and Perspectives, *c*.1500–1650

2

Early Tudor Humanism

Mary Thomas Crane

There are so many problems with 'humanism' both as a term and a concept that one hesitates to use it. For one thing, the noun 'humanism' actually dates from the nineteenth century (although 'humanist' – *umanista* in Latin – occurs in the fifteenth century). In the Renaissance various Latin phrases – *bonae litterae*, *litterae humaniores*, etc. were used to describe the scholarly and educational field that we now call humanism. There has been much scholarly debate over many years about how 'humanism' in general is to be defined, and about its nature and scope in Tudor England and elsewhere.

Central questions in these debates include: what was the relationship between Italian humanism and its northern European versions? Is the Protestant reformation in northern Europe an outgrowth and close associate of humanism, as James McConica and Douglas Bush suggested, or did it destroy humanism proper, as argued by Frederic Seebohm? Was English humanism essentially politically conservative (as suggested in different ways by Fritz Caspari, Anthony Grafton and Lisa Jardine), or did it lead to political reform and eventually to republicanism (as Arthur B. Ferguson and McConica have argued), or was it essentially irrelevant outside the classroom (as Daniel Javitch holds)? Was humanism mainly a philosophical, literary or pedagogical movement? Was it truly innovative, or was it an outgrowth of medieval tendencies and practices, or merely a product of its own public relations efforts? Was it enabling for women, or, with a few extraordinary exceptions, implicated in the structures and institutions that excluded them from public life? Debate continues on all of these topics. More recent writers like Grafton and Jardine point out our own implication in ideologies of humanism, as students, scholars and teachers who work within institutions derived, even indirectly, from humanist ideals and practices, and would therefore question the self-interestedness of any of our investigations of it.

In general, earlier scholars tended to take humanism seriously as a successful reform movement, to take it on its own terms and to believe the claims of its early champions (although, these earlier scholars were not, perhaps, quite as naïve as some revisionist scholars suggest). More recently, there has been a tendency to emphasize early humanists' lack of sophistication, their political conservatism or even political irrelevance, and to point out the gap between their claims that a humanist education could create virtuous and effective leaders and reform human society and the often brutal and dangerous actuality of political life during the period. In this chapter I want to accord with Rebecca Bushnell in making a modest claim for the usefulness, sophistication and significance, both intellectually and socially, of early Tudor humanism in England. I believe that humanism in sixteenth-century England effectively shaped practices of reading, writing and thought as well as the ways in which subjects imagined themselves and their social and political roles. Some scholars have also argued that, although humanism bore few immediate political fruits in England, we can nevertheless trace tenuous links between earlier humanism and the emerging republicanism of the seventeenth century.

As is well known, the humanist reform movement began in Italy, appearing there in the late thirteenth century, much earlier than its first beginnings in England. Scholars have charted a number of basic differences between Italian humanism and its later northern European versions. Italian humanism emerged out of opposition to the technical philosophical and logical programmes of late medieval scholasticism, which humanists accused of narrowness and sterility. Humanism sought to replace a scholastic curriculum focused on complex and highly specialized systems of philosophy, theology and logic with a broader, more 'humane' training in literature and rhetoric. According to Grafton and Jardine, Italian humanism was largely propagated by charismatic and influential writers and teachers rather than through widespread curricular change. It introduced two intertwined programmes: an interest in the recovery, restoration and translation of classical texts from Greek and Latin antiquity; and a focus on training in writing and speaking elegant Ciceronian Latin (rather than the 'debased' medieval Latin of the schoolmen).

Scholars have suggested that Italian humanism differed from its northern European manifestations in several important ways. The Italian movement is often characterized as 'pagan' in contrast to the Christian humanism of the northern Renaissance, because it grew out of opposition to the logical, exegetical and stylistic practices of the late medieval church and because it advocated a return to classical texts without sharing to the same extent northern concerns to make them compatible with Christianity. Italian humanism also seemed 'pagan' in its emphasis on the virtuous secular life in the context of the political controversies of Italian cities rather than (as in the north) on reform of the church.

Italian civic humanism was meant to be of use not only to specialists but to all citizens. Humanism has thus been linked by some scholars to the civic ideals of city states such as the Venetian and Florentine republics, although humanism continued as an influential pursuit under other regimes (such as the Medici in Florence). In Italy, the humanist movement was fuelled in part by a patriotic and quasi-nationalist desire to reclaim and re-establish a link between contemporary Italy and ancient Rome. Although training in Latin was predominant, the study of Greek also had a role in

Italian humanism and some have argued that the conquest of Constantinople by the Turks in 1453, which caused many Greek scholars to flee to Italy, was a formative event. The role of Greek learning was especially significant in the revival of interest in Plato (countering the medieval tradition of Aristotelianism). However, it remained true in Italy as well as in England that claims about the importance of Greek learning often exceeded actual knowledge of the Greek language and its literature.

One of the earliest important Italian humanists was Francesco Petrarca, a classical scholar who revived interest in Cicero as a model for prose style, and who was also the author of important works in both Latin and Italian. Petrarch's Florentine follower, Giovanni Boccacio, and later such scholars as Collucio Salutati, Leonardo Bruni, Poggio Bracciolini (who visited England) and Lorenzo Valla, continued to produce translations of important classical works and to recover lost manuscripts from classical antiquity, searching monastery libraries for these neglected treasures. Angelo Poliziano and Pietro Bembo continued the work of the previous generation of humanist scholars. Other Italian humanists turned to the works of Plato to provide an alternative to medieval Aristotelianism. Nicholas of Cusa, Marsilio Ficino and Giovanni Pico della Mirandola were especially known for their development of neoplatonic thought. Most important for the development of humanism in England were the famous Italian teachers who spread humanist learning to rest of Europe. Guarino Guarini in Verona and Ferarra (1374–1460) was an especially important figure in this regard. Finally, the writings of Niccolò Machiavelli exerted a profound influence on historical and political thought and it is through his writings that humanism can be tied most explicitly to republicanism.

Humanism spread north from Italy in the fourteenth and fifteenth centuries but did not have widespread influence in England until the sixteenth. As humanism reached northern Europe, influencing scholars and teachers in France, Germany, the Low Countries, England and elsewhere, its outlines were altered by new and inextricable connections with religious reform movements and, as scholars such as Elizabeth Eisenstein, Walter Ong and Lisa Jardine have stressed, by the invention of the printing press with movable type in Germany (around 1450). The printing press made possible a wider and more accurate dissemination of texts and thus was an important tool for furthering humanism, across geographical space and also across class lines (as printed books made texts available not only to wealthy patrons who could afford hand-copied manuscripts, but also, increasingly, to ordinary people). But the printing press also shaped the forms through which humanism was expressed, advocated and dispersed. Erasmus gained international stature as a humanist not, like Guarini and other Italians, as a charismatic teacher who attracted students from all over Europe, but through the strategic publication of widely read texts. In her biography of Erasmus, Jardine points out how much time he spent carefully seeing his manuscripts through humanist presses (such as Froben in Basel or the Aldine in Venice). A volume like Thomas More's *Utopia* (seen through yet another humanist press in Louvain by Erasmus himself) represents a case in point, since, its elaborate front matter – including letters from More to Peter Giles, from Giles to Jerome Busleiden, from

Erasmus to John Froben, and commendatory verses in Latin by other European humanists – works to establish the prominence of the whole More–Erasmus circle of humanists. In general this group used publication quite effectively to create themselves as a pan-European intellectual movement.

Although England was not home to any learned humanist press to rival Froben or the Aldine, the publication of vernacular humanist works (such as Sir Thomas Elyot's *Book Named the Governor* and Roger Ascham's *Schoolmaster*) gained a wider audience for the movement. The humanist reliance on print publication in England contrasted sharply with an aristocratic disdain for the stigma of print which lingered in England into the seventeenth century. Thus, courtly writers in England eschewed publication in favour of circulation of their works in manuscript among a small elite audience, a practice quite at odds with humanists' enthusiastic embrace of publication. Some scholars have argued that the very form of a printed book, and the possibilities that it offered for organizing and indexing its contents, led to an increasing emphasis on rational 'method' in humanist theories of composition and education. The French rhetorician Petrus Ramus who popularized an organizational 'method' of dichotomy can be said to have emerged from humanism and to have been strongly influenced by the book as a material object, as Walter Ong has shown.

Different countries in northern Europe developed different versions of humanism. France became a centre for serious textual scholarship. Its most influential figures, Jacques Lefèvre d'Étaples and Guillaume Budé, were important scholars of classical and religious texts. Lefèvre was, like Erasmus, interested in religious reform and produced a French version of the New Testament. The reformer Jean Calvin began his career, like many Protestants in the period, with strong interests in classical scholarship, but, like others, eventually turned away from humanism to focus more exclusively on religious matters. Budé was one of the best Greek scholars of the period and also contributed important work on Justinian's *Digest*, the central legal work of Roman antiquity. In the next generation, the essayist Michel de Montaigne was greatly influenced by humanist ideas but, as became increasingly common among later generations of humanist-trained writers, wrote in the vernacular rather than in Latin.

In Germany and the Netherlands, Desiderius Erasmus, emerged as the central figure of the northern renaissance and exerted a profound influence over the forms that humanism was to take, through publication and the foundation of schools, in those countries and in England. Scholarly arguments have been waged over whether there is a definable Erasmian humanism, and, if so, how it might be defined. Erasmian humanism was basically centred on the reform of school curricula and methods of teaching, and also on ideals for the reform of church and state. Unlike Italian and French humanism, which was based in the writing and teaching of a few influential scholars, Erasmian humanism had a broad impact on the education of many (eventually most) young men who were educated in the countries – and England was one – where it became a dominant force. Erasmian humanism has been especially associated with values such as pacifism (most famously expressed in Erasmus's critique of the warrior Pope Julius II in his *Julius Exclusus* and in Thomas More's *Utopia*), and with the idea of a return to the original and unadorned text of the scriptures, eschewing the complex apparatus of specialized scholastic commentary. Erasmian humanism can thus be linked to the reformist idea of making Christianity more directly available to ordinary people in a vernacular translation based on a biblical text understood in more literary (rather than specialized theological) ways.

Like most humanists at the time, Erasmus did not hold a position in a university, but instead gained his reputation through his correspondence and publications. Although he was a member of a Roman Catholic religious order, Erasmus never lived in one place for very long. His ideas about reformed religion were at least initially similar in some ways to those espoused by the Protestant Reformation, and it is often said that 'Erasmus laid the egg that Luther hatched'. Certainly Erasmus's controversial 1516 translation of the New Testament shared such reformist ideas as the need to return to 'original' Greek texts and interpret them literally, without recourse to the tradition of scholastic commentary. But when Martin Luther (also deeply influenced by humanist ideas) broke with the Catholic church, Erasmus, like Thomas More in England, refused to join him, ultimately disagreeing with Luther on his more pessimistic Protestant ideas about lack of free will and the innate sinfulness and imperfectibility of human nature.

As an itinerant scholar without any permanent teaching position, Erasmus, as Lisa Jardine has shown, made a career out of networking, strategic publication and friendships with other prominent humanists all over Europe (including John Colet and Thomas More in England). The effectiveness of Erasmus's self-promotion – as Jardine argues, he even constructed a retrospective career for his own mentor Rodolphus Agricola – does not negate his real and lasting influence on education and on the concept of the publishing public intellectual. Erasmus's published works range from the translation of the New Testament, the life and letters of St Jerome, the *Enchiridion militis christiani* (*Handbook of a Christian Soldier*), *Institutio principis christiani* (*Education of a Christian Prince*) as well as educational works such as the *Adagia* (*Adages*), *Colloquia* (*Colloquies*), *De Copia* (*On Copious Expression*), *De ratione studii* (*On the Method of Study*, written for John Colet's new humanist school) and his famous *Encomim moriae* (*Praise of Folly*).

Erasmus championed the work of Rodophus Agricola, who provided a 'logic' to form the basis for the Erasmian ideal of copious expression. Agricola's dialectic offers ways to generate and organise ideas for composition rather than a rigorous method of logical proof. We can sense behind Agricola's work an underlying anxiety, about first, the difficulty of thinking of things to say, especially in Latin; but also, anxiety about an uncontrolled proliferation and profusion of language, especially if it was based on promiscuous reading of pagan authors. Agricola's logic offers rules and aids for generating commonplace ideas and also offers a systematic way to classify both the rules and the ideas that they produce. Thus, Agricolan dialectic provided the ideal basis for a school curriculum designed to provide matter for invention, as well as ways to keep it under control.

English humanism first began to emerge, in tentative and piecemeal ways, in the fifteenth century. It did not really take root until the Tudor monarchy discovered the usefulness of humanist-educated men in meeting two crucial needs: for propaganda to legitimize a rather tenuous claim to the throne, and for educated personnel to staff the centralized bureaucracy forged to strengthen its position in relation to the feudal aristocracy. English humanism was, at least at the beginning, closely linked to Italy, with travel occurring in both directions: English men went to study in Italy, and Italian scholars came to teach and write in England. Roberto Weiss, in his important study of *Humanism in England During the Fifteenth Century*, traces the earliest beginnings of humanist influence in England before the accession of Henry VII in 1485, although he notes that at first, humanist learning was simply assimilated to existing scholastic methods and only very gradually brought about a transformation of attitudes and approaches to education. When the noted Italian humanist Poggio Bracciolini joined the household of Henry Beaufort, Bishop of Winchester, in 1418, he was disheartened to find that England was, from a humanist's point of view, a cultural backwater. There was virtually no interest in humanist education, no adequate libraries to be found, nor did English monasteries contain interesting manuscripts.

Humphrey, Duke of Gloucester, son of King Henry IV, first brought serious enthusiasm for humanism to England. He came to know a number of prominent Italian scholars and began, with their help, to build a library of classical and humanist works, much of which he donated to Oxford University. Although he did not read Greek himself, he commissioned translations of important works from that language into Latin, thus planting the first seeds of interest in Greek learning at Oxford. During the fifteenth century, some graduates of Oxford and Cambridge began to undertake postgraduate studies in Italy (rather than, as was formerly common, in France) and as a result came under the influence of humanist teachers like Vittorino da Feltre, and, especially, Guarino da Verona. Returning to England, they were then able to transmit humanist learning to a new generation of English students, who were soon able to gain adequate training in *bonae litterae* without leaving the country.

Henry VII took a greater interest in humanism and humanist scholars than had any previous English monarch. He discovered, as noted above, the value of humanist writers as propagandists for his regime. It was important to shore up the somewhat shaky Tudor claim to the throne by careful re-telling of the history of the Wars of the Roses, emphasizing the providential accession of Henry in bringing an end to a long period of violence and unrest. The Italian scholar Polydore Vergil, for example, came to England as part of a papal delegation and stayed on to write a history of England, the *Anglia historia*, which Henry commissioned. Henry also provided a humanist education for his children, hiring John Skelton and Bernard André, among others, to tutor them. Thus, when Henry VIII became king in 1509, humanists, with some justification looked forward to increased patronage and support from someone who had himself been educated in humane letters. Thomas More, for instance, greeted the accession of Henry VIII with several Latin epigrams, praising his humanist education:

Quid enim non principe fiat ab illo,
Cui cultum ingenuis artibus ingenium est,
Castalio qum fonte nouem lauere sorores,
Imbuit et monitis Philosophia suis?

('What could lie beyond the powers of a prince whose natural gifts have been enhanced by a liberal education, a prince bathed by the nine sisters in the Castalian fount and steeped in philosophy's own precepts?') More offers proleptic praise of Henry for providing jobs for humanists: 'Ille magistratus et munera publica, uendi / Quae sueuere malis, donat habenda bonis. / Et uersis rerum uicibus feliciter, ante / Quae tulit indoctus praemia, doctus habet.' ('He now gives to good men the honours and public offices which used to be sold to evil men. By a happy reversal of circumstances, learned men now have the prerogatives which ignoramuses carried off in the past.') (Yale Edition of *The Works of Thomas More*, Vol 3, 106–7). '*Doctus*' was the word used by English humanists to describe those who had received a humanist education, while '*indoctus*' could designate either those who had been educated according to late medieval scholastic principles or the relatively uneducated feudal aristocracy. More, of course, would be one of the '*docti*' or learned men preferred by Henry, and would come to learn that such appointments did not always end '*feliciter*' (happily).

While the patronage of important figures at court helped encourage interest in humanism, it could not gain a real foothold until curricula at both universities and schools in England were altered to incorporate humanist approaches. The earliest institutional changes came at Oxford, and especially New College, where, by the second half of the fifteenth century, the teaching of grammar began to follow the newer methods of Lorenzo Valla and Greek was beginning to be taught as well. William Grocyn (*c*.1446–1519), one of the so-called 'Oxford Reformers' studied by Seebohm and perhaps the first true English humanist, had, according to Weiss, begun to learn Greek before he went to study in Italy around 1488. Grocyn, along with Thomas Linacre (1460–1524, a fellow of All Souls, court physician, and tutor to Prince Arthur), and John Colet (1466–1519) brought the fruits of study in Italy back to England, where they influenced a new generation of humanists, including Thomas More. Humanist learning was further encouraged by the foundation of new colleges expressly dedicated to its principles: St John's College, founded at Cambridge (where interest in humanism also began to appear) in 1511 and Corpus Christi College, Oxford, founded in 1516. Regius professorships in Greek and Hebrew came into being at both universities in 1542.

John Colet was the most important of the early humanists, advocating an influential blend of religious and educational reform. He exercised his influence primarily through his sermons, his friendship with Erasmus, and most especially in founding St Paul's School, which became the model for humanist grammar schools in England. His lectures on the New Testament, delivered at Oxford in 1496, advocated the application to the Bible of scholarly methods which humanists had applied to establishing and re-editing classical texts, eschewing the medieval practice of elaborate glosses and commentaries for more direct attention to the immediate contexts for, and language and style of, the text itself. Erasmus, who visited England at least six times, living there at one point (1509–14) for almost five years, heard some of Colet's lectures on the Pauline letters and was strongly influenced by his ability to combine classical learning with a reformed Christian faith.

Colet's greatest influence probably came through the founding of St Paul's School in 1510 in London, a grammar school with a strongly humanist curriculum which extended educational reform to the earliest levels of schooling and became a model for grammar schools throughout England. Colet, Erasmus and the school's first headmaster, William Lily, collaborated in establishing the curriculum of the school and in writing a new Latin grammar (Lily's *Grammar*). The Magdalen College School also adopted a humanist curriculum, as, soon, did many other schools throughout England.

Northern European (Erasmian) humanism, as exemplified in English grammar schools, took further a technique already present in Italian educational practice. This technique involved teaching students to excerpt aphorisms, commonplaces, and striking *sententiae* from all classical works read, to collect them in a notebook, and to use them as the raw material for 'invention' (in the literal Latin sense of 'finding') of their own compositions. In its reaction against medieval scholasticism, Italian humanism had shifted its focus from logic (with its goal of epistemological certainty) to rhetoric (with more modest goals of plausibility and persuasion). Rodolphus Agricola's humanist 'dialectic', offered a method for classifying gathered fragments so that they could be 'framed' into original compositions. Erasmus, in his *De copia* and other works, furthered this method, and Colet's school codified it as the basis of the humanist grammar school curriculum in England.

This pedagogical method was especially appealing to Christian humanists like Erasmus and Colet because it provided a way to make classical literature more compatible with Christianity. Students were instructed to fly over the fields of classical literature like bees, selecting only the most wholesome and moral flowers from which to collect their nectar of learning. This 'notebook method' of collecting and recycling moral fragments also provided a way, at least in theory, to bridge the gap between humanist claims that education made people morally better and the realities of grammatical education. Latin was taught in the late middle ages in England through a method which emphasized the memorization of rules (found in the grammar) and of examples of the rules (found in a *Vulgaria*). These examples were coined by the writer of the text and consisted of useful phrases for daily life (since students were usually required to speak Latin at certain parts of the day). Lily, on the other hand, de-emphasized, to some extent, memorization of rules (though this was still a large part of learning Latin), stressing instead the assimilation of exemplary sentences taken from classical authors (found in a new *Vulgaria* written by William Horman). Horman's examples tend to be moralizing *sententiae*, and they reflect humanist ideals of hard work, diligence and sober moral probity. The Grammarians War of 1520, over the attempt to replace Whittinton's traditional vulgaria with Horman's new one as an accompaniment to Lily's *Grammar* marked an important victory for the humanist curriculum at the grammar school level. Lily's *Grammar* was officially recognized as the standard textbook in 1542.

As a humanist education gained ascendancy over older scholastic methods and was established as a valid credential for preferment at court, many writers began to contrast humanist education in *bonae litterae* with its emphasis on such modest virtues as prudence and using time wisely with an aristocratic training in fencing, dancing, hunting and other pastimes designed to reveal the aristocrat's graceful indulgence in the leisure that was his right. Before long, virtually all grammar schools in England used some version of St Paul's curriculum, and private tutors (to Edward VI and Elizabeth) used it too. Humanist education manifested itself through a copious style (in Latin, or, increasingly, English) larded with moralizing quotations from classical authors. Writing in this manner became a way to reveal possession of the 'cultural capital' (to use Pierre Bourdieu's phrase) afforded by a humanist education, as aristocrats revealed their own 'capital' by dancing, fencing, hunting, hawking and other such pursuits. It succeeded in part because it also created an alternative stance for upwardly mobile seekers of position at court. As Tudor monarchs, beginning with Henry VII and especially Henry VIII, sought to protect their position by reducing the power (and numbers) of the powerful aristocratic families, 'new men' were needed to fill positions at court that nobles had previously filled. Although some scholars have argued that the Protestant Reformation, with its more pessimistic view of human nature and distrust of secular art effectively ended humanism in England, others have suggested that there were significant continuities between the religious humanism of Colet, Erasmus and More, and later English Protestants. Certainly Henry's break with the Roman church in the 1530s intensified the ascendancy of humanist-educated men at court, since it necessarily removed some previously influential clergy from power (and also provided lands formerly owned by the church to establish new men as landed gentry). Humanist education appeared at just the right time to provide an alternative set of credentials for preferment: rigorous rhetorical training and discipline in hard work, organization and diligence. Men trained in this way provided ideal bureaucrats and many were preferred by Henry VIII and by his advisers More, Thomas Wolsey and Thomas Cromwell. However, the idealistic rhetoric of educational theory which argued that humanist education produced virtuous citizens who could improve society by advising the prince, yielded to reality: the need to ingratiate, to compromise and to sway with prevailing winds.

Sir Thomas More was, perhaps, the most prominent humanist at the court of Henry VIII, although some have questioned whether he is to be considered a humanist in the purest sense of the term, since his strongly Catholic religious faith eventually led away from his position as adviser to Henry VIII to martyrdom and sainthood, and from writing elegant humanist works to vehement religious polemic. His education was mixed, involving a strong humanist influence but he also followed the aristocratic custom of spending time serving at table in the home of an important and wealthy figure, Cardinal John Morton. In addition, More was strongly attracted to Catholic ideals of a cloistered and celibate life, spending time at Charterhouse in London, and he seriously considered entering the order of Franciscan friars. Deciding instead on marriage and public life, he practised law and entered into friendships with Erasmus and his circle of continental humanists.

More's most important published works were his *The History of King Richard III* (with versions in both Latin and English) and *Utopia*. The life of *Richard III* follows the trend of Tudor historiography in depicting Richard (whose defeat by Henry VII marked the beginning of the Tudor regime) as a figure of monstrous evil. More follows English humanist principles in the strongly moralistic tenor of the work, which represents and criticizes the evils of tyranny and pride, but also in its strong narrative sense. However, More's brand of humanist historical writing differs greatly from an Italian humanist historian such as Machiavelli, who emphasized the realities of political life rather than its relation to moral ideals.

More's *Utopia*, written in Latin and published in 1516, continues to be a very controversial work. Critics have been unable to agree on such basic questions as whether Utopia, as More describes it, is intended to be a truly ideal society or an example of the opposite of an ideal (a dystopia). If it is meant to be a true utopia, critics have wondered why the Utopians are not Christian, and why the narrator, Hythlodaeus (whose name means 'speaker of nonsense'), is such a questionable figure. On the other hand, if it is dystopic, why does it advocate so many reforms dear to both Erasmus and More? Critics have also questioned the relationship between the so-called dialogue of counsel in book 1 and the description of Utopia in book 2. Hytholodaeus's praise of Utopian communism has also been much questioned and discussed. It seems clear that the answers to these questions lie both in More's deeply humanist nature and also in those aspects of his character and background that led him to depart from humanism in important ways. *Utopia*'s dialogue form and playful use of rhetoric are important, and deeply humanist features. In accordance with the humanist practice of argument '*in utramque partem*', the work does not advocate a single view but explores multiple possibilities. It is thus not intended to be read as a straightforward political treatise, but, like Erasmus's *Praise of Folly*, is inflected with multiple ironies.

On the other hand, those ironies both reflect, and question, humanist beliefs. Stephen Greenblatt's influential reading of the work has emphasized the way in which it reveals More's belief in humanist programmes of public service and reform, but also his equally strong distrust of human nature and the imperfectons that make successful reform virtually impossible in the real world. The first book joins with the elaborate prefatory matter to place the work clearly in relation to Eramus's humanist circle. The 'dialogue', in which a character named More urges a reluctant Raphael Hythlodaeus to serve as an adviser to some prince so that his humanist learning will lead to reform, offers both a humanist critique of contemporary social ills and a critique of humanist optimism that educated men can find a way to solve them. The description of Utopia in book 2 presents a society that is superior in many ways to contemporary European states (offering freedom from poverty and avoidance of war) but ultimately buying those benefits at the cost of a system of constant surveillance and public shame.

Written when More was considering whether to accept a position at the court of Henry VIII, *Utopia* directly confronts the gap between humanist hopes and ideals and the realities of human nature, especially when it is in close proximity to absolute power. Although the character 'Morus' argues that some good can be done by a humanist adviser who is able to compromise and bend with prevailing winds, More, who rose to the position of Lord Chancellor, found himself unable to accept Henry's divorce, marriage to Anne Boleyn, and break with Rome. He was executed for treason on 6 July 1535.

Thomas More is not the only sixteenth-century Englishman whose credentials as a humanist can be questioned, for along with arguments over how to define humanism, are arguments over who in early Tudor England is to be considered a humanist. Scholars generally agree that Sir Thomas Elyot, Roger Ascham and Sir John Cheke can be placed in the humanist camp. Elyot was about ten years younger than More and wrote in English rather than Latin, as later generations of English humanists were increasingly to do. He was the author of *The Book Named the Governor*, published in 1531, which offered an account in the vernacular of a humanist educational programme for prospective 'governors' or public officials similar to Erasmus's *Institutio principis christiani*. Elyot's writing also transfers from Latin to English the humanist 'copious' style of writing interspersed with frequent citation of fragments from classical authors. Although Elyot did not have a successful political career, he was important as a popularizer of the humanist educational programme.

Sir John Cheke and Roger Ascham were both products of St John's, Cambridge, and both were tutors to the children of Henry VIII. Cheke (along with Richard Cox) was tutor to Edward VI and supervised Edward in a curriculum involving such rigorous (and tedious) instruction in Latin and Greek, both reading and composition, that scholars have wondered whether it contributed to his early death. Some of the boy king's compositions survive, preserving his dutiful application of humanist methods to such topics as '*Amor maior causa obedientiae timor*' ('Love is a greater source of obedience than fear'). Accounts of Edward's rigorous education can be found in works by T. W. Baldwin, Grafton and Jardine). Roger Ascham, in turn, supervised the education of the future Elizabeth I, and his programme of 'double translation' from Latin into English, and English back into Latin, is set forth in an influential educational treatise, *The Schoolmaster* (1570).

Other figures from the courts of Henry VII and VIII are more tenuously connected with mainstream humanism. John Skelton served as tutor to Henry VIII and produced some typically humanist works, writing poems in Latin and translating classical works into English. However, his English poems, for which he is mostly known today, imitate native medieval, rather than classical models. More tellingly, in the so-called Grammarians War of 1520, Skelton sided with the anti-humanist faction and expresses these sentiments in his poem 'Speke Parrott'. The poet Thomas Wyatt presents a similarly mixed allegiance, translating both classical and Italian humanist authors, yet his translations of Petrarch and other lyric poems are steeped in the aristocratic milieu of Henry's court. Many of Wyatt's poems express the speaker's anxious engagement with aristocratic and humanist systems that seem equally attractive but finally incompatible. Once humanist education became widespread, and once it offered a widely accepted source of cultural capital for preferment at court and in other areas, most prominent figures were influenced by it in some way, even when they were opposing some aspect of it. Whether or not humanist ideas about political reform had much practical effect, by the end of the sixteenth century almost every educated man in England was shaped to some extent by humanist practices, if not principles. Thus, rather than attempting to decide whether Skelton, Wyatt, Christopher St German, Reginald Pole or Thomas Lupset are true humanists in the Erasmian mould, it might be more fruitful to trace the place of humanism in the complex mix of religious, educational and political ideologies that shaped them.

Readers may have noticed that all of the humanists discussed in this chapter so far have been men. The question whether humanism was beneficial to women in the early modern period has been much debated. Joan Kelly Gadol famously argued that women did not really experience a 'renaissance' in the early modern period because they had more social and economic freedom under the social structures which predominated in the late middle ages. Whether or not humanist educational reforms were a positive force for women is a slightly different question. Certainly, only a very few women were able to benefit from this new kind of education; the newly founded schools and universities were not open to women, so only those whose families could provide private tutors were exposed to the new learning. With a very few exceptions, women were educated with the expectation that they would used their learning in an exclusively private sphere – to train and influence their children, to serve as companions and aids to their husbands, to read scriptures and engage in devotional writing. Careers of public service or teaching were completely unavailable to women who were not Queen of England.

Nevertheless, there were women in this period who received humanist training and became famous for their learning. Thomas More made his household into a school of sorts, where his daughters were educated in Latin along with his son. More's eldest daughter Margaret was especially known for her learning. However, More's serious attention to his daughters' education coexisted with his belief in the intellectual inferiority of women and an assumption that they could have no role in public life. The daughters of Sir Anthony Cooke, Margaret, Elizabeth, Katharine, Anne and Mildred, were also afforded a humanist education and, although they were also barred from public life, two of them in particular came to exercise considerable influence through their marriages to influential men and in the course of their efforts on behalf of their son's careers. Mildred Cooke married William Cecil, later Lord Burghley, and was the mother of Robert Cecil; Anne married Nicholas Bacon who reportedly owed some of his success at court to her position and connections. She later worked tirelessly to advance the careers of her sons Anthony and Francis.

Only those women who were in the possible line of succession to the throne were educated with the goal of developing the eloquence and prudence necessary for successful public leadership. Lady Jane Grey, who was executed in 1554 because of Protestant support for her claim to the throne, was praised by Ascham as a model student. Elizabeth I was also taught by Ascham and received a full humanist education with the idea that it might lead to public service. Although she is mostly known for her assumption of roles like a Petrarchan mistress, Gloriana, or Astraea, she also did sometimes lay claim to the authority of her humanist education, when she delivered addresses in Latin, continued to translate classical works throughout her life and assumed a stance of moral authority in her speeches. Although Elizabeth is also perhaps most commonly associated with aristocratic courtly favourites like Robert Dudley, Earl of Leicester, and Robert Devereux, Earl of Essex, she relied on men with humanist training such as William Cecil and Sir Nicholas Bacon for advice throughout her reign.

Although self-conscious devotion to the humanist programme of educational, religious and social reform did not survive the generation of More and Erasmus in its purest form (if, indeed, it ever existed in a pure form), its influence extended through the reign of Elizabeth and beyond. An education based on the study of classical literature remained an important credential for public service careers in England well into the twentieth century. More importantly, the rhetorical training and the habits of recycling bits of commonplace wisdom from classical authors instilled by humanist education mark the writing of British authors from Shakespeare through Milton and into the eighteenth century. Sir Philip Sidney, educated at the Shrewsbury School and Christ Church, Oxford; Edmund Spenser, of the Merchant Taylor's School and 'sizar' or poor scholar at Pembroke Hall, Cambridge; Christopher Marlowe, a 'poor boy' at King's School at Canterbury and holder of a scholarship at Corpus Christi College, Cambridge, all represent examples of the widespread influence of humanism throughout England and across class lines. All three, in different ways, produced literary works shaped by humanism. Shakespeare, indeed, may have learned 'smalle Latine and lesse Greeke' in the grammar school at Stratford, but his writings are strongly marked by the rhetorical methods that would have been taught there. There is no question that humanist education, however limited its direct effect on political reform, had a crucial formative influence on English literature, in the early Tudor period and for many years to come.

REFERENCES AND FURTHER READING

Bush, Douglas (1939). *The Renaissance and English Humanism*. Oxford: Oxford University Press.

Bourdieu, Pierre (1977). *Outline of a Theory of Practice*, tr. R. Nice. Cambridge: Cambridge University Press.

Bushnell, Rebecca (1996). *A Culture of Teaching: Early Modern Humanism in Theory and Practice*. Ithaca: Cornell University Press.

Carlson, David (1993). *English Humanist Books: Writers and Patrons, Manuscript and Print, 1475–1525*. Toronto: University of Toronto Press.

Caspari, Fritz (1954). *Humanism and the Social Order in Tudor England*. New York: Columbia University Press.

Crane, Mary Thomas (1993). *Framing Authority: Sayings, Self, and Society in Sixteenth-century England*. Princeton: Princeton University Press.

Eisenstein, Elizabeth (1979). *The Printing Press as an Agent of Change*. 2 vols. Cambridge: Cambridge University Press.

Ferguson, Arthur B. (1965). *The Articulate Citizen and the English Renaissance*. Durham, NC: Duke University Press.

Ferguson, Wallace K. (1948). *The Renaissance in Historical Thought: Five Centuries of Interpretation*. Cambridge, MA: Riverside.

Fox, Alistair and Guy, John (1986). *Reassessing the Henrician Age: Humanism, Politics, and Reform, 1500–1550*. Oxford: Blackwell.

Goodman, Anthony and MacKay, Angus (eds) (1990). *The Impact of Humanism on Western Europe*. London: Longman.

Grafton, Anthony and Jardine, Lisa (1986). *From Humanism to the Humanities: Education and the Liberal Arts in Fifteenth- and Sixteenth-century Europe*. Cambridge, MA: Harvard University Press.

Halpern, Richard (1991). *The Poetics of Primitive Accumulation: English Renaissance Capital and the Genealogy of Culture*. Ithaca: Cornell University Press.

Jardine, Lisa (1993). *Erasmus, Man of Letters: The Construction of Charisma in Print*. Princeton: Princeton University Press.

Javitch, Daniel (1978). *Poetry and Courtliness in Renaissance England*. Princeton: Princeton University Press.

Jordan, Constance (1986). 'Feminism and the Humanists: The Case for Sir Thomas Elyot's Defense of Good Women'. In Margaret W. Ferguson, Maureen Quilligan and Nancy J. Vickers (eds), *Rewriting the Renaissance: The Discourse of Sexual Difference in Early Modern Europe* (pp. 242–58). Chicago: University of Chicago Press.

Kahn, Victoria (1985). *Rhetoric, Prudence, and Skepticism in the Renaissance*. Cornell: Cornell University Press.

Kelly-Gadol, Joan (1976). 'Did Women Have a Renaissance?' In Renate Bridenthal and Claudia Koonz (eds), *Becoming Visible: Women in European History* (pp. 139–64). Boston: Houghton Mifflin.

McConica, James (1965). *English Humanists and Reformation Politics under Henry VIII and Edward VI*. Oxford: Oxford University Press.

Ong, Walter (1958). *Ramus, Rhetoric, and the Decay of Dialogue*. Cambridge, MA: Harvard University Press.

Pocock, J. G. A. (1975). *The Machiavellian Moment: Florentine Political Thought at the Atlantic Republican Tradition*. Princeton: Princeton University Press.

Rabil, Albert (ed.) (1988). *Renaissance Humanism: Foundations, Forms and Legacy, Vol 2: Humanism Beyond Italy*. Philadelphia: University of Pennsylvania Press.

Stewart, Alan (1997). *Close Readers: Humanism and Sodomy in Early Modern England*. Princeton: Princeton University Press.

Weiss, Roberto (1957). *Humanism in England During the Fifteenth Century*. Oxford: Blackwell.

3
English Reformations
Patrick Collinson

I

The pluralization of 'Reformation', a departure from the traditional concept of '*the* English Reformation', a major watershed in national history, is a recent historiographical development, as in a survey by Christopher Haigh which insists that the Reformation must be 'broken up, or deconstructed'.[1] His 'English Reformations' implies that the process of Protestantization occurred in irregular and inconsistent stages and was not coincident with a state reformation consisting of piecemeal measures to reconstruct the church institutionally and constitutionally; and that both the official restoration of Catholicism under Mary I (1553–8) and unofficial efforts to sustain and reinvent English Catholicism in the ensuing reigns of Elizabeth I and her Stuart successors were episodes and movements which also deserve to be called 'reformations' in their own right. Replacement of the term 'Marian Reaction' by 'Marian Reformation' is equally indicative of a shift in historical perspective away from the Protestant, or 'Whig', assumption that the old religion was a doomed cause, with England almost predestined to assume its modern greatness in the world as a Protestant nation. But it is important that revisionism should not be taken too far. The English Reformation, in the traditional sense, did happen. One of the most Catholic countries in western Europe did become, within a hundred years, if not one of the most Protestant nations, culturally and politically profoundly anti-Catholic, an alteration of global significance.

All this is reflected in the religious literature of this age of reformations. The first point to be established is that there was a lot of it. 'Religious books' is almost an anachronism, a category hard to define exactly or to measure with statistical precision, for religious and moral values and intentions pervaded a great many literary genres, just as 'religion' itself was not a discrete phenomenon but something which permeated virtually all areas of early modern culture. Politics in particular was inseparable from religion. When a lawyer called John Stubbes wrote a bold and even seditious book attacking the proposed marriage between Queen Elizabeth I and the Duke of Anjou it was obvious that the author was motivated by his ardent Protestantism. It would be not so much political folly as 'a sin, a great and mighty sin', 'to couple a Christian lady, a member of Christ, to a prince and good son of Rome, that anti-Christian mother city'.[2] Even the cheap broadsheets and pamphlets conveying 'true' reports of the latest hideous murder or monstrous birth claimed a religious motivation. But taking a more conventional view of what constituted a religious book, it appears that religion was the great staple of the sixteenth-century book trade, making up roughly half its total output.[3] Much of this huge output, for example some hundreds of different catechisms and other didactic works, lie beyond the scope of this literary and cultural survey.[4]

Protestantism, it has been assumed, was a religion of the book, its devotees people of the book in a sense that Catholicism never was. Martin Luther called printing 'God's ultimate and greatest gift', through which He would instruct 'the whole world' in 'the roots of true religion', and the English martyrologist John Foxe said similar things. 'God hath opened the press to preach, whose mouth the Pope is never able to stop with all the puissance of his triple crown.'[5]

There was much in this. Pre-Reformation Catholicism was a religion of orality and visuality, polemically caricatured by Protestants as a contrivance to keep the people in a state of ignorance, 'the mother of devotion'. If the English Reformation was nothing else, it was a massive onslaught on the concrete apparatus of that kind of religion, an iconoclastic holocaust of imagery.[6] Luther's principle of *sola scriptura*, the Bible replacing the church as the only authority for doctrine and for life, put a premium on the printed word, to the extent that more radical reformers would regularly accuse the Protestants of having made a 'paper pope'. In Germany, if print made Protestantism possible, Protestantism made the fortune of many printers, a benign symbiosis.

If we want to explain how it was that in England Protestantism took firm root in the sixteenth century, whereas the Wycliffite heresy of the fourteenth century, the religion of the so-called Lollards, had proved a premature and abortive reformation, it may be sufficient to point to the mass production of printed New Testaments in English within ten years of the first copy coming off the press in Worms in 1526. For these were not religiously neutral publications. Efforts to suppress William Tyndale's Testament, smuggled into England and sold at about three shillings a copy, were futile. When the authorities bought up copies in order to burn them, good money was thrown after bad, to pay for more. In a liberal age we say that if you can't beat them you must join them. But two generations would pass before English Catholics would overcome their resistance to the principle of scripture in the vernacular to the extent of printing their own New Testament (Rheims, 1582), hedged about with health warnings.

But some revisionary adjustment to this conventional scenario is called for. On the one hand, Protestantism as propaganda, polemic and evangelism was by no means limited to the printed page. Oral communication in the form of the sermon (admittedly a Bible-based sermon) was primary. Many Protestants even insisted that it was *only* through hearing the Word preached, not through 'bare reading', that saving faith could be obtained, for St Paul had decreed: 'Faith cometh by hearing, and hearing by the Word of God' (Romans 10:17). The 2,300 sermons which John Calvin is known to have preached in Geneva were not intended for publication, and some of the most celebrated of the English preachers of the age never appeared in print. Nor was the sermon the only medium through which the Protestant message was communicated, especially to the illiterate majority. Psalms and so-called 'scripture songs' (often songs of anti-Catholic protest), pictures, stage plays and street demonstrations were all exploited. Some of these 'popular' media were more typical of the culture of Lutheran Germany than of the kind of Protestantism which came to prevail in late sixteenth-century England, but metrical psalm-singing endured as a powerful and popular religious affirmation.[7]

On the other hand, Catholicism proved that it too could be a religion of the book. This was not new. Long before Luther and Foxe, churchmen had recognized the value of print, and the press had been used on a large scale for all kinds of religious purposes, including the production of indulgences, lists of relics and reports of miracles at shrines of pilgrimage, but also the encouragement of lay devotion. This was an established tradition which the Reformation could be said to have hijacked. In England, the Bridgetin monk Richard Whitford was the first popular spiritual writer to exploit the medium of print, in *A Work for Householders* and other handbooks of practical divinity published in the 1530s.

With the political entrenchment of Protestantism, printed books for English Catholics became a simple necessity. Protestantism as the state religion enjoyed all the resources of an established and relatively well-endowed church, including its pulpits, whereas Catholicism was a proscribed and clandestine faith, its human agents thin on the ground and living under cover. To a considerable extent, books took their place. Secret presses operated in England, and large quantities of printed books were smuggled into the country from abroad, including an English version of the little book by St Charles Borromeo called *The Last Will of the Soul*, to which Shakespeare's father put his name before concealing it in the roof of his house in Henley Street, Stratford-upon-Avon.[8] This was an enterprise on a larger and more highly organized scale than the better publicized activities of dissident Protestants. A catalogue of Catholic imprints between 1558 and 1640 lists 932 items in English and no fewer than 1,619 in other languages.[9]

II

We may locate the spirit of all Protestant literature in the principle which Janel Mueller has called 'scripturalism'.[10] And we may further define scripturalism as a religious and literary aesthetic of the plain, literal and open sense; but also, almost conversely, as a bottomless well of metaphor and allegory on which the entire range of

human emotion and experience could draw. John Donne wrote: 'There are not so eloquent books in the world as the Scriptures.' Barbara Lewalski provides examples from
seventeenth-century religious poetry of some of the Bible's 'richly tentacular tropes':
sin as sickness, Christ as physician; sin as darkness or blindness, Christ as light; human
life as warfare, pilgrimage, childlikeness; the tropes of sheep and shepherding; of the
husbandry of seed, plant, figure tree, vine; the metaphors of marriage, the body, the
temple, the heart.[11]

The beginnings of the scripturalist imperative are to be found in the activities of
the translators of the fourteenth-century Wycliffite Bible. Nicholas Purvey (in about
1395) declared his purpose 'to make the sentence as true and open in English as it is
in Latin, either [or rather] more true and more open than it is in Latin.'[12] The claim
which Mueller makes on Purvey's behalf is audacious: that the preference for an 'open',
sense-determined version of the Bible was almost the same thing as an instinct for
a natural, truly vernacular English as the proper mode for written as well as oral
expression. There was to be a long unfulfilled appetite for religion to be enjoyed and
expressed in these accessible terms, since in England (and the situation was not the
same in Germany and the Low Countries) the association of translated scripture with
heresy held back the publication of a vernacular Bible long after the invention of
printing, until the advent of Tyndale.

Tyndale was the fulfilment of what Purvey had promised, a man heaven-bent to
make the Bible freely available to lay readers and hearers, driven by the urgent and
Protestant conviction that the Bible contained what he called 'the pith of all that pertains to the Christian faith', which was faith itself, 'a living thing, mighty in working,
valiant and strong, ever doing, ever fruitful'.[13] Sir Thomas More took exception to his
tendentious translation of certain key scriptural terms ('all these Christian words',
which, as someone else complained, were lost in his translation): 'congregation' rather
than 'church' for *ecclesia*, *presbyteros* no longer 'priest' but 'elder', *metanoia* not 'do
penance' but 'repent'. To suggest 'that all England should go to school with Tyndale
to learn English is a very frantic folly'.[14]

More chose to miss the point that Tyndale had himself gone to school with all
England to learn the language of his translation, which is essentially the language
which we use today. How it was that a native of the remote hill country of the Forest
of Dean, where presumably an impenetrable dialect was spoken, should have discovered our language will always remain a mystery.[15] But it is relevant that Tyndale was
a precocious classical philologist, not only an expert Grecian but learned enough in
Hebrew to be able to detect the Hebrew implied in New Testament Greek; and that
he was convinced, at least at first, of the perfect affinity of both Hebrew and Greek
with English. 'The manner of speaking is both one. So that in a thousand places thou
needest not but to translate it into English, word for word.' (Later, as he grappled
with the Old Testament, much of it almost untranslatable, Tyndale was not so sure.)
For the typical word order of the original biblical languages was a significant source
for what would become standard English syntax.[16]

Tyndale's one-eyed resolve to put the Bible into the hands of the people had huge historical importance. Whereas Erasmus of Rotterdam had said 'would that' (*utinam*) the farmer at the plough and the weaver at his loom should know the New Testament (and had said it in Latin, in the Preface to an edition in Latin and Greek), Tyndale boasted (his famous 'vaunt') that he would cause the ploughboy to know scripture better than the ignorant clergy.[17] But as an exile from Henry VIII's England, about to be kidnapped, imprisoned and executed, he had conveyed to his king the message that if he would only make the Bible available to his subjects, printed in their own language, he would be content 'never to write more', as it were to cease to exist.[18] This is what happened. Tyndale's name was all but forgotten, but 80 or 90 per cent of the words in versions of the English Bible for a hundred years were his, for the New Testament and those parts of the Old Testament which he was given time to translate. It was Tyndale who gave us 'the burden and heat of the day', 'filthy lucre', 'God forbid', 'the salt of the earth', 'the powers that be'. Tyndale's English is actually more English, more demotic, than the so-called Authorized Version of 1611, where a committee has smoothed over many rough edges to produce something safer and more ecclesiastical: once again 'charity' in 1 Corinthians 13, rather than Tyndale's 'love'.

As for the effect on English civilization of the direct exposure to scripturalism which Tyndale made possible, it is sufficient to quote from the official Homily of the Reformed Church of England, 'On the Scripture': the reader who will profit the most is the one who is 'turned into it, that is . . . in his heart and life altered and changed into that which he readeth'.

Tyndale was also the inaugurator of the torrents of religious polemic which were to accompany every stage of the English Reformations. His most notable controversial work was *The obedience of a Christian man and how Christian Rulers ought to Govern* (1528). The full title is of some importance. Henry VIII, reading perhaps only the first half of the book, duly noted the assertion that the prince is in this world without law and may 'at his lust' do as he pleases without correction. This, said Henry, was a book for all Christian princes to read, an ideological cornerstone, we might say, for royal supremacy. But if the king had read on he would have found Tyndale instructing him, publicly and in print, in what rulers ought to do, and this pointed forward to the critique of monarchy which would be mounted by religious writers from both sides of the Reformation debate, whenever they disagreed with official policy. Christopher Goodman's home thoughts from abroad, *How Superior Powers ought to be Obeyed of their Subjects* (Geneva, 1558), written against the Marian regime, seems to have a 'not' missing from its title.

The first major battle of the books of the English Reformation pitted Tyndale against Sir Thomas More. More opened fire in *A Dialogue concerning Heresies, or Dialogue against Luther and Tyndale* (1529), a modest 175,000 words; to which Tyndale responded in the mere 80,000 words of his *Answer unto Sir Thomas More* (1531), which provoked the interminable *Confutation of Tyndale's Answer* (1532), weighing in at half a million words.[19] Both men were outstanding English stylists, and what was at stake was the right language in which to express the religion of the English people as much as the theological rights and wrongs of the matters in dispute. More began gracefully, deploying the rhetorical art of *concessio* by telling scandalous and even dirty stories about ecclesiastical abuses to show that he was not unaware of the need for religious reform. Tyndale, who was not amused, defended his corner with the plain dignity which was his trademark. But in the *Confutation* More lost it, at least to the satisfaction of Janel Mueller, who writes that his efforts to domesticate an authoritative Latinate manner of expression in English was a failure. He was now resorting to intimidation rather than persuasion.

> It is hard to avoid the conclusion that More deliberately resigns to Tyndale and the Protestants generally the exercise of native resources for prose composition. He is conceding that the open, vernacular style is a suitable mode for undermining the authority of the Church, not for defending it.[20]

Presently this would apply equally to the prose styles deployed by Puritans in their attacks on the church, when the established church was Protestant, and by their opponents. Authority tended to rely upon authority rather than on the cut and thrust of vernacular argument; although it has to be said that, towards the end of the century, the decorous polemic of Richard Hooker made a huge difference in this respect.[21]

The adoption of a plain English vernacular as the appropriate medium for religious expression, even in the very words with which Almighty God was to be addressed in worship, was powerfully reinforced by the *Book of Common Prayer*, a text as inexorably linked with the name of Archbishop Thomas Cranmer as the Bible was with Tyndale. Cranmer's Prayer Book, in the first version of 1549 and even in the more radically reformed recension of 1552, was not an original composition but a skilful reworking of an inherited liturgical tradition, leaving a deep and permanent mark on English religious experience in the slender economy of the short prayers known as 'collects': 'Lighten our darkness we beseech thee, Oh Lord, and by thy great mercy defend us from all perils and dangers of this night.' But Cranmer combined, uniquely, the instincts of a liturgist with the Tyndale-like conviction that everything said and done in worship should be 'understanded of the people', who were also given a significant participatory role in the 'responses' which punctuated the two new and standard services of Morning and Evening Prayer. The minister was to face the congregation and to read 'distinctly, with a loud voice, that the people may hear'. When parts of the service were sung, a 'plain tune' was to be used, 'after the manner of distinct reading'. However, Cranmer thought it appropriate that for such solemn purposes plain English should be weighed down with 'doublings', which for the purpose of sense were strictly redundant, such as 'devices and desires', 'sins and wickednesses', 'all good counsels and all just works'.[22]

The demotic inclusiveness of these new services was compromised, at least in the perception of a more liberal age, by their uncompromisingly compulsory nature. Uniformity was the name of the game, and successive parliamentary acts of uniformity (the last of these, in 1559, achieving virtual perpetuity) both required the regular attendance of the entire population and made illegal even the slightest departure from the text of the Prayer Book and its 'rubrics' (or stage directions). For centuries to come it would be possible to check one's watch at 11.08 on a Sunday morning, and to be certain that at that moment everyone in the land was intoning the psalm known as the *Venite*.

Bible and Prayer Book were the foundations for the Protestant 'plain style' which, as Nicholas Udall explained, was preferable to 'elegancy of speech', out of 'a special regard to be had to the rude and unlettered people'. But 'plain' is deceptive. Udall also insisted that if divinity 'loveth no cloaking' it did not necessarily 'refuse eloquence'. Roger Ascham repeated an Aristotelian dictum: 'speak as the common people do', 'think as wise men do'. Some of the best examples of the Protestant plain style will be found in the sermons of Bishop Hugh Latimer, full of homely imagery, loose and anecdotal in structure, and printed in the 'black letter' preferred by relatively illiterate readers: which in the very appearance of the thing was to put a populist spin on the content. The Word of God was not strawberries 'that come but once a year, and tarry not long but are soon gone.' It was 'meat, . . . no dainties'. Lurking in the arras, as it were, was the living ghost of *Piers Plowman*, who was accorded honorary Protestant status and printed for the first time in 1550 by the evangelical publicist Robert Crowley. And *Piers Plowman* was behind Edmund Spenser's *The Shepheardes Calender*.[23]

III

Soon the history of the events we call the Reformation became in itself a major bone of contention, with each side presenting its own version of the story in the context of two radically different understandings of the nature and destiny of the church. The Protestants got in first, with a potent mixture of martyrology and the apocalyptic vision of the meaning of time and its end which we find in the mind-blowing imagery of the last book of the Bible. A former Carmelite monk, John Bale, led the way in the exploration of these genres. *The Image of both Churches, after the Revelation of Saint John* (1545?) created for English Protestants a radically dualistic ecclesiology, Christ against Antichrist, True Church in historic contention with False Church, ostensibly almighty but destined to fall. 'Babylon is fallen, that great city' – which, of course, was Rome. And Bale's edited accounts of the trials and execution of Anne Askew, a Lincolnshire gentlewoman burned at the stake in the dying days of Henry VIII's regime, was the overture to a whole opera of English martyrology. The witty, incorrigible Askew was presented as the author of her own testament, but the second of these books, *The Latter Examination of Anne Askew* acknowledged *The Elucidation of J. Bale* (1547). Askew's sex was significant, and not only to modern feminists and historians of 'gender'. Bale's 'elucidation' identified her with the second-century martyr Blandina, a type of the church itself, the spouse of Christ, an apocalyptic image.[24]

Bale's lead was followed by his friend John Foxe in one of the most stupendous literary achievements of the age, *Acts and Monuments or The Ecclesiastical History*, known to generations of readers as 'Foxe's Book of Martyrs', a book which grew through four successive editions published in Foxe's lifetime (1563, 1570, 1576, 1583) into a vast but skilfully constructed compilation of some millions of words.[25] It is significant that an Exeter worthy of the early seventeenth century whose daily spiritual diet was a chapter of the Bible and a chunk of Foxe had, after some years, read the Bible twenty times over, but Foxe, which was altogether more demanding, a mere seven times.[26] Foxe's engraved title page turned into virtual reality Bale's 'image of both churches', an adaptation of the medieval doom painting, with Christ in glory. On his left hand, devils, with the shaven tonsures of Catholic ecclesiastics, are cast down to hell; on his right, the martyrs, tied to their stakes but wearing crowns, are praising him with trumpets. On earth, the Catholics are depicted in their fond religious exertions; while the godly Protestants sit quietly with open Bibles under a pulpit occupied by a grave and bearded divine. Through apocalyptic spectacles, this was the scenario spelt out through the entire history of the church, but thickening in texture and detail as the chronology approached the events of Foxe's own time and that of his readers. Foxe was a scrupulous historian and editor, faithfully reproducing his sources, whether the contents of a bishop's register or the eye-witness account of the burning of Ridley and Latimer at Oxford. But this was also history as propaganda, with much inconvenient evidence airbrushed out of sight, and stunning woodcuts deployed to dramatize events in themselves sufficiently dramatic.

Large assumptions have been made about Foxe's impact. He is justifiably regarded as a major progenitor of the virulent Anti-Catholicism which was the most powerful political ideology of the seventeenth and even the eighteenth centuries, fuelling a sense of xenophobic exceptionalism. If it was never Foxe's intention to elevate England to the rank of a uniquely favoured, elect nation, he cannot be held responsible for the effect of his book on generations of readers. However, the serious, unprejudiced, study of the reception of Foxe has only just begun. On the one hand, it can be demonstrated that such a large and expensive book, with restricted print runs in all its editions, cannot have been as widely promulgated as it has been conventional to suggest. But on the other the 'Book of Martyrs' generated many 'little foxes', slim, ephemeral, debased but culturally significant bastard sons of the majestic original.[27]

Catholic historical polemicists were not slow to catch up. Already, before Foxe, the reign of Mary had seen the construction of a version of recent events interpreted in terms of disorder, corruption and social upheaval, with their roots in Henry VIII's carnal lust for Anne Boleyn. For heresy itself was a false harlot. An anonymous *Life of John Fisher*, the bishop whom Henry had executed, exploited to the full the imagery of filthy carnality. Henry VIII 'in ripping the bowels of his mother, the holy Church and very spouse of Christ upon earth', had torn her in pieces, monstrously taking it upon him to be her supreme head. It was fitting that when his own body accidentally fell to the floor while being prepared for burial, there issued forth 'such a quantity of horrible and stinking filthy blood and matter'. Another writer exclaimed: 'What a restless evil heresy is!' It was common ground for both Catholic and Protestant historical polemicists to smother their opponents in more than metaphorical ordure and to credit them with gross physical deformities, while the very language they were made to utter was suggestive of radical disorder.[28]

John Foxe did not have to wait long to be answered by Catholic controversialists, and at appropriate length. Nicholas Harpsfield, who in Mary's reign had played an active role in the making of Foxe's martyrs, led the way in attacking '*Joannis Foxi mendacia*' in his *Dialogi sex contra . . . oppugnatores et pseudomartyres* (Antwerp, 1566), a work of formidable scholarship which might be better known if it had not remained untranslated, followed a generation later by the Jesuit Robert Persons's *Treatise of three conversions of England* (1603–4). The aim of all this industry was to prove Foxe a liar. Persons claimed to have found no less than 120 lies in less than three pages. While the 'Book of Martyrs' was officially and conventionally regarded as virtually infallible, 'a book of credit' second in status only to the Bible itself, its author was sensitive and responsive to this criticism, often correcting his mistakes, to the extent that his detractors may be counted paradoxically among his collaborators.[29] But some of the most telling criticism was of a more subtle order. In the Preface to his translation of the Venerable Bede, *The History of the Church of England* (1565), the learned Thomas Stapleton asked why Foxe should take such exception to the legends of Catholic miracles, since his own martyr stories were full of miraculous and improbable happenings. Some modern commentators on Foxe, who have exaggerated the extent to which his work was part of the 'disenchantment of the world', would do well to pay attention to Stapleton, for Foxe's Protestant world was very much a world of wonders.[30]

IV

Meanwhile, the first decade of Elizabeth's reign had witnessed what has been called 'The Great Controversy' between more or less official spokesmen for the church of the Elizabethan Settlement, and especially John Jewel, Bishop of Salisbury, and some leading Catholics who, like the Protestant cadres in the reign of Mary, had now departed into continental exile.[31] In a sermon preached from the national pulpit of Paul's Cross on 29 November 1559, Jewel appealed to history, turning on its head the familiar Catholic taunt: where was your church before Luther? He challenged the Catholics to demonstrate that four principal articles of their belief and practice had been known in the first six Christian centuries: communion in one kind, prayers in a language unknown to the people, the papacy and transubstantiation. If they could prove their credentials on these terms, he undertook to 'give over'. Thomas Harding, whose career, until they had divided confessionally, had curiously shadowed Jewel's own, responded in an *Answer to Master Jewel's Challenge* (Antwerp, 1564), which met with *A Reply* from Jewel (1565), duly provoking Hardings's *A Rejoinder to Master*

Jewel's Reply (1566). As if this were not enough, a parallel debate between the same authors was set in motion by Jewel's all but official *Apologia ecclesiae anglicanae* (1562), which the mother of Francis Bacon translated into impeccable English. Harding published a *Confutation* of the *Apology*, to which Jewel responded. No fewer than sixty-four distinct books were perpetrated in the course of this controversy. Their literary merits, consisting to a modern eye of a depressing mixture of scholastic tedium and vulgar abuse, is conveyed in Harding's denunciation of Jewel for his 'impudency in lying', 'his continual scoffing', 'his immoderate bragging'; and in Jewel's more icy plea: 'If ye shall happen to write hereafter, send us fewer words and more learning.'[32]

This was only the beginning. The confutation of Catholicism became a major industry in Elizabethan and Jacobean England, the life work of such university men as John Rainolds in Oxford and William Fulke and William Whitacre in Cambridge, and, eventually, it was institutionalized, not very successfully, in a College of Controversy at Chelsea. Andrew Willett's *Synopsis papismi* (1592) addressed itself to 'three hundreds of popish errors'. These became 400 in the second edition (1594) and 500 in the third (1600). Peter Milward in his *Religious Controversies of the Jacobean Age* (1978) lists 764 titles. Of these no fewer than 526 were engagements across the Catholic–Protestant divide.

Even these figures conceal the full extent of the Catholic polemical input, since many ostensibly devotional works had a hidden, controversial purpose.[33] And the Catholic exiles, especially the brilliant publicist Richard Verstegan, living on a generous Spanish pension in Antwerp, produced their own martyrologies, with illustrations which surpassed Foxe's woodcuts in making visual what Verstegan called the *Theatrum crudelitatum*, a book published in Latin and French, for the European Counter-Reformation. After all, death by hanging, drawing and quartering, the fate of Catholic clergy and their supporters convicted of treason under the Elizabethan penal laws, provided opportunities even more voyeuristic and pornographic than incineration.

Meanwhile, what one Elizabethan called 'civil wars of the Church of God'[34] were productive of parallel controversies between critics of a Protestant Settlement condemned as both deficient and defective – people who were beginning to be labelled 'Puritans' – and its defenders, the bishops and their subalterns. The opening salvoes contested what on the surface appeared to be trivial matters, such as the costume prescribed for the clergy in their ministrations, a white linen surplice, and the head covering for outdoors known to later generations as a mortar board. Hence what church historians call, awkwardly, 'the Vestiarian Controversy'.[35] But not only were these items of attire, which no one supposed to have any doctrinal significance, symbols of the old order, signifiers of a 'popish' priesthood, but their compulsory retention was intended to blur the distinction between sheep and goats in a church which one contemporary defined as 'a constrained union of protestants and papists'.[36] A number of obstreperous London 'gospellers', veterans of the underground congregation which had functioned in Mary's reign and now reluctant to remain in parish churches where something looking like the mass was still celebrated, assured their judges in 1567 that there was still 'a great company of papists' in the city 'whom you do allow to be preachers and ministers'. As for surplices and caps, 'it belongeth to the papists, therefore throw it to them'.[37]

The year 1566 saw what we may call the first printed Puritan manifesto, *A brief Discourse against the Outward Apparel of the Popish Church*, to which a conformist, who may have been none other than Archbishop Matthew Parker, promptly responded in *A Brief Examination for the Time*. The manifesto was the work of the printer preacher Robert Crowley, editor of *Piers Plowman*, but assisted, or so it was said, by 'the whole multitude of London ministers', evidence of how far Puritanism was already a movement, with a sense of being a 'church within the Church', a voice of its own, and a programme.[38]

However, the next major manifesto, which announced an escalation of the programme, spoke for a more extreme, and younger element, from which some of the original nonconformists were careful to distance themselves. This proclaimed itself *An Admonition to the Parliament*, although the title was a thin cover for what was in reality a populist appeal to the public at large. The authors were two young London preachers, Thomas Wilcox and John Field, who in his letters to one of the veterans of nonconformity, Anthony Gilby, complained that his seniors had limited their concern to 'shells and chippings of popery', neglecting matters which were fundamental. These were the Prayer Book, not merely in a rubric or a ceremony here and there but in something like its structural entirety, 'an unperfect book, culled and picked out of that popish dunghill the mass-book, full of all abominations'; and the retention of an episcopal and essentially popish hierarchy with all its attendant offices, institutions and laws. To apply a word not yet invented, these were some of the first Presbyterians. In his portion of the pamphlet, Wilcox declared, soberly, that England was so far from having a church rightly reformed, 'according to the prescript of God's word' that as yet it had not come 'to the outward face of the same'. (As an afterthought 'not' was prudently altered to 'scarce', a better indication of the marker which Puritans, who were not Separatists, put on the Elizabethan church. 'Scarce' kept them inside the tent, if only just.)

Field's contribution, a 'View of popish abuses yet remaining in the English Church' was more witty and vituperative, a landmark in the history of English satire. Caricaturing Sunday worship in the Church of the Elizabethan Settlement, he wrote that 'they toss the Psalms in most places like tennis-balls', 'the people some standing, some walking, some talking, some reading, some praying by themselves'. When Jesus was named, 'then off goeth the cap and down goeth the knees, with such a scraping on the ground that they cannot hear a good while after'. Field was proud to take responsibility for 'the bitterness of the style'.[39]

The immediate literary sequel to the *Admonition* was not more satire, although the subversive potential for that was never far distant, but another tedious exchange of weighty tomes rivalling the Jewel–Harding exchanges, the so-called 'Admonition Controversy'. It was John Whitgift, master of Trinity College Cambridge and a future archbishop, who assumed the mantle of Jewel and wrote an *Answer to a certain Libel*, a large hammer to crack a chestnut. The academic ideologue of Presbyterianism, Thomas Cartwright, whom Whitgift was in the course of expelling from Trinity and Cambridge, wrote *A reply to an Answer*, to which Whitgift responded in *The Defence of the Answer*, which invited from Cartwright not only *The Second Reply*, but *The Rest of the Second Reply*, itself a fat little book of some hundreds of pages. No one now reads the Admonition Controversy, but it is different from Richard Hooker's *Of the Laws of Ecclesiastical Polity* (first four books published 1593), a still living work sufficiently philosophical and magisterial to persuade generations of Anglicans, quite incorrectly, that Hooker had the last word in the ongoing debate with Puritanism.[40]

In the Armada year, 1588, the satirical potential bottled up in the Puritan movement finally exploded in the series of pamphlets published in the name of a pseudonymous and clown-like figure, Martin Marprelate.[41] In his own way, 'Martin' did have the last word on so much tedious religious controversy. The conformist tome to which he was ostensibly replying, John Bridges' *A Defence of the Government Established in the Church of England*, was 'a very portable book, a horse may carry it if be not weak'. Although contemporaries may have enjoyed Martin's jokes at the expense of the bishops as much as we do, in the eyes of officialdom the tracts were seditious and criminal. That they were published at all is an indication of desperation among radical Puritans whose literary and political efforts to bring about 'further reformation' had come to nothing, thanks above all to Queen Elizabeth, and they have been compared to the use of chemical weapons in warfare. Poison gas is liable to blow back in the faces of those who use it, and Martin invited not only the heavy hand of the law but a spate of anti-Martinist tracts, written 'in the same vein' by Thomas Nashe, John Lyly as well as other less talented writers, and even anti-Martinist jigs performed in the public theatres.

Much of the scholarly literature devoted to the Marprelate tracts has concerned, as with other anonymous serial publications, the problem of authorship, which is the least interesting thing to ask about them (The principal author seems to have been a Warwickshire squire and outspoken MP, Job Throckmorton.[42]) What the tracts tell us about is the interaction of print with the living street culture of Elizabethan England, in which it was common practice to pursue private and public quarrels by means of defamatory libels or 'ballads', 'cast abroad' or stuck up in public places. They are also evidence of the interplay of reality and polemically distorted perceptions of reality, theatre and life. For the anti-Martinist reaction served to create the stock figure of the stage puritan which we encounter in Ben Jonson or, through the Shakespearean prism, in the character of Malvolio. It is hardly an exaggeration to say that the Martinist affair created the idea and image of the hypocritical Puritan and gave it half a century and more of life, reaching a kind of climax in the 1650 in Samuel Butler's *Hudibras*. 'Marry,' says one actor to another in a jest-book by Thomas Dekker, 'I have so naturally played the Puritan that many took me to be one.'[43]

VI

By now the reader may want to know what the religious literature of this age of Reformations had to offer by way of spiritual nourishment. Was it a case of the hungry sheep looking up unfed? The first generation of Protestants growing up under Elizabeth was perhaps rather poorly nourished. But its grandchildren would reap a bountiful harvest of 'practical divinity' in best-sellers like the Essex preacher Richard Rogers's *Seven Treatises* (five editions between 1602 and 1629, and six abridgements of what was a large and expensive book), the enormously popular works of applied theological learning by the prince of English Calvinist theologians, William Perkins, and the more modest *The Plain Man's Pathway to Heaven* (1601, twenty-five editions by 1640) by another Essex preacher, Arthur Dent, which prefigured *Pilgrim's Progress*.

The seed had been sown in the letters of spiritual comfort addressed to the distressed consciences of individuals familiar to all readers of Foxe and of a companion text, *Letters of the Martyrs* (1564), gathered and edited by Foxe's collaborator Henry Bull and published under the name of Bishop Miles Coverdale. *Certain Godly and very Comfortable Letters* by the exemplary Puritan divine Edward Dering, posthumously published in 1590, were mostly addressed to religiously troubled gentlewomen. What did it mean to write 'comfortably'? Dent's *Plain Man's Pathway* was written, or so says its title, in order that every man may clearly see whether he shall be saved or damned. But practical divinity was about much more than that simple, if odious, Calvinist distinction, with predestination looming less large than many have supposed. To know that one was on the pathway to salvation was not to press a magic switch but to engage in unremitting spiritual endeavour, guided by these practical and increasingly systematic manuals. Salvation was not so much an event as a process.[44]

But when it came to books which actually nurtured the pious practice of religion, it was the Catholics who were in the van, especially writers touched by the circumstantial spirituality of the Society of Jesus and its founder, Ignatius Loyola. Here was instruction in how to pray, how to confess, how to receive the sacrament. English Protestant religion was a native plant, its 'practical' divines internationally acknowledged in the seventeenth century as an unusual religious resource. But English Catholics were part of a pan-European book culture, to which they made a significant contribution. Edmund Campion's *Rationes decem*, first clandestinely printed at Stonor Park in Oxfordshire in 1581, ran to no fewer than forty-five editions in the original Latin, with translations into Czech, Dutch, Flemish, French, German, Hungarian and Polish.[45] Ignatian spirituality was given notable lyrical expression in the poems of the English Jesuit Robert Southwell, written in the course of a mission which was to end on the scaffold and the source of a tradition which has been called English Catholic baroque, which Southwell bequeathed to one of the most neglected poets of the age, Richard Crashaw.[46]

The best evidence of the quality of the spiritual sustenance offered by the English Counter-Reformation was its appropriation by Protestants, and the most celebrated example of cross-confessional cross-fertilization was *The First Book of the Christian Exer-*

cise, an adaptation by Robert Persons of an Italian Jesuit text. In 1584, a Protestant minister in Yorkshire, Edmund Bunny, published a version of Persons which removed all references to such distinctively Catholic doctrines as purgatory, but still retained 90 per cent of the original. Bunny's bowdlerized version went through many more versions than the original, and by 1623 the ratio was 24:1. The fact that no fewer than sixteen editions of Bunny / Persons were published in the single year 1585 suggests that the most generous springs of Christian spirituality were still Catholic, even if they were made to pass through a Protestant filter.[47] There were, of course, paths between the religious traditions which were rougher and more painful. John Donne wrote in 'Satire III':

> On a huge hill,
> Cragged and steep, Truth stands, and he that will
> Reach her, about must, and about must go.

But truth and falsehood were 'near twins', and what we regard as Donne's apostasy was also a kind of fulfilment and dénouement.

NOTES

1 See Haigh.

2 Lloyd E. Berry, ed., *John Stubbs's Gaping Gulf* (1579) (Charlottesville, 1968), especially p. 6.

3 See Klotz. See also Maureen Bell's statistical analysis of STC imprints in John Barnard and D. F. McKenzie, eds, *A History of the Book in Britain*, vol. 4 (Cambridge University Press, forthcoming.) For the wider scope of 'religious' print, see Walsham, (1999).

4 On catechisms, see Green.

5 See Gilmont, pp. 1–2, 266; S. R. Cattley and G. Townsend, eds, *The Acts and Monuments of John Foxe*, iii (London, 1837), 720. And see also Andrew Pettegree, 'Books, Pamphlets and Polemic', in A. Pettegree, ed., *The Reformation World* (London and New York, 2000), pp. 109–26.

6 See Duffy.

7 See Watt; Patrick Collinson, 'Protestant Culture and the Cultural Revolution' in Collinson (1988); and Temperley.

8 See Walsham, 'Domme Preachers' (2000). For John Shakespeare and Borromeo, see Samuel Schoenbaum, *William Shakespeare: A*

Documentary Life (New York: Oxford University Press, 1975), pp. 41–6.

9 See Allison and Rogers.

10 See Mueller.

11 Lewalski: Donne quoted at p. 84.

12 Mueller, pp. 111–12.

13 For 'pith', see Henry Walter, ed., *Doctrinal Treatises by William Tyndale*, Parker Society (Cambridge, 1848), p. 507. See especially 'A Prologue Upon the Epistle of St Paul to the Romans (closely following Martin Luther)', in Schuster Duffield, pp. 119–46.

14 Pollard, p. 124; Schuster et al., pp. 206–7, 212.

15 For most aspects of Tyndale's life, see Daniell. But that his origins were not on the western scarp of the Cotswolds but west of the Severn in the Forest of Dean is a new and persuasive suggestion made by Andrew J. Brown in *William Tyndale on Priests and Preachers With New Light on his Early Career* (1996). I owe this reference to Diarmaid MacCulloch.

16 This draws on a number of papers communicated to the 1994 Oxford International

Tyndale Conference and published in *Reformation*, 1 (1996), and on the papers read to a Tyndale Conference in Washington, DC, in 1994 and published as John T. Day, Eric Lund and Anne M. O'Donnell, eds, *Word, Church and State: Tyndale Quincentenary Essays* (Washington, DC, 1998).

17 Erasmus, Paraclesis, in J. C. Olin, ed., *Christian Humanism and the Reformation* (New York, 1965), p. 97; *Acts and Monuments of Foxe*, v. 117.

18 Daniell, p. 216.

19 Lawler; Walter and Schuster et al.

20 Mueller, pp. 220–2.

21 Brian Vickers, 'Public and Private Rhetoric in Hooker's Lawes', in A. S. McGrade, ed., *Richard Hooker and the Construction of Christian Community* (Tempe, AZ, 1997), pp. 95–145.

22 See MacCulloch.

23 King, ch. 3, 'Vox Populi, Vox Dei'.

24 *The first examinacyon of Anne Askew* (Wesel, 1546), *The lattre examinacyon of Anne Askewe* (Wesel, 1547), both edited by Beilin; Betteridge, pp. 80–119; King, pp. 73–4.

25 The British Academy John Foxe Project aim to produce a modern, critical, electronic edition of the four versions, and has already published a facsimile edition of 1583 on CD-ROM (Oxford, 1999). The first two John Foxe colloquia have been published in Loades (1997) and Loades (1999).

26 Patrick Collinson, 'Truth and Legend: The Veracity of John Foxe's Book of Martyrs', in Collinson (1994), p. 151.

27 Leslie M. Oliver, 'The Seventh Edition of John Foxe's "Acts and Monuments"', *Papers of the Bibliographical Society of America*, 37 (1943), 243–60; Eirwen Nicholson, 'Eighteenth-century Foxe: Evidence for the Impact of the Acts and Monuments in the "Long Eighteenth Century"', in Loades (1997). See also Linda Colley, *Britons* (London, 1992).

28 Betteridge, pp. 120–60.

29 Collinson, *Elizabethan Essays*, pp. 151–2; Ceri Sullivan, '"Oppressed by the Force of Truth": Robert Persons Edits John Foxe', in Loades, *John Foxe: An Historical Perspective*, pp. 154–66. These remarks are also reliant on forthcoming work by Dr Thomas Freeman of the Foxe Project.

30 Walsham (1999).

31 Southern, esp. pp. 60–6; Milward (1977), ch. 1, 'Anglican Challenge'.

32 J. Ayre, ed., *The Works of John Jewel*, iv. Parker Society (Cambridge, 1850), 1,092.

33 Walsham, 'Domme Preachers'. See also Walsham (2000).

34 Patrick Collinson (1967), pp. 165–6.

35 John H. Primus, *The Vestments Controversy* (Kampen, 1960).

36 Henry Ainsworth, *Counterpoison* (Amsterdam, 1608), p. 228.

37 *A part of a register* (Middelburg, 1593), pp. 23–37.

38 Collinson (1967), pp. 77–8.

39 Ibid., pp. 101–21; Patrick Collinson, 'John Field and Elizabethan Puritanism', in Collinson (1983), pp. 332–70. *The Admonition* and associated pamphlets, including the anonymous *Second Admonition to the Parliament*, are printed in Frere and Douglas.

40 Lake; McGrade.

41 A modern, student, edition of the Marprelate Tracts is much needed. They were edited by William Pierce in 1908 as *The Marprelate Tracts*, 1588, 1589, and were printed in facsimile by the Scolar Press in 1967.

42 Carlson.

43 Patrick Collinson, 'Ecclesiastical Vitriol: Religious Satire in the 1590s and the Invention of Puritanism', in John Guy, ed., *The Reign of Elizabeth I: Court and Culture in the Last Decade* (Cambridge, 1995), pp. 150–70; Patrick Collinson, 'Ben Jonson's *Bartholomew Fair*: The Theatre Constructs Puritanism', in D. L. Smith, R. Strier and D. Bevington, eds, *The Theatrical City: Culture, Theatre and Politics in London, 1576–1649* (Cambridge, 1995), pp. 157–69.

44 Forthcoming work on practical divinity by Dr Jason Yiannikkou; Dr Thomas Freeman's forthcoming edition of the *Letters of the Marian Protestants* for the Church of England Record Society; Patrick Collinson, 'John Knox, the Church of England and the Women of England', in Roger A. Mason, ed., *John Knox and the British Reformations* (Aldershot, 1998), pp. 74–96.

42   *Patrick Collinson*

Allison and Rogers, i pp. 24–9; Birrell.
46 Shell, pp. 56–104.
47 Gregory; and, for a different interpretation, Victor Houliston, 'Why Robert Persons Would Not be Pacified: Edmund Bunny's Theft of the Book of Resolution', in Thomas M. McCoog, ed., *The Reckoned Expense: Edmund Campion and the Early English Jesuits* (Woodbridge, 1996), pp. 159–77.

REFERENCES AND FURTHER READING

Allison, A. F. and Rogers, D. M. (1989, 1994). *The Contemporary Printed Literature of the English Counter-Reformation between 1558 and 1640*. 2 vols. Aldershot: Scolar.

Beilin, Elaine V. (ed.) (1996). *The Examinations of Anne Askewe*. Oxford: Oxford University Press.

Betteridge, Thomas (1999). *Tudor Histories of the English Reformations, 1530–83*. St Andrews Studies in Reformation History. Aldershot: Ashgate.

Birrell, T. A. (1994). 'English Counter-Reformation Book Culture', *Recusant History*, 22, 113–22.

Carlson, Leland H. (1981). *Martin Marprelate, Gentleman: Master Job Throkmorton Laid Open in his Colours*. San Marino, CA.: Huntington Library.

Collinson, Patrick (1967, 1990). *The Elizabethan Puritan Movement*. London and Berkeley: Jonathan Cape and University of California Press; Oxford: Oxford University Press.

——(1983). *Godly People: Essays on English Protestantism and Puritanism*. London: Hambledon Press.

——(1988). *The Birthpangs of Protestant England: Religious and Cultural Change in the Sixteenth and Seventeenth Centuries*. Basingstoke: Macmillan.

——(1994). *Elizabethan Essays*. London and Rio Grande, AZ: Hambledon Press.

——(1995). 'Ecclesiastical Vitriol: Religious Satire in the 1590s and the Invention of Puritanism'. In John Guy (ed.). *The Reign of Elizabeth I: Court and Culture in the Last Decade*. Cambridge: Cambridge University Press.

——(1997). 'The English Reformation, 1945–1995'. In Michael Bentley (ed.), *Companion to Historiography*. London and New York: Routledge.

Collinson, Patrick, Hunt, Arnold and Walsham, Alexandra (forthcoming). 'Religious Publishing in England 1557–1640'. In John Barnard and D. F. McKenzie (eds), *The History of the Book in Britain*, vol. 4. Cambridge: Cambridge University Press.

Daniell, David (1994). *William Tyndale: A Biography*. New Haven and London: Yale University Press.

Day, John T. Lund, Eric and O'Donnell, Anne M. (eds) (1998). *Word, Church and State: Tyndale Quincentenary Essays*. Washington, DC: Catholic University of America Press.

Dickens, A. G. (1989). *The English Reformation*, 2nd edn. London: Batsford.

Duffield, Gervase (ed.) (1964). *The Work of William Tyndale*. Appleford: Sutton Courtenay Press.

Duffy, Eamon (1992). *The Stripping of the Altars: Traditional Religion in England c.1400–c.1580*. New Haven and London: Yale University Press.

John, Foxe (1583). *Actes and monuments of matters most speciall in the church. Newly reuised and recognised, partly also augmented, and now the fourth time published*. London: John Day. (Published by Oxford University Press on CD-ROM, 1999.)

Frere, W. H. and Douglas, C. E. (eds) (1907, 1954). *Puritan Manifestoes: A Study of the Origin of the Puritan Revolt*. London: SPCK.

Gilmont, J.-F. (1998). *The Reformation and the Book*, tr. K. Maag. St Andrews Studies in Reformation History. Aldershot: Ashgate.

Green, Ian (1995). *The Christian's ABC: Catechisms and Catechising in England, c.1530–1740*. Oxford: Oxford University Press.

——(forthcoming). *Print and Protestantism in Early Modern England*. Oxford: Oxford University Press.

Gregory, Brad S. (1994). 'The "True and Zealouse Service of God": Robert Persons, Edmund Bunny and the First Booke of the Christian

Exercise', *Journal of Ecclesiastical History*, 45, 238–68.

Haigh, Christopher (1993). *English Reformations: Religion, Politics and Society under the Tudors*. Oxford: Oxford University Press.

Haller, William (1964). *Foxe's Book of Martyrs and the Elect Nation*. London: Jonathan Cape.

King, John N. (1982). *English Reformation Literature: The Tudor Origins of the Protestant Tradition*. Princeton: Princeton University Press.

Klotz, Edith L. (1938). 'A Subject Analysis of English Imprints for Every Tenth Year from 1480 to 1640', *Huntington Library Quarterly*, 1, 417–19.

Lake, Peter (1988). *Anglicans and Puritans? Presbyterianism and English Conformist Thought from Whitgift to Hooker*. London: Unwin Hyman.

Lawler, Thomas M. C. Marc'hadour, Germain and Marins, Richard C. (eds) (1981). *A Dialogue Concerning Heresies, Complete Works of St Thomas More*, vol. 6. New Haven and London: Yale University Press.

Lewalski, Barbara (1979). *Protestant Poetics and the Seventeenth-century Religious Lyric*. Princeton: Princeton University Press.

Loades, David (ed.) (1997). *John Foxe and the English Reformation*. St Andrews Studies in Reformation History. Aldershot: Ashgate.

——(1999). *John Foxe: An Historical Perspective*. Aldershot: Ashgate.

MacCulloch, Diarmaid (1996). *Thomas Cranmer: A Life*. New Haven and London: Yale University Press.

McGrade, A. S. (ed.) (1997). *Richard Hooker and the Construction of Christian Community*. Tempe AZ: Medieval and Renaissance Texts and Studies.

The Marprelate Tracts (1967). Leeds: Scolar.

Milward, Peter (1977). *Religious Controversies of the Elizabethan Age: A Survey of Printed Sources*. London: Scolar.

——(1978). *Religious Controversies of the Jacobean Age: A Survey of Printed Sources*. London: Scolar.

Mueller, Janel (1984). *The Native Tongue and the Word: Developments in English Prose Style 1380–1580*. Chicago: University of Chicago Press.

A part of a register (1593). Middelburg: Richard Schilders.

Pollard, A. W. (ed.) (1911). *Records of the English Bible*. London: Oxford University Press.

Reformation, 1 (1996).

Schuster, L. A. et al. (eds) (1973). *The confutacyon of Tyndales answere, Complete Works of St Thomas More*, vol. 8. New Haven and London: Yale University Press.

Shell, Alison (1999). *Catholicism, Controversy and the English Literary Imagination*. Cambridge: Cambridge University Press.

Southern, A. C. (1950). *Elizabethan Recusant Prose 1559–1582*. London and Glasgow: Sands and Co.

Temperley, Nicholas (1979). *The Music of the English Parish Church*. 2 vols. Cambridge: Cambridge University Press.

Walsham, Alexandra (1999). *Providence in Early Modern England*. Oxford: Oxford University Press.

——(2000). *Church Papists: Catholicism, Conformity and Confessional Polemic in Early Modern England*, 2nd revd edn. Woodbridge: Boydell and Brewer.

——(2000). '"Domme Preachers": Post-Reformation English Catholicism and the Culture of Print', *Past and Present*, November.

Walter, H. (ed.) (1850). *William Tyndale, An Answer to Sir Thomas More's Dialogue*. Parker Society. Cambridge: Cambridge University Press.

Watt, Tessa (1991). *Cheap Print and Popular Piety, 1550–1640*. Cambridge: Cambridge University Press.

4

Platonism, Stoicism, Scepticism and Classical Imitation

Sarah Hutton

One of the distinguishing features of the Renaissance was the new valuation of classical culture, known now as (but not so-called then) the humanist movement. As a programme of recovery and rediscovery of the textual sources of Latin and Greek culture, humanism originally entailed proficiency in those languages. Nevertheless, its secular emphasis, its central concern with literary, linguistic and historical issues ensured that humanism had enormous impact on vernacular cultures across Europe. Humanist focus on rhetoric has obscured its important impact on philosophy, where the enterprise of recovery and discovery resulted in a wider knowledge of the classical philosophy than ever before in post-classical times: in particular, the expanded knowledge of the corpus of Platonic and Stoic writings, and the new access to the sources of Scepticism significantly widened philosophical horizons still dominated by Aristotelianism.[1] In the longer term, the philosophical pluralism to which they contributed resulted in the displacement of Aristotelianism as the chief component of European philosophy.

The impact of the recovered corpus of ancient philosophy was not confined to professional philosophy, but extended well beyond into all aspects of vernacular literary culture. Humanism played a key part in this process. First of all, humanism made these new aspects of philosophy available to a wider audience than the professional philosophy of the universities, with the result that part of the lasting contribution of humanism to philosophy was the development of secular philosophy. This shift from technical to lay philosophy exposed humanists to the jibe that they were ignorant of philosophy. An inevitable, longer-term consequence of the process of laicization which they initiated was the assimilation of classical thought as the stock-in-trade of Renaissance secular culture. These developments are as true of the English Renaissance as of the rest of Europe – the main difference being that England was, if anything, a latecomer to the cultural developments that define the Renaissance as a period.

When singling out individual philosophies for discussion, we should bear in mind that they were received and studied in a pluralistic setting. For this, the Renaissance had both classical precedent and humanist example. One of the most important sources for ancient philosophy was the writings of Cicero, the Roman author most admired by Petrarch and other humanists. In the Renaissance, Cicero was admired not just as a master of eloquence, but as a philosopher in his own right. Just as Cicero had mediated Greek philosophy to the Romans, so also his writings were of incalculable importance as a conduit of ancient philosophy to the Renaissance. Cicero was not a mere doxographer or mere reporter of the ideas of others, but his writings record the interaction of philosophical positions with one another, including his own. In philosophy he may be described as an eclectic, since he drew on the Stoics, Plato and Aristotle. Furthermore, he was an example of a philosophical amateur, not a professional. An eminent lawyer, and man of public affairs, his was a philosophy for the active life, not a life of meditation. The appeal of his philosophy to the thinking layman was increased by his choice of genre, namely the dialogue or private letter. In his introductory letter to his edition of Cicero's *Tusculan Disputations*, Erasmus recommends Cicero for his moral philosophy, and for making philosophy relevant to everyday life, by adopting a style 'that even an uneducated audience could applaud'.[2]

Although Platonism, Stoicism and Scepticism were recognized by the humanists as distinct branches of philosophy, they were not treated as the self-contained, mutually exclusive philosophical alternatives they are today. Accommodation is the hallmark of their assimilation into Renaissance culture. As with other areas of the Renaissance classical revival, the newcomers to the philosophical corpus were adopted and adapted to the needs and expectations of a different culture. To make an obvious point, part of the appeal of Stoicism and Platonism to the Renaissance was the moral emphasis of these philosophies which struck a chord with humanism's own preference for moral philosophy. Plato's concern with the nature of true eloquence likewise echoed humanist interest in rhetoric. One of the most significant ways in which the receiving culture of the Renaissance transformed the classical past was in the accommodation of pagan philosophy with the requirements of Christianity: the most striking example of reinvention of this kind is the transformation of Plato into a proto-Christian sage, the divine Plato, the seer of the soul most famously celebrated in Milton's 'Il Penseroso'. In seeking an accommodation between philosophy and faith humanist thinkers were continuing an established tradition: Seneca, for example, had been revered as the acceptable face of Stoicism in the middle ages, on account of his piety, sobriety and moral fortitude. The Renaissance interpretation of Seneca continued in this vein, following the lead given by Petrarch's immensely popular *De remediis utriusque fortunae*. Even Francis Bacon acknowledged that Seneca 'seemeth . . . to have some approach to the state of a Christian' (*Essays*: 'Of Adversity'). What was new was the expanded vista on Stoic thought, which made it less easy to ignore those aspects of Stoicism which did not fit this proto-Christian model. Scepticism had long been known through the writings of Cicero, but the recovery of Pyrrhonism through the writings of the rediscovered Sextus Empiricus opened the way for new applications for scepticism as a weapon against dogmatism in the religious crisis of the Reformation.

The recovery and dissemination of classical philosophy, would not, of course, have been possible without the humanist linguistic skills that gave access to original sources. Most obviously, humanist knowledge of Greek made the rediscovery of Plato, early Stoicism and Greek Scepticism possible. Furthermore, humanist educational programmes ensured that readers had the linguistic skills to read both Latin and Greek philosophy. And humanist translations brought classical texts a wide public. In the case of classical philosophy, vernacular translation was less significant than translation into Latin, but this did not mean that philosophy was accessible only to the university elite. As the *lingua franca* of Europe, in this period, Latin was the language of educated lay readers, as well as clerics, even if, at its most basic, a grammar-school education equipped Elizabethans, with 'smale Latine and lesse Greeke'. The evidence of Elizabethan library collections is that bilingualism in Latin and the vernacular was fairly standard. Latin texts were therefore relatively accessible: Cicero and Seneca, for example, were normally read in Latin. And, indeed, there were a number of Latin editions of their works printed in England in the sixteenth and early seventeenth centuries. By contrast, since Greek was less widely known, Latin translations of Greek texts were the key to their dissemination across Europe. Ficino's Latin translation of Plato is perhaps the best example of this. Far from being an indicator of narrow readership, the fact of a text's being printed in Latin gave it a wide audience Among the key works of Renaissance intellectual culture, the popularity of More's *Utopia* (1516) owes much to the language in which it was written, namely Latin. And Baldessare Castiglione's *Il Cortegiano* was more widely read in England in Bartholomew Clerk's Latin translation (1571) than in Sir Thomas Hoby's English one, *The Courtier* (1561). The use of Latin for intellectual discussion means that translation into the vernacular (e.g. English) is not the best indicator of diffusion. But to recognize this is not to belittle the importance of vernacular translation. Rather, it is to put it in perspective. The overall trend of the period was towards the full development of the vernacular as the chief medium of written expression. Latin permitted an international readership, though, in a national context, vernacular writing reached a wider social spectrum than Latin. Promotion of the vernacular was a dimension of the humanist enterprise. And indeed one of the best known English translations of classical texts – North's translation of Plutarch – was actually made from another vernacular translation, the French translation of Plutarch by Jean Amyot. The first printed English translation of Epictetus' *Enchiridion*, John Stanford's *The Manual of Epictetus* (1567), was translated from French, not Greek.

Part of the appeal to the humanists of classical philosophy outside the Aristotelian tradition was its philosophical style and diversity of genres used for philosophizing. Erasmus admired Plato as the 'most eloquent of philosophers' and Plutarch for combining learning with eloquence. For Petrarch, Cicero was unrivalled for his eloquence. In contrast to Cicero, the brevity of Seneca's written style was part of his appeal, though it did not become fashionable until the late sixteenth century. The philosophers commended by Sidney in his *Apology for Poetry* are those who employed 'poetical helps' to express their thoughts, namely Plato and Cicero. As Francis Bacon notes, the ability to communicate is an asset in a philosopher, and he commends the Stoics and Plato in this regard: 'it is a thing not hastily to be condemned, to clothe and adorn the obscurity even of philosophy itself with sensible and plausible elocution. For hereof we have great examples in Xenophon, Cicero, Seneca, Plutarch, and of Plato also in some degree' (*Advancement of Learning*, 1.4.4). Indeed, according to Thomas Elyot, the philosophers who most aptly exemplified Horace's judgement that the best writing combines instruction with pleasure were Plato and Cicero:

> what incomparable sweetness of words and matter shall he [the student] find in the said works of Plato and Cicero; wherein is joined gravity with delectation, excellent wisdom with divine eloquence, absolute virtue with pleasure incredible.
>
> (Elyot, *The Governor*, 1.12)

The genres preferred by the Stoics, Platonists, Sceptics and their spokesmen contrasted with the formal treatises in which medieval philosophers had expounded their theories. Cicero, Plato, Seneca and Plutarch had made use of the dialogue, the personal letter, and the essay as the preferred medium of intellectual discussion and they were widely imitated by humanists themselves. The choice of such genres was undoubtedly a recommendation to lay readers. For example, Plutarch's collection of ethical reflections known as the *Moralia*, printed in Greek in 1509, and translated into English by Philemon Holland in 1603, was not just a conduit of Stoic and Platonic moral philosophy, but the *Moralia* helped to popularize the loose philosophical essay as a form for private philosophical reflection which was imitated by, among others, Montaigne and, after him, Bacon.

Humanist aesthetics and literary theory actively encouraged the practice of using classical models. This was enshrined in the doctrine of 'imitation' or following examples. As a teaching technique for inculcating classical standards in the writing of Latin and Greek, this entailed copying the style of recommended authors. The ultimate aim was not slavish copying, but emulation. Ben Jonson was echoing classical precedent and humanist opinion when, in his *Discoveries*, he defined imitation as a kind of creative adaptation and cautions against mere servile reproduction. To imitate, he writes is

> to be able to convert the substance or riches of another poet to his own use. To make choice of one excellent man above the rest and so to follow him as the copy may be mistaken for the principal. Not, as a creature that swallows, what it takes in, crude, raw or undigested, but, that feeds with an appetite and hath a stomach to concoct, divide and turn all unto nourishment.
>
> (*Discoveries*, 'Of Imitation')

Erasmus's satire, *Ciceronianus* (1528) was famously directed against imitation of the first type – the self-conscious reproduction of Ciceronian-style Latin. As exemplified by Erasmus' *De copia*, imitation as a method for acquiring a richer, more expressive written style, entailed a process of selection and re-combination of examples drawn from a variety of classical sources. It was a method which encouraged eclecticism, in philosophy no less than other fields: in *The Schoolmaster* (1570) Roger Ascham cites as a commendable example of imitation, his friend Sturm's recommendation that 'examples out of Plato and other good Authors' should be used to illustrate the precepts of Aristotle.[3] Perhaps the most striking English example of such eclecticism in practice is Robert Burton's *Anatomy of Melancholy* (1621), where ancient philosophy is treated as a repository of *sententiae* and the discussion of melancholy takes the form of a patchwork of quotations.

The object of classical imitation, according to Renaissance theory, was not mere faithful reproduction of the original, but the transformation of the models imitated to present use. A prime example of imitation resulting in creative adaptation is More's *Utopia* (1516): the book owes much to his reading of Plato's *Republic* and the satires of Lucian. The result is neither Platonist nor Lucianic, but an entirely new genre, that raises serious political issues in a light-hearted way. The book was, furthermore, directed at a non-academic audience, and its success in reaching that audience may be explained in terms of the way it is written. And indeed, the extra-mural diffusion of philosophy in vernacular culture initiated by the humanists owed much to mediation in non-philosophical formats. Castiglione's *Il Cortegiano*, for example, functioned as a compendium of Platonic wisdom. Another source of philosophical doctrine were discursive works like Duplessis Mornay's *De la verité de la religion chrétienne* (translated by Sir Philip Sidney and Arthur Golding), or compendia like La Primaudaye's *L'Académie Françaize* (translated into English by Thomas Barnes in 1586). In the case of Seneca, the popularity of his drama gave prominence to the ethos of Stoicism.

Platonism

In the Middle Ages, Plato's philosophy had been known in imperfect translation, via only a handful of dialogues. Knowledge of the works of other Platonists was partial. The works of Plotinus were unknown. In the fifteenth century, one man changed all that: the Florentine, Marsilio Ficino (1433–1499). Ficino's Latin translation of the thirty-six extant dialogues of Plato (commissioned by Cosimo de' Medici and published in 1484) ensured that the philosophy of Plato was more widely known in the Renaissance than at any time since classical antiquity. Ficino also translated other important thinkers in the Platonic tradition, most important of whom was Plotinus, whose *Enneads* Ficino translated and published in 1492. As part of the same programme of translation, Ficino also translated the writings of Hermes Trismegistus, the supposed Greek sage whose writings were believed to be a key interface between pagan philosophy and biblical religion. Ficino's legacy was not just access to hitherto 'lost' philosophical works, but an interpretative approach for reading them. He regarded the Platonic tradition as a continuous one, and interpreted Plato through his later followers, notably Plotinus. He also presented Plato's dialogues as a unified system of philosophy. In recommending Platonism to his Renaissance readers, he stressed compatibilities between Platonism and Christianity, as well as parallels between Platonism and other philosophy in the European tradition. For Ficino, Plato stood as first among philosophical equals, with special insight into religious truth. One of Ficino's most enduring contributions to Renaissance literature was his virtual invention of the concept of 'Platonic love' in his commentary on Plato's *Symposium*. By reinterpreting the implicit pederasty of Plato's dialogue as amatory idealism, Ficino obliterated the unacceptable face of Greek social practices, opening the way to the creative adaptations of Platonic love popularized by *dialoghi de' amore*, and central to the vocabulary of subjectivity in Renaissance love poetry.

Ficino's translation of Plato retained its currency well into the eighteenth century. The first Greek edition of Plato's dialogues was published by Aldus Manutius in 1513. In 1578 the Hugenots Henri Estienne and Jean de Serres dedicated their edition of Plato to Queen Elizabeth I. However, none of Plato's dialogues was translated into English. There was an English translation of the pseudo-Platonic dialogue *Axiochus* (London, 1592). And the only dialogue to be printed in Greek in England was the *Menexenus* (Cambridge, 1587). This is in striking contrast to contemporary France, where there were numerous editions and translations. Indirect knowledge of Platonism in Tudor England was, of course, available through Latin sources, such as Cicero, and popular manuals of contemporary culture, such as Castiglione's *The Courtier*.

An interest in Platonism was, nevertheless, fostered in England in a number of ways. Early on, in the mid-fifteenth century, Leonardo Bruni and Pier Candido Decembrio dedicated their translations of Plato to Humphrey Duke of Gloucester, benefactor of the present Bodleian Library. By the early sixteenth century, interest in Platonism is evident at Tudor universities. Plato's works were acquired by the new colleges founded along humanistic lines, notably Corpus Christi College, Oxford, and St John's College, Cambridge. Indeed, Cardinal Wolsey's unachieved plans for a Cardinal College at Oxford included the making of transcriptions of all of Cardinal Bessarion's Greek manuscripts. Visiting humanists such as Erasmus and Juan Luis Vives helped to promote the study of Plato. Indeed, Erasmus's own Christian humanist Platonism owed much to his English friend, the humanist, John Colet, who had in his turn corresponded with Ficino. Tudor humanists, like John Cheke, Nicholas Carr, Roger Ascham and John Aylmer were among the first to encourage the study of Plato. Aylmer's pupils included Jane Grey, who studied Plato's *Phaedo*. Ascham's reading of the *Phaedrus* is evident in his *Toxophilos*. Elyot's *The Book Named the Governor* (1561) is in many ways a reflection on Plato's *Republic* and More's translation of the life of Giovanni Pico della Mirandola (1510) is testimony of his interest in the Platonist humanists of Italy.

The influence of Platonism on English Literature was pervasive, but diffuse. In many texts, including some by Shakespeare, Platonism is a presence, even though it is difficult to pinpoint specific sources and doctrines. In most cases literary Platonism is mediated by other literary sources in Italian and French literature: notably Petrarch, Tasso, Du Bellay and the poets of the Pléiade. A central theme of the literary Platonism of the Renaissance was the idealization of secular love through the doctrine of spiritual beauty and what has come to be called 'Platonic love'. Subsumed within Petrarchism, Platonic love was celebrated in lyric poetry, especially sonnet sequences like Spenser's *Amoretti* and Drayton's *Idea*, and given more critical treatment in Sidney's *Astrophil and Stella*. It was also incorporated into pastoral romance made popular by Honoré d'Urfé's *Astrée*. Underlying these literary manifestations of Platonism, was the courtly Platonism of the kind expounded in Castiglione's *The Courtier*. When Sidney opens sonnet 71 of *Astrophil and Stella* with the question 'Who will in fairest book of nature know / How virtue may best lodged in beauty be', and answers it by declaring Stella to be the outward manifestation of inward beauty, he is expounding Platonic doctrine as done by Bembo in the fourth book of Castliglione's *The Courtier*. There Bembo declares, 'outward beauty' to be 'a true sign of the inward goodness, and in bodies this comeliness is imprinted more and less, as it were, for a mark of the soul, whereby she is outwardly known' (*The Courtier*, tr. Hoby, book 4). The writer whose Platonism is best documented and most complex is Edmond Spenser, who drew on wide variety of sources including Macrobius, Boethius, Alain de Lille and Dionysius the Aereopagite as well as Ficino's *De Amore* (especially important for his *Fowre Hymnes*). One writer who turned to the text of Plato was Ben Jonson, who owned Jean de Serres' translation and probably drew directly on Ficino in his treatment of Platonic love in his masques *The Masque of Beauty* (1608) and *Love's Triumph through Callipolis* (1630) and in his play, *The New Inn* (1629).

By the end of the sixteenth century, we have the first examples of indigenous English Platonic thought in the work of Everard Digby (*c.*1550–92) and Thomas Jackson (1579–1640). Both exhibit the syncretic tendencies of Ficinian Platonism. Digby's *Theoria analytica ad monarchiam scientiarum demonstrans* (1579) was the first serious philosophical work was to be published in post-Reformation England. Digby attempts an accommodation between Platonism and Aristotelianism by combining Aristotelian syllogistic with Platonic dialectic. This is subsumed within a Platonist system of metaphysics according to which all things, including the human mind derive from the divine ideas in the mind of God. Jackson's Platonism, too, was syncretic, but more overtly theological in its application. A younger contemporary of Richard Hooker, at Corpus Christi College, Jackson wrote twelve books of commentaries on the Apostles Creed, published singly from 1613. Like Ficino, he treats Platonism as an ancient philosophy. In this respect he anticipates the so-called Cambridge Platonists who flourished at the University of Cambridge in the mid-seventeenth century.

Although not a close-knit school of thinkers, Cambridge Platonism is the most important example of Platonist philosophy produced in the English language. Philosophically, the most prominent members of this group were Henry More (1614–87) and Ralph Cudworth (1617–88). Other members of the group were Benjamin Whichcote (1609–83), Nathaniel Culverwell (1619–33), John Smith (1618–52), and Peter Sterry (1613–33). They all studied at Emmanuel College, Cambridge, except for Henry More, who studied at Christ's College, where he was a younger contemporary of Milton. They were exponents of a syncretic Platonism, reminiscent of Florentine Platonism and informed by the evangelical humanism of Erasmus. But they were also receptive to other currents of thought, both ancient (e.g. Stoicism) and contemporary (e.g. Cartesianism). With the exception of More and Cudworth, most of their writings were published posthumously: Smith's *Select Discourses* in 1659, and Sterry's *Discourse of the Freedom of the Will* in 1675, Culverwell's *An Elegant and Learned Discourse of the Light of Nature* in 1652, and Whichcote's *Moral and Religious Aphorisms* in 1703. They were masters of poetic prose, who, while valuing reason, acknowledged the communicative power of metaphor. In this they followed the example of Plato, who used allegory to convey metaphysical truth, and who, like Ficino, they believed to have had special insight into matters divine. Their Christian Platonism has literary analogues in the poetry of Thomas Traherne, Thomas Vaughan and Andrew Marvell. The only poet of their number, Henry More, was an admirer of Spenser, whose stanzaic pattern he adopted for *Psychodia platonica* and other allegorical poems on the soul.

Scepticism

The form of Scepticism best known in the early Renaissance was the academic Scepticism of Cicero. According to this mitigated form of Scepticism, it is impossible to know anything with absolute certainty. All knowledge-claims are, therefore, at best provisional. The name, 'academic' derives from its origins in the Platonic Academy of the third century BC, where it was taught by Arcesilas and Carneades. These Greek sources were unknown in the middle ages. Cicero was the main source for academic Scepticism in medieval times, and remained an important source throughout the Renaissance. However, knowledge of Ciceronian Scepticism was enlarged first by Petrarch's commendation of the Cicero's *Academica*, and second by the fuller knowledge of Cicero's Greek sources acquired from doxographies such as Diogenes Laertius' *Lives of the Philosophers* and the writings of Sextus Empiricus. The first printed edition of Cicero's *Academica* appeared in 1548. It was the work of Omer Talon, friend of Pierre la Ramée (Ramus).

Of even greater impact than these additions to the corpus of academic Scepticism was the recovery of the second school of Greek Scepticism, Pyrrhonism, obtained from the same doxographies by Diogenes Laertius' *Life of Pyrrho* and Sextus Empiricus's *Outlines of Pyrrhonism*. Pyrrhonian Scepticism, which originates with Pyrrho of Elis (*c.*360–352 BC), is a more radical form of Scepticism since it doubts even Sceptical judgement. Pyrrhonists hold that there is insufficient and inadequate evidence to determine or deny whether any knowledge is possible. We should suspend judgement on all questions of knowledge, as the only way to obtain tranquillity of mind, or *ataraxia*. Although Greek manuscripts of Sextus Empiricus circulated in the fifteenth century, the first printing of a work by Sextus was Henri Estienne's Latin translation of the *Outlines of Pyrrhonism* in 1562. This was followed in 1569 by the edition of

Gentian Hervet which included both the *Outlines* and *Against the Mathematicians*. There was no Greek printing of Sextus's works until 1621.

   Academic Scepticism was available to the Renaissance largely through the writings of Cicero, but it does not appear to have made much impact beyond supplying *exempla* for humanist discussion. For example, in *The Praise of Folly* (translated by Sir Thomas Chaloner in 1569), Erasmus light-heartedly commends the academicians as the least assuming of the philosophers who have correctly recognized that nothing is certain. An early instance of the use of Pyrrhonism is Henry Cornelius Agrippa's *De incertitudine et vanitate scientiarum* (1526) (*On the Uncertainty and Vanity of the Sciences*). Agrippa's position is more fideistic and anti-intellectual than sceptical, but he draws on Pyrrhonism, for which he was ridiculed by Rabelais in *Gargantua et Pantagruel Le Tiers Livre* (1542). In fact it was not until the mid-sixteenth century, when Pyrrhonian Scepticism was applied as a weapon against philosophical and religious dogmatism, that Scepticism became a current of thought to be reckoned with. Scepticism was first invoked as a polemical weapon during the controversies generated by Pierre de Ramée's (Petrus Ramus) attack on Aristotelian dogmatism. Ramus himself had little more than stylistic comments to make about academic Scepticism. But his ally Omer Talon noted the anti-dogmatic application of the arguments of Cicero's *Academica* in his own work of that name (1547). In the ensuing controversy, the Ramists were branded academic Sceptics by Pierre Galland and Guy de Brués. Shortly afterwards, Scepticism was employed in the more dangerous arena of confessional controversy. This time it was the more devastating scepticism of Pyrrho that was deployed, recently made available in the Latin translations of Sextus Empiricus by Henri Estienne (*Outlines of Pyrrhonism* in 1562) and Gentian Hervet (*Against the Mathematicians*). Hervet undertook his translation of Sextus's interest in Pyrrhonism specifically in the service of the counter-Reformation. Quite how extensively these Reformation applications of Scepticism made an impact in England is difficult to tell. But Elizabethans were undoubtedly aware of them on account of the Ramist controversies at Cambridge.[4] The writings of Sextus Empiricus do not appear to have been well known in Tudor England, though there are known cases of people who owned them – for example John Dee. There was manuscript of English translation of Sextus attributed to Sir Walter Ralegh. Pyrrhonism was probably known through secondary sources, such as Henry Cornelius Agrippa's *De vanitate et incertitudine scientiarum* of 1526, a popular work which was translated into English in 1569 as *Of the Vanity and Uncertainty of the Sciences*. The most important source for Pyrrhonian Scepticism was of Michel de Montaigne (1533–92), for whom Sceptical doubt was encapsulated by the question he took for his motto: 'Que sçays-je? ('What do I know?'). In his *An Apology of Raymond Sebond* contained in the second book of his *Essays* Montaigne undertakes an exercise in Pyrrhonism to demolish the truth claims of human reason and philosophy. The dogmatisms that he attacks include the 'prince of dogmatists', Aristotle, but also Stoicism and Platonism. His purpose is not, as with Hervet or Talon, polemical, but is closer to the original aim of Pyrrhonism to use doubt (*epoche*) as a means to achieve tranquillity of mind. As Montaigne explains in his *Apology*, 'the profession of the Pyrrhonians is ever to waver, to doubt, and to enquire; never to be assured of any thing, nor to take any warrant of himself' with the result that they are lead 'unto their Ataraxie, which is the condition of a quiet and settled life, exempted from the agitations which we receive by the impression of the opinion and knowledge we imagine to have of things' (*Essays*, translated by Florio, Book 2, no. 12). Originally published between 1580 and 1588 Montaigne's three books of *Essais* were translated into English by John Florio in 1603. Although Florio's translation does not do justice to Montaigne's style, the *Essays* had wide appeal on account of their relaxed combination of urbanity and sardonicism, which ensure that they wear their extensive erudition lightly. The same combination of learning, Scepticism and religious faith exhibited by Montaigne is evident in John Donne. As with Montaigne, the bewildering variety of philosophy – exacerbated by the appearance of novel theories – 'throws all in doubt' (*Anatomy of the World. The First Anniversary*, l. 205). For Donne, however, the weakness of human reason is unsettling: we are 'oppressed with ignorance' (*The Progress of the Soul. The Second Anniversary*, ll. 254). Montaigne's sceptical question is posed as an interrogation of the soul, 'what dost thou know?'

> Poor soul, in this thy flesh, what dost thou know?
> Thou know'st thyself so little, as thou know'st not,
> How thou didst die, nor how thou wast begot.
> *(The Progress of the Soul. The Second Anniversary,*
> ll. 255–8)

Stoicism

The availability of the writings of Cicero and Seneca in the middle ages meant that there was some knowledge of Stoicism before the Renaissance. Through Seneca's dialogues (e.g. *De constantia*) and letters (*Epistulae morales*) and writings such as Cicero's *De officiis*, *De finibus* and *Tusculan Disputations*, the Stoics were known largely as moral philosophers, admirable for the parallels with Christian ideals which they appeared to exhibit – their moral seriousness and apparent piety, their recommendation of forbearance in the face of adversity, their contempt of worldly goods, their asceticism and their subscription to the doctrine of four cardinal virtues, prudence, temperance, justice and fortitude. Other, less comfortable aspects of Stoicism – e.g. their advocacy of suicide, their ideal of the suppression of the emotions (apathy), their belief in determinism – were conveniently ignored or glossed over. The early humanists enriched the corpus of Stoic writings, and established the Stoic canon. The partial knowledge of earlier Greek Stoicism available via Cicero and Plutarch, was increased by the publication of doxographies like Diogenes Laertius' *Lives of the Philosophers*. Epictetus' manual of Stoic moral philosophy, his *Enchiridion*, was translated into Latin and printed in 1547. The medieval view of Stoicism as congruent with Christian piety did not substantially change until the late sixteenth century. Ironically, perhaps, it was the humanist leader, Petrarch, who perpetuated the medieval view of Seneca in imitation of a work misattributed to Seneca: Petrarch's *De remediis utriusque fortunae* of 1366 was a Renaissance bestseller, the most frequently reprinted of all his writings. (An English translation by Thomas Twyne, *Physic against Fortune, as Well Prosperous, as Adverse* was printed in 1579.) The work is a set of consolatory dialogues in which Stoical reason debates with the emotions, in order to find remedies for the ill effects of fortune, whether good or bad. Petrarch's work did much to recommend Stoicism as a repository of moral *sententiae* and Seneca as a lay moralist fit for Christian consumption. Stoicism had other powerful advocates among leading humanists, notably Erasmus, who admired and edited Seneca. Although his *Praise of Folly* mocks the Stoics, it nonetheless retains the 'Stoic definition' of wisdom as the rule of reason. By virtue of having a place in the humanist school curriculum, Stoicism remained a familiar throughout the Renaissance: Cicero's richly Stoic *De officiis* and *De senectute*, were widely used as introductory texts in moral philosophy. Epictetus's *Enchiridion* was used as a school textbook of Greek. Seneca's writings were widely available in numerous editions. Another source of Greek Stoicism was Plutarch's *Moralia* (translated into English and published in 1603 by Philemon Holland) which drew on Stoic moral philosophy, illustrations of which might be found in some of the biographies, such as that of Cato the Younger, contained in Plutarch's *Lives of the Noble Grecians and Romans* (English translation 1579).

In the latter half of the sixteenth century this positive image of Stoicism was redrawn thanks to the scholarly investigations and the re-reading of Stoicism by the Flemish humanist historian, Justus Lipsius (Joest Lips) (1547–1606). Lipsius's main contribution to Renaissance Stoicism is his influential treatise, *De constantia ab publicis malis* (*On Constancy*) of (1584). Presented as a dialogue in time of civil war, this enunciates a practical moral philosophy for the man of public affairs. Seneca is held up as a model of conduct in the face of despotism and corruption. The only remedy in such a situation is to accept fate unswervingly, through steadfastness or fortitude (*constantia*), that is, by applying the Stoic principle of indifference to adversity through subordination of the passions to reason. Lipsius's concept of fortitude (*constantia*) is more positive than the ancient Stoic prescription of apathy (emotionlessness). Lipsius sought to redraw the boundary with Christianity in order to render Stoicism acceptable. The new reading of Stoicism which he initiated entailed fuller acknowledgement of some of the aspects of Stoicism that were difficult to reconcile with Christian piety. For example, he subordinated Stoic fate to God and interpreted the Stoic concept of destiny as the decree of divine providence. The resulting accommodation of Stoicism and Christianity has come to be known as neo-Stoicism. In his *Politicorum sive civilis doctrinae libri sex* (1590), translated into English by Sir W. James as *Six Books of Politics or Civil Doctrine* (1594), Lipsius's political philosophy combines Stoicism with his interest in the Roman historian Tacitus. Lipsius also edited Seneca (1605) and was one of the first to emphasize the importance of Stoic natural philosophy as the basis of Stoic ethics, in his *Physiologia stoicorum* (*Physics of the Stoics*) (1604).

Lipsius's view of Stoicism was taken up by his French admirers, Guillaume du Vair and Pierre Charron. The translation of their writings into English is one measure of

English interest in Stoicism. Sir John Stradling's translation of Lipsius's *De constantia* as *Two Books of Constancy* in 1594, was followed in 1598 by Thomas James's publication, his translation of Du Vair's, *Philosophie morale des Stoiques* (1594) as *The Moral Philosophie of the Stoics*. Charron's *De la Sagesse*, was printed in Samson Lennard's English translation, *The Moral Philosophy of the Stoics* in 1606 which saw five editions by 1640. It was in the wake of Lipsius that Thomas Lodge made his English translation of Seneca which was published as *The Works of Lucius Annaeus Seneca, both Moral and Natural* (1614).

Among Stoic writers, Seneca had, of course, always been popular as a dramatist and was imitated by English dramatists writing in both Latin and English. Thomas Newton's, *Seneca his Ten Tragedies* (1581) is testimony to the vernacular interest in Seneca's plays. The formative impact of Senecan drama on English Renaissance tragedy is well attested. But the prominence of Stoic models in the subject matter of the plays may be attributed in large measure to the reinvigorated Stoicism of Lipsius. In the drama of the late Elizabethan and early Jacobean period, Stoicism furnishes the model of the virtuous 'antique Roman', be he Brutus in Shakespeare's *Julius Caesar* or Horatio, 'that man who is not passion's slave' in *Hamlet*. Likewise, Pandulpho in Marston's *Antonio's Revenge* (performed 1599) is a mouthpiece of Stoicism, and Rusticus in Massinger's, *Roman Actor* (performed 1626), is a model of Senecan fortitude. It is in the plays of George Chapman that Stoicism is most fully drawn: *Bussy d'Ambois* (performed 1604), Clermont d'Ambois *Revenge of Bussy d'Ambois* (performed *c*.1610) or Cato in *The Wars of Caesar and Pompey* (*c*.1613), the righteous statesman who commits suicide to preserve his liberty. Among English playwrights, Ben Jonson owned and annotated Lipsius's *Politicorum . . . libri*, drawing on him in his tragedies, *Catiline* (performed 1603) and *Sejanus* (performed 1611).

Another important mediator of Stoicism in England were the *Essays* of Montaigne, translated by John Florio in 1603. Montaigne was an admirer of Lipsius. He cites Seneca frequently, and many of his essays are devoted to Stoic themes, e.g. 'That to philosophise is to learn how to die' (*Essays*, 1: 20). (This essay opens with a quotation from Cicero's *Tusculan Disputations*.) Montaigne was, as we have already noted, a stringent critic of Stoicism: in his *Apology for Raymond Sebond* Stoicism is one of the dogmatisms he attacks in his Pyrrhonist refutation of philosophy. In his attack on Stoic moral philosophy, Montaigne rejected the Stoic equation of passion with vice, and argued that the ideal of impassivity is unattainable and the exaltation of virtue presumptuous. His critique of Stoicism was, however, neither doctrinaire nor total. Nor does it undermine the evident Stoicism of other essays. For example, his essay, 'Of Experience', written after the *Apology*, returns to Stoic themes, enunciating the Stoic principle of fortitude in the face of adversity, 'A man must endure that patiently which he cannot avoid conveniently' (*Essays*, Book 3, 13). Montaigne's Pyrrhonist refutation of Stoicism certainly did not discourage other essayists from turning to Stoicism. Among Francis Bacon's *Essays*, 'On Death' and 'Of Adversity' draw extensively on Seneca. The value of Stoicism as a moral preparation to Christianity continued to be recognized. Among devotional writers, Joseph Hall (1547–1656) was dubbed 'our

English Seneca' for His *Heaven upon Earth or of True Peace and Tranquillity of Mind* (1606). The sobriquet is echoed by the Latin translator of *Heaven upon Earth*, who calls him 'Seneca Christianus' and in the title of the French translation of the same work, *Le Seneque Chrestien* (1610).

As we have already seen in the example of Montaigne, Stoic moral philosophy was not without its critics. In fact two of the main sources of Stoicism, Cicero and Plutarch, were also sources for anti-Stoic arguments. In his *Praise of Folly* Erasmus derides the Stoics for denigrating the emotions, thereby reducing the human subject to a mere marble statue. The Stoics are, moreover, guilty of pride for making them-selves equal to the gods. An influential critic of Stoicism was John Calvin, whose edition of Seneca's *De clementia* (1532), while acknowledging some parallels between Stoicism and Christianity, attacks the Stoic doctrine of virtuous apathy and fatalism. These criticisms are echoed in Milton's *Paradise Regained*, where Christ scorns as mere human pride the Stoic concept of virtue as equal to God, the Stoic ideal of self-sufficiency, asceticism and trust in suicide as liberation.

> The Stoic last in philosophic pride,
> By him called virtue; and his virtuous man,
> Wise, perfect in himself, and all possessing,
> Equal to God, oft shames not to prefer,
> As fearing God nor man, contemning all
> Wealth, pleasure, pain or torment, death and life,
> Which when he lists, he leaves, or boasts he can,
> For all his tedious talk is but vain boast,
> Or subtle shifts conviction to evade.
> *(Paradise Regained* IV. 297–321)

As the culmination of the humanist synthesis of antiquity with contemporary culture, Milton stands at the point of intersection between the Renaissance and the Enlight-enment. The critique of Stoicism which Milton here puts into the mouth of Christ echoes traditional Christian antipathy towards Stoicism. At the same time, in so far as they acknowledge the unassimmilable alterity of Stoicism, these words presage change. By the time *Paradise Regained* was published in 1671, humanism was in the process of radical transformation, with profound implications for the status of the philosophies it had fostered. On the one hand, the authority of the ancients in matters of wisdom had been challenged by Bacon. On the other hand, Pyrrhonism had dis-solved the old certainties of philosophy. The new philosophies of the seventeenth century declared their modernity by rejecting the past. With the success of Carte-sianism, the laicization of philosophy was now complete – Descartes, in his answer to Scepticism, having explicitly appealed to 'common sense' rather than tradition. The old currents of thought brought into view by humanism had become the province of history and imagination. It is perhaps no coincidence that the first English history of philosophy was written at this time, albeit one greatly indebted to classical sources – Thomas Stanley's *History of Philosophy* (1655–62). The scene was now being set for the so-called 'battle of the books', in the course of which humanism was revised as neo-classicism according to standards laid down by the likes of Bentley and Boileau.[5]

NOTES

1 The best account of Renaissance philosophy is Copenhaver and Schmitt (1992). For Renaissance Humanism, Kraye (ed.) (1996) contains a very useful collection of essays on a wide range of topics. See especially Bolgar (1954) for the European background. A shortcoming of Gilbert Highet's classic study, *The Classical Tradition* (Oxford: Oxford University Press, 1949) is that his focus on genre overlooks the intellectual and cultural impact of the texts discussed.

2 Letter to John Vlatten, tr. Martindale (1985), p. 127.

3 Ascham, *The Scholemaster*, in *Elizabethan Critical Essays*, ed. G. G. Smith (Oxford: Clarendon Press, 1904), vol. 1, p. 21.

4 See N. W. Gilbert, *Renaissance Concepts of Method* (New York: Columbia University Press, 1960), ch. 9.

5 See Grafton (1991) and Highet (1949).

REFERENCES AND FURTHER READING

Allen, D. C. (1964). *Doubt's Boundless Sea: Skepticism and Faith in the Renaissance*. Baltimore, MD: Johns Hopkins University Press.

Baldwin, A. and Hutton, S. (eds) (1994). *Platonism and the English Imagination*. Cambridge: Cambridge University Press.

Binns, J. W. (1990). *Intellectual Culture in Elizabethan England*. Leeds: Francis Cairns.

Copenhaver, B. P. and Schmitt, C. B. (1992). *Renaissance Philosophy*. Oxford: Oxford University Press.

Bolgar, R. R. (1954). *The Classical Heritage and its Beneficiaries*. Cambridge: Cambridge University Press.

Ellrodt, R. (1960). *Neoplatonism in the Poetry of Spenser*. Geneva: Droz.

Evans, R. C. (1992). *Jonson, Lipsius and the Politics of Renaissance Stoicism*. Durango, CO: Longwood Academic.

Grafton, A. (1991). *Defenders of the Text*. Cambridge: Cambridge University Press.

Hankins, J. (1990). *Plato and the Italian Renaissance*, 2 vols. Leiden: Brill.

Highet, G. (1949). *The Classical Traditions*. Oxford: Oxford University Press.

Jayne, S. (1995). *Plato in Renaissance England*. Dordrecht: Kluwer Academic Publishers.

Kraye, J. (1996). *The Cambridge Companion to Renaissance Humanism*. Cambridge: Cambridge University Press.

Martindale, J. (1985). *English Humanism, Wyatt to Cowley*. London: Croom Helm.

Monsarat, G. D. (1984). *Light form the Porch: Stoicism and English Renaissance Literature*. Paris: Didier.

Nelson, J. C. (1958). *Renaissance Theory of Love*. New York: Columbia University Press.

Popkin, R. H. (1964). *The History of Scepticism from Erasmus to Descartes*. New York: Humanities Press.

Patrides, C. A. (ed.) (1980). *The Cambridge Platonists*. Cambridge: Cambridge University Press.

Schmitt, C. B. (1972). *Cicero scepticus. A Study of the Influence of the Academica in the Renaissance*. The Hague: Nijhoff.

5

History

Patrick Collinson

I

In his *Apology for Poetry* Sir Philip Sidney had fun at the expense of the historian, 'loaden with old mouse-eaten records, authorising himself (for the most part) upon other histories, whose greatest authorities are built upon the notable foundation of hearsay'. And yet the historian boasted that it was he who held the key to 'virtue and virtuous actions'. Sidney, who was making the case for fiction as more useful than history, dismissed such claims. The historian was tied 'not to what should be but to what is', 'to the particular truth of things and not to the general reason of things'.[1] He might as well have said that history is a tale told by an idiot, signifying nothing.

That was not a conventional opinion. Sidney was parodying what every preface to every work of history said in defence of its subject, and such apologies were merely repetitive of old classical tropes. Sidney was quoting Cicero when he wrote of history as 'the witness of times, the light of virtue, the life of memory, the mistress of life'. Soon Sir John Hayward, ignoring Sidney's *Defence*, which had appeared in print in 1595, would introduce his *Life and Reign of Henry IV* (1599) with the same familiar words. Cicero, himself only following Aristotle, had said that the first requirement of a historian was that he should not be a liar (*De oratore*, II.xii.51). William Camden, a friend of Sidney, wrote in the preface to his *Annals of Elizabeth* (1615) that to take away truth from history was to poison the mind of the reader. As for the didactic usefulness of historical truth, the Protestant historian John Foxe told his readers that he took pity on 'the simple flock of Christ' who knew so little of the 'true descent of the church', 'and all for ignorance of history'.[2] Commending a history of their own county to the gentlemen of Kent, Thomas Wootton wrote:

> There is nothing either for our instruction more profitable, or to our minds more delectable . . . than the study of histories: nor for the gentlemen of England, no history so meet as the history of England.[3]

(nor, naturally, for the gentlemen of Kent, the history of Kent).

Such high-flown sentiments often failed to connect with what historians actually did. It is significant that the words 'story' and 'history', which for us mean rather different things, were for this period interchangeable. 'Truth' was a slippery commodity. From a ballad of 1565, *The true description of two monstrous children born at Herne in Kent* to *The true history of the tragic loves of Hipolito and Isabella, Neapolitans* (1628), the word 'true' was almost a health warning. Ben Jonson in *The Staple of News* said of such 'true' reports: 'no syllable of truth in them'. Sidney admitted that often the historian did make up his stories, or made sense of them only by 'borrowing weight' from poets, so that there was no absolute difference between history and fiction. And more than merely 'authorising' himself on other histories, many a sixteenth-century historian indulged in what we should regard as plagiarism on a massive scale. If Livy or Tacitus had already said it, why trouble to tell it differently? Hayward in his book on Henry IV's usurpation took the Ciceronian trope as a licence to lift almost everything from older historians, word for word. The book was political dynamite and got its author into serious trouble, but when Queen Elizabeth asked whether Hayward could be done for treason, Francis Bacon thought not, but said that he had committed 'very apparent theft', 'for he had taken most of the sentences of Cornelius Tacitus and translated them into English, and put them in his text'. Actually Bacon flattered Hayward, since his source was Sir Henry Savile's translation of Tacitus (1591).[4]

The history of history in the English Renaissance has been written as a slow upward progression from such dubious practices to something like our modern idea of what history ought to be.[5] Camden's *Annals of Elizabeth* was a history of the reign based on, as it were, the Public Record Office, its author making much of his Herculean labours in 'great piles and heaps of papers and writings of all sorts'. He also claimed to be an impartial witness to the times: 'Prejudices I have shunned.' So he gets a pat on the head for placing history, in Hugh Trevor-Roper's words, 'on a new base of scientific documentation'.[6] Fritz Levy called this the 'new history', new in its dispassionate, analytical purposes as well as in its method. But in keeping our ears cocked, as it were, for the first cuckoo in spring, we are in danger of not bothering to understand what the Renaissance historians themselves thought that they were about, and we may well misjudge even Camden.

What did the sixteenth century understand by history? For Francis Bacon, 'history', if not the same thing as the whole of knowledge, was the empirical basis of all knowledge. A linguistic fossil of this classical taxonomy survives in our 'natural history'. But for others the term was more restricted. The study of antiquity was not the same thing as history, and Camden, the historian of Elizabeth, did not consider his great work of antiquarianism, *Britannia* (1584), which explored such evidences of the British past as placenames, ancient ruins and buried coins, to be history. The essence of history lay in literary composition, which had no place in 'mere' antiquarianism. Cicero had asked in his treatise, *De oratore*: 'Do you not see how far history must be a job for the rhetorician?'(II.xv.62.). So it was that Bacon left to mere 'factors' the gathering of the necessary facts and documents. The historian was above such a menial task. Bacon's *History of the Reign of King Henry the Seventh* (1622) did not dispense entirely with 'research', but in its most essential respects it was a work of literary invention. It was also a prescriptive political treatise, written for the instruction of James I and the future Charles I. History was present as well as past politics.[7]

The poor antiquary continued to be fair game for the caricaturist. John Earle drew his picture in the collection of 'characters' he called *Microcosmography* (1628): 'A great admirer he is of the rust of old monuments . . . Printed books he contemns as a novelty of this latter age, but a manuscript he pores on everlastingly.' Yet antiquarians had serious business in hand, until the government of James I stepped in to stop them reading scholarly papers to each other in the Society of Antiquaries. This was where we might hope to find the critical testing of evidence which we associate with historical protocols. In this respect the historians were lagging behind.[8]

Arthur Ferguson even suggests that if we hope to find examples of historical consciousness and a sense of historical perspective, the political narratives formally designated as 'histories' are almost the last place that we should look.[9] An understanding of historical process was more likely not as an end in itself but when history was used to illuminate particular issues, such as law, theology, and, above all, language. It was with a sense of language as a social and historical phenomenon that Richard Mulcaster could write in his *Elementary* (1582), a book on the teaching of English grammar, that whereas the English of his own day was at the peak of its development, like Greek in the time of Demosthenes, or Latin in Cicero's day,

> when the age of our people, which now use the tongue so well, is dead and departed, there will another succeed, and with the people the tongue will alter and change.[10]

It is not that Renaissance historians did not know that good history ought to transcend mere antiquarianism. Thomas Blundeville in his *The true order and method of writing and reading histories* (1574) disparaged those who 'having consumed all their life time in histories' knew nothing except useless dates, genealogies 'and such like stuff'.[11] Camden quoted with approval the ancient historian Polybius:

> Take away from history why, how, and to what end things have been done, and whether the thing done hath succeeded according to reason, and all that remains will rather be an idle sport and foolery than a profitable instruction.[12]

But it remains a question how far these historians practised what they preached. They had more interest in teaching from the past, or what purported to be the past, than in learning from it, or rather, learning about it.

II

All that being said, 'history' for the educated classes of the later sixteenth and seventeenth centuries would have meant not English history but the Greek and especially the Roman historians. When Savile translated some of the *Histories* of Tacitus as *The end of Nero and beginning of Galba*, a story of imperial monarchy degenerating into tyranny, the impact on political consciousness, and perhaps practice, was immense.[13] Yet educated Elizabethans were not dependent upon translations. Sallust, author of *The Conspiracy of Catiline* and a model for Tacitus and who, unlike Tacitus, wrote easy Latin, was published several times, but not in English until 1608. The standard editions of these classics were products not so much of the underdeveloped English book trade as of the great continental printing houses. Tutors in Oxford and Cambridge, who were giving up more and more time to educating the sons of the gentry and aristocracy, introduced them to 'history' as a soft but useful option, and that normally meant Roman history.

For all his posturing against history in the *Defence*, Philip Sidney was himself a serious student of the subject, who had prepared for a diplomatic mission by reading some of the *Decades* of Livy. Gabriel Harvey recorded in the margin of the copy they used (an edition printed in Basle in 1555, now preserved at Princeton) that he and Sidney had 'privately discussed these three books of Livy, scrutinising them so far as we could from all points of view, applying a political analysis'. Such shared experiences were typical of the pedagogical and reading practices of the age. Harvey had conducted readings of Livy with others, much as a modern musician might conduct master classes.[14]

Another kind of history which was familiar to all dedicated Bible readers, and even to the much greater numbers who heard the Bible read, Sunday by Sunday, in church, was sacred, Old Testament history, which must have been more accessible and familiar than many events closer in time. Ever since Eusebius of Caesarea invented the subject in the fourth century, ecclesiastical history, a continuation of the biblical record, had been considered a distinct subject, separate from civil history. When Camden endowed a chair of history at Oxford, the first professor, Degory Wheare, was alarmed to be told that he would have to lecture on ecclesiastical history, a subject of which he claimed to be ignorant. Camden reassured him that it was his intention that he should profess only civil history.[15]

Archbishop Matthew Parker made a notable contribution to the genre in his history of the seventy archbishops of Canterbury, *De antiquitate Britannicae ecclesiae* (1572–4), but the ecclesiastical history with which Protestant Elizabethans were most familiar, and generations after them, was John Foxe's *Acts and Monuments*, popularly known as 'Foxe's Book of Martyrs', an account of 'matters ecclesiastical passed in the Church of Christ, from the primitive beginnings to these our days'. Defending the distinctive importance of his subject, Foxe remarked that men delighted in the chronicles of war, 'the hurly-burlies of realms and people'. But how much better for Christians to recall the lives, acts, and doings, not of bloody warriors, but of mild and constant martyrs. 'For doubtless such as these are more worthy of honour than an hundred Alexanders, Hectors, Scipios and warlike Julies . . . Such as these are the true conquerors of the world.'[16]

Foxe's book began life as a modest text in Latin, written to instruct a European audience about the history of persecutions in England from the time of John Wycliffe.

The first, greatly expanded, English edition appeared in 1563, with further enlarged editions in Foxe's lifetime in 1570, 1576 and 1583. This was not only the largest book ever published in England. It was a protean text which changed its shape, content and even purpose, from edition to edition, growing in density and detail as Foxe approached his own times, the years of the Marian Persecution.[17] This was virtually contemporary history, with an appeal which invites comparison with Louis de Jong's multi-volume history of the Nazi occupation of the Netherlands, which attracted tens of thousands of Dutch readers.

Foxe was the ultimate historical revisionist, turning the received history of the Church on its head, and identifying truth with the suppressed and almost invisible martyr minority, falsity with the pomp and pride of the Roman Church. Although he was capable of suppressing inconvenient truths, he made almost nothing up, following his sources (the 'monuments' of the title) very closely. Many of Foxe's informants were the victims themselves, or the eyewitnesses of their sufferings, so that it could be said that the book was written by the people to whom it belonged, the product of the godly community which it constructed.

According to an influential reading of Foxe, his book also instilled into the whole English nation a sense of its special status as the elect nation.[18] That was far from Foxe's purpose, although no author can hope to control the use which generations of readers will make of a book of several million words. It may be symbolic that Foxe's friend Sir Francis Drake took the 1576 edition on board the *Golden Hind* when he circumnavigated the world, and made use of it.[19] However, very exaggerated claims have been made about the capacity of this huge and expensive tome to penetrate extensively even the literate population, let alone 'the unlearned sort' for whom Foxe ostensibly wrote. Its bulk was self-defeating, and it is unlikely that as many as 10,000 copies were printed of all editions up to the Civil War.[20]

Yet another dimension of history, 'popular' rather than learned, was to be found in the memories of common people, connecting time, locality and present needs. 'We old men are old chronicles', says a character in a dialogue of 1608; and John Aubrey called such village patriarchs 'living histories'. It has been said that the English landscape was 'a vast repository of memory', a memory bank which endlessly interacted with written records and stories, such as the tales of Robin Hood, so that there may have been no purely oral historical traditions. Aubrey himself remembered that his nurse 'was excellent at these old stories', and 'had the history from the conquest down to Carl. I [Charles I] in ballad'. Could Shakespeare assume at least some basic knowledge when he wrote his English history plays?[21]

At the other extreme from localized memory, Elizabethan readers were introduced to more exotic places. William Thomas produced the first English *History of Italy* (1549), and 1591 saw the publication of Giles Fletcher's *Of the Russe common wealth*. In this literature 'the other' was often deployed patriotically and xenophobically. In *The Glory of England* (1615), Thomas Gainsford drew comparisons with China, India and Turkey: 'My joy exceedeth for not being a native amongst them.' In the huge book which he called *The principal navigations of the English nation* (1589) which, like

Foxe, grew in successive editions, continued by Samuel Purchas, Richard Hakluyt explored an empire which as yet did not exist.

III

By now it is apparent that the scope of 'history' in the literature and culture of the English Renaissance was very wide indeed. But in what remains of this chapter we shall restrict the term to the history of Britain and its parts. John Pocock has written that there have been as many pasts as there were social and professional groups with an interest in recalling it. The lawyer's past was not the same thing as the cleric's, or the herald's, who all owned different pasts, nor, we might add, the past of the Derbyshire lead miner.[22] Pocock asks whether we can speak of a national past in the early modern period? The answer has to be given by the writers of various kinds of English history, national and local.

We may begin with the chronicles. Archbishop Parker feared that Queen Elizabeth would be 'strangely chronicled',[23] implying that there would be, or ought to be, only one, more or less authoritative account of her reign, rather like the practice in imperial China where even the original archives were shredded to leave a single, official history. It was said that chronicles 'do carry credit'.[24] Chronicles were also, in principle, universal histories, covering the whole of time. Sir Walter Ralegh's *History of the World* (1614) was, in the tradition of the chronicles, only the introduction and groundwork for an intended history of England which never got written although its 'Preface' ran through the history of the Tudors into the reign of James I.

In practice, sixteenth-century English chronicles multiplied and jostled for space in a fiercely competitive market. Daniel Woolf has counted 220 editions of 79 different chronicles between 1475 to 1699.[25] This tells us something about the devolved diversity of early modern English society and culture (quite unlike China). The chronicles of the sixteenth century derived, in part, from town chronicles which were organized on the principle of the local civic year, consisting, as Thomas Nashe complained, of nothing but 'Mayors and Sheriffs, and the dear year [year of dearth] and the great frost'.[26] But the chronicle was also shaped by the centralizing tendencies of Tudor England. Although provincial towns such as Worcester and Shrewsbury continued to be served by their own self-appointed chroniclers, their books were not printed.[27] London took over. It is also significant that with the chronicle of Edward Halle, entitled *The union of the two noble and illustre families of Lancaster and York* (1548), the great theme (hitherto chronicles had had no themes) was political and royal, the coming of unity and peace through the union of the red and white roses in the Tudor dynasty.

But if the chronicles were in competition, they also ingested material from each other and from more literary sources, so that the story is one of complex agglomeration. There were three books coming from outside the tradition which fed into the mid-Tudor chronicles. Polydore Vergil was an erudite Italian who was engaged by

Henry VII to compose an ambitious *Anglica Historia*. It was complete in manuscript
up to 1513 in that year, but not printed until successive editions appeared in Basle
in 1534 and 1546 (covering events up to 1509), and 1546 (now reaching as far as
1538). Polydore introduced a critical and dispassionate standard to English history,
as well as the formal organizing principle of devoting a chapter to each reign, and the
fact that he was incorporated into the chronicles was to their advantage.[28] There was
an interactive relationship between Polydore's enterprise and Sir Thomas More's *The
History of King Richard III*, completed in about 1518. More's searching and ironical
interrogation of his subject has aroused almost as much discussion as *Utopia*, written
concurrently, and it has even been suggested that part of his intention was to parody
the historical search for 'truth'.[29] Nevertheless, the transcendent merits of *Richard III*
were widely acknowledged, one Elizabethan considering it 'the only story worthy of
reading',[30] while it was left to Shakespeare to pay it the most enduring of compli-
ments. A book which deserves much more admiration than it has ever received was
the *Life and Death of Cardinal Wolsey* by his gentleman usher, George Cavendish,
(1554–8) (modern edition, Early English Text Society, no. 243, 1959), which
remained unprinted until 1641, but which was reproduced in several chronicles.
Shakespeare and Fletcher could not have contrived the brilliant masques which light
up the stage in *Henry VIII* without Cavendish.

The 1560s saw something of a climax in the war of the chronicles. Edward Halle
had died, leaving his friend Richard Grafton to complete his work. Grafton published
in his own right *An abridgement of the Chronicles of England* (1562), which ran into
several editions. But a far more ambitious *Chronicle at large . . . of the Affairs of England
from the Creation of the World unto the First Year of Queen Elizabeth* (1568) was a flop,
seen off the turf by John Stow, who published a more successful *Summary of English
Chronicles* (nineteen editions in two different versions between 1565 and 1618), and
his bumper *Chronicles* (1580) which, unlike Grafton, achieved several editions and was
continued into the next century by Edmond Howes. Stow, a self-made and autodi-
dactic London tradesman, derided Grafton as one who 'hath but picked feathers from
other birds next in his reach'.[31]

But then, in 1577, the trump card was played with the publication of the *Chronicles of England, Scotland, and Ireland*, which would always be known after the leading
figure in the syndicate that planned it as 'Holinshed', Raphael Holinshed; but perhaps
unfairly, since the original idea belonged to the immigrant printer Reginald Wolfe,
and Holinshed was dead before the second edition appeared in 1587. 'Holinshed',
the main source for Shakespeare's history plays, was a vast and somewhat chaotic
agglomeration, much 'castrated' by official censorship in 1587. But it included a
number of virtually self-contained works of considerable merit, such as the 'Description of England', written against ever-pressing deadlines by a rather odd cleric called
William Harrison, whose real interest lay in a vast and unpublishable chronology of
the whole of human history.[32] Chronicles have been disparaged for their mindless
inconsequentiality. But more recently Annabel Patterson has drawn attention to the
'protocols' which determined the shape and arrangement of Holinshed, which she calls

'an important and inventive cultural history', including a very deliberate 'multivocality' which allowed all interests, social and religious, to be heard. This was not 'state history' but history for the citizen, and Patterson has even risked a considerable anachronism by calling its values 'liberal'.[33]

Were chronicles on the way out? It has been argued that they were becoming mere 'artefacts', while their practical functions were taken over by several other genres, including better organized and more manageable histories and cheap and expendable pamphlets, the early precursors of newspapers.[34] Their massive size was perhaps self-defeating, and it made little sense to continually update their contents, always beginning with the creation of the world. But that is not to say that Holinshed and Stow were not still read, in different ways and for different purposes, throughout the seventeenth century. And it was a regular and cyclical process for large books to ingest smaller books, and then in their turn to spawn still more derivative and even ephemeral publications.[35] So the chronicles fed into both cheap ballads and the more respectable historical and political poems known as *A Mirror for Magistrates*, first published by William Baldwin and other poets in 1559 and kept in print in variant versions until the 1620s.[36]

How far a wide public maintained its interest in the kind of history the chronicles contained is a different but related question, and one not easy to answer. The 1590s witnessed nothing short of a craze for history plays. Of the 266 known titles of plays performed in the London theatres in the 1590s, a good proportion were history plays, not all of which were written by Shakespeare, but it proved to be a somewhat transient fashion. Shakespeare's contribution to the genre was once seen as patriotic and straightforwardly affirmative of the shared values of the Elizabethan age. These were, after all, wartime plays. 'Come the three corners of the world in arms / And we shall shake them.' (*King John*, 5.7.124–7.) Recently, rather more has been made of Shakespeare's critical interrogation of regal and martial pretensions, even in *Henry V*. Since those who impersonated kings on the stage were commoners of low social status, historical drama could even be said to have had a subversive potential, although, conversely, it has been argued that it was also a vehicle for the social aspirations of its creators, especially Shakespeare, lifting him and his art out of the world of base mechanicals.[37]

IV

But there is no mistaking the fervently expressed patriotism which resounds in so much of the historical and topographical literature of Renaissance England. Shakespeare's 'This blessed plot, this earth, this realm, this England' (*Richard II*, 2.1.50) is a typical rather than exceptional sentiment. Holinshed had climaxed with a paean of praise for 'the commonwealth of England, a corner of the world, O Lord, which thou hast singled out for the magnifying of thy majesty', while Camden declared that 'the glory of my country' had been his motivation.

The glory of England, as of other emergent nations reaching for their identity in the Renaissance, was partly a matter of origins. The dominant origins myth (British rather than English) told of the foundation of civilized society in these islands by Brutus, the grandson of Aeneas, from whom the very name Britain was derived; and of the British hero and all-conquering emperor, Arthur.[38] These stories had passed into the chronicles from a twelfth-century work of imaginative invention, Geoffrey of Monmouth's *Historia Regum Britanniae*, the value of which as history was doubted even in its own time. Polydore Vergil, as a detached foreigner, was in a good position to pour cold water: 'Truly there is nothing more obscure, more uncertain or unknown than the affairs of the Britons from the beginning.' Since it was possible to see the cliffs of Dover from France, it was likely that the island had always been inhabited. As for Arthur, it was conclusive for Polydore that the Roman historians knew nothing of his exploits. His tomb had been 'discovered' at Glastonbury Abbey, but Glastonbury had not been founded in Arthur's day.[39] A friend of Sir Thomas More, John Rastell, joined in the fun in *The Pastime of People* (1529). Visitors to Westminster Abbey were shown Arthur's seal. But Westminster, too, had not existed in those days, the wax of the seal would long since have decayed, and, in any case, charters before the Conquest were not sealed.

According to conventional ideas of what the Renaissance was about, the 'British History' should now have evaporated like morning dew. Not so. Anthony Grafton has taught us that the not inconsiderable critical powers of the humanists could function in strange and paradoxical ways. The best critics made the best forgers, and even great scholars were capable of believing what they wanted to believe.[40] John Leland, who was far more learned than John Rastell, firmly believed in the historicity of Arthur, invoking the same evidence which Rastell had rubbished.[41] It became a matter of national, and soon of Protestant, honour to defend these old stories, which were actually supplemented from a highly dubious source by Foxe's learned friend John Bale, author of the first English bibliography, *Illustrium maioris Britanniae scriptorum* (1548). The Welsh, or 'Cambro-Britons' were particularly defensive of traditions which still flourished in their bardic culture. Humfrey Lhuyd affirmed in his *Breviary of Britain* (published, posthumously, in translation, 1573): 'I do believe that Brutus came into Britain with his train of Trojans.' When Camden came to write *Britannia* he reduced the wonderful world of Geoffrey of Monmouth to a pile of rubble, but still declined to pronounce absolutely on the issue. Let Brutus be taken for the father and founder of the British nation. 'I will not be of a contrary mind.'[42]

The old legends now had a future as 'poetical histories', as in Michael Drayton's epic poem *Poly-Olbion* (1612, 1622), which devoted 236 lines to the British History. John Selden wagged a pedantically reproving finger in his marginal notes, but this was no more than a friendly flyting between the scholar and the poet. Meanwhile, Camden had discovered the true ancestors of the English and their language in the Saxons, 'a warlike, victorious, stiff, stout and vigorous nation'.[43]

Local and regional patriotisms were at least as powerful as national sentiment in an England which functioned as a kind of federation of partly self-governing communities. The relation between the whole and its parts is demonstrated in one of the major cultural achievements of the age, the great *Atlas* associated with the name of Christopher Saxton (1579) which, it has been said, gave Englishmen 'visual and conceptual possession of the physical kingdom in which they lived'.[44] For Saxton's *Atlas* depicted England, for the first time, as a collection of 'coloured counties', and included separate maps of individual counties and groups of counties. This was the climax to a cartographical enterprise which accompanied the application to the English landscape and its history of 'chorography', a now forgotten art located somewhere between geography and history, invented in Renaissance Italy by Flavio Biondo in his *Italia Illustrata* and taken up by German humanists whose ambition was to produce a *Germania Illustrata*.

The pioneer of English chorography was John Leland, a philologist and Latin poet whose boundless ambition was to travel the length and breadth of England, on foot, first to survey and rescue the threatened monastic libraries, and then to take stock of the country itself, in all its rich physical and historical detail. He told Henry VIII that he would present him with a survey of 'your whole world and empire of England'.[45] But Leland bit off more than he could chew, became insane, and left to John Stow and other successors the vast accumulations of paper which we know as Leland's 'Itineraries'.

Leland's legacy was delivered piecemeal, in a number of regional studies which together amounted to what A. L. Rowse called 'the Elizabethan discovery of England'. William Lambarde led the way in his *Perambulation of Kent* (1576), to be followed by John Stow's *Survey of London* (1598), Richard Carew's *Survey of Cornwall* (1602), and the ambitious plan of John Norden to complete an entire *Speculum Britanniae*, which got little further than some of the counties closest to London. These books bear a strong authorial impression. Whereas Stow's book was suffused with backward-looking nostalgia for the lost world of merry and Catholic England, Lambarde wrote as a fierce Protestant, while Carew wrote optimistically, and entirely in the present tense.[46]

The consummation came with Camden's *Britannia*, which began (1586) as a stubby little book in Latin, intended to introduce a learned and cosmopolitan audience to a neglected province of the Roman Empire, but became in Philemon Holland's translation (1610) a sumptuous, illustrated folio for English gentlemen, the foundation for generations to come of topographical and antiquarian history in the same tradition. Just as Shakespeare put Holinshed into verse, so Michael Drayton versified Camden in the 12,000 lines of *Poly-Olbion*, a deification, almost, of 'Albion's glorious Isle'. When he reached the last frontier of Cumberland, Drayton wrote: 'My England doth conclude, for which I undertook this strange Herculean toil.'

NOTES

1 Geoffrey Shepherd, ed., *An Apology for Poetry*, (London, 1965), pp. 105–12.

2 G. Townsend and S. R. Cattley, eds, *Acts and*

Monuments of John Foxe, i (London, 1841), p. 514.

3 *A Perambulation of Kent . . . by William Lam-*

barde (Chatham, 1826, repr. Bath, 1970), pp. vii–x.

4   J. J. Manning, ed, *The First and Second Parts of John Hayward's The Life and Raigne of King Henry IIII*, Camden 4th ser. 42 (1991), Introduction. But see forthcoming work by Dr Lisa Richardson, who has for the first time established the true extent of Hayward's borrowings.

5   Especially in Levy.

6   MacCaffrey, pp. 3–8; Collinson.

7   Vickers, pp. 150–1.

8   John Pocock, *The Ancient Constitution and the Feudal Law* (Cambridge, 1987), p. 6.

9   Ferguson (1979).

10 E. T. Campagnac, ed., *Mulcaster's Elementarie* (Oxford, 1925), pp. 83, 179.

11 Quoted Woolf, p. 5.

12 MacCaffrey, p. 6.

13 J. H. Salmon, 'Seneca and Tacitus in Jacobean England', in L. L. Peck, ed., *The Mental World of the Jacobean Court* (Cambridge, 1991), pp. 169–88; Blair Worden, 'Ben Jonson among the Historians', in K. Sharpe and P. Lake, eds, *Culture and Politics in Early Stuart England* (Basingstoke, 1994), pp. 67–89.

14 Lisa Jardine and Anthony Grafton, ' "Studied for Action": How Gabriel Harvey Read his Livy', *Past and Present*, 129 (1990), 30–78.

15 H. Stuart Jones, 'The Foundation and History of the Camden Chair', *Oxoniensa*, viii, ix (1943–4), 175.

16 *Acts and Monuments of Foxe*, i. 521–2.

17 Loades; David Loades, ed., *John Foxe: An Historical Perspective* (Aldershot, 1999).

18 William Haller, *Foxe's Book of Martyrs and the Elect Nation* (London, 1964). But see Katherine R. Firth, *The Apocalyptic Tradition in Reformation Britain 1530–1645* (Oxford, 1979).

19 Glyn Parry, 'Elect Church or Elect Nation? The Reception of *The Acts and Monuments*', in Loades, *Foxe: An Historical Perspective*, pp. 167–81.

20 Leslie M. Oliver, 'The Seventh Edition of John Foxe's "Acts and Monuments" ', *Papers of the Bibliographical Society of America*, 37 (1943), 243–60.

21 Adam Fox, 'Remembering the Past in Early Modern England', *Transactions of the Royal Historical Society*, 6th ser., 9 (1999), 233–56.

22 John Pocock, 'England', in Orest A. Ranum, ed., *National Consciousness, History and Political Culture in Early Modern Europe* (Baltimore, 1975, p. 99); Andy Wood, *The Politics of Social Conflict: The Peak Country 1520–1770* (Cambridge, 1999).

23 BL, MS. Lansdowne 15, fol. 66.

24 Raphael Holinshed, *The first volume of the Chronicles of England, Scotland, and Ireland* (London, 1577), p. 766.

25 D. R. Woolf, 'Genre into Artefact: The Decline of the English Chronicle in the Sixteenth Century', *The Sixteenth Century Journal*, 19 (1988), 346.

26 A. B. Grosart, ed., *The Complete Works of Thomas Nashe* (London, 1884), ii. 62.

27 See the essays on Worcester and Shrewsbury in P. Collinson and J. Craig, eds, *The Reformation in English Towns 1500–1640* (Basingstoke, 1998).

28 See Hay.

29 Alistair Fox, *Thomas More* (Oxford, 1982), pp. 75–107; Alistair Fox, *Politics and Literature in the Reigns of Henry VII and Henry VIII* (Oxford, 1989), pp. 108–27; Hanham, pp. 152–90, 188–219.

30 Francis Alford to Sir Francis Walsingham, n.d., Inner Temple Library, MS, Petyt 538.10, fol. 11v.

31 Kingsford, i. x–xii.

32 Edelen; G. J. R. Parry (1987).

33 See Patterson.

34 Woolf, 'Genre into Artefact'.

35 Alexandra Walsham, *Providence in Early Modern England* (Oxford, 1999).

36 Lily B. Campbell, ed., *The Mirror for Magistrates* (New York, 1938).

37 Helgerson, ch. 5, 'Staging Exclusion'.

38 Kendrick; Ferguson (1993).

39 Sir Henry Ellis, ed., *Polydore Vergil's English History*, Camden Society (1846), pp. 31–3, 121–2.

40 Anthony Grafton, *Forgers and Critics: Creativity and Duplicity in Western Scholarship* (Princeton, 1990); Anthony Grafton, 'Traditions of Invention and Inventions of Tradition in Renaissance Italy: Annius of Viterbo',

in Grafton, *Defenders of the Text* (Cambridge, MA 1991), pp. 76–103.

41 John Leland, tr. R. Robinson, *A Learned and true Assertion of the Original Life, Acts and Death of . . . Arthur, King of Great Britain* (1582) (repr. ed. W. E. Mead, Early English Text Society, 165 (1925).

42 Camden, pp. 8, 10, 22.

43 Leslie Dunkling, ed., William Camden, *Remains of a Greater Work, Concerning Britain* (Wakefield, 1974), pp. 24–5.

44 Helgerson, p. 107; J. B. Harley, 'Meaning and Ambiguity in Tudor Cartography', in S. Tyacke, ed., *British Map-Making 1500–1650*; V. Morgan, 'The Cartographic Image of "The Country" in Early Modern England', *Transactions of the Royal Historical Society*, 5th ser., 29 (1979), pp. 129–54.

45 'Leland's Newe Yeares Gyfte to King Henry the viii', in Lucy Toulmin Smith, ed., *The Itinerary of John Leland*, 5 vols (Oxford, 1907, repr. Carbondale, IL., 1964), i. xxxvii–xliii.

46 Ian Archer, 'The Nostalgia of John Stow', in D. L. Smith, R. Strier and D. Bevington, eds, *The Theatrical City: Culture, Theatre and Politics in London, 1576–1649* (Cambridge, 1995), pp. 17–34; Patrick Collinson, 'John Stow and Nostalgic Antiquarianism', in Julia Merritt, ed., *Imagining Early Modern London* (Cambridge, forthcoming).

REFERENCES AND FURTHER READING

Camden, William (1610). *Britannia*, tr. P. Holland. London.

Collinson, Patrick (1998). 'One of Us? William Camden and the Making of History: The Camden Society Centenary Lecture', *Transactions of the Royal Historical Society*, 6th ser., 8, 139–63.

Edelen, Georges (ed.) (1968, 1994). *The Description of England: The Classic Contemporary Account of Tudor Social Life by William Harrison*. Washington, DC and New York: The Folger Shakespeare Library and Dover Publications.

Ferguson, Arthur B. (1979). *Clio Unbound: Perception of the Social and Cultural Past in Renaissance England*. Durham, NC: Duke University Press.

——(1993). *Utter Antiquity: Perceptions of Prehistory in Renaissance England*. Durham, NC: Duke University Press.

Foxe, John (1583). *Actes and Monuments of Matters Most Speciall in the Church*. London: John Day. (Facsimile edition, CD-ROM, Oxford: Oxford University Press, 2000.)

Hanham, Alison (1975). *Richard III and his Early Historians, 1483–1535*. Oxford: Clarendon Press.

Hay, Denys (1952). *Polydore Vergil: Renaissance Historian and Man of Letters*. Oxford: Clarendon Press.

Helgerson, Richard (1992). *Forms of Nationhood: The Elizabethan Writing of England*. Chicago and London: University of Chicago Press.

Holinshed, Raphael (1587). *The First and Second Volumes of Chronicles*. London.

Jardine, Lisa and Grafton, Anthony (1990). ' "Studied for action": How Gabriel Harvey Read his Livy', *Past and Present*, 129, 30–78.

Kelley, Donald R. and Harris Sacks, David (eds) (1997). *The Historical Imagination in Early Modern Britain: History, Rhetoric, and Fiction, 1500–1800*. Cambridge: Cambridge University Press.

Kendrick, T. D. (1950). *British Antiquity*. Oxford: Clarendon Press.

Kingsford, C. L. (ed.) (1908). *A Survey of London by John Stow Reprinted From the Text of 1603*. Oxford: Clarendon Press.

Levy, F. J. (1967). *Tudor Historical Thought*. San Marino, CA: The Huntington Library.

Loades, David (ed.) (1997). *John Foxe and the English Reformation*. Aldershot: Ashgate.

MacCaffrey, Wallace T. (ed.) (1970). *William Camden, The History of the Most Renowned and Victorious Princess Elizabeth Late Queen of England: Selected Chapters*. Chicago and London: University of Chicago Press.

Manning, John J. (ed.) (1991). *The First and Second Parts of John Hayward's The Life and Raigne of*

King Henrie IIII. Camden 4th ser. 42. London: Royal Historical Society.

Parry, Graham (1995*). The Trophies of Time: English Antiquarians of the Seventeenth Century*. Oxford: Oxford University Press.

Parry, G. J. R. (1984). 'William Harrison and Holinshed's Chronicles', *Historical Journal*, 27.

——(1987). *A Protestant Vision: William Harrison and the Reformation of Elizabethan England*. Cambridge: Cambridge University Press.

Patterson, Annabel (1994). *Reading Holinshed's Chronicles*. Chicago and London: University of Chicago Press.

Sylvester, Richard S. (ed.) (1959). *The Life and Death of Cardinal Wolsey by George Cavendish*. Early English Text Society, no. 243.

Vickers, Brian (ed.) (1998). *Francis Bacon, The History of the Reign of King Henry VII*. Cambridge: Cambridge University Press.

Woolf, D. R. (1990). *The Idea of History in Early Stuart England: Erudition, Ideology, and 'The Light of Truth' from the Accession of James I to the Civil War*. Toronto: University of Toronto Press.

6

The English Language of the Early Modern Period

N. F. Blake

In reviewing the English language from 1550 to 1642, we must look both backwards and forwards; backwards, because that represents the foundation upon which the language of this period was built; and forwards, because, to understand the language of this period, we have to look through developments which have taken place in the language since then, particularly the rise of grammatical correctness from the late seventeenth century onwards. These are necessary steps, for as Granville-Barker (1932, p. 7) noted: 'The literature of the past is a foreign literature. We must either learn its language or suffer it to be translated.'

Let us begin by looking forwards. When you read a modern edition of a work written within this period, play, poem or prose text, there is a good chance that it will have its language modernized, with the spelling and punctuation made to fit modern conventions. The occasional word may retain an 'archaic' form, such as *holp* for the preterite or past participle instead of modern *helped*, though even such forms may be altered by some editors. The result is a text which seems to be modern, and inexperienced readers assume that, as the text looks modern, they may read it in the same way as a contemporary text. This can mislead the reader, especially as most editors of texts from this period are not expert in its language and so may fail either to realize the implications of their modernization with its potential ambiguities or to alert their readers to them. Take a simple example. The modern verbs *to price* and *to prize* were not distinguished in spelling at this time; to all intents and purposes they were the same verb. A modernizing editor has to make a choice as to which of the two is meant in any given context, on the assumption that the author meant one or the other rather than possibly both. A modern reader coming across either of the words in its modern spelling will not realize that the editor may have made the wrong choice or even that a choice is damaging, for to read the text one way or the other could have an impact on the general sense of the context.

Another difficulty was referred to in the first paragraph. During the course of the eighteenth and nineteenth centuries rules for the grammar of the English language were codified and, especially during the nineteenth century, their implementation was made prescriptive. The concept of correctness became important and is still influential today. As a professor of English language I am frequently asked what is the correct way of writing or saying something. This codification had not taken place in the Elizabethan–Jacobean period so there was much greater flexibility in usage and tolerance of diversity. Today we have clear ideas as to what is standard and what is non-standard, and we tend to look down on those who habitually use non-standard forms because to employ the standard is a mark of education and status. Hence those who do not use it are often considered uneducated and ignorant. These attitudes were beginning to emerge in this earlier period, but they were very far from being widely accepted. Provincial language may have been recognized as provincial, but that recognition did not carry with it the same lack of status as non-standard language does today. Sir Walter Ralegh is said to have used the Devon dialect throughout his life. As an example of flexibility one may note the way in which different prefixes and suffixes were freely attached to roots. An adjective like *wise* could be turned into a noun as *wiseness, wis(e)dom, wisehood* etc. We have reduced this variation to a single form, in this case *wisdom*. The earlier freedom was exploited by authors for the sake of variety and euphony – or simple unawareness. This means that the characters in literary works who commit malapropisms are only doing what everyone else did, but sometimes attached an inappropriate prefix or suffix to a root. The difference between what they were doing and what everyone else did was relatively small, and in some cases it may be difficult today to determine whether a malapropism was intended or not. We often assume today that characters who commit malapropisms were ignorant and stupid, but audiences or readers at that time may rather have thought that they were simply trying to emulate what everyone else was doing and occasionally overdoing it – a procedure which many of us follow even today! Especially with texts other than plays it is difficult to decide whether the form of a word with an unusual affix, which strikes us as 'incorrect', is to be taken at face value.

In syntax the language tolerated both double negatives and double comparatives, though these were being frowned on by some such as Ben Jonson and have since been eliminated from the standard written language, though not from speech. Thus it was perfectly acceptable to have such constructions as 'nor openly durst not command the murdering of his brother' (R. Greneway, *The Annals of Tacitus* (1597) 13.4.183) and 'other most ancientest authors' (G. Legh, *The Accedens of Armoury* (1597) preface). These constructions were subsequently regarded as illogical, because in Latin two negatives make a positive and because you cannot have the 'most' of something which is already superlative. But such constructions were freely used at this time for rhetorical ends, though forms with single negatives and comparatives were otherwise the norm. But the point to remark is that the variety in language use which existed then was accepted without any of the derogatory implications that have since become attached to variant, non-standard forms.

Our modern punctuation is grammatical and is intended to introduce clarity into the written language. The assumption is that what is written has a single meaning and the punctuation is designed to make that single meaning absolutely clear to the reader. Punctuation in the earlier period was often more rhetorical than grammatical, and ambiguity in meaning was appreciated and even cultivated. Furthermore, the development of certain grammatical words had not progressed as far as it has today so that the ability to indicate the interrelationship of clauses was not so easily achieved. This is still true of spoken English, but written English is something quite different. In spoken English we can still understand a causal relationship in 'Keep quiet; he's coming' and this was common in earlier written English. When in *Eastward Ho* Gertrude says 'I tell you I cannot endure it; I must be a lady' (1.2.17), we recognize the causal link despite the modern semi-colon, but other examples may be more difficult to recognize. We look for the same grammatical clues that we know today, and where they do not exist we either make faulty assumptions about the language or force it into an inappropriate grammatical strait-jacket. Assumptions about our own written language reinforced by modernization in editions may make us miss layers of meaning which writers in this period could achieve and aimed for.

It is time now to look backwards from this period to earlier stages of the language. In the Middle English period there was essentially no standard English, for if there was a standard it was Latin. French was used in many occupations, especially law. The onset of humanism meant that classical Latin replaced vulgar Latin so that Latin became a dead language, essentially with no spoken variety. As such it remained unchanging, and became a model for vernacular languages like English to emulate. But emulation was an unachievable goal, because speech means change and diversity; English could never be as fixed as Latin. At the same time French had ceased to be the first language of any Englishmen and it became a taught language, so it too ceased to be a competitor to English at the spoken level. But English speakers tended to regard their language as inferior to Latin and French, because they believed the former was regulated and fixed and the latter was more sophisticated and literary. They thought that English had to be improved and made a suitable vehicle for the highest literary expression. This led to an outpouring of comments about the shortcomings of English and to the publication of numerous books on rhetoric, spelling and grammar. The English language was a matter of great interest and concern to most educated speakers, but how to improve it was more difficult to agree on.

These factors influenced speech and spelling. People were becoming more conscious of linguistic varieties and their impact on status, and this was particularly so in London with its continuing influx of settlers from the provinces. All English varieties could be found there. This encouraged some to put a distance between themselves and their less desirable neighbours. French, which had been one way to exhibit linguistic and social superiority, was no longer viable as few people used it, and Latin was only for the highly educated. Hence speakers had to exploit the resources within the English language. One way of doing this was through pronunciation, as has remained true ever since. The movement in vowel sounds at this time, now referred to as the Great Vowel Shift, may represent attempts by established families in London to distance themselves from newcomers by altering the pronunciation of their long vowels. This change, by which long vowels were raised and the two high vowels diphthongized, is characteristic of this period, and has left the relation between English sounds and spellings out of line with those found in other European languages. The spelling of English vowels and diphthongs no longer represents a difference in length: the <ee> of *meet* (no longer [e:] but [i:]) is not a long form of the <e> of *met* [e]. But this change was erratic in its implementation and by no means a universal phenomenon, so there remained a plethora of different pronunciations in London with some speakers trying to distance themselves from others, not always successfully. This variety in pronunciation is significant, for poets exploited differing sounds for their rhymes and puns without necessarily attaching any suggestion of impropriety to these variants. Although some sounds were being preferred, it took time to make the rest seem unacceptable. Representations of different pronunciations are found from time to time, but the status of most variant forms is often difficult to ascertain, apart from the stage rustic dialect assumed by Edgar when faced with Oswald in *King Lear*.

As for spelling, one may note a bifurcation in usage between private and public documents. Compositors in printing houses gradually adopted preferred spellings, though each may have had a slightly different set of preferences, as is true of the compositors for Shakespeare's First Folio. But individuals writing privately were less motivated by the incipient standardization of spelling found in printed material. Queen Elizabeth's letters show an extraordinary range of spellings. The printing houses tended to reduce the number of variants in spellings, especially eliminating forms which were grossly provincial such as *xal* for *shall*. The amount of variation was reduced but not eliminated, and this reduction continued the process of standardization associated with two factors.

The first was the development of Chancery English, the spelling characteristic of Chancery documents. Documents issuing from the Chancery became increasingly homogeneous in their spelling through the elimination of unacceptable variants rather than through the promotion of preferred ones, and as such documents found their way throughout the country their conventions became well known. This spelling system gradually displaced the other systems which had been used in London, such as that found in the better Chaucerian manuscripts, and slowly made its way into much printed material. But this process was not completed till later in the seventeenth century. The second was the development of printing. Introduced into England by William Caxton in 1476, printing soon became the most important means of reproducing the written word, though copying of manuscripts still continued. However, the growth of printing was expedited with the dissolution of the monasteries by Henry VIII, since they had been the usual centres of producing the written word until then. Printing, it could be said, replaced the monastic scriptorium. It made the written word much cheaper, because more plentiful, and more uniform in its spelling. It also led to the greater disparity between what might be thought of as the preferred spelling system and other spellings. Official, public documents showed a higher degree of standardization, whereas private letters were more diverse in their spellings. This standardization in public writing meant that a distinction arose between the standard system and other systems, which were increasingly regarded as non-standard. It became possible to distinguish in writing among different speakers and registers by the use of variant spellings, for the approved spellings were increasingly regarded as the norm. In the texts of this period we see the use of various clipped or abbreviated forms, such as *spital* 'hospital' or *ne're* 'never', and some of these may be intended to promote a colloquial style to the language, though some forms were also used in poetry for their convenience in the metre.

To indicate that variety existed in the language of this period is not to imply that there were no preferred patterns of usage, for no language can be understood unless there is a consensus on the basic grammatical pattern behind it. We have variety today, though it is mostly manifest in the spoken language. The difference in this period is that the variety which existed was in a different relation to the preferred forms than is true of the relation between standard and non-standard varieties today. In order to understand how this may affect the way texts are edited we need to consider some aspects of the language.

In spelling the possessive or genitive of the noun was rarely indicated in writing through an apostrophe. This led to two interesting situations. After a word ending in <-s>, such as *Charles*, the genitive ending <-s> would be pronounced [iz], as it is today. But initial [h] at this time was regularly dropped in pronunciation by all speakers of the language so that the possessive pronoun *his* was also pronounced [iz]. In Modern English most people pronounce *Charles's* with [iz] and the *his* of 'What's his name' also as [iz], although many pretend that for the latter they actually say [hiz]. It is hardly surprising, therefore, that in this period many writers would spell the possessive of *Charles* as *Charles his*, for the spelling *Charles's* did not exist, as the apostrophe was not used for the possessive singular or plural. Any other spelling, such as *Charles* by itself or *Charless*, would have been ambiguous. The spelling *Charles his* is perfectly rational in this period but, because we think we always pronounce initial [h], we may regard it today as an aberration arising through ignorance. The second situation is the interpretation of final <-s> in the possessive at this time. This <-s> could represent both the subjective and the objective possessive and, as the apostrophe was not used for the possessive, there was no way of telling whether it represented the singular or plural possessive. Thus *my brothers murder* had four potential meanings: 'the murder by my brother', 'the murder by my brothers', 'the murder of my brother' and 'the murder of my brothers'. The context might help to elucidate which is meant, but in many texts the necessary clues may not be given, because the author knew what he meant. Even today most people are uncertain whether *wits* in the saying *at my wits end* is singular *wit's* or plural *wits'*. Modern editors make a choice when interpreting the possessive and there is often no way of guaranteeing that they have made the right one.

Let us now consider some aspects of syntax and morphology at this time. The Elizabethan period inherited a variety of forms from different parts of the country.

The old southern ending of the third person singular present indicative was <-(e)th>, but by the beginning of the sixteenth century the northern ending in <-(e)s> had made great inroads into southern writing so that two forms were available: *bringeth ~ brings*. The form in <-(e)th> was old-fashioned, but was used by dramatists and poets for rhyme, metre and possibly also to give a higher tone to a particular passage. It is difficult to decide how far a stylistic implication was attached to one ending compared with the other, though <-(e)s> is found more often in prose and <-(e)th> in verse. A pronunciation representing the written form <-(e)th> was evidently not usual in everyday speech, for many writers on the language noted that a word like *cometh* was pronounced as though written *comes*, but that would not prevent it having a certain prestige in written texts.

Another aspect of the verb forms is the use of the second person singular pronoun *thou* with its associated verb ending <-(e)st>. This was being replaced by *you* and the base form of the verb: *thou comest ~ you come*. It is frequently stated that there is a significant distinction in these two forms at this time, with *you* being the unmarked or neutral form and *thou* the marked one which was used to express intimacy, a threat or an insult. It is certainly possible to find examples which fall into this pattern, but there are also examples where it is difficult to find any justification for the use of one rather than the other. Furthermore, where plays exist in more than one contemporary edition, as is true of those Shakespeare plays which exist in quarto(s) and First Folio, compositors felt free to alter the occurrence of *you* or *thou* just as they did the endings <-(e)s> and <-(e)th>. Interpretation of these forms needs to be done cautiously, for it cannot be proved that all examples reflect the differences in politeness which is assumed today.

Syntactically, many of the expanded verb forms were not yet fully grammaticalized. This applies especially to forms with *do* and progressive forms like *he is coming*. Today we distinguish sentence types by restricting how a question, a command or a statement can be framed. Because so many inflections of the verb dropped out of the language, the base form of the verb became overloaded. Today a question must have either *do* or a part of the verb 'to be' with inversion of the subject: *Did he do it?*, *Was he doing it?* A command cannot have a subject, though it can have *do*: *Come here, Do come here*. A statement has its subject before the verb and the object after it. In other words *do* forms in all tenses and parts of the verb 'to be' in progressive tenses have been grammaticalized in negative and interrogative sentences so that one must use them in sentences like *He didn't do it* and *Is he coming?* In the earlier period both *do* and progressive forms were common but not yet obligatory, and it is not possible to tell whether they had a stylistic implication, though they were undoubtedly useful at a metrical level since they could provide an extra syllable. It is possible to think that the *do* forms were used to emphasize a point and thus to give it greater weight, for they occur frequently with verbs like *think* and *believe*, although as it seems that these forms grew through their use at a colloquial level it is possible to think that they had a colloquial tone. Because the *do* and the progressive forms were not yet grammaticalized and because a subject could still be used with imperatives, it was possible to have a question *Come you tonight?*, and an imperative *Come you tonight*. Equally it is possible to have a question *Do you speak?*, meaning 'Are you speaking?', and a command *Do you speak*, meaning 'Do speak'. This may make it difficult to interpret whether particular sentences in texts of this period are one or the other, for the context can often be interpreted in either way. But the interpretation which is chosen will naturally affect the way the context is understood. Similarly, the verb form *I come* can be interpreted as a simple present or as the progressive present 'I am coming', as is still true of many other modern European languages. To some today this use of *I come* can seem more decisive and authoritative than *I am coming*, but this might not be how the Elizabethans understood it.

The fall of inflections had another effect upon English. The old subjunctive was gradually dying out because, as it lost its inflections, most forms were the same as the indicative. At this time it differed from the indicative only in the second and third persons singular (though the first of these was also on its way out). This meant that the base form of the verb, say *hold*, could be used as the present subjunctive (often in expressions of wishing), the imperative, most forms of the present tense indicative, and the infinitive itself. This functional overload can make the interpretation of some clauses ambiguous and this too can affect the way passages are interpreted. In a sentence like *I pray you hold this cloak*, the *hold* could be understood as the infinitive '(to) hold', an imperative 'hold' or even a subjunctive 'may you hold', though this last is perhaps least likely. As the subjunctive lost its distinctive features, its functions were increasingly taken over by the modal auxiliaries, whose role was expanded. The preterites *could, might, should* and *would* drew away in meaning from their present forms *can, may, shall* and *will* to be used to indicate hypothetical situations or to express a wish. The development of modals was not without its own difficulties. These verbs were originally full lexical verbs and they retained these original meanings in part so that *can* meant 'to know (something)'. *Shall* implied obligation and *will* volition, but they gradually adopted the role of indicating futurity as well without entirely losing their former meanings. This led to a difficulty that is already evident in this period by which two verbs, *shall* and *will*, had to express three different concepts: obligation, volition and futurity; and this is one reason why later grammarians attempted to distinguish which person should be used with which verb to indicate futurity.

Another effect of the fall of the inflectional system was that word order became increasingly significant for the meaning of any clause so that the order subject–verb–object became the norm. However, the old order in English with, for example, the subject after the verb in clauses beginning with an adverb and the new influence of Latin which encouraged the object to precede the verb left their mark on the English of this period. A pattern was emerging for the approved structure of an English sentence, but the pull of that pattern was not so strong that it was followed universally. To break away from the pattern did not have the same implications as it does in Modern English. Subject, verb and object may appear in different places, and even in the verb group the auxiliary may come before the subject and object with the lexical verb after them. This created difficulties in comprehension which were compounded by another feature of the language so characteristic of the period, functional shift. As endings dropped out of the language, there were no endings which distinguished a noun from an adjective, an adjective from an adverb, or a noun from a verb. Today we expect an adjective to come before a noun, the subject to precede the verb which is then followed by the object, and an adverb to have an ending in <-ly>, though none of these features occurs regularly. But at this time authors were experimenting with the language and expanding the word stock through functional shift, by which they could use a noun as a verb, an adjective as an adverb, and so on. We accept *wondrous* as an adverb more readily in a clause like *He is wondrous clever*, than in *He does it wondrous*. Furthermore, the possibility of ordering the different elements of a clause in another order means that one cannot always tell which word is the subject and which the verb. In verse, whether in poetry or plays, this can be a problem as in the following passage:

> This Entertainment
> May a free face put on: deriue a Libertie
> From Heartinesse, from Bountie, fertile Bosome,
> And well become the Agent.
> > *(Winter's Tale*, 1.2.113–16)

I have quoted this passage from the First Folio as its spelling and punctuation make the passage more complicated to understand. Which is the subject of the first clause *Entertainment* or *free face*? Either would make sense. The second half of the sentence suggests that *free face* is the subject, though it is not absolutely decisive, and without this second clause the ambiguity could hardly be resolved. This type of difficulty is common enough in more elaborate verse, and is one reason why later periods insisted on a more regulated word order.

The significance of Latin as a dead language and its role as a model for English meant that some of its structures and lexis were imitated in English. This led to the growth in the number of conjunctions, especially subordinating ones, and the overall development of hypotaxis in sentence structure. Earlier English had tended to be paratactic in structure so that there were few subordinate clauses, but mainly main clauses either linked by a coordinate conjunction or by some punctuation which could suggest some form of subordination. Sentences in English became longer as the rise of subordination became more marked and this had the effect of making written English, especially prose, quite different from spoken English, and this distinction has remained with us. Equally, various constructions like the Latin ablative absolute were imitated in English so that the role of participles became more significant.

The feature of the language which strikes readers of texts from this period is the inventiveness of the vocabulary. This can be attributed in part to the growth of science and technology, such as new discoveries geographically and intellectually, and in part to the wish to make English as rich a language as Latin or French. The former introduced new words of a latinate nature or from modern languages in the old or new worlds. The latinate words often reduplicated words which already existed in the language, such as *vision* for *sight*. In addition to an increase in vocabulary through functional shift, many words were imported from other languages, new compounds were formed, and new affixes were attached to existing words. The growth in the English vocabulary shows a curve of expansion which peaked about 1600. It is not possible to give precise figures because what constitutes a new word is contentious, but this period witnessed the fastest growth in new vocabulary in the English language. The effect of this expansion was to produce a language with a very rich vocabulary and which often had more than one word for the same thing. At first there may simply have been a stylistic difference between a word of Latin origin and one of Anglo-Saxon origin so that *see* and *perceive* meant more or less the same thing, though they might occur in different contexts. But gradually the connotations would have led to a restriction in usage and overall meaning of these words. In other cases the new words drove the old words out of the language altogether, so that this period sees an increase in the obsolescence of native English words. A word like *swink* 'to work, labour' was in competition with *labour* itself. It first became restricted to the meaning 'to have intercourse' and, presumably as a result of this meaning, disappeared from the language altogether. Other examples of this process include *elde* ~ *age* and *siker* ~ *iwis* ~ *certainly*. Earlier poetry had been alliterative and this had encouraged a special type of vocabulary, often with many words with different initial sounds meaning the same thing. As rhyme and blank verse became the standard forms of poetic composition, this older vocabulary was no longer needed and this older vocabulary was abandoned. English as a language is not rich in rhymes, and this also led to the introduction of many words which were needed for poetic composition. Furthermore, the loss of inflections and the weakening of unstressed syllables meant that many English words ended up as monosyllables, and this also caused some problems for poetic composition, since monosyllables would usually carry stress. The need to create the interplay of stressed and unstressed syllables encouraged the import of foreign words which were usually polysyllabic and had this variety within themselves. There was also a growing interest in special vocabularies, inspired in part by dictionary making. The first monolingual dictionary did not appear till 1602 and, significantly, it dealt with the so-called 'hard words', usually learned and long words. Many early dictionaries were modelled on Latin–English dictionaries, and they simply Anglicized the Latin word and gave the English equivalent as the meaning. How far these words were used in the language is debatable. But these dictionaries encouraged the idea that long latinate words were desirable.

Perhaps the message of this chapter is that the language at this period was going through considerable changes in all aspects of grammar and vocabulary. Attitudes towards the language encouraged diversity and experimentation, which led to the inevitable reaction in a call for more regulation. We today have inherited that sense of regulation and we often approach texts from this period from that standpoint. It is necessary to understand the language of the period in its own terms if one is to appreciate the texts fully, which is the only way to come to an appreciation of the culture which produced them.

REFERENCES AND FURTHER READING

Abbot, E. A. (1870). *A Shakespearian Grammar*, 3rd edn. London: Macmillan.

Barber, C. (1997). *Early Modern English*, 2nd edn. Edinburgh: Edinburgh University Press.

Blake, N. F. (1983). *Shakespeare's Language: An Introduction*. London: Macmillan.

—— (1996). *Essays on Shakespeare's Language*. 1st Series. Misterton: Language Press.

Blank, P. (1996). *Broken English: Dialects and the Politics of Language in Renaissance Writings*. London: Routledge.

Bolton, W. F. (1992). *Shakespeare's English: Language in the History Plays*. Oxford: Blackwell.

Brook, G. L. (1976). *The Language of Shakespeare*. London: Deutsch.

Cercignani, F. (1981). *Shakespeare's Works and Elizabethan Pronunciation*. Oxford: Clarendon Press.

Cusack, B. (1998). *Everyday English 1500–1700: A Reader*. Edinburgh: Edinburgh University Press.

Dobson, E. J. (1968). *English Pronunciation 1500–1700*, 2nd edn. Oxford: Clarendon Press.

Donawerth, J. (1984). *Shakespeare and the Sixteenth-Century Study of Language*. Urbana and Chicago: University of Illinois Press.

Görlach, M. (1991). *Introduction to Early Modern English*. Cambridge: Cambridge University Press.

Graham-White, A. (1995). *Punctuation and its Dramatic Value in Shakespearean Drama*. London: Associated University Presses.

Granville-Barker, H. (1932). *Associating with Shakespeare*. London: Oxford University Press.

Hope, J. (1994). *The Authorship of Shakespeare's Plays: A Socio-Linguistic Study*. Cambridge: Cambridge University Press.

Houston, J. P. (1988). *Shakespearean Sentences: A Study in Style and Syntax*. Baton Rouge and London: Louisiana State University Press.

Hulme, H. (1962). *Explorations in Shakespeare's Language: Some Problems of Word Meaning in the Dramatic Text*. London: Longman.

Hussey, S. S. (1992). *The Literary Language of Shakespeare*, 2nd edn. London: Longman.

Jacobsson, B. (1951). *Inversion in English with Special Reference to the Early Modern English Period*. Uppsala: Almqvist and Wiksell.

Partridge, A. C. (1964). *Orthography in Shakespeare and Elizabethan Drama*. London: Edward Arnold.

Ronberg, G. (1992). *A Way with Words: The Language of English Renaissance Literature*. London: Edward Arnold.

Rudanko, J. (1993). *Pragmatic Approaches to Shakespeare: Essays on 'Othello', 'Coriolanus' and 'Timon of Athens'*. Lanham, New York and London: University Press of America.

Salmon, V. and Burness, E. (1987). *Reader in the Language of Shakespearean Drama*. Amsterdam: Benjamins.

Sugden, H. W. (1936). *The Grammar of Spenser's Faerie Queene*. Philadelphia: Linguistic Society of America.

Wyld, H. C. (1936). *A History of Modern Colloquial English*, 3rd edn. Oxford: Blackwell.

7

Publication:
Print and Manuscript

Michelle O'Callaghan

From Print to Manuscript?

In the mid-fifteenth century Johannes Gensfliesch zum Gutenberg invented movable type and the printing press in Mainz and the first printed book came off the press around 1455. This innovation in book production is recognized as one of the defining moments in the history of the west. Elizabeth Eisenstein has termed it a 'communications revolution' that radically altered the shape of early modern societies.[1] Print profoundly transformed social relations and systems of ideas and facilitated the religious, social, and economic changes that characterize the early modern period. Protestant reformers were quick to realize the potential of print in the propaganda war with the established church and claimed print as their own, a sign of God's grace. John Foxe spoke of 'the excellent art of printing most happily of late found out . . . to the singular benefit of Christ's Church' which would restore 'the lost light of knowledge to these blind times' and renew those 'wholesome and ancient writers whose doings and teachings otherwise had lien in oblivion' (Eisenstein 1979: 1.304). Early printed books were often distributed through the same channels and markets as other commodities and slowly transformed the exchange of information on which the new market economy depended. Print transformed the way that people thought about knowledge itself. It gave rise to new models of authorship, of literature, and made possible the concept of a national culture by standardizing and homogenizing vernaculars into mechanically reproduced print languages.

Print was introduced to England over a decade after it reached the major European cities. On 30 September 1476, the merchant William Caxton, who had already been trading in manuscript books and possibly early printed books in Bruges, opened a shop in the precincts of Westminster Abbey. His press in England was at work by 13 December 1476 and the next year he published *Dicts or Sayings*, the first known English printed book.[2] In this initial phase of print in England there was a great deal of continuity between manuscript and print publication. Although it is possible to talk about a print revolution, it would be mistaken to see this new technology as immediately sweeping away earlier methods of book production. In fact, the early printed book used the technology of manuscript production.[3] Printed books were prepared according to the same hierarchy of formats that had governed manuscript production: the folio was reserved for presentation copies and works intended for serious study; the quarto was more manageable and tended to be used for classical and new works; and the portability of the octavo made it ideally suited for secular and devotional works that were consulted every day.[4] The printed books produced by William Caxton imitated the form of the manuscript so that the early printed book in many cases looked physically similar to a manuscript book. It even seems to have been a common practice in the fifteenth century to produce manuscript copies of printed books; it is appropriate that there is a manuscript presentation copy of the first English book in print, *Dicts or Sayings*, that seems to have been made from the printed copy (Blake 1989: 413).

The growth of a print industry in England did not result in the demise of a manuscript culture. Nor should manuscript publication in the sixteenth and early seventeenth centuries be seen as the residue of an older marginal scribal culture that doggedly persisted alongside a new dominant print culture. Arthur Marotti has pointed out that the majority of literature written during the English Renaissance was produced for manuscript circulation rather than for print. Rather than print superseding manuscript, these two modes of publication 'not only competed but also influenced each other, and to a great extent, coexisted by performing different cultural functions'.[5] Manuscript provided a conscious alternative to print publication and a number of writers chose to circulate their poems in manuscript rather than commit them to print.

Manuscript Publication

The production and circulation of literary manuscripts in the Renaissance was part of the social life of the elite.[6] A folio manuscript book might be presented to a social superior to attract patronage, or a single sheet or small booklet of poems could be exchanged with a peer to reinforce a friendship. Harold Love has identified three distinct modes of publication within a manuscript economy: author publication, referring to texts written in the author's hand; entrepreneurial publication, designating works copied by a professional scribe; and user publication, those texts copied for the owner's use.[7] A representative case of author publication is that of John Donne whose poems were often written for and circulated amongst a circle of friends and patrons and were then transmitted through a process of copying to a wider audience. This type of social exchange functioned to bond individuals according to shared interests, be they literary or political, and was also part of the patron–client relationship.[8] A single poem or a volume of poems could be presented to a patron as a gift that the patron was required to acknowledge. Entrepreneurial publication had a different social value and function. Professional scribes worked either for patrons or for the book trade and they tended to produce specialist texts. Authors could commission copies of their poems for presentation to a patron and the high quality of the transcription would give the work the status of a work of art. Professional scribes also produced manuscript texts on a commercial basis: parliamentary speeches and proclamations, for example, were copied and sold at stationers' shops alongside printed legal texts.

Manuscript offered an alternative to print, but it would be misleading to distinguish between the two by confining manuscript publication to a private sphere and reserving the public sphere for print. Manuscript, as Love's model suggests, offered authors a variety of modes of publication. User publication would seem to indicate that the text was intended primarily for personal use and not for circulation outside the user's intimate social circle. At the other end of the spectrum, are the elaborate manuscript books, modelled on the form of the printed book, with title pages, dedications, page numbers, tag words, and so on, and produced either by professional scribes or authors. These books were typically presented as gifts to patrons and were often intended for circulation in the wider public domain. They were 'private,' as Margaret Ezell has argued, 'only in the sense that the author, not the bookseller, had control of the manuscript'.[9] This has particular implications for our understanding of the woman writer's participation in a manuscript culture. As Marotti points out, women writers 'were much more active in the system of manuscript transmission than in print' (p. 49).[10] He goes on to argue that women chose manuscript over print because manuscript maintained a degree of privacy and print culture was hostile to women (p. 61). Yet, this is not the argument that Ezell offers. She suggests that women writers' choice of manuscript was more complex and related to attitudes towards print that were as much class-based as determined by gender (p. 65). In the sixteenth century, the majority of women who published their verses in manuscript belonged to the elite and therefore shared the prejudices towards print of their male counterparts. Ezell concludes, on the basis of her study of Katherine Philips, that women's choice of manuscript was not due to a gender bar on print, but because of 'conservatism, the preference for an older form of literary transmission which left control of the text in the author's hand rather than signing it over to the bookseller' (p. 100).

Patterns of manuscript circulation can be mapped on to the pre-existing elite communities from which they originated. Moreover, it is argued that poems produced within a manuscript culture actively participate in the social world in which they were produced and retain the impression of this environment in a way that texts produced for a print market do not. Love uses the term 'scribal community' to refer to this phenomenon and argues that 'author and user publication, in such cases, was often a mode of social bonding whose aim was to nourish and articulate a corporate ideology' (Love 1993: 80–1). Verse miscellanies, which were often produced communally and circulated within families, literary circles, the universities, and Inns of Court, provide fruitful territory for mapping scribal communities (Marotti 1995: 17–25). The Inns of Court, in particular, provided an environment that was highly conducive to communal literary activity and many of the early seventeenth-century manuscript miscellanies can be traced to the Inns. Inns of Court men dominated the tavern societies that met at the nearby Mermaid, Mitre, and Devil and St Dunstan taverns. This is the context of a poem that records a *convivium philosophicum* held at the Mitre tavern around 1611 in honour of Thomas Coryate which was circulating in manuscript in this period. Authorship has been attributed to John Hoskins or Thomas Coryate but it is arguably more usefully viewed in terms of the collaborative activity of a scribal community. Guests at the *convivium philosophicum* included John Hoskins, Richard Martin, Christopher Brooke and John Donne, among others. This community was not a professional literary society but a political circle that brought together Members of Parliament, lawyers, members of Prince Henry's household and businessmen.[11] The verses associated with this scribal community dramatize the meetings of a group of like-minded men brought together by a mutual interest in wit, wine and politics. The exchange of texts amongst its participants describes a sphere of dialogue and debate in which there is a certain freedom of association because it takes place in manuscript and not in print. This type of liberty is encapsulated by Ben Jonson, who was closely associated with this community, in his 'Inviting a Friend to Supper'. Friendship, in this poem, describes a semi-private sphere where like-minded men can air political views that would be dangerous to voice in public.

Manuscript could be used not only to establish the type of relational networks described by scribal communities, it could also be used to gain and pass on information that was particularly sensitive or privileged and so restricted to a selected readership or its origin kept anonymous (Love 1993: 177). Publication through manuscript channels offered a way of getting material into the public domain that would have been censored if printed. Political libels, satires and epigrams that attacked figures in the public eye were often more suited to circulation in manuscript in a practical sense since they tended to be short and pithy, like this epitaph on Henry Howard, Earl of Northampton, 'Here lies my Lord of Northampton, His Majesty's earwig / With a papistical bald crown, and a Protestant periwig', and therefore easier and quicker to copy by hand than to commit to the printing press. These verses had a broader circulation that went beyond the confines of an elite culture. Pauline Croft has described libels as the 'spontaneous expressions of popular culture' that belonged to the 'tavern world of pamphlets, epigrams and satires rather than among factious courtiers'.[12] These two worlds were perhaps not so distinct, and verse libels were able to appeal to a range of social classes. Libels were often left in public places, nailed to the doors of public buildings, where they could be memorized or copied and so disseminated to a wider audience. They frequently employed a generalized language of sexual or political corruption that did not require a sophisticated grasp of politics to comprehend the general tenor of the libel, although others did require an insiders' knowledge of court politics.[13] For Pauline Croft, the 'multitude of spontaneous political libels', circulating amongst a socially diverse audience, demonstrates the existence of a public that was becoming increasingly interested in current affairs to the extent that one can begin to talk about an active public opinion that could be mobilized at particular historical moments (Croft 1991: 63, 68). Tom Cogswell has pushed this argument much further by suggesting that this market in political gossip 'was as close to a mass media as early Stuart England ever achieved'.[14]

It is not possible to talk of a socially homogeneous manuscript culture in the late sixteenth and early seventeenth centuries. As the circulation of political libels testifies, individuals and communities drawn from different social classes were able to participate in this type of politicized manuscript culture. Literacy was not necessarily a barrier to access to either a manuscript or a print culture since texts could be read aloud to a non-literate audience or repeated from memory and transmitted by word of mouth. There were other more socially exclusive scribal communities such as those that flourished at the court, but just as importantly there were forms of manuscript publication that participated alongside printed texts in the formation of the early modern public sphere.

Print Publication

By the early sixteenth century, St Paul's Churchyard in the City of London was the centre of the book trade. Booksellers had their stalls or shops in the churchyard and nearby streets and would be known by their device: Wynkyn de Worde's shop, for example, was to be found at the sign of the Sun in Fleet Street. They would advertize their wares by fixing the title pages of books to the wall or a nearby post.[15] Books were sold outside London at provincial markets and fairs, at shops established in the major provincial towns, and cheap pamphlets were sold by travelling peddlers along with other wares from the mid-sixteenth century. The availability of books encouraged literacy which in turn increased the demand for books. There was a rapid increase in the number of books published from the mid to the end of the sixteenth century: in the period from 1558 to 1579 3,850 titles were published which rose to 7,430 titles in the next two decades. This figure steadily increased to 9,740 titles in the years from 1605 to 1,624, and declined slightly in the period from 1625 to 1640 to 9,680.[16] This new market for books stimulated new print genres. The mid-seventeenth century, as Tessa Watts has pointed out, 'first saw the development of a specialist trade in books which were purposefully small, in order to reach a market of potential readers who had been hitherto unlikely to purchase the printed word, except in the form of a broadside ballad'.[17]

Print transformed early modern literary culture, giving poetry a new value as a national institution and generating new models of authorship. The beginning of the process of turning poetry into 'Literature' has been traced to the *Songs and Sonnets, written by the right honorable Lord Henry Howard late Earl of Surrey, and others*, published by Richard Tottel in 1557 and usually referred to as *Tottel's Miscellany*.[18] Tottel printed the lyrics of Wyatt, Surrey, and other early Tudor poets that had previously only circulated in manuscript. The movement from manuscript into print changed the relationship between the poem and the social context of its production. Print distanced these poems from the relatively cohesive scribal community that gave them meaning by making these poems available to a wider and more diverse print public. Because these poems tended to be context-oriented, when they were recontextualized within a print culture it became necessary to give them titles or preface them with explanatory material that would enable the reader to make sense of the fictional world of the poem. For example, Tottel gave Wyatt's poem, 'What needeth these threatening words and wasted wind?', the headnote 'To his love from whom he had her gloves' (Hedley 1988: 44). Other titles were of a more generic nature and related the poem to a set of stylized conventions associated with the lyric, such as 'The aged lover renounceth love', so that these conventions then became the context for interpreting the poem. The poem is thus distanced from its immediate social context and turned into 'Literature', an institution with its own sets of rules and conventions that give it authority (Marotti 1991: 219).

The Renaissance, Michel Foucault has argued, was 'the privileged moment of *individualization*' when the 'author' came into being.[19] For Elizabeth Eisenstein this modern concept of the author is made possible by print since it is dependent on the fixity and materiality that print confers on the book as opposed to the ephemerality of the compositions of a manuscript and oral culture (Eisenstein 1979: 21–2). Print did transform the relationship between the author and the text but models of authorship in the early modern period must be distinguished from the modern concept of the author who, in the words of Mark Rose, 'is conceived of as the originator and therefore the owner of a special kind of commodity, the work'.[20] For Rose the key term is 'proprietorship' which defines the author in terms of their ownership of their intellectual labour and was given an institutional and legal reality in modern copyright laws which date from the 1710 Statute of Anne.

In the early modern period, copyright, and the concept of literary property in general, took a different form which arguably had more to do with the business of the book trade than the literary creations of authors. The print trade gave the question of the ownership of books a particular urgency. Printing was an expensive business and the printer-bookseller needed to ensure that there was a viable market for the multiple copies the presses were producing that was not compromised by competition from other printers. A system of privileges and patents based on the royal prerogative began to be introduced in England in the early sixteenth century which were designed to regulate the book trade both in the interests of the crown and the printer-bookseller. The sole right to print was granted for whole classes of books, such as law books, Bibles, prayer books, almanacs and music books or for a single book. These class patents were taken out of the hands of individual printer-booksellers in 1603 to form the English stock which was controlled by the Stationers' Company. In 1557 a royal charter had been granted to the Worshipful Company of Stationers which gave the Stationers' Company a monopoly over the print trade that they vigorously policed over the next two hundred years (Feather 1988: 15–16, 29). From the mid-sixteenth century, the copyright to individual texts was also established through entry of the work or copy in the Stationers' Register. The majority of patents were granted to printer-booksellers, although there were a few cases where an author was granted a patent for an individual book. Samuel Daniel, for instance, was granted a ten-year exclusive right to print his *History of England* in 1612 by James I. This was not a recognition of the author's property rights over his own work, but rather the rewards of patronage (Rose 1993: 11–17). The author owned the physical manuscript of his work, but once it was sold to a printer-bookseller he or she had no further rights in the text. The printer-bookseller would then have the text or copy entered in the Stationers' Register which conferred exclusive rights of publication. It was usual in England in the sixteenth century to pay authors in kind rather than money, in other words, to give authors a number of copies of the printed work, which they could then sell on or use as presentation copies to attract patronage (Plant 1974: 217–18).

It has been argued that, because there was such a small return for authors from the print trade, the patronage system continued to dominate literary production in the sixteenth and seventeenth centuries (Rose 1993: 16–17). It was the case that the payment authors received was not enough to live on. That said, it was an income, and as such had its own professional value, and could be used to supplement other ventures (Feather 1988: 27). This is the period that sees the emergence of the professional writer who laboured with his pen and had a cultural as well as economic investment in the print trade. One such writer was George Wither. He did participate in a patronage economy, dedicating a number of his poems to patrons, yet he also envisioned a mode of literary production and a model of authorship that he saw as not just distinct from a patronage culture but fundamentally opposed to it. The epistles before the 1615 and 1617 editions of his *Fidelia* and his *Fair Virtue* (1621) offer accounts of the publishing process that begin to conceptualize a working relationship between the author and the print trade. The epistle, 'The Occasion the Private Impression of this Elegy', prefacing the first edition of *Fidelia*, describes a form of publishing that is financed by subscriptions from friends.[21] If a bookseller was unwilling to cover the cost of having an edition printed then an author could look to friends or other well-wishers to finance the publication. Wither privileges subscription publishing over aristocratic patronage since by '*this means . . . I shall be sure to be beholding to none, but those that love virtue or Me, and preserve the unequalled happiness of a free spirit: Whereas else being forced to accept some particular bounties . . . I might fall into the common baseness incident to flatterers*'.[22] Credit no longer derives from the author's ability to identify his name with a powerful patron, but from the author's own intellectual labour, from his cultivation of '*the Little World of my Mind*' (A5r), as Wither puts it, to make it profitable to others.

The venture did not go according to plan and the second edition of 1617 was put out by the bookseller George Norton who placed a new preface before the work explaining how Wither gave him permission to publish *Fidelia*. According to this epistle, Wither decided against collecting the subscriptions because he realized '*how far it would be from his disposition to lay claim to the proffered gratuities*'.[23] This sounds like a version of the conventional 'the stigma of print'. Since manuscript rather than print was deemed to be the proper channel of publication for gentlemen, writers attached explanatory epistles to their texts which related how they were forced to commit their writings to print against their better judgements and so were able to maintain or lay claim to the status of gentleman.[24] Rather expressing a true reluctance to print, it is perhaps best read as a trope that enables the writer to negotiate his entry into the literary marketplace by asserting the cultural value of his text. Norton goes on to explain that Wither then sold him the copy on the strict condition that in the printing of the text he '*carefully respect his credit*', that is, his name and reputation invested in the quality of the printed text. The sale of the copy to Norton does not seem to have ended Wither's interest in the text and this epistle acts as a type of contract between author and publisher. John Marriot's epistle, 'The Stationer to the Reader', appended to *Fair Virtue*, can also be read as an informal contract and, in fact, was ghost written by Wither. Marriot explains how he entered the copy in the Stationers' Register and intended 'to publish it, without further inquiry', however the book bore 'so much resemblance of the Maker' and he discovered 'to whom it most properly belonged' that he felt obliged to get the author's permission to publish his book. These 'stationer' epistles do not have the status of accurate reflections of the publishing process, although they do have an authenticity. Rather, they construct an idealized professional relationship between the author and the bookseller that is offered as a model for future practice. These epistles replace the dedication to the patron so that Wither's primary relationship is no longer to a patron but to his publisher, and they construct a publishing history in which the author takes on a new professional agency.

In 1623, Wither was offered an opportunity to make a substantial income from the print trade when he was granted a royal patent by James I which gave him the rights to his *Hymns and Songs of the Church* for fifty years and required that it be bound with every copy of the English Psalter.[25] The granting of the patent was an act of patronage, but Wither's vigorous defence of it was an expression of his own professional interest in the book trade. Stationers refused to comply with the patent as it added to the cost of the psalter and Wither was to receive the same amount for each sheet of his *Hymns and Songs* as they did for each sheet of the psalter. Yet, Wither's battle with the Stationers' Company over his patent appears to have been fought for more than profit. The patent to the English Psalter itself was part of the English Stock whose shares were controlled by the Master and Wardens of the Stationers' Company (Feather 1988: 34–7). Wither may have had a hand in a 1621 petition to Parliament by freemen and journeymen printers against this monopoly which concentrated power and wealth in the hand of the company elite to the exclusion of the majority.[26] His *The Scholars' Purgatory, Discovered in the Stationers' Commonwealth*, printed by the 'Honest Stationers', likened the Stationers' Company's control over the print trade to a tyranny over learning and formulated an account of the author's right to his intellectual labour based on a model of property inheritance – the rights to the book should first go to the elder brother, the author, then to the younger brothers, the printer, bookbinder and bookseller (p. 31).

It has long been argued women's gender acted as a constraint on their entry into the public domain of print. One version of this argument is that women by making their writings public transgressed the dictum of 'chaste, silent, and obedient', which rests on an analogy between women's speech and female sexuality, and so were left open to accusations of promiscuity. This negative view of women who printed their writings was available in the Renaissance; however, we perhaps should see it as the 'extreme end of an ideological spectrum', as Margaret Ferguson has suggested, rather than accepting it as the norm.[27] As we have seen in relation to manuscript, the relationship between gender and publication is more complex than this type of repressive hypothesis suggests. 'Patriarchal sentiments', as Ezell has pointed out, 'may have dissuaded some women from publishing their writings – along with reasons of geography, social status, and expense, which also deterred male writers – but it did not stop the act of writing itself' (p. 82). As this suggests, when looking at the woman writer's relationship to print, it is necessary to consider the way that gender is mediated by geography, particularly since the print trade in this period was centred in London, socially determined attitudes towards print, and financial constraints, given that in order to get a publisher to take on the expense of publishing a text either there needed to be a market or the author had to subsidize the cost of publication, often with the support of a patron.

The first professional woman literary writer, Isabella Whitney, who published two poetry collections, *The Copy of a Letter Lately Written in Meter, by a Young Gentlewoman: to her Unconstant Lover* (1567) and *A Sweet Nosegay: or Pleasant Posy: Containing a Hundred and Ten Philosophical Flowers* (1573), appears to have been particularly well placed socially and geographically to take advantage of the new print culture. Like George Wither, Isabella Whitney came from a lower gentry family and moved from Cheshire to London to work as a lady's companion, a position that she later lost. Although she claimed to have turned to print out of financial necessity, her motivations seem to have been more complex and may have included literary ambitions since a number of the verse epistles addressed to friends and fellow authors, such as Thomas Berry, in *A Sweet Nosegay* indicate that she was part of a circle that engaged in literary exchanges. Other members of her family had literary pretensions; her brother, Geoffrey Whitney, followed in her footsteps, publishing his *A Choice of Emblems* in 1586. Isabella Whitney appears to have had a very good working relationship with her printer, Richard Jones, who published both her collections, and unusually for authors of this period she declared her respect for those in the print trade, saluting 'all the bookbinders by Paul's / because I like their art', in her London poem, 'Will and Testament', which ends *A Sweet Nosegay*, although her greatest debt is to 'my Printer' to whom 'I will my friends their books to buy of him, with other ware'.[28] Jones specialized in popular manuals and poetic miscellanies, genres that had a wide readership ranging from the gentry and merchant classes to the urban artisans. Whitney's volumes were similarly designed to appeal to this broad audience; they were printed in cheap pamphlet form and she tends to popularize formal literary genres by adopting a didactic, moralizing tone, simple verse forms, and a plain and often colloquial style. It is possible that Jones may have commissioned Whitney to write her second collection *A Sweet Nosegay*, a versification of Hugh Plat's collection of proverbs, *The Flowers of Philosophy*, published in the previous year. Plat's volume may have attracted both Jones and Whitney as these type of collections of moral commonplaces were popular with readers and so highly profitable.

It should be said that Whitney is a relatively unusual figure for this period in that it was rare for women to publish original volumes of poetry, although Aemilia Lanyer, who came from a similar social background, does offer an interesting parallel to Whitney.[29] Religious and devotional works make up the largest category of women's printed texts, in keeping with their role as spiritual guides within the household. One of the growth areas in women's publications in the seventeenth century was the advice and skills book, which included books on cookery, medicine, household management and midwifery. Although before the mid-seventeenth century, the vast majority of these books were written by men for a female readership, after 1640 they began to be written by women in increasing numbers. The seventeenth century saw a dramatic increase in the number of women in print. This was due to the rapid expansion of the public sphere during the English Revolution and, more generally, to improvements in literacy rates amongst women, which gave more women access to print both as producers and consumers as the century progressed.[30]

Censorship

As the number of presses increased and books became available to a wider audience both the state and those involved in the print trade pushed for regulation of the new industry. The royal charter granted to the Stationers' Company in 1557 formalized the company's role in the censorship of 'scandalous, malicious, schismatical and heretical' books by restricting the ownership of presses to members of the company, which effectively centralized the print trade in London making it easier to control, and by involving the company in pre-publication licensing. This latter arrangement was clarified by the injunctions issued by Elizabeth I in 1559 which required that all new books had to be approved by either six Privy Councillors or the Archbishop of Canterbury and the Bishop of London, or the Vice Chancellors of Oxford or Cambridge, if this was the place of publication (Feather 1988: 31–2). In theory, this meant that the stationer was required to take the manuscript to the official licenser to get it authorized before entering it in the Stationers' register to secure the copyright. The charter also granted the company the right of search and seizure of illegal books. This right, however, tended to be used not in the pursuit of seditious works but in cases where copyrights or patents were being contravened or non-members were operating illegal presses. This has led Sheila Lambert to argue that regulation of press in this period had less to do with censorship than with the economics of the book trade and she criticizes the studies of Annabel Patterson and Christopher Hill for adopting a repressive model of censorship that assumes that there was 'a government policy of all-pervasive censorship to prevent all expression of unorthodox opinion' (Lambert 1987: 1).[31] Cyndia Clegg similarly argues that press censorship should not be seen as the expression of a coherent crown policy but as a fragmentary and 'pragmatic situational response to an extraordinary variety of events', and she points to the gap between mechanisms for the control of the press and the practice of systematically using these mechanisms. Stationers, for example, frequently violated licensing ordinances by not getting texts authorized or even entering them in the register, yet fines were rarely imposed.[32]

For Clegg, Elizabethan press censorship is characterized by its heterogeneity rather than uniformity; she describes it as a 'crazy quilt of proclamations, patents, trade regulations, judicial decrees, and Privy Council and parliamentary actions patched together by sometimes common and sometimes competing threads of religious, economic, political and private interests' (Clegg 1997: 5). This line of argument can be elaborated to suggest that censorship itself was multiform in the sense that there was not one censorship that served the whole state but rather multiple censorships that operated in the service of a range of interest groups including the crown, the peerage, the City of London, and extending to other individuals and communities operating at a local level.[33] This decentred model also implies that censorship did not only operate through the regulation of the press, particularly since books tended to come to the attention of the authorities after they had been published rather than before, but also operated through other mechanisms, such as laws relating to defamation. The authorities were particularly concerned with open criticism of those in the public eye, such as Privy Councillors and other peers. Sir Edward Denny, for example, was able to get Lady Mary Wroth's *Urania* withdrawn on the grounds of libel. Henry Howard, the Earl of Northampton, was notoriously sensitive to criticism in the years before his death in 1614 and brought a number of cases before the Star Chamber according to the statute of *scandalum magnatum* which enabled actions to be brought by peers who had been defamed. Censorship in these cases was directed against the spoken word and Northampton seems to have been particularly concerned with sermons. It has been claimed that no professional author was punished for libel under James (Wheale 1999: 72), however there does seem to be at least one exception. In 1614, George Wither was imprisoned by order of the Privy Council for an unnamed offence. In his defence, *A Satire: Dedicated to his Most Excellent Majesty*, Wither says he was punished for libelling a 'great man' at court in his *Abuses Stript, and Whipt* – probably the Earl of Northampton, given that the warrant was issued from Northampton House. It is possible to argue that this demonstrates how censorship operated at a local level, in this case in the interests of an individual peer, rather than in the service of the crown, since Northampton was more concerned with his reputation than in protecting the state against subversion. Yet, Northampton saw his interests as a peer of the realm as closely allied with those of his sovereign, moreover, *scandalum magnatum* itself was an extension of the royal prerogative.

Although censorship was multiform, one can trace broad patterns of interest that coa-
lesce into a loose ideology.

Critics, such as Janet Clare, have similarly argued for a 'dynamic censorship' in
relation to the theatre.[34] The main responsibility for the censorship of plays lay with
the Master of the Revels. The office had been extended by Elizabeth I in 1581 to
include the regulation of the new commercial theatres and the Master of the Revels
was given new powers to license and suppress plays and to imprison offending players
and playwrights. Censorship, in this case, was pre-production in that it was the play-
book and not the play in performance that was examined by the Master of the Revels.
This meant that there were opportunities for evasion. Plays could be performed in a
quite different form than the play that went before the censor, or the text could be
given topical inflections in performance through gesture, mimicry and so on (Clare
1990: 213). In these instances, censorship was post-performance. The Privy Council
attempted to control the theatres by issuing proclamations prohibiting playing and
ordering playhouses to be closed or even demolished. Topics that would draw the
attention of the Master of the Revels and the Privy Council were those which touched
on the authority of the crown, in ascending order, sedition and rebellion, foreign policy
and the reputation of the court. Despite these areas of political sensitivity, theatrical
censorship did not operate according to a coherent and consistently maintained ideological agenda. Clare has argued that there were 'no consistent political, moral, or
cultural criteria to be discerned; instead, the historical moment determined the
censor's response in each case' (Clare 1990: 211–12). The result is a fluid and historically located model of censorship.

There are dangers in completely rejecting a model of state censorship. As a result,
censorship can become so anatomized and depoliticized, reduced to the micro-level of
individual interests, that the wider picture is lost; or censorship is deemed to be so
inefficient that one is left with the impression of a state that is by default capable of
tolerating all dissenting viewpoints. The early modern state did act against treason
and religious dissent and Puritans and English Catholics were subject to constant
policing. As we have seen, libellous verses circulated widely and anonymously in manuscript rather than print as a means of avoiding detection and prosecution. Radical
political and religious texts were printed in the Low Countries and then smuggled
back into England (Wheale 1999: 76–7). It is necessary to retain a sense of censorship as a repressive force, but we also need to recognize how it could be productive.
Clegg's study of the Martin Marprelate pamphlets of 1588 to 1589 offers a vivid
example of how writers and communities were not passive subjects of censorship but
actively interpreted laws, in this case laws on libel, and constructed models of censorship in order to provoke public debate (Clegg 1997: 170–97). As she recognizes,
a repressive model of censorship first began to appear in the texts of religious reformers and writers such as Spenser and Milton (and Wither) who counterposed censorship to ideals of free expression and liberty of conscience (p. 218) and in doing so
began to construct a model of a public sphere. It is in this sense, just as much as in
terms of regulation, that censorship is central to the formation of a print culture.

NOTES

1 Eisenstein, Vol. 1, p. 44.
2 Feather, pp. 8–11.
3 For a comparison of print and manuscript production, see Blake.
4 Chartier, 'Introduction', p. 2.
5 Marotti, pp. xii, 1.
6 See COURT AND COTERIE CULTURE.
7 Love, pp. 46, 51–83.
8 See DONNE AND HIS CIRCLE.
9 Ezell, pp. 66–8.
10 See DIARIES and LETTERS.
11 On this scribal community, Shapiro; Michelle O'Callaghan (1998), '"Talking politics": Tyranny, parliament, and Christopher Brooke's *The ghost of Richard the third* (1614)'. *The Historical Journal*, 41, 102–5.
12 Croft, pp. 62–3.
13 Bellany, pp. 289–92.
14 Cogswell, p. 287.
15 Bennett, pp. 260–1.
16 Wheale, p. 6.
17 Watts. p. 258; see POPULAR VERSE.
18 On print culture's institutionalization of lyric poetry, see: Marotti, pp. 212–90; and Hedley.
19 Foucault, p. 141.
20 Rose, p. 1.
21 Lindenbaum has singled out Wither as the author 'who *almost* invented the subscription method of publication' with this edition of *Fidelia* (p. 135).
22 George Wither (1615), *Fidelia* (A5v–6r) London.
23 Wither (1617), *Fidelia* (A3r) London.
24 J. W. Saunders. 'The Stigma of Print: A Note on the Social Bases of Tudor Poetry'. *Essays in Criticism*, 1, 139–64.
25 Pritchard; Creigh.
26 Sheila Lambert (1987), 'The Printers and the Government, 1604–1637', in Myers and Harris (1987), p. 12.
27 Krontiris, pp. 17–19; Ferguson, p. 145.
28 See THE LITERATURE OF THE METROPOLIS.
29 See Lanyer's 'DESCRIPTION OF COOKHAM' and Jonson's 'TO PENSHURST'.
30 Tebeaux. Literacy rates are notoriously difficult to determine and means of assessment can be biased against women (Ferguson, pp. 146–8). It should also be remembered that literacy levels for both men and women remained low in social groups below that of the urban artisan and the rural yeoman. See Literacy and Education.
31 See also the criticisms of new historicism's treatment of censorship in Clare (1997).
32 Clegg, pp. xii, 4–5, 7, 19.
33 Leeds Barroll (1998), 'Inventing the Unspeakable: Censorship as a Cultural Practice', unpublished paper delivered at Reading Conference.
34 Clare (1990), p. 211, and Clare (1997), pp. 174–5.

REFERENCES AND FURTHER READING

Beal, Peter (1998). *In Praise of Scribes: Manuscripts and Their Makers in Seventeenth-century England*. Oxford: Clarendon Press.

Bellany, Alastair (1994). '"Raylinge Rymes and Vaunting Verse": Libellous Politics in Early Stuart England, 1603–1628'. In Kevin Sharpe and Peter Lake (eds), *Culture and Politics in Early Stuart England* (pp. 285–310). Basingstoke and London: Macmillan.

Bennett, H. S. (1965). *English Books and Readers, 1558 to 1603*. Cambridge: Cambridge University Press.

Blake, N. F. (1989). 'Manuscript to print'. In Jeremy Griffiths and Derek Pearsalls (eds), *Book Production and Publishing in Britain, 1375–1475* (pp. 403–32). Cambridge: Cambridge University Press.

Chartier, Roger (ed.) (1989). *The Culture of Print: Power and the Uses of Print in Early Modern Europe*. Princeton: Princeton University Press.

Clare, Janet (1990). *'Art Made Tongue-tied by Authority': Elizabethan and Jacobean Dramatic Censorship*. Manchester and New York: Manchester University Press.

—— (1997). 'Historicism and the question of censorship in the Renaissance', *English Literary Renaissance*, 27, 155–76.

Clegg, Cyndia Susan (1997). *Press Censorship in Elizabethan England*. Cambridge: Cambridge University Press.

Cogswell, Thomas (1995). 'Underground Verse and the Transformation of Early Stuart Political Culture'. In Susan Amussen and Mark Kishlansky (eds), *Political Culture and Cultural Politics in Early Modern England* (pp. 277–300). Manchester and New York: Manchester University Press.

Creigh, Jocelyn (1980). 'George Wither and the Stationers: Fact and Fiction'. *Papers of the Bibliographical Society of America*, 74, 49–57.

Croft, Pauline (1991). 'The Reputation of Robert Cecil: Libels, Political Opinion and Popular Awareness in the Early Seventeenth Century', *Transactions of the Royal Historical Society*, 1, 43–69.

Dutton, Richard (1991). *Mastering the Revels: The Regulation and Censorship of English Renaissance Drama*. London: Macmillan.

Eisenstein, Elizabeth (1979). *The Printing Press as an Agent of Change: Communications and Cultural Transformation in Early Modern Europe*. 2 vols. Cambridge: Cambridge University Press.

Ezell, Margaret (1987). *The Patriarch's Wife: Literary Evidence and the History of the Family*. Chapel Hill and London: University of North Carolina Press.

Feather, John (1988). *A History of Book Publishing*. London, New York and Sydney: Croom Helm.

Ferguson, Margaret (1996). 'Renaissance Concepts of the "Woman Writer"'. In Helen Wilcox (ed.), *Women and Literature in Britain, 1500–1700* (pp. 143–68). Cambridge: Cambridge University Press.

Foucault, Michel (1979). 'What Is an Author?' In Josué V. Harari (ed.), *Textual Strategies: Perspectives in Post-structuralist Criticism* (pp. 141–60). London: Methuen.

Hedley, Jane (1988). *Power in Verse: Metaphor and Metonymy in the Renaissance Lyric*. University Park, Pennsylvania and London: Pennsylvania State University Press.

Krontiris, Tina (1992). *Oppositional Voices: Women as Writers and Translators of Literature in the English Renaissance*. London and New York: Routledge.

Lindenbaum, Peter (1991). 'John Milton and the Republican Mode of Literary Production', *Yearbook of English Studies*, 2, 121–36.

Love, Harold (1993). *Scribal Publication in Seventeenth-century England*. Oxford: Clarendon Press.

Marotti, Arthur (1995). *Manuscript, Print, and the English Renaissance Lyric*. Ithaca and London: Cornell University Press.

Myers, Robin and Harris, Michael (eds) (1987). *Aspects of Printing from 1600*. Oxford: Oxford Polytechnic Press.

—— (eds) (1992). *Censorship and the Control of Print in England and France 1600–1910*. Winchester: St Paul's Bibliographies.

Plant, Marjorie (1974). *The English Book Trade*, 3rd edn. London: Allen and Unwin.

Pritchard, Alan (1963). 'George Wither's Quarrel with the Stationers: An Anonymous Reply to *The Schollers Purgatory*', *Studies in Bibliography*, 14, 27–42.

Rose, Mark (1993). *Authors and Owners: The Invention of Copyright*. Cambridge, MA and London: Harvard University Press.

Shapiro, I. A. (1950). '"The Mermaid Club"', *Modern Language Review*, 45, 7–10.

Saunders, J. W. (1951). 'The Stigma of Print: A Note on the Social Bases of Tudor Poetry', *Essays in Criticism*, 1, 139–64.

Tebeaux, Elizabeth (1997). 'Women and Technical Writing, 1475–1700: Technology, Literacy, and Development of a Genre'. In Lynette Hunter and Sarah Hutton (eds), *Women, Science and Medicine 1500–1700* (pp. 29–59). Stroud: Sutton Publishing.

Watts, Tessa (1991). *Cheap Print and Popular Piety, 1550–1640*. Cambridge: Cambridge University Press.

Wheale, Nigel (1999). *Writing and Society: Literacy, Print and Politics in Britain, 1590–1660*. London and New York: Routledge.

Woudhuysen, H. R. (1996). *Sir Philip Sidney and the Circulation of Manuscripts, 1558–1640*. Oxford: Clarendon Press.

8
Literacy and Education
Jean R. Brink

We do not know how many people could read in the sixteenth and early seventeenth centuries. There is virtually no reliable evidence enabling us to draw statistical conclusions about mass literacy in the English Renaissance. We do know that William Shakespeare – and those fortunate enough to attend an Elizabethan or Jacobean grammar school were well educated. They were literate in English when they entered school, and at school they learned Latin, were introduced to Greek, and in some instances were exposed to Hebrew. They studied Greek and Roman history and literature in texts written in those languages and were trained to write and speak Latin.

The printed word fascinated early modern society in part because of the phenomenal impact of the printing press; books previously produced laboriously in scriptoria and monasteries could be mass produced for the first time. Religion also offered incentives for literacy. The Protestant Reformation coincided with and fuelled the development of printing. Sectarian reformers, or even Puritan critics of the established clergy, could enlist print in their service, produce 1,500 copies of a pamphlet, and so rapidly disseminate their views to a popular audience. In the aftermath of the translation of the Bible into English, the Protestant clergy urged their congregations to learn to read so that they would have access to the Holy Scripture; if literacy could not insure their salvation, reading texts might make their parishioners less susceptible to error. Knowledge of the Bible was a blessing to the ungodly as well as the godly. A thief or murderer could plead 'benefit of clergy' and have his sentence commuted.

For a criminal, the capacity to read and translate a sentence from the Latin Bible could figure literally as a matter of life or death. The illiterate were sent to the gallows while the literate were merely branded. Lawrence Stone estimates that 47 per cent of the criminal classes were literate, but David Cressy, in his extremely influential study of literacy, has revised this estimate arguing that the Middlesex records show that 32 per cent of the capital felons under Elizabeth and 39 per cent under James successfully claimed benefit of clergy.[1] Even these revised statistics suggest that criminals were as, or more, literate than the population at large.

Benefit of clergy may even have had a lasting impact on literary history. Early in his career, two days after the opening of his *Every Man in His Humour*, Ben Jonson killed Gabriel Spencer, who was a member of the Lord Admiral's Men, the company of Philip Henslowe. Henslowe, whose *Diary* is the source of much that we know about Renaissance drama, reported news of the duel to Edward Alleyn, his son-in-law. He describes Jonson, not as a playwright, but as a bricklayer, an uncelebrated occupation even among the trades: 'I have lost one of my company, which hurteth me greatly – that is, Gabriel, for he is slain in Hogsden Fields by the hands of Benjamin Jonson, bricklayer.'[2] Jonson was convicted and left the prison a branded felon but, because he could read Latin, escaped the gallows.

Renaissance educators, most of whom had received the traditional Christian humanist education in the Bible and the classics, were biased in favour of their own educational background. They also advocated educating the poor as well as the rich, women as well as men. In his *Utopia* Sir Thomas More envisions an educated society in which all classes study literature. Less than a century later, however, Sir Francis Bacon counsels James I against increasing educational opportunities. By 1611 Bacon subscribed to the opinion that were too many grammar schools and that an excessive number could be dangerous: 'Many persons will be bred unfit for other vocations, and unprofitable for that in which they are brought up, which fills the realm of indigent, idle and wanton people which are but *materia rerum novarum*' (revolutionaries, lit. 'innovators').[3] In the decades after the Civil War most people were even less progressive about educating the poor. They feared that to overproduce intellectuals by educating the humbly born beyond their station in life would breed social unrest. Lawrence Stone has concluded that in quantitative terms, it was not until World War I that English higher education was as egalitarian as it was in the 1630s and that it was not until after World War II that social elites were as committed as they had been in the sixteenth and early seventeenth centuries to educating the lower classes.[4]

Substantive answers to social questions, such as who should be educated and to what ends, are not always easy to find, but the answers, even when they appear to be factual, are always difficult to interpret. For example, in the 1543 'Act for the Advancement of True Religion' the government of Henry VIII spelled out the dangers of extending literacy to women and the lower classes: 'No women nor artificers, prentices, journeymen, serving men of the degrees of yeomen or under, husbandmen, nor labourers' were to be permitted to read the Bible in English.[5] Unless there were a threat to religious and social stability because increasing numbers of women and labourers had become literate, a decree of this kind seems pointless. It is also possible that literacy was a class and gender marker and that specific prohibitions against female literacy were reminders of status and endorsements of the principle that women were to be subordinate to men just as servants were subject to their masters and the lower classes were expected to defer to the gentry.

David Cressy's statistical study of literacy in the English Renaissance has suggested that 70 per cent of the men were illiterate on the eve of the Civil War, and that nearly all women and labourers were illiterate (pp. 55–9). An influential study of playgoing in Shakespeare's London uses these statistics to claim that women were a significant presence in the theatres and that their presence indicates that audiences were illiterate:

> The high proportion of women at the playhouses testifies to the popularity of playgoing for the illiterate, since few women of any class, even in London, could write their names. Illiteracy among women in the country as a whole approached 90%, and did not drop significantly until the last quarter of the seventeenth-century.[6]

Cressy's figures derive from statistical analysis of the relative percentages of people signing their names with a mark or signature in public documents (Cressy, 55–9). A signature is interpreted as evidence of functional literacy – the ability to read. Conversely, it is assumed that the illiterate signed with their marks. John Shakespeare, William's father, for example, is usually assumed to be illiterate because he signed documents with a mark.

Conclusions drawn from these statistical studies have been widely accepted but need to be critically evaluated. It is generally assumed that the majority of people were illiterate and that nearly all women were. These data have been legitimately criticized on the grounds that reading and writing were taught separately and that many more people may have been able to read than to write. In addition, when the statistics are based on wills, it is important to consider that people drawing up their wills were likely to be elderly or infirm and so more likely to sign with a mark than a signature. When statistics are derived from marks on political testimonials, such as loyalty oaths, marks may have been preferred over signatures because they conferred more anonymity.

While it seems reasonable to assume that lower-class women, like lower-class men, were illiterate, the assumption that women were illiterate irrespective of class is troubling. Occupations, such as printer, baker, bricklayer, can be used to differentiate men, but are of less value in differentiating women who were more likely to have been employed in the home. The assumption that over 90 per cent of the women were illiterate would be more persuasive if it were based on selected samples. It would be significant, for example, if it could be shown that 90 per cent of the women named as executors of their husband's estates were illiterate or if a high percentage of maids of honour serving at court were unable to write their own names. It is also important to keep in mind that women are likely to be under-represented in most data collected from public documents. Women made up only one-fifth of the legal depositions in rural areas, but the figures for London are much higher. Nearly 50 per cent of the depositions in London courts were made by women, the majority being described as wives or widows (Cressy, 145–7).

Even in studies of male literacy we lack data samples that would enable us to differentiate one decade from another. In consequence, the sixteenth and seventeenth centuries are sometimes treated as a vast and unchanging backdrop to social change. As David Cressy acknowledges, no public documents survive from the sixteenth century, which can be used for generalized statistical studies of literacy. The oath for the establishment of the king's succession of 1534 was not universally administered. It is not until over a century later that suitable evidence is forthcoming. The Protestation Oath of 1641 is the starting point for most discussions of seventeenth-century literacy. By March 1642 almost everyone, *who was a male* and over eighteen, had been given an opportunity to sign his name or mark to the Protestation Oath (Cressy, 66–8). This oath merely supported Protestantism, but the more radical vow and convenant which followed held that there had been a traitorous and popish plot to subvert reformed religion and liberty. Summarising this data, Cressy concludes that the evidence for male literacy in the 1640s is based on the signatures and marks of more than 40,000 men from over 400 parishes in twenty-five counties; however, he adds the important qualification that this sample was not scientifically constructed and that the resulting statistics probably underestimate the literacy in urban as opposed to rural England. According to Cressy, statistical studies indicate an overpowering stratification by social class and gender: 'The gentry and clergy were overwhelmingly literate; tradesmen and yeomen fell in the middle; husbandmen, labourers, and women were massively illiterate' (Cressy, 106).

Statistical studies of literacy are based on incomplete data, but the same holds true for other quantitative approaches to estimating the numbers of those receiving an education in the sixteenth and seventeenth centuries. We need to be careful about using figures on book production, book ownership or opportunities for schooling to assess either the level of education or its ease of access. More than one observer lauded the availability of grammar schools in England, but expressed reservations about the accessibility of those same grammar schools. In *The Description of England*, chapter 3, 'Of Universities' (1577), William Harrison states that in addition to the universities, 'there are a great number of Grammar Schools throughout the realm, and those very liberally endowed for the better relief of poor scholars, so that there are not many corporate towns now under the queen's dominion, that have not one Grammar School at the least, with a sufficient living for a master and usher appointed to the same'.[7] Earlier in the same chapter, Harrison is less optimistic about the number of fellowships likely to trickle down to the lower classes: 'it is in my time a hard matter for a poor man's child to come by a fellowship (though he be never so good a scholar, and worthy of that room) . . . In some grammar schools likewise, which send scholars to these universities, it is lamentable to see what bribery is used . . . such bribery is made, that poor men's children are commonly shut out, and the richer sort received'. Although in 1577 Harrison is sceptical about how fairly educational opportunities are in practice distributed, neither he nor his contemporaries question the principle that the poor should be educated. A century later in 1678 Christopher Wase is forced to acknowledge that there is widespread opposition to educating the lower classes. He concedes that 'there is an opinion commonly received that the scholars of England are overproportioned to the preferments for lettered persons':

Hereupon the constitution of free-schools cometh to be questioned, as diverting those, whom Nature or Fortune had determined to the plough, the oar, or other handicrafts, from their proper design, to the study of the liberal arts' and 'multiplying . . . foundations is . . . represented as dangerous to the government'.[8]

The quality and quantity of educational opportunities available to the lower classes and to women decreased as the seventeenth century came to an end.

Our picture of what actually occurred in the Renaissance educational system and of its impact on all classes of people remains uncertain, but we are remarkably well informed about theory as opposed to practice. Renaissance handbooks on education range from philosophical theories of government and social control, such as More's *Utopia* (1516) and Machiavelli's *The Prince* (1513, printed in 1532) to the moral programs such as Erasmus's *Education of a Christian Prince* (1517) and Sir Thomas Elyot's *Book named the Governor* (1531). Sir Thomas Hoby's translation of Castiglione's *The Courtier* (1528, translated and printed 1561), was a courtesy book offering a portrait of the ideal courtier that also influenced books intended for those who aspired to be gentlemen. In the *Schoolmaster* (1570) Roger Ascham, who had been the pupil of Sir John Cheke, the best teacher, and the schoolmaster of Queen Elizabeth, the best student, outlined the principles of a humanist education. Ascham's programme was aimed at the landed gentry and assumed a tutorial setting. In contrast, Richard Mulcaster, headmaster of Merchant Taylors' School and master of St Paul's, wrote two handbooks, *Positions* (1581) and the *Elementary* (1582) concerned more directly with teaching the children of merchants and tradesmen to read and write. In *The First Part of the Elementary, Which Entreateth Chiefly of the Right Writing of our English Tongue* (1582) he explains what skills are to be taught – reading, writing, drawing, singing and playing – and how and when these skills are to be introduced. As Mulcaster's emphasis on fine arts suggests, students from the Merchant Taylors' School frequently performed at court in the decade between 1574 and 1584.

These and other educational manuals indicate that there was considerable agreement on curriculum and methodology. Children first attended a petty school where they learned reading, writing and counting, but girls might be taught needlework instead of writing and arithmetic. The child was to begin by learning his ABC, probably from a hornbook, and then, in 'good reformation style', read the Catechism, Psalter and Primer. The petty school was under the jurisdiction of the church, but that mattered little in terms of curriculum since church and state were in practice inseparable: in injunctions of 1536 and 1538 Henry VIII decreed that everyone should be taught the basic articles of faith, the Pater Noster, Ave Maria, Credo and Decalogue, in English. The drive toward religious uniformity deeply influenced early education. In 1545 King Henry's authorized Primer was published in English to supply 'one uniform manner or course of praying throughout all our dominions'.[9] A translation was made available for those who knew Latin. All agreed that the ABC and Catechism should be the first text and that religious uniformity was essential; there was less consensus concerning which religious doctrines and practices should be uniform.

As T. W. Baldwin concludes about the curriculum of the petty school: 'The emphasis here is on Reformation, not on Renaissance' (32).

Nowell's Catechism, existing in three Latin versions of increasing difficulty, was approved by the bishops in 1562, but was not published until eight years later. Between 1570 and 1647 this work went through forty-four editions in Latin, English and Greek and so had a major impact on the way texts were interpreted. The master asks a question to which the student supplies a memorized answer. In addition, to inculcating specific doctrines, such as justification by faith, the catechism led the student to pay attention to correspondences between the Old and New Testaments. In Romans 5:14, 'type' is used in a strict theological sense when Paul calls Adam the *typos* of Christ, literally, 'the figure of him that was to come'. A type in the Old Testament foreshadows its antitype in the New. If, for example, the master asks why the Decalogue refers to the Christians of the New Testament as well as the Israelites of the Old Testament, then the student is supposed to reply that the pharaoh of Egypt is a type of the devil and that Moses' delivery of the Israelites from bondage in Egypt is a type of Christ's delivery of the faithful Christian from the bondage of sin. This system of reading influenced metaphysical poets such as George Herbert and affected the design of Milton's *Paradise Lost*. The catechism helped to establish typology as a system for reading the Bible, but as was true of four-fold allegory, its approach to allusions also influenced the reading and writing of secular texts.

Nowell's Largest Catechism was written in Ciceronian Latin, but no doubt was left as to the primacy of religion in the educational scheme of things:

> I see it belongeth to the order of my duty, my dear child, not so much to instruct thee civilly in learning and good manners, as to furnish thy mind, and that in thy tender years, with good opinions and true religion.[10]

The schoolmaster was to prefer Christian over humanist objectives: 'For this age of childhood ought to less, yea, also much more, to be trained with good lessons to godliness, than with good arts to humanity' (216). It is understandable that in a sixteenth-century hierarchy religion would be ranked over civility and learning, but these comments in the catechism go further and set godliness in opposition to humanity and civility.

Humanist educators view the education of women positively, but very little is known about schools for women. From the comments of Renaissance schoolmasters who discuss contemporary practice, it is clear that women were involved in disseminating the basic literacy fostered by the petty school system. In *Ludus Literarius or the Grammar Schoole* (1612), John Brinsley says that basic skills should be learned before admission to a grammar school and comments that this might be a good job for a poor man or woman: 'it would help some poor man or woman, who knew not how to live otherwise'.[11] He repeats his description of a woman as a possible instructor in a petty school: 'Thus may any *poor man or woman* enter the little ones in a town together (20). In his *New Discovery of the Old Art of Teaching School*, Charles Hoole says:

The petty school ... deserveth that more encouragement should be given to the teachers of it than that it should be left as a work for poor women or others whose necessities compel them to undertake it as a mere shelter from beggary.[12]

We know very little about the gender of the students attending schools, but women were employed to teach children to spell, read, write and cast accounts.

Following the petty school, a student who had aptitude and parental support, would enter a grammar school. Ben Jonson's disparaging comment about Shakespeare's grammar school education, that he had 'little Latin' and 'less Greek', stimulated twentieth-century interest in the curriculum and pedagogy of the Elizabethan and Jacobean grammar schools. The Latin word play in *Love's Labours Lost* and the French puns in *Henry V* suggest that Shakespeare was well educated and allow us to infer that the audience was linguistically sophisticated. In assessing Jonson's deprecatory comment on Shakespeare's learning, we need to keep in mind that Jonson was himself a formidable classical scholar who was awarded honorary master of arts degrees by both Oxford and Cambridge.

The uniformity prized in religious instruction in the petty school extended into the grammar school curriculum. In addition to authorizing a prayer book, Henry VIII decreed that William Lily's *Grammar* was to be the standard introduction to Latin, and this *Grammar* remained the standard grammar school text throughout the sixteenth and seventeenth centuries. Renaissance educators regarded innovation with suspicion and used the term 'newfangled' to express this resistance to change. In the Convocation of Canterbury in 1664 and again in 1675 in the House of Lords attempts were made to end the privileged status of Lily's *Grammar*, but it retained its official authority.

After concentrating on Lily's *Grammar* in the lower grammar school (approximately the first three years), the study of rhetoric began in the fourth form. Students composed elegant letters in Latin and began Greek. The dramatist Terence was particularly important as a text. Charles Hoole says that students must make him 'wholly their own':

> Terence, of all the school-authors that we read, doth deservedly challenge the first place, not only because Tully [Cicero] himself hath seemed to derive his eloquence from him ... The matter of it is full of morality, and the several actors therein most lively seem to personate the behaviour and properties ... of people, even in this age of ours.
>
> (137–8)

In *The Staple of News* Jonson satirises schoolmasters for not spending enough time on the catechism and for letting the children speak plays and act fables, but Terence is exempted from this censure: 'We send them to learn their grammar and their Terence, and they learn their play-books' (Intermean 3 after 3.4).

In terms of methodology, throughout all the forms most schoolmasters used the 'double translation' method advocated by Roger Ascham in *The Schoolmaster* (1570).

Students would be given verses from a text, such as Ovid's *Metamorphoses*, and asked to parse it grammatically, identify tropes and figures and mention synonyms in Latin. Then, the student would turn the passage into English prose and then translate it back into Latin, taking care to ensure that each word was correctly placed grammatically and rhetorically; finally, the passage was turned into English verse. In some schools, grammatical translations were used. Students were asked to translate words and phrases into normal English word order before they returned the passage to Latin. From this work with Latin grammar, students learned to exploit fully the syntax of the English sentence. The double translation method involved very close reading and caused students to pay more attention to specific word choice than to overall design or structure.

The fifth form introduced the comparative grammar of Latin and Greek and focused on oratory, especially Demosthenes, Isocrates, and the all-important Cicero. Poetry was not neglected: students read Virgil's *Eclogues* and *Georgics* with their schoolmasters. Hoole comments that after they have memorized sections of the *Eclogues* and worked with their schoolmaster on the *Georgics*, they may be left to read the *Aeneid* by themselves (180). In the fifth form students also prepared a commonplace book, a kind of mini-Bartlett's *Quotations*, in which witty or apt phrases were arranged under headings such as friendship, liberty and law. These sayings and stylistic set pieces could later be used in compositions and speeches. It is important to remember that, for the educated, Latin was a spoken language in the Renaissance. Montaigne, for example was not allowed to speak vernacular French until he was six; his family, servants, and tutors spoke only Latin to him.

If Hebrew were to be included in the curriculum, it was introduced in the sixth form along with Homer and a long list of Greek writers including Pindar, Euripides, Sophocles and Aristophanes. Latin authors, such as Horace, Lucan, Martial, Persius, Seneca and Plautus, were also studied. The sheer concentration of the method limited the number of texts that could be read, and those texts appearing in the curriculum were read selectively as they are in modern anthologies. Hoole concludes his section on 'The Master's Method' in A *New Discovery of the Old Art of Teaching Schoole* by announcing that he has described what is 'commonly *practised*' in England and foreign countries and that the curriculum and pedagogy are '*proportioned to the ordinary capacities of children* under fifteen years of age' (204–5).

Medieval universities were intended to train the clergy, and Renaissance universities retained this focus. Many fellowships were specifically limited to those who intended to enter the church. Universities offered undergraduate degrees, but they concentrated upon the professions – theology, medicine, law and music. In addition to clerical training, the university also promoted social mobility. All university graduates were considered gentlemen; nearly one-half of those enrolled at Oxford and Cambridge at the turn of the century were members of the gentry or the nobility. Women were not allowed to take degrees until the twentieth century, nor was a female presence encouraged. Married men were not allowed to hold fellowships, and Elizabeth was reluctant to promote the careers of university dons who married.

After studying at either Oxford or Cambridge, young men might enter one of the four law schools located in London, known as the Inns of Court. A university degree was not a prerequisite to entrance; it was possible to go immediately from a grammar school to the Inner Temple, Middle Temple, Gray's Inn or Lincoln's Inn. Students attending the Inns of Court might study the common law and actually pursue a career as a lawyer. The Inns also served as a lodging place for those who may have had as much interest in the London theatres as the common law and who planned to spend some time in London before settling down to the management of a country estate.

We are inclined to conceive of the history of education in terms of the development of institutions, the petty school, grammar school and university. We can assess the importance of societies, such as the Society of Antiquaries, whose papers have survived. We know that great collections of manuscripts, books and art were put together by private collectors and preserved as part of family traditions. The climate of a culture is more difficult to assess, but the Renaissance seems to have fostered intellectual curiosity and aspiration. In his *Novum Organon* Sir Francis Bacon set out to write the new 'organon', the replacement for the corpus of Aristotle surviving from the ancient and medieval worlds. We have examples of extraordinary intellectual energy including numerous translations of texts from classical and modern languages, These translations, some of which have become classics in their own right, were produced not by professional scholars, but by those with an interest in culture: Sir Thomas North's Plutarch, George Chapman's Homer, Lucy Hutchinson's Lucretius, John Florio's Montaigne, Sir Thomas Hoby's translation of *The Courtier*, Arthur Golding and George Sandys' *Ovid*, Sir John Harington's *Ariosto*. Those committed to the active life also respected intellectual endeavours: the explorer Sir Humphrey Gilbert, who drew up an elaborate plan for an idealized Elizabethan academy, sat on the deck reading More's *Utopia* as his ship sank. We know that Sir Walter Ralegh, Gilbert's half-brother, whiled away his years of imprisonment in the Tower writing a history of the world. Commitment to education even helped to shape Renaissance literature. In a letter to Ralegh about *The Faerie Queene*, Edmund Spenser acknowledges that his aim is 'to fashion a gentleman or noble person in vertuous and gentle discipline' ('Letter of the Author's').

NOTES

1   Stone, (1964). p. 43; Cressy, p. 17. All further references to this statistical study will be cited parenthetically in the text.

2   *Ben Jonson*, ed. C. H. Herford and Percy Simpson (Oxford: Clarendon Press, 1925), I, 18.

3   Sir Thomas More, *Yale Edition of the Complete Works of St. Thomas More: Utopia* (New Haven: Yale University Press), 4, 158–9.

Letters and Life of Francis Bacon, ed. J. Spedding, (London, 1868), 4:252–53.

4   Stone (1969).

5   34 and 35 Henry VIII.c.1. Cited in Cressy, p. 44. The following authors interpret this as evidence of widespread literacy: J. W. Adamson, *The Illiterate Anglo Saxon* (Cambridge: Cambridge University Press, 1946), 44 and Richard Altick, *The English Common*

Reader: A Social History of the MA Reading Public, 1800–1900 (Chicago: University of Chicago Press, 1957), 16, 25. H. S. Bennet, *English Books and Readers, 1445–1557* (Cambridge: Cambridge University Press, 1969), 27.

6   Gurr, p. 55.

7   Cited from Holinshed's *Chronicles of England, Scotland, and Ireland*. Collected and Published by Raphael Holinshed, William Harrison (London, 1807), Book 2, ch. 3, 254, 252.

8   Christopher Wase, *Considerations concerning Free Schools as Settled in England* (Oxford:

Theater and London, Mr Simon Millers, 1678), 1.

9   Baldwin (1943), p. 44.

10   *A Catechism. Written in Latin by Alexander Nowell, Dean of St. Paul's: Together with the Same Catechism Translated into English by Thomas Norton*, ed. G. E. Gorrie. Parker Society 32. (Cambridge: Cambridge University Press, 1853), 113 for English translation, 1 for Latin.

11   Brinsley, p. 17.

12   Hoole, p. 157. Further references will be to this edition; page numbers will be cited parenthetically in the text.

REFERENCES AND FURTHER READING

Ascham, Roger (1570). *The Schoolmaster*, ed. Lawrence V. Ryan. (Published for Folger Shakespeare Library.) Ithaca, NY: Cornell University Press.

Atkins, S. H. (1970). *Aids to Research in Education: A Select Check-list of Printed Material on Education Published in English to 1800*. Willerby, Hull: University of Hull Institute of Education.

Baldwin, T. W. (1943). *William Shakspere's Petty School*. Urbana: University of Illinois Press.

——(1944). *William Shakspere's Small Latine & Lesse Greeke*. 2 vols. Urbana: University of Illinois Press.

Benedict, Barbara M. (1996). *Making the Modern Reader: Cultural Mediation in Early Modern Literature*. Princeton: Princeton University Press.

Brinsley, John (1612; 1627; rpt 1917). *Ludus Literarius, or the Grammar Schoole*, ed. E. T. Capagnac. Liverpool and London: Liverpool University Press. New York. Scholars' Facsimiles

——(1622; rpt 1943). *A Consolation for our Grammar Schooles*. New York: Scholars' Facsimiles and Reprints.

Bushnell, Rebecca W. (1996). *A Culture of Teaching: Early Modern Humanism in Theory and Practice*. Ithaca and London: Cornell University Press.

Crane, Mary Thomas (1993). *Framing Authority:*

Sayings, Self, and Society in Sixteenth Century England. Princeton: Princeton University Press.

Cressy, David (1980). *Literacy and the Social Order: Reading and Writing in Tudor and Stuart England*. Cambridge: Cambridge University Press.

Elsky, Martin (1989). *Authorizing Words: Speech, Writing, and Print in the English Renaissance*. Ithaca: Cornell University Press,

Grafton, Anthony and Jardine, Lisa (1986). *From Humanism to the Humanities: Education and the Liberal Arts in Fifteenth and Sixteenth-century Europe*. Cambridge: Cambridge University Press.

Gurr, Andrew (1987). *Playgoing in Shakespeare's London*. Cambridge: Cambridge University Press.

Hoole, Charles (1659; rpt 1913). *A New Discovery of the Old Art of Teaching Schoole, in Four Small Treatises*, ed. E. T. Campagnac. Liverpool: Liverpool University Press.

Jagodzinski, Cecile M. (1999). *Privacy and Print: Reading and Writing in Seventeenth-century England*. Charlottesville: University Press of Virginia.

Moss, Ann (1996). *Printed Commonplace-Books and the Structuring of Renaissance Thought*. Oxford: Clarendon Press.

Mulcaster, Richard (1582; rpt 1925). *The First Part of the Elementarie, which entreateth chefelie of the right writing of our English tung*, ed. E. T. Campagnac. Tudor and Stuart Library. Oxford: Clarendon Press.

——(1581; rpt 1887). *Positions: . . . Which Are Necessarie for the Training vp of Children,* ed. Robert Hebert Quick. London: Longmans, Green, and Co.

Raven, James, Helen Small and Naomi Tador (eds) (1996). *Practice and Representation of Reading in England.* Cambridge: Cambridge Univ. Press.

Sanders, Eve Rachele (1998). *Gender and Literacy on Stage in Early Modern England.* Cambridge: Cambridge University Press.

Spufford, Margaret (1982). *Small Books and Pleasant Histories: Popular Fiction and Its Readership in Seventeenth-century England.* Athens, GA: University of Georgia Press.

Stone, Lawrence (1964). 'The Educational Revolution in England, 1560–1640', *Past and Present,* 28, 41–80.

——(1969). 'Literacy and Education in England, 1640–1900', *Past and Present,* 42, 69–139.

Watson, Foster (1908). *The English Grammar Schools to 1660.* New York: August M. Kelley; London: Frank Cass and Co.

Watt, Teresa (1991). *Cheap Print and Piety, 1550–1640.* Cambridge, Cambridge University Press.

9
Court and Coterie Culture
Curtis Perry

The courtly elite in Tudor and Early Stuart England consisted of important office-holders in the royal household together with those men and women fortunate enough to be granted access to the monarch by virtue of family prestige, connections or personal charm. Royal favour brought enormous rewards, so access to the monarch was a prize highly sought after. Recipients of royal favour were much courted in turn, for they were influential and had the opportunity to broker suits for others. The ability to reap benefits for clients was one way of demonstrating and maintaining prestige, and so much of the wealth doled out through the court was distributed to various associates of successful courtiers. As a result, the social and political world of the upper classes organized itself into shifting and overlapping networks of patronage that served among other functions as conduits to distribute royal bounty in the forms of grants, patents and offices. A great courtier would tend to have a sizeable number of dependants and clients, whose reciprocated services helped to cement the social and political importance of their patron. These affiliations were the very stuff of public life in a society that imagined government as more personal than bureaucratic.

Some offices within the royal household were specially coveted because they guaranteed access to the monarch. For example, the Earls of Leicester and Essex, two of Queen Elizabeth's great favourites, served as Masters of the Horse, a position that ensured access to the queen during her excursions. In a system built on personal intimacy, however, patronage relationships were frequently less official than such titles would suggest. Moreover, though official administrative positions were held by men, there are numerous cases in which well-placed women were able to exert considerable influence within networks of court patronage. The women who served in Elizabeth's Chamber used their access to the queen to obtain suits for clients, for example, and Lucy, Countess of Bedford became one of the more influential power brokers of the Jacobean period, as well as being an important literary patron.[1] The importance of personal intimacy within this social organization also helps explain why the theme of sexual corruption should be so common in negative accounts of court life. As Alan

Bray has argued, patronage relations between men that were seen by contemporaries as socially corrupt tended also to attract accusations of sodomy. And in literary texts as diverse as Sir Thomas Wyatt's 'They Flee From Me' and Christopher Marlowe's *Edward II* (1591–92) the unruliness of sexual desire stands in for the troubling instability of personal intimacy and the anxieties built into a social system predicated upon it.[2]

The practice of patronage ensured that something like a court culture extended well beyond those men and women who attended the monarch in any immediate capacity. Moreover, the premium placed within this system upon personal relationships put a tremendous amount of pressure on the behaviour and taste of courtiers and aspirants alike. Personal charm could be of the utmost importance, which in turn encouraged the cultivation of virtuosity in matters of fashion and taste. Even those who hoped for patronage at several removes from the monarch were eager to follow changes in fashion that ultimately emanated from the court. Court culture, then, was somewhat larger and more nebulous than was the court itself. Its reach included members of extended patronage networks eager to reap the benefits of the court's bounty, active aspirants of all kinds and various hangers-on.

As the government of England became increasingly centralized in the Tudor period and beyond, success at court came to rival family pedigree as a vehicle for prestige. This explains the resentment generated by men like Cardinal Wolsey (1475–1530) or George Villiers, Duke of Buckingham (1592–1628), who were able to parlay success at court into wealth and social prominence despite having come from relatively obscure families. As a result, courtliness took on greater importance as a marker of rank, and the ambitious became increasingly eager to keep up. The desire among those outside the inner circle to seem courtly in manner and taste contributed to the popularity of courtesy books promising to offer guidance on matters of courtliness. Thomas Hoby's translation of Castiglione's elegant *Book of the Courtier* (1561), for example, was published with a brief epitome designed to offer a checklist of courtly virtues for those whose interest was more practical than literary. Eagerness on the part of outsiders to copy the taste and manners of the court could, however, be self-defeating. If a particular manner or style were to be successfully copied by aspirants outside of the inner circles of the court, it would cease to be useful as means of distinction. Fashions had to be endlessly changeable in order to maintain their function as a marker of the difference between insiders and outsiders. For aspirants, the pursuit of courtly elegance could thus be fraught with uncertainty and anxiety (Whigham).

The impact of court culture on the literature of the period is pervasive as to be unavoidable. For one thing, a lot of literature was produced either by courtiers like Sir Walter Ralegh or Sir Philip Sidney or for their immediate entertainment. Masques, plays, tournaments and pageants were put on regularly at court, and courtiers were interested in many forms of poetry and prose. For another, most writers sought some form of support or preferment from the wealthy and well connected. It was nearly impossible to make a living from the pittance a writer might receive from a printer or theatrical company, and it was traditional for educated young men to aspire to serve the commonwealth either in the church or the state. Court preferment was important for success in either arena. Consequently, a great deal of what we today think of as literature was written in the hopes of obtaining money or position from a patron with court connections.

Beyond such immediate connections, the anxious and competitive nature of court performance made it a fertile breeding ground for fashions and mannerisms that manifest themselves in literary practice as well as in things like clothing or behaviour. The publication of George Puttenham's *The Art of English Poesie* (1589) – a how-to book for would-be court poets – attests to the desire among writers to copy courtly styles. A demonstrated facility with the latest literary manner might help a writer secure the patronage of a courtier who admired literature or who had need of a tutor or a secretary. Moreover, since the court provided a highly visible focus for the dreams and aspirations of the educated and literate, identifiably courtly styles were frequently copied in texts produced far from the centres of patronage. For instance, the vogue for pastoral in late Elizabethan England – fuelled by the cultural prestige of the courtier Sir Philip Sidney – spurred imitators who enjoyed little or no connection to the courtly elite. The publication of the pastoral miscellany *England's Helicon* in 1600 testifies to the spread of the mode's popularity; the book contains poems by Sidney as well as poems by non-courtly writers like Robert Greene and Anthony Munday. This process of imitation ensured that the influence of the court on literary culture extended beyond the limits of actual patronage networks. Court culture generated a good deal of the literary fashion of Tudor and early Stuart England.

Because court culture and patronage shaped literary production in so many subtly different ways, understanding Renaissance literature typically involves understanding the social situation of its production. Dedicatory epistles marking actual or wished-for patronage can be an invaluable starting point for this, though further biographical research is often required in order to understand the nature of the relationship between writer and dedicatee. Looking beyond the patron–client dyad, many literary texts were written with a specific circle of acquaintances in mind. These literary communities, or coteries as they are sometimes called, could have a profound effect on the types of texts produced within them. The notion of coterie production offers a useful way to think about the kinds of networks that provided the social occasions for a great deal of literary production.

Coteries took a number of forms, from extended family circles to patronage networks to other kinds of institutionally determined groupings. One example of a literary coterie is the sizeable group of writers associated with the Sidneys. Philip Sidney, his brother Robert, and his sister Mary, the Countess of Pembroke, were all active both as writers and in encouraging others to write. The cultural prestige of Sir Philip, the family's connections with other intellectually ambitious gentlemen like Fulke Greville, and the Countess of Pembroke's active patronage of poets like Samuel Daniel combined to establish a network of writers with interrelated interests. The fact that members of this extended circle experimented with many of the same forms –

devotional and amatory lyric, for example, and Senecan closet drama – demonstrates the kind of give and take typical of coterie literature.

A more institutionally structured example of coterie production is provided by the literary gamesmanship indulged in by gentlemanly aspirants within the different Inns of Court. The Inns served simultaneously as law schools for would-be common lawyers and finishing schools for would-be courtiers. A significant percentage of the young men who were members of these institutions saw them as a leaping-off point for careers at court, and such men competed with one another in the mastery of courtly manners and taste (Prest). The display of writerly wit was part of this rivalry, which means that texts produced within these circles tended to be written in order to demonstrate virtuosity for and among peers. Many of John Donne's early poems, for instance, were written while he was at Lincoln's Inn. Their witty playfulness, sophistication, erotic content and satiric bite can all be understood as part of Donne's social performance within this coterie of ambitious young men (Marotti 1986: 25–95). Other kinds of literary production likewise show the influence of this milieu: it can be seen, for example, in the combination of knowing political cynicism, erudition and artistic sophistication in the plays of John Marston, a member of the Middle Temple (Finkelpearl).

Because Renaissance texts were written for a variety of kinds of audiences – patrons and coteries as well as the larger reading public – not everything was intended for print publication.[3] Too much has been made of the idea that courtiers avoided the crass commercialism of print publication – courtiers like Sir Walter Ralegh and Edward De Vere, the Earl of Oxford, did not hesitate to have their works printed – but texts written for a limited courtly readership were frequently circulated in manuscript. In the case of material written for a limited audience, this would have been by far the most efficient means of distribution. Manuscript circulation may have appealed to courtly writers for other reasons as well. For one, the informality of manuscripts made it possible to circulate politically charged or libellous writings that would have been too dangerous for the more public mechanisms of print publication. The anonymous libel known as *Leicester's Commonwealth* (1584) was printed abroad and smuggled into England. But the text, which describes Elizabeth's great favourite as a sexually corrupt poisoner, was vigorously suppressed. Though only a handful of printed copies exist, its modern editor has tracked down upwards of fifty handwritten copies, a survival rate that attests to a rather wide manuscript circulation (Peck 1985: 222–7). Similarly, there is an enormous body of political libel dealing with Jacobean political figures that has survived only in manuscript form (Bellany). This material seems to have been exchanged and collected by a broad cross-section of literate English men and women with an interest in court politics. For another, it may be that manuscript circulation sometimes appealed to courtly elites as a way of keeping their thoughts and observations out of the hands of social inferiors. Since manuscripts are copied from one reader to the next, manuscript circulation tends to follow pre-existing lines of social acquaintance. The readership of a text produced for manuscript circulation is thus more likely to be limited to a specific coterie or class.

Though the administrative efficiency of Henry VII's reign (1485–1509) was instrumental in the establishment of a stable Tudor dynasty, it was Henry VIII (1509–47) who brought the conspicuous magnificence of continental courts to England. To some degree this was probably a matter of personality – the young king enjoyed entertainments and liked to demonstrate his prowess in tournaments – but there is also an element of careful calculation behind Henry's magnificence. Ambassadors from abroad saw the splendour of the court, and came away impressed with England and the king. Henry, who dramatically increased England's involvement in the military and diplomatic world of continental Europe, was eager to establish a commensurate prestige on this international stage. An ambassadorial description of the English court from 1517 demonstrates England's poor reputation and attests to the effectiveness of Henry's magnificence:

> The wealth and civilization of the world are here; and those who call the English barbarians appear to me to render themselves such. I here perceive very elegant manners, extreme decorum, and very great politeness; and amongst other things there is this most invincible King, whose acquirements and qualities are so many and excellent that I consider him to excel all who ever wore a crown.
>
> (quoted in Anglo, 123)

Demonstrating 'the wealth and civilization of the world' meant among other things spending tremendous amounts of money on the arts. Henry was an energetic builder, for example; he also employed the great German painter Hans Holbein as a member of his household. Likewise, much of the literature produced by Henrician courtiers displays a sophisticated internationalism that is both innovative and clearly related to the magnificence of Henry's court. Writers like Sir Thomas More and Sir Thomas Elyot are typically credited with bringing the accomplishments of European humanism to English letters. Sir Thomas Wyatt and Henry Howard, Earl of Surrey, adapted the elegant lyric poetry of Petrarch and his European imitators to the English vernacular. Surrey also translated Virgil into English blank verse. Though the lyric poems of Wyatt and Surrey were circulated in manuscript during their lifetimes, many were printed in 1557 in Richard Tottel's verse miscellany *Songs and Sonnets*. Their prosody and style thus provided a template for court poetry that was influential during the reign of Queen Elizabeth. Sir Philip Sidney found in Surrey's lyrics 'many things tasting of noble birth, and worthy of a noble mind' (64).

The administrative style of Henry VII emphasized the king's distance. By holding himself aloof he was able to manage his court with an even hand. Because Henry VIII was always an active participant in the life of the court, however, his personal relationships took on a tremendous political importance. The difference would have been immediately obvious to contemporaries, for the youthful Henry VIII made splashy appearances in court entertainments and surrounded himself with a group of young noblemen who accompanied him everywhere. Referred to by contemporaries as the king's minions, these men parlayed their intimacy with the king into considerable influence within Henry's court. Until 1518, this intimacy was informal. Then, in imitation of a similar title bestowed upon the intimates of King Francis I of France, the minions were made into Gentlemen of the Privy Chamber. This gave them control of access to the king's suite of private rooms, and provided an institutional structure to match the king's penchant for government by intimacy. The exclusivity of access gave the minions an important political advantage over courtiers whose contact with the king was more limited. Members of the Privy Chamber also took on important administrative duties, managing the finances of the Privy Purse and obtaining the king's signature to authorize official documents. These institutional innovations helped shape the nature of court politics well into the seventeenth century.[4]

The minions' influence was matched for a time by that of Cardinal Wolsey, whose administrative talents made him indispensable to the king. Wolsey recognized the threat that Privy Chamber favourites represented to his position, and used his own influence to limit theirs until 1529. He was finally brought down in the factional intrigue surrounding his attempts to obtain an annulment for Henry's first marriage to Catherine of Aragon. From this point on, Henry's reign was characterized by intense factional infighting over royal intimacy. Anne Boleyn, Henry's second wife who led a powerful faction with connections in the Privy Chamber, was tried and executed in 1536. Thomas Cromwell, whose faction helped push Anne from favour, fell victim to the vicissitudes of factional politics in 1540. He was convicted of heresy and treason and executed. The large number of Henry's intimates who wound up in prison or executed testifies to the instability of royal favour as a basis for power. To be sure, the tumultuous nature of Henry's domestic and political life – his many wives, the break from Rome – created ample opportunity for reversals of favour and alliance at court. Viewed from the Olympian perspective of the survey, however, the reign of Henry VIII looks like a series of cautionary tales about the problematics of government by intimacy.

It is not surprising, therefore, that the literature of the Henrician court should demonstrate an obsessive interest in these problems as well. The description of the ideal state in book 2 of Sir Thomas More's *Utopia* (1516), for example, is ironized by a rather pessimistic discussion of court service in book 1. Raphael Hythlodaeus, one of More's personae in that complex fiction, argues that idealism and courtliness are incompatible, since the courtier is forced to please the ruler instead of serving the state. As he puts it, 'there is no room for philosophy with rulers' (99). More's eventual execution is a bitter irony in light of such concerns. A similar ambivalence about court service runs through Wyatt's lyrics, and though Wyatt was a successful courtier, he was also imprisoned for over a month in the contretemps surrounding Anne Boleyn in 1536 (Zagorin).

There are also some biting satires of court written by Henry's courtiers. The best known are probably Wyatt's – especially 'Mine own John Poynz' – but those of John Skelton deserve mention as well. Skelton, who had been tutor to the young Henry, was the most successful of the would-be court poets during the first years of his reign. Henry even granted him the title *orator regius* sometime around 1512. Skelton's signature verse form – short rhyming lines, now know as skeltonics – is ideally suited to boisterous vituperation, and much of his extant poetry lampoons the favourites of the Henrician court. His one extant play, *Magnificence* (1519) satirizes Henry's minions, and several of his poems – 'Speak, Parrot' (1521), 'Colin Clout' (1522) and 'Why Come Ye Not to Court' (1522) – attack Wolsey. Though traditional literary history treats Skelton as primitive precursor to the elegant vernacular poetry of Wyatt and Surrey, they all share an insider's concern with the problems of favour in the court of Henry VIII.

When Henry VIII died, in 1547, he was succeeded by his nine-year-old son, Edward, who was King Edward VI for a mere six years. Edward's older sister, Mary I, then ruled for five years (1553–1558) before herself succumbing to illness. Mary was never particularly concerned with entertainments or the display of courtly magnificence, and the most active periods for shows and tournaments occurred when her husband, Philip II of Spain, came to England (Anglo, 281–343). After these two short reigns, the sheer duration of the reign of Elizabeth I (1558–1603) helped to ensure the development of an elaborate court culture with its own distinct pressures and conventions.

Unlike her father, Henry VIII, Elizabeth managed factions so as to minimize hostility among her inner circle of courtiers. There were rivalries, to be sure, but the cast of characters at the centre of the court was remarkably stable and fairly homogeneous. Kinship ties among the courtiers were thick, and many of them came from families with previous ties to Tudor courts. Though her stinginess with wealth and titles aroused plenty of frustration, the literature produced by and for Elizabeth's court featured less of the pessimism and ambivalence characteristic of Henrician court literature (Adams).

Elizabeth's ability to balance the politics of favour may have had something to do with her unusual position as an unmarried queen. Because her most intimate chamber service had to be performed by women – who could use their influence to obtain suits for others, but who were themselves shut out of administration – Elizabeth avoided the kind of institutionalized intimacy that featured so prominently in the factionalism of the Henrician court. The administrative duties built up for the Privy Chamber under Henry were handled for Elizabeth by ministers like William Cecil, Baron Burleigh. Instead, the queen's entourage of women helped to insulate her from the demands of the court. This in turn gave Elizabeth flexibility in the management of access to her person, for no powerful favourite could bolster his position by means of an official position in the monarch's intimate chamber service. Though Elizabeth's favour was never as mercurial as that of her father, the resulting uncertainty of access and favour contributed to the frustration of her courtiers. Even Elizabeth's own godson Sir John Harington complained about her distance from the court, describing her in 1602 as 'a lady shut up in a chamber from her subjects and most of her servants, and seldom seen but on holy days' (quoted in Adams, 77).

This change in the institutionalization of access put added pressure upon less immediate means of catching and holding Elizabeth's attention. Since intimacy with the queen was for the most part no longer secured by position, active courtship of her favour seemed more important than ever. Fiction-making was one way of casting for the queen's attention, and indeed one cannot help but be struck by the elaborate web of literary conceits developed in pageants and entertainments, poetry, and even direct addresses to the queen. An example will serve to demonstrate the overlapping social functions of such fictions within the world of Elizabethan court politics. In April of 1581, as part of the entertainment for a French delegation, Sir Philip Sidney, Fulke Greville, and two other knights used the tilt-yard to stage an allegorical spectacle: in the personae of four foster children of desire, they laid siege to the queen, whose gallery was figured as an impregnable fortress of perfect beauty. In these roles, bedecked in sumptuous armour and equipment, the knights participated in a tournament, before finally offering a ritualized apology for their violent courtship. Such a tournament serves many purposes simultaneously. Though its primary function was to entertain the court and its visitors while displaying English magnificence, it also served as an occasion for participants to exhibit themselves before the queen. The pageant's emphasis on the queen's inviolable chastity may also have been intended to comment obliquely upon the marriage proposals that were the occasion of the French visit. Finally, since Sidney had a hand in it, the show may also have been designed to express his ambition and frustration in Elizabeth's service. The symbolic complexity of the event is indicative of the highly sophisticated fiction-making of Elizabeth's court. Elizabeth herself was learned, literate and highly sensitive to nuances of representation. As a result, many of her courtiers either cultivated or hired literary talent, and used allegorical conceits to entertain and entreat the monarch.

This in turn was a major impetus behind the creation of the vast allegorical vocabulary of praise for the queen that has come to be known as the cult of Elizabeth (see Strong; Frye). Moreover, though Steven May is correct to differentiate between fully fledged courtier poets like Sidney and Ralegh and mere aspirants, interest in poetry and allegorical fiction among the Elizabethan elite clearly helped to stir and shape courtly ambition among a less elevated class of ambitious and literate men. Elizabethan writers like George Gascoigne, John Lyly, Samuel Daniel and Edmund Spenser (to name a few of the better known examples) inhabited the periphery of the world of court while attempting to use their writing to catch its attention. The cultivation of literary taste within the Elizabethan court is one of the reasons for the remarkable flowering of literature during Elizabeth's reign.

As the tilt-yard pageant suggests, the gender of the unmarried queen helped shape the kinds of fictions that surrounded her. In addition to the countless personae used to embellish Elizabeth's image, writers drew heavily upon the analogy between the desire of the courtier to serve his queen and the desire of the lover to serve his lady. It is no coincidence that the literary genres associated with the Elizabethan period in standard literary histories – romance, pastoral, love lyric – should feature amatory fictions so prominently. Of course, figurations of the queen and literary responses to her court changed during the course of her long reign. The familiar image of Elizabeth as the Virgin Queen, for example, became prominent only in the late 1570s as the possibility of her marrying became increasingly remote. Much of the best-known Elizabethan literature was produced during the 1580s and 1590s, as the queen herself moved from her late forties to her sixties. The enormous popularity of sonnets and stories of unrequited love during these years attests in part to the growing frustrations of the court, which grew restless with the notorious stinginess of the ageing queen.

Elizabeth, of course, had no heirs. James VI of Scotland, who had been in clandestine negotiations with the leading statesmen in Elizabeth's government, became James I of England (1603–25) upon Elizabeth's death. He was welcomed by a court grown weary of Elizabethan parsimony, and wasted no time demonstrating his own largesse with both wealth and titles. In his first four months as King of England, for example, James granted more knighthoods than had been given in the whole of Elizabeth's reign. His generosity with money was similarly striking. While it is possible that the foreign king misunderstood English finances, his generosity had a purpose. James urgently needed to secure loyalty in his new country.

But James also wanted to create a court that would mirror his dual position as king of both England and Scotland. While he retained most of the officials from Elizabeth's court, he created the office of Gentlemen of the Bedchamber and filled it with his own Scottish entourage. The Bedchamber supplanted the Henrician Privy Chamber as the key site of the king's intimate service, and Gentlemen of the Bedchamber got the lion's share of the king's generosity.[5] To the English, James and his imported Scottish favourites seemed uncouth, and their prominence at court seemed a shocking departure from Elizabethan decorum. The diary of Lady Anne Clifford records such feelings in a memorable account of her first visit to the new king's court: 'we all saw a great change between the fashion of the Court as it is now and of that in the queen's time, for we were all lousy by sitting in the chamber of Sir Thomas Erskine' (3). The allegedly infested Erskine was First Gentleman and Groom of the Stool in James's Scottish Bedchamber. Generally, English courtiers resented seeing English wealth flow into the coffers of the lousy Scots.

James was much more loyal to his personal favourites than Henry VIII had been, and as a result they were able to use their positions to dominate royal patronage. English courtiers did not like it, but they had to play along. One can find evidence of resulting dissatisfaction with the court from very early in the reign, in personal letters as well as in the lurid depictions of court corruption featured in numerous Jacobean plays (Tricomi). In 1615–16, when Robert Carr – Earl of Somerset and Gentleman of the Bedchamber – his wife, and their associates were convicted of poisoning Sir Thomas Overbury, the scandal seemed to confirm people's deepest suspicions about the moral corruption of James's court. The Scottish Carr had been James's favourite, and a huge number of manuscript news items and poems commenting upon the scandal were circulated among those interested in the court. In fact, some contemporary accounts of the scandal – such as 'The Five Years of King James' – make the denizens of James's court sound like characters in a lurid Jacobean tragedy.[6] Though the Scottish hold on the Bedchamber gave way in 1615 with the rise of

George Villiers, his domination of royal patronage also provoked enormous resent-ment. Commentary and libel dealing with Villiers (who became Duke of Bucking-ham) is also a staple of the period's manuscripts. It is not an overstatement to say that the rise of political verse libel in the early seventeenth century is an important liter-ary manifestation of the dissatisfaction with favouritism in James's court (Bellany).

Like Elizabeth, James was learned and literate. As King of Scotland, he had pub-lished two volumes of poetry and learned treatises on subjects as diverse as kingship and witchcraft. He admired and encouraged scholarship, but did not welcome the kind of elaborate allegorical fictions that Elizabethan writers so frequently used to explore political topics. Poets, he declared in a treatise on verse published in Scotland in 1584, should not presume to meddle with or advise about affairs of state. James is often criticized, in fact, for failing to promote the kind of cultural embellishments that lent lustre to the monarchy in the eyes of subjects. Writers eager to attract James's attention traded in Elizabethan allegories for a plainer style, emphasized their learn-ing, and were careful not to seem to be telling the king what to do. Ben Jonson, whose poems in praise of the king appeal to him as a fellow scholar while celebrating his self-sufficiency, was able to make himself into the central literary spokesman for the Jacobean court. He and the architect Inigo Jones, for example, prepared the lion's share of the masques put on before king and court. So closely was Jonson identified with courtly entertainment that when James announced plans to dine with the Mer-chant Taylors of London in 1607, the company felt that it had to hire Jonson to orga-nize the evening's entertainment (Perry, 194). Outside of Jonson and the masque, characteristic literary productions encouraged by James are typically scholarly or reli-gious: sermons, the Bible translation that bears the king's name (1611), Sir Francis Bacon's *Advancement of Learning* (dedicated to James in 1605).

James's family also played an important role in the shaping of Jacobean court culture, as his sons and his wife Anne set up households of their own. Before his death in 1612, Prince Henry became the focal point for a brand of Protestant imperial nationalism associated with the memory of Sir Philip Sidney, the Earl of Essex and Elizabethan chivalry. His court at St James became an alternative cultural centre fos-tering values antithetical to King James's policy of negotiated peace with Spain. One literary manifestation of this tension is Michael Drayton's *Poly-Olbion* (1612): dedi-cated to Prince Henry, this massive work celebrates England's imperial destiny and rather pointedly snubs King James from time to time. There has been debate about the nature of the relationship between Prince Henry's court and that of his father. On the one hand, Henry clearly fostered a militarism that tended to chafe under James. On the other, it is possible that this alternative centre may have helped contain hos-tility to Jacobean policies: so long as writers like Drayton could look forward to the accession of Henry they were less likely to risk opposing the pacific policies of James. Anne and her court provided yet another cultural centre, and were particularly active as patrons of literature (Barroll; Lewalski, 15–43). Anne organized and danced in court masques, for example, and Lucy, Countess of Bedford, her most important associate, was active as a patron to writers like Donne and Daniel. Anne, like Prince Henry, sometimes encouraged literary production that would never have been supported by James. Anne's patronage thus made it possible for the Children of the Queen's Revels, under the licensing authority of Samuel Daniel, to present a series of scandalously topical anti-court plays at Blackfriars between 1603 and 1608.

With its competing households and its dual nationalities, Jacobean court culture can seem like something of a hodge-podge. It is much easier to identify specific styles and tastes associated with the court of Charles I (1625–49). To a considerable degree, this is the result of the active interest that Charles and his French wife Henrietta Maria took in poetry and drama. Indeed, as the involvement of the royal couple with painters like Rubens and Van Dyck suggests, they were actively interested in the arts as an integral part of courtly elegance. Charles had a theatre built at Whitehall to accommodate court performances of plays, and he and his wife both actively encouraged the cultivation of poetic talent. The poet Thomas Carew was given a position among Charles's entourage, and writers like Sir William Davenant, Sir John Suckling and Edmund Waller enjoyed positions at court largely on the basis of their literary talents (Smuts, 183–213). Though Charles and Henrietta Maria maintained separate household staffs and patronized different writers, the couple's famous domestic happiness prevented the kind of conflicting court cultures typical of Jacobean England.

Charles's interest in the arts can be understood as part of his larger concern with the formal and ceremonial aspects of government. Perhaps in reaction to his experience with the informal decorum of his father's household, Charles aggressively sought to reform the manners and administrative protocols of the court. Especially after the assassination of the Duke of Buckingham in 1628, the king was careful to insist upon the ceremonial aspects of monarchy and made efforts to separate intimate friendship from public policy. Caroline reform of the court was itself the subject of Carew's great masque *Coelum Britannicum* (1634). A related interest in decorum and restraint informs both the themes and styles of Caroline court literature. Accordingly, in addition to literature and art celebrating the achievement of peace, harmonious government, idealized nature, and neo-platonic love, Caroline court culture produced an aesthetic predicated upon neo-classical orderliness and controlled elegance. In art, as in government, Charles put a premium upon formal control.

Students of literary history will most likely associate Caroline culture with the poetry of writers like Carew, Robert Herrick or Richard Lovelace, men typically lumped together in anthologies as cavalier poets. Though recent scholarship has demonstrated that generalizations about this group can be misleading (Sharpe, 1–53), it is nevertheless clear that much of their poetry shares an interrelated set of aesthetic and social values which in turn reflects the influence of the Caroline court. This is not surprising, since many of these writers had active ties to the court: Herrick was a Buckingham client, for example, and Carew was Sewer in Ordinary to Charles himself. To generalize, their poems celebrate liberty without licentiousness, the social harmony of good fellowship, hostility to puritanical abstemiousness, and a natural order that includes both plenty and hierarchy. Even those poems whose erotic frankness might seem antithetical to the austere manners of the Caroline court qualify their erotic abandon with the evident self-discipline of artistic decorum. The result – in poems like Carew's 'The Rapture' or Herrick's 'Upon Julia's Clothes' – is mixed: they celebrate desire and self-control at once, the former contained and made acceptable by the latter.

Self-control is also thematically central to many of the masques and poems designed explicitly to celebrate the royal family. Time and again the self-command and domestic order of the royal couple are depicted as mirror and model for social harmony on a national scale. The realm, in such fictions, enjoys and participates in the peace, plenty and liberty secured at the top by personal virtue. As his household reforms suggest, Charles attempted to live up to this image, and he was also eager to use it as propaganda in order to secure the love and loyalty of subjects (Smuts, 245–76).

There is some irony in the fact that Charles's court, with its emphasis on order, civility and peace, should have been destroyed by civil war. Perhaps this decisive event tells us that the image of Charles promulgated within the court was ineffective in securing loyalties outside it. Perhaps, however, it tells us merely that even the sacred image of a king was no longer sufficient to forestall political crisis brought on by other factors. At any rate, though the royal court was restored with the king in 1660, the monarch's personal favour would never again play such a dominating and central role in the administration of the state and the dispersal of its wealth. The court of Charles II was suitably lavish, and its writers celebrated the achievements of Elizabethan and early Stuart culture, but for all of its nostalgia the restored court was no longer quite the same kind of political or cultural institution.

NOTES

1 On Elizabeth's Ladies, see P. Wright, 'A Change in Direction: The Ramifications of a Female Household, 1558–1603', in Starkey, pp. 147–72. On Bedford, see Lewalski 1993, pp. 95–123. See also David Bergeron, 'Women as Patrons of English Renaissance Drama', in Lytle and Orgel, pp. 274–90.

2 Since Wyatt's lyrics were circulated in manuscript, it is often impossible to date them precisely. For further remarks on the language of eros and court see Lerer.

3 See also PUBLICATION: PRINT AND MANUSCRIPT.

4 See D. Starkey, 'Intimacy and Innovation: The Rise of the Privy Chamber, 1485–1547' in Starkey et al., 71–118.

5 See N. Cuddy, 'The revival of the entourage: the Bedchamber of James I, 1603–1625', in Starkey et al., 173–225.

6 This libel, which was finally printed in 1643, appears in several manuscripts from the 1620s and 1630s.

REFERENCES AND FURTHER READING

Adams, S. (1987). 'Eliza enthroned? The Court and Its Politics'. In C. Haigh (ed.), *The Reign of Elizabeth I* (pp. 55–77). Athens: University of Georgia Press.

Anglo, S. (1969). *Spectacle Pageantry, and Early Tudor Policy*. Oxford: Oxford University Press.

Bellany, A. (1993). ' "Raylinge Rymes and Vaunting Verse": Libellous Politics in Early Stuart

England, 1603–1628'. In K. Sharpe and P. Lake (eds), *Culture and Politics in Early Stuart England* (pp. 285–310). Stanford: Stanford University Press.

Bray, A. (1994). 'Homosexuality and the Signs of Male Friendship in Elizabethan England'. In J. Goldberg (ed.), *Queering the Renaissance* (pp. 40–61). Durham and London: Duke University Press.

Barroll, L. (1991). 'The Court of the First Stuart Queen'. In L. L. Peck (ed.), *The Mental World of the Jacobean Court* (pp. 291–08). Cambridge: Cambridge University Press.

Clifford, A. (1997). *The Diary of the Lady Anne Clifford, 1590–1676,* ed. Isabella Barrios. Boulder, CO: Aardvark Press.

Finkelpearl, P. J. (1969). *John Marston of the Middle Temple: An Elizabethan Dramatist in His Social Setting.* Cambridge: Harvard University Press.

Frye, S. (1993). *Elizabeth I: The Competition for Representation.* New York and Oxford: Oxford University Press.

Lerer, S. (1997). *Courtly Letters in the Age of Henry VIII.* Cambridge: Cambridge University Press.

Lewalski, B. K. (1993). *Writing Women in Jacobean England.* Cambridge: Harvard University Press.

Lytle, G. F. and Orgel, S. (eds) (1981). *Patronage in the Renaissance.* Princeton: Princeton University Press.

Marotti, A. F. (1986). *John Donne, Coterie Poet.* Madison: The University of Wisconsin Press.

——(1995). *Manuscript, Print, and the English Renaissance Lyric.* Ithaca and London: Cornell University Press.

May, S. W. (1991). *The Elizabethan Courtier Poets: The Poems and Their Contexts.* Columbia and London: University of Missouri Press.

More, T. (1965). *Utopia,* eds J. H. Hexter and E. Surtz. New Haven: Yale University Press.

Peck, D. C. (ed.) (1985). *Leicester's Commonwealth:*

The Copy of a Letter Written by a Master of Art of Cambridge (1584) and Related Documents. Athens, OH, and London: Ohio University Press.

Peck, L. L. (1990). *Court Patronage and Corruption in Early Stuart England.* Boston: Unwin Hyman.

——(ed.) (1991). *The Mental World of the Jacobean Court.* Cambridge and New York: Cambridge University Press.

Perry, C. (1997). *The Making of Jacobean Culture: James I and the Renegotiation of Elizabethan Literary Practice.* Cambridge: Cambridge University Press.

Prest, W. R. (1972). *The Inns of Court under Elizabeth I and the Early Stuarts, 1590–1640.* London: Longman.

Sharpe, K. (1987). *Criticism and Compliment: the Politics of Literature in the England of Charles I.* Cambridge: Cambridge University Press.

Sidney, P. (1966). *A Defence of Poetry,* ed. J. A. Van Dorsten. Oxford: Oxford University Press.

Smuts, R. M. (1987). *Court Culture and the Origins of a Royalist Tradition in Early Stuart England.* Philadelphia: University of Pennsylvania Press.

Starkey, D. et al. (1987). *The English Court: From the Wars of the Roses to the Civil War.* London and New York: Longman.

Strong, R. (1977). *The Cult of Elizabeth: Elizabethan Portraiture and Pageantry.* London: Thames and Hudson.

Tricomi, A. (1989). *Anticourt Drama in England, 1603–1642.* Charlottesville: University of Virginia Press.

Whigham, F. A. (1984). *Ambition and Privilege: The Social Tropes of Elizabethan Courtesy Theory.* Berkeley: University of California Press.

Zagorin, P. (1993). 'Sir Thomas Wyatt and the Court of Henry VIII: The Courtier's Ambivalence.' *Journal of Medieval and Renaissance Studies,* 23, 113–41.

10
The Literature of the Metropolis
John A. Twyning

Economic growth, a vast shift of people from the country to the city, and an increase
in the structure and function of government, are among the major forces which made
London a metropolis during the sixteenth century.[1] As London burgeoned it enabled
and required different forms of representation – to itself, to the nation and to the rest
of the world. The reshaping and redrawing of London during this process was often
fraught and always complex. When the court and its administration took up more or
less permanent residence as Westminster, the Tudor–Stuart monarchy and the upper
aristocracy supported and defined itself through the masque. Classically inspired,
masques were incredibly lavish forms of costumed drama staged exclusively for the
court and its milieu. As if to rival the masque, the dozen or so trade, or liveried, companies which comprised the ruling civic elite of the City of London funded and produced ever more ostentatious pageants. Staged annually, the most prestigious of these
was the Lord Mayor's inaugural pageant which sought to circumscribe the city both
morally and topographically. With inspirational titles like Thomas Middleton's *The
Triumphs of Truth*, mayoral pageants moved around the city stopping for various theatrical interludes at key points in the city. Competition with the court was not the
only engine driving the prestige of mayoral and other city pageants, rivalry between
the premier companies to stage them led to an increase in grandeur and an accelera-
tion of costs. Displays of civic and courtly pride provided opportunities for all kinds
of writers: Ben Jonson and Inigo Jones designed several classic masques for the
Jacobean court, whilst Middleton along with Anthony Munday, Thomas Dekker, John
Webster, Thomas Heywood and others all wrote pageants for the city. By the late sixteenth century representing London in a variety of genres was becoming increasingly
popular and political. All kinds of encomiastic writing came to incorporate London's
topography. From celebratory poetry and drama heralding the arrival in London of
some dignitary to panegyrical verse describing and praising urban life, new ways of
seeing the city flourished. As early as 1501 William Dunbar dubbed London 'thou
lusty Troynovant', or New Troy, an epithet which was endorsed and popularized by

later writers like Edmund Spenser and Thomas Dekker. But as London's official profile expanded and diversified, the demographic forces which created such a bright new metropolitan culture also generated a darker aspect of the New Troy: the urban underworld. Many of the writers who charted London through its official texts also crafted what came to be seen as a threatening unofficial realm inhabited by tricksters, parasites and rogues of all kinds.

Much of our sense of what constituted London's underworld has been and still is shaped by the cony-catching pamphlets which developed during the latter half of the sixteenth century. These cheaply produced pamphlets contributed to the huge expansion of London's printing industry which rode the demand for newer kinds of entertaining urban literature. Initially, the pamphlets purported to offer admonition and instruction into the nefarious ways of London's rogues and tricksters, such as Gilbert Walker's *A Manifest Detection of Dice-Play* (1552) and John Awdeley's *The Fraternity of Vagabonds* (1561). But whatever the moralizing content, such literature of exposure was laced with sensational and salacious material which detailed the activities of the unscrupulous poor, or 'masterless men'.[2] Lurid and alliterative titles such as Thomas Harman's *A Caveat for Common Cursitors Vulgarly Called Vagabonds* tempted the browsing client who frequented the numerous bookstalls which had begun to proliferate around St Paul's Cathedral. As the city expanded, the roads and alleys around St Paul's, including its long thoroughfare (Paul's Walk), became a kind of Elizabethan Grub Street and bazaar. The area became a place of cheap delights where twopenny pamphlets, almanacs and romances, competed with gewgaws, tobacco and other catchpenny products, for the attention of the metropolitan consumer. Pamphlets were thus being bought and sold in the very milieu about which the reader was being warned.

Writing by Gilbert, Awdeley and Harman exemplifies the first phase of cony-catching literature. Ostensibly, they were morally upright authors who offered inside knowledge of certain nefarious activities or a comprehensive catalogue of the various types who inhabited the underworld. Usually the author claimed access to the information either through personal observation or, more often, direct interlocution. The rhetorical strategy of the writing worked to structure the reliability of the observer and the veracity of the witness. Whether any punters of cony-catching pamphlets actually went to play dice armed with a copy of *A Manifest Detection of Dice-Play* is difficult to say. The reader was first made curious by his apparent ignorance only to be proffered the consolation that the unknown really could be deciphered by the purchase of the pamphlet.

Most cony-catching literature was based on the 'detection' or 'discovery' of things which were, by that process of revelation, proved to be already there. Thus the sense of a vast ineffable army of rogues and vagabonds became, through these accounts, both definable and comprehensible. But assuaging anxieties by categorizing the rogue, and seeking to fix knowledge about their activities, proved to be a double-edged sword which many writers exploited to the hilt. As the reader defended himself by learning all the ways in which he could be conned at cards, dice, on the street or in the ordinary, the more he realized he needed to increase his knowledge. The more the underworld was taxonomized through arcane terms like 'ruffler', 'whipjack', jarkman', or 'swigman', the more complexly populated it appeared to be. The more it was comfortingly ordered into categories, the more it appeared to be threateningly organized. If the underworld was potentially unfathomable, how much ease could be bought by knowing the difference between, say, 'a wild rogue' and 'an Abraham man'? For the perplexed reader, the pamphlets generated as much anxiety as they assuaged. But what was the writer's role, and how did such literature affect London's topography and structures of urban experience? More than one critic has noted that the cony most caught was the one who bought the pamphlet.

Not everyone shares this view: some scholars adopt a positivist approach to the literature. In *The Canting Crew: London's Criminal Underworld*, John McMullan echoes the pamphlets' claims: 'to lay bare the nature of criminal group formation, the features of a wider criminal infrastructure, and the operation of criminal markets'.[3] McMullan recognizes the problems of 'validity and reliability' of such sources but does he fall into the trap set by the writers by simply trying to corroborate roguish and criminal behaviour 'by seeking out different kinds of evidence'?[4] Adding to such evidential difficulties is the fact that cony-catching literature was implicated in exploiting the same anxieties as the authorities who were in the business of redefining what constituted illegal behaviour. As Craig Dionne says:

> McMullan's ambitious socio-historical account is meant to settle the score, to find out the truth about these criminal gangs, but his own discourse of criminology objectifies the cony-catching manuals by reading them as an instance of an ahistorical entity called 'crime', a term whose social meaning is contingent upon changing historical perspectives.[5]

And such perspectives did change during the sixteenth century as legislation on vagrancy both increased and diversified. Phrased around the deserving or undeserving poor, the organizing principles which governed such legislation were founded upon defining the itinerant's relationship to work. Therefore, the primary distinction made was between the 'sturdy beggar' – 'mighty in body and able to labour' – and those who were legitimately disabled.[6] Although a plethora of categories arose later, most legislation was aimed at defining the differences between these two groups: 'the civic counterpart of the sturdy beggar was but a species – with an infinite number of varieties – of the genus *rogue*'.[7] To put it crudely, unemployment became a crime because the authorities had no way to deal with what Arthur Kinney calls 'the Tudor dispossessed' other than by demarcating them from the rest of society through branding and whipping, eradicating them altogether by hanging, or by sending them back to the very place where they had been evicted or disenfranchised.[8]

The question arises: what part did the writing of Walker, Awdeley, Harman, Greene and others, play in all this? According to Dionne:

The cony-catching pamphlets used stereotypes of sloth and indolence to incite anger in their readers about the transient poor. In so doing they worked as ideological handmaids to the legal reforms that attempted to deal with the effects of severe social and economic shifts at root in the dislocation of manorial production: rapid industrial expansion, dispossession of tenant farms, debasement of currency, periods of uncontrolled inflation, a doubling of population, all this during a time of 'heavy government expenditures for defense, exploration, and an expansionist economy'.[9]

That the pamphlets were intimately connected to the vast socio-economic upheavals of the sixteenth century cannot be ignored, but to cite the pamphlets as 'ideological handmaids' depends upon accepting that in some sense the pamphlets are what they purportedly claimed to be: caveats against cony-catchers. Sandra Clark's view is that the pamphlets are 'moralistic' whose 'primary function . . . was to inform rather than to entertain, and they are presented as factual accounts of the deceptions currently practised by rogues and vagabonds'. Clark continues:

> But it does not do to take them entirely at face value; undoubtedly they are factual, truthful, realistic to different degrees – but none of them is without an element of literary artifice, and the desire to tell the truth is modified by pressures conscious and unconscious, to entertain, to moralize, to conform to traditional ways of telling a tale.[10]

Clark seeks to maintain a distinction here between facts, truth and 'literary artifice' which the cony-catching pamphlets do not uphold. Yet, for the most part, the pamphlets have been taken at face value – not least because there is so much corresponding evidence which appears to support the content of their writing. Its worth remembering, too, that moralizing, even when taken at face value, is no more an ahistorical or apolitical category than crime. So convincing is the air of veracity attached to this literature that the editors of *Crime and Punishment in England: A Sourcebook* cite the cony-catching pamphlets as an authentic 'contemporary view on crime in Tudor England'.[11] Harman's 'very detailed account' of 'the case of Nicholas Jennings' is deemed to be 'the best we have of such criminals . . . it illustrates the skill and success of such counterfeit-cranks'.[12]

Is the case of Nicholas Jennings as good as its word? Let us explore some of the rhetorical structure of the story. Harman, a JP from Kent, is interrupted one day when his 'book was half printed', upon which he tells us how he came upon 'early in the morning a Counterfeit Crank under my lodging at the Whitefriars'. At this stage, though, according to the story, he does not know that the Crank is an impostor. The man appears 'loathsome', covered in blood, with a 'horrible countenance'. After striking up a conversation, Harman demands to know what is wrong with him, whereupon he is told the man has 'the falling sickness' (epilepsy). Harman notices that he refuses to be cleaned by an 'honest poor woman' and when asked why, the Crank claims that he should fall to 'bleeding afresh again'. In Harman's account, 'These words made me more to suspect him', though of what we are not yet told. Immediately, Harman interrogates him: 'Then I asked him where he was born, what his name was, how long he had this disease, and what time he had been here about London, and in what place.' Upon receiving the information from the man he now knows as Nicholas Jennings he swings into action: sending the 'printer of this book to Bethlem to understand the truth' of the illness.[13] Meanwhile, two boys are employed to 'diligently and vigilantly' follow him as he goes about his begging business. They observe him refreshing his disguise of blood and dirt, and taking a lot of money begging. Following such detective work, the 'zealous printer' finds a 'Constable' and Jennings is charged with being a 'malefactor and a dissembling vagabond'. Upon arrest, he is literally exposed. 'They stripped him stark naked, and as many as saw him said they never saw a handsomer man, with a yellow flaxen beard, and fair skinned, without any spot of grief.' Jennings is summarily punished:

> where he was stripped stark naked, and his ugly attire put upon him before the masters thereof, who wondered greatly at his dissimulation. For which offence he stood upon the pillory at Cheapside, both in his ugly and handsome attire. And after that went in the mill while his ugly picture was a drawing. And then [he] was whipped at a cart's tail through London, and his displayed banner carried before him unto his own door and so back to Bridewell again, and there remained for a time, and at length let at liberty, on the condition he would prove an honest man, and labour truly to get his living. And his picture remaineth at Bridewell for a monument.[14]

In this case urban fact and literature correspond: a man fitting the description of Jennings *'alias* Blunt . . . appeared before the Court of Aldemen in January 1567'.[15]

In many ways, the case of Nicholas Jennings is the paradigmatic cony-catching account. Undoubtedly the country and the streets of London offered plenty of 'proof and precedent of Bedlam beggars', but that does not mean we should simply read such texts as straightforward evidence.[16] Despite the correspondence between fact and fiction, they should not be collapsed into one another, read separately, or teased apart. Harman's writing is reflexive about the fiction and evidence which it offers. He interrupts the very 'book' you are reading in order to interpolate the 'counterfeit crank' immediately putting its textual quality into play. The ensuing story of detection, in which his 'printer' plays detective, reveals what the author already knows: that Jennings is not as he appears. Undermining his own purported claim to an authentic account, the disconcerting truth which Harman eventually reveals is that the world is full of 'artificial persons,' and that counterfeiting and writing are infrangibly intertwined.[17] The cony-catching pamphlet was both an authentic description of a social fiction and a fictive account of a cultural fact. Significantly, Jennings is punished in both his 'ugly and handsome attire' as if neither persona could denote him truly. Ironically, Harman's literature of detection discovers dissimulation in order to disguise it again. It is the act of punishment by the authorities which ultimately seeks to prove Jennings' faking, only later to define him as 'an honest man'. But the whip which seeks authority through its authenticating zeal, in effect, only rationalizes its own sense of failure. What Harman discovers is that Jennings's crime is one of dissimulation: of not being who you really are. But everyone who was unemployed – evicted from the land, demobbed from the army, every vagrant and masterless man – was no longer who they were. In effect, every crank was a counterfeit crank; every vagrant was an idle rogue. Through Harman's account we can see how the casualties of a changing economic system quickly become its scapegoats. And Jennings' story – that an unemployed beggar could make more money than his sturdy hard-working counterpart – quickly became part of capitalist apocrypha and of literary history.[18]

A generation after Harman's *Caveat*, the prolific author Robert Greene turned to writing cony-catching pamphlets just before he died around 1591–2. With a dazzling display of wit and rhetoric, Greene wrote *A Notable Discovery of Cozenage*, *The Second Part of Cony-Catching*, *The Third and Last Part of Cony Catching* and *A Disputation Between a He Cony Catcher and She Cony Catcher* which, for Clark, form the 'heart' of the cony-catching genre.[19] Reworking material from the earlier pamphlets, Greene effectively restructured the components of prose-narrative as he redefined notions of authorship. In this sense, Italo Calvino's concept of an author perfectly suits Robert Greene: 'The author of every book is a fictitious character whom the existent author invents to make him the author of his fictions.'[20] Before the benefits of copyright, and at a time when the writer was poorly paid and barely recognized, Greene developed an extraordinary metafictional and authorial persona. This has led to the paradoxical situation whereby the more we find out about Greene from his contemporaries and from Greene himself, the less clear our picture of him becomes. Such a lack of definition has continuously troubled critics and scholars. Paucity of evidence has led many to agree with Charles Crupi that 'there is much uncertainty about the facts of Greene's life'. Despite this, Crupi feels compelled to rely on scant accounts and hearsay; reluctantly concluding that Greene 'was a notorious character in literary London'.[21] After 'sorting through the various sources' and evidence, Crupi's 'verdict' is that the case for Greene's character is 'not proven'.[22] Although he proffers the hope that there will be found 'some certainties in the end', he finally impeaches Greene and finds him guilty of not being securely himself.[23] Somewhat disconcertingly, even by his assiduous biographer, Greene appears to be as much an 'artificial person' as Nicholas Jennings is. Yet, ironically, the credibility of the characters cited by Greene depend upon the author being an authentic witness.

To understand Greene's mystique means coming to terms with the complex way in which he was embedded in the forms and function of his writing. As he begins *A Notable Discovery of Cozenage*, Greene quickly sets up a mock distinction between continental erudition and native English custom and wit, one which turns into a discourse upon 'the Art of *Cony catching*'.[24] Writing in this form created a new urban style, a 'comic prose' which, according to Manley, 'depended foremost on its contamination of the traditional humanistic canons of Ciceronian prose with the base element of popular idiom, marketplace, and theatre'.[25] This interrelationship between high and low discourse gives Greene's writing a dynamic hybridity. According to Kinney, in a *Notable Discovery*, there is 'a bifurcation of perspective' which is due to Greene's position as 'active narrator . . . and the moral commentator'.[26] As Greene deploys the tropes of classical learning, the plain speech of urban moralism, the idiomatic language of the underworld like canting and other slang, it becomes impossible to find a single authoritative voice in, or through, his writing. Underwriting this is what Constance C. Relihan has identified, in *Fashioning Authority*, as a 'split between the narrative voice and the authorial voice'.[27] For Relihan, Greene's departure from earlier writers is pivotal:

> The differences between Harman's narrative approach and that Robert Greene adopts in his criminal pamphlets is clear. As we shall see, Greene allows the reader to doubt the veracity of his narrative voices much more overtly than does Harman, and Greene even actively causes his readers to perceive a gap between authorial and narrative voice. Instead, Harman repeatedly refers to his role as an auditor of criminal anecdotes, to criminals who have appeared before him when he was 'in Commission of the Peace' . . . [his] emphasis throughout is to present allegedly factual information in an impersonal narrative voice.[28]

This perception of authority and veracity in Harman's narrative voice is crucial to Stephen Greenblatt's highly influential account of the role of rogue literature in Renaissance culture which he explores in 'Invisible Bullets'.[29] According to Greenblatt: 'in *A Caveat for Common Cursitors* (and in much of the cony-catching literature of the period in England and France) printing is represented in the text as a force for social order and the detection of criminal fraud.' Greenblatt goes on to claim that:

> The subversive voices are produced by and within the affirmations of order; they are powerfully registered, but they do not undermine that order. Indeed . . . the order is neither possible nor fully convincing without both the presence and perception of betrayal.

Much is at stake in this monological paradigm: dissenting or subversive voices are undermined by 'broken promises' only to become subsumed in the fictions which founded 'the modern state'.[30] Such an account depends upon a contractual distinction of voices within the very structure of the literature. Yet, if such a pattern can be discovered in Harman, any sense of betrayal is obscured if not lost in Greene.

A 'University wit', Greene put a wide variety of voices and discourses into play as he borrowed, manipulated and developed the tradition of rogue literature. Even his early cony-catching text, *A Notable Discovery*, was 'not designed to reveal cony-catchers but to play games with language as cony-catchers do', says Kinney. Instead 'the author is transformed by the pamphlet into a cony-catcher himself; and we in turn teased into becoming conies by buying this book, tricked into thinking it was the exposé it proposed to be'.[31] As the 'book keeps turning in on itself and turning us in on ourselves' the bounds between cony and catcher, fiction and non-fiction, authorial voice and subversive voice, become increasingly commingled and confused.[32]

In *A Disputation Between a He Cony Catcher and She Cony Catcher*, Greene adopts an unusual narrative style: a dialogue between 'Nan' and 'Laurence' who attempt to discover that which is 'most prejudicial to the commonwealth'. This dialogue speculates whether the stability of the modern state is more threatened by male or female rogues.[33] It's a mockery, of course, one which seems reflexively aware of Greenblatt's pattern of containment.[34]

Significantly, the narrative voice in the 'disputation' operates between 'Greene', 'Nan', 'Laurence', and a disembodied third person. At one point the two rogues are discussing their fellow crossbiters but, with a stylized sense of self-consciousness, refuse to name them, whereupon 'Nan', somewhat ambiguously, invokes Greene's authorial persona: 'I fear R. G. will name them soon in his *Black Book*. A pestilence on him! They say he hath set down my husband's pedigree, and yours too, Laurence.'[35] The apparent moralistic impulse of the pamphlet – that rogues should cease their activities because 'R. G.' will discover them – is undercut by the text itself. 'Laurence' takes him on: 'Nan, Nan, let R. G. beware!', he says as he condemns him to dissolution and infamy (charges eerily echoed by Greene's biographers). A similar pattern of representational reflexivity emerges in *The Defence of Cony-Catching* whereby the narrator, 'Cuthbert', begins: 'I cannot but wonder master R. G. what poetical fury made you so fantastic, to write against cony-catchers?'[36] Somewhat disconcertingly, then, the credibility of 'R. G.' to write authentically about London's rogues depends upon Greene's own fictional characters. Not only is the contractual distinction between betrayer and betrayed increasingly difficult to locate in Greene, but he develops a fiction that tends to conceal rather than discover its own origins and purpose – such that neither subversion nor containment seems possible or relevant. Through fictionalizing his authorial persona, Greene, like the cony-catching pamphlets of which he was a part, generated fictions beyond the simple confines of authorship. Such was the force of this literary centrifuge that Greene's actual death could not gainsay his death as a fiction.

Greene's deathbed output was only surpassed by his posthumous writing. From *The Repentance of Robert Greene* and *Greene's Groatsworth of Wit* to *Greene's News Both from Heaven and Hell* and *Greene's Ghost Haunting Cony Catchers*, 'Greene' proved that it was both possible and profitable to publish after he had perished. That Greene was popular and others wanted to cash in on his reputation goes some way towards explaining this phenomenon, but few characters have had such an extensive career after their death.[37] Undaunted, some scholars are determined to discover the 'authentic Greene', often through various kinds of textual taxonomy. From scrutinizing biographical evidence to crunching his words and those of others through a computer, attempts are continually made to identify the real Greene and distinguish him from 'forgers' like Henry Chettle. This is the scope of D. Allen Carroll's edition of *Greene's Groatsworth of Wit*.[38] But Carroll's hope that we are approaching the time when 'all questions of attribution may one day be settled by statistical analysis (stylometry)' perhaps misses the point. It is Greene's very style, itself produced through quoting the fictions of others and himself, that enables him to be 'copied', 'forged', 'plagiarised'. Did Greene forge

Greene? At least some of the titles above suggest that readers were more interested in the authenticity of Greene's style than the security of its origins. Whichever way you look at it, Greene appears – somewhat precociously – as the consummate metropolitan. He became, as Manley says, a posthumous luminary because he 'successfully negotiated the preexisting boundaries between life and art, entertainment and literature, outlaw urban setting and in-law society'.[39]

In the first decade of the seventeenth century, Thomas Dekker adopted Greene's mantle as writer of London's underworld. Like Greene, Dekker was a skilful picklock of his predecessor's work. Both Kinney and E. D. Pendry see Dekker as Greene's 'closest' and 'self-appointed heir'.[40] With a pragmatism born of necessity, Dekker turned to pamphleteering because the relatively more lucrative activity of writing for the stage was continuously disrupted by theatre closures due to increased outbreaks of the plague. Early professional writers like Greene and Dekker usually received a one-time payment for their work. The rate for a pamphlet was somewhere between £1–2, whilst a play script could be double that or more. Without the financial security of copyright, or the consistent support of a patron, writers who sustained themselves solely by the pen lived precariously – usually on the verge of bankruptcy. Dekker (like Greene), for example, had no consistent patron and spent more than seven years in prison for debt. Consequently, he continually sought to establish a viable relationship with the pamphlet-buying public by generating a wide constituency of readers. In so doing, Dekker appealed directly to his customers by developing a popular and intimate type of urban literature.[41] To cast Dekker, then, as a 'hack' writer inevitably obscures the important contribution he makes to the development of prose literature, narrative structure and metropolitan stylistics.

In his three main cony-catching pamphlets – *The Bellman of London, Lantern and Candlelight*, and *O per se O* – Dekker plays up Greene's Diogenical conceit of becoming a quasi-moral observer carrying a lantern by daylight trying to find an honest man in the city of London.[42] More openly than earlier writers, Dekker undercuts the purported moralism and edification of his pamphlets in order to proselytize the value of entertainment: 'Read and laugh; read and learn; read and loathe. Laugh at the knavery; learn out the mystery; loathe the base villainy.'[43] Tongue-in-cheek, perhaps, but Dekker's metropolitan writing worked across a tense contradiction embedded in a literature of discovery. The 'attempt to mystify London, to present it as an alien realm honeycombed with shadowy sub-communities' was matched by the narrator's claim to shed light – by candle, lantern, or perspicacity – upon that realm's denizens.[44] Dekker plays both ends against the pamphlet-buyer:

> Give me leave to lead you by the hand in a wilderness where are none but monsters – whose cruelty you need not fear, because I teach the way to tame them. Ugly they are in shape and devilish in conditions. Yet to behold them far off, may delight you, and to know their qualities if ever you should come near them may save you from much danger.[45]

Anyone seeking to arouse their thrills by quelling their anxieties was in considerably more danger of losing twopence than of palpably facing cruel monsters. A new kind of reader-customer was drawn by the paradoxes which made this kind of urban fiction. The delights of taming one's fears were, however, somewhat short-lived as Dekker, like those before him, zealously generated ever more enormities to be discovered. Whilst London's underworld was 'based on a true story' of poverty, vagrancy and prostitution, its organizing principles rest more on the developing structures of metropolitan literature than on the collective criminal conspiracies of the urban dispossessed.

Dekker produced a new form of metropolitan prose by expanding Greene's style to include a huge grab-bag of voices, discourses and social registers. This extravagant mix included, among other things, allegory, realism, classical allusions, canting and other slang, erudite, bawdy, homily, colloquy, sentimentalism, satire, moralism, mockery, parody and piety – often in close and contaminating proximity. Dekker created a rich and dense narrative medium through which he laid the foundations for the urban prose of later writers like Defoe and Dickens. Ironically, that for which Dekker is most condemned – lack of coherence and structural inconsistencies – is inextricably linked to that which made him so innovative. Dekker's stylistic tours de force stem from his ability to blend social landscape and London's topography through an imaginative panoramic narrative in which the writer was embedded. In *The Wonderful Year*, 'Death' appears 'like a Spanish leaguer' and 'Plague' sports his 'purple colours' as both form an army to attack London. Dekker, as writer, places himself in the midst of the urban fray:

> Join all your hands together, and with your bodies cast a ring about me: let me behold your ghastly visages, that my paper may receive their true pictures: echo forth your groans through the hollow trunk of my pen, and rain your gummy tears into mine ink, that even marble bosoms may be shaken with terror, and hearts of adamant melt into compassion.[46]

Writing, perception and situation becomes fused in layers of metaphor and figurative language. Dekker's 'true pictures' are complex 'structures of feeling' produced by melding experience and narrative. Through this Dekker can be seen as a both transparent 'painter of London life' and a powerful 'social critic'.[47]

Dekker's 'favourite device' and chief innovation was 'the panoramic sentence' which, as Pendry notes, should not be confused with realism.[48] Rather, the variation of styles, multiplicity of forms, compromise the very ways of seeing it purports to set up. Such writing, accordingly, is able to 'respond sensitively and experimentally to a wide range of different aesthetic promptings that may indeed be irreconcilable one with another'.[49] This sense of a 'multiconsciousness', or the juxtaposition of consciousnesses, brings to mind Mikhail Bakhtin's concept of 'polyphony'.[50] A crucial term for Bakhtin's notion of prosaics, polyphony refers to the effect in writing whereby the author's voice is just one of many competing and unmerged voices in the text. One of the principal functions of a polyphonic text is its 'unfinalizability': that is, being continuously and open-endedly dialogic. This not only explains why critics chastise Dekker for his unevenness and lack of originality, but also why terms like plagiarism, copying or even theft, are inappropriate concepts through which to think about cony-catching literature. Writers like Harman, Greene and Dekker integrated the reproductive potential of narrative prose with that which it seamlessly generated and represented: metropolitan literature and London's underworld. To distinguish between these two would be as fruitless as identifying the authentic Greene, defining Dekker's plagiarism or detecting a 'real' counterfeit crank. To grasp the significance of this style in the development of (early) prose, it might be more productive to see the cony-catching literature as part of an integrated, unfinalizable, whole rather than as the province of distinct and separate authors.

If Dekker's unfinalized observations of London touched upon almost every aspect of metropolitan culture, from another contemporary perspective John Stow's *The Survey of London* (1603) was no less panoramic. Although written from a different position than that which generated the cony-catching pamphlets – Stow was supported and patronized by London's civic elite – *The Survey* grapples with some of the same issues concerning the way in which London appeared to itself. When *The Survey* was published at the very end of the sixteenth century, London's economic growth and huge demographic increase meant that it had overwhelmed its medieval boundaries. The city's Liberties (its extended suburbs) became increasingly populated by poor immigrants from all over England and continental Europe seeking refuge and a livelihood. Semi-official and often poorly regulated living areas, increasingly inhabited by the itinerant poor, spread out from the ancient walls of the city and incorporated once distinct villages and parishes. The relentless attempts to distinguish sturdy beggars as indolent workers ensured that the suburbs constituted and remained a vast army of cheap labour. By exploiting and deploying its wealth gained from commercial enterprise, London's mercantile class steadily expanded and appropriated civic government by regulating poverty, vagrancy, and prostitution. At the same time London became an intimate witness to the centralization of state power as the Tudor court consolidated its hold on a post-feudal aristocracy, its customs and social resources, including control of the church and confiscation of its lands during the Reformation.

Although Stow's *Survey* is thoroughly embedded in the confluence of forces and circumstances outlined briefly here, it cannot be reduced to one particular point of view. Son of a tallow-chandler, and member of the Merchant Taylors' Company, Stow was intimately connected to the mercantile class. This caste were the chief beneficiaries of London's economic growth and they constituted an oligarchy which could, at times, rival the crown. Most identifiable in Stow is the reconstruction of London's history as one of bourgeois benefaction. In Stow's account, civic pride – founded on London's citizen worthies – comes to be built on patricianism, charity and other good works. With a compelling mix of rhetorical allusion and antiquarian discovery, Stow suggests that nowadays such values are in decline and the fabric of the city is under threat. This sense of impending dilapidation in the city's social and material infrastructure underpins a discontinuity in the trajectory of *The Survey*. According to Manley, 'Stow confronted a register of change at odds with the temporal continuities stressed at the beginning of the work.'[51] Thus, the story of London's development in *The Survey* is not one of progression. The catalogue of changes amounted to a diminution of community and an undermining of London's edificial values. Stow's record, then, could be seen as an indictment of the incumbent city fathers who spent less on charity than they could and more on feasts and pageants for their own glory than they should.

Stow's compendious taxonomy in *The Survey* tends to stabilize and define a city which, for many, was transgressing all its bounds.[52] As he charted, catalogued, and named the various sites of London, Stow gave his readers a much looked for sense of order. Moreover, Stow reorganized urban space as he reclassified London's history. At times it seems as if Stow echoes the city government's attempt to bring order to the streets through containment and control. William Fleetwood – who was aptly entitled London's Recorder – was an ardent fan and supporter of Stow, and spent many hours locating, identifying and punishing vagrants and others in the city. Although both men organized London in very different ways, Stow's compassion and wider sense of social responsibility meant that the form of *The Survey* was often at odds with its content. Fleetwood attempted to regulate and purify the metropolitan body politic, to expunge its unruly elements, whereas Stow's writing articulated a conflicted and political reminiscence, one which harked back to a time of charity, hospitality and an all-inclusive harmony.

The rifts and contradictions in Stow's London generate some extraordinary literary effects. Most noticeable is the way in which *The Survey*, according to Archer, is 'suffused with nostalgia'.[53] This appears to contradict both Stow's avowed intention (often taken at face value) that what he attempts is 'the discovery of London', and how *The Survey* is often used simply as an evidential source and factual historical account.[54] But to read *The Survey* in such a straightforward way would radically diminish its purpose. What Stow's text sets up is the discovery of the reader's longing for London's past. *The Survey* uniquely creates this effect, not least because the past he invites the reader to imagine is one which could never be reconciled with his contemporary London. Stow's metropolitan present was underwritten by an ideological clash between residual feudal principles and the vigour of a mercantile ethos. Ironically, one of the most enduring aspects of *The Survey* is the way in which it meticulously articulates the irrevocability of its own longings. As Stow chastises those responsible for not upholding the principles of charity, the nostalgia generated by *The Survey* could also be read as an anxiously muted critique of the growing absolutism of the late Tudor state. Either way, Stow's nostalgic discoveries – an escape from the future into the past – set the tone for much English literature to come.

NOTES

1 See Beier and Finlay.
2 See Beier.

3 McMullan, p. 2.
4 Ibid., pp. 2–3.

5   Dionne, p. 31.
6   Beier, pp. 1–12 and 107–44.
7   Judges, p. xxxvii.
8   Kinney, p. 5.
9   Dionne, p. 37.
10 Clark, p. 41.
11 Barrett and Harrison.
12 Ibid., p. 36. (A counterfeit crank was deemed to be a person who pretended to be an epileptic in order to justify their status as a beggar.)
13 Bethlem, Bethlehem Hospital, Bedlam, was London's infamous asylum, one of the first for those troubled in the mind.
14 Judges, p. 90. (The mill to which Harman refers was a giant corn-grinding machine in Bridewell powered by a dozen men or more who were whipped to exhaustion or death.)
15 Beier, pp. 117–18.
16 Edgar becomes a counterfeit crank in Shakespeare's *King Lear* (2.2.184–5).
17 Agnew, especially ch. 3, 'Artificial Persons', pp. 101–48.
18 See Conan Doyle, especially 'The Man with the Twisted Lip', pp. 123–48, where Holmes is called in to investigate the death of a city gentleman who turns out to be prospering as a counterfeit beggar. In Doyle, as in Harman, the 'crime' is one of dissimulation.
19 Clark, p. 46.
20 Calvino, Italo (1981) *If On a Winter's Night a Traveler*, San Diego: Harcourt Brace Jovanovich, p. 180.
21 Crupi, p. 47.
22 Ibid., p. 2.
23 Ibid.
24 Kinney, p. 164.
25 Manley, p. 321.
26 Kinney, p. 158.
27 Relihan, p. 56.
28 Ibid., p. 61.
29 Greenblatt, pp. 21–65.
30 Ibid., pp. 50–2.
31 Kinney, p. 158.
32 Ibid.
33 Judges, p. 206.
34 Such containment being one of the principles of new historicist readings of Renaissance culture, of which Greenblatt was an early exponent. Drawing upon Michel Foucault's concepts of power, new historicism accounts often claim that oppositions to authority, rather than subverting its power, are necessary for its strength and maintenance.
35 Judges, p. 220.
36 Salgado, Gamini (1972) *Cony-Catchers and Bawdy Baskets: An Anthology of Elizabethan Low Life*, Harmondsworth: Penguin, p. 345.
37 More recently, for example, Greene has appeared as Nick Greene in *Orlando* by Virginia Woolf.
38 Carroll.
39 Manley, p. 326.
40 Kinney, p. 209 and Pendry, p. 17.
41 See Twyning, especially ch. 4, 'Breaking Loose from Hell: Devils, Despair, Dystopia', pp. 129–201.
42 Diogenes appears as an inspiration to the writers of cony-catching pamphlets. An ancient Greek philosopher *c*.400 BC, he was a playful moralist and an acute satirist. Diogenes had a reputation for being an eccentric and colourful character, so it is easy to see why he would have been a hero to a university wit like Greene. According to legend, he used to walk around Athens carrying a lantern by daylight looking for an honest man – an image which underscores much of London's underworld literature including Thomas Dekker's *Lantern and Candlelight*.
43 Pendry, p. 183.
44 Twyning, p. 63.
45 Pendry, p. 177.
46 Ibid., p. 43.
47 For contrasting views on the function of Dekker's observations see Twyning and Jones-Davies.
48 Pendry, p. 11.
49 Ibid., p. 21.
50 For an exploration of this complex concept see Bakhtin.
51 Manley, p. 162.
52 See Archer, Agnew and Twyning.
53 Archer, Ian W., 'The Nostalgia of John Stow', in. Smith, Strier and Bevington, pp. 17–34 (p. 21).
54 Stow.

REFERENCES AND FURTHER READING

Agnew, Jean-Christophe (1986). *Worlds Apart: The Market and the Theater in Anglo-American Thought, 1550–1750*. Cambridge: Cambridge University Press.

Archer, Ian W. (1991). *The Pursuit of Stability: Social Relations in Elizabethan London*. Cambridge: Cambridge University Press.

Bakhtin, Mikhail (1963). *Problems of Dostoevsky's Poetics*, ed. and tr. Caryl Emerson. Minneapolis: University of Minnesota Press.

Barrett, Andrew and Harrison, Christopher (1999). *Crime and Punishment in England: A Sourcebook*. London: University College London Press.

Beier, A. L. (1985). *Masterless Men: The Vagrancy Problem in England 1560–1640*. London and New York: Methuen.

Beier, A. L. and Finlay, Roger (1986). *London 1500–1700: The Making of the Metropolis*. London and New York: Longman.

Carroll, D. Allen (ed.) (1994). *Greene's Groatsworth of wit: bought with a million of repentance (1592) attributed to Henry Chettle and Robert Greene*. New York: Binghampton.

Clark, Sandra (1985). *The Elizabethan Pamphleteers: Popular Moralist Pamphlets 1580–1640*. Rutherford: Fairleigh Dickinson University Press.

Conan Doyle, Arthur (1993). *The Adventures of Sherlock Holmes*. Oxford: Oxford University Press.

Crupi, Charles W. (1986). *Robert Greene*. Boston: Twayne Publishers.

Dionne, Craig (1998). 'Playing the "Cony": Anonymity in Underworld Literature'. *Genre*, 30, 29–50.

Greenblatt, Stephen (1992). *Shakespearean Negotiations*. Berkeley: University of California Press.

Greene, Robert (1881–3). *The Life and Complete Works in Prose and Verse of Robert Greene*, ed. Alexander B. Grosart. 15 vols. London: The Huth Library.

Jones-Davies, Marie Thérèse (1958). *Un Peintre de la Vie Londonienne: Thomas Dekker circa 1572–1632*. Paris: Didier.

Judges, A. V. (1930). *The Elizabethan Underworld*. London: Routledge.

Kinney, Arthur F. (1990). *Rogues, Vagabonds, and Sturdy Beggars*. Amherst: University of Massachusetts Press.

Manley, Lawrence (1995). *Literature and Culture in Early Modern London*. Cambridge: Cambridge University Press.

McMullan, John L. (1984). *The Canting Crew: London's Criminal Underworld, 1550–1700*. New Brunswick: Rutgers University Press.

Miller, Edwin Haviland (1959). *The Professional Writer in Elizabethan England*. Cambridge, MA: Harvard University Press.

Pendry, E. D. (ed.) (1968). *Thomas Dekker*. Cambridge, MA: Harvard University Press.

Relihan, Constance C. (1994). *Fashioning Authority: The Development of Elizabethan Novelistic Discourse*. Kent, OH, and London: Kent State University Press.

Salgado, Gamini (1984). *The Elizabethan Underworld*. Totowa, NJ: Rowman and Littlefield.

Smith, David L., Strier, Richard and Bevington, David (eds) (1995). *The Theatrical City: Culture, Theatre and Politics in London 1576–1649*. Cambridge: Cambridge University Press.

Stow, John (1908). *A Survey of London*, ed. C. L. Kingsford from the text of 1603. Oxford: Clarendon Press.

Twyning, J. A. (1998). *London Dispossessed: Literature and Social Space in the Early Modern City*. Basingstoke: Macmillan Press.

Williams, Raymond (1977). *Marxism and Literature*. Oxford and New York: Oxford University Press.

11
Playhouses and the Role of Drama
Michael Hattaway

In order to understand the nature of dramatic representation in sixteenth- and seventeenth-century England the location and dating of theatres may be less important than we think.

A narrative of English theatre predicated entirely upon 'Renaissance' might single out one event: the year 1576 when James Burbage, a joiner turned player, constructed in Shoreditch, just to the north of the City of London, the most significant permanent construction dedicated to dramatic performance in England since Roman times, a twenty-sided polygonal building with three levels of galleries and a covered stage.[1] Its name, 'the Theatre', proclaimed both commercial enterprise and classical emulation. The next year another playhouse, the Curtain, was erected close by. But records abound for performances well before this. Not only does it now seem that there was an earlier playhouse, the Red Lion in Whitechapel from about 1567, but we know of a myriad of earlier performances: at court and at inns, in the halls of Oxford and Cambridge colleges and the Inns of Court, as well as in great houses of the gentry and aristocracy. Groups of boys from schools or choirs had also provided dramatic entertainment: around 1600 they were to become fashionable enough for their masters to house them in their own theatres. Plays not performed on the stages of theatres were often designated as 'interludes': groups of entertainers could comprise tumblers and minstrels as well as actors, and their songs, mummings, allegorical plays or 'morals', and farces were given hall performances as part of banquets and feasts. The drama was always associated with music, dance and non-mimetic entertainment – one of the London theatres, the Hope, doubled as a bear-baiting pit.

In some contexts, the dates not only of the constructions of playhouses but of the first performances of plays may not be of special significance. 'Occasional' plays commissioned for professional companies for private performances could be and were given later for further monetary gain, whether in London amphitheatres ('public' playhouses) or indoors ('private' playhouses), in halls adapted from ecclesiastical use or, in the Caroline period, in theatres that catered to London's elites. *Love's Labour's Lost* may have been written for a coterie around 1594, was probably performed at court at Christmas 1597, and in 1598 was performed at a public playhouse. This is a play of great verbal intricacy: its revival in a popular playhouse may suggest that Hamlet's opinion of the groundlings, 'for the most part . . . capable of nothing but inexplicable dumb shows and noise' (3.2.11–12) may have been patronizing. Although many may have been illiterate, habits of listening, to sermons as well as plays, may have given them a serviceable kind of education. In 1610 *King Lear* was performed in Gowthwaite Hall in Yorkshire: given that this performance took place in the house of a recusant family, it may be that this revival, like many revivals, for a student of cultural history is as significant as the occasion of its first performance (1605–6).[2]

Some players formed companies of 'sharers' under the patronage of wealthy aristocrats, and it was such a group, Leicester's Men, who first occupied the Theatre, while further companies were housed in the other playhouses that entrepreneurs like Philip Henslowe built soon afterwards. Sharers owned their companies and paid a proportion of their takings to the syndicates that owned the playhouses. The status of players as 'servants' to the nobility was a legal fiction that protected them from being whipped out of the parish by unfriendly Justices of the Peace as 'rogues, vagabonds, and sturdy beggars' – as a statute of 1598 categorized the unlicensed members of their profession. It was the sharers who commissioned plays from playwrights and, when these were delivered, owned them outright. Despite many complaints from the godly and industrious – which the players could counter by making contributions to parish relief[3] – large profits were to be made, and there was a huge demand for new plays which was often met by pairs or teams of playwrights working collaboratively. Henslowe's 'Diary' reveals that, for example, from February to June 1592 Lord Strange's Men 'in nineteen weeks . . . gave 105 performances of twenty-three plays'.[4]

The playhouses were situated on the thresholds of London, in 'liberties' that were outside the jurisdiction of the City, their geographic marginality suggesting to some interpreters a cultural marginality that, it has been assumed, might be inscribed upon our readings of the texts performed in them.[5] The Corporation of London considered that the crowds that frequented plays not only generated frays but drew workers from their trades and kept congregations from attendance at evensong. Sir Nicholas Woodrofe, Lord Mayor in 1580, in a letter to the Lord Chancellor designated the players 'a very superfluous sort of men'.[6] Such complaints were only partially taken up. In 1582 we learn one of the reasons why: the Privy Council requested the Lord Mayor to allow 'certain companies of players to exercise their playing in London . . . [that] they might attain to the more dexterity and perfection in their profession, the better to content Her Majesty'.[7] Other troupes toured the provinces, performing when appropriate on the scaffolds of portable theatres of the sort we see illustrated in engravings from the Low Countries (no illustration of such an English occasion has survived). When the London playhouses were closed, notably by outbreaks of plague in the 1590s, the London professionals were also forced into the provinces on tour. The text of Marlowe's *Doctor Faustus* exists in two forms, both published long after Marlowe's death in 1593. The first, dated 1604 (the A text) derives from provincial performance. Stage directions reveal that no actors appeared above the stage or aloft in the playhouse 'Heavens'. The B text, however, printed in 1616, derives from performances in a fully equipped London playhouse. There the Devils 'aloft' watch Faustus on the stage below as he conjures and later prepares for death. A (spectacular?) dragon seems to appear in the middle of Faustus's conjuring. Their presence ironizes those parts of the stage action, generates a different effect for the play, taking away from the hero's stature and revealing the depth of his self-deception.[8] The Induction to Marston's *Malcontent* (1603), originally written for boys, reveals that the play was appropriated by the King's Men who were taking revenge on boy players who had 'stolen' from them a play called '*Jeronimo*', probably *The Spanish Tragedy*. From these we may deduce two things: the theatre of Renaissance England was not simply a metropolitan theatre but a national theatre, and the 'meaning' of any play text must have been shaped in part by particular conditions of theatrical performances.

London, however, was undoubtedly the centre for theatrical production. A few years after the building of the Theatre, William Shakespeare wrote a three-part sequence concerning the reign of *Henry VI* (1589–92?) that ambitiously and daringly presents the politics and struggles of the Wars of the Roses as well some of the battles of the Hundred Years War. It must have been not only a reminder to Elizabethan audiences of the perils of aristocratic factionalism and the horrors of civil war but of the precariousness of civil order. There is evidence of censorship in the sequence involving Jack Cade in *2 Henry VI*: Shakespeare in fact used for this episode the chroniclers' accounts of the Wat Tyler rebellion that had taken place earlier, in the reign of Richard II, to show how rebels might penetrate to the heart of the city.[9] Such plays, in the words of one describing Fletcher and Shakespeare's *Henry VIII* (1613), made 'greatness seem familiar'. That was at the end of Shakespeare's career: at the beginning, at the time of the Henry VI plays, his endeavour may also have appeared 'oppositional': on 12 November 1589 the Privy Council had written to the Archbishop of Canterbury, the Lord Mayor of London and the Master of the Revels asking them each to appoint someone to scrutinize all plays performed in and about the City of London because the players had taken upon themselves 'without judgement or decorum to handle in their plays certain matters of divinity and state'.[10] The fact that such orders were often repeated is yet another example of the way the reach of the Tudor state exceeded its grasp. Thirty-five years later Middleton's *A Game at Chess* (1624) notoriously satirized James' attempts to broker a match between his son and the Spanish Infanta.[11]

Those Henry VI plays were performed in one of Henslowe's theatres, the Rose which was in use from 1587 to 1603, one of the first theatres to be built south of the Thames, in the Liberty of the Clink, conveniently just across the river from the Inns of Court, students from which were playhouse habitués.[12] From 1599 the Rose was to be eclipsed by the first Globe, built out of the timbers of the Theatre on the Bankside just to its east, and home to the Lord Chamberlain's Men, later to become 'servants' of James himself and known as the King's Men. In 1600 Henslowe built a new theatre, the Fortune, for another of his companies, the Admiral's Men, whose star player, Edward Alleyn, had taken the principal roles in the plays of Marlowe.

When the foundations of the Rose were laid bare in 1989 the tapered stage seemed small (twenty-five feet across the yard at its front, thirty-seven feet at the rear, and about eighteen feet deep), yet experience in replica spaces indicates that epic effects that seem to be demanded by plays like those that comprise the Henry VI sequence do not depend upon illusion – large theatrical spaces or *trompe l'oeil* scenery to hold 'the vasty fields of France' – but can be generated by processions and duels, costumes, drums and trumpets. The generic word in the period for a theatre is 'playhouse' (the first recorded use of the word in *OED* is from about 1000), for actor, a 'player', and it is useful to remember the similarity between games and Renaissance plays. When Coleridge, near the beginning of the nineteenth century, famously wrote of the need for any artist to create 'A semblance of truth sufficient to procure for these shadows of imagination that willing suspension of disbelief for the moment, which constitutes poetic faith' (*Biographia Literaria*, 1817, II. xiv) he was drawing upon dramatic experience in theatres equipped for bourgeois realism where 'fourth wall' sets were made as far as was possible to resemble the realities of rooms, but where the experience of being in a theatre easily created that 'suspension of disbelief'. Nothing in a Renaissance playhouse was ever designed to persuade a spectator to 'believe in' a place or a character; everything on stage proclaimed its status as a sign. Plays were enacted in distinctive fictive worlds that were created within the frames of specifically theatrical architecture. These frames were always visible, essential signs of those conventions for game and revelry that govern the action. Although they traded in *spectacle*, Renaissance playhouses had no mechanism for *illusion*. Indeed dramatists encouraged their audiences to join in a collaborative endeavour of imaginative play, proclaiming the impossibility of a literal 'representation':

> The scene is now transported, gentles, to Southampton,
> There is the playhouse now, there must you sit.
> (Shakespeare, *Henry V*, 2. Chorus 35–6)

The spectators know that the 'scene' (or representation) can no more be 'changed' than the playhouse itself be transported to Southampton. When movable scenery was eventually used, notably in Jacobean court masques, the art of the scene painters' perspective would have drawn attention to itself – what was depicted was neither drawn from 'nature' nor did it represent an actual city location but was a timeless place out of literature or mythology, akin to what Mikhail Bakhtin termed a 'chronotope'.[13] Moreover, it was a feature of such entertainment for the scenes to be changed before the spectator's eyes, kindling not an illusion of change of place but of admiration for the mechanical art that could substitute one kind of mythic space for another.

This absence of illusion made it possible for playwrights to deploy a wide variety of registers. The opening of *Titus Andronicus* is a very emblematic pageant using the two basic axes of the stage, its width and the height of the tiring-house gallery situated above the tiring-house doors. This offered a playing space 'aloft' that could signify the walls of a besieged city, be used as a 'music room', or simply be a place from which those in authority, like the new emperor Saturninus in Shakespeare's play, might survey the scene. Other scenes contain on-stage violence which, given the excess, it is tempting to place in a loose category of 'naturalism'. Yet others are allegoric: in 5.2, Tamora, entering in a chariot, designates herself as 'Revenge' and her two sons 'Rape' and 'Murder'. Absence of illusion generated freedom of allusion: Shakespeare's 'Rome', here a 'wilderness of tigers' (3.1.53), was a displacement of other Renaissance concepts of 'Rome' and possibly referred to myths of court politics that could be applied to the moments of the play's productions. The mode of representation politicized the historical action: it was neither locked up in a historical time isolated from the audience by signs of the past nor located in a place separated from them by anything serving the function of a proscenium arch. A drawing survives that may record a stage production of this play: intriguingly the actors are garbed both in togas and Elizabethan dress.[14]

Plays themselves were classed not only according to hierarchies of literary decorum but within the categories of sports and games. An example: *Robin Hood and the Friar*, printed between 1553 and 1569,[15] which notes 'Here beginneth the play of Robin Hood, very proper to be played in May Games.' Playhouses were cheek by jowl with the bear-baiting arenas and brothels of Bankside, and texts were often prepared for or featured among the calendrical games of popular culture:

SLY: Is not a comonty a Christmas gambold or a tumbling trick?
BARTHOLOMEW: No, my good lord, it is more pleasing stuff.
SLY: What, household stuff?
BARTHOLOMEW: It is a kind of history.

(Shakespeare, The Taming of the Shrew, Ind. 2.132–6)

Sports, one category of games, take place on playing fields. It is best to think of Renaissance stages as spaces rather than places, as fields of play, places for supposing, spaces where ideas might be explored: of the tyranny of the senses in *A Midsummer Night's Dream*, of the relationship between authority and power in *King Lear*. The 'forest' of *As You Like It* signifies a condition – or state of mind – rather than a location.

Like sports, plays have 'rules' or conventions. There were conventions for battles, conventions of language (Petrarchism and Euphuism, for example) for the celebration of love. Texts that entail play create an implicit contract between players and spectators to enjoy not only, on occasion, physical knockabout, but sets of wit and virtuoso flourishes of *verbal* artistry – the display of recognized theatrical styles. Ben Jonson made the contract explicit in the Induction to his *Bartholomew Fair* (1614). He also usefully likened dramatic personages to heraldic figures, iconic rather than lifelike: he offers 'a Justice of the Peace *meditant* . . . a civil cutpurse *searchant* . . . and as fresh an hypocrite as ever was broached *rampant*' (*Bartholomew Fair*, Ind. 125–8). There are often invisible inverted commas around each speech act in the theatre, and its style is as important as the sentiments it evokes. Speeches can veer towards pastiche, are sometimes so obviously 'theatrical' that they become metatheatrical. Lots of games involve 'dressing up': so does theatre. Some of the most memorable moments of Renaissance drama are based around on-stage investiture – Tamburlaine's famous substitution of his shepherd's weeds with the cutlass and armour of the warlord (*1 Tamburlaine*, 1.2) – or disinvestiture – as when King Lear strips himself of his 'lendings', the vestments of authority (3.4). Both moments have something to say about the theatricality of politics. As Donne wrote in his verse epistle to Sir Henry Wotton: 'Courts are theatres where some men play / Princes, some slaves, all to one end and of one clay.'

Tamburlaine's is an image not just of bravado but of political challenge: by his self-fashioning the shepherd Tamburlaine defies the sumptuary laws which maintained what Shakespeare called 'degree' and we would call a status system – that was the theory. The fact that these laws existed at all suggests how for from absolute was the Elizabethan state. Tudor attempts to control the dress of their subjects suggest some degree of phobia on the part of the political elite. Well might they fear: some of the most notorious transgressors of the sumptuary code were the players themselves, their own licensed servants. Tamburlaine's dressing up draws attention to the ease and dangers of self-fashioning and social climbing, the instability of political hierarchies, for all of which the theatre provided a model.

It is significant that the same courtier responsible for providing recreation at court, the Master of the Revels, was responsible for 'seeing and allowing' the play-books of the companies, licensing plays for performance, in effect acting as censor. Cuts were made of scenes or sequences deemed seditious, as of the deposition scene (4.1) of Shakespeare's *Richard II*, a revival of which was staged at the request of followers of the Earl of Essex the day before he staged his fatal uprising. *Richard II* is an encouraging play for a would-be usurper in that it enacts a rebellion against a partially corrupt regime and shows no sign of divine displeasure being visited upon the successful rebels.

The presence of ritual moments like these does not mean that many parts of the action of these plays were not localized. The wrestling in *As You Like It* takes place 'at' Duke Frederick's court, and Rosalind opens the forest sequence with a proclamation 'Well, this is the forest of Arden' (2.4.13) – which encouraged generations of theatre directors to stage the play amid painted forests. ('Forest' in the period in fact designates a domain for hunting.) Yet this instance is more complex than we may imagine. Shakespeare's source, Thomas Lodge's prose romance *Rosalind* (1590), set the action in 'Ardenne', uncertainly situated near either Bordeaux or Belgium. This green world could be in Warwickshire or in France. Shakespeare gave some of his characters French names, others English ones, and the text evokes yet another kind of space, the 'pleasance' (*locus amoenus*) of classical literature, as well as a mythic world with lions and hermits out of medieval romance. 'Arden' so becomes a mythic forest world.

One thing, however, is certain: the playhouses and those who were associated with them were not just part of an 'entertainment industry'. Certainly going to the theatre provided a form of recreation, but it is notable that the players were regarded equally as chroniclers of the time, anatomizers of the age, fulfilling some of the functions of journalists or political commentators. In 1592 Thomas Nashe boasted of 'Our representations . . . not consisting like [those of foreigners] of a pantaloon, a whore, and a zany [comedian attending upon a clown], but of emperors, kings, and princes.'[16] Plays addressed public issues – indeed from about the 1580s theatres took forward the cause of 'reform' at about the very moment that church reformers ceased to deploy godly plays, ballads and images, and turned from iconoclasm to iconophobia.[17] Theatre is *re*-presentation: kings become 'subjects' – the monarchy and many other institutions become the subjects of the playwrights' analytic endeavours. If we remember that the stages were not illusionistic we can recognize the plays performed on them not as 'historical' but as 'political', demanding to be 'read' and not just seen. Dramatists traded not just in ideas but in ideology. St Paul had proclaimed that 'All power is of God' (Romans 13:1): Marlowe may be remarkable for making explicit the way that authority may derive from secular power rather than from divine ordination.

Player kings strutted and fretted in the very centre of the playhouse on a scaffold raised above the yard to about head height, around three sides of which groundlings might stand. Around the yard ran tiered galleries where sat spectators who had paid a supplement to enter the galleries from the yard, admission to which seems to have cost a penny. From the galleries, the audience below must have been part of the spectacle: later it became possible for gallants to pay for stools to sit on the stage itself, thus presenting themselves as part of the show. This is important: there was no physical separation between players and spectators, no suggestion of two separate worlds. Sometimes the relationship must have resembled that between spectators and players in modern vaudeville or pantomime. When appropriate, actors would have exchanged lines with spectators – there are tales of the great Elizabethan clown Richard Tarlton, a well-known London figure and a favourite jester of the queen. He was known for his skills at improvisation.

> At the Bull in Bishopsgate Street where the Queen's Players oftentimes played, Tarlton coming on the stage, one from the gallery threw a pippin at him. Tarlton took up the pip and, looking on it, made this sudden jest:
>> Pip in, or nose in, choose you whether,
>> Put yours in, ere I put in the other.
>> Pippin you would have put in: then, for my grace,
>> Would I might put your nose in another place.[18]

In a bourgeois theatre players who spoke more than was set down for them would have broken the illusion: in the Renaissance there was no illusion to break.

Plays in performance may have been based on texts very different from those with which we are familiar. In the 'bad Quarto' of *Hamlet* the following abbreviated version of the flyting match between Hamlet and Corambis (the name mysteriously given in that text to the Polonius figure) appears. Hamlet has just vilified Ophelia, bidding her betake herself to a nunnery (probably a brothel): in the good Quarto and Folio versions this sequence comes much later. The way this version runs suggests a style of playing with Hamlet sharing his jests at Corambis' expense with spectators, perhaps on one side of the stage, while Corambis who, *pace* Nashe, seems here to play the role of Pantaloon, the stock old man from *Commedia dell'arte*, may have given as good as he got by inviting support from spectators on the other:

> *Enter Hamlet*
> CORAMBIS: . . . Now, my good lord, do you know me?
> HAMLET: Yea, very well, y'are a fishmonger.
> CORAMBIS: Not I, my lord.
> HAMLET: Then, sir, I would you were so honest a man,
>   For to be honest, as this age goes,
>   Is one man to be picked out of ten thousand.
> CORAMBIS: What do you read, my lord?
> HAMLET: Words, words.
> CORAMBIS: What's the matter, my lord?
> HAMLET: Between who?
> CORAMBIS: I mean the matter you read, my lord.
> HAMLET: Marry, most vile heresy:
>   For here the satirical satyr writes
>   That old men have hollow eyes, weak backs,
>   Grey beards, pitiful weak hams, gouty legs,
>   All which, sir, I most potently believe not:
>   For sir, yourself shall be old as I am,
>   If, like a crab, you could go backward.
> CORAMBIS: How pregnant his replies are, and full of wit!
>   Yet at first he took me for a fishmonger:
>   All this comes by love, the vehemency of love,
>   And when I was young, I was very idle
>   And suffered much ecstasy in love, very near this –
>   Will you walk out of the air, my lord?
> HAMLET: Into my grave.
> CORAMBIS: By the mass, that's out of the air indeed –
>   Very shrewd answers –
>   My lord, I will take my leave of you.
>
>   (Sig.E1ᵛ–E2ʳ)

This reads like a rehearsed clowns' cross-talk routine; the characters are both 'on-' and 'off-stage', within the 'scene' and outside it. Moreover it is notable that Corambis' oath 'By the mass' appears in neither of the other texts, being the sort of language that the 'Act to Restrain Abuses of Players' of 1606 (3 Jac.I, c.21) was supposed to extinguish. Literary and generic decorum was subject to a particular kind of theatrical decorum.[19]

If such a (provincial?) version of *Hamlet* is a consequence of popularization, other performances were graced by grand surroundings. Visitors to London and those who execrated the playhouses on religious or commercial grounds, are practically unanimous in describing their opulence. 'The gorgeous playing-place erected in the fields . . . as they please to have it called a "Theatre"'[20] is a typical description, and it is indeed the splendour of the structures surrounding the stage that impresses first-time visitors to the replica Globe built in the 1990s on London's South Bank. Above the stage was a canopy, the underside of which was painted with the signs of the zodiac, and behind the stage was the façade of the tiring-house which must have matched in elaborateness the stage pillars which, according to an early visitor to the Swan, 'were painted in such excellent imitation of marble that it is able to deceive even the most cunning'.[21]

Early historians of Renaissance playhouses were under the impression that the space behind the hangings at the back of the stage, now generally termed 'the discovery space', served as an 'inner stage', becoming more prominent as the seventeenth century progressed, its frame serving as a prototype for proscenium arch theatres which emerged as men of the theatre adopted Renaissance principles of perspective for scenic design. This 'inner stage', it was surmised, served to represent interiors, rooms that lacked their fourth wall, prototypes of the stage rooms in which were set over two hundred years of bourgeois drama. However, no actor would want to confine himself within the place behind the stage with an empty space gaping before him. He would want to come out onto the platform to share with the audience the pleasures of discharging his part. Editors of play texts who suggest to their readers that the action of a scene 'takes place' 'in Macbeth's castle', 'in Rosillion at the Count's Palace' or, desperately, 'in another part of the forest', are misleading them and indeed encouraging them to create in their mind's eye characters of the same sort that inhabit 'classic realist texts' of the nineteenth century – or real people. Actors in plays of the period were called upon to play roles that may not equate with individuals. A character could indeed impersonate an individual, but could also, as we have seen, figure in an allegory, moral or psychological, or could, in particular parts of a play, take on the role of a chorus. Actors had to sing, to dance, to play the fool, to fight. In order to understand a sequence from a Renaissance play it is not necessary to localize it: the action takes place on the stage.

The playhouses did, however, contain mechanical devices for spectacle. The 'hut' above the stage seems to have housed, in some of the larger playhouses, a crane that could have been used for spectacular descents like that of Jupiter in 5.4 of *Cymbeline* (1610): Ben Jonson had disparaged the use of 'creaking thrones let down the boys to please' (*Every Man in his Humour*, Prologue). Actors could be flown on wires: it is conceivable that in public playhouse performances the Weird Sisters in *Macbeth* appeared in this manner. Fireworks, attached to wires, were used to accompany thunder effects for scenes of tempest. Where appropriate, scenic properties were used, three-dimensional devices similar to those allegorical devices that were used for processions. Thrones and beds provide obvious examples, but Henslowe's *Diary* gives examples of emblematic devices such as 'one hell mouth', 'the city of Rome'. More functional ones include rocks, cages tombs, stairs, trees, altars, 'the cauldron for *The Jew* [*of Malta*]', and a 'frame for the [be]heading in *Black Joan*'. Such scenic devices as were used served to establish genre rather than place – the 'mossy banks' of the sort that may have been employed in *As You Like It* presumably signalled not 'forest' but 'pastoral'. It is difficult to believe that scenic devices were ever meant to deceive: they were designed to be read. Portable objects included musical instruments, armour and weaponry, regalia – an example would be the 'warder', the staff used to signal the beginning of a tournament, carried by Richard II in 1.3 of his play, as well as devices that served as a kind of theatrical shorthand. A character entering bearing a riding-crop had obviously just got off a horse.[22] If Renaissance playwrights treated of illusion they were concerned to treat of the effects of illusion upon characters rather than creating chimeras for the audience.

Costumes were important elements in theatrical languages. Henslowe's *Diary* reveals that costumes could be the most expensive parts of productions: 'Henry the Fifth's velvet gown', 'Tamburlaine's coat with copper lace', 'six green coats for *Robin Hood*', a 'fool's coat, cap, and bauble [a stick surmounted with a head with the ears of an ass]', a 'yellow leather doublet for a clown', 'Eve's bodice', 'a little doublet for [a] boy', 'four torch-bearers' suits', and a 'robe for to go invisible' are among those listed, along with devices such as 'Cerberus' three heads', lions' and bears' skins, and that 'dragon in [*Doctor*] *Faustus*'. Thomas Platter, a Swiss traveller to London, narrates that it was a custom for the rich to pass on costumes to their servants who then would sell them to the players. This meant that a rich cloak which had served to fashion the image of an important courtier before the monarch one week could have appeared on stage the next – and it is conceivable that such practice could have been part of a system of political reference. But if some costumes evoked the historically specific, others evoked the allegoric: Henslowe had a group of what he listed as 'antic' suits, including 'two leather antics' coats with bosses [possibly humped backs]', a category which presumably also included the costume to be worn by Rumour, prologue to Shakespeare's *2 Henry IV*, which was *'painted full of tongues'*.[23]

All of these devices, with modification, could have been adapted for the 'private' (indoor) playhouses that became very popular, the habitats of Hamlet's 'little eyases' (2.2.337), among them the short-lived Whitefriars then the Blackfriars, where coterie audiences were prepared to pay more to be admitted. Later the Blackfriars was taken over by the King's Men. There is no evidence that private theatres offered scenes that were more spectacular than those in the public playhouses. There, however, as in other indoor performance spaces, artificial lighting was used, instrumental music may have been more prominent, and, as is revealed in a Blackfriars play, Beaumont's *The Knight of the Burning Pestle* (1607) there was music and dancing between the acts.

As with so many institutions of early modern England an understanding of hierarchy may be one of the best ways of appreciating the nature of the playing companies. Some actors began their careers by becoming, in effect, apprentices under the tutelage of the company. They might then progress to become the equivalent of 'journeymen', qualified to work for a day's wages, but occupying a rank below that of 'master', the equivalent of which was a 'sharer'. Famously, women's parts were taken by males, but it may be erroneous to imagine in all performances pre-pubertal youths with unbroken voices boying the greatness of the great female roles. A boy's apprenticeship might extend until he was about twenty, so that women's parts could be in effect taken by young men. It is difficult to know how much this aspect of representational form was an important constituent of the meaning of performances. There are accounts of spectators on the prowl for 'ingles' (male lovers),[24] ogling the 'boys', which may have given a homo-erotic effect to certain performances. The boys dressed lavishly and wore gorgeous wigs – the letting down of hair was a sign of female madness. But it may have been the case that cross-dressing, although in theory a species of deviancy, was by and large an invisible convention: it was present in many of the sports of Tudor and Stuart England. Ben Jonson in *Bartholomew Fair* enjoyed his mockery of Zeal-of-the-Land Busy who, because he believed that actors were of no lawful calling and that the puppets were violating biblical injunction against crossdressing, would pluck down the prophanity of their stall, only to have it revealed to him that the puppets had no genitals (5.5). Only fools or the obsessed took shadow for the substance. (Recently evidence has come to light of some acting by women, although not in playhouses.[25])

In addition to their representational skills, exhibiting fictive others, players used the skills of presentation, exhibiting themselves. First, were their skills of speaking, that would have derived in part from their rhetorical study of classical texts and patterns of discourse.[26] This was an aural culture, audiences would have been used to listening – and enjoyed listening to verbal art as is nicely suggested by the reactions of audiences to performance in John Madden's 1998 film *Shakespeare in Love* (which also gives a good idea of the nature of the Rose playhouse). Some playhouses had resident troupes of musicians or professional groups of wind instrumentalists ('waits') played at some performances. Surviving play texts often provide very little evidence of the amount of music that was required: significant affective moments may be signalled only by the direction 'song' with no words specified; 'flourishes' and 'sennets' were probably used more than is recorded to magnify entrances and exits. On occasion music was used in the manner of imagery in verse – an example would be the music that is played during Richard II's soliloquy in prison.

Presentational parts of the plays, songs, dances, fights, must have been fully rehearsed, probably under the tutelage of the an important member of the company: 'He that telleth the players their part when they are out [have "dried"] and have forgotten, the book-holder'[27] – who, among other duties, functioned as a prompter. The 'book' of the play was an important and precious document: like a modern stagemanager's script it could be marked up to record the need for properties or to complete stage directions that were often missing from authorial manuscripts. A second document was the 'plot', a paper, sometimes stiffened so it could be hung up, presumably in the tiring-house, which recorded the players required for each scene. Players, as we remember from the rehearsal of 'Pyramus and Thisbe' in *A Midsummer Night's Dream* (3.1), were not given copies of the whole play but only their 'parts', long strips of paper containing their own lines with necessary cues.

New plays were added to the repertory on average every three weeks, and it took about the same time for the text to be prepared for performance. Companies were comparatively small: there seem to have been between six and eleven sharers in each, which means that, even with about four hired men, boy apprentices, and the possible use of stage-keepers for bit parts, doubling must have been extensive. Sixteen players for *Doctor Faustus* would have had to play forty-five named parts.[28] With regard to particular plays it is possible to work out patterns for this, but we do not know whether companies deployed their members as Peter Brook did in his production of *A Midsummer Night's Dream* of 1970 when he doubled Theseus and Hippolyta with Oberon and Titania to make a point about the dark side of a marriage union. Players were trained to have good memories, but there was no time for the kind of intensive rehearsal we expect to lie behind modern productions, and there was no one to research for accurate costumes, control the whole production, no one moderating pace, making sure the Bottoms among the players did not hog the space or quieten any player who thought it rich 'To hear the wooden dialogue and sound / 'Twixt his stretched footing and the scaffoldage' (*Troilus and Cressida*, 1.3.156). On the other hand authors like Shakespeare were also sharers in the companies with which they were associated and would have been on hand on occasion to clarify intention or see to necessary revisions to their texts. Much of the effect, as in all good theatre, must have been generated by interaction with the audience, on the players' capacities to exploit their own appearances or personalities, and their ability to improvise themselves out of a situation when things went wrong: as Tarlton did when a player missed his entrance during a performance of *The Famous Victories of Henry V*,[29] or, as in Beaumont's *The Knight of the Burning Pestle*, when a spectator, witty or otherwise, interrupted the play. Clowns could be notorious for speaking more than was set down for them and presumably had distinctive catch-phrases and patter: it came to be known as 'gag'.

It is difficult to generalize about acting styles. Some parts, declamatory passages in Marlowe, for example, were probably delivered with a formality of gesture to match the sententiousness of the verse. Certain players (Tarlton provides a famous example) would have been taken on for their distinctive appearance or skills at repartee – like stand-up comics today. Clowns and fools must have had verbal and physical skills like the *lazzi* or stock comic routines of the Italian *Commedia dell'arte*. In the coterie theatres boys may have gained effect by emphasizing discrepancies between their size and youth and outsize roles or aged roles, creating a kind of pastiche. But there are praises for personations to the life, and when Shakespeare in his prime was writing roles that suggest characters thinking aloud as they speak, the role of his star player, Richard Burbage, was probably to play down the gestures and extremes of modulation in order to have the crowd within the wooden O share in his concentration.

It is probably wrong to conceive of spectators 'identifying' with characters. The concept is anachronistic, and in many plays characters gain their 'identity' from representativeness rather than individuality. Soliloquies, which we tend to think of as being a revelation of inwardness, were probably directed for the most part at the audience. Certainly Richard III begins his play with a sophistical attempt to justify his actions to the spectators that is analogous to the way that, in love poems of the period, male figures reason with the women they address to get them to capitulate to desire. In some texts one 'personality' could be shared among several players: the Good and Bad Angels in *Doctor Faustus* may be read as projections of the hero's consciousness, the Weird Sisters are both interior and exterior to Macbeth. Then as now spectators would have come to see actor X as character Y, taking pleasure or satisfaction from the 'two distincts, division none' of the personation.

Audiences could be large. The Globe may have held up to 3,000 spectators, and there is evidence that people of all ranks attended plays, the higher prices of admission to the indoor playhouses deterring the poorest. Women, not only prostitutes but many from leisured groups, formed a significant segment of the audiences, a topic of comment by travellers from countries where women had less freedom. It is difficult not to believe that the sight on stage of women rebuking kings, debating with magistrates, tutoring green young men in the arts of love did not make many think that Renaissance injunctions against female transgressions were indeed cages of rushes.

Then as now playhouses were among the main attractions for travellers to London. Few detailed accounts survive, but here is Thomas Platter, a Swiss traveller:

> And . . . every day at two o'clock in the afternoon in the city of London sometimes two sometimes three plays are given in different places, which compete with each other and those which perform best have the largest number of listeners. The places [i.e. playhouses] are so constructed that [the actors] play on a raised scaffold, and everyone can see everything.

Platter reminds us of the variety of entertainment available, and interestingly designates what we would call 'spectators' as 'listeners': contemporaries often speak of going to 'hear' a play, suggesting perhaps a desire to be instructed as much as entertained. He also describes a performance on 21 September 1599 of what may have been Shakespeare's *Julius Caesar* at the Globe:

> After dinner . . . about two o'clock, I went with my companions over the water [i.e. the Thames] and in the straw-thatched house saw the tragedy of the first Emperor Julius with at least fifteen characters very well acted. At the end . . . they danced according to their custom with extreme elegance, two in each group dressed in men's and two in women's apparel.[30]

Modern editions seldom record the possibility of terminal jig – more evidence of the convention is provided by the Bergamask at the end of 'Pyramus and Thisbe' in *A*

Midsummer Night's Dream. Perhaps, at the Globe, at the end of *King Lear*, the actor who had played the broken old man got up and danced . . .

NOTES

1 A useful survey of London playhouses is given by Andrew Gurr, 'Shakespeare's Playhouses', Kastan (1999), 362–76.

2 J. L. Murphy, *Darkness and Devils: Exorcism and 'King Lear'* (Athens, OH, 1984), p. 106.

3 Rutter, p. 39.

4 Ibid., p. 57.

5 See Mullaney.

6 Rutter, p. 12.

7 Chambers, IV, 287.

8 Michael Hattaway, 'Christopher Marlowe: Ideology and Subversion', *Christopher Marlowe and English Renaissance Culture*, ed. Darryll Grantley and Peter Roberts (London, Scolar, 1996), 198–223.

9 See William Shakespeare, *The Second Part of King Henry VI*, ed. Michael Hattaway (Cambridge, Cambridge University Press, 1991), pp. 219–20.

10 Chambers, IV, 306.

11 See TALES OF THE CITY.

12 Quarto versions of the second and third parts indicate provincial performances as well.

13 M. M. Bakhtin, *The Dialogic* Imagination, trs Caryl Emerson and Michael Holquist (Austin, University of Texas Press, 1981).

14 See Hattaway (1982), pp. 193–4 and figure 10.

15 See LOCAL AND CUSTOMARY DRAMA.

16 *Pierce Penniless his Supplication to the Devil*, quoted in Chambers, IV, 239.

17 See Patrick Collinson's 1985 Stenton Lecture, *From Iconoclasm to Iconophobia: The Cultural Impact of the Second English Reformation* (Reading, 1986).

18 R. Tarlton, *Tarlton's Jests*, ed. J. O. Halliwell (London, 1884), pp. 13–14.

19 I am indebted to my students at Sheffield whose practical work on this sequence illuminated it for me.

20 Chambers, IV, 200.

21 Hattaway (1982), p. 26.

22 See Dessen.

23 Rutter, pp. 133–7; see also Peter Stallybrass, 'Worn Worlds: Clothes and Identity on the Renaissance Stage', *Subject and Object in Renaissance Culture*, ed. Margreta de Grazia, Maureen Quilligan and Peter Stallybrass (Cambridge, Cambridge University Press, 1996), 289–320.

24 See Jonson's *Poetaster*: 'What? shall I have my son a stager [actor] now? an ingle for players?' (1.2)

25 Ann Thompson, 'Women / "women" and the stage', *Women and Literature in Britain 1500–1700*, ed. Helen Wilcox (Cambridge, 1996), 100–16.

26 See Rhetoric.

27 John Higgins *The Nomenclator* (London, 1585), p. 501 (cit. *OED*); William B. Long, '"Precious Few": English Manuscript Playbooks', Kastan (1999), 414–33.

28 Rutter, p. 22.

29 Hattaway (1982), p. 89.

30 Ibid., p. 68.

REFERENCES AND FURTHER READING

Baskervill, C. R. (1929). *The Elizabethan Jig and Related Song Drama*. Chicago: University of Chicago Press.

Bentley, G. E. (1941–68). *The Jacobean and Caroline Stage*. 7 vols. Oxford: Clarendon Press.

Chambers, E. K. (1923). *The Elizabethan Stage*. Oxford: Clarendon Press.

Dessen, A. C. (1984). *Elizabethan Stage Conventions and Modern Interpreters*. Cambridge: Cambridge University Press.

Dillon, J. (2000). *Theatre, Court and City 1595–1610: Drama and Social Space in London.* Cambridge, Cambridge University Press.

Dutton, R. (1991). *Mastering the Revels: The Regulation and Censorship of English Renaissance Drama.* London: Macmillan.

Foakes, R. A. (1985). *Illustrations of the English Stage 1580–1642.* London: Scolar.

Galloway, D. (ed.) (1969–70). *The Elizabethan Theatre.* London: Macmillan.

Gurr, A. (1980). *The Shakespearean Stage 1574–1642.* Cambridge: Cambridge University Press.

—— (1987). *Playgoing in Shakespeare's London.* Cambridge: Cambridge University Press.

—— (1996). *The Shakespearian Playing Companies.* Oxford: Clarendon Press.

Harte, N. B. (1976). 'State Control of Dress and Social Change in Pre-industrial England'. In D. C. Coleman and A. H. John (eds), *Trade, Government and Economy in Pre-Industrial England* (pp. 132–65). London: Weidenfeld and Nicholson.

Hattaway, M. (1982). *Elizabethan Popular Theatre.* London: Routledge.

Howard, J. E. (1993). *The Stage and Social Struggle in Early Modern England.* London: Routledge.

Hodges, C. W. (1968). *The Globe Restored.* London: Oxford University Press.

Hunter, G. K. (1997). *English Drama 1586–1642: The Age of Shakespeare.* Oxford: Clarendon Press.

Kastan, D. S. (ed.). (1999). *A Companion to Shakespeare.* Oxford: Blackwell.

King, T. J. (1992). *Casting Shakespeare's Plays: London Actors and their Roles, 1590–1642.* Cambridge: Cambridge University Press.

Klein, D. (1963). *The Elizabethan Dramatists as Critics.* London: Peter Owen.

Laroque, F. (1991). *Shakespeare's Festive World,* tr. Janet Lloyd. Cambridge: Cambridge University Press.

MacLean, S.-B. (1988). 'Players on Tour: New Evidence from Records of Early English Drama', *Elizabethan Theatre,* 10, 155–72.

Mann, D. (1991). *The Elizabethan Stage Player: Contemporary Representation.* London: Routledge.

Maus, K. E. (1995). *Inwardness and Theater in the English Renaissance.* Chicago: University of Chicago Press.

Montrose, L. (1996). *The Purpose of Playing: Shakespeare and the Cultural Politics of the Elizabethan Theatre.* Chicago: University of Chicago Press.

Mullaney, S. (1988). *The Place of the Stage: License, Play and Power in Renaissance England.* Ann Arbor: University of Michigan Press.

Orrell, J. (1983). *The Quest for Shakespeare's Globe.* Cambridge: Cambridge University Press.

Rowan, D. F. (1986) 'Inns, Inn-Yards, and Other Playing Places'. In G. R. Hibbard and Jill L. Levenson (eds), *The Elizabethan Theatre IX.* Port Credit, Ontario.: P. D. Meany.

Rutter, C. C. (ed.) (1984). *Documents of the Rose Playhouse.* Manchester: Manchester University Press.

Shapiro, M. (1994). *Gender in Play on the Shakespearean Stage: Boy Heroines and Female Pages.* Ann Arbor: University of Michigan Press.

Streett, J. B. (1973). The Durability of Boy Actors, *NQ,* 208, 461–5.

Sturgess, Keith. (1987). *Jacobean Private Theatre.* London: Routledge.

Thomson, P. (1983). *Shakespeare's Theatre.* London: Routledge.

Weimann, R. (1978). *Shakespeare and the Popular Dramatic Tradition in the Theater,* tr. Robert Schwartz. Baltimore: Johns Hopkins University Press.

Wickham, G. (1959–72). *Early English Stages 1300 to 1660.* 3 vols in 2. London: Routledge and Kegan Paul.

Wiles, D. (1987). *Shakespeare's Clown: Actor and Text in the Elizabethan Playhouse.* Cambridge: Cambridge University Press.

12

The Writing of Travel

Peter Womack

In the first of the role's great set-pieces, Shakespeare's Othello tells the story of his travels (*Othello*, 1.3.126–67). It is the third telling, in fact: first he told Brabantio, and then Desdemona, and now he 'runs it through' yet again for the senators and the audience. The traveller's tale is a repeatable performance; it is as the exponent of a distinctive kind of talk that Othello acquires his dramatic substance and allure. Shakespeare constructs this performance by mixing a cocktail of discursive conventions: the commonplaces, you could say, of the writing of travel.

Most obviously, the traveller tells of wonders: ''twas strange, 'twas passing strange'. He has been to places which are strange in the simple early modern sense of the word – foreign – but then that sense has others attached to it – bizarre, other, contrary to expectation. As the bearer of strange news, he has an obscure magic: the closing allusion to witchcraft is not only a sideswipe at Brabantio's accusation, but also an ironic reflection on the narrative's capacity to enchant. The traveller appears as someone who has been not only to other countries, but to other worlds, and who returns with some of their power to fascinate and disturb.

But the play also offers another account of Othello's telling of his story – Iago's: 'Mark me with what violence she first loved the Moor, but for bragging and telling her fantastical lies' (2.1.225). Precisely because the traveller has been so far away, his story is uncheckable; so the sense of him as a carrier of numinous intimations is close to the rougher proverbial sense of him as a liar. This suspicion, voiced by Othello's enemy, infiltrates his own speech too. The opening encodes the traveller's insistence on his own truthfulness. Telling the whole story 'to th' very moment that he bade me tell it', he offers himself as his own authentication: the man to whom all these wonderful things happened stands before you. But the Anthropophagi and the misplaced heads are bywords for the implausibility of travellers' tales, and the phrases which introduce them – 'it was my *hint* to speak – such was my *process*' – refer them not so much to experience as to genre (this is the kind of thing one says when telling this kind of story). The ideas of authenticity and fabrication clearly go together: the writing of travel in the period is making particular truth claims, and is open to particular accusations of falsehood.

If there is doubt about whether the traveller is to be believed or not, there is a related uncertainty about whether he is to be admired or pitied. Iago thinks Othello was bragging, and his story does indeed suggest that his having been so far makes him a man to love. Travel confers renown. But the conclusion insists on the idea of pity. In conformity with an assumption that goes back to the *Odyssey*, travelling appears as exposure to the 'disastrous chances' of the world. The traveller is a victim of misfortune; the happy man stays at home and enjoys his inheritance in peace.

The traveller is thus hero and victim and, in a common image which contains elements of both these, pilgrim. Any Christian life is a 'pilgrimage'; but the conventional metaphor is refocused when the life in question is literally one of travel and vicissitude. It intimates that the traveller's random exposure to fortune has a larger meaning; but in the absence of a devotional framework (Protestant English travellers are of course not literally pilgrims), the meaning is metaphorical and suggestive.

Characteristically, then, Shakespeare provides an abstract and brief chronicle of the returned traveller: bearer of strange news; liar; pilgrim. These may be taken as the headings for an anatomy of the genre.

Strange News

The appetite for foreign marvels shown by Desdemona is a conventional object of mockery:

> The brain-sick youth that feeds his tickled ear
> With sweat-sauced lies of some false traveller,
> Who hath the Spanish *Decades* read a while;
> Or whetstone leasings [fabrications][1] of old Mandeville.[2]

The satirist Joseph Hall is here, as often, better at bibliography than at rhyme. The 'Spanish Decades' are the *De Novo Orbe* of Pietro Martire d'Anghiera, partially translated by Richard Eden in 1555 as *The Decades of the New World*. The book is one source of the convention of calling the Americas 'the New World', with the implication that the Iberian voyages discovered not only new lands but a new world, perhaps even an earthly paradise. And Sir John Mandeville's *Travels*, a fabulous compilation originally written in the fourteenth century, was still being excerpted and reprinted at the end of the sixteenth, and mentions many of the phenomena Hall goes contemptuously on to itemize: the bird that can carry off large animals, the nation of people with no heads, and the inevitable cannibals.[3]

The humanist contempt is partly a matter of class: for Hall, as for a writer like Jonson, travellers' tales form part of the gaudy repertoire of vulgar credulity. But there is also a more sophisticated way of reading 'old Mandeville', which is to point out that in his day the idea of a nation beyond the western ocean was no less fantastical than the men whose heads do grow beneath their shoulders – and yet it has turned out to be the case. There are no good grounds, then, for dogmatism about what can and cannot possibly exist:

> Who ever heard of th'Indian *Peru*?
> Or who in venturous vessell measured
> The *Amazons* huge river now found trew?
> Or fruitfullest *Virginia* who did ever view?
>
> Yet all these were, when no man did them know;
> Yet have from wisest ages hidden beene:
> And later times things more unknowne shall show.
> Why then should witlesse man so much misweene [misjudge]
> That nothing is, but that which he hath seene?
>
> (Spenser, *The Faerie Queene*, Book II, sts 2–3)

This is Spenser arguing the conceivability of 'the happy land of Faery', and although the argument is logical, it moves in a curious direction. After all, the allegorical terrain of *The Faerie Queene* does not exist in the same way as America, and a reader who thought it did would be misunderstanding the poem; Spenser is not really maintaining that we might one day sail to Fairy Land in a ship. His point is Platonic rather than progressive: the fact that the Americas were there all the time when no one had seen them is an emblem of invisible realities, places that exist for the mind as opposed to the senses.

But then to affiliate the newly discovered parts of the world to this counter-factual logic is to apprehend them as, precisely, intellectual entities: speaking fictions, utopias. This is what Montaigne does in his famous essay 'Of the Cannibals', one of the sources for Shakespeare's *The Tempest*. His Indians form a philosophical critique of European civilization in the noble simplicity of their lives, the disinterested honour code by which they fight, their incomprehension of the social inequalities they observe on visiting France, and so on. 'Surely in respect of us these are very savage men: for either they must be so in good sooth, or we must be so indeed: There is a wondrous distance between their form and ours.'[4] The act of comparing is what constitutes the image: it is as the opposite of us, or as our reprovingly purified reflection, that the 'cannibals' impress themselves upon us. Our brazen age makes theirs golden, and a series of classical quotations, thematically apposite but of course evidentially irrelevant, confirms that Montaigne perfectly understands the literary trope he is working. But then the essay is also sprinkled with earnests of empirical enquiry – Montaigne goes out of his way to outline the trustworthy character of his informant, or to mention that one or two objects from the culture he describes are in front of him as he writes. Apparently he is concerned, after all, to show that his details are substantial rather than speculative. Two modes of writing the exotic – fictional reflection and factual report – remain in tension, playfully set against one another by the essay form.

More functional kinds of prose are of course less free to indulge in the ironies of 'utopian' writing, but strange places still tend to resolve into strange messages about familiar places. Take for instance the work of Giles Fletcher, who travelled to Russia in 1588 on an embassy from Elizabeth, and later published the tract *Of the Russe Common Wealth* (1591). The purpose of the book is informative: based on direct and recent observation, it describes an empire of some political and mercantile importance to Elizabethan England, and so addresses a constituency with a practical need for information. What it also becomes, however, as Fletcher develops his political analysis, is a contrast with the state of things at home: this 'true and strange face of a tyrannical state' will, Fletcher hopes in the dedication, increase Elizabeth's happiness 'in that you are a Prince of subjects, not of slaves, that are kept within duty by love, not by fear'.[5]

Governed by these antitheses, Fletcher's account of the Russian polity, for all its empirical detail, develops an internal logic. The unrestrained power of the emperor leads to a general absence of public justice; consequently, no one has any security for their property; consequently, the people have no incentive to enrich themselves, and arts and manufactures decay. Again, the oppression of the people causes their oppressors to look on them as potential enemies, and therefore to desire their weakness, from which it follows that education is almost non-existent, and organized religion corrupt and superstitious. These pervasive themes of slavery and fear produce the image of a *systematic* opposite of the good commonwealth. Fletcher's casual pairing, 'true and strange', starts to seem distinctly charged. 'Strange' because it is the reverse of what is right and natural, but then also 'true' because every placename and anecdotal instance insists that this is not, as it increasingly appears to be, a mere hypothetical worst case in political theory, but an actual country. As in Montaigne, idea and information come together, and it is that coincidence that constitutes the fascination of the message, its capacity to arouse wonder.

The shaping power of the idea is most strikingly seen in the chapter about the Tartars, the nomadic Asian tribes who are the Russian Empire's main adversaries. Although they appear to Fletcher as barbarous and Islamic, whereas the Russian commonwealth is civilized and Christian, his account of them takes on the outlines of a paradoxical idealization: their poverty can be read as a disdain for riches, their violence as a form of directness in contrast with Russian deviousness, their fierce exclusiveness as an admirable fidelity amongst themselves, and so on. The source of this surprising romance of the steppes is the demonization of Moscow: that the Russian centre embodies every political vice fashions the otherwise unpromising material of its barbaric margin into an image of virtue. It is then not altogether 'strange' to find Fletcher, later in his life, advancing the theory that the Tartars are the descendants of the ten lost tribes of Israel.

This pattern of utopian and dystopian projection informs a great deal of early modern travel writing, but it is unusually easy to trace in the texts I have mentioned so far because their relation to their materials is, by and large, contemplative and disinterested. This is not typical. Most of the news that reached England from foreign lands came with much more readily identifiable interests attached to it. It is in that context, then, that I turn to the next character suggested by Othello: that of the liar.

Truth and Lies

The most significant single figure in Elizabethan travel writing is Richard Hakluyt, who devoted some twenty years to collecting accounts of global travel by Englishmen. Altogether he amassed about two hundred such narratives. Many of them appeared in what are effectively successive editions of a steadily expanding book, from the single-volume *Divers Voyages to America* in 1582 to the immense *Principal Navigations, Voyages, Traffics and Discoveries of the English Nation*, published in three volumes in 1598–1600. Even this did not use up all Hakluyt's material: more was published in 1625 by his disciple and successor Samuel Purchas in *Hakluytus Posthumus*, a still larger collection which also contains many journeys collected or described by Purchas himself.[6]

Hakluyt was neither a traveller nor a writer: rather, he was a compiler, editor and translator. Expeditions to lesser-known parts of the world would consult him for guidance in advance, and report back with any new information afterwards. In the character of a clearing house, then, he naturally presents himself under the sign of unadorned truth:

> I have referred every voyage to his author, which both in person hath performed and in writing hath left the same: for I am not ignorant of Ptolomy's assertion, that *peregrinationis historia*, and not those weary volumes bearing the titles of universal cosmography . . . is that which must bring us to the certain and full discovery of the world.[7]

Academic cosmographies lead to no certain discovery because they merely rehearse what has already been written; their 'authorities' are canonical authors. Hakluyt's typical informant, on the other hand, is an 'author' himself, who has been to the places he describes, and has the authority not of erudition but of experience. If that contrast sounds Baconian, it is hardly a coincidence: Bacon repeatedly points to the maritime discoveries of the sixteenth century as a model for the scientific discoveries he expects from the seventeenth; and by the time *The Advancement of Learning* appeared in 1605 the definitive English source of knowledge about maritime discoveries was Hakluyt. And certainly the project of a 'universal cosmography' was a particularly inappropriate one at this point of England's, and Europe's, overseas expansion. The 'discovery of the world' that Hakluyt was able to present was neither certain nor full. The globe had been circumnavigated, the coasts of Africa and the Americas had been imperfectly charted; but the continental interiors were largely unknown, the theory of northern passages to China had neither been confirmed nor confuted, and the possibility of a fifth continent, a vast *Terra Australis*, was a matter of almost pure speculation. European geographers knew enough to know how much they did not yet know; the world as it appeared to Hakluyt (or to Bacon, or to Drake) was in a specific sense incomplete, transitional, not susceptible of totalization.[8] *Peregrinationis historia* (the story of travel), anecdotal as it might be, was nevertheless the appropriate material for this cosmography-under-construction.

This commitment to the circumstantial is inscribed on Hakluyt's collection in the form of its miscellaneity. He accepts anything that relates to voyaging, and arranges it mechanically – grouping documents by regions of the world, and, within the regions, chronologically. So that, for example, the documents relating to Alexandria include both an exciting story about imprisonment and escape from the Turks, and a memorandum setting out the conditions that govern trading in the port (V, 153–67; 272–4). Or again, Sir Walter Ralegh's description of Guyana, one of the few Hakluyt texts with any literary reputation, comes immediately after a collection of accounts of the Caribbean which are essentially 'ruttiers' – that is, verbal route-checks written down as aids to navigation: texts which are not designed to be read at all, but to be used (X, 280–337; 338–431). Victorian ideologists sought to establish Hakluyt as 'the prose epic of the English nation',[9] but the book resists such a reading. It is less epic than archive; its structuring is not poetic but classificatory.

The effect is an air of epistemological innocence, as if these raw materials, bafflingly heterogeneous as they may be, are at any rate free from the sophistications that would be entailed by rhetorical coherence. However, the purpose of the *Principal Navigations* is not reducible to the neutral accumulation of data. Hakluyt himself did have an indiscriminate passion for maps and voyages, but he was also a lobbyist, pressing for investment in exploratory and colonial enterprises, for public recognition of such enterprises as there had been and for an endowment to teach the art of navigation. All these themes are nationalistic: nearly all Hakluyt's work was done during the Anglo-Spanish war (1585–1605), and the repeated implication of his accumulation of evidence is that England has the resources, the opportunity and the right to acquire a commercial and colonial network on a par with Spain's American Empire.[10] Publishing accounts of voyages forms part of this patriotic project: on the one hand it honours the English voyagers of the past and the present, and on the other it seeks to offer at once encouragement and information to the voyagers of the future.

The trouble then is that not much of the information was encouraging. For one thing, England was not yet the proto-imperial power which hindsight tends to project. In America, the English presence was a scattering of toe-holds in comparison with the well-established Hapsburg operation. In India and the East Indies, English commerce had neither the extent nor the historical depth of the Dutch and the Portuguese.[11] Eastward overland, the English traveller encountered at least three imperial principalities – the Ottoman, the Persian and the Mogul – each of which was greater and richer than the realm of Elizabeth and James I.[12] English forces could not assume, as they could for most of the eighteenth and nineteenth centuries, that they would be major players in any world theatre they entered. And second, most of the expeditions Hakluyt commemorates ended in failure. The repeated searches for the north-west passage failed to find it; the hopes of gold and silver mines were not realized; attempts to hurt Spanish sea-power were inconclusive. Even privateering – the nationally licensed piracy which was probably the most cost-effective form of voyaging in the 1590s – was a lottery with more blank tickets than prizes.[13] Pacifying disappointed investors was a regular function of travel narrative. Under these circumstances, the need for accurate information is at odds with colonial and mercantile promotion; the record of the past is pulled out of shape by the requirements of the future. And if these tensions run through the compilation as a whole, they also shape individual documents – none more than Sir Walter Ralegh's pamphlet, reprinted by Hakluyt, *The Discovery of the large, rich, and beautiful Empire of Guyana*.

Ralegh returned empty-handed from the Orinoco in 1595, and presents his account as the report of a 'wasteful factor [agent]' (X, 338). His apologetic strategy is twofold. First, it is that the fabulous city of gold was *just* out of reach. Always a few days further up river, tantalizingly beyond the limits of what the expedition could safely undertake, was 'the first town of apparelled and rich people' (411), where gold images are manufactured, and where the discovery would really begin. The whole narrative is shaped by this trope of 'almost there'; with whatever labour and enterprise Ralegh's expedition presses on into the interior, it remains on the fringes of its true object; the people whom Ralegh actually meets are understood to be *borderers* of the golden empire. The second strategy is grounded in this threshold imagery. There were, it seems, several opportunities for short-term gain, but Ralegh declined them because he considered himself the representative, on behalf of the queen, of a greater enterprise. So his penniless return is partly a matter of aristocratic disdain – 'It became not the former fortune in which I once lived, to go journeys of picory [plundering]' (340) – and partly the logic of a longer-term policy. For example, Ralegh hears about a cacique [native prince] who recently died and was buried with a finely wrought gold chair – a specimen of Manoan craftsmanship which would have gone some way to dispel public scepticism; 'but if we should have grieved them in their religion at the first, before they had been taught better, and have digged up their graves, we had lost them all' (425). Similar considerations interdict an immediate attack on the rich and apparelled people:

> I thought it were evil counsel to have attempted it at that time, although the desire of gold will answer many objections; but it would have been in mine opinion an utter overthrow to the enterprise, if the same should be hereafter by her Majesty attempted: for then (whereas now they have heard we were enemies to the Spaniards, and were sent by her Majesty to relieve them) they would as good cheap have joined with the Spaniards at our return as to have yielded unto us, when they had proved that we came both for one errand: and that both sought but to sack and spoil them. But as yet our desire of gold or our purpose of invasion is not known to them of the empire, and it is likely that if her Majesty undertake the enterprise, they will rather submit themselves to her obedience than to the Spaniards, of whose cruelty both themselves and the borderers have already tasted.

(413–14)

The conditional constructions hold a tortuous pathos. Ralegh has described his delightfully courteous dealings with the people he met: they offered him hospitality, and he gave them presents and assured them that his distant mistress was a powerful empress who wished only their good. Now he admits that he was lying to them: actually, he suggests, there is no difference between the English and the cruel Spaniards, but the English are concealing their purpose until the time is ripe, so as to extract as much advantage as possible from the Guyanans' friendship before betraying it. But in practice nobody in England is likely to reproach Ralegh for lying to his South American contacts. The real suspicion is that he is lying to his readers – that the whole El Dorado story is a fantasy, and that the reason he has returned with no gold is that he found none, or even that he was never there. It is to buttress his credibility as a narrator that he presents himself as a ruthless Machiavellian. And even as he develops this persona, his narrative makes clear the exposure of his party to the vastness of the territory he speaks so easily of controlling: struggling with torrential rivers, lost, dirty, frequently dependent on their future subject peoples for enough food to stay alive, the Englishmen appear as the manipulators of the situation only by a huge leap of imagination. So the ostensible brutality of Ralegh's waiting game reads ultimately like a rationalization: we suspect that the narrator is not so vicious and powerful as he would like us to believe.

A further possibility appears within this ambiguous suspension. What is being deferred, Ralegh repeatedly says, is the satisfaction of the 'desire of gold'. Not that he holds himself superior to this desire, but, on the contrary, that he is forgoing thousands now for the sake of millions later. His account of the latter rises to degraded heights that foreshadow Sir Epicure Mammon:

> The common soldier shall here fight for gold, and pay himself instead of pence with plates of half a foot broad, whereas he breaketh his bones in other wars for provant [a soldier's allowance of food] and penury. Those commanders and chieftains that shoot at honour and abundance shall find there more rich and beautiful cities, more temples adorned with golden images, more sepulchres filled with treasure, than either Cortez found in Mexico or Pizarro in Peru; and the shining glory of this conquest will eclipse all those so far extended beams of the Spanish nation.
>
> (425–6)

This is passionately and polysemically about gold: the shining glory is at once that of the conquerors' reputation and that of the actual material. But what the golden vision both intimates and obscures is that this future moment – not here, but there; not now, but in the deferred time when all this 'shall' come about – is one of catastrophic violence: the commoners will earn their gold plates by fighting over them, and the ambitious commanders are drawn to the temples and sepulchres because they hope to sack them. 'Guyana', Ralegh famously concludes, 'is a country that hath yet her maidenhead' (428): unquestionably his plan is that the English rape her before the Spaniards get the chance. *Then*, the large, rich, and beautiful Empire of Guyana will be pillaged, but for the moment, it is still intact: the beauty of its abundant promise can still be enjoyed, the dignified native leaders one meets can still be treated honourably. The attempt to conquer the world is saved by its failure from the gross criminality which would constitute its success. The utopian possibility, then, is that we could somehow really prove to be different from the Spaniards: that the flattering words addressed to the indigenous people could magically turn out to be true. Bragging and telling fantastical lies, Ralegh at once substantiates and protects the golden world which, despite his title, he has not so much discovered as intensely imagined.

Pilgrims

In the winter of 1609–10, the Scots traveller William Lithgow was wandering the Aegean in a Greek boat which was chased into a creek by two Turkish ships. Until the Turks went away, Lithgow was prevailed upon to stand sentinel each night on a promontory above the bay, an experience 'which did invite my Muse to bewail the tossing of my toilsome life'.[14] The lengthy result begins:

> I wander in exile,
> > As though my pilgrimage:
> Were sweet comedian scenes of love
> > Upon a golden stage.
> Ah I, poor I, distressed,
> > Oft changing to and fro,
> Am forced to sing sad obsequies
> > Of this my swan-like woe.
> A vagabonding guest,
> > Transported here and there,
> Led with the mercy-wanting winds
> > Of fear, grief, and despair.

What is formally striking about this moment is its theatricality. The promontory is a stage, and Lithgow a character soliloquizing upon it. The poem is in this respect the literary equivalent of the woodcuts that adorn his book, depicting him in remarkable costumes and circumstances: 'The Author in the Libyan Desert', 'The Author beset with six murderers in Moldavia' (328, 364). For Lithgow as for Othello, the narrating of travel is among other things a presentation of himself. This self-display affiliates him to a curious genre in which a journey is a kind of performance. Sometimes this was literally a matter of show business, like Will Kempe's famous dance from London to Norwich in 1600. But it also includes two self-conscious eccentrics of Jacobean society: Thomas Coryate and John Taylor. Coryate was a minor figure on the fringes of Prince Henry's household who in 1608 undertook a journey to Venice and back, largely on foot. His account appeared in 1611 as *Coryate's Crudities*, an inflated volume whose main distinction lies in the commendatory verses that preface the text – over a hundred pages of them, since what clearly happened in the interval between travel and publication was that writing encomia on Coryate became a literary craze. Mostly devoid of geographical interest, the book works to construct a public character – loquacious, clownish, at once hapless and pretentious: a poor learned wretch.[15] Taylor, the 'Water Poet', is discussed elsewhere in this volume,[16] but from our point of view here he is a comparable type: in his hands the unorthodox journey (to York in a wherry, to Scotland with no money) became something between a public show and a bet.

The journey in these cases is a kind of stunt: a pointlessly difficult undertaking which generates publicity, and whose appeal rests on the idea that the traveller is a fool. Travelling any distance was after all a risky business, given the seventeenth-century state of navigation, medicine and law enforcement. When the journey is necessary, a reasonable person accepts the risks; but the man who chooses to travel is doing something conspicuously and as it were liberatingly daft. The consistency of this pattern can be understood via something else that Lithgow has in common with both Coryate and Taylor: all three write in two distinct styles. One style is flatly informative – plain, itemizing, fairly dull – and the other is floridly rhetorical, a sort of verbal fancy dress. The distinction to which this rather absurd alternation corresponds is between travel as a practical activity and travel as a gratuitous performance. The traveller in the latter sense is in every sense making an exhibition of himself, and so keys into the familiar ambiguities of the theatrical fool: he is an entertainer, he is vain and lacking in wisdom, and he may just possibly be in a state of grace inaccessible to those of us who organize our lives more sensibly.

If the traveller's life is a kind of folly, it is also, as Desdemona says, 'wondrous pitiful'. Lithgow's accidental situation is a metaphor for his essential condition: the traveller is in some sense always alone, benighted, exposed, dependent on strangers. The sea in front of him embodies the 'tossing' of his 'toilsome life'; the winds signify the turbulence of his feelings; he speaks as an exile. This is not literally true: although Lithgow hints at injustices which drove him away from his native land, he also admits to an insatiable appetite for seeing the world. He is in the Aegean by choice; and although he does seem eventually to have met with genuine disaster, being imprisoned and tortured in Malaga in 1620, his career before that was not marked by anything worse than the usual vicissitudes of early modern travel.[17] Rather, the association between travel and misfortune has the character of a literary convention. The traveller, like the lover, is a generic figure of woe.[18]

However, if there is an acknowledged rhetorical place for the 'unfortunate traveller',[19] there is another, equally well established, for the praise of travel. It is the nursery of virtue; it shows us the varieties of religion and government; and through encounters with a diversity of men and manners, it affords a kind of wisdom that cannot be derived from books. It is also associated with the commerce between nations, valued, equally conventionally, as the means of civility, prosperity and the diffusion of the Gospel.[20] The traveller, then, is an exemplary humanist as well as a poor wretch, and Lithgow is typical if untypically extreme in simply running the two incompatible models side by side: 'all in all', he declares confusingly, 'what I found was more than ordinary rejoicing, in an extraordinary sorrow of delights' (9).

An analogous contradiction shapes many of the less individualistic travel narratives found in Hakluyt. Take for example the account of Martin Frobisher's unsuccessful Canadian voyages of 1576–8. At one point, the ships are nearly lost after entering a bay and getting caught by a gale that pushes floating ice in behind them, so that it is equally dangerous to stay or to leave. The narrator, George Best, puts this crisis firmly into the framework of heroic narrative – 'in greatest distress, men of best valour are best to be discerned' – and continues:

> And amidst these extremes, whilst some laboured for defence of the ships and sought to save their bodies, other some of milder spirit sought to save the soul by devout prayer and meditation to the Almighty, thinking indeed by no other means possible than by a divine miracle to have their deliverance; so that there was none that were either idle or not well occupied.
>
> (VII, 331)

Valour and devotion, the labours of spirit and of soul, are here equally praised, and equally responses to the 'extremes' of the situation. The atrocious conditions elicit fundamental values of the culture. But then neither author nor editor is in control of the irony, which is that their more immediate purpose is to promote the hope of finding the north-west passage. It seems that these northern waters are *both* so perilous as to form the ultimate testing ground of the explorers' faith and greatness of mind *and* so open that they offer a straightforward commercial route to China. The contradiction runs through the entire account: Best more than once argues from the freshness of the water from melting icebergs that salt water does not freeze, so that the northern route will be open when it is found; but he also explains the expedition's eventual decision to return home by noting that 'the ice began to congeal and freeze about our ships' sides a night'(224, cp. 266) – that is, they knew that if they stayed too long they risked getting stuck in the (saltwater) ice. Travel is narrated in the codes of suffering and of success at the same time.

The opposed conventions correspond to opposing views of the world. The equation of travel with misfortune is implicitly religious – hence its association, in both Lithgow and *Othello*, with the idea of life as a pilgrimage. The traveller is the type of the Christian soul on earth, lodging here and there, comfortlessly, because heaven is its home. By contrast, the praise of travel is secular and humanistic, locating virtue not in a form of *contemptus mundi*, but in the accumulation of practical knowledge of the world – with a view, in the colonialist writings, to its ultimate domination. The textual doubleness is the trace of a historical conjunction: on the eve of the globalization of English interests, a traditional ethos which views travelling as an evil (albeit a sometimes necessary one) sits uneasily next to a 'venturing' ethos which views it as a route to profit and glory (albeit a sometimes delusive one). The sense of transition, of an unresolved contest of paradigms, recurs in these writings, and illuminates the sheer difficulty of what travel writers were trying to do as they improvised ways of representing their irregularly expanding world.

However, if the older paradigm is religious in its sense of the world as a place of distressful exile, the aggressive worldliness which beats against it cannot simply be described as secular. In the terms of militant protestantism, after all, to subjugate the inhabitants of, say, the New World, is to save them at once from their own heathen darkness and from the false Christianity of Spain. Hakluyt's informants repeatedly scrutinize the aims and outcomes of expeditions to establish whether they either deserved or received the endorsement of Providence. Even for a modern reader, schooled by an influential historical sociology, the unembarrassed intimacy of the connection between religion and the rise of capitalism is startling. Take for example the richest prize of the privateering war, the *Madre de Dios*, captured in 1592. The anonymous account published by Hakluyt lists the Indian and Chinese treasures found on board, and comments:

> And here I cannot but enter into the consideration and acknowledgement of God's great favour towards our nation, who by putting this purchase into our hands hath manifestly discovered those secret trades and Indian riches, which hitherto lay strangely hidden and cunningly concealed from us; whereof there was among some few of us some small and unperfect glimpse only, which now is turned into the broad light of full and perfect knowledge. Whereby it should seem that the will of God for our good is (if our weakness could apprehend it) to have us communicate with them in those East Indian treasures, and by the erection of a lawful traffic to better our means to advance true religion and his holy service.
>
> (VII, 116)

The obscure echo of Corinthians is only the finest touch in this suave benediction of piracy. All the same, writing of this kind is not simply readable as hypocritical. Rather, it records a habit of mind which works out political and economic imperatives by considering them as coded messages from God. Bizarrely, the figure of the pilgrim fuses with that of the entrepreneur.

That fusion, we could say, was the shape of the future. Now, looking back at early modern travel from the far side of both empire and enlightenment, we find the performances of the journeying fool culturally remote, while the emollient providentialism of the colonial projectors seems all too familiar. The vitality of Renaissance travel writing consists in its failure to achieve the ideological closure which imperialism would later necessitate. It is a *pre*-colonial genre: there is no stable discourse for representing Englishmen's relations with the rest of the world, and the attempts to develop one are exasperatingly but enliveningly hit-and-miss.

NOTES

1   Alluding to the custom of hanging a whet-
    stone round the neck of a liar.

2   Joseph Hall, *Virgidemiarum*, Lib IV, Sat vi,
    ll. 58–61, in *Collected Poems*, ed. A. Daven-

port, Liverpool: Liverpool University Press, 1949.

3   *Mandeville's Travels*, ed. M. C. Seymour, London: Oxford University Press, 1968. See for example ch. 22 (pp. 154–62).

4   *The Essays of Michael Lord of Montaigne, done into English by John Florio*, ed. Thomas Seccombe, 4 vols, London: Grant Richards, 1908, I, 268.

5   *The English Works of Giles Fletcher, the Elder*, ed. Lloyd E. Berry, Madison: University of Wisconsin Press, 1964, pp. 169–70.

6   The complicated bibliography of Hakluyt's work is indispensably charted in *The Hakluyt Handbook*, ed. D. B. Quinn, 2 vols, London: The Hakluyt Society, 1974, and *The Purchas Handbook*, ed. L. E. Pennington, 2 vols, London: The Hakluyt Society, 1997.

7   Richard Hakluyt, *The Principal Navigations Voyages Traffiques and Discoveries of the English Nation*, 12 vols, Glasgow: James MacLehose and Sons, 1903–5, I, xxiv. All subsequent references to this work are given as volume and page numbers in the text.

8   This state can be seen vividly in the world map appended to the second volume (1599) of the *Principal Navigations* (endpaper to vol. I of the Glasgow edition). Produced by Edward Wright, it employs both the new information available from Drake's world voyage of 1577–80 and the path-breaking projection devised in 1569 by Gerardus Mercator. It centres on the Atlantic, and the lands around it look astonishingly similar to what one sees in a modern atlas. Away from this centre, however, the detail either loses in accuracy or else fades out into the criss-cross lines of the projection itself: a mathematical schema visibly waiting for further news.

9   The phrase is J. A. Froude's, from an essay published in 1852. See L. E. Pennington, 'Secondary Works on Hakluyt and His Circle', *Hakluyt Handbook*, pp. 576–610.

10 Hakluyt's own ideological position is most clearly set out in the 'Discourse of Western Planting', which was written for the Privy Council in 1584, and not published until the nineteenth century. Available in *The Original Writings and Correspondence of the Two Richard Hakluyts*, ed. E. G. R. Taylor, 2 vols, London: The Hakluyt Society, 1935, pp. 211–326.

11 Portugal really did produce the maritime epic Froude tried to find for England in Hakluyt: the *Os Lusiadas* of Camoens (1572).

12 This point is forcefully made by Kenneth Parker in the introduction to his anthology *Early Modern Tales of Orient*, London: Routledge, 1999.

13 The authoritative study of the privateering war is still Andrews.

14 William Lithgow, *The Totall Discourse of the Rare Adventures and Painefull Peregrinations of Long Nineteene Years Travayles*, Glasgow: James MacLehose, 1906, p. 99.

15 Thomas Coryate, *Coryate's Crudities*, 2 vols, Glasgow: James MacLehose and Sons, 1905.

16 See The Neglected Genres of Popular Verse.

17 Lithgow, pp. 392–427. The account of his tortures, like much of his detail, is not entirely credible, but as we have seen, that is not quite the point.

18 The identification is visible in Lithgow's not uncommon spelling: his 'travayles' are both 'travels' and 'troubles'.

19 The phrase is, of course, the title of Thomas Nashe's picaresque narrative of 1594 – itself a further sign of the conventional nature of the association, since his hero is as it turns out at least as lucky as he is unfortunate.

20 Coryate translates a formal oration on the theme (I, 122–48), but its commonplaces are found everywhere, from top to bottom of the culture. For a 'high' example, see *Profitable Instructions, describing what observations are to be taken by travellers in all nations* (London, 1633), a book in handily tiny format which prints letters of advice to a young aristocratic traveller by Essex, Sidney and Davison. A wonderfully 'low' counterpart is John Taylor's poem *The praise of hemp-seed*, in *All the Workes of Iohn Taylor The Water Poet* (London, 1630), facsimile reprint, Aldershot: Scolar, 1973. Since hemp is an essential constituent of ropes, sails and paper, the praise of hemp-seed is tantamount to the praise of communication.

REFERENCES AND FURTHER READING

Andrews, Kenneth R. (1964). *Elizabethan Privateering: English Privateering during the Spanish War, 1585–1603*. London: Cambridge University Press.

Capp, Bernard (1994). *The World of John Taylor the Water-Poet 1578–1653*. Oxford: Clarendon Press.

Fuller, Mary C. (1995). *Voyages in Print: English Travel to America, 1576–1624*. Cambridge: Cambridge University Press.

Greenblatt, Stephen J. (1991). *Marvelous Possessions: The Wonder of the New World*. Oxford: Clarendon Press.

Hadfield, Andrew (1998) *Literature, Travel, and Colonial Writing in the English Renaissance 1545–1625*. Oxford: Clarendon Press.

Haynes, Jonathan (1986). *The Humanist as Traveller: George Sandys's 'Relation of a Journey Begun An Dom. 1610'*. London: Associated University Presses.

Hulme, Peter (1986). *Colonial Encounters: Europe and the Native Caribbean, 1492–1797*. London: Methuen.

Maczak, Antoni (1995). *Travel in Early Modern Europe*. Cambridge: Polity Press.

Maquerlot, Jean-Pierre and Willems, Michèle (eds) (1996). *Travel and Drama in Shakespeare's Time*. Cambridge: Cambridge University Press.

Nicholl, Charles (1995). *The Creature in the Map: A Journey to El Dorado*. London: Cape.

—— (1999). 'Field of Bones'. *London Review of Books*, 21 (17), 3–7.

Parker, Kenneth (1999). *Early Modern Tales of Orient: A Critical Anthology*. London: Routledge.

Parr, Anthony (ed.) (1995). *Three Renaissance Travel Plays: The Travels of the Three English Brothers, The Sea Voyage, The Antipodes*. Manchester: Manchester University Press.

Pennington, L. E. (ed.) (1997). *The Purchas Handbook*. 2 vols. London: The Hakluyt Society.

Quinn, D. B. (ed.) (1974). *The Hakluyt Handbook*. 2 vols. London: The Hakluyt Society.

Stoye, John (1989). *English Travellers Abroad, 1604–1667*. New Haven: Yale University Press.

Strachan, Michael (1962). *The Life and Adventures of Thomas Coryat*. Oxford: Oxford University Press.

Taylor, E. G. R. (1934). *Late Tudor and Early Stuart Geography 1583–1650*. London: Methuen.

PART THREE
Readings

13

Translations of the Bible

Gerald Hammond

SHYLOCK: When Jacob grazed his uncle Laban's sheep –
   This Jacob from our holy Abram was,
   As his wise mother wrought in his behalf,
   The third possessor; ay, he was the third –
ANTONIO: And what of him? Did he take interest?
SHYLOCK: No, not take interest; not, as you would say,
   Directly int'rest; mark what Jacob did:
   When Laban and himself were compromised
   That all the eanlings which were streaked and pied
   Should fall as Jacob's hire, the ewes, being rank,
   In end of autumn turned to the rams;
   And when the work of generation was
   Between these woolly breeders in the act,
   The skilful shepherd pilled me certain wands,
   And, in the doing of the deed of kind,
   He stuck them up before the fulsome ewes,
   Who, then conceiving, did in eaning time
   Fall parti-coloured lambs, and those were Jacob's.
   This was a way to thrive, and he was blest;
   And thrift is blessing, if men steal it not.
ANTONIO: This was a venture, sir, that Jacob served for;
   A thing not in his power to bring to pass,
   But swayed and fashioned by the hand of heaven.
   Was this inserted to make interest good?
   Or is your gold and silver ewes and rams?

(*Merchant of Venice*, 1.3.66–90)

Taunting Antonio with the implication that because he is a Christian he is unlikely to know the Old Testament in any detail, Shylock, in Shakespeare's most extensive biblical allusion, tells in loving detail a story from Genesis 30. By contriving the unlikely birth of many parti-coloured lambs which the contract between them had promised to him, Jacob, whose name means 'cunning', outfoxes his wily relative Laban. Such trickery, Shylock implies, may act as a precedent for his own guile in making excessive profits when opportunity offers itself. Antonio opposes this argument with an emphatic denial that the Genesis story is any kind of precedent. It reveals only God's grace at work in the world, to be interpreted as a one-off act of Providence rather than as a pattern for human action.

This exchange shows how creatively Shakespeare read his Bible, its text and its margins. Twice in their annotations the translators of the Geneva Bible indicate that this episode should not be taken as a justification for deceit, in words which clearly inform Antonio's response. To the story itself the marginal note reads, 'Jacob herein used no deceit: for it was God's commandment'; and in the next chapter, when Laban's sons complain that they have been cheated, the note alongside Jacob's claim that it was an act of God re-emphasizes the point: 'this declareth that the thing which Jacob did before was by God's commandment and not through deceit'. The Geneva margins might even have generated the dramatic scene, for in their double annotation the translators reveal their anxieties about how the story might be interpreted, a response which would have registered with a careful reader like Shakespeare on the look out for ways to dramatize the collision of Old with New Testament values.

Not only Shakespeare, but probably every literate Elizabethan owned and read the Geneva Bible, making it perhaps the single most influential English book ever published. First printed in 1560, soon after Elizabeth's accession, it ran through multiple editions right into the 1640s.[1] Reliable estimates calculate that over half a million copies were sold in the sixteenth century, a figure high enough in proportion to the total population to put into question our assumptions about Elizabethan literacy levels. It was cheaply printed, generally affordable and read by the highest and lowest in the kingdom. Its copious annotation helped fulfil the demands of the early sixteenth-century Reformers, that Scripture alone should sit at the centre of the national culture, to be accessible to everyone without the mediation of priest and bishop. It was the first English Bible to be divided into chapters and verses thereby encouraging its readers to become their own interpreters, to play with the text by matching verse with verse from one end of the Bible to the other. In essence, its text and notes gave them control over their own reading.

James I certainly sensed the threat to authority from such freedom to read and interpret. At the Hampton Court Conference, called at the beginning of his reign to help assuage the tensions between Anglicans and Puritans, the one concession which he allowed the Puritan party was for a new translation of the Bible which would embody the most recent research of Protestant scholars into Old Testament Hebrew and Aramaic and New Testament Greek.[2] But James's concession was characteristically duplicitous for he not only kept outspoken Puritan scholars like Hugh Broughton off the translation committees but he also forbade the new version to include interpretative notes in its margins. The model to avoid was the Geneva Bible's.

It was, James thought, 'the worst of all' English Bibles; strong criticism since in his opinion they were a generally poor bunch. In particular, its notes were grievously seditious. He claimed to have

> found in them annexed to the Geneva translation . . . some very partial, untrue, seditious, and savouring too much of dangerous and traitorous conceits, as, for example, Exod 1:19 where the marginal note alloweth *disobedience to kings*.
>
> (Pollard, 46)

But with a Geneva Bible in every household this was a case of bolting the stable door too late; and even when the new Bible appeared in 1611, it failed to replace the earlier version in popular affection. Not for two generations, after the Restoration, did the Geneva Bible cease to be printed, leaving the field clear at last for the Authorized Version (also known as the King James Version) to become the accepted English Bible for the next three hundred years.[3]

James clearly intended the Authorized Version to be translated in opposition to the Geneva version, ordering the translators to rely primarily upon the Bishops' Bible of 1568; but there are clear signs that his wishes were subverted from within. In overall charge of the project was Archbishop Bancroft, the author of the brief dedication to James which can still be found in today's reprints, while day-to-day coordination of the work seems to have been the responsibility of Miles Smith, the writer of the extensive and celebrated preface to the version. These men and their documents make an interesting contrast. Bancroft, theologically Calvinist, used his dedication to attack the Puritan opposition within the country; but Smith's preface emphasized the external Catholic threat and, significantly, guided its readers into seeing this version as merely the finishing touch to the collaborative and accumulative achievement of nearly a hundred years of Protestant translation. Smith, it seems, was a closet Puritan, as his post-1611 career bears out. Appointed Bishop of Gloucester in 1612, he behaved in a very unbishoplike way, being eventually reprimanded by Archbishop Laud for his contempt for ceremony and his neglect of the fabric of his cathedral.[4]

Whatever their politics, however, Smith and his fellow translators were scholars too accomplished to rely heavily on the Bishops' Bible, a ramshackle, patchy effort by the Elizabethan church establishment to rival the potentially subversive and highly popular Geneva version. In practice, the Authorized Version's text is highly dependent upon the Geneva text, and where it does use other versions, particularly in the New Testament, it is as likely to use the scholarly respectable Catholic Rheims version (1582) as the Bishops' Bible. And Smith's preface makes the vital point that this 'new' version is really only a revision. In words designed to contradict James I's proclaimed view of the inferiority of earlier English Bibles, he wrote

> we never thought from the beginning that we should need to make a new translation, nor yet to make of a bad one a good one . . . but to make a good one better, or out of many good ones one principal good one.
>
> (Pollard, 369)

Conceivably, the preface's insistence upon the continuity of English translation might well have irritated the king, for it remains a puzzling fact that there exists no record at all that the Authorized Version was ever actually authorized.

The first and most important of the Protestant translators in the line leading up to the Authorized Version was William Tyndale, who turned to Bible translation after having run into trouble among his local clergy for his supposedly heretical teaching. Tyndale had naively assumed that their hostility to what he regarded as evident truth could only be based upon his opponents' ignorance of Scripture. Equally naively he then made his way to the Bishop of London in 1523 to seek his permission to translate the Bible into English.[5] His need to do this reveals much about the political and cultural concerns which inform the whole issue of Bible translation in early modern England. While there were, for example, vernacular German Bibles in existence, all of them translations of the Latin Vulgate, there was no English Bible. There had been one: a version translated by the followers of John Wyclif in the 1380s, before the age of printing, whose popularity is borne out by the many manuscripts which survive. But its association with the Lollards, an embryonic Protestant movement with politically subversive tendencies, had led to its suppression. Throughout the fifteenth century and into the sixteenth the English people, uniquely in western Europe, were forbidden to own, translate, or even read a vernacular Bible without their bishop's permission.[6] The Bishop of London's contemptuous treatment of Tyndale and plain refusal to countenance a translation soon revealed the hollowness behind the pretence that there could ever be an officially sanctioned English Bible. As Tyndale later put it, he

> understood at the last not only that there was no room in my Lord of London's palace to translate the New Testament, but also that there was no place to do it in all England.
>
> (Pollard, 97–8)

The New Testament which Tyndale published from the continent in 1525 began the process which culminated nearly a century later in the Authorized Version. Indeed, in any estimation of cultural influence Tyndale's may be thought the greatest of all, for in those parts of the Bible which he lived to translate, the whole of the New Testament and half of the Old, his versions supply the skeleton and much of the flesh for the Bibles which followed. Here is his translation of one of the New Testament's most poetic passages, 1 Corinthians 13:

> Though I spake with the tongues of men and angels, and yet had no love, I were even as sounding brass: or as a tinkling cymbal. And though I could prophesy, and understood all secrets, and all knowledge: yea, if I had all faith so that I could move mountains out of their places, and yet had no love, I were nothing. And though I bestowed all my goods to feed the poor, and though I gave my body even that I burned, and yet had no love, it profiteth me nothing.

Love suffereth long, and is courteous. Love envieth not. Love doth not frowardly, swelleth not, dealeth not dishonestly, seeketh not her own, is not provoked to anger, thinketh not evil, rejoiceth not in iniquity: but rejoiceth in the truth, suffereth all things, believeth all things, hopeth all things, endureth in all things. Though that prophesying fail, or tongues shall cease, or knowledge vanish away, yet love never falleth away.

For our knowledge is imperfect, and our prophesying is imperfect. But when that which is perfect is come, then that which is imperfect shall be done away. When I was a child, I spake as a child, I understood as a child, I imagined as a child. But as soon as I was a man, I put away childishness. Now we see in a glass even in a dark speaking: but then shall we see face to face. Now I know imperfectly: but then shall I know even as I am known. Now abideth faith, hope, and love, even these three: but the chief of these is love.

A few words are different, but in its rhythms, syntax and much of its language this is immediately familiar to anyone who knows the Authorized Version text. It bears out Smith's claim that the 1611 translation committees were essentially doing a work of revision; and we might reflect that the most significant presence on those committees was the long dead Tyndale's. Stylistically, the main result of such an intense reliance upon the translators of the past was that in a period of radical language change and experimentation the English Bible which emerged in 1611 was both archaic and simple. It preserved the syntax and language forms of the 1520s and 1530s and it retained the plain untheological and unscholarly language of the man whose aim was for every ploughboy to sing psalms as he worked. It is easy to measure the effects of this policy today. A modern reader needs the help of a historical dictionary or editorial gloss much less often to make sense of the Authorized Version than when reading other early seventeenth-century texts, by Shakespeare, Donne or Bacon, for instance.

In spite of the simplicity of his language, Tyndale's achievement was as much a scholarly as a literary one, for unlike other Protestant translators in Reformation Europe, who tended mainly to translate Luther's German Bible into their own vernacular, he had mastered Greek and Hebrew and translated from those original languages.[7] In 1530 he used his Hebrew knowledge to translate an English Pentateuch and he then revised his New Testament in 1534, not long before he was executed by Henry VIII's allies in Belgium. Soon after his death Henry embraced the Reformation and with great historical irony encouraged the first of a succession of English versions which all built on Tyndale's work. The first complete English Bible was translated by Miles Coverdale in 1535. Then the Matthew Bible in 1537 included more of Tyndale's Old Testament work which had survived, followed by the Great Bible, the first 'authorized' version in 1539. All of these Bibles maintained Tyndale's basic text, revising it in the light of the burgeoning biblical scholarship going on all over Europe, in Catholic as well as Protestant centres, a process continued by the Geneva Bible, the base text of the Authorized Version.

As with Tyndale's translations, smuggled into the country and read and owned clandestinely at great risk, the main concern for state and church authority in rela-

tion to all of these English versions was to keep control over their use. The initial
Reformation impulse, encouraged by Thomas Cranmer the Archbishop of Canterbury,
had been permissive, to get an English Bible into the peoples' hands; but this was
soon countermanded by other powerful figures who were concerned that unmediated
access to God's word might be used to validate all kinds of seditious and heretical
attitudes. Something of this conflict can be perceived a few years earlier in the attitudes of major Humanist figures like Erasmus and Thomas More. Erasmus, the pioneer
of a modern textual scholarship of the New Testament, would never approve a vernacular translation: it was far safer to keep God's word in Latin. More also set his face
against an English version, taking time off from his state duties to write attacks upon
Tyndale and his associates. He argued that Tyndale's English New Testament had been
designed to destroy the power of the church, citing its use of 'congregation' and
'senior' in preference to 'church' and 'priest'. But behind this specific charge lay a
deeper concern about the cheapening effects of translation exemplified in Tyndale's
preference for 'love' rather than 'charity' to translate the Greek word *agape*, as in the
passage from 1 Corinthians quoted earlier.[8] Tyndale's reply was disarmingly direct,
pointing to the impossibility of translating according to More's demands:

> And when Mr More sayeth 'every love is not charity', no more is every apostle Christ's
> apostle, nor every angel God's angel, nor every hope Christian hope, nor every faith or
> belief Christ's belief, and so by an hundred thousand words, so that if I should always
> use but a word that were no more general than the word I interpret [i.e. translate], I
> should interpret nothing at all.[9]

The argument goes right to the heart of possession of the biblical text. 'Charity',
Tyndale argues, is a technical term removed from common speech, so that even an
English version which uses it still requires a gloss. 'Love', More fears, throws the Bible
open to all and reduces its mysteries to the level of common worldly experience. And
to add to More's discomfort there was the flagrancy of Tyndale's use of his versions to
support his polemical purposes, for in his margins was a succession of notes designed
to delight the public by their anti-Papal invective. Not all of the people, however,
were prepared to see their traditional faith treated so cavalierly and there are strong
indications that among the general population there was a generational divide, the
youth of England embracing a vernacular Bible which their parents feared, even
despised. William Maldon's account of his youthful experience, derived from Foxe's
papers, is a case in point. He describes a situation in which at one end of the church
the official service in Latin was being conducted while at the other end the younger
members of the congregation were crowding round one of their own who was reading
an English testament out loud. Stimulated by this, he and his father's apprentice put
their money together to buy a New Testament which they hid in their bed straw,
William teaching himself to read so that the two of them might study it together.
His mother, fearing for his soul, informed on him to his father, leading to a terrible
scene in which his father tried to strangle him.[10] In the domestic milieu as much as

the political the English Bible was a means of self-assertion and resistance to authority in the early modern period.

Bible translation had a major cultural role in areas other than English Bible versions. Translations and paraphrases of the Psalms, for instance, repeatedly embodied significant personal and national issues. At the end of the period John Milton first translated a set of psalms which addressed the national situation at a time of civil war and then another set which related to his own concerns, including his blindness. Over a hundred years earlier Cranmer's Book of Common Prayer contained the Psalms from the Great Bible which accordingly formed the central element in the liturgy of the newly founded Anglican Church. At around the same time Thomas Wyatt used his paraphrase of the so-called Penitential Psalms as a means of making covert criticism of Henry VIII's behaviour. Interleaved between the Psalms is a verse narrative which fixes them into the context of David's adulterous liaison with Bathsheba, offering a salutary model for the even more adulterous king of England.

In the Elizabthan period Mary Herbert, Countess of Pembroke took up her brother Philip Sidney's translation of the Psalms (he ended at Psalm 43; she began at Psalm 44) and wrote versions which are more experimental and daring than her brother's efforts, but which have only recently begun to be appreciated. In her explorations of the original's imagery, often taking the form of expansions, the English reader may begin to see how the Psalms gave a strong impulse to the fashion for personal and meditative lyric poetry in the late sixteenth century. So, in the first two verses of Psalm 139, thirteen Hebrew words become twenty-two in the Authorized Version: 'O Lord, thou hast searched me, and known me. / Thou knowest my downsitting and mine uprising, thou understandest my thought afar off.' In the first two stanzas of her translation Herbert expands the verses to forty words and introduces her own domestic imagery, but without any loss of simplicity or directness:

> O Lord in me there lieth nought
> But to thy search revealed lies:
>   For where I sit
>   Thou markest it;
> No less thou notest when I rise.
> Yea, closest closet of my thought
>   Hath open windows to thine eyes.
>
> Thou walkest with me when I walk;
>   When to my bed for rest I go,
>   I find thee there,
>   And ev'rywhere;
>   Not youngest thought in me doth grow,
> No, not one word I cast to talk,
>   But yet unuttered thou dost know.
>
> (Davie, 77)

And a little later in the Psalm it is clear that her creativity far outgoes the cumbrousness of the later Authorized Version translation. Here is first the Authorized Version text of vv. 13–16, followed by Herbert's paraphrase.

> For thou hast possessed my reins: thou hast covered me in my mother's womb.
> I will praise thee: for I am fearfully and wonderfully made: marvellous are thy works: and that my soul knoweth right well.
> My substance was not hid from thee, when I was made in secret, and curiously wrought in the lowest parts of the earth.
> Thine eyes did see my substance, yet being unperfect; and in thy book all my members were written, which in continuance were fashioned, when as yet there was none of them.

> Each inmost piece in me is thine:
>   While yet I in my mother dwelt,
>   All that me clad
>   From thee I had.
>   Thou in my fame hast strangely dealt;
> Needs in my praise thy works must shine,
>   So inly them my thoughts have felt.

> Thou, how my back was beam-wise laid
>   And raft'ring of my ribs, dost know;
>   Know'st ev'ry point
>   Of bone and joint,
>   How to this whole these parts did grow,
> In brave embroid'ry fair arrayed
>   Though wrought in shop both dark and low.

> Nay, fashionless, ere form I took,
>   Thy all-and-more beholding eye
>   My shapeless shape
>   Could not escape;
>   All these, time framed successively
> Ere one had being, in the book
>   Of thy foresight enrolled did lie.

While Mary Herbert's Psalms embody art of a high order, by far the most popular texts in Renaissance poetry were the metrical psalms of Sternhold and Hopkins which from the mid-sixteenth century were commonly attached to English Bibles. A byword for doggerel in later centuries and nearly beneath contempt for a modern reader, these 'poems' were loved, learned by heart and sung by successive generations of England and Scotland's increasingly Puritan communities. This is their version of those verses just quoted from Psalm 139:

> For thou possessed hast my reins,
>   And thou hast covered me,
> When I within my mother's womb
>   Enclosed was by thee.
> Thee will I praise, made fearfully
>   And wondrously I am:
> Thy works are marvellous, right well
>   My soul doth know the same.
>
> My bones they are not hid from thee,
>   Although in secret place
> I have been made, and in the earth
>   Beneath I shaped was.
> When I was formless, then thine eye
>   Saw me: for in thy book
> Where written all, wrought was before
>   That after fashion took.[11]

The monotonous metrical regularity is carefully designed for communal chanting, in line with an ethic which regarded the only proper art as one which was plain and functional.

The future for such verse as this lay largely in America, in the New England psalters and perhaps in the black spiritual. In England the Methodist hymn was its eventual development, but by then the Bible's grip upon the popular imagination had been radically attenuated. With the Restoration a new way of looking at the world regarded the early modern Bible as an increasingly grotesque and misleading object; as when John Locke, trying to make his own sense of the Pauline Epistles, expressed his irritation at the way the English Bible had been misleadingly divided into chapters and verses. 'They are so chopped and minced, as they are now printed', he complained, and

> stand so broken and divided, that not only the common people take the verses usually for distinct aphorisms, but even men of more advanced knowledge in reading them, lose very much the strength and force of the coherence, and the light that depends on it.[12]

But for a hundred and fifty years of the early modern period the English Bible, largely in the form of the chapters and verses of the Geneva Bible, had dominated the country's cultural, political and religious life; and in its Psalms it had provided a stimulus both for the period's great achievements in lyric poetry and for the rise of militant Puritanism.

NOTES

1   At least 144 editions according to Darlow and Moule, p. 62.

2   For details of the conference, see Hammond, 1993.

3 See volume 2 of Norton for an account of the AV's influence.

4 See the article on Smith in the *DNB*.

5 See the account in Daniell, 82–107.

6 According to the prohibition issued by the Provincial Council in Oxford, 1408; see Pollard, 79–81.

7 For Tyndale's Hebrew knowledge, see Hammond, 1981.

8 More's sustained attack upon Tyndale is in the third book of his *Dialogue Concerning Heresies*, 1529.

9 From *An Answer Unto Sir Thomas More's Dialogue*, 1531, ed. H. Walter, The Parker Society, Cambridge, 1850.

10 For the details of William's story, see Pollard, 268–71; for popular resentment towards the Reformation, see Duffy *passim*.

11 Text taken from my own copy, attached to a 1609 Geneva Bible. For a mature poet's imitation of a metrical psalm, see Andrew Marvell's 'Bermudas'.

12 From *A Paraphrase and Notes on the Epistles of Paul*, 1705, ed. Arthur Wainwright, Oxford, Clarendon Press, 1987, p. 105.

References and Further Reading

Allen, Ward (1969). *Translating for King James.* Kingsport, TN: Vanderbilt University Press.

Alter, Robert and Kermode, Frank (eds) (1987). *The Literary Guide to the Bible.* Cambridge, MA: Harvard University Press.

Benjamin, Walter (1973). 'The Task of the Translator'. In Hannah Arendt, ed., and Harry Zohn, tr. London: Fontana.

Buber, Martin and Rosenzweig, Frank (1994). *Scripture and Translation.* Bloomington: Indiana University Press.

Butterworth, C. C. (1941). *The Literary Lineage of the King James Version, 1340–1611.* Phildalphia: University of Pennsylvania Press.

Daniell, David (1994). *William Tyndale: a Biography.* New Haven and London: Yale University Press.

Darlow, T. H. and Moule, H. F. (1968). *Historical Catalogue of Printed Editions of the English Bible 1525–1961*, revised by A. S. Herbert. London: British and Foreign Bible Society.

Davie, Donald (ed.) (1996). *The Psalms in English.* London: Penguin.

Duffy, E. (1992). *The Stripping of the Altars.* New Haven and London: Yale University Press.

Freer, Coburn (1972). *Music for a King: George Herbert's Style and the Metrical Psalms.* Baltimore and London: Johns Hopkins University Press.

Hammond, Gerald (1981). 'William Tyndale's Pentateuch: Its Relation to Luther's German Bible and the Hebrew Original', *Renaissance Quarterly*, 33, 351-85.

——(1982). *The Making of the English Bible.* Manchester: Carcanet.

——(1993). 'The Authority of the Translated Word of God: A Reading of the Preface to the 1611 Authorized Version of the Bible', *Translation and Literature*, 2, 17-36.

Hill, Christopher (1993). *The English Bible and the Seventeenth-century Revolution.* London: Allen Lane.

McEachen, Claire and Shuger, Debora (eds) (1997). *Religion and Culture in Renaissance England.* Cambridge: Cambridge University Press.

Norton, David (1993). *A History of the Bible as Literature.* 2 vols. Cambridge: Cambridge University Press.

Opfel, Olga (1982). *The King James Bible Translators.* Jefferson and London: McFarland.

Pollard, Alfred W. (ed.) (1911). *Records of the English Bible.* Oxford: Oxford University Press.

Schwarz, W. (1955). *Principles and Problems of Biblical Translation: Same Reformation Controversies and Their Background.* Cambridge: Cambridge University Press.

Shuger, Debora (1994). *The Renaissance Bible: Scholarship, Sacrifice and Subjectivity.* Berkeley: University of California Press.

Watt, Tessa (1991). *Cheap Print and Popular Piety, 1550–1640.* Cambridge: Cambridge University Press.

Williams, Arnold (1948). *The Common Expositor: an Account of Commentaries on Genesis, 1527–1637*. Chapel Hill: University of North Carolina Press.

Zim, Rivka (1987). *English Metrical Psalms: Poetry as Praise and Prayer 1535–1601*. Cambridge: Cambridge University Press.

14

A Reading of Wyatt's 'Who so list to hunt'

Rachel Falconer

A master of verse translations, songs, sonnets and satires, Sir Thomas Wyatt is now widely recognized as one of the most technically versatile and original poets of the Tudor period. But it is his abrupt, plain-speaking persona which has captured critical attention, and which sets his work apart from the measured elegance of other courtly 'makers'.[1] Mason, for example, says in reading Wyatt, 'we are convinced that we have been hearing the authentic voice of a man of much experience and humanity' (p. 11). And Greenblatt writes that 'Wyatt captures the authentic voice of early English Protestantism, its mingled humility and militancy, its desire to submit without intermediary directly to God's will, and above all its inwardness' (p. 115). If critics as methodologically diverse as Greenblatt and Mason agree to describe Wyatt's poetic voice as 'authentic', it seems to me that this phenomenon of 'authenticity' merits closer investigation. 'Who so list to hunt' is one of Wyatt's best-known imitations of Petrarch; it is also much quoted as an example of Wyatt's characteristically forthright, honest, Protestant, independent and English personality. In this chapter, I would like to analyse the textual dynamics that give shape and audibility to such a distinctive persona and voice.

We might begin by remarking how unusual it is that Wyatt's writing, including his ballad lyrics and translations, should strike so many twentieth-century readers as authentic, unmediated by convention or formulaic thinking. A literary text (which is, after all, a representation and by definition not the 'real thing') might be said to be authentic, in one of two senses. It could be 'referentially authentic', that is, it could refer with verifiable accuracy to an actual, material event or situation. It could also, or otherwise, be described as 'emotionally authentic', appearing to transcribe the sincere thoughts of a particular individual in a specific situation. In this latter case, the more closely the 'I' of the text appears to resemble the biographical author, the greater will be the impression of 'emotional authenticity'. Wyatt's sonnet, 'Who so list to hunt', appears to fulfil both these criteria to the letter. The poem is full of pointed and insistent hints that suggest an actual, specific context that would be recognizable to a contemporary reader. The emotional state of the speaker is also inescapable; in the space of twelve lines, he refers to himself not less than twelve times. We seem to hear the 'authentic' Wyatt, expressing his weariness with this courtly game of pursuit:

> Who so list to hounte: I know, where is an hynde.
> but, as for me: helas, I may no more.
> the vayne travaill hath weried me so sore,
> I ame of theim, that farthest cometh behinde.
> yet, may I, by no meanes, my weried mynde
> drawe from the Diere: but as she fleeth afore
> faynting I folowe. I leve of therefore:
> sithens in a nett I seke to hold the wynde.
> Who list her hount: I put him owte of dowbte:
> as well, as I: may spend his time in vain.
> and, graven with Diamondes, in letters plain:
> there is written, her faier neck round abowte:
> noli me tangere: for Cesar's I ame:
> and wylde for to hold: though I seme tame.

Before considering its substance, it might be appropriate to comment on the appearance of the text, which I reproduce here in its original spelling and punctuation. In the *Collected Poems of Sir Thomas Wyatt*, Muir and Thomson modernize the punctuation of the Egerton MS 2711, in which 'Who so list' appears. To justify this editorial decision, they comment that 'it is by no means certain that Wyatt was responsible for all or most of the two hundred punctuation marks in the first hundred lines of the MS' and in any case that the heavy pointing 'would be misleading to a modern reader' (p. xxvi). But Joost Daalder questions this decision, and objects that Muir and Thomson's modernized version does 'not seem to do justice to Wyatt's syntax'.[2] But is the pointing in the MS Wyatt's, or someone else's? Hughey discusses Nicholas Grimald's corrections to the Egerton MS, which frequently involved the insertion of colons and other heavy pointing, such as we see in the sonnet above.[3] But, while the MS punctuation might represent the hand of Grimald, or an unknown scribe, it might equally be Wyatt's. In the final analysis, the Egerton was Wyatt's manuscript; he approved and authorized the text as it there appeared. Thus, since its pointing contributes to the sonnet's meaning, and especially, its remarkable rhythmic structure, I would argue that it is best studied with pointing and spelling unmodernized.[4] Certainly in the present context, where we are pursuing the image of Wyatt as a poet of authenticity, it makes sense to begin with the text as it would have appeared to readers in Wyatt's own day.

The sonnet certainly invites us to consider it in terms of a particular historical context. A long-standing critical tradition holds that the Diere (deer, dear) to which the text refers is Anne Boleyn, that 'Cesar' is Henry VIII, and that 'noli me tangere' (let no one touch me) refers to the sexual prohibition surrounding Anne, after it

became clear that she was the king's new favourite.) Interestingly, the critical tradition associating Wyatt with Anne Boleyn dates back to Wyatt's own time. Mason
quotes a Spanish chronicler who reports the contents of a letter from Wyatt to the
king, in which Wyatt admits to having slept with Anne on one occasion, at the lady's
own encouragement (p. 147). In May 1536, Wyatt and half a dozen other men were
arrested for treasonous involvement with Anne. Wyatt was kept in the Tower of
London for several months, while Anne Boleyn and those men found guilty by association with her, were put to death. A later poem, 'Who lyst his welthe', suggests
that Wyatt may have witnessed Anne's execution from his prison window ('The bell
towre showed me suche syght / That in my hed stekyss day and nyght' (CP 187)).

But the question is, does 'Who so list' refer specifically to the period (*c*.1527) in
which Wyatt learned of the king's interest in Anne? And if so, does the sonnet 'authentically' express Wyatt's own disappointment and frustration as a former, perhaps still
interested, lover of Anne Boleyn? The Egerton MS is dated *c*.1535, long after Wyatt's
alleged involvement, but before his imprisonment in 1536. Mason claims that the
sonnet must have been written several years after Wyatt first heard news of the king's
interest in Anne, and that therefore the poem's situation and emotional content must
be fictional (Mason, p. 136). But any former lover of Anne's might justifiably retain
his anxiety and resentment over a long period. After all, by the time Wyatt was
arrested, whatever treasonous affair he'd had with Anne would already have been ten
years old. It seems most likely that the poem addresses itself to courtiers who had
some association with Anne, or knew of those who did, during the period (the 1520s)
when Henry made clear his interest in her.

I stress this point because recent criticism tends to be sceptical towards overly referential interpretations of such highly wrought works as 'Who so list'. For example,
Elizabeth Heale writes that Wyatt 'makes it impossible to decide whether the 'her'
of this poem is a particular woman (Anne Boleyn), any woman as prize . . . or woman
as a figure for worldly favour' (p. 58). Greenblatt writes that the sonnet expresses the
frustration and anxiety not of an individual, but of a social class. To read more specifically into the historical context would, Greenblatt argues, detract from 'the poet's
immense power of implication . . . its restraint and suggestiveness' (p. 146). But this
is to ignore the way the text invites its readers to raise specific questions about its referential content. Its opening line makes reference to a common social activity with
which the text's narratees are evidently very familiar. This appeal to a familiar audience, engaged in a specific social activity, is repeated again in line nine. It is equally
clear that the hunt is being used as a metaphor for the courtly game of amorous
pursuit. The deer's precise identity is a riddle which this texts invites its readers to
untie. For a modern, critical reader, determining the sonnet's exact referential object
is perhaps less important than recognizing the text's referential dynamic, its gesture
towards, its pursuit of, concrete meaning within the text's verbal maze.)

It is similarly more to the point to recognize that the speaker of 'Who so list' presents himself as emotionally sincere and direct, than to determine the extent to which
this fictional character resembles the text's biographical author. Wyatt's speaker

renounces the courtly hunt in which only 'Cesar' will win the prize (lines 2, 10). But he also candidly admits that he cannot desist, even though he knows he should (lines 5–6). The picture he presents to the reader, then, is of a man caught between conflicting desires and social pressures. Between the attraction of the Diere (the feminine other) and the prohibition of Cesar (paternal authority), Wyatt's speaker struggles to find a neutral space in which to 'be' or 'address' himself. Whether or not he is an entirely or partially fictional persona, the speaker presents himself and his situation with no obvious inflection, no indication of a significant difference between narratorial voice and implied author. Thus if critical analysis of Wyatt's sonnet tends to slide from the speaker's persona to assumptions about Wyatt's personality, this too is partly a function of the text's narrative structure.

From this critical distance, we may begin to see how and why Wyatt's verse *represents* this particular stance of 'authenticity'. Greenblatt suggests that courtier-diplomats like Wyatt made a cult of rebellious forthrightness, because their marginal status in an absolutist court denied them any exercise of real power or agency. In the Tudor world, Greenblatt comments, 'conversation with the king must have been like small talk with Stalin' (pp. 136–7). But this model of subjectivity seems to deny the Renaissance poet-courtier any degree of agency. And yet Wyatt's persona might be interpreted as itself absolutist, when viewed from the perspective of those subjectivities his verse works to control. For example, Estrin argues that the speaker of 'Who so list' attempts to impose tyrannical control over its female subject, the silenced and absent Diere. In Estrin's view, 'Who so list' represents the strategies by which the silenced female subject rediscovers her own voice and agency. This seems to me an overly idealistic reading of the sonnet which has the detrimental effect of effacing the more probable, though, more limited signs of female agency in the text, as I hope to show. But both these readings are valuable in the way they reveal the sonnet's dynamic construction of an 'authentic' subjecthood.

In my view, 'Who so list' signals its 'authenticity' by means of a textual *turn*, not only a *turning away* from Petrarch, from the Diere and Cesar, but also a *return to* the alliterative and accentual verse of 'native' English traditions. In the sestet, we shall also find evidence of a *return of* the Diere, and of Petrarch's source-text, which the octave represses with only partial success.[7] Wyatt's 'authentic' *persona* should always be understood as a polemically conceived subject position. The 'I' of 'Who so list' is always also 'not him', 'not her', or 'not you'. Above all, the 'I' is 'not Petrarch', whose sonnet sequence to Laura provided Wyatt with the material for his own experimentation with the sonnet form. This is Petrarch's famous sonnet, 'Una candida cerva', which Wyatt freely translates in 'Who so list to hunt':

> Una candida cerva sopra l'erba
>   verde m'apparve, con duo corna d'oro,
>   fra due riviere, all'ombra d'un alloro,
>   levando'l sole a la stagione acerba.
> Era sua vista si dolce superba

ch'i' lasciai per seguirla ogni lavoro,
come l'avaro che'n cercar tesoro
con diletto l'affanno disacerba.

'Nessun mi tocchi' al bel collo d'intorno
  scritto avea di diamanti e di topazi,
  'libera farmi al mio Cesare parve'.
Et era 'l sol già volto al mezzo giorno,
  gli occhi miei stanchi di mirar, non sazi,
  quand'io caddi ne l'acqua, et ella sparve.

A pure white doe upon green grass
Appeared to me, with two horns of gold,
Between two streams, in the shade of a laurel,
While the sun was rising, in the bitter season.
Her appearance was so sweetly proud,
That to follow her I abandoned all work;
Like the miser who in seeking treasure
With delight makes his work less bitter.

'Let no one touch me' round about her beautiful neck
was written with diamonds and topazes;
It pleased my Caesar to set me free'
And already the sun had turned to midday,
My eyes wearied with gazing, not satiate,
when I fell into the water, and she disappeared.[8]

Petrarch's sonnet is structured as a series of oppositions and oxymora. The entire visionary experience is mapped out between two extremes, the sacred purity of the deer ('candida') and the profanity of the speaker (who in the last line, falls into water, 'io caddi' and betrays his fallen nature). With her two horns of gold, and appearing between two rivers, the deer is the visual symbol of the speaker's irreconcilably dualistic universe. To the poet's world belongs labour ('lavoro') in the bitter season ('la stagione acerba'); to the deer's, freedom ('libera') and the power to transcend bitterness ('disacerba'). The prohibition ('Nessun mi tocchi') in Petrarch's sonnet does not lead to the onlooker's despair; on the contrary, it increases the creature's desirability. In other words, Cesare is a benevolent force in the poem; 'it pleases' ('parve') God to let the deer roam freely, and to grant 'Petrarch' a fleeting glimpse of her ('apparve'). If God owns the deer, she also expresses possessiveness towards 'her' deity. But if the vision of the collared deer is itself positive, it is also foreign to the speaker's own world. In this dualistic schema, there is no bridge between the sacred and the profane.

This dualism can also be seen in the sonnet's temporal organization, a feature that is effaced in Wyatt's translation. 'Una candida cerva' unfolds in the simple (completed) past tense. The white doe first appears to inhabit a timeless realm; in the fourth line, we then hear that she appears to the speaker at dawn. The vision lasts the space of a morning, then disappears as the sun approaches mid-day. Petrarch brilliantly conveys the speaker's sense of temporal suspension while the vision lasts, and then the return of post-fall temporality at the end of the sonnet ('Et era 'l sol gia volto'). But the key temporal marker, upon which the whole of the sonnet turns (this is *Petrarch's* distinctive *turn*) is the 'quando' of the final line. It is this 'when' that divides the time of the speaker into a then and a now, a pre- and post-fall consciousness. The 'when' is the decisive temporal split which divides Petrarch's dreaming from his waking self and the desiring 'io' from the 'ella' he so desires. But it is also the temporal split that makes the vision narratable. Looking back at the time before 'when', Petrarch is able to frame his vision within a specific temporal sequence. More importantly, he is able to stand outside and beyond the self who gazes wearily at the untouchable deer. The speaker's unfortunate fall into the water is also, simultaneously, a conversionary baptism which permits the 'new self' to speak of the 'old self' as a separable identity. The temporal break signified by 'quando' allows Petrarch to plot desire along a single trajectory, with a final resolution.[9] Although, of course, Petrarch re-narrates and re-plots Laura's unattainability many times in his *Rime*, here in 'Una candida cerva' the deer appears to the speaker once and then is gone.

By contrast, Wyatt's sonnet takes place in a present tense of indefinite duration. His most decisive turn away from Petrarch is his refusal to emplot his knowledge of the deer into the narrative structure of a single, conversionary experience. Estrin argues that the chronological sequence of octet and sestet are reversed in Wyatt's sonnet (p. 138). She claims that the speaker glimpses the deer in the final six lines, and that this prior event explains the emotional outpouring of the first eight lines. But can we even assume that Wyatt's speaker actually sees, or has seen, the deer of which he speaks? If so, when does this happen? Wyatt's sonnet lacks chronological coherence. As Greenblatt writes, 'The reader is left with the impression that, despite the poet's attempts a decisiveness, he never quite "leaves off", that he is incapable of fully drawing him mind from the "deer"' ' (p. 147). There is no decisive 'when' to distinguish the present time of *narrating* from the time of *narration* in which the deer may actually have been glimpsed.[10] Thus, unlike Petrarch's, Wyatt's sonnet conspicuously lacks the conversionary point which breaks past from present speakers, and turns vision into narratable experience.

Wyatt's *turn away* from Petrarchan temporal organization (in Bakhtinian terms, his reordering of Petrarch's visionary chronotope) must be seen alongside other, more noticeable thematic changes. Wyatt's Cesar is secular, possessive and tyrannous, but his Diere is also secular and arguably powerful herself. Wyatt's added description of her as 'wylde for to hold: though I seme tame' hints at a powerful duplicity not present in Petrarch. There is a suggestion that this duplicity might equally be exercised against the speaker, his rivals, or Cesar himself. If the sonnet was composed in *c.*1527, it may record a belief in Wyatt's circle that Anne Boleyn wielded an independent, possibly rebellious, power at court.

In Petrarch's sonnet, Cesar and the deer belong to the sacred world, in contrast to the poem's fallen speaker. In Wyatt's, we discover unlooked for affinities between both the deer and the speaker, and the speaker and Cesar. As others have noted, Wyatt's speaker is feminized by the hunt (see Heale, p. 57). In the line, 'as she fleeth afore, / faynting I folowe', both hunter and hunted lack agency; both are victims of the courtly chase. But the speaker's vain attempt 'to hold the wynde' (line 8) is also an imitation of Cesar's possessive act of 'holding' the deer by collaring her (line 14). Thus the speaker identifies by turns with feminine and masculine, with the Diere and Cesar, with possessed and possessing subjects in the poem. In Bakhtin's terms, his subjectivity is 'unfinalized'; he hovers between the positions of self and other. He is 'unfinalized' in terms of gender, social class, and, as we have seen, 'address' in time.[11]

But if Wyatt's speaker is an unfinalized subject, it might be objected that the text itself is finalized; it has a definite beginning, middle and end. So the subject achieves closure insofar as it is enclosed in a finished poem. But I would argue that Wyatt's sonnet conceals a further layer of conflict, this time at the intertextual level of its relation to Petrarch. Just as Wyatt's speaker turns, or attempts to turn from the Diere. So Wyatt as translator attempts a turn away from his Petrarchan 'original' (although Petrarch's poem in itself is a translation / turn from Ovid), Wyatt's turn from Petrarch includes a *return to* alternative traditions of prosody and verse form. As J. W. Lever has shown, Wyatt gradually evolved his own sonnet structure, evolving from Petrarch's two-part to his own tripartite division, three quatrains concluded by a rhyming couplet (p. 34). After Wyatt's death, Surrey developed this form, which became known as the 'English', as opposed to 'Italian', sonnet; here again we find a connection with Wyatt and 'Englishness'.

In 'Una candida cerva', we can see that the octave and sestet form two halves of a diptych which together represent a 'finalized' visionary experience. Muir and Thomson arrange Wyatt's sonnet in similar form on the page, although the MS contains no stanzaic division (CP, p. 5). The editors further guide the reader's eye towards the Petrarchan model by indenting Wyatt's text to create two quatrains within the octet, and two triplets within the sestet (producing the Petrarchan rhyme scheme, ABBA ABBA CDD CEE). But this editorial arrangement obscures the obvious *textual* emphasis on the final couplet, Cesar's 'don't touch', which functions as a 'twist in the tail', a retort or rebuke to what has come before. Arranged differently, Wyatt's sonnet might read as a sonnet of the new English type, with the rhyme scheme ABBA ABBA CDDC EE. The objection to this reading is that the third quatrain (CDDC) does not stand alone syntactically or semantically. Taking into account both the couplet, and the 'weak' third quatrain, we might conclude that 'Who so list' is neither wholly 'English' nor wholly 'Italian' in structure; rather, it hesitates between alternatives. Structurally, Wyatt here attempts but does not finalize his *turn away* from Petrarch.

The intertextual conflict with Petrarch is evident, not only in the sonnet's structure, but also in its play of syllabic versus accentual metres. Here again, we find evidence of Wyatt's authentically 'English' rhythm being expressed as a turn away from the Italian, or in this case, away from Wyatt's approximation of Italian rhythm. This conflict over rhythm is especially evident when we retain the manuscript's original system of punctuation (as I have reproduced it above). Taking the punctuation marks as indicators of rhythmic rather than syntactic breaks, we find that each of the first twelve decasyllabic lines of the sonnet contains five accents or stresses. But as the heavy pointing shows, each five-beat line is further divided by mid-line caesurae into widely varying rhythmic combinations. The most striking examples of rhythmic, as opposed to syntactic, punctuation, occur in lines 5 and 10. Here the ungrammatical pointing serves to emphasize the speaker's attempts to break away from the chase; his failure to break free is marked by a change to lighter pointing, and a faster, unchecked iambic beat. A reader presented with the poem's original MS punctuation thus might be equipped to *hear* the rhythms of a subject in crisis.

Thus far, however, I have discussed variation of rhythm within the regular ten-syllable, five-beat line, which Wyatt employed in imitation of Petrarch's eleven-syllable lines. His real break with Petrarch comes in the final two lines of the sonnet, where he abandons the five-beat syllabic line altogether, in favour of the four-beat accentual line of the traditional English lyric. Although the couplet may be scanned as two ten-syllable lines ('wylde' is disyllabic, according to Mason), its heavy mid-line and end-stopped punctuation permits of no ambiguity as regards its stress-pattern. Each half-line unit contains two accentual beats, regardless of the number of syllables in the half-line. In traditional English accentual metre, the number of beats in a line are counted, rather than the number of syllables (as in the four beat line: *baa* baa *black* sheep, *have* you any *wool?*). Wyatt's songs and ballads regularly employ this traditional, accentual metre. After his visit to Italy in 1527, Wyatt began experimenting with versions of quantitative and syllabic metres, in which, retrospectively, the length of vowels, and number of syllables in a line are counted. But as Lever argues, and 'Who so list' demonstrates, Wyatt continues to make dramatic use of English accentual metre. Analysing the juxtaposition of metres in another sonnet, Lever raises this clash of rhythms to the level of political conflict: 'Beneath this artificial conformity the old English stress patterns with their turbulent beat fought hard to reassert themselves, like feudal barons under the yoke of Tudor despotism' (p. 18).

Lever's suggestion of political conflict worked out at the level of prosody, however, seems to me a little too fanciful in places. For example, if this struggle of barons and despots applies to 'Who so list', then it applies in the wrong way. It is the despotic Henry / Cesar who employs the 'turbulent beat' of the accentual metre, and Wyatt's speaker who imposes a decasyllabic 'conformity' on the sonnet's preceding lines. More generally, it might be questioned whether Wyatt's continued use of accentual metre could be construed as a sign of vigorously independent 'Englishness'. On one hand, Wyatt's songs are as convention-bound as his sonnets; the conventions are simply different (they lack, for example, the sonnet's individualized narrator). Wyatt's 'authenticity', in this context, consists of his ability to play one literary convention against another, thus illuminating, even ironizing each genre from within. On the other hand, true 'Englishness' in Wyatt's day would not necessarily have been expressed as faithfulness to native verse traditions. George Puttenham felt Wyatt's contribution to English literature was that he injected foreign class into the 'rude and homely manner of vulgar [English] Poesie'.[12] We must also take into account Wyatt's profession as a diplomat in the court of Henry VIII. Given that his function was to maintain Henry's dignity and reputation amongst fierce competition at home and abroad, his sense of 'Englishness' must have been much more dialogically conceived; that is to say, to be English was to be agonistically other than French or Spanish or Italian.

But if the couplet's accentual beat does not represent the triumph of Englishness, as Lever's approach suggests, it certainly seems to represent a twist on the sonnet's preceding twelve lines. The couplet's ostentatiously chiming beat reads like an imposition of order on the 'wylde' and dramatically varied rhythms of the quatrains. Each four-beat, accentual line is severed by a mid-line caesura; thus the poem concludes with a formal self-enclosed, double chiasmus. Nothing could be more different from Petrarch's final, intensely personal decrescendo. Wyatt's sonnet therefore has it both ways. Its speaker tries and fails to assert his own subjective agency, by rejecting both Cesar and the Diere; his dilemma appears 'authentic' because it is unfinalized and irresolvable. But the text also imposes a 'vigorous' 'English' closure on its theme of the subject in crisis; and here the text becomes 'authentically' Wyatt's in the sense that it successfully escapes what Wyatt remaps as a Petrarchan impasse.

In this precariously balanced, two-tiered resolution, Wyatt's speaker participates in the successful 'Englishing' of Petrarch; by association, he thus acquires a measure of the 'English' Cesar's authority over the Diere. After all, it is he who transcribes the diamond letters for the reader to see; it is he who narrates the authoritative line, 'noli me tangere'. To this conscious Englishing of Petrarch might be added the poem's traditional alliterative lines (especially the six f's of 'fleeth afore / faynting I folowe. I leve of therefore') and Wyatt's signature use of homely aphorism ('sithens in a nett I seke to hold the wynde'). But how complete is this act of Englishing Petrarch? How stable is the couplet's resolution to the formal, thematic and structural crises of the sonnet? I would suggest, finally, that the couplet raises as many questions as it appears to resolve. First, while Wyatt adds a second line to (and thus 'Englishes') the Petrarchan inscription, what does the final line actually mean? Should it surprise us that the deer turns out to be wild? Were we expecting it to be tame? Is 'tame' a positive attribute (chaste, obedient) or a negative one (as of a prostitute, owned, appropriated); is 'wylde' negative (foreign, other, unruly) or positive (untouched, pure)? Furthermore, is the couplet as self-contained and finalized as it seems on first reading? Do the 'letters plain' on the collar really clarify anything? It is only paratactically connected (by 'and') to the previous phrase; '*for* [because], graven' would have given a stronger sense than 'and, graven' that here, finally, is an explanation for the deer's untouchability. Because of that fatally weak link, 'and', the couplet reads as one more detail in a disturbingly ongoing experience. The couplet does not, though it first seems to, exert an apotropaic power over (a power to ward off) the traumatic memory. Wyatt's *return to* accentual stress may thus equally be interpreted as a *return of* the repressed – the speaker's unsatiated desire, the undifferentiated presence of Petrarch in Wyatt's poem. The 'authenticity' of Wyatt's 'Who so list to hunt' consists of the provisionality of its resolution. Whether Wyatt's speaker succeeds or fails to establish an independent subjectivity depends, finally, on the interpretative *turn* of the reader.

NOTES

1 For Wyatt's particular achievements in lyric, satire and sonnet see, respectively, Mason (p. 29), Starkey (p. 232) and Ferry (p. 118).

2 See Daalder, *Notes and Queries* 216 (1971), p. 214. For further comments on Wyatt's punctuation see Parkes, *Pause and Effect: An Introduction to the History of Punctuation in the West*, p. 107.

3 See Hughey, 'The Harington manuscript at Arundel Castle and related documents', *The Library* 15 (1934–5), pp. 388–444.

4 Hughey provides a facsimile of the Egerton MS (*The Library* pp. 414–15), from which I have reconstructed the printed version here.

5 See Nott, Chambers, Baldi, cited in CP, p. 267.

6 See R. A. Rebholz, *Sir Thomas Wyatt: The Complete Poems*, pp. 22–3, and H. A. Mason, *Sir Thomas Wyatt: A Literary Portrait* (Bristol: Bristol Classical Press, 1986), p. 95 and *passim*.

7 On the return *to* origins and return *of* the repressed in narrative, see Brooks, and Kristeva.

8 My translation of Petrarch draws on existing translations by d'Amico, p. 145, Musa and Mason.

9 The psychoanalytic approach to plotting desire in narrative is the subject of Brooks's *Reading for the Plot*.

10 The time of narrating (*Erzahlzeit*) and narrated time (*Erzahlte Zeit*) are discussed by Ricoeur, pp. 78ff.

11 In Kristevan terms, he might be analysed as the subject-in-process and the subject-on-trial, repeated enacting the thetic break between semiotic and symbolic realms; access to the phallic mother, the Diere's 'faier neck' is denied by Cesar's paternal prohibition (cf. Kristeva, pp. 46–7).

12 See Puttenham, 'Art of English Poesie' in *Elizabethan Critical Essays*, Vol. 1, p. 60.

REFERENCES AND FURTHER READING

Bakhtin, M. (1984). 'Forms of Time and of the Chronotope in the Novel'. In *The Dialogic Imagination* (pp. 85–258), trs C. Emerson and M. Holquist. Austin: University of Texas Press.

Brooks, P. (1984). *Reading for the Plot: Design and Intention in Narrative*. Oxford: Clarendon Press.

Crewe, J. (1988). *Trials of Authorship: Anterior Forms and Poetic Reconstruction from Wyatt to Shakespeare*. Berkeley and Los Angeles: University of California Press.

d'Amico, J. (1979). *Petrarch in England: An Anthology of Parallel Texts from Wyatt to Milton*. Ravenna: Longo (*Speculum artium* 5).

Estrin, B. L. (1994). *Laura: Uncovering Gender and Genre in Wyatt, Donne, and Marvell*. London: Duke University Press.

Ferry, A. (1983). *The 'Inward' Language: Sonnets of Wyatt, Sidney, Shakespeare, Donne*. Chicago: University of Chicago Press.

Freccero, J. (1986). *The Poetics of Conversion*, ed. R. Jacoff. Cambridge, MA: Harvard University Press.

Greenblatt, S. (1980). *Renaissance Self-fashioning from More to Shakespeare*. Chicago: University of Chicago Press.

Heale, E. (1998). *Wyatt, Surrey and Early Tudor Poetry*. London: Longman.

Kristeva, J. (1983). 'Revolution in Poetic Language'. In K. Oliver (ed.), *The Portable Kristeva* (pp. 27–92). Chichester: Columbia University Press.

Lever, J. W. (1956). *The Elizabethan Love Sonnet*. London: Methuen.

Mason, H. A. (ed.) (1986). *Sir Thomas Wyatt: A Literary Portrait*. Bristol: Bristol Classical Press.

Muir, K. and P. Thomson (eds) (1969). *Collected Poems of Sir Thomas Wyatt*. Liverpool: Liverpool University Press.

Musa, M. (1985). *Selections from the Canzoniere and Other Works*. Oxford: Oxford University Press.

Ricoeur, P. (1985). *Time and Narrative, vol. 2*, trs K. McLaughlin and D. Pellauer. Chicago: Chicago University Press.

Southall, R. (1964). *The Courtly Maker: An Essay on the Poetry of Wyatt and His Contemporaries*. Oxford: Blackwell.

Starkey, D. (1982). 'Castiglione Ideal and Tudor Reality', *Journal of the Warburg and Courtauld Institutes*, 45, 232–9.

Waller, M. (1989). 'The Empire's New Clothes: Refashioning the Renaissance'. In S. Fisher and J. Halley (eds), *Seeking the Woman in Late Medieval and Renaissance Writings: Essays in Feminist Contextual Criticism* (pp. 160–86). Knoxville: University of Tennessee Press.

15

Courtship and Counsel: John Lyly's *Campaspe*

Greg Walker

John Lyly's *Campaspe* was performed before Elizabeth I at Whitehall on 1 January 1584. In it, as in each of Lyly's early plays, a classical figure undergoes a sea change into a form which more directly addressed the preoccupations of the court of England's Virgin Queen. In Lyly's source for *Sapho and Phao*, Sapho, the Lesbian poetess is metamorphosed from the ageing bawd who was converted from the love of women by her lust for the supernaturally beautiful ferryman Phao. In the play, Sapho is transmuted into a chaste young maid who resists her own desires and rejects the advances of the amorous boatman. In *Campaspe*, Alexander the Great is transformed into a chaste heterosexual who, although temporarily floored by desire for a young Theban captive, Campaspe, is restored to his senses when he discovers she loves another, his favourite artist Apelles. In the somewhat perfunctory denouement Alexander blesses the union of prisoner and painter before departing to pursue his greater destiny.

In each of these dramas, Lyly depicts a prince who is tempted to abandon political duties in favour of a sexual relationship with an inappropriate commoner, but eventually thinks better of it. To strengthen this similarity of situation Lyly elevates Sapho from a poetess to a queen, and – to remove any last trace of sexual impropriety – shifts her from Lesbos to Syracuse, so making her probably the least Sapphic Sapho in literary history. The political resonance of presenting this theme of unwise, unequal dalliances at court when Elizabeth I was controversially considering marriage to a non-royal catholic, Francis, Duke of Anjou, has been noted by a number of critics, and does not need labouring here.[1] But it is important to stress at this stage that these plays, and *Campaspe* in particular, do touch upon issues of intense political importance to their contemporary audiences, and so Lyly was inevitably flying close to the wind.

Direct intervention in politics by writers outside the charmed court circle was always a perilous business if the rules of engagement were not carefully followed. A powerful reminder of this fact had been delivered some five years earlier on 31 August 1579 when John Stubbes had his right hand publicly severed as punishment for publishing a pamphlet, *The Discovery of A Gaping Gulf*, critical of the Queen's willingness to consider marriage to Anjou. Lyly's play seems, however, to have been carefully designed to avoid the sort of ill-judged political canvassing that Stubbes's tract represents. Indeed, it takes as its theme the very issues which Stubbes's case raised, the nature of political counsel and the manner in which criticism of the sovereign might be expressed in a personal monarchy. In this respect Lyly's choice of protagonist and the form in which he is represented are tailored to highlight the theory and practice of princely government

For scholars of the Renaissance, the life of Alexander brought philosophy and politics into conjunction in their most obvious and extreme forms. Alexander was, of course, tutored by Aristotle, and so could be presented as a humanist icon, a type of Plato's ideal philosopher king, mingling the martial and political skills of the governor with the intellectual and moral training of the philosopher. And not only was Alexander trained by the greatest philosopher of the classical period, but he subsequently came into contact with others at key moments in his career, most notably Diogenes the Cynic, whose robust rejection of authority and refusal to flatter were the source of many anecdotes exemplifying the problems of reconciling princes with their outspoken subjects.[2] Thus exemplary stories accumulated around Alexander as no other classical figure during the middle ages and the early Renaissance, not least because the model of a martial prince that he provided was more readily applied to early modern monarchies than stories set in Republican Rome. As Chaucer's Monk remarks in *The Canterbury Tales*:

> The storie of Alisaundre is so commune
> That every wight that hath discrecioun
> Hath herd somwhat or al of his fortune.
> (*The Monk's Tale*, 2631–4)[3]

He was even made the hero of a number of medieval romances which transformed his historical campaigns into the stuff of fantasy, involving encounters with mythical beasts, space flights and submarine journeys among their itinerary.[4]

And yet there was also sufficient information in circulation about the historical Alexander to confirm that he had actually been far from the ideal sovereign that Plato imagined.[5] His killing of a number of his companions, one in a drunken rage, another through the ignoble employment of an assassin, created problems for those who wished to use Alexander as a model of princely wisdom and enlightened patronage.

As the heir of both the medieval romance tradition and the more critical legacy of the Renaissance historians, Lyly consequently inherited a profoundly ambivalent figure as the protagonist of his first courtly play, and he exploited that ambivalence to the full.[6] As Michael Pincombe has observed, although the Alexander we see onstage commits no acts of violence, and eventually behaves with admirable political correctness in resolving the dilemma created by his actions, the other characters around him act as if they were aware of the Alexander of history, whose behaviour is less predictable and potentially more threatening.[7] In this phenomenon lies one of the play's most interesting features, its conscious deployment of anachronism. The action is ostensibly set early in Alexander's reign, immediately following the destruction of Thebes in 335 BC, but characters speak and act as if they had a knowledge of their king's entire career. Chryssipus alludes to his apparent aspirations towards divinity, a feature of his conquest of Egypt in 332 BC, and Alexander himself refers to the death of Callisthenes, which occurred even later, during his central Asian campaign in spring 327 BC, while other judgements of his character sound like retrospective summations of his life as a whole.[8]

Perhaps the most strikingly anachronistic role is played in this respect by the soldiers Clitus and Parmenio, who behave oddly like the citizens of a modern totalitarian regime, conducting their conversations in anxious, semi-public tones and spicing their talk with assurances of their loyalty to the state. When the opportunity to speculate directly about the causes of what the audience knows to be Alexander's love-sickness, Parmenio rejects it outright in terms which make his political anxieties clear.

> In kings' causes I rather love to doubt than conjecture, and I think it better to be ignorant than inquisitive; they have long ears and stretched arms, in whose heads suspicion is a proof and to be accused is to be condemned.
>
> (3.4.6–10)[9]

The unsettling effect that this has upon the play is clearly deliberate, and relies upon irony. For, as those members of the audience familiar with the Alexander story would know, Clitus and Parmenio were historically, along with Callisthenes, the best-known victims of the king's anger, each being killed (in 329 BC and 330 BC respectively) for just such 'suspicions' of disloyalty as they are here so anxious to dispel.

Such allusions play upon the audience's familiarity with the Alexander story, drawing upon their knowledge of his life and legacy to create ironic resonance at key moments in the plot. The drama thus takes on the aspect of an academic exercise, the philosophical dissection of a problem through the application and study of a historical analogue. Alexander is represented whole, as the sum of his achievements and reputation, as he provides an extreme example of the problem of statecraft that Lyly is exploring. What if he were the exemplary philosopher king that many of the humanist anecdotes imply? How might he react to the emotional stress created by love? Could civic virtue stand up to the potential for Ovidian psychological metamorphosis brought about by extreme emotion? And yet Lyly is also able to deploy the rest of the Alexandrian narrative by implication, alluding metatheatrically to the threat of what might happen if hypothetical virtue was to give way under the promptings of passion.

The capacity of the true prince to discipline his or her own natural instincts in the interests of the commonweal through the application of philosophical detachment and the will to virtue is, of course, the 'point' of *Campaspe*. The key to Lyly's portrayal of his ideal Alexander is restraint, his capacity to resist in peacetime those urges to decisive, brutal action which characterized his 'terrible' leadership in time of war. The threat to that restraint is provided by his passion for Campaspe. What brings the king back to reason and self-control is his relationship with his advisers, and in particular, not the horrified reaction of Hephestion to the very idea of Alexander in love, still less the overarching criticisms of Diogenes, but the amiable personality and gentle conduct of Apelles the painter, and of Campaspe herself.

The moral is itself celebrated in the final scene.

> ALEXANDER: Let the trumpet sound, strike up the drum, and I will presently into Persia. How now, Hephestion, is Alexander able to resist love as he list?
> HEPHESTION: The conquering of Thebes was not so honourable as the subduing of these thoughts.
> ALEXANDER: It were a shame Alexander should desire to command the world if he could not command himself.
>
> (5.4.163–9)

This translates precisely Pliny's reading of the 'original' story of Alexander's 'giving up' of Campaspe: the King 'in this act of his . . . won as much glory as by any victory over his enemies: for now he had conquered himself'.[10] This victory of self-control and the reconquest of the self which it enables, is deeply inscribed in *Campaspe*, not only in the narrative, but in the very form in which it is presented, Lyly's characteristic euphuistic prose.

For Lyly, euphuism, with its careful balancing of phrases and poised antithetical tropes, was not simply a stylistic innovation but the linguistic embodiment of an entire classical philosophical tradition. In *Campaspe*, the best state of human existence is presented in the embrace of the Aristotelian mean, the ideal mid-point between antithetical extremes of conduct. Hence Alexander's characteristic magnanimity is defined as the condition in which niggardliness and profligacy are held in equal disdain, just as good government is the ideal accommodation between the rival tendencies towards anarchy and tyranny, the virtuous point at which powerful and malevolent forces are brought to a benevolent and productive equilibrium.

The linguistic equivalent of this philosophy is precisely Euphuism, with its self-conscious deployment of the tropes of equipoise: *isocolon* (the balancing of equally long parallel clauses), *paramoion* (the even balancing of parallel clauses repeating key sounds), and *parison* (the even balancing of parallel clauses employing a repeated pattern of the parts of speech). Thus, in *Sapho and Phao*, Phao reveals his happy, balanced state in the very language which he employs to describe the advantages of his humble condition.

> Thou art a *ferryman*, Phao, but a *free man*, possessing for riches content, and for honours quiet . . . Thy *heart's thirst* is satisfied with thy *hands' thrift*, and thy gentle *labours* in the day turn to sweet *slumbers* in the night.
>
> (1.1.1–2, 5–7, my italics)

When he came to write drama, Lyly found a theatrical equivalent for euphuism, and thus for the exploration of his Aristotelian philosophy, in a stagecraft of balanced locations. As critics have frequently noted, Lyly's plays are not packed with action, nor do they conspicuously develop their characters. Rather, their interest lies in the alignment, and periodic realignment, of the philosophical and emotional principles at their core, a process which Lyly plots with almost geometrical precision through the movement of characters between the onstage locations or 'mansions' (three-dimensional structures placed about the hall or stage, visible throughout the performance, and where characters congregated for particular sequences),[11] and sometimes of the real or imagined movement of those mansions themselves. In each of his earliest plays there are three symbolic locations, each at odds in some way with the others, and each representative of an important aspect of the play's central problem.

In *Campaspe* the problem involves the proper relationship between government and philosophy, itself merely a more politically charged rehearsal of the medieval opposition of the active and contemplative lives, the ways of Martha and Mary. Government, the active life, is represented by the court of Alexander, philosophical withdrawal by Diogenes' 'cabin' or tub. The impossibility of reconciling service in the court with the extreme form of the contemplative life is demonstrated physically by the impossibility of bringing the court and the tub together. Although Alexander tells Hephestion, 'Were I not Alexander, I would wish to be Diogenes' (2.2.167), his duties as a governor and general prevent him from embracing the stoic life: similarly Diogenes' rejection of the world prevents him embracing the life of the court. When in 1.3, Alexander summons the philosophers to court, Diogenes pointedly refuses to attend. When the king subsequently attempts to bring about a reconciliation by shifting the symbolic geography of the stage, he meets with no greater success.

> ALEXANDER: Diogenes, I will have thy cabin removed near to my court, because I will be a philosopher.
> DIOGENES: And when you have done so, I pray you remove your court further from my cabin, because I will not be a courtier.
>
> (5.4.78–83)

Ultimately, the two can only rehearse the absolute positions that they had adopted in their earlier encounter.

> ALEXANDER: I have the world at command.
> DIOGENES: And I in contempt.
>
> (2.2.161–2)

Diogenes' uncompromising criticism of Alexander's position is theoretically admirable but politically ineffective, and it is ineffective precisely because it is uncompromising. In courtly politics the essence of political engagement was an unequal, hard-won and continually renegotiated compromise between ruler and ruled. At its simplest it involved the prince's willingness to mitigate his own power in order to address the needs of his subjects, and his subjects' willingness to present those needs in a range of prescribed and acceptable forms. The medium in which this compromise was achieved was courtliness, one of the most effective of the enabling fictions of early modern political culture.

In *Campaspe* this political theory is given a concrete form. The median point, the compromise location between the court and the cabin, is Apelles' workshop – the site at which loyal service of the crown can be reconciled with independence of mind and the practice of virtue. Unlike Diogenes, Apelles is able to tell the king unwelcome truths without entirely rejecting everything for which he stands. The painter's integrity, and his refusal to flatter, are presented in a scene in which Alexander seeks to try his hand as an artist.

> ALEXANDER: Where do you first begin, when you draw any picture?
> APELLES: The proportion of the face, in just compass as I can.
> ALEXANDER: I would begin with the eye as a light to all the rest.
> APELLES: If you will paint as you are, a king, your Majesty may begin where you please; but as you would be a painter you must begin with the face.
>
> (3.3.81–7)

When Alexander takes a charcoal to test his skill, Apelles similarly mingles courtesy with a refusal to disguise the truth, a quality that effectively communicates to the king his lack of real aptitude in the artistic sphere.

> ALEXANDER: How have I done here?
> APELLES: Like a king.
> ALEXANDER: I think so, but nothing more unlike a painter.
>
> (3.4.126–8)

Apelles' workshop gives three-dimensional form to the semi-private theoretical space created by good counsel. Unlike the public rebukes delivered by Diogenes from his tub – symbolically located in the marketplace, the most common of civic spaces, the artist's workshop is a private space which Alexander chooses to enter of his own volition, and in which he willingly agrees to suspend the normal rules of public deference and decorum. There, Apelles has the initiative and can exercise his own authority to criticize (albeit employing the protocols of courteous exchange) the weaknesses or presumptions of his sovereign. Thus good princes forestalled the tendency to slide into tyranny by willingly subjecting themselves to criticism, and loyal subjects reinforced the public honour of their princes by offering in private the sound guidance which prevented their acting inappropriately in public.

Exactly this interplay of the private and public personae of the sovereign is evident in Pliny's account of Alexander's relationship with Apelles. The historian describes how the king, being in [Apelles'] shop, would seem to talk much and reason about his art, and many times let fall some words to little purpose, bewraying his ignorance, Apelles after his mild manner would desire his grace to hold his peace, and said, 'Sir, no more words, for fear the prentice boys there, that are grinding of colours, do laugh you to scorn'.[12]

Alexander, seeing the good intentions behind the painter's advice, accepts the tacit rebuke gracefully.

So reverently thought the king of him, that being otherwise a choleric prince, yet he would take any word of his hands in that familiar sort spoken in the best part, and never be offended.[13]

In Diogenes we thus see a model of the wrong use of counsel, a dramatic analogy to John Stubbes's presumption in launching his criticism of Elizabeth's marriage nego-tiations in the very public medium of print. In Apelles we see a model of how princely government works in its ideal form. The good counsel of the courtier, appropriately delivered, prompts the well-educated prince to discover within himself the strength of character necessary to conquer his own baser instincts and desires.[14]

There is, as I have suggested, something of the schoolroom about *Campaspe*, with its exemplary exposition of clear and absolute positions, and the ease with which the emotional complications are ultimately swept away and order restored once everyone reverts to type and behaves in the way that the textbooks say they should. It is some-thing of a laboured lesson in the foundations of good kingship and sound government that the play offers. In part, no doubt, its rather ponderous deference to courtly sen-sibilities (evident in both the portrayal of Alexander and the short shrift finally given to Diogenes' principled objection to courtliness[15]) was a response to circumstances, a conspicuous attempt to stay with Sir Andrew Aguecheek on 'the windy side of the law' in the wake of Stubbes's case, with its grotesquely fitting punishment for a par-ticularly inept intervention in court politics. Yet in part it is also a conscious strat-egy to draw the audience's attention to the play's own method of representing political issues, for Apelles' decorous use of counsel is similar, of course, to that employed by Lyly himself, who took to court, at the royal request, plays which touched decorously on political themes. *Campaspe* loyally pointed out the inappropriateness of publicly rebuking the sovereign on an issue which was felt, by Queen Elizabeth at least, to be among those 'kings' causes' not open to general discussion, yet the play nonetheless also manage to imply to her by decorous analogy the need to refrain from unwise marriages.

NOTES

1   R. Warwick Bond, ed., *The Complete Works of John Lyly* (3 vols, Oxford, 1902), II, pp. 366ff; A. Feuillerat, *John Lyly* (Cambridge, 1910), pp. 107ff; T. A. Jankowski (1991). Pincombe (1996) and Bevington (Hunter and Beving-ton (1991) pp. 165–7) are more sceptical.

2   *The Apophthegms of Erasmus*, tr. Nicholas
    Udall (London, 1542); J. L. Lievsay,
    'Some Renaissance Views of Diogenes the
    Cynic', in J. G. McManaway, et al., eds, *J.
    Q. Adams Memorial Studies* (Washington, DC,
    1948).
3   L. D. Benson, ed., *The Riverside Chaucer* (3rd
    edn, Oxford, 1988).
4   See David J. Salter, 'The Representation of
    Animals and the Natural World in Late-
    medieval Literature', University of Leicester
    D. Phil. thesis, 1998; G. Cary, *The Medieval
    Alexander* (Cambridge, 1956).
5   'Alexander', in *The Lives of the Noble Greeks
    and Romans*, tr. Sir Thomas North (1579).

6   Pincombe, p. 29.
7   Pincombe, pp. 29–30.
8   See, for example, 3.4.21–3.
9   All references are to the edition in Hunter
    and Bevington (1991).
10 Philemon Holland, tr., *The History of the
    World, Commonly Called the Natural History of
    C. Plinius Secundus* (2 parts, London, 1601),
    p. 539.
11 See Saccio, pp. 12–14.
12 Holland, II, pp. 538–9.
13 Ibid.
14 Hunter, 'Introduction', pp. 7–8, in Hunter
    and Bevington.
15 Pincombe, p. 34.

References and Further Reading

Best, M. R. (1968). 'Lyly's Static Drama', *Renaissance Drama*, 1, 75–86.

Bevington, D. (1966). 'John Lyly and Queen Elizabeth: Royal flattery in *Campaspe* and *Sapho and Phao*', *Renaissance Papers*, 1, 56–67.

Hunter, G. K. (1962). *John Lyly: The Humanist as Courtier*. London: Routledge and Kegan Paul.

Hunter, G. K. and Bevington, D. (eds) (1991). *John Lyly, Campaspe and Sapho and Phao*. Manchester: Manchester University Press.

Jankowski, T. A. (1991). 'The Subversion of Flattery: The Queen's Body in John Lyly's *Sapho and Phao*', *Medieval and Renaissance Drama in England*, 5, 69–87.

Jeffery, Violet M. (1928, reprinted 1969). *John Lyly and the Italian Renaissance*. New York: Russell and Russell.

Pincombe, Michael (1996). *The Plays of John Lyly: Eros and Eliza*. Manchester: Manchester University Press.

Saccio, Peter (1969). *John Lyly: A Study in Allegorical Drama*. Princeton: Princeton University Press.

Walker, Greg (1998). *The Politics of Performance in Early Renaissance Drama*. Cambridge: Cambridge University Press.

16
Spenser's *Faerie Queene*, Book V: Poetry, Politics and Justice
Judith H. Anderson

Until quite recently, it would have been inconceivable to focus the chapter on Spenser in a companion to the literature and culture of the English Renaissance on the fifth book of *The Faerie Queene*, the book treating Justice and concluding with efforts to impose an effective political order on England's unruly colony Ireland.[1] By traditional moral and aesthetic standards, the fifth book is deeply flawed: as C. S. Lewis memorably asserted of its morality, 'Spenser was the instrument of a detestable [colonial] policy in Ireland, and in his fifth book the wickedness he had shared begins to corrupt his imagination' (p. 349). This book also doubly disappoints readers' normal expectations of structural closure: both the hero Artegall's quest to establish justice and his prophesied union with Britomart, the heroine of a love quest spanning the two preceding books, are summarily aborted, the latter never to be mentioned again in the poem.

By comparison, the four earlier books of *The Faerie Queene* further magnify the shortcomings of Book V. Like this book, the first two – Holiness and Temperance – have a single major hero and a dominantly linear structure; the allegory in them is fairly tight and a moralistic reading, while grossly oversimplified, is possible. Although the linear structure of the fifth book invites comparison with these, comparison highlights not only its problematical ending but also the persistent strains between metaphorical and material dimensions of meaning, between concept and history, word and thing, throughout it. Instead of a linear structure, the two books immediately preceding the fifth, Chastity (pure married love) and Friendship, have a romance structure in which the related experiences of many characters revolve around a mythological and thematic core; rather than linearity, the interlacing or entanglement of several stories characterizes these books. Allegory in them is looser, more suggestive, and relatively closer to symbolism. Indeed, the fourth book is so loosely or experimentally structured as to challenge the assumptions and methods that underlie Books I and II. When we work our way through Book IV and then reach Book V, the linearity and superficially tight allegory of the later book are made to look and feel like the forceful, arti-

ficial imposition of order they are, and the strains of their reimposition are both everywhere evident and essential to interpretation.

Even as order becomes conspicuous, indeed thematic, within Book V, the concerns
of this book engage history, first conceived as the general materialisms of social issues,
such as crime, taxation, corruption, inheritance, patriarchy and equity, and then
history conceived more specifically as current political problems in England, on the
continent, and in Ireland. This combination of the messiness of history and tight
order, whether theoretical, structural or allegorical, is a recipe for trouble and, to my
mind, for deliberated trouble on the part of the poet who penned Book V. Besides the
clear signs of deliberation (or intention) I have mentioned to this point, the literary
theory of the Renaissance and particularly of the Italians would have alerted Spenser
to the dangers (and to the shock value) of treating current history, and he appears to
reflect its cautions when he notes in the letter to Ralegh published with the 1590
instalment of *The Faerie Queene* that he 'chose the historye of king Arthure [for the
general frame of the poem], as . . . furthest from the daunger of enuy, and suspition
of present time'.[2] Closer to home, the representative views of the idealizing Sidney
and the materializing Bacon would further have guaranteed Spenser's awareness of the
necessary difference between the immediate, specific concerns of history and the more
general, fictive concerns of poetry. Sidney considers real poetry, or fiction, 'truer' than
history because it is not restricted to what actually happened but necessarily is more
nearly perfect or ideal; in contrast, Bacon distinguishes sharply between 'true history'
and untrue history, which he dismissively terms poetry and which in his negative
view, too, is necessarily an idealizing fiction.[3]

But if Spenser's fifth book engages current history, as poetry it still remains at some
distance from *A View of the Present State of Ireland*, the political tract presumably
written by Spenser in the 1590s to persuade the English court to adopt severely repressive measures in order to establish a stable government in Ireland and thus to ensure
peace and prosperity there.[4] Far more deeply and extensively than the tract, Book V
examines the abstract principle of justice as it relates to human experiences and material conditions, often questioning the principle itself and exposing the inadequacy or
cruelty of its unqualified application. As poetry, Book V has different purposes, or
ends, from the tract and deals more hypothetically and conceptually than practically
and immediately with the historical problems it addresses. Whether from a modern
or a Renaissance view, it is finally a hybrid – what Shakespeare's Perdita would consider a bastard – of poetry and history that threatens conventional moral, political and
aesthetic categories of interpretation. Precisely because this book is so fundamentally
problematical, in an age suspicious of easy answers and neat solutions, especially
political ones, it claims our attention.

The problems of Book V begin with its titular virtue of justice. Unlike the virtues
of the earlier books, justice, 'Most sacred vertue she of all the rest,' is impersonal and
external, committed to an objective world that is outside the subject (pro.x). The justicer, according to such traditional definitions as those of Aristotle and Aquinas, is 'a
sort of animate justice,' a 'personification of justice', 'a living justice' (Anderson 1970:

74). He must abstract himself from respect of persons, maintaining objectivity at the expense of emotion and empathy. Not surprisingly, the hero of Book V, Artegall (art equal, art of equality, Arthur's equal) is often torn between his roles as romance knight and rational justicer. The contrary vices of cruelty and vain pity alike threaten the objectivity of his virtue, and his personal life as Britomart's lover, while not irrelevant to our conception of him, stands apart from his quest as Justice.

But even before the action begins in Book V, the length and anxiety of its proem (prologue) to it signal a difference in orientation from the earlier books of the poem. This is the first of the proems with a truly dramatized speaker, one whose voice is not conventionally that of the poet describing his song. In the first two lines of the proem, the speaker laments the 'state of present time', comparing it unfavourably with the 'image of the antique world', the latter a recurrent figure of a lost age of virtue, and thus he introduces a contrast between past and present, poetic image and actual temporality, idealizing fiction and material history. He substantiates his near-despair by reference to morality, the conditions of meaning, and physical mutability – more exactly, to an erosion of virtue, a lack of congruence between word and thing ('that which all men then did vertue call, / Is now cald vice') and to apparently irrational movements in the heavens, such as the precession of the equinoxes, the obliquity of the ecliptic, and the seemingly retrograde orbits of the planets. Since these phenomena were largely susceptible of rationalization in the sixteenth century, we might suspect that the poet is merely setting his speaker up as a fin de siècle worry-wart, were it not that the speaker's awareness of degeneration emerges recurrently in Book V, as well as in Book VI, where it has the last word, and in the mutability cantos, where it refers to the inexplicable presence of a new star and similarly worrisome appearances of comets in the seemingly unchanging heavens (Meyer, 118–19). Perhaps the appropriate response is to recognize that the proem represents the historically prevalent claims of degeneration for our consideration and, temporarily suspending an evaluative judgement, read on.[5]

Seeking refuge from despair, the proem's speaker pivots from the retrograde planet Saturn to myth, recalling the golden age of mythic Saturn's reign before Jove supplanted him, a time when justice sat 'high ador'd with solemne feasts' (pro.ix). Abruptly and not entirely convincingly, in the proem's final stanza the speaker waxes idealistic and hopeful, addressing the 'Dread Souerayne Goddess' whose just instrument 'here' is Book V's hero Artegall. Blurring the identities of the mythic Astrea, Goddess of Justice in Saturn's reign on earth, and Queen Elizabeth, he leaves open whether 'here' is on earth or in Faerie, here in the present or in the mythic past. Clearly, however, Artegall is introduced with fanfare that discords with the proem's dominant pessimism. Not an isolated effect, such dissonance recurs in the early cantos, which repeatedly pair hyperbolic praise of the justicer with questionable justice (e.g., i.2–3, ii.1, iv.2).

The history of the justicer, recounted at the beginning of the first canto, itself gives us reason for pause. As a child Artegall is lured from human company with gifts and kind speeches by Astrea and then brought up by her in a cave, where he is taught the discipline of justice, 'which, for want there of mankind, / She caused him to make experience / Vpon wyld beasts'. By the time he reaches manhood, wild beasts fear the sight of him, 'and men admyr'd his ouerruling might; / Ne any liu'd on ground, that durst withstand / His dreadfull heast, much lesse him match in fight' (i.7–8). Notably, force, not authority, is at the beginning his strongest suit. Nonetheless, to ensure even greater dread of him, Astrea, 'by her slight', steals from Jove the sword he used against the Titans, now to become the sword of earthly justice (i.7–9). Her justicer educated and equipped, if somewhat dubiously for human society, Astrea makes her servant the implacable iron man Talus (Latin *talus*, 'heel', *talio*, 'an eye for an eye') her final gift to him and flees the sinful earth, metamorphosing into the heavenly sign associated with her, the virgin in the zodiac (see also Hamilton, ed., 532n V.v.12).

Once on his own, Artegall's first exploit is to adjudicate the conflicting claims of the knight Sanglier and a squire, both of whom claim possession of one lady and disavow responsibility for the decapitation of a second. To solve this mystery, Artegall imitates the biblical judgment of Solomon, proposing to divide the living lady between the two claimants. The murderer quickly accepts his offer, but the squire, her true love, as quickly rejects it, preferring to spare his lady's life and to accept the Artegallian penalty to be imposed on the murderer, namely, bearing the dead lady's head for a year. Now satisfied that the squire is innocent, Artegall proceeds to judgement: the guilty knight gets the head, the guiltless squire 'adore[s]' Artegall for his great justice, and the latter takes his leave, 'Ne wight with him but onely Talus went. / They two enough t'encounter an whole Regiment' (i.30). Fanfare swiftly follows (ii.i).

Tonal dislocations, the result of pacing and the juxtaposition of incongruous details, slightly skew Artegall's initial triumph. His resolution of the conflict is correct, but the punishment he metes out hardly seems adequate to the crime, which greatly exceeds that in his biblical model. His justice reduces the decapitated lady to the level of a dead albatross. While it might be argued that the Artegallian penalty is appropriate to romance, it ill suits the virtue of justice in a real world of men and women. In actuality, Artegallian justice in this instance mimics the barnyard, where a dog that kills a domestic animal such as a goose is first beaten with its carcass and then bears this around its neck, a folk remedy for the killer instinct. The knight Sanglier's name, 'Wild Boar', his initial apprehension by Talus, who seizes him in his 'iron paw,' and Sanglier's assuming his burden, the lady's head, 'for feare' 'As [does a] rated Spaniell' all suggest that Artegall's training among the beasts has enduringly marked him (i.22, 29).

Artegall's next exploit takes him to a bridge where Pollente, a powerful but corrupt lord exacts unjust tolls from any who would pass over it. Although Artegall rectifies this injustice by killing Pollente and executing his daughter Munera (Latin *munus*, 'office, duty, favour, gift'), he does so at some cost to his own ideality. His defeat of Pollente comes with mundane and material detail that at moments gestures towards mock epic. These include a emphasis on his swimsmanship ('But Artegall was better breath'd beside') that is digressive in length and focus and descriptions of battle that disappoint heroic expectation. When Artegall and Pollente meet at close quarters, for example, 'They snuf, they snort, they bounce, they rage, they rore', thus expressing the sounds of mortal combat between a dolphin and a seal (ii.15–17).

The execution of Lady Munera affords tonal dissonance still more pronounced. On the one hand, Munera is said to have metal hands and feet, which suggest that she is merely an allegorization of social corruption and more specifically of bribery. On the other hand, she is described a little too much as an attractive but erring young woman, led astray by her wicked father. From the latter point of view, we can read her 'hands of gold' as richly adorned like those of her prototype Lady Meed, rather than as gold-dispensing, and see her feet similarly furnished with jewellery or net-work slippers of 'trye', that is, 'choice' silver. In fact, the word 'trye' itself intimates that the silver of the slippers carries a symbolic or an aesthetic meaning. To make matters worse, Lady Munera's hands and feet are first 'Chopt off, and nayld on high' even while she is 'Still holding vp her supliant hands on hye, / And kneeling at his [ambiguously Artegall's or Talus'] feete submissiuely' (ii.26). The rest of her, 'in vaine loud crying', is cast over the castle wall to drown in the 'durty mud'. And the dissonance does not end even here: in a biblical echo of purgation by water, the stream is said to have 'washt away . . . [Munera's] guilty blood', suggesting the mercy she is denied. Just before, her plight has been described as 'seemelesse': 'unseemly', 'seamless', 'unseeming', or real; this single word summarizes the inseparability of her plight into human and abstract parts – parts of flesh and parts of theory (ii.25, 27). The whiff of parody that accompanied the justicer's victories over Sanglier and Pollente has given way to questions more probing: how far can the objectivity and externality of justice be carried without denying the humanity of the justicer and reducing human beings to objects?

Within the same canto, Artegall next encounters the levelling giant, who would reduce hierarchical distinctions to equality and distribute all wealth accordingly. Given the size of the giant, he is somewhat ironically an equalizer, and he is fundamentally a materialist in the literal sense, since he bases his arguments exclusively on quantity and sight: 'The sea it selfe doest thou not plainely see / Encroch vppon the land there vnder thee' (ii.37)? Yet his pessimistic view of present conditions accords with that of the speaker of the fifth proem, and the reassertion of this view within the fiction itself attests to its historically real pressure, owing not only to irrational movements in the heavens but also to persistent crop failures, rampant inflation, further enclosures of land and consequent poverty and vagrancy in England, as well as to anxieties about the spread of the economic communism of religious radicals on the continent, such as the Anabaptists, and about uprisings and invasions in Ireland.[6] Debating the materialistic giant and the mutability his view necessarily entails, Artegall takes an equally extreme position, however, arguing that nothing really changes and that 'All change is perillous, and all chaunce vnsound' (ii.36). His position recalls the unnatural impasse in Book II, where Guyon and the Palmer attempt to keep Occasion fettered, in effect stopping time and the forward movement of their own quest. As Mutability will declare in the Cantos bearing her name 'all that moueth, [that is, all that lives,] doth mutation loue' (VII.vii.55). Notably, Mutability is the offspring of the giant Titans and, like the levelling Giant, a natural enemy of the Jovian force invested in Artegall's sword.

But Artegall himself is more immediately caught in contradictions. Although he argues for intangible values and tells the Giant that 'in the mind the doome of right must bee', his justice relies conspicuously on physical signs, on spectacle (Pollente's head on a pole, Munera's extremities nailed on high), and above all, on physical force (ii.47). His high-minded debate with the giant ends when Talus abruptly shoulders the giant off a cliff to destruction 'in the sea' below (ii.49):

> Like as a ship, whom cruell tempest driues
>   Vpon a rocke with horrible dismay,
>   Her shattered ribs in thousand peeces riues,
>   And spoyling all her geares and goodly ray,
>   Does make her selfe misfortunes piteous pray.
>   So downe the cliffe the wretched Gyant tumbled;
>   His battred ballances in peeces lay,
>   His timbered bones all broken rudely rumbled.
>   (V.ii.50)

Ironically, this stanza celebrates Artegall's victory in the very terms the giant embraced, not only levelling him but also drowning him in the punning of 'sea' with 'see.' Although Talus is the immediate agent of this levelling, his charge from Astrea is to do whatever Artegall intends (i.12); the adjective 'cruell' in the simile therefore participates in the increasing association of Artegall with cruelty, traditionally the vice opposed to justice, prior to his crucial encounter with Radigund, the Amazon Queen.

Leaving the seaside, Artegall next appears in the very different context of a tournament celebrating the spousals of Marinell and Florimell (the fruitful conjunction of water and earth, the harmonious union of a Mars with a Venus). Both characters are holdovers from the two preceding books of romance, and Artegall's appearance in their romance world foreshadows his experiences at Radigund's hands, in Radegone, her city of women. Here, he acts less as a justicer, an animate abstraction, and more as a knight. Indeed, to participate in the tournament, he borrows another's shield and thereby his identity, disguising his own as a justicer. His doing so enables his knightly rescue of Marinell but soon after actually furthers injustice until he reassumes his identity as justice. Once he reassumes it, however, his choler has to be calmed by the Knight of Temperance, a personal, inner virtue that by definition has no necessary relation to the impersonal, outer nature of justice yet obviously affects it – and I intend the word 'affects' for all it's worth. The paradox, indeed the bind, is that temperance is different in nature from justice and cannot be channelled directly into a quest for it. At the same time, Artegall's human, knightly response to the abuse of his honour threatens to affect his ability to administer justice impartially. This whole romance episode takes 'vsurie of time forepast'; it lingers in memories of earlier times and earlier books of the poem (iii.40). It also serves as a paradigm – a 'fore-conceit,' in Sidney's term – for the central cantos of Book V, Artegall's adventures among the Amazons and Britomart's rescue of her lover.

Artegall might be said to fall into full humanity in the fifth canto of Book V when he battles Radigund, who challenges men to battle, subdues them 'by force or guile', clothes them in shameful 'womens weedes', and sets them to spin in her prison (iv.31). He first overcomes her, but stooping to behead her, he discovers in her face 'A miracle of natures goodly grace' and experiences, as if for the first time, 'his senses straunge astonishment' (v.12). Suddenly torn between insensitive cruelty and vain pity, he throws away his Jovian sword (which Radigund subsequently breaks) and yields himself to her. While hardly right, his response, like that of Milton's Adam, is all too human. Had he decapitated the beautiful Radigund after experiencing passion for her, his act would have been perversely cruel and inescapably vicious, far worse than the death of Lady Munera, since he, not Talus, would have been the executioner of a woman about whose humanity there is no ambiguity. Although the poet reflects here ironically on Artegall's 'goodwill' in yielding, he offers no viable alternative to it, and indeed he cannot without denying history in the biblical Garden (v.17).

Only when Artegall falls into the selfish city of Radegone – for him a city of the subject (in both senses) – does his history in the preceding books become relevant to him. Before this point it is treated as if it were non-existent, as it is for his impersonal quest, and indeed it would be hard to square with the figure we see operating in the early cantos. Now suddenly, his Britomart enters the picture and does so with a vengeance. Learning of Artegall's capture by another woman, she sets out to rescue him. In her own eyes she is simply and literally rescuing her lover, not the personification of justice, but her route to him is a conspicuous process of suppression and transference. In it, the poem asks her to change from an immoderate woman, raging at the disloyalty of her lover, to a myth, a goddess of equity to complement her Jovian justicer. At the same time, however, the poem exposes and questions what is lost in her progress – namely her personal identity, which is synonymous with her own quest for chaste love in marriage. This loss is most evident in the episode in Isis church, where Britomart has a richly mythopeic 'dream of sexuality, death, and birth' that as a myth of procreative power is matched nowhere else in the poem (Miskim, 32–3). She dreams that she is the goddess Isis and that the phallic crocodile beneath her feet but enfolding her middle with his tail impregnates her. First she feels from below 'an hideous tempest' that scatters the holy fire 'Vppon the ground, which kindled priuily, / Into outragious flames vnwares did grow':

> With that the Crocodile, which sleeping lay
>   Vnder the Idols [statue of Isis's] feet in feareless bowre,
>   Seem'd to awake in horrible dismay,
>   As being troubled with that stormy stowre;
>   And gaping greedy wide, did streight deuoure
>   Both flames and tempest: with which growen great,

And swolne with pride of his own peerelesse powre,
He gan to threaten her likewise to eat;
But that the Goddesse with her rod him backe did beat.

(V.vii.15)

Resisted, the crocodile becomes humble, throws himself at her feet, and sues for grace and love: 'Which she accepting, he so neare her drew, / That of his game she soone enwombed grew, / And forth did bring a Lion of great might' (v.viii). The morning after, Isis' priest rationalizes all this fire and fear and potency into a dynastic allegory of justice, utterly failing to acknowledge or account for 'The troublous passion' in Britomart's 'pensiue mind' (vii.19). Her personal experiences are reduced or sublimed into an externalized allegory of justice, even while the text demands another reading.

When Britomart finds and battles Radigund, she is wounded to the bone by her, allegorically suggesting not only her vulnerability to the tyranny of affection (emotion, passion) Radigund represents but also its depth. Yet there is a disturbing excess to their battle that is wasteful in a specifically sexual sense: 'But through great fury both their skill forgot, / And praticke vse in armes: ne spared not / Their dainty parts, . . . Which they now hackt & hewd, as if such vse they hated' (vii.29). As they fight on, the blood flows from their sides and gushes through their armour, so that they tread in blood and strew their lives on the ground, 'Like fruitles seede, of which vntimely death should grow' (vii.31). After this battle, Britomart is purged of more than her affections; she is fitted to perform as agent of a purely symbolic love to free fallen man, Artegall the justicer, from Radegone. What I would stress, however, is the extent to which the poem has made the sacrifice of her personal self visible.

Freed from Radegone by love, Artegall returns to his quest for justice. Symbolically at least, he is now a whole person, 'inly' a human being with operative affections and not simply a personification of externalized justice. His virtue, moreover, is presumably charged with a significance more specifically Christian, a justice more forgiving than Talus's identity — an 'eye for an eye' — symbolizes. But now it is Artegall's task to realize his redeemed virtue in a real world, or at least in a world that refers openly, at times even blatantly, to Tudor history, including the defeat of the Spanish Armada (the Suldan and his chariot), the execution of Mary, Queen of Scots (Duessa), Henri de Navarre's apostasy to gain the throne of France (Burbon and Fleurdelis), Spanish tyranny in the Netherlands (Belge and her seventeen sons) and rebellion, abetted by Spain and the papacy, in Ireland (Irena's island).

After leaving Radegone, accompanied only by Talus, Artegall encounters Prince Arthur, best and most Christian of Princes, who mistakes the justicer for the pagan villain he is pursuing. Both knights prepare to fight until the maiden Samient (sameness, togetherness) intercedes to stop them. Raising their ventails and thus exposing what is within, the knights recognize their kinship: Artegall, 'touched with intire affection,' yields allegiance to Arthur, who for his part apologizes for having 'mistake[n] the liuing for the ded' — the redeemed for the pagan, the saved for the lost – and enters into alliance with Artegall. This episode testifies to the inner transformation of Artegall after Radegone and introduces the cooperation of the two knights in the following cantos. At the same time, Arthur's initial misrecognition dramatizes that from the outside, Artegall's virtue still looks as unredeemed as ever.

While Arthur and Artegall travel together, the course of justice runs smoothly because they can divide the tasks that would otherwise have pulled Artegall simultaneously in two directions. Arthur deals with the Suldan, the explicit historical threat, and Artegall with the Suldan's wife Adicia, the principle of wrong he has wed. Arthur also deals with Malengin as a specific manifestation of guile in Ireland, be it rebel Irish or Jesuit priests and missionaries, and Artegall, through his agent Talus, eliminates Malengin when he turns into the metamorphic principle of Guile itself[7] (*The Works of Edmund Spenser: A Variorum Edition*, Edwin Greenlaw, Charles Grosvenor Osgood, Frederick Morgan Padelford (eds), 11 vols. Baltimore: The Johns Hopkins Press). In each of these exploits, Artegall has the more mythic task and represents the principle of Justice without encountering the dissonant strains of realism. The advantages of his cooperation with Arthur are perhaps most obvious when the two knights stand like balances in the scale of justice on either side of Mercilla during the trial of Duessa. Arthur responds as would any knight to a damsel in distress; he is so 'sore empassionate' in heart that 'for great ruth his courage gan relent'. Precisely because he is so, Artegall does not have to be. Instead, the justicer 'with constant firme intent, / For zeale of Iustice was against her bent' (ix.46, 49).

Once Arthur and Artegall separate, however, their stories differ sharply. Arthur goes off to a fairy tale success in Belge's land, one that is very much at odds with the actual history of English attempts to intervene against the Spanish power in the Netherlands. Meanwhile, Artegall returns to his original quest to assist the Lady Irena in reclaiming her kingdom (Ireland) and, unhappily, to the contradictions between his humanity and his principle, his knighthood and his justice, that earlier beset him. If anything, these are exacerbated by his having recovered the wholeness of his identity in his fall and redemption. Encountering Burbon and Fleurdelis (France) under attack by a lawless mob, Artegall shifts abruptly back and forth between the responses of a knight and those of a virtue. Now he sees Burbon's shield as merely a piece of armour and now as the emblem that morally and religiously defines him; now he regards Burbon as a fellow knight in need and now as a shameless apostate. There is no uncompromising way for him either to assist Burbon and his lady or to abandon them to the mob. The demands of virtue simply do not coincide here with those of history.

Generously choosing to help Burbon, Artegall is further delayed in his quest on behalf of Irena, whose side he finally reaches just in time to stay her execution. He battles and defeats her oppressor, but when he tries radically to reform her country, pursuing and punishing those who resist, he is summoned back to Faerie Court. On his way there, the hags Envy and Detraction revile him and set on him the Blatant Beast, monster of slander, accusing him of having abused his honour and having stained the sword of justice with cruelty. Their words return us to the early cantos of Book V as if Artegall, our judgement of him, and our awareness of the dilemmas of justice had never been affected. Artegall's ending is like – indeed, equal to – that of Arthur, Lord Grey de Wilton, whom Spenser served as secretary in Ireland and to whom the figure of Artegall unmistakably alludes in canto xii. In deliberate contrast to the providential version of history granted Arthur in canto xi, the version Artegall gets testifies loudly and discordantly to the injustice of a real world.

NOTES

1 This chapter draws on the various discussions of Book V of *The Faerie Queene* I have published: 1970, 1976, 1990, 1996. For additional extension and substantiation, these might be consulted.

2 *Works*, I, 167. All further reference is to this edition.

3 Anderson 1984, 124–5, 164–5.

4 Brink has argued that Spenser was not the author of *A View*. The jury is still out on this issue: Many Spenserians remain convinced on

the basis of internal evidence of Spenser's authorship.

5 My view of an appropriate response has shifted in emphasis from 1976, 184–6, to 1996, 172–3. My effort to settle on an appropriate response is in Anderson 1998, e.g., 97–8.

6 See Anderson 1996, 173; 167–89 are more generally relevant.

7 On the relevance to Malengin of laws against Catholic missionaries, see Clegg, 250–5.

REFERENCES AND FURTHER READING

Anderson, J. H. (1970). '"Nor Man it is": The Knight of Justice in Book V of Spenser's Faerie Queene', *Publications of the Modern Language Association of America*, 85, 65–77.

——(1976). *The Growth of a Personal Voice: 'Piers Plowman' and 'The Faerie Queene'*. New Haven: Yale University Press.

——(1984). *Biographical Truth: The Representation of Historical Persons in Tudor-Stuart Writing*. New Haven: Yale University Press.

——(1987). 'The Antiquities of Fairyland and Ireland', *Journal of English and Germanic Philology*, 86, pp. 199–214.

——(1990). 'Artegall' and 'Britomart' entries. In A. C. Hamilton (ed.), *The Spenser Encyclopedia*. Toronto: University of Toronto Press.

——(1996). *Words that Matter: Linguistic Perception in Renaissance English*. Stanford: Stanford University Press.

——(1998). 'Narrative Reflections: re-envisaging the poet in 'The Canterbury Tales'

and 'The Faerie Queene'. In T. Krier (ed.), *Refiguring Chaucer in the Renaissance* (pp. 87–105). Gainesville: University Press of Florida.

——(2000). 'Better a Mischief Than an Inconvenience: 'the saiyng self' in Spenser's View, or, How Many Meanings can Stand on the Head of a Proverb?' In P. Cheney and L. Silberman (eds), *Worldmaking Spenser: Explorations in the Early Modern Age* (pp. 219–33). Lexington: University of Kentucky Press.

Aptekar, J. (1969). *Icons of Justice: Iconography and Thematic Imagery in Book V of 'The Faerie Queene'*. New York: Columbia University Press.

Baker, D. J. (1997). *Between Nations: Shakespeare, Spenser, Marvell, and the Question of Britain*. Stanford: Stanford University Press.

Berger, H. (1961). 'The Prospect of Imagination: Spenser and the Limits of Poetry', *Studies in English Literature*, 1, 93–120.

Brink, J. R. (1997). 'Appropriating the Author of The Faerie Queene: The Attribution of the

View of the Present State of Ireland and A Brief Note of Ireland to Edmund Spenser'. In P. E. Medine and J. Wittreich (eds), *Soundings of Things Done: Essays in Early Modern Literature in Honour of S. K. Heninger, Jr* (pp. 93–136). Newark: University of Delaware Press.

Clegg, C. S. (1998). 'Justice and Press Censorship in Book V of Spenser's Faerie Queene', *Studies in Philology*, 95, 237–62.

Coughlan, P. (ed.) (1989). *Spenser and Ireland: An Interdisciplinary Perspective*. Cork: Cork University Press.

Fowler, E. (1995). 'The Failure of Moral Philosophy in the Work of Edmund Spenser', *Representations*, 51, 57–86.

Hadfield, A. (1997). *Spenser's Irish Experience: Wilde Fruit and Salvage Soil*. Oxford: Clarendon.

——(1998). 'Was Spenser a republican?', *English*, 47, 169–82.

Hamilton, A. C. (ed.) (1977). *The Faerie Queene*. Longman: London.

Lewis, C. S. (1936). *The Allegory of Love: A Study in Medieval Tradition*. Oxford: Oxford University Press.

Maley, W. (1997). *Salvaging Spenser: Colonialism, Culture and Identity*. London: Macmillan.

Meyer, R. J. (1984). '"Fixt in heauens hight": Spenser, Astronomy, and the Date of the Cantos of Mutabilitie', *Spenser Studies*, 4, 115–29.

Miskimin, A. S. (1978). 'Britomart's Crocodile and the Legends of Chastity.' *JEGP*, 77, 17–36.

O'Connell, M. (1977). *Mirror and Veil: The Historical Dimension of Spenser's 'Faerie Queene'*. Chapel Hill: University of North Carolina Press.

Patterson, A. (1993). *Reading between the Lines*. Madison: University of Wisconsin Press.

17
Kyd's *The Spanish Tragedy*
A. J. Piesse

Theatre conveys meaning through language, through display, and through the inter-action of language and display. Like any other literary text, the dramatic text also creates meaning referentially, by assuming shared sets of knowledge about the way a literary text works. Kyd's *Spanish Tragedy* is important in the chronological canon because of the degree to which it draws attention to its own meaning (in terms of both text and action), and the ways in which that meaning is constructed.[1] Written in a period where the robustness of the English language is in question,[2] the play is also a timely interrogation into the nature of language and the relationship between the signifier and the signified.[3] Moreover, exchanges of letters throughout the text draw attention to kinds of communication, alerting the audience to ways in which written language and spoken language might motivate or delay.

Kyd writes out of the Senecan tradition, where the plays are characterized by a plot pivoting around revenge, with a supernatural presence of some kind or another, usually in the form of a ghost, a tragic protagonist and a great deal of blood and violence. The antiquity of the medium, in Renaissance rewritings, is signalled by a markedly formal style and the interspersing of classical quotations.

But Kyd signals his intention to problematize at least some of these givens from the outset of the play by setting up a double supernatural presence, in the form of the allegorical figure of Revenge and the liminal figure of the ghost of Andrea. This could be interpreted as an acknowledgement of the mixed origins of the play; it is quite plainly coming out of the Senecan tradition, but the invocation of the allegor-ical moral protagonist connects it too with the still extant traditions of the English morality play and moral interludes.

By juxtaposing a purely allegorical figure with the classical go-between between the living and the dead, Kyd creates a complex series of frameworks for the play. The audience watches allegory informing a character who inhabits a half-life between the living and the dead; watches a doubly effective figure instructing both reflection and action. The audience is invited to consider which of these protagonists is most likely to construct an accurate representation of meaning.[4] Is meaning conveyed by that which is abstract and notional, or is it conveyed by that which is active and effective?

The allegorical figure signals the dislocation between the figure and the meaning of language. That is, Revenge functions as a physically real operator in connection with Andrea's ghost, in that particular layer of the drama, but as a motivating word – if you like, a word that has not been made flesh – within the main action of the play. By constructing the choric figure, the truth-teller, in this way, Kyd indicates the liminal nature of meaning and the complex relationship between signified and signifier in this play. Simultaneously, he complicates the role of the ghost to load it with teleological meaning. Andrea has been real, has been able to operate physically within the main action, but is now an impotent observer. The audience thus watches a play being introduced by a once functional character that is now impotent to act. This character must rely on a purely notional figure, that is either an allegory or just a lexical unit, to affect the action of the play in a way that the supposedly 'real' character cannot. In this way, Kyd sets up a whole series of questions about meaning, action, and ability to act, questions that are at least as important to the final moments of the play as the resolution of the action itself.

Once this framework is established – and it is set up visibly too, since Andrea and Revenge must inhabit a playing space that is clearly at a tangent, quite literally, to the main action – the relationship between word and action is elaborated upon in a far more explicit fashion as the play begins to reveal its meaning. The General's description of battle at 1.2, a rhetorical set-piece, is a mechanism by which the broad principles of the execution of the Senecan tradition becomes localized. The physical battle is evoked at a distance through a sanitized formal rhetoric:

> There met our armies in their proud array:
> Both furnished well, both full of hope and fear,
> Both menacing alike with daring shows,
> Both vaunting sundry colours of device,
> Both cheerly sounding trumpets, drums and fifes,
> Both raising dreadful clamours to the sky . . .
> While they maintain hot skirmish to and fro,
> Both battles join and fall to handy blows,
> Their violent shot resembling th'ocean's rage,
> When, roaring loud, and with a swelling tide,
> It beats upon the rampiers of huge rocks,
> And gapes to swallow neighbour-bounding lands.
> And while Bellona rageth here and there,
> Thick storms of bullets rain like winter's hail,
> And shivered lances dark the troubled air.
>   *Pede pes et cuspide cuspis;*
>   *Arma sonant armis, vir petiturque viro.*
>   (1.2 24–9, 46–56)

The repetitive structure suggests the even match, and moves from sight to sound, where voicing of the battle cry suggests imminent action. The extended metaphor of the ocean suggests that such violence is natural, but cannot prepare the audience for the gory detail of the next twenty or so lines ('Here lies a body scindered from his head, / There arms and legs lie bleeding on the grass, / Mingled with weapons and unbowelled steeds' 59–61). The Latin tagging, as carefully balanced as the opening quotation, at once authorizes the English account and reminds the audience of the form's origins. Kyd continually draws attention to the fact that this is something new being made out of something traditional.

This specific report of the battle is pulled into a still sharper focus when the battle between the two sides becomes a localized and individual battle of words between Lorenzo and Horatio over the capture of Balthazar. Even as the form of the play follows a particular progression – the movement from the universal to the particular – Kyd problematizes his material, suggesting that truth depends on point of view:

> KING: But tell me, for their holding makes me doubt,
>   To which of these twain art thou prisoner?
> LORENZO: To me, my liege.
> HORATIO: To me, my sovereign.
> LORENZO: This hand first took his courser by the reins.
> HORATIO: But first my lance did put him from his horse.
> LORENZO: I seized his weapon and enjoyed it first.
> HORATIO: But first I forced him lay his weapons down.
> KING: Let go his arm upon our privilege.
>   Say, worthy prince, to whether didst thou yield?
> BALTHAZAR: To him in courtesy, to his perforce:
>   He spake me fair, this other gave me strokes:
>   He promised life, this other threatened death;
>   He wan my love, this other conquered me;
>   And truth to say, I yield myself to both.
>
>   (I. ii. 152–65)

The stichomythic exchanges – where one line immediately follows another, turn about, between or among two or more characters – mimic the closeness of the argument. But expectations are undermined, roles are reversed. The prisoner is called upon to be judge. He is also the character who will be revealed as simultaneously both at the mercy of a rote-bound rhetoric and the least rhetorically able. His language will be seen to be empty, lacking a connection with reality, but here, in the early stages of the play, he is being treated as a referent for the truth. So far in this play, then, the truth-tellers are tangential (as in the case of Andrea and Revenge), or they are in a position of inferiority, by dint of being prisoners or through their ineptitude with language. On a broader scale, the movement of the structure of the play is also deliberately destabilizing. The reported battle is believed to be real, but now exists only as a report. It also functions as a signifier of the adherence to Senecan rules, by which violence, no matter how graphically described, only happens offstage. The report is replaced by the march past of the troops, a present action which signifies – physically – the past triumph. The march past in its turn is superseded by the argument over Balthazar, a specific, immediate dispute between two individuals. This is an early instance of the kind of experiment with representation that will characterize the play – in this case a movement from the historical (but reported) to the representative (but present) to the immediate, individual and specific. Each attempt at accurate representation is qualified by its circumstances. It is the same kind of deliberate uncertainty that we have already seen between Revenge as an allegorical, tangential character and revenge as an effective, consequence-provoking lexical unit, where paradoxically a word has more power to effect physical action than a figure that is at once a character and a moral imperative.

Kyd explores the relationship of words to action in far more explicit ways. Stichomythic exchange can be used, as we have seen, to mimic the closeness of debate. In Balthazar's exchanges with Bel-Imperia, Kyd uses the accepted form to demonstrate the distance between the thinking of the two, and to imply that although the formal situation suggests they might be suited, the inner persona of each could not be more different. Bel-Imperia's impatience with the outward form increases as the play progresses. In 1.4, she is gently mocking, exposing his shallowness by deliberately refusing the particular mindset that allows metaphor to operate:

BALTHAZAR: What if conceit hath laid my heart to gage?
BEL-IMPERIA: Pay that you borrowed and recover it.
BATHAZAR: I die if it return form whence it lies.
BEL-IMPERIA: A heartless man, and live? A miracle!

And ending the exchange finally, wearily, by stating the obvious:

BEL-IMPERIA: Alas my lord, these are but words of course.

By 2.4, by which time revenge for Horatio's death is being planned, Kyd writes her as distracted and far more impatient:

BALTHAZAR: Come, Bel-Imperia, Balthazar's content,
    My sorrow's ease and sovereign of my bliss,
    Sith heaven hath ordained thee to be mine;
    Disperse those clouds and melancholy looks,
    And clear them up with those thy sun-bright eyes,
    Wherein my hope and heaven's fair beauty lies.
BEL-IMPERIA: My looks my lord are fitting for my love,
Which new-begun can show no brighter yet.
BALTHAZAR: New kindled flames should burn as morning sun.
BEL-IMPERIA: But not too fast lest heat and all be done.
    I see my lord my father.

(3.14)

Dismissing him, she replaces the wordplay with a real entrance.

In some cases in the play the relationship between word and action is more pointed. When Lorenzo forces Pedringano to swear fidelity on the cross-shaped hilt of his sword, the metaphor of language into action is made plain, suggesting that fidelity is to be demonstrated by action rather than by words:

> LORENZO: Swear on this cross that what thou sayest is true,
>   And that thou wilt conceal what thou hast told.
> PEDRINGANO: I swear to both by him that made us all.
> LORENZO: In hope thine oath is true, here's thy reward,
>   But if I prove thee perjured and unjust,
>   This very sword on which thou took'st thine oath,
>   Shall be the worker of thy tragedy.

> (II. i. 87–93)

This metatheatrical recognition of the interaction of language and action is so fully integrated as part of the scene that it does not really draw attention to itself. But when Kyd works with the emblem of the bower at 2.2, 2,4, 3.5 and 4.2, he is anxious that the audience recognize the stylized games that are being played. The manipulation of the emblem is a pointed marker that the outward form is being wrenched out of shape in order to accommodate the disjuncture of the times.

The exchange between Bel-Imperia and Horatio at 2.2 is heavily charged, both emotively, as the stichomythia featly reveals their intimacy, and prophetically, in terms of the motifs they use, of war and love. The juxtaposition of the motifs mimics the dangerous proximity of the two sets of observers, Andrea and Revenge, and Lorenzo's group. There is a sense of Horatio taking on the mantle of Andrea, and the presence of the two liminal figures is far from comforting. Balthazar's echoings rapidly become annoying and are a confirmation of what Kyd has already more gently demonstrated, that Horatio's silences and thoughtfulness make him clearly more fit for Bel-Imperia. The underlying mutuality of understanding that drives the exchanges reveals more about the relationship than the words themselves. The momentary alignment of Lorenzo's group with Andrea and Revenge (they are each observers) signals that a dangerous degree of power will be available to Horatio's enemies. The continued motif of a loving battle at 2.4 augurs ill for Horatio, recalling as it does the ominous presences in the previous scene. The dramatic irony reaches an almost unbearable crescendo as Horatio arrives at the obvious Renaissance pun on *le petit mort*:

> O stay a while and I will die with thee,
> So shalt thou yield and yet have conquered me.

and the metaphoric dying is made literal not in the act of procreation but conversely at the hands of murderers.

Hieronimo's generalized head-shaking over the inappropriate setting for an act of murder ('This place was made for pleasure, not for death') is similarly oxymoronic, similarly coloured by dramatic irony. In this brilliantly written and justly famous scene the audience experiences with Hieronimo the space between spoken puzzlement and active discovery. Beginning 'What outcries pluck me from my naked bed?', Hieronimo's words and actions are exactly consonant throughout his soliloquy, describing his journey from bewilderment ('I did not slumber, therefore 'twas no dream') through fear ['A man hanged up and all the murderers gone, / And in my bower to lay the guilt on me.'] to the slow dawning of realization ['Those garments that he wears I oft have seen –'] betokening a man whose innermost thoughts and outward behaviour are utterly integral with each other.

Given this steady consequentiality, Hieronimo's subsequent tendency to remake himself emblematically (as when he appears as a suicide), referentially *(Vindicta mihi!)*, or to slide into metaphor or apparent madness, simultaneously creates a self-referential theatre that draws attention to its own ways of constructing meaning, and a self-conscious audience aware that meaning is being made for it. The embedded metaphorical understanding of the bower, and of these subsequent appearances by Hieronimo, suggest that Kyd relies in no small measure upon a shared understanding of emblem and literary meaning, using these tools to create a depth of mutuality between playwright and audience both within and across the confines of the text. The slide into allegorical mode is especially spectacular, not least because it is entirely unexpected. Having been asked for physical directions to the court, Hieronimo begins to reply, but the two theatrical conventions of assumed realism and allegorical representation suddenly elide:

> O, forbear,
> For other talk for us far fitter were,
> But if you be importunate to know
> The way to him, and where to find him out,
> Then list to me, and I will find him out.
> There is a path upon your left-hand side,
> That leadeth from a guilty conscience
> Unto a forest of distrust and fear,
> A darksome place, and dangerous to pass:
> There shall you meet with melancholy thoughts,
> Whose baleful humours if you but uphold,
> It will conduct you to despair and death;
> Whose rocky cliffs when you have once beheld,
> Within a hugy dale of lasting night,
> That, kindled with the world's infirmities,
> Doth cast up filthy and detested fumes,
> Not far from thence, where murderers have built
> A habitation for their cursed souls,
> There, in a brazen cauldron, fixed by Jove
> In his fell wrath upon a sulphur flame,
> Yourselves shall find Lorenzo bathing him
> In boiling lead and blood of innocents.

It appears that the only appropriate response to such an astonishing shift in register is an inarticulate one:

> PORTINGALE: Ha, ha, ha!
> HIERONIMO: Why, ha, ha, ha! Farewell, good, ha, ha, ha!

(III. xi. 10–31)

Hieronimo is closely aligned with the playwright from this moment onwards. By aligning him with different kinds of expression – assimilation, allegorization – Kyd prepares the way for Hieronimo to become provider of the theatrical creation that will reveal truth through manipulation of different kinds of texts.

When the final scene reveals that, within the context of the play, language is finally useless to a nation intent on being bound by convention rather than meaning, Hieronimo's pilgrimage through the various forms of representation reveals itself for what it is. In setting up the play within the play, he completes a significant trio of entertainments, each of which has been in keeping with his position at the moment at which it takes place. In this final, astonishing invocation of self-conscious, analytical observation, Kyd sets up his audience to watch an audience that believes it is participating in an illusory convention. The 'sundry languages' demonstrate that where language is meaningless – as it has been proven to be throughout the play – action must tell the story; and action, in this case, does not lie. The onstage audience is informed only by the action, and cannot therefore profit from the multiplicity of meanings that language can offer; the audience beyond the notional proscenium arch is privileged with the text in a recognizable language and so is allowed the convention of stage deaths. Hieronimo goes on to make his meaning dramatically plain as he bites out his tongue, signifying an end to spoken language, and stabs himself with a penknife, killing himself with the very instrument by which his revelatory inventions were transcribed into an accessible life.

But as Frank Ardolino has recently and very persuasively argued, this final scene reveals its universal will to meaning by its invocation of Babel. In a play where the investigation of mediums for meaning have been at least as important as internal meaning itself, this final exposition of truth through the medium of incomprehensibility and the double take on suspension of disbelief renders up the notion of language as obfuscatory in its unredeemed state. Catholic Spain cannot access revealed New Testament meaning, because it seeks its meaning in words rather than the Word. Hieronimo's movement from acquiescence to the workings of the state, to a painful coherence of language and action, through a retracing and recasting of meaning through allegory and assimilation of ancient texts, finally arrives at the representation of truth by rejecting language in all its forms and allowing the action, the thing itself, to represent itself without a linguistic medium.

It seems to me that Ardolino's thesis is particularly apposite to its time, apocalyptic revision being a favourite occupation of the late 1990s. It is particularly seductive as a reading encompassing many of the essential investigations that went before it, and opening up the way for work such as Hillman's on the revised scenes that were added to the play at a later stage.[4] Early, essential interrogations of form, emblem and intertextual reference, however, highlight steadily and clearly each of the mechanisms by which the play might be seen, at this moment in history, to be synechdochic signifiers of the Protestant desire for clear communication of theological truth.

NOTES

1 The play was hugely popular in its own time, being performed twenty-nine times between 1592 and 1597, and running to ten editions in various forms before 1633. (Smith, viii; Rowan, 112–13). Hattaway remarks how 'the number of references to the play or affectionately parodic quotations from it show that it occupied the collective consciousness of the Elizabethans' (Hattaway, p. 101). Mehl comments on this 'first attempt to combine rhetorical and popular drama' (Mehl, p. 64) and suggests that characters' awareness of the significance of the dumb show instigates a new dramatic form (Mehl, pp. 70–1), while Clemen agrees that 'many diverse influences contribute to the creation of a new kind of drama' (Clemen, p. 63).

2 See THE ENGLISH LANGUAGE OF THE EARLY MODERN PERIOD.

3 The criticism of the play during the last thirty years of the twentieth century suggests an increasing predisposition to view it in these terms. Broude develops a formulaic representation of 'the Time, Truth and Right topos' (p. 132) in his historical alignment of the play's preoccupations with the relationship between England and Spain, concluding that 'Viewed in this way, *The Spanish Tragedy* must have offered welcome comfort to Englishmen of the 1580s, reassuring them that no matter how precarious their situation might seem, Divine Providence would punish their enemies' wickedness and Time would vindicate the truth and justice of the English cause' (145). Mulryne, Hattaway, Ardolino (1990) and Hillman, of which more below, have seen a more embedded historical and cultural context operating to reveal meaning, while Hill is among the first to announce the play as 'a deeply self-conscious work' (164).

4 This point has been addressed in recent productions of the play. Smith provides an interesting overview in her introduction to the Penguin edition (1998). In the 1978 Glasgow production directed by Robert David Macdonald, 'the final tragedy of "Soliman and Perseda" was staged in English as a shadow-play behind a bloody sheet' (xxvi), suggesting, it seems to me oddly, that language in the play is finally clear, but vision obscured or at least on another plane. In 1997, with the RSC at Stratford under Michael Boyd, Andrea observed throughout, sometimes seated, 'at other points moving unseen among the characters' (xxviii), and Revenge was finally revealed to be Hieronimo, as the play was made to end by beginning its first scene again, the words being drowned in increasingly loud music (xxix). Hattaway deals with issues of staging throughout (pp. 101–28).

REFERENCES AND FURTHER READING

Ardolino, F. (1995). *Apocalypse and Armada in Kyd's Spanish Tragedy*. Kirksville: Sixteenth Century Essays and Studies, Vol. 29.

Broude, R. (1971). 'Time, Truth and Right in *The Spanish Tragedy*', *Studies in Philology*, 68, 130–45.

Clemen, W. ([1961] 1980) *English Tragedy Before Shakespeare*, tr. T. S. Dorsch. London and New York: Methuen.

Hattaway, M. (1982). *Elizabethan Popular Theatre*. London: Routledge and Kegan Paul.

Hill, E. D. (1985). 'Senecan and Vergilian perspectives in *The Spanish Tragedy*', *English Literary Renaissance*, 15, 143–65.

Hillman, R. (1997). *Self-speaking in Medieval and Early Modern English Drama*. Basingstoke: Macmillan.

Kerrigan, J. (1996). *Revenge Tragedy: From Aeschylus to Armageddon*. Oxford: Oxford University Press.

Kyd, T. ([?1597, 1970] 1984). *The Spanish Tragedy*, ed. J. R. Mulryne. New Mermaids. London / New York: A. and C. Black Ltd. / W. W. Norton and Company Inc.

McGinnis Kay, C. (1977). 'Deception Through Words: A Reading of *The Spanish Tragedy*', *Studies in Philology*, 74, 20–38.

Mehl, D. ([1965] 1982). *The Elizabethan Dumbshow: The History of a Dramatic Convention*. London: Methuen.

Mulryne, J. R. (1996). 'Nationality and Language in Thomas Kyd's *The Spanish Tragedy*'. In Jean-Pierre Maquerlot and Michele Willems (eds), *Travel and Drama in Shakespeare's Time* (pp. 87–105). Cambridge: Cambridge University Press.

Rowan, D. F. (1975). 'The Staging of *The Spanish Tragedy*', *The Elizabethan Theatre*, 5, 112–23.

Smith, E. (ed.), (1998). 'Introduction'. In Thomas Kyd, *The Spanish Tragedie*. London: Penguin.

18

Donne's 'Nineteenth Elegy'

Germaine Greer

For Marlowe who translated Ovid's *Amores*, Campion who imitated them in Latin, and Donne who imitated them in English, the project was transgressive; the three books of the *Amores* were not among the Ovidian texts studied by Elizabethan schoolboys and could be published with impunity only in Latin. One printing of Marlowe's translation of the elegies was burnt by order of the bishops in 1599. Donne's performance was to be assessed only by those who could not be corrupted by it, among which select company his elegies circulated in manuscript, inspiring many more exercises in the genre. Helen Gardner's observation

> The great popularity of the Elegy from 1595 to 1640 is rather overlooked in literary histories because the work of gentlemen writers in this genre has not been collected or anthologized as their songs and lyrics have been. Much of it is still in manuscript.
>
> (p. xxxiii, n)

still holds good. Donne's first publisher printed only eight of his elegies in the first edition; this number was expanded in the second edition of 1635; more Ovidian elegies more or less likely to have been by Donne were added in subsequent editions. Elegy Nineteen (following Grierson's numbering) did not appear in print until 1669, thirty-eight years after the poet's death, when it was given the title 'To his Mistress Going to Bed'. During the seventy or so years that the poem had circulated in manuscript under the title 'Elegy' the text had destabilized to some extent but the contested readings from the fourteen manuscripts that survive are not crucial.

The precedent of the *Amores* allows a poet to interrogate his own sexuality in a disabused, wry, even embittered fashion, whether mildly amazed at his own perfidy or disgusted by the reality of abortion. Anthony La Branche has argued that what Donne inherited from the classic elegiac tradition is an 'awareness of self-deception' (pp. 362, 366). M. L. Stapleton (pp. 2–6) identifies the speaker of the *Amores* as *desultor amoris*, who is always outsmarted by the women he seeks to use and abuse, though he may not be aware of the fact: 'We can see much more about the *desultor* than he can see himself, a lesson of the master not lost on the pupil Donne.'

The subject of Ovidian elegy is not the woman who is its apparent occasion, but the man who is sniffing around her. Donne's speaker is more aware of the sophistry of phallic arguments even than Ovid's, because he lives and acts in the world within worlds of Protestant Christianity. His erotic concerns are compromised and complicated in ways that Ovid's Latin lover would not understand. The elegist may ostensibly address his mistress, his mistress's maid, the go-between, his rival, Cupid, the gate-keeper, or none of the above, but they are given no space for a reply. The Ovidian lover's imagination projects its own states on to the objects of his interest; it is up to the reader to assess the degree of solipsism in his account of situations and events. The Ovidian lover may confess anything from impotence or premature ejaculation to priapism or inflicting actual bodily harm; it is up to the reader to grant or refuse absolution.

The first of Donne's elegies is an imitation of Elegy iv of Book I of the *Amores* but as the series progresses, the Ovidian situations are left behind. Elegy Nineteen, purporting to be an address from a man who is already abed to the woman he expects to join him there, has no direct Ovidian model, though it may be an allusion, by way of contrast, to I. v. in the person of the lover describing his mistress's naked body:

> ut steatite ante oculos posito velamine nostros,
>   in toto nusquam corpore menda fuit.
> quos umeros, quales vidi tetigique lacertos!
>   forma papillarum quam fuit apta premi!
> quam castigato planus sub pectore venter!
> quantum et quale latus! quam iuvenale femur!

[In Marlowe's translation:

> Stark naked as she stood before mine eye,
> Not one wen in her body could I spy:
> What arms and shoulders did I touch and see,
> How apt her breasts were to be pressed by me!
> How smooth a belly under her waist saw I,
> How large a leg, and what a lusty thigh!]

This is what the lover in Donne's elegy does not get to see, and for which he pleads, beginning in peremptory vein –

> Come, madam, come,

This repeated urging in the imperative is followed by a curiously inverted statement in the indicative mood, which could be misconstrued at first hearing as another instruction to the woman:

> all rest my powers defy.

To get the sense right the reader has to flip the clause over to read 'my powers defy all rest'. 'All rest' implies that neither man nor woman will be allowed to rest by the speaker's 'powers', a curiously aggrandizing way of referring to his virility, evidenced one may suppose by his erection. 'All rest' implies all rest for everybody ever, as if this mighty penis could unhinge the very spheres. The feeling of upside-downness or back-to-frontness is reflected by the inversion in which it is the male speaker who is on his back, 'brought to bed' as it were, seeing himself as in travail from which he must be delivered. The repetition of 'labour' contrasts the different meanings of the verb and the noun, and both are contradicted by the double-meaning verb 'lie'.

> Until I labour, I in labour lie.

Both birth and death haunt the poem as invisible presences, which the switchback syntax seems pettishly to deny. This is a man totally intent upon the release of his own genital tension. The lovelessness of the opening turns to actual enmity in the next couplet:

> The foe oft-times having the foe in sight,
> Is tired with standing, though he never fight.

The battle metaphor reinforces the suggestion that intercourse may involve more risk than pleasure for the woman. The male speaker is already tired with 'standing' though, as we discover in the next line, she has not even begun to undress. The peremptoriness of the opening 'Come, . . . come' returns in the next couplet which seems almost to snatch at her, only to reel backwards in a skyey figure:

> Off with that girdle like heaven's zone glittering,
> But a far fairer world encompassing.

A new motif has made its appearance, of the woman as unexplored globe, the new world itself. The woman's silence and distance dehumanize her; the lover is now as it were 'silent on a peak in Darien', marvelling at the beauties of a distant unconquered realm. The woman is next invoked as a blazon that is undoing itself:

> Unpin that spangled breast-plate which you wear,
> That th'eyes of busy fools may be stopped there.

We do not know whether these instructions are being followed or even whether they have been heard; the previousness of the speaker is the only certainty. The description of the woman's stomacher as a 'spangled breast-plate' revives the suggestion of sexual warfare; in a reversal of the epic machinery the female warrior is being unarmed for combat. The gaze of 'busy fools' are presented as assaults to be warded off by her stomacher; without it she is vulnerable to the voyeur in bed. She will inform him of her approach no more consciously than if she were a clock.

> Unlace yourself, for that harmonious chime,
> Tells me from you that now it is bedtime.

Though he uses the present tense, we do not know if he has in fact heard the clinking of her points; his present tense may be the present habitual, reinforcing the impression that this is a domestic scene. If this woman's bedtime ritual has been witnessed so many times that it can be securely imagined now, we might suspect that the speaker's erection is just as habitual. From the beginning of the poem the lover has sounded insensitive; the hint of incontinence becomes more than a hint when he tells the reader that he envies her busk, her stiff corset, because it can be so close to her for so long and still stand, that is, not ejaculate and detumesce. Among his concerns is anxiety about the maintenance of his erection; one of the functions performed by his roving fantasy is keeping that erection entertained. The woman is relevant only as the object of his fantasy; her silence, distance and obliviousness are masterfully inferred.

> Your gown going off, such beauteous state reveals,
> As when from flow'ry meads th'hills shadow steals.

To appreciate the way the shadows of the upland retract as the sun climbs higher the viewer must be at some distance. Whatever the 'beauteous state' may denote, it is not a revelation of the woman's body or of enjoyment to be gained from it. We have had the hint of woman as landscape before, in the verb 'labour' which originally means to plough, a commonplace for sexual intercourse; the still-to-be-enjoyed woman is an untilled meadow full of wild flowers which the ploughshare would destroy.

Catherine Ginelli Martin identifies the speaker's purpose in this poem as 'at once objectifying, shaming and figuratively raping his "new-found-land"' thus satisfying Freud's description of the function of obscene wit, 'linking himself to a host of phallic allies who receive his "gift", the shared exploitation of woman' (p. 80). The person exposed in the poem is not the woman but the aroused man. Martin's claim that Donne details 'not only each garment he would have his mistress discard but also precisely what it should conceal' (p. 79) cannot be substantiated. Donne's speaker would be desperately envious of Chapman's Ovid in *Ovid's Banquet of Sense* (printed in 1595) gazing his fill on Julia / Corinna (Stanza 58).

> Now as she lay, attired in nakedness,
> His eye did carve him on that feast of feasts:
> Sweet fields of life which Death's foot dare not press,

Flowered with th'unbroken waves of my Love's breasts,
  Unbroke by depths of those her beauties' floods:
See where with bent of gold curled into nests
  In her head's grove the spring-bird lameate [?] broods:
Her body doth present those fields of peace
Where souls are feasted with the soul of ease.

And so on for several stanzas which develop an extended parallel of the woman's body with the Garden of Eden. Donne certainly knew Chapman's poem, and may in fact be ironically alluding to it. Donne's speaker, like the reader, sees nothing and must imagine all.

The behaviour of Donne's woman is not that of Ovid's Corinna, a complaisant mistress seizing amorous opportunity, but of a woman going to bed for the night. The man observing her as it were through the bed curtains, as post-modern man might listen for sounds beyond the bathroom door, is acting less as a lover than as a husband. His addressing the woman as 'madam, and nothing else' as Sly is instructed to call the page masquerading as his wife in *The Taming of the Shrew*, reinforces the suggestion that the object of his lust is indeed the speaker's wife. If he were as interested in raping and colonizing as is often suggested, it is the more remarkable that he lies naked in his bed imagining the woman undressing rather than undressing her himself. By instructing her to remove her clothes, as it were *sotto voce*, he enacts passivity; his aggression is all in the mind. She will come bedward, as any decent woman would, in her shift.

In such white robes heav'n's angels used to be
Received by men: thou angel bringst with thee
A heaven like Mahomet's Paradise

The irruption of a reference to exotic carnal pleasures with soulless female houris underlines the independence of his fantasies from the couple's shared reality. He develops his conceit to revel in its apparent perversity. His witticism that he knows her for a good angel because she sets his flesh rather than his hair on end drives him further into his solipsism.

Licence my roving hands and let them go,
Before, behind, between, above, below.

The imperative 'Licence' is also a noun with transgressive connections; Albert C. Labriola has pointed out that the lover expresses himself furthermore as if he were a privateer begging the queen's permission to sack and plunder in her name:

The word 'licence' was the technical expression for the queen's favour or approval of a maritime expedition. The word 'roving' has a two-fold significance: wandering and robbing . . . In accounts of voyages, such language is commonplace for navigating against or across lines of latitude and longitude; traveling between, below and above points of reference on the terrestrial globe.

(p. 56)

Intrusion, invasion, and spoliation are all implied. The non-cooperation of the woman remains the still centre-point of the turning poem, assailed again and again by the man's restless fantasy.

> O my America, my new-found-land,
> My kingdom, safeliest when with one man manned,
> My mine of precious stones: my empery,
> How blest am I in this discovering thee!

It is Donne's achievement to strike us with the wonder and elation produced by the lover's mounting sexual excitement, without compromising the unassailability of the woman. She is a continent, and therefore continent; as Donne reminded Sir Francis Nethersole in his wedding sermon, 'the fitness that goes through all is a sober continency; for without that "*matrimonium jurata fornicatio*", Marriage is but a continual fornication sealed with an oath'. The insistence on the woman's unimaginable vastness cannot but carry with it the ironic suggestion of her lover's comparative tininess. Donne jolts the reader even harder by allowing the transported lover suddenly to disquisit upon monarchy as the best form of government, implying the usual parallels of the husband's role with that of a monarch, only to collapse the grand proprietorial metaphor into ownership of a single mine before inflating it again to encompass empire. The reader leaps from couplet to contrasting couplet over anything but solid ground, briefly knocking against the legal contract between spouses, which endorses the husband's authority and his right over her, '*in coniugio transactis*' as Donne's epitaph for his wife has it (Hester, p. 517).

> To enter in these bonds is to be free;
> Then where my hand is set my seal shall be.

The speaker may be admitting some form of reciprocity, a partnership, and by implication the bonds or bands of wedlock, but there is no consultation. His partner in the sexual activity has dwindled to an abstraction. The lover suddenly interrupts himself with a peal of praise to nakedness, which he follows with an unprovable and unmistakably argumentative statement.

> As souls unbodied, bodies unclothed must be
> To taste whole joys.

This bald assertion begins a typically masculine dispute with 'you women' who wear jewels to attract male concupiscence. A bejewelled woman is likened to an illustrated book made for illiterate 'lay-men', while the sacerdotal husband claims the right to read the mystery itself. As consciously transgressive as the assertion that we may know good angels because they cause erections (as the succubus does) is the equation of self-revelation with the shifting of the shift.

> Then since that I may know
> As liberally as to a midwife show
> Thyself: cast all, yea, this white linen hence.

The spectre of pregnancy now at centre stage, the shift becomes the white garment in which individuals taken in adultery were ordered to stand at the church door in partial expiation of their sin. The woman's modesty having been speciously parlayed into evidence of guilt, he absolves her in his own interest only to deny her innocence too.

There is no penance, much less innocence.

In his marriage sermon for the wedding of Sir Francis Nethersole, Donne quoted St Jerome '*Nihil foedius, quam uxorem amare tanquam adulteram,*' glossing it 'There is not a more uncomely, a poorer thing, than to love a wife like a mistress'. The chaste wife does not capitulate to her husband's importunity; she remains hidden from both speaker and reader. The last couplet is almost petulant.

> To teach thee, I am naked first; why then
> What needst thou have more covering than a man?

The ambiguity reaches to a pun on 'covering'. As a woman needs no more covering than a man does, a woman needs no more than a man to cover her. The idiom derives from animal husbandry, and once more implies mating and ensuing pregnancy. Ending on a question implies a lack of closure; the woman, and perhaps the speaker's orgasm, have eluded him after all. A further nuance is more difficult for modern readers to intuit. In *The Order of Household Government* (1592) Fenner uses 'cover' in a special sense:

> The proper care for the wife is to cover her, that is, to provide all things meet for a mate so nearly joined in full blessing to him and thus according to their condition, to give honour to her, as the fittest to him in heaven and in earth, with a patient covering or bearing of her infirmities.

Ovid's elegies provide the precedent for a man's presenting his sexuality as unpredictable, peremptory and occasionally degrading, at the same time that it provides him with his only glimpses of heaven. For Donne sex is more specifically anagogical, as in Christian teleology sacred things can only make themselves known through physical signs. The sacramental bond of matrimony is made flesh in the act of copulation. The naked body of the woman becomes the emblem of truth and as such, paradoxically, the embodiment of sacred love. The contradictions are relentless. The woman's body is only exciting because it is so seldom disclosed; the elation of exploring it is only possible because it is not laid open to the lover's view. Husband and wife may be one flesh only in the spirit.

The poem was not written to a woman, is not a negotiation with a woman, but is an exploration of a paradigmatic confrontation between the overt, obvious sexuality of a man and the elusive and inscrutable object of his desire. That desire, clearly carnal and specific, is sanctified by divine mandate at the same time as it is bedevilled by fantasy and human perversity. What sex is not is intercourse; the object of desire is a projection of the desire itself. Not only is the female figure of the elegy silent, she is unresponsive in every way. She does not do as she is told, but as she always does, as the voiceless speaker watches and gives instructions that are no more than predictions. Elegy Nineteen is so teasingly ambiguous that learned critics have on the one hand seen it as Donne's epithalamium for himself and on the other refused to accept it as having any relevance whatsoever to marriage. Yet all readers of Donne know that the contradictions in his work are the contradictions of the human condition with which, both conceptually and actually, marriage is replete. The love expressed in Elegy Nineteen is 'begotten by despair upon impossibility', captious and captivating, occasionally cruel, heated to irresistibility by what distinguishes a great lover according to all the imitators of Ovid, the flame not of lust but of wit.

References and Further Reading

Armstrong, Alan (1977). 'The Apprenticeship of John Donne: Ovid and the *Elegies*', *English Literary History*, 44, 319–42.

Benet, Diana Treviño (1994). 'Sexual Transgression in Donne's Elegies', *Modern Philology*, 92 (1), 14–35.

Carey, John (1981). *John Donne, Mind, Life and Art*. Oxford: Oxford University Press.

Donne, John (1956). 'Preached at a marriage'. In Evelyn M. Simpson and George R. Potter (eds), *The Sermons of John Donne* (vol. ii, pp. 241–55). Berkeley and Los Angeles: University of California Press.

——(1956). 'Preached at Sir Francis Nethersole's marriage'. In Evelyn M. Simpson and George R. Potter (eds), *The Sermons of John Donne* (vol. iii, pp. 335–47). Berkeley and Los Angeles: University of California Press.

——(1956). 'A Sermon preached at the Earl of Bridgewater's house in London at the marriage of his daughter, the Lady Mary, to the eldest son of the Lord Herbert of Castle-Island,

November. 19, 1627'. In Evelyn M. Simpson and George R. Potter (eds), *The Sermons of John Donne* (vol. viii, pp. 94–109). Berkeley and Los Angeles: University of California Press.

Gardner, Helen (ed.) (1965). *John Donne. The Elegies and the Songs and Sonets*. Oxford: Clarendon Press.

Gill, Roma (1972). 'Musa Iocosa Mea: Thoughts on the Elegies'. In A. J. Smith (ed.), *John Donne: Essays in Celebration*. London.

Grierson, Herbert J. C. (ed.) (1912). *The Poems of John Donne*. Oxford: Oxford University Press.

Guibbory, Achsah (1990). '"Oh, Let Mee Not Serve So": The Politics of Love in Donne's *Elegies*', *English Literary History*, 57, 811–33.

Hester, M. Thomas (1995). '"miserrimum dictu": Donne's Epitaph for his Wife', *Journal of English and Germanic Philology*, 94 (4), 513–29.

La Branche, Anthony (1996). '"Blanda Elegeia": The Background to Donne's "Elegies"', *Modern Language Review*, 61, 357–68.

Labriola, Albert C. (1996). 'Painting and Poetry of the Cult of Elizabeth I: The Ditchley Portrait and Donne's "Elegy: Going to Bed", *Modern Philology*, 93 (1), 22–41.

Lerner, Laurence (1988). 'Ovid and the Elizabethans'. In Charles Martindale (ed.), *Ovid Renewed: Ovidian influences on literature and art from the Middle Ages to the twentieth century* (pp. 121–35). Cambridge: Cambridge University Press.

Mann, Lindsay (1985–6). 'Sacred and Profane Love in Donne', *Dalhousie Review*, 65, 534–50.

Marotti, Arthur F. (1988). *John Donne, Coterie Poet*. Madison: University of Wisconsin Press.

Martin, Catherine Ginelli (1995). 'Pygmalion's Progress in the Garden of Love, or The Wit's Work Is Never Donne'. In Claude J. Summers and Ted-Larry Pebworth (eds), *The Wit of Seventeenth-Century Poetry*. Columbia, MO: University of Missouri Press.

Ricks, Christopher (1988). 'Donne after Love'. In Elaine Scarry (ed.), *Literature and the Body: Essays on Population and Persons*. Baltimore: Johns Hopkins University Press.

Selden, Raman (1975). 'John Donne's "Incarnational Conviction"', *Critical Quarterly*, 17, 55–73.

Stapleton, M. L. (1996). '"Why should they not alike in all parts touch": Donne and the Elegiac Tradition', *John Donne Journal*, 15, 1–22.

Turner, Grantham (1987). *One Flesh: Paradisal Marriage and Sexual Relations in the Age of Milton*. Oxford: Clarendon Press.

19

Lanyer's 'The Description of Cookham' and Jonson's 'To Penshurst'

Nicole Pohl

In 1956 G. R. Hibbard published his article 'The Country House Poem of the Seventeenth Century' where he catalogued a 'homogeneous body of poetry', united by common social and political ideals (Hibbard 159). Recent scholarship has taken Hibbard's work as point of departure but has identified a much larger formal and ideological diversity within the body of texts.[1] However, while poems such as Aemilia Lanyer's 'The Description of Cookham' (1611), Ben Jonson's 'To Penshurst' (1616), and 'To Sir Robert Wroth' (1616), Thomas Carew's 'To Saxham' (1640) and Marvell's 'Upon Appleton House' (1681) might be formally distinct, they all present ideals of community, simplicity, responsible use of wealth and property, good housekeeping and hospitality. The poems' rich classical ancestry ranges from Martial, Horace, Statius and Virgil's *Georgics* to Pliny's *Epistle II, 6.* which pre-empted significant seventeenth-century debates. Indeed, the early modern dissension around the country vs. the city / court, the change from a feudal to a monetary land ownership, the emergence of 'possessive individualism', accompanied by the introduction of the representational Palladian building styles for country houses determined the formation of this distinctive literary tradition.[2] 'Through the logic of the metonym', the country estate has come to represent these profound ideological conflicts (Duckworth 396). Furthermore, as Hugh Jenkins suggests, since 'the country-house poem occupies the uneasy, shifting ground between a popular, residual, and communal ideology and a more egalitarian, emerging bourgeois ideology, so too does it place itself between two dominant literary forms: Renaissance drama and the bourgeois form of the novel' (Jenkins 12). By calling upon mythological resonances of the Golden Age and Arcadia, the estate becomes a mythical place 'in which dwelling is the relationship with others, without denial or deprivation of one's own being, and of such a place as a model for human relationships on a larger social scale' (Wayne 173). This mythical quality explains why aspects of the estate poetry heritage are perpetuated from the seventeenth century into the modern age with manifestations in Jane Austen's *Pride and Prejudice* (1813), *Emma* (1816) and *Mansfield Park* (1814), Daniel Defoe's *Tour through the Whole Island of Great Britain* (1724–26), Vita Sackville-West's *The Land* (1926) and *The Garden* (1946) and Evelyn Waugh's *Brideshead Revisited* (1945). The longevity of the myth has led critics such as Lewis Mumford to believe that the country house ideal is indeed a social myth, a 'collective utopia' that springs from 'a collective consciousness' (Mumford 193).

It is necessary to distinguish the thematic shape and poetic structure of this genre.[3] Critics still differ on the question of the former. Whilst Raymond Williams and William McClung identify the country-house poetry as 'quasi-pastoral' and 'neopastoral', Alistair Fowler argues for the georgic as the basic configuration. A reading of the poetry as pastoral highlights the idealizing and exclusive aspects of the tradition. A classification of the poetry as English georgic emphasizes the theme of the agricultural estate as a working community. This conflict is settled if one acknowledges that the estate poem implicates an ideal community in its very critique of the historical and social reality. It is this ideological incongruity which gives the tradition its fundamental political impetus.

The external form of the estate poetry is less disputed and ranges from verse epistles, elegies (Lanyer's 'To Cookham'), valedictions, to encomiastic epigrams such as Jonson's 'To Penshurst'. In addition to these formal divisions, Fowler suggests definite sub-genres which include: (1) invitations; (2) welcomes; (3) entertainment poems; (4) appreciations; (5) retirement poems; (6) park poems; (7) closet and gallery poems; (8) building or reconstruction poems; (9) hunting poems; (10) satires (Fowler, *The Country House Poem* 15–16).

The following sections will investigate Aemilia Lanyer's 'The Description of Cookham' and Ben Jonson's 'To Penshurst' as two of the earliest estate poems.

Aemilia Lanyer, 'The Description of Cookham' (1610)

In 1611, Aemilia Lanyer published a small volume of verse, the *Salve Deus Rex Judæo-rum*.[4] It is a religious work, preceded by several dedicatory verses. All of these are addressed to women, clearly to warrant patronage: Princess Elizabeth, Queen Anne, the Countesses of Kent, Pembroke, Bedford, Cumberland and Dorset and 'all virtuous Ladies in general'. The title page suggests four separate poems: (1) *The Passion of Christ*; (2) *Eves Apology in defence of Women*; (3) *The Tears of the Daughters of Jerusalem*; (4) *The Salutation and Sorrow of the Virgin Marie*. However, the poems are linked through a iconoclastic re-reading of the Bible and the creation of a virtual female community. In this sense, biblical events such as the Fall are reinterpreted and, more radically, the figure of Christ is appropriated as an exemplary icon for women.

The concluding poem of this collection is 'The Description of Cookham', an estate poem written at the request of Lanyer's patron Margaret Clifford, Countess of Cumberland. It precedes Jonson's 'To Penshurst' in publication, and possibly in creation.[5] This makes Aemilia Lanyer's work possibly the first estate poem in English literary history. Formally, 'The Description of Cookham' is an elegiac valediction with both elements of the pastoral and the georgic, mourning the loss of a female community at the estate of Cookham. Margaret and Anne Clifford were given this royal manor in Berkshire as temporary accommodation between 1603 and 1605 while Margaret Clifford was fighting a legal battle against her estranged husband George Clifford and his brother to secure her and her daughter's rights to the Clifford estates.[6] Aemilia Lanyer joined the two women for an indefinite period of time, probably as a tutor to Anne.[7] The whole oeuvre of *Salve Deus Rex Judæorum* is deeply indebted to the patronage and spiritual inspiration of Margaret Clifford.

'A Description of Cookham' celebrates the existence and at the same time, mourns the loss of a unique paradise:

> Farewell, sweet place, where virtue then did rest,
> And all delights did harbour in her breast:
> Never shall my sad eyes again behold
> Those pleasures which my thoughts did then unfold.
>
> (7–10)

The estate, the personified natural surroundings and indeed the women of the place blend into a *locus amoenus*:[8]

> The walks put on their summer liveries,
> And all things else did hold like similes:
> The trees with leaves, with fruits, with flowers clad,
> Embraced each other, seeming to be glad,
> Turning themselves to beauteous canopies
> To shade the bright sun from your brighter eyes;
> The crystal streams with silver spangles graced,
> While by the glorious sun they were embraced;
> The little birds in chirping notes did sing,
> To entertain both you and that sweet spring.
>
> (21–30)

Still, as Susanne Woods has pointed out, the personification of nature is inferred through 'the poetry of surmise' which not only 'distances the poem's pathos' but also highlights the role of the poet in the depiction of this earthly paradise (Woods 119):

> Oh how me thought each plant, each flower, each tree
> Set forth their beauties then to welcome thee.
>
> (33–4)

This bliss, though, is transient:

> And you, sweet Cookham, whom these ladies leave,
> I now must tell the grief you did conceive

At their departure: when they went away,
How everything retained a sad dismay;
Nay long before, when once an inkling came,
Methought each thing did unto sorrow frame:
The trees that were so glorious in our view
Forsook both flowers and fruit; when once they knew
Of your depart, their very leaves did wither,
Changing their colours as they grew together.
But when they saw this had no power to stay you,
They often wept, though, speechless, could not pray you;
Letting their tears in your fair bosoms fall,
As if they said 'Why will ye leave us all?'

(127–40)

With the departure of the three women, the paradise withers away, 'The house cast off each garment that might grace it, / Putting on dust and cobwebs to deface it' (201–2), but the poet remains to celebrate and eternalize these blissful times and herself in poetry:

This last farewell to Cookham here I give:
When I am dead, thy name in this may live.
(205–7)

This couplet epitomizes the process of poetic self-fashioning which Stephen Greenblatt has developed in his *Renaissance Self-Fashioning*. Greenblatt has conspicuously ignored the issue of women's subject formation. However, Kari Boyd McBride suggests 'that the poetic construction of virtuous female community is the first step in her [Lanyer's] poetic self-fashioning. But within that female community, Lanyer fashions herself as a poet by using material that traditionally had silenced women, manipulating features of Petrarchism, the pastoral, and the country house genre to construct her poetic vocation' (McBride, 'Engendering' 14–15).

In the tradition of the genre, the estate Cookham becomes a mythical place, a model for human relationships and at the same time, it provides a profound socio-political critique. The legal system of patrilinear descent is overturned by a creation of a pastoral separatist community. Unlike women in later, male-authored poems, Margaret Clifford, as the (temporary) mistress of the estate, is not the mere adjunct of the master of the house but, as much as the self-fashioned poet Lanyer, is a subject in her own right. It is interesting in this context that the actual architecture of the house is irrelevant. However, while the exclusion of men guarantees a feminocentric *locus amoenus* in 'Cookham', a very well-defined class division between writer and patron remains intact:[9]

Unconstant Fortune, thou are most to blame,
Who cast us down into so low a frame,

> Where our great friends we cannot daily see,
> So great a difference is there in degree.
>
> (103–16)

This deep social separation is finally resolved in the context of the whole of *Salve* where, as McBride has shown, Lanyer 'bows to authority in her patronage poems and at the same time condemns social privilege by invoking the greater authority of Christ. She both decries her weakness of her social position and makes use of it by allying herself to Christ, occupying both positions of authority, that of holy poverty and that of holy power' (McBride, 'Engendering', 17). Cookham metonymically represents not the political integrity or good stewardship of its owner, but the empowered subjectivities of its female guests and chronicler.

Ben Jonson, 'To Penshurst'

Ben Jonson published his estate poem, 'To Penshurst' in *The Forest* in 1616, but probably composed it sometime in 1612.[10] It certainly established the genre although, as we have seen, the first English example may have been Lanyer's 'A Description of Cookham'.[11] Formally, 'To Penshurst' is an encomiastic epigram. Unlike, Lanyer's poem, it epitomizes the metonymic employment of the estate and especially its architecture. The different legal relations to landed property has led critics to suggest that 'the country-house genre was gendered at its interception' (Grossmann 131).

Jonson's celebration of Penshurst is framed by a historical and aesthetic comparison between this Old Hall and more representational country houses:

> Thou art not, Penshurst, built to envious show,
> Of touch, or marble; nor canst boast a row
> Of polished pillars, or a roof of gold:
> Thou has no lantern whereof tales are told,
> Or stair, or courts; but standst an ancient pile,
> And these grudged at, art reverenced the while.
>
> (1–6)
>
> . . .
>
> Now, Penshurst, they that will proportion thee
> With other edifices, when they see
> Those proud, ambitious heaps, and nothing else,
> May say, their lords have built, but thy lord dwells.
>
> (99–102)

The change implied in these lines from the archaic Old Hall to the fashion of grand Elizabethan country houses 'suggests many metaphors and analogies: from community to the individual, from anonymous to idiosyncratic design, from utility to display,

from timelessness to 'modernity', and stylistically, from horizontal to vertical thrust'
(McClung 90):

> Where comes no guest but is allowed to eat,
> Without his fear, and of thy lord's own meat:
> Where the same beer, and bread, and self-same wine
> That is his lordship's, shall be also mine;
> And I fain to sit (as some, this day,
> At great men's tables) and yet dine away.
>
> (61–4)

Penshurst represents the good stewardship and social virtue of Robert Sidney who
nurses an organic, self-sufficient but, as the above quote also shows, still hierarchical
community. It is he who is not 'envious to show', who does not boast and who is
neither proud nor ambitious. This specific endorsement of Penshurst is continued in
a rather different vein:

> Thy Mount, to which the Dryads do resort,
> Where Pan and Bacchus their high feasts have made,
> Beneath the broad beech, and the chestnut shade;
> That taller tree, which of a nut was set,
> At his great birth, where all the Muses met.
>
> (10–14)
>
> . . .
>
> And thence, the ruddy Satyrs oft provoke
> The lighter Fauns to reach thy Lady's Oak.
>
> (17–18)

Penshurst, the historically specific place is blended with Penshurst, the mythologized
social model. It is worth pointing out that Jonson's realistic description of the estate
was already tainted by this utopian desire. By the time Jonson wrote the poem, Penshurst was more than a humble medieval Hall. In 1594, state rooms and the long
gallery were added to the original structure and Jonson's contemporary, Robert Sidney,
planned to turn Penshurst into a 'prodigy house'. Rathmell argues that Jonson perhaps
warned Sidney not to become a proud owner of an 'ambitious heap' (256–8).[12] This
warning is also echoed in the hyperbolic *sponte sua* motif which reminds Sidney of his
commitment to hospitality and generosity:

> The purpled pheasant, with the speckled side:
> The painted partridge lies in every field,
> And, for thy mess, is willing to be killed.
>
> (28–30)
>
> . . .
>
> Bright eels, that emulate them, and leap on land
> Before the fisher, or into his hand.

> Then hath thy orchard fruit, thy garden flowers,
> Fresh as the air, and new as are the hours.
>
> (37–40)

It is not only the land and the wild life that offer themselves to the good of Penshurst's community. Lady Sidney is herself an ideal host, an eager provider for the guests, her husband and her children. In the manner of the poem, she is naturalized as 'fruitful':

> These, Penshurst, are thy praize, and yet not all.
> Thy lady's noble, fruitful, chaste withal.
> His children thy great lord may call his own:
> A fortune, in this age, but rarely known.
>
> (89–92)

Her daughters are represented in the same manner:

> By their ripe daughters, whom they would commend
> This way to husbands; and whose basket bear
> An emblem of themselves, in plum, or pear.
>
> (53–6)

Wayne interprets this comparison as a depiction of a 'natural' chain of events, where 'the land gives of itself, animals give themselves, ripe daughters give of themselves, ladies give of themselves to lords, lords give of themselves to kings. Moreover the giving is voluntarily and constitutes an equivalent exchange in kind, hence, nothing and no one is exploited' (Wayne 75). Jenkins adds that Lady Sidney's body is indeed the site where residual (feudal) and emerging (bourgeois) ideologies are negotiated and subsumed (Jenkins 56–62).

Whilst Jonson, as shown above, presents his model of an ideal commonwealth, he also presents a critique of the socio-political status quo of the early seventeenth century. His reading of history however is itself prejudiced by a utopian blueprint. Jonson therefore sets up a dialectic between social reality, as perceived by him, and the ideal. This dialectic is the basis for poems such as 'To Penshurst' with their intricate framing structure and their internal ideological contradictions. It is the poet's voice that embodies these conflicts and his own struggle between being 'the ideal self of the good man / good poet, and the alienated satirist of urban comedies' (Jenkins 7).

NOTES

1 See References.
2 I borrowed this term from C. B. Macpherson (1962). *The Political Theory of Possessive* *Individualism: Hobbes to Locke.* Oxford: Oxford University Press.

3 On the question of genre, subgenre and literary mode, see GENRE.

4 Lanyer. The work was entered in the Stationers' Register on 2 October 1610. Quotes are from Fowler, *The Country House Poem*, 45–52.

5 See Susanne Woods on this question.

6 See Barbara Lewalski's work on the biography of Margaret and Anne Clifford.

7 See Woods, p. 30.

8 See Curtius, pp. 195–200.

9 On the aspect of patronage and class, see Krontiris; Coiro and Lamb. On the erotic aspect of this relationship, see Goldberg, 1997.

10 See Woods, 184. 'To Penshurst' is quoted from Fowler, *The Country House Poem*, pp. 53–62.

11 Hugh Jenkins ranks Ben Jonson as the originator of the estate poem and 'To Penshurst' as the most complex model for the genre. Susanne Woods on the other hand presents an analysis of 'The Description of Cooke-ham' which suggests that Jonson learnt from Lanyer's poem.

12 Malcolm Kelsall indeed suggests that 'Thou art not' 'carries with it a sense of "Thou shalt not", as if the house were a Biblical commandment reified' (Kelsall 35).

REFERENCES AND FURTHER READING

Chedgzoy, Kate, Sanders, Julie and Wiseman, Susan (eds) (1998). *Refashioning Ben Jonson: Gender, Politics and the Jonsonian Canon.* Basingstoke: Macmillan.

Coiro, Anne Baynes (1993). 'Writing in Service: Sexual Politics and Class Position in the Poetry of Aemilia Lanyer and Ben Jonson', *Criticism*, 35, 357–76.

Curtius, Ernst Robert (1953). *European Literature and the Latin Middle Ages*, tr. Willard R. Trask. London: Routledge and Kegan Paul.

Duckworth, Alistair (1989). 'Gardens, Houses, and the Rhetoric of Description in the English Novel'. In Gervaise Jackson-Stops, Gordon J. Schochet, Lena Cowen Orlin and Elizabeth Blair MacDougall (eds), *The Fashioning of the British Country House* (pp. 395–417). Hanover, NH: University Press of New England for the National Gallery of Art, Washington.

Fowler, Alistair (1994). *The Country House Poem: A Cabinet of Seventeenth-century Estate Poems and Related Items.* Edinburgh: Edinburgh University Press.

——(1986). 'Country House Poems: The Politics of Genre', *The Seventeenth Century*, 1 (3), 1–14.

Goldberg, Jonathan (1997). *Desiring Women Writing: English Renaissance Examples.* Stanford: Stanford University Press.

——(1983). *James I and the Politics of Literature: Jonson, Shakespeare, Donne, and Their Contempo-*

raries. Baltimore: Johns Hopkins University Press.

Greenblatt, Stephen (1980). *Renaissance Self-Fashioning: From More to Shakespeare.* Chicago; University of Chicago Press.

Grossman, Marshall (ed.) (1998). *Aemilia Lanyer: Gender, Genre and the Canon.* Lexington: University Press of Kentucky.

Hibbard, G. R. (1956). 'The Country House Poem of the Seventeenth Century', *Journal of the Warburg and Courtauld Institutes*, 19, 159–74.

Jenkins, Hugh (1998). *Feigned Commonwealths: The Country-House Poem and the Fashioning of the Ideal Community.* Pittsburgh: Duquesne University Press.

Kelsall, Malcolm (1993). *The Great Good Place: The Country House & English Literature.* New York: Columbia University Press.

Krontiris, Tina (1992). *Oppositional Voices: Women as Writers and Translators of Literature in the English Renaissance.* New York: Routledge.

Lamb, Mary Ellen (1998). 'Patronage and Class in Aemilia Lanyer's Salve Deus Rex Judaeorum'. In Jane Donawerth, Mary Burke, Linda Dove and Karen Welson (eds), *Women, Writing and the Reproduction of Culture.* Syracuse, NY: Syracuse University Press.

Lanyer, Aemilia (1611). *Salve Deus Rex Judæorum.* London: printed by V. Simmes for R. Bonian.

Lewalski, Barbara Kiefer (1989). 'The Lady of the Country-house Poem'. In Gervaise Jackson-Stops, Gordon J. Schochet, Lena Cowen Orlin and Elizabeth Blair McDougall (eds), *The Fashioning of the British Country House* (pp. 261–75). Hanover, NH: University Press of New England for the National Gallery of Art, Washington.

——(1993). *Writing Women in Jacobean England*. Cambridge, MA: Harvard University Press.

McBride, Kari Boyd (1994). 'Engendering Authority in Aemilia Lanyer's *Salve Deus Rex Judaeorum*'. Dissertation, University of Arizona.

——(1998). 'Remembering Orpheus in the Poems of Aemilia Lanyer', *Studies in English Literature*, 38, 87–108.

McClung, William A. (1977). *The Country House in English Renaissance Poetry*. Berkeley: University of California Press.

Macpherson, C. B. (1962). *The Political Theory of Possessive Individualism: Hobbes to Locke*. Oxford: Oxford University Press.

Mumford, Lewis (1963). *The Story of Utopias*, 3rd edn. New York: Viking Press.

Rathmell, J. C. A. (1971). 'Jonson, Lord Lisle, and Penshurst', *English Literary Renaissance*, 1, 250–60.

Wayne, Don E. (1984). *Penshurst: The Semiotics of Place and the Poetics of History*. London: Methuen.

Williams, Raymond (1973, 1993). *The Country and the City*. London: Hogarth Press.

Woods, Susanne (1999). *Aemilia Lanyer: A Renaissance Poet in Her Context*. Oxford: Oxford University Press.

20

Bacon's 'Of Simulation and Dissimulation'

Martin Dzelzainis

For over three-quarters of a century, the agenda for interpreting Francis Bacon's *Essays* (1597, 1612, 1625) has been set by a handful of commentators, notably R. S. Crane and Morris W. Croll, whose articles originally appeared together in 1923, and Stanley Fish, whose 'Georgics of the Mind: The Experience of Bacon's *Essays*' was published in 1971 and then expanded into a chapter of his *Self-Consuming Artifacts* (1972). Fish begins by endorsing Crane's suggestion that many of the essays which appeared for the first time in the editions of 1612 and 1625 were written specifically to fulfil the scientific programme Bacon had announced in *The Advancement of Learning* (1605). According to Fish, however, the fact that several of these new essays appear to address the deficiencies in the state of moral and civil knowledge identified in 1605 is not what gives them their scientific quality. For this we must look to the experience of reading them, since 'this experience, rather than the materials of which it is composed, is what is scientific about the *Essays*'. The keynote of this experience is that the reader is left more uncertain and puzzled at every turn – a strategy designed to promote 'a more self-conscious scrutiny of one's mental furniture' and hence to 'foster the curious blend of investigative eagerness and wary skepticism which, according to Bacon, distinguishes the truly scientific cast of mind' (Fish 1972: 81, 95).

For Fish himself, the *Essays* are a crucial exhibit in the case for a phenomenological approach to criticism; that is, 'a method of analysis which focuses on the reader rather than the artifact'. Instead of making a fetish of the 'objectivity of the text', we should accept literature as a form of kinetic art which only operates by virtue of 'the actualizing role of the observer'. The task of criticism accordingly is to analyse 'the developing responses of the reader in relation to the words as they succeed one another in time' (Fish 1972: 387–8, 400–1).

While this has proved a very influential method of reading Bacon's later essays in particular, it also has severe drawbacks. Firstly, it means that no particular significance attaches to the essay topics in themselves, since a title 'merely specifies the par-

ticular area of inquiry within which and in terms of which the reader becomes involved
in a characteristic kind of activity, the questioning and testing of a commonly received
notion'. For these purposes, an essay on, say, received notions of love, is indistinguishable from one on, say, received notions of adversity. Fish also equivocates on the
issue of authorial intentions: on the one hand he maintains that it is entirely possible to 'analyze an effect without worrying about whether it was produced accidentally or on purpose', but on the other hand the question does not arise since it so
happens that he is dealing with 'texts in which the evidence of control is overwhelming' (Fish 1972: 92, 409). He is therefore quite certain that what Bacon
intended to achieve by writing as he did was to induce a state of confusion in the
reader as a preliminary step towards acquiring a more open and 'scientific cast of
mind'. One difficulty with this view is that by the time Bacon came to prepare a new
edition of the *Essays* in 1625 he had arguably abandoned the project of a demonstrative civil science – if he ever thought it was feasible in the first place (see Box;
Peltonen 1996: 292–5). Another difficulty is that this account of Bacon's aims is hard
to reconcile with his intentions in writing as he did (on the distinction between intentions *in* and *by* writing, see Skinner, 260–1). The 1625 volume was clearly a contribution to the genre of the advice book, as is underlined by the two presentation copies
intended for the Duke of Buckingham (the dedicatee) and the Prince of Wales (see
Bacon 1985: xix–xxxi). But if Bacon's intention in writing and publishing the work
was to offer immediately useful political advice, then it is hard to see why he chose
to do so in what is, according to Fish at least, a 'style that confuses and unsettles'
(Fish 1972: 378).

At the last moment, Fish appears to recoil from his own thesis by revealing that
notwithstanding 'their provisionality the *Essays* are finally objects; they are not used
up in the reading but remain valuable as source material for future consultation' (Fish
1972: 154). But it is the *Essays* that have failed, not the theory. For as artefacts which
are not altogether 'used up in the reading', they fall short of the theoretical ideal of
total self-consumption. And even as 'objects' they are drearily literal stuff, 'valuable'
only for reference purposes.

The most direct way of challenging this somewhat depressing verdict on the *Essays*
is to re-contextualize them and thereby restore their historical identity. Of the essays
from the 1625 collection which are discussed by Fish, the one which would benefit
most from such an approach is 'Of Simulation and Dissimulation' (for the text, see
Bacon 1996: 349–51). The origins of this essay on simulation (pretending to be what
you are not) and dissimulation (not seeming to be what you are), lay not in any scientific programme but in the so-called new humanism of the late sixteenth century.
The complicated alignment of leading figures like Lipsius, Montaigne and Bacon in
relation to each other and to their classical mentors, the Stoic philosopher Seneca and
the historian Tacitus, was first sketched by Croll. But he was looking largely at the
prose style(s) that characterized the new humanist configuration, whereas recent scholars have been more interested in the intellectual programme that underpinned it.
According to Richard Tuck, the years following the Massacre of St Bartholomew's Eve

in 1572, were the time 'when scepticism, Stoicism and Tacitism came together to make a mixture as powerful and soon as all-pervasive as the Ciceronian humanism of the Quattrocento had been' (63).

The crucible for these developments – at least in northern Europe – was the French court, presided over by the Queen Mother, Marie de Medici, the daughter of the ruler of Florence to whom Machiavelli had dedicated *The Prince*. Italian émigrés were prominent in these circles, and one of their number, the historian Davila, later described how King Henri III would retire

> every day after dinner with Baccio de Bene, and Giacopo Corbinelli, both Florentines, men exceedingly learned in the Greek and Latin studies, making them read unto him Polybius and Cornelius Tacitus; but much more often *The Discourses* and *Prince* of Machiavel; whose readings stirring him up, he was so much the more transported with his own secret plots.
>
> (Quoted in Tuck, 42)

The least surprising item here is Machiavelli's *Prince*, a work that systematically inverts orthodox political morality (see Machiavelli, xix–xx). For example, whereas the Roman moral philosopher Cicero advised in his *De officiis* (*On Duties*) that the force and deceit typified by the lion and the fox are alien to human nature, Machiavelli urges in chapter 18 ('How rulers should keep their promises') that the ruler 'should imitate both the lion and the fox'. And whereas Cicero decreed that pretence and concealment ought to be eliminated from the whole of our lives (*ex omni vita simulatio dissimulatioque tollenda est*), Machiavelli positively insists that one must be a great feigner and dissembler (*gran simulatore e dissimulatore*) (Cicero, 44–5 (1.13.41), 330–1 (3.15.61); Machiavelli, 62). Having in effect rejected Cicero, it is no surprise that this group embraced Tacitus. The writings in which he dissected imperial Rome were increasingly regarded as a storehouse of political techniques to be employed for the purposes both of setting up a tyranny and surviving under one. Thus the account of Tiberius in the *Annals* dwells repeatedly on his power to manipulate others through the art of dissimulation (see 1.4, 4.71, 6.50). Moreover, in 1574 the Stoic scholar Justus Lipsius published a definitive new edition of Tacitus, and followed this up in 1589 with a political handbook (translated from the Latin in 1594 as *Six Books of Politics or Civil Doctrine*) which quoted Tacitus no fewer than 547 times. Lipsius agreed fully with Machiavelli about the importance of simulation and dissimulation; a prince *'having to deal with a fox'* should *'play the fox'* (113). Finally, Jacopo Corbinelli's involvement suggests that the work of Francesco Guicciardini, another admirer of Tacitus, was also read by this group since in 1576 he published the first edition of Guicciardini's *Ricordi* (maxims) as *Piu consigli et avvertimenti* and dedicated it to the Queen Mother. What made this a key text in the new humanism as much as anything was its aphoristic style; indeed Guicciardini was soon hailed by Francesco Sansovino as 'il primo inventore di queste Propositioni, Regole, Massime, Assiomi, Oracoli, Precetti, Sentenze, Probabili' (Sansovino, 100b).

As a member of the entourage of Sir Amias Paulet, the English ambassador to the French court, Bacon was able to observe this milieu for himself between 1576 and 1579, a period he came to regard as formative in his own development. His awareness of the influences at work on the French monarchy would have been sharpened in 1577 when his brother Edward became one of the dedicatees of the Latin edition of Innocent Gentillet's *Anti-Machiavel*, which, as its title suggests, systematically denounced the Machiavellianism of the Queen Mother and her acolytes (Jardine and Stewart, 62). At one point in 'Of Counsel', drafted after 1607 and first published in 1612, Bacon canvassed various solutions to 'inconveniences' such as the lack of secrecy, noting that 'the doctrine of Italy, and the practice of France, in some kings' times, hath introduced *cabinet* councils', which he thought 'a remedy worse than the disease'. Although Kiernan suggests that Bacon was thinking especially of Henri IV, the particular conjunction of doctrine and practice is actually more redolent of his predecessor. Indeed, Bacon's fascination with this Franco-Italian brand of politics shows itself even at the level of etymology. Thus the use here of 'cabinet' in a political sense is one of the earliest recorded, but while in 1612 this appears to reflect the influence of the French *cabinet*, the 1638 Latin translation of the essay employs the Italianate form *cabinetti* (properly *gabinetti*, first used in its political sense in Italian by Davila) (Bacon 1996: 380; 1985: 216). And the same conjunction is writ large in the title of the 1625 edition: *The Essays or Counsels Civil and Moral*; just as *Essays* gestures towards Montaigne's *Essais*, so *Counsels* gestures towards Guicciardini's *Consigli*. For although Bacon is often associated most closely with just the two genres of essay and aphorism, he was actually familiar with the full repertoire which Sansovino identified as appropriate to civil knowledge; advertisements (*avvertimenti*), rules (*regole*), axioms (*assiomi*), maxims (*massime*), precepts (*precetti*), and sentences (*sentenze*) (for examples, see Bacon 1996: 265, 267, 270, 286).

Judged by its title alone, 'Of Simulation and Dissimulation' identifies itself as a contribution to a well-established discourse, the parameters of which were set by Cicero's earnest repudiation of these complementary forms of deceit, and Machiavelli's satirical endorsement of them. However, Bacon does not wish to sanction either of these positions but to explore a rather different range of possibilities. This is signalled by the opening words of the essay:

> Dissimulation is but a faint kind of policy or wisdom; for it asketh a strong wit and a strong heart to know when to tell the truth, and to do it. Therefore it is the weaker sort of politiques that are the great dissemblers.
>
> (Bacon 1996: 349)

What makes this gambit so arresting is that Bacon emphatically chooses to focus on dissimulation alone. That is to say, he splits apart the double formula that was entrenched in the literature both conceptually and linguistically (*simulatio et dissimulatio, simulazione e dissimulazione, simulación y dissimulación*, and so on), and discards one element of it. Indeed it should be noted that, other than in the title, the two terms are only considered together as a pair in the concluding paragraph of the essay (and arguably not even then). Considered singly, dissimulation is then dismissed as the hallmark not of the strong but of the 'weaker sort of politiques'.

In the next phase of his argument, Bacon persists with dissimulation but now treating it in apposition to 'arts or policy' rather than, as might have been expected, simulation. This new pairing is decisively established on the authority of Tacitus, with a pulverizing battery of quotations from the *Annals*, the *Histories* and the *Agricola* (it is likely that these were taken from the 1595 Lipsius edition; see Bacon 1985: 250):

> Tacitus saith, 'Livia sorted well with the arts of her husband and dissimulation of her son'; attributing arts or policy to Augustus, and dissimulation to Tiberius.
>
> (Bacon 1996: 349)

Once again, however, dissimulation comes off worse, as Bacon finds in favour of the Augustan rather than the Tiberian mode of conduct. This is because those who have 'that penetration of judgment' which enables them to decide what matters are appropriate 'to be laid open, and what to be secreted, and what to be showed at half lights', would actually be hampered in their conduct of affairs by a constant 'habit of dissimulation'. While for those lacking in judgement dissimulation is 'generally' the safest option, it is merely one of the choices open to the more able:

> Certainly the ablest men that were have had all an openness and frankness of dealing; and a name of certainty and veracity; but . . . at such times when they thought the case indeed required dissimulation, if then they used it, it came to pass that the former opinion spread abroad of their good faith and clearness of dealing made them almost invisible.
>
> (Bacon 1996: 350)

In short, openness incorporates dissimulation.

However, that is not quite the end of it. For Bacon also appears to be suggesting that openness is not merely inclusive of, but itself actually *is*, a form of dissimulation. This becomes clearer when we consider some of the materials upon which this passage is based. The first is one of Guicciardini's maxims:

> A truthful, open nature [*natura vera e libera*] is universally liked and is, indeed, a noble thing; but it can be harmful. Deception [*simulazione*], on the other hand, is useful and sometimes even necessary, given the wickedness of man; but it is odious and ugly. Thus, I do not know which to choose. I suppose you ought ordinarily to embrace the one without, however, abandoning the other. That is to say, in the ordinary course of events practice the former so that you will gain a reputation for being a sincere person [*el nome di persona libera*]. And nevertheless, on certain important and rare occasions, use deception. If you do this, your deception will be more useful and more successful because, having a reputation for sincerity, you will be more easily believed.
>
> (Guicciardini 1970: 107; 1951: 114; see 1576: 39–40)

Here Guicciardini coolly opens up a distinction between nature and reputation, suggesting that, whether or not you actually are sincere, acquiring a reputation for sincerity will certainly facilitate deceit. The second source is Bacon's Latin portrait of Julius Caesar ('Imago Civilis Julii Caesaris'), of unknown date but first published posthumously in 1658. Caesar, Bacon observes,

> was taken to be by no means cunning or wily, but frank and veracious [*apertus et verax*]. And though he was in fact a consummate master of simulation and dissimulation [*summus simulationis et dissimulationis artifex esset*], and made up entirely of arts, insomuch that nothing was left to his nature except what art had approved, nevertheless there appeared in him nothing of artifice, nothing of dissimulation; and it was thought that his nature and disposition had full play and that he did but follow the bent of them.
>
> (Bacon 1870: 336, 342)

Caesar's sincerity, however, can have been nothing other than a matter of reputation because his *persona* was artificial through and through. In his case, apparent sincerity was not so much a means of facilitating deceit as the ultimate instance of it – the art which conceals art. The paradox Bacon thus arrives at is that to be open and truthful (or *apertus et verax* or *libera e vera*) is in fact the best way to render oneself and one's dissimulation 'almost invisible'.

For the next phase of argument, Bacon's model is not Tacitus but Lipsius, whose work he clearly admired. (In a letter of *Advice to Fulke Greville on his Studies*, nominally from the Earl of Essex but actually from Bacon, Greville was urged to make use of epitomes such as Lipsius' *Politicorum sive civilis doctrinae libri sex* (1589) or *Six Books of Politics or Civil Doctrine* (see Bacon 1996: 102). When discussing political prudence, Lipsius discriminates between 'light', 'middle', and 'great' deceit, of which he urges the first, tolerates the second and condemns the third (Lipsius, 115). Bacon now adopts the same triple structure, considering secrecy, dissimulation and simulation in turn. The first, secrecy, is

> when a man leaveth himself without observation, or without hold to be taken, what he is. The second, Dissimulation, in the negative; when a man lets fall signs and arguments, that he is not that he is. And the third, Simulation, in the affirmative; when a man industriously and expressly feigns and pretends to be that he is not.
>
> (Bacon 1996: 350)

Secrecy he finds 'both politic and moral', while dissimulation can hardly be avoided if secrecy is to be maintained, but simulation is 'more culpable'.

The simple arithmetical progression that governs the essay is maintained to the end. Thus the last paragraph rather insistently considers three advantages and three disadvantages of simulation and dissimulation, treated for these purposes not as a complementary pair but as completely synonymous terms. Only in the very last sentence, which recapitulates the argument of the essay as a whole, is its full quadruple structure finally revealed:

The best composition and temperature is to have openness in fame and opinion; secrecy in habit; dissimulation in seasonable use; and a power to feign, if there be no remedy. (Bacon 1996: 351)

The four elements are thus folded into one 'composition'. At no point, however, has Bacon allowed the essay to come to rest on the conventional pairing of simulation and dissimulation as promised in the title. But that of course is the point of the essay.

A re-contextualized reading may not seem very different from Fish's; in both Bacon is intent on rearranging the reader's 'mental furniture'. From the phenomenological point of view, however, there can be no consequences other than purely mental ones, such as being confused or troubled. But for Bacon and his readers challenging the conventional categories might well give them an edge in the practical world of politics. After all, what they were living through was not only the era of the Reformation and the Counter-Reformation, but, as Zagorin aptly terms it, the 'Age of Dissimulation' (Zagorin 1990: 330).

REFERENCES AND FURTHER READING

Bacon, Francis (1870). *The Works of Francis Bacon*, ed. James Spedding, Robert Leslie Ellis and Douglas Denon Heath, vol. 6. London: Longman.

——(1985). *The Essayes or Counsels, Civill and Morall*, ed. Michael Kiernan. Oxford: Clarendon Press.

——(1996). *Francis Bacon*, ed. Brian Vickers. Oxford: Oxford University Press.

Box, Ian (1982). Bacon's *Essays*: From Political Science to Political Prudence, *History of Political Thought*, 3, 31–49.

Bradford, Alan T. (1983). 'Stuart Absolutism and the 'Utility' of Tacitus', *Huntington Library Quarterly*, 46, 17–55.

Burke, Peter (1991). 'Tacitism, Scepticism and Reason of State'. In J. H. Burns (ed.), *The Cambridge History of Political Thought 1450–1700*. Cambridge: Cambridge University Press.

Cicero (1975). *De officiis*, ed. Walter Miller. Cambridge, MA and London: Harvard University Press and William Heinemann Ltd.

Crane, Ronald S. (1968). 'The Relation of Bacon's *Essays* to His Program for the Advancement of Learning'. In B. Vickers (ed.), *Essential Articles* (pp. 272–92).

Croll, Morris W. (1971). 'Attic Prose: Lipsius, Montaigne, Bacon'. In S. E. Fish (ed.), *Seventeenth-Century Prose* (pp. 3–25).

Fish, Stanley E. (1971). 'Georgics of the Mind: The Experience of Bacon's Essays'. In Stanley E. Fish (ed.), *Seventeenth-Century Prose: Modern Essays in Criticism*. New York: Oxford University Press.

——(1972). *Self-consuming Artifacts: The Experience of Seventeenth-century Literature*. Berkeley, CA: University of California Press.

Guicciardini, Francesco (1576). *Piu consigli et avvertimenti*, ed. Jacopo Corbinelli. Paris.

——(1951). *Ricordi*, ed. Raffaele Spongano. Firenze: G. C. Sansoni.

——(1970). *Maxims and Reflections of a Renaissance Statesman (Ricordi)*, tr. Mario Domandi, intro. Nicolai Rubinstein. Gloucester, MA: Peter Smith.

Jardine, Lisa and Stewart, Alan (1998). *Hostage to Fortune: The Troubled Life of Francis Bacon*. London: Victor Gollancz.

Levy, F. J. (1986). 'Francis Bacon and the Style of Politics', *English Literary Renaissance*, 16, 101–21.

Lipsius, Justus (1594). *Six Bookes of Politickes or Civil Doctrine*, tr. William Jones. London.

Machiavelli, Niccolò (1988). *The Prince*, eds Quentin Skinner and Russell Price. Cambridge: Cambridge University Press.

Peltonen, Markku (1995). *Classical Humanism and Republicanism in English Political Thought*

1570–1640. Cambridge: Cambridge University Press.

——(ed.) (1996). *The Cambridge Companion to Bacon.* Cambridge: Cambridge University Press.

Salmon, J. H. M. (1989). 'Stoicism and Roman Example: Seneca and Tacitus in Jacobean England', *Journal of the History of Ideas,* 50, 199–225.

Sansovino, Francesco (1583). *Propositioni, overo considerationi in materia di cose di stato.* Vinegia.

Skinner, Quentin (1988). *Meaning and Context: Quentin Skinner and His Critics,* ed. James Tully. Cambridge: Polity Press.

Smuts, R. Malcolm (1987). 'Court-centred Politics and the Uses of Roman Historians, c.1590–1630'. In Kevin Sharpe and Peter Lake (eds), *Culture and Politics in Early Stuart England* (pp. 21–43). Basingstoke: Macmillan.

Tuck, Richard (1993). *Philosophy and Government 1572–651.* Cambridge: Cambridge University Press.

Vickers, Brian (1968). *Essential Articles for the Study of Francis Bacon.* Hamden, CN: Archon Books.

Zagorin, Perez (1990). *Ways of Lying: Dissimulation, Persecution, and Conformity in Early Modern Europe.* Cambridge, MA and London: Harvard University Press.

——(1998). *Francis Bacon.* Princeton, NJ: Princeton University Press.

21

Lancelot Andrewes's Good Friday 1604 Sermon

Richard Harries

The major sermons of Lancelot Andrewes (1555–1626) were preached at the courts of Elizabeth and James I. The importance of the setting has been established by McCullough. The preacher, raised in a pulpit, faced the sovereign in a closet in the west gallery. The closet windows both advertised and guarded the royal presence and the iconographical features surrounding it accentuated the monarch's role as head of both church and state. Sovereigns could interrupt the sermon, as when Queen Elizabeth told a preacher to stop railing against images. Below the gallery the court was arranged with Lords on one side and Ladies on the other, all seated according to rank. Monarchs lived a hidden life and preachers had privileged access which could be used for criticism as well as praise. Against the background of turbulent political events and court intrigues, this setting created an atmosphere of immediacy and drama. Preaching of a high standard was expected and appreciated. 'The sermon – not Shakespearean drama, and not even the Jonsonian masque – was the pre-eminent literary genre at the Jacobean court' (McCullough p. 125).

Andrewes spent much of his academic life in Cambridge, eventually becoming master of his college, Pembroke, in 1589. Cambridge was being increasingly influenced by Puritanism but, as John Aubrey recounts in a waspish anecdote against Puritan hypocrisy, Andrewes 'was not of the brotherhood'. Andrewes turned down two bishoprics but in 1605 became Bishop of Chichester, then Bishop of Ely before becoming Bishop of Winchester, where he remained from 1619 until he died in 1626. This Good Friday sermon was preached when he was Dean of Westminster, which he became in 1601. He was famed as a preacher in his own time and much appreciated by Elizabeth and especially James I. But from the end of the seventeenth century until mid-way through the nineteenth century his style went out of fashion (Chadwick). Samuel Johnson, whose high Anglicanism was akin to that of Andrewes, and who had read omnivorously, never refers to him. It was the Catholic revival (the Oxford Movement) that brought about a new appreciation of Andrewes and his eleven-volume *Works* were published in the Library of Anglo-Catholic Theology. T. S. Eliot, in his

1926 essay on Andrewes, re-established the position of Andrewes as a prose stylist. Eliot wrote of the sermons that 'They rank with the finest English prose of their time, of any time'. In addition to recent historical work on Andrewes there has been an emphasis on the affinity between the theology of Andrewes and that of the Orthodox church and an appreciation of him as a person who unites in his outlook both western and eastern Christianity.

Andrewes was called upon to preach for the court on the major festivals of Christmas, Easter and Whitsun as well as the special thanksgivings for deliverance from the gunpowder plot (5 November) and the Gowrie conspiracy (5 August) but we know that he was deeply immersed in the liturgical cycle of the church from his remarkable private prayers in Latin, Greek and Hebrew (the *Preces Privatae*). Each sermon sets out the whole scheme of salvation but around the axis of the particular festival being celebrated (Lossky). Among the ninety-six of his sermons published three years after his death by royal command three Good Friday sermons are preserved, those for 1597, 1604 and 1605. The text for the 1604 sermon is Lamentations 1:12:

> Have ye no regard, O all ye that pass by the way? Consider and behold, if ever there were sorrow like my sorrow, which was done unto me, wherewith the Lord did afflict me in the day of the fierceness of his wrath.

This text is the refrain of the reproaches used at the traditional liturgical service on Good Friday, again indicating Andrewes's feeling for the liturgical year. As these had been excised from the reformed rite part of the thrill of hearing the sermon would have been the slightly dangerous reference to a pre-Reformation liturgy. Even more significant, this text, like others used by him, was the exact opposite of a peg on which to hang a few thoughts. All through the sermon he stays close to the text, unwrapping layers of meaning, digging deeper and deeper into its significance. There is in Andrewes no trace of self-indulgence, no gimmicks, no rhetoric for its own sake, no concession to fashion. He is wholly given over to the text and what it seeks to communicate. He does not play with words, as Aubrey suggested, nor does he use his enormous erudition (besides Latin, Greek and Hebrew he came to know Aramaic, Syriac and Arabic among the oriental languages and no fewer than fifteen modern languages). His philology is always at the service of the text and its message. As T. S. Eliot wrote:

> When Andrewes begins his sermon, from beginning to end you are sure that he is wholly in his subject, unaware of anything else, that his emotion grows as he penetrates more deeply into his subject.

Andrewes read and prayed from 07.00 to 12.00 every day. Indeed 'He doubted they were no true scholars, that came to speak with him before noon.' The sermon that is considered here is one of the fruits of that kind of prolonged intellectual and spiritual attention over many years.

The central theme and image, the point on which the whole sermon revolves, is the notion of regarding. The text begins 'Have ye no regard' and continues 'Consider and behold'. To regard is to look, to turn away from ourselves and behold what is actually there. But it also indicates a proper valuation of what is there, so opening ourselves to it that it matters to us. These words, as used in the liturgical tradition of the church and as treated by Andrewes, are ones which are in effect spoken by Jesus from the cross. They are spoken not so much to the historical figures associated with the crucifixion as to the listeners before him in the chapel of Whitehall Palace.

> Be it then to us, as to them it was, and as most properly it is, the speech of the Son of God, as this day hanging on the cross, to a sort of careless people, that go up and down without any manner of regard of these his sorrows and sufferings, so worthy of all regard.[1]

'A sort of careless people, that go up and down without any manner of regard' well conjures up the image of courtiers walking up and down the spacious rooms of the Palace, gossiping, perhaps even sneaking in late to the royal gallery, which they could do relatively unobserved. He knows that some who pass by come to church because they have little else to do but others have great matters on their mind, especially great personages. But they too must stay and consider: 'The regard of this is worthy the staying of a journey. It is worth the considering of those, that have never so great affairs in hand.' Then, with pastoral affirmation, he makes the point that those before him have stayed.

If the axle or pivot is regard, the method Andrewes chooses in order to bring about a proper regard is that of comparison. So the refrain that runs through the sermon is 'if ever there was . . . *si fuerit sicut*'. In a series of comparisons and considerations he shows that there is nothing comparable *non sicut*. What emerges here is the clear, logical ordering of the sermon. Andrewes presents a structure, like some Renaissance building, with a proper symmetry and elegance. Yet the image of a classical building going up does not do justice to the ever-increasing depth of analysis of the text, with an accompanying intensity of emotion to those following the analysis. It is remarkable but understandable for those drawn into the logic of the sermon that Eliot should use a phrase like 'ecstasy of assent' for the culmination of this logical learned analysis.

Andrewes describes the physical suffering of Christ but does not indulge in this. He dwells more on the anguish of spirit, focusing on Luke 22:44 when Jesus, in the Garden of Gethsemene was said to be in an agony.

> No manner of violence offered him in body, no man touching him or being near him; in a cold night, for they were fain to have a fire within doors, lying abroad in the air and upon the cold earth, to be all of a sweat, and that sweat to be blood; and not as they call it *diaphoreticus*, 'a thin faint sweat' but *Grumosus*, 'of great drops;' and those so many, so plenteous, as they went through his apparel and all; and through all stream to

the ground, and that in great abundance; read, enquire and consider, *sic fuerit sudor sicut sudor iste*; 'if ever there were sweat like this sweat of his'. Never the like sweat certainly, and therefore never the like sorrow.

It is interesting that he relates Jesus in a sweat in the Garden of Gethsemene to the story of the denial of Peter, when the gospels say that Peter came close to the fire to keep warm, hence the cold. We are reminded of the line in the famous Christmas sermon of Andrewes, on the three kings, which Eliot incorporated into a poem 'A cold coming they had of it at this time of the year.'

Andrewes then goes on to consider the third aspect of distress, that in all this sorrow Jesus had no one to comfort him. Even God had apparently abandoned him and left him like a weather-beaten tree, all desolate and forlorn.

'My God, my God, why hast thou foresaken me?' [Matthew 27:46] Weigh well that cry, consider it well, and tell me, *sic fuerit clamor sicut clamor iste*, 'if ever there were cry like that of his;' never the like cry, and therefore never the like sorrow.

Although the strength of a sermon by Andrewes lies in its cumulative effect there are individual sentences which themselves have extraordinary poetic qualities. The one just quoted is an example. There is alliteration and assonance. There is a musical contrast between the deep 'weigh well . . . , consider it well, and tell' . . . with the rising, interpolated pain of . . . *sic fuerit clamor sicut clamor iste* 'cry . . . never the like cry'. There is also the sense of solemnity brought out by the balance of particular sentences 'never the like cry, and therefore never the like sorrow'.

Having considered the suffering of Jesus on the cross Andrewes then goes on to examine who it is that really suffers. This is not just a human being, nor even a prince or king, however noble. This is the Son of God. This is not just an innocent person but an innocent God who is suffering. Andrewes is appalled and awestruck.

Then in a nice pastoral touch which again brings home the immediacy of the sermon, a sense that real people are being addressed and their very souls struggled with Andrewes adds 'Men may drowsily hear it and coldly affect it, but principalities and powers stand abashed at it.'

The preacher goes on to consider why all this happens and draws out the meaning of the last part of the text 'wherewith the Lord did afflict me in the day of the fierceness of his wrath'. This suffering is nothing less than the wrath of God, wrath visited on human sinfulness but voluntarily borne by the innocent Jesus on our behalf.

Andrewes emphasizes that this is for every single human being. Quoting Isaiah 53:6, 'All we as sheep were gone astray, and turned every man to his own way; and the Lord has laid upon him the iniquity of us all' he continues "All," "all" even those that pass to and fro, and for all this regard neither him nor his passion'.

To bring home the fact that it is human sin that has brought Jesus to this state he cleverly uses the story in 2 Samuel 12 about King David and Nathan. David wanted some land owned by one of his military commanders, Uriah, so David arranged for him to go to the front line and be killed. Nathan the Prophet comes to David and tells a story about a rich man who stole a poor man's single lamb. David was angry when he heard this story and said that the rich man deserved to die. At which point Nathan tells David that he is the man. It is an indication of the background biblical knowledge which could be assumed by Andrewes that he does not need to tell the incident or story at all. He simply refers to Nathan's *tu es homo* 'Thou the man'.

Although it was human sin that brought Christ to the cross it was also God's love in order that he might rescue us from the effects of that sin both now and in eternity. In a fine phrase, Lancelot Andrewes refers to that from which Christ delivers us as 'a never dying death'. Out of his compassion Christ went to the cross. 'Even then in his love he regarded us, and so regarded us that he regarded not himself, to regard us.'

Andrewes pleads with his congregation. The court of James I was often a pretty coarse and lewd affair. It is said that Andrewes was held in very great respect and that people put aside some of their coarseness when he was around. He knew much of what went on. They knew that he knew. He wrestles with them for their eternal salvation.

> Yes sure, his complaint is just, 'Have ye no regard?' None? and yet never the like? None? and it pertains unto you? 'No regard?' As if it were some common ordinary matter, and the like never was? 'No regard?' As if it concerned you not a whit, and it toucheth you so near? As if He should say, Rare things you regard, yea, though they no ways pertain to you: this is exceeding rare, and will you not regard it? Again, things that nearly touch you you regard, though they be not rare at all: this toucheth you exceeding near, even as near as your soul toucheth you, and will you not yet regard it? Will neither of these by itself move you? Will not both these together move you? What will move you? Will pity? Here is distress never the like. Will duty? Here is a Person never the like. Will fear? Here is wrath never the like. Will remorse? Here are sins never the like. Will kindness? Here is love never the like. Will bounty? Here are benefits never the like. Will all these? Here they be all, all above any *sicut*, all in the highest degree.

Then he comes to the final thrust, a last desperate attempt to pierce their hearts: the complaint of Jesus on the cross 'Have ye no regard, all ye that pass by the way?' is indeed just.

> Sure it moved Him exceeding much; for among all the deadly sorrows of His most bitter Passion, this, even this, seemeth to be His greatest of all, and that which did most affect Him, even the grief of the slender reckoning most men have it in; as little respecting Him, as if He had done or suffered nothing at all for them.

This complaint moves heaven and earth but will it move us?

> The sun in Heaven shrinking in his light, the earth trembling under it, the very stones cleaving in sunder as if they had sense and sympathy of it, and sinful men only not moved with it.

Andrewes ends his sermon on two notes which bring to the fore his long experience as a pastor and confessor. For he knows that our motives are always mixed and he knows that however intense the protestations of our love for Christ, they quickly fade. Yet, though they may fade, though we can offer but little in that Whitehall Chapel in the way of concentration or devotion, nevertheless that little is still better than nothing.

> But God help us poor sinners, and be merciful unto us! Our regard is a *non sicut* indeed, but it is backward, and in a contrary sense; that is, no where so shallow, so short or so soon done. It should be otherwise, it should have our deepest consideration this, and our highest regard.

But if that cannot be had, our nature is so heavy, and flesh and blood so dull of apprehension in spiritual things yet at leastwise some regard. Some I say; the more the better, but in anywise some, and not as here no regard, none at all.

Most of the characteristic features of sermons by Andrewes are apparent in this one. First, his understanding of the Hebrew scriptures, the Old Testament, as providing types or figures which find their focus and fulfilment in Jesus. Andrewes was not primarily interested in the literal or historical understanding of the text or its allegorical interpretation. He saw Christ speaking in the Old Testament in ways that could be recognized as such in the New. So, for example, he does not deny that the text on which he preaches appears in the Book of Lamentations which people believed was written by the prophet Jeremiah. But he argues that these words are most properly understood as words of Jesus from the cross spoken to every generation. This highlights Andrewes's understanding of time and history. For him the past is brought into the present through an anamnesis, a remembrance which is not just confined to the eucharist. Scriptural history has been raised into a universal contemporanety. Lossky believes that this influenced Eliot in the *Four Quartets*.

This way of interpreting scripture was not individualistic but belongs to the mind of Christ in the church. Andrewes is steeped in the early fathers. But he does not use their sayings as proof-texts. Instead he sees them as part of a living tradition of which he also is a part. In this there is a particular affinity with the eastern Fathers (Lossky).

Andrewes also has a profound sense of the limitation of words, a sense of the apophatic way, a proper reticence before the appalling mystery of Christ's death. Reflecting on the anguish of soul in the Garden of Gethsemene he says

> That hour, what His feelings were, it is dangerous to define; we know them not, we may be too bold to determine of them. To very good purpose it was, that the ancient fathers of the Greek church in their liturgy, after they have recounted all the particular pains, as they are set down in His passion, and by all, and by every one of them, called for mercy, do after all shut up all with this, . . . 'By thine unknown sorrows and sufferings felt by thee, but not distinctly known by us, have mercy upon us, and save us!'

Then before the cry on the cross, developing a meaning of a Hebrew word he said

> His soul was even as a scorched heath-ground, without so much as any drop of dew of divine comfort; as a naked tree – no fruit to refresh him within, no leaf to give him shadow without; the power of darkness let loose to afflict him, the influence of comfort restrained to relieve him. It is a *non sicut* this, it cannot be expressed as it should, and as other things may; in silence we may admire it, but all our words will not reach it.

Mention was made earlier of the drama, the genuine drama, of Andrewes wrestling for the soul of his Sovereign and the souls of the Sovereign's sycophants. The playwright John Osborne was once quoted as saying that he would far rather go to church on Sunday than to attend a play in the west end. During the 1970s, frustrated with passive middle-class audiences, he sought to shock and engage them in new ways. He failed. In the Royal Chapel of Whitehall, performer and audience were engaged in a struggle of life and death, everlasting life and everlasting death. For a preacher who went too far in his criticism could, at the very least, end in prison. A sovereign who did not go far enough in the way of righteousness would, in the conviction of the preacher, end up in everlasting darkness, 'a dying death'. The audience would want to turn it into a play, one which they could applaud or execrate, from which they could stand apart or to which they could be indifferent. The preacher sought always the existential engagement, the point of personal responsibility, *tu es homo*.

When it comes to Andrewes's style an equally surprising modern comes to mind, though this time someone who succeeded, Samuel Beckett. Beckett achieved his effects in part through a culmination of subtle, complex, poetic repetitions. Andrewes does the same both in individual paragraphs and in the sermon as a whole, especially in the variations he rings on the theme of *non sicut*. He asks 'If ever there were sorrow like my sorrow'. But in respect of *dolor* there is nothing comparable, *non sicut*; nothing comparable either to Christ's sweat in the Garden of Gethsemene, no *sudor*; nor to the cry from the cross, no *clamor*. And above all there is no comparable love, no *amor*. Always there is a *non sicut*.

Few have preached on this theme with the power of Andrewes. No one has done so with his combination of precision and passion; a passion totally contained in and expressed through such carefully ordered learning; learning wholly given over to its subject. There is *a non sicut* here too.

NOTE

1   The text used is Seymour-Smith, M (1976) *The English Sermon, Volume I: 1550–1650*. Cheadle; Carcanet (capitals have been kept only for the divine names). The eleven-volume *Works* ed. J. P. Wilson and James Bliss was published in the Library of Anglo-Catholic Theology, Oxford 1841–54. There is a selection of sermons edited with an introduction by G. M. Story, 1967, and one by P. E. Hewison, 1995.

References and Further Reading

Allchin, A. B. (1992). 'Lancelot Andrewes'. In Geoffrey Rowell (ed.), *The English Tradition and the Genius of Anglicanism* (pp. 145–64). Wantage: Ikon.

Aubrey, J. (1975). *Brief Lives*. London: The Folio Society.

Chadwick, O. (1999). 'A Defence of Lancelot Andrewes' Sermons', *Theology*, Nov./Dec.

Eliot, T. S. (1928). *For Lancelot Andrewes: Essays on Style and Order*. London: Faber.

Lake, P. (1991). 'Lancelot Andrewes, John Buckeridge and Avant-garde'. In Linda Levy Peck (ed.), *The Mental world of the Jacobean Court* (pp. 113–33). Cambridge: Cambridge University Press.

Lossky, N. (1991). *Lancelot Andrewes the Preacher (1555–1626)*. Oxford: Clarendon.

McCullough, P. E. (1998). *Sermons at Court, Politics and Religion in Elizabethan and Jacobean Preaching*. Cambridge: Cambridge University Press.

——(1998). 'Making Dead Men Speak, Laudinism, Print and the Works of Lancelot Andrewes 1636–1643', *The Historical Journal*, 41 (42), 401–24.

Welsby, P. A. (1958). *Lancelot Andrewes*. London: SPCK.

Miller, E. C. Jr (1984). *Toward a Fuller Vision*. Wilson, CN: Morehouse Barlow.

22
Herbert's 'The Elixir'
Judith Weil

Teach me, my God and King,
In all things thee to see,
And what I do in any thing,
To do it as for thee:

Not rudely, as a beast,
To run into an action;
But still to make thee prepossest,
And give it his perfection.

A man that looks on glass,
On it may stay his eye;
Or if he pleaseth, through it pass,
And then the heav'n espy.

All may of thee partake:
Nothing can be so mean,
Which with his tincture (for thy sake)
Will not grow bright and clean.

A servant with this clause
Makes drudgery divine:
Who sweeps a room, as for thy laws,
Makes that and th'action fine.

This is the famous stone
That turneth all to gold:
For that which God doth touch and own
Cannot for less be told.[1]

George Herbert's lyric takes its title from the 'famous stone' stressed in its final stanza – that substance sought by alchemists which would supposedly change baser metals into purest gold. In her influential study, *The Metaphysical Poets*, Helen C. White analysed the process by which Herbert revised an earlier version of 'The Elixir' entitled 'Perfection'. She argued that his new final stanza containing the 'somewhat rigid alchemical figure brilliantly sums up the whole poem, with the completeness and firmness of arc that is one of the characteristic movements of Herbert's mind' (p. 181). White's reading provides a useful point of departure because she misses the surprise of finding an 'elixir' among the qualities she so values in Herbert's poetry, 'the little passages of daily life and the small passages of our common environment' (p. 182). How could a notorious metal-changer/tester have slipped into Herbert's *Temple*? And does this metaphor behave with the fixity or finality that White perceives?

'Elixir', according to the *OED*, derives from a compound of Arabic 'al' with Greek 'xerion', a 'desiccative powder for wounds'. It may refer, in addition to the 'stone' or alchemical processes, to a drug or essence which prolongs life indefinitely, to a 'strong extract or tincture' (including a quintessence, soul, or kernel), and to a pharmaceutical concoction. Herbert's 'stone' could be dry and wet, a dust and a rock, a core principle and a boiled-down reduction, an occult cause and an ordinary domestic medicine. While scarcely so paradoxical, other words in this remarkable poem also seem to have been touched into mobility. I begin with *OED*'s gathering of senses available to Herbert because his poem activates and increases its significations by compressing them or by turning restrictive figures of speech into conduits and connectors. Through a closer reading of the poem I will try to account for the propriety of its final metaphor, the 'famous stone'. I will also surmise that a specific cultural context, housekeeping or hospitality, helps to clarify the work being done by the language of the poem.

Like other poems near the conclusion of *The Temple*, 'The Elixir' communicates a joyful, straightforward trust in the speaker's reciprocal relationship with God. It exhibits that simplicity of representation which the following poem, 'A Wreath', identifies with God's ways, as opposed to the 'crooked winding ways' of a sinful Herbert. Arnold Stein comments that 'Most of what he has to say to God and himself is relatively unhandicapped by the forbidding prestige of pure intellect' (p. 204). Following the method suggested by Herbert's own desire to understand sacred texts in 'The H. Scriptures. II' – 'Oh that I knew how all thy lights combine, / And the configurations of their glory!' – Herbert's readers often place individual poems like 'The Elixir' within patterns descried throughout *The Temple*. We can begin to understand Herbert's lyrics by treating them as their author treated 'constellations of the story' in Old and New Testaments: 'Thy words do find me out, and parallels bring, / And in another make me understood'.

Because of its emphasis on behaviour and action informed by God's presence, 'The Elixir' might be linked with 'The Windows': there Herbert compares the fusion of precept and practice within an effective minister to the story of Christ annealed in stained glass. If poems concerned with the preacher and his calling (cf. 'The Odour. 2. Cor. ii. 15.') shine out as an obvious configuration in which to view 'The Elixir', words and phrases within the poem can also draw our attention to other broad patterns of emphasis in *The Temple*. Herbert's opening personal address to 'my God and King' employs a form repeated in the Psalter as well as in *The Temple*, sounding a note of psalm-like sincerity. His third stanza could affiliate 'The Elixir' with more visionary ontological lyrics like 'The Glance'. Through the emphatic first line of the fourth stanza, 'All may of thee partake', he invokes the eucharist, celebrated by many of his lyrics and often taken by more Anglican commentators to be 'the marrow of Herbert's sensibility' (C. A. Patrides, 17). With his references to polishing something 'mean' or to the 'drudgery' of sweeping a room, Herbert seems to repudiate elitism in theology and society, inviting a scholar like Richard Strier to group 'The Elixir' with poems strongly motivated by a Protestant sense of grace: 'A true Hymn', 'Faith' and 'The Forerunners'.

When we read through 'The Elixir', we discover, I think, not a biographical or parabolic narrative but an interpenetrating set of constellations which shift as the poem becomes more familiar. The speaker whose first two lines address God with such urgent humility, chiming the vowel sounds of 'Teach' with those of its object and effects, appears to need no more instruction by the third stanza, which matter-of-factly counsels readers on how visions may be had. Not, in this case, by seeing through a glass darkly (1 Corinthians 13:12), but rather by passing through the 'glass' at will ('if he pleaseth'). Northrop Frye has observed that when Emily Dickinson 'meets an inadequacy in the English language she simply walks through it, as a child might do' (p. 203). Herbert seems to walk through laws of grammar which could indicate whether the eye or the man can 'pass' through the 'glass' and whether the pronoun 'he' in 'if he pleaseth' is human or divine. A heaven 'then' to be spied is accessible to 'Man' as it once was to Adam, according to 'The H. Communion': 'He might to heav'n from Paradise go, / As from one room t'another'. It seems ordinary, like the New Jerusalem glimpsed in the First Book of Edmund Spenser's *The Faerie Queene*: Angels descending 'to and fro' can 'wend' into 'that Citie' as 'commonly as friend does with his friend' (X, lvi, 2–5).

Using the figure of a passage through glass, Herbert connects his almost detachable and oracular third stanza to other types of movement in 'The Elixir': the repeated 'do's of stanza one, the perfected 'action' of stanza two, the implied work of purifying or cleaning in stanza four, the 'drudgery' of the servant who sweeps a room in stanza five, and the final transforming agency of the stone, whose power to 'touch and own' may both echo and answer the initial 'Teach me' prayer. Within 'The Elixir', 'perfection' acquires a dynamism latent in its Latin root, the verb 'perficio', meaning to 'carry out, accomplish, perform, finish, complete'. This sense of sufficient action emerges with special force in the vivid image of the sweeping servant whose work 'as for [with respect to] thy laws' seems to create the space of its own completion. Herbert's swept 'room' removes the legal grime and abstraction from 'clause' – referring back to the parenthesis which circumscribes and stipulates the significance of 'tincture' in the preceding stanza. It also suggests that 'clause', connoting enclosure and the ending of a grammatical period, has been opened up and made ready for new purposes.

Perhaps because the servant's sweeping offers the only action within the poem which can easily be visualized, it has often been noted by readers alert to material circumstances. For Marion Singleton, mindful of how Herbert the aristocratic courtier struggled to reform himself, the servant image suggests 'a descent to lowliness' as part of an unremitting 'effort' (p. 159) on which real change depended. 'Only a thoroughly worldly courtier of the late Renaissance could so sharply model a pattern of loyal service that fully incorporates the interior and exterior limits to "perfect freedom"' (11). Michael Schoenfeldt, also adept at recognizing anxiety about courtship in Herbert, cites Christopher Hill's opinion that the 'servant' stanza 'represented a point of view more common among employers and independent craftsmen than among employees' (p. 94). Schoenfeldt implies that Hill is pointing to Herbert's elitism, whereas Hill in fact argues that 'Puritans and others' were 'evolving a doctrine of the dignity of labour' ('property in a man's own labour and person') even as the English working class was demonstrating its 'hatred of wage labour' (pp. 234–5). Schoenfeldt himself regards the 'tincture (for thy sake)' as 'a kind of magical spell' and concludes that 'mortal agency is a necessary but misleading fiction under the rule of an omnipotent deity' (p. 179).

Surprisingly, those who emphasize Herbert's Puritan faith find little more dignity or freedom in his evocations of labour. Chana Bloch believes that he selected the servant image for its 'lowliness' rather than for its intrinsic value: 'the dignity of all vocations in the eye of God [was] a favourite theme of the Reformers'(p. 227). The 'aristocratic Herbert', she observes, probably never held a broom. In *Love Known*, Strier denies both that 'The Elixir' concerns preparation for a visionary ascent (Stein's opinion) and that it is even about 'actually doing things well' (p. 207). Strier reminds us (in connection with 'The Temper', 227–38) that Herbert generally treats spaces as metaphors; in *Resistant Structures* he takes Schoenfeldt and other new historicists to task for a 'systematic confusion of the vehicle with the tenor of metaphors' (p. 110). Nevertheless, his Reformation Protestant reading of 'The Elixir' (a strong influence on Schoenfeldt's material one) shrinks the dynamic expansiveness of Herbert's housekeeping tropes by making 'as for thee' a mere 'fiction', a 'tincture' that has become little more than a tint. God, Strier insists, does not supply a lack but accepts a 'frame of mind' (*Love Known*, 208).

It seems to me that Herbert has indeed dignified his servant figure, not only by brightening the dark glass of Christian dualism in his third stanza but also by equivocating on 'prepossest' in his second. According to Patrides, Herbert would have understood God's grace as 'above all "prevenient", anticipatory of man's behaviour by virtue of Christ's presence in history' (pp. 18–19). To 'prepossess' is to seize upon or to influence in advance – actions which seem impossible unless we imagine human agents as capacities preoccupied by God. When Herbert vows 'to make thee prepossest', he boldly anticipates divine ends with human means. If such theology were more logical, Stanley Fish might be right to argue that Herbert's human agents have 'no room to manoeuvre' (p. 160). But in this poem theology becomes unusually elastic. Herbert's prepossessing may explain why 'The Elixir', for all of its verbal movement, has almost no narrative. It also explains why his 'drudgery' is free from suggestions of political or magical coercion. Can it be coincidental that when Christ refers to a house as 'empty, swept, and garnished' in Matthew 12:44, he is describing a case of demonic possession? Such possession often coincides, in early modern texts, with awareness of servility and enslavement. 'The Elixir' may gesture toward a reciprocity between master and servant rarely glimpsed in paternalistic laws or in the discourse of household guides teaching total subordination of the servant's agency and will. To identify a biographical development (with Helen Vendler, 270–1) from a loftily 'intellectualised' second stanza to a humble fifth one may be to ignore a seventeenth-century constellation of meanings and to lose the active, creative force of the verb 'make(s)', shared between the agents of these two stanzas.[2]

As mentioned above, poems like 'The Windows' which refer to the services of a priest form an obvious group through which to approach 'The Elixir'. Such poems have also invited students of Herbert to enter his own *Rule of Holy Life for A Priest to the Temple, or The Country Parson*. For example, Stanley Stewart turns from 'Prayer II', an 'extemporaneous' private exercise characterized by '*Ease*' (p. 36), to Herbert's 'Anglican' approval of public ceremonial prayers, and he cites (pp. 37–8) from *A Priest* this sentence which also resonates with 'The Elixir':

> This is that which the Apostle calls a reasonable service, *Rom.* 12. when we speak not as parrots, without reason, or offer up such sacrifices as they did of old, which was of beasts devoid of reason; but when we use our reason, and apply our powers to the service of him that gives them.
>
> (p. 232)

Bloch compares Herbert's 'homely' poetic images with his comment that the country parson 'neither disdaineth . . . to enter into the poorest Cottage, though he even creep into it, and though it smell never so loathsomely' (p. 229, citing *Works*, 249). Equally pertinent are Herbert's reflections on Christ as the 'true householder' who used 'familiar things' to teach and uplift the 'meanest' of hearts and minds, 'even in the midst of their pains' (p. 261). Or his advice that pastors imitate Scripture by naming 'things of ordinary use', thereby showing 'they are not only to serve in the way of drudgery, but to be washed, and cleansed, and serve for lights even of Heavenly Truths' (p. 257). In her fine essay on 'The Windows', Judy Z. Kronenfeld writes that 'The Windows' is 'like a private, meditative version of "The Author's Prayer before Sermon"' (p. 65). This prayer with which Herbert ends *A Priest* includes an obvious parallel to 'The Elixir' – his direct appeal, 'Lord Jesu! teach thou me, that I may teach them' (p. 289).

Why add yet another dimension of meaning to the structures troped by 'glass' and 'room', to the richly semiotic 'houses', biblical or ecclesiastical, through which Herbert shapes his awareness of God in the human heart? If I propose that early modern hospitality might be relevant to 'The Elixir' it is because this practice, often mentioned in other poems, helps to explain its distinctive mood. 'Lent' ends with a surprising image for abstinence: the sin-starved soul joins the 'poor' being given a banquet at his own door. The speaker of 'Unkindness' has let 'the poor / And thou within them, starve at door'. Herbert imagines his prayers as noisy beggars both in 'Gratefulness' ('Perpetual knockings at thy door, / Tears sullying thy transparent rooms') and in 'Longing', but in the latter poem he also writes, 'Thy board is full, yet humble guests / Find nests'.

It is difficult to find in such poems the 'vision' which, in Schoenfeldt's view, prompted Herbert to represent noble hospitality: his 'profound insight into the power and prestige bestowed by the capability to feed others' (p. 201). Schoenfeldt cites the research of Felicity Heal to support his interpretation of 'Love III' as a strategic power struggle between courtly host and guest. But he omits her emphasis on the vigour of hospitality as a continuing, lived ideal in the seventeenth century (see Heal, 3–4, 89–90, 221–2). *All* men, she demonstrates, were expected to act as hosts within their means, providing food, drink and accommodation for neighbours and strangers, rich and poor. When 'harbingers' mark his door (and head) with white in 'The Forerunners', Herbert makes room for God, imagined as a lord or king approaching on progress, by parting with his 'beauteous words'. But when he writes about the well-ordered soul as God's household in 'The Family' ('where thou dwellest all is neat') or in 'Christmas' tropes on 'My dearest Lord' as an innkeeper offering 'all passengers most sweet relief', prestigious courtship seems far beside the point.

This innkeeper offers yet another example of prevenient grace on the part of a Lord who, in 'Holy Baptism II', 'didst lay hold, and antedate / My faith in me'. Within a few lines, the 'Christmas' passenger or traveller is praying 'Furnish and deck my soul, that thou mayst have / A better lodging then a rack or grave'. Hospitable house-keeping gives Herbert a trope for reciprocity between God and Humanity which fore-grounds the conditions of mutual trust. How beautifully he writes in 'Providence' about the 'curious art' filling God's 'house': 'Light without wind is glass: warm without weight / Is wool and fur: cool without closeness, shade.' In 'The Elixir' Herbert creates a temper of welcome and readiness without belabouring the work of preparation (as he does in his Latin poem, 'Martha: Maria'). Helen Wilcox has suggested that because Herbert turns his readers into participants, seventeenth century women were involved with his poetry 'at every stage of the transmission and reception of a text' (204). Perhaps children and servants as well as women would quickly have sensed the calmly festive mood of 'The Elixir' or have seen themselves in the 'glass' of its actions.

Compared with a house trope, that of an elixir, which Herbert uses only once, is surprisingly strange. But Herbert's 'stone' does not astonish or enchant in any way. As Singleton shows (p. 159), it replaces the hardness of graves and hearts so evident in the poems that begin *The Temple*. I may have taken Helen White too literally when she commends Herbert's final stanza for a 'precision and economy of statement that does justice to but also hides the fine elaboration of the thought' (p. 182). Economy, however, once meant 'oeconomy', the arts of managing a household. 'The Elixir' turns 'little passages of daily life' and narrow passages of theology into neat, hospitable song.

NOTES

1 All citations of Herbert's poetry and prose refer to the edition of his works by F. E. Hutchinson. See Herbert (1941).
2 In the poem 'Perfection' corrected by Herbert in the Williams Manuscript, the original third stanza read:

He that does ought for thee,
Marketh yt deed for thine:
And when the Divel shakes ye tree,
Thou saist, this fruit is mine.

See Hutchinson's notes 184–5 and commentary 541–2.

REFERENCES AND FURTHER READING

Asals, Heather (1981). *Equivocal Predication: George Herbert's Way to God.* Toronto: University of Toronto Press.

Bloch, Chana (1985). *Spelling the Word: George Herbert and the Bible.* Berkeley: University of California Press.

Burnett, Mark Thornton (1997). *Masters and Servants in English Renaissance Drama and Culture: Authority and Obedience.* London: Macmillan.

Charles, Amy M. (1977). *A Life of George Herbert.* Ithaca: Cornell University Press.

Fish, Stanley (1978). *The Living Temple: George Herbert and Catechizing.* Berkeley: University of California Press.

Frye, Northrop (1963). *Fables of Identity: Studies in Poetic Mythology.* New York: Harcourt, Brace and World.

Heal, Felicity (1990). *Hospitality in Early Modern England.* Oxford: Clarendon Press.

Heaney, Seamus (1995). *The Redress of Poetry.* New York: Farrar, Straus and Giroux.

Henderson, Diane (1997). 'The Theater and Domestic Culture'. In John D. Cox and David Scott Kastan (eds), *A New History of Early English Renaissance Drama* (pp. 173–94). New York: Columbia University Press.

Herbert, George (1941). *The Works of George Herbert,* ed. F. E. Hutchinson. Oxford: Clarendon Press.

——(1965). *The Latin Poetry of George Herbert: A Bilingual Edition,* tr. Mark McCloskey and Paul R. Murphy. Athens, OH: Ohio University Press.

Hill, Christopher (1974). 'Pottage for Freeborn Englishmen: Attitudes to Wage Labour'. In *Change and Continuity in Seventeenth-century England* (pp. 219–38). London: Secker and Warburg.

Kronenfeld, Judy Z. (1985). 'Probing the Relation between Poetry and Ideology: Herbert's "The Windows"'. *John Donne Journal,* 2, 55–80.

Laslett, Peter (1983). *The World We Have Lost: Further Explored.* London: Methuen.

Orlin, Lena Cowen (1994). *Private Matters and Public Culture in Post-Reformation England.* Ithaca: Cornell University Press.

Patrides, C. A. (1974). 'A Crown of Praise: The Poetry of Herbert'. In C. A. Patrides (ed.), *The English Poems of George Herbert* (pp. 6–25). London: Dent.

Robbins, Bruce (1986). *The Servant's Hand: English Fiction from Below.* New York: Columbia University Press.

Schoenfeldt, Michael C. (1991). *Prayer and Power: George Herbert and Renaissance Courtship.* Chicago and London: University of Chicago Press.

Singleton, Marion White (1987). *God's Courtier: Configuring a Different Grace in George Herbert's Temple.* Cambridge: Cambridge University Press.

Stein, Arnold (1968). *George Herbert's Lyrics.* Baltimore: Johns Hopkins University Press.

Stewart, Stanley (1986). *George Herbert*. Twayne Publishers: Boston.

Strier, Richard (1983). *Love Known: Theology and Experience in George Herbert's Poetry*. Chicago: University of Chicago Press.

——(1995). *Resistant Structures: Particularity, Radicalism, and Renaissance Texts*. Berkeley: University of California Press.

Vendler, Helen (1975). *The Poetry of George Herbert*. Cambridge, MA: Harvard University Press.

White, Helen C. (1962, first published 1936). *The Metaphysical Poets: A Study in Religious Experience*. New York: Collier Books.

Wilcox, Helen (1996). 'Entering *The Temple*: Women, Reading, and Devotion in Seventeenth-century England'. In Donna B. Hamilton and Richard Strier (eds), *Religion, Literature, and Politics in Post-Reformation England, 1540–1688* (pp. 187–207). Cambridge: Cambridge University Press.

23

The Heart of the Labyrinth: Mary Wroth's *Pamphilia to Amphilanthus*

Robyn Bolam

I . . .
Since I exscribe your sonnets, am become
A better lover, and much better poet.

(Ben Jonson, Sonnet 'To the noble Lady, the Lady Mary Wroth')

Lady Mary Wroth was the first Englishwoman to publish a long work of fiction and a complete sonnet sequence. In the 1620s, she was also probably the first female to create a dramatic comedy, *Love's Victory*, though its text was not printed until 1988.[1] Her range is striking for any author, but particularly so for a Renaissance woman: she is now widely recognized as one of the most exceptional and outstanding writers of her day. In 1621 her controversial 558-page prose romance, *The Countess of Montgomery's Urania*, appeared with a separately numbered, 48-page sequence of sonnets and songs, entitled *Pamphilia to Amphilanthus*, appended to it.[2] Pamphilia, the fictional writer of the sonnet sequence and Amphilanthus, her inconstant lover, are characters in *Urania*, where examples of their poetry appear. Although the appended sonnets are linked to *Urania*, they can be read successfully on their own.

Born Mary Sidney, like her greatly respected aunt and godmother, Wroth had an impressive family heritage to which she drew readers' attention on the title page of *Urania*. She had a female mentor and role model in her aunt, but did not follow her 'rare and pious example'[3] as a translator of religious literature, choosing instead to concentrate on traditionally male-dominated genres and original, secular texts. Her father, Sir Robert Sidney, though not as celebrated as his siblings for literary accomplishments, nevertheless left a manuscript of 66 poems (including an incomplete corona of sonnets), which his daughter appears to have read and recalled during the writing of *Pamphilia to Amphilanthus*.[4] It is also possible to see her adoption of the Elizabethan romance and sonnet sequence favoured by her uncle, Sir Philip Sidney, as attempts to revive and continue Sidneian literary tradition at a time when these genres were no longer fashionable. While many features of her verse are conventional, she is even more experimental than he in her treatment of the Petrarchan sonnet, experimenting with sestet and octet variations and often deviating from tradition in subject and style, particularly in her use of enjambment between stanzas. Philip Sidney's *The Countess of Pembroke's Arcadia* and *Astrophil and Stella* are echoed in her *The Countess of Montgomery's Urania* and *Pamphilia to Amphilanthus*, but although Wroth identified her work with that of her uncle, she also demonstrated their differences. She followed and revered her aunt, yet showed that she was a new kind of Renaissance female writer. Like Urania (a lost, lamented, and significantly absent shepherdess in *Arcadia*, who is given a prominent place as Wroth's title figure in her own romance), Wroth was involved in a quest – not, as in the case of her character, for lost origins, but for a place in literary tradition which she could call her own. It is significant that, in *Urania*, Pamphilia, the character most associated with Wroth, inherits her kingdom from her uncle rather than her father, suggesting a parallel with Wroth's literary inheritance.

Mary Wroth wrote 105 sonnets in all: the published *Urania* contains 19, there are 3 in a manuscript of the second part of *Urania*, which was not completed or published, and 83 comprise the published *Pamphilia to Amphilanthus*. It is possible that, as well as being a literary friend of Jonson, she exchanged manuscripts with Donne and others.[5] A holograph manuscript of *Pamphilia to Amphilanthus*, corrected and revised in Wroth's hand, is held today in the Folger Library.[6] This contains five sonnets and a song which were not printed elsewhere, and two sonnets and seven songs which were later incorporated into *Urania*. The fourth sonnet in the published *Pamphilia and Amphilanthus* does not appear in the manuscript. Wroth corrected her manuscript to make minor changes to language, particularly to improve grammar or metre. When the poems were published, spelling was modernized, punctuation altered (often to avoid enjambment), the order of the poems was changed, and some were not printed. As the 1621 version includes changes (particularly to punctuation) which are not necessarily Wroth's, and some which may be printer's errors, I have followed Josephine Roberts in using the selection and sequence of the printed edition with the Folger manuscript's versions of the poems, modernizing spelling and punctuation as lightly as possible. As well as Wroth's separate numbering for each part of the sequence, I have cited Roberts's continuous system for clarity.[7]

Roberts suggests that the paper on which the manuscript was written can be dated as early as 1587,[8] the probable year of Wroth's birth, but the exact time of writing is unknown, although it seems likely to have been after her husband's death in 1614. (Robert Wroth left her with large debts and a month-old son, who died two years later, taking her last claims to his father's estate with him, and perhaps prompting her to consider writing for publication.) The 1621 published version of *Pamphilia to Amphilanthus* contains four numbered sequences of sonnets interspersed with songs. Between the sequences are two transitional sections of unnumbered sonnets and songs and a third of four numbered songs. The name 'Pamphilia' appears at the ends of the first and last sonnet sequences, as if to authenticate her fictitious authorship.

Pamphilia to Amphilanthus: A Matter of Names

Wroth's choice of the persona, Pamphilia, suggests the double role of female writer and constant lover. The Greek-based reading of 'Pamphilia' is 'all-loving', while Amphilanthus, her unfaithful lover and cousin, has a name meaning 'lover of two'.[9] May Nelson Paulissen suggests Latin derivations: 'one who loves everyone' or is 'beloved of all' (from Pamphilus) and 'one who scatters light all around' for Amphilanthus (a combination of 'amphi', 'all around' and 'lanthus', light or lantern). Additionally, Wroth's persona shares her name with Pamphilia, the prolific poet and prose writer, who lived during the reign of Nero, but in *Urania*, Pamphilia is a queen and writes her poetry and tales privately. Roberts speculates that the name may 'be a witty conflation' of Sidney's Pamela and Philoclea, or may 'ironically recall Sidney's philandering character, Pamphilus, who abandons women' in the *New Arcadia*. She also notes that 'Pamphilus' is a 'common name for a male lover mistreated by women . . . in sixteenth-century ballads and romances'.[10]

Despite its melancholic tone, such ironies suggest that *Pamphilia to Amphilanthus* is not tragic. Pamphilia suffers trials in her love for Amphilanthus, but she survives and, in the published version, finally seems stronger, if resigned. The work charts the speaker's progress in exploring the nature of love and the virtue of constancy that Pamphilia champions. The choice of her characters' names indicates the multiplicity of approaches Wroth demonstrates throughout, which makes her a rewarding subject for feminist criticism. Jeff Masten points to 'absence as a palpable presence'[11] in these sonnets and Naomi J. Miller focuses on the 'multiplicity of speaking positions for women' in Wroth's texts.[12]

Puns on the poet's name or on the semi-disguised named of a loved one were popular in Elizabethan sonnets. In Wroth's case possible examples have been discerned which may refer to herself and her lover, William Herbert, third earl of Pembroke (1580–1630), her cousin and a man 'immoderately given up to women'.[13] As a young widow, she had two children by him – William and Catherine. In sonnet 8 of her Crown of Sonnets (P84), Wroth follows a contemporary practice of punning on her own name (Wroth / worth):

> He that shuns love doth love himself the less
> And cursèd he whose spirit not admires
> The worth of love, where endless blessedness
> Reigns, and commands, maintained by heavenly fires
>
> Made of virtue, joined by truth, blown by desires
> Strengthened by worth.
>
>   (lines 1–6)

This can be read as an assertion of the part love plays in the development of the self. To love is to be beloved, as Pamphilia's name suggests. Love brings self-esteem: constant love brings 'endless blessedness' and is 'maintained by heavenly fires', not the destructive fires of desire fanned by Cupid in the very first sonnet. 'Virtue' which originally appeared as 'vertu', like the pun on worth / Wroth and its link with the character of Pamphilia, brings the divine power of love into play with the finest aspects of art and self.

Earlier, in Sonnet 48 (P55), the final poem of the first sequence, Pamphilia / Wroth appears to be punning on the name, 'Will', possibly alluding to Herbert's Christian name. Again, images of fire portray the strength of her consuming passion:

> How like a fire doth love increase in me,
> The longer that it lasts, the stronger still,
> The greater purer, brighter, and doth fill
> No eye with wonder more, then hopes still be
>
> Bred in my breast, when fires of love are free
> To use that part to their best pleasing will . . .
>
> My breath not able is to breathe least part
> Of that increasing fuel of my smart;
> Yet love I will till I but ashes prove.
>
> (ll. 1–6, 12–14)

The last line implies eventual destruction, but up to that point the speaker describes a love with the fierce intensity of a heavenly phenomenon – surpassing the experience of the senses and showing no sign of abating. It is a fitting end to the first part of the sequence, creating a bridge between physical lust and the enduring nature of constant love which transcends transitory worldly passion. There is clearly an autobiographical element to *Pamphilia to Amphilanthus* but it would be unwise to think that the sequence is no more than a literary working out of Wroth's complex personal life. The references to herself and perhaps, Pembroke, are not at the forefront. A continuous reassessment of the nature of love is the true subject, and while this is carried out by a woman, she appears to be appealing to lovers of both sexes.

A Woman's Voice

Mary Wroth was not the first woman poet to speak through a female persona, but she was the first writer of an English sonnet sequence to do so.[14] At times her approach is ungendered, but there are also moments when the fact that a woman is speaking helps to intensify the pathos and courage of the work; however, the subject is still as relevant to men as to women, as Jennifer Laws has shown.

If it were not for the title of the sequence, a reader would not immediately identify the speaker as female. We hear a voice conjuring up the deepest darkness of night to describe the speaker's temporary dislocation from her conscious self and the onset of a vivid dream, which takes total possession of her thoughts. In this dream 'winged Desire', rather than the traditional Ovidian doves, draws Venus's chariot, in which Cupid intensifies the heat of burning hearts, held aloft by his mother (as portrayed on the title page of *Urania*). When Venus places a heart 'flaming more than all the rest' against the speaker's breast and commands Cupid to enclose it within her body ('now shut, said she, thus must we win') he obeys and the speaker's original heart is 'martyred'. On waking, the speaker discovers that the legacy of her dream remains; the flaming heart has consumed her own and burns on in its place, making her a lover against her will. Thinking of Cupid's arrow (which is not mentioned in the sonnet), several critics and editors substitute 'shoot' for 'shut', but the latter is in both manuscript and printed versions of the poem and expresses love's seizure of control in a more graphic image of the body's violation than can be expressed solely by a wound from an arrow-head.

Wroth begins her sequence with allusions to Petrarch's *Trionfi d'Amore*, Ovid's *Metamorphoses*, Dante's *Vita Nuova*, and conventional Renaissance tropes, such as 'sleep (death's image)', but we are also aware, from the title, that her helpless lover is not the traditional male. Nor is the object of desire chastely unattainable, as was the usual Petrarchan beloved. Like Shakespeare's Dark Lady, he is only unattainable to the speaker because he is lavishing his favours temporarily on others. Amphilanthus is rarely addressed and is always physically absent. He is not given a voice (even Sidney's Stella and Spenser's Elizabeth speak briefly). Pamphilia does not create a blazon of his physical attributes and when she briefly portrays his appearance it is in the conventional imagery of former sonneteers, seeing his eyes as 'Two stars of Heaven' (sonnet 2). Her unconventionality is in applying such Petrarchan tropes to a man.

In her sonnets Pamphilia writes almost therapeutically – to obtain 'some small ease' – but putting her grief into 'lines' only increases her pain and makes her conclude: 'grief is not cured by art' (sonnet 8 (P9)). In sonnet 39 (P45), she portrays herself as one long used to sorrow who is able to suffer in silence, being unable to 'enjoy / My own framed words' which are inadequate, 'For where most feeling is, words are more scant'. In this she is set apart from the ready wits of whom she says, 'your plenty shows your want'. True feeling, then, is privately expressed to the self in 'purer thoughts' than words can express: it is not for public consumption. The reader therefore feels privileged to be party to such private explorations and the poems we are reading are experienced as if they were the speaker's most inward thoughts. By this means Wroth draws her audience into Pamphilia's mind, encloses us in her thoughts.

Images of enclosure abound. In the first poem the newly enclosed heart is associated with negative aspects of desire – destruction, pain and danger. Later, Wroth demonstrates the positive aspects of enclosure which allow the reader to share Pamphilia's thoughts and Pamphilia to find comfort in the private world of her own mind. Far from being limited, this is an enclosed world which brings freedom with its endless potential for expansion of thought – both enabling Pamphilia to dwell on thoughts of Amphilanthus and allowing her to continue her analysis of love in a movement towards self-knowledge, as in sonnet 23 (P26).

Like the personae of the male sonneteers, the speaker focuses mostly on her own state but, unlike many of them, does so mainly to concentrate on the nature of love itself. In this, Wroth seems closer to Shakespeare than other, nearer contemporaries. From the outset Pamphilia is shown to be singled out by love against her will. Amphilanthus is introduced in the second sonnet solely as the object of her desire in order to demonstrate the strength of the passion she now has to combat, and all responsibility for her predicament is shown to rest with love itself, rather than the beloved. Pamphilia's plea is for justice and responsibility on love's part. In sonnet 3, addressed to love, she introduces a link with the third part of the sequence, 'A Crown of Sonnets Dedicated to Love': 'Think but on this; / Who wears love's crown, must not do so amiss, / But seek their good, who on thy force do lie.' Both lover *and* beloved are helpless victims in this view.

These first poems of Pamphilia's show her joy in the loved person alongside the pains produced by his indifference and are concerned with her fluctuating moods as she struggles with the effects of love. Pamphilia staves night off in sonnet 4 but welcomes her in sonnet 15 (P17); within sonnet 16 (P18) she switches from trying to hold back sleep to abandoning herself to it,' let me for ever sleep, / And so forever that dear image keep, / Or still wake, that my senses may be free'. In both cases the plea is for control – and it is love rather than Amphilanthus who has taken that control from her.

The secret nature of her love is also a source of pain. In sonnet 22 (P25), which incorporates images apparently associated with Jonson's *Masque of Blackness* (in which Wroth performed), Pamphilia considers the Indians 'who . . . to blackness run' as 'better' than her pale, grieving self because they have sight of the sun they worship and, as was believed, carried evidence of its power in the colour of their skin, whereas she has to carry the power of her love hidden in her heart. Jeff Masten sees Wroth as privatizing the essentially public Petrarchan genre and suggests that she is opposed to the kind of gestures of theatrical display in her verse which her male counterparts used. Sonnet 22 suggests the opposite, with Pamphilia's regret that her sacrifices are 'hid as worthless rite'. This surfaces again in sonnet 36 (P41), in which she addresses her 'poor heart', whose 'chief pain' is that she must hide her love 'From all save only one who should it see'. Her need to conceal enables her to produce an internal drama far more intense than any public play; nor does Pamphilia wholly escape the public gaze. Bemoaning love's blindness in sonnet 42 (P48), she reasons:

> For had he seen, he must have pity showed;
>
> I should not have been made this stage of woe
> Where sad disasters have their open show
> O no, more pity he had sure bestowed.

It is not open display alone which is the problem, but the state of her unhappiness, which she would prefer to keep from the eyes of the world.

Through their perceived role as transmitters of light to produce sight, and as trans-mitters of love, eyes are powerful images throughout. Pamphilia complains of Cupid's lack of vision, but she is nevertheless able to find joy in the arms of the blind female, Fortune, who tells her to trust them both in sonnet 31 (P36). Eyes or lack of them help to characterize all the main figures, but such bodily features are often used to infer far more than the physical. In sonnet 6, 'the depth of my heart-held despair' recalls the first sonnet in its Sidneian compound 'heart-held' – both despair because Pamphilia's heart is held by Venus and because it is a heart full of despair. In sonnet 13, her emotional struggles are expressed in terms of bodily survival. Here, a lover, once fed on love, is now starved of it; she is an easy victim whose blood is constantly being shed because she allows it, wishing (as she does in sonnet 6) for death as the only hope of release. Her suffering is graphically evoked through metaphors of the physical body which are used paradoxically to negate the physical and describe a spiritual state. In sonnet 26 (P30) Pamphilia alludes to the Petrarchan exchange of hearts in her request to Amphilanthus to, 'Send me your heart which in mine's place shall feed / On faithful love to your devotion bound.' Her own heart is now in his breast and without his in its place she cannot survive. Importantly, she hopes that, once in her body his heart, feeding on her 'faithful love', will realize 'the sacrifices made / Of pure and spotless love which shall not fade / While soul and body are together found'.

In sonnet 33 (P38) Pamphilia briefly looks ahead to the Crown of Sonnets when she temporarily dismisses criticism of Cupid because humans neglect to consider their own folly. She makes the case for admiring his 'sacred power' rather than treating it as a child's mischief – for if love takes offence humans will 'be born without fire' into a passionless existence. To make the best of the human predicament Cupid needs to be praised not mocked. The sequence is constantly turning and enclosing, looking back and then moving forwards in a labyrinth of emotional struggles and reasoning.

The Labyrinth as Image, Metaphor and Style

Following Petrarch, like many English sonnet writers before her, Wroth made use of the image of a labyrinth in her poetry.[15] Nancy Miller draws attention to the fact that in his sonnet sequence, transcribed some time after 1596 (the date of the manuscript's watermark), Robert Sidney wrote of a 'saving thread' of the lady's faults which allowed the lover to come to his senses and escape the 'maze' of love. She concludes that, just as, in one version of the myth, Ariadne 'provided Theseus with the thread, only to be abandoned by him . . . on . . . Naxos to commit suicide in despair', 'embedded' in Robert Sidney's use of these images 'is a trope of masculine abandonment of the feminine other, justified as masculine escape from female wiles, with the understated possibility that female sexuality is perceived as the monstrous power lurking at the centre of the maze of male desire'.[16] Countering this, in the first published English defence of women possibly written by a woman, Jane Anger writes of a labyrinth 'At the end of men's fair promises' in *Her Protection for Women* (1589). She urges women to 'shun men's flattery, the forerunner of our undoing' as men's rule 'is to flatter: for Fidelity and they are utter enemies. Things far fetched are excellent, and that experience is best which cost most: Crowns are costly, and that which cost many crowns is well worth God thank you, or else I know who has spent his labour and cost, foolishly'.[17] Wroth follows neither writer directly, but is closer to Anger's line in her choice of 'A Crown of Sonnets dedicated to Love' which spring from Pamphilia's costly experience, i.e. her suffering because of Amphilanthus's inconstant behaviour and her struggle with her own emotions. Dubrow suggests that she stresses the labours of love from a female perspective, even to the point of her spelling of 'labourinth' in the Folger's holograph manuscript. Love's complexities present Pamphilia with her biggest challenge and opportunity for heroism: 'In this labyrinth, where shall I turn?' – as well as her best consolation – that it is not a maze with dead-ends, but an ongoing journey which leads to the heart of the labyrinth and constant love itself, 'the soul's content'. The problem for her is not knowing how much further she needs to twist and turn in these labours before she will be delivered from her task. She must also keep hold of the thread: 'As the final line of each sonnet in the corona is repeated in the first line of the successive sonnet, Pamphilia's voice becomes her thread of love expressed, revealing her chosen path through the labyrinthine turns of her male beloved's fluctuating behavior.'[18] The repetitions demonstrate the extent of her perseverance and either a growing weariness or a strengthened conviction, depending on her state of mind at a particular point. Mary Moore draws together many labyrinthine aspects of Wroth's style, pointing out that her crown of sonnets 'represents perplexity even as it perplexes'.[19] What Moore sees as deliberately labyrinthine style, a male critic held up as a weakness: 'Each sonnet really should be grammatically self-contained, but Wroth did not manage that. In fact, she often has difficulty with her grammar; her sentences frequently lose direction, impetus and clarity.'[20] Like Moore, I prefer to give her credit for innovation.

Pamphilia's dilemma infuses style as well as content. The repeated lines at the beginning and ends of each sonnet finally enclose the crown completely when the last line of the final sonnet repeats the first line of the first. This appears to be enclosure without closure, for Pamphilia leaves the reader with her unanswered question, 'In this strange labyrinth how shall I turn?' In the printed version the opening use of this phrase is punctuated with a comma which contrasts with the emphatic question mark at the end of the final stanza. This works against the symmetrical circularity of the manuscript in Wroth's hand, which has a question mark in both places, suggesting either that the speaker is in the same state at the end of the sequence as at the beginning – and that no progress has been made, or that the way she turned initially was inwards – to an exploration of the nature of love itself and her relation to it, and that the final question mark therefore indicates an even greater awareness of the complexities of her dilemma, but still provides no answer to it.

Of course, if she cannot turn to right, left, move forward or go back, the only other way is upwards – and by the end of the sequence it could be argued that Pamphilia has turned in this direction, i.e. a spiritual one, via her inward explorations. She now looks 'To truth, which shall eternal goodness prove' to give her everlasting joy. There is resignation and maturity as well as newly found contentment in her final resolution to 'Leave the discourse of Venus and her son / To young beginners' who will use 'stories of great love', such as hers, as their muse 'and from that fire / Get heat to write the fortunes they have won'. The fire of Pamphilia's physical passion has finally become a fire of inspiration for other writers and lovers. A woman's poetic art, rather than the woman herself, is the new muse.

NOTES

1 Brennan, Michael G. (ed.) (1988). *Lady Mary Wroth's Love's Victory*. London: Roxburghe Club.
2 British Library 86.h.9 and G.2422. Editions of *Pamphilia to Amphilanthus* have been edited by Gary F. Waller (1977), Josephine A. Roberts (1983), and R. E. Pritchard (1996).
3 Sir Edward Denny to Lady Mary Wroth, 26 February 1621–2. Reproduced in Roberts, Josephine A. (ed.) (1983). *The Poems of Lady Mary Wroth*. Baton Rouge and London: Louisiana State University Press, p. 239.
4 Croft, P. J. (ed.) (1984). *The Poems of Robert Sidney*. Oxford: Clarendon.
5 From Margaret Quilligan's unpublished paper (1992 MLA convention), cited in Miller, Naomi J. (1996), p. 34.
6 Folger MS V.a.104, Folger Shakespeare Library, Washington, DC.
7 Signified by (P-). For alternative views to Roberts's assumptions about Wroth's manuscript see Jeff Masten, '"Shall I turne blabb?": Circulation, Gender, and Subjectivity in Mary Wroth's Sonnets'. In Miller, Naomi J. and Waller, Gary (eds) (1991), pp. 68–9.
8 Roberts (1983), p. 62.
9 Wroth, Mary (1621). *Urania*, First Part, Book II, p. 250.
10 Roberts, Josephine A. (ed.) (1995). *The First Part of the Countess of Montgomery's Urania*. Renaissance English Text society Seventh series, vol.17. Binghampton, NY: Medieval and Renaissance Texts and Studies, pp. xxv–xxvi.
11 Masten, Jeff in Naomi J. Miller and Gary Waller (eds) (1991), p. 74.
12 Miller, Naomi J. (1996), p. 5.
13 Macray, W. Dunn (ed.) (1888). Edward Hyde, First Earl of Clarendon's *History of the Rebellion I*, p. 73. See Roberts (1983), p. 43 and Roberts (1982), 1 (1).
14 Miller, Naomi J. (1996), p. 35.
15 John, Lisle C. (1938). *The Elizabethan Sonnet Sequences*, p. 65 and note 94. New York: Columbia University Studies in English and Comparative Literature, 133.
16 Miller, Naomi J. (1996), p. 42.
17 Anger, Jane (1589). *Her Protection for Women*, London: Richard Jones and Thomas Orwin, C4 verso.
18 Miller, Naomi J. (1996), p. 42.
19 Moore, Mary (1998). 'The Labyrinth as Style in *Pamphilia to Amphilanthus*', *Studies in English Literature*, 38, 109.
20 Pritchard, R. E. (ed.) (1996). *Lady Mary Wroth: Poems, a Modernized Edition*, Keele: Keele University Press, p. 11.

REFERENCES AND FURTHER READING

Beilin, Elaine (1981). 'The Onely Perfect Vertue: Constancy in Mary Wroth's *Pamphilia to Amphilanthus*', *Spenser Studies*, 2, 229–45.

——(1987). *Redeeming Eve: Women Writers of the English Renaissance*. Princeton: Princeton University Press.

Dubrow, Heather (1995). *Echoes of Desire: English Petrarchism and Its Counterdiscourses.* Ithaca and London: Cornell University Press.

Farrell, Kirby, Hageman, Elizabeth H. and Kinney, Arthur F. (eds) (1990). *Women in the Renaissance: Selections from English Literary Renaissance.* Amherst, University of Massachusetts Press.

Harvey, Elizabeth D. and Maus, Katharine Eisaman (eds) (1990). *Soliciting Interpretation: Literary Theory and Seventeenth-century English Poetry.* Chicago; London: University of Chicago Press.

Haselkorn, Anne M. and Travitsky, Betty S. (eds) (1990). *The Renaissance Englishwoman in Print: Counter-balancing the Canon.* Amherst: University of Massachusetts Press.

Jones, Ann Rosalind (1990). *The Currency of Eros: Women's Love Lyric in Europe, 1540–1620.* Bloomington: University of Indiana Press.

Lamb, Mary Ellen (1990). *Gender and Authorship in the Sidney Family Circle.* Madison, WI: London: University of Wisconsin Press.

Laws, Jennifer (1996). 'Gender and Genre in the Sonnet Sequences of Philip Sidney and Mary Wroth', *Deep South*, 2, 1–7.

Lewalski, Barbara Kiefer (1993). *Writing Women in Jacobean England.* Cambridge, MA and London: Harvard University Press.

MacArthur, Janet (1989). ' "A Sydney, though un-named": Lady Mary Wroth and Her Poetical Progenitors', *English Studies in Canada*, 15, 12–20.

Miller, Naomi J. (1996). *Changing the Subject: Mary Wroth and Figurations of Gender in Early Modern England.* Lexington: University Press of Kentucky.

Miller, Naomi J. and Waller, Gary (eds) (1991). *Reading Mary Wroth: Representing Alternatives in Early Modern England.* Knoxville: University of Tennessee Press.

Moore, Mary (1998). 'The Labyrinth as Style in *Pamphilia to Amphilanthus*', *Studies in English Literature*, 38, 109–25.

Pacheco, Anita (ed.) (1998). *Early Women Writers 1600–1720.* London and New York: Longman.

Paulissen, May Nelson (1982). *The Love Sonnets of Lady Mary Wroth: A Critical Introduction.* Salzburg: Institut fur Anglistik und Amerikanistik, University of Salzburg.

Pritchard, R. E. (1996). 'George Herbert and Lady Mary Wroth: A Root for "the Flower"?', *Review of English Studies*, New Series, 47, 386–9.

——(ed.) (1996). *Lady Mary Wroth Poems: A Modernized Edition.* Keele: Keele University Press.

Randall, Martin (ed.) (1997). *Women Writers in Renaissance England.* London: Longman.

Roberts, Josephine A. (1982).'The Biographical Problem of *Pamphilia to Amphilanthus*', *Tulsa Studies in Women's Literature*, 1, 43–53.

——(ed.) (1983). *The Poems of Lady Mary Wroth.* Baton Rouge and London: Louisiana State University Press.

——(1996). ' "Thou maist have thy *Will*": The Sonnets of Shakespeare and His Stepsisters', *Shakespeare Quarterly*, 47 (4), 407–23.

Walker, Kim (1996). *Women Writers of the English Renaissance.* New York and London: Twayne and Prentice-Hall International.

Waller, G. F. (ed.) (1977). *Pamphilia to Amphilanthus.* Salzburg: Institut fur Englische Sprache und Literatur, University of Salzburg.

Wilcox, Helen (ed.) (1996). *Women and Literature in Britain 1500–1700.* Cambridge: Cambridge University Press.

24

The Critical Elegy

John Lyon

At the turn of the millennium an elegiac view of English literature is especially apposite, and in critical elegies – poems written by one poet on the death of a contemporary or near contemporary – we find a distinctively concentrated and complex history of English writing, 'the heart of literary history' (Lipking (1981) p. 138). Typically such poems characterize the main literary concerns specific to the times in which they were written. W. H. Auden's elegy for W. B. Yeats, for example, spoke of anxieties particular to the twentieth century – a century of wars and atrocities but also of remarkable emancipations – in worrying about the political responsibilities and efficacy of literature. By contrast, in the nineteenth century, poets as diverse as Shelley writing of Keats, Matthew Arnold elegizing his friend Arthur Hugh Clough, and Swinburne lamenting the loss of Baudelaire were all exercised by the possibility (or impossibility) of belief, and religious belief in particular. The concern which dominated the elegy of the Renaissance – coinciding with a culture increasingly aware of print as a means of preserving its poetry for posterity[1] – was the English language itself: the question, repeatedly posed and diversely answered, was whether English might serve as the medium for an enduring and major literature.

Critical elegies were particularly prevalent in the earlier half of the seventeenth century when 'an English writer's death would almost automatically occasion poetic tributes from mourning fellow citizens of the literary world' (Murphy (1972) p. 75). The rewarding concentration and the interpretative difficulty of such poems arise from the same source. The views of one poet, expressed in verse, on the works of another are usually altogether richer and more intense than mere discursive commentary of non-practitioners. Yet poems, addressed to the writings of contemporary poets, may be about many complex things, diverse things which prove difficult to disentangle: such poems may appear as true and accurate tributes, but also may represent the workings of anxiety, hostility, rivalry, appropriation and rewriting. No less a figure than John Dryden affords evidence of the difficulty of reading such concentrated critical elegies when he described and dismissed the most important of them all – Ben

Jonson's poem on Shakespeare – as 'an insolent, sparing, and invidious panegyric.'[2] Yet again, in contrast to such general interpretative complexity, these elegies are often remarkably direct and particular in offering the nearest thing to what we presently think of as practical criticism or close reading: through 'mirror technique' (Murrin (1968) p. 203), where the elegist mimics the style of the poet whom he mourns, we gain highly specific illustrations of what the poet's contemporaries may have regarded as the defining characteristics of the poet's style.

John Cleveland, Abraham Cowley, Richard Crashaw, John Donne, John Fletcher, Ben Jonson, Richard Lovelace, Katherine Philips and William Shakespeare are among the poets who were the subjects of such poems; Thomas Carew, Abraham Cowley, Sidney Godolphin, Ben Jonson, Henry King, Henry Vaughan and Edmund Waller among those who wrote them. Critical elegies, often in great numbers, prefaced posthumous editions of individual poets. An entire volume, *Jonsonus Virbius* (1637), was devoted to Ben Jonson. Registering the elegiac prolixity which Jonson's death occasioned, Sir Thomas Salusbury began his tribute 'Shall I alone spare paper?'[3] while Sidney Godolphin's fine elegy celebrated Jonson's superlative status as a sociable poetic influence, fathering a lucid and plain style to be practised by Jonson's successors, the whole 'tribe of Ben':

> The Muses' fairest light in no dark time,
> The Wonder of a learned age; the line
> Which none can pass; the most proportioned wit
> To nature, the best judge of what was fit;
> The deepest, plainest, highest, clearest pen;
> The voice most echoed by consenting men.[4]

In the poem above, Jonson's supremacy is acknowledged appropriately in the very poetic form which Jonson himself, paradoxically in elegizing Shakespeare, had sought to make his own. His 'To the memory of my beloved, The Author, Mr. William Shakespeare: And what he hath left us'[5] – the very title has the characteristic, detailed precision of a Jonsonian inventory – is a poem of great affection and admiration, but also a poem whose true subject is contentious. Is Jonson's poem really about Shakespeare? Or an idealized Shakespeare? Or Shakespeare refashioned in Jonson's own image? The poem's original context is as part of the prefatory writings to the great and posthumous Shakespeare folio of 1623, but that context is already as Jonsonian as it is Shakespearean, since Jonson's own earlier folio stands as precursor of and model for the present Shakespearean volume. In 1616, Jonson had had the audacity to publish – in turn after the model of the then current Works (*Opera*) of the Latin poets – an edition of his own *Works*: but Jonson's works were in English and provocatively included the ephemera of the theatre – 'but plays',[6] as the poet John Suckling put it scornfully, plays now boldly invested by their author with greater permanence and status. Moreover, in respect of drama, Jonson's move into print places textuality above theatricality, and the writer above the players. And so, prefacing the folio of 1623, Jonson's elegy on Shakespeare reminds readers of the Jonsonian example which precedes the volume in hand; thus reverses the priority of the two writers' careers, declaring Jonson's primacy; and recasts the Shakespearean playwright as a Jonsonian author. We must recognize, then, that if Shakespeare endures as the greatest English writer it is, in part at least, as a result of a process which Ben Jonson's aggressive elegiac prediction, 'He was not of an age, but for all time!' (line 43) initiated. We must recognize too that if Shakespeare endures it is, again at least in part, as *Jonson's* Shakespeare: '*my* beloved', '*My* Shakespeare, rise' (title and line 19; italics added).

Yet Jonson's own views of Shakespeare appear complex, if not contradictory. In his prose writings, *Timber, or Discoveries*, Jonson lamented Shakespeare as a writer who 'never blotted out line' and 'flowed with that facility, that sometime it was necessary he should be stopped.'[7] The record of Jonson's conversations with William Drummond includes the abrupt view that 'Shakespeare wanted art'.[8] In contrast, Jonson's elegy goes out of its way to emphasize Shakespeare as reviser and improver:

> Yet must I not give nature all: thy art,
>   My gentle Shakespeare, must enjoy a part.
> For though the poet's matter, nature be,
>   His art doth give the fashion. And, that he,
> Who casts to write a living line, must sweat,
>   (Such as thine are) and strike the second heat
> Upon the muses' anvil; turn the same,
>   (And himself with it) that he thinks to frame;
> Or for the laurel, he may gain a scorn,
>   For a good poet's made, as well as born.
> And such wert thou.
>
> (ll. 55–65)

As a characterization of Ben Jonson at work, the above is and has always been entirely persuasive. In contrast, how plausible we have found Jonson's picture here of the hard-working striker of second heats as an accurate account of Shakespeare has varied greatly over time. Nonetheless, what is perhaps more interesting here is how the second parenthesis above insists that a turning or transforming of language is also a turning or transforming of the artistic self: Jonson is here continuing an emphasis on the intimate interrelatedness of Shakespeare's art, nature and the English language, an emphasis literally central to the poem. Jonson sees a perfect and permanent fit between Shakespeare and nature, in which one cannot readily discern where one ends and another begins:

> Nature herself was proud of his designs,
>   And joyed to wear the dressing of his lines!
> Which were so richly spun, and woven so fit,
>   As, since, she will vouchsafe no other wit.
>
> (ll. 47–50)

We underread these lines if we see in them only an example of the familiar neo-classical notion of language as dress, and assume that here Jonson cedes priority to nature, and conceives of Shakespeare and Shakespearean language as secondary and subsequent. In insisting on a perfect and enduring fit of language and nature, Jonson is presenting Shakespearean language as *shaping* as well as *dressing* nature. Indeed Jonson remarkably anticipates some of the best twentieth-century accounts of Shake-speare's power to endure in his suggestion that Shakespeare not merely reflected but changed nature, so much so that previous artists' representations are rendered obso-lete, untrue and denatured:

> The merry Greek, tart Aristophanes,
>   Neat Terence, witty Plautus, now not please;
> But antiquated, and deserted lie
>   As they were not of nature's family.
>
> (ll. 51–4)

In these lines we find examples of another audacious aspect of this audacious poem – favourable comparisons with, and indeed dismissals of 'all, that insolent Greece or haughty Rome / Sent forth, or since did from their ashes come' (lines 39–40). Though Shakespeare had 'small Latin, and less Greek' (line 31), the great classical tragedians are summoned to honour Shakespeare, and the classical comedians dismissed as inad-equate. Time has rendered true and commonplace what was at the time an extraor-dinary and daring move by the classicist Jonson – the claims for an English writer's legitimate and enduring place in the largest of literary contexts, and the declaration of the triumph of English:

> Triumph, my Britain, thou hast one to show,
>   To whom all scenes of Europe homage owe.
> He was not of an age, but for all time!
>
> (ll. 41–3)

In writing his elegy for Shakespeare, Jonson established the model for the way in which his own death was to be received. The many elegies for Jonson play and replay the tropes which Jonson had himself deployed in writing of Shakespeare: the national pride; favourable comparison with the classics; the works a more enduring monument than any tomb; the combining of art and nature; the poet born and made . . . and, above all, the declaration of Jonson's poetic immortality. What also recurs repeatedly in these poems is the surprised and proud recognition that Jonson the classicist who boasted to Drummond that he 'was better versed, and knew more in Greek and Latin, than all the poets in England'[9] was wholeheartedly and unequivocally committed to English as his sole literary medium. 'Yet he wrote English'[10] declared the water-poet, John Taylor. Whatever the realities of the matter, this period seems still to have felt acutely the precariousness and vulnerability of English, particularly as a medium for literature. In 1635 Sir Francis Kynaston translated Chaucer's *Troilus* into Latin in order to preserve the poem's intelligibility. Theodore Bathurst performed a similar service for Spenser's *The Shepheardes Calender*. Edmund Waller advised poets who sought 'last marble' to 'carve in Latin, or in Greek'; English poets merely 'write in sand'.[11] More persuasive perhaps than these quirky examples, are the facts that both Bacon's and Milton's literary achievements equivocate between English and Latin; that Latin exerted a claim on literature well into the eighteenth century; and that Samuel Johnson, despite his famous English Dictionary, continued often to favour Latin as a poetic medium. In contrast, Ben Jonson was from the outset patriotically loyal to English. His elegists celebrate his particular pure English:

> that spring,
> To whose most rich and fruitful head we owe
> The purest streams of language which can flow.
> For 'tis but truth; thou taughtst the ruder age,
> To speak by grammar . . .
> (Henry King, 'Upon Ben Jonson', ll. 22–6)

> Our canting English (of itself alone)
> (I had almost said a confusion)
> Is now all harmony; what we did say
> Before was tuning only; this is play.
> (Richard West, 'On Mr. Ben Jonson', ll. 79–82)[12]

If Jonson insisted on the intertwining of Shakespeare and the English language, and predicted Shakespeare's literary immortality, he had harsher predictions for another writer whom he nevertheless much admired. For Jonson, Donne's poetic wit was not in any easy relationship with English, and consequently Jonson took the view that Donne, 'for not being understood, would perish'.[13] (And since it was truly only in the twentieth century that Donne again received the admiration and attention comparable to that which his contemporaries afforded him, the evidence of time for the prediction of Donne's obscurity is still on Jonson's side.) Jonson also feared the damage which the influence of Donne's highly idiosyncratic strong lines might do to English poetry:

> Others, that in composition are nothing, but what is rough and broken [. . .] And if it would come gently, they trouble it of purpose. They would not have it run without rubs, as if that style were more strong and manly, that struck the ear with a kind of unevenness. These men err not by chance, but knowingly, and willingly [. . .] And this vice, one that is in authority with the rest, loving, delivers over to them to be imitated: so that oft-times the faults which he fell into, the others seek for. This is the danger, when vice becomes a precedent.[14]

Perhaps the most remarkable aspect of the critical elegy in the Renaissance is the way in which Thomas Carew, a 'son of Ben', took this Jonsonian poetic form – the critical elegy – and Jonson's negative views of John Donne, and transformed them into an elegiac celebration of Donne. Carew effected subtle but crucial shifts in Jonson's argument, transforming Jonsonian censure into praise. For Jonson, Donne will not survive the test of time, and that is an indictment of Donne. For Carew, Donne will not survive, and that is an indictment of time and language. For Jonson, Donne is the bad example who *should not* be imitated. For Carew, Donne is the unique poet who *cannot* be imitated. Thus Carew's poem celebrates Donne as the coterie poet who never had his *Works* printed and who, indeed, often cultivated obscurity rather than lucidity. Carew seizes a Pyrrhic victory from Donne's predicted defeat at the hands of time, seeing such defeat as a measure of Donne's exceptional and fleeting greatness. Carew makes virtues out of Donne's exclusiveness and out of his imperious wrenching of the English language to serve his poetic will:

> Thou shalt yield no precedence, but of time,
> And the blind fate of language [. . .]
> > Yet thou mayst claim
> From so great disadvantage greater fame,
> Since to the awe of thy imperious wit
> Our stubborn language bends, made only fit
> With her tough-thick-ribbed hoops to gird about
> Thy giant fancy, which had proved too stout
> For their [other poets'] soft melting phrases.
> > ('An Elegy upon the death of the Dean of Paul's,
> > Dr John Donne', ll. 45–6 and 47–53)[15]

Momentariness rather than endurance is here a measure of greatness.

A further enriching complication – typical of the complexity of the critical elegy genre – is that despite the vehemence of his insistence that Donne is inimitable, Carew, in his elegy, does imitate Donne's poetic style. Indeed, the brilliance of Carew's characterizations of Donne's verse is unlikely ever to be surpassed. In the moment of lamenting the irrecoverable loss of Donne, Carew audaciously elaborates and audaciously controls a parenthesis worthy of Donne himself:

> > But the flame
> Of thy brave soul, (that shot such heat and light,
> As burnt our earth, and made our darkness bright,
> Committed holy rapes upon our will,
> Did through the eye the melting heart distil;
> And the deep knowledge of dark truths so teach,
> As sense might judge; what fancy could not reach;)
> Must be desired forever.
> > (ll. 14–21)

Here the violent compression of Carew's own 'holy rapes' captures something of Donne's typical and provocative transposition of the erotic and the spiritual. The insis-

tence on Donne as the poet of the dark and the deep, the far from obvious, is reinforced here by the conceit of distillation and later in the poem by the notion of Donne
opening us 'a mine / Of rich and pregnant fancy' (lines 37–8). The illumination which
Donne affords, the scorching heat of lightning which 'made our darkness bright', contrasts precisely with the characterization of Jonsonian light offered by Sidney Godolphin in his tribute cited above: Donne works violently and suddenly in the dark, while
Jonson's is a steady sociable illumination, a superlative example yet continuous with
the other poetic talents of his time – 'The Muses' fairest light in no dark time'.

More persuasive perhaps than even Carew's explicit descriptions of Donne's verse
is the way that some passages of Carew's elegy – including those quoted above –
mimic, in run-on lines of 'masculine expression' (line 39), the characteristic movement of Donne's strong-lined verse. But, insofar as Donne is imitated in Carew's elegy,
it is imitation locally controlled and confined. It is valedictory imitation and reveals
Donne's influence growing feeble by the poem's close, as the conceit of the turning
wheel explains and justifies:

> Oh, pardon me, that break with untuned verse
> The reverend silence that attends thy hearse,
> Whose awful solemn murmurs were to thee
> More than these faint lines, a loud elegy,
> That did proclaim in a dumb eloquence
> The death of all the arts, whose influence
> Grown feeble, in these panting numbers lies
> Gasping short winded accents, and so dies:
> So doth the silent turning wheel not stand
> In the instant we withdraw the moving hand,
> But some small time maintain a faint weak course
> By virtue of the first impulsive force.
>
> (ll. 71–82)

By the end of Carew's elegy, true to Carew's own argument that Donne and Donne's
influence will not survive, the Donnean voice has gone and Donne's epitaph is pronounced, with greater poetic propriety, in closed couplets:

> Here lies a king, that ruled as he thought fit
> The universal monarchy of wit;
> Here lie two Flamens, and both those, the best,
> Apollo's first, at last, the true God's Priest.
>
> (ll. 95–8)

An introduction such as this can only begin to suggest something of the complexity
of the critical elegy, a particularly intense form of poetic criticism whose own medium
is itself poetry. Readers interested in pursuing this complexity might begin by noticing the important rhyme of 'fit' and 'wit' – to be found in the passage just quoted,

in other passages cited in this chapter and in many other critical elegies of the seventeenth century: such a noticing is one way of registering how intimate and attentive a dialogue these poems are engaged in, one with another, and how that dialogue is often furthered by poetic, non-discursive means, such as rhyme.

NOTES

1 See PUBLICATION: PRINT AND MANUSCRIPT.

2 John Dryden, 'A discourse concerning the original and progress of satire', *Essays*, ed. W. P. Ker (Oxford: Clarendon Press, 1900), Vol. 2, p. 18.

3 Sir Thomas Salusbury, 'An elegy meant upon the death of Ben Jonson', *Ben Jonson*, eds C. H. Herford, Percy Simpson, and Evelyn Simpson, 11 vols (Oxford: Clarendon Press, 1925), Vol. 11, pp. 485–6, line 1. All references to Ben Jonson and to elegies on Ben Jonson are to this edition.

4 Sidney Godolphin, 'On Ben Jonson', *Ben Jonson*, 11, p. 450, lines 1–6.

5 *Ben Jonson*, 8, pp. 390–2.

6 John Suckling, '"The Wits" or "A Session of the Poets"', *The Non-Dramatic Works*, Vol. 1 of *The Works of Sir John Suckling* edited by Thomas Clayton (Oxford: Clarendon Press, 1971) pp. 71–6, line 20.

7 *Ben Jonson*, 8, pp. 583–4.

8 *Ben Jonson*, 1, pp. 128–78, line 50.

9 Ibid., lines 622–3.

10 John Taylor, 'A Funeral Elegy, In Memory of the rare, Famous, and Admired poet, Mr Benjamin Jonson deceased'. In *Ben Jonson*, 11, pp. 421–8, line 71.

11 All these pro-Latin examples are taken from Richard Foster Jones, *The Triumph of the English Language* (Stanford: Stanford University Press, 1953) pp. 263–6. See also The English Language of the Early Modern Period.

12 Respectively *Ben Jonson*, 11, pp. 440–1 and pp. 468–70.

13 *Ben Jonson*, 1, pp. 128–78, line 196. On Donne and Jonson see also Poets, Friends and Patrons.

14 *Ben Jonson*, 8, p. 585.

15 Thomas Carew, *Poems*, ed. Rhodes Dunlap (Oxford: Clarendon Press, 1949) pp. 71–4.

REFERENCES AND FURTHER READING

Primary materials

Jonson's elegy on Shakespeare may be found in *Ben Jonson* edited by C. H. Herford, Percy Simpson, and Evelyn Simpson, 11 vols (Oxford: Clarendon Press, 1925), Vol. 8; and elegies on Ben Jonson in Vol. 11.

Elegies on Donne, including Carew's, are in *John Donne: The Epithalamions, Anniversaries and Epicedes*, ed. W. Milgate (Oxford: Clarendon Press, 1978). Further bibliographical information about other elegies may be found in the article by Avon Jack Murphy cited below.

Secondary material

Donaldson, Ian (1997). *Jonson's Magic Houses: Essays in Interpretation*. Oxford: ClarendonPress.

Gottlieb, Sidney (1983). 'Elegies upon the Author: Defining, Defending, and Surviving John Donne', *John Donne Journal*, 2, 23–38.

Lipking, Lawrence (1981). *The Life of the Poet: Beginning and Ending Poetic Careers*. Chicago: University of Chicago.

Lyon, John (1997). 'Jonson and Carew on Donne: Censure into Praise', *Studies in English Literature 1500–1900*, 37, 97–118.

——(1999). 'The Test of Time: Shakespeare, Jonson, Donne', *Essays in Criticism*, 49, 1–21.

Murphy, Avon Jack (1972). 'The Critical Elegy of Earlier Seventeenth-century England', *Genre*, 5, 75–105.

Murrin, Michael (1968). 'Poetry as Literary Criticism', *Modern Philology*, 65, 202–7.

Peterson, Richard S. (1981). *Imitation and Praise in the Poems of Ben Jonson*. New Haven: Yale University Press.

25

Ford, Mary Wroth, and the Final Scene of *'Tis Pity She's a Whore*

Robyn Bolam

The most sensational piece of staging in John Ford's *'Tis Pity She's a Whore*, and perhaps in the whole of Caroline drama, is Giovanni's entrance in Act V scene vi with his sister's heart upon his dagger. His brother-in-law, Soranzo, having discovered his wife's incestuous affair with Giovanni, impatiently awaits the opportunity to murder him at a banquet in the presence of the 'good' citizens of Parma and their cardinal. Giovanni's triumphant confession of incest and murder is swiftly followed by his father's death (apparently from a heart seizure), by Soranzo's murder ('see this heart which was thy wife's; / Thus I exchange it royally for thine', lines 72–3), and by Giovanni's death at the hands of the banditti and Soranzo's servant, Vasques. Giovanni welcomes death because, after the killing of his lover and their unborn child, as he passionately declares to the assembly when he shows them Annabella's heart, he believes that his own is already 'entombed' inside hers (line 27).

As Giovanni's extravagant actions mount, an audience may well find its sympathy for the sacrificed and censured sister increasing. In her stimulating essay, *'Tis Pity She's a Whore*: Representing the Incestuous Body', Susan Wiseman notes that until 1650, when it was declared a felony, incest, like adultery and fornication, was dealt with by the church rather than the state, and she quotes Lawrence Stone's view that the penalties were 'surprisingly lenient'.[1] The way the cardinal glosses over the exact nature of the crime in his final words: 'Of one so young, so rich in Nature's store, / Who could not say, *'Tis pity she's a whore?*', putting Annabella in the 'dangerous (but less dangerous) general category for the desirous female' and indicating that, as Wiseman suggests, the point 'at which the irreconcilable nature of the conflicting claims of church, state, family and economics on the body – particularly the reproductive body – fail to be resolvable and fail to verify and stabilize the meaning of incest'[2] has been reached. Understanding the problem is not the church's concern, as the friar demonstrates throughout. It is clear where the cardinal's priorities lie: 'Take up these slaughtered bodies; see them buried; / And all the gold and jewels, or whatsoever, / Confiscate by the canons of the Church, / We seize upon to the Pope's proper use' (lines 144–7).

A whole family line has been wiped out and, once the dead have been plundered, a cardinal who harbours murderers at his pleasure will 'talk at large of all' with Richardetto, whose only answer to the dangers of bodily passion is to place his niece permanently in a convent. The status quo has been resumed but this tragedy shows how shakily it is maintained.

Our final image of Annabella is not necessarily the cardinal's. Ford's sympathetic treatment of her plight leaves us, like Giovanni, with an image of her face (line 106) superimposed on the mutilated body we are left to imagine as there is no direction to indicate that her remains are brought onstage, and Vasques' return within seconds of being despatched to verify her state, would support this. As a victim she is a star-crossed lover, represented onstage at this point only by a bleeding heart, which has the additional parodic resonance of a biblical sacrifice. But what happens to Annabella's heart once it has served its shocking purpose at the beginning of the scene? Giovanni taunts Soranzo with it at line 10 before the latter realizes that it *is* a heart, far less, that of his wife. It is possible that, because he is covered in blood and brandishing a dagger, Soranzo suspects Giovanni has already wounded himself and may deprive him of his revenge: 'Shall I be forestalled?' (line 15). The opening stage direction clearly states that the scene is a banquet, that the Cardinal, Florio, Donado, Soranzo, Richardetto, Vasques and attendants *'take their places'*. Soranzo, presumably, is standing to welcome his last guest, but the others may be already seated and eating. Soranzo invites the Cardinal: 'Pleaseth your grace / To taste these coarse confections?' (line 4) just before Giovanni enters to thrust the heart before the assembly with: '*'Tis* a heart, / A heart, my lords, in which is mine entombed. / Look well upon't; d'ee know't?' (lines 25–7). The most likely place for Annabella's heart to rest is on the banquet table, as performances testify.

Donald K. Anderson pronounced:

> In the climactic fifth act . . . Ford's heart and banquet imagery are literal: Giovanni tears out Annabella's heart and brings it to Soranzo's feast. This spectacular action is foreshadowed throughout the play, for the heart and the banquet often appear figuratively. With the final scene in mind, one finds in the earlier imagery irony and unity.[3]

Since this article almost forty years ago, critics have debated the 'heart's riddle', as Michael Neill terms it, at length. The best summary of their progress can be found in Neill's essay, '"What strange riddle's this?": deciphering *'Tis Pity She's a Whore*', where he argues persuasively that explaining the spectacle as 'a way of representing Giovanni's diseased inner condition', 'as an emblem of the hidden corruption beneath the surface of Parmesan social order', or as 'a piece of self-conscious symbolization contrived by the hero himself[4] in a grotesque biblical parody, does not provide the full picture.

Picking up Giovanni's description of himself as 'a most glorious executioner' (line 32), Neill draws attention to the custom, at public executions, of cutting out the victim's heart to be exhibited 'for the execration of the crowd'.[5] In a striking reversal, the assembly in the last scene of *'Tis Pity* reserves curses and abhorrence for the executioner rather than the trophy he brings. Neill also links Giovanni's action to scenes involving impaled, entombed, or apparently extracted hearts in Robert Wilmot's *The Tragedy of Tancred and Gismund* and John Fletcher's *The Mad Lover*, which might have been known to a contemporary audience. He views Ford's play as a complex 'startling re-vision[s] of his predecessors' and in teasing out its meanings draws attention to the close links between the 'iconography of Love's Cruelty'[6] and that of religious devotion – a line followed more recently by Alison Findlay who suggests: 'The bringing of Annabella's heart into the play's last supper completes her progress through the key icons in the biblical story of creation, fall, virgin birth and sacrifice.'[7] The Petrarchan conceits which are both mocked and revered in plays which Ford reworks, such as *Romeo and Juliet* and *The Duchess of Malfi*, also provide him with a fusion of the erotic and the divine here.

In V.v., Giovanni describes his frequent tears as the tribute which his 'heart / Hath paid to Annabella's sacred love' and as he tearfully prepares to murder her, bids: 'Pray, Annabella, pray. Since we must part, / Go thou, white in thy soul, to fill a throne / Of innocence and sanctity in Heaven. / Pray, pray, my sister' (lines 63–6), before begging successfully for first one, then a second kiss. His last request is accompanied by a plea for forgiveness which Annabella grants, believing it to be for things past, when it is for the killing yet to come. At this point, although she does not realize it, Giovanni has become 'a most glorious executioner' (V.vi. 33), whose request for his victim's forgiveness is a matter of course just before the event takes place. Despite its final twist, parallels and contrasts between this scene and the sonnet Romeo and Juliet create at their first meeting (in I.v.) are several. Annabella, like Juliet, is elevated to saintly status by her lover, but Romeo takes his two kisses in a playful bartering: first sinning with a kiss, then having that sin purged by taking the sin back in the second embrace. Ford's character, however, moves beyond the Petrarchan metaphors which are literalized so safely in Shakespeare's play by way of touching palms and lips in loving devotion. Annabella repents prior to Giovanni's last visit and her strict treatment of herself – writing her letter to him in her own blood and tears, as the Friar directed – puts her in the role of repentant fallen woman rather than saint; yet her newly found religious devotion *is* saintly and her sacrificial death casts her as an unsuspecting martyr for the cause of forbidden love. Annabella's abrupt repentance in V.i., which many find implausible and a betrayal of her earlier spirited encounter with Soranzo,[8] is necessary to fulfil the Friar's wish: 'My blessing ever rest / With thee, my daughter; live to die more blessed!' (V.i. 55–6) and to enable Ford to bring her closer, at her end, to a liberalisation of the adored passive beloved, whose love is considered sacred.

When Giovanni leaves his sister's body in V.v. he takes from it the organ which, in metaphor, bears witness to the truth of its owner's feelings: 'Here I swear / By all that you call sacred, by the love / I bore my Annabella whilst she lived, / These hands have from her bosom ripped this heart' (V.vi. 56–9). To Giovanni, Annabella's heart is a physical token of their love, reassuring him of her forgiveness:

GIOVANNI: Kiss me again – forgive me.
ANNABELLA: With my heart.

(V.vi. 78)

To the banqueting assembly, it is an unwelcome addition to their table, a bloody piece of human meat amongst the 'confections' or sweetmeats they were invited to enjoy. It offends, horrifies, and reproaches them: they cannot be blind to it. When Annabella predicted, 'Brother . . . know that now there's but a dining time / 'Twixt us and our confusion' (V.v. 16–17) she did not know that her forgiving heart would be the feast, though she rightfully saw the banquet as 'an harbinger of death'. In 1997 Michael Neill returned to analysing this scene, arguing that Giovanni's 'display . . . gives hallucinatory life to the recurrent imagery of the human heart as the repository of tormenting secrets', and that it 'carries to its frenzied extreme the anatomical will-to-knowledge that informs the bodily dismemberments of the Renaissance stage; but what it discovers is only an impenetrable enigma'.[9]

Packed with 'the welter of competing definitions and explanations it invites',[10] this heart carries too much, rather than too little meaning. As an object on the stage it is used to show that none of the characters, not even Giovanni himself, are able to appreciate its full significance. It has symbolic value but this, significantly, does not register in the horror of the moment. This noticeable failure on the part of the characters' understanding causes the object to have a strong impact on an audience in the final scene because, as Terri Clerico argues, 'the heart has served so capably as the central referent in a struggle intended to remind us of the ineffable and mysterious contiguity of body and speech – of nature and culture – and of our equally mysterious desire to force the two apart'.[11] The heart's literary and philosophical associations conflict with its physical presence, but the exposure of the latter leads to a re-examination of the former.

Nathaniel Strout noticed that, although Annabella speaks fewer lines than Giovanni, she speaks more often than any other character in the play, usually in response to conversation addressed to her. Unlike Giovanni, she rarely has the opportunity to talk at will, but is the recipient of wooing or interrogation throughout: 'For most of the play, Annabella is a woman more spoken to than speaking.'[12] The heroine who 'enters the play quietly "above" the action rather than as immediately part of it'[13] in I.ii., also goes out quietly, being the centre of attention in the final scene, yet tantalisingly absent from it. When Vasques tells the Cardinal about Putana, 'an old woman, sometimes guardian to this murdered lady' (V.vi. 122), Annabella's body is, apparently, elsewhere, so does he gesture at her heart, physically small and silent but, nevertheless, a powerful reminder of both her and her fate? Strout reminds us that Romeo was willing to give up his freedom to Juliet, but Giovanni always considered himself in control of Annabella and, here, his literal possession of her heart emphasizes the extent to which she was subject to his will.

If Ford had wanted a fitting epigram for this scene, the sonnet from which the following lines are taken expresses the absent Annabella's predicament perfectly:

> I am the soul that feels the greatest smart;
> I am that heartless trunk of heart's depart
> And I, that one, by love, and grief oppressed;
>
> None ever felt the truth of love's great miss
> Of eyes, till I deprivèd was of bliss;
> For had he seen, he must have pity showed;
>
> I should not have been made this stage of woe
> Where sad disasters have their open show
> O no, more pity he had sure bestowed.[14]

When Mary Wroth wrote this as part of a much longer Petrarchan sonnet sequence (probably sometime between 1614 and its publication in 1621), she and John Ford were almost the same age. (Ford was christened in April 1586 and Wroth was born in either October 1586 or, more probably, 1587.) Ford has been criticized for looking back to the Elizabethans, but he does so in order to differ from them in important ways, and it should be remembered that he was not alone in this practice. A Sidney by birth, Wroth had her own reasons for continuing and adapting the Petrarchan tradition. In writing 'Tis Pity, Ford reworked Romeo and Juliet, not only in his transformation of characters and plot, but also in his treatment of the Petrarchan elements of Shakespeare's play. This was only a few years after Wroth had, herself, re-examined and transformed the Petrarchan sonnet.

Ford's connections with the Sidney family have been perceptively detailed by Lisa Hopkins[15] but links with Wroth have so far escaped attention. In 1606 Ford published Honour Triumphant, a prose pamphlet on love and beauty, dedicated to the Countesses of Pembroke and Montgomery: the first was Wroth's aunt and the second, her close friend to whom the volume in which her sonnet sequence appeared was dedicated. In 1613, a long poem, Christ's Bloody Sweat, was published by 'I. F.', believed by many to be John Ford: the poem was dedicated to the Earl of Pembroke, Wroth's cousin and lover. Some suspect that her liaison with William Herbert predated the death of her husband in 1614 and he also had a wife whom, according to Gary Waller, he married 'to acquire money and lands'.[16] Wroth bore him two children after her husband's death, although they never married, and her position at court was adversely affected both by the relationship and the scandal caused by the publication of her romance, Urania, to which her sonnet sequence was appended. She agreed to cease its distribution and recall existing copies, but the work was already well known and there is no evidence that the recall actually took place. Pembroke's mother was Wroth's godmother as well as her aunt and, as Waller explains,

> To complicate it further, Mary Wroth was in a sense Pembroke's sister, since when his own father died, William transferred much of his battle against his father for independence to Mary's father. A sister is frequently the focus of an adolescent boy's voyeuristic sexual experiences – and both William and Mary grew up in an atmosphere

permeated by the voyeuristic gaze of the court, epitomized in that most scopophiliac of poetic forms, the sonnet, which both wrote to and about each other. In the classic Freudian pattern, the son is beaten back by the father from the mother, so transfers his desire from the mother to some other woman, and thereafter the incestuous desires for the mother are projected upon her replacement – in this case, a cousin who is not, legally, a forbidden blood relative, but one who stands in for the forbidden sister and mother.[17]

Pembroke died in 1630, the approximate date at which Ford began to write *'Tis Pity*.[18] Her sonnets show that Wroth could write feelingly about the pains of secret love and whether or not her relationship with Pembroke was a subliminal influence in the writing of *'Tis Pity* (much as the story of her uncle's first love, Penelope Devereux, has been cited as a possible source for his play, *The Broken Heart*, which was published the same year) cannot be verified.

However, a mutual concern with revising use of the Petrarchan tradition and challenging its assumptions, a preoccupation with the 'truth' of love and a knowledge of its nature,[19] along with a feminizing of 'tragic heroism',[20] can be demonstrated in the work of both writers. The sonnet quoted above, with its graphic reference to a female body ('trunk') whose heart has been removed, love's blind irresponsibility and lack of concern for her plight, and the repetition of the word 'pity', juxtaposed with her complaint that she 'should not have been made this stage of woe / Where sad disasters have their open show', have strong associations with *'Tis Pity*.

Of a fifteenth-century German woodcut representing the 'Tortures of Love', Michael Neill comments: 'that print may also serve to highlight one striking difference between conventional representations of Love's Cruelty and Ford's climactic tableau: in the iconographic tradition the victim is almost invariably male'.[21] Such was the case in the English poetic tradition until the work of Mary Wroth. Neill continues, 'In Ford's version of the motif . . . the roles are strikingly reversed'.[21] Wroth's *Pamphilia to Amphilanthus* and Ford's *'Tis Pity* are surprisingly alike in their unconventionality.

NOTES

All act, scene and line references to *'Tis Pity* are taken from Marion Lomax (ed.) (1995). *'Tis Pity She's a Whore and Other Plays*. Oxford: Oxford University Press.

1   Wiseman, Susan J. (1990). *'Tis Pity She's a Whore*: Representing the Incestuous Body'. In Lucy Gent and Nigel Llewellyn (eds), *Renaissance Bodies*. London: Reaktion Books, p. 184.
2   Ibid., p. 195.
3   Anderson, Donald K. (1962). 'The Heart and the Banquet: Imagery in Ford's *'Tis Pity*

and *The Broken Heart*', *Studies in English Literature, 1500–1900*, 2, 209.

4   Neill, Michael (1988). '"What Strange Riddle's This?": Deciphering *'Tis Pity She's a Whore*'. In Michael Neill (ed.), *John Ford: Critical Re-Visions*. Cambridge: Cambridge University Press, pp. 155–6.
5   Ibid., p. 157.
6   Ibid., p. 161.
7   Findlay, Alison (1999). *A Feminist Perspective on Renaissance Drama*. Oxford: Blackwell, p. 31.
8   Strout, Nathaniel (1990). 'The Tragedy of

Annabella in *'Tis Pity She's a Whore'*. In David G. Allen and Robert White (eds), *Traditions and Innovations: Essays on British Literature of the Middle Ages and the Renaissance*. Newark, London and Toronto: University of Delaware Press and Associated University Presses, p. 167.

9   Neill, Michael (1997). *Issues of Death: Mortality and Identity in English Renaissance Tragedy*. Oxford: Clarendon, p. 373.

10 Neill (1988), p. 165.

11 Clerico, Terri (1992). 'The Politics of Blood: John Ford's *'Tis Pity She's a Whore'*, *English Literary Renaissance*, 22, 433–4.

12 Strout (1990), p. 163.

13 Ibid., p. 170.

14 Wroth, Mary (1621). *Pamphilia to Amphilanthus*. Sonnet 42.

15 Hopkins, Lisa (1994). *John Ford's Political*

Drama. Manchester and New York: Manchester University Press and St Martin's Press, pp. 7–34.

16 Waller, Gary (1991). 'Mary Wroth and the Sidney Family Romance: Gender Construction in Early Modern England'. In Naomi J. Miller and Gary Waller (eds), *Reading Mary Wroth: Representing Alternatives in Early Modern England*. Knoxville, University of Tennessee Press, p. 50.

17 Ibid., p. 51.

18 See Neill (1988), pp. 159 and 176, note 20.

19 Ibid., p. 174.

20 See THE HEART OF THE LABYRINTH and Lisa Hopkins (1998). 'Knowing Their Loves: Knowledge, Ignorance, and Blindness in *'Tis Pity She's a Whore'* Renaissance Forum, 3 (1), 1–14.

21 Neill (1988), pp. 173–4.

REFERENCES AND FURTHER READING

Anderson, Donald K. (1962). 'The Heart and the Banquet: Imagery in Ford's *'Tis Pity* and *The Broken Heart*', *Studies in English Literature 1500–1900*, 2, 209–17.

——(ed.) (1986). *'Concord in Discord': the Plays of John Ford 1586–1986*. New York: Ams Press.

Barker, Simon (ed.) (1997). *'Tis Pity She's a Whore*. London: Routledge.

Boehrer, Bruce Thomas (1992). *Monarchy and Incest in Renaissance England: Literature, Culture, Kinship, and Kingship*. Philadelphia: University of Pennsylvania Press.

Clerico, Terri (1992). 'The Politics of Blood: John Ford's *'Tis Pity She's a Whore'*. *English Literary Renaissance*, 22, 405–34.

Findlay, Alison (1999). *A Feminist Perspective on Renaissance Drama*. Oxford: Blackwell.

Gibson, Colin (ed.) (1986). *The Selected Plays of John Ford*. Cambridge: Cambridge University Press.

Hopkins, Lisa (1994). *John Ford's Political Theatre*. Manchester and New York: Manchester University Press and St Martin's Press.

——(1994). 'A Source for John Ford's *'Tis Pity She's a Whore'*, *Notes and Queries*, 41, 520–1.

——(1995). ' "Speaking sweat": Emblems in the

plays of John Ford', *Comparative Drama*, 29, 133–46.

——(1998). 'Knowing Their Loves: Knowledge, Ignorance, and Blindness *in 'Tis Pity She's a Whore*, *Renaissance Forum*, 3 (1), 1–14. <http://www.hull.ac.uk/renforum/v3no1/hopkins.htm>

Lomax, Marion (1987). *Stage Images and Traditions: Shakespeare to Ford*. Cambridge: Cambridge University Press.

——(ed.) (1995). *'Tis Pity She's a Whore and Other Plays*. Oxford: Oxford University Press.

McCabe, Richard A. (1993). *Incest, Drama and Nature's Law 1550–1700*. Cambridge: Cambridge University Press.

Morris, Brian (ed.) (1968). *'Tis Pity She's a Whore*. London: Benn.

Neill, Michael (ed.) (1988). *John Ford: Critical Re-visions*. Cambridge: Cambridge University Press.

——(1997). *Issues of Death: Mortality and Identity in English Renaissance Tragedy*. Oxford: Clarendon.

Roper, Derek (ed.) (1975). *'Tis Pity She's a Whore*. Manchester: Manchester University Press.

Rosen, Carol (1974). 'The Language of Cruelty in

Ford's *'Tis Pity She's a Whore'*, *Comparative Drama*, 8, 356–68.

Sawday, Jonathan (1995). *The Body Emblazoned*. London: Routledge.

Smith, Molly (1998). *Breaking Boundaries: Politics and Play in the Drama of Shakespeare and his Contemporaries*. Aldershot: Ashgate.

Strout, Nathaniel (1990). 'The Tragedy of Annabella in *'Tis Pity She's a Whore'*. In David G. Allen and Robert A White (eds), *Traditions and Innovations: Essays on British Literature of the Middle Ages and the Renaissance* (pp. 163–76). Newark, London and Toronto: University of Delaware Press and Associated University Presses.

Wiseman, Susan J. (1990). *'Tis Pity She's a Whore*: Representing the Incestuous Body'. In Lucy Gent and Nigel Llewellyn (eds), *Renaissance Bodies* (pp. 180–97). London: Reaktion Books.

Wymer, Rowland (1995). *Webster and Ford*. Basingstoke: Macmillan.

PART FOUR
Genres and Modes

26

Theories of Literary Kinds

John Roe

As in most periods, literary performance in the Renaissance tends to outrun the theories constructed for and around it. The reasons for this differ from age to age; but at this time most statements about literature reveal two limiting approaches: critics either look for contemporary literature to fulfil the tenets established by ancient, mainly Aristotelian principle, which is to concentrate on questions of form, or they restrict literature to what is morally acceptable (a concern originating with Plato in *The Republic*, and renewing itself through contemporary religious scruple). The disadvantage of applying Aristotle is that he restricts himself to certain genres, concentrating his remarks on epic and in particular tragedy, while making only passing references to comedy and saying virtually nothing about the lyric.[1] But even were Aristotle to have given a fuller account of literary kinds, the case of the Renaissance theorist would not have been helped all that much, as developments within genre still required a corresponding evolution of descriptive and definitive terms. For their part, the guardians of public morality, inevitably opposed to the free expression of art in virtually all its forms, habitually try to restrict activity to only the most carefully regulated performance or production. In the Renaissance, the question was further complicated by the fact that some of the chief theorists of style, including practising poets, were themselves instinctive moralists.

What I aim to do here is to examine reasons for critics' offering the advice they did about literary forms, assess their value in understanding and 'placing' the literary work, and establish the degree to which their discussion is either helpful or negative. Since my subject is the 'theory of kinds' I shall try to avoid saying much about contemporary criticism (for which, see The Position of Poetry), but inevitably the question of criticism coincides with discussions of genre, as almost any Renaissance statement about poetry makes clear. What I shall not undertake is to attempt to devise a theory of genres that will retrospectively make sense of Renaissance practice. Apart from sinking into the mire of endless subdivision along with Polonius,[2] there seems little point in our attempting to arrive at definitions that would have mystified contemporary practitioners or theorists. Besides, it is more illuminating to dwell on the *aperçus* or shortcomings of Elizabethan commentators than to supplement their comparatively meagre findings with a more sweeping, systematic analysis.[3]

Anyone who reads even a little Elizabethan commentary on literary forms will be struck by the degree to which eloquence and style predominate over other concerns. Many commentators explore literary texts almost exclusively for examples of speaking well and eloquently, and in particular they find their models in the works of Sir Philip Sidney, himself a supreme theorist. Hence, Abraham Fraunce, in the *Arcadian Rhetoric* (1587), takes many of his examples from the poetry and prose of Sidney, recently dead and receiving special posthumous celebrity as a hero of English military and literary life. Similarly, John Hoskins, in *Directions for Speech and Style* (1599?), treats the reader as an aspiring gentleman who could do no better than to consult Sidney's literary works as a manual which teaches the art of deportment in words. Spenser, for his part, assumes 'gentilnesse' in his reader, and recommends the right sort of poem as a means of strengthening his virtue, rather in the manner of the humanist education-of-princes tradition:

> The generall end therefore of all the book is to fashion a gentleman or noble person in vertuous and gentle discipline: Which for that I conceived should be most plausible and pleasing, being coloured with an historicall fiction, the which the most part of men delight to read, rather for variety of matter, then for profite of the ensample.[4]

The question of how best a gentleman should speak and behave brings together two issues that invariably occur in any discussion of Renaissance literary theory, the social and the moral. A significant word here is the Horatian one, 'decorum', which signifies the kind of speech or description appropriate to a fictive character or situation. Sidney gives English equivalents, when he cautions strongly against such things as the 'mongrel tragi-comedy',

> But besides these gross absurdities, how all their plays . . . thrust in clowns by head and shoulders, to play a part in majestical matters, with neither decency nor discretion.[5]

Sidney himself shows the correct way, as his admirer Hoskins eagerly declares to the reader:

> What personages and affections are set forth in *Arcadia*. For men: pleasant idle retiredness in King Basilius, and the dangerous end of it; unfortunate valour in Amphialus; proud valour in Anaxius; hospitality in

Kalander; the mirror of true courage and friendship in Pirocles and

> Musidorus; fear and fatal subtlety in Clinias; fear and rudeness, with ill-affected civility, in Dametas.[6]

On the one hand, Hoskins cites his examples with Horatian aesthetic precepts in mind: each character should be drawn according to clear stylistic principle with no messy confusion of attributes. For example, it would be inappropriate for Clinias suddenly to show courage. On the other hand he makes use of that aspect of Horace which helped Renaissance poets through the thicket of moral watchfulness: the examples should be capable of instructing as well as delighting: *aut prodesse volunt aut delectare poetae*.[7] Renaissance theory bound these two aspects more closely to each other, as Sidney himself testifies eloquently when describing the pleasing yet cautionary tale of Ajax:

> Anger, the stoics say, was a short madness: let but Sophocles bring you Ajax on a stage, killing and whipping sheep and oxen, thinking them the army of the Greeks, with their chieftains Agamemnon and Menelaus, and tell me if you have not a more familiar insight into anger than finding in the schoolmen his genus and difference.
>
> (Shepherd, p. 108)

However, this justification, though well enough expressed, sells poetry a bit short. To emphasize the instructive nature of such examples understates the emotive power they exert on an audience. Though acknowledging Aristotle's authority and his powerful analysis of drama in *The Poetics*, Sidney shies away from discussing the cathartic function of tragedy, and emphasizes, rather, its ideal nature. He notes approvingly Aristotle's observation that even ugly things may be beautified in artistic representation (Shepherd, p. 114), a comment that implies a preference for a genre that more decisively extols the noble over the base. Consequently Sidney parts company with Aristotle by promoting the epic, or heroic, form over the tragic:

> all concurreth to the maintaining the heroical, which is not only a kind, but the best and most accomplished kind of poetry. For as the image of each action stirreth and instructeth the mind, so the lofty image of such worthies most inflameth the mind with the desire to be worthy.
>
> (Shepherd, p. 114)

Sidney gives the example of Aeneas bearing his aged father from the ruins of Troy, and he even commends his abandonment of Dido (conduct regarded by many Renaissance readers as unworthy) as an act of self-government and religious obedience (Shepherd, p. 114). In Sidney's own works self-discipline does not always determine the behaviour of his heroes, most controversially perhaps in the *Old Arcadia*, where according to strict morality Pyrocles may be accused of having seduced the princess Philoclea, while contributing by his self-indulgence to the problems of her father Duke Basilius.[8] But if the plot grows subtle, and the authority of the princes seems undermined by the ironies of their situation, the narrative exonerates them. As the princes appear before the public on the day of their trial, Sidney describes them in terms that reflect his commendation of the epic mode's representation of virtue in the *Apology*. Their physical presence compels the gaze of everyone around them, Musidorus 'promising a mind much given to thinking' and Pyrocles's 'look gentle and bashful, which bred more admiration having showed such notable proofs of courage'. The effect is such that:

> the more they should have fallen down in an abject semblance, the more, instead of compassion, they should have gotten contempt; but therefore were to use (as I may term it) the more violence of magnanimity, and so to conquer the expectation of the onlookers with an extraordinary virtue.
>
> (Robertson, p. 377)

The power of epic to redeem its heroes, even late in the day, and to inspire its audience with attractive descriptions of virtue incarnate – what Sidney, invoking the precepts of Plato and Cicero, calls 'virtue in her holiday apparel' (Shepherd, p. 119), persuades him and other Renaissance theorists (as we have seen) to elevate the heroic form over tragedy. Tragedy suffers in the comparison because, as we have seen, it inspires mainly by negative example, showing what not to do (as in the case of Ajax's misguided anger). Also, still persisting in conceptions of tragedy is the medieval *de casibus* (or fall of great ones) tradition, which the *Old Arcadia* evokes in the description of the threat hanging over Gynecia:

> a lady of known great estate and greatly esteemed, the more miserable representation was made of her sudden ruin, the more men's hearts were forced to bewail such an evident witness of weak humanity,
>
> (Robertson, p. 377)

which brings together both the *de casibus* motif and the principle of teaching by admonition. Epic, by contrast, was a genre that enjoyed more freedom, being capable not only of fulfilling the precepts laid down by morally concerned humanist commentators but also of exploring the possibilities of the imagination in a larger sense than the partly old-fashioned terms describing tragedy allowed. In some respects epic was *the* characteristic Renaissance literary mode in that it advanced ideals on all fronts, not only those of moral inspiration, as we have already observed, but also ones of national achievement. The development of humanism throughout western Europe led to national ambitions within the sphere of poetry (the acme of linguistic performance), and nothing suited this better than the epic genre, established by Virgil as the poetry of national destiny, and imitated as such during the whole course of the Renaissance.[9]

While Italian commentators such as J. C. Scaliger argued for the superiority of the epic for its comprehensiveness,[10] others like Antonio Minturno furthered the idea (*De Poeta*, 1559; 1563) that all poetry moved its audience towards acts of virtue. The later Italian post-Tridentine theorists[11] developed arguments for the moral value of poetry that greatly helped their Protestant and Puritan counterparts in both France and England. Sidney especially drew on Minturno for his defence of the moral character of the poet, and seems to have derived his ideas of admiring poetic example, and wishing to emulate the virtuous actions it describes, both from him and from the neo-platonist commentator Benedetto Varchi (*Lezzioni della poesia*, 1549).[12]

Nothing contributes more towards the moral credentials of a genre than demonstrating its use of allegory.[13] Spenser, in the letter to Ralegh, speaks famously of his poem as a 'continued Allegory, or darke conceit', by which he means that whatever occasional delight the images offer there should be no doubting their underlying seriousness. As well as satisfying moralists (including the Lord Chancellor) who might have raised an eyebrow at some of the ideas treated in the poem,[14] to emphasize its allegorical intention and nature helped resolve some tricky questions of form, or at least made them subordinate to the main purpose. *The Faerie Queene* rambles, and demonstrates that mixing of epic and romance that had caused some classically minded Italian critics, worrying about the confusing of genres, to condemn the work that so inspired Spenser, the *Orlando Furioso* of Ariosto. The debate was largely settled by the time of Spenser's epic, and questions regarding shape and proportion (which, as we see below, continued to exercise Sidney) mattered less than whether the content and purpose of a work appeared serious.

The use of allegory to interpret form once again reveals the likely influence of Scaliger, who more than anyone insisted on decorum, emphasizing that subject-matter defines kind. In turn, this leads to mode as dominant over genre, so that style influences form rather than the reverse.[15] For example, pastoral while it is a genre also functions as a mode, and as such finds expression in other genres, notably the epic and the comic. Sidney, though disdaining 'mongrel' forms elsewhere, follows Scaliger in this respect:

> Some have mingled matters heroical and pastoral. But that cometh all to one in this question, for, if severed they be good, the conjunction cannot be hurtful.
>
> (Shepherd, p. 116)

Allegory is exclusively a mode, but derives its importance in this period from its ability, as we have observed, to strengthen the moral hand of poetry. When Bacon in *The Advancement of Learning* argued for the primacy of the 'fable', and dismissed poetry's allegorical exposition as something simply added on afterwards by concerned moralists, he both liberated the poetic imagination from the constraints of ethical purpose and yet inevitably reduced its claim for serious consideration – a situation that prevailed until the Romantic period.[16] Notwithstanding, the habit of allegory trained readers, for better or worse, in the subtleties of imaginative response and interpretation.

Lyric poetry is similarly a mode without a definite form. Sidney, Puttenham and other theorists treat it fairly slightly, partly because Aristotle did not bother with it, and was therefore unable to provide the Renaissance humanists with a helpful classification, and partly because they were nervous of discussing it. Lyric poetry is the mode of the erotic; but Sidney felt that as with all modes of writing it should have a fitter subject. Consequently he introduces the lyric principally as a suitable mode for the praise of God, and only secondarily as a means of lauding one's mistress (Shepherd, p. 137). His own poetic practice in *Astrophil and Stella* differs notably from his precept.

As for tragedy, Sidney, it is well known, made his pronouncements before the great age of drama in England. We now smile to think of his testing his prescription on such works as *Gorboduc* (1561), and expressing concern that, excellent in so many ways, the play fails to observe Aristotle's requirements for unity:

> yet in truth it is very defectious in the circumstances, which grieveth me, because it might not remain as an exact model of all tragedies. For it is faulty both in place and time, the two necessary companions of all corporal actions.
>
> (Shepherd, p. 134)

What, then, would Sidney have made of those many dramas of Shakespeare which violate the 'laws' of time and place? Think of *Antony and Cleopatra* which has thirteen scene changes in the third act and fifteen in the fourth, or a late play such as *The Winter's Tale*, with its interval of sixteen years between significant actions. *Cymbeline* seems to have been written partly, and perversely, to demonstrate that Polonius's 'tragical-comical-historical-pastoral' need not be an absurdity.

Sidney, however, would probably have been more disturbed by what goes on in some of the plays. *King Lear* shows us a king reduced to penury, and even physically stripping himself in humility; it is a lame conclusion that finds only a moral caution here. The play's own ending expresses the idea of avoiding an unhappy example, but assumes that we shall do this not through the exercise of our discretion but because, by the nature of things, we are unlikely to experience the repetition of such large-scale misery:

> The oldest hath borne most; we that are young
> Shall never see so much nor live so long.
> (*King Lear*, 5.3.325–6)

The persistent ill treatment of the king from the middle of the first act onwards would cause concern to anybody expecting to find in a work of literature the comforting endorsement of the social and political order, as would the desperate intimacy the king shares first with his own fool and then with an apparent madman whose language is largely gibberish. Contemporary theoretical applications of Aristotle reveal an emphasis on tragedy not as cathartic or questioning but as more straightforwardly normative and edifying. Aristotle assumed a king to be a serious, elevated character; but Renaissance theorists' further insistence that the king should maintain dignity throughout the enactment of his tragedy collapses under the example of Lear.[17]

The humanist aspiration, reflected in the dramas of the academy in Italy, and in the court in England, to apply Aristotelian principles of unity in order to regulate creativity in a dignified, socially useful manner, contrasts vividly with the practice of the professional stage. This is true of comedy as much as tragedy, perhaps even more so, especially given comedy's natural tendency towards the unbridled.[18] In the Blackfriars Prologue to *Campaspe* (1580–1, printed 1584) John Lyly congratulates himself on achieving balance and proportion in his play:

howsoever we finish our work we crave pardon if we offend in the matter and patience if we transgress in the manners. We have mixed mirth with counsel, and discipline with delight, thinking it not amiss in the same garden to sow pot-herbs that we set flowers.[19]

This blends perfectly Aristotelian and Horatian precept according to the recommendations of humanist education, which saw play-acting (practised by schoolboys) as useful for elocution and deportment.

On the professional stage, however, such civilizing aspirations invariably gave way to a more vigorous kind of comedy, which interacted with an audience that wanted its humour to mix the rough with the delicate. Exactly the same thing had taken place in Italy, but there a more rigorous division was observed between theatres: the academy, heedful of Counter-Reformation strictures, practised a thoughtful, reflective drama, whereas the *Commedia dell'arte* performed a kind of street theatre, which traded in irreverent assaults on pretensions to dignity and respectability. In the earlier pre-Tridentine part of the century, the plays of Machiavelli, Aretino and Bibbiena had been freely scurrilous, but later humanists, under the urgings of the church, tended to favour a theatre in which laughter was oddly selective, the poorer classes being fair game, while gentlemen and clerics were not admitted as subjects into the circle of ridicule. Such restrictions strained the Italian comic theatre to the point of collapse.[20]

One of the key spokesmen on comedy in Italy was Gian Giorgio Trissino, who developed a one-sided but influential theory in his *Poetica* (1549, published 1561); in the course of his argument – which draws partly on Cicero's *De Oratore* – he contends that the objects of laughter deserve mockery because of their moral shortcomings. He makes no allowance for sympathetic or approving laughter (at witticisms, for instance), or simply laughter as release.[21] Trissino partly revives and intensifies ancient theories of comedy, notably comedy as satire, and his arguments most show up in English stage satire, or in comedies that include strong satirical elements. As we might expect, Sidney responds to the gravity of Trissino's argument, finding in it an endorsement of the principles of decorum he advocates in his own treatise. However, he modifies Trissino is an important way, distinguishing much more than his Italian source between a malicious, essentially misanthropic laughter and a more generous kind:

> But our comedians think there is no delight without laughter;
> which is very wrong, for though laughter may come with delight,
> yet cometh it not of delight, as though delight should be the cause
> of laughter; but well may one thing breed both together.
>
> (Shepherd, p. 136)

The subtlety of Sidney's argument would do justice to that balance of effects Shakespeare achieves in his greatest comedies; and in commenting on the cross-dressing of Hercules, which the hero lends himself to out of love for Omphale, Sidney shows himself capable of accounting for the complexity of feeling engendered by the predicament of Viola in *Twelfth Night*, when she disguises herself as a boy:

> For the representing of so strange a power in love procureth
> delight: and the scornfulness of the action stirreth laughter.
>   (Shepherd, p. 136)

While Sidney (characteristically for his age) inclines towards the conservative and restrictive in his discussion of literary kinds, at moments such as these he is ahead of his time. As Geoffrey Shepherd observes, Sidney seems on the brink of identifying that aesthetic sense that only properly came to be discussed a couple of centuries later.[22]

There is no knowing how well acquainted Shakespeare was with Trissino's writings, but it is likely that Jonson knew of him (perhaps through Sidney's mediation), if only because aggressive, reproving laughter distinguishes so much of his comedy. *Volpone* fits Trissino's theory of laughter very well up to a point: the avaricious figures, Corvino, Corbaccio, etc., receive the comic punishment they deserve; but what of the rogues who gull them, and who indeed take the play's principal roles, Volpone and Mosca? Next to Corvino's miserably obsessive greed, Volpone's acquisitiveness cannot but seem quite palatable. Though exploitative themselves the fox and his parasite prey upon the others only in so far as the play chooses to exploit the laughter rising from their victims' vicious folly: their function is determined by the drama's function. Volpone and Mosca are not new, for they derive from such rascally figures as Arlecchino and Zani in the *Commedia dell'arte*. Yet there was nothing in theory, ancient or modern, that was able to account for an audience's delight in their kind of villainy, in its ability to find therapeutic release in the depiction of behaviour that in life would be morally and socially unacceptable.[23]

In dismissing that 'mongrel tragi-comedy' Sidney confirms the impression that in England such drama grew up in a shapeless, uncontrolled manner without any theoretical underpinning. He acknowledges ancient authority for the form (Apuleius, Plautus) but sees no continuity between then and the present times. However, again within Italy, a serious plea for tragi-comedy was to be advanced by such practitioners as Battista Guarini, author of the influential pastoral play *Il Pastor Fido*. In his prefaces, where he debates the ever-worrying topic of decorum,[24] Guarini asserts:

> there results a poem of most excellent temperament, not only very fitting to the human complexion . . . but much more noble than simple tragedy and comedy . . . a poem which does not bring us the atrocity of misfortunes, blood and deaths, which are horrible and inhuman sights, and on the other hand does not make us so dissolute in laughter that we sin against modesty and against the decorum of the well-behaved man.[25]

Responding to the kind of prescriptive pressure exerted by Trissino, Guarini is keen to demonstrate that the virtue of tragi-comedy lies in its avoiding anything that might offend a cultivated sensibility. The advantage of this appeal was not lost on John Fletcher, who adapted Guarini's play as *The Faithful Shepherdess*; in his preface (the play had a disappointing reception when first performed) Fletcher offers this definition – and justification – of the genre:

> A tragi-comedy is not so called in respect of mirth and killing, but in respect it wants deaths, which is enough to make it no tragedy, yet brings some near it, which is enough to make it no comedy.[26]

John Lyly, using a more colourful, more disarming, idiom seems to have in mind Sidney's objection to those that 'have mingled matters heroical and pastoral', when he declares:

> If we present a mingle-mangle, our fault is to be excused, because the whole world is become an hodge-podge.[27]

Such descriptions, proceeding by negatives and disclaimers, offer a narrow rather than expansive sense of the possibilities of the form. Arthur C. Kirsch comments aptly that the effect on Fletcher is that he cultivates virtuosity at the expense of substance. For his part, Guarini, while making cautious claims for his theatrical practice, in execution reveals something more: a belief in art's capacity to trace a providential pattern with the dramatist acting as its agent.[28] Despite the lack of evidence that he drew on Guarini, and despite the absence of any theoretical statement from him, Shakespeare more than Fletcher resembles the Italian dramatist, particularly in a late work such as *The Winter's Tale*, in the large matter of representing providence.[29]

Renaissance humanist theoreticians of genre were often in thrall to Aristotle, or more accurately to their interpretation of Aristotle, who by naming and categorizing genres offered the security of a workable system, one that included the possibility of applying social and moral norms. Some humanist commentators on style (Hoskins, Fraunce) welcomed this for particular reasons, seeing in it the triumph of eloquence – often regarded as a mere attribute of rhetoric – and its determining influence on the mode of heroic poems or romances, notably Sidney's *Arcadia*. Gentlemanliness, social cohesion, and literary purpose all combined well together. Nonetheless, many works, including those of Sidney himself, point to a discontinuity between their instinctive tendency and what may be claimed for them morally. Purely in the matter of form, a good many Elizabethan poems or dramas observe the precepts of Aristotle or Horace quite naturally. After all, ancient theory developed from either the experience or practice of art, unencumbered by moral or social legislation. All that came later. Rosalie L. Colie puts the proper case for the value of genre: 'significant pieces of literature are worth more than their kind, but they are what they are in part by their inevitable kind-ness'.[30] Sidney understands the importance of this, but errs as a critic in attempting to construct a hierarchy of kinds in accordance with a moral sense of hierarchy. Renaissance example shows that any good formulation of genre depends more on observing what is practised than on insisting what it must be.

NOTES

1 Renaissance commentary on Aristotle, which is mainly Italian, infers his views on comedy from his discussion of tragedy (Clubb, 1989, pp. 40–1).

2 'The best actors in the world, either for tragedy, comedy, history, pastoral, pastoral-comical, historical-pastoral, tragical-historical, tragical-comical-historical-pastoral, scene undividable, or poem unlimited' (*Hamlet*, 2.2.392–6). But see also Pearson (1965).

3 This is not to detract from the celebrated achievements of grand synthesizers such as Northrop Frye in his magisterial, innovatory system of categorization, *Anatomy of Criticism*. However, the difficulties of trying to be comprehensive are set out clearly by Earl Miner (Lewalski, 1986), pp. 15–44.

4 'A Letter of the Authors' (*The Faerie Queene*, ed. A. C. Hamilton, London: Longman, 1977) p. 737.

5 *An Apology for Poetry*, ed. Geoffrey Shepherd (London: Nelson, 1965), p. 135. However, elsewhere Sidney argues in favour of mixed modes (Shepherd, 1965, p. 116; see below, p. 4).

6 *Directions for Speech and Style*, ed. Hoyt H. Hudson (Princeton: Princeton University Press, 1935), p. 41.

7 *Horace, Art of Poetry*, l. 333.

8 See the events of the third book: *Sir Philip Sidney: The Countess of Pembroke's Arcadia (The Old Arcadia)*, ed. Jean Robertson (Oxford: Clarendon, 1973).

9 See EPIC.

10 *Poetices* 1.3 (Shepherd, 1965, p. 192).

11 The Council of Trent met intermittently between 1545 and 1563.

12 See Shepherd (1965), p. 181.

13 See ALLEGORY.

14 Lord Burghley is thought to have obliged Spenser to change the lascivious-seeming ending to the Third Book, as it was published in 1590. See the Proem to Book Four.

15 See Colie (1973), p. 28.

16 See Bacon, *Advancement of Learning* (Spingarn, p. 276).

17 See also Horace, ll. 228–9. Chubb (1989, pp. 191–203) argues for Shakespeare's sophisticated experiments in tragic genre in *Hamlet*.

18 See Horace, ll. 281–3.

19 *Works*, ed. R. Warwick Bond (Oxford: Clarendon, 1902), II, p. 315.

20 See Andrews (1993), esp. ch. 6, 'Obstacles to Comedy', pp. 204–26.

21 See Andrews (1993), pp. 208–11.

22 See Shepherd (1965), pp. 224–5.

23 Andrews (1993), p. 211. In *Discoveries*, Jonson somewhat resembles Trissino in his comments on audience and comedy. See Wimsatt (1969), pp. 34–7.

24 Andrews remarks that 'the distinction between *decorum* as appropriate style and as moral and social orthodoxy was . . . constantly being blurred' (p. 216).

25 Battista Guarini, *The Second Verrato* (1593); in Weinberg, p. 1,087.

26 *The Works of Beaumont and Fletcher*, ed. A. Glover and A. R. Waller, 10 vols (Cambridge: Cambridge University Press, 1906–7), II, 522.

27 Prologue to *Midas*, in Lyly, III, 115.

28 Kirsch, p. 39.

29 See Chubb's chapter ('Pastoral Nature and the Happy Ending') for links between *The Winter's Tale* and Italian pastoral. Kirsch (pp. 57–64) approaches the complexities of *All's Well That Ends Well* – especially their providential resolution – through an analysis of Guarini.

30 Colie (1973), p. 128.

REFERENCES AND FURTHER READING

Andrews, Richard (1993). *Scripts and Scenarios: The Performance of Comedy in Renaissance Italy*. Cambridge: Cambridge University Press.

Clubb, Louise George (1989). *Italian Drama in Shakespeare's Time*. New Haven and London: Yale University Press.

Colie, Rosalie L. (1973). *The Resources of Kind: Genre-Theory in the Renaissance*, ed. Barbara K. Lewalski. Berkeley, Los Angeles and London: University of California Press.

Doran, Madeline (1954) *Endeavors of Art: A Study of Form in Elizabethan Drama*. Madison: University of Wisconsin Press.

Dubrow, Heather (1982). *Genre*. London: Methuen.

Estrin, Barbara L. (1994). *Laura: Uncovering Gender and Genre in Wyatt, Donne, and Marvell*. Durham, NC: Duke University Press.

Fowler, Alastair (1982). *Kinds of Literature: An Introduction to the Theory of Genres and Modes*. Oxford: Clarendon.

—— (1987). *A History of English Literature: Forms and Kinds from the Middle Ages to the Present*. Oxford: Blackwell.

Frye, Northrop (1957). *Anatomy of Criticism*. Princeton: Princeton University Press.

Hall, Vernon (1945). *Renaissance Literary Criticism: A Study of its Social Content*. New York: Columbia University Press.

Kirsch, Arthur C. (1972). *Jacobean Dramatic Perspectives*. Charlottesville: University Press of Virginia.

Lewalski, Barbara Kiefer (ed.) (1986). *Renaissance Genres: Essays on Theory, History, and Interpreta-tion*. Cambridge, MA and London: Harvard University Press.

Miner, Earl (1986). 'Some Issues of Literary "Species, or distinct kind"'. In Lewalski (pp. 15–44).

Orgel, Stephen (1979). 'Shakespeare and the Kinds of Drama'. *Critical Inquiry*, 6, 107–23.

Pearson, Norman Holmes (1965). 'Literary Forms and Types; Or, a Defence of Polonius', *English Institute Annual 1940*. New York: AMS.

Reichert, John (1978), 'More Than Kin and Less Than Kind: The Limits of Genre Theory'. In Strelka (pp. 57–79).

Spingarn, Joel E. (1908). *A History of Literary Criticism in the Renaissance*, 2nd edn. New York and London: Columbia.

Strelka, Joseph P. (ed.) (1978). *Theories of Literary Genre (Yearbook of Comparative Criticism*, vol. 8). University Park and London: Pennsylvania State University Press.

Todorov, Tzvetan (1976). 'The Origin of Genres', *New Literary History*, 8, 159–70.

Weinberg, Bernard (1961, 1974). *A History of Literary Criticism in the Renaissance*. 2 vols. Chicago: University of Chicago Press.

Wimsatt, W. K. (1969). *The Idea of Comedy*. Englewood Cliffs, NJ: Prentice-Hall.

27

Allegory

Clara Mucci

As figures be the instruments of ornament in every language, so be they also in sort abuses or rather trespasses in speech, because they pass the ordinary limits of common utterance, and be occupied of purpose to deceive the ear and also the mind, drawing it from plainness and simplicity to a certain doubleness, where by our talk is the more guileful and abusing. For what else is your Metaphor *but an inversion of sense by transport, your* allegory *by a duplicity of meaning or dissimulation under covert and dark intendments; one while speaking obscurely and in riddle called* Enigma; *another by common proverb or Adage called* Paremia; *then by merry scoff called* Ironia; *then by bitter taunt called* Sarcasmos.[1]

This is how, in his *Art of English Poesie*, George Puttenham defines allegory. The passage occurs in his catalogue of figures of speech immediately after 'metaphor', and it is interesting that Puttenham categorizes allegory as 'an inversion . . . by a duplicity of meaning'. Moreover, figures of speech, although in Puttenham's opinion the 'ornament of every language', 'abuse' or 'trespass' speech itself, a claim that points at an unstable or disquieting power of language to disguise and deceive. Allegory is a 'duplicity of meaning or dissimulation under covert and dark intendments'.

The tendency of allegory to expose polysemy in language is a feature confirmed by the etymology of the word, which derives from the Greek *'allos'* ('other') and *'agoreuo'* ('to speak openly, to speak in the 'agorà' or marketplace') – to 'say' something 'other', i.e., something different from what is said literally. Like puns, therefore, allegories dispel the illusion that our words mean what they say.[2] As the most important of rhetorical figures ('the chief ringleader and captain of all other figures, either in the poetical or oratory science', Puttenham 1589, p. 186), allegory exemplifies a deceitful practice at work in all tropes:

We dissemble again under covert and dark speeches, when we speak the way of riddle (Enigma).

(p. 188)

Ye do likewise dissemble, when ye speak in derision or mockery, and that may be many ways: as sometime in sport, sometime in earnest, and privily, and apertly, and pleasantly, and bitterly: but first by the figure Ironia.

(p. 189)

Nevertheless ye have yet two or three other figures that snatch a spice of the same false semblant, but in another sort and manner of phrase, whereof one is when we speak in the superlative and beyond the limits of credit, that is by the figure which the Greek call Hyperbole . . .

(p. 191)

Then have ye the figure Periphrasis, holding somewhat of the dissembler, by reason of a secret intent not appearing by the words . . .

(p. 193)

As a 'radical linguistic procedure' (Fletcher 1964, p. 3), allegory can appear in a range of literary contexts, while in a wider sense it might define a distinctive feature of literature itself, revealing literature's self-reflexivity, and calling attention to the implied 'medium', leaving meaning to linger in the very distance between literal and metaphorical. As Northrop Frye has pointed out, all literary commentary is more or less allegorical, while 'no pure allegory' will ever be found.[3]

Implied in verse as well as prose, allegory is ubiquitous in drama too – ancient, Medieval, Renaissance, or modern drama. Allegory was a time-honoured rhetorical method for preaching, used in the priest's homily, and was the foundation of morality plays or medieval dream visions in verse (such as William Langland's *The Vision of Piers Plowman*). During the Renaissance, it was more and more marginalized in popular drama, although it retained a pivotal role in the masque, i.e. in a courtly, aristocratic dramatic form celebrating the monarch, the court and regal power. Allegory also persisted in lyrical and metaphysical verse and in epic or pastoral (the genres that were combined in Spenser's *Faerie Queene*) as a fundamental vehicle for a form of representation, although it was ultimately destined to a political and cultural twilight, unless revived in satirical forms, for instance in Swift's *A Tale of a Tub* in the eighteenth century.

Recent critics have analysed allegory ahistorically, concentrating on theoretical considerations of genre[4] or mode of discourse,[5] but for the writers of the early modern period allegory was simply a rhetorical figure involving a substitution or transference of meaning. Puttenham, however, specifically related it to politics and the court:

The use of this figure is so large and his virtue of so great efficacy as it is supposed no man can pleasantly utter and persuade without it, but in effect is sure never or very seldom to thrive and prosper in the world, that cannot skilfully put in ure, insomuch as not only every common courtier, but also the gravest councillor, yea and the most noble and wisest prince of them all are many times enforced to use it, by example (say they) of the great emperor who had it usually in his mouth to say, *Qui nescit dissimulare nescit regnare.*

(p. 186)

Puttenham calls allegory both 'the figure of false semblant' and 'the courtier': 'the courtly figure *Allegoria* is . . . when we speak one thing and think another, and that our words and our meanings meet not' (p. 186, emphasis in the text). In his peroration to the queen, Puttenham writes that the courtier should 'dissemble his conceits as well as his countenances, so as he never speak as he thinks, or think as he speaks, and that in any matter of importance his words and his meanings very seldom meet'; and that 'our courtly poet' should 'dissemble not only his countenances and conceits but also his ordinary actions of behaviour, or the most part of them, whereby the better to win his purposes and good advantages' (pp. 229–300). In other words, Puttenham equates the courtly poet with the courtier.

For sixteenth- and seventeenth-century courtly culture, irony, allegory and impersonation are fundamental concepts, with a common denominator – what might be termed 'tropicity', that is, direct or monosemic signification replaced by indirect or polysemic signification.[6] In his treatise Puttenham points to the moral ambiguity that is generated by the aestheticism of court culture, a feature that is apparent in the masque where power is figured in rituals which, although ostensibly celebrative, could also unmask aberration. To him, decorum persists in the delicate balance between virtue and vice. The moral question becomes very complex since, if all figures are transgressive of the norm which Puttenham calls 'ordinary' language, that which is in itself unnatural and deceitful might result in a sort of 'cure' for the defects of nature.

As the court seemed to be the place where rule and disguise, or Machiavellian dissimulation, went hand in hand, allegory as 'false semblant' was the courtly figure' *par excellence*, able as it was simultaneously to reveal and conceal the truth. The more refined the Renaissance reader was, the deeper the pleasure in the verbal disguise, while the naive reader had to be contented with the *'litera'*. If, in the wake of the widely read *Institutio Oratoria* by Quintilian, obscurity for Renaissance rhetoricians was a fatal flaw, to reveal and to conceal remained a fundamental trait of courtly aesthetics.[7]

In *The Faerie Queene*, Edmund Spenser incorporated in the heroic frame of the poem what he terms a 'continued Allegory, or dark conceit'. In his dedicatory epistle to Ralegh, the author gives a crucial definition of allegory, emphasizing its variability of signification and placing his work in the context of the allegorical tradition: 'I have followed all the antique Poets historical, first Homer . . . then Virgil . . . after him Ariosto . . . and lately Tasso.' While imitating the heroic conception of his work, he is nonetheless aware that:

> To some I know this method will seem displeasant, which had rather have good discipline delivered plainly in way of precepts, or sermoned at large, as they use, then thus cloudily enwrapped in allegorical devises.[8]

Even more interestingly, Spenser adds that this characteristic veiling or 'cloudily enwrapping' is appropriate to an age which admires ideal fictions and things not as they are but 'as might best be' (Herron). The explicit purpose of his work is 'to fashion a gentleman or noble person in virtuous and gentle discipline' (p. 407).

Stressing duality in interpretation, Spenser gives two different definitions of Gloriana: 'In that Faery Queene I mean glory in my general intention, but in my particular I conceive the most excellent and glorious person of our sovereign the Queen and her kingdom in Faery Land.' Later he adds: 'And yet in some place else I doe otherwise shadow her. For, considering she beareth two persons, the one of a most royal queen or empress, the other of a most virtuous and beautiful lady, this latter part in some places I do express in Belphoebe' (II. 486). He therefore warns against seeking one-to-one correspondences between his fictive characters and the historical personages or abstract ideas.

In drama, allegory, although having ostensibly fallen out of favour at the end of the sixteenth century, survived as a structuring principle in play texts for the public playhouses by virtue of its presence in inductions, inserted masques, emblematic scenes, and sub-plots. Particular sub-genres, such as city comedy, the most topical form of drama, retained structural allegorical features (as is the case, for example, with *Volpone, A Chaste Maid in Cheapside*).

Not only can it be argued that 'there is an allegorical dimension to all verse drama'[9] but an allegorical mode of thinking was structural in Renaissance and baroque culture, finding its expression in the 'textualization' of the world. In such a cultural system rhetoric becomes in effect a sort of metatext, pervading all forms of what Manfred Windfuhr calls this 'tropical court-society'.[10] The aesthetic precept *ars est celare artem*, transferred from court life to the writing of texts, served the purpose of helping the artist to avoid censorship or to keep an official position. As a courtly code of behaviour the courtier was urged to 'use in every thing a certain disgracing to cover art withal, and seem whatsoever he doth and saith, to doe it without pain, and (as it were) not minding it' – this is the explanation Castiglione offered of his key notion of *sprezzatura*.[11] But if courtly rhetoric aims at presenting the artificial as natural, the opposite tendency is present as well, since the natural is presented, described and depicted (in a word, represented) as artificial, to be read continuously and problematically.

In this process of textualization of the world – with the moral dangers the duplicity of any figure posits – allegory follows the general Renaissance philosophical attitude of reading the patterns of both nature and art as analogical constructions. The book of nature was there for poets and scientists to uncover an ordered and interrelated universe. The microcosm was a reproduction of the macrocosm, in politics or in the social order of the family as well as in the arts. If God spoke to human beings through tropes and signs, the world-as-emblem-book required allegorical representation and decodification.[12]

The *theatrum mundi* metaphor is just one example – even if a major one – of this coalescence of reality and iconography at the time: the very shape of the amphitheatre playhouses similar to the Globe illustrates this desire for a convergence between human and divine order. As Frances Yates, drawing a hypothetical plan which represents the stage as world, concludes:

this suggested plan draws near to the Vitruvian image of man within the square and the circle, basic Renaissance image which Dee knew very well and popularised in his Preface, as a statement in symbolic geometry of man's relation to the cosmos, of man the Microcosm whose harmonious constitution relates him to the harmonies of the Macrocosm.

(*Theatre of the World*, 1969, p. 133)

The construction of the Globe playhouse recalls the recently discovered rotundity of the earth, which probably Shakespeare had in mind while writing sequences such as the famous one containing Jaques' speech beginning 'All the world's a stage' in *As You Like It* (2.7.139–65), or the dark allusion to the 'great globe' itself which 'shall dissolve' leaving 'not a rack behind' (*The Tempest*, 4.1.153–6).[13] Shakespeare draws the allegorical *topos* of the *theatrum mundi* from the stage into the sonnets, as in sonnet XXIII ('As an unperfect actor on a stage, / Who with his fear is put besides his part, / Or some fierce thing replete with too much rage, . . . / So I, for fear of trust, forget to say / The perfect ceremony of love's rite'). Likewise Spenser, in Sonnet LIV of his *Amoretti*, borrows images of the *theatrum mundi* for his lover who plays 'all the pageants' while the audience take the role of the loved one 'who idly sits' and is 'but a senseless stone'. The same emblematic vision informs two short poems by Sir Walter Ralegh which are constructed through a pattern of analogies recalling the stage. To quote just one of them:

> What is our life? a play of passion,
> Our mirth the music of division.
> Our mother's wombs the tiring-houses be,
> Where we are dressed for this short comedy.
> Heaven the judicious sharp spectator is,
> That sits and marks who still doth act amiss.
> Our graves that hide us from the searching sun,
> Are like drawn curtains when the play is done.
> Thus march we playing to our latest rest,
> Only we die in earnest: that's no jest.

(Sir Walter Ralegh, *Poems*, ed. Agnes Latham.
Routledge and Kegan Paul (London, 1951), pp. 51–2.)

Even in anti-theatrical pamphlets an allegorical structure can be detected: the theatres are called, variously, 'Synagogue of Satan,' 'church of infidelity,' 'bastard of Babylon', and 'hellish device'.[14]

If we read Elizabethan courtly culture through Renaissance eyes as a sequence of allegorical texts requiring interpretation, an important role is played by pictorial and iconographic representation. In the figurative arts allegory was predominant; but even in the description of ceremonial events, such as Elizabeth's entry to the city, or her summer progresses, the visual-pictorial aspects are encoded with allegorical traits. As we read in a passage from a description of the progress in print a few days after

Elizabeth's entry to the city, a spectator 'could not better term the city of London that time than a stage wherein was showed the wonderful spectacle of a noble-hearted princess toward her most loving people, and the people's exceeding comfort in beholding so worthy a sovereign, and hearing so prince-like a voice' (cited in Montrose 1996, p. 26). In fact we could maintain that all aesthetic forms of the period, literature as well as painting, music, as well as architecture and ceremonial, have an allegorical dimension by virtue of their ideological focus on the queen and the legitimization of the House of Tudor.[15]

Renaissance portraits are indeed interesting 'icons', to use Roy Strong's term, concerned more with religious and political allegorical views than with actual likeness.[16] An example might be the well-known 'Rainbow Portrait' (*c*.1600–3), which, according to Strong, is 'above all a composite portrait which has, like the 'Sieve' portraits, to be read as a series of separate emblems as well as collectively' (1987, p. 158). More than depicting an individual, the ruler's portrait was intended to reproduce the abstract principles of that power, evoking at once aesthetic, religious, literary and political concepts.

The highly refined technical features of the painting were intended to distract the viewer from the composite artifices that are keys to an allegorical interpretation of the portrait. Firstly, the queen is always represented in her youth, with an allegorical dissimulation of the decay of her body. In her case, the allegorical representation of an ageless body politic disguises not simply the decadence of a monarch's body natural, but hides the flaws and weaknesses to which, according to cultural constructs, a female body is prey. Triumph over age meant triumph over a sexual body which had to be ideologically preserved as pure and virgin and intact as the Virgin Mary's body.[17] The distance between the literal and the figurative body of the queen recalled a miraculous integrity and immutability in the sovereign which denied both the narrative of the Edenic Fall and the feminine destiny attached to it. In a sense, it gave pictorial voice to Elizabeth's motto, '*Semper Eadem*', and to her declaration: 'I know I have the body of a weak and feeble woman, but I have the heart and stomach of a king, and of a King of England too' (cited in Montrose 1986, p. 315). Escaping normative constructions of the feminine, the iconic representation of the monarch's two bodies was made even more complicated by other details (the coiled snake and ears and eyes suggesting the queen's vigilance; the colourless, cylindrical rainbow in her hand, possibly a suggestion of masculine attributes or in any case an emblem of power and autonomy), details which underline the 'essentially iconic nature of Renaissance interpretive codes'.[18] The very lack of colour of the rainbow, while seemingly a subversive undercutting of Elizabeth's symbolic brilliance, might suggest that her magnificence is in decline or, on the contrary, that her splendour is such that no rainbow can shine in comparison to her. The allegory implied, therefore, both hides and simultaneously reveals contradictory features,[19] in a manner similar to the punning motto displayed right over the queen's hand holding the rainbow: *Non sine sole Iris*, which might be read as 'there is no Rainbow without the Sun' but also, (since Iris was one of the ancient names for Ireland), 'there is no Ireland without her Queen'. This might identify her symbolic link with the demonized Irish 'other' (as the symbols on her mantle could also signify).[20]

There is always a potential alternative reading lurking behind representation, as another famous painting, Holbein's *The Ambassadors*, exemplifies. Here the use of anamorphosis (perspectivism) hints at the hidden text of the painting – the impermanence of material things and the fragility of human destiny – with the skull as sub-text creating an allegorical reading of the surface of the main plot. (The skull is visible only when the painting is viewed awry, from the side.) In the gap between main plot, so to speak, and sub-plot, the inverted space of the subjacent allegory – death pervading everything, leaving not a rack behind – lies open, with its message subversive of the main plot, so establishing a punning commentary on the duplicity and deceitfulness of the spectacle presented to the viewer's eyes.

To conclude, as John Bunyan wrote, allegories are 'dark and cloudy' (p. 144) and they 'shadow' meaning in unstable and overlapping ways. But reading the court and the world as text *sub specie allegorica* for the post-modern critic might nonetheless prove that:

> full-fledged allegory . . . recognises the same 'duplicity' of language that propels deconstructionist theory, but allegory rejoices in it, finding in it a source of connection and a mire of undiscovered meaning . . . For deconstruction, all language puns, and all puns are disjunctive, driving the mind to disparate and intolerable extremes . . . For allegory, all puns are conjunctive, weaving the universe together . . . Conjunctive punning makes a fair metaphor for the way allegory says one thing and means another.[21]

In other words, if the Renaissance world puns, the distance opened by allegory between language and the world seems analogical rather than oppositive, which might be consistent with Foucault's view that the turn of the seventeenth-century signals the point when the main 'activity of the mind' ceased to 'consist in *drawing things together*, in setting out on a quest for everything that might reveal some sort of kinship, attraction, or secretly shared nature within them, but, on the contrary, [it turned towards] *discriminating*, that is, in establishing their identities' (emphasis added).[22]

NOTES

1 Puttenham, p. 128.
2 See Fletcher.
3 Frye, p. 89.
4 See, for example, Quilligan.
5 Fletcher applies the repetition compulsion principle in psychoanalysis to personified universals in famous allegorical texts; see also Caldwell.
6 Plett, p. 607.
7 Quintilian, VII.vi.50–3, 'When . . . allegory

is too obscure, we call it a riddle. Such riddles are, in my opinion, to be regarded as blemishes, in view of the fact that lucidity is a virtue.' This work set the pattern for future rhetoricians from Wilson to Day, to Raynolde, Puttenham and Peacham. George Chapman, however, elevates what is difficult over what is merely perspicuous (see George Chapman, *Poems*, ed. Phyllis Brooks Bartlett, (1941). New York: MLA, pp. 49–50.)

8 Cited in Herron, pp. 181–2.

9 Hattaway. My thanks to the author for having shared with me his ideas on the topic.

10 Cited in Plett, p. 607. Pett concludes his article with an interesting point, between theory and history: 'Research has shown that the symptoms of a courtly decadence were on the increase during the final years of Queen Elizabeth's reign. It is also the period when the discrepancy between appearance and reality becomes an increasingly frequent topic of Shakespeare's plays. Whatever may be the causes of this development – the boundless ambition of a new generation of politicians, the upper-class need for status and luxury, the decline of traditional concepts of order – the 'crisis of the aristocracy' makes the socio-aesthetic problem of allegory, the duality of *'beau semblant'* persistently apparent' (p. 612).

11 Castiglione, p. 46.

12 Grzegorzewska.

13 See also Richard Dutton, *'Hamlet, An Apology for Actors*, and the Sign of the Globe', *Shakespeare Survey*, 41 (1988), 35–43.

14 See Thomas Nashe, *Pierce Pennilesse his Supplication to the Devil*, in *The Works of Thomas Nashe*, ed. R. B. McKerrow, 5 vols. Oxford: Blackwell, 1966–74, vol.1, p. 212. See also

Diane Purkiss (1996). *The Witch in History. Early Modern and Twentieth Century Representations.* London and New York: Routledge, p. 181.

15 In this connection, see Fischlin.

16 Strong.

17 For the Marian iconography of Elizabeth, see Frances Yates (1985). See also Montrose (1980).

18 Breitenberg, p. 4. In the following page he affirms: 'The proliferation and popularity of emblem books . . . allows us to realize the sixteenth-century perception of the interconnectedness of pictorial representation, allegorical tableaux and rhetorical figuration.'

19 It is A. Fletcher's s contention that allegory expresses 'conflict between rival authorities, as in time of political oppression' similar to 'symbolic power struggles' (pp. 22–3); even if this might be true for some cases, I nonetheless see an analogical trait structuring most allegories at root.

20 For this interpretation, see Fischlin and Neill.

21 Maresca.

22 Foucault, M. (1973). *The Order of Things: An Archeology of the Human Sciences.* New York: Vintage Books, p. 55.

REFERENCES AND FURTHER READING

Attridge, D. (1988). *Peculiar Language: Literature as Difference from the Renaissance to James Joyce.* New York: Cornell University Press.

Breitenberg, M. (1986). ' ". . . the hole matter opened": Iconic Representation and Interpretation in "The Queenes Majesties Passage" ', *Criticism*, 28, 1–26.

Bunyan, J. (1966). *Grace Abounding to the Chief of Sinners and The Pilgrim's Progress*, ed. Roger Sharrock. Oxford and London: Oxford University Press.

Caldwell, M. K. (1977). 'Allegory: The Renaissance Mode', *English Literary History*, 44 (4), 580–99.

Castiglione, B. (1928; rpt. London 1959). *The Book of the Courtier*, tr. Sir Thomas Hoby, intro. W. H. D. Rouse.

Fabiny, T. (1984). ' "Theatrum Mundi" and the Ages of Man'. In T. Fabiny (ed.), *Acta Universitatis Szegediensi De Attila Jozsef Nominatae, Shakespeare and the Emblem: Studies in Renaissance Iconography and Iconology* (pp. 273–331). Szegeb: Attila Jozsef University.

Fischlin, D. (1997). 'Political Allegory, Absolutist Ideology, and the "Rainbow Portrait" of Queen Elizabeth I', *Renaissance Quarterly*, 50, 1, 175–206.

Fletcher, A. (1964). *Allegory. The Theory of a Symbolic Mode.* Ithaca, NY: Cornell University Press.

Frye, N. (1967). *Anatomy of Criticism.* New York: Atheneum.

Grzegorzewska, M. (1993). 'Theatrum Orbis Terrarum on the Court Stage'. In Jerzy Limon and Jay L. Halio (eds), *Shakespeare and His Contemporaries: Eastern and Central European Studies* (pp. 219–42). Newark: University of Delaware Press, Associated University Presses; London and Toronto: Associated University.

Hattaway, M. (2000). 'Allegorising in Drama and the Visual Arts'. In P. Happé (ed.), *Allegory in the Theatre*. Theta, 5, 187–205. Berne: Peter Lang.

Herron, D. (1970). 'The Focus of Allegory in Renaissance Epic', *Genre*, 3 (1), 176–85.

Maresca, T. E. (1993). 'Personification vs. Allegory'. In Kevin L. Cope (ed.), *Enlightening Allegory, Theory, Practice, and Contexts of Allegory in the Late Seventeenth and Eighteenth Centuries*. New York: AMS Press.

Montrose, L. A. (1980). ' "Eliza, Queene of shepheards", and the Pastoral Power', *English Literary Renaissance*, 10, 2.

—— (1986). 'The Elizabethan Subject and the Spenserian Text'. In P. Parker and D. Quint (eds), *Literary Theory / Renaissance Texts* (pp. 303–340). Baltimore: Johns Hopkins University Press.

—— (1996). *The Purpose of Playing: Shakespeare and the Cultural Politics of the Elizabethan Theatre*. Chicago and London: University of Chicago Press.

Neill, M. (1994). 'Broken English and Broken Irish: Nation, Language, and the Optic of Power in Shakespeare's Histories', *Shakespeare Quarterly*, 45, 1–32.

Plett, H. F. (1983). 'Aesthetic Constituents in the Courtly Culture of Renaissance England', *New Literary History*, 14 (3), 597–621.

Puttenham, G. (1589). *The Art of English Poesie*, ed. Gladys D. Willcock and Alice Walker (1936). Cambridge: Cambridge University Press.

Quilligan, M. (1979). *The Language of Allegory. Defining the Genre*. Ithaca and London: Cornell University Press.

Quintilian (1920). *Institutio Oratoria*, ed. H. E. Butler. Cambridge: Loeb Classical Library.

Spenser, E. (1961). *The Faerie Queene*, ed. J. C. Smith (1961). 2 vols. Oxford: Clarendon Press.

Strong, R. (1987). *Gloriana: The Portraits of Queen Elizabeth I*. London: Thames and Hudson.

Yates, F. (1969). *Theatre of the World*. London: Routledge and Kegan Paul.

—— (1985). *Astraea: The Imperial Theme in the Sixteenth Century*. London and Boston: Routledge and Kegan Paul.

28

Pastoral

Michelle O'Callaghan

The earliest kind of poetry was of course the product of one of the earliest stages of life, either the pastoral stage, the hunting, or the agricultural . . . As Varro states, and Thucydides implies, the pastoral stage preceded the agricultural; and the fact that the farmer lives a life of toil, but the shepherd of leisure, is additional evidence.[1]

Pondering which poetic kind came first, pastoral or georgic, Julius Scaliger in his *Poetics* articulates a common assumption in the Renaissance that genres are social rather than purely literary constructs and do not merely reflect culture but are constitutive of it. This view of genre was enshrined in the classical theory of decorum favoured in the Renaissance which posited a correspondence between style and subject matter based on hierarchical models of social behaviour.[2] Michael Drayton set out this principle in his 1619 essay on pastoral: just as the 'subject of Pastorals', that is, shepherds, are 'worthily therefore to be called base, or low', so too 'the language of it ought to be poor, silly, and of the coarsest woof in appearance'.[3]

Louis Montrose has argued in his seminal essay 'Of Gentlemen and Shepherds: The Politics of Elizabethan Pastoral Form', that the equation between literary form and social status is particularly acute in pastoral, and its popularity during the English Renaissance was due to the way that it naturalized the class distinctions that structured Elizabethan society at a time when this system was being placed under pressure through social mobility and the successes of the new humanist education system.[4] As a consequence, towards the end of the century there was a generation of well-educated young men of relatively lowly status on the margins of the court seeking advancement. Elizabethan pastoral provided these men with a culturally recognizable form in which they could gracefully voice their ambitions not only because it was at the bottom of the Renaissance hierarchy of poetic kinds, and therefore appropriate to young men at the start of their careers, but more importantly because of the way that the shepherd's life was aestheticized in Elizabethan pastoral fictions. As Scaliger argued, the pastoral life was one of leisure as opposed to the farmer's life of toil, so that the absence of labour was one of the defining features of the classical pastoral world. During the Renaissance, leisure became one of the key social markers of the gentry and aristocracy in distinction to the labouring classes. Italianate pastoral, in particular, is populated by courtly shepherds who live a life of ease, free from the taint of labour. Pastoral is therefore predicated upon an elision of the agrarian labour that structures pastoral societies which enables the 'metaphorical identification between otiose shepherds and leisured gentlemen' (p. 431). For Montrose, Elizabethan pastorals are elegant courtly performances whose primary function is to affirm the civility and gentility of the courtier-poet.

Montrose's essay has become a classic of new historicist criticism, a theoretical approach that is apparent in his emphasis on the way that pastoral works to contain the contradictions that it articulates. One of the problems of this model is that it tends to close down the doubleness of the pastoral form:

> Is the poor pipe disdained, which sometime out of Meliboeus' mouth can show the misery of the people under hard lords or ravening soldiers? And again, by Tityrus, what blessedness is derived to them that lie lowest from the goodness of them that sit highest.[5]

Sir Philip Sidney's definition of pastoral in his *An Apology for Poetry* derives from Servius's commentary on Virgil's *Eclogues*, written at the end of the fourth century AD, which established a way of reading Virgil that dominated the middle ages and the Renaissance.[6] The key pastoral text was the first *Eclogue*. The fortunate shepherd Tityrus, who enjoys a life of ease through the favour of the gods, was understood to be the pastoral persona of the poet Virgil, protected by the patronage of Augustus, while his friend Meliboeus, who is exiled from his homeland, represented the victims of the new regime, those farmers whose lands were expropriated by Augustus to reward his soldiers following the civil war. The contrast between the situation of the two representative shepherds, Tityrus and Meliboeus, produced a version of pastoral that was double coded; simultaneously available for panegyric and for satire, and able to describe the dependency of patronage relations and the paradoxical freedom of exile.[7]

This paradigmatic reading of the first *Eclogue* attributed an ethical and political weight to pastoral that was belied by its simplicity. Drayton was careful to remind his readers that although the language and subject matter of pastoral was low, 'Nevertheless, the most high, and most noble matters of the world may be shadowed in them' (p. 517). George Puttenham in *The Arte of English Poesie* (1589) made a similar point, arguing that Virgil wrote his *Eclogues* 'not of purpose to counterfeit or represent the rustical manner of loves and communication: but under the veil of homely persons and in rude speeches to insinuate and glance at greater matters'. He did not leave it there but went on to give this allegorical dimension of pastoral a certain inflection, suggesting that such veiling was a political necessity given that it may not have 'been safe to have been disclosed in any other sort'.[8] Annabel Patterson, in her *Pastoral and Ideology*, takes Puttenham's emphasis on what 'had not been safe' as the key to the uses of pastoral in this period. Like Montrose, she sees pastoral as providing a language for the expression of courtly ambitions and their attendant anxieties, but it is the possibilities that pastoral metaphor offers for writing under cover that holds her critical attention. Montrose's ambitious courtier-poets become troubled humanist-intellectuals living under an all-pervasive censorship in Patterson's account. Her critical sympathies lie with Meliboeus rather than Tityrus so that the value of the Virgilian eclogue lies 'in its capacity to embody ideals of free speech and free thought in a hostile cultural environment' (p. 134).

Virgil's *Eclogues* were not the only pastoral model available in the English Renaissance. The period inherited a rich native tradition of vernacular pastoral which modified the way that the Virgilian eclogue was read and emphasized the tendency of pastoral towards satire and complaint. The principal influence on this vernacular tradition was the Bible, and it had the effect of re-evaluating the pastoral life. Shepherds no longer lived a life of ease and leisure, retiring to a Virgilian *vmbra* (shade), but were instead hard at work tending to their flocks. This Christianized georgic emphasis on pastoral care meant that issues to do with government – personal, political and ecclesiastical – were foregrounded within the pastoral form. The figure of the shepherd merged with that of the ploughman to produce a distinctive tradition of ploughman literature modelled on Langland's *Piers Plowman* and was given a new impetus with the Reformation in works such as *Pierce the Ploughman's Creed*, *The Plowman's Tale* (often ascribed to Chaucer) and *The Prayer and Complaint of the Plowman unto Christ*.[9] It was primarily a literature of social and religious protest and its values were those of poverty, hard work, piety and humility. The plain-speaking ploughman had long been a spokesman for the oppressed peasant – John Ball wrote under the name 'Piers Plowman' during the Peasants' Revolt. The demotic energies of this literature gave a harder, satiric edge to pastoral and often found their expression in a form of pastoral realism which drew attention to the hardships of rural working life.

Elizabethan Pastoral: Spenser, Sidney and Shakespeare

Spenser's *The Shepheardes Calender* defined the standard for English pastoral for his own and subsequent generations of writers, so much so that Drayton in 1619 could confidently proclaim that '*SPENSER* is the prime *Pastoralist* of *England*' (p. 518). With *The Shepheardes Calender*, Spenser consciously set out to establish his name as the English Virgil and to provide contemporaries with a definitive pastoral handbook suitable for imitation. He used the resources newly made available by print to produce an elaborate eclogue book complete with woodcuts, extensive prefatory epistles giving a defence of the English language, the history of the eclogue and the form of the calendar, and glosses on each eclogue in the manner of medieval commentaries on Virgil's *Eclogues*. The definition of the eclogue that E. K. provided in 'The generall argument of the whole booke', on the assumption that its etymology was 'vnknowen to most, and also mistaken of some of the best learned',[10] educates its readers in pastoral theory and so sets out a standard against which they can judge the new poet's achievements as the founder of a tradition of English pastoral which would rival that of the classics. Spenser's book of eclogues aims for a certain exhaustiveness in the effort to perfect the pastoral form in English. E. K. divides the twelve eclogues into 'three formes or ranckes': the plaintive, exemplified by the January, June, November and December eclogues; the recreative, which treat 'of love, or commendation of special personages', the latter epitomized by his April eclogue, written in 'honor and prayse of our most gracious souereigne Queene Elizabeth'; and the moral, which incorporates the satiric, and is exemplified by the February, May, July, September and October eclogues.[11] Pastoral has an expansiveness in the *Shepheardes Calender* and Spenser is attune to the double perspective in the Virgilian eclogue, its ability to speak for those in power and the marginal and dispossessed.

One of the most distinctive and innovative features of the volume is its language. E. K.'s epistle to Gabriel Harvey is primarily a defence of the 'straungenesse' of Spenser's 'good and naturall English words, as haue ben long time out of vse and almost cleane disherited' (p. 417). It did not convince Sir Philip Sidney who criticized the language of the *Calender* in his *Defence of Poesie*. It is Spenser's English, his revival of 'such old and obsolete words . . . most used of country folk' (p. 416), that most clearly speaks of his debt to a native tradition of pastoral satire, particularly the Plowman literature of the Reformation (King, 369–98; Chaudhuri, 123–5). The May, July and September eclogues self-consciously model themselves on this tradition, offering stories of wolves in sheep's clothing, 'good shepheardes' and 'proude and ambitious Pastours', and the corruption and 'loose liuing of Popish prelates', and so dramatize the religious debates following the Elizabethan settlement. This populist and polemical aspect of *The Shepheardes Calender* made it attractive to Puritan writers, such as Henoch Clapham, who appended 'A Pastoral Epilogue, between Hobbinoll, and Collin Clout' to his *Error on the Left Hand* (1608). Spenser's 'English' is not just confined to these satiric eclogues but is used throughout. This gives the impression that his English shepherds do not lead an Italianate life of aristocratic leisure but feel the cold in winter and endure the hardships of seasonal labour (King, p. 376). Labour is at the centre of *Calender*'s value-system. Its twelve eclogues correspond to the labours of the months in the tradition of almanacs and calendars, often appended to psalters and books of hours, that displayed human activity within a providential framework (Chaudhuri, 450–6). Shepherds's 'swinck' is the marker that distinguishes the godly and the unregenerate, the virtuous and the corrupt, and has the Reformation connotations of church and self-government. Godly labour frequently turns into poetic labour and the shepherd-pastor merges with the shepherd-poet so that the ethical and political responsibilities of the poet become a prominent theme of the eclogues.

Critical attention has typically concentrated on Colin Clout, the solitary singer of the January eclogue. Yet, while *The Shepheardes Calender* introduces the new English poet, this self-presentational gesture is made possible by the community that is figured not only in the eclogues but in the machinery of the volume, the prefatory epistle addressed from E. K. to Gabriel Harvey and E. K.'s glosses, which give the impression that the volume was not the product of an individual author but more of a communal effort. E. K. explains to Harvey that his glosses were made possible by his friendship with the author, so that 'I was made priuie to his counsell and secret meaning in them' (p. 418), and his glosses themselves foreground a communal model of textual production by establishing a dialogue between author and reader and between fellow writers. The reader is encouraged to identify the loose community of shepherds that populate the eclogues with a circle gathered around Spenser and Harvey, who are said to appear under the names of Colin and Hobbinol, 'As also by the names of other shepheardes, he couereth the persons of diuers other his familiar freendes and best acquanytance' (p. 455). Yet, E. K. frequently withholds information, drawing attention to that which cannot be said openly. William Webbe in his *A Discourse of English Poetry* (1586) recognized that there was 'much matter uttered somewhat covertly, especially the abuses of some whom he would not be too plain withal' which meant that 'his special meaning' was not 'apparent to every one'.[12] The secrecy that often shrouds figures in the eclogues has the effect of politicizing the motif of pastoral community. These dual imperatives of secrecy and openness describe a semiprivate space in which like-minded friends can freely meet and speak with each other under the cover of pastoral metaphor.

Spenser's volume of pastoral elegies, *Astrophel*, was largely responsible for the transformation of Sir Philip Sidney from courtier-soldier into shepherd poet in the pastorals of the early seventeenth century. This transformation elides the tensions between the soldier and the shepherd that are played out in Sidney's version of pastoral. As we have seen, Sidney provided one of the key definitions of pastoral in his *Defence of Poesie* and critics have recognized the interplay between his *Defence* and his *Arcadia*.[13] Like Spenser, Sidney promoted an ethical pastoral but even more so than Spenser he expanded its political and philosophical range. His Arcadia is no longer an abstract mythical world but a Renaissance state governed, or more to the point, misgoverned by the Duke Basilius.[14] Sidney's *Defence* read the Virgilian story of Meliboeus and Tityrus dialectically as a tale of tyrannical and virtuous government that drew particular attention to the responsibilities of rulers towards their subjects. The *Arcadia* opens with Basilius abandoning his seat of government and retiring with his family to the countryside because he accepts the 'soothsaying sorceries' of the oracle over the wise counsel of his adviser Philanax. This analogy between rule of oneself and rule of a kingdom is elaborated in the story of the princes Musidorus and Pyrocles who succumb to the tyranny of love and abuse their princely natures, epitomized by their adoption of the disguises of the shepherd Dorus and the Amazon Cleophila in order to gain access to the Arcadian princesses, Pamela and Philoclea. 'Sometimes under the pretty tale of wolves and sheep, can include the whole considerations of wrong doing and patience; sometimes show that contentions for trifles, can get by a trifling victory.' This second pastoral story of patience and suffering that Sidney provides in his *Defence* can again be found in the *Arcadia*, and is an element of the aristocratic virtues that underpin its value system. Yet Sidney's 'trifles' would seem to give his *Arcadia* a sharper edge notable not only in the theme of the vanity of princes, with Basilius's mind 'corrupted with a prince's fortune',[15] but also in the sense that even virtuous young men, such as Musidorus and Pyrocles, deprived of their proper aristocratic occupation as soldiers of the realm and forced to compete for court trifles, necessarily abuse their own natures and, more importantly, symbolize the dangerous degeneration of the state.

Sidney transformed the dialectical structure of Virgilian pastoral into a mode of humanist debate in his *Arcadia*. At the same time, he opened pastoral to other genres which enabled the incorporation of a greater range of political and philosophical themes. This type of generic mixing also has another effect in that it creates a certain instability of perspective that works to undermine the ethical certainties on which the text seems to depend. Stephen Greenblatt has drawn attention to the way that the shifting generic perspectives 'can call into question the nature of ethical judgement', so that, for example, in the climactic scene, adultery is not adultery and murder is not murder.[16] The *Arcadia* itself is not a stable text but exists in two versions – the earlier *Old Arcadia*, which circulated in manuscript from the 1580s, and the *New Arcadia*, published posthumously by Sidney's friend Fulke Greville in 1590. Generically, the pastoralism of the *Old Arcadia* turns into chivalric romance in the *New Arcadia*. This generic shift is encapsulated by the transformation of Sidney's pastoral persona, Philisides, who is a shepherd-poet in the *Old Arcadia*, into a knight in the *New*. The ethical and political dimension of pastoral is accordingly strengthened in the *New Arcadia* which may owe something to the editorial influence of Fulke Greville who himself is responsible for the earliest reading of the *Arcadia* as Sidney's treatise on government in his *Life of Sidney*.

The pastoralism of Shakespeare's *As You Like It*, performed around 1600, has affinities with the ethical and revisionary pastorals of both Spenser and Sidney. *As You Like It* is highly eclectic in its use of pastoral, juxtaposing Italianate and native modes of pastoral in the interaction between its courtier-lovers, Rosalind and Orlando, its Petrarchan shepherd lovers, Phoebe and Silvius, and clown lovers, Touchstone and Audrey (Chaudhuri, p. 358). The Forest of Arden is simultaneously a place of aristocratic leisure and, like *The Shepheardes Calender*, populated by shepherds who feel cold and hunger and articulate the plight of the labouring rural poor. This eclecticism encourages a revision of the various modes of pastoral and the social, moral and political perspectives that they encode. Rather than pastoral enacting a retreat into an enclosed and static world, pastoral in *As You Like It* is an open process that keeps in play competing cultural models.

Pastoral in the Seventeenth Century

A number of recent studies have argued for a major ideological reorientation of pastoral under the Stuarts in the seventeenth century. Patterson speaks of pastoral 'going public' and merging with georgic to provide a language for addressing issues to do with the land (Patterson 1988, pp. 133–4). Virgil's first eclogue was re-read to concentrate on the land of exile, Britain, 'A Race of Men from all the World disjoin'd'. In Jacobean panegyric, Britain's insularity was taken as a sign of divine grace and assimilated to James's neo-Augustanism whereby Britain's self-sufficiency became analogous to the golden age of peace and plenty ushered in by the new Stuart king.[17] Leah Marcus has equated pastoral with absolutism in this period, arguing that pastoral was closely tied to Stuart policy in a way that exerted an ideological pull on the genre as a whole.[18]

It is, however, too restrictive and misleading to see pastoral as a predominantly royalist form in the early seventeenth century. During James's reign, the ideological possibilities of pastoral remained open and the type of royalist reorientation of pastoral that Marcus describes did not take effect until the 1630s with the personal rule of Charles I. Pastoral in the earlier period was arguably dominated by the Spenserian poets, Michael Drayton, Samuel Daniel, John Fletcher, William Browne and George Wither, who maintained the ethical responsibilities of the Elizabethan shepherd poet.[19] These poets' indebtedness to Elizabethan political pastoral did not preclude innovation, as is often assumed. The pastoral eclogues of Drayton, Browne and Wither, in particular, loosened the form's ideological ties to the court and isolated and developed the anti-courtliness of pastoral satire to produce an effective oppositional poetic. This is evident in Drayton's revisions to his *The Shepheardes Garland*, first published in 1593, in his *Pastorals* (London, 1606). Rowland's love lament is sharpened into a complaint against a corrupt court and Sidney, the original shepherd poet, has turned satirist in the sixth eclogue, 'laughing even kings, and their delights to scorn / and all those sots them idly deify' (F1r). The vitality of pastoral satire in the early seventeenth century is suggested by the way that the new editor of the second edition of the Elizabethan pastoral anthology *England's Helicon* chose to reformulate pastoral in 1614. The new motto to the collection took an aggressively anti-court tone; English pastoral found its true home in a virtuous commonwealth that is defined through its opposition to the court, 'The court of kings hear no such strains / As daily lull the rustic swains'.

Browne's *The Shepheard's Pipe* (1614), which incorporates eclogues by Christopher Brooke, Wither, and John Davies of Hereford, and Wither's *The Shepherd's Hunting* (1615) are similarly conscious revivals of pastoral satire. Yet what is remarkably innovative about these eclogue books is their expansion of the pastoral metaphor of the shepherd poet to incorporate a wider community or public.[20] Browne, Brooke and Wither feature throughout *The Shepheards Pipe* under the names of Willy, Cuddy and Roget, who are then reunited in Wither's *The Shepherd's Hunting*. This effectively turns these two volumes into sequels whereby they become part of an ongoing intellectual exchange rather than the discrete products of individual authors. The energies of both volumes are directed towards establishing communities and investing them with a collective agency. Pastoral friendship is used to express communal values and to project an idealized social space where friends meet to exchange ideas freely. Because these exchanges are not only attributed to actual individuals – Browne, Wither, Brooke and their associates – but also often located in a recognizable London environment, and so given a specific spatial and historical location, the pastoral metaphor of the shepherd poet becomes metonymic. The semi-private space of pastoral metaphor is in the process of being turned into a print public in these eclogue books and the pastoral takes on a generic suppleness as it is made responsive to a print rather than a court culture.[21]

Pastoral tragi-comedy was another site of generic innovation in the early seventeenth century. When Daniel and Fletcher 'Englished' Guarini's pastoral tragi-comedy, *Il Pastor Fido*, they emphasized the ethical dimension of this new mixed form: the practice of *genera mista*, the artistic control over various genres and multiple plots, mirrored the way that passions are brought under the sway of reason in the action of the play, and gave a lesson in temperance that likened the proper rule of the body to the government of the commonwealth.[22] Daniel's pastoral tragi-comedy for Queen Anne's court, *The Queen's Arcadia* (1606), opens Arcadia to forces of corruption and discord so that pastoral becomes a space for the trial of virtue in a situation of adversity. The main vehicles of corruption, colax (flattery) and techne (art) have a self-reflexivity that draws attention to the dangers of undiscriminating praise of the court. Although they are exiled in the final act, the play does not close with a compliment to the court but with a warning to guard against abuses. Fletcher's pastoral tragi-comedy, *The Faithful Shepherdess*, is presided over by the Elizabethan virgin priestess Clorin. Again, the pastoral world is not a secluded place of retirement and ease but constituted through trial and the active pursuit of virtue and the emphasis is firmly placed on ethical and political responsibility.[23]

W. W. Greg has described Browne's *Britannia's Pastorals* as 'the longest and most ambitious poem ever composed on a pastoral theme'.[24] Browne consciously set out to produce a pastoral epic not of Arcadia but of his 'native home'. Pastoral in *Britannia's Pastorals* has 'gone public' and in the process has become expansive: various genres, tragi-comedy, Spenserian allegory, epic, elegy, satire, georgic, lyric and romance, are incorporated in the effort to give shape to the native land. Genres are used for different ideological effects in the poem. Pastoral tragi-comedy structures the first three songs of Book I which trace the loves and misfortunes of Celadine, Marina, Doridon, Redmond and Fida. The metamorphosis of Fida's deer into Aletheia / Truth neatly triggers a generic shift into Spenserian allegory which is nonetheless incorporated within the tragi-comic imperative and this book closes by imagining a consensus between 'court' and 'country'. By the second book, published in 1616, this consensus has been shattered and the poem's vision of the landscape of Britannia is dominated by satire and a romance instability. The poet wanders in exile and looks to his 'native soil' for alternative sites of poetic validation. Yet, the pastoral landscape itself is in a constant state of flux. The poem's radical formlessness is partly an effect of its generic expansiveness which in turn is a marker of its sensitivity to the protean form of pastoral, its capacity to accommodate other genre and to turn into other things.

Arguably, the history of pastoral is a history of generic accommodation and transformation rather than a story of a essentially pure form that is transmitted from poetic fathers to their sons. As Greg reminds us, 'pastoral is not capable of definition by reference to any essential quality; whence it follows that any theory of pastoral is not a theory of pastoral as it exists, but as the critic imagines it ought to exist' (p. 417).

NOTES

1 Scaliger, p. 20.
2 See THEORIES OF LITERARY KINDS.
3 Drayton, V, p. 417.
4 Montrose (1983).
5 Sidney (1595), p. 116.
6 On this reading of the Virgilian eclogue, see Patterson (1988), pp. 19–59.
7 On patronage, see PUBLICATION: PRINT AND MANUSCRIPT and POETS, FRIENDS AND PATRONS.
8 Puttenham, p. 38.
9 On a tradition of ploughman literature, see: King; Chaudhuri, pp. 116–25.
10 Spenser, p. 419.
11 For a reading of *The Shepheardes Calender* in relation to patronage, see Montrose (1979).
12 Webbe, Vol. 1, p. 264.
13 See, in particular, Patterson (1984), pp. 24–43.
14 Cooper, p. 146.
15 Sir Philip Sidney, *The Old Arcadia*, ed. Katherine Duncan-Jones. Oxford and New York: Oxford University Press, 1985, p. 5.
16 Greenblatt, p. 274.
17 MacLean, pp. 64–96.
18 Marcus.
19 On the Spenserian poets, see Grundy.
20 O'Callaghan, pp. 26–62.
21 See PUBLICATION: PRINT AND MANUSCRIPT.
22 James Yoch (1987). 'The Renaissance dramatization of temperance: The Italian revival of tragicomedy and *The Faithful Shepherdess*'. In Nancy Klein Maguire (ed.), *Renaissance Tragicomedy: Explorations in Genre and Politics*. (pp. 115–30). New York: AMS Press, pp. 115–23.
23 Gordon McMullan (1994), *The Politics of Unease in the Plays of John Fletcher*. Amherst, MA: University of Massachusetts Press.
24 Greg p. 131. See also O'Callaghan, pp. 86–146.

REFERENCES AND FURTHER READING

Chaudhuri, Sukanta (1989). *Renaissance Pastoral and its English Developments*. Oxford: Clarendon Press.

Cooper, Helen (1977). *Pastoral: Mediaeval into Renaissance*. Ipswich: D. S. Brewer; Totowa, NJ: Rowman and Littlefield.

Drayton, Michael (1619; 1941). 'To the reader of his Pastoralls', *Pastorals*. In J. Hebel. (ed.), *The Works of Michael Drayton*. 5 vols (Vol. 5, pp. 417–18). Oxford: Basil Blackwell.

Greenblatt, Stephen (1973). 'Sidney's *Arcadia* and the Mixed Mode', *Studies in Philology*, 70, 269–78.

Greg, W. W. (1906). *Pastoral Poetry and Pastoral Drama: A Literary Inquiry with Special Reference to the Pre-Restoration Stage in England*. London: A. H. Bullen.

Grundy, Joan (1969). *The Spenserian Poets: A Study in Elizabethan and Jacobean Poetry*. London: Edward Arnold.

Hunter, William B. (ed.) (1977). *The English Spenserians: The Poetry of Giles Fletcher, George Wither, Michael Drayton, Phineas Fletcher and Henry More*. Salt Lake City: University of Utah Press.

King, John N. (1986). 'Spenser's *Shepheardes Calender* and Protestant Pastoral Satire'. In B. K. Lewalski (ed.), *Renaissance Genres: Essays on Theory, History, and Interpretation*. (pp. 369–98). Cambridge, MA and London: Harvard University Press.

MacLean, Gerald M. (1990). *Time's Witness: Historical Representation in English Poetry, 1603–1660*. Madison, WI: University of Wisconsin Press.

McMullan, Gordon (1994). *The Politics of Unease*

in the Plays of John Fletcher. Amherst, MA: University of Massachusetts Press.

Marcus, Leah (1994). 'Politics and Pastoral: Writing the Court on the Countryside'. In Kevin Sharpe and Peter Lake (eds), *Culture and Politics in Early Stuart England* (pp. 139–59). Basingstoke and London: Macmillan.

Montrose, Louis Adrian (1979). '"The perfect paterne of a poete": The Poetics of Courtship in *The Shepheardes Calender*', *Texas Studies in Literature and Language*, 21, 34–67.

——(1983). '"Of gentlemen and shepherds": The Politics of Elizabethan Pastoral Form', *English Literary History*, 50, 415–59.

Norbrook, David (1984). *Poetry and Politics in the English Renaissance*. London: Routledge and Kegan Paul.

O'Callaghan, Michelle (2000). *The 'Shepheards Nation': Jacobean Spenserians and Early Stuart Political Culture*. Oxford: Oxford University Press.

Patterson, Annabel (1984). *Censorship and Interpretation: The Conditions of Writing and Reading in Early Modern England*. Madison, WI: University of Wisconsin Press.

——(1988). *Pastoral and Ideology: Virgil to Valéry*. Oxford: Clarendon Press.

Puttenham, George (1589; 1936; repr. 1970). *The Arte of English Poesie*, eds Gladys Doidge Willcock and Alice Walker. Cambridge: Cambridge University Press.

Scaliger, Julius Caesar (1905). 'Pastoral poetry'. In Frederic Morgan Padelford (ed.), *Select Translations from Scaliger's Poetics*. Yale Studies in English, 26.

Sidney, Sir Philip (1595; 1965). *An Apology for Poetry*, ed. Geoffrey Shepherd. London.

——(1985). *The Old Arcadia*, ed. Katherine Duncan-Jones. Oxford and New York: Oxford University Press.

Spenser, Edmund (1916; 1966). *Poetical Works*, eds J. C. Smith and E. De Selincourt. London, New York, Toronto: Oxford University Press.

Yoch, James (1987). 'The Renaissance Dramatization of Temperance: The Italian Revival of Tragicomedy and *The Faithful Shepherdess*'. In Nancy Klein Maguire (ed.), *Renaissance Tragicomedy: Explorations in Genre and Politics*. (pp. 115–30). New York: AMS Press.

Webbe, William (1586; 1902). *A Discourse of English Poetrie*. In G. Gregory Smith (ed.), *Elizabethan Critical Essays*. 2 vols. Oxford: Oxford University Press.

29

Romance

Helen Moore

In 1577, Thomas Underdowne prefaced the second edition of his translation of Heliodorus' Greek romance, the *Ethiopica* (third century BC), with the following observation:

> If I shall commend the reading of it to any, I might find other better to be commended. If I shall compare it with other of like argument, I think none cometh near it. *Morte Darthur*, *Arthur of Little Britain*, yea, and *Amadis of Gaule*, etc. account violent murder, or murder for no cause, manhood: and fornication and all unlawful lust, friendly love. This book punisheth the faults of evil doers, and rewardeth the well livers.[1]

Underdowne's judgement is typical of sixteenth-century attitudes to romance in its simultaneous fascination with, and rejection of, the stuff of romance, and also in its desire to find a legitimate means of engaging with romance narrative. Anxieties about romance-reading are not just restricted to the matter of romance: one of the reasons for rejecting romance with quite such vehemence lies in the imaginative delight it exercises, and the pleasure its reading provides. As well as indicating the sites of anxiety associated with romance, Underdowne's preface also demonstrates a very accurate sense of the sub-divisions of romance in Renaissance England: he lists the best-known examples of medieval Arthurian romance, Tudor translated romance and Spanish chivalric romance. With the addition of Greek romance, we have here a catalogue of four of the major groupings into which sixteenth-century romances fall. The only groups missing are epic romance and pastoral romance, which in 1577 had not yet reached their full potential in English.

As Underdowne's comments make clear, there was an extensive range of romance reading available in the sixteenth century. Much of it was inherited from the late medieval period via the presses of printers such as Wynkyn de Worde and Richard Pynson. Malory's *Morte Darthur*, originally published by William Caxton in 1485, was also printed in 1498 and 1529 (by de Worde), 1557 (by William Copland) and *c*.1578 (by Thomas East). Malory's text was by no means the only medieval romance to extend its influence into the Renaissance period: de Worde, who took over the Westminster press on Caxton's death in 1491, actively continued his predecessor's interest in printing romances. As well as reprinting Caxton texts such as the *Morte Darthur*, de Worde published verse romances extant in earlier manuscripts (for example *Bevis of Hampton*, *c*.1500), romances such as *Valentine and Orson* (*c*.1510) which do not exist in earlier forms, and translations from French such as *Helyas, the Knight of the Swan* (1512). Translations from French had been one of the staple items of Caxton's printing output, and the influence of French narratives continued to be as important in the reign of Henry VIII as it had been under Henry VII. The writer most responsible for the continuance of continental romance in England during the Tudor period was John Bourchier, Lord Berners, who translated the chivalric romances *Arthur of Little Britain* and *Huon of Bordeaux* from French (published *c*.1534 and *c*.1555). Berners's work also anticipated the influence to be exerted later in the century by Spanish fiction: he translated the Spanish sentimental romance *Carcel de amor* as the *Castle of Love* (the earliest extant edition is dated 1549). Berners is most renowned as the translator of Froissart's *Chronicles* (1523 and 1525), which illustrates the considerable overlap, in both style and substance, between the genres of romance and historical narrative in early Renaissance writing. A comparison of Berners's prefaces to *Arthur of Little Britain* and the *Chronicles* reveals a common interest in chivalry, the exercising of virtue, and the stirring of the reader to emulation of these noble deeds. Both prologues envision the translations as acts of recollection; in the words of the *Chronicles* prologue this prevents the knowledge of chivalrous deeds going 'clean out of remembrance', and manifests, 'by example of old antiquity, what we should enquire, desire, and follow'.[2] The source for this prologue (the *Historical Library* of Diodorus Siculus) was also used by Caxton: other similarities of phrasing in Berners's prologues point to a close knowledge of Caxton's work, and possibly even to a self-modelling in the Caxtonian mould.[3] Another link between the two is provided by their mutual indebtedness to the traditions of allegorical romance and learned chivalry that were popular in the court of the Dukes of Burgundy. Another Tudor romancer, Stephen Hawes, the author of *The Pastime of Pleasure* (1517) and *The Squire of Low Degree* (*c*.1520) manifests a similar Burgundian influence.

The writing of romance had been closely allied with the writing of history since Geoffrey of Monmouth used the legend of Arthur as a major component in his *Historia Regum Britanniae* (completed in 1136). In the Tudor age, the historicity of romance – and of Arthur in particular – became a talking-point, as antiquarians and chroniclers re-assessed the evidence for the historical Arthur. They were stimulated in part at least by the desire of Henry VII to associate himself with Arthurian legend. Renaissance scepticism about some aspects of the Arthurian legend began with Robert Fabyan's *New Chronicles of England and France*, written in the early 1490s but not published until 1516. Whilst Geoffrey of Monmouth remained a major source for Tudor chroniclers, there was a growing sense that elements of his history were untrustworthy. John Rastell's *The Pastime of the People, or The Chronicles of Divers Realms, and especially England* (1529) adopts Fabyan's scepticism about the reliability of Geoffrey as a source, whilst not denying the story of Arthur outright. Polydore Vergil, whose *Anglicae Historiae* was written at the request of Henry VIII and published in 1534, goes further in condemning the way in which Geoffrey praised the Britons 'above the nobleness of Romans and Macedonians, enhancing them with most impudent lying'. He rejects the 'soothsayings of one Merlin' as historical evidence but he does allow that Arthur was a historical figure, albeit one who is over-praised by 'the common people'.[4] Polydore's scepticism stimulated John Leland into writing his Arthurian defence, *Assertio Inclytissimi Arturii Regis Britanniae*, published in 1544. Leland is keen to assert not only the historicity of Arthur, but also the British history within which he belongs and which has been threatened by Polydore's scepticism. After surveying the evidence for Arthur's knights, his battles, and even his round table, Leland takes refuge in the witness of the landscape: 'unthankful persons I utterly eschew and I betake me unto those rocks and monuments, the true witnesses of Arthur's renown and majesty'.[5]

Just as chroniclers questioned the veracity of Arthurian material, so sixteenth-century humanists debated the moral and intellectual effects of reading fictional material, which in this period largely means romances. Whilst it is difficult to separate conviction from rhetorical tradition in this debate – the abuse of romance reading becomes so widespread as to be formulaic – it is clear that there was a body of opinion which held that reading romances was a morally dangerous pastime. The primary target of Roger Ascham's *The Schoolmaster* (1570) is Italian fiction, but he is equally suspicious of the medieval and Roman Catholic associations of romance. Ascham also shares Underdowne's misgivings about the matter of romance, as his comments on the *Morte Darthur* make clear: the 'whole pleasure' of Malory's book 'standeth in two special points – in open manslaughter and bold bawdry'.[6] Like Underdowne, Ascham is concerned about the examples of masculinity and femininity encountered in romance: the fear among humanist intellectuals was that romances perpetuated not only sexual licence but also unduly military models of heroism and government. The magical content of romance, and its attractions for youthful readers, sometimes came under attack as well, as in François de la Noue's discourse 'That the reading of the books of Amadis de Gaule, and such like is no less hurtful to youth, than the works of Machiavel to age'. De la Noue is also prepared, however, to acknowledge the imaginative lure of romance reading: after having censured the fantasy, the 'cutting one another's throat for frivolous matters' and the 'dishonest lusts' of the romance, he concludes,

> Here might I allege many other vanities wherewith these books are stuffed, were it not that I fear to bring myself too far in liking with them, whiles I seek to bring others out of taste thereof.[7]

The debate about the historical veracity of Geoffrey's Arthurian material, and the vocal opposition of a number of humanist thinkers and educators, does not seem to have dampened the mid-century enthusiasm for Arthurian and other romances. The best source of information about romance reading habits in the Elizabethan period is Robert Laneham's letter describing the entertainment of the queen at Kenilworth in 1575. Included in his account of the festive activities is a pen-portrait of Captain Cox, a mason who is 'hardy as Gawain' and who has 'great oversight . . . in matters of story'.[8] Laneham then gives an extensive list of the romances, ballads and almanacs owned by Captain Cox, which include 'King Arthur's book' (probably the *Morte Darthur*) and *Huon of Bordeaux*, as well as many other metrical and prose romances first printed by Caxton and his successors, such as *Sir Eglamour* and *The Four Sons of Aymon*.

At the time of Laneham's letter the reprinting of metrical romances such as those owned by Captain Cox was in slow decline. Prose romance, on the other hand, received an invigorating boost from translations of Italian novellas and Spanish chivalric romances in the 1560s and onwards. William Painter's *Palace of Pleasure* (1566), Geoffrey Fenton's *Certain Tragical Discourses* (1567) and George Pettie's *A Petite Palace of Pettie his Pleasure* (1576) were all novella collections which enjoyed a wide popularity in England and which introduced Italian narrative styles and material into Elizabethan romance. The main features of the Italian novella taken up in English fiction are the intricately plotted love affairs (often with some moral message) and the depiction of witty talk; the tales are also located within recognizable, rather than fantastic or magical, narrative contexts. The influence of the Italian novella tradition is seen clearly in Barnaby Riche's collection, *Riche his Farewell to Military Profession* (1581), in the ease with which the narrative *topoi* of romance, such as separated lovers and fractured families, can be absorbed into the contemporary world of the novella.

Even more significant than the translations of Italian novellas, however, were the numerous translations of Spanish romance, which indicate a resurgence of interest in chivalric fiction during the last twenty years of the sixteenth century. The vogue for Spanish romance began with Margaret Tyler's translation of the first book of *The Mirror of Princely Deeds and Knighthood* in 1578, and it continued into the first two decades of the seventeenth century with translations of the romances *Palmerin of England*, *Palmerin de Oliva*, *Primaleon of Greece*, *Gerileon of England*, *Palladine of England* and *Amadis de Gaule*. In many respects, the success of Spanish romance in England is attributable to the efforts of one man, Anthony Munday, who translated all of these texts. Munday died in 1633, but his translations of the Spanish books of chivalry continued to be printed into the 1660s. The reasons for translating Spanish romance, as given in Tyler's preface, reprise those of Caxton and Lord Berners: she offers the reader the traditional pairing of 'profit and delight', praises the romance's rhetorical style, and hopes that 'by liking of the virtues herein commended' (that is, magnanimity and courage) the reader may be moved to 'hazard thy person and purchase good name' in the service of his prince.[9]

The wording of Tyler's preface is very close to the back-handed compliment paid to *Amadis de Gaule* by Sir Philip Sidney, in *A Defence of Poetry* (printed 1595, possibly composed 1579). *Amadis* 'wanteth much of a perfect poesy' but Sidney has known men who on reading it 'have found their hearts moved to the exercise of courtesy, liberality, and especially courage'.[10] The courage and magnanimity argument is vital to the late sixteenth-century rehabilitation of romance, in that it rescues the genre from the charge of being given over to imaginative pleasure rather than moral worth. The idea that poetry can be both pleasurable and useful is adopted from Horace's *Ars poetica*, in which praise is accorded to the poet who can ally these two aims. Sidney was not alone in his belief in the potential of romance to be both delightful and instructive: George Puttenham, in his *Arte of English Poesie* (1589) accounts the matter of Arthur, Guy and Bevis to be a part of 'poetry historical', which, even when it mixes truth with fiction, can stir people up to the emulation of valiant deeds. To this end, he admits having written 'for pleasure a little brief romance or historical ditty in the English tongue of the isle of Great Britain'.[11] Once again, ideas about the writing of romance and the writing of history are interwoven.

It is in Spenser's *Faerie Queene* that this combination of historical narrative, poetic pleasure and moral worth reaches its full potential. The first three books of *The Faerie Queene* were published in 1590, and books four to six appeared in 1596. In his letter to Sir Walter Ralegh, printed with the first part in 1590, Spenser expresses his purpose as being 'to fashion a gentleman or noble person in virtuous and gentle discipline'. To the end that his poem should be 'plausible and pleasing' he couches it in terms of a 'historical fiction, the which the most part of men delight to read, rather for variety of matter, then for profit of the example'. Spenser names his models in this enterprise as being Homer, Virgil and the Italian poet Torquato Tasso. Tasso was the author of the epic romance *Gerusalemme Liberata* (1581), which was later translated into English by Edward Fairfax as *Godfrey of Bulloigne* and published in 1600. Spenser borrows heavily from Tasso for his depiction of the Bower of Bliss,

> In which what euer in this worldly state
> Is sweet, and pleasing vnto liuing sense,
> Or that may dayntiest fantasie aggrate, [i.e. please]
> Was poured forth with plentifull dispence,
> And made there to abound with lavish affluence.[12]

The idea of the earthly paradise, a place where the lover can linger in aesthetic enjoyment of nature, is a staple feature of Italian epic romance: another example is Ariosto's description of Alcina's isle in *Orlando Furioso* (1516). The Bower of Bliss is not just an earthly paradise, however, but a dangerously artful garden, a place where 'fantasie' is allowed free rein and where pleasure and beauty are to be found in excess. For these ideas Spenser is particularly indebted to Tasso's depiction of Armida's isle, where the Christian knight Rinaldo lies in the 'sweet prison' of sensuous pleasures.[13]

For Spenser as for Tasso, the garden of earthly beauty is the site of allegorical as well as actual enslavement. Allegorical meaning, like heroic purpose, helps in the task of making serious the narrative pleasures of romance. When Spenser includes Tasso as one of his models in his letter to Ralegh, he is alluding not only to the heroic matter of the Italian poem, but also to the allegorical purpose elucidated by Tasso in his own preface. As Tasso explains his poem, Jerusalem stands for civil happiness, Godfrey represents reason and Rinaldo signifies 'ireful power'. When Rinaldo returns to the service of Godfrey, after pursuing his own deeds of arms and then languishing in Armida's isle, this reconciliation teaches us that 'Reason commandeth Anger, not imperiously, but courteously and civilly' (p. 92). The aim of epic romance is the uniting of reason and action: hence it is ideally suited to the task of fashioning noble minds at the same time as entertaining and inspiring them.

The serious purposes of pleasure are also evident in Sir Philip Sidney's *Arcadia*. The *Arcadia* in its original form is a pastoral romance and is modelled on ancient Greek romance and Renaissance Italian pastoral, specifically Heliodorus's *Ethiopica* and Jacopo Sannazaro's *Arcadia* (1504). Sidney called this version, which circulated in manuscript, a 'trifle',[14] and the pleasurable aspects of romance are evident in its convoluted love plots, disguisings, reversals, restorations and poetic interludes. Beneath the surface of the *Arcadia*'s pastoral simplicity, however, lie the threats of sexual intemperance, civil unrest and the unseating of reasonable rule by passion. These sombre concerns, more akin to chivalric romance and epic than to pastoral romance, are given greater prominence by Sidney in the revised version of his romance, nowadays called the 'new' *Arcadia* in contrast to the manuscript 'old' version. Sidney's revision was still in progress when he died in 1586, and so the version that was printed in 1590 is incomplete. In 1593, Sidney's sister, the Countess of Pembroke, brought out another edition, which is an amalgam of the 'new', revised parts of the first two and a half books, and the final two and a half books of the 'old' version. A transitional passage to link the 'new' and 'old' texts in this composite version was written by Sir William Alexander and first appeared in some issues of the edition of 1613; another supplement, by James Johnstoun, also accompanied the 1638 edition.

Sidney's *Arcadia* stands on the cusp of sixteenth- and seventeenth-century romance. On the one hand, it is the most accomplished representative of the fashion for Greek romance which was current in the last two decades of the sixteenth century, and which spawned a cluster of English pastorals, such as Robert Greene's romances *Pandosto* (1588) and *Menaphon* (1589), and Thomas Lodge's *Rosalynde* (1590). On the other hand, the revised *Arcadia* also anticipates the uses to which romance will be put in the seventeenth century, when the innocent enjoyments of pastoral love are put aside in favour of intensely allegorized erotic and political romances. The status of the *Arcadia* as a pivot between the Elizabethan and the Stuart worlds of romance is also seen in its frequent reprinting (it had reached nine editions by 1638) and in the fashion for continuations of Sidney's romance. This fashion was encouraged by the closing paragraph of the *Arcadia*, which invites 'some other spirit to exercise his pen in that wherewith mine is already dulled' (p. 417) and to continue the stories of, among others, Pyrophilus (son of Pyrocles) and Melidora (daughter of Pamela). The first to offer such a continuation was Gervase Markham, with *The English Arcadia, Alluding his Beginning from Sir Philip Sidney's Ending*, which was published in two parts in 1607 and 1613 and described the fortunes of this second generation. The next continuation, by Richard Beling, was appended to the 1627 edition of the *Arcadia* and was called a 'Sixth Book', although it had appeared separately in Dublin in 1624. Beling continues the stories of characters, such as Helen and Amphialus, who were already known to readers of the *Arcadia*. The story of Helen and Amphialus forms part of the matter of the 'new' *Arcadia*, and it is the 'new' text which also offered the inspiration for Anna Weamys to write *A Continuation of Sir Philip Sidney's Arcadia* (1651). Weamys adopts the romance convention of presenting narrative resolution as erotic union, which in this case entails a multiple marriage ceremony tying up the plots of the four main protagonists, plus Plangus, Erona, Helen and Amphialus, so that 'the former cruelty of fortune was ever after turned into pity'.[15] Cruelty does persist, however, in the form of unrequited love: the nuptials are marred by Claius's dying with the name of the shepherdess Urania on his lips, and the body of the 'despairing shepherd' Philizides is discovered soon afterwards on Claius's tomb (p. 104).

Whilst Weamys uses the cruelty of love as a coda to her continuation of the *Arcadia*, Lady Mary Wroth, Sidney's niece, gives it pride of place in her romance, *The Countess of Montgomery's Urania* (1621). Love in Wroth's romance brings distraction, despair and violence in its wake, and is often featured as a form of imprisonment. This is seen most clearly in the episode of the Throne of Love, which is a building with three towers, guarded by figures of Cupid, Venus and Constancy. In book one, Urania and her servant are trapped in the second tower and become 'prisoners in the throne of Love: which throne and punishments are daily built in all human hearts'.[16]

Wroth's depiction of human hearts, whilst owing a great debt to her uncle's *Arcadia*, is rooted in the contemporary events and personalities of the Jacobean court. The *Urania* is a *roman à clef*, and as such provoked an angry reaction from Edward Denny, who identified members of his family within it. This highlights the increasingly close relationship between romance and the royal circle in the seventeenth century, a point that is reinforced by the uses of romance for political allegory. Two unpublished Caroline continuations of *The Faerie Queene*, Ralph Knevett's *Supplement to the Faery Queene* and Samuel Sheppard's *The Faerie King*, adopt the guise of romance for the purposes of monarchical praise. In the Stuart period, the example of French romance becomes increasingly influential: John Barclay's romance *Argenis*, published in Latin in 1621, and in English in 1625, casts its political commentary on the French court in an allegorical format. Similarly, the dominant fictional form in mid-century is the refined and emotional *roman de longue haleine* imported from France and exemplified by the works of Madame de Scudéry.

In England, the transition from sixteenth- to seventeenth-century romance can be seen most clearly in the abandonment of Arthurian fictions in favour of stories which reflect the political and social concerns of Stuart court culture. Whereas for Malory, Berners, Spenser and Sidney the knight is the agent of virtuous action, in Stuart romance, as in the court masque, the knight becomes a symbol of social finesse and erotic refinement. A similar process can be seen in the treatment of romance themes on the stage, as plays derived from Arthurian material (such as *The Misfortunes of Arthur* (1587) give way to the mythic and magical world of Shakespearean romance, exemplified by the enchanting art of *The Tempest* (c.1611). Whilst the general tendency of seventeenth-century romance is towards the stylized and allegorical, chivalric – and essentially medieval – forms of romance still show themselves to be remarkably tenacious. Chaucer's *Knight's Tale* is the source for *The Two Noble Kinsmen*, written by Shakespeare and John Fletcher (performed 1613–14), and the translation of *Amadis de Gaule* continued unabated either by the fashion for allegorical romance, or the translation into English in 1612 of Cervantes' chivalric parody, *Don Quixote* (1605). Don Quixote's madness is engendered by his excessive devotion to the books of Amadis and his like: the satire thereby pays tribute to the genre's imaginative fascination at the same time as warning of the mental perils lying in wait for readers of romance. The reading of romance also became a favourite topic in English comedies, witnessing to the continuing popularity of romance (especially among the artisan classes) at the same time as parodying it. Jonson and Dekker both betray an extensive knowledge of *Amadis* and its relatives, and Francis Beaumont captures the enthusiasm of the middling sort for romance in his depiction of Rafe, the grocer's apprentice turned knight errant in *The Knight of the Burning Pestle* (c.1607).

Exaggerated though Rafe's attraction to romance may be, it was not untypical in this period, nor was it restricted to those who had little choice of other reading matter. The eighteenth-century churchman, Bishop Richard Hurd, in his *Letters on Chivalry and Romance* (1762), described Milton and Spenser as being 'more particularly rapt with the Gothic fables of chivalry' than with classical stories, albeit that their 'poetic fire' was kindled from the classics.[17] Throughout this period, the rapture of romance is feared and yet desired, imitated and yet scorned. Renaissance romance licences dangerous narrative pleasures, but it is also the period's most versatile mechanism for profitable allegory, and for the fashioning of virtuous and gentle readers.

See also Early Tudor Humanism, Pastoral, Epic, Caroline Drama, Prose Fiction, History

NOTES

1   Thomas Underdowne, *An Aethiopian History, written in Greek by Heliodorus*, London, 1577, sig. ¶3ʳ.

2   *The Chronicle of Froissart, Translated out of French by Sir John Bourchier Lord Berners annis 1523–1525*. With an introduction by William Paton Ker (The Tudor Translations 27–32), 6 vols, London: David Nutt, 1901, p. 4.

3   Blake, p. 130.

4   Sir Henry Ellis (ed.), *Polydore Vergil's English History, from an early translation preserved among the manuscripts of the Old Royal Library* in the British Museum, vol. I, London: Camden Society, 1846, pp. 29 and 121–2.

5   William Edward Mead (ed.), *The Famous Historie of Chinon of England by Christopher Middleton to which is added The Assertion of King Arthure translated by Richard Robinson from Leland's Assertio Inclytissimi Arturii together with the Latin Original*, EETS original series 165, London: Early English Text Society, 1925, p. 54.

6   Roger Ascham, *The Schoolmaster*, edited by Lawrence V. Ryan, Ithaca: Cornell University Press, 1967, pp. 68–9.

7 *The Politic and Military Discourses of the Lord de la Noue . . . translated out of the French by E.A.*, London, 1587, sig. G8^r.

8 F. J. Furnivall (cd.), *Robert Laneham's Letter: Describing a Part of the Entertainment unto Queen Elizabeth at the Castle of Kenilworth in 1575*, London: Chatto and Windus, 1907, p. 29.

9 Margaret Tyler, *The Mirror of Princely Deeds and Knighthood*, London, 1578, sig. A3^r.

10 Sir Philip Sidney, *A Defence of Poetry*, edited by J. A. Van Dorsten, Oxford: Oxford University Press, 1966, pp. 40–1.

11 George Puttenham, *The Arte of English Poesie*, edited by Gladys Doidge Willcock and Alice Walker, Cambridge: Cambridge University Press, 1936, p. 42.

12 Edmund Spenser, *The Faerie Queene*, edited by A. C. Hamilton, London: Longman, 1977, II.xii.42.

13 Kathleen M. Lea and T. M. Gang, *Godfrey of Bulloigne, A Critical Edition of Edward Fairfax's translation of Tasso's Gerusalemme Liberata, together with Fairfax's Original Poems*, Oxford: Clarendon Press, 1981, argument to book sixteen, p. 448.

14 Sir Philip Sidney, *The Countess of Pembroke's Arcadia (The Old Arcadia)*, edited by Jean Robertson, Oxford: Clarendon Press, 1973, p. 3.

15 Anna Weamys, *A Continuation of Sir Philip Sidney's Arcadia*, edited by Patrick Colborn Cullen, New York and Oxford: Oxford University Press, 1994, p. 68.

16 Lady Mary Wroth, *The Countess of Montgomery's Urania*, London, 1621, sig. G1^r.

17 Richard Hurd, *Letters on Chivalry and Romance* (1762), edited by Hoyt Trowbridge, Augustan Reprint Society 101–2, Los Angeles: William Clark Memorial Library, 1963, p. 54.

References and Further Reading

Adams, Robert P. (1959). 'Bold Bawdry and Open Manslaughter: The English New Humanist Attack on Medieval Romance', *Huntington Library Quarterly*, 23, 33–48.

Blake, N. F. (1971). 'Lord Berners: A Survey', *Medievalia et Humanistica*, new series, 2, 119–32.

Bornstein, Diane (1976). 'William Caxton's Chivalric Romances and the Burgundian Renaissance in England', *English Studies*, 57, 1–10.

Burrow, Colin (1993). *Epic Romance: Homer to Milton*. Cambridge: Cambridge University Press.

Cooper, Helen (1997). 'Romance after Bosworth'. In Evelyn Mullaly and John Thompson (eds), *The Court and Cultural Diversity: Selected Papers from the Eighth Triennial Congress of the International Courtly Literature Society, 1995* (pp. 149–57). Cambridge: D. S. Brewer.

Fletcher, Robert Huntington (1966). *The Arthurian Material in the Chronicles*, 2nd edn expanded by a bibliography and critical essay for the period 1905–65 by Robert Sherman Loomis. New York: Burt Franklin.

Hamilton, A. C. (1982). 'Elizabethan Romance: The Example of Prose Fiction', *Journal of English Literary History*, 49, 287–99.

Hayes, Gerald R. (1926). 'Anthony Munday's Romances of Chivalry', *The Library*, fourth series, 6, 57–81.

Hays, Michael L. (1985) 'A Bibliography of Dramatic Adaptations of Medieval Romances and Renaissance Chivalric Romances First Available in English through 1616', *Research Opportunities in Renaissance Drama*, 28, 87–109.

Helgerson, Richard (1991). 'Tasso on Spenser: The Politics of Chivalric Romance', *Yearbook of English Studies*, 21, 153–67.

Kay, Dennis (ed.) (1987). *Sir Philip Sidney: An Anthology of Modern Criticism*. Oxford: Clarendon Press.

Kipling, Gordon (1977). *The Triumph of Honour: Burgundian Origins of the Elizabethan Renaissance*. Leiden: Leiden University Press.

Logan, George M. and Teskey, Gordon (eds) (1989). *Unfolded Tales: Essays on Renaissance Romance*. Ithaca and London: Cornell University Press.

Meale, Carol M. (1992). 'Caxton, de Worde, and

the Publication of Romance in Late Medieval England', *The Library*, sixth series, 14, 283–98.

Merriman, James Douglas (1973). *The Flower of Kings: A Study of the Arthurian Legend in England between 1485 and 1835.* Lawrence: University Press of Kansas.

Millican, Charles Bowie (1932). *Spenser and the Table Round: A Study in the Contemporaneous Background for Spenser's Use of the Arthurian Legend*, Harvard Studies in Comparative Literature 8. Cambridge, MA: Harvard University Press.

Moore, Helen (1999). 'Jonson, Dekker, and the Discourse of Chivalry', *Medieval and Renaissance Drama in England*, 12, 121–65.

Ní Cuilleanáin, Eileán and Pheifer, J. D. (eds) (1993). *Noble and Joyous Histories: English Romances, 1375–1650.* Dublin: Irish Academic Press.

Parker, Patricia (1979). *Inescapable Romance: Studies in the Poetics of a Mode.* Princeton: Princeton University Press.

Patterson, Annabel (1984). *Censorship and Interpretation: The Conditions of Writing and Reading in Early Modern England.* Madison, WI: University of Wisconsin Press.

Salzman, Paul (1985). *English Prose Fiction 1558–1700: A Critical History.* Oxford: Oxford University Press.

Scanlon, Paul A. (1978). 'A Checklist of Prose Romances in English', *The Library*, fifth series, 33, 143–52.

Schlauch, Margaret (1963). *Antecedents of the English Novel 1400–1600.* Oxford: Oxford University Press.

Worden, Blair (1996). *The Sound of Virtue: Philip Sidney's Arcadia and Elizabethan Politics.* New Haven and London: Yale University Press.

30

Epic

Rachel Falconer

In 1941, Mikhail Bakhtin defined epic as a genre formally oriented toward the distant past: it is a world of 'beginnings' and 'peak times' in the national history, a world of fathers and founders of families, a world of 'firsts' and 'bests' . . . 'The formally constitutive feature of the epic as a genre is . . . the transferral of a represented world into the past, and the degree to which this world participates in the past . . . the authorial position immanent in the epic and constitutive for it (that is, the one who utters the epic word) is the environment of a man speaking about a past that is to him inaccessible, the reverent point of view of a descendent.'[1]

Bakhtin describes epic in this way so as to set the scene for the emergence of a new and very different genre; the paragraph quoted above concludes, 'To portray an event on the same time-and-value plane as oneself and one's contemporaries (and an event that is therefore based on personal experience and thought) is to undertake a radical revolution, and to step out of the world of epic into the world of the novel' (*EN*, p. 14). In reaction to the polemical bias of this essay, some critics have rejected Bakhtin's views outright, while others have attempted to reverse his terms, or have cited their favourite epics as exceptions.[2] But the serious implications of his analysis are sometimes too easily overlooked. The point, for Bakhtin, is not that epics deal with past subject matter (though many do), but that they project everything of value into the past. Thus it is the past that contains a society's truths, its ethical systems, its modes of evaluating itself and the world. From this complete and finalized world, the contemporary listener and poet are forever cut off, the only appropriate attitude to the past being one of humble reverence. In his essay, 'Epic and Novel', the term 'epic' becomes virtually synonymous with unificatory, hierarchized discourse which Bakhtin contrasts negatively with the joyous, democratic, polyphonic discourses of the novel. It is not surprising that critics have taken umbrage at this polarisation of genres, even if elsewhere Bakhtin analyses epic poetry in more nuanced terms.

Here I would like to suggest three aspects of Bakhtin's description in 'Epic and Novel' that are fundamental to the study of epic, particularly European, literary

Renaissance epic. First, Bakhtin places the listener and the poet on the same plane of experience (I will refer to the reader, rather than the listener, as we are discussing literary not oral epic). So if epic poetry deals with elevated subjects, with first causes of evil, and grand narratives of history, the epic poet himself is not morally elevated above his audience; he is 'a man speaking about a past that is to him inaccessible'. This immediately introduces a dynamic and unstable element to the relation between the epic narrator and his material; it explains why the narrator so frequently voices anxiety about whether he is equal to the task at hand (as, for example, in Milton's *Paradise Lost*: 'Me of these / Nor skilled nor studious, higher argument / Remains, . . . unless an age too late, or cold / Climate, or years damp my intended wing / Depressed'.. (*PL*.9.41–6)) We might say that the epic *story* is sacred, monologic and unified; but the epic *text* is necessarily dialogic because it is uttered by a narrator who inhabits the 'post-fall', contemporary world of his audience.

Secondly, the 'one who utters the epic word' (I think we should understand this to mean the text's narrator) adopts the point of view of a descendent towards his subject matter. So epic provides the narrator and his audience with an extended time frame; epic situates the human subject in 'great time' rather than in the immediacy of the present tense. This elongated temporal perspective need not work in only one direction, as Bakhtin suggests, but may require the narrator, hero or reader to picture himself as an ancestor as well as a descendent. In fact, a reader's temporal engagement with epic is more closely related to the way s / he reads a novel, than other genres of poetry, simply by virtue of the novel's and epic's comparable length. But even considering the formal constitution of time in epic, without reference to the reader's experience, what we find are not finalized certainties about a golden age, but shifting, sliding perspectives on historical process.

Finally, epic represents 'the environment of a man speaking about a past': a man, rather than a woman (unless we redefine the boundaries of epic to include prose romances, such as Mary Wroth's *Urania* or the Countess of Pembroke's continuation of Sidney's *Arcadia*). This 'man' who speaks of the 'world of fathers and founders of families' nevertheless addresses himself to women and men in his contemporary world. Edmund Spenser dedicated his *Faerie Queene* to 'The Most High, Mighty and Magnificent Empress Renowned for Piety Virtue, and All Gracious Government Elizabeth by the Grace of God Queene of England France and Ireland and of Virginia'.[3] Even if Queen Elizabeth was regarded as an exceptional case, rather than as a model of female authority, Spenser still faced the task of translating his contemporary, female-centred court, into a masculine, epic world-view. As we shall see, the *representation* of women plays a crucial part in the fashioning of a mythic world of 'fathers and founders'.

When we turn to Renaissance theories of epic (or as they also termed it, heroic verse), we will find many similarities with Bakhtin's view.[4] Although of course the Renaissance theorists meant it in a positive sense, they too stressed epic's 'firstness', its elevated subject matter, its capacity to instruct the present age in the higher virtues of the ancient past. Poetry in general was defended on the grounds that it could teach virtue more effectively than theology, history or philosophy, because its method, imitation of real life, was more pleasurable than unmediated instruction (see, for example, Sidney's *A Defence of Poetry*, p. 25, which echoes the standard line from Horace's *Ars Poetica*, p. 106[5]). But because epic poetry imitated only the most noble and heroic actions from the past, its virtuousness (rather than its virtuosity) was the most easily defended of all the literary genres. Thus Sir Philip Sidney argues that the very name of 'heroical' poetry 'should daunt all backbiters: for by what conceit can a tongue be directed to speak evil of [the epic poet] . . . who doth not only teach and move to a truth, but teacheth and moveth to the most high and excellent truth; who maketh magnanimity and justice shine through all misty fearfulness and foggy desires' (*DP*, p. 47). Sir John Harington is no less confident of the special powers of 'heroical poesie, that with her sweet stateliness doth erect the mind and lift it up to the consideration of the highest matters, and allureth them that of themselves would otherwise loath them to take and swallow and digest the wholesome precepts of philosophy, and many times even of the true divinity.'[6]

We move closer to the Bakhtinian concept of unificatory, hierarchized discourse, when we hear that epic poetry aims to educate only the highest classes of society, and that this education consists of learning how to be a good Prince (male or female) or a good courtier. Thus the often cited Aristotle admitted that epic is 'directed to a cultivated audience . . . , tragedy to a low-class one'.[7] This observation did not prevent him from defending tragedy as the superior genre, but amongst the English epicists, we hear echoes of the same assumptions about epic's elect readership. Spenser, for example, declares that his aim in *The Faerie Queene* is 'to fashion a gentleman or noble person in virtuous and gentle discipline:' ('A Letter of the Authors Expounding the Whole Intention', *FQ*, p. 15). Since this is Spenser's aim, he naturally chooses to write in epic verse. Renaissance theorists accepted without much reservation the classical view that poetry could be ranked high (epic), middle (georgic), and low (pastoral); Tasso, for example, approvingly borrows and amplifies this three-tiered classification from Cicero.[8] Moreover, Renaissance editions of Virgil's *Aeneid* were commonly prefaced with four lines referring to the poet's progression from pastoral to georgic to epic verse. These lines were adopted as the *cursus honorum*, or career path, appropriate to the serious poet. Spenser thus signals that he has reached the highest rung of the ladder, when he echoes the 'Virgilian' preface, in the opening lines of the *Faerie Queene*:

> Lo I the man, whose Muse whilome did maske,
> As time her taught in lowly Shepheards weeds,
> Am now enforst a far vnfitter taske,
> For trumpets sterne to chaunge mine Oaten reeds.
> (*FQ*, I.1.1–4)

'Oaten reeds' belong to the pastoral poet, trumpets to the epicist. But when we recall Bakhtin's observation that the epic poet stands on the same plane as his audience, a *lower* plane with respect to his elevated subject matter, we will discover a much less monologic, less harmonious relationship amongst the three constituent parts of epic narration: the poet, the text and his audience. In the first place, the poet may intend an ironic contrast between the ideal heroes of his epic and the real-life courtiers to whom his text is addressed. Thus when Spenser declares that in *The Faerie Queene*, he means particularly to represent Elizabeth I ('A Letter', *FQ*, p. 16), this can be taken either as flattery or as a warning to his royal audience not to fall below the heroic ideal. Even the heroes *within* Renaissance epic rarely embody the perfected ideals to which they aspire. Both Tasso and Spenser represent their knights acquiring heroic virtue painfully and laboriously; the knight provides a model for the reader, in that *both* must strive for a perfection that seems beyond mortal reach.

Moreover, while the epic poet may aim his poem at an elevated audience, he has no guarantee that this audience of powerful, influential people will actually listen to him. Colin Burrow has shown that the decline of regal patronage under Charles I drastically changed both the substance and the function of epic poetry (*Epic Romance*, pp. 235–6). While Spenser, Fairfax and Harington all dedicated their volumes to the queen, the later epicists, Giles and Phineas Fletcher, Gorges and Slayter, all lacked powerful patrons. Rather than continue the fiction that 'personal passions have a direct application to political life' they chose to 'invert the Spenserian model, and to appropriate government as a metaphor for self-regulation.' (*Epic Romance*, p. 236). Epic turns away from its elevated audience, when that audience ceases to hear.

Furthermore, the epic poet is as far below the heroic ideal as his audience is. Like them, he approaches the high truths of heroic poetry indirectly, via the pleasures of the text. Thus Spenser does not offer us 'virtuous and gentle discipline' delivered 'plainly in way of precepts,' but rather, 'cloudily enwrapped in Allegorical devises.' ('A Letter', *FQ*, p. 16; for the double-edged, ambivalent effects of allegory, see ALLEGORY). This is perhaps why, although theoretically epic stood *above* the other poetic genres, in practice it tended to embrace all other genres within itself. In order to fashion the heroic ideal, epic continues to make use of the 'lower', more devious, strategies of pastoral and georgic, not to mention the dramatic genres, and most contentiously of all, the conventions of romance. To a modern reader, Renaissance epic may appear to speak with the voice of unchallenged, regal authority. But when we turn to the poems themselves, we find that the heroic ideal takes shape in the midst of bitter and polemical argument with contemporaries, by means of narrative strategies that call into question the very efficacy of epic poems as vehicles for heroic virtue.

Chapman's *Homer*

The dynamic interplay between the idealized *image* of epic and its concrete realization is nowhere more evident than in the business of translation. George Chapman prefaces the 1611 edition of his *Homer's Iliads* with a letter to the reader which begins, 'Of all books extant in all kinds, Homer is the first and best'.[9] There can be no doubt in any reader's mind how highly Chapman elevates his beloved Homer above himself; his 'silly endeavours' can never hope to match 'Homer's far more right and mine own earnest and ingenious love of him' (*Iliads*, p. 18). While a second preface, 'Of Homer', treats of the man (or rather, the myth of the man), it is clear from Chapman's first sentence that Homer's excellence is indivisible from the excellence of his work: Homer is the first and best *book*. From this original source of heroic virtue, the reader of Chapman's translation will be twice removed, by distance in time and place, and by language.

This situation does not, however, produce the reverent consensus between poet and audience that Bakhtin describes. Chapman borrows the mantle of Homer to berate any mere contemporary who might criticize his work:

> let my best detractor examine how the Greek word warrants [justifies] me. For my other fresh fry, let them fry in their foolish galls – nothing so much weighed as the barkings of puppies or foisting hounds, too vile to think of our Homer or set their profane feet within their lives' lengths of his thresholds.
>
> (*Iliads*, p. 15)

If the distance between Homer and his English readers gives Chapman the right to reject any criticism, it does not, surprisingly, require him to be slavishly deferential to his great original. On the contrary, Chapman considers it his right and duty as a translator to *interpret* Homer for a different age: 'how pedantical and absurd an affectation it is in the interpretation of any author (much more of Homer) to turn him word for word, when . . . it is the part of every knowing and judicial interpreter not to follow the number and order of words but the material things themselves' (*Iliads*, p. 17). The freedom of the translator to adapt his original lies at the heart of the Renaissance conception of imitation as emulation. But even by the standards of his own age, Chapman was remarkably liberal in his 'interpretations'.

Chapman derives his authority from Homer, then, but Homer is to be 'Englished' for his own times; the translation, in that case, occupies an unstable position neither wholly in one world nor the other. The potential hybridity of the translated work becomes chronic when we realize how multi-layered and heteroglossic the world of Renaissance translation was; not only were Greek epics being translated into English, but they were being translated through the filter of Latin, French and Italian versions. Chapman strenuously denies the allegations of 'a certain envious windfucker, that hovers up and down, . . . affirming I turn Homer out of the Latin only' (*Iliads*, p. 17); in this retort, we hear the polemical note of a translator whose Janus-faced authority crucially depends on the reader's belief in his linguistic competence.

And yet, despite feeling universally criticized, Chapman remains marvellously flexible and open-minded towards his text. The 1611 edition announces that the first two books of Chapman's original edition ('Seven Books of *The Iliads*', published in 1598) have been systematically revised, while due to lack of time, the other five have been reproduced without further revision. Books 3 through 6 and 12 are reproduced from the 1608 edition, and the whole second half of the *Iliad*, Books 13 through 24, have been newly translated for the 1611 edition. Such a gradual evolution is not unusual in the history of translation; what *is* unusual is how Chapman himself lays bare the inconsistencies among the various parts of the work. If we want to see him at his best, his least 'paraphrastical' and most Greek, Chapman tells us, we should read the last books of the translation. With such frank and extensive notation about the text's genesis, it is impossible to read Chapman's Homer monologically; we are always aware of the varying degrees of licence, of estrangement from the Greek world-view in the unrevised books, or estrangement from English idiom in the first two and final twelve books.

Thus much might be said about the relation of the poet to his audience and his text, but surely, it might be argued, the text itself depicts idealized, heroic characters far removed from the context of its early seventeenth century readers? But the extra-ordinary aspect of Chapman's Homer is that it manages to be both archaic and con-temporary at once. In the first book of the *Iliad*, Achilles takes offence at the way Agamemnon, King of the Greeks, demands recompense from his own soldiers when he is forced to give up a slave he has won in battle:

> King of us all, in ambition
> Most covetous of all that breathe, why should the great-souled Greeks
> Supply thy lost prise out of theirs?
>
> (*Iliads*, I.120–2, 1611 edn)

Agamemnon is incensed at this and replies that he'll have what slave he likes, from any of the Greek captains. Achilles calls him impudent and reminds him that it was only for the sake of the Atrides brothers that the Greeks came to war in the first place,

> Thine and thy brother's vengeance sought (thou dog's eyes) of this Troy
> By our exposed lives – whose deserts thou neither dost employ
> With honour nor with care.
>
> (*Iliads*, I.161–3, 1611 edn)

Colin Burrow has analysed the particular resonance this passage would have had in the context of the Earl of Essex's rebellion against Queen Elizabeth (*Epic Romance*, p. 215). Essex suffered insult from the Queen in 1598, and attempted a *coup* against her in 1601. Chapman's *Seven Books* were dedicated to the Earl of Essex, in 1598; the com-plete *Iliads* (1611) were dedicated to Prince Henry. One might expect that in the later edition, Chapman was dissociating himself from the disgraced Essex, and from the theme of 'injured merit', which the rebellion came to represent. But as Burrow has shown, Chapman actually underlines Achilles' resentment, lengthening and sharpen-ing his speeches in the 1611 edition. By comparison with the lines quoted above, the response of Chapman's Achilles in 1598 is quite mild ('our kind arms are lifted to release / (Thou senseless of all Royalty) thine and thy brother's fame'). Under the veil of translation, Chapman was able to develop a much sharper criticism of ungrateful royalty than epicists like Samuel Daniel and Michael Drayton, poets writing directly in English.

But if it is fiercely topical, Chapman's *Iliads* also aims for, and intermittently achieves, an estranging archaism. We may be encouraged to make comparisons between Achilles' resentment and English baronial pride in the opening books of the *Iliads*, but in the final books, the hero cannot be so easily assimilated to an early modern context. The *aristeia* of Achilles (that is, the book in which he slaughters innumerable Trojans) concludes starkly,

> Thus to be magnified,
> His most inaccessible hands in humane blood he dyed.
> (*Iliads*, 20.449–50)

Here the translation invites the reader neither to identify with, nor to repudiate Achilles, but rather to contemplate him as a manifestation of the otherness of classical culture. The more Chapman revised his work, the more he appears to have been captivated by the strangeness of the Greek martial ethos. But at the same time, his revisions sharpened the references in his translation to the particular, political disputes of his times. The result is a split time-sense in Chapman's Homer, a sense of the work standing *there* and *here* at once.

Epic and the Marvellous

Chapman's translation of Homer's *Odyssey*, printed in 1614 and 1615, reads like a different work entirely.[10] In place of the weighty fourteener (fourteen syllable lines), Chapman substitutes the more sprightly decasyllabic couplet. The opening lines announce a different kind of project:

> The Man, O Muse, inform, that many a way
> Wound with his wisdom to his wished stay;
> That wandered wondrous far when He the town
> Of sacred Troy had sacked and shivered down.
> (*Odysseys*, I.1–4)

Renaissance critics, notably Pigna and Cinzi, assimilated the *Odyssey* to the genre of romance, in contrast to the epic *Iliad*.[11] Chapman's choice of words, 'wandered wondrous far' together with his marginal gloss about Odysseus' 'necessary (or fatal) passage' in this 'miraculous Poem', signals his awareness of the critical tradition. In contrast to epic, chivalric romances typically depicted the wandering of a knight-hero, whose journey was shaped by chance, rather than destiny. Romances were structured episodically, with several plot lines interleaved in one text, in contrast to the teleological (end-directed), linear narrative of epic, which typically followed the fate of a single, national hero.[12] Accommodating an endless variety of 'marvellous' incidents, romances aimed to inspire their readers with wonder, rather than (perhaps) nationalistic duty. But the boundaries between the genres were by no means clear-cut. The

Odyssey, for example follows the fate of a single hero, while the *Iliad* celebrates many different heroes, not only Achilles but also Hector, Agamemnon, Ajax, Odysseus, Diomedes and Patroclus. Aristotle states that the distinctive characteristic of epic is that it is 'tolerant of the prime source of surprise, the irrational [*to alogon*]' (*Poetics*, p. 83), which is exactly the distinguishing characteristic of romance in Renaissance criticism. The event that seems to have sparked the major critical debate about epic and its relation to romance, was the publication of Ariosto's *Orlando Furioso* in 1516. Interlacing the adventures of Orlando and Angelica (a Carolingian knight and an eastern princess) with those of Ruggiero and Bradamante (legendary ancestors of the Ferraran house of Este, the poet's patrons), Ariosto created a new kind of work that threatened to upstage the more traditionally defined epic narrative. Significantly, the *Furioso* came out several decades before the first Italian commentaries on Aristotle's *Poetics*, and it may be that Ariosto would have broken fewer epic rules if he had been aware of what was at stake.[13] But coming after him, Torquato Tasso worked painstakingly to contain the energies Ariosto had unleashed, redefining the principles of post-Ariostan epic in his *Discorsi* (1587), and reforging romance as epic in his own ground-breaking poem, *Gerusalemma Liberata* (1575). In the *Discorsi*, he argues that all poetry should profit and delight, but that epic poetry should do it by moving the reader to wonder (*Discorsi*, p. 15). Not content to invoke Aristotle as the last word, Tasso admits that this 'new genre', represented by '*Orlando Furioso* and the like', can produce more marvels, more variety, more surprise, than traditional epic, and consequently is preferred by the modern, sixteenth-century reader (*Discorsi*, pp. 68, 76). But, and this is where Tasso draws the line, 'I do deny . . . that multiplicity of action is more apt to delight than unity' (*Discorsi*, p. 76). *Variety* is acceptable, even 'laudable up to the point where it turns into confusion', but a true epic poem must serve a unified purpose; its moral and aesthetic objectives should be clear (*Discorsi*, p. 77). Thus romance enters epic as moral and aesthetic errancy; it is allowed in to delight the reader, but in the end its centrifugal energies must be reigned in to serve the teleological aims of epic. In twentieth-century criticism, the history of epic as a genre self-riven by its introjection of the marvellous, has been told with a bewildering number of permutations. For example: in '*Mirabile Dictu*', Biow argues that Ariosto reigns in the power of the marvellous, which originates in epic with Virgil's bleeding branch episode. In *Poets Historical*, Fichter writes that Ariosto fights back to epic sternness (pp. 4–5), thus providing one example of the way Virgil's 'tragically incomplete' narrative is given an epic ending in the Renaissance (p. 12). In *Epic Romance*, Burrow argues conversely that Ariosto liberates the repressed remorse of Virgil's poem, while in turn Spenser corrects and contains Ariosto. In *Milton, Spenser and the Epic Tradition*, Cook's formulation is that romance 'revitalises epic' in Ariosto. And finally, in *Epic and Empire*, Quint argues that Tasso and Virgil are imperial 'winners' in epic's war with romance (see Further Reading). John Watkins argues in *The Specter of Dido* that Ariosto resists Virgilian closure, while Tasso romances the imperialist Latin poet. According to some recent commentators, then, Ariosto is as seriously epic as Tasso is traditionally held to be; according to others, Tasso is as romance-torn as Ariosto.

Spenserian critics commonly cite the Tasso-like (linear epic) structure of the second book of the *Faerie Queene* as opposed to the Ariostan (multi-plotted) structure of the central books, three and four. But again there is disagreement about how (or whether) Spenser resolved these conflicting narrative drives. In these most recent accounts of Renaissance epic, Virgil is a particularly changeable figure. In some accounts, he is represented as the founder of 'imperial' epic, while in others he figures as the romancer whose tragically limited hero finds fulfilment within the moral framework of subsequent, Christian epic.

Fairfax, Harington and Spenser

Many critics have discussed the debate over romance errancy and epic high seriousness in the context of English epic. But one problem with such critical discussion is the failure to acknowledge that the grounds of the debate shift markedly when imported from the continent. Again, this shift emerges most clearly in the context of epic translation. In translating Tasso's *Gerusalemma Liberata* into *Godfrey of Bulloigne* (1600) a decade or so before Chapman's *Iliads*, Edward Fairfax is clearly influenced by his reading of *The Faerie Queene*.[14] Tasso's careful, duty-bound hero becomes subject to a surprising range of feeling in Fairfax's hands. At the death of a fellow-knight, Tasso's Goffredo shows restraint: 'he reigned in his emotion, the dutiful Bulloigne, and was silent' (frena il suo affetto il pio Buglione, e tace (*GL*, III.67.5–7)).[15] But Fairfax's Godfrey weeps inwardly, and the reader is allowed to know it: 'His rueful looks upon the coarse he cast / Awhile, and thus bespake'. But Fairfax does not simply romanticise Tasso's epic; he also develops Spenser's theme that courtly virtue must be learned and practised. In Rinaldo's shield, which might, in the Italian tradition, be taken as a symbol of empire, Fairfax finds an apt symbol of ancestral virtue. His hero is urged to follow 'this true course of honour, fame and praise' (the Italian reads more simply, 'let what I paint here be a goad and spur to your valour' (al tuo valore / sia sferza e spron quel ch'io colà dipingo (*GL*, XVII.64–5)).[16] Honour, fame and praise are the trio of civic virtues to which Fairfax's heroes aspire, but they are earned in the epic journey, rather than bestowed by birthright.

When Sir John Harington translated Ariosto's *Orlando Furioso* into English (1591), he may not have known *The Faerie Queene*.[17] But like Spenser, he adapts continental epic to English idiom and English political concerns. Ariosto's female characters are figured as objects of desire, endlessly out of reach. As such, they embody the (dis)organizing principle of romance narrative itself, in which closure is endlessly deferred. Indeed, Quint claims that the subordination of romance to epic teleology is 'identical to the Western mastery – achieved by the Western male's self-mastery – of a feminised East whose disorder tends toward self-destruction' (p. 40). But in Harington's translation, virtuous female characters (as opposed to their demonized counterparts) are desired for their concrete and attainable attributes – their rank, good name and fortune. The contrast is evident, for example, in the scene where the warrior-heroine

Bradamante, takes off her helmet after battle. In Guido Waldman's modern prose translation of Ariosto, the passage reads:

> Now Bradamant started to disarm. She set down her shield and drew off her helmet, but a golden band with which she concealed and contained her long tresses came off with the helmet, so that her hair fell loosely over her shoulders, all at once revealing her for a maiden no less beautiful than fierce in battle. / As when the curtains part to reveal the scene – arcades, sumptuous buildings, statues, painting, gilding everywhere, all lit with a thousand lamps; or when the Sun shows his face, clear and serene, through the clouds: so the damsel, lifting the helmet from her face, showed as it were a glimpse of paradise.[18]

In Harington's translation, the act of taking off her helmet reveals not only Bradamante's beauty, but her name:

> Now when the Lady did disarm her head,
> Off with her helmet came her little call,
> And all her hair her shoulders over spread,
> And both her sex and name was known withal
> And wonder great and admiration bred
> In them that saw her make three Princes fall;
> For why, she showed to be in all their sight
> As fair in face as she was fierce in fight.
>
> (*Harington OF*, 32.74)

Ariosto's morally ambiguous gilded palaces with their 'glimpse of paradise' are sealed shut in a neat antithesis: 'as fair in face as she was fierce in fight'. The Englished courtiers gaze in wonder, not on a half-revealed, female *body*, but on Bradamante's heroic *act* of making 'three Princes fall'. In Harington's translation, Bradamante and her lover Ruggiero demonstrate the epic characteristics of 'alta gentilezza' (high nobility) throughout the text, whereas in the Italian, these qualities only come to the fore in the final cantos (see, for example, *OF*, 26.2.4[19]). Romance error, figured as female desire (both the desired, and the *desiring* female), is more subtly contained in *The Faerie Queene*. This is Spenser's description of Britomart (his Bradamante) after battle, when the men are taking their hats off (the spelling is Spenser's):

> . . . the braue Mayd would not diasarmed bee,
> But onely vented vp her vmbriere,
> And so did let her goodly visage to appere.
>
> As when faire *Cynthia*, in darkesome night,
> Is in a noyous cloud enueloped,
> Where she may find the substaunce thin and light,
> Breakes forth her siluer beames, and her bright hed
> Discouers to the world discomfited;
> Of the poore traueller, that went astray,
> With thousand blessings she is heried;

Such was the beautie and the shining ray,
With which faire *Britomart* gaue light vnto the day.
(*FQ*, III.1.42–3)

The most obvious contrast is of course that Britomart does not remove her helmet (perhaps we are meant to think of Hector, kissing his wife and child goodbye through his visor). In addition, Spenser's heroine is strikingly beautiful, and out of reach, but her beauty is sublimated from flesh to moral worth; she becomes a guiding light to the poor traveller. Echoes of other texts, however, introduce traces of more errant desires (a reader might be expected to remember Dido, glimpsed in the moonlight of Virgil's hell; as an overly passionate lover, she is a negative *exemplum* of Britomart's longing for Artegall). Britomart moves warily through her romance encounters; in this section of *The Faerie Queene*, female disguise is virtuous and necessary.

When Spenser turns directly to Elizabeth I, in the Ariostan centre of his work, to address her as the 'Queene of loue, and Prince of peace', it becomes clear that Spenser is attempting, not so much to turn romance into imperial epic, as to deflect desire into love and honour. Or as Burrow writes, his aim is 'to create a language which might obliquely persuade a queen . . . that there are times to follow the law, and not the clement instincts of the monarch' (p. 102). For writers of the 1580s and 1590s, it might be said that the discourses of power were *too* romance-infected; English epic had to express, not the will of the monarch, but the merit of the courtier. When Chapman sides with Achilles over King Agamemnon in his *Iliads* of 1611, he is expressing a similar concern, that monarchs should recognize merit and reward it. In the hands of Chapman, Spenser, Harington, Fairfax and others, epic poetry is made to criticize present government even as it reveres the mythic past.

NOTES

1 Mikhail Bakhtin, 'Epic and Novel', in *The Dialogic Imagination: Four Essays by M. M. Bakhtin*, ed. Michael Holquist, trs Michael Holquist and Caryl Emerson (Austin, TX: University of Texas Press, 1981), p. 13. Further references cited in the text as *EN*.

2 For Bakhtin and epic, see Cook; Colin Graham's (less convincing) *Ideologies of Epic: Nation, Empire and Victorian Epic Poetry* (Manchester: Manchester University Press, 1998); and Falconer.

3 Edmund Spenser, *The Faerie Queene*, ed. by Thomas Roche, Jr (Harmondsworth: Penguin, 1984), p. 38. Further references cited in the text as *FQ*.

4 For Renaissance commentaries on epic poetry, see J. E. Spingarn, *A History of Literary Criticism in the Renaissance* (New York: Columbia University Press, 1954). Renaissance theorists frequently cited Latin and Italian commentaries on Aristotle's *Poetics*, plus Horace's *Ars Poetica*, and for examples they most commonly drew on Homer's *Iliad* and *Odyssey*, Virgil's *Aeneid*, Statius's *Thebaid* and Lucan's *Pharsalia*.

5 Sir Philip Sidney, *A Defence of Poetry* (Oxford: Oxford University Press, 1984), cited here as *DP*; Horace, 'The Art of Poetry' in *Classical Literary Criticism*, eds D. A. Russell and M. Winterbottom (Oxford: Oxford University Press, 1989), cited as *AP*.

6   Sir John Harington, 'A Brief Apology for
    Poetry' in *Elizabethan Critical Essays*, ed. G.
    Gregory Smith (Oxford: Clarendon Press,
    1904), Vol. 2, p. 198.

7   Aristotle, 'Poetics' in *Classical Literary Criti-
    cism*, eds D. A. Russell and M. Winterbot-
    tom (Oxford: Oxford University Press,
    1989), p. 88. Cited as *Poetics*.

8   Torquato Tasso, *Discourses on the Heroic Poem*,
    trs Mariella Cavalchini and Irene Samuel
    (Oxford: Clarendon Press, 1973), pp. 129ff.
    Cited as *Discorsi*.

9   George Chapman, *Chapman's Homer: The
    Iliad, the Odyssey and the Lesser Homerica*, ed.
    Allardyce Nicoll (Princeton, NJ: Princeton
    University Press, 1967), Vol. I, p. 14. Cited
    as *Iliads*.

10 George Chapman, *Chapman's Homer: The
    Iliad, the Odyssey and the Lesser Homerica*, ed.
    Allardyce Nicoll (Princeton, NJ: Princeton
    University Press, 1967), Vol. II. Cited as
    Odysseys.

11 Giovanni Pigna, *I romanzi* (Venice, 1554);
    Giovambatista Giraldi Cinzi, *Discorsi*
    (Venice, 1564). For the *Odyssey* as romance,

see Patricia Parker, *Inescapable Romance*, pp.
42–3, and David Quint, *Epic and Empire*, p.
376, n.1.

12 In addition to Parker and Quint, see Ker,
    Epic and Romance, Fichter.

13 Steadman, p. 130.

14 Edward Fairfax, *Godfrey of Bulloigne: The
    Fairfax Translation of Tasso's Gerusalemme Lib-
    erata* (Oxford: Clarendon Press, 1981).

15 Torquato Tasso, *Gerusalemme Liberata*
    (Milano: Rizzoli Editore, 1963), my
    translation.

16 For further discussion of this passage, see
    Burrow, p. 175.

17 Burrow, p. 152. Sir John Harington,
    *Ludovico Ariosto's Orlando Furioso Translated
    into English Heroical Verse by Sir John Haring-
    ton*, ed. Robert McNulty (Oxford: Oxford
    University Press, 1972). Hereafter cited as
    Harington OF.

18 Ludovico Ariosto, *Orlando Furioso*, tr. Guido
    Waldman (Oxford: Oxford University Press,
    1974), p. 392.

19 Ludovico Ariosto, *Orlando Furioso* (Torino:
    Guilio Einaudi, 1966).

REFERENCES AND FURTHER READING

Bellamy, E. (1994). 'From Virgil to Tasso: The
Epic Topos as an Uncanny Return'. In V.
Finucci and R. Schwartz (eds), *Desire in the
Renaissance: Psychoanalysis and Literature* (pp.
207–32). Princeton, NJ: Princeton University
Press.

Biow, D. (1996). *'Mirabile dictu': Representations of
the Marvelous in Medieval and Renaissance Epic*.
Ann Arbour, MI: University of Michigan Press.

Burrow, C. (1993). *Epic Romance: Homer to Milton*.
Oxford: Clarendon Press.

Colie, R. (1973). *The Resources of Kind: Genre
Theory in the Renaissance*. Berkeley, CA: University of California Press.

Cook, P. (1996). *Milton, Spenser and the Epic
Tradition*. Aldershot: Scolar Press.

Falconer, R. (1997). 'Bakhtin, Milton and the
Epic Chronotope'. In C. Adlam, R. Falconer, A.
Renfrew and V. Makhlin (eds), *Face to Face:
Bakhtin Studies in Russia and the West*. Sheffield:
Sheffield Academic Press.

Fichter, A. (1982). *Poets Historical: Dynastic Epic in
the Renaissance*. New Haven, CT: Yale University Press.

Gregerson, L. (1995). *The Reformation of the Subject:
Spenser, Milton and the English Protestant Epic*.
Cambridge: Cambridge University Press.

Hainsworth, J. B. (1991). *The Idea of Epic*.
Berkeley, CA: University of California Press.

Lewalski, B. (1985). *Paradise Lost and the Rhetoric
of Literary Forms*. Princeton, NJ: Princeton University Press.

Looney, D. (1996). *Compromising the Classics:
Romance Epic Narrative in the Italian Renaissance*.
Detroit, MI: Wayne State University Press.

Martindale, C. (1986). *John Milton and the Transformation of Ancient Epic*. London: Croom Helm.

Murrin, M. (1994). *History and Warfare in Renaissance Epic*. Chicago: University of Chicago Press.

Parker, P. (1975). *Inescapable Romance: Studies in
the Poetics of a Mode*. Princeton, NJ: Princeton
University Press.

Quint, D. (1993). *Epic and Empire*. Princeton, NJ: Princeton University Press.

Steadman, J. (1996). 'Principles of Epic: Problems of Definition, Renaissance and Modern', *The Ben Jonson Journal*, 3, 127–46.

Treip, M. (1994). *Allegorical Poetics and the Epic: The Renaissance Tradition to 'Paradise Lost'*. Lexington, KY: University of Kentucky Press.

Vickers, B. (1983). 'Epideictic and Epic in the Renaissance', *New Literary History: A Journal of Theory and Interpretation*, 14 (3), 497–537.

Watkins, J. (1995). *The Specter of Dido: Spenser and Virgilian Epic*. New Haven, NJ: Yale University Press.

Webber, J. (1979). *Milton and His Epic Tradition*. London: University of Washington Press.

Weller, B. (1999). 'The Epic as Pastoral: Milton, Marvell and the Plurality of Genre', *New Literary History*, 30, 143–57.

31

The Position of Poetry: Making and Defending Renaissance Poetics

Arthur F. Kinney

'The profession and use of Poesie is most ancient from the beginning, and not, as many erroneously suppose, after, but before, any civil society was among men', George Puttenham claims in *The Art of English Poesie* (1589). His narrative history of poetry became commonplace in the Renaissance. He goes on,

> For it is written that poesie was th'original cause and occasion of their first assemblies, when before the people remained in the woods and mountains, vagrant and dispersed like the wild beasts, lawless and naked, or very ill clad, and of all good and necessary provision for harbour or sustenance utterly unfurnished, so as they little differed for their manner of life from the very brute beasts of the field. Whereupon it is feigned that Amphion and Orpheus, two poets of the first ages, one of them, to wit Amphion, builded up cities, and reared walls with the stones that came in heaps to the sound of his harp, figuring thereby the mollifying of hard and stony hearts by his sweet and eloquent persuasion. And Orpheus assembled the wild beasts to come in herds to hearken to his music, and by that means made them tame, implying thereby, how by his discreet and wholesome lessons uttered in harmony and with melodious instruments he brought the rude and savage people to a more civil and orderly life, nothing, as it seemeth, more prevailing or fit to redress and edify the cruel and sturdy courage of man than it.
>
> (ed. Smith, II, 6–7)

The argument is deliberately forceful: civilization began with and depends on poetry. A few pages later he underscores his position: 'for that they were aged and grave men, and of much wisdom and experience in th'affairs of the world, they were the first lawmakers to the people, and the first politicians, devising all expedient means for th'establishment of common wealth, to hold and contain the people in order and duty by force and virtue of good and wholesome laws, made for the preservation of the public peace and tranquillity' (pp. 7–8). To us, phrases like 'all expedient means' and 'hold and contain' are troubling. But so is their method: 'Poets were also from the beginning the best persuaders, and their eloquence the first rhetoric of the world' (p. 9).

But Puttenham has been slippery all along: poets and poetical history began, he says, with the 'feigning' of Amphion and Orpheus. Traced to its historic roots, Puttenham says, poetry is *sui generis*. Later poets made earlier poets who made poetry.

What causes Puttenham to walk his own rhetorical tightrope – and what permits later critics taking up the same narrative – is the need to dodge and mend the questionable practices of any kind of language. For it is at precisely this moment in history – the moment of Sidney and Spenser and Shakespeare – that battles raged over not merely the function but the foundation of language itself. We have come to call the two warring camps naturalism and conventionalism. The *locus classicus* for the first of these was found in a text recently revived by Renaissance humanists, Plato's *Cratylus*. Plato argues that words and names must be 'as much as possible like the things which they are to represent' (Loeb tr. 433D–E). Such a position resonated in the sixteenth century with Ficino's translation of Hermetic texts – those philosophical and occult texts attributed to Hermes Trismegistus – with Pico's pioneering syncretism, with scriptural tradition and the traditions of Zoroaster and Neoplatonism. Cabalistic formations of natural language, in fact, drew on biblical sources; the three most common practices were *gematria* (the interchange of words on the basis of numerical equivalence), *notarikon* (an acrostic system of creating new words from old ones, and *Themurah* (employing anagrams of Hebraic words). Denying such essentialism, conventionalism was derived from Books I–III of Aristotle's *De Interpretatione* which argues the arbitrariness of language. Whereas naturalism posited a vertical narrative of language, Aristotle defended scientific empiricism, an investigation cutting through horizontal time. His scepticism was dramatically advanced in the sixteenth century by Sextus Empiricus whose work would deeply influence both Bacon and Montaigne. For Sextus, poetry, like any language practice, was necessarily rhetorical, and 'Rhetoric declares this to be its main task: how, for instance, we are to make small things great and great things small' (*Against the Professors*, Loeb tr. 46). Plato's reply comes in the *Gorgias* (463A–C) where he aligns rhetoric with sophistry, comparing them not with art and poetry but with such trades as cookery, face painting, fawning and bewitching – that is, trades that employ trickery, deceit, immorality and superficiality.

Throughout the sixteenth century, such matters of language could be momentous. In the schoolroom Latin was slowly being displaced by English; in the pulpit, the mass was superseded by English sermons and services. Statutes, proclamations and the Acts and debates of parliament all relied on a linguistic precision that could guarantee widespread understanding and compliance; in a time of expanding international trade and imperialistic colonization, of international conflicts over religion and territory, an emerging nation state such as England had to have a usable means of communication. In such a climate, an increasingly literate public saw poetry – that is, imaginative writing – as neither elitist nor marginal. 'Among the innumerable sorts of English books, and infinite fardles of printed pamphlets, wherewith this country is pestered, all shops stuffed, and every study furnished', William Webbe remarks at the outset of his *Discourse of English Poetry* (1586), 'the greatest part I think, in any one kind, are such as are either mere poetical, or which tend in some respect (as either in matter or form) to poetry' (ed. Smith, I, 226–7). Poets sustained such production and influence because, defending themselves as others too defended them, language was not either natural nor conventional (socially constituted) but always both. Such a line of argument is explicit or implicit in all the defences (or apologies) of the period, but arguably the best statement, growing out of a descriptive human psychology, is Juan Huarte's pioneering *Examen de Ingenios*, Englished by Richard Carew as *The Examination of Men's Wits* in 1594. Huarte combines a general anatomy of the intellect with the faculty of speech. He cannot therefore subscribe to a single original but instead sees language as the product of an agreement among members of a community. According to Huarte,

> tongues were devised by men, that they might communicate amongst themselves, and express one to another their conceits, without that in them there lie hid any other mastery or natural principles: for the first devisers agreed together, and after their best liking, (as Aristotle saith) framed the words, and gave to every each his signification. From hence so great a number of words, and so many manners of speech so far beside rule and reason, that if a man had not a good memory, it were impossible to learn with any other power.
>
> (Scholars Facsimiles and Reprints, Gainesville, 1959, pp. 103–4).

Huarte then proceeds to merge this Aristotelian position with Plato's in dialectical balance, combining empirical data with biblical sanction:

> the one saith that there are proper names, which by their nature carry signification of things, and that much wit is requisite to devise them. And this opinion is favoured by the divine scripture, which affirmeth that Adam gave every of those things which God set before him, the proper name that was best fitting for them. But Aristotle will not grant, that in any tongue there can be found any name, or manner of speech, which can signify ought of its own nature, for that all names are devised and shaped after the conceit of men. Whence we see by experience, that wine hath above sixty names, and bread as many, in every language his, and of none we can avouch that the same is natural and agreeable thereunto, for them all in the world would use but that.
>
> (p. 118)

In the end, Huarte returns to Plato.

> But for all this, the sentence of Plato is truer: for put case that the first devisers fained the words at their pleasure and will, yet was the same by a reasonable instinct, communicated with the ear, with the nature of the thing, and with good grace and well sounding of the pronunciation, not making the words over short or long, nor enforcing an unseemly framing of the mouth in time of utterance, settling the accent in his convenient place, and observing the other conditions, which a tongue should possess, to be fine, and not barbarous.
>
> (p. 118)

To this syncretic use of language, widely subscribed to by the poets of Shakespeare's age, the poets themselves widened the act of making poetry to employ either of two variant approaches. As Puttenham has it,

> In some cases we say Art is an aid and coadjutor to Nature, and a furtherer of her actions to good effect, or peradventure a mean to supply her wants, by reinforcing the causes wherein she is impotent and defective, as doth the Art of physic . . . In another respect art is . . . a surmounter of her skill, so as by means of it her own effects shall appear more beautiful or strange and miraculous, as in both cases before remembered.
>
> (pp. 187–8)

From such a perspective as this, 'feigning' Amphion and Orpheus is not making them up but rather remembering them, recalling and recollecting them, as names (or images) of shared historical constructs that make sense through conventional appeal to essentialist names. Puttenham is not really writing history; he is positing concepts through images.

Puttenham is a critic, to be sure, but his criticism relies on his seizing the poet's recognized special medium in the Renaissance – that of the feigned example as meaningful image (embodying a concept, whether literally true or not). It appeals to the mind's eye; it is what the poet envisions so that the reader can envision it too. A little later, Puttenham adds to this: 'Poesie is a pleasant manner of utterance, varying from the ordinary of purpose to refresh the mind by the ears' delight' (p. 24): both the mental eye and the physical ear reinforce each other to allow the poet to produce 'pleasant' and 'purposeful' meaning. Actually, this is Puttenham's more sophisticated development of ideas already expressed in George Gascoigne's *Certain Notes of Instruction* (1575). Although Gascoigne really concentrates on rhyme and tropes in his brief statement, he too begins by remarking that 'The first and most necessary point that ever I found meet to be considered in making of a delectable poem is this, to ground it upon some fine invention' or initial idea, and then to add 'some good and fine device, showing the quick capacity of a writer' (ed. Smith, I, 47). Puttenham continues to expand on Gascoigne by adding an entire second book to his treatise on proportion or sound and an entire third book on ornament or figures to which he gives creative (because mnemonic) names, such as *hyperbaton* or the trespasser and *parenthesis* or the insertor (chapter 13), or *anaphora* or report; *antistrophe* or the counterturn, *ploche* or the double, and *episeusix* or the underlay or cuckoo-spell (chapter 19).

Gascoigne, Webbe and Puttenham are important stages in the institution and criticism of a Renaissance poetics, in part because they represent and expand on currents of thought among their contemporaries, thoughts that address directly the various crucial issues concerning language – and the place of poetry in such a context – that we have been identifying. But none of them has the stature nor had the effect of Sir Philip Sidney's treatise, composed in 1579 but not published until 1595 and then in two versions, as the *Defence of Poesie* (for the printer William Ponsonby) and as the *Apology for Poetry* (for the printer William Ponsonby) and as the *Apology for Poetry* (for the printer Henry Olney). S. K. Heninger Jr's estimate of Sidney is now universal:

'Since its composition . . . it has remained, without abatement, a potent force in determining the course of English letters' (p. 225). This is due not only to the wit and high spirits of Sidney's treatise but to Sidney's very special talent for synthesis, finding ways to make *poesis* (theory) and *praxis* (application) relatively seamless. Within the shape of a formal oration, Sidney proposes that poetry rests

> in that *idea* or fore-conceit of the work, and not in the work itself. And that the poet hath that *idea* is manifest, by delivering them forth also is not wholly imaginative, as we are wont to say by them that build castles in the air; but so far substantially it worketh, not only to make a Cyrus, which had been but a particular excellency as nature might have done, but to bestow a Cyrus upon the world to make many Cyruses, if they will learn aright why and how that maker made him.
>
> (Katherine Duncan-Jones and Jan van Dorsten (ed.),
> *Miscellaneous Prose of Sir Philip Sidney*, Oxford, Clarendon Press, 1973, p. 79)

The Platonic idea, conceived with an imagined 'excellency' that surpasses any earthly (and thus partial) embodiment, is nevertheless so powerfully and substantially conceived (not simply castles in the air) that it stands as exemplary, inviting others to pattern behaviour on the superiority of that image. At first it would seem that such behaviour is, like its source, ideational and imagined an thus excellent. Conceptually, readers 'will learn aright why and how that maker made him'. But only a few lines later, Sidney pointedly adds that 'Poesy therefore [also] is an art of imitation, for so Aristotle termeth it in the word μιμεσις [mimesis] – that is to say, a representing, counterfeiting, or figuring forth – to speak metaphorically, a speaking picture – with this end, to teach and delight' (pp. 79–80). The key common term is *representation*: the re-presentation of a mental image of the poet will induce a re-presentation in the behaviour of his audience. In remaking the poet's image or fore-conceit, the reader both counters with his own creation (counterfeits) and extends the poet's image (figures it forth). That he does so successfully is judged by the result: it will both teach (that is, train and educate, instruct) and delight (give pleasure in that very instruction). Sidney's poet is thus both the creator of an idea or fore-conceit and mediator of it. To prepare his reader properly for such a definition of poetry as word and object, idea and act, he has noted that 'There is no art delivered to mankind that hath not the works of nature for his principal object, without which they could not consist, and on which they so depend, as they become actors and players, as it were, of what nature will have set forth' (p. 78). Yet, at the same time for Sidney,

> the poet, disdaining to be tied to any such subjection [to the 'depth of nature'], lifteth up with the vigour of his own invention, doth grow in effect another nature, in making things either better than nature bringeth forth, or, quite anew, forms such as never were in nature, as the Heroes, Demigods, Cyclops, Chimeras, Furies, and such like: so as he goeth hand in hand with nature, not enclosed within the narrow warrant of her gifts, but freely ranging only within the zodiac of his own wit. Nature never set forth the earth in so rich tapestry as divers poets have done; neither with so pleasant rivers, fruit-

ful trees, sweet-smelling flowers, nor whatsoever else may make the too much loved earth more lovely. Her world is brazen, the poets only deliver a golden.

(p. 78)

What at first may seem a hopelessly confused amalgam of the essentialist and conventional definitions of language finds its common element where Puttenham too places it – in the feigning of the invention which pulls together both idea and (concrete) image that figures forth a creating, created nature. The golden world grows out of the brazen one (or it would be so personal ad bizarre it would not communicate). It elevates, but it does not deny and it does not contract the brazen world which suggests it and which, in the end, must convey and test it. Poetry for Sidney is not an individual's mere fancy – not castles in the air – nor exacting realism – which lacks the distance to inspire and instruct. Put the other way, Sidney's golden world contains the brazen world; it does not ignore it. It is as macrocosm to microcosm, vehicle to tenor. The poet mimetically recovers the idea which relates to but is never limited to realism (as history is). Nor does the poet wish to convey the idea without transforming it (philosophy deals with untranslated ideas). Rather, poetry bridges idea and reality; Platonism and Aristotelianism are irrevocably merged through the poetic act of choosing right images. As Sidney comments, poets are at once makers and seers (although such ideas had once separated Greek thought from Roman) because the poet is a visionary in order to make something (the poem, or work of art) and the maker to make anything must be a visionary (to 'see' the concept or fore-conceit). Or, as Alan Hager has it, 'He is neither pure imitator of nature nor pure prophet, but both, an inspired maker of likenesses or a mimetic inventor of fictions' (p. 128).

'Imagination bodies forth The forms of things unknown,' Shakespeare's Theseus remarks in *A Midsummer Night's Dream*, 'and gives to airy nothing A local habitation and a name' (5.1.14–17). But this is Theseus speaking – not Shakespeare, and surely not Sidney. For them the poet's imagination is not called forth by 'airy nothing' but by a golden world analogous to a brazen one, discovering a play-world that touches the lives of playgoers at the Globe. Both Shakespeare and Sidney gain licence to do this – sharing their pedigree with all other poets – because the analogous worlds they create only mimic God's First Creation. Etymology then as now links 'imagination' with 'image' and 'imitation,' sharing the same root, and as the biblical God creates His world *ex nihilo* according to Ideas within Himself, so the right poet 'with the force of a divine breath,' as Sidney has it, 'bringeth things forth' (p. 79). As God breathes life into man and into man's world, so the poet is 'lifted up with the vigour of his own invention' (p. 78). Limited in intellect and in possibility to God's known world, the poet finds limitless possibilities, making what is brazen golden, yet allowing the traffic of this bridging to go both ways, without end. The power, then, centres on the image that is that bridge. This is Sidney's idea of poetry, but it is also a more widespread phenomenon: images of Elizabeth I, for instance, could show a virgin, a monarch or a soldier; portray her as Diana, Astraea, Venus, Minerva or Cynthia. For John Foxe, opening his *Acts and Monuments* to martyrs, Elizabeth was Constantine (representing authority over the pope); for Edmund Spenser, she was Gloriana, inviting an entire faery landscape analogous in its golden presentation to the brazen world of his readers and susceptible to all of the brazen world's shortcomings, so that Ruddymane's pledging with bloody hands in *The Faerie Queene* represents the fall, sacrifice, and the possibility of redemption (II.i.37.6–9), and Sidney's *Arcadia*, in the resurrection of Basilius to those of faith and innocence (Book V) finds its model in the gospels.

Sidney, then, sees no difference in didactic force between the verity and the verisimilar; a feigned example has as much (and as much power) to teach as a true example and is not as limited. For all his praise of the poet's golden world, Sidney's poetics, like those of others in his time, is stubbornly anti-mystical, severely practical as A. C. Hamilton has commented (p. 120). Thus 'the highest-flying wit [must] have a Daedalus to guide him. That Daedalus', moreover, 'hath three wings to bear itself up into the air of due commendation: that is, art, imitation, and exercise' (pp. 111–12).[1] Poetry may inspire and create, but it must also be corrective, curative, and educational. The Cyruses of the poet's fore-conceit are what Aristotle calls *paradeigma* (*Rhetoric*, 1.2.8), behavioural models. They work through what Sidney calls *enargia* that leads to 'the knowledge of a man's self, in the ethic and politic consideration, with the end of well-doing and not of well-knowing only' (pp. 82–3). This is done through instructive narratives, such as that of Menenius Agrippa's story of 'mutinous conspiracy' (p. 93) later used by Shakespeare in *Coriolanus* or by the story of Nathan's tale of David's lust for Bathsheba (pp. 103–4). Genres, with their own conventions, also suggest and regulate the lessons which poetry teaches: Puttenham identifies the purpose of comedy and tragedy as 'the good amendment of man by discipline and example' (p. 33) and yet such conventions can also liberate as when the eclogue is used 'not . . . to counterfeit or represent the rustical manner of loves and communication, but under the veil of homely persons and in rude speeches to insinuate and glance at greater matters, and such as perchance had not been safe to have been disclosed in any other sort' (p. 40). Here too the liberating zodiac of the poet's wit is restricted through conventions that guarantee the performance of poetry: Sidney is quick to insist on the rules of genres, and criticizes works, like *Gorboduc*, that break the rules (p. 113). The conventions that regulate poets also guide readers and help them to measure the models they are to follow. This sense also lies behind Webbe's more simplistic and sunnier conclusion that 'The end of poetry is to write pleasant things, and profitable' (p. 295).[2]

But Thomas Nashe took a dimmer view. 'I account of poetry', he warns in *The Anatomy of Absurdity* (1589) 'as of a more hidden and divine kind of philosophy, enwrapped in blind fables and dark stories' (ed. Smith, I, 328) where fallen man obscures the poet's golden world, perhaps through limited insight or misunderstanding, perhaps wilfully. Puttenham shares Nashe's concern when he speaks of allegory: '*allegory* [works] by a duplicity of meaning or dissimulation under covert and dark intendments'; working with 'a certain doubleness', allegory and other obscure writing 'is the more guileful and abusing' (160; III.18). Loosened from true poetic purpose and convention, the fallen poet, Henry Peacham claims, 'may set forth any matter with a goodly perspicuity, and paint out any person, deed, or thing, so cunningly with these colours [of rhetoric], that it shall seem rather a lively image painted in tables, than a report expressed with the tongue' (quoted Heninger, 225). 'Filed speech', 'elegancy of phrase', 'vain affection of eloquence' (quoted Javitch, 112), when unmoored from a poet's true purpose, could lead to the kind of dissimulation and manipulation Sextus saw as inherent in any rhetorical practice, practice which came, for Elizabethan critics generally, to represent false art because it deliberately sought dishonest ends. Such fallen acts were, for them, likewise condemned by scripture. 'Thou shalt destroy them that speak lies', the Psalmist writes; 'The Lord will abhor the bloody man and deceitful' (Geneva Bible, Psalms 5:6); 'Keep thy tongue from evil, and thy lips, that they speak no guile' (Ps. 101:7). Proverbs echoes Psalms: 'Lying lips are an abomination to the Lord, but they that deal truly are his delight' (12:22); 'The bread of deceit is sweet to a man: but afterwards his mouth shall be filled with gravel' (20:17). It is a tangled problem, one which appears insoluble because it arises from degree, perhaps, and not necessarily kind.

Of all the major critics writing in the Renaissance, it is Sidney who faces this problem head on. He acknowledges that poetic abstraction leads to an autonomous world of exemplary discourse, where Pylades stands for constancy or Orlando for valour (p. 79), but just because it is autonomous it fails to join with the brazen world and thus resorts, finally, to something analogous to castles in the air. In its autonomy, it fails to make connections with its audience; it retreats instead into the obscurity which Nashe also condemns. But the function of the poet is to build bridges through images and fore-conceits; the job of poetry is to attract through feigned examples that have practical outcomes. The poet's idea and the reader's discretion and application must join. True poetry binds. There is never a breach between the world of the poem and the world of the reader (see Heninger, 249). In his understanding of poets as legislators of human behaviour, Sidney prefigures Shelley; in this, he prefigures Wordsworth's understanding of poetry as 'Reason in her most exalted mood' (quoted Kimbrough, 45). Sidney's lively treatise – his widely acknowledged and admired *sprezzatura* of casual sophistication – never sacrifices moral commitment or an earnest sense of reality; the *Defence* concludes, in fact, by warning readers that those who dismiss poetry and its power of immortality dismiss their own epitaphs and therefore their own immortality.

Sidney is decisively inclusive in seeing poetry as the Aristotelian *mimesis* of Platonic *Idea*; he is equally inclusive over versification:

> Now of versifying there are two sorts, the one ancient, the other modern: the ancient marked the quantity of each syllable, and according to that framed his verse; the modern, observing only number (wit some regard of the accent), the chief life of it standeth in that like sounding of the words, which we call rhyme. Whether of these be the more excellent, would bear many speeches: the ancient (no doubt) more fit for music, both words and time observing quantity, and more fit lively to express diverse passions, by the low or lofty sound of the well-weighed syllable; the latter likewise, with his rhyme,

striketh a certain music to the ear, and, in fine, since it doth delight, though by another way, it obtains the same purpose: there being in either sweetness, and wanting in neither majesty. Truly the English, before any vulgar [i.e. vernacular] language I know, is fit for both sorts.

(pp. 119–20)

His admiration of the capacity and dexterity of English picks up William Harrison's observation, in his *Description of England*, that 'ours is a mean language and neither too rough nor too smooth' (ed. Georges Edelen, 1968, p. 416). But Sidney embraces both sides of a debate, as Harrison does, that essentially begins with Gascoigne, 'the acknowledged master of English poetry for his generation' (Woods, 110) and is keenly fought at least through Samuel Daniel's *Defence of Rhyme* (?1603). For Gascoigne, poetry depends on syllabic regularity and the maintenance of strophic patterns whether or not they rhyme. For Puttenham, who devotes Book II of his *Art* to metre (or proportion), the subject is divided into five topics: 'Staff, Measure, Concord, Situation and figure' (p. 68). Both Gascoigne and Puttenham are, then, apparently as tolerant as Sidney. For the musician Thomas Campion, however, in his *Observations in the Art of English Poesie* (1602), poetry must be quantitative since his lyrics are set to music; in this, he revives an interest in the metre of the ancients that the Areopagus circle of poets – Spenser, Harvey, Dyer and Greville – had proposed and briefly pursued in the 1580s. In a sense, Richard Helgerson notes, this could be viewed, in a time when England was emerging as a self-conscious nation, as part of a larger rivalry 'between active self-making . . . and passive acceptance of time and custom' (p. 281). For Daniel, however, who had the last word n the battle over quantitative versus qualitative meter, rhyme was essential.

Rhyme (which is an excellency added to this work of measure, and a harmony far happier than any proportion antiquity could ever show us) doth add more grace, and hath more of delight than ever bare numbers, howsoever they can be forced to run in our slow language, can possibly yield.

(ed. Smith, II, 360)

Such an understanding of English poetry confronts Campion's advocacy of classical quantitative meter directly.

For as the Greek and Latin verse consists of the number and quantity of syllables, so doth the English verse of measure and accent. And though it doth not strictly observe long and short syllables, yet it most religiously respects the accent; and as the short and the long make number, so the acute and the grave accent yield harmony. And harmony is likewise number; so that English verse then has number, measure, and harmony in the best proportion of Music.

(II, 360)

In time, Daniel's viewpoint would triumph, but for Sidney, friend to Spenser, the English language could supply both quantitative and qualitative poetry.

Yet, for all of Sidney's desire to be inclusive – of Plato and Aristotle, of two kinds of meter, of profit and pleasure as the ends of poetry – his own wit characterizing moral philosophers 'with a sullen gravity, as though they could not abide vice by daylight' and historians 'laden with old mouse-eaten records' (p. 83) sees poetry as that which by its very nature 'cometh unto you, with a tale which holdeth children from play, and old men from the chimney corner' (p. 92). Poetry is inseparable from delight. Puttenham, too, allows poetry 'being used for recreation only' (II, 25): 'Poesie is a pleasant manner of utterance, varying from the ordinary of purpose to refresh the mind by the ears delight' (II, 24). But that physical, immediate pleasure is not all poetry offers for Sidney, Puttenham, Webbe, or even Gascoigne. There is also the deeper, more thoughtful pleasure that informs the moral understanding. Sir John Harington sees this too in allegory in his 'Brief and Summary Allegory' preceding his translation of Ariosto's *Orlando Furioso* (1591): 'Thus much I thought good to note of the general allegory of the whole work to give you occasion to ruminate, as it were, and better to digest that which you before in reading did perhaps swallow down whole without chewing' (quoted Kintgen, 95–6). Perhaps the most famous formulation of the period for thoughtful reading as the truest and highest end of poetry is in Bacon's essay on books: 'Read not to contradict, and confute; nor to believe and take for granted; nor to find talk and discourse; but to weigh and consider' (quoted Kintgen, 186).

Still the most famous definition of poetry in this period comes not from a poet or a critic but from a playwright, from the Hamlet of Shakespeare. Poetry, he tells the players, is what holds 'the mirror up to nature, to show virtue her own feature, scorn her own image, and the very age and body of time his form and pressure' (3.2.23–5). The Renaissance mirror was, however, dioptric and prismatic; it opened images to a range of interpretations. But in all of them it bound together the poet and the reader, freeing their imaginations to converse with each other, holding the brazen world within the golden one while freeing them from the vicissitudes and tyrannies of actuality. At the same time it brought both together into meaning, it awakened them to the liberty of new comprehension, and it did so, always, with pleasure and profit, with instruction toward a new response to life itself.

NOTES

1   As late as *Discoveries* (?1603–35; published during the interregnum), Ben Jonson still defines the poet as 'a maker, or a fainer; his art, an art of imitation, or faining; expressing the life of man in fit measure, numbers, and harmony, according to Aristotle' and continues, 'Now, the poesy is the habit, or the art: nay, rather the queene of arts: which had her original from heaven ... And, whereas they entitle philosophy to be a rigid, and austere poesie: they have (on the contrary) styled poesy, a dulcet, and gentle philosophy, which leads on, and guides us by the hand to action with a ravishing delight, and incredible sweetness ... And not think, he can leap forth suddenly a poet by dreaming he has been in Parnassus ... For to nature, exercise, imitation, and study, art must be added, to

make all these perfect . . . For . . . without art, nature can never be perfect, and without nature, art can claim no being' (*Works*, ed. Herford and Simpson, VIII, 635–8).

2 'For [the ancients],' Ben Edwin Perry claims, 'the world was primarily a world of ideas, which could be put to practical use in the instruction and edification of living men, rather than a world of facts valued only as such, and thereby useless. What moral or spiritual good is there in a mere fact? On some occasions the ancients became antiquarians and were at pains to distinguish what was probably true in the distant past from what was mythical and false; but this was not their habitual way of looking at traditional data, and least of all when they were concerned with *belles lettres*. With all his critical zeal, not even Thucydides

challenges the historical reality of Deucalion and the patently eponymous Hellen; and from the Greek poetical point of view (which was that of drama and romance) Inachus, Candaules, Xerxes, Alcibiades, Ninus, Nireus, and Daphnis are alike historical and belong in the same category' (quoted Nelson, 2–3). It is instructive to remember that Cicero classified *fabula*, *historia*, and *argumentum* all as *narratio*, although *fabula* meant something neither true nor verifiable; *historia* an account of actions in a remote past; and *argumentum* a fictional action that was nonetheless possible (see *De Inventione*, I.27ff; *Ad Herennium*, I.8.13; as well as the *Institutes* of Quintilian, II.iv.2). The humanists were citing such definitions as a basis for poetics as early as the 1510s; the Elizabethan critics all knew this legacy.

References and Further Reading

Berger, Harry Jr (1988). *Second World and Green World: Studies in Renaissance Fiction-Making*, ed. John Patrick Lynch. Berkeley: University of California Press.

Connell, Dorothy (1977). *Sir Philip Sidney: The Maker's Mind*. Oxford: Oxford University Press.

Eden, Kathy (1986). *Poetic and Legal Fiction in the Aristotelian Tradition*. Princeton: Princeton University Press.

Ferguson, Margaret W. (1983). *Trials of Desire: Renaissance Poetry*. New Haven: Yale University Press.

Hager, Alan (1991). *Dazzling Images: The Masks of Sir Philip Sidney*. Newark: University of Delaware Press.

Hamilton, A. C. (1977). *Sir Philip Sidney: A Study of His Life and Works*. Cambridge: Cambridge University Press.

Helgerson, Richard (1988). 'Barbarous Tongues: The Ideology of Poetic Form in Renaissance England'. In Heather Dubrow and Richard Strier (eds), *The Historical Renaissance* (pp. 273–92). Chicago: University of Chicago Press.

Heninger, S. K. Jr (1989). *Sidney and Spenser: The Poet as Maker*. University Park: Pennsylvania State University Press.

Javitch, Daniel (1978). *Poetry and Courtliness in Renaissance England*. Princeton: Princeton University Press.

Kimbrough, Robert (1971). *Sir Philip Sidney*. New York: Twayne Publishers.

Kinney, Arthur F. (1972). 'Parody and Its Implications in Sidney's *Defence of Poesie*', *Studies in English Literature*, 12, 1–19.

——(1987). *Humanist Poetics: Thought, Rhetoric, and Fiction in Sixteenth-century England*. Amherst: University of Massachusetts Press.

Kintgen, Eugene R. (1996). *Reading Tudor England*. Pittsburgh: University of Pittsburgh Press.

Levao, Ronald (1987). 'Sidney's Feigned *Apology*'. In Dennis Kay (ed.), *Sir Philip Sidney: An Anthology of Modern Criticism*. Oxford: University of Oxford Press.

Miller, Jacqueline T. (1986). *Poetic Licence: Authority and Authorship in Medieval and Renaissance Contexts*. Oxford: Oxford University Press.

Myrick, Kenneth O. (1938; repr. 1965). *Sir Philip Sidney as Literary Craftsman*. Lincoln, WI: University of Nebraska Press.

Nelson, William (1973). *Fact or Fiction: The Dilemma of the Renaissance Storyteller*. Cambridge, MA: Harvard University Press.

Patterson, Annabel (1984). *Censorship and Interpretation: The Conditions of Writing and Reading in Early Modern England*. Madison, WI: University of Wisconsin Press.

Smith, G. Gregory (1904; repr. 1964). *Elizabethan Critical Essays*. 2 vols. Oxford: Oxford University Press.

Taylor, Barry (1991). *Vagrant Writing: Social and Semiotic Disorders in the English Renaissance*. New York, London: Harvester Wheatsheaf.

Tribble, Elizabeth B. (1996). 'The Partial Sign: Spenser and the Sixteenth-century Crisis of Semiotics'. In Douglas F. Routledge (ed.), *Ceremony and Text in the Renaissance* (pp. 23–34). Newark: University of Delaware Press.

Ulreich, John C. Jr (1986). In Arthur F. Kinney (ed.), *Essential Articles for the Study of Sir Philip Sidney* (pp. 135–54). Hamden, CN. Archon Books.

Woods, Susanne (1984). *Natural Emphasis: English Versification from Chaucer to Dryden*. San Marino: Huntingdon Library.

32

The English Print, c.1550–c.1650

Malcolm Jones

Unaccountably neglected by scholars until very recently, the corpus of woodcut and engraved broadside prints issued in England during our period has much to offer the student of English Renaissance culture. If for convenience we divide these sheets into secular and religious, we may be surprised by the number of the former. The overall tone of so many prints is satirical, whether at the expense of women, social types, or – in this era, in particular – the Roman Catholic clergy.

From the 1620s come a number of prints of traditional misogynist type: especially the popular striking European monsters, known in their English manifestation as *Bulchin and Thingut* (engraved version), or *Fill Gut and Pinch belly* (woodcut version), the latter with verses by John Taylor and the explanatory sub-title, *One being Fat with eating good Men, the other Lean for want of good Women.*[1] *The Several Places Where You May Hear News* issued at much the same time is the title given to a late sixteenth-century composition which also enjoyed Europe-wide popularity. In a series of unified scenes, *A new year's gift for shrews* [figure 8] depicts the traditional nagging wife eventually beaten by her husband and ultimately chased off by the devil, and is accompanied by the following traditional rhyme:

> Who marrieth a wife upon a Monday,
> If she will not be good upon a Tuesday,
> Let him go to the wood upon a Wednesday,
> And cut him a cudgel upon the Thursday,
> And pay her soundly upon a Friday;
> And she mend not, the Devil take her on Saturday   [And = if]
> Then may he eat his meat in peace on the Sunday

A *Good Housewife* of *c*.1600 [figure 6] is now lost, but depicts a paragon who spins while her son reads and her daughters sew, and the maid sweeps her well-regulated household, seated beneath a picture of Time with his *Occasio*-forelock, while outside we see a hive of symbolically busy bees. She is matched by the bust of the prudent *Good householder*, subject of a bold woodcut sheet dated 1607. A unique series of twelve engraved sheets issued in 1628 includes suggestive images as well as a characteristic English emphasis on the cuckold's horns, the latter significantly having no continental source. Another of the prints shows a woman walking with her lover who places horns on her old husband's head; a second woman holding her distaff rides on her old husband's back, two spindles are stuck in his hat forming another pair of horns. A third [figure 7b] depicts a virago belabouring her husband with her key-bunch. This 'unnatural' inversion of the marital power relations is publicly satirized by a skimmington-ride in the background, and the verse. Another depicts a smoking, drinking woman with her young lover, whom she allows to fondle her breasts behind her elderly husband's back, who holds a distaff and rocks the baby's cradle with his foot. *The foot on the cradle and the hand on the distaff is the sign of a good housewife* was a proverbial admonition addressed to seventeenth-century women [Tilley F563]. She is also shown directing the lateral 'horns' gesture at the old man: to the implication of cuckoldry is added that of effeminacy in that the husband is depicted spinning, that quintessentially feminine occupation, as well as rocking the cradle. Smoking was the sort of habit affected only by 'roaring girls', of the sort found personifying *Taste* in Jan Barra's contemporary set of the *Five Senses*, which were used, incidentally, as the model for wall-paintings at Hilton Hall in Huntingdonshire in 1632.

Another of the suite is the only English representative of the motif of *Woman and the Men of the Four Elements*. It is clear from antecedent continental versions that this English version of 1628 has been somewhat bowdlerized; the woman's hand rests innocuously enough on her belly, but in the earlier continental versions she points to her crotch as the real object of the men's industrious searching.[2] There is reason to believe that another from the series, which may be termed *The Four (Sexual) Ages of Man*, has been similarly bowdlerized, or rather, adapted. A young couple on the far left of the engraving are regarded by three men who increase in age and beard-length – a symbolic indicator of their age – as we look towards the right. A rare piece of wholly secular Tudor wall-painting in the lodge of West Stowe Manor in Suffolk reveals the 'proper' import of this print (which German evidence confirms), for the characters speak thus:

YOUNGEST MAN EMBRACING WOMAN: Thus do I all the day.
MIDDLE-AGED MAN: Thus do I while I may.
MATURE MAN: Thus did I when I might.
OLD MAN: Good Lord will this world last for ever.

The last print from the series to be discussed [figure 7a] depicts a wife putting on her husband's breeches while he spins wearing an apron, accompanied by the following verse:

The world is turned upside down
When wives so on their husbands frown,

> As by their wheels to gain least riches,   [i.e. spinning-wheels]
> Shall forced give leave to wear the breeches

Here is the 'nightmare scenario' of the *monde renversé*, the man so *un*manned that he does 'woman's work' and bears her quintessential attribute — do we not still speak of 'the distaff side' of the family? — while it is she who 'wears the breeches'. The image is certainly attested in the late middle ages on the continent, but the expression and image appear remarkably late in England, not certainly before the Elizabethan era, after which it is frequently quoted. In 1613, for example, Elizabeth Edwardes told Alice Baker, 'I would be ashamed to have a husband and wear the breeches', and apparently posted a paper at her door repeating the words.[3]

If women came in for some tediously predictable criticism, men were not wholly exempt either. Men's dress was attacked in at least two sheets, *The Funeral Obsequies of Sr. All-in-New-Fashions* (*c.*1630) [figure 19], a reversed copy of one of the German *Allamodo* sheets of 1629, and *The Picture of an English Antic* (1646); and the fashion for smoking is similarly satirized in a burlesque coat-of-arms entitled *The arms of the tobacconists* [i.e. smokers] (1630). The horns of the complaisant cuckold, only too happy to live off his wife's 'immoral earnings', become cornucopias in a late sheet copied from a French engraving, *Le Cornard Contant*, the title pun of which is lost in translation [figure 11]. Gambling is the subject of at least two sheets of a very popular appearance engraved *c.*1650, the one featuring a lawyer and soldier playing cards to the former's evident discomfiture, the other, a monkey and a cat — an engraving by John Droeshout (*d.c.*1652) of a gambler and his girl cheating a youth at cards is now missing. The vices to which young men were felt to be particularly prone were further admonished in an image accompanying *A Looking-Glass for Lascivious Young Men: or, the Prodigal Son Sifted*, a broadside ballad issued *c.*1690 but, as so often, illustrated with a woodcut which must belong to the Jacobean era. *The Prodigal Son Sifted* is the central subject of prints issued in the late 1670s showing his mother and father literally sieving him of his vices, symbolized by the bastards, wine-glasses, lace cuffs, dice, cards, pipes, tennis-rackets, etc. which pour through the sieve. One of the miniature bordering scenes to this print depicts "the device of the Horn", referred to in Chapman, Jonson and Marston's comedy *Eastward Ho* (1605): 'I had the horn of suretyship ever before my eyes. You all know "the device of the horn", where the young fellow slips in at the butt-end, and comes squeezed out at the buccal [i.e. mouthpiece]' (1.1.51–4). The device is found as the subject of a panel painting as early as the mid-sixteenth century and appears, for example, on the engraved title-page of *The Unlucky Citizen* (1643) — it was clearly a visual commonplace throughout the period, and yet how few of us would know it today.[4]

An untitled sheet engraved by Cross *c.*1650 [figure 20] satirizes the pursuit of money and depicts a winged coin on legs fleeing from a party hunting it on foot labelled *Frugality, Flattery, Prodigality* and *Covetousness*, and their dogs, named respectively *Diligence, Industry* and *Labour, Rapine* and *Hazard*, [none], and *Deceit* and *Usury*; it is copied from an original engraving by Goltzius (*d.*1617).

A fashion for numerical series of prints is reflected in George Glover's output, who alone, *c.*1635 engraved *The Four Complexions* (= 'Humours'), *The Four Virtues*, *The Seven Liberal Arts and Sciences*, *The Seven Deadly Sins* and *The Nine Women Worthies*; the virtues and vices are often represented by figures of women (William Marshall's contemporary *Four Complexions* with their unflattering couplets are reproduced here as figures 9 and 10). Robert Vaughan's *The Twelve Months . . . in habits of several nations* depicts couples of various nationalities above verses which are, incidentally, a good indication of how Jacobeans regarded various foreigners: the French who 'love to wench' represent March, and are 'given to bulling, horns, and cuckoldry'; the Spanish represent June (Zodiac sign Cancer) whose 'canker God grant that we may well . . . miss'; while 'September's temperate season here is shown / By the well-tempered English Nation'. Sets of circular engravings in dozens or half-dozens are occasionally found pasted to banqueting trenchers – compare Middleton's *No Wit, no Help Like a Woman's* (1612), 2.1.62ff, which refers to 'Twelve trenchers, upon every one a month . . . and their posies under 'em'. A unique half-dozen circular emblems engraved by Marshall specifically for trenchers and dated also 1650 survives.[5] Other such sets known to have been pasted to trenchers include Martin Droeshout's copies of twelve Crispin van de Passe engravings of the *Sibyls*, and an anonymous engraver's *Twelve Aesop's Fables* after Marcus Gheeraerts the Elder, both issued *c.*1630.

Twenty named social types are criticized in the little-known *Pack of Knaves* etched by Hollar *c.*1640; the title-card, The whetstone, depicts the notorious liar, 'in allusion to the former custom of hanging a whetstone round the neck of a liar; esp. in phr. "to lie for the whetstone", to be a great liar' (*OED* s.v.), while the scatological All-hid is shown seated, head in hands, on the close-stool. On the other hand, *The Cries of London*, of which there were several versions by *c.*1650, is the English representative of the European tradition of prints depicting numbers of itinerant tradespeople together with their characteristic advertising cries.[6] *All* social types are criticized in Elstrack's satirical engraving, *All do ride the ass* (1607) [figure 14][7] in which various ranks and types all seek to ride an ass which is given four stanzas of moralizing protest. Droeshout's *Doctor Panurgus* (1620s) is another generalized satire also dependent on a Continental source, in which the Doctor purges his well-dressed patients of all the 'strange chimaera crotchets' which make them mad, and which we see being voided by one patient (under the influence of a purgative labelled *Wisdom*) into a close-stool, and escaping from a gallant whose head is shown entering a furnace; a small inset picture of two churchmen, bearing several churches on their shoulders, more specifically aims at pluralists.

The taste for prodigies and portents so evident in the broadside ballad repertoire, and popularly interpreted as a sort of supernatural social criticism, is reflected in the print record too. As early as 1531, *This Horryble Monster / Diss Monstrum* is a remarkable sheet with front and back-view woodcut images of conjoined piglets born in Germany, with a bilingual text. Monstrous fish (including beached whales) abound, as do portraits of Siamese twins, such as the sheet bearing front- and back-view woodcuts of the twins born at Middleton Stoney in 1552, or *The two inseparable brothers* who appear as a woodcut heading the ballad of this name by Martin Parker issued in 1637, clearly copied from the rather more upmarket engraving which heads *Historia aenigmatica de gemellis Genoae connatis*. The previous year Glover had engraved the broadside, *The Three Wonders of this Age*, with text by Thomas Heywood, depicting three superlative human phenomena, William Evans the giant, Jeffrey Hudson the dwarf, and Thomas Parr, reputedly 153 years old.

The popular Jacobean proverbial notion that it is 'A mad world, my masters' (Tilley W880), enshrined in the title of Middleton's play published in 1608, was literally interpreted in a Dutch sheet engraved in Antwerp *c*.1590 [figure 12], but one of the many Dutch engravings now known to have been circulating in England at this time, and specifically referred to in Robert Burton's vastly learned *Anatomy of Melancholy* (1621):

> all the world is mad . . . is melancholy . . . is (which Epicthonius Cosmopolites expressed not many years since in a map) made like a fool's head (with that motto, *Caput helleboro dignum*).
>
> ('Democritus Junior to the Reader')

but one of the many Dutch engravings now known to have been circulating in England at this time.

Thomas Nashe's incidental comment that 'It is no marvel if every alehouse vaunt the table of the world upside down, since the child beateth his father, and the ass whippeth his master'[8] is a valuable confirmation of the popularity of such *monde renversé* sheets in Elizabethan England, and of the fact that they might be seen along with broadside ballads pasted up on the walls of taverns. Some of the captions from a recently discovered, unique late sixteenth century sheet entitled *A Pleasant History of the World Turned Upside Down* will suffice to describe the many small scenes represented: *the hog singest the butcher; horses ride on their masters' backs; ships and galleys float on hill tops; wives go to war and husbands sit in* [= by] *the fire; the servant calleth his master to reckoning; the child rocketh his father in the cradle the country man sits on a horse and the king follows him; beasts of chase pursue the greyhounds; fishes come out of the air to angle for fowls in the water; stones do swim.*

A far less threatening topsy-turvy world was the medieval Land of Cockaigne, known to the Elizabethans as Lubberland; *The Map of Lubberland or the Isle of Lazy* was issued by Stent (before 1653) and contains twelve lines of descriptive verse below a copy in reverse of a Dutch engraving from the 1560s by Pieter Baltens. A similarly popular pan-European subject was the *Cat's castle besieged and stormed by the rats* also issued by Stent. While there is some reason to believe that this subject was sometimes capable of a political interpretation, it seems that for the majority of viewers most of the time it was a purely humorous image. The carnivalesque subject of the battle between personifications of Shrovetide and Lent, companion prints with accompanying verses by John Taylor, were first issued in 1636 [figures 16 and 17]. The following year the *Stationers' Register* licensed *a pamphlet called we be seven &c by John Taylor*

– though not extant, this would undoubtedly have carried on its title-page a version of the popular European joke at the viewer's expense which depicts a group of *six* foolish animal and human figures, leaving the viewer by his puzzled inquiry to make himself the seventh. From Stent's earliest advertisement (1653) we learn that he was selling a similar sheet entitled *Sumus septem, we are seven* which survives.

A numerical variant of this popular visual joke is the picture of *'we three'* alluded to by Sir Toby in *Twelfth Night* (1601) which, by the same logic, features two fools – contemporary continental prints survive, but the closest English representative is a painting entitled *Wee Three Logerh{ea}ds* acquired by the Shakespeare Birthplace Trust, Stratford-on-Avon, which depicts two fools with ass-eared hoods, one carrying a 'bauble' [figure 13]. Another Shakespearian reference to *the picture of Nobody* (*The Tempest*, 3.2.124) alludes to another joke picture which was clearly very popular in the first decade of the seventeenth century. A pun available only in English, this Nobody is depicted with *no body*, i.e. as a head on legs; it was famously the sign under which the popular publisher John Trundle traded; he seems to have specialized in the popular end of the market,[9] and so it is not surprising to see entered to him in the *Stationers' Register* on 8 January 1606, *The picture of No body*, as well as *no body and some body* later the same year. The earliest detailed allusion to the figure appears in Ben Jonson's *Entertainment at Althorp*, also known as *The Satyr* (1603), in which 'the person of Nobody appeared, attired in a pair of breeches which were made to come up to his neck, with his arms out at his pockets, and a cap drowning his face' but *six pictures of Nobody* was one of the outstanding items for which payment was claimed by the London printer and bookseller Abraham Veale in Michaelmas term 1571.[10]

Another sort of visual trick is represented by the 'anthropomorphic landscape' in which the recumbent human form is reinterpreted by the artist as a landscape – one such (after Merian) was being issued by Stent *c.*1650. When reference is made in *Richard II* (1593) to 'perspectives, which rightly gazed upon Show nothing but confusion, eyed awry, / Distinguish form' (2.2.18–20), it is to anamorphoses, the best known of which is the distorted picture of Edward VI in the National Portrait Gallery, which has to be viewed from the edge – in Ben Jonson's words – 'as you'd do a piece of perspective, in at a key-hole' (*Every Man out of His Humo*ur, 4.4. (1599)). Ironically, the only such engraved print of this type to survive is a head of Charles I.

By the late sixteenth century the establishment had begun to commemorate some of its non-monarchic institutions in print-form, and engraved pictures of parliament survive from 1628 and 1640, of the Convocation of the Church of England from 1623–4, of the Lord Mayors of London from 1601, *The Arms of the Earls Lord Barons and Bishoprics according to the degrees in parliament* from *c.*1600, *The arms of all the chief corporations of England with the Companies of London* . . . (1596), and *The Arms* . . . *of all the several Companies and Corporations* . . . *of London* (*c.*1635). Similarly, the loyal citizen might have on his wall tributes to the army and navy in the shape of *The true portraiture of the valiant English soldiers* (1588?), or the *table* of drill postures engraved by Cockson and first issued in 1619, or perhaps a magnificent ship, such as the large woodcut sheet of the *Ark Royal* (1588), which led the fleet against the Armada, or Payne's engraving of *The Sovereign of the Seas* (1637).

The domestic political event of the period – with international implications – was, of course, the Gunpowder Plot. *The Papists' Powder Treason* was engraved some time between 1606 and 1613 but probably closer to the latter date; similarly anonymously engraved is *A Plot with Powder 1605*, but Michael Droeshout's *Powder Treason* is probably to be dated *c.*1621, the year in which Samuel Ward's iconic composition, 'The Double Deliverance 1588: 1605' (i.e. from the Armada and the Gunpowder Plot) was published in Amsterdam.

At the very end of our period came the great disruption of the Civil War and a spate of associated prints. The title-page woodcut of another of John Taylor's productions, draws on the 'World Turned Upside-Down' topos we have already noted above: *Mad fashions, Odd Fashions, All out of Fashions, Or The Emblems of these Distracted times* (1642) depicts a man who wears gloves on his feet, boots on his hands, trousers on his arms and a jacket on his legs, while a mouse chases a cat, a hare chases a dog, fish swim in the air, a church hangs upside down in the air, as does a flaming candle, a wheelbarrow pushes a man and a cart pulls a horse. Marshall's engraving to the broadside *Heraclitus' Dream* (1642) also invokes this *monde renversé* imagery in the shape of the shepherd whose hair and beard are shorn by his sheep. Similarly proclaiming itself *An Emblem of the Times* is a broadside issued five years later which *presents our isle's late misery*, and shows Libertines and Anti-Sabbatarians, in company with a literally two-faced Hypocrisy, fleeing before an armoured War and a cloud-borne Pestilence. At the beginning of our period the emblem-book had not yet been born, and yet it was to become the publishing sensation of the time, so that by the end of the era, any artist wishing to suggest that his picture was to be understood in anything other than a purely literal manner would reach for the fashionable term; thus it is that in 1646 appeared *England's Miraculous Preservation Emblematically Described*, in which England's ark containing the Lords, Commons and Assembly is about to make land safely, while in the stormy seas various prominent royalists drown. In the somewhat similar *The Invisible Weapon, or Truth's Triumph and Errors* (1648), probably by the same (anonymous) engraver, the ship of the Church is attacked by Nero, the Pope, a Turk, a Shaker, an Arminian, and so on. This is also the period in which the internationally famous engraver Wenceslaus Hollar begins to issue prints commercially, and naturally, several concern the Civil War; although the majority appear to support the parliamentarian cause (*Parliamentary Mercies* (1642), and *Solemn League and Covenant* (1644)), his comparison of the Bohemian and English wars of 1642–3 has a more neutral elegiac tone. Similarly non-partisan is his etching for a broadside entitled *The World is Ruled and Governed by Opinion* (1642), with verses by the emblematist Henry Peacham.

Two other impressive and not overtly partisan broadsides are *Syon's Calamity or England's misery hieroglyphically delineated* (1643), and *The Commonweal's Canker Worms, or the Locusts both of Church, and State* (*c.*1650): in the latter, ten human types (each provided with an inset emblem) describe their relations with the previous persons arranged in a circle round a grotesque devil issuing from a hell-mouth (*And Satan* *cheats the cheating world at last*). The former engraving includes satire of the many radical sects which sprang up during the Civil War period, while another engraved broadside, *These Tradesmen are Preachers* (1647) is headed by twelve images of tradesmen plying their trades in order for the text to scoff at the presumption of mere artisans in daring to preach. From the same year comes *The Picture of an English Persecutor or a Fool-Ridden Anti-Presbyterian Sectary*. *The Committee Man* (earlier issued as *Fanatic Madge*) which also appears to be a satirical sheet belonging to this period, depicts a large owl wearing glasses and reading by candlelight, copying an engraving by Cornelis Bloemart (after a lost painting by his brother Hendrick) which is captioned (in Dutch), *What use candle and glasses if the owl will not see?*

Clearly partisan sheets include *The Sound-Head; Rattle-Head, and Round-Head* (1642) in which the parliamentarian is the *Sound-Head* and rejects the epithet *Round-Head* by applying it here to the tonsured crown of a royalist Jesuit priest, and *a Picture of the Malignants' treacherous and bloody Plot* (1643) which takes the form of a large sheet, divided into three picture-strips of four frames each, detailing the discovery and prevention of a plot against the parliamentarians. A comparable pro-royalist sheet is *The Royal Oak of Britain* in which the *Incertum vulgus* chops and pulls down the symbolic royal tree over-seen by Cromwell.

Prints satirizing individuals before the Civil War period are not as common as might have been expected, though *The Description of Giles Mompesson late Knight censured by Parliament the 17th of March Anno 1620* (?Amsterdam, 1621) is one such, and the three frames depict the hated monopolist firstly persecuting the landlady of the Bell Inn, then fleeing to France, and finally ruing his folly as a lame and penniless exile. The effects of such pictorial attacks on prominent individuals may be exemplified by the case of Archbishop Laud who complained of libels and ballads 'sung up and down the streets . . . as full of falsehood as gall, [and of] base pictures of me, putting me into a cage and fastening me to a post by a chain at my shoulder and the like. And divers of these libels made men sport in taverns and ale-houses'.[11] He was committed to the Tower on 1 March 1641, and the former caged picture alludes to one of the woodcuts illustrating *A new play called Canterbury His Change of Diet* (another shows his nose being literally held to the grindstone), while the latter picture was in the form of a small half-length portrait engraved by Marshall and used as the frontispiece to Fuller's *The Argument*, both published that year. A full-size engraved print of Laud vomiting books, his head held by Henry Burton, whom he had imprisoned and whose ears he had had cut off, also exists.

As for international politics, in 1609 Thomas Cockson engraved a sheet entitled the *Revels of Christendom* showing the English view of the settlement between Spain and the States General of Holland (the Twelve Years Truce), though once again copied from one of continental (probably German) origin. It depicts the Protestant monarchs playing cards against the pope and Catholic clergy. The breakdown of that settlement was satirized by *Treves endt. The funeral of the Netherlands peace. Anno 1621*, depicting a mock-funeral, a copy of the original Dutch *Testament van't Bestand, Treves Endt*, an etching by Claes Jansz Visscher, printed in the Netherlands with English letterpress verses in the same year. *Great Britain's Noble and worthy Council of War* is an anonymous engraving issued in 1624 portraying ten of the country's top soldiers and seamen around a table clearly showing Britain's preparedness for war, while Cockson's the *Revels of Christendom* was copied in reverse for the different political situation of 1627. Throughout the Jacobean era broadsheets of notable battles and sieges were issued, e.g. of the Isle of Rhé in 1627, or John Droeshout's *Siege of Magdeburg* by Tilly (1631) copied in reverse from a contemporary German sheet, or his father, Michael Droeshout's *Plan of the Battle of Leipzig, 1631* (1632), similarly copied. Capitalizing on more recent political realities, Vaughan engraved *The Portraitures at large of Nine Modern Worthies of the World* [STC24602] (1622), among which the most modern are Charles V, Henri IV, Scanderberg and William of Orange.

Even before the Armada, the Spanish were perhaps the favourite target for English xenophobia, pictorial no less than literary. One of the retrospective print-lists of 1656 records *The nature and condition of the Spanish senor with verses* which does not survive, but must be intimately related to *A pageant of Spanish humours wherein are naturally described and lively portrayed, the kinds and qualities of a senor of Spain Translated out of Dutch by H.W.* (1599) with its prefatory list of *The natural kinds of a Senor of Spain* enumerating the same sixteen derogatory qualities in the same order as are attributed to the Spaniard in the early seventeenth-century German and French broadsides which have two rows of eight small engraved cuts at the head of the sheet keyed to explanatory verses below.

Large allegorical engravings entitled the *Laurel of Metaphysic* and *The Tree of Man's Life* survive from 1638, and *memento mori* sheets are found throughout our period. *The dance and song of death* (1569), for example, and most striking broadsheet (*c.*1580?), really a version of the popular *Five Alls* motif, the actors here being identified as bishop, king, harlot, lawyer, country clown [i.e. peasant] and, of course, Death, who 'kill[s] you all'. A fascinating detail of the background is the trellised arbour within which a banquet is taking place, the table quite literally supported by the back of a peasant kneeling on all fours. Stylistically, this sheet is clearly of French origin. What must have been a most impressive *memento mori* sheet, which would have been 52 × 44 cm when complete, appears in Stent's 1653 advertisement as *Death his Anatomy*, but survives now only in fragments, minus the skeleton, the *anatomy* of the title.

Sheets of a neutral Christian content are in a minority, but such are *The broad and narrow way, or, St Bernard's ladder to heaven and hell* (before 1616), another European type. In the same year that Martin Droeshout engraved his celebrated portrait of Shakespeare for the first Folio edition of the poet's works, he also engraved a broadside entitled *Spiritual Warfare* (1623), depicting the massed armies of the Devil besieging a *Fort of Stone*, in the middle of which we see the *Christian Soldier bold* with *Faith* (symbolized by the Cross) and *God's Word* (symbolized by an open Bible) before him, flanked by sixteen Christian virtues, and with *Good Works* guarding his rear. Two other such 'godly tables' from the 1620s are *The Christian's jewel fit to adorn the heart and deck the house of every Protestant* (1624), and *Come ye Blessed, &c. Go ye Cursed, &c* (1628?). A broadside with a large woodcut of the Nativity, entitled *Christus natus est*, was issued in 1631 and reprinted throughout the seventeenth century; the Pepys Collection, however, possesses what looks like the original cut signed with the initials I. B., which may perhaps be those of the Elizabethan woodcut-engraver John Bettes. Simple but striking, is *an Emblem called Sin's discovery by the Emblem of a Toad* (1638), with its fashionably dressed *Reprobate* and outsize but somehow benevolent toad.

In this era of Reformation, however, the print is more often the vehicle of denominational polemic than piety, especially in the form of attacks on the pope and the Catholic clergy, especially the friars. The pope came under attack as early as the lost *picture of the Devil and the Pope* (early 1560s), and in the iconic Protestant composition which confronted Christ on an ass with the pope on his steed (1620s), and in *Rome's Monster*, a broadside issued in 1643 with a dramatically apocalyptic engraving depicting the pope mounted on a barrel-bellied Beast [figure 5], above a verse description of the scene by John Vicars. A broadside ballad, *A New-year's-gift for the Pope* (1624), is headed by a woodcut of the popular image, found also in the third, 1576 edition of Foxe's *Acts and Monuments*, which depicts a blindfold Justice weighing a Bible in one scale-pan labelled *Verbum Dei*, attended by Christ and the disciples, against the Papal Decretals, Decrees, crucifixes, rosaries, coins, etc., attended by the pope, cardinals, bishops and friars, and a devil who clings bodily to the lighter scale-pan – all to no avail, of course. The same image but minus Christ and the Protestants on the heavier side, and the Pope and his clergy on the lighter side (but including the useless friar), was used as the device of a Civil War banner by the Parliamentary party in 1642.[12]

The Marian martyrs, of course, were to be memorialized for all time in the woodcut images illustrating what is still popularly known as Foxe's *Book of Martyrs*. The two-volume 1570 second edition includes an elaborate and gruesome three-page fold-out cut suitable for pasting up on the wall entitled, *A Table of the X. First Persecutions of the Primitive Church*; the same cutter was responsible for the large *Spanish Inquisition* woodcut (27 × 36 cm) bound at the end of a book published the previous year. Another anti-Catholic woodcut in the form of a branching tree, formerly thought to have been issued independently, has recently been identified as made as a fold-out (53 × 35.5 cm) inserted at the end of Barthlet's *The pedigree of heretics* (STC 1534) (1566), and is of evidently foreign (German?) workmanship. It is similarly satisfying to learn that the extraordinarily violent *The Lamb speaketh* [figure 1] was originally inserted as a fold-out into William Turner's *The hunting of the Romish wolf* (STC 24356) (Emden, 1555?), the Bodleian copy uniquely preserving the original Latin texts, traces of which may still be discerned in the English copies. A panel painting closely copying the engraving but with the Devil's scroll bearing the inscription, *Yone are my victims anno 155{6?}* turned up at auction some twenty years ago.[13] We are afforded a rare glimpse into late Elizabethan attitudes to this war of images ('counter-picturing') in the form of a letter written in 1597 by the radical Yorkshire preacher Giles Wigginton to Lord Burghley, in which he enclosed *two homely Emblems* of his own invention entitled *A pair of riddles against the philistines of Rome*; a pictorial woodcut sheet issued in 1623 survives, portraying four such emblematic riddles, four animal and human encounters of a literal or metaphorically predatory nature, e.g. the goose between two foxes, and the *maid between two friars* [figure 3].[14]

As the riddle-sheet hints, the friars were perhaps the most popular target of Protestant attack, from as early as *c.*1580 (?) in *A new sect of friars called Capichini*. Of course, one of the vices most frequently alleged against the mendicant orders, in particular, was that they made sexual advances to laywomen, and *The shepherd in distress* portrays the dilemma of the eponymous shepherd who must decide whether to abandon his flock to the ravening wolf, in order to rescue his wife (or, rather, his honour) from the amorous friar who presses his attentions on her, or to save his flock from the wolf and resign himself to the name of cuckold.

A Nest of Nun's Eggs, strangely Hatched . . . (before 1626) is a most curious broadside headed by a piece of engraved grotesquerie of probable late sixteenth-century German origin. The central motif depicts a monk and nun sitting on a last basket of eggs from which further tiny monks and nuns are hatching – the scene is observed by a pope who shines a lantern on them and wears the tiara and a pair of spectacles.[15] Above the central hatching scene a burlesque joust is depicted: on one side *Bacchus on his Tun in state doth sit, / Armed with a Roasted Goose, upon a Spit: / Drawn by two Clowns*, while on the other a cleric seated on a wickerwork construction is drawn by the nun and friar – another version apparently of the Battle of Shrovetide / Carnival (on the secular left-hand side) and Lent (represented by the Catholic religious on the right-hand side).

As often as not, however, Protestant image-makers could not resist the spectacle of monks and nuns engaged in mutual sexual activity. Stent's 1662 advertisement included a *Friar whipping a nun*, a *Friar and nun*, a *Friar teaching cats to sing*, and *Cornelius of Dort brings Parsons to Confession*, but can we know what any of these would have looked like? It seems to have been the idea of corporal chastisement by friar confessors which afforded Protestant controversialists a particular frisson. While giving directions, the speaker in the second part of Heywood's *If you know not me you know nobody* (1605) names two inn-signs to be seen in the street: 'there's the Dog's head in the pot, and here's the Friar whipping the Nun's arse'. A lost print which may be dated 1618–23, and depicts two naked female penitents with switches in their hands while a seated confessor, the notorious Brother Cornelius of Dort, names the penance to be undergone by a third clothed woman who squats before him. Cornelius's notoriety had prompted earlier images but it was presumably the important Synod of Dort held in 1619 that accounts for this topical publication.

In *Histriomastix* (1633) William Prynne inveighed against 'obscene pictures', as well as many other evils, including lascivious songs, bonfires, grand Christmases, long hair and laughter.[16] It is certain that Prynne would have considered Marcantonio Raimondi's notorious engraved 'Postures' [*I Modi*] to Aretino's sonnets 'obscene pictures', as had Goodman the previous year, in the preface to his *Holland's Leaguer* (1632): 'Virtue is seldom found to spring from Lacedaemonian Tables, and Chastity much less from Aretine's pictures.' Puritans like Prynne had time (and censorship) on their side; in a late twentieth century sense, not a single piece of visual pornography from this period, at least, of native manufacture, is known to survive. Trying to account for the resort of so many people to the Alchemist's house in the opening scene of act five of Jonson's play, Lovewit opines

> . . . Sure he has got
> Some bawdy pictures to call all this ging: [crowd, company]
> The Friar and the Nun, or the new motion   [puppet-play]
> Of the knight's courser covering the parson's mare;
> The boy of six year old, with the great thing . . .
>   (Jonson, *The Alchemist* (1610) 5.1.20–4)

We do not know much about print erotica in England at this period (though we can assume that Aretine's pictures or 'Postures' circulated clandestinely in some form), but it is interesting that the suspicion of 'bawdy pictures' immediately suggests *The Friar and the Nun* to Lovewit – perhaps the very *Friar and Nun* sheet that Stent was still selling fifty years later. The *Friar teaching cats to sing* is known only from a nineteenth century collector's description: *A monk stands in the centre of the engraving with one cat on either shoulder, another on his head, and three on a table in front of him, their front paws on sheets of music whereon are inscribed their familiar cries: below are the lines,*

> That organs are disliked I'm wondrous sorry,
> For music is our Romish Church's Glory.
> And ere that it shall music want, I'll try
> To make these cats sing and that want supply.

A Pass for the Romish Rabble To the Pope of Rome through the Devil's Arse of Peak (c.1624) [figure 4], an incidentally scatological broadside exulting in the (repeated) banishment of Jesuits from England, engraved and published by another Dutch artist, Claes Jansz Visscher, survives uniquely in Paris. *A picture called The Man of Sin revealed or a Map of the kingdom of Antichrist and the Ruins thereof* is an impressive panoramic engraving issued in 1622. As we have seen, from 1563, Foxe's *Acts and Monuments* kept images of the martyrs burned by Mary ever before the eyes of English Protestants and included large pull-out woodcuts clearly intended for wall-display. A similarly commemorative and impressive broadside, engraved anonymously and depicting the martyrs amid flames, was issued in 1630 entitled, *Faith's Victory in Rome's Cruelty*. Nor should it be forgotten, of course, that throughout the first quarter of the century, the occasional prints issued referring to the Gunpowder Plot of 1605 (see above), added more fuel to anti-Catholic sentiment.

Extant from *c.*1640 is another image which became iconic for the whole of Protestant Europe, and probably originated in England early in the century, in the form of a painting of fourteen Reformers with Luther at their centre gathered round a table on which a burning candle is set; this was soon turned into a more explicitly anti-Catholic image by the addition of the Devil, the pope, a cardinal and a monk, all trying unsuccessfully to blow the candle out, accompanied in England by the inscription, *The candle is lighted, we cannot blow {it} out*, recalling the Apocryphal *Esdras* xxiv.25, but more directly for an English audience, Latimer's echoing of the verse addressed to Ridley at their burning on 16 October, 1555: 'We shall this day light such a candle by God's grace in England, as I trust shall never be put out.' A Dutch version is significantly labelled, *na de copy van Londe* [after the copy in London], and for once, reverses the direction of influence in a medium in which, it would seem, almost all new graphic ideas were imported from the continent.

In closing, we should at least mention two kinds of printed image which there has not been space to discuss here. The woodcuts adorning broadside ballads were probably the most popular kinds of printed image, carried into the very heart of the countryside by many an Autolycus, and evidently valued as much for their pictures as their texts: 'Prithee give me threepence in ballads, pick me out those with the best pictures', Sim commands his servant in Randolph's unpublished play, *The Drinking Academy* (1620s).[17] We have similarly passed over the huge number of small engraved portraits of monarchs and other notables which, in fact, constitute the greater part of all the engravings catalogued in Hind's three volumes, but perhaps the following note will serve as a reminder of how very precarious and new is our knowledge of the prints of this era.

It is not surprising that there should have been considerable interest in any foreign suitor for the hand of the Virgin Queen, and in his *Annals* under the year 1581, John Stow recorded how 'by this time his picture, state, and titles, were advanced in every stationer's shop, and many other public places, by the name of Francis of Valois, Duke of Alençon, heir apparent of France, and brother to the French King: but he was better known by the name of Monsieur, unto all sorts of people, then by all his other titles'. Here we learn both of the popularity of the portrait print and of the ready and prompt availability of topical licences at stationers' shops – all the more chastening, then, to reflect that not a single English print of the suitor Elizabeth called her 'little frog' has come down to us. In 1596, however, in his provocative work which takes as its ostensible subject a flush-toilet [a jakes], cunningly entitled *The Metamorphosis of Ajax*, John Harington recalled a famous political cartoon, the *Flanders Cow*, which must have enjoyed considerable popularity throughout Europe *c.*1583, and which depicted the Netherlands as a cow being fed, ridden, milked and squabbled over by representatives of several European countries, including the same 'Monsieur d'Alençon who . . . would have pulled her back by the tail, and she [de]filed his fingers'. With slight variants in the personnel, so as to include Leicester milking the animal (who had been forced to abandon his ill-fated expedition to the Netherlands in December 1587), it was issued as an engraving, probably in Cologne, in 1588, and was surely known in England too, for two contemporary paintings of this scene survive – one with accompanying English verses, beginning 'Not long time since I saw a cow Did Flanders represent', and ending, 'The cow did shit in Monsieur's hand While he did hold her tail'.[18]

It is doubtless not how the Duc d'Alençon would have chosen to be remembered by history, but we in England have been shamefully careless of our visual history, and

'Monsieur' is fortunate that any likeness of him has come down to us at all. It is to be hoped that there is now a new awareness of the importance of the visual heritage of the English Renaissance abroad, and a realization, on the part of younger students of the period, at least, however well read, that a proper understanding of the culture of the period is not possible so long as culture is understood to be coterminous with literature.

NOTES

1 For full details see Hind, *Part II James I* (Cambridge, Cambridge University Press, 1955), 210–13; recently 'rediscovered' by Sheila O'Connell – see S. O'Connell, 'The Peel Collection in New York' in *Print Quarterly* 15:i (March, 1998), 66–7.

2 Apparently one-off versions are found in woodcut by Hans Weiditz *c.*1521 and Balthasar Jenechem (1580s) and engraved by Wierix, but more to the point, this composition is to be found as one of the series of engravings collected together in the *Pugillus facetiarum* (Strasbourg, 1608), reversed in the original *Jeucht Spieghel* of 1610 and reused in the *Nieuwen Jeucht Spieghel* (Arnhem, 1617).

3 Cit. L. Gowing, 'Gender and the Language of Insult in Early Modern London', in *History Workshop* 35 (1993), 11.

4 See M. Jones,'The Horn of Suretyship' in *Print Quarterly* 16 (1999), 219–28.

5 P. Daly and M. Silcox, 'William Marshall's Emblems (1650) Rediscovered', in *English Literary Renaissance*, 19 (1989), 346–74.

6 See S. Shesgreen, *The Criers and Hawkers of London* (Aldershot, 1990), and especially the same author's 'The Cries of London in the Seventeenth Century' in *The Papers of the Bibliographical Society of America*, 86 (1992), 269–94.

7 This derives, possibly via some intermediary, from a German woodcut sheet of *c.*1525 which was in the Berlin Kupferstichkabinett early this century, when reproduced as Abb.666 in E. Diederichs, *Deutsches Leben der Vergangenheit in Bilder* (Jena, 1908). I hope to publish a note on this shortly in *Print Quarterly*.

8 *Preface* to Greene's *Menaphon* (1589), A3v–A4 [ed. R. B. McKerrow, *The works of Thomas Nashe* (London, 1905), III.315, 18–21]. McKerrow is uncharacteristically mistaken in supposing that by *table* Nashe here means (*tavern*) *sign*; not only are no taverns of this name recorded in the city before the eighteenth century [see B. Billywhite, *London Signs* (London, 1972), s.n.], but *table* in the sense of 'pictorial broadside' was certainly available in 1589; in the self-same year, for example, appeared Bucke's *Instructions for the vse of beades . . . Vvere vnto is added a figure or forme of the beades portrued* [sic] *in a table . . .* i.e. the large fold-out sheet (301 × 225 mm) engraved with images of the rosary and other devotional pictures.

9 See G. D. Johnson, 'John Trundle and the book-trade 1603–26' in *Studies in Bibliography*, 39 (1986), 177–99.

10 H. R. Plomer 'Some Elizabethan book sales' in *The Library* 3rd Series, 7 (1916), 318–29, esp. 323.

11 Quoted in Griffiths, 157.

12 See Alan Young's fascinating *Emblematic Flag Devices of the English Civil Wars 1642–1660* (University of Toronto Press, 1995), 60, no. 0111.0.

13 The version with labels in the vernacular survives loose in the British Museum, Department of Prints and Drawings, and in the Herzog August Bibliothek, Wolfenbuttel – see W. Harms, *Illustrierte Flugblatter*, Bd. II, 8. The original site of its publication was first noted by E. Ingram in D. Loades (ed.), *John Foxe and the English Reformation* (Aldershot, 1997). I discuss this print in some detail in M. Jones, 'The Lambe Speaketh. An Addendum', in *JWCI* (forthcoming). The painted version was sold at Christies on 11 April, 1980.

14   Earlier texts of the riddle alone may be found in a manuscript jotting datable to 1581 made in a Scots Register of Signatures – cit. M. H. B. Sanderson, *Mary Stewart's People: Life in Mary Stewart's Scotland* (Edinburgh, 1987), 89, and in the famous (and also Scots) Bannatyne manuscript (1568).

15   W. Harms, *Deutsche illustrierte Flugblätter des 16. und 17. Jahrhunderts* (Niemeyer, Tübingen, 1985–), Bd.IV.19, 34. Harms was evidently unaware that there is a closely related panel painting dating from the second quarter of the seventeenth century in the Rijksmuseum Het Catharijneconvent,

Utrecht, reproduced and discussed by P.D. *Geloof en satire anno 1600* [ex. cat.] (Utrecht, 1981), 43–7.

16   Cit. R. Thompson, *Unfit for modest ears* (London, 1979), 176–7.

17   (Malone Society edition), p. 22, lines 459ff.

18   For a full discussion of these pictures, see M. Bath and M. Jones, '*Dirtie Devises*: Thomas Combe and the *Metamorphosis of Ajax* (with an appendix on *The Flanders Cow*)' in P. M. Daly and D. S. Russell (eds), *Emblematic Perceptions: Essays in Honor of William S. Heckscher on the Occasion of His Ninetieth Birthday* (Baden-Baden, 1997), 7–32.

REFERENCES AND FURTHER READING

Aston, M. (1993). *The King's Bedpost: Reformation and Iconography in a Tudor Group Portrait*. Cambridge: Cambridge University Press.

Barker, N. (forthcoming). *Thomas Trevilian's Great Book*. For the Roxburgh Society.

Globe, A. (1985). *Peter Stent: London Printseller, circa 1642–1665*. Vancouver: University of British Columbia Press.

Griffiths, A. (1998). *The Print in Stuart Britain 1603–1689*. London: British Museum Press.

Hind, A. M. (1952–64). *Engraving in England: Part I The Tudor Period; Part 2 James I; Part III Charles I*. Cambridge: Cambridge University Press.

Hodnett, A. E. (1973). *English Woodcuts 1480–1535*. Oxford: Oxford University Press.

Jones, M. H. (forthcoming). 'Prints Recorded in

the Stationers' Registers 1562–1656', *Journal of the Walpole Society*.

Luborsky, R. S. and Ingram, E. M. (1998). *A Guide to English Illustrated Books 1536–1603*. Tempe, AZ: Arizona State University.

O'Connell, S. (1999). *The Popular Print in England 1550–1850*. London: British Museum Press.

Stephens, F. G. (1870). *Catalogue of Personal and Political Satires in the British Museum, Volume 1*. London: British Museum.

Watt, T. (1991). *Cheap Print and Popular Piety 1550–1640*. Cambridge: Cambridge University Press.

Wells-Cole, A. (1997). *Art and Decoration in Elizabethan and Jacobean England*. New Haven and London: Yale University Press.

Plates

Plate 1 'The Lambe speaketh'. A dramatic attack on the Marian Catholic Persecutions, bound into William Turner's *The huntyng of the romyshe vuolfe*, printed in Emden in 1555. Archbishop Stephen Gardiner identified here as *The Winchester wolfe*, quite literally 'leads by the nose' several of the simple laity, while a group of older men seek to pull him back, and devours the Lamb of God while the Devil looks on approvingly. He is supported by the wolf-headed Bishops Boner and Tunstall 'in sheep's clothing', with six dead sheep bearing the names of the Protestant martyrs at his feet. A contemporary painting of the subject was sold at Christie's on 11 April 1980 as lot 135. Thomas Trevilian copied various elements from this sheet into his *Great Book* in 1616. British Museum, London.

Plate 2 'The pope suppressed by King Henry the Eighth', anonymous woodcut, illustration to Foxe, *Actes and monuments* (London, 1570). An iconic allegory of the English Reformation. Henry VIII enthroned treads on the body of the fallen Pope Clement VII, below whom are shown the Catholic clergy in disarray, Bishop Fisher leaning over the prostrate pope; the side-note reads 'The lamentable weeping and howling of all the religious rout for the fall of their god the Pope'. King Henry hands a Bible to Archbishop Cranmer (Cromwell, the Lord Chancellor, stands behind him). This cut clearly recalls earlier images depicting demonstrations of papal supremacy which were a commonplace of Protestant polemic – Pope Alexander III's humiliation of Frederick Barbarossa (shown with his foot on the emperor's neck), and Pope Celestine III's similar treatment of Emperor Henry VI (shown kicking the crown of the emperor who kneels before him): cf. 'The Popes have as well made Foot-balls of the Crowns of Emperors as Foot-stools of their Necks' [Henry More, 'Divine Dialogues', (1668)]. Contemporary English Bibles use the phrase 'making one's enemies one's foot-stool', and the use of the motif in Marlowe's *1 Tamburlaine* (1587) reflects its popularity in Elizabethan England: cf. 'Sapores when he had conquered Valerianus the Roman emperor used him afterward most villainously, as his foot-stock [stool]' from Bishop John Jewel's 'Defence of the Apology' (1567). British Library, London.

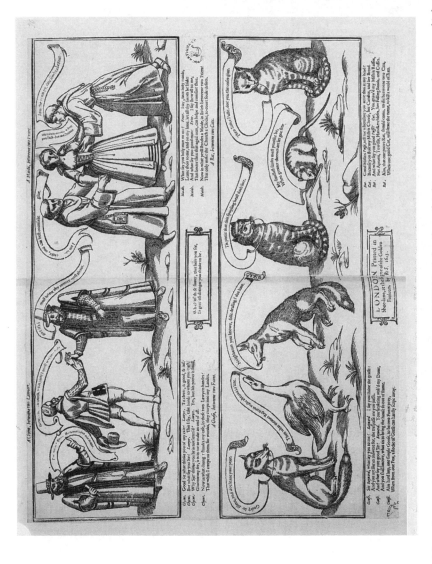

Plate 3 'Which of these fower . . .' (London, 1623). The viewer is asked *Which of these fower that here you see,* / *In greatest daunger you thinke to be,* and shown four animal and human encounters of a literal or metaphorically predatory nature: the goose between two foxes, the rat between two cats, the client between two lawyers, and the *maid between two friars*. It is a depiction of a traditional riddle (found in two late sixteenth-century Scots manuscripts), but in an English Jacobean context, it is clear that it is part of anti-mendicant, anti-Catholic polemic. Leach was granted a retrospective licence to reprint the sheet in 1656. Society of Antiquaries, London.

Plate 4 'A pass for the Romish rabble' (Amsterdam, 1624). The central image (deriving immediately from a German sheet of 1621) is a horned devil wearing a mitre devouring Jesuit priests and excreting them as soldiers. The pope and priests kneel ?imploringly before it. At the right edge another priest reads a copy of James I's Proclamation of 6 May 1624 attached to a broken column (the conventional attribute of Fortitudo, here symbolizing Strong Rule) charging all Catholic priests to leave England by 14 June. Behind him real 'pastors' look on in bewilderment. Bibliothèque nationale, Paris.

Plate 5 'Behold Romes monster on his monstrous beast' (?London, 1643). A Dutch engraving (with Dutch labels and evidently secondary English translations beneath them) heading a broadside with verses signed by John Vicars. The pope is mounted on the barrel-bodied, scorpion-tailed Beast of the Apocalypse, its seven heads labelled as the Seven Deadly Sins but all wearing the headgear of the Roman clergy. It excretes skulls and bones (saints' relics) into vessels held by other clergy who offer them to kneeling kings, but the pope has been shot by one of Death's skeletons and he and the Beast are about to plunge into the abyss of hell.

Plate 6 'A Good Housewife', anonymous woodcut sheet (?London, *c*.1600). An important image of the ideal housewife. This paragon who spins while her son reads and her daughters sew, and the maid sweeps her well-regulated household, sits beneath a picture of Time (with his *Occasio*-forelock – 'Seize time by the forelock'), while outside we see a hive of symbolically busy bees (right) and industrious ants (left, 'Go to the ant, thou sluggard'). British Museum, London.

The world is turned, vpside downe — As by their wheeles to gaine least riches,
When wiues so on their Husbands frowne, Shall forst giue leaue, to weare ẙ breeches:

Plates 7a and 7b Satires on marriage, anonymous engraved sheets (London, 1628).
7a: The wife puts on ('wears') her husband's breeches while he spins from the distaff – that quintessential attribute of femininity – and wears her apron, making him an 'apron-husband', cf. Middleton and
Dekker, *The Roaring Girl* (1611), 'I cannot abide these apron husbands: such cotqueans [wimps]' (3.2.30).
To early modern Englishmen this is seriously unnatural gender role-reversal, which the caption-verse
describes as 'The world . . . turned upside down'. Folger Shakespeare Library, Washington.

Well worth to scurge, so weake A patch, And cause the Bayes thereat make games,
Who wth so strong, A whore would match, By ryding thus, to both their shames:

7b: in the foreground a virago beats her husband (whose hands are held in the praying pose) with her
key-bunch, while in the background, this 'unnatural' inversion of marital power relations is being
publicly satirized by a skimmington-ride accompanied by 'rough music' (here a drummer) and derisive
pointing: the couple are represented sitting back to back on a horse, so that the husband faces and holds
the tail, holding aloft his wife's distaff and wearing a horned hat (symbol of the cuckold), while she
holds aloft his breeches, symbol of the masculine power she would usurp. Folger Shakespeare Library,
Washington.

Plate 8 'A New yeares guift for Shrews' (London, *c.*1630). In a series of unified scenes, the 'traditional' nagging wife is shown being beaten by her husband, and ultimately chased off by the Devil (for caption text of the traditional rhyme, see p. 352), leaving him free to spend Sunday 'in peace' down 'The Swan' eating and drinking! Apart from the pub sign, a board painted with a swan, note the 'lattice' (which signified an inn), and cf. *Arden of Faversham* (1592): 'He had been sure to have had his sign pulled down, and his lattice borne away the next night' (sig.H2). British Museum, London.

Faire and Foolish.

Phlegmaticke.

In Beauty I haue share of Rose and Lilly
But I lack Breeding, and my wit is silly.

Little and Lovd.

Cholerick.

Nature because Shee would not doe Mee wrong
In stead of Stature hath afforded Tongue.

THE
foure
Complexions
Sold by
Tho: Ienner
at the
Exchange

Long and Lazie.

Melancholy.

When I am forcd to worke my Senses droope
For I am tall, and doe not like to stoope.

Black and Proud.

Sanguine.

I was not at my Birth with Beautie blest
But I as coy and proud am, as the best.

Plates 9a–d

The Contented Cuckold.

Sould by Iohn Ouerton at the white horse neare the fountaine tauern without Newgate

How bleſt am I, and what a happie life, in my conceite; hees more then mad, that
doe I injoy; well godamercie wife; (ſtore to weare ſuch pretious, profitable hornes,
tis thou haſt raiſd my fortune, all this To be a cuckold, why ſhoold I repine;
thy occupation brings; and ten times more the diſgrace is my wife's, the profit mine

Plate 10 'The Contented Cuckold' (?London, *c*.1660). Not only does this cuckold have the traditional horns, but they shower forth coins and jewellery – they are cornucopias. Smilingly he counts the money and jewels he has acquired from his wife's 'occupation' (as the caption punningly puts it) and cynically concludes, 'the disgrace is my wife's; the profit mine'. It is a copy of a French sheet entitled 'Le Cornard Contant', the last word punning on 'contant' [counting] and 'content' [contented]. A version with verses in Dutch and French is also known. Overton also sold a second version (New York, Library of Congress), and it was copied in woodcut to illustrate various broadside ballads of the 1680s. British Museum, London.

Plates 9a–d 'The Foure Complexions' (London, 1630s). One of the 'numerical' series of prints popular at this period in which abstractions were personified as half- or three-quarter-length female figures, mostly with far from flattering verses; here each temperament is a woman labelled according to the misogynist proverb, *Faire and foolish, little and loud, long and lazie, blacke and proud* (Tilley F28 (from *c*.1600)), i.e. Phlegmatic, Choleric, Melancholic and Sanguine. They are accompanied by a fish, a cockerel, a cat and stringed instruments, respectively, which 'speak' the names of their temperaments. Kunstsammlungen der Fürsten zu Waldburg-Wolfegg.

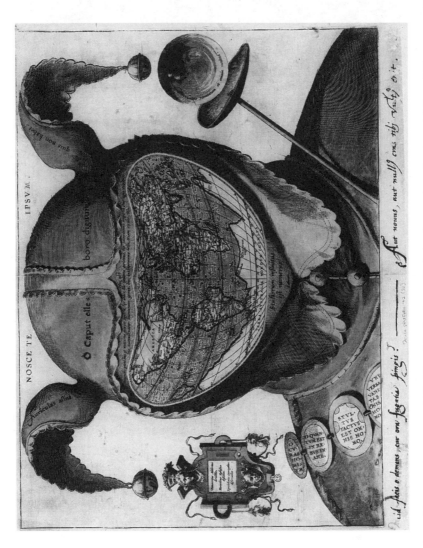

Plate 11 ('Fool's Head World Map') (?Antwerp, c.1590). The globe is given a fool's hood as a token of universal folly and blows a soap-bubble as a symbol of the transience and vanity of human existence ('homo bulla'). Alluding specifically to this print in his *Anatomy of Melancholy* (1621) Burton noted that 'all the world is mad'; a Jacobean (and earlier) commonplace (Tilley W880) enshrined, for example, in the title of Middleton's play, *A Mad World, My Masters* (1608). Bodleian Library, Oxford.

Plate 12 'Wee three Logerh[ea]ds' (?*c*.1650). A visual joke at the viewer's expense (a 'logger-head' is a blockhead or fool). The third loggerhead is the viewer who is tricked into asking where the third fool is. Continental prints of this trick survive from Shakespeare's era, but no English examples survive before the date of this painting. This is the sort of picture to which the clown Feste alludes in *Twelfth Night* (1601) as the picture of 'we three' (2.3.16). Shakespeare Birthplace Trust Museum, Stratford-upon-Avon.

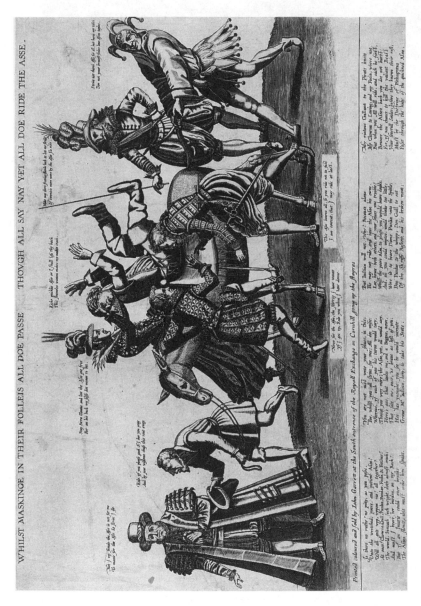

Plate 13 'All doe ride the ass' (London, 1607). Based on a German original, this is a general rather than a particular satire in which, with the exception of the judge (far left), all social ranks and types of early Jacobean society (including Dame Punk, Don Pandar, Don Gull and a Gallant) are associated with asinine folly. Though unrecorded elsewhere, Burton appears to use the idiom in the same sense in his *Anatomy of Melancholy* (1621): 'that they may go "ride the ass," and all sail along . . . in the "ship of fools"'. Compare the title-page woodcut to 'The Fool's Complaint to Gotham College' (1643) which depicts a fool riding on an ass which says 'The fool rides me'. British Museum, London.

SHROVETYDE

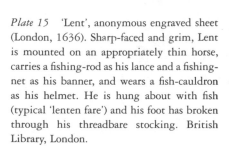

You that hate Fasting, Dearth, and starting Lowes . SHROVE: *Behold your Champion Shrovetyde in this fray*
.Spits bright hand up, and Teeth and Platters Chimes TYDE *Would murder Lent, and every fasting day.*

Plate 14 'Shrovetyde', anonymous engraved sheet (London, 1636). One of a pair of prints, the earliest English representatives of the 'Battle between Carnival (Shrovetide) & Lent' (with verses by John Taylor). For a marginally earlier reuse of a German version of the Battle on a sheet published in England, see the discussion of 'A Nest of Nuns' Eggs' (before 1626) in the text. The present sheet shows a plump Shrovetide, wearing a cooking-pot as helmet, mounted on a stout ox carrying a broom from which a 'cook's foul apron' flutters as his banner, and armed with a roasting-spit as his lance on which various pieces of meat are skewered; a grid-iron hangs over his shoulder by a string of sausages and a bottle and two bags are slung at his side, two 'plump capons' behind him. British Library, London.

Plate 15 'Lent', anonymous engraved sheet (London, 1636). Sharp-faced and grim, Lent is mounted on an appropriately thin horse, carries a fishing-rod as his lance and a fishing-net as his banner, and wears a fish-cauldron as his helmet. He is hung about with fish (typical 'lenten fare') and his foot has broken through his threadbare stocking. British Library, London.

LENT,

You that love flesh, or to the flesh are given LENT. *In warlike manner here's to Combat come*
By Lent, unto your shifts you shall be driven *And unto (many) welcome like Jack-Drum*

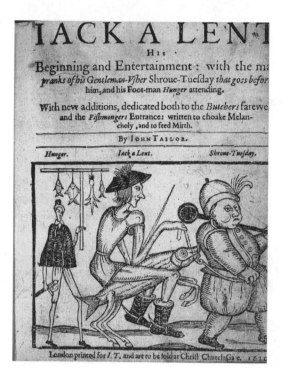

Plate 16 'Jack a Lent' by John Taylor, anonymous title-page woodcut (2nd edn, London, 1620). A thin Jack-a-Lent, so poor that his 'hair grows through his hat' (Tilley H17var.) rides a herring (typical 'Lenten fare'), led by a fat Shrove Tuesday carrying a ladle over his shoulder. Behind them walks the skeletal figure of Hunger carrying a pole from which fish and an onion dangle. The figures of Jack-a-Lent and Shrove Tuesday derive from an engraving of Bruegel's 'Thin Kitchen' published in 1569, a rare testimony to the familiarity with Bruegel's work in Jacobean England. It further shows how dangerous it is for modern historians to make assumptions about seventeenth-century English popular culture (e.g. that this title-page represents a contemporary London carnival procession) when they are not as familiar as they might be with the extent of the visual record. British Library, London.

Plate 17 'A continued inquisition against paper-persecutors' by Abraham Holland, engraved title page (London, 1625). This is the title page to the second part of 'A scourge for paper-persecutors' (by John Davies), a diatribe against trivial literature such as ballads and news-sheets, and their authors who thus waste paper. The engraving depicts Wit whipping one of these 'paper-spoilers' who is lifted off the ground on Time's back (note the same Occasio-forelock as in plate 6) and Time's scythe and hour-glass attributes which he has had to put on the ground. The offending author's trousers have been pulled down exposing his bare buttocks to Wit's lash and he wears the three-pointed belled hat of a fool. British Library, London.

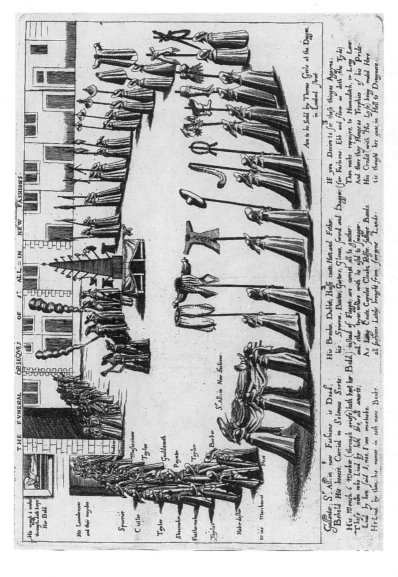

Plate 18 'The funeral obsequies of Sir-all-in-new-fashions', anonymous engraved sheet (London, 1630). A satire on male fashion *c*.1630, but actually copied from a German sheet issued in 1629. The mourners include the dandy's poet, painter and musician, and a large number of the tradespeople he patronised (the verses imply he died owing them money), including four tailors, a haberdasher, a shoemaker, a feathermaker, a spurrier, a fencing-master, and a number of laundresses and their maids. The mourners leading the procession hold aloft many of the deceased's clothes and other accoutrements. Bodleian Library, Oxford.

Plate 19 (Hunting money), sheet engraved by Thomas Cross, London, *c*.1650. Based on an original engraving by Goltzius (*d*.1617), this untitled sheet satirises the pursuit of money, and depicts a winged coin on legs fleeing from a party hunting it on foot with dogs. Frugality walks barefoot and carries his shoes and socks over his shoulder (to save shoe-leather!), Flattery wears a cockerel-headed hat (he is a 'cock's comb / coxcomb'), the dandified Prodigality throws money into the air while trampling on the sword and scales of justice, a crouching Covetousness lets slip the dogs, Deceit and Usury. A gallows is visible on a hill in the background. British Museum, London.

33

Traditions of Complaint and Satire

John N. King

In *An Apology for Poetry* (composed *c*.1583), Sir Philip Sidney emulates the genial urbanity of Horace in describing the satirist as a sportive wit who makes readers 'laugh at folly'. Although George Puttenham shares Sidney's Horatian principles, the normative definition of early modern English metrical satire in his *Art of English Poesie* (1589) veers toward 'bitter invective against vice and vicious men' associated with Juvenal. Puttenham goes on to extend from drama to poetry the view of Aelius Donatus, a Roman grammarian, that satire derived from vicious personal attack in ancient Greek satyr plays.[1] The fashion for stylistic roughness and invective in early modern English satire accords with a false etymology that identified *satyr* with both verse satire and lustful woodland inhabitants who combined human form with that of goats.[2]

Puttenham confers a place of honour upon *The Vision of Piers Plowman*, the fourteenth-century alliterative allegory commonly attributed to William Langland, as the outstanding instance of native English satire. Homage to Langland acknowledges the medieval origins of English verse satire at a time when Latinate and Italianate practices were undergoing importation late in the reign of Queen Elizabeth I. In accepting the 'hard and obscure' language of Langland's archaic dialect, Puttenham deems it equivalent to the 'rough and bitter speeches, and . . . invectives' of the Roman satirists, Lucilius, Juvenal and Persius.[3]

Because complaint and satire are literary modes rather than genres, one cannot differentiate between them with precision. Rooted in medieval practices, the more unambiguous and oratorical mode of complaint gives way over time to the more indirect play of satirical irony. During the early modern era, complaint encompassed attacks on worldly vanity (e.g., Edmund Spenser's *Complaints, Containing Sundry Small Poems of the World's Vanity* and Sir Walter Ralegh's 'The Lie') and moralistic verse concerning the tragic falls of illustrious individuals (e.g., *The Mirror for Magistrates*).

Because satire has never corresponded to any particular genre, that problematic mode can inform a variable array of external formal characteristics.[4] The reader encounters attitudes that range from delicate Horatian laughter at human folly capable of reform to Juvenalian grief at irredeemable vice. Not limited to rough language associated with Langland's middle English verse, the satirical mode infuses instances of different genres to produce, for example, parodies of Petrarchan convention in poems such as Shakespeare's 'My mistress' eyes are nothing like the sun' (sonnet 130) or epic convention during the war in heaven in Milton's *Paradise Lost*.

The satiric mode encompasses vilification, ridicule or mockery of recognizable historical targets. Attack by means of linguistic appropriation, imitation or innuendo is a distinctive feature of literary, political, social and religious satire. It encompasses puns and quibbles; beast fables that veil allegorical attack; and parody, burlesque or travesty of recognizable literary styles, devices and forms. We may think in terms of a satirical spectrum that ranges from invective complaint coloured by rhetorical figures that stop short of fictiveness, to constructions that are more or less fictive, to a point where satire shades into comedy unconcerned with discernible historical particulars.[5] The remote family resemblances associated with the satirical mode link texts in the manner of distant cousins within a far-flung clan.

Puttenham's *Art of English Poesie* grants John Skelton a place second to Langland as 'a sharp satirist, but with more railing and scoffery than became a Poet Laureate'. Falling short of the prophetic visions of *Piers Plowman*, in Puttenham's view, Skelton applied his wit 'to scurrilities and other ridiculous matters'.[6] During service as tutor to Prince Henry (later Henry VIII), Skelton composed *The Bowge of Court*, a satire on courtly vices in the form of a late medieval ship of fools allegory. After departing court to serve as rector at Diss in East Anglia, Skelton composed satirical poems in idiosyncratic meters that came to be known as Skeltonics. They are notable for breathless monorhyme leashes that run on line after line. Avoiding rhetorical adornment for the sake of native plain style, he exploited a jarring mixture of high and low styles, puns and obscure allegory. Among his secular satires is *The Tunning of Elinour Rumming*, a rollicking portrayal of a rowdy alewife.

Drawing upon medieval traditions of anticlerical complaint and satire, Skelton's religious satires afforded a flimsy basis for Protestant reformers who attempted to appropriate Skelton as a proto-Protestant satirist. The objects of anticlerical satire (e.g., simony, priestly avarice and clerical ignorance) were non-doctrinal in nature. 'Ware the Hawk' incorporates parody of transubstantiation and the mass not in order to mock the eucharist, but to defend its sanctity and that of the clerical vocation by satirizing a profligate priest whose attentiveness to hunting results in sacrilege when his hawk sheds blood upon an altar.

During the early 1520s, Skelton composed virulent satires on the excesses of Cardinal Thomas Wolsey, Archbishop of York and Lord Chancellor of England: *Speak, Parrot, Colin Clout*, and *Why Come Ye Not to Court?* They attack a prelate, born a butcher's boy, whose princely magnificence subverted clerical humility and outshone the grandeur of Henry VIII. Written in rhyme royal, the first poem veils attack by exploiting the persona of a parrot who utters a seriocomic mixture of sense and nonsense. Employing Skeltonics, the second satire assumes the persona of a rural truth-telling malcontent. The third attacks the archbishop for subversion of the Bible, the liturgy, and other bases for worship and devotion.

Also notable for allegiance to the 'old religion', John Heywood thrived under Henry VIII, Edward VI and Mary I. A dramatist, musician and versifier of proverbs, Heywood defended traditional devotional practices such as pilgrimages and the sale of pardons in farces written under King Henry: *Pardoner and Friar, Four PP* and *Johan Johan*. Beginning with *An Hundred Epigrams* (1550), Heywood versified ever-expanding collections of poems notable for brevity and wit. Early modern readers regarded the epigram as a species of satire. Pro-clerical bias produced poems such as 'A Man of the Country Shriven in Lent Late', which mocks the ignorance of laypeople. During an age when monarchs determined the official religion of England, 'Of Turning' satirizes those who recant in order to avoid execution for heresy: 'Half turn or whole turn, where turners be turning, / Turning keeps turners from hanging and burning'. When Mary I reversed the schism from the Church of Rome effected by Henry VIII and continued under Edward VI, Heywood published *The Spider and the Fly* (1556), an obscure allegory that personifies Protestantism as a spider that attempts to prey upon a Catholic fly until the Queen as a divine handmaid cleanses England's house. Refusing to 'turn' when Elizabeth I restored Protestantism, Heywood went into exile.

We remember Sir Thomas Wyatt chiefly for domesticating the Italian sonnet and, in company with Henry Howard, the Earl of Surrey, importing techniques and conventions of romantic love derived from Petrarch, the fourteenth-century Italian humanist poet. Nonetheless, Wyatt is notable for cultivating the geniality of Horatian wit in a set of three epistolary satires that harmonize Chaucerian style with imported techniques and conventions derived from Horace and Luigi Alamanni, a contemporary Italian follower of the Roman poet. Wyatt's unadorned plain style reflects Horatian practice, but his poems also exemplify characteristics of native English tradition including moralistic sentiment and heavy use of aphorisms.

Addressed to Sir Francis Brian, Wyatt's 'A spending hand that always poureth out' dramatizes courtly failures including flattery and avarice. Modelled upon Alamanni's tenth satire, Wyatt's 'Mine own John Poins' is addressed to another Henrician courtier. Apparently composed during the poet's 1536 withdrawal from court, the poem hinges upon the conventional identification of courtly life as a breeder of hypocrisy and vice in contrast to country life as a repository of moral virtue. The speaker adopts the conventional satirical persona of a plain-spoken truth-teller:

> My Poins, I cannot frame my tune to feign,
>   To cloak the truth, for praise without desert,
>   Of them that list all vice for to retain.
>
> (ll. 19–21)

Verging upon republican opposition to monarchical tyranny, the speaker aligns his rural pursuit of hunting, reading and writing with both liberty and religious faith. Also addressed to Poins, Wyatt's reworking of Aesop's fable of the country mouse and the city mouse continues his satire on life at court.

Satires on Roman Catholic doctrine and ritual, notably transubstantiation and the mass, poured from the printing press when the militantly Protestant regime of Edward VI relaxed censorship. They are important as a seedbed for religious satire by poets such as Edmund Spenser and John Milton. The prominence of parody and lampoon (exaggerated mockery grounded in malice) in writings by Robert Crowley, Luke Shepherd, William Baldwin (see discussion of *Beware the Cat* in PROSE FICTION, below), and others, contradicts the stereotyped view of early Protestants as humourless opponents of poetry and drama. Writers modelled satirical verse upon *Piers Plowman*, the pseudo-Chaucerian *Plowman's Tale*, and Skelton's *Colin Clout*. Texts include dialogues in which sceptical laypeople mock the mystifying ignorance of pompous clerics and allegorical analyses of the Reformation.

Notable for editing the first printed editions of *Piers Plowman* (1550), Crowley incorporated an influential commentary that interprets that medieval allegory as both a satire on religious and social abuses and a prophecy of the Protestant Reformation. Langland's poem afforded a model for the versification and subject matter of Crowley's own 'gospelling' poems, which include a pair of estates satires that address lessons to different levels of the social hierarchy ranging from beggars to magistrates: *The Voice of the Last Trumpet* and *A New Year's Gift, Wherein Is Taught the Knowledge of Our Self and the Fear of God*. Showing a particular concern for social welfare, the poems issue apocalyptic warnings to avaricious landlords, rack renters, and wealthy idlers who ignore the plight of the poor. Crowley's *One and Thirty Epigrams* affords a precedent for Puttenham's identification of the 'bitter taunts, and privy nips or witty scoffs, and other merry conceits' of epigram as a species of satire.[6] The collection includes satires on institutions including alehouses and brothels and social estates personified by examples that include a bribe-taking bailiff, a wealthy coal miner who yearns to be a knight, and a friar who travels to Louvain in order to wear his habit once again.[7]

The most interesting of Crowley's satires is *Philargyry of Great Britain* (1551), an appeal for completion of religious reforms blocked by Henry VIII's failure to redistribute the wealth of dissolved monasteries to the poor. The gold-eating giant Philargyry personifies avarice in general, but the personified vices who serve in sequence as his chief minister, Roman Catholic Hypocrisy and Protestant Philaute (self-love), align him with Henry VIII's ecclesiastical policy. The conclusion looks to a millennial king to redress oppression of the poor common people.[8]

Like Crowley, Luke Shepherd works within native traditions of late medieval verse satire. Sharing Skelton's predilection for vigorous colloquial vocabulary, macaronic diction, copious verse catalogues and scatological innuendo, Shepherd stands alone as a successful imitator of Skeltonics. Among nine satires published during the reign of Edward VI, *John Bon and Master Parson* stands out as a memorable fusion of medieval English and Lutheran satirical traditions.[9] On the model of polemical dialogues composed by Hans Sachs and other German Lutherans, a rural malcontent descended from Piers Plowman cannily confutes an ignorant cleric. The satire hinges upon the commonsense rationality of John Bon, who denies transubstantiation because he can neither taste nor see it. *Doctor Double Ale* ridicules a London priest who neglects parish affairs in order to haunt alehouses. Exemplifying the appeal lodged by Desiderius Erasmus and William Tyndale for the laity to read the Bible in vernacular translation, a cobbler's boy risks execution as a heretic when he opposes subversive scriptural interpretation to the drunken ignorance of a Catholic priest who mistakes an ale pot for his mass book.

The *Piers Plowman* tradition endured until midway during the reign of Elizabeth I[10] in the form of satires such as Thomas Churchyard's *Davy Diker's Dream* (1552), a blunt truth-teller's vision of a millennial time of social justice. The poet models that speaker on a poor ditch-digger whose prophesied death by starvation is cited in Langland's attack on avaricious clergy and landlords. George Gascoigne employs Piers Plowman as a satirical voice in *The Steel Glass* (1576), a complaint against social ills that assumes the form of late medieval estates satire. It shares the moralistic perspective of mid-century satirists such as Crowley and Shepherd.[11] Although Gascoigne casts the poem in blank verse, its plain style and alliterative manner link it to the native tradition.

Classical and humanistic elements underwent infusion into native satire when Edmund Spenser composed pastoral eclogues (i.e., short monologues or dialogues spoken by shepherds) that followed precedents set by Virgil, Petrarch and Mantuan (i.e., Baptista Spagnuoli). Not only did Petrarch originate the attribution of speeches to *pastors* in the double sense of shepherds and clergymen, he redirected Virgilian eclogue to denounce the alleged depravity of the Avignon papacy. Later poets grounded anticlerical satire on pastoral eclogues by Petrarch and Mantuan, who imitated both Virgil and Petrarch. Mantuan's eclogues, which were on the curriculum of English grammar schools, found favour with Protestant readers because of their stringent satire on clerical corruption.

The unconventional use of simple English names establishes a vernacular context within which Spenser's own pseudonym, Colin Clout, invokes the authority of John Skelton, whose satires on Cardinal Wolsey underwent anachronistic interpretation as proto-Protestant polemics. Combination of sophisticated verse with paradoxically humble character and setting affords a thin mask in the view of Puttenham, who notes that poets compose eclogues 'under the veil of homely persons and in rude speeches to insinuate and glance at greater matters'.[12]

According to the General Argument supplied by E. K., five out of twelve months in Spenser's *Shepheardes Calender* are 'moral [eclogues], which for the most part be mixed with some satirical bitterness'.[13] 'February' and 'October' are non-controversial in nature, but 'May,' 'July' and 'September' satirize alleged clerical corruption in a Mantuanesque manner. Piers Plowman and the narrator of the pseudo-Chaucerian *Plowman's Tale* live on in the guise of Piers, the austere shepherd who attacks surviving Roman Catholic practices in 'May'. By inviting the reader to identify the interlocutors, Piers and Palinode ('counter-song'), respectively with 'two forms of pastors or ministers, or the Protestant and the Catholic', the Argument announces that the eclogue allegorizes contemporary religious controversy. Piers's fable concerning a Kid who foolishly falls victim to a 'false Foxe' (l. 279) assimilates the Protestant satirical tradition that Roman Catholic clerics conceal themselves as wily Foxes or ravenous Wolves. In his railing attack on May games, Piers also attacks the ignorance of avaricious clerics who, under the guise of shepherds, 'playen, while their flocks be unfed' (l. 44). That diatribe against both hirelings and those who abandon their flock by putting them out for hire (i.e., non-resident holders of benefices) attacks a long-standing clerical abuse.

Spenser's July eclogue allegorizes the disgrace of Algrind, a thinly veiled figure for Edmund Grindal, Archbishop of Canterbury, whose official powers underwent suspension by Queen Elizabeth when he rejected her order that he discipline Puritan clergy who engaged in unauthorized scriptural interpretation. The eclogue takes the form of a debate between Thomalin, a humble shepherd, and Morrell, a goatherd whose name offers an anagram for John Aylmer, Bishop of London. Thomalin's humble dedication to pastoral care aligns him with Grindal's advocacy of a preaching ministry. Morrell's extravagant attire and prideful arrogance associate him, by contrast, with the survival of prelatical pomp in the Elizabethan Church of England:

> They bene yclad in purple and pall,
>   so hath theyr god them blist,
> They reigne and rulen over all,
>   and lord it, as they list:
> Ygirt with belts of glitter and gold.
>   (ll. 173–7)

That description echoes the *Plowman's Tale*.

In the September eclogue, the native persona of Davy Diker undergoes metamorphosis into Diggon Davy, a shepherd who narrates a story that idealises Spenser's patron, John Young, Bishop of Rochester, as a model cleric attentive to pastoral care. He assumes the guise of Roffy, a watchful shepherd-pastor who protects his flock by killing 'a wicked Wolfe . . . / Ycladde in clothing of seely sheepe' (ll. 184, 188). Roffy's protection of the laity from a wolf in sheep's clothing, a Gospel figure for 'false' clerics, recalls the role of Jesus Christ as the Good Shepherd. Diggon Davie is a penitent prodigal recently returned from 'a far country' where he became disillusioned by the prideful greed of bad shepherds. The headnote's reference to the 'abuses . . . and loose living of Popish prelates' identifies that locale with Rome, thus situating Roffy's vigilance within the context of a hunt for a crypto-Catholic cleric in a diocese of the Church of England.

In their application of beast fable as a genre appropriate for satire, 'May' and 'September' are in the tradition of polemical dialogues by John Bale and William Turner. Those tracts employed allegorical hunts for 'Romish' foxes and wolves as devices for satirizing Bishop Stephen Gardiner, leader of the anti-Protestant opposition. Spenser's eclogues also concur with Sidney's moralistic interpretation of Aesop's fables: 'whose pretty allegories, stealing under the formal tales of beasts, make many, more beastly than beasts, begin to hear the sound of virtue from these dumb speakers'. Even though

An Apology for Poetry formally disallows Spenser's 'framing of his style to an old rustic language' as a violation of pastoral decorum,[14] Sidney adopts archaic language in his own Ister Bank eclogue. Sung in the *Old Arcadia* by Philisides, a persona for Sidney as a shepherd-poet, that beast fable employs the gathering of a parliament of animals to satirize the increasingly authoritarian and repressive reign of Elizabeth I.

Spenser appears to agree with Sidney's position in *Prosopopoia: Or Mother Hubberd's Tale* (1591), the composition of which may date from the time of *The Shepheardes Calender*. On the model of medieval versifications of the story of Renard the Fox, the Spenserian allegory features an unscrupulous Fox and Ape, who wreak havoc upon a kingdom that mirrors England. Although the poem's meaning is obscure, the indolent slumber of the regal Lion seems to allegorise militant Protestant allegations concerning the religio-political negligence of Queen Elizabeth. The beast fable functions as a vehicle for estates satire through its exposure of the vices and follies of husbandmen, clerics and courtiers as the Ape and Fox prey upon a misgoverned realm. Courtly vices are at issue in Colin's complaint in *Colin Clout Come Home Again* (composed in 1591, ll. 680–730).

From the Red Cross Knight's opening encounter with monstrous Error in Book One of *The Faerie Queene* (1590, 1596), religious and political satire recur within the encyclopaedic array of genres and modes that constitute Spenser's romantic epic.[15] Satire inheres in the historical level of a poem whose multiple allegorical senses also encompass more general ethical, poetic, and social concerns. Error's dragonets, who 'sucked up their dying mothers blood' after her slaughter by the clumsy knight, bring to mind Protestant slurs concerning Jesuit missionaries or clandestine priests. The youngling monsters' cannibalistic feast upon the body and blood of their parent constitutes a blasphemous parody of the mass offered by the Roman Church conceived of as an unholy mother. Archimago's ensuing deception of the knight and his lady, Una, derives from that shape-changer's personification of hypocrisy both as archmagician and as maker of dissimulating images. The false hermit functions as the butt of Protestant satire on recusant priests as wizards and necromancers.

The Red Cross knight's infidelity to Una and dalliance with Duessa ('duplicity'), whose scarlet attire misrepresents her as Fidessa ('faith'), affords an allegory for England's abandonment of the 'true' church for the Church of Rome as the whore of Babylon. Following Una's abandonment by Redcross, her sojourn at the house of Corceca satirizes abuses associated with 'blind' devotion personified in the form of a sightless mother who ceaselessly performs acts of formulaic piety. Allegations that convents breed irregular sexual practices satirize both the vow of celibacy and monasticism, which undergo personification in Abessa, Corceca's daughter, who functions as *abbess* of a disorderly house. Her lover, Kirkrapine ('church robbery'), personifies an ambiguous cluster of allegations concerning misappropriation of ecclesiastical wealth and excesses of Protestant iconoclasts who destroy church ornaments and other holy things. The low point in Redcross's fall involves anti-Catholic satire at the Castle of Orgoglio. The lover of Duessa as the whore of Babylon, that giant seems to associate Spanish Catholicism with 'spiritual fornication' in the historical allegory. Duessa's wearing of a papal tiara and brandishing of a golden chalice as she rides her seven-headed beast mock the papacy and the mass.

After the trial and execution of Duessa in Book Five (see LANCELOT ANDREWES'S GOOD FRIDAY 1604 SERMON, above), which contains extended satire on female mis-government associated with the Catholic Queens, Mary I and Mary, Queen of Scots, and on Spanish Catholicism, a return to estates satire marks the conclusion of Book Six ('The Legend of Courtesy'). Renewing the slanderous onslaught that began in Book Five, the blatant beast ranges 'through all estates' before its rampage through a monastery and 'sacred Church' satirizes both abuses of monasticism abuses and failures of Protestant iconoclasm (6.12.23–5).

In contrast to Spenser's harmonization of classical, Italianate and native English precedents, most late Elizabethan poets turned to the Roman satirists, Horace, Juvenal, Persius and Lucilius, as models for formal verse satire that came into fashion during the 1580s and 1590s. Its conventions include obscure allusions, ambiguity and abrupt and unclear transitions. Following Spenser's practice in *Mother Hubberd's Tale*, Thomas Lodge helped to establish the pentameter couplet as a normative satirical meter in *A Fig for Momus* (1595), a collection that features epistolary satires in addition to pastoral eclogues. Also important are Edward Guilpin's *Skialetheia, Or a Shadow of Truth, in Certain Epigrams and Satires* (1598) and sardonic epigrams by Ben Jonson and Sir John Harington.

Among contemporaries of Lodge and Spenser, the pre-eminent satirists were John Donne, Joseph Hall and John Marston, the last of whom joined Jonson in compos-ing satirical plays that crabbedly attack social foibles and vices. Although Marston builds upon classical models, obscure passages in his *Certain Satires* (1598) and *Scourge of Villainy* (1598) remain in touch with the stylistic roughness of Tudor satire. Fusing the role of malcontent with the newly fashionable pose of the melancholy satirist, Marston accepts the theatrical convention that the persona of the satirist rails against vice that he exemplifies.

Composed circa 1593 to 1598, five satires by Donne circulated in manuscript until posthumous publication of his verse in 1633. The censor's original refusal to license the poems for publication affords evidence concerning their controversial character. The notoriously difficult sense and irregular prosody of the poems exemplify satirical roughness. The satires mock the fashionable excesses of Elizabethan costume, hyper-bole in romantic poetry, courtly flattery and corruption in law courts. Most often read among those poems, satire III concerns the speaker's search for 'true' religion. It anatomises the failures of those who decline to undertake that quest or unite with 'false' churches (e.g., the Church of Rome and Genevan Calvinism) personified in the form of women. Sceptical of organized religion, the speaker instead identifies 'truth' with the strenuous process of his spiritual search:

> To adore, or scorn an image, or protest,
> May all be bad; doubt wisely; in strange way
> To stand inquiring right, is not to stray;
> To sleep, or run wrong, is.

(ll. 76–9)

Joseph Hall, who later gained prominence as a conservative bishop, claimed to be the originator of English satire in *Virgidemiarum Six Books* (1597–8). Despite that declaration, the subject matter of the collection's two volumes is largely conventional. 'Of Toothless Satires' incorporates Horatian criticism of vices and foibles, whereas 'Of Biting Satires' contains Juvenalian attacks. His greatest innovation lies both in imitation of Juvenal and Persius and in inclusion of academic topics and literary criticism. Objects of attack include the fashion for blank-verse drama and elaborate poetic conceits. Mid-sixteenth-century precedents exist for the project of purging bawdiness from poetry in 'Of Toothless Satires'. Hall cites Thomas Nashe's frankly pornographic *Choice of Valentines*, composed for circulation in manuscript, but his attack also includes titillating verse such as Donne's 'To His Mistress Going to Bed' (elegy 19) and Sir John Davies' obscene parody of romantic love, 'Faith (wench) I cannot court thy sprightly eyes.'

Marston and John Milton contested Hall's attempt to redefine verse satire. Although Milton shares Hall's moralism, his *Apology for Smectymnuus* (c.April 1642) would ridicule the aged bishop's composition of formal verse satire on the model of 'the Latin, and Italian satirists' and his definition of *toothless* satire:

> For if it bite neither the persons nor the vices, how is it a satire, and if it bite either, how is it toothless, so that toothless satires are as much as if he had said toothless teeth.[16]

Emulating Spenser's archaic language and allegory, Phineas Fletcher emulated *The Faerie Queene* as a model for anti-Catholic satire in *The Locusts, Or Apollyonists* (1627). Lucifer's worldly guise as Equivocus (i.e., equivocation) recalls the mastery of disguise and slippery speech of Archimago. Jesuitical locusts who swarm in Hell under the tutelage of Lucifer recall the offspring of Spenserian Error, with whom they share common antecedents in the Book of Revelation. Echoes of Spenser's Cave of Error also resonate in the apocalyptic conclusion of Fletcher's *Purple Island* (1633).

Milton's *Lycidas* (1637) features a satirical outburst in the manner of Spenser's 'May' and eclogues by Spenserian poets including William Browne, George Wither and John Davies of Hereford. In the manner of Spenserian shepherd-clerics, St Peter employs rough-hewn language akin to Tudor verse satire to utter a jeremiad against prelatical wolves who abandon pastoral care and misappropriate church wealth:

> Besides what the grim wolf with privy paw
> Daily devours apace, and nothing said,
> But that two-handed engine at the door,
> Stands ready to smite once, and smite no more.
> (ll. 128–31)

A headnote added to the 1645 edition guided revolutionary readers to discover a prophecy of the downfall of Archbishop William Laud and his associates: 'And by occasion foretells the ruin of our corrupted clergy then in their height.'[17]

Scholars have acknowledged scattered instances of political satire in *Paradise Lost*, but a prevailing engagement with religious complaint and satire has received little attention until now. Before the Fall, polemical innuendoes focus heavily, but not exclusively, on Satan in the demonic world of Hell and Chaos. Thus the initial gathering of fallen angels in Hell takes on anti-papal shading when they converge upon a secret *conclave* (that term generally denotes a gathering of cardinals to elect a pope) at Pandaemonium, where they proclaim Satan their leader. Sin and Death reunite with their father, Satan, in a problematic intrusion of Spenserian allegory that shares common ground with seventeenth-century Protestant satire. Satan's ensuing sojourn at the Paradise of Fools affords an occasion for the epic's most explicit outburst of ecclesiastical satire. Satan's wolfish predation in Eden, which affords a precedent for 'lewd hirelings' who will intrude 'into his [God's] church' (4.193), prepares the way for the Edenic meal shared by Adam and Raphael, a repast that hints at Protestant anxieties concerning the Roman-rite mass. Parodies of Roman Catholic devotional formulae and hymns infuse the intrusion of idolatry in Eden at the time of the Fall. Books 11 and 12 foretell despoliation of the Christian church by ravening clerical 'wolves,' a stock target of anticlerical satire.

Paradise Lost underwent publication during the Restoration, but it resorts to time-honoured traditions of complaint and satire rather than the newly fashionable mode of neo-classical satire composed in heroic couplets. Although *A Satire Against Mankind* (1679) by John Wilmot, the Earl of Rochester, and John Dryden's *Mac Flecknoe* (1682) recall the harsh voice of the Tudor satyr-satirist and the pentameter couplets of Spenser's *Mother Hubberds Tale*, they also anticipate eighteenth-century satirical practices notable in poems such as Alexander Pope's *The Dunciad*. Andrew Marvell's satires, notably *The Last Instructions to a Painter*, observe Restoration fashion. By 1700 the homely voices of malcontents descended from Piers Plowman, Colin Clout and other agrarian radicals had fallen silent. Eighteenth-century readers encountered not shepherd-hunters and prelatical wolves, but neo-classical voices modelled more strictly upon Virgilian eclogues.

See also Prose Fiction, English Reformations, Theological Writings and Religious Polemic, Spenser, *Faerie Queene V*

NOTES

1   G. Gregory Smith, ed., *Elizabethan Critical Essays*, 2 vols (London: Oxford University Press, 1904), 1 (176), 2: 32. Quotations are modernized with the exception of passages from verse by Edmund Spenser and Spenserian poets such as Phineas Fletcher. Unless otherwise noted, quotations are from David Norbrook and H. R. Woudhuysen, ed., *The Penguin Book of Renaissance Verse,* *1509–1659* (London: Penguin, 1992); or Richard Sylvester, ed., *English Sixteenth-century Verse: An Anthology* (New York: Norton, 1984).

2   See Alvin Kernan, *The Cankered Muse: Satire of the English Renaissance* (New Haven: Yale University Press, 1959), pp. 54–5.

3   *Elizabethan Critical Essays*, 2 (27), 64–5. See Kernan, *Cankered Muse*, p. 59.

4   Alastair Fowler, *Kinds of Literature: An Introduction to the Theory of Genres and Modes* (Cambridge, MA.: Harvard University Press, 1982), pp. 106–7, 110.

5   Edward W. Rosenheim, *Swift and the Satirist's Art* (Chicago: University of Chicago Press, 1963), p. 31.

6   *Elizabethan Critical Essays*, 2 (65).

7   Ibid., 2 (56).

8   Robert Crowley, *Select Works*, ed. J. M. Cowper, e.s. 15 (London: EETS, 1872).

9   John N. King, ed., 'Philargyrie of Greate Britayne by Robert Crowley,' *English Literary Renaissance*, 10 (1980), 47–75.

10 Janice Devereux's edition of Shepherd's satires is forthcoming from the Renaissance English Text Society.

11 After its 1561 publication, the poem remained out of print until 1813.

12 Hallett Smith, *Elizabethan Poetry: A Study in Conventions, Meaning, and Expression* (Cambridge: Harvard University Press, 1952), pp. 210–12.

13 *Elizabethan Critical Essays*, 2 (40).

14 Edmund Spenser, *The Yale Edition of the Shorter Poems of Edmund Spenser*, eds William Oram, et al. (New Haven and London: Yale University Press, 1989) p. 23.

15 *Elizabethan Critical Essays*, 1 (167), 196.

16 Edmund Spenser, *The Faerie Queene*, ed. A. C. Hamilton (London: Longman, 1977).

17 *Complete Prose Works of John Milton*, eds Don M. Wolfe, et al., 8 vols (New Haven: Yale University Press, 1953–1982), 1, 915–16.

REFERENCES AND FURTHER READING

Crane, Mary Thomas (1993). *Framing Authority: Sayings, Self, and Society in Sixteenth-Century England*. Princeton: Princeton University Press. Consideration of aphoristic poetry touches upon satirical epigram.

Fowler, Alastair (1982). *Kinds of Literature: An Introduction to the Theory of Genres and Modes*. Cambridge, MA: Harvard University Press. An indispensable study.

Hadfield, Andrew (1994). *Literature, Politics, and National Identity: Reformation to Renaissance*. Cambridge: Cambridge University Press. Helpful discussion of the vernacular Protestant tradition.

Kernan, Alvin (1959). *The Cankered Muse: Satire of the English Renaissance*. New Haven: Yale University Press. Concerned largely with drama, Kernan's account of early modern theory of satire has not been superseded.

King, John N. (1982). *English Reformation Literature: The Tudor Origins of the Protestant Tradition*. Princeton: Princeton University Press. Focuses on early native traditions of English Reformation literary culture.

——(1990). *Spenser's Poetry and the Reformation Tradition*. Princeton: Princeton University Press. Considers religious satire in *The Shepheardes Calender* and *The Faerie Queene*.

——(2000). *Milton and Religious Controversy: Satire and Polemic in 'Paradise Lost'*. Cambridge: Cambridge University Press. The first consideration of a neglected subject.

Norbrook, David G. E. (1984). *Poetry and Politics in the English Renaissance*. London: Routledge and Kegan Paul. Contains the best account of the Spenserian poets.

Peter, John (1956). *Complaint and Satire in Early English Literature*. Oxford: Clarendon Press. Dated but sometimes useful.

Anne Lake Prescott (2000). 'The Evolution of Tudor Satire'. In Arthur F. Kinney (ed.), *The Cambridge Companion to English Literature: 1500–1600* (pp. 220–40). Cambridge: Cambridge University Press.

Smith, Hallett (1952). *Elizabethan Poetry: A Study in Conventions, Meaning, and Expression*. Cambridge: Harvard University Press. Contains the best account of early modern English verse satire.

34

Love Poetry

Diana E. Henderson

Was love poetry being written in Renaissance England? The obvious answer is a resounding yes: this was the age of Shakespeare's sonnets and John Donne's metaphysical lyrics, of Cavalier invitations to 'gather ye rosebuds' (and have sex), and of elegies to dead beloveds of all ages and varieties. Recently however, a school of criticism has answered the question differently. Certainly, they grant, much poetry spoke of desire, but was the subject really 'love'? And even if so, did the writer actually feel such emotions? Because much lauded love poetry was generated at and for the court of Queen Elizabeth I, sceptics have argued that its rhetoric was primarily a cover for social advancement or special pleading within a system headed, unconventionally, by a female authority. In instances such as Sir Walter Ralegh's 'Ocean to Cynthia', the masking was slight indeed: Elizabeth had nicknamed him 'Water', and Cynthia was one of the chaste goddesses with whom the queen was routinely identified. Furthermore, given the general misogyny characteristic of Renaissance thought, honouring non-royal women as an actual (as distinct from fictional) audience might be regarded as debasing rather than elevating for male courtiers. Why hold themselves up to ridicule? Certainly, traces of conventional contempt for women can be found in poems by Ben Jonson and Donne. Women poets writing to male beloveds would not face this particular problem, but their access and practice of writing was itself deeply vexed, and their expression of desire constrained. So, what is the proper answer to the question with which we began? Alas, a more qualified 'yes . . . sometimes'. But often it was very good indeed – arguably the greatest body of lyric poetry in the English language, in quality as well as quantity. And for all our distance and potential cynicism about the gendered relations represented therein, we may continue to learn much about love as well as poetry from studying these verses.

While in many cases it remains uncertain whether an actual beloved inspired verse, sometimes beloveds did; sometimes but not always that beloved was female. And while one might debate the contours and depths of various affections, some can be elevated by the name of love. Just because the general codes of conduct dismissed or condemned behaviour did not make it disappear. Even if a young man were not truly in love, he could not produce such verse without being conscious that he was writing poetry: at least the artistic craft had to be genuine. The majority of Elizabethan and Stuart writers were well versed in the traditions of classical and European love poetry, and all were aware of the ballads and folk songs of their own land. They drew on all sources to create fresh, vital lyrics.

As the English language began to settle into its modern systems of syntax and sound, amateur poets were already there, ready to express feelings of love in the developing vernacular. 'Western wind,' one of the briefest anonymous lyrics of the early Tudor period, is also among the most poignant. It remains a starting point for accounts of English lyric, and may stand here for the large body of unattributed or anonymous verses that provided background music for those poets whose names endure:

> Western wind, when will thou blow?
> The small rain down can rain –
> Christ, if my love were in my arms
> And I in my bed again!
> (Hebel and Hudson, p. 42)

Holding in tension the seeming antitheses of specificity and abstraction, self and landscape, emotional yearning and formal control, and immediacy and invisibility, this quatrain's exquisite balancing act foreshadows, in microcosm, one great achievement of Renaissance love poetry. As is true of many sonnets by Shakespeare, its simple diction and melancholy urgency make it appear timeless and portable. Thus it continues to echo centuries later, its lines reappearing in such seemingly unlikely places as Virginia Woolf's *The Waves*. In that high modernist novel, 'Western wind' serves both as an expression of a character's deep feeling and as a nostalgic wish for connection with others and with the past in a harsh, fragmented world. These desires, among others, continue to draw twenty-first-century readers back to Renaissance poetry. But there they encounter other, less immediately accessible, verse as well – verse just as remarkable and beautiful, but requiring some knowledge of its context and project to gain our own readerly affections.

What were the traditions upon which the English poets constructed their own? Especially with the expansion of humanist-inspired programs of education, classical Latin verse provided examples for every schoolboy to imitate. Hence the pervasive influence of Ovid on Christopher Marlowe and Shakespeare. The sensuality and playfulness of Ovid's language had wide appeal, as did his investigation of the psychological twists and torments of desire (often presented in Renaissance editions with Christian allegorizations and moralizing glosses to tame the Roman's wantonness – which nevertheless remained discernible). Marlowe translated Ovid's *Amores*, the autobiographical representation of an illicit love affair, as a sequence of scandalous English *Elegies*. In doing so, Marlowe challenged the usual philosophical 'excuse' for memorializing sexual desire, as championed by Renaissance neoplatonists. They likewise drew upon the writing of the ancients, such as the philosopher Plotinus, to argue that contemplation of earthly beauty led one up the 'ladder of love' to the idea of beauty itself, and hence ultimately to the good and to God. By contrast, Marlowe's Ovid remained earthbound and lustful, achieving sexual union with the married Corinna yet still obsessed and tormented, sublimating nothing. The volume in which the *Elegies* were published alongside Sir John Davies's satires (after Marlowe's death) fell victim to the Bishops' ban and was burned in 1599; while the ostensible reason was concern that topical satires were having corrosive effects upon social stability at a fractious moment, no doubt the clergy was pleased to see Marlowe's libidinous verse going up in flames as well. Learning too much from the Romans had its dangers.

Closer to home, poets looked back to the fourteenth-century Englishman Geoffrey Chaucer, who was admired primarily for his *Troilus and Criseide* and courtly poems. Published along with *The Testament of Cresseid* (a continuation of Chaucer's narrative by the fifteenth-century Scots poet Robert Henryson, but often presented as if by Chaucer himself), the *Troilus* story of courtly love betrayed and punished by fate provided another influential narrative for Elizabethan poets. Edmund Spenser also imitated Chaucer's *The Book of the Duchess* when writing of the deep grief caused by love – specifically, by a wife's death – in *Daphnaida*, a poem for and about the widowed Sir Arthur Gorges. Here, as in his own sonnet sequence the *Amoretti*, Spenser played a pivotal role in adapting courtly traditions to address marital love. A generation later, Bishop Henry King would take the next step in this direction by writing a vivid elegy on his own wife's death, 'The Exequy'. It likewise presages western modernity's emphases on autobiography and the ideological involvement of love and marriage.

But before this move toward bourgeois family values, and providing the most important model of all, came Petrarch. Poet of the *Canzoniere* and *Trionfi*, the fourteenth-century Italian poet Francesco Petrarca was the Renaissance embodied. He 'revived' a romanticized notion of antiquity, crowning himself poet laureate (complete with laurel wreath) and writing a Latin epic about Scipio Africanus. At the same time, in his vernacular poetry he made himself – *pace* his love for the idolized, unattainable Laura – his own supreme poetic subject. Building upon the achievements of Dante (in *Vita Nuova*) and other proponents of the *dolce stil nuovo* in developing a flexible lyric form and style, Petrarch made the sonnet and a model of courtship synonymous with his own name. When he moved to Provence, he began the transmission of that figure and style across western Europe (despite his personal aim of retreat), in effect initiating the modern cult of celebrity authorship. A sceptic might say he also began, through his poetic self-exploration, the modern cult of narcissism. But Petrarch and his *rime* were more than just a fad or phenomenon. He was a remarkable craftsman of sound and sense who made the love lyric seem capable of capturing all that mattered most in human experience. Grouping his sonnets thematically (approximately half to the living Laura, half after her death), he gave stature to the free-standing sonnet sequence. His poems, and those of the sixteenth-century French *Pléiade* school whom he inspired and which included du Bellay and Ronsard, drew upon classical learning but created something truly new: a non-classical form that could be successfully adapted to several European languages, the sonnet; and an innovative representation of the poet / lover's experience of heterosexual desire, focusing on his internal struggles and subjectivity.

The story of the sonnet's gradual rise to become the dominant form of Elizabethan love poetry is also the story of the shift from manuscript to print culture[1] and the enlargement of the audience for written poetry. It epitomizes the change from 'lyric' understood as words set to music (as is still true in popular music) to 'lyric' as a genre of short poem, often written in the first person and primarily contemplative or emotive rather than narrative in emphasis. The different illusions of a 'speaker' conveyed by diverse sonneteers reflect changing attitudes toward love and poetic expression, and suggest what options were available to writers who would present, or even self-consciously fashion, a self for wider consumption.

Two 'courtly makers' of love poetry during Henry VIII's reign stand pre-eminent, in part because they were well represented after their deaths in one of the most influential poetry anthologies of any day. Richard Tottel's *Songs and Sonnets* (1557; also known as Tottel's Miscellany) contained numerous poems by Sir Thomas Wyatt and Henry Howard, Earl of Surrey, including the earliest versions of Petrarch's sonnets published in English. Having spent time abroad as a diplomat, Wyatt returned with a continental taste for vernacular love poetry, and translated Petrarch's eleven-syllable lines into (often irregular) iambic pentameter sonnets of internal struggle, such as 'My galley charged with forgetfulness' and 'I find no peace'. He captured Petrarch's emphasis on the lover's split psyche and torment, and adapted images to fit his own uncertain position as the blunt, outspoken servant of a notoriously temperamental monarch.

Wyatt's achievement in the Petrarchan sonnets was to meld continental trends with his own distinctive, rough-edged 'voice,' in the process providing a model of vernacular English love poetry. A brilliant instance is his adaptation of Petrarch's 'una candida cerva', figuring the beloved as an elusive deer, in his sonnet 'Who so list to hunt'.[2] Wyatt also drew on traditional lyric forms, as in his lute songs ('Blame not my lute', 'My lute awake') which recall the close connection between words and music at Henry's court. Many are songs of love betrayed or denied, with the ability to versify becoming a form of release and revenge (publicizing the beloved's treachery). Despite his poetic innovation, Wyatt usually presents himself pining for the good old days, unable to understand or master 'newfangledness'. In the spectacular three-stanza rime royal 'They flee from me that sometime did me seek', Wyatt merges medieval form and new sophistication, again mixing erotics and images of animals tame and wild, in a fantasia from which the speaker's voice emerges baffled, righteous and wounded. Some (including later poets) have identified the plain-speaking scepticism about love in such poetry as the English contribution to Petrarchism, or even as an anti-Petrarchan antidote to Italianate worship of the inaccessible madonna-love. But Wyatt – like the Elizabethans George Gascoigne, Ralegh and Donne, all dubbed 'plain stylists' by certain scholars – is not so easy to schematize. More accurately, a struggle persists throughout the century between the extremes of veneration and debasement, belief and scepticism, played out stylistically within single poems and more broadly by schools of poetry that tend either towards rough disruption or smooth sound and metrics. In this larger scheme, Wyatt's younger peer and admirer Surrey becomes his stylistic foil: where Wyatt stresses resistance, anger and confusion, Surrey glosses over the rough edges with more regular, sonorous versification, greater attention to the relationship between self and landscape, and muted expressions of love as melancholy. Setting Wyatt's Petrarchan translation 'The long love that in my thought doth harbour' alongside Surrey's alternative 'Love that doth reign', the smoothness of the younger poet is self-evident. And Surrey's more controlled, understated manner was long regarded not only as truer to Petrarch's subtleties but also as the more perfect poetry in its own right. Especially given what we know of Surrey's tempestuous arrogance (which contributed to his beheading shortly before Henry VIII's death), his achievement is the more classical, subordinating at least some aspects of his personality to the task of translation. Only with our contemporary emphasis on individuality and struggle has Wyatt's reputation eclipsed Surrey's.

Tottel's miscellany played a crucial role in establishing their respective positions as forerunners for Elizabethan sonneteers. As aristocrats whose poetry circulated in manuscript, their words remained closely connected to that courtly context and moment. Only when Tottel transferred their poetry from the manuscript to print medium did it have a broader impact. Tottel also regularized Wyatt's metre – an infamous act in the eyes of many now, yet at the time, a necessary step to update an older poet's style for a new audience. (As the early Elizabethan Gascoigne lamented, the regular iambic line had become the 'tyrant' of his day.) Such editing played an important part in establishing the iambic norm of modern English poetry, moving away from the four- and five-stress lines of fourteenth-century verse to a metrical system that considered both accent and the number of syllables. Although Surrey's metrics were impeccable, Tottel 'improved' his manuscripts too, giving sonnets biographical titles (such as a 'description and praise of his love Geraldine'). Tottel thereby generated an apocryphal love story of Surrey and Geraldine that provided fodder for Elizabethan writers. Thus modified in medium, metre and narrative context, the Petrarchan adaptations of Wyatt and Surrey exemplify the difficulties inherent in asserting an authentic personal 'voice' on paper. The tension between the lover's desire and what is actually expressed by his poem becomes a central topic for Sir Philip Sidney in his influential sonnet sequence, *Astrophil and Stella*, which in turn generated many more sequences – and parodies, such as Shakespeare's mockery of courtly sonneteers in the comedy *Love's Labour's Lost*.

Sidney's poetic achievement becomes all the more dazzling when understood in historical context. For while Tottel provided models for those wishing to adapt continental innovations, his immediate impact was to generate readers rather than a flourishing school of such poets. Even within his anthology, Petrarchan poetry collides with the moralistic native tradition of other mid-century writers. In their poems, love is distanced, the stuff of a prodigal youth now viewed through more mature eyes. Lord Vaux's 'The Agèd Lover Renounceth Love' exemplifies what could be achieved in this vein, using broken poulter's measure (alternating seven and six-beat iambic lines).

Gascoigne, the early Elizabethan who developed love poetry and many other genres the farthest, plays with the moralizing convention in lyrics such as 'The lullaby of a lover' and 'The green knight's farewell to fancy.' In each case, the speaker professes to be abandoning love – but its emotional power remains vivid. Again a split self emerges, allowing a struggle of perspectives between the 'mature' speaker and his own bodily desires (here addressed in the second person):

> With lullaby your looks beguile:
> Let no fair face, nor beauty bright,
> Entice you eft with vain delight.
> (Gascoigne I, p. 44)

Repeating the word 'beguile,' the poem suggests that self-deception lies in the present renunciation just as much as in past 'vain' delights. Similarly, when the Green Knight says farewell to 'fancy', it embraces poetry as well as love – yet the putative farewell is of course itself a poem (and not Gascoigne's last). In fact, Gascoigne was among a growing number of poets, including Barnabe Googe and George Turberville, making new claims as authors, either publishing their work directly or announcing themselves as producers of volumes, rather than contributing single poems in anthologies or manuscripts only. Love lyrics were gradually becoming detachable from their stated audience as well as from manuscript or accompanying melodies: published anthologies recontextualized them, different mixes of words and song were suggested, and readers with no personal familiarity with the writer copied verses into commonplace books. Sonnets and court lyrics in this way resembled ballads and more widely popular songs, some authored, some anonymous. Gascoigne plays with the very idea of the poetic speaker, at times implying autobiographical allusions (referring to 'George' within a verse or including 'Gascoigne' in the title); using personae such as the Green Knight, Master F. J., or Dan Bartholomew of Bath; and claiming in the preface to his voluminous collection *The Posies*, 'if ever I wrote a line of love for my self in causes of love, I have written ten for other men in lays of lust' (Gascoigne I, p. 16). For all his playfulness and desire, however, it remains true that Gascoigne classifies love as a comparatively light, unworthy topic, and most of his love stories end in sadness and disillusionment. Ultimately, like most of his Protestant contemporaries, he turns away from amorous affairs to moral and religious themes.

One might almost say the same of Sir Philip Sidney – except that his emphasis on love is so extensive, his defence of poetry so much stronger, and his innovative treatments of the topic so vivid, that it is the love poetry rather than his deathbed renunciation that must be taken seriously. While Thomas Watson's *Hekatompathia* (1582) can claim the prize as the first extensive sequence of love sonnets published in English, Sidney's *Astrophil and Stella* showed what variety and drama could be produced within the form; moreover, the mythologizing of Sir Philip after his death from battle wounds (and gangrene) in the lowlands gave his writings almost unmatched cultural power. Again, the move from manuscript to print was crucial. As an aristocrat, Sidney did not offer his writings for general consumption, but after his death they were published and then imitated by middle-class poets hoping for advancement and fame. Thomas Nashe railed against the cheap ubiquity of ballad-makers and sonneteers, but Sir Philip's sonnets even when printed communicated the aura of a privileged, coterie world, and gave the form social distinction. By the 1590s, almost every aspiring poet seemed to be writing a sonnet sequence.

Sidney spent time on the continent, and familiarity with French Protestant humanism in particular melded with his knowledge of classical and European literature. His lengthy prose romance, *Arcadia*, was modelled on the Spaniard Montemayor's *Diana*, and includes love poems written using classical metrics and elaborate forms such as the double sestina. Similar formal innovation and mastery appears in *Astrophil and Stella*, which begins with an unconventional sonnet in alexandrines (a twelve-syllable line usually more successful in French) even as it speaks of imitation and 'other's feet' impeding the poet's expression of love. The sequence dramatizes the struggle to make the Petrarchan tradition one's own, and adds another layer by sustaining the semi-fiction that the speaker is Astrophil (star-lover) – who is and is not Sidney. Like the actual poet, Astrophil jousts well, frequents the court and is smitten with a black-eyed woman married to a man named Rich. Yet Astrophil is presented by the intelligent, urbane Sidney as being fitfully absurd in his logic, buffoonish and immoral in his attempts to justify his sexual longings. In a sense, Sidney makes himself into a fictive spectacle of the sort Stella is said to enjoy; desperate to win his beloved's attention, Astrophil concludes 'I am not I; pity the tale of me' (no. 45). Sidney's desired audience clearly includes many besides Stella, with some poems addressed to courtier friends, and all implicitly requiring a coterie that would understand the myriad allusions and coy self-referentiality. As a frustrated advocate of radical Protestant positions Queen Elizabeth chose to subdue, Sidney provides one of the best cases for those who argue that love poetry was a rhetorical means to political ends: his romantic hopes, rejection, and marginalization nicely figure his tenuous hold on courtly power and position.

Yet Sidney's artistic control and wide-ranging allusiveness make it hard to reduce *Astrophil and Stella* to any single agenda or allegorical reading. The 108 sonnets show the influence of the *Pléiade* poets, as in a sub-sequence of *baiser* poems seeking a kiss from the beloved. As in Petrarch, songs are interspersed, sometimes advancing the narrative, sometimes adding another perspective (see the pastoral ninth song, or song eight's third-person account of Astrophil and Stella's brief tryst). Out of all this, Sidney creates a seriocomic drama in which Astrophil attempts to climb the ladder of love but instead finds himself gradually debased by desire. Despite his familiarity with Neoplatonic theories of love's elevating influence, he finds that lust overpowers sublimation: 'But ah, Desire still cries, give me some food' (no. 71). Loving a married woman encounters more impediments at Elizabeth's court than it had in Ovid's Rome, leaving Astrophil disconsolate and unfulfilled. The language of the last sonnets echoes Sidney's own theoretical discourse in defence of poetry, with a twist: whereas in theory he argues that the poet creates a golden world which teaches and edifies more effectively than brazen reality can, his sonnet sequence shows a man deploying the resources of poetry for corrupt ends, left all the more mired in dross as he pines for lost gold. Scholars still debate the tone, moral claims and levels of irony in this sequence, some believing that Sidney's additional sonnets which turn explicitly to God ('Leave me, o love, that reaches unto dust') indicate a resolution and / or absolute split between Astrophil's position and Sidney's; others are less sure that Sidney's practice is so schematic. His sheepish, partial defence of love poetry in *An Apology for Poetry* implies that the militant Protestant courtier sometimes found himself holding inconsistent, if not untenable, positions. What is indubitable is that *Astrophil and Stella* presented a marvellously skilful puzzle, meditation, drama and set of lyrics all in one, and had a deep and wide influence on other composers of sonnet sequences, including Henry Constable (*Diana*), Samuel Daniel (*Delia*), Michael Drayton (*Idea*), Barnabe Barnes (*Pathenophil and Parthenope*), Philip's niece Lady Mary Wroth (*Pamphilia to Amphilanthus*) and his best friend and biographer Fulke Greville (*Caelica*). All built on Sidney's model but added their own twists, from the more integral neoplatonism of Constable and philosophical contortions of Greville to the gender reversals of Wroth.

Comparing Sidney's sequence with that of another great Elizabethan lyricist, Edmund Spenser, demonstrates how the form had become capacious enough for two quite different narratives and conceptions of love. Like blank verse in drama, the sonnet sequence provided these poets with a malleable verse form and framework in which to pursue their own philosophical and social meditations, to tell a story or express emotion. Rather than emphasize social constraints and self-incrimination, Spenser's *Amoretti* foregrounds the vagaries of a developing relationship between the poet-speaker and his proud beloved, and hearkens to the seasonal and religious calendar to chart its 'natural' evolution towards marriage. The sequence, as published, concludes with an *Epithalamion* celebrating the poet's marriage, a *tour de force* of natural, ceremonial and mythical imagery contained within an elegant metrical and numerological system. Nevertheless, even here – as in the sonnets themselves – the poet worries whether time is on his side: mutability and mortality loom large. As if playing Surrey to Sidney's Wyatt, Spenser sonorously subdues rather than accentuates his struggle through elegant technique, while nevertheless presenting a conflicted speaker. As with the earlier pair of poets, seeing them only as foils is an oversimplification: Sidney had an impeccable sense of proportion and number, and Spenser's poet-lover had his rages. Both make the question of how one reads (a lover's gesture, a word, a poetic line) into a major theme, stressing the partiality of interpretation even as they argue their case. What emerges from reading their sequences, nevertheless, is a more vivid awareness of distinctive sensibilities and adjustments to the social, philosophical and religious quandaries occasioned by erotic desire.

Amoretti 67 ('Like as a huntsman after weary chase') captures not just another deer in the love-hunting tradition but also Spenser's particularity. Although beginning with a typical Petrarchan comparison, the sonnet reverses expectations in the second quatrain:

> So after long pursuit and vain assay,
> When I all weary had the chase forsook,
> The gentle dear returned the self-same way,
> Thinking to quench her thirst at the next brook.
>
> (Sylvester, p. 378)

Rather than draw the obvious parallel between the exhausted hunter of the first quatrain and himself, the speaker here makes the simile with a huntsman apply – at least grammatically – to 'the gentle dear', placing himself in a subordinate modifying clause. After one has read hundreds of poems beginning 'Like as a hunter. . . . so I' or 'Like as a ship . . . so I', the effect is profound, and accords exactly with the poem's own wonder at the shifting power relations between the first-person writer and his object of his desire:

> There she beholding me with milder look,
> Sought not to fly, but fearless still did bide:
> Till I in hand her yet half trembling took,
> And with her own goodwill her firmly tied.
> Strange thing me seemed to see a beast so wild,
> So goodly won with her own will beguiled.

Who is the hunter, who is the hunted? Who leads, who follows, whose will? As the ambiguous modifier 'half trembling' indicates, the sonnet alters convention by mingling the two parties grammatically and thereby merging their sensibilities. Like Spenser's epic *The Faerie Queene* (whose stanza is itself an expanded version of his distinctive interlocking *ababbcbccdcdee* rhyme scheme in these sonnets), *Amoretti* 67 is fascinated by doubling and gender-bending, tensions between masculine action and passive receptivity to the good, between courtly love schema and the intimacy of marital love, and between female chastity (so fetishized in this period) and fully realized sexuality. As in the epic, it remains debatable which kind or level of allegory should be emphasized in this clearly figurative story: some say erotic love between man and woman, others stress Christian love of God. Symbolizing Christ as a deer was not Spenser's innovation. Wyatt's 'Who so list' also plays with the association when his deer's neck proclaims Christ's warning, *Noli me tangere* – before adding that she belongs to Caesar. Poems by Tasso and especially Marguerite de Navarre echo in Spenser's sonnet: in the sixth lyric of the Frenchwoman's *Chansons Spirituelles*, the deer stands for the crucified Christ and may be caught by the net of a humble heart only (see Prescott). Whereas Marguerite has a wise woman so instruct her young hunter, however, Spenser mystifies the process (and mutes Marguerite's gendering of wisdom) by representing only the intimate scene between speaker and 'beast'. The ironies of so naming the gentle creature / Creator recoil, like so much in the *Amoretti*, upon the speaker, creating an effect of comic humility for all Spenser's poetic mastery and ultimate masculine self-assertion.

The fact that the *Amoretti* do not leave the earthly world of gendered bodies, despite their religious overtones and allusions, arguably creates a sense of greater power for 'real' women. Though still only represented during the period of courtship, and drawn from the elevated lady-love of courtly tradition, Spenser's beloved is praised for her pride and goodness even as she figuratively comes down from her pedestal and eventually marries him. The fears that haunt much Renaissance love poetry when women become sexual are not entirely erased, but the usual diatribes against female fickleness and weakness do not come to the fore and drown out the *Epithalamion's* song of wedded love. And indeed, 'real' women – those few with the access and education to write their own poetry – also saw potential in the sonnet tradition, as had continental poets Louise Labé and Vittoria Colonna. Women wrestled with the conventions that positioned them as the silent, obscure objects of desire (the *petit objet* in a modern Lacanian's reading), and added their own voices. Sometimes they enlarged the types of love (both maternal and the love between female friends in Katherine Philips' seventeenth-century lyrics). Sometimes they took conventional associations and made them resonant, as Mary Wroth did when claiming darkness, stasis and confinement as expressive of her experience. She might have less social mobility, but found consolation in familiar forms: 'When others hunt, my thoughts I have in chase' (Norbrook, p. 341).[3] Like men, women writers found in love poetry a vehicle for confronting social, religious, gender, and authorial struggles – and sometimes, a way to express feelings of love as well.

What comes after Sidney and Spenser is too diverse and multitudinous to summarize. The possibilities established, poets worked to distinguish themselves from the conventional mass. It is within this context that Shakespeare's sonnets can be read as more than an autobiographical account of vexed love for a fair youth and a dark lady; from his seemingly simple vocabulary and looser English form (three quatrains and a couplet, seldom carrying a rhyme beyond four lines) emerges not only an accessible set of exquisite poems but a strenuous attempt to triangulate familiar dichotomies and further invert expectations. In de-historicizing Shakespeare, readers get portable quotations and lovely lines, but miss much of the force and newness of his sonnets. They also miss his debts and links with other poets, and the power of his unconventional address to the beloved male (Richard Barnfield being the other poet to use the sonnet to express male–male desire explicitly). One may turn from Shakespeare's 'dark lady' poems to Michael Drayton's later revisions of *Idea* (1619) and see how far the sonnet has come from a courtly tribute to idealized femininity: dismissing the pride of 'painted things' (ladies riding in their carriages), Drayton makes it clear that true power lies with the hyper-masculine writer who can give his poetic subject 'eternity'. Shakespeare is not alone in upholding his black lines of ink as more powerful than time's lines and marble monuments. Nor was he, despite the bardolatry of Harold Bloom or the compelling Lacanian reading of Joel Fineman, the only begetter of modern subjectivity or 'the human'. Self-creation was a group achievement.

With the new century and a new king making courtly subordination to a high and mighty woman a thing of the past, the floodgates of seventeenth-century reaction against Elizabethan Petrarchism opened wide:

> A libertine, fantastically I sing;
> My verse is the true image of my mind,
> Ever in motion, still desiring change . . .
> My muse is rightly of the English strain,
> That cannot long one fashion entertain.
>   (Sylvester, p. 583)

Drayton's lines pave the way for Stuart Cavaliers, for Robert Herrick, Sir John Suckling and the witty licentiousness of Thomas Carew. Eroticism became, more than ever, a form of individuated self-expression. But these writers too had sixteenth-century forerunners, not to be forgotten when telling the dominant story of sonnets and love songs. In addition to the putatively 'English' scepticism within the tradition from Wyatt through Sidney and beyond, there were those like Marlowe who stood apart from the Petrarchan model entirely. As well as Marlowe's Ovid, he produced one of the most delightful and oft-imitated lyrics, 'Come live with me and be my love', which offered conditional bliss in an aestheticized future in exchange for love now. Sir Walter Ralegh took up his challenge in a sceptical companion poem, in which a nymph reminds the Marlovian 'shepherd' that time matters:

> If all the world and Time were young,
> And truth in every shepherd's tongue
> Your pretty pleasures might me move
> To live with thee, and be thy love.
>   (Sylvester, p. 331)

Reality bites poet. In short, here is the playful volleying between the *carpe diem* invitations of salacious suitors and the pragmatic resistance of vulnerable maidens that will be elaborated by Stuart poets for a century to come. Marvell's 'To his coy mistress' rolls the tradition into a ball and shoots it into eternity, after which a new era, the Restoration, would see coyness crumble in a libertine triumph (for both sexes and all orientations in the erotic poems of Aphra Behn). But that short time soon passed as well, to be followed by the reiteration and recontextualization of the narrative Edmund Spenser first created as the stuff of poetry: the seemingly endless monumentalization of monogamous love culminating in marriage.

To others in this volume, I leave the wit and passion of John Donne, only noting here his dramatic reworking of the relationships between the holy and metaphysical and the erotic in a volume borrowing its title from Tottel, *Songs and Sonnets*.[4] He could not have rebelled and yet reworked the tropes of love poetry so effectively, nor made the transition from blasphemous sexuality to sexualized worship in his *Holy Sonnets*, had it not been for the patterns – distinct from one another and from his own – laid forth by Sidney and Spenser. From the woman as conquered prey to the woman as (conquered) New Found Land, topographies and scientific metaphors would change, but not always or entirely the gendered and philosophical relationships upon which they were constructed. Donne might cast himself as the sceptic rebel in regard to what came before, but those after would also see his involvement in similar social relations. When Katherine Philips later wondered why an unmarried friend would wish to marry given the poetry written to woo her, she challenged the endpoint of the Spenserian narrative most obviously:

> She is a public deity,
> And were't not very odd
> She should depose her self to be
> A petty household god?
> (Norbrook, p. 378)

Why let go of the moment of symbolic power? Nor does Philips's comic questioning stop here. Her mockery embraces the metaphysical as well as Spenserian lyricists when she orders the youth to 'make the Sun in private shine . . . That so he may his beams confine / In complement [compliment?] to you'. Anticipating his inability to do so, she then chastizes his presumption:

> Think how you did amiss
> To strive to fix her beams which are
> More bright and large than his.

The now-dead John Donne, and the Draytons and Shakespeares who likewise perceived their poetic powers as fixing and hence enlarging their beloved's value, now face the revenge of the mutable: life, Philips says, triumphs over art. His poem is (to invert Drayton) the 'paltry, foolish, painted thing' that cannot compete with the living woman's worth. One might well imagine a friend saying to Philips, as Don Pedro says to Shakespeare's Beatrice in *Much Ado*, 'You have put him down, lady, you have put him down'.

Should we put these love poets down, as we begin a new millennium? Deeply embedded in their cultures as we must all be, Renaissance poets now alienate many readers – be it for their narrow images of the 'fair' or their dissecting catalogues 'blazoning' female beauty as fetishized parts while the speaker revels in dominating the imagined whole; for their repetitious turning back to certain figures, tropes, and metaphors; or for simply acting as if erotic love were all-important when we know that history tells a different story. I think we should still pick these poems up rather than put them down – and not only because of the historical and cultural stories they reveal, which are of indubitable interest to scholars. At the same time, I don't think we (who have time and space to do so) should simply wonder and delight in the artistic game and mastery, as do those who would entirely forget the historical context.

Rather, this poetry matters now because it addresses and combines both the imperatives implicit above: it makes us aware of how people have imagined their worlds and interactions; *and* it simultaneously aspires to free itself from those worlds through its own internal systems, shapes and beauties. To the extent that we still value the worlds they imagined or participate in similar systems, the game is one requiring serious reflection about what to preserve and what to discard. To the extent we have left the dreams and assumptions of these poems behind, they force us to examine what has taken their place, and whether their paradises are well lost or suggest new pastures. (And finally, while we sort through the representations and meanings of 'love', we cannot help but recover something of their excitement at creating a new language and control over poetic expression, writing at a moment when with sudden energy and ubiquitousness, the word was love.)

NOTES

1 See PUBLICATION.
2 See WYATT'S 'WHO SO LIST TO HUNT'.
3 See THE HEART OF THE LABYRINTH.

4 See DONNE'S 'NINETEENTH ELEGY', POETS, FRIENDS AND PATRONS.

REFERENCES AND FURTHER READING

Braden, Gordon (1999). *Petrarchan Love and the Continental Renaissance*. New Haven: Yale University Press.

Dubrow, Heather (1995). *Echoes of Desire: English Petrarchism and its Counterdiscourses*. Ithaca: Cornell University Press.

Fineman, Joel (1986). *Shakespeare's Perjured Eye: The Invention of Poetic Subjectivity in the Sonnets*. Berkeley: University of California Press.

Gascoigne, George (1907; 1910). *The Complete Works of George Gascoigne*, ed. John W. Cunliffe. 2 vols. Cambridge: Cambridge University Press.

Greene, Roland (1991). *Post-Petrarchism: Origins and Innovations of the Western Lyric Sequence*. Princeton: Princeton University Press.

Hebel, J. William and Hudson, Hoyt H. (1929). *Poetry of the English Renaissance 1509–1660*. New York: F. S. Crofts and Co.

Helgerson, Richard (1976). *The Elizabethan Prodigals*. Berkeley: University of California Press.

Henderson, Diana E. (1995). *Passion Made Public: Elizabethan Lyric, Gender, and Performance*. Urbana: University of Illinois Press.

——(1997). 'Female Power and the Devaluation of Renaissance Love Lyrics'. In Yopie Prins and Maeera Shreiber (eds), *Dwelling in Possibility: Women Poets and Critics on Poetry* (pp. 38–59). Ithaca: Cornell University Press.

Javitch, Daniel (1978). *Poetry and Courtliness in Renaissance England*. Princeton: Princeton University Press.

Johnson, William C. (1990). *Spenser's 'Amoretti': Analogies of Love*. Lewisburg: Bucknell University Press.

Jones, Ann Rosalind (1990). *The Currency of Eros: Women's Love Lyric in Europe, 1540–1620*. Bloomington: Indiana University Press.

Kermode, Frank (1971). "The Banquet of Sense". In *Renaissance Essays* (pp. 84–115). London: Routledge and Kegan Paul.

Marlowe, Christopher (1971). *The Complete Poems and Translations*, ed. Stephen Orgel. New York: Penguin Books.

Marotti, Arthur (1982). ' "Love is not love": Elizabethan sonnet sequences and the social order', *ELH*, 49, 396–428.

Norbrook, David and Woudhuysen, H. R. (eds) (1992; 1993). *The Penguin Book of Renaissance Verse 1509–1569*. London: Penguin.

Prescott, Anne Lake (1985). 'The Thirsty Deer and the Lord of Life: Some Contexts for *Amoretti* 67–70', *Spenser Studies*, 6, 33–76.

Roche, Thomas P. (1989). *Petrarch and the English Sonnet Sequence*. New York: AMS Press.

Sidney, Sir Philip (1970). *Apology for Poetry*, ed. Forrest G. Robinson. Indianapolis: Bobbs-Merrill.

Stephens, Dorothy (1998). *The Limits of Eroticism in Post-Petrarchan Narrative*. Cambridge: Cambridge University Press.

Sylvester, Richard S. (ed) (1974). *English Sixteenth-century Verse: An Anthology*. New York: Norton.

Vickers, Nancy (1981). 'Diana Described: Scattered Woman and Scattered Rhyme'. *Critical Inquiry*, 8, 265–80.

Wall, Wendy (1993). *The Imprint of Gender: Authorship and Publication in the English Renaissance*. Ithaca: Cornell University Press.

Waller, Gary (1986). *English Poetry of the Sixteenth Century*. New York: Longman.

35
Erotic Poems
Boika Sokolova

In 1589, Thomas Lodge published *Scylla's Metamorphosis*, a narrative Ovidian tale about tragic love and metamorphic transformation told in appropriately domesticated circumstances on the banks of the Isis. Clearly the piece touched a vibrant vein in the artistic air of the times as the next decade or so saw an outburst of erotic metamorphic poems on subjects derived from Ovid and older Greek models. These dealt with the love games of mythological gods, nymphs and mortals, the delights of watching and touching beautiful bodies, the consummation of sex or the impossibility of it, and with a final (more often than not tragic) transformation into a natural form, plant or animal. Outstanding examples of the genre, known as *epyllion* (minor epic), are Christopher Marlowe's *Hero and Leander* (published 1598)[1] and Shakespeare's *Venus and Adonis* (published 1593). Though not metamorphic in the strict sense, George Chapman's *Ovid's Banquet of Sense* (1595) can also be related to this group, because of its classical narrative and stylistic features. This witty fluid poem, where metamorphosis is a structural principle rather than a narrative event, has been long committed by criticism to the realm of the philosophically inscrutable and has only lately made a comeback as the lively, erudite and ironical piece which it is.

The aristocratic vogue for exquisite voyeuristic narratives was mediated through the printing presses to coteries of well-educated aspiring professionals relishing the subtleties of courtly pleasures, as the five reprints of *Venus and Adonis* in the six years following its first publication testify. This catching fashion proved the existence of a considerable interest, and poems would soon be discarding mythological paraphernalia to focus only on sex. Such is Thomas Nashe's wittily obscene *Choice of Valentines* (1600?).[2] These, however, were not to appear in print until much later. The popularity of the erotic poem can be read as an indication of the processes of commodification of sex and the body, made intentionally titillatingly voyeuristic for the burgeoning male market.[3]

The new vogue of the erotic in Renaissance England was not unique. The lines of its genesis can be traced back to Italy of the 1520s and are connected with the name of Pietro Aretino (Aretine) (1492–1557), a poet, art critic and publicist. In 1527, Aretino published *I sonnetti lussuriosi* as a response to the suppression of sixteen engravings of sexual poses, *I Modi,* by his painter friend Giulio Romano.[4] The sonnets are an explicit compendium on sexual technique and the thrill of sex as well as a slap in the face of the 'hypocrites' to whom they were dedicated, 'out of patience with their villainous judgement and with the hoggish custom that forbids the eyes what most delights them'.[5] Though demonized by Protestants, just like his older contemporary Niccolò Machiavelli Aretino was well known in England not only for his erotic writings. One of the most influential art critics of the sixteenth century, his voice had been formative in arguing the identity of poetry and painting / art due to their imitation of nature and the objectivity of the seeing eye. He stressed the fact that the visual also resides in the mind, traditionally considered the domain of poetry. Imitation, on its part, was conceived as a 'form of male control over the alluringly female' nature and, as a result, poetry and painting were thought of as 'brother' rather than 'sister' arts.[6] The powerful illusionism of the art of perspective painting and chiaroscuro prompted poets to develop fresh techniques and push the limits of linguistic representation in new directions.[7]

The 1590s were a time of political and religious restraint. After the Puritan attacks of the 1580s on the theatre and the episcopacy, in which Nashe became the acerbic paid hack of the episcopal cause, there were several theatre closures, most notably in 1592–3. Catholic and Puritan religious propaganda was ruthlessly stamped out.[8] In 1597, Nashe was in trouble with the authorities over the contents of a play.[9] Chapman escaped harsher treatment under Elizabeth but was imprisoned in 1605, also for a play. In 1593 Christopher Marlowe met his violent death, engineered by the Queen's Secret Service, and the close of the 1590s saw his translations of Ovid's *Amores* officially sequestered and burnt on account of its licentiousness. Arthur Golding's moralized and bowdlerized 1565 translation of the *Metamorphoses* became the preferred text. In the context of hardening Protestant debate on the family and the consequent strictures on women's behaviour, discussing illicit erotic pleasure offered a position for exploring attitudes to licit familial, gender and power roles.[10]

The instability of the theatre and the general tightening of censorship made patronage an important element in the survival of a poet. Shakespeare wrote his sonnets and erotic poems for the Earl of Southampton and is known to have designed an *impresa* for the Earl of Rutland. In the conditions of the sixteenth century, patronage provided more than security and a little money. It helped create an *author* status, something the writing of plays did not.[11] Materialized in the printed book, the erotic poem, originally dedicated to an aristocratic patron, joined the circulation of cultural capital as its author became a participant 'in the collective consciousness of publishing individuals' and in this way, in the *dissemination* of authority over the creation of meanings.[12] Expensively gift-wrapped in layers of dedicatory sonnets and prefatory letters, the epyllia were instrumental in shaping the author as a subject and in spreading specific interest among coterie readers.[13]

The Elizabethan taste for the sensual could not be modelled on Aretino's explicitness because of the strictures of the cultural and political climate in Reformation England. The subtle heritage of Ovid however, whose *Metamorphoses* and *Ars Amatoria* were used in schools well into the 1580s, provided a convenient classical blueprint for exploring the erotic. Ovid's rapport with refined sixteenth-century audiences bore an air of elegant courtship between author and reader, be he noble by birth or intellectually ennobled through education. His legacy offered an eroticism accommodating the male, female and the androgynous, the heterosexual and homoerotic. Its dazzling descriptive exuberance delighted the mind with complex allusiveness, its self-conscious artistic virtuosity complemented the achievement of the poet, its never-ending fluid reversals invariably addressed issues of power.

While ostensibly using Ovid as an *exemplum*, the erotic poems 'made novel use of language and ideology by wresting them in a new direction and conscripting them into a project peculiar to them alone'.[14] In this sense, they are specific to their time in negotiating a position of artistic freedom and autonomy in constrictive historical and political circumstances.

The Ovidian provided a meeting point of the apposite classical with current artistic debate. The intricate linguistic strategies of the erotic poem tallied with new aesthetic developments. The 'knowingly fallacious visual conceit' of the *trompe l'oeil* in painting was matched by the epyllion's fascination with the imaginative and sexual stimulation of its knowledgeable reader, controlled by the poet's mastery of form.[15]

Marlowe's two sestiads of *Hero and Leander* and their continuation, by George Chapman (sestiads 3–6), exhibit an enhanced painterly awareness of the position of the onlooker, take great care in providing aesthetic and intellectual pleasure, and maintain the position of the authorial voice as the single-handed manipulator of the overall effect.

The first sestiad offers a feast of stunning descriptive passages, meant 'for men to gaze upon' (I, l. 8). Profound irony is sustained throughout by reversing received patterns of expectation. The idealistic Petrarchan layout of gender roles is consciously invoked by the rhetoric, only to be made a butt of irony. Chaste 'Hero the fair', though outwardly a piece of sonnet statuary, is an undercover agent of love's passions, while Leander, fully endowed with the persuasiveness of the Petrarchan lover, is a comic failure in the first test of love's consummation (II, ll. 1–86). Hero, conceived as a highly ornate object of desire, a mystery veiled in 'artificial flowers and leaves / Whose workmanship both man and beast deceives' (I, ll. 19–20) is a perfect *trompe l'oeil*. The real Hero is teasingly hidden from the male gaze under a breathtaking blazon of an artifice of wrappings, arousing sensual fantasies for what lies underneath and comically undermining her position as 'Venus' nun' (I, l. 45).

On its part, Leander's nakedness is also meant to gratify 'the loves of men' (l. 70). The 'vent'rous youth of Greece', 'Jove', 'wild Hippolytus' (I, ll. 77–8), 'the barbarous Thracian soldier', are all 'moved by him' as if he were 'a maid in man's attire' (I, ll. 49–90). Leander's body is a site of teasing sexual contest between Hero and a male world of erotic desire exemplified by Neptune which promises the reader gratification, whoever the winner. This dynamic is sustained to the end by Chapman who has Leander lose his life in an inept attempt by Neptune to rescue him from the Fates (VI, l. 231).

These shifting perspectives on the characters are enhanced by other deliberate effects like the heroics of the verse, resounding at every step with Hero's name and the intricate interplay of feminine and masculine rhyme generating epigrammatic sharpness.[16]

Another level of authorial control is demonstrated through the direct comments flung at the reader by the wry ironic narrator. These vary from banal wise saws – 'Love deeply grounded hardly is dissembled' (I, l. 185), to 'helpful advice' for male readers – 'Women are won when they begin to jar' (I, l. 332), knowing fraternal misogynist 'winks' like 'All women are ambitious, *naturally*' (l. 428), or confidence-inviting direct addresses: 'Harken awhile, and I will tell you why' (I, l. 85).

The ambience in which the principal narrative progresses is saturated with references to erotic gratification, and the authorial voice never fails to provide anything less than a feast for the aroused imagination. Whether invented or borrowed, the inserted narratives about Mercury (I, ll. 386–484), or Neptune's lascivious tale, cut short by Leander (II, 192–201), keep the focus ultimately on sex. Like Hero's elaborate display of clothes, they prevent the viewer from getting too soon to the lovers' bed, and whet his appetite. In the seamless flow of narrative invention the authorial voice briefly gestures at 'divine Musaeus' (I, l. 52), not only to signal respect for his noble source, but also to show how it can be outdone by a contemporary masterpiece. Thomas Nashe, confirmed this new poetic self-confidence by speaking of 'divine Musaeus . . . and a diviner Muse than him, Kit Marlowe'.[17]

The heavily ornate background is fraught with erotic suggestiveness. Innocent Hero makes her offerings in Venus's 'church' with its intensely thrilling pictures, presenting 'the gods in sundry shapes, / Committing heady riots, incest, rapes' (I, ll. 143–4). The position of the virgin officiating in this temple of decadent art is both ironical and deeply touching. Leander is placed in similar sexually aggressive surroundings as he swims across the Hellespont to Hero's tower, and old Neptune plays around him enacting lascivious sexual poses (II, ll. 153–80). The second sestiad opens with Hero fainting and Leander 'breathing life into her lips' (II, l. 3) then throwing herself on top of him 'like light Salamacis' (II, l. 46). These prefigurative sexual poses culminate in his comic 'Petrarchan' inability to consummate the relationship and the realization that during the first night of lovemaking 'some amorous rites or other were neglected' (II, l. 4).

Marlowe's elaborate transferral of reference from one medium to another was consciously sustained by George Chapman who undertook the difficult task of continuing the poem in its tragic part. As compared to the amused, voyeuristically minded persona of the first two sestiads, Chapman's authorial figure is more compassionate to the lovers and questions the reasons for their tragedy, pinpointing its source in the power struggles of the Goddesses Venus and Diana. Elements of the larger discourse of the relationship of art and poetry are also significantly highlighted.

Chapman's Hero, unlike Marlowe's, is not only an ornate voyeuristic object or a character viewed merely with irony and amusement, but is given artistic subjectivity. Her embroidery is presented as a perfect act of craftsmanship in which she translates into pictures her hopes and fears (IV, ll. 37–101). Suggestively pricking with her needle Leander's image on the silk, Hero acquires the masculine connotations of the creative artist. She becomes a creator of meanings – while 'working of his eye / She thought to prick it out to quench her ill; / But as she pricked, it grew more perfect still' (IV, ll. 65–7). Love, sex and art, are inextricably bound together in Hero's effort as through an elegant allusion to the sexual act, the passage offers a comment on the emotional interplay of artistic subject and object, of sexual roles and the inherent instability of the interaction of intention and effect.

Hero's efforts to 'create' a Leander and a comprehensible narrative of her fears and forebodings are 'Arachnean', feminine and, as such, they fail to assuage Venus's anger. Leander's picture which she holds 'as a Persian shield' (IV, l. 346) to protect herself is of little avail. But where Hero's feminine art fails against the adversities of mythical history, the Renaissance male poet rescues her from 'devil Venus' (VI, l. 290) and restores the glory of the lovers, first sung by the father of all poets, divine Musaeus himself.

The poem closes with an exquisite series of shifts of thought suggesting the metamorphic reversibility of art into poetry when in the hand of a male subject. As the dead lovers are turned by Neptune into thistle-warps, the focus narrows on the colour symbolism of their feathers (VI, l. 288) and on the power of poetry to express, implicitly, like painting, the 'true honour' of love (VI. l. 292) in resistance to the ravages of history.

Chapman's other poem, *Ovid's Banquet of Sense*, places voyeurism and the control of the seeing male subject at the heart of eroticism.[18] The poem plays with optical reversal, sophisticated transfer of signification, extended digressions, similes and metaphors linking together 'eroticism, metamorphosis and the writing of poetry itself'.[19] It tells the story of Ovid's falling in love with Julia / Corynna, Augustus Caesar's daughter, presented as a process of awakening of the different senses. Originally, he is drawn to Corynna's secluded bower by her song and fragrance, then his eye is captivated by her beauty, then he tastes her by persuading her to grant him a kiss, and finally touches her, as she willingly bares her breasts. At this moment the lovers are disturbed by distant voices and further voyeuristic gratification is suspended, but the poem has long before reached its erotic climax in the depiction of Corynna's impact on Ovid's sight.

'Eye' images are consistently conjured up. To begin with, Corynna's bower itself has the structure of an eye whose pupil is a statue of 'Niobe, shedding tears' (stanza 2) placed in a pool.[20] The statue changes depending on the light and the position from which it is observed: from afar 'it showed a woman's face / Heavy and weeping; but more nearly viewed, / Nor weeping, heavy, nor a woman showed' (stanza 3).[21] In stanza 7, 'In a loose robe of tinsel', Corynna steps into the bower to redefine it from Niobe's disempowered tragic eye to an eroticized space, the powerful subject / object eye of the sonnet mistress (stanza 9). In the watery centre of the bower eye, naked Corynna, still invisible to the poet, is an object of admiration in full view of the reader.

The sublime moment of Ovid's seeing (stanza 49) is prepared by a brilliant digressive epic simile comparing his hesitation to look with the womanish movements of the Thames (stanzas 44 and 45) before she embraces her lover the Ocean. Amorous Ovid merges into the eroticized landscape through feminine images until he finally, like an Actaeon, charges 'the arbour with his eye' (stanza 49). This effects a crucial reversal. The ancient poet acquires the privileged position of the narrator and the male reader. This position, promising even 'chapmen all eternity', links through a self-reflexive pun the author's name and Ovid's position, just before expounding a very Renaissance theory of perspective. This privileged seeing, whose source is in the eye of the artist, is used for the argument of the interchangeability of poetry and art:

> Betwix mine eye and object, certain lines,
> Move in the figure of a pyramis,
> Whose chapter in mine eyes gray apple shines,
> The base within my sacred object is:
> On this will I inscribe a golden verse
> The marvels reigning in my sovereign bliss,
> The arks of sight, and how her arrows pierce:
> This in the region of the air shall stand
> In Fame's brass court, and all her trumps command.
>
> (stanza 64)

Once seen, Corynna undergoes a series of imageal transformations constructing her as a map of paradise, her body as the Elysian fields, her arms, legs and fingers as rivers and brooks (stanzas 58–63). These recall Ovid's earlier feminised inscription in the forms of nature before he acquires a point of seeing and suggest that the position of the observing subject is the one conferring erotic meaning on the observed object.

As Ovid and Corynna vanish, the poem calls on the imagination and knowledge of its reader to construe for himself what has been left out in a masterly figure aligning sexual enjoyment, poetic organization and the rules of perspective painting. Ovid, the author and the reader are offered the central position to view the 'royal hand' (of the painter / poet?), as metaphor for artistic creation:

> But as when expert painters have displayed,
> To quickest life of monarch's royal hand
> Holding a sceptre, there is yet bewrayed [shown]
> But half his fingers; when we understand
> The rest not to be seen; and never blame
> The painter's art, in nicest censures stand:
> So in the compass of this curious frame,
> Ovid well knew there was much more intended,
> With whose omission none must be offended.
>
> (stanza 117)

The erotic, the poetic, and the visual, are thus subsumed under similar principles, transcending the limits of individual arts and unambiguously commending their achievement as the product of a male subjectivity.

Shakespeare's *Venus and Adonis* adds to the discourse of the erotic and creative, a specific flavour and nuance. Judged against Marlowe's seamless narrative flow which teasingly delays the gratification of the reader's curiosity but never falters – it certainly does not offer an example of smoothness. Instead, the story is deliberately interrupted by striking self-contained medallion-like animal scenes used as *exempla* of natural behaviour: the horses (stanzas 42–53) in the rapture of ecstatic sex, and the hare (stanzas 114–18) in apprehensive flight from danger. The narrative is further diffused by elaborate extended metaphors and similes, deflecting attention from the story towards their own embedded pictures (stanzas 39–41; 101–2; 172–6). The ironic misogynist authorial interventions are there (stanza 52), but counterbalanced by strong commiseration with Venus, a frustrated lover endowed with artistic imagination.

On the level of 'event', except for a few sweaty embraces, there is precious little. The poem generates its tension from what does not happen. Like a sonnet sequence run out of proportion, it expands the space for expressing frustration, pain and the explosiveness of suspended sexual gratification. This inversion produces an effect, which is dramatic rather than ironical. In spite of her presentation as a comically muscular deity, who can easily manhandle Adonis, the Goddess of love is treated with compassion and her voice is heard throughout the poem along with that of the narrator. Venus's monumental figure squares with the new aesthetics defined for her by Aretino 'because this goddess imparts her qualities in the desire of the two sexes' and can accommodate in her female body a 'male musculature' 'moved by virile and womanly feelings through an artifice of elegant vivacity'.[22]

Apart from physical strength, which she does not hesitate to use (ll. 31–42), Venus possesses the linguistic sophistication of the sonnet lover. Her failure to put Adonis into words signals the impossibility to talk him into loving her – Adonis is 'above compare' and 'more lovely than a man' (ll. 7–9) – beyond description he is also beyond sex, an elusive ideal, an illusion.

The gap between Venus's status as Goddess of love and the reality of her frustration is made even wider by the anti-Petrarchan adjectives comprising her auto-blazon: 'Were I hard-favoured, foul or wrinkled-old, / Ill-nurtured, crooked, churlish, harsh in voice, . . . rheumatic . . . barren, lean and lacking juice – Then mightst thou pause' (ll. 132–145). Even when describing herself at her best and lightest, the language conveys heaviness (stanza 26). As she is, Venus is a match for heroic Mars whom she led 'in a red-rose chain' (l. 110), not for boyish Adonis.

Venus's presence in the poem is not constructed only of incompatibilities. There is a basic harmony between her femininity, the benign forms of nature and images of protective beauty, as when Adonis is offered the pleasures of her body turned park for him to feed upon (39–40). Venus is wholesome and whole, while Adonis appears in fragments seen as if through a magnifying lens, leaving a disturbing sense of optical aberration, which meaningfully corrects Venus's excessive praise. As in a close-up, the dimples on his cheeks show like 'lovely caves', 'enchanting pits' with 'mouths' ready to 'swallow Venus' liking' (ll. 246–7). In her frustrated words he comes across as a 'lifeless picture, cold and senseless stone / Well-painted idol, image dull and dead' (ll. 211–12) as his own well-worded but trite defence of celibacy testifies (ll. 411–26). Ironically, he will gain a natural dimension only through death and metamorphosis. While alive, this 'thing like a man' (l. 214) is fatally fascinated with male strength, which, like sexuality and love, proves beyond his grasp. Like Leander's, his body is a site of contest between female (Venus) and male (the boar) desire, but unlike it, the only gratification it brings or experiences is death. Beyond sex and language, Adonis is 'a statue contending but the eye alone' (l. 213), an object, never a subject of either love or art.

Venus, on the other hand, has the full-blown subjectivity of a lover and a gift of seeing, which though deluded, is artistically productive. Her construction of Adonis and his courtship are feats of imaginative seeing in which he is unable to engage. In the 'war of looks' between them 'His eyes saw her as they had not seen them' (ll. 357–8). Unseeing Adonis cannot appreciate female attraction or the dangers of the boar's masculinity, or the natural beauty of his horse's passion for the jennet (ll. 259–318).

This exquisite cameo digression does not only thematically parallel Venus's argument and passion. It offers an intricate comment on the nature of perfect achievement as a controlled, forcefully focused act of seeing. The horse creates nothing less than a masterpiece of sexual prowess: he 'sees his love and nothing else he sees / For nothing else with his proud sight agrees' (l. 288–9). Like a painter trying to 'surpass the life', 'His art with Nature's workmanship at strife / As if the dead the living should exceed: / So did this horse excel a common one' (ll. 291–3). The horse is both a worthy object of poetic description and a subject-creator of his passion, an artist bursting constraints, achieving sexual / artistic subjectivity never to be experienced by unseeing Adonis.

Almost in the exact middle of the poem's 199 stanzas, in stanza 101, the theme of seeing as central to love and art resurfaces. Venus's final unsuccessful effort to make love to Adonis and save him from the boar is rendered as a moment when, like an artist whose craft has outdone nature, she is taken in by a *trompe l'oeil*. The reference is to one of Pliny's popular anecdotes of ancient painters:[23]

> Even as poor birds deceived with painted grapes
> Do surfeit by the eye, and pine the maw:
> Even so she languished in her mishaps
> As those poor birds that hapless berries saw.
>
> (ll. 601–4)

Loving Venus's artistic imagination has conjured up an Adonis who is nothing but a *trompe d'amour*, a bunch of painted grapes, life-like, yet totally unreal.[24] The artist has fallen into the trap of her own creation, which like Leander's picture, protectively held up by Hero, offers no help against history. Not surprisingly, the fellow poet is the first to offer compassion to the frustrated lover / artist, for he knows that it is 'all in vain', 'it will not be' (l. 607). Art cannot change life, though, in itself, it offers a form of life.

The last part the poem consistently foregrounds Venus's eyes as the centre of her emotion. In pain she 'veiled her eyelids, who like sluices stopped / The crystal tides', then her crystalline eyes engage in a dialogue with her tears: 'Both crystals, where they viewed each other's sorrow', suggesting an optical amplification of sadness. These brittle sorrowful eyes are soon shattered by the sight of dead Adonis in a cuttingly poignant simile, of vulnerable softness, based on another animal image:

> as the snail, whose tender horns being hit,
> Shrinks backward in his shelly cave with pain,
> And, there all smothered up, in shade doth sit,
> Long after fearing to creep forth again:
> So at his bloody view her eyes are fled
> Into the deep recesses of her head.
>
> (ll. 1,033–8)

Venus's internalized scream, rendered as blindness, directs the readers' emotion towards her and deflects it from Adonis. The lover's loss, irreversible as an artist's loss of sight, leaves the poet as the only 'voice' to bring the narrative to its statuesque finale. Alienated like her shattered eyes, the Goddess retreats from the human world as the poem takes leave of a reader captivated by the delicate equilibrium and passionate grandeur of creativity, be it love, poetry or art.

While the epyllia sustained the vogue of the erotic under the shadow of Ovidianism, Nashe's *Choice of Valentines*, represents the process of forfeiting the already set convention in favour of Aretinian explicitness. Just as the epyllion mocked the sonnet by flaunting, overturning and overexploiting its conventions, so does Nashe's narrative consciously engage with the epyllion. It offers erotic stimulation as tongue-in-the-cheek advice for sexually active males, disguised as authorial experience. The dedicatory sonnet resounds with Aretino's attack on hypocrisy:

> Ne blame my verse for loose unchastity
> For painting forth the things that hidden are,
> Since all men act what I in speech declare,
> Only induced by variety.

This is followed by a series of hard snapshots of events in a 'house of venery', be they the feeling of the body of a mistress, the rhythms of love-making, the revival of a suddenly reluctant penis, or the blazon of a new object in the economy of love – the dildo. In describing the function of this 'eunuch' and 'counterfeit' the poem goes through the technicalities of a sexual act by ironically suspending the male organ and substituting for it the dildo, which acquires an independent existence. Unlike most of the epyllia, Nashe's text allows not simply for a sexual difference, but for the expression of an 'independent [female] sexuality, which needs to be satisfied'.[25] For all its explicitness however, the poem manages to diffuse the pornographic through sparkling wit, literary allusion and self-conscious mock-seriousness.

The erotic poem, Ovidian or Aretinian, was a powerful venue for Elizabethan *fin-de-siècle* pursuits, and opened up a world of wonder created by the poet and artist of the new epoch. The potential of classical narratives was untapped to explore the transformative powers of sexual desire, the limits of artistic convention, gender and power roles, and to negotiate for the author the privileged status of creator of a world, not only reflecting but informing real life, a synaesthetic reality, whose laws are exclusively in the artist control of the master.

NOTES

1 The dating and the history of *Hero and Leander* need some explanation. The first two sestiads (two of six parts) were written by Christopher Marlowe perhaps in 1591. The poem must have had a manuscript circulation though, judging by the take-offs in Shakespeare's *Venus and Adonis,* which suggest knowledge of Marlowe's text. After his death in 1593, George Chapman added four more sestiads so as to bring the story to an end and had the whole poem published in 1598 as a commemoration of his friend.

2 The dating is not clear. The piece exists only in manuscripts and was first published in the twentieth century. See Thomas Nashe, *The Unfortunate Traveller and Other Works,* edited by J. B. Steane, Harmondsworth, Penguin Books, 1972 (2nd edition 1978).

3 About the development of similar processes in France during the first half of the sixteenth century see Nancy Vickers, 'Hecatomphile, The Flowers of French Poetry, and Other Soothing Things', in Margareta De Grazia, M. Quilligan and Peter Stallybrass, eds, *Subject and Object in Renaissance Culture*, Cambridge, Cambridge University Press, 1996, pp. 166–89.

4 For the dissemination of Romano's images and their influence specifically on Andrew Marvell, see James Graham Turner, 'The Libertine Abject: The 'Postures' of *Last Instructions to a Painter*. In Warren Cherniak and Martin Dzelzainis, *Marvell and Liberty,*

Basingstoke and London, Macmillan, 1999, pp. 217–48.

5 *The Works of Pietro Aretino,* translated into English from the original Italian by Samuel Putnam, Vol. 1, Covici–Friede Publishers, New York, 1933, this quotation is on p. 24.

6 Clark Hulse, *The Rule of Art. Literature and Painting in the Renaissance*, Chicago and London, The University of Chicago Press, 1990, p. 108. See particularly ch. 3, pp. 103–14.

7 Lucy Gent, *Picture to Poetry 1560–1620*, Leamington Spa, James Hall, 1981, an excellent book on the relationship of aspects of Renaissance art to the poems under discussion here. See particularly Chapters 2–3, pp. 6–66.

8 See Robbins: The poet John Donne lost his brother in 1593 for helping a Jesuit priest and members of his family had been in the Tower for the same reason.

9 His co-author Ben Jonson was imprisoned.

10 For an interesting discussion of Aretino's erotic writings and the debate of civic morality and the family see Guido Ruggiero, 'Marriage, love, sex, and Renaissance civic morality', in James Graham Turner, editor, *Sexuality and Gender in Early Modern Europe, Institutions, Texts, Images*, Cambridge, Cambridge University Press, 1993, pp. 10–30.

11 See Robbins about Jonson in particular.

12 Louis Montrose, 'Spenser's Domestic Domain: Poetry, Property and the Early

Modern Subject', in Margareta De Grazia, M. Qulligan, Peter Stallybrass, eds, *Subject and Object in Renaissance Culture*, Cambridge, Cambridge University Press, 1996, p. 85.

13 See R. Robbins for a similar point concerning John Donne and Ben Jonson.

14 Pierre Macherey, *A Theory of Literary Production*, translated from the French by Geoffrey Wall, London, Routledge and Kegan Paul, 1978, p. 52.

15 For an interesting discussion of the influence of Mannerist art on Shakespeare see John Greenwood, *Shifting Perspectives and the Stylish Style, Mannerism in Shakespeare and His Jacobean Contemporaries*, Toronto: University of Toronto Press, 1988, p. 22.

16 Sandra Clark, ed., *Amorous Rites, Elizabethan Erotic Narrative Verse*, Everyman, 1994, Introduction, p. xl. Good also for further bibliographical reference.

17 This reference I owe to Lucy Gent, *Picture to Poetry 1560–1620*, p. 5.

18 For an excellent discussion of the poem, not as turgidly philosophical, but as erotic and artistic see G. Snare, *The Mystification of George Chapman*, Durham and London, Duke University Press, 1989. The present section is indebted to this study for many insightful observations.

19 See G. Snare, p. 113.

20 Quotations from Phyllis Bartlett, ed., *The Poems of George Chapman*, New York, Russell and Russell, 1962.

21 See Lucy Gent, p. 47.

22 Aretino's statement is quoted in Mary Pardo 'Artifice as seduction in Titian', in James Graham Turner, ed., *Sexuality and Gender in Early Modern Europe, Institutions, Texts, Images*, Cambridge, Cambridge University Press, 1993, p. 77.

23 The reference is to the Greek Zeuxes and his painting of a bunch of grapes, which deluded birds who came to peck.

24 For an illuminating interpretation see Catherine Belsey, 'Love as Trompe-l'oeil', *Shakespeare Quarterly,* 46 (Fall, 1996), pp. 257–76, reprinted in Philip C. Kolin, ed., *Venus and Adonis, Critical Essays*, New York and London, Garland Publishing Inc., 1997.

25 Stephen Orgel, 'Gendering the Crown', in Margareta De Grazia, M. Qulligan, Peter Stallybrass, eds, *Subject and Object in Renaissance Culture*, Cambridge, Cambridge University Press, 1996, p. 161.

REFERENCES AND FURTHER READING

Texts

Alexander, Nigel (ed.) (1967). *Elizabethan Narrative Verse*. London: Edward Arnold.

Clark, Sandra (ed.) (1994). *Amorous Rites: Elizabethan Erotic Verse*. London: Everyman.

Donno, Elizabeth Story (ed.) (1963). *Elizabethan Minor Epics*. London: Routledge.

Nashe, Thomas (1978). *The Unfortunate Traveller and Other Works,* ed. J. B. Steane. London: Penguin Books.

Reese, M. M. (1968). *Elizabethan Verse Romances*. London: Routledge and Kegan Paul.

Critical works

Bate, Jonathan (1963). *Shakespeare and Ovid*. Oxford: Oxford University Press.

Bradbrook, Muriel (1951). *Shakespeare and Elizabethan Poetry*. Cambridge: Cambridge University Press.

Bush, Douglas (1932; revd edn 1963). *Mythology and the Renaissance Tradition in English Poetry*. New York: Norton.

Dubrow, Heather (1987). *Captive Victors: Shakespeare's Narrative Poems and Sonnets*. New York: Ithaca.

Gent, Lucy (1981). *Lucy Gent, Picture to Poetry 1560–1620*. Leamington Spa: James Hall.

Hulse, Clark (1981). *Metamorphic Verse: The Elizabethan Minor Epic*, Princeton: Princeton University Press.

Keach, William (1981). *Elizabethan Erotic Narrative*. New Brunswick, NJ: Rutgers University Press.

Kermode, Frank (1971). *Shakespeare, Spenser,*

Donne: Renaissance Essays, London: Routledge and Kegan Paul.

Kolin, Philip C. (ed.) (1997). *Venus and Adonis, Critical Essays.* New York and London, Garland Publishing Inc.

Smith, Bruce (1991). *Homosexual Desire in Shakespeare's England: A Cultural Poetics.* Chicago and London: Chicago University Press.

Snare, Gerald (1989). *The Mystification of George Chapman.* Durham and London: Duke University Press.

Steane, J. B. (1964). *Marlowe: A Critical Study,* Cambridge: Cambridge University Press.

Wilkinson, L. P. (1955). *Ovid Recalled.* Cambridge: Cambridge University Press.

36
Religious Verse
Elizabeth Clarke

In the early seventeenth century there was intense consideration of the nature of holy poetry. The pioneers of the Reformation had identified a need for sacred verse to replace profane song in the vocabulary of ordinary men and women: the frantic translation and paraphrase of biblical verse which marked the late sixteenth century was part of an answer to that perceived problem. At the court of King James, who had himself ventured into poetic composition, there was also keen interest in what a holy poetry might be: David Norbrook has traced the subtle interactions of poetry, religion and politics at court in the early seventeenth century (Norbrook). Part of the problem was with the character of classical rhetoric, the dominant force in education and writing in the sixteenth century in England, which was implicated in self-display to an extent thought unworthy of the practice of a religious poet. The closer to biblical language a poet kept his verses, the purer they were considered to be: since it was axiomatic to Protestant theology that the Bible was perspicuous, biblical verse had to be simple, and preferably unrhetorical. Thus the execrable psalm paraphrases of Sternhold and Hopkins held sway in church liturgy throughout this period, as more literary alternatives were considered indebted to merely human invention. On a more positive note, the gorgeous manuscripts of psalm paraphrases by Philip and Mary Sidney circulated widely at the turn of the century seem to have formed many poets' ideas of what sacred poetry looked like: at least seventeen of these manuscripts are still extant. Critics' attitudes towards this joint authorship tend to polarize along predictable lines: traditional reverence for Philip Sidney versus feminist valorization of Mary Sidney's work. Susanne Woods has suggested that this volume and its enormous influence should be attributed entirely to Mary Sidney, who revised the forty-three psalm versions left by her brother at his death, and composed the other paraphrases, over two-thirds of the entire work.[1] Various critics have noticed Mary Sidney's feminizing of the biblical text, in the Protestant tradition of annexing psalms for the experience of an individual: distinctively female events such as marriage, pregnancy, childbirth and gender restrictions are emphasized and even inserted into her paraphrases.[2] Devotion to the biblical text meant that the work could be enlisted in the Sidney–Dudley project to persuade the queen to greater Protestant radicalism, as Margaret Hannay has argued (Hannay, pp. 89–98). Moreover, Sidney engages in a deliberate and daring experimentation with the lyric form, which is modelled on the metrical variation of the 1562 French Psalter.[3] Her work clearly inspired many writers of religious verse, not least George Herbert, whose characteristic combination of long and short lines owes something to the verse forms of the Sidney Psalter.

John Donne wrote a poem in praise of the Sidney sonnets, but he does not seem to have been troubled by a Puritan attitude to the religious poetry: his sermons show a sensitivity to metaphor that is theologically conceived. In the 1580s, Philip Sidney had suggested, in his *Defence of Poetry*, a straightforward substitution of sacred subject matter for profane as the strategy of a true Protestant lyric poet: 'that lyrical kind of songs and sonnet . . . Lord, if He gave us so good minds, how well it might be employed, and with how heavenly fruit both private and public, in singing the praises of that god who giveth us hands to write and wits to conceive'. John Donne's religious poetry, likewise, seems to reflect his choice of a religious subject but not a completely different direction as a poet, despite his instruction to mortify rhetorical gifts, in 'The Cross':

> So when thy brain works, ere thou utter it,
> Cross and correct concupiscence of wit.[4]

Unlike other poets of this period, there is no attempt to modify the exercise of wit discernible in Donne's religious poetry, apart from his biblical paraphrase, 'The Lamentations of Jeremy', which is in the Reformed poetic tradition of simple form and metre. Unlike Herbert and Marvell's crowns of praise to God, Donne's 'La Corona' of holy sonnets does not deconstruct itself but ends its meditations on the life of Christ with the completion of a complex form: the expressed hope is that the graceful interlocking of first and last lines is acceptable technique for a heavenly muse. Critical opinion has differed as to whether there is a deliberate order to the rest of Donne's holy sonnets, but their subject matter – death of a loved one, difficulties with the doctrine of original sin, the struggle to be holy, the confrontation with death itself – is the stuff of the religious vocation. It has allowed many devotees of Donne to endow the figure of the rather austere Dean of St Paul's with a complex and troubled inner life apparently continuous with the Donne of the secular poems, although critical opinion dates the sonnets from the period 1608 to 1610, well before Donne took up ecclesiastical appointment. The problem with famous religious poems, however, is that readers tend to remake their authors in their own image, which means that they have been read at one extreme as thoroughly Calvinist in tone, at the other as evidence that the Catholicism into which Donne was born is still troubling him. Rather than view these poems in isolation, it is salutary to place them in an English tradition of holy sonnets, as William Stull does, suggesting a comparison between Donne's sonnets and those of Protestant writers such as Fulke Greville as well as Catholic sonneteers such as Alabaster,[5] a project on which Susanne Woods has made a start (Woods, pp. 133–5).

'Good Friday, 1613. Riding Westward' is a brilliantly complex 'occasional' poem – it is dated and located – which is also an Ignatian meditation, a form of Catholic spirituality which was well-known in this period, and which Donne in particular would have been familiar with. Ignatian 'composition of place' demanded the imaginative re-creation of biblical scenes, especially from the Passion: the believer then placed himself within the scene. In a typical subversion of this process, Donne turns his progress westward into a flight from the imaginatively conceived scene of the Crucifixion, which he locates in the east. The whole poem becomes a refusal to locate himself at the Passion of Christ, an ironic refusal since the scene is vividly present in his mind:

> Could I behold those hands which span the poles,
> And turn all spheres at once, pierced with those holes?
> (Donne, p. 330)

Even the half-presence of riding away from this scene, however, has the spiritual benefit offered by proponents of this kind of meditation: at the end of the poem Donne can envisage a point at which he can wholly confront the dying Christ, a sight which threatened him with annihilation at the start of the poem, as long as the work of redemption and regeneration has been performed for him by God.

Like many of the secular lyrics, Donne's hymns stage elaborate rehearsals for death, and have been appropriated from Isaac Walton's *Life* onwards for biographical purposes. Perhaps the most complex is 'Hymn to God, my God, in my Sickness', said by Walton to have been composed on his deathbed, but which scholars think probably dates from his illness in 1623, eight years before his death. It employs his rhetorical habit, familiar from the secular lyrics and sermons, of applying the chosen metaphor in as many extended variations as possible. In this case, the metaphor is his prone body as a map:

> Whilst my physicians by their love are grown
>   Cosmographers, and I their map, who lie
> Flat on this bed, that by them may be shown
>   That this is my south-west discovery
>   *Per fretum febris*, by these straits to die,
>
> I joy, that in these straits, I see my west;
>   For, though their currents yield return to none,
> What shall my west hurt me? As west and east
>   In all flat maps (and I am one) are one,
>   So death doth touch the resurrection.[6]

A reader delighting in poetic justice might see this as a rather pleasing reversal of his geographical exploration of the woman's body in elegy 19, 'To His Mistress Going to

Bed'. It is characteristic of Donne's method of argument that he proceeds from metaphor to metonymy to produce a triumphant conclusion: 'what shall my west hurt me?'. The one religious poem with impeccable claims to lyric (Donne had it set to music in his lifetime) is 'A Hymn to God the Father', which is as sparse and simple as any Puritan poetic might demand – except for the incessant playing on the poet's name.

George Herbert

George Herbert's 1633 volume, *The Temple*, has often been contrasted with Donne's religious poetry as being more serene, and less troubled. This may simply be a feature of the different choice of forms. All the poems of 'The Church', the central part of *The Temple,* are lyrics, with a corresponding smoothness of technique and lack of intellectual difficulty: even when Donne wrote lyrics, the absence of such qualities in his poetry was often commented on. Occasionally Herbert engages in something like a traditional meditation on biblical events, as in 'The Sacrifice': what his poems typically chart, however, are the vicissitudes of the Reformed Christian's spiritual life. Even his sonnet on 'Redemption' is not an excursion into Christ's Palestine but a translation of the Gospel story into the terms of Jacobean property-letting. When Herbert confronts Christ, it is not in the imaginative space of a vividly realized meditation, but in the circumstances of his own spiritual life: the Cross in his poem of that name has been uprooted from Golgotha and planted firmly in his seventeenth-century path. The reluctant progress towards eye-contact with Christ Himself is conducted in terms which are nothing like Ignatian in tone: Michael Schoenfeldt has represented the rhetoric of 'Love (iii)' as a courtly exchange of the Jacobean era charged with eroticism (Schoenfeldt, pp. 200–29, 263–4).

Unlike Donne Herbert is haunted by the inadequacy and even the iniquity of representing the Divine in poetry. His poetry is extremely biblical in character but what marked it as holy to a seventeenth-century readership was probably the Calvinist obsession with failure expressed there: not simply failure as a Christian, but failure as a Christian poet. His poems such as 'A true Hymn' chart the difficulty of matching the motion of the Holy Spirit, always non-rhetorical, often non-verbal, with the sophisticated verbal 'motions' of rhetoric: the two poems entitled 'Jordan' seem to reject the contemporary practice of lyric poets for something altogether plainer, and more severe.

> When first my lines of heav'nly joys made mention,
> Such was their lustre, they did so excel,
> That I sought out quaint words, and trim invention;
> My thoughts began to burnish, sprout, and swell,
> Curling with metaphors a plain intention,
> Decking the sense, as if it were to sell.
>
> . . .

> As flames do work and wind, when they ascend,
> So did I weave my self into the sense.
> But while I bustled, I might hear a friend
> Whisper, *How wide is all this long pretence!*
> *There is in love a sweetness ready penned:*
> *Copy out only that, and save expense.*[7]

The complication here is that these lines from 'Jordan ii' are also a parody of Sidney's sonnet 3. Herbert's famous 'simplicity' is always relative.

One way to avoid the besetting sin of poets, self-glorification, was to make gestures in the direction of failure, as Herbert does with lack of rhyme in 'Denial', or with the use of the ballad form in 'Submission'. A brilliant stroke by whomever gave *The Temple* its subtitle was to invoke the theology of ejaculatory prayer, which in early seventeenth-century England meant spontaneous prayer in response to an impulse from God. To call a volume *Sacred Poems and Private Ejaculations* is to claim the complex verbal artefacts of *The Temple* as the results of spontaneous religious inspiration. Again, the poetry reinforces this impression with intensely emotional and verbally stark pieces such as 'Longing' and 'Discipline', and with motions towards wordlessness in 'Love iii' and 'Love unknown'. It is this apparently self-destructive movement that was noted in Stanley Fish's *Self-consuming Artifacts*, an essay which has had huge influence on treatments of the religious lyric at the end of the twentieth century. Andrew Marvell, who wrote one exquisite religious lyric, 'The Coronet', seemed to think that the essence of the genre was the writing of a poem about the impossibility of writing Divine poetry:

> When for the thorns with which I long, too long,
>   With many a piercing wound,
>   My Saviour's head have crowned,
> I seek with garlands to redress that wrong:
>   Through every garden, every mead,
> I gather flowers (my fruits are only flowers),
>   Dismantling all the fragrant towers
> That once adorned my shepherdess's head.
> And now when I have summed up all my store,
>   Thinking (so I myself deceive)
>   So rich a chaplet thence to weave
> As never yet the King of Glory wore:
>   Alas, I find the serpent old
>   That, twining in his speckled breast,
>   About the flowers disguised does fold,
>   With wreaths of fame and interest.
> Ah, foolish man, that wouldst debase with them,
> And mortal glory, Heaven's diadem!
> But Thou who only couldst the serpent tame,
> Either his slippery knots at once untie;

And disentangle all his winding snare;
Or shatter too with him my curious frame,
And let these wither, so that he may die,
Though set with skill and chosen out with care:
That they, while Thou on both their spoils dost tread,
May crown thy feet, that could not crown thy head.[8]

This poem is a distillation of the language and ideas of three of Herbert's poems: the
two entitled 'Jordan' and 'The Wreath'. The flowers for such garlands are of course
the 'flowers' of rhetoric, which the poet intends to weave into a poem. However, the
very intention to produce something worthy of God is suspect: hiding in the rhetoric,
as Herbert found in 'Jordan ii', is the snake of human pride. The only solution is for
God himself to destroy the 'curious frame' which is the complex rhetorical structure.
This God apparently does in 'Jordan ii' as the Divine voice interrupts Herbert's poem.
However, the sacrifice both poets gesture towards is only a theoretical one: for each,
a complex poem survives intact, even though it is not, apparently, the perfect song of
praise each set out to write.

The influence of Herbert's poetic strategy on religious poets of this period is apparent in the subtitles of volumes for the rest of the century, which constitute a veritable 'school of Herbert'. Henry Vaughan chose the title for his 1650 volume as an
explicit act of homage: *Silex Scintillans, or, Sacred Poems and Private Ejaculations*. In a
volume which resounds with allusions to Herbert's poetry, Vaughan's openings often
have the force of ejaculation: 'They are all gone into the world of light!'. What
Vaughan seems to take from Herbert is a directly expressed but profound sense of
religious emotion. Some opening lines are enigmatic, their reference only explicated
later in the poem: 'And do they so?'[9] (p. 188), 'Peace, peace; it is not so' ('Affliction
(1), p. 219), 'Sure, it was so' ('Corruption', p. 196). This sense of 'ejaculation' draws
on the Anglican use of the term, derived from Continental Catholic spirituality, as
response to some kind of external stimulus; sometimes Vaughan provides scriptural
verses as epigraphs to his poems, which represent the spiritual starting-point for his
poem (pp. 188, 281). Other poems are a response to observation of the external world
('The Water-fall', p. 306, 'The Timber', p. 261). In effect these become occasional
meditations, another genre in which Anglican spirituality expressed itself in the seventeenth century. However, the connection between Nature and the spiritual life is
often represented in terms which go far beyond the typology which was the conventional Reformed manner in which to cast their relationship, and which gave the priority firmly to biblical hermeneutic. The hermetic philosophy of Henry and his
brother Thomas has often been commented on, and its influence is obvious in lyrics
such as 'The Night' and 'Cock-Crowing':

Father of lights! What sunny seed,
What glance of day hast thou confined
Into this bird? To all the breed
This busy ray thou hast assigned;

Their magnetism works all night,
And dreams of Paradise and light.
('Cock-Crowing', p. 251)

Less than metaphorical illustrations of a biblically based aspect of the Divine, these
poems reveal a perception of the Divine in Nature beyond the place of the natural
world in Reformed theology. Given this theological embracing of a broad spectrum
of natural phenomena, it is not surprising that there is none of the deep-rooted suspicion of the poetic process in Henry Vaughan's poetry, despite the Herbertian sentiments of a poem like 'Idle Verse' (p. 204).

Henry Vaughan's poetry is that of a royalist and Church of England conformist in
retirement, celebrating his particular brand of spirituality within the formal complexity that is the religious lyric, which took the place of external ceremony during
the interregnum, as Nigel Smith has argued.[10] Christopher Harvey's 1640 work *The
Synagogue: Sacred Poems and Private Ejaculations* also made explicit its debt to Herbert,
so much so that it was bound with Herbert's *The Temple* in 1647, and reprinted in
this joint format twelve times before 1709. This volume is an explicit celebration of
Laudian churchmanship In a way that *The Temple* is not; the second edition includes
an additional section on ' Church-utensils', an attention to external detail rather out
of harmony with Herbert's poetry, where the Temple is usually a spiritual and inward
construction. Although the format in which many readers read Herbert's poetry was
thus an explicitly royalist one, devotion to his particular kind of religious lyric was
widespread in the seventeenth century. The parliamentary general Robert Overton
and Dudley, Lord North, at opposite ends of the political spectrum in the interregnum, both found Herbert's poetry profoundly congenial. Herbert's ubiquitous popularity has allowed the religious lyric to become the site of what Gene Veith calls,
humorously, a re-enactment of the Civil War amongst critics. This has not only
involved the attempt to pin down poets' precise political and religious position, but
to claim a context of Protestant or Catholic texts as essential for understanding religious verse. Thus Louis Martz offers continental texts of meditation as the authentic
context for the religious lyric, whilst Barbara Lewalski offers a biblical poetics infused
by Puritan doctrine.

The Epigram and the Lyric

The study of the religious lyric has of course been dominated by the discipline of
English literature: it is one of the first distinctively English genres to evolve. However,
attention to the related pan-European genre of Latin epigram, often employed in a
religious context, is enlightening. Although the condensed wit of the epigram, which
was often employed in religious polemic between Catholic and Protestant, or in
England between various wings of the Church of England, seems far from the lyric
form, a study of Herbert's treatment of the Latin epigram shows many formal features

in common with his English lyrics. It was as a Latin poet that Herbert was first known. The first publication of Richard Crashaw, another Cambridge poet who participated in the neo-Latin tradition, was a collection of Latin and English epigrams, *Epigrammata Sacra* (Cambridge, 1634). It was published to fulfil the terms of a scholarship, and its origins in the academic curriculum which included the epigrams of Martial and *The Greek Anthology* are rather more obvious than those of Herbert, who shares many of the same sources. But the practice of extravagant conceit noted by contemporary and later critics as characteristic of 'metaphysical' poetry is very obvious in Herbert's Latin epigram 'In Arund. Spin. Genuflex. Purpur.' (Herbert, *Works* p. 405), and Crashaw's English epigram 'On our crucified Lord Naked, and bloody', which share one vivid image:

> Thee with thy self they have too richly clad,
> Opening the purple wardrobe of thy side.
> O never could be found garnets too good
> For thee to weave, but these of thine own blood.[11]

Herbert's epigrams occur in manuscript collections, and show features of manuscript culture such as answer-poetry. Many practitioners of the religious lyric – Donne, Herbert and Herrick – were primarily manuscript poets, at least in their lifetime. Peter Beal's *Index of Literary Manuscripts* offers many manuscript contexts for religious lyrics. In this context Arthur Marotti has drawn attention to the importance of the posthumous editions of Donne and Herbert's verse in 1633. He argues that the presentation of printed volumes of poetry as serious works by sober churchmen helped to overcome 'the stigma of print' and paved the way for other collections of religious verse (Marotti, pp. 246–59). 'The aristocratic and conservative associations of poetry within the manuscript system carried over into the medium of print when, in the middle third of the seventeenth century, lyric texts moved from one medium to the other.' He characterizes this printing enterprise as 'a manifestation of Royalism' (Marotti, p. 259).

Historicist Approaches

The new historicist criticism has drawn attention to the politicization of what could look like a personal, spiritualized form. George Herbert's poetry has been re-read by Michael Schoenfeldt as participating in secular court rhetoric as much as in the devotional discourse of Reformed Protestantism, an interpretation which offers new critical insight into the poems. The poetry of Richard Crashaw in particular has benefited from attention to the micro-history of Cambridge under the influence of Archbishop Laud as well as to the texts of Counter-Reformation devotion to which his lyrics explicitly pay homage. The explicit corporeal imagery and spirituality rather more typical of Catholic devotion have isolated him among the English religious poets:

words like 'baroque' and 'mannered' have been used of him, without, as Thomas Healy points out, much justification. Healy's careful study starts from the premise that Crashaw clearly situated himself within the 'school of Herbert', as indicated by the title of his 1646 volume *Steps to the Temple*. Much of his poetry's devotion to the Virgin Mary and sensual spirituality which has been read in the light of Crashaw's later conversion to Catholicism was in fact current in the practice of the chapel at Peterhouse in the 1630s. Healy comments that Crashaw is not only interested in typological interpretations of Biblical stories, a characteristically Puritan approach, but in dramatizing the experience of those who knew Christ (Healy, 1985, p. 121).

Another poet who has been characterized by retirement from religious controversy and immersion in a mystical devotional spirituality, although of a more Protestant tradition, is Thomas Traherne. Traherne, like Crashaw, seems to have no problem with figuring the body in his poetry: his first 'Thanksgiving' is for the body, and the thanksgiving for the soul comes second. Unlike Crashaw, however, he opts for a simple style which is everywhere reminiscent of George Herbert, and his statement of poetic intention owes much to Herbert's 'Jordan' poems;

> No curling metaphors that gild the sense,
> Nor pictures here, nor painted eloquence
>
> . . .
>
> An easy style drawn from a native vein,
> A clearer Stream than that which Poets feign.[12]

However, this perception of Traherne is likely to change, thanks to recent manuscript discoveries by Jeremy Maule which show him thoroughly engaged in contemporary theological debates such as the Calvinist/Arminian controversy.[13] The stage is set for a thorough-going historicizing of Traherne's poetry.

The religious lyric not only features in the Cavalier miscellanies which kept alive the nostalgic spirit of pre-war royalism, but in the journals and commonplace books of nonconformists under persecution. Henry Pinnell used Herbert's poems in a 1650s defence of antinomianism,[14] and a Herbert lyric was sung by a Westcountry dissenter about to be executed for his part in the Monmouth Rebellion in 1685. However, it is royalist conformists such as Robert Herrick and less familiar poets such as Cardell Goodman who practised the religious lyric as opposed to reading it.[15] Sophisticated lyric form, even when it is religiously directed, is not congenial to a Puritan spirituality. George Wither, whose poetry had been neglected until David Norbrook's treatment of his work in *Writing the English Republic*, wrote one ejaculation, but its title showed that he was unwilling to participate in the fictions that enabled less scrupulous poets to imply spontaneous composition for their highly wrought poetry: 'An Interjection, occasioned by a sudden Ejaculation, whilst this Review of Neglected Remembrances was transcribing, which shall here stand inserted, though it be no part of what was heretofore experienced, or intended to be hereunto added. And in such Language as may evidence the truth, without affected Eloquence.'[16] An Collins's 1653 volume, *Divine Songs and Meditations*, which celebrates the triumph of the religious party of Independents in government, may be an attempt to impose a Puritan aesthetic on the religious lyric.[17] She experiments with various forms, but there is clearly an attempt to subordinate form to content in a way that often interferes with conventional aesthetic value. Nigel Smith, who has argued for the lyric form as 'an instrument of religious policy',[18] has traced a Dissenting practice of the religious lyric as simple stanza form with vivid imagery as practised by the Welshman Morgan Llwyd, which eventually produced the hymns of Isaac Watts. The poetry of Julia Palmer, which exists in a manuscript of 200 poems in the Clark Library dated 1671–3, fits into this history: it is simple, emotional and biblical.

The Gendering of Religious Verse

Religious poetry was favourite and recommended reading matter for women in this period, as seen by the frequent mentions of Herbert and, particularly, Quarles, in women's manuscripts. Susanna Countess of Suffolk is commended in her funeral sermon for knowing all of Herbert's poems off by heart. It would be surprising, therefore, if women did not in their first ventures into poetry try their hand at this perhaps most approved form. This acrostic tribute from the manuscripts of Anne, Lady Southwell (1573–1636), credits Francis Quarles with inspiration for her own efforts:

> Fain would I die whilst thy brave muse doth live
> > Quaintest of all the Heliconian train
> Raised by thy artful quill, that life doth give
> > Unto the dullest things, thy fiery strain
> Adds immortality, maugre privation
> > And by thy power brings forth a new creation.
> Unhappy they that poesy profess
> > Raising their thoughts by any star but thine
> Nor let them think celestial powers will bless
> > Loose ballads or hyperbolising rhyme
> Curst be those sulph'rous channels that make stink
> > Each crystal drop that in their crannies sink
> Enthrone thy Phoenix in Jehovah's breast
> > Since she approves herself bird of that nest
> So shall she live immaculate and blest.[19]

The contempt for extravagant secular poetry, and the need for an alternative muse, is typical of religious poetry of the period. The figuring of inspiration as divine liquid channelled through poetic form is typical of a strand of seventeenth-century imagery probably triggered by the recent installation of piped water supplies in English cities. Less common is the confidence in a woman's poetic authorship expressed here: Anne Southwell has produced a critique of seventeenth-century poetics from the standpoint of one engaged in the same process, although she represents herself as vastly inferior to Francis Quarles.

There is very little poetry by women extant from the early modern period: most of this is in manuscript, as publication by women seems to have been regarded as little short of prostitution. In a poetic discursion on authorship Anne Southwell expresses total contempt for those who publish their poetry (Southwell, p. 151). In this hostile climate Aemilia Lanyer published *Salve Deus Rex Judaeorum* in 1611,[20] an extraordinary religious poem apparently inspired by the Sidney Psalter, which begins with dedicatory epistles to various learned and well-born Stuart women from one who, as wife to a court musician and distinctly non-aristocratic, would not normally be expected to engage in poetic authorship. The poem has been both celebrated as a construction of a community of learned women, and dismissed as an unsuccessful attempt to gain patronage: it does not appear that her addresses gained her any favours from the women she considered as potential patrons, although her principal dedicatee, Margaret Clifford, Countess of Cumberland, presented a copy to Prince Henry (Lewalski, p. 32). Lanyer's version of the Passion of Christ is interrupted by several set pieces of rhetoric, all highly gendered: a 'Defence of Eve', which is a reinterpretation of the Genesis story to Adam's disadvantage, and a version of a 'blazon' from the Song of Songs in which the beauty of Christ is celebrated from an explicitly feminine perspective. The prominence given to female characters in the biblical story such as Pilate's wife and the women who accompanied Christ to his death have led some feminist critics to claim her work as 'proto-feminist'. Susanne Woods aligns her Christianized neoplatonism with that of Spenser, and her treatment of the red and white topos with Shakespeare's use of it in *Venus and Adonis*: she compares Donne's 'First Anniversary' with Lanyer's poem, published in the same year. This integration of a woman's writing into the Renaissance canon is part of the phase in feminist scholarship which follows the recovery of much unknown women's writing of the period. However, this enterprise is fraught with methodological difficulty, not least because major works by men have been thoroughly edited and modernized over centuries to produce something that looks very different from a newly discovered woman's text, which often emerges with her own idiosyncratic spelling, and without a tradition of interpretation behind it.

One of the few manuscript poets who has been published in a modern edition is Anne, Lady Southwell. Even within the protected medium of manuscript she seems to feel the need to defend her own practice of writing religious verse: a prose letter to her friend Cecily Ridgeway is, in effect, her own elegant 'Apology for Poetry' (Southwell, pp. 151–2, 4–5). She takes for granted, of course, that it is religious verse that she is defending. In the Folger manuscript entitled 'The workes of the Lady Ann Sothwell', some of which seem to have been collected by her husband after her death, there are a few shorter poems (some of them transcribed from other writers) including her own defence of Eve which wittily reinterprets the Genesis story to exonerate Eve from male prejudice (p. 42). She is particularly talented at verse epistles, as evidenced by her letters to the Bishop of Limerick and the Countess of Londonderry.

What she considered her major work, however, seems to be a series of long poems on the Ten Commandments. These are less restricted in scope than might appear by the title: taking as her point of departure a particular commandment, she ranges over a great deal of philosophical and moral opinion. She defends her particular choice of religious verse with a rather simple form, repudiating the kind of rhetorical competition which was the basis for much courtly poetry. This statement is particularly interesting in view of the probability that she was the 'A. S.' who, in younger days, engaged in rhetorical games at court with the likes of John Donne.[21] Her criticisms of seventeenth-century culture include the relentless sexualization by men of women's bearing and behaviour. The plight of the woman poet (and later, interestingly, of the woman prophet), is lamented in witty but forthright terms:

> Dare you but write, you are Minerva's bird
> the owl at which these bats and crows must wonder,
> they'll critickize upon the smallest word
> this wanteth number case, that tense and gender
>   then must you frame a pitiful epistle
>   to pray him bee a rose was borne a thistle.
>   (Southwell, p. 156)

It can be no coincidence that this stanza is taken from the British Library manuscript which bears a dedicatory poetic epistle to James I, the Scottish thistle trying hard to become an English rose. Religious verse in manuscript was not necessarily an exercise in private devotion: Lady Southwell's poetry was circulated at the very highest level.

One woman who left a major body of poetry in a recently uncovered manuscript is Lady Hester Pulter, sixth daughter of the Earl of Marlborough (1596–1678).[22] As well as political poems, philosophical poems, a series of emblems and an unfinished prose romance her work contains many religious lyrics in which the debt to George Herbert is clear. Such female poetic confidence is, however, rare in this period. The few male-sanctioned volumes of women's writing published pre-1640 are usually prose treatises: several of them, however, do have verses by the author affixed to the volume, as if to show that she is competent at a limited, authorized style of poetry, which invariably consists of conventional religious content in a pedestrian form. Only women from the highest aristocratic contexts with access to elite literary circles experiment further: Jane Cavendish (1624–67) is one woman whose manuscript writing shows a subversion of some of the common tropes of the religious lyric, especially the complete submission to God expected of all religious poets, and women in particular.[23]

The religious lyric has been noted as a feminized form by Helen Wilcox because of its characteristic stance of dependence on God, and its debt to secular love poetry. Research such as that by Michael Schoenfeldt have begun to explore this highly gendered aspect of the religious lyric, which introduces a kind of eroticism into Herbert's poetry, despite its contemporary reputation for holiness. Sexuality is more of an issue in religious verse which explicitly adopts a feminine subject position in relation to God, in accordance with the sacred poetry of the Song of Songs. Yet to be explored is the significance of women themselves using this feminized form: Aemilia Lanyer, Anne Southwell, An Collins and other female poets of the seventeenth century seem to find an authorized feminine subjectivity in the biblical voice of the Bride of Christ. The anonymous author of 'Eliza's Babes' (1656) has used this biblical type in conjunction with the conventional 'offspring' trope for poetry to present her verses as divinely engendered children. However, use of this rhetoric is complicated for women, as Lorna Hutson has perceptively investigated for Aemilia Lanyer. The female voice in the secular love lyric of the Renaissance has been already appropriated as a vehicle for the display of male rhetorical skill; and the voice of the bride in the Song of Songs is not straightforwardly gendered female, as it has been interpreted in many biblical commentaries of the Reformation as the voice of the individual male Christian.

Those critics who refuse to spiritualize all the sexual imagery of seventeenth-century religious verse have begun to investigate its complex gendering. Richard Crashaw, who often uses the tropes of the Song of Songs, has been identified as a poet whose lyrics manifest an instability of gender roles: many critics are uncomfortable with what Healy calls his 'indecorous' rhetoric. Richard Rambuss has highlighted the explicit eroticism of his poetry, along with that of Traherne and other religious poets, disputing the tendency to allegorical interpretation that would de-sexualize the imagery. He notes the figuring of the religious ecstasy of St Teresa, in one of Crashaw's most famous poems, as the ecstasy of a male body possessed by his male lover:

> O how oft shalt thou complain
> Of a sweet & subtle PAIN.
> Of intolerable IOYES;
> Of a DEATH, in which who dyes
> Loves his death, and dies again.
> And would forever so be slain.
> And lives, & dyes; and knows not why
> To live, But that he thus may never leave to DIE.
> How kindly will thy gentle HEART
> Kiss the sweetly-killing DART!
> And close in his embraces keep
> Those delicious Wounds, that weep
> Balsam to heal themselves with.
>   (Crashaw, pp. 319–20)

Such cross-gendering raises the question of whether the model for the relationship between Christ and the believer is always the heterosexual one of mystical marriage. Rambuss draws links between the seventeenth-century imagery of wounds which pervades so many religious lyrics and modern gay pornography, pointing out that a number of Crashaw's sacred epigrams are concerned with 'lyricising the various implements that had been employed at one time or another to open or enter Jesus' body'

(Rambuss, 1998, p. 26). He highlights the figuring of the believer as Ganymede in Traherne's 'Love' soon after a heterosexual rape topos reminiscent of one of Donne's bolder conceits (Rambuss, 1998, pp. 54–7). Rambuss is concerned not to impose modern categories of gender orientation, but the very process of gesturing towards twentieth-century gay culture tends to elide differences from, and between, early modern sexualities. Suspicious of an ahistorical psychoanalytic criticism, the dominant new historicism has yet to find a convincing way of dealing with gendered writing in the Renaissance, an issue which is particularly pertinent to the religious lyric.

NOTES

1   Woods, S. (1984). *Natural Emphasis: English Versification from Chaucer to Dryden*. San Marino, CA: Huntingdon Library, pp. 169–82.

2   Hageman, E. H. (1996).'Women's Poetry in Early Modern Britain'. In H. Wilcox (ed.), *Women and Literature in Britain 1500–1700*. Cambridge: Cambridge University Press, p. 193.

3   Waller, G. (1979). *Mary Sidney, Countess of Pembroke: A Critical Study of her Writings and Literary Milieu*. Salzburg: University of Salzburg, p. 159.

4   Donne, J. (1970). *John Donne: The Complete English Poems*. A. J. Smith (ed.), Harmondsworth: Penguin, p. 327.

5   Stull, W. (1982). 'Why are not *Sonnets* Made of Thee?' A New Context for the 'Holy Sonnets' of Donne, Herbert, and Milton'. *Modern Philology*, 80, pp. 129–35.

6   Donne, J. (1970). *John Donne: The Complete English Poems*. A. J. Smith (ed.), Harmondsworth, Middlesex: Penguin, pp. 347–8.

7   Herbert, G. (1941). *The Works of George Herbert*. F. E. Hutchinson (ed.). Oxford: Clarendon Press, pp. 102–3.

8   Marvell, A. (1972). *Andrew Marvell: The Complete Poems*. E. Story Donno (ed.), Harmondsworth: Penguin, p. 54.

9   Vaughan, H. (1976). *Henry Vaughan: The Complete Poems*. A. Rudrum (ed.), Harmondsworth: Penguin, p. 188.

10 Smith, N. (1994). *Literature and Revolution in England 1640–1660*. New Haven: Yale University Press, p. 274.

11 Crashaw, R. (1957). *The Poems, English, Latin and Greek of Richard Crashaw*. L. C. Martin (ed.). Oxford: Clarendon Press, p. 100.

12 Traherne, T. (1958). *Centuries, Poems and Thanksgivings*. G. M. Margoliouth (ed.). Oxford: Clarendon Press, vol. 2, p. 2.

13 Inge, D. and McFarlane, C. (2000). ' "Seeds of Eternity": A New Traherne Manuscript'. *TLS*, 2 June, p. 14.

14 Smith, N. (1984). 'George Herbert in Defence of Antinomianism'. *Notes and Queries*, 229, NS 31, pp. 334–5.

15 Wilcox, H. (1994). ' "Curious Frame": The Seventeenth-century Religious Lyric as Genre'. In J. R. Roberts (ed.). *New Perspectives on the Seventeenth-Century Religious Lyric*. Columbia: University of Missouri Press, p. 10.

16 Wither, G. (1668). *Fragmenta Propheticae: Or, The Remains of George Wither Esq*. London, p. 111.

17 Collins, A. (1996). *Divine Songs and Meditacions*. S. Gottlieb (ed.). Tempe, AZ: Medieval and Renaissance Texts and Studies, pp. 45–6.

18 Smith, N. (1994). *Literature and Revolution in England 1640–1660*. New Haven: Yale University Press, p. 276.

19 Anne, Lady Southwell, (1997). *The Southwell-Sibthorpe Commonplace Book: Folger MS. V.b.198*. J. Klene (ed.). Tempe, AZ: Medieval and Renaissance Text Society, pp. 20–1. I have removed the deletions which are shown in this edition.

20 See Lanyer's 'The Description of Cookham' and Jonson's 'To Penshurst'.

21 Schleiner, L. (1994). *Tudor and Stuart Women*

Writers. Bloomington: University of Indiana Press, pp. 113–18.

22   University of Leeds Brotherton MS Lt q 32–c 1645–65.

23   Bodleian MS Rawlinson poet. 16: Beinecke MS b. 223.

REFERENCES AND FURTHER READING

Clarke, E. R. (1997). *Theory and Theology in George Herbert's Poetry: 'Divinitie, and Poesie, Met'*. Oxford: Clarendon Press.

Doelman, J. (1994). 'The Accession of King James I and English Religious Poetry', *Studies in English Literature*, 34, 19–40.

Fish, S. (1974). *Self-consuming Artifacts: The Experience of Seventeenth-century Literature*. Berkeley: University of California Press.

Hannay, M. P. (1990). *Philip's Phoenix: Mary Sidney, Countess of Pembroke*. New York: Oxford University Press.

Healey, T. (1986). *Richard Crashaw*. Leiden: E. J. Brill.

Hutson, L. (1992). 'Why the Lady's Eyes Are Nothing Like the Sun'. In C. Brant and D. Purkiss (eds), *Women, Texts and Histories 1575–1760* (pp. 13–38). London: Routledge.

Lewalski, B. K. (1970). *Protestant Poetics and the Seventeenth-century Religious Lyric*. Princeton: Princeton University Press.

Marotti, A. F. (1995). *Manuscript, Print and the English Renaissance Lyric*. Ithaca, NY: Cornell University Press.

Martz, L. (1962). *The Poetry of Meditation: A Study in English Religious Literature of the Seventeenth Century*, red edn. New Haven: Yale University Press.

Norbrook, D. (1984). *Poetry and Politics in the English Renaissance*. London: Routledge and Kegan Paul.

Rambuss, R. (1998). *Closet Devotions*. Durham: Duke University Press.

Ray, R. H. (1986). 'The Herbert Allusion Book: Allusions to George Herbert in the Seventeenth Century', *Studies in Philology*, 83, 1–182.

Roberts, J. R. (ed.) (1994). *New Perspectives on the Seventeenth-century English Religious Lyric*. Columbia and London: University of Missouri Press.

Schoenfeldt, M. C. (1991). *Prayer and Power: George Herbert and Renaissance Courtship*. Chicago: University of Chicago Press.

Summers, C. J. and Pebworth, T.-L. (eds) (1987). *'Bright Shootes of Everlastingnesse': The Seventeenth-Century Religious Lyric*. Columbia: University of Missouri Press.

Veith, G. E., Jr (1988). 'The Religious Wars in George Herbert Criticism: Reinterpreting Seventeenth-century Anglicanism', *George Herbert Journal*, 11, 19–33.

Wilcox, H. E. (1990). 'Exploring the Language of Devotion in the English Revolution'. In T. Healy and J. Sawday (eds), *Literature and the English Civil War*. Cambridge: Cambridge University Press.

——(2000). 'Whom the Lord with Love affecteth'. In D. Clarke and E. Clarke (eds), *'This Double Voice': Gendered Writing in Early Modern England*. Basingstoke: Macmillan.

Woods, S. (1999). *Lanyer: A Renaissance Woman Poet*. New York: Oxford University Press.

Zim, R. (1987). *English Metrical Psalms: Poetry as Praise and Prayer 1533–1601*. Cambridge: Cambridge University Press.

37

Poets, Friends and Patrons: Donne and his Circle; Ben and his Tribe

Robin Robbins

Invention and Imitation, Art and Values

Thomas Carew's 'Elegy upon the Death of the Dean of Paul's, Dr John Donne' laments firstly the loss of England's pre-eminent preacher, who 'Committed holy rapes upon our will; Did through the eyes the melting heart distil'. Similarly, Izaak Walton's hagiography prefixed to the *LXXX Sermons* in 1640 is of an antitype of St Augustine, the profligate youth becoming a saint of the church. Donne himself had fostered this image, for example in his letter of 1619 to Sir Robert Ker asking him to regard the treatise on suicide, *Biathanatos*, written before his ordination, as 'by Jack Donne and not by Dr Donne'. Ben Jonson reported to Drummond in the same year that Donne, 'since he was made Doctor, repenteth highly and seeketh to destroy all his poems' (HS (Herford and Simpson) 1. 136). But though Carew finally falls in with this change of identity in his last line, 'Apollo's first, at last the true God's priest', he devotes the intervening three-quarters of his 98-line poem to Donne's achievement for English poetry. Carew sees Donne as throwing off the dominance of what young men were made to read at school and university, principally Latin poets:

> The Muses' garden, with pedantic weeds
> O'erspread, was purged by thee, the lazy seeds
> Of servile imitation thrown away,
> And fresh invention planted.

Donne has 'opened us a mine Of rich and pregnant fancy, drawn a line Of masculine expression'. To claim that the dead person is inimitable is usual in funeral orations, but Carew foresaw rightly that

> thy strict laws will be
> Too hard for libertines in poetry:

> They will repeal the goodly exiled train
> Of gods and goddesses which, in thy just reign,
> Were banished nobler poems.

Ironically, though he echoes Donne's Holy Sonnet 'Batter my heart' with that meta-physical conceit (not an 'image' but the adducing of abstract similarities between things materially different) of 'holy rapes', Carew looks back to Greece and Rome in 'Promethean breath . . . Delphic choir . . . The Muses' garden . . . good / Old Orpheus . . . crown of bays . . . two flamens . . . Apollo'. Moreover, while Donne was inventive in his imagery and diction, he deployed them in the classical genres of epigram, verse-epistle, elegy, lyric, satire, epicede (commemorative poem), hymn and epithalamion, as well as a Renaissance form, the sonnet. Classical writers such as Ovid provided some of the stock figures in his earlier poems, such as the libertine woman of 'Confined Love'.

'Go and Catch a Falling Star' derives ultimately from a classical tradition, that of likening the breach of love or friendship to a list of impossibilities (*adunata*). In the Christian era the device was diverted onto female fidelity, as in the fifteenth-century example (Robbins 1952, p. 101): 'When nettles in winter bear roses red . . . Then put in a woman your trust and confidence.' Another example, beginning 'Embrace a sunbeam', is printed in Osborn (p. 299) as possibly by Donne's contemporary at Oxford and the Inns of Court, John Hoskyns. In octosyllabics, as Donne's is pre-dominantly, both might derive from a contest of wit among a group of young courtier-wits in the early 1590s. Donne's itself became a classic, copied and recopied in numerous collections of his poems and miscellanies, and imitated by other poets. William Habington (1605–54) at last turned the tables 'Against them who Lay Unchastity to the Sex of Women' in *Castara*, 1635 (Donne 1965, pp. 152, 157).

Donne, Carew implies, challenges head-on the ideals of Jonson, who in his *Poetaster*, satirizing the satirist John Marston, has Virgil prescribe a corrective diet of classical authors. To the Scots poet-laird William Drummond in 1619 Jonson boasted that 'He was better versed and knew more in Greek and Latin than all the poets in England, and quintessenced their brains'. Moreover, so central and sufficient for him was Horace's 'Ars poetica' that when his 1604 translation was affected by a new critical text from the continent in 1610, he meticulously revised it, and wrote a commentary (destroyed in the burning of his library in 1623). Jonson's poetic work, like Donne's, is largely in the traditional genres, with the difference that he is concerned to emulate but not go far beyond them. Rosalind Miles (1990, pp. 278–9) defends his classicism as 'never mere pedantry . . . He strove always for the timeless classical virtues of unity, symmetry, clarity and proportion'. Accordingly, he opined to Drummond 'That Donne for not keeping of accent deserved hanging . . . that Donne himself for not being understood would perish' (HS 1. 133, 138).

This is a selective version, however, of 'classical values': Jonson does not often display in his poems Plato's rationalism, Horace's urbanity or Seneca's stoical avoid-ance of emotion. In his longest poem, 'On the Famous Voyage', the concentration on the filthy side of London life is far from Horatian in its deliberate excess, though as an overt burlesque of the underworld journeys of classical myth, it follows an alternative classical precedent, that of parody such as the Homeric *Batrachomyomachia*, 'The Battle of the Frogs and Mice', and works by Aristophanes and Lucian, Horace, Ovid and Petronius. It was because Greek and Latin cultures contained so much variety and contradiction that they provided rich opportunities for imitation and development.

Begging the question of his own qualification, Jonson asserted 'the impossibility of any man's being the good poet without first being a good man' so as 'to be able to inform young men to all good disciplines, inflame grown men to all great virtues' (Epistle to the two universities prefixed to *Volpone*). For 'being' read 'seeming': it is by the persona he constructs, by what Miles (1990, p. 175) calls 'a consistent self-imaging along the wished-for lines', screening his own vigorous indulgence in all seven deadly sins (except, perhaps, sloth), that he achieves the sound of moral authority. In life, as he makes clear to Drummond, no Horatian ethos of civilized restraint regulated the actual proud, ambitious, lustful, envious, greedy, irascible Jonson. His frank self-portrait in 'Epistle to my Lady Covell' as 'Laden with belly, and doth hardly approach His friends, but to break chairs or crack a coach. His weight is twenty stone' – this and the claim to Drummond that he was 'in his youth given to venery: he thought the use of a maid nothing in comparison to the wantonness of a wife, and would never have another mistress' – his illegitimate offspring, his drunkenness, his gluttony, undercut his habitually moralistic posture in, for example, 'On Gut' (*Underwood*, 9, 56; *Epigrams*, 118; HS 1. 140).

The high valuation of male friendship instilled at school through Cicero's *De amicitia* was often voiced but inconstantly practised by Jonson, especially with fellow-dramatists such as Marston, Chapman and Brome. His favourite pupil, Nat Field, had to go to law to recover a large loan. Another classical attitude he could not share was the relaxed acceptance of same-sex love by Plato (when young), innumerable Greek writers, and his esteemed Catullus, Tibullus, Ovid, Horace and Martial. But same-sex killing was to be celebrated: Jonson enthusiastically echoed for England the Roman belief in the inferiority of all other nations, the militarism of Julius Caesar, the imperialism of Augustan Rome as expressed in Virgil's *Aeneid*. Jonson's vividly eloquent 'Epistle to a Friend to Persuade him to the Wars' sees peace as 'vicious ease' and soon becomes an unrestrained satire in a prophetic vein, Juvenalian-cum-Jewish, a denunciation of gluttony, lust, fine clothing, and, at length, women who

> firk and jerk, and for the coachman rail,
> And, jealous of each other, think it long
> To be abroad, chanting some bawdy song,
> And laugh, and measure thighs, then squeak, spring, itch,
> Do all the tricks of a salt lady bitch.
>
> (*Underwood*, 15)

In 'To the Immortal Memory and Friendship of that Noble Pair Sir Lucius Cary and Sir Henry Moryson' (*Underwood*, 70), who set out to fight in Ireland, Jonson celebrates

Moryson's death as 'a soldier to the last right end, A perfect patriot and a noble friend', though he died in bed of smallpox in Wales. The poem was presumably written to please not Jonson's feelings but Cary's: he fulfilled Jonson's ideal of a soldier-poet, an intelligent man of action, as passionate as Jonson in love and hate, and himself idealizing his beloved Moryson as poet, soldier, classicist and admirer of Jonson (Peterson, pp. 195–9). Cary was proud in his 'Epistle to his Noble Father, Mr Jonson' to call himself a poetic 'Son of Ben' – a title also claimed by Edmund Gayton, James Howell, William Cartwright, Thomas Randolph, Richard Lovelace, and Robert Herrick (Miles 1986, p. 292), and loosely applied to other younger poets of the 1620s and 1630s such as Carew. Jonson responded not only to such verbal tribute but to Cary's material generosity: Clarendon recorded in his autobiography that Lord Falkland, as he became, 'seemed to have his estate in trust for all worthy persons who stood in want of supplies and encouragement, as Ben Jonson and many others of that time' (Riggs, p. 316).

Jonson's easy intimacy with classical writers appears in his sophisticated rework-ing of them. Many of his most spontaneous-seeming poems, such as 'To Penshurst' (*The Forest*, 2) and the songs 'To Celia' (*The Forest*, 5, 6, 9), are tissues intricately woven from classical poems. From an aesthetic point of view, the reused materials are so com-pletely merged that they are integral parts of new work. He shows his discrimination and control in choosing a highly apt non-classical allusion in 'To Penshurst', the reminiscence of Kalander's house in Philip Sidney's *Arcadia*, showing his brother Robert's accord with traditional values, Roman and English, in his maintenance of hospitality (in particular, his unstinting provision of food and drink for Jonson). With this poem and 'To Sir Robert Wroth', Jonson started a fruitful tradition in English poetry, that of the 'country-house poem', emulated by Herrick in 'Panegyric to Sir Lewis Pemberton', and Carew in 'To Saxham' and 'To my Friend, G. N., from Wrest', and transformed by Marvell in 'Upon Appleton House'. Modern continental writers, too, he reworked, as in a more overtly artful poem (very popular with manuscript-miscellany compilers – Marotti 1986, p. 127), 'The Hour-glass' (*Underwood*, 8):

> Do but consider this small dust
> Here running in the glass,
> By atoms moved:
> Could you believe that this
> The body ever was
> Of one that loved?
> And in his mistress' flame playing like a fly,
> Turned to cinders by her eye?
> Yes, and in death as life unblessed:
> To have't expressed
> Even ashes of lovers find no rest.

Like a jeweller, Jonson exquisitely resets the gem of a conceit that he owes to a Renais-sance Latin poet in an English poem with point, force and whimsical humour. Word-choice and verse-form work together to produce between flow and restraint an engaging tension, just as the wit, jarring between frivolity and grim truth, gives both pleasure and pause for thought. Such crafting of tensions is as frequent an excellence in Jonson's poems as in his plays. The reader who tires of strenuous abuse, moralizing and wit can find feeling and calm in equilibrium in his tenderly eloquent epitaphs (a genre in which his 'son' Herrick also excelled), such as 'On my First Daughter', 'On my First Son', on the boy-actor Salomon Pavy, 'On Elizabeth, L. H.', and on Vincent Corbett, the nurseryman father of Jonson's poetic 'son' Richard Corbett (*Epigrams*, 22, 45, 120, 124; *Underwood*, 12).

Reference to classical models functioned in various ways in the relationship between writer and reader. It borrowed authority for the new writing from the old that was taught as exemplary in school and university; it established, if perceived, that writer and reader shared membership of the educated minority, and thence, because these groups were largely congruent, the ruling gentry. Moreover, if a satire, or a tragedy such as Jonson's *Sejanus*, could claim to follow closely a classical source, it might even manage to leave open (and so avoid prosecution) whether it was really aimed at contemporary people and institutions. But Elizabethans were instructed by their preachers in the application of old texts, in that case biblical, to themselves and their society, and the authorities were never short of perceptive, sometimes over-ingenious denouncers: in 1603 he was nevertheless summoned before the Privy Council for *Sejanus*.[1]

Some of Donne's chosen classical genres put him in danger too: the new wine he put in old bottles could be explosive. In 1599, alarmed by the uneasy public situation concerning the succession to the aged queen, the Archbishop of Canterbury and the Bishop of London had ordered that all printed copies of Hall's, Marston's and Guilpin's satires, Marlowe's elegies of Ovid and Sir John Davies's epigrams, all books by Nashe and Gabriel Harvey, and various others, should be confiscated and burned, and 'That no satires or epigrams be printed hereafter'. Donne voices anxiety about his poems in a letter of *c*.1599–1601 (Simpson 1948, p. 316): 'To my satires there belongs some fear, and to some elegies and these [paradoxes] perhaps shame . . . Therefore, I am desirous to hide them, without any over-reckoning of them or their maker'. There are manuscript versions of satire V and some epigrams with and without possibly original proper names.

Satire I is an innocuous imitation of Horace, reapplied to a universally ridiculed target, the fatuous, obsequious, quarrelsome devotee of fashion. Satire II, however, though its generalized target, the swindling professional lawyer, was despised by the gentry and hated by many more, chooses risky analogies for his lying, 'Like a king's favourite – yea, like a king', and with his squalid law-practice compares royal bastardy and churchmen's corruption (lines 65–76). That the reigning monarch was a queen, not a king would be no defence, since Elizabeth was notorious for her sometimes disastrously misjudged favouritism. Even more seriously, Donne went directly against the compulsory Oath of Allegiance in implicitly echoing the pope's decree that Henry VIII's divorce from Catherine of Aragon was invalid and Elizabeth consequently illegitimate.

Satire III interrogates the various brands of Christianity on offer in western Europe: Roman Catholicism, Genevan Calvinism, Anglicanism, independence and eclecticism. Refusing to fall into any, yet feeling that 'To stand enquiring right is not to stray, To sleep or run wrong is', Donne is nonetheless not impartial, coming out vehemently against the teaching and law of Elizabethan England:

> Some preachers – vile, ambitious bawds – and laws
> Still new, like fashions, bid him think that she
> Which dwells with us is only perfect.
> . . .
> Fool and wretch! Wilt thou let thy soul be tied
> To man's laws, by which she shall not be tried
> At the last day?
>
> (ll. 56–8, 93–5)

His fourth satire depicts treacherous machination at court, where a probable double agent tries to involve him in treasonous talk (lines 119–20, 129–33). In line 216, some manuscripts read 'Topcliffe' (the officer Richard Topcliffe was notorious as a torturer) for 'pursuivant', suggesting a possibly earlier version prudently emended – not necessarily by the author, since anyone who owned manuscripts containing criticism of the authorities would be in danger. Even in satire V (written when Donne is presumed to have converted to Anglicanism and become secretary to Lord Egerton), he denounces in lines 63–8 false accusations and extortion perpetrated by the government's enforcers.

Coteries

It would be wrong to regard Donne and Jonson as conscious leaders of opposing poetic factions, innovators versus classicists. As well as using classical forms and materials, both showed that multivalent power esteemed as 'wit': mental sharpness, verbal ingenuity, fertile imagination, wide knowledge, and so on. Jonson declared in epigram 23, 'To John Donne' that 'every work of thy most early wit Came forth example, and remains so yet', praising his 'language, letters, arts, best life'. To Drummond he showed he treasured an image in 'The Calm' and knew by heart the epigram 'Phryne' (HS 1. 135). Before readying his own epigrams for publication, he sent them to Donne

> That so alone canst judge, so alone dost make.
> . . . and if I find but one
> Marked by thy hand and with the better stone,
> My title's sealed.
>
> (*Epigrams*, 96)

Moreover, though a rival seeker of patronage, Jonson not only fulfilled the Countess of Bedford's wish to see Donne's satires (perhaps prompted by Henry Goodyer), but added a poem lauding both them and her as 'of the best' (though one suspects no unwillingness to displace from Lady Bedford's favour that Samuel Daniel whom he deemed 'a good honest man . . . but no poet' (HS 1. 132)). It may only have been in return for this favour that Donne provided the commendatory Latin verses prefixed to *Volpone* in 1607, but Jonson was the only living poet whose skill he ever praised.

Both Donne and Jonson demanded acceptance as gentlemen: the son of a prosperous ironmonger, Donne used the arms of the ancient family of Dwn of Kidwelly in Carmarthenshire. In 1604 Jonson claimed gentle ancestry and a coat of arms, telling Drummond later that 'His grandfather came from Carlisle and he thought from Annandale to it; he served King Henry VIII and was a gentleman. His father lost all his estate under Queen Mary, having been cast in prison and forfeited, at last turned minister, so he was a minister's son. He himself was posthumous, born a month after his father's decease, brought up poorly, put to school by a friend'. Jonson thus lacked Donne's advantageous education at Oxford and Lincoln's Inn, where he got to know lifelong friends among the gentry such as Henry Wotton and Christopher Brooke. Instead, Jonson was taken away from Westminster School early, and set to work. In 1590–1 he preceded Donne at Lincoln's Inn, not as a student but helping his bricklayer stepfather on a wall. Both served briefly against Spain, Donne as a gentleman-volunteer with the Earl of Essex to Cadiz and the Azores, Jonson in the Low Countries. From then on their courses differ: whereas there is no evidence that Donne was more than a spectator of the action, Jonson boasted of having killed and despoiled a Spaniard in single combat. Donne became secretary to the chief law officer of the crown, Sir Thomas Egerton, Jonson one of Henslowe's actors at the Rose. Both got into trouble, Jonson by killing a fellow-actor in a duel in 1598, and frequently over his plays, Donne ruining his prospects for a dozen years by eloping in 1601 with his employer's niece by marriage. Jonson failed as an actor, and turned to writing plays, at first collaborating on hack-work that has perished. Donne probably exhausted his inheritance in the early 1590s, emulating the habits of his gentleman friends: a fellow-student remembers him as 'not dissolute, but very neat; a great visitor of ladies, a great frequenter of plays, a great writer of conceited verses' (Sir Richard Baker, in Bald 1970, p. 72).

Jack Donne, young man about town in the early 1590s, seems to have popped like a cork from the dark bottle of an oppressive upbringing in the 'old religion' of Roman Catholicism. His maternal grandfather John Heywood, was distantly related to the writer and martyr, Sir Thomas More. Himself a courtier and epigrammatist, John and his son Jasper Heywood were exiled. The latter, one-time page to Princess Elizabeth and translator of Senecan plays, was caught after landing to head the Jesuit mission in England and imprisoned for two years under sentence of death in the Tower, where Donne as a twelve-year-old may have visited him in the autumn of 1584. In May 1593, his brother Henry Donne was arrested by Topcliffe's chief assistant, Richard Young, and died in prison, for harbouring a priest who was hanged, cut down alive, castrated, disembowelled and chopped into quarters at Tyburn. This was normal

English practice in the fearful years when extreme Jesuits such as Robert Persons sought to bring about the death of Elizabeth and her replacement with the Spanish Infanta so as to fulfil the pope's release of English Roman Catholics from their allegiance. Donne was telling no more than the truth in the preface to *Biathanatos* (1984, p. 29): 'I had my first breeding and conversation with men of a suppressed and afflicted religion, accustomed to the despite of death.'[2]

Henry Donne was arrested in Thavies Inn: if elder brother John had not moved on to Lincoln's Inn, he might have shared his fate. But at Lincoln's Inn a new life opened. Here, as with his last poem, the Hymn to Hamilton, he started to write poems that were given only to friends in manuscript. The liberation he experienced at this time is expressed in the vigour and freedom of expression in his epigrams, lyrics and love-elegies. His earliest surviving poems include, for example, several erotically phrased verse-letters. In one, 'To Mr T. W.', enjoining his verses to 'Haste thee . . . to him my pain and pleasure', the latter clause and lines 5–6 and 8–10,

> Plead for me and so, by thine and my labour,
> I'm thy Creator, thou my Saviour.
> Tell him, all questions which men have defended
> Both of the place and pains of Hell are ended,
> And 'tis decreed our Hell is but privation
> Of him, at least in this earth's habitation:

– these lines so outraged some later Christian fanatic and homophobe that he or she heavily inked them over in the manuscript compiled for the Earl of Westmoreland by Donne's friend and contemporary at the Inn, Rowland Woodward. The next poem but one in this Westmoreland manuscript, again 'To Mr T. W.', begins 'Pregnant again with the old twins Hope and Fear', and is followed by one from T. W. 'To J. D.', which develops a lesbian image of his 'sinful Muse . . . rubbed and tickled with thine' in 'mystic tribadry . . . oh strange and holy lechery.' It is evident that Donne and his set were not too pious to mix Christian and sexual metaphors for their private amusement.[3]

Donne's coterie included more than the Woodwards, possibly including someone not suspected until recently. Curiously enough, between those two early poems to T. W., Rowland Woodward placed one he titled 'To L. of D'. This appeared in the posthumous printed edition of Donne's *Poems* in 1633 as 'To E. of D. with six holy sonnets', an alternative title found in two out of the four surviving manuscripts, neither having the authority of Woodward's. *Poems* itself is based on manuscripts at several removes from the author, so Dennis Flynn (1988) has argued plausibly that 'L. of D.' could denote 'Lord of Derby', referring either to Ferdinando, fifth earl from 1593 to 1594, or his brother William, sixth earl, and Donne's fellow-student at Lincoln's Inn. The similarity of its sexual metaphors for writing poems to those in Donne's early verse-epistles suggests it accompanied a group of poems much earlier than the Holy Sonnets:

See, sir, how, as the sun's hot, masculine flame
> Begets strange creatures on Nile's dirty slime,
> In me your fatherly yet lusty rhyme
(For these songs are their fruits) have wrought the same.
But though the engend'ring force from whence they came
> Be strong enough, and nature do admit
> Seven to be born at once, I send as yet
But six: they say the seventh hath still some maim.

If the printed title is ignored in favour of the more authoritative manuscript, the poem itself gives no hint of 'holy sonnets', and, unsurprisingly, Woodward placed the poem between those two 'To Mr T. W'. Both poet and patron, Ferdinando was celebrated as 'Amyntas' by Spenser in 'Colin Clout's Come Home Again', and his taste for erotic verse is presumed from Thomas Nashe's dedicating his 'wanton elegy' 'A Choice of Valentines' to 'Lord S.': he was summoned to parliament as Lord Strange in his own right in 1589 and thus styled until he succeeded to the earldom on 25 September 1593. He himself punned on his name with the words 'my lines strange things may well suffice' in the poem 'Of my Unhappy State of Life' (printed by May, pp. 370–1). Donne punned on names too (see below), so could well have intended a quibble in likening the offspring of Ferdinando's 'fatherly yet lusty rhyme' to 'strange creatures'.

Rather than hypothesize some lost (Roman Catholic) sonnets, we might more economically assume that by 'these songs' Donne refers to lyrics such as are found in the collection that was first entitled 'Songs and Sonnets' by the unknown editor of the second edition of Donne's poems in 1635. One surviving manuscript (called the Dolau Cothi MS, pp. 100–5) does indeed group six lyrics as 'Songs that were made to certain airs that were made before': 'The Message', 'The Bait', 'Community', 'Confined Love', 'Song: Sweetest Love, I do not Go' and 'Song: Go and Catch a Falling Star'. It was, perhaps, this group of poems that was given to Lord Derby. Contemporary but subsequent musical settings exist for the first two and the last two, as well as for 'The Expiration' and 'Break of Day', either of which (among numerous others) might have been 'the seventh' Donne alludes to.

Whether or not that is so, these poems typify verse-production by young wits and courtiers in the 1590s: imitations, responses, parodies, poems on shared themes. 'The Bait' is one of numerous rejoinders to Marlowe's 'The Passionate Shepherd to his Love', with its promise of an unflawed pastoral idyll. There are parodies by Marlowe himself in *The Jew of Malta* (4. 2. 97–8), and by Shakespeare in *The Merry Wives of Windsor* (1597? 3. 1. 16–19). In *England's Helicon* (1600) it was followed by 'The Nymph's Reply' (anonymous, but generally ascribed to Ralegh), a detailed rejoinder pointing out the evanescence of all the promised pleasures, and by an anonymous parody which, as Gardner pointed out (Donne 1965, pp. 155–6), may have sparked off Donne's piscatorial version.

In reading his poems, whether sacred or secular, we may understand them better, or at least not construct a false image of Donne, if we remember their status as fictions for particular readers. He is not seeking 'to perplex the minds of the fair sex with nice speculations in philosophy' (Dryden). No seducer as intelligent as Donne would expect results from handing to a woman a poem such as 'The Flea', 'Love's Alchemy' with its 'Hope not for mind in women', the utterly callous 'Anagram', the crudely boastful 'Comparison', or 'The Perfume' with its frank admission that 'Thy beauty's beauty, and food of our love' is the speaker's desire for her father's wealth: to call them 'love-poems' blurs their original function in entertaining and winning admiration from male friends. Similarly, his disappointed hope in a letter to Goodyer of 1615 (*Letters*, p. 149) that Lady Bedford would have forgotten his earlier life and believe in his reformation, can warn us that when we read the Holy Sonnets, written probably during the period when he was actively courting her favour with the seven verse-letters and funeral elegies on her friends Lady Markham and Cecilia Bulstrode, we should be as wary as perhaps she was of accepting them as transparent autobiography.[4]

Donne's ability to vary his poems to suit their recipients matches the varied roles he plays in his portraits. He had at least five made. First came a miniature (surviving as engraved frontispiece to the 1635 *Poems*) painted in 1591, in his eighteenth year, showing him dressed as a dapper courtier with a sword and a Spanish motto meaning 'Sooner dead than changed' – whether in religion or love is left to the imagination: he wears crosses in his ears, but the words come from a love-story. In life-size oils in 1595 he is the melancholy lover with folded arms, a wide black hat and a Latin motto turned from the Prayer-Book's 'Lighten our darkness, O Lord' into '. . . O Lady'. Another miniature shows him in 1616, the year after his ordination, as a smart gentleman with ruff and pointed beard. In 1620, the year before he won the Deanship of St Paul's, he was again painted in oils (still in the Deanery) as a bare-shouldered ancient philosopher. In his last days he had the picture drawn which may have been the original of the frontispiece to his last sermon, *Death's Duel*, 1632, and the monumental effigy in St Paul's, which survived the cathedral's destruction in the 1666 Fire of London. His poems are similarly dramatic portraits, ventriloquizing, posing as various personae, cynic, wit, seducer, lover, penitent and more. Two at least are put in the mouth of a woman, 'Break of Day' and 'Confined Love'.

Readers have noticed some poems where Donne does introduce an autobiographical fact, his wife Anne's maiden name, More. In the 1617 sonnet 'Since she whom I loved hath paid her last debt', asserting that 'Wholly on heavenly things my mind is set', he vacillates in this conviction, introducing the conflict that usually tautens his poems, when he hints at inability to forsake his earthly love entirely: 'But why should I beg more love whenas thou Dost woo my soul, for hers off'ring all thine?' Before he departed as chaplain to the Earl of Doncaster on an embassy in 1619, he still demands God's help in this: 'Thou lov'st not till from loving more thou free My soul' ('A Hymn to Christ, at the Author's Last Going into Germany'). Seriously ill and expecting to die in 1623, he tells God thrice in 'A Hymn to God the Father' that he has not freed Donne from his dominating self or from his human love until he has promised salvation: 'When thou hast done, thou hast not done, For I have more' (in manuscript, 'done' was sometimes spelt 'donne').

In the past, readers seeking to idealize Donne as an exemplary figure tended to read all the songs and sonnets as addressed to Anne before and after marriage. That seems unlikely, but there are love poems that, like the three later religious poems quoted, echo her maiden name. One such is 'A Valediction: Of my Name in the Window' (for dating in 1599 see Kline, Robbins). This poem's closing image of 'dying men' is the starting point of 'A Valediction: Forbidding Mourning' with its contrastingly quiet deathbed, which perhaps followed immediately on the same occasion, though the mutual love, described in religious terms, differs from the imagining of her 'inconsiderate hand' flinging open the window to greet a rich or witty lover. 'A Valediction: Of the Book' similarly uses religious terms, 'faith', 'schismatic', a treatment most intensely applied to love in 'The Canonization'. In 'A Valediction: Of Weeping', the departing man says of her tears:

> For thy face coins them, and thy stamp they bear.
> And by this mintage they are something worth,
>> For thus they be
>> Pregnant of thee.
> Fruits of much grief they are, emblems of more:
> When a tear falls, that thou fall'st which it bore.

Later he asks her to 'forbear To teach the sea what it may do too soon', suggesting fearful anticipation of a sea-crossing such as he made with Sir Walter Chute for a continental tour in 1605.

Some of the songs and sonnets may thus have arisen from real occasions, but may well have been written with the coterie reader in mind. Whether they were intended for Anne More's eyes, or for hers alone, is doubtful: Sir Henry Wotton concludes a letter from Ireland in April 1599, 'May I after these kiss that fair and learned hand of your mistress, than whom the world doth possess nothing more virtuous' (Bald 1970, p. 104). If Wotton is referring to Anne rather than Lady Egerton, he was party to Donne's secret affair, and a likely recipient of poems stemming from it.[5] Some of the most literally 'metaphysical' poems, containing abstract philosophical arguments, such as 'Air and Angels' and 'The Ecstasy', are also likely to have been written for male readers, such as Sir Edward Herbert, who wrote three poems entitled 'Platonic Love' (though one or more of them perhaps much later during the cult of it at King Charles's court) and 'An Ode upon a Question Moved, Whether Love should Continue for Ever'. Like 'The Ecstasy', this last poem is set in a spring landscape, with two unmoving lovers in a long embrace before they debate their love in octosyllabic quatrains in terms similar to Donne's, but conclude, unlike his pair, by resuming 'a moveless, silent peace'. The verbal similarities are such as to put beyond doubt that one poet had read the other's work, and Donne's closeness to a known source suggests he wrote first (Donne 1965, pp. 259–65). As to Wotton and to Goodyer, Donne wrote a verse-epistle to Herbert at the siege of Juliers in 1610, confirming that they were all three in his poetic circle, though too concerned in worldly affairs to devote themselves in the same way to poetry.

Identifying the probable contexts and recipients of Donne's poems modifies his and his hagiographer Walton's absolute distinction between rambling Jack the youthful author of erotica and the Doctor of Divinity devoting himself to sermons and hymns. The overlap and intermingling of categories is shown by poems associated with Sir Edward Herbert from 1610 to 1613. These might include 'The Ecstasy':[6] Gardner (Donne 1965, pp. 256–7) augments the close parallels with Herbert's 'Ode upon a Question Moved' by noting Donne's rare use of flower symbolism here and in 'The Primrose'. To the latter's title the 1635 second edition of Donne's poems added 'being at Montgomery Castle, upon the hill on which it is situate'; as Gardner (Donne 1965, pp. 219, 255) observes, this is 'too circumstantial not to be given credence'. Between 'The Ecstasy' and 'The Primrose' probably came the poem titled in the 1633 *Poems* 'Good Friday, 1613. Riding Westward'. We thus see a sequence of love poem, verse epistle, religious poem, love poem. We also have a picture of Donne circulating among his friends, repaying their hospitality with poetic currency.

Donne and Jonson were members between about 1605 and 1615 of overlapping circles of acquaintances, largely comprising Inns of Court men, lawyers, parliamentarians, officers of government and court, men who appreciated wit and were capable of indulging in it themselves as a sideline. Both Donne and Jonson wrote epistles to Sir Henry Goodyer, for example, patron of Drayton, Gentleman of the Privy Chamber, Donne's weekly correspondent, entertainer at his country home of not only Donne and Drayton but Jonson and Inigo Jones. Both Donne and Jonson were remembered among his circle of friends by Thomas Coryat (Bald 1970, pp. 190–5). They include Christopher Brooke (addressee of Donne's 'Storm' and 'Calm' and a verse-letter), Hugh Holland (poet and, like Jonson, Old Westminsterian convert to Roman Catholicism), Inigo Jones, and two Inns of Court wits and MPs Richard Martin and John Hoskyns. The latter took a leading part in composing one of the century's most popular poems on a response to the king's wishes during the House of Commons debate on the Union of England and Scotland, 'The Parliament Fart'.[7]

Towards the end of their lives, Donne and Jonson when not at court moved in largely different circles. Donne had among his acquaintance fellow-members of the Privy Council and other poet-clergymen such as Joseph Hall, Henry King and George Herbert, while Jonson ended up in taverns (and after a stroke in 1629, in bed) domineering over younger poets, his 'sons', who could tolerate his dogmatic assertions and rhodomontades. One loyal 'son', James Howell, reported on a supper with Jonson in 1635 'that B[en] began to engross all the discourse, to vapour extremely of himself, and, by vilifying others, to magnify his own muse. T[om] Ca[rew] buzzed me in the ear that though Ben had barrelled up a great deal of knowledge, yet it seemed he had not read the *Ethics*, which, among other precepts of morality, forbid self-commendation, declaring it to be an ill-favoured solecism in good manners' (HS 11. 429). Whereas Donne was regarded as a supreme preacher, Jonson did not achieve the universal literary dictatorship he would have liked: there were other gatherings of literary men without him in London in the 1620s: the playwright Philip Massinger, with his 'Order of Fancy', and Edward Hyde, later Earl of Clarendon, politician and historian, both had their circles, the latter's including William Davenant and Thomas Carew (Hobbs, pp. 45, 100). And where Jonson was tolerated he was not given free rein if those present were more substantial men than his 'sons': at a gathering comprising 'Sir John Suckling, Sir John Davies, Endymion Porter, Mr Hales of Eton, and Ben Jonson, . . . Mr Hales . . . hearing Ben frequently reproaching him [Shakespeare] for the want of learning and ignorance of the Ancients, told him at last, 'That if Mr Shakespeare had not read the ancients, he had likewise not stolen anything from them (a fault that the other had made no conscience of)' (Miles 1986, pp. 293, 262). Endymion Porter emphasized the difference in an epigram 'upon Ben Jonson and his Zany Tom Randolph':

> But after times, with full consent,
> This truth will all acknowledge:
> Shakespeare and Ford from Heaven were sent,
> But Ben and Tom from college.[8]
>
> (Miles 1986, p. 262)

The backhanded conclusion to Owen Felltham's 'To the Memory of Immortal Ben', was justified:

> But he
> Of whom I write this has prevented me,
> And boldly said so much in his own praise,
> No other pen need any trophy raise.
>
> (HS 11. 462)

Poets, Patrons and Publication

Such members of the gentry were men whom Donne considered, like the recipients of his early verse letters, fellow-students and young men about town, to be on his own social level: his relationship with later addressees of verse letters, funeral elegies and epithalamia between 1607 and his ordination in 1615, is that of client to patron. Jonson was forced from the start to write for a living, a course which Donne, until he had spent his inheritance and forfeited his job, could disdain: as a student presuming on his own fine prospects, he asked in satire II (20–1), 'they who write to lords rewards to get, Are they not like singers at doors for meat?' (He also sneers at 'law practice for mere gain', and in satire I has the speaker portray himself as happily 'consorted' with books of theology, philosophy, political theory, history and poetry – though the frivolous friend who lures him out into the town may well be a recognition of another side of the real Donne). Contemporary opinion was voiced by a friend of both Donne and Jonson, John Selden, in his *Table-talk*:

'Tis ridiculous for a Lord to print verses; 'tis well enough to make them to please himself, but to make them public, is foolish. If a man in a private chamber twirls his band-strings or plays with a rush to please himself, 'tis well enough; but if he should go into Fleet Street and sit upon a stall and twirl a band-string or play with a rush, then all the boys in the street would laugh at him.

(Marotti 1995, p. 228)

When the need to pay debts forced Donne to crawl to the king's favourite (the channel for most jobs and rewards), the soon to be disgraced Earl of Somerset, he wrote to his close friend Henry Goodyer just before Christmas 1614:

One thing more I must tell you, but so softly that I am loath to hear myself, and so softly that if that good lady [Bedford] were in the room with you and this letter, she might not hear. It is that I am brought to a necessity of printing my poems and address-ing them to my Lord Chamberlain [Somerset]. This I mean to do forthwith, not for much public view, but at mine own cost, a few copies. I apprehend some incongruities in the resolution, and I know what I shall suffer from many interpretations, but I am at an end of much considering that; and if I were as startling ['nervous'] in that kind as ever I was, yet in this particular I am under an unescapable necessity, . . . I must do this, as a valediction to the world, before I take orders.

(*Letters*, p. 196)

(In the event, he escaped this indignity, his poems not being printed until 1633, after his death, and not from his own copies.)

Donne continued to write poems, but, like his earlier efforts, for transmission (and, almost unpreventably, circulation) only in manuscript. Even in this mode he for a time nursed the idea of restricting his output to the most useful recipient, Lady Bedford. When in 1609–10 his friend Henry Goodyer solicited complimentary verses for the Countess of Huntingdon, whom Donne had known as Egerton's step-daughter, Elizabeth Stanley, he initially demurred: 'I have these two reasons to decline it. That that knowledge that she hath of me was in the beginning of a graver course than that of poet, into which (that I may also keep my dignity) I would not seem to relapse. The Spanish proverb informs me that "He is a fool which cannot make one sonnet, and he is mad which makes two."' He then undermines his supposed disdain for poetry by admitting that 'The other, stronger reason is my integrity to the other Countess . . . for her delight (since she descends to them) I had reserved not only all the verses which I should make, but all the thoughts of women's worthiness' (*Letters*, pp. 103–4). However, with typical inconstancy, he encloses verses to Lady Huntingdon (two verse-epistles to her survive) as the 'picture' of Lady Bedford, to whom he later proposed the similar excuse that the others to whom he had written verses were 'copies, not originals'. In 1612, Donne found that Lady Bedford was indeed offended by such disloyalty when he published the *Anniversaries* written for Sir Robert Drury. (Donne's necessities had driven him, with some misgivings, to accept Drury's offer to be his companion and secretary on a foreign tour.) His remorse was qualified:

'Of my *Anniversaries*, the fault that I acknowledge in myself is to have descended to print anything in verse . . . I confess I wonder how I declined to it, and do not pardon myself' (*Letters*, p. 255) – he regrets not the broken promise but the social descent. This was no eccentric prejudice: when in 1625 he acceded to Sir Robert Ker's request for verses on the death of the Marquess of Hamilton, disguising it as a 'Hymn' less inappropriate for a Dean of St Paul's to write, it was soon copied and circulated widely enough for the private newsletter writer John Chamberlain to observe the next month that 'though they be witty, and reasonable well done, I could wish a man of his years and place to give over versifying'.

Indeed, 'Upon the Translation of the Psalms' was embarrassingly obvious ammunition in his campaign for the Deanship in 1621 (Bald 1970, pp. 370–81) after Lady Pembroke's death (God 'hath translated these translators', line 53). She herself had sent the translation in hopeful tribute to Queen Elizabeth with an accompanying poem (*Penguin Book of Renaissance Verse* no. 31, p. 131); in turn her son, the Third Earl of Pembroke, one of the most influential patrons in the land after Buckingham (whom Donne also courted) would have appreciated the tribute to his mother and famous uncle. Bald thinks it likely (1970, p. 376) 'that Donne had sedulously enlisted the aid of everyone who was capable of influencing the King in his favour'.

Jonson was held back by no such scruples as the churchman. He sought publication to augment his reputation and income. Unlike Shakespeare, he himself prepared his plays for the printers from *Every Man out of his Humour* in 1600 onward, ignoring any rights the players might have in the script, or, as with *Sejanus*, circumventing them by rewriting it so as to exclude his collaborator. When he claimed the status of classical authors, theologians, and the like by publishing selected plays and poems as *The Works of Benjamin Jonson* in 1616, he was mocked for presumption, an attitude later embodied in Sir John Suckling's 'Session of the Poets':

> The first that broke silence was good old Ben,
> Prepared before with canary wine,
> And he told them plainly, he deserved the bays,
> For his were called works, when others were but plays.

The status of both printing and poetry were thus contested: Drayton in the general preface to his *Poly-Olbion*, 1612, complains against the privileging of manuscript circulation: 'Verses are wholly deduced [removed] to chambers, and nothing esteemed in this lunatic age but what is kept in cabinets, and must only pass by transcription.' Donne, on the other hand, in a Latin poem to Dr Richard Andrews, who had punctiliously replaced a book borrowed from Donne and damaged by his children, warmly thanks him on the grounds that manuscripts are to be more greatly venerated. In contrast to Donne's not wanting Lady Huntingdon to remember him as a poet, Jonson's epigram 10, 'To My Lord Ignorant', snaps 'Thou call'st me poet as a term of shame: But I have my revenge made in thy name' (perhaps a riposte to Lord Rutland's sarcastic accusation of his wife, 'that she kept table to poets', related to Drummond, HS 1. 141).

The bleak truth for Donne was that though Jack would be a gentleman, having destroyed his career in December 1601 by eloping with Anne More, he had to sing for his supper. The spendthrift Lady Bedford, leader of the queen's ladies at court, revelling in prodigiously expensive masques, gorgeous clothes and high living, patron of poets such as Samuel Daniel, Michael Drayton and Ben Jonson, was a good prospect for a substantial handout. Thus he promised her that his last verses would be for her, his 'Obsequies to the Lord Harington' her brother, but alluded in the accompanying letter to 'your noble brother's fortune being yours', and elicited an 'offer to pay my debts' before he entered holy orders. To his chagrin, he told Henry Goodyer in March 1615, she sent him only £30, far short of what he wanted, with the excuse that her immediate debts were 'burdensome', and a promise of good intentions 'on all future emergent occasions'. Donne acknowledged her sincerity on both counts: apart from his having so trusted her earlier promise as to fix times with his creditors (*Letters*, pp. 218–19, 149), what really stung was her 'suspicion of my calling, a better memory of my past life than I had thought her nobility could have admitted'. The would-be Doctor Donne was still haunted by Jack.

We have seen how capable Donne was of evoking imaginary situations, so it is no surprise that poems associated with Lady Bedford are outstandingly skilful and inventive examples of their kind. Addressing love poems to a woman with whom no real erotic relationship can be envisaged is now a strange mode: in England it had been normalized at the court of Queen Elizabeth. That the central source of status, wealth and power should be praised was to be expected; it is the terms in which the queen was presented, the idealizing analogues and conceits that are remarkable. Just as the styles of royal portraiture were followed in paintings and engravings of non-royal subjects, so their literary equivalents were applied by Donne, Jonson and a host of others to potential or actual patrons. E. C. Wilson (pp. 239–55) gives multitudinous examples of courting the favour of the queen in the posture and with the images of Petrarch wooing Laura. Donne's verse letters to ladies, mostly to Lady Bedford but also to Magdalen Herbert (for whom he also wrote the sequence of devotional sonnets, *La Corona*), to Lady Huntingdon, to the daughters of Sidney's (later scandalously adulterous) Stella, to Lady Carey and Essex Rich, and to Lady Salisbury (sister of the also scandalous Frances Howard, Countess of Essex and then of Somerset), all adopt a posture of humble devotion, praising, as such poems conventionally did, not just those qualities which the ruling-class might be thought to need, prudence, insight and so on, but their beauty, making them neoplatonic types whose looks are the outward expression of inner goodness.

The limited possibilities of the genre are suggested by the repetition of material from one author to another. Samuel Daniel, in 'To the Lady Lucy, Countess of Bedford', printed in 1603, lauded her as 'So good, so fair; so fair, so good', and praised her studiousness: 'you run the rightest way'. In 'To the Countess of Salisbury', Donne praises her too as 'Fair, great and good', and in 'To the Countess of Bedford: Honour is so sublime perfection', he thus supports her religious conduct: 'Go thither still; go the same way you went'. When Jonson wrote 'To Lucy, Countess of Bedford, with Mr Donne's Satires', he punned on her name:

> Lucy, you brightness of our sphere, who are
> Life of the Muses' day, their morning-star!

Donne too alludes, with a pious reservation, to the etymological significance of her name (line 21): 'But one, 'tis best light to contèmplate you'. Even Daniel's unusual 'clearness' of her heart may also be a play on her name.

But Donne ingeniously varies the routine, at least with Lady Bedford, drawing on his learning and imagination to adduce analogies for her excellences from the sun, religion, an epigram by Martial (on the bee), and a celebrated temple in ancient Rome that was built of translucent stone.

Masquerading as a lower being addressing a higher in 'Twickenham Garden' (the Countess's current Home County seat) he flatteringly laments the sin of carnal longing aroused by such beauty as hers:

> But oh, self-traitor! I do bring
> The spider love, which transubstantiates all,
> And can convert manna to gall,
> And that this place may thoroughly be thought
> True paradise, I have the serpent brought.

As in many of his poems, the tension between society's laws and forbidden desire makes a little drama even of a poem suing for patronage.

Other songs and sonnets, such as 'The Fever' and 'The Relic', may relate to Lucy Bedford. One of the most likely is 'A Nocturnal upon St Lucy's Day', its seasonal setting functional, as in 'Twickenham Garden', but in tune with the mood. Lady Bedford was so seriously ill in 1612 that on 23 November she was described by Lord Dorset as 'speechless, and . . . past all hopes'. The intensity of this poem's language, which Marotti (1986 p. 233) compares to 'the vivid hyperboles of the *Anniversaries*', might seem, as it does there if misunderstood, to be inappropriate, but the sense of being 'nothing' which it so forcefully expresses usually related not to Donne's wife (thought by some to be the subject) but to his lack of position in the world, as in a letter to Goodyer of September 1608:

> I would fain do something, but that I cannot tell what it is is no wonder. For to choose is to do, but to be no part of any body is to be nothing. At most, the greatest persons are but wens and excrescences, men of wit and delightful conversation [such as he could claim to be] but as moles for ornament, except they be so incorporated into the body of the world that they contribute something to the sustentation of the whole.
>
> (*Letters*, pp. 50–1).

With the countess all his worldly hopes of being something might die. Moreover, if Donne did not, for once, expect her to be able to read and reward the poem, that might well explain the focus on himself, even more intense than in 'Twickenham Garden', because more serious. Although Lucy Bedford may have been better by her name-day, 13 December, Donne could have anticipated it as an appropriate occasion for his lament.

Panegyrics to patrons may now seem not just tedious but distasteful. Donne, Jonson and most other poets of their time praised those they knew to be unworthy because there was no alternative for anyone who wished not just to rise in society but even to survive. Lady Bedford was interested in and capable of writing verse herself (see Donne 1978b, pp. 235–7), and might welcome some enhancement of her current image at court as an intriguer and extravagant pleasure-lover. But those with the power to assign the means of earning a living found it easy to keep petitioners at their mercy: as Robert Evans points out, the transaction was not one of guaranteed fairness; the supply of writers from the universities, expanded in the later sixteenth century to produce a literate clergy, far exceeded the available patronage. The very unreliability of patronage reinforced subservience, keeping people such as Donne and Jonson dangling in hope. Poetry was a central concern of poets, not those whose money and influence the poets wanted in exchange. Moreover, rivals *were* dependable in their hostility (Evans 1989, pp. 29–33, 178). Nor was it only material reward that poets needed: Jonson was saved from hanging for homicide by being able to repeat the psalm-verse requisite to prove his literacy, but when arraigned for his writings[9] he depended on the favour of members of government and those who might influence them. After *Eastward Ho!* his gratitude to James, Salisbury, Monteagle, Suffolk and Aubigny was expressed in epigrams, 35, 43, 60, 67 and 127. The incentive to keep in favour is made plain by the rumour that the prisoners 'should then had their ears cut and noses', so that his mother was ready to provide poison, he told Drummond, and kill herself with him (HS 1. 140). Sheavyn and Saunders (p. 61) list a couple of dozen writers of the period who suffered interference by the authorities. Without powerful protectors, Jonson would have been treated like the scholar of Merton College, Oxford, who in 1602 'was whipped in London and lost his ears in Oxford for libelling the Vice-Chancellor and the Council' (Marotti 1995, p. 93).

As Riggs puts it, following Jonson's release from prison after *The Isle of Dogs* in 1597, he set his mind on acceptance as a man of letters, not a mere 'playwright' (his own derisory coinage for the lowly, ill-paid labour of a dramatist), 'and patronage was the common denominator of all his new undertakings' (Riggs, p. 63). He took *Every Man out of his Humour* to a bookseller located, exceptionally, in Fleet Street, the main road between the City and the Inns of Court. He wrote poems to various noblemen and women, centring on the clan connected with Sir Philip Sidney, many of whose members were both patrons and writers: his brother, Sir Robert at Penshurst, his daughter the Countess of Rutland, his nephew the Earl of Pembroke, his niece Lady Wroth, his distant cousin Lucy Harington, Countess of Bedford. Pembroke and Lady Bedford were generous patrons of poets such as the sonneteers Daniel and Drayton, and the pastoralist William Browne of Tavistock. In 1602 Thomas Overbury told the diarist John Manningham that 'Ben Jonson the poet now lives upon one [Sir Robert] Townshend, and scorns the world' (Riggs, p. 92). He then made a better catch than this heir of a Norfolk squire in the person of Lord Aubigny, one of the six gentlemen of the bedchamber, and thus intimate with the king. For Lady Bedford and the Queen, Jonson wrote court masques, and in dedicating his epigrams to Lord Pembroke in 1612 as 'the ripest of my work' announced that he had risen clearly above the rank of playwright to that of man of letters, on familiar terms with the nobility, a status further enhanced by the almost unprecedented publication of them and choice plays in the grand folio of 1616. He was substantially rewarded, telling Drummond in 1619 that 'every first day of the New Year he had £20 sent him from the Earl of Pembroke to buy books' (HS 1. 141). After the death of Salisbury, and temporary eclipse by the Howards and Somerset of the Pembroke–Lady Bedford faction, until they groomed and put before James's eye young George Villiers (soon to be Buckingham), Jonson worked for Sir Walter Ralegh on the latter's *History of the World*, and gained the position of tutor to his son Wat on a continental tour.[10]

So, despite Donne's youthful scorn of poetic clientage and Jonson's boast to Drummond that if made a churchman he would preach to the king, and 'not flatter, though he saw death' (HS 1. 141), their urge to survive prevailed. The humiliation was covered by claiming a didactic role: in *Essays in Divinity* (1952, p. 34) Donne points out that 'over-praising is a kind of libelling'. After three epigrams praising Salisbury's virtues, Jonson places (prudently, for publication in 1612 after Salisbury's decline and death) 'To my Muse', pointedly regretting his 'fierce idolatry' of 'a worthless lord' but in conclusion consoling himself that 'Whoe'er is raised For worth he has not, he is taxed, not praised' (*Epigrams*, 43, 63–5). (He seems to have seen no irony in his complaint to Drummond that 'Salisbury never cared for any man longer nor he could make use of him' – exactly Jonson's way with patrons.) In a commendatory poem of 1612 to a friend, the jurist John Selden (*Underwood*, 14), he admits that

> I have too oft preferred
> Men past their terms, and praised some names too much;
> But 'twas with purpose to have made them such.

However, this humanist precept of teaching by praising, in the hope that recipients would try to live up to the image made by the poet, and be shamed by publicly visible discrepancies, was effective more in saving the self-respect of poets than in preventing or reforming abuses of power. So desperate was Donne for employment that in 1613–14 he abased himself to Somerset, suing for any and every government job possibly available, whether ambassador to Venice or clerk to the Privy Council or personal secretary. This last post was vacant because Somerset had contrived to get his then secretary Sir Thomas Overbury imprisoned in the Tower, so that he could not interfere with the Countess of Essex's scheme to divorce her husband and marry Somerset. Donne's project for dedicating a collection of poems to the latter came to nothing, but he wrote a 235-line eclogue and epithalamion celebrating the marriage. Jonson provided a eulogy of 'virtuous Somerset' (*Ungathered Verse* 18, excluded from his later collection, *The Underwood*), *A Challenge at Tilt* and (to suit the taste of those honoured) the bawdy *Irish Masque*. In the latter he exhorted Frances Howard to 'Outbe that *Wife*, in worth, thy friend did make', referring to the popular poem by his friend Overbury, whom the Somersets were later convicted of murdering (but let off their sentences by King James).

Jonson had been fortunate in arousing some feeling of affinity in James: apart from the former's claim to Scots ancestry, both were irresponsible, scornful of the people, unashamedly lascivious, coarse or downright filthy in their personal habits, and addicted to alcohol (Riggs, p. 112). And although Jonson, like Donne, gloried in being a self-confessed practising heterosexual, and denounced all other orientation, he brought himself to flatter the king's physical attraction to young men with the sexual innuendo of the Porter's invitation into Buckingham's Burley-on-the-Hill in *The Gypsies Metamorphosed* (1621): 'The house your bounty built, and still doth rear . . . The master is your creature as the place . . . please you enter Him and his house, and search him to the centre.' That earned Jonson £100, rather better than the £5 to be expected from playhouse or bookseller. To earn such rewards, he had to concur with 'the half-baked whims of his capricious patrons' (Miles 1990, p. 153), but also with central doctrines of royal power. From the start he deified James and Charles as God on earth, as in the courtiers' song of *Pan's Anniversary* (1620): 'by him we breathe, we live, We move, we are', reapplying the description of God in Acts 17:26–8. Donne as Dean of St Paul's had likewise to remember that he was put there to serve king and government: Jeanne Shami (Donne 1996, pp. 24–35) has shown the differences between a sermon prepared by Donne for posthumous publication and the more circumspect version he actually delivered from the pulpit and then sent to the king to be vetted before printing (which, even so, did not take place).

Donne managed his performance as the reformed Doctor at St Paul's, as a preacher who could 'through the eyes the melting heart distil', including his final appearance in the pulpit as a dying man preaching on death, with the skill of an actor-manager. Ben Jonson in the end played a less admired part. On this praiser in his poems to patrons of all the traditional virtues of temperance, prudence, fortitude, and so on, Drummond's verdict, after days of conversation, is borne out by Jonson's life:

> He is a great lover and praiser of himself, a contemner and scorner of others; given rather to lose a friend than a jest [a joke Jonson had made of himself as 'Horace' in *Poetaster* 4. 3]; jealous of every word and action of those about him (especially after drink, which is one of the elements in which he liveth) . . . For any religion, as being versed in both. Interpreteth best sayings and deeds often to the worst. Oppressed with fantasy, which hath ever mastered his reason (a general disease in many poets). His inventions are smooth and easy, but above all he excelleth in a translation.
>
> (HS 1. 151)

In his strenuous self-assertion and competitive denigration of others, he was perhaps over-compensating for the humble occupation of his stepfather, which dogged him till the end. Henslowe wrote to his partner Edward Alleyn that 'Gabriel [Spencer is] slain in Hoxton Fields . . . by the hands of Benjamin Jonson, bricklayer' (HS 1. 164) – not 'fellow-actor and poet'. His self-praise and sneering at others inevitably prompted reminders of bricklaying from Dekker in *Satiromastix* (1601), a Paul's Cross preacher in 1612 (Riggs, p. 195), a courtier, Nathaniel Brent, in 1618 (HS 10. 576–7), and Alexander Gill in 1632 (HS 11. 348). Though buried in Westminster Abbey, that was because he lived in the precinct; though followed to his grave by a throng of nobility and gentry, he had died almost destitute; writer of gracious epitaphs, his was simply 'O rare Ben Jonson' – and that possibly the mason's error for 'Orare . . .', 'Pray for . . .'. Donne arranged his own commemoration in inscription, effigy and the publication of his sermons, perhaps even Walton's biography emphasizing the Christian, not the poet. As writer of the play of his own life, he rivalled Jonson's creations for the theatre and Banqueting House. Jonson in his poems bore the standard for the classicism that after the Restoration was to dominate English writing for a century. Donne's came into their own with the twentieth century's preference for the innovator and inventor, evoker not of communal ideals but individual psychology. Both still fascinate as skilled writers and for the way they interacted as such with a society so foreign to the twenty-first century, yet sharing the human strengths and failings they brought vividly to life.

Notes

1 See Herford and Simpson, Vol. 11, 253.

2 Dennis Flynn 'Donne and the Ancient Catholic Nobility'. *English Literary Renaissance*, 19 (1989) pp. 305–23, has advanced the intriguing hypothesis (which hangs primarily on identifying the names 'Donnes' and 'Downes' with Donne) that only three months after matriculating from Hart Hall, Oxford, the twelve-year-old Donne was taken to Paris in the ambassadorial train of the Roman Catholic Henry Stanley, fourth earl of Derby, in order to avoid his being made to swear to the articles of the Church of England. However, such a short stay at Oxford would have made unlikely the gathering of the wide range of acquaintance he is supposed by others to have made there, and he shared his exact name, let alone 'Downes', with other recusants (Bald 1970, p. 23). Sir Richard Baker, who shared rooms at Donne's Oxford College with their friend in common Henry Wotton, then read law in London, says that Donne, 'leaving Oxford, lived at the Inns of Court', implying no interval.

3 Conversely, a later Donne applies the language and ideas of physical human love to religion, but in deep seriousness. The educated Christian reader knew the biblical Song of Songs, on whose originally erotic purpose had been imposed a religious reading as the courtship of Christ and his bride, the universal church, for instance of verse 5. 2: 'Open to me, my sister, my love, my dove, my undefiled.' Donne's more violent religious eroticism was to be found in the Spanish Counter-Reformation poet, St John of the Cross.

4 That Lady Bedford saw at least one of the Holy Sonnets is indicated by the opening of her elegy on Cecilia Bulstrode: 'Death, be not proud' (Donne 1978b, pp. 235–7).

5 Wotton's own freer morality is suggested by an anecdote told by Jonson to Drummond: 'Sir Henry Wotton, before His Majesty's going to England, being disguised at Leith [as 'Octavio Baldi'; sent in 1602 via Norway by Duke of Florence to warn James of assassination plot – Pearsall Smith, 1. 40–2], on Sunday when all the rest were at church, being interrupted of his occupation by another wench who came in at the door, cried out 'Pox on thee, for thou hast hindered the procreation of a child!' and betrayed himself' (HS 1. 146).

6 A verbal link occurs in the opening of what is evidently one of Donne's Tuesday letters from Mitcham to Henry Goodyer (*Letters*, p. 11), dated merely '9 October', but falling on a Tuesday in 1610 (its other echoes of 'To Sir Edward Herbert at Juliers', 1610, and *Ignatius his Conclave*, written in 1610, supporting this year): 'I make account that this writing of letters, when it is with any seriousness, is a kind of ecstasy, and a departure and secession and suspension of the soul, which doth then communicate itself to two bodies.'

7 See Marotti 1995 pp. 93, 127–8. One of the longer versions is printed from manuscripts in Whitlock, pp. 288–92).

8 Shakespeare himself was alleged to have exacted a jest from this too in the anonymous *Shakespeare's Jests, or, The Jubilee Jester* (*c*.1769): 'Shakespeare seeing Jonson in a necessary-house with a book in his hand, reading it very attentively, said he was sorry his memory was so bad that he could not shite without a book' (Miles 1986, p. 169).

9 He was imprisoned for *The Isle of Dogs* and *Eastward Ho!* in 1597 and 1605; cited before the Lord Chief Justice for *Poetaster*, 1601; summoned before the Privy Council for *Sejanus*, 1603; 'accused' for *The Devil is an Ass*, 1616; examined by the Privy Council for alleged verses of his on Buckingham's death, 1628; and cited before the Court of High Commission for *The Magnetic Lady*, 1632.

10 For Jonson's ridiculous humiliation when drunk, see Riggs, p. 207.

REFERENCES AND FURTHER READING

Bald, R. C. (1959). *Donne and the Drurys*. Cambridge: Cambridge University Press.

——(1970). *John Donne: A Life*. Oxford: Clarendon Press.

Bates, Catherine (1992). *The Rhetoric of Courtship in Elizabethan Language and Literature*. Cambridge: Cambridge University Press.

Berman, Ronald (1964). *Henry King and the Seventeenth Century*. London: Chatto and Windus.

Bradley, J. F. and Adams, J. Q. (1922). *The Jonson Allusion Book: A Collection of Allusions to Ben Jonson from 1597 to 1700*. New Haven, Oxford and London: Yale University Press.

Brennan, Michael G. (1988). *Literary Patronage in the English Renaissance*. London and New York: Routledge.

Brown, Meg Lota (1995). *Donne and the Politics of Conscience in Early Modern England*. Leiden, New York and Köln: E. J. Brill.

Carew, Thomas (1949). *The Poems, with his Masque: 'Coelum Britannicum'*, ed. Rhodes Dunlap. Oxford: Clarendon Press.

Carey, John (1986). *John Donne: Life, Mind and Art*. London: Faber and Faber.

Di Cesare, M. A. and Fogel, E. (1978). *A Concordance to the Poems of Ben Jonson*. Ithaca, NY and London: Cornell University Press.

Donne, John (1912). *The Poems*, ed. J. C. Herbert Grierson. 2 vols, Oxford: Clarendon Press.

——(1952). *Essays in Divinity*, ed. E. M. Simpson. Oxford: Clarendon Press.

——(1965). *The Elegies* and *The Songs and Sonnets*, ed. Helen Gardner. Oxford: Clarendon Press.

——(1967). *The Satires, Epigrams* and *Verse Letters*, ed. W. Milgate. Oxford: Clarendon Press.

——(1974). *Letters to Severall Persons of Honour (1651)*, facsimile. Hildesheim and New York: Georg Olms Verlag.

——(1978a). *The Divine Poems*, ed. Helen Gardner, 2nd edn. Oxford: Clarendon Press.

——(1978b). *The Epithalamions, Anniversaries* and *Epicedes*, ed. W. Milgate. Oxford: Clarendon Press.

——(1983). *The Songs and Sonets*, ed. Theodore Redpath, 2nd edn. London: Methuen.

——(1984). *Biathanatos*, ed. E. W. Sullivan. Newark: University of Delaware Press; London and Toronto: Associated University Press.

——(1990). *John Donne* (the poems with a selection of the prose), ed. John Carey. Oxford and New York: Oxford University Press.

——(1996). *John Donne's 1622 Gunpowder Plot Sermon: A Parallel-text Edition*, ed. Jeanne Shami. Pittsburgh: Duquesne University Press.

Evans, Robert C. (1989). *Ben Jonson and the Poetics*

of Patronage. Lewisburg, PA: Bucknell University Press; Toronto and London: Associated University Presses.

——(1994). *Jonson and the Contexts of His Time*. Lewisburg, PA: Bucknell University Press; Toronto and London: Associated University Presses.

Flynn, Dennis (1988). '"Awry and Squint": The Dating of Donne's Holy Sonnets', *John Donne Journal*, 7, 35–46.

——(1989). 'Donne and the Ancient Catholic Nobility'. *English Literary Renaissance*, 19, 305–23.

Hammond, Gerald (1990). *Fleeting Things: English Poets and Poems, 1616–1660*. Cambridge, MA and London: Harvard University Press.

Herford, E. F. and Simpson, P. E. (eds) (1925–52). *Ben Jonson*. Oxford: Clarendon Press.

Hobbs, Mary (1992). *Early Seventeenth Century Verse Miscellany Manuscripts*. Aldershot: Scolar; Brookfield, VT: Ashgate Publishing Co.

Jonson, Ben (1925, 1952). *The Works*, ed. in 11 vols by C. H. Herford and Percy Simpson. Volume 1: Appendix 1, Conversations with William Drummond of Hawthornden; Volume 11: Jonson's Literary Record. Oxford: Clarendon Press. Referred to in the text as HS.

——(1975). *Poems*, ed. Ian Donaldson. London, New York, Toronto: Oxford University Press.

King, Henry (1965). *The Poems*, ed. Margaret Crum. Oxford: Clarendon Press.

Lewalski, B. K. (1973). *Donne's Anniversaries and the Poetry of Praise: The Creation of a Symbolic Mode*. Princeton, NJ: Princeton University Press.

Love, Harold (1993). *Scribal Publication in Seventeenth-century England*. Oxford: Clarendon Press.

McClung, W. A. (1977). *The Country House in English Renaissance Poetry*. Berkeley, Los Angeles and London: University of California Press.

McEuen, Kathryn (1968). *Classical Influences upon the Tribe of Ben*. New York: Octagon Books.

Marotti, A. F. (1986). *John Donne, Coterie Poet*. Madison: University of Wisconsin Press.

——(1995). *Manuscript, Print, and the English Renaissance Lyric*. Ithaca and London: Cornell University Press.

May, Steven W (1991). *The Elizabethan Courtier Poets: The Poems and Their Contexts*. Columbia: University of Missouri Press.

Miles, Rosalind (1986). *Ben Jonson: His Life and Work*. London and New York: Methuen.

——(1990). *Ben Jonson: His Craft and Art*. London and New York: Routledge.

Montrose, L. A. (1977). 'Celebration and Insinuation: Sir Philip Sid and the Motives of Elizabethan Courtship', *Renaissance Drama*, 8, 3–35.

Osborn, Louise Brown (1937). *The Life, Letters, and Writings of John Hoskyns 1566–1638*. New Haven: Yale University Press; London: Oxford University Press.

Pask, Kevin (1996). *The Emergence of the English Author: Scripting the Life of the Poet in Early Modern England*. Cambridge: Cambridge University Press.

Patterson, Annabel H. (1984). *Censorship and Interpretation: The Conditions of Writing and Reading in Early Modern England*. Madison: University of Wisconsin Press.

Peterson, R. S. (1981). *Imitation and Praise in the Poems of Ben Jonson*. New Haven: Yale University Press.

Riggs, David (1989). *Ben Jonson: A Life*. Cambridge, MA and London: Harvard University Press.

Robbins, Rossell Hope (1952), ed. *Secular Lyrics of the Fourteenth and Fifteenth Centuries*. Oxford: Clarendon Press.

Sharpe, Kevin (1987). *Criticism and Compliment: The Politics of Literature in the England of Charles I*. Cambridge: Cambridge University Press.

Sheavyn, Phoebe (1967). *The Literary Profession in the Elizabethan Age*, 2nd edn, rev. J. W. Saunders. Manchester: Manchester University Press; New York: Barnes and Noble.

Simpson, Evelyn M. (1948). *A Study of the Prose Works of John Donne*, 2nd edn. Oxford: Clarendon Press.

Sloane, Thomas O. (1985). *Donne, Milton, and the End of Humanist Rhetoric*. Berkeley, Los Angeles, London: University of California Press.

Summers, Joseph H. (1970). *The Heirs of Donne and Jonson*. London: Chatto and Windus.

Whitlock, Baird W. (1982). *John Hoskyns, Serjeant-at-Law*. Washington, DC: University Press of America.

Wilson, Elkin Calhoun (1966). *England's Eliza*. Harvard Studies in English, Vol. 20. London: Frank Cass.

38

'Such pretty things would soon be gone': The Neglected Genres of Popular Verse, 1480–1650

Malcolm Jones

In recent times there have at long last been moves to extend the canon of 'approved authors' of English literature during our period, though rarely to extend the canon of approved genres. There has, for example, been surprisingly little interest in the parodic forms,[1] and almost none in inscriptional and functional verse, for all its ubiquity.

In *A Dialogue full of Pith and Pleasure* (1603), Nicholas Breton wrote that 'Verses are so common that they are nailed upon every post',[2] and, surprisingly, we have a fair idea of what such ephemeral verses were like thanks to the litigious nature of an age in which an attack on a man's honour, or a woman's *honour*, which usually implied an attack on her sexual reputation, was likely to end up in court. Hundreds of such libels survive in our county and national record offices. Many of these 'railing rhymes' are halting in the extreme: they stutter and splutter, but nothing better conveys the passion, the immediacy, of personal or group antagonisms. At the beginning of the third millennium it is not easy for us to understand why these squibs are invariably in verse, albeit often ill-scanned and otherwise imperfect, but for us, prose is the 'default position'; we live in a culture that is, literally, more prosaic. The early modern *mentalité*, if it had something urgent to say, naturally expressed itself in rhyme – small wonder that Chapman's eponymous hero, *Monsieur d'Olive* (1606) was moved to say, 'I am afraid of nothing but I shall be balladed', for, given some of the 'ballads' that follow, he was right to be afraid. Of course, the production of such libellous ballads was not without risk, and Fox suggests that the poetaster whose tongue is nailed to the post in book 5 of *The Faerie Queene*, who 'lewd poems . . . did compile . . . and railing rymes had spread', would have been 'quite a familiar sight' to his Elizabethan contemporaries.[3] In 1619, for instance, a group of aggrieved Lancashire tenants composed a 'scandalous libel in rhyme and fasten[ed] and pinn[ed] it to the common whipstock [whipping-post] standing in the most public place', and were furthermore ready to 'read and sing the said libel as a ballad'.

Only very exceptionally would one of these essentially local ballads ever reach print, but on the other hand, some bear a distinct resemblance to published ballads. Martin

Ingram pointed out that the following defamatory verse, found in the Essex village of Earls Colne in 1588,

> Woe be unto Kendal
> that ever he was born
> He keeps his wife so lustily
> she makes him wear the horn
>
> But what is he the better
> or what is he the worse
> She keeps him like a cuckold
> with money in his purse

is clearly closely related to a rhyme published in *Tarlton's Jests* (1613):

> Woe worth thee, Tarlton,
> That ever thou wast born;
> Thy wife hath made thee cuckold,
> And thou must wear the horn.
>
> What and if I be, boy,
> I'm ne'er the worse;
> She keeps me like a gentleman
> With money in my purse.

Ingram further noted an elaborated version which appeared at Bremhill, Wiltshire, in 1618; it seems safest to assume that a traditional mocking verse, circulating below the level of print, was eventually fathered on Tarlton by the compiler of his (posthumous) *Jests* in exactly the same way many of 'his' equally traditional jests themselves were. From another Wiltshire village, Ogbourne St Andrew, comes the following scatological verse dated 1626:

> O hark a while and you shall know
> Of a filthy beast did her breech show . . .
> Although she be never so brave and fine
> I say her breech is not the moonshine,

in which we are surely entitled to see some adumbration of the modern English sense of the verb *moon*, 'to expose the buttocks'. It should be pointed out that these 'libels' are of great importance for filling out the record of the language. It is particularly in the taboo areas of the lexicon, of course, that such verse can most usefully supplement the printed record, not least, because the majority of such cases to reach the courts concern illicit sexual relations or the imputation of such. The following verse relates to Bath in 1614–15; the clerk, to whom we must be grateful for what follows, finally gave up his transcription in disgust, remarking that 'the residue and other part of the said libel rhyme and verses is so obscene and foul as it is not fit herein to be written or remembered, neither is the same fitting for any modest eyes to read or ears to hear'. To judge from what he did transcribe, it must have been very strong meat indeed:

> Of all the whores that I have known,
> from court that came unto our town,
> There's none compares with Muddy Mall,
> That plays the whore from spring to fall:
> from spring to fall was never see[n],
> A pocky jade worse than Marie,   [infected with the pox]
> All honest women do her scorn,
> because she was a bastard born,
> A bastard born of noble race,
> which makes her wear a brazen face,
> A brazen face of opal hue,
> An arrant whore fit for a stew,   [brothel]
> If you have gold she shows her arse,
> if you have none she burns your tarse,   [infects your penis]
> She keeps her self just like a punk,   [prostitute]
> and lays her heels against a trunk,
> Against a trunk she lays her feet,
> And wipes her cunt with a foul sheet.[4]

In an era of such awful penalties for *lèse-majesté*, rarely do we come across such outrageous verses as the following quatrain apparently circulating in the little Welsh village of Llansilin in 1612:

> The Bible is a bauble,
> the lord Chamberlain is a fool,
> The old Queen a bastard,
> the Lord Treasurer a long tool.   ['prick'][5]

No Puritan, presumably, would have countenanced the following abuse of biblical authority in the form of this parodic Decalogue entitled, *Andrew Abington's Commandments*, from Trent, Somerset, in 1616:

> Thou shalt do no right nor thou shalt take no wrong
> Thou shalt catch what thou canst
> Thou shalt pay no man
> Thou shalt commit adultery
> Thou shalt bear false witness against thy neighbour
> Thou shalt covet thy neighbour's wife
> Thou shalt sell a hundred sheep to Henry Hopkins after
> Thou shalt draw the best of them

Thou shalt sell thy oxen twice
Thou shalt deny thy own hand[6]

A typically scurrilous verse from Worcestershire in 1605 shows the value of such authentically popular rhyme in illuminating our knowledge of colloquial usage:

> I can no more:
> This is the whore
> Of cowardy George Hawkins;
> He got with child
> In a place most wild,
> Which for to name
> it is a shame.
> Yet for your satisfaction
> I will make relation:
> It was in a privy,
> A place most filthy
> As, gent, you may judge,   [gentleman]
> Yet nothing too bad
> For a knave and a drab,
> And so they pray go trudge.[7]

The colloquial adjective 'cowardy' is not recorded in the *OED* until 1836, but the final words of this verse provide an interesting parallel by which to gauge the colloquiality of Falstaff's dismissal of his cronies in the third scene of *The Merry Wives of Windsor* (1598), 'Go! / Trudge, plod away o'th'hoof: seek shelter, pack!' (1.3. 71–2).

A verse from the village of Beckington near Berkley in Somerset of 1611–12 alludes to an ancient folkloric ritual by which a man might be insulted by cutting off his horse's tail, preparatory to a skimmington ride – a satirical parade in which a community conveyed its disapproval of one of its number, usually for some marital irregularity or other sexual offence felt to outrage local mores. At Beckington the animal was prepared by having a large pair of horns bound to its head (thereby implying that the procession was conceived as an attack on a cuckold), and having the hair cut off its ears, mane, and tail, whereupon, thus mutilated, it was led through the village accompanied by loud shouts and outcries – interestingly, the word used to describe what was done to the horse is 'disgraced', though this is clearly a transference of the disgrace done thereby to its owner, the target of the skimmington.

> William Swarfe, I heartily commend
> your mare; tail she hath spended.
> I pray take it for no scorn,
> for in her head there hangs a horn;
> because your mare is somewhat pied,
> she is finely trimmed for you to bide.[8]   [? ride]

Occasionally, as in the case of the disturbances in Wells in 1607, the verses recorded belong rather more obviously in a (para-)dramatic context. O'Conor has masterfully reconstructed the circumstances attending the parodic sermon preached against the Earl of Lincoln with satirical intent at South Kyme in Lincolnshire in 1601, with at the end of a play, *{an interlude} termed and named the Death of the Lord of Kyme*, as the Earl's Bill of Complaint has it.[9] It was further alleged that Cradock 'in frown of religion and the profession thereof, being attired in a minister's gown and having a corner-cap [as worn by divines] on his head, and a book in his hand opened, . . . in a pulpit made for that purpose, [did] deliver and utter a profane and irreligious prayer . . . and did . . . read a text out of the book of Mabb, as he then read it'. The form of verse used here is a delightful farrago of liturgical parody and sheer nonsense:

> *De profundis pro defunctis.* Let us pray for our dear Lord [i.e. Summer Lord]
> that died this present day,
>
> Now blessed be his body and his bones:
> I hope his legs are hotter than gravestones,
> And to that hope let's all conclude it then,
> Both men and women pray, and say, Amen.

A little later, 'he . . . did read a text which he said was taken out of the twenty second chapter of the book of Hitroclites,[10] which text was',

> *Cesar Dando,*
> *sublivando,*
> *ignoscendo*
> *gloriam adeptus est*   [meaningless pseudo-Latin]

On examination, the sermon's author, Talboys Dymoke, was able to give the text of the preacher's parodic blessing, with the alliteration of which he was, perhaps, particularly pleased: 'The mercy of mustard seed and the blessing of bullbeef and the peace of potluck be with you all. Amen.'

   There is not space here to exemplify all the parodic genres, but perhaps we might just take two examples of the parodic prescription from both ends of our period; *c.*1520 we find the anonymous 'Good medicine if a maid have lost her maidenhead to make her a maid again',[11] and from *c.*1647, one of Katherine Philips' juvenilia, surviving in the form of 'A recipe to cure a Love sick Person who can't obtain the Party desired':

> Take two oz. of the spirits of reason
> three oz. of the Powder of experience
> five drams of the Juice of Discretion
> three oz. of the Powder of good advice
> and a spoonful of the Cooling water of consideration.[12]

Popular verse has long been at the service of political protest, of course, and one of the best known of such verses, which saw its author executed, is the rhyming couplet which William Collingbourn fixed to the doors of St Paul's in 1484:

> The Cat, The Rat and Lovel our dog,
> Rule all England under a hog.   [= Richard III]

Often such political protest was couched in prophetic verse. In Norfolk in 1549 the peasants who followed Kett were encouraged by a prophecy which they openly proclaimed in public places:

> The country knaves, Hob, Dick, and Hick
> With clubs and clouted shoon   [patched shoes]
> Shall fill up Dussindale
> With slaughtered bodies soon.[13]

In the 1530s, according to Cavendish, his biographer, Wolsey had been impressed by the prophecy 'When this cow rideth the bull / Then, priest, beware thy skull' – popularly interpreted to allude to Anne Boleyn's influence over King Henry VIII and the Dissolution of the Monasteries. The following verse from Wye in Kent dates from 1630 and voices popular protest at high prices, as well as threatening retribution on those in authority:

> The corn is so dear,
> I doubt many will starve this year;   [fear]
> If you see not to this,
> Some of you will speed amiss;
> Our souls they are dear,
> For our bodies have some care,
> Before we arise
> Less will suffice.[14]

An apparently increasing anxiety throughout the early modern era as to 'who shall wear the breeches' is reflected in unsophisticated verse of the type found in Plat's *The Flowers of Philosophy* (1592), in which John says to Joan, 'if thou wilt wear thy husband's gear, then shalt thou be above me', and

> make me promise never more
> that thou shalt mind to beat me.
> For fear thou wear the wisp,[15] good wife,
> and make our neighbours ride.   [act out a skimmington ride]

In the same poem Joan envisages a topsy-turvy world in which

women then must play the men,
and ride about the land,
And men must reel, and wind the wheel   [i.e. spinning-wheel]
with distaff in their hand,

exactly like the hapless man shown in one of the engravings from a series first issued in 1628 [figure 7a or 7b].[16]

Located somewhere between literary and inscriptional verse is the quite unresearched genre of 'trencher poetry' – though the literary men were quite sure at which end of that spectrum it belonged. In his *Art of English Poesy* (1589), however, Puttenham is not judgemental, neutrally stating that 'We call them [sc. epigrams] posies, and do paint them nowadays upon the backsides of our trenchers of wood, or use them as devices in arms or in rings', but Joseph Hall refers to 'hunger-starved trencher poetry' (Satires (1598), I. i. 13). Milton couples such verses with ring-posies: 'Instead of well sized periods, he greets us with a quantity of thumb-ring posies. *He has a fortune therefore good / because he is content with it.* This is a piece of sapience not worth the brain of a fruit-trencher (*Apollo Smectymnus* (1642), 28). Middleton has one of his characters in *The Old Law* (*c*.1618) refer sneeringly to 'running admonitions / Upon cheese-trenchers, as

Take heed of whoring, shun it;
'*Tis* like a cheese too strong of the runnet [rennet].
(2.1.126ff)

Maybe it is the contempt of the seventeenth century *litterati* that has led to the unaccounted scholarly neglect of the genre which, however, has much to reveal about contemporary *mentalité*. John Davies's *Verses given to the Lord Treasurer* [Thomas Sackville, Lord Buckhurst] *upon New Year's Day upon a Dozen of Trenchers*, commonly known as *The XII Wonders*, represent twelve social types with corresponding painted figures. At least three copies of this original set which must have been presented *c*.1600 survive, and the following lines are taken from the verse accompanying the twelfth of the dozen stereotypes depicted, *The Maid*:

I marriage would forswear but that I hear men tell,
That she that dies a maid must lead an ape in hell,   [Tilley M37]
Titles and lands I like, yet rather fancy can,
A man that wanteth gold, than gold that wants a man   [Tilley M361]

It is perhaps not without a certain significance that the majority of trencher-sets to survive are painted with verses which relate to marriage and relations between the sexes. From a set of a dozen trenchers dated 1599, I excerpt three quatrains, the first well exemplifies the sententious nature of these verses:

A quiet life surmounteth gold,   [see Tilley L244]
Though goods great store thy coffers hold;

Yet rather death I do beseech,
Than most masters to wear no breech[es].   [Tilley M727]

These trencher marriage-debates are very reminiscent, stylistically too, of Thomas Tusser's *Dialogue between two Bachelors, of wiving and thriving* (*Five hundred* . . . 1580 ed.). The third trencher of this set, for example, reads:

What needs such cares oppress thy thought,
For Fortune saith that hap is naught:
A shrew thy chance is for to keep,
But better a shrew, say, than a sheep.

– which may be compared with Tusser's verse,

She may in something seem a shrew,
Yet such a housewife as but few,
To help thee, sir, to thrive:
This proverb look in mind ye keep,
As good a shrew is as a sheep,
For you to take to wive.

The idiom of 'wearing the breeches' turns up again:

I shrew his heart that married me;   [beshrew, curse]
My wife and I can never agree;
A knavish quean, by Jys, I swear,   [shrew] [by Jesus!]
The goodman's breech she thinks to wear.

Two verses from another set dated 1595 clearly refer to the stereotypical idle housewife or sloven, with more than a hint of sexual excess in the second:

Early rising shall do me no harm,   [I shan't allow rising early to harm me]
Till ten or eleven I keep my bed warm;
Knitting and spinning I lay both aside,
The smoke of the kitchen I cannot abide.

You are a good housewife and careful to gain
A world of goods by travail and pain;
For all that you lose at night by your play,   [i.e. love-making]
You get it up again by sleeping all day.   [1 you recover; 2 your husband recovers
                                                                           his erection]

The majority of such verses are typically misogynist, and the 'curst' or 'shrewish' wife is the target of many such (and note in this next the traditional prejudice against the red-haired):

> A woman that is wilful is a plague of the worst,
> As good live in hell as with a wife that is curst

> Pick out a shrew that will serve you a choice,
> With a red head, a sharp nose, and a shrill voice.

The passage berating women at *Othello* 2.1.110ff is shown for the commonplace it is [Tilley W702] by its incidental (and incomplete) occurrence on one of these trenchers:

> A widow that is wanton, with a running head,   [giddy]
> Is a devil in the kitchen, and an ape in her bed.

Another writer of such 'trencher poetry' when composing couplets to accompany a now lost set painted with plants, could not resist, for 'pea', employing the suggestive word, 'peascod'; one A. M. R. published the couplet in question thus in no. 64 of the *Gentleman's Magazine* (1794):

> Peascods are restorative, and hardly found,
> When for [*] some women give a pound,

with a note that the asterisk replaced a word 'so indelicate that it is not worth supplying' – presumably the inverted 'codpieces'.

One such trencher couplet, not dated unfortunately, seems to come close to the title of one of Shakespeare's plays, perhaps strengthening the case for considering it – like so many others of that era – proverbial:

> Thy love that thou to one hast lent:
> In labour lost thy time was spent:[17]

More 'popular' writers like Brathwaite, however, were not above 'composing Posies upon bracelets' ['The Courtier' in *Strappado for the Devil* (1615), 128], and from *c*.1630 survives a broadside ballad entitled, '*A delicate new Ditty composed upon the Posie of a Ring being, "I fancy none but thee alone": sent as a New Year's Gift by a Lover to his Sweetheart.*' It is interesting to note that, even then, the literary elite lumped such posies together with the verses to be found on painted cloths and knives as beneath their dignity: Jonson has his sneer in *Every Man in his Humour* (1598), where the foolish Stephen is seen composing a ring-posy, 'The deeper the sweeter, I'll be judged by St Peter', and lamely explains that he put in the saint's name, 'to make up the metre' [2.4].

Knife-handles were another site for inscriptions, and we may recall Gratiano's contemptuous reference to the ring given him by Nerissa in *The Merchant of Venice* (5.1.147ff):

a hoop of gold, a paltry ring
That she did give me, whose posy was
For all the world like cutler's poetry
Upon a knife, 'Love me, and leave me not'

Real non-literary examples of such 'cutlers' poetry' include the following knife-handle inscription dated to the second quarter of the sixteenth century:

BETTER IT IS A POOR HOUSE TO HOLD
THAN TO LIE IN PRISON IN FETTERS OF GOLD[18]

From the very end of our period, the British Museum possesses a pair of wedding-knives dated 1676, one of which is inscribed

My Love is fixed I will not range,
I like my choice I will not change[19]

which must be one of the most popular of all amatory couplets and is later found, for example, embroidered on a pair of garters also bearing the date 1717 (but with a heart symbol in place of the word 'Love').[20] Another very popular inscription found on posy-rings (but also on a piece of Metropolitan slipware dated 1650)[21] is

The gift is small,
good will is all.

The earliest printed collection of such amatory posies appears to be *Love's garland, or Posies for Rings, Hand-Kerchieves, and Gloves, and such pretty Tokens that* Lovers send their Loves (1624), but earlier John Manningham jotted down some 'Posies for a jet ring lined with silver' in his diary. An ingenious semi-rebus type is included in *Cupid's Posies* (1642), and actually survives on a poke-dial found near Petworth:

The love is true that I.O.U.
As true to me then C.U.B.   [i.e. see you be]

Others use tiny images either to represent the word itself (e.g. a heart or a hand) or to suggest it (e.g. a skull = death). Seventy years ago Joan Evans catalogued a large number of posies both from manuscripts and the rings themselves,[22] and a few follow:

That heart that hopeth hath no rest.
If hope were not my heart would burst
(on a mid-sixteenth century. armillary-sphere ring found at Bodwrdda)

True Love hath led my heart to choose
My heart is dead if you refuse   [Harleian MS 6910, *c*.1596]

My joy will die
If you deny   [Sion College MS English 65, *c*.1605]

a wedding ring with this posy in it, viz.:

you have my heart
till death depart[23]   (1596–7)

Forever or never:
love is all   [ring in Museum of London]

Hurt not his heart
whose joy thou art   [ring found at Sullington, Sussex]

More utilitarian objects might also be inscribed – with more utilitarian messages: a pair of bellows bearing the date 1645 was inscribed

DO. YOUR. WORK. AS. WELL. AS. I
AND. YOU'LL. HAVE. FIRE. BY. AND. BY.[24]

A church bell formerly at Martham, Norfolk, and made by Thomas Brend in 1660 is inscribed:

God amend what is amiss
and send love where none is   (TB 1660)

– a proverbial sentiment only recorded earlier as the title or first line of a (lost) ballad entered in the *Stationers' Register* to John Allde in 1567/8.

Pottery of this period is frequently inscribed, but it can speak for itself: a Metropolitan slipware jug in the Museum of London reads

BREAK ME NOT PRAY IN YOUER HASTE   [NB: spelling seems to suggest
                                                                               your is]
FOR I TO NONE WILL GIVE DISTASTE 1645[25]   [to be pronounced as a disyllable
                                                                   as required by the couplet metre]

A beautiful majolica jug of *c*.1630, made at a pottery in Lambeth or Southwark, sounds like another lover's gift; a young man in the conventional melancholic pose – not unlike Hilliard's famous miniature of the young man amongst the roses – is surrounded by an inscription which reads:

I AM NO BEGGER I CANNOT CRAVE
YOU KNOW THE THING THAT I WOULD HAVE.[26]

However spiritually we may be inclined to interpret the 'thing' the young man would have, there can be no doubting the suggestiveness of the legend, *See my conny 1657*, on a mug in the Victoria and Albert Museum, with a rabbit [i.e. *con(e)y*] painted inside on the bottom which loomed into the drinker's view as the contents were drunk – a familiar period innuendo.[27]

Rather more wholesome is the inscription borne by a majolica plate made in London and dated 1600:

> THE ROSE IS RED THE LEAVES ARE GREEN
> GOD SAVE ELIZABETH OUR QUEEN.[28]

The earliest surviving samplers date from the latter part of our period, and include such verses as

> is my name,
> and with my nedell I rought the same,   [needle I wrought]
> and if my skil had beene better,
> I would have mended every letter[29]

evidenced on an American sampler of *c*.1630.

Weever's interest in *Ancient Funeral Monuments* (1631) reminds us that epitaphs, of course, frequently consist of short poignant verses, and one such is recorded on the Judd funeral monument (1560):

> THE WORD OF GOD
> HATH KNIT US TWAIN
> AND DEATH SHALL US
> DIVIDE AGAIN

Many of the verses we call nursery rhymes are of some antiquity. Although, of the 550 rhymes in the *Oxford Dictionary of Nursery Rhymes*, the Opies were able to trace only a very few (mostly riddles) as far back as the late middle ages, almost a quarter of the rhymes were known before 1600, and half of the 550 by 1700. Certainly of seventeenth-century date, for example, is *I do not love thee Dr Fell*, and although political and personal satires are far rarer than some popular authors have claimed, *Jack Spratt* may ridicule a seventeenth-century Archdeacon Pratt, and the couplet

> Cocka doodle dooe,
> Peggy hath lost her shooe

is found in *The Most Cruel And Bloody Murder.* (1606), and is probably the opening of a bawdy ballad, 'losing one's shoe', being an earlier idiom for 'losing one's virginity', when used of women. Although – like the reference to the master's lost 'fiddling stick' of the following couplet of 'Cock-a-doodle-doo' – 'I had a little nut-tree' is not recorded before the late eighteenth century, it too may well be a sexual innuendo, when we consider the close verbal parallels with an early fifteenth-century erotic lyric, 'I have a new garden':

> In the midst of my garden is a pear-tree set
> and it will no pear bear but a St John's pear
> The fairest maid of this town prayed me
> to give her a graft of my pear tree

The singer gives the maid a good 'grafting', and twenty weeks later she gives birth. A couplet in the Skeltonic *Image of Hypocrisy* (c.1533) seems similarly familiar:

> As wise as a gander,
> Wots not where to wander   [knows]

appearing to adumbrate 'Goosey, goosey gander', which the Opies could not find before 1784.

In Wager's *The Longer thou livest the more fool thou art* (written c.1559), Moros enters singing snatches of songs he was taught by his mother's maid as he used to sit on her lap and – by way of excuse – says, *Such pretty things would soon be gone, If I should not sometime them remember*. He sings a fragment of one song which is not known again until printed in an early nineteenth century nursery-rhyme book:

> Tom-a-lin and his wife, and his wife's mother
> They went over a bridge all three together,
> The bridge was broken, and they fell in,
> 'The Devil go with all!' quoth Tom-a-lin.

'John Cook's mare' is also hinted at in Moros's 'I laid my bridle upon the shelf, If you will any more sing it your self' – implying two and a half centuries' survival in the oral tradition – and 'Broom broom on Hill', also alluded to by Moros, is included amongst Captain Cox's *ballets and songs, all ancient* (1575). The 'inexpressibility topos' represented by 'If all the world were paper', is first found in print in *Wit's Recreations* 1641, but not found in print again until 1810, which suggests it was kept alive by the oral tradition through the intervening two and a half centuries; a similar period in the solely oral tradition is inferred for a verse collected by Halliwell in 1842, 'I went to the toad that lies under the wall, I charmed him out, and he came at my call', which is only known earlier as spoken by one of the witches in Jonson's *Masque of Queens* (1609). A catch given in the play the *Pinder of Wakefield* (1632), 'The hart he loves the high wood', is similarly not heard of again until 1846.

Painted cloths, a cheap substitute for tapestry, are another genre of artefact almost entirely neglected by scholars – admittedly very few are extant – but their ubiquity, as confirmed by the evidence of inventories, for example, means that an ignorance of their iconography and literary content seriously misrepresents the popular visual culture of the era. A lengthy passage in William Bullein's *A Dialogue against the fever Pestilence* (1564)[30] records 'a comely parlour, very neatly and trimly apparelled, London-like, the windows . . . well glazed, and fair cloths with many wise sayings painted upon them . . . in golden letters', several of which he goes on to specify. The sententiousness of such verses had already fallen from favour amongst the elite by the end of the sixteenth century, so that it should not surprise us to find John Hoskins in his *Directions for Speech and Style* (1599), asking rhetorically, 'why should the writers of these days imprison themselves in the straitness of these maxims? . . . and doth not he vouchsafe to use them that [are called] posies conned from goldsmith's rings'.[31] A similar disdain is implied in *The Rape of Lucrece* (1594),

> Who fears a sentence or an old man's saw   [proverb]
> Shall by a painted cloth be kept in awe,

and it is an opinion voiced elsewhere by Shakespeare, in Jaques' sparring with Orlando, in *As You Like It* (written *c*.1599):

> J: You are full of pretty answers; have you not been acquainted with goldsmiths' wives and conned them out of rings?
> O: Not so; but I answer you right painted cloth, from whence you have studied your questions.

In similarly dismissive vein, the vastly learned Robert Burton in his *Anatomy of Melancholy* (1621) concludes a long list of entirely serious maxims and adages with 'Look for more in Isocrates, Seneca, Plutarch, Epictetus, etc., and for defect, consult with cheese-trenchers and painted cloths'.[32] John Taylor the Water Poet, who may surely be termed a popular writer, lodged at an inn called the Star in Rye in 1653, as he records in *The certain travels*, and records five such sententious couplets from painted cloths:

> And as upon a bed I musing lay,
> The chamber hanged with painted cloth, I found
> My self with sentences beleaguered round . . .
> Thus truly, lying, I transcribed them all
> *No flower so fresh, but frost may it deface,*
> *None sits so fast, but he may lose his place:*
> *'Tis Concord keeps a realm in stable stay,*
> *But Discord brings all kingdoms to decay.*
> *No subject ought (for any kind of cause)*
> *Resist his prince, but yield him to the laws.*
> *Sure God is just, whose stroke, delayed long,*
> *Doth light at last, with pain more sharp, and strong,*   [alight]

> *Time never was, nor ne'er I think shall be,*
> *That Truth (unshent) might speak, in all things free.*   [unharmed]
> . . . And 'tis supposed, those lines written there
> Have in that room been, more than 40 year

In Sir Thomas More's house when he was a boy was a 'goodly hanging of fine painted cloth, with nine pageants on the Ages of Man', and *c.*1490 the young More composed 'verses over every of those pageants', which were duly printed in Rastell's 1557 edition of his English works.[33]

We do not know much about the *latrinalia* and other graffiti of this period, but there is no reason to suspect they differed much in kind from their modern descendants. Graffiti were not above the notice of Sir Thomas More, either, who coyly cites the following example in his *Treatise . . . upon these words of holy Scripture, Memorare novissima* (1522):

> Men are wont to write a short riddle on the wall, that DC hath no P. Rede [interpret] ye this riddle I cannot: but I have heard say, that it toucheth the readiness that woman hath to fleshly filth, if she fall in drunkenness. And if ye find one that can declare it, though it be no great authority, yet have I heard say that it is very true.[34]

and 'A drunken cunt has no porter' is still listed as one of Howell's *Proverbs or Old Said-Saws and Adages in the English Tongue* published in 1659. In much the same vein, Lovewit complains of 'Madame, with a Dildo, writ o' the walls' in Jonson's *Alchemist* (1610), a presumably bawdy rhyme (unless a pictorial graffito – *writ* still retaining the possible sense, 'scratched, incised' at this period). In a more respectable vein, a glass quarry formerly at Smither's Farmhouse, Sutton, Essex, was inscribed with the dates 1581 and 1594, some initials, and the legend:

> I favour as I find
> And love as I like

both lines are to be found (albeit separately) amongst the list of ring-posies written in a commonplace book of *c.*1596.[35]

More earnest verses were, of course, inscribed more officially on walls. In the first decade of the seventeenth century, John Smyth, estate steward, at North Nibley, Gloucestershire, jotted down a list of 'moral notes and sayings' to be painted 'above the wainscot' in his house, including,

> They that perceive not deceit are often deceived themselves
> Crows will not peck a man till he be dead, but flatterers
>   will devour a man being alive

Happy is he that wooeth virtue, but more happy is he that is contracted to her.[36] Dating from *c.*1597, another sentiment also on Smyth's list is still extant on the wall of a farmhouse at Bazings, Sussex:

For he that will not hear the cry of them that stand in need
Shall cry himself and not to be heard when he doth hope to speed.

Among published authors, it is perhaps the verse of the East Anglian farmer, Thomas Tusser, which best represents the sort with which we are concerned here, and, indeed, in his *The points of housewifery* (1570) he includes sample *Posies for the parlour*, *Posies for the guests' chamber*, *Husbandly posies for the hall*, and decidedly pious *Posies for thine own bed chamber*. In the presumably 'comely decked guest-room', Tusser's guests were greeted by

The sloven and the careless man, the roinish nothing nice,   [scabby, scurvy]
To lodge in chamber comely decked, are seldom suffered twice.

With curtain some make scabbard clean, with coverlet their shoe,
All dirt and mire some wallow bed, as spaniels use to do.   (dirty the bed as
                                                                                     spaniels do)

It is to be hoped they could take such broad hints as to appropriate behaviour.

A significant proportion of the popular verse produced during our period had a mnemonic function – Tusser's *Five hundred points of good husbandry* (1573) is the classic example of this habit of mind, and the fact that much of it is arranged according to the agricultural yearly round no co-incidence, for mastering the calendar has long taxed the ingenuity of popular versifiers. Even today, we still recite *sotto voce* an only slightly modernized version of this verse, found already in a fifteenth century manuscript:

Thirty days hath November
April June and September
Of eight-and-twenty is but one
And all the remnant thirty and one

and later in Holinshed's *Chronicles* (1577). The absolute apogee of ingenuity, however, must surely be granted to the *Cisiojanus*, a set of mnemonic verses, one for each month of the year, more or less sensible, and designed to recall the feasts of the Church calendar; the example excerpted here was published in a Book of Hours printed for the English market by Regnault in Paris in 1527:

MARCH:
Da.vid.of.Wales.lo.veth.well.leeks.   [1st, St David]
That.will.make.Gre.go.ry.lean.cheeks.   [12th, St Gregory the Great]
if.Ed.ward.do.eat.some.with.them.   [18th, St Edward King and Martyr]
Ma.ry.send.him.to.Bed.lem.   [25th, Feast of the Annunciation]

APRIL:

In.A.pril.Am.brose.is.fain.	[4th, St Ambrose + St Isidore [is]]
To.see.us.wa.shed.with.rain.	[15th, Oswald of Worcester, translation]
Os.wald.forth.with.sent.vic.tore.	[20th, Pope Victor]
With.George.and.Mark.to.do.so.no.more.[37]	[23rd, St George; 25th, St Mark]

According to Deloney's set of rules for the 'gentle craft', as well as being able to 'bear his part in a three-man's song', the cobbler must also be able to readily 'reckon up his tools in rhyme[38] and such a verse composition listing all the tools of the trade, opening 'Listen lords verament [verily]', does indeed survive from the beginning of our period, in a late fifteenth-century manuscript,[39] while a similar rehearsal of the tools of his trade (though politicised) is given in a ballad entitled 'The Cobbler's Last Will and Testament', printed *c*.1660.

Blason populaire is a folklorists' term which includes rhymes about particular localities and their inhabitants. Howell's *Proverbs* (1659) and Fuller's *Worthies* (published posthumously in 1662) are two of the earliest sources to record such material. Rivers' reputations are summed up in the following couplets:

> Between Trent-fall and Whitten-ness,   [Yorkshire, the Humber]
> Many are made widows and fatherless

as is the unsavoury reputation of

> Salisbury Plain,
> Never without a thief or twain.

Similarly uncomplimentary are rhymes of the sort which seem first to have been published by Ray in his *Collection of English Proverbs* (1670), but which we may presume were around earlier, and purport to itemize the characteristics of the inhabitants of various towns and villages in a particular county, such as these two referring to Essex and Suffolk respectively:

> Beckles for the Puritan
> Bungay for the poor,
> Halesworth for a drunkard
> and Bilborough for a whore.

Traditional epithets for the inhabitants of particular counties, e.g. 'Wiltshire moonrakers', 'Hampshire hogs', etc., also emerge during our period, several being found as early as *c*.1500 in a poem on the counties of England.

There was something almost numinous, an aura of magic perhaps, that still hung about the use of rhyme in our era, and we mistake if we take Rosalind's sophisticated reference to being 'never so berhymed since Pythagoras' time that I was an Irish rat', as representative of contemporary popular attitudes to rhymed blessings and cursings.[40] The 'White Paternoster' is a charm which survived into this century as a children's prayer. Writing in *A Candle in the Dark* (1656), Thomas Ady noted that 'An old woman in Essex who . . . had lived . . . in Queen Mary's time, had learned thence many Popish Charms, one whereof was this; every night when she lay down to sleep she charmed her Bed, saying;

> Matthew, Mark, Luke and John,
> The Bed be blest that I lie on.'[41]

The apocalyptic feel of a charm recorded in mid-seventeenth century Devon, must strike us at this distance as bathetic, when we learn that it was used merely to relieve a scald:

> Two angels came from the West.
> The one brought fire, the other brought frost.
> Out fire! In frost!
> In the name of the Father, Son and Holy Ghost[42]

but there are hundreds more such unaccountably neglected charms still to be found in manuscripts.

Like most other genres of popular orality, the riddle is not one we look on with much favour today, yet riddle collections were published throughout our period, beginning with the *Demands Joyous* printed by Wynkyn de Worde in 1511 (much of it translated from a late fifteenth-century French collection), which contains all the usual obscenity and curiously post-modern wit associated with the genre, e.g. 'Which was first the hen or the egg?' Riddles are to be found, of course, scattered incidentally throughout the literature of the period. The grave-digger in *Hamlet* (1601), for example, poses the riddle, 'What is he that builds stronger than either the mason, the shipwright or the carpenter?'and his interlocutor does well to respond with 'The gallows-maker; for that frame outlives a thousand tenants?' However, the grave-digger is not satisfied with this solution and eventually solves the riddle himself: 'a grave-maker. The houses he makes last till Doomsday.'

What was the *Book of Riddles* that Master Slender lent to Alice Shortcake in the opening scene of the *Merry Wives of Windsor*? The earliest extant edition of the *Book of Merry Riddles* was printed *c*.1600, but was not the first, and Shakespeare might well have known it.

In 1939 J. J. Graham published a book of local folklore entitled *Weardale* and in it included this riddle which he had collected orally:

> Little bird of paradise,
> She works her work both neat and nice;
> She pleases God, she pleases man,
> She doe the work that no man can,

last published in the seventeenth century in the *Book of Merry Riddles* (1631), but even earlier in the first printed English riddle-book of 1511 in the form

> What is it that is a wright and is no man,
> and he doth that no man can,
> and yet it serveth both god and man?

Randle Holme copied another oral version of this bee-riddle into his manuscript collection *c*.1645.

Riddles have always gone in for the scatological and the *risqué*, and riddlers seem particularly to enjoy the 'catch riddle' in which the guesser is embarrassed into refusing to offer the indecent solution, only to be rebuked by the riddler, who offers some innocuous answer, for being so dirty-minded. A classic instance of this technique is to be found in a typically unhealthy erotic exchange between Ferdinand and his sister, the Duchess of Malfi, in Webster's eponymous play published in 1614:

> FERDINAND: Women like that part, which, like the lamprey, Hath never a bone in't.
> DUCHESS: Fie, sir!
> FERDINAND: Nay, I mean the tongue . . . Farewell, lusty widow.

Extraordinarily, the 'boneless beast' would appear to be an erotic motif of Indo-European antiquity.

Nonsense verse is a perhaps understandably neglected genre,[43] but one which, paradoxically, has something to teach us. It is a truism that it is very difficult to write complete nonsense, that fragments of sense will, as it were, keep breaking through; and nonsense has its own clichés. The Tudor playwright-publisher John Rastell seems to have had an affection for such verse, and in his *Nature of the Four Elements* (1520), Yngnoraunce sings a song which opens

> Robin Hood in Barnsdale stood
> And lent him to a maple thistle,
> Then came our lady and sweet Saint Andrew,
> Sleep'st thou, wak'st thou, Geoffrey Coke?

The final line of this opening stanza recurs in a round or canon printed in Ravenscroft's *Pammelia* (1609), but the verses were discovered written in a roughly contemporary hand on a mid-fifteenth century fragmentary Exchequer Issue roll.[44] The same issue roll also contains a scrap of sixteenth-century verse of an – at first sight – apparently similar nature:

To-morrow alleluia shall be locked	[see MED s.v. to lock alleluia; during
And in the stocks fast stocked	Lent the 'Alleluia' is not sung; it is sung
fast by the legs,	again at Easter which marks the end of
he shall never come out of sorrow	Lent, i.e. of the period during which

till goose and pigs be his borrow, (security)   meat and dairy produce may not be
butter cheese and eggs   eaten]

This apparent nonsense is not nonsense at all, but a valuable scrap of tradition relating to popular English attitudes towards the dietary restrictions of Lent with its
'Lenten fare'. It is a matter for regret that none of the rhymes 'set forth to deprave
Lent' reported by Bishop Gardiner in 1547 have survived, nor *Jack of Lent's testament*
which he complains is aimed at him and being openly sold in Winchester market,[45]
mock-testaments being another most entertaining and usually satiric verse-type.[46]
Entered in the *Stationers' Register* on 15 February 1636 were 'Lent and Shrovetide with
verses to them by John Taylor, Two Pictures' which survive as a pair of engraved prints
[see figures 16 and 17] – English representatives of the European 'Battle of Carnival
and Lent' tradition familiar from Bruegel's great painting. Curiously, the woodcut on
the title-page of Taylor's *Jack a Lent* (1620) which shows this personification of Lent
as an emaciated figure riding on a herring behind a fat Shrove Tuesday [figure 18],
derives not from this painting but from another of Bruegel's works, the engraved print
of his 'Thin Kitchen'.

That historians of English literature have not for the most part been familiar with
the sort of popular verse discussed here is not a testimony to their refinement but to
an ignorance which has compounded the suppression of a popular culture available to
both high and low, and seriously distorted our modern perception of the era, and, if
much of what is snapped up here is unconsidered, it is far from being all trifling.

NOTES

1   But see my 'The Parodic Sermon in Medieval
    and Early Modern England', *Medium Aevum*
    66 (1997), 94–114; 'The Abbot of Evil
    Profits (1530)' [edition and commentary
    of a mock-proclamation], *Medieval English
    Theatre* 20 (2000). I am currently preparing
    an edition of a newly discovered English
    version of *The Pig's Last Will and Testament*.

2   Ed A. B. Grosart, *The Works in Verse and Prose
    of Nicholas Breton* (Edinburgh, 1879), ii, j,
    p. 6.

3   Fox, A. (1992), pp. 211–12, 224.

4   Ed. J. Stokes and R. J. Alexander, *Somerset.
    I The Records* (Records of Early English
    Drama) (Toronto, 1996), 24 (Bath,
    1614–15).

5   Ed. Somerset, J. A. B., *Shropshire. 1 The
    Records* (Records of Early English Drama),
    (Toronto, 1994), 69 (Llansilin, 1612).

6   Fox, (1994), 78 (Trent, Som., 1616 PRO
    STAC8/42/14).

7   Fox (1992), p. 206ff (Worcestershire, 1605).

8   Ed. J. Stokes and R. J. Alexander, *Somerset.
    I The Records* (Records of Early English
    Drama), (Toronto, 1996), 35 (Berkley,
    1611–12); see further, Ingram, 1998 and
    1984; M. Ingram., 'Juridical Folklore in
    England Illustrated by Rough Music' in
    C. W. Brooks and M. Lobban (eds), *Commu-
    nities and Courts in Britain, 1150–1900*
    (London and Rio Grande, 1997), 61–82.

9   The whole affair has been masterfully recon-
    structed by N. J. O'Conor, as 'The Dymoke
    Case', in *Godes Peace and the Queenes* (London,
    1934), ch. 6, 108–26.

10 *OED* citations for *heteroclite* adj., sense 2, and
    heteroclital, show that the three earliest cita-
    tions of these words, all belonging to the

final decade of the sixteenth century, are associated with the figure of the fool.

11 Printed in T. Wright and J. O. Halliwell, *Reliquiae Antiquae* (London, 1841), I. 250ff.

12 C. Limbert, 'Two Poems and a Prose Receipt' in *English Literary Renaissance*, 16 (1986), 383–90, esp. 390.

13 Cit. K. Thomas, *Religion and the Decline of Magic* (London, 1971), 478.

14 P. Clark 'Popular Protest and Disturbance in Kent, 1558–1640', *Economic History Review* 29 (1976), 369–70.

15 See *OED wisp* n. 1, sense 2b 'A twist or figure of straw for a scold to rail at', and citations: *He writhed a litell wipse of strawe, and sette it afore her, and saide, ladi, yef that ye will chide more, chide with that straw.* [*Knight de la Tour Landry* (1450), xv. 21]; *Women Whose tatling tongues, had won a wispe* [Drant, *Horace, Satires* (1566) vii. D 7 b]; Shakespeare, *3 Hen. VI* (1593), ii. ii. 144; *Theres nothing mads her* [sc. a scold] *more then but the very naming of a wispe* [H. Parrot, *Cures for the Itch* (1626), B 5 b].

16 See the fuller discussion in *The English Print c.1550–c.1650*.

17 See J. Florio, *First Frutes* (1578), 71: *it were labour lost to speake of Loue*; and see further R. W. Dent, *Shakespeare's Proverbial Language An Index* (Berkeley, 1981), L551.1.

18 *Masterpieces of Cutlery and the Art of Eating* (Victoria and Albert Museum, London, 1979), cat. no. 15, from a private collection. There is only one other known instance of this proverbial couplet, found scribbled in the margin of a manuscript of Hoccleve's verse a generation or so earlier.

19 Evans, xix, n. 2.

20 Reproduced as pl. 12 in M. Spufford, *The Great Reclothing of Rural England* (London, 1984).

21 J. E. Hodgkin *Examples of Early English Pottery* (London, 1891), 25.

22 Evans; the earliest example is in the 1596 Harleian MS 6910: 'Though a guifte be smale, yet good will is all.'

23 Cit. O'Hara, 'The Language of Tokens' in *Rural History*, 3 (1992), 1–40. For the second line, see *Book of Common Prayer, Matrimony* (1548–9): *Till death vs departe* [altered to *do part* in 1662].

24 Reported in *Proceedings of the Society of Antiquaries*, 2 (1849–53), 215.

25 B. Rackham and Read, figure 55.

26 Ibid., plate V.

27 For a full discussion, see M. Jones, 'Folklore Motifs in Late Medieval Art III: Erotic Animal Imagery', *Folklore*, 102 (1991), 192–219.

28 For this rhyme see Opie and Opie, no. 417.

29 E. S. Bolton and E. J. Coe, *American Samplers* (Boston, 1921), no. 128

30 I hope shortly to publish a discussion of this passage.

31 Ed. H. H. Hudson, *John Hoskins, Direction for Speech and Style* (Princeton, 1935), 39–40.

32 Ed. H. Jackson, *Robert Burton. The Anatomy of Melancholy* (London, 1932), Pt. 2 Sec. 3 Mem. 8.

33 Ed. W. E. Campbell et al., *The English Works of Thomas More* (London, 1931), I. 332–5.

34 B. J. Whiting and H. W. Whiting, *Proverbs, Sentences, and Proverbial Phrases from English Writings Mainly before 1500* (Cambridge, MA, 1968), C619.

35 Cit. B. Hooper, 'Graffiti on Windows' in *FLS News*, 30 (November 1999), 11, from *Transactions of the Essex Archaeological Society* NS 5 (1895), 72.

36 *Social History* 12 (1987), 326–8.

37 The most recent full discussion of this class of text is by R. M. Kully, 'Cisiojanus. Studien zur mnemonischen Literatur anhand des spätmittelalterlichen Kalender-gedichts' in *Schweizerisches Archiv für Volkskunde*, 70 (1974), 93–123.

38 Cit. B. Pattison, *Music and Poetry of the English Renaissance* (London, 1948), 286.

39 Published as *A Shoemaker's Verse Testament* by E. Wilson in *Notes and Queries. New Series* (1980).

40 Shakespeare, *As You Like It* (1600), iii. ii. 186, and Jonson, *Poetaster* 'An Apologetical Dialogue', line 163. See further, D. Gray, 'Rough Music: Some Early Invectives and Flytings', in C. Rawson and J. Mezciems (eds), *English Satire and the Satiric Tradition*, (Oxford, 1984), 21–43.

41 Opie and Opie, 303.

42 K. Thomas, *Religion and the Decline of Magic*

(London, 1971), 212, citing F. Glanvile et al., *The Tavistocke Naboth proved Nabal* (1658), 40–1.

43 But now see Malcolm (1998), which at long last specifically addresses the nonsense verse of the seventeenth century.

44 J. C. Holt and T. Takamiya, 'A New Version of "A rhyme of Robin Hood"' in *English Manuscript Studies*, 1 (1989), 213–21.

45 Cit. Baskervill, 47.

46 For which, down to 1565, see E. Wilson, '*The Testament of the Buck* and the sociology of the text', in *Review of English Studies*, New Series 45 (1994), 157–84.

REFERENCES AND FURTHER READING

Baskervill, C. R. (1929). *The Elizabethan Jig and Related Song Drama*. Chicago: Chicago University Press.

Edwards, A. S. E. (1997). 'Middle English Inscriptional Verse Texts'. In J. Scattergood and J. Boffey (eds), *Texts and their Contexts* (pp. 26–43). Dublin: Four Courts Press.

Evans, J. (1931). *English Posies and Posy Rings*. London: Oxford University Press.

Fox, A. (1992). 'Aspects of Oral Culture and Its Development in Early Modern England', unpublished PhD thesis, Cambridge University.

——(1994). 'Ballads, Libels and Popular Ridicule in Jacobean England', *Past and Present*, 145, 47–83.

Gowing, L. (1993). 'Gender and the Language of Insult in Early Modern London', *History Workshop Journal*, 35, 1–21.

Ingram, M. (1984). 'Ridings, Rough Music and the "Reform of Popular Culture" in Early Modern England', *Past and Present*, 105, 79–113.

——(1988). 'Ridings, Rough Music and Mocking Rhymes in Early Modern England'. In B. Reay (ed.), *Popular Culture in Seventeenth-century England* (pp. 166–97). London: Routledge.

Jones, M. (1997). 'The Parodic Sermon in Medieval and Early Modern England', *Medium Aevum*, 66, 94–114.

Malcolm, N. (1998). *The Origins of English Nonsense*. London: Fontana.

Northall, G. F. (1892). *English Folk-rhymes*. London: Kegan Paul and Co.

Opie, I. and Opie, P. (1975). *Oxford Dictionary of Nursery Rhymes*. Oxford: Oxford University Press.

Rackham, B. and Read, H. E. (1924). *English Pottery: Its Development from Early Times to the End of the Eighteenth Century*. London: Ernest Benn.

Simpson, C. M. (1966). *The British Broadside Ballad and its Music*. New Brunswick: Rutgers University Press.

Willcock, G. D. and Walker, A. (1589; 1936). *The Arte of English Poesie*. Cambridge: Cambridge University Press.

Sisson, C. J. (1936). *Lost Plays of Shakespeare's Age*. Cambridge: Cambridge University Press, esp. pp. 184–185 for Wells May Day verses.

Tilley, M. P. (1950). *A Dictionary of the Proverbs in England in the Sixteenth and Seventeenth Centuries*. Ann Arbor: University of Michigan Press.

Wurzbach, N. (1990). *The Rise of the English Street-ballad 1550–1650*. Cambridge: Cambridge University Press.

39

Local and 'Customary' Drama

Thomas Pettitt

Renaissance England saw the emergence, out of local, customary traditions, of the professional skills, practices and ambitions that ultimately become the national, commercial, 'popular', theatre of Marlowe and Shakespeare. But in their time the detachment never became absolute, and in 1591 we find Samuel Cox, secretary to Sir Christopher Hatton, wishing that the trend could be reversed:

> that players would use themselves nowadays, as in ancient former times they have done, which was only to exercise their interludes in the time of Christmas, beginning to play in the holidays and continuing until twelfth tide, or at the furthest until Ash Wednesday.

Alongside 'such as were in wages with the king', Cox correctly identifies the two major classes of players under the older dispensation and the local, customary auspices of their performance. The first were household players:

> such as pertained to noblemen, and were ordinary servants in their house, and only for Christmas times used such plays, without making any profession to be players to go abroad for gain.

the second had community affiliations:

> certain artisans in good towns and great parishes, as shoemakers, tailors, and such like, that used to play either in their town-halls, or some time in churches, to make the people merry.[1]

The story of the professional players and their popular theatre will be told elsewhere in this volume: here it is those antecedent, but persisting traditions of household and community theatre which are the focus of attention. Their significance lies both in their persistence, as a characteristic feature of English Renaissance culture, and in the persistence with which dramatists inserted material of this kind (mummings, masques, May-games, morris dances) into stage plays: a topic which with regret, and with one major exception, has not been included here. In this field the distinction between theatre, pageantry and folklore is largely anachronistic: most late-medieval drama (and most medieval and Renaissance pageantry) was 'customary' in the sense of being performed as, or in the context of, a traditional, recurrent observance or activity, be it a seasonal festival or an occasional celebration, and it is also a feature of its embeddedness in custom that this drama as often as not comprises less or other than a fully fledged, rounded play involving the achievement of a distinct, fictional play-world.

Disruptions and Continuities: Miracles, Mysteries and Moralities

It is in the nature of tradition both to persist through time and change over time, but the sixteenth century saw more abrupt dislocations than usual. However given the affiliation of local, customary drama to wider social and cultural activities, including Christian worship and celebration, the Reformation (on which see Patrick Collinson's chapter (3) in this volume) inevitably had a vastly more decisive impact than the Renaissance, whose major contributions (say the influence of classical authors) occurred more within the emerging theatre as an independent cultural system. The Edwardian regime in particular, in its doctrinal extremism and its liturgical interventions effectively destroyed the quintessentially medieval and Catholic miracle plays (enactments of the lives, martyrdoms and miracles of saints, or miracles achieved by the host); and in putting down guilds and votive lights it similarly destroyed the institutional auspices, the physical context and the *raison d'être* of numerous customary observances. Those that survived faced a new barrage of attacks from the Elizabethan Puritans. In the seventeenth century there was some alleviation through royal support expressed in the *Book of Sports* of 1618 and 1633, but the attacks culminated in the cataclysm of the mid-century Civil War and the Cromwellian interregnum: village wakes and church ales were prohibited, maypoles destroyed, Christmas abolished. After a brief resuscitation to welcome the Restoration of the monarchy in 1660, the older customs survived, if at all, without the benefit of official, institutional auspices, in the unofficial, plebeian traditions destined to be rediscovered as 'popular antiquities' and 'folklore' by the educated elite in the eighteenth and nineteenth centuries.

Against this background the great mystery cycles, and the tradition of civic plays of which they were the apotheosis, despite additional stresses from the demographic and economic crises of sixteenth-century urban communities, impress by the obstinacy with which they persisted. Compromising with metropolitan politics and theology where necessary (for example in cutting deferential references to the Pope and plays on the Virgin Mary), this essentially provincial tradition survived in several places into the 1570s, and in remote Kendal (Westmorland) just made it into the seventeenth century. The strength of commitment to civic cycle-plays in Coventry led briefly in the 1580s and 1590s to experiments replacing the biblical plays with more secular material: the Destruction of Jerusalem; the Conquest of the Danes; the History of King Edward the Fourth.

But while the mystery cycles finally succumbed, leaving only occasional memories (for example Hamlet's complaint that an overdone acting style 'out-Herods Herod'), the flexibility evinced by the morality plays, combined with their association, as 'moral interludes', with household players, ensured both their persistence and their influence on the emerging popular theatre. The medieval, Catholic paradigm of a mankind figure influenced by agents of redemption (mainly personified virtues) and damnation (vices), succumbing to temptation but ultimately repenting and finding salvation through confession and penance (as in *Mankind*, rather than the more celebrated but atypical *Everyman*), could be adapted to other topics and beliefs: how a king should rule his kingdom (*Magnificence*); Reformation polemics (*Lusty Juventus*; *Respublica*); education (*Wit and Science*); Calvinist doctrines on predestination (i.e. dual mankind figures, respectively saved and damned, as in *The Trial of Treasure*). The morality apparatus could also be combined with an existing narrative (*Cambises*), which brings us within reach of Marlowe's *Doctor Faustus*, and the morality's characteristic vice-figure pursued a highly successful independent career on the Elizabethan stage.

These major genres (mystery plays and moralities), although the date of the surviving texts and contextual evidence would qualify them (at least chronologically) as Renaissance drama, are conventionally treated under medieval theatre, and their influence on the emerging professional stage is explored in Michael O'Connell's essay in this volume. The focus here will therefore be on less familiar (but perhaps more typical) forms. It is also appropriate that these be presented not in terms of their literary genre (as determined by content), but in relation to the customary auspices in which they featured.

Household Theatre and Custom

As Samuel Cox observed, traditional entertainments within households showed an incidence clustering around the series of great midwinter festivals at Christmastide, but analogous customary revelry would make an out-of-season appearance at major life-cycle celebrations within the household concerned, particularly weddings. Such revels would have taken place in the hall that was the central room in most dwellings, with the pastimes and entertainments, at least the seasonal ones, organized by a lord of misrule, appointed by the householder for the season, or in some cases chosen by lot for a given festival.

At almost any social level, such a household group, under festive auspices, would play traditional games, ranging from contests of physical strength and skill to almost unstructured horseplay, for which the standard term seems to have been 'gambols'. Some had a mimetic element qualifying them as simple forms of customary drama, for example the game called 'shoeing' or sometimes 'riding' the 'mare' (or 'wild mare'), frequently mentioned in Renaissance evocations of Christmas revelry. One participant was designated as the mare, whom others as riders or blacksmiths were to attempt ride or shoe: evidently a token mimetic frame for a rough and tumble. Rather more complex is the combat game known (in later tradition) as 'skewer the goose' of which we have a precious early account as a 'gambol' (*jocum sive gambolium*) performed during the Christmas revels of an Elizabethan gentleman's household in County Down, Ireland, in 1602:

> Two servants squatted on the ground in the way women do . . . when they defecate in open field . . . Their hands were tied together so that they embraced their knees between them, and a stick was placed between the bend of their arms and legs so that they could not move their arms in any way. Between forefinger and thumb of each hand they held a certain small stick of about a foot in length and sharpened at the further end. These two servants are placed in the following way: one faces the other at about an ell's distance. When these things have been arranged, the two start to approach each other, and tackling with his feet, each tries to topple his opponent; for once thrown over he can never recover himself, but he offers his backside to be prodded with the small stick previously mentioned.[2]

The household accounts of Princess Mary for 1522 record a payment of 8d to 'a man of Windsor, for killing of a calf before my Lady's grace behind a cloth': since it persisted (as 'Killing the Calf') into the late eighteenth century, we know this – an entertainment rather than a pastime – comprised a dialogue-with-sound-effects (performed by a single man hidden behind a curtain or door) between a butcher and his reluctant victim.[3]

Given the longevity of these two examples (and the private nature of the tradition) it is very likely that the semi-dramatic games recorded in the nineteenth century at English harvest homes and (notoriously) Irish lyke-wakes [night-time vigils by the corpse between death and funeral] preserve earlier traditions. They, together with some early texts suggest Elizabethan households also saw the performance of wooing games or dance-songs with a clear distribution of roles and dialogue between a girl and her suitor, say 'Joan and John', perhaps in the manner of children's wooing games and dance-songs.

There is likely to have been an uncertain boundary (and perhaps a history of development) between the more elaborate of such dramatic games and entertainments and the 'interlude' which features in these same household auspices in the sixteenth century. George Puttenham's *The Wooer*, which he explicitly terms an 'Enterlude', does not survive as a whole, but to judge from the summary and extract he gives to illustrate a couple of points in his *Arte of English Poesie* (1589), it must have been closely related to the traditional wooing gambols:

the country clown came and wooed a young maid of the city, and being aggrieved to
come so often, and not to have his answer, said to the old nurse very impatiently.

    Iche ['I' in stage Mummerset] pray you good mother tell our young dame,
    Whence I am come and what is my name,
    I cannot come a wooing every day.
Quoth the nurse.
    They be lubbers not lovers that so use to say.[4]

The relationship is also underlined by the tendency of the more conventionally dramatic interludes to encompass simpler gambols (sometimes apologised for as 'toys').
For example Henry Medwall's celebrated *Fulgens and Lucres* (1495), despite its humanist message on the nature of true nobility, incorporates, under the name of 'fart prick
in cule [buttocks]', the skewer the goose combat mentioned earlier, as a mock joust
between two servants competing for the favours of a servant-girl. Thanks to an
enhanced awareness of contextual perspectives and the increasing availability of historical records, there has been considerable success of late in providing persuasive
argument or evidence for the original production of individual late-medieval and
sixteenth-century interludes in specific noble or institutional households.

An interlude, however, was rarely performed alone. Given its revels context it
would need a good strong 'presentation' (at the least a spoken prologue) to gain attention and to transform the revellers into an audience, and it was also often followed by
a sub-dramatic spectacle for which the contemporary term was 'disguising'. In the
instructions set down for the conduct of the household of the Earls of Northumberland in the early sixteenth century, the disguising, following the play presented before
the Lord and Lady in the hall at Twelfth Night, is specified as comprising the entry,
accompanied by torchbearers, of the disguisers, and their (many) dances, interrupted
by a separate group of morris dancers, who come on concealed in a tower or other
device, emerge from it, perform, and withdraw again.[5] But no amount of scholarly
reconstruction can match the living recreation by that first and highly perceptive
student of local, customary drama, William Shakespeare, at the end of *A Midsummer
Night's Dream*. Shorn of the quirks deriving from other agendas, the show performed
by the Mechanicals of the city for the wedding revels of their Duke resolves itself into
the classic three-part sequence of presentation (the spoken prologue, the parading on
of the characters and their description), interlude ('Pyramus and Thisbe') and disguising (the 'bergomask' which will have comprised a spectacular and probably
grotesque display by – evidently masked – dancers).[6]

Community Theatre and Custom

Communities, as Cox infers, did sometimes follow households in electing Christmas
lords and in celebrating winter revels but, as normally outdoor activities, community
custom and drama were mainly associated with the great festivals of the summer

season, from St George's Day (23 April), through May Day, Midsummer, Whitsun and Corpus Christi, to the village wakes of the late summer and early autumn. There is little documentation that English communities matched their continental European analogues in extensive Shrovetide (carnival) festivity, except for an extraordinary record from fifteenth-century Norwich. According to a claim by the civic leaders, in 1443, a certain John Gladman:

> of disport as hath been accustomed in any city or borough through all this realm, on Tuesday in the last end of Christmas, viz., Fastingong Tuesday [Shrove Tuesday] . . . having his horse trapped [decorated] with tinfoil and other nice disguising things, crowned as king of Christmas, in token that all mirths that season should end, with the twelve months of the year afore [before] him, each month disguised after the season required, and Lent clad in white and red herrings' skins, and his horse trapped with oyster shell after him, in token that sadness should follow, and an holy time, and so rode in diverse streets of the city, with other people with him disguised, making mirth and disports and plays.[7]

This would give English cities a tradition of carnival parades, and even perhaps (in the 'disports and plays') carnival versus lent conflicts familiar from the continent, but as yet there is little independent confirmation of the custom elsewhere, and the Norwich authorities are here defending themselves against the charge that the parade was insurrectionary. We are on much safer ground with the better-documented 'ridings' of St George and the dragon performed, mainly by the local St George's guild, in provincial cities. Sometimes the parade demonstrably paused for a conflict between the two figures. In some cities there was a major mustering and parade of the 'Watch', with varying degrees of accompanying pageantry, on Midsummer Eve, while of course prior to the Reformation the feast of Corpus Christi (the Thursday after Trinity Sunday) was characterized by significant processions honouring (and displaying) the host.

In many communities, particularly in the north, the parading season would end with the procession which brought newly harvested rushes – on a decorated cart accompanied by musicians and dancers – to strew the floor of the parish church. It was often associated with the parish 'wake', technically celebrating the anniversary of the church's dedication, in practice a late-summer or autumn holiday. This in turn provides an example of the major (and simpler) alternative to the parade as a characteristic context for community drama, the congregation of the inhabitants at some traditional venue (churchyard; play-field) for banqueting, pastimes and entertainment. That the latter could include dramatic items is suggested by Robert Herrick's mid-seventeenth-century evocation, which lists, alongside the reappearance (from festivals earlier in the season) of Maid Marian and her morris dancers:

> a mimick to devise
> Many grinning properties [peculiarities].
> Players there will be, and those

> Base in action as in clothes:
> Yet with strutting they will please
> The incurious [uncritical] villages.[8]

Earlier, on 29 July 1557, the diarist Henry Machyn recorded what was evidently a rather pleasant summer evening in London:

> The same day, being saint Olave's day, was the church holiday in Silver Street; and at eight of the clock at night began a stage play of a goodly matter, that continued until xij at midnight, and then they made an end with a good song.[9]

Other 'summer games' also combine the parade and the assembly. First in the season is the 'Maying', but the term refers as much to the activity as the date: the fetching in of 'may' (foliage and flowers, but particularly whitethorn blossom), which might well take place on May Day, but just as likely occur at Whitsun or midsummer or some locally traditional date in between. Its distinctive feature was the early-morning parade from the woods to the community bearing greenery and, often, a maypole, and early records suggest the parade could be enlivened by the presence of drummers, musicians and morris dancers. This parade culminated in effectively establishing the venue for the games and festivals of the upcoming summer festivals (setting up the pole; building summer 'bowers'), the first of which ensued immediately, and this assembly too would provide a suitable context for dramatic entertainments. In a retrospective account (1603) of London mayings John Stow notes both the pageantry of the procession and the drama of the ensuing festival:

> I find also, that in the month of May, the citizens of London of all estates, lightly in every parish, or sometimes two or three parishes joining together, had their several mayings, and did fetch May-poles, with divers warlike shows, with great archers, morris dancers and other devices, for pastime all the day long; and towards the evening they had stage plays and bonfires in the streets.[10]

While it could have a wider application, the ubiquitous term 'may-game' was sometimes used synonymously with the Maying, and early usage suggests the presence of a dramatic element. For example the notorious Act ('to Restrain the Abuses of Players') of 1605–6 forbids profanity 'in any stage play, interlude, show, May-game or pageant', and in John Fletcher's *The Woman's Prize*, having been locked up as mad, and seeing a doctor brought to examine him, a character (Petruchio) exclaims, 'Death, gentlemen, doe ye make a maygame on me?'[11] That there was indeed a traditional festive routine involving a doctor and patient (as in the modern mummers' plays) is suggested by the use by a contemporary of the term 'Maygame' to refer to a notorious stage merriment of 1589 in which a figure representing the Puritan propagandist Martin Marprelate was subjected to grotesque surgery.[12]

Perhaps the classic summer festival scenario is provided by the church-ale. Most often it is associated with Whitsun, but the procedures involved could be deployed in connection with any of the summer festivals (and even some winter ones). Designed to raise funds for good purposes within the parish through sale of the proverbial cakes and ale, the business side of the ale was overseen by the church wardens, while the jollifications themselves were organized by an annually chosen leader, the 'lord of misrule', or 'Summer King', 'May King', or 'Robin Hood'. To the degree that this temporary ruler, his 'Queen' (or 'Maid Marian') and his officers were dressed in part and behaved accordingly the custom as a whole had a distinctly mimetic element, but more substantial and conventionally dramatic performances might feature as an additional attraction at the ale. We may never come closer to the spirit of such occasions than the epilogue to a play recorded (probably in the 1470s) in his commonplace book by a Robert Reynes, who as a parish official (of Acle, Norfolk) might well have had the task of thanking the audience for their attention, apologising for shortcomings in the performance, and urging them to stay and drink:

> Sovereigns all insame [together],
> Ye that are come to see our game,
> We pray you all in God's name
>   To drink ere [before] ye pass [depart];
> For an ale is here ordained by a comely assent
>   For all manner of people that appear here this day,
> Unto holy church to be increasement [a benefit to]
>   All that exceedeth the costs of our play.[13]

On some occasions the play may have overshadowed or even ousted the drinking in an occasion which nonetheless retains the character of a community money-raising festival in which drama is still a means to an end. For example at Braintree, Essex, in 1523, a play of St Swithin was performed in the church, the churchwardens recording money 'gathered for' and 'paid at' the play, the profit in excess of production costs 'due to the church'.[14]

As this instance reminds us, while the culmination of the ale was the communal feast with accompanying revelry and plays, a definitive preliminary was the 'gathering' of money and provisions in a festive perambulation of the host and neighbouring communities. And just as the feast could be made more attractive by the performance of a play, so the likelihood is that gatherers drew attention to themselves by some kind of display: a morris or sword dance, most likely, and the cavorting of grotesques in the form of beasts, a man–woman (e.g. Maid Marian) and fools, and even a brief dramatic item: to the extent it also advertises the performance at the ale such a perambulation concurrently has the status of the of 'banns' for the play.

It is in this connection that it is appropriate to invoke the Robin Hood plays. In many early records, reference to a Robin Hood 'game' or 'play' may mean no more than the doubtless colourful and raucous spectacle he provided in parading from one venue to another to make his 'gathering'; others may suggest rather more, for example when the churchwardens of St John's Bow parish, Exeter (which had a 'play' of Robin

Hood from at least 1426–7), in 1507–8 record expenditure on 'the repair of St
Edmund the martyr's arrow for Robin Hood',[15] which looks very much like the re-
application of a property previously used in a saint's play (the Anglo-Saxon St Edmund
was martyred by the arrows of marauding Vikings). The question is fortunately
decided by the chance survival of three texts of fully fledged (if brief) plays of Robin
Hood. The earliest, 'Robin Hood and the Sheriff', preserved (as lines of unattributed
and uncontextualized dialogue) in a manuscript of *c*.1475, was probably performed at
the ale itself, comprising somewhat too elaborate action to be suitable for peram-
bulatory performance. It opens with a series of contests (archery, stone-throwing,
wrestling) between Robin and a knight, culminating in a sword fight which Robin
wins. He decapitates his opponent, puts on his clothes, and goes off carrying the head.
In further scenes (difficult to reconstruct precisely) Robin's followers (Little John,
Scarlet, Friar Tuck) confront the Sheriff and are captured. The two other plays, printed
(as one piece) in *c*.1560 by William Copland as 'The Playe of Robyn Hoode, verye
proper to be played in Maye Games', are short and simple enough to have been performed in the course of a money-gathering perambulation. 'Robin Hood and the Friar'
effectively comprises a confrontation between the protagonists, first verbal, then
violent, broadening into a general mêlée between their followers. They are reconciled,
and the friar is rewarded with a lady (probably Maid Marian), and the show ends with
the two of them dancing together. The second piece similarly pits Robin against the
potter (after a preliminary, largely verbal, encounter with the latter's comic servant)
in a sword-and-buckler fight which Robin loses. There follows a confrontation
between the potter and Little John whose outcome is not clear.[16]

The summer assemblies also provided a convenient venue for the performance of
plays satirizing local people who had fallen foul of the community. In south Kyme,
Lincolnshire, in 1601, at the last (late August) festival of the season a play was performed ostensibly dramatizing the death and funeral of the outgoing summer lord,
but apparently satirizing an unpopular local magnate, the Earl of Lincoln (he claimed
it included a dirge in which all the whores of the neighbourhood were called on to
pray for his soul).[17]

Customary Encounters

But while the assemblies of households and communities for, respectively, their winter
(or wedding) revels and their summer festivals provide major auspices for the performance of dramatic custom and customary drama, equally or more significant is a
second type of contextual scenario, which involves traditional, contrived, structured
encounters between two such groups. We have indeed just seen one variant of the customary encounter in the gatherings of the church-ales, which involve the exaction of
money and resources by one group from another, the community through whose territory they perambulate. Other customary encounters function as a demonstration by
one group to another, a feature that is particularly discernible if the demonstration is

condemnatory. In early modern communities, breaches of the traditional code of domestic behaviour not punished by the judicial system (typically the shrewish or adulterous wife) could be dealt with by the 'folklaw' of the charivary, which conventionally took the form of a spectacular and raucous 'riding'. In this shaming ritual the offender, or more often a surrogate, was paraded through the community on a horse or plank, ignominiously facing the rear, and accompanied by the 'rough music' of pans and kettles, the firing of guns and raucous shouts. Some features seem consciously to express the perceived unnaturalness of the relationship condemned, and other inversionary symbolism might include the holding aloft on poles of a skirt (female dominance) or a reversed sword (male subservience), and the scattering among spectators of grains mixed with dung (reversing the wedding custom in which spectators threw grains on the procession of bride and groom). In a regional (west country) variant the male figure might be joined by a female (a man dressed as a woman representing the shrewish wife), beating him with the ladle or 'skimmington' which gave the form its traditional name.

Within the important category of house-visit customs the most familiar is the 'mumming' of the Christmas season, an interactive rather than a demonstrative encounter, in which disguised and visored visitors penetrated households in order to indulge with them in pastimes, usually gambling with dice. In small communities (as in modern Newfoundland 'mummering') or among members of an elite coterie (as in Henry VIII's notorious visit to Cardinal Wolsey, dramatized by Shakespeare), the fun can include trying to recognize the resolutely 'mum' visitors (as in modern Newfoundland 'mummering'), but in the anonymity of cities a custom facilitating the entry of disguised strangers into private space was open to abuse, prompting local and national legislation banning the use of masks in its observance. Beyond the display of their costumes and masks, and their dancing entry (accompanied by a pipe and drum), mummers offered little by way of entertainment. It is just possible that in the later middle ages, by gradually acquiring first an introductory prologue then mimetic action and finally dialogue, one variety of the mumming developed into the more elaborate and conventionally dramatic masque, but it is equally likely that the latter developed from an originally and essentially distinct house-visit custom involving not so much convivial interaction as demonstrative courtesy by subordinates (say manorial tenants) who in connection with a winter feast or wedding revels brought a show to honour and entertain their lord (who reciprocated with hospitality and largesse). The financial accounts of provincial households contain payments at Christmas time to 'the men of' specified communities of which the householder was manorial lord offering an entertainment which is rarely specified beyond a tantalising 'singing and dancing'.

The Mummers' Plays

Twenty years ago, pride of place in a survey of this kind would have been assigned to the mummers' plays: the Christmas custom, recorded in hundreds of Victorian communities, in which a group of rural labourers or urban youths, in outlandish garb, perambulated the locality performing at street corners or in private and public houses a play whose central acts were the combat between St George and a varying antagonist (the King of Egypt; Bold Slasher; the Turkish Knight), the death of one of them, and his 'revival' by a garrulous Quack Doctor. A mummers' play however comprised more than this dramatic action (which we may therefore distinguish as the play-proper). The show opened with a presentation which invoked the season's goodwill and (often) called on the characters, and ended with a non- or sub-dramatic entertainment usually comprising a miscellany of odd speeches by supernumerary characters (often including a club-bearing Beelzebub), then perhaps songs, or dances, and (if it hadn't come at the start) a request for largesse and / or refreshment.

Mummers' plays were long believed to be the survivals of a primitive, pre-Christian ritual, the death-and-revival originally intended, in accordance with the principles of sympathetic magic identified by Sir James Frazer's *The Golden Bough* (1890), to ensure the continued fertility of crops, herds and men.[18] Some theatre historians claimed this ritual actually constituted the origins of the theatre in the west (in the manner of its Dionysian cousin in ancient Greece); for others it persisted as a tradition of semi-dramatic folklore liable at any time to exert some influence on individual genres or specific plays in 'regular' theatre history. Neither view is now tenable, the evolutionary anthropology and the survivalist folklore underpinning them having been abandoned in the respective disciplines themselves decades ago, exposing the scenarios to the simple historical fact that there is no direct and convincing evidence for the mummers' plays as we know them from before the middle of the eighteenth century.

But that does not exclude the possibility that our extensive documentation of the mummers' plays in recent, living tradition could be of use in supplementing our often rather dry historical records of local and customary drama in the Renaissance period. While some parts (say the individual plays) may be new, other parts – the host customs; the non-dramatic features of the traditional show – may be older, and the situation may vary as between different types of tradition. As they have been recorded over the last couple of centuries, the mummers' plays fall fairly clearly into three broad categories: the ubiquitous hero combat plays (as just described); the sword dance plays of the north of England (in which a slaying-and-cure sequence provides a dramatic interlude amidst the sections of a skilled dance-display); the wooing plays of the east midlands (in which a slaying and cure can supplement a distinct plot in which a lady is wooed by one or more suitors), often performed in the context of a begging custom (*quête*) in which a decorated plough is perambulated through the community on 'Plough Monday' (the first Monday following epiphany).

There is little doubt that the host customs (respectively sword-dance and plough-trailing *quêtes*) of the last two forms are survivals, under unofficial auspices, of late medieval and Tudor 'gatherings' in support of guild or parish funds of the kind discussed above (if of the Christmas season rather than Whitsun), but it is far from certain that the earlier forms of the custom had the 'folk play' attached to them (and play-less traditions of both customs have also been recorded in recent times). In the case of the hero combat plays it is more difficult to identify an analogous but playless host custom: it may have been (like the tradition just suggested as lying behind the masque) a now otherwise defunct courtesy visit to the household of a lord by representatives of a neighbouring, dependent community: Victorian village traditions showed a distinct predilection for gentry households, and sometimes put on a more elaborate show for the squire. Whatever the exact original auspices and the complications of historical development, it is striking that in the modern hero combat mummers' play, with its emphatic structure of presentation, play-proper and entertainment, we have if not a derivative, then a living analogue of the three-part show (affectionately parodied in *A Midsummer Night's Dream*) of the household winter revels. As the most dramatic of recent customs it would be appropriate if the mummers' plays, taken together, could be seen to match and illuminate significant features of both the household and community traditions, and the encounters of communities with households, that constituted the bulk of the local, customary drama of the Renaissance period.

NOTES

1 E. K. Chambers, *The Elizabethan Stage*, 4 vols (1923; repr. London: Oxford University Press, 1965), IV, 237.

2 Fletcher, 135–6 (original Latin and Alan Fletcher's translation quoted here).

3 *Letters and Papers, Foreign and Domestic, of the Reign of Henry VIII*, III.ii, ed. J. S. Brewer (London: HMSO, 1867), pp. 1,098–1,100, no. 2,585; Madeleine Hope Dodds, 'Northern Minstrels and Folk Drama', *Archaeologia Aeliana*, 4th ser., 1 (1925), 121–46, at pp. 124–5.

4 George Puttenham, *The Arte of English Poesie*, ed. G. D. Willcock and A. Walker (1936; repr. Cambridge: Cambridge University Press, 1970), p. 203.

5 Lancashire, pp. 34–5.

6 William Shakespeare, *A Midsummer Night's Dream*, ed. Peter Holland, Oxford Shakespeare (Oxford: Oxford University Press, 1994), 5.1.106ff: 'Pyramus and Thisbe' is referred to as an 'interlude' at l. 154.

7 Cited in Tydeman, p. 19.

8 'The Wake', ll, 9–14, in *The Complete Poetry of Robert Herrick*, ed. J. Max Patrick (New York: University Press, 1963), H-761.

9 *The Diary of Henry Machyn*, ed. J. G. Nichols (London: J. B. Nichols for Camden Soc., 1848), p. 145.

10 John Stow, *A Survey of London* (2nd edn, 1603), ed. H. B. Wheatley, (1912; repr. London: Dent, 1987), pp. 90–1.

11 Chambers, *Elizabethan Stage*, IV, 338–9; *The Woman's Prize*, ed. G. B. Ferguson (The Hague: Mouton, 1966), III.v.65.

12 Thomas Nashe, attrib., *Martins Months Minde*, in Chambers, *Elizabethan Stage*, IV, 230.

13 *Non-Cycle Plays and Fragments*, ed. Norman Davis, EETS. st 1 (London: Oxford University Press, 1970), item XIII, 'The Reynes Extracts', B, 'An Epilogue', ll. 24–31.

14 Robert R. Wright, 'Medieval Theatre in East Anglia', Dissertation (University of Bristol, 1970–1), p. 178.

15 *Records of Early English Drama: Devon*, ed. John Wasson (Toronto: Toronto University Press, 1986), p. 118 (translation p. 393).

16 David Wiles, *The Early Plays of Robin Hood* (Cambridge: Brewer, 1981), Appendix 4, 'Original Play-texts'.

17 Barber, pp. 37–50.

18 James G. Frazer, *The Golden Bough. A Study in Magic and Religion*, 2 vols (Cambridge: Cambridge University Press, 1890; 3rd edn, 12 vols 1913).

REFERENCES AND FURTHER READING

Barber, C. L. (1959; 1972). *Shakespeare's Festive Comedy: A Study of Dramatic Form in its Relation to Social Custom*. Princeton: Princeton University Press.

Bevington, David (1962). *From 'Mankind' to Marlowe: Growth and Structure in the Popular Drama of Tudor England*. Cambridge, MA: Harvard University Press.

Cawte, E. C. (1978). *Ritual Animal Disguise: A Historical and Geographical Study of Animal Disguise in the British Isles*. Cambridge: Brewer.

Cox, John D. and David Scott Kastan (eds) (1997). *A New History of Early English Drama*. New York: Columbia University Press.

Fletcher, Alan J. (1986). '"Farte Prycke in Cule": A Late-Elizabethan Analogue from Ireland'. *Medieval English Theatre*, 8 (2), 134–9.

Forrest, John and Heaney, Michael (1991). 'Charting Early Morris', *Folk Music Journal*, 6 (2), 169–86.

Greenfield, Peter H. (1999). 'The Carnivalesque in the Robin Hood Games and King Ales of Southern England'. In Konrad Eisenbichler and Wim Hüsken (eds), *Carnival and the Carnivalesque* (pp. 19–28). Amsterdam and Atlanta: Rodopi.

Happé, Peter (1999). *English Drama before Shakespeare*. London: Longman.

Hutton, Ronald (1994). *The Rise and Fall of Merry England*. Oxford: Oxford University Press.

Ingram, M. (1984). 'Ridings, Rough Music, and the 'Reform of Popular Culture' in Early Modern England', *Past and Present*, 105, 79–113.

Johnston, Alexandra F. and Wim Hüsken (eds) (1996). *English Parish Drama*. Amsterdam and Atlanta: Rodopi.

——(1991). 'English Puritanism and Festive Custom', *Renaissance and Reformation*, NS, 15, 289–97.

Lancashire, Ian (1980). 'Orders for Twelfth Day and Night circa 1515 in the Second Northum-

berland Household Book', *English Literary Renaissance*, 10, 6–45.

Laroque, François (1991). *Shakespeare's Festive World: Elizabethan Seasonal Entertainment and the Professional Stage*. Cambridge: Cambridge University Press.

Pendleton, Thomas A. (1995). 'Mystery's Addenda: Secular Drama in Late Sixteenth-century Coventry', *Mediaevalia*, 18, 341–65.

Pettitt, Thomas (1984). 'Tudor Interludes and the Winter Revels', *Medieval English Theatre*, 6 (1), 16–27.

——(1995). 'Customary Drama: Social and Spatial Patterning in Traditional Encounters', *Folk Music Journal*, 7 (1), 27–42.

——(1997). 'Folk Drama'; 'Mumming'. In Thomas A. Green (ed.), *Folklore: An Encyclopedia of Beliefs, Customs, Tales, Music and Art* (vol. I, pp. 205–12; vol. II, pp. 566–7). Santa Barbara: ABC–CLIO.

Tillis, Steve (1999). *Rethinking Folk Drama*. London: Greenwood Press.

Tydeman, William (1978). *The Theatre in the Middle Ages*. Cambridge: Cambridge University Press.

Weimann, Robert L. (1978). *Shakespeare and the Popular Tradition in the Theatre*. Baltimore: Johns Hopkins University Press.

Westfall, Suzanne R. (1990). *Patrons and Performance: Early Tudor Household Revels*. Oxford: Clarendon Press.

White, Paul Whitfield (1993). *Theatre and Reformation: Protestantism, Patronage, and Playgoing in Tudor England*. Cambridge: Cambridge University Press.

Wickham, G. (1959). *Early English Stages 1300 to 1660, Vol. i: 1300 to 1576*. London: Routledge and Kegan Paul.

Wright, Robert R. (1970–1). 'Medieval Theatre in East Anglia'. Dissertation, University of Bristol.

40
Continuities between 'Medieval' and 'Early Modern' Drama
Michael O'Connell

The Elizabethan drama has generally been characterized as something new in the history of European theatre, the beginning of a theatrical tradition that, while interrupted by the closing of the public theatres in 1642 (and their subsequent destruction in the following years), continued on in the performing of Shakespeare and his contemporaries in the Restoration and beyond, down to the present day. This beginning is generally marked with the opening of the Theatre, James Burbage's purpose-built playhouse in Shoreditch in 1576 – though the Red Lion (1567), a converted inn, may contest its claim as the first actual public theatre. It is doubtless true that the establishment of fixed playing spaces in London enabled an extraordinary expansion in the writing and the production of new plays. The subsequent opening of the Curtain, the Rose, the Swan, the Globe, the Fortune, the Boar's Head, and the Red Bull certainly indicate the economic advance prompted by Burbage's enterprise. But the emphasis on newness and beginnings has obscured the fact that the Elizabethan and Jacobean theatre was heir to vibrant theatrical and performance traditions reaching back more than two hundred years, traditions that playwrights, companies and audiences were well aware of. An understanding of these traditions allows modern interpreters a richer sense of how this 'new' theatre was transmuting and transposing formal and ideological structures from those previous two centuries. The present chapter aims briefly to describe those traditions and to suggest their relationship to some representative dramatic texts of the Elizabethan and Jacobean theatre.

One theatrical moment in particular points up the awareness the playwrights themselves had of being part of a tradition. *Sir Thomas More*, a play written initially, it appears, by Anthony Munday, then revised by a committee of playwrights that included Shakespeare, has at its centre a scene in which a play is performed before More and his guests by 'My Lord Cardinal's Players'. The play is called *The Marriage of Wit and Wisdom*, which exists in several versions, but goes back to John Redford's *Wit and Science* in the 1530s. Like Hamlet when he is confronted by a travelling troupe,

More questions the players about their company, then queries their repertory: 'I prithee tell me, what plays have ye?' The player responds:

> Diverse, my Lord: *The Cradle of Security,*
> *Hit the Nail o' th' Head, Impatient Poverty,*
> *The Play of the Four P's, Dives and Lazarus,*
> *Lusty Juventus*, and *The Marriage of Wit and Wisdom.*
> (III.ii.59–63)

All but *Hit the Nail o' the Head* are plays known from other sources, and *Impatient Poverty, The Play of the Four P's* (by John Heywood, who was associated with the More circle), *Lusty Juventus* and *The Marriage of Wit and Wisdom* survive as play texts. Except for *The Four P's*, these were not plays that the historical Thomas More could have known, but they were all works known to the Elizabethan playwrights, and probably to their audiences as well, as representing an earlier theatrical generation. Printed some forty to fifty years earlier, the play titles evoke the repertory of a small troupe, like ones that travelled through the country, but also played in London. More enthusiastically chooses *The Marriage of Wit and Wisdom* and, again like Hamlet, shows himself knowledgeable about theatre and playing – so knowledgeable in fact that he steps in and plays the part of Good Counsel when one of the players misses his entrance, an act that recalls what William Roper tells of More's actual practice as an adolescent in the house of Cardinal Morton a century before. What the company plays is in fact a pastiche of several plays that Munday had available to him in print, mostly *Lusty Juventus* but with a prologue taken in part from Thomas Ingelond's *The Disobedient Child* and elements of a couple of other mid-Tudor plays. Of the scene David Bevington says, 'The impression is one of a playwright in the 1590s looking back on his professional ancestors with a certain amount of humorous condescension, portraying an average troupe of the early or middle century' (*Mankind to Marlowe*, p. 19).

This is not, of course, the only moment of self-consciousness about earlier theatrical traditions in late Elizabethan and Jacobean plays. When in *1 Henry IV* Falstaff offers to take on the role of King Henry so Prince Hal may practise the answer he must give the king about his escapades, he says he will play the part 'in King Cambyses' vein' (II.iv.390); that is, he will perform in the manner of Thomas Preston's 'lamentable tragedy mixed full of pleasant mirth' from some thirty or forty years earlier. And so he does in the creaking verse of the old play. Part of the fun rests in the fact that in Shakespeare's play Falstaff himself has the role of the morality vice in relation to Hal, something both he and Falstaff are aware of. A similarly amused, though less specific, *homage* to earlier theatre comes in the play that Bottom and the mechanicals perform in *A Midsummer Night's Dream*. While the subject matter of their *Pyramus and Thisbe* may seem Ovidian and classical, the description of Pyramus as 'a wandering knight' would have tipped off an Elizabethan audience that Bottom and his troupe are performing a romance of the previous theatrical generation. Here the reference is to the more recent vogue of the romances from the 1570s, works like *Clyomon and Clamydes, Common Conditions* and *The Rare Triumphs of Love and Fortune*, plays whose dominant verse form is also, like *Cambyses*, the creaking fourteener. Also with a similar lack of specificity, Edmund in *King Lear* jokes about the opportune entrance of Edgar just as he mentions his name: 'Pat! he comes like the catastrophe in the old comedy' (I.ii.137). Here in fact the reference to the morality tradition may signal a more profound connection. Similarly, in *Macbeth* the drunken gate keeper of Macbeth's castle plays at being 'porter of hell gate' (II.iii.1), and as Macduff knocks vigorously at the gate the porter ends up replicating the role of the devil who kept the gate of hell in the mystery-cycle pageant of the Harrowing of Hell. Macbeth's castle, the site of a murder that is like a 'breach in nature', has in effect become a version of hell. Clearly the playwrights were conscious of their inheritance of a long theatrical tradition, and while they might sometimes gently mock outdated fashions, they were as aware as any modern film director that their art had a history that could be invoked and exploited for a variety of effects and meanings.

In these examples of plays in the consciousness of Elizabethan playwrights, at least two types of earlier theatre can be identified. The morality interludes and the romances were a public theatre that was performed by professional troupes that may have been based in London but also maintained travelling itineraries, the immediate predecessors of the later Elizabethan companies. Such troupes may initially have been small, 'four men and a boy', but later grew in size, playing in inn yards and other public spaces in towns and villages as well as in private venues, like the hall of a nobleman's household or at the universities. The other type of theatre was the large-scale civic production that was performed at religious festivals, typically the feast of Corpus Christi, in cathedral cities and regional centres. These were amateur productions whose auspices were frequently the craft guilds, but this should not be taken to mean amateurism or naiveté in performance; in fact production values were high and performances elaborate. A third type of theatre, not alluded to in the above examples but more important to the Elizabethan and Jacobean theatre than has frequently been recognized, is drama that might be understood as a small-scale version of the civic cycles, plays performed by towns and parishes that were part of local festivity and, in conjunction with 'church-ales', often used for local fund-raising. These were frequently termed 'miracles', plays centring on a saint's life or concerned, like the fifteenth-century Croxton *Play of the Sacrament*, with some miraculous event. Folk drama was part of this local tradition, and references to Robin Hood are found in parish records, though no contemporary play texts survive that could give a firm sense of what exactly this was.

Each of these types of theatre might be understood to have a particular dramatic genre associated with it. The professional companies were associated with interludes, the allegorical morality plays that the troupe in *Sir Thomas More* had in its repertory. The civic theatre performed a kind of epic drama centred, in the surviving examples, on biblical history from creation to doomsday (though Coventry's Corpus Christi play appears to have focused solely on the events of Christ's life). And the parish drama has been identified with the careers of saints and the miraculous deeds associated with them. But this impression comes mainly from the texts that survive, and here it should be emphasized that the surviving texts of drama preceding the Elizabethan public playhouses represent merely the tip of an iceberg. Drama flourished at the local level, and from the late fifteenth century, touring companies performed widely. Together they represent a vast tradition of performance throughout England and indeed throughout Britain. But the corpus of surviving dramatic texts has not increased in tandem with our knowledge of performance, so we are left to imagine the kinds of theatre from a comparatively small number of texts. It appears, for example, that many saints' plays, enactments of the lives and miracles of saints who were the patrons of parishes and guilds, were performed at the local level. But only three saints' plays survive from the fifteenth century, the elaborate *St Mary Magdalen* and, from the same Digby manuscript, *St Paul*, and *St Meriasek* in Cornish. (Lewis Wager's mid-sixteenth-century, *Mary Magdalen*, represents a rather pale survival of the tradition, grafted onto a morality structure.) Similarly *Mankind* is the sole text surviving from the fifteenth century that indicates performance by a travelling troupe of players, but many more such texts must have existed. Because this play and later plays associated with travelling companies are morality interludes, we may be tempted to assume that their repertories were exclusively such plays. But it is possible that they also performed saints' lives or even biblical narratives. Similarly, it is also known that a 'Creed Play' was performed at York, as an apparent alternative to the biblical play, but its character and subject matter are not known. We are left, then, with a sense of a large and various tradition of performance in the period before the public theatres, but with only a comparatively small number of texts to stand for the whole.

Part of the reason for the small number of texts has to do with the nature itself of theatre: texts were scripts to be performed, subliterary and only subject to the preservation of print after the early decades of the sixteenth century. Many such plays as survive do so frequently in unique manuscripts or single surviving copies of printed books. The major winnowing force in the period is the Reformation – and a far more significant demarcation than the constructions of 'late medieval' and 'renaissance' or 'early modern' by modern cultural historians. While very little of the theatre had specifically religious auspices – it is important to realize that the mystery cycles were sponsored by the craft guilds and lay oligarchies of the towns – a large part of it was religious in sentiment and purpose. In fact, in the two centuries before the public theatres, theatre as an institution can be understood as serving religious ends. Saints' plays, of course, served the cult of saints, and the civic theatre was centred, initially at least, on the feast of Corpus Christi. Both became targets of the Reformation, like the visual art that also served devotional ends.

At the same time it is important to note that traditional period divisions between 'late medieval' and 'early modern' may not be entirely useful in the understanding of this theatre. Humanist ideas and a sophisticated dramaturgy appear in some late fifteenth-century texts; for example, the two plays of Henry Medwall, and the experimental drama of John Heywood in the 1520s can appear more interesting and sophisticated than Elizabethan morality drama written in the 1560s and 1570s. But just as importantly, some dramatic genres generally assumed to be 'late medieval', like the mystery cycles, were in fact performed well into Elizabeth's reign. The York cycle, the earliest cycle text (in its surviving form dating from 1463–77) was performed until 1569, after which it was suppressed. The Chester cycle, whose surviving text certainly dates from the sixteenth century was given for the last time in 1575. And the most famous cycle of all, Coventry, whose two surviving pageants were also written, or re-written, in the sixteenth century, was last performed in 1579. Coventry, in its proximity to Stratford upon Avon, is the cycle that Shakespeare certainly saw during his boyhood and adolescence. Parish drama, which doubtless included many saints' plays, was still being performed in the 1560s, though no texts survive. And because the cycle drama, and no doubt the parish drama too, was subject to constant revision during these last decades of its performance, the distinction between 'late medieval' and 'early modern' theatre can become both hard to fix and misleading.

As the episode in *Sir Thomas More* suggests, the dominant tradition behind the public theatres was the allegorical and quasi-allegorical morality play, or 'interlude' as it was termed. And this is the tradition that has been most thoroughly explored by twentieth-century scholarship into the roots of the late-Elizabethan drama. The result of this exploration has been an understanding of its pervasiveness in the drama of the late Elizabethan and Jacobean playwrights. 'But that your royalty / Holds idleness your subject', Shakespeare's Antony says to Cleopatra, 'I should take you / For Idleness itself' (I.iii.91–3). Antony thus constructs Cleopatra momentarily as the vice figure idleness, who led youth astray on the morality stage. If this could be ironic in view of Antony's age, it accords rather precisely with what the audience understands of his captivation by the queen and his dereliction of active, Roman duty. If not youth, he is middle age drawn off by idleness. Morality structures are to be found in large and small elements of the mature Elizabethan and Jacobean theatre. Since Bevington's classic study, Christopher Marlowe's structural use of the morality has been well known. Barabas in *The Jew of Malta* is an evident vice character in both dramaturgy – his confident relationship with the audience established in soliloquies and asides – and in the tenor of his character. As a vice, Barabas' role descends most immediately from mid-century homiletic tragedy, plays like Wager's *The Longer Thou Livest the More Fool Thou Art*, that displayed a vicious character whose dramatic progress is to become hardened in villainy until he is carried off by Satan in the end. Marlowe's accomplishment is not only to meld this pattern with a non-allegorical narrative, but to introduce a pervasive moral irony into the apparent triumph of good in the final destruction of the vice; it is not evident that the supposed forces of good represent significant moral advance over the corruption centred in Barabas. In plot *Doctor Faustus* may also replicate homiletic tragedy, but here the morality structure is if anything even more evident. In part a psychomachia, the play even introduces good and evil angels vying for the attention of the protagonist, but at the same time Marlowe's potent verse internalizes the struggle within Faustus's soul. Modern experience of the play has frequently found the comic scenes – servants imitating Faustus's conjuring, Faustus himself snatching the pope's dinner and boxing him on the ear, or tricking a horse dealer – unworthy of the play's best moments. These scenes are the ones most directly related to the interludes earlier in the century and, on the evidence of *Mankind*, to the moralities of the fifteenth century.

Shakespeare's use of morality structures, while perhaps less pervasive than Marlowe's, is no less purposeful. A clear example of a local structure occurs in the scene of *Othello* (II, iii) when Cassio is turned from a sober officer of the watch to a drunken fool by the vice-like temptation of Iago. The scene is like a miniature morality interlude in which the vice tempts the protagonist, first to lechery, and when that is not successful, to drunkenness. In the larger play as well, Iago's role shares much with the morality vice: his wit, his intimate relation to the audience, and his overall purpose of corrupting and ruining the central figure. The fact that the temptation is transposed to a psychologically persuasive mode does not obscure its relation to the essential pattern stemming from the allegorical interlude. A different kind of morality can be seen to inhere in the basic structure of *King Lear.* As Freud recognized in his essay 'The Theme of the Three Caskets', a summons of death seems implicit in Cordelia's refusal to flatter the aged king in the play's opening scene. In structural terms the scene is strikingly like the opening of a fragmentary fifteenth-century morality, *Pride of Life* (which Shakespeare is unlikely to have known), where a king is similarly confronted with a choice of listening to flattery or a truthful statement of his human mortality. Lear soon banishes his good counsel in the person of the truth-telling Kent. The best known example of this type of morality is *Everyman*, a summons-of-death allegorical play, originally Dutch, that illustrated the stripping away of all that is inessential in human life before the grim fact of death. While the dramatic mode of *King Lear* is not allegorical, the tragedy follows a similar pattern as the king is successively stripped of all the social supports of his existence until he discovers 'unaccommodated man' in the mad beggar that Edgar plays. Lear then turns himself into 'such a poor, bare, forked animal' as he sees in Poor Tom – and in so doing embarks on the discovery of basic human values.

But the issue of dramatic antecedents to Elizabethan and Jacobean theatre is broadened and complicated by another analogue to *King Lear. King Robert of Sicily*, lost as a play but known through prose narratives, tells of a king who is converted from self-absorbed indifference to the plight of the poor by being cast out of his court and made to endure the life of a beggar. Generically different from a morality, *King Robert* is a blend of saint's life and romance, narrating the protagonist's conversion. Shakespeare's tragedy may be more directly related to Thomas Lodge's prose romance *Robert the Devil*, but plays on the subject were known in England. Such plays on the lives of saints may indeed have been the most commonly performed dramatic genre before the Reformation, but because of the attack on the cult of the saints, far fewer texts would survive than in any other genre. From performance records alone it is known that at least 66 plays on 38 different saints existed and that 44 towns and villages in England produced such plays (Wasson, 'Secular Saint Plays,' pp. 241–2). And this may be just the tip of the iceberg. *The Conversion of St Paul* and *Mary Magdalen*, both in the Digby manuscript, and the Cornish *Life of Meriasek* are the only extant texts from this tradition that flourished in the previous century. But mid-sixteenth-century plays like Bale's *King Johan* and William Wager's *Conversion of Mary Magdalen*, and, later, *The Comedy of Virtuous Susanna* represent Protestant transformations of the saint's play. In the early seventeenth century Thomas Heywood's play on the life of Queen Elizabeth, *If You Know Not Me You Know Nobody* and the anonymous *Thomas Lord Cromwell* and *Sir John Oldcastle* are further developments of the Protestant saint's play. But the most extraordinary survival of the genre is Thomas Dekker and Philip Massinger's *The Virgin Martyr* (1620), which, in its portrayal of the torture and mar- tyrdom of St Dorothea of Caesarea, seems strikingly Catholic in its baroque dra- maturgy. If nothing else, *The Virgin Martyr* suggests that the genre of the saint's life had not been erased from consciousness, but remained a possibility for dramatic exploitation.

The dramatic genre on which the saint's life exerted the greatest influence was the romance, which had never been absent from the longer and more elaborate late medieval saints' plays. The self-conscious archaism of Shakespeare's *Pericles* perhaps constitutes a direct acknowledgement of that influence, and its miraculous preserva- tion of the queen and the heroic virtue of Marina surely suggest its affinities with hagiographic dramatic conventions. If *Cymbeline* too presents a heroically persevering woman, certainly *The Winter's Tale* shows the most powerful secular elaboration of a saint's life in Hermione's endurance, her apparent death and seeming resurrection. Perdita's veneration of her as a seeming statue in the final scene even momentarily heightens the sense that Hermione's heroism represents a transmuted response to the cult of the saints. *The Tempest* may seem less evidently tied to this tradition, but from such a perspective on romance it might be called *The Conversion of Prospero* in its enact- ment of a turn from embittered memory and the renunciation of Faustus-like power.

The influence of the mystery cycles is perhaps the most difficult to gauge – and it has been the least discussed among the 'medieval' influences on the Elizabethan drama. The medieval character of the cycles, while real, must remain bracketed because although the origins of the genre go back to the late fourteenth century, the texts of Chester and what survives of the Coventry play are clearly sixteenth century. The Wakefield text too derives from early in the century, and the fifteenth-century text of York was subject to revision down to the final performance of 1569. These are medieval plays that continued to be written, revised, and played into the period we identify as 'early modern', and clearly they were part of Elizabethan consciousness. Shakespeare is the only Elizabethan playwright who appears to have been deeply touched by the cycles, no doubt because of his origins in the midlands, where the Coventry play was still performed as late as 1579. If some portion of his 'lost years' was spent in Lancashire, as has recently been argued, he may also have known the 'Corpus Christi Play' that John Weever (*Ancient Funeral Monuments*, 1631) records having seen played at Preston. Playwrights bred in London or southern England would not have known any local cycles in the latter half of the sixteenth century. But Shakespeare's references to elements of the plays suggest that they remained a general cultural memory some two or three decades after they ceased being performed. The best known allusion to the cycle drama occurs in Hamlet's advice to the players: a player who overacts a passionate role offends him greatly: 'I would have such a fellow whipt for o'erdoing Termagant, it out-Herods Herod' (*Hamlet*, III, ii 13–14). The audience is clearly expected to understand this reference to the over-the-top ranting of the mystery-cycle role; it is not a private allusion, but shared even among those geographically and chronologically removed from direct contact with the performances. *Macbeth* may contain the most obviously purposeful uses of the mystery-play tradition. As noted above, the drunken porter plays comically at being the doorkeeper of Hell, transposing a scene in the Harrowing of Hell pageant. Other elements of the play ground Macbeth's tyranny in the character of Herod. Here as elsewhere Shakespeare appears to allude to the biblical theatre to adumbrate relations that lie in and beneath narrative and character patterns. With an open-endedness that does not coerce meaning or demand theological reading, these allusions can, momentarily and transiently, open a scene to larger ways of understanding or constructing it. Male sexual jealousy is another frequently occurring thematic in Shakespeare that can be understood as linked to cycle traditions. Male protagonists in both comic and tragic plots accuse their innocent wives of betrayal – thereby re-enacting Joseph's confrontation of Mary in the nativity sequences. Coventry's pageant of the Shearmen and the Taylors contains a particularly vivid enactment of the scene. In all Shakespearean cases, as in the cycle narratives, it is the innocence of the wife and the futility of the jealousy that become a central thematic focus.

One of the projects of criticism in the next century will be to query the boundaries of 'medieval' and 'early modern' drama and to explore the significance of their interpenetration in the late sixteenth century. The Records of Early English Drama project has been systematically amassing detailed records of theatre and festivity for the regions of England. One result is that the topography of performance now appears a good deal more complex and diffuse, less centred on London. Scholars are less inclined to evolutionary and teleological models that see theatre developing inevitably toward Elizabethan glories. What is needed are new theatre histories that will acknowledge both continuities and discontinuities in the complex traditions that extend from the late fourteenth century.

REFERENCES AND FURTHER READING

Beadle, Richard (ed.) (1994). *The Cambridge Companion to Medieval Theatre*. Cambridge: Cambridge University Press.

Bevington, David (1962; rpt 1968). *From Mankind to Marlowe: Growth of Structure in the Popular Drama of Tudor England*. Cambridge: Harvard University Press.

Bishop, T. G. (1996). *Shakespeare and the Theatre of Wonder*. Cambridge: Cambridge University Press.

Cox, John D. (1989). *Shakespeare and the Dramaturgy of Power*. Princeton: Princeton University Press.

Cox, John D. and Kastan, David Scott (eds)

(1997). *A New History of Early English Drama.* New York: Columbia University Press.

Emmerson, Richard (1998), 'Eliding the "Medieval": Renaissance "New Historicism" and Sixteenth-century Drama'. In James J. Paxton, Lawrence Clopper and Sylvia Tomasch (Eds), *The Performance of Middle English Culture* (pp. 25–41). Cambridge: D. S. Brewer.

Freud, Sigmund (1913; 1958). 'The Theme of the Three Caskets'. In James Strachey (ed.), *The Standard Edition of the Complete Psychological Works.* Volume 12. London: Hogarth Press.

Gardiner, Harold C. (1946). *Mysteries End: An Investigation of the Last Days of the Medieval Religious Stage.* New Haven: Yale University Press.

Hamilton, Donna B. (1974). 'Some Romance Sources for *King Lear*: Robert of Sicily and Robert the Devil', *Studies in Philology*, 71, 173–91.

Jones, Emrys (1977). *The Origins of Shakespeare.* Oxford: Clarendon Press.

Norland, Howard B. (1995). *Drama in Early Tudor Britain 1485–1558.* Lincoln, NE; London.

O'Connell, Michael (1999). 'Vital Cultural Practices: Shakespeare and the Mysteries', *Journal of Medieval and Early Modern Studies*, 29, 149–68.

——(2000). *The Idolatrous Eye: Iconoclasm and Theater in Early Modern England.* New York: Oxford University Press.

Potter, Robert (1975). *The English Morality Play: Origins, History, and Influence of a Dramatic Tradition.* London: Routledge.

Wasson, John (1986). 'The Secular Saint Play of the Elizabethan Era.' In Clifford Davidson (ed.), *The Saint Play in Medieval Europe.* Kalamazoo: Medieval Institute Publications.

White, Paul Whitfield (1993). *Theatre and Reformation: Protestantism, Patronage, and Playing in Tudor England.* Cambridge: Cambridge University Press.

Wickham, Glynne (1969). *Shakespeare's Dramatic Heritage.* London: Routledge and Kegan Paul.

Womack, Peter (1992). 'Imagining Communities: Theatres and the English Nature in the Sixteenth Century'. In David Aers (ed.), *Culture and History, 1300–1600: Essays on English Communities, Identities, and Writing.* Detroit: Wayne State University Press.

——(1997). 'Medieval Drama'. In Simon Shepherd and Peter Womack (eds.). *English Drama: A Cultural History.* Oxford: Basil Blackwell.

——(1999). 'Shakespeare and the Sea of Stories', *Journal of Medieval and Early Modern Studies*, 29, 169–87.

41

Political Plays

Stephen Longstaffe

Whether a play is a 'political play' is not simply a function of its content. The relationship between play-about-a-polity and the wider polity itself must also be considered, in both general and specific aspects. One influential presentation of the place of the stage in general sees the theatre, situated at London's unruly geographical and symbolic margins, as having a liberty 'at once moral, ideological, and topological – a freedom to experiment with a wide range of available ideological perspectives and to realize, in dramatic form, the cultural contradictions of the age' (Mullaney, ix–x). This freedom sometimes produced subversive plays – 'radical tragedy' – demystifying political and power relations, interrogating providentialism and the essentialist subjectivity it entails (Dollimore, 4). Demystification, in turn; was not merely Brechtian show business. David Scott Kastan argues that

> In setting English kings before an audience of commoners, the theater nourished the cultural conditions that eventually permitted the nation to bring its king to trial, not because the theater approvingly represented subversive acts but rather because representation itself became subversive. Whatever their overt ideological content, history plays inevitably, if unconsciously, weakened the structure of authority: on stage the king became a subject – the subject of the author's imaginings and the subject of the attention and judgement of an audience of subjects.
>
> (Kastan, 111)

Louis Montrose extends Kastan's point to encompass a theatre whose power

> did not lie in the explicit advocacy of specific political positions but rather in the implicit but pervasive suggestion – inhering in the basic modalities of theatrical representation and dramatic conflict – that all such positions are relationally located and circumstantially shaped and that they are motivated by the passions and interests of their advocates. In this precise and limited sense, Shakespearean drama as enacted in the

Elizabethan theatre *formally* contested the dominant ideological assertions of the Elizabethan state.

(Montrose, 105)

Other accounts draw very different conclusions about what the theatre's marginality meant, and how much it contested or subverted the state or the structure of authority. Alan Somerset questions Mullaney's assumption that the area outside London's walls conferred a kind of transgressive marginality on both the new theatres built there and on playing itself. He argues that theatre-builders operated on the margins of London simply because taxes were less and land was cheaper there, and that the predominant associations of the environs were therefore commercial. Burbage's and Brayne's decision to locate the Theatre on the south bank of the Thames in 1576

was similar to decisions in any modern city, observable as one drives towards the country through the inevitable ring of shopping malls, golf driving ranges, big-box retail outlets, car dealerships, garden centers, and what have you, by which the land makes a good income, often temporarily while awaiting more intensive development.

(Somerset, 53–4)

Paul Yachnin argues that producing plays we can now read as subversive was not in itself a subversive act, and that though 'between about 1590 and 1625, the stage persistently represented the issues of the moment . . . these representations were usually seen to subsist in a field of discourse isolated from the real world . . . such representations were seen as incapable of intervening in the political arena' (Yachnin, 3). Certainly the London theatre was tolerated, in sharp contrast to the determined suppression of the great civic religious play cycles of the sixteenth century. Transgressive players or writers were sometimes punished; but these punishments were mild compared to, for example, the Privy Council's arrest and torture of the playwright Thomas Kyd in 1593 on suspicion of stirring up anti-immigrant sentiments (Yachnin, 90–1).

Yachnin's concern with actual responses (or non-responses) to plays (what was 'usually seen') seems incompatible with Montrose or Kastan's downplaying of 'overt ideological content' or 'explicit advocacy' and their focus on the deep structural functions of the theatre (operating, for example, on the level of 'formal contestation'). It is possible, however, to find some common ground in the concept of genre, through which both necessarily conscious response and its not necessarily conscious conditions can be explored.

The broad generic distinction through which I will read political drama is that between plays with historical and fictional subject matter. Any play focusing strongly on a past polity is a history play, whether the polity be Old Testament, Greek, Roman, pagan, popish or Anglican British, or near-contemporaneous European. In non-theatrical political discourse, at one end of the spectrum is writing focusing on prece-

dent, predominantly biblical, but secondarily European political history. Much political writing on the law, the constitution and religion is of this nature. At the other
end of the spectrum is the political writing which makes use of invented polities such
as pastoral, romance and fable.

The distinction between fictional and historical subject matter is important because
discourse on politics, as opposed to the polity, was predominantly historically
based. Guidance on practical politics was sought in case histories rather than fiction
(or religious principle). The reverse was also true. Historiography, in whatever
mode, was often read for its applications to, or as a comment upon, contemporary
politics, that is to say the political actions of living and influential people. Elizabeth
Tudor was Deborah or Richard II. The Earl of Essex was Henry IV, Philotas,
or Jack Cade. Of course, it was possible to interpret fiction as indirect commentary
on politics, but unlike history it was not automatically read for its political
application.

One sign that the history play as defined above was carefully read for such applications is the regulatory attention it attracted. Though the evidence is not always conclusive, it suggests that the history play was far more censored than any other dramatic
genre, and certainly more so than other political genres such as tragedy; the only
element of comparable concern to the Master of the Revels was personal satire (Dutton,
1991; Clare, 1999).

Many critics of the history play continue to be misled by Thomas Nashe's famous
comment in *Piers Penniless* on Shakespeare's *1 Henry VI*:

> How it would have joyed brave Talbot, the terror of the French, to think that after he
> had lain two hundred years in his tomb, he should triumph again on the stage and have
> his bones new embalmed with the tears of ten thousand spectators at least (at several
> times), who, in the tragedian that represents his person, imagine they behold him fresh
> bleeding!

Nashe proposes that this kind of empathetic response to realism leads brave spirits to
emulate the heroes of the past. But this not the only response he reports. Talbot is
deployed as part of a wider critique of the *wrong* kind of response to such a scene, and
the attitudes from which it springs.

> What talk I to them of immortality, that are the only underminers of honour, and do
> envy any man that is not sprung up by base brokery like themselves? They care not if
> all the ancient houses were rooted out, so that . . . they might share the government
> amongst them . . . and be quarter-masters of our monarchy . . . if you tell them what a
> glorious thing it is to have Henry the Fifth represented upon the stage, leading the
> French king prisoner, and forcing both him and the Dolphin to swear fealty, 'Aye, but,'
> will they say, 'what do we get by it?', respecting neither the right of fame that is due
> to true nobility deceased, nor what hopes of eternity are to be proposed to adventurous
> minds, to encourage them forward, but only their execrable lucre, and filthy, unquench-
> able avarice.

The conflict Nashe notes is played out in many history plays, in which power is contested via forms of display. In the first scene of Marlowe's *Edward II* (1593), the king's favourite Gaveston fantasizes classical scenarios to accompany Edward's everyday routines; these entertainments are later said by Mortimer Junior to have 'drawn thy treasury dry and made thee weak' (1:1, 50–71; 2:2, 158). Gaveston himself, according to Mortimer, 'wears a short Italian hooded cloak / Larded with pearl, and in his Tuscan cap / A jewel of more value than the crown' (1:4, 412–14). Gaveston's preferred forms of display are Italianate (foreign, fashionable and implicitly effeminate). On going to war, his troops are said to have 'marched like players, / With garish robes, not armour' (2:2, 182–3); he himself is said to have been 'bedaubed with gold' and covered in women's favours (2:2, 184–6). G. K. Hunter's comment on Edward II nicely points up the conflict of styles in the plays; the king would turn 'a feudal warriors' hall into a Renaissance pleasure dome' (Hunter, 197).

Against the court's 'pleasure dome' is set a different kind of display, based in the forms of power of the ancient houses. On Gaveston's return, the nobles express their opinion of him via their shield devices for the king's celebratory triumph:

> Pliny reports there is a flying fish
> Which all the other fishes deadly hate,
> And therefore, being pursued, it takes the air;
> No sooner it is up, but there's a fowl
> That seizeth it; this fish, my lord, I bear;
> The motto this: *Undique mors est.* [i.e., 'On all sides there is death']
> (2:2, 23–8)

The king, exasperatedly, protests 'Can you in words make show of amity / And in your shields display your rancorous minds?' (2:2, 32–3). But the barons' choice of this chivalric rather than courtly channel for communication in itself signifies. Even a herald is identified in a stage direction as 'from the Barons, with his coat of arms' (3:1, 151). The play ends with a resolution of the contest between the two kinds of power-in-display. The young Edward III's coronation begins with a ritual exchange with his champion, whom he toasts (though the ceremony is interrupted by the haling in of his uncle Kent, prior to his execution). The play ends with another ceremony, the young king commanding, as Mortimer's head is brought in by an attendant, 'Go fetch my father's hearse, where it shall lie, / And bring my funeral robes' (5:6, 93–4). These traditional ceremonies – however compromised by their context – offer some closure to the play's visual contestations.

The anonymous play *Woodstock* (not printed, possibly never performed), survives in a manuscript marked by the censor. The play stages the conflict between great nobles and a young Richard II, focused on Richard's defiance of, and eventual disposal of, his uncle Woodstock, in which display metonymically signifies the difference between the two sides. On his first entry, Woodstock is specified as *'in frieze'*, a plain woollen cloth. When the Duke of York chides him for 'this country habit / For which the

coarse and vulgar call your grace / By th' title of Plain Thomas', calling for him to
be seen 'in bravery', Woodstock replies 'my heart in this plain frieze sits true and
right' (1:1, 197–9, 201, 203). In the next scene before the king, dressed in 'bravery',
Woodstock makes plain how fashionable attire is paid for:

> There's honest plain dealing in my t'other hose.
> Should this fashion last I must raise new rents,
> Undo my poor tenants, turn away my servants,
> And guard myself with lace; nay, sell more land
> And lordships too, by th' rood. Hear me, King Richard:
> If thus I jet in pride, I still shall lose;
> But I'll build castles in my t'other hose.
>
> (1:3, 103–9)

Luxury in this play is not, as in *Edward II*, particularly un-English; rather, it signifies a willingness to extort money from subjects in order to satisfy trivial wants.
Richard and his cronies' finery metonymically indicates their willingness to tax and
tax again. One direction specifies they enter *'very richly attired in new fashions'* (3:1, 1).
Whole days are spent in devising these fashions; Richard says he will ride 'through
London only to be gazed at'. Woodstock, meanwhile, is mistaken for a groom by a
courtier, whose explanation of his shoe with a chain linking toe and knee mocks both
the fashion and the courtier's misplaced ingenuity:

> For these two parts, being in operation and quality different, as for example: the toe a
> disdainer, or spurner: the knee a dutiful and most humble orator; this chain doth, as it
> were, so toeify the knee and so kneeify the toe, that between both it makes a most
> methodical coherence, or coherent method.
>
> (3:2, 217–21)

As with *Edward II*, the dissonant styles of clothing and attitudes towards display indicate an underlying political division, which eventually leads to the nobles taking the
field against the king. Woodstock himself is captured during a masque put on by
Richard and his minions *'like Diana's knights, in green, with horns about their necks and
boar-spears in their hands'* and carried out disguised in a masquing suit and vizard, to
be murdered soon afterwards.

This brief discussion shows the ways in which history plays refract aspects of late
Elizabethan social contestation (here exemplified in Nashe's comparison) through
late medieval politics. This practice both historicizes (by showing the specificity of
late medieval forms) and universalizes (because sometimes such specificity is no obstacle to posing a direct equivalence). This need not preclude the kind of identification
Nashe claims, for both the realism and the emotional intensity necessary for such
involvement are patchy in most histories (particularly those with a comic element).

The kind of comic interaction between Woodstock and the courtier quoted above
is not unusual in history plays. What is unusual is the involvement of a noble, for

comedy tends to be confined to commons characters. Most history plays present a mixed polity, in which at least the wishes of the commons are a material factor, even if only expressed through intermediaries. In addition, whether they have power or not within the world of the play, comic commoners could affect an audience as profoundly as a Talbot. Richard Helgerson splits history plays into those focusing upon the problematics of kingship and those concerned with an equally problematic subjecthood, in which, 'caught between their loyalty to the crown and their adherence to a set of values that the crown regularly violated, the protagonists of the Henslowe history plays repeatedly find themselves forced into making choices where either alternative is equally ruinous' (Helgerson, 239). These ruinous choices are often gendered, one of the crown's regular transgressions being the desire of the monarch for a married woman subject. Helgerson's split between plays focused on monarch and on subjection, whilst subject to qualification, is a useful reminder that the stage's concern with political agency extended to the problems posed by its lack.

Not all political problems found a ready mirror in the political history of late medieval England. Roman political plays offered the example of a civilization in which rhetoric and the arts were embedded, and whose own history – as mediated through these arts, rather than through chronicles – was a basic reference point for political action. In contrast, the history play offered a model of society in which this kind of participatory political culture was peripheral at best.

Ben Jonson's *Sejanus* (1603), set in Rome during Tiberius's reign, focuses on the rise and fall of the emperor's favourite, Sejanus. Jonson's Rome self-consciously takes its own past for a touchstone. Even Sejanus, describing the faction and discontent in the city, says 'Our city's now / Divided, as in time o' th' civil war' (2:369–70). This sense of a past 'Rome' as a living political presence is strongly presented in two scenes. One is the accusation of the historian Cordus in the Senate, mid-way through the play. The other is the very first scene, in which Jonson shows how 'Rome' enables political action in Rome. The opposition to Tiberius is informed by a sense of a more equitable past, as Silius says

> We, that (within these fourscore years) were born
> Free, equal lords of the triumphed world,
> And knew no masters but affections,
> To which betraying first our liberties,
> We since become the slaves to one man's lusts.
> (1:59–63)

But given this sense of a divided political culture, publicly presenting the past by writing a history is immediately shown potentially to implicate the writer in factional politics. Cordus's work deals with this past, and even though no character knows his own opinions – whether he is 'or Drusian? or Germanican? / Or ours? or neutral?' (1:80–1) – Natta comments that 'Those times are somewhat queasy to be touched' (82).

The play is fundamentally concerned with tyranny, and Jonson's placing of historiography as one of the first subjects mentioned is explained when Tiberius, in his first speech to the senate, refers to the historical record as the only thing that a prince cannot manipulate. 'Fame' (the verdict of history) is ultimately the only thing the tyrant fears; when he no longer cares about fame, there is no barrier to his actions. After praying to the gods to inspire him, Tiberius asks 'men'

> to vouchsafe us after death
> An honourable mention, and fair praise,
> T'accompany our actions, and our name.
> The rest of greatness princes may command,
> And (therefore) may neglect; only a long,
> A lasting, high, and happy memory
> They should, without being satisfied, pursue.
> Contempt of fame begets contempt of virtue.
> (1:495–502)

The stability of the historical record asserted by Tiberius is later shown to be contingent and manipulable. Cordus is accused before the Senate, and his books are ordered to be burned.

Though he is not linked to either faction in the state, Cordus's subject matter is 'queasy' because it is appropriable by either. In the first scene, Sabinus asserts there are no parallels between Cordus's subject and the present ('But these our times / Are not the same' (1:85–6)), to which Arruntius retorts that the times are, but the men are not: 'we are base, / Poor, and degenerate from th'exalted strain / Of our great fathers' (1:87–9). Arruntius then goes on to praise Cato, Brutus and Cassius, and, finally, Cordus's history, which he reads as topical commentary: *"Tis* true, that Cordus says, / "Brave Cassius was the last of all that race"' (1:103–4). At Cordus's accusation, however, these same figures signify differently. Brutus is 'a parricide, an enemy of his country' (3:397), and in 'comparing men, / And times, thou praisest Brutus, and affirm'st / That 'Cassius was the last of all the Romans', thereby insulting all subsequent Romans, including the emperor (3:390–2). Cordus has 'brought in parallel' (396) to the present the past of which he writes.

However much Cordus insists that he is merely repeating other historians' judgements, the play shows that his production of a particular history at a particular time is viewed as an intervention into a polity in which historical reference is part of the discourse of public justification and critique. The fact that the performance of the play itself led to Jonson being called before the Privy Council for questioning on the request of the Earl of Northampton in 1604 confirms that this was not just an antiquarian point. Jonson's substantial revision of the play for its printing in 1605, and his supporting it against hostile interpretation by marginal references to the authorities he had consulted, is clearly a response to this, though it has not deterred scholars from interpreting the play as topical comment upon the demises of such fallen favourites as Ralegh or Essex.

Philip Massinger's *The Roman Actor* (1626), also explores the interface between culture and politics. This play, based, like *Sejanus*, upon Tacitus's accounts of first-century Rome, both stages a tyranny (Domitian's) and explicit meditations upon the role of the theatre (rather than that of the historian) in such a circumstance. One of the play's two plots concerns the actor Paris, who begins the play defending the theatre to the senate. In the course of the play he puts on three dramatic presentations, during the last of which he is killed by Domitian.

Paris first appears defending the theatre against the accusation that the emperor's government is 'Depraved and scandalized by meaner men / That to his favour, and indulgence, owe / Themselves and being' (1:3, 28–30). The actors are 'libellers against the state and Caesar' (1:3, 34). This 'libel' is more of a breach of (an albeit symbolically vital) decorum than a threat to the polis. The players transgress by showing 'under feigned names on the stage . . . / actions not to be touched at', and 'traduce / Persons of rank', satirically making 'even the senators ridiculous / To the plebeians' (1:3, 38–40, 42–3).

Paris's response is firstly that the theatre is a deterrent from personal vice, so that the 'sad end' of a 'man sold to his lusts' persuades 'careless youth, by his example, / From such licentious courses' (1:3, 60). Politically, the theatre also encourages civic virtue. Philosophy delivers 'cold precepts' on 'the active virtue':

> But does that fire
> The blood, or swell the veins with emulation
> To be both good, and great, equal to that
> Which is presented on our theatres?
> (1:3, 80–3)

In addition, theatrical 'wicked undertakings' are 'mulcted so in the conclusion that / Even those spectators that were so inclined / Go home changed men' (1:3, 104–6). Paris's oration concludes with a disclaimer: if audience members think they are 'of the same mould' as vicious characters in a play, that is conscience's work, not the theatre's accusation. He ends by applying the point directly to his audience:

> If any of this reverend assembly,
> Nay, e'en yourself, my lord, that are the image
> Of absent Caesar, feel something in your bosom
> That puts you in remembrance of things past,
> Or things intended, 'tis not in us to help it.
> (1:3, 136–40)

This defence of the theatre's monitory and reformative functions is not answered by Paris's accusers. However, the three dramatic performances within the play undermine Paris's arguments. In the first, the players present *The Cure of Avarice* to try and change a miserly father. Significantly, Paris's claims to the son beforehand are expressed much more equivocally than those before the senate:

> Nor can it appear
> Like an impossibility, but that
> Your father, looking on a covetous man
> Presented on the stage, as in a mirror
> May see his own deformity, and loathe it.
>
> (2:1, 95–9)

The miser remains unrepentant, even after an epilogue directly pointing the moral of the play in his own case. In the second presentation, far from being encouraged toward virtue, Domitia falls in love with Paris (who is acting a lover's part) and pursues him outside the performance. It is for this that a jealous Domitian himself later kills Paris onstage, as he plays *The False Servant* at the emperor's request.

Massinger's play shows both a notorious tyranny and a relationship between this tyranny and the theatre. The three examples of playing which follow Paris's oration contradict its claims for the theatre's role to such a degree that, as Martin Butler comments, 'it is hard to understand the plays-in-the-play in any other way than as a demonstration of the speciousness, danger even, of the arguments of I.iii' (Butler, 159). The key to this contradiction is the problematic concept of emulation, which Paris presents as one of the main hortatory effects of showing honourable deeds.

The English history play, which staged few tyrants and fewer tyrannicides, did not have to confront the possibility that tyrannicide was one of these honourable deeds. Roman history plays, however, could not avoid the issue, for (as *Sejanus* indicates) the example of Brutus and Cassius as honoured tyrant-killers placed the issue of 'emulation' in a very different light. Paris's list of the deeds which the theatre might present to fire emulation only includes uncontroversial examples of martial virtue, but the early foregrounding of the relationship between theatrical 'example' and act, in a play which ends with the death of a tyrant, raises the possibility that Massinger's theatre might itself be seen to incite tyrannicidal desire in its audience. This model of the political functions of the theatre is, however, almost immediately disrupted by the working of actual performances. Despite what are carefully shown to be the actors' best intentions, those watching persistently miss the point. The theatre does not incite to virtue – including, implicitly, the particularly Roman virtue of tyrannicide.

This 'theatre of incitement' was most clearly produced in topical and satirical plays, the most famous of which – Thomas Middleton's *A Game at Chess* – ran for nine consecutive days at the Globe in the summer of 1624, and would have run longer but for the intervention of the Spanish ambassador, who prevailed on the king to order the closure of the theatre. *A Game*'s success was largely due to its satirical representation of unpopular Spaniards, within an allegorical format concerning the manoeuvring of black (Spanish) and white (English) chess pieces. The main targets of the play's anti-Spanish and anti-Jesuit animus were Gondomar, the Spanish ambassador to James's court between 1613 and 1622, who appears as the Black Knight, and De

Dominis, a Spanish archbishop who spent some time at the court in the years up to 1622, who is the Fat Bishop. As with the earlier moral plays, upon whose dramaturgy it draws, the play's choice of villain exploited rather than challenged the political commonplaces of its time (Howard-Hill, 108).

Tragi-comedy, the major political genre after about 1610, though it sometimes shared the history play's focus on tyranny and tyrants, was free to redefine them. Unburdened either by uncomfortably unavoidable examples of successful – even honourable – tyrannicide or usurpation, or by the immediate assumption that it was taking a place in a tradition of commentary on historical politics, the genre explored both the limits of stageable political disruption and the regenerative, compensatory power of non-tragic closure.

Beaumont and Fletcher's tragi-comedy *Philaster* (1609) begins with a political injustice: Philaster, the rightful heir of Sicily, has been dispossessed by the usurping king of Calabria, who plans to marry his daughter Arethusa, who loves Philaster, to the Spanish prince Pharamond. For much of the plot, the focus is Pharamond's unchaste behaviour with a lady in waiting, and Philaster and Arethusa's constancy. Philaster is an unruly presence at court, taunting Pharamond, but does little but rail, refusing to claim his right because it would mean challenging Arethusa's father, even though, in the words of another noble,

> The gentry do await it, and the people
> Against their nature are all bent for him
> And, like a field of standing corn that's moved
> With a stiff gale, their heads bow all one way.
> (3:1, 18–22)

This virtuous stasis is eventually disturbed by Philaster's growing and unfounded conviction that Arethusa is cuckolding him with his servant. All three flee to the woods, Philaster wounds Arethusa and his servant, and is himself wounded by a 'country fellow' ('Hold, dastard, strike a woman?'). Philaster is condemned to death, and marries Arethusa in prison. The king sentences her to death as well. But the city rises in support of Philaster; Pharamond returns to Spain; and the troublesome servant turns out to be a woman. The king resigns his throne to Philaster, blesses his union with Arethusa, and concludes the play with the words

> Let princes learn
> By this to rule the passions of their blood,
> For what heaven wills can never be withstood.
> (5:5, 223–5)

The play's focus on romantic love clearly offers a vision of the polity and political action different from that of the history play, where lust is more likely to be the focus. Even though the decisive political action is a rising in support of Philaster by citizens of the city at the point of his execution, Philaster himself remains committed to virtuous inaction, dispersing them with assurances that he will be all right, as indeed he is.

Though tragedy might seem to be better suited to portraying political disruption and its consequences, this is not necessarily the case. Beaumont and Fletcher's *The Maid's Tragedy* (c.1611) explores tyranny as it impinges upon the private life of the subject, rather than the public life of the polis. Its tyrannical (and unnamed) king of Rhodes breaks the engagement of Amintor ('a noble Gentleman') to Aspatia, and forces him to marry the royal mistress Evadne, in order to avoid scandal should she become pregnant. This private tyranny is revenged not by Amintor, but by Evadne, who half-persuaded, half-intimidated by her brother, Amintor's friend Melantius, kills the king, and then herself when Amintor rejects her. Amintor himself kills Aspatia, who picks a fight with him while disguised as a man, and then commits suicide.

In this play, court stands for polis. This court is powerfully inclined toward equilibrium, the only threat to which is initiated by the monarch himself. In its commitment to an absolutist king-centred perspective, *The Maid's Tragedy* breaks with the polities of the Roman and the English historical political plays. In these plays, supreme political power (if such a thing exists at all) is provisional, to be negotiated, to be produced and reproduced, often in the shadow of the past. The world of *The Maid's Tragedy* has no past. Political power is non-negotiable, in several senses of the word. The sexual honour of individuals and families replaces the various reflexive 'honour communities' of the medieval and Roman worlds as the testing ground of royal power. It is a scaled-down world, in which personal revenge is what civil war or large-scale rebellion are to the English history play, the decisive indicator of a polity broken down.

In a world without history, conclusive closure is easier to imagine (though not, modern critics insist, to achieve). At the play's end, king and king-killer are dead. So too are Amintor and Aspatia. Melantius, whose provocation of Evadne to regicide and securing control of the fort to safeguard himself in anticipation of the king's death argued some Machiavellian *virtù*, is restrained from suicide upon seeing Amintor's corpse, but makes it clear that he is now interested only in willing himself to die. King-killing is presented as the seventeenth-century version of taking the nuclear option during a battle, indirectly (providentially?) assuring the destruction of deployer, victim and innocent bystanders. But the equilibrium of the court/polis is not itself disturbed, because the deaths will lead no faction or family to further action. The dead king's brother smoothly takes over, having earlier issued a blanket pardon, pausing over the last-scene corpses only to point a 'just say no' moral similar to that of *Philaster*:

> May this a fair example be to me
> To rule with temper, for on lustful kings
> Unlooked-for sudden deaths from God are sent;
> But cursed is he that is their instrument.
>
>   (5:292–5)

The plays of Beaumont and Fletcher discussed here are not fully representative even of these dramatists' output of political plays, let alone the genres of tragi-comedy or tragedy. Rather, they are examples of political plays which, freed from the constraints of historical plots, imagine a static polity in which the monarch has absolute power, and explore how that power can be both abused and compensated for. In this, they engage optimistically with emergent forms of absolutist-tending royal power. Their divergence from the political plays covering Roman, medieval British or other histories can be seen not as a refusal to face the essential, ahistorical truths of politics, but an engagement with a modernity seemingly breaking with old patterns, issuing in a radically discontinuous polity and politics for which 'history' (as embodied in the forms of politics embodied in the historical play) was at an end. Absolutist monarchy turned out not to be the future of Britain; but the Civil War was not a replay of the Wars of the Roses either.

REFERENCES AND FURTHER READING

Bevington, D. (1968). *Tudor Drama and Politics*. Cambridge, MA: Harvard University Press.

Burt, Richard (1988). ' " 'Tis Writ by Me": Massinger's *The Roman Actor* and the Politics of Reception in the English Renaissance Theatre', *Theatre Journal*, 40 (3), 332–46.

——(1993). *Licensed by Authority: Ben Jonson and the Discourses of Censorship*. Ithaca and London: Cornell University Press.

Butler, M. (1984). *Theatre and Crisis 1632–1642*. Cambridge: Cambridge University Press.

——(1985). 'Romans in Britain: *The Roman Actor* and the Early Stuart Classical Play'. In D. Howard (ed.). *Philip Massinger: A Critical Reassessment* (pp. 139–70). Cambridge: Cambridge University Press.

Clare, Janet (1999). *Art Made Tongue-tied by Authority: Elizabethan and Jacobean Dramatic Censorship*. Manchester: Manchester University Press.

Dollimore, J. (1984). *Radical Tragedy: Religion, Ideology and Power in the Drama of Shakespeare and his Contemporaries*. Brighton: Harvester Press.

Dutton, R. (1991). *Mastering the Revels: The Regulation and Censorship of English Renaissance Drama*. London: Macmillan.

Heinemann, M. (1980). *Puritanism and Theatre: Thomas Middleton and Opposition Drama under the Early Stuarts*. Cambridge: Cambridge University Press.

——(1990). 'Political drama'. In A. R. Braunmuller and M. Hattaway (eds), *The Cambridge Companion to English Renaissance Drama* (pp. 161–205). Cambridge: Cambridge University Press.

Helgerson, R. (1992). *Forms of Nationhood: The Elizabethan Writing of England*. Chicago and London: Chicago University Press.

Howard-Hill, T. H. (1995). *Middleton's 'Vulgar Pasquin': Essays on 'A Game at Chess.'* London and Toronto: Associated University Presses.

Hunter, G. K. (1997). *English Drama 1586– 1642: The Age of Shakespeare*. Oxford: Clarendon Press.

Kastan, D. S. (1999). *Shakespeare after Theory*. New York and London: Routledge.

Limon, Jerzy (1986). *Dangerous Matter: English Drama and Politics 1623/4*. Cambridge: Cambridge University Press.

Montrose, L. (1996). *The Purpose of Playing: Shakespeare and the Cultural Politics of the Elizabethan Theatre*. Chicago and London: Chicago University Press.

Mullaney, S. (1998). *The Place of the Stage: License, Play and Power in Renaissance England*. Chicago and London: Chicago University Press.

Orgel, Stephen (1975). *The Illusion of Power: Political Theater in the English Renaissance*.

Berkeley and London: University of California Press.

Patterson, Annabel (1984). *Censorship and Interpretation: The Conditions of Reading and Writing in Early Modern England*. Madison: Wisconsin University Press.

Pitcher, J. (1998). 'Samuel Daniel and the Authorities', *Medieval and Renaissance Drama in England*, 10, 113–48.

Purkiss, D. (1998). *Three Tragedies by Renaissance Women*. London: Penguin.

Randall, D. (1995). *Winter Fruit: English Drama 1642–1660*. Lexington: University Press of Kentucky.

Sharpe, K. (1987). *Criticism and Compliment: The Politics of Literature in the England of Charles I*. Cambridge: Cambridge University Press.

Somerset, A. (1999). 'Cultural Poetics, or Historical Prose? The Places of the Stage', *Medieval and Renaissance Drama in England*, 11, 34–59.

Walker, G. (1991). *Plays of Persuasion: Drama and Politics at the Court of Henry VIII*. Cambridge: Cambridge University Press.

Yachnin, P. (1997). *Stage-Wrights: Shakespeare, Jonson, Middleton and the Making of Theatrical Value*. Philadelphia: University of Pennsylvania Press.

42

Women and Drama

Alison Findlay

In *The Tragedie of Antonie* (1592), Mary Sidney Herbert's translation of Garnier's *Marc Antonie*, Cleopatra tells her dead lover she is 'most happy in this hapless case, / To die with thee, and dying thee embrace' (5.171–2). Drawing on the Renaissance pun for death as orgasm, Cleopatra creates a paradoxical fusion between pleasure and despair, love and loss, absence and presence, a connection that Freud was to theorize later as a relationship between two basic instincts in human life: the sex-drive (Eros) and the death-drive (Freud 1950: 47–8). Following from this, Bataille argued 'anguish, which lays us open to annihilation and death, is always linked to eroticism; our sexual activity finally rivets us to the distressing image of death, and the knowledge of death deepens the abyss of eroticism' (Bataille 1997: 245). Women and female bodies have been a site on which desire and death have frequently been focused, partly because of the analogy between 'mother' and 'earth' that defines her as both womb and tomb. It is therefore not surprising to find these opposite poles linked closely in Renaissance plays for and about women. Sex and death-drives point towards conception and dissolution, liminal states at the origin and end of earthly human existence, bourns from which no traveller can bring an accurate description. The feminization of desire and death in Renaissance drama thus attempts to give shape and form to what is beyond representation, beyond the symbolic order or social systems of signification within which we live.

For women, the situation is doubly complex. Luce Irigaray has argued that these systems are inadequate to represent female sexuality at all and that 'women's desire most likely does not speak the same language as man's desire, and it probably has been covered by the logic that has dominated the West since the Greeks' (Irigaray 1981: 101). In the case of mainstream drama, women's desire was literally covered by male forms of representation, since the performers and writers were exclusively male. Nevertheless, Renaissance women did write and perform in other arenas: court and household drama offered them opportunities to represent their desires and fears themselves. This chapter offers a comparative analysis of several plays about desire and mortality, which were written about, for, and by women. Discussing texts by John Lyly and Thomas Heywood alongside translations and original drama by aristocratic women, I will examine how woman becomes a trope for masculine insecurities and how female dramatists rewrite the fusion of death and love to undo fixed boundaries which appear to dictate human existence.

Representations of virgin sacrifice have been a classic form of aestheticizing, containing, and so disempowering female sexuality, enacting in symbolic terms the connection between death and marriage. In John Lyly's *Gallathea* (*c*.1585), the 'fatal virgin' (5.2.1) Hebe outlines the destructive nature of possessive male eroticism in terms which perhaps gave voice to women's fears: 'thou insatiable monster of maiden's blood, and devourer of Beauty's bowels, glut thyself till thou surfeit, and let my life end thine' (5.2.48–50). In Lyly's play, however, sacrifice becomes a catalyst to alternative forms of feminine desire. The heroines Gallathea and Phillida are disguised as boys to escape the role of fairest virgin tribute to Neptune. It is their fathers who instigate the deception, out of a disturbingly possessive love, yet Gallathea and Phillida's adoption of masculine habits and their fathers' names allows them to claim ownership of their sexualities. The ever-present threat of sacrifice heightens their self-awareness; Phillida makes use of bawdy innuendo to remark 'say what they will of a man's wit, it is no second thing to be a woman' (2.1.25–6). In a remarkably erotic scene, the heroines move through a process of metaphorical undressing to recognition of same-sex passion. Male disguise and imaginative role play provide a gateway to alternative forms of desire in which women can begin to find a voice. The play's exploration of homoerotic possibilities looks forward to Shakespeare's *As You Like It* (1599), another play in which women are invited to 'like as much of this play as please you' (Epilogue). In *Gallathea*, disguise spares the heroines the shame of being a maiden suitor 'a thing hated in that sex' (3.2.13–14), yet ironically leads to the tentative uncovering of lesbian desire. Their physical disguises are a material representation of the difficulties of articulating such feelings within a phallocentric erotic discourse:

> PHILLIDA: Suppose I were a virgin . . . and that under the habit of a boy were the person of a maid, if I should utter my affection with sighs, manifest my sweet love by my salt tears, and prove my loyalty unspotted, and my griefs intolerable, would not then that fair face pity this my true heart?
> GALLATHEA: Admit that *I* were as you would have me suppose that *you* are, and that I should with entreaties, prayers, oaths, bribes and what ever can be invented in love, desire your favour, would you not yield?
>
> (3.2.18–25)

Each suspects that the other is, in fact, the same – one 'as I am' (3.2.29), and by the end of the scene the pair seek to move beyond cultural knowledge: '*Phil.* Come let us into the grove, and make much of one another, that cannot tell what to think one of another. *Exeunt.*' (3.2.58–9). Significantly, this will happen off stage, beyond the representation by boy actors.

Gallathea and Phillida's determination to absent themselves from the sacrifice and 'wander into these Groves' (4.4.32), disempowers the symbolic father / husband figure Neptune. Hebe is released and Neptune rages 'do men begin to be equal with Gods, seeking by craft to over-reach them that by power over-see them' (5.3.10–11). Although Neptune blames the fathers, it is in fact the daughters who have thwarted his tyrannical control of female sexuality. When they are brought to judgement before Neptune and unmasked, they refuse to sacrifice their love:

GALLATHEA: I will never love any but Phillida: her love is engraven in my heart, with her eyes.

PHILLIDA: Nor I any but Gallathea, whose faith is imprinted in my thoughts by her words.

NEPTUNE: An idle choice, strange and foolish, for one virgin to dote on another; and to imagine a constant faith, where there can be no cause of affection.

(5.3.124–130)

Although Venus promises to transform one of the lovers into a man, apparently reinforcing Neptune's view of female same-sex love, this resolution is not enacted in the play. The fathers' attempts to reclaim ownership of their daughters is thwarted; only Gallathea and Phillida can be certain of satisfaction (5.3.170–4) and by deferring the male transformation, the play suggests that satisfaction is already within their grasp. It is not only the heroines whose love challenges the heterosexual status quo in *Gallathea*. Diana's nymphs maintain a chaste independence rather than subjecting themselves to Cupid's arrows (1.2.28–9). They are thinly disguised versions of the ladies of Queen Elizabeth's court, for which the play was written, and Michael Pincombe has argued that its presentation of Diana is highly critical of the queen's vehement dictation of a cult of virginity (1996: 136). The epilogue, encouraging the ladies to yield to love, certainly flies in the face of royal disapproval of sexual dalliance.

Queen Elizabeth was an obvious icon for early modern women, even though her royal status made her a remarkable exception to many of the dictates on female behaviour. Her own desires and duties are explored in Lyly's *Sappho and Phao* (1584), presented at court and at the Blackfriars' theatre. In this play eroticism is combined with a less violent sense of mortality: the simple process of ageing. Bataille writes that 'the curse of decay recoils on sexuality, which it tends to eroticise; in sexual anguish there is a sadness of death, an apprehension of death which is rather vague but which we will never be able to shake off' (Bataille 1997: 245). Such a cloud hangs over love in the presentation of three generations of women: the young Sappho, the ageing Venus and the ancient Sibylla. Through this triumvirate, the drama plays out in oblique form the Queen's sacrifice of passion in favour of duty to her country.

The relationship between the rivals Venus and Sappho and the low-born ferryman Phao may contain a local allegorical meaning; it has been suggested that Phao is a portrait of the Duke of Alençon, or of Robert Dudley, the Earl of Leicester. Elizabeth openly displayed her affections for both but did not commit herself to marry either (Lyly 1967: 366; Reese 1942). The latter seems more likely; the play can be read as a melancholy, retrospective commentary on Elizabeth's troubled relationship with

Leicester. The idealized ruler, Sappho, is an image of the young Elizabeth whose unrestrained display of love for Leicester led many at court to believe he would become king in 1561–2 (Jones and White 1996). Phao's doubts about his own ambitions – 'can'st thou not be content to behold the sun, but thou must covet to build thy nest in the sun' (2.4.3–5) – reiterate the suspicions surrounding Leicester's interests in the queen. Sappho engages in a highly public and controlled flirtation with Phao. Their love scenes are stylized like graceful dances, a performance style appropriate to the boy actors but also to the court environment where hints and allusions form a secret code of courtship. When Phao is summoned to prescribe herbs to cure Sappho's love sickness, for example, both Princess and courtier use the word 'yew' with deeply flirtatious double entendre (3.4.79–89).

Sappho and Phao makes the audience privy to a ladies' world of courtly gossip, alluding to the power such women wielded behind the scenes. Ismena and Mileta and the other ladies-in-waiting point out the irony of their supposed status as the 'weaker vessel' (1.3.31–4). It is only by being admitted to this private feminine world, and to the royal bedchamber, that the audience can appreciate the emotional depth of Sappho's suffering. She confesses that 'glutting myself on the face of Phao I have made my desire more desperate' (3.3.109), and spectators witness her struggle to suppress her passion. Her own self-penned epitaph, like that of Elizabeth, celebrates how her wisdom and honour 'was such as love could not violate' (3.3.121). Nevertheless, she remains physically and emotionally disturbed and 'can take no rest' (3.3.124–5). To soothe her passion, she asks for a lute, and ends the scene singing of a love characterized by frustration ('prison-mates, groans, sighs and tears' (3.3.151)), and 'fantastic passions, vows and rhymes' (3.3.152–3). Jean Howard has convincingly argued that playing the viol can be read as a form of female masturbation in *The Roaring Girl*, and in this play, where the lute performance happens on Sappho's bed, the autoeroticism is all the more obvious (Howard 1992: 185, 189). Sappho's song climaxes with an address to the absent Phao: 'in thee poor Sappho lives, for thee she dies' (3.3.161). The scene displays the pain and pleasure of a passion which must be confined behind the curtains of a lonely bed in the interests of duty. Female spectators at court or at Blackfriars may not have been bound by a queenly role or national politics, but the need to suppress one's desires for the sake of dynastic politics was probably shared by many of them.

Fantasy is the only escape route and the prologue at court, which recommends 'your Highness imagine yourself to be in a deep dream' draws explicit parallels between the dreams of the Sappho and her ladies and those of the female audience. In act 4 scene 3, Sappho's ladies recount fantastic visions of common female experiences: passion, constancy, covetousness in marriage and love. The dreams function as a courtly code for articulating desires and fears, to simultaneously disguise and reveal them. *Sappho and Phao* responds to women's needs to release such suppressed emotions in safe narratives like the dream or like the play itself.

Its depiction of lost love is all the more poignant in the light of what happened to the Leicester–Elizabeth relationship. Through the character of Venus, the play dramatizes a bitter rivalry for Phao's affections which seems to comment darkly on Elizabeth's furious reaction, in 1579, to Leicester's clandestine marriage to Lettice Knollys. In Pliny's *Varia Historia*, one of Lyly's sources, Phao, is 'hidden of Venus among lettise which sprung up and grew very rankly' (Lyly 1991: 154), and the jealous Venus of the play remarks 'when I nursed thee, Sappho, with lettuce, would it had turned to hemlock' (4.1.10–12), a poison. Venus seems to personify both Lettice, the rival who enjoys Phao, and the ageing, jealous Elizabeth who has lost him to a ravishing beauty. The Spanish ambassador commented that Lettice was 'one of the best-looking ladies of the court' and Elizabeth never forgave her or allowed her to return. In 1584, the year of the play, Leicester thanked Lord Burghley for dealing 'so friendly and honourably with my poor wife. For truly my Lord, in all reason she is hardly dealt with. God must only help it with her Majesty' (Perry 1990: 139, 177–8). In *Sappho and Phao* Jealousy dominates Venus's comments on Sappho:

> Sappho forsooth, because she hath many virtues, therefore must have all the favours. . . . Venus waxeth old . . . now the crow's foot is on her eye, and the black ox hath trod on her foot. But were Sappho never so virtuous, doth she think to contend with Venus to be as amorous? Yield Phao, but yield to me, Phao. I entreat where I may command; command thou, where thou should'st entreat . . . Venus must play the lover and the dissembler, and therefore the dissembler because the lover.
>
> (4.2.20–30)

The ageing Venus gives voice to the fears of women governed by a culture in which physical beauty and attractiveness to the opposite sex are a measure of female self-worth. Naomi Wolf points out that women experience a double death, first of their beauty and then of their bodies. Thus, women spectators 'in the full bloom of beauty keep a space always in mind for its diminution and loss' and their consciousness of its fragility acts like a *momento mori*, keeping them subservient and maintaining in them 'a fatalism' more intense than that experienced by men (Wolf 1990: 80). Venus's awareness of the death of her beauty combines with an increased sexual appetite, attesting to Bataille's idea that the curse of decay acts as an erotic charge: 'Venus, though she be in her latter age for years, yet is she in her nonage for affections' (4.2.42–4). As a figure of decay and unsatisfied desire, Venus represents the nightmare of herself which Queen Elizabeth endeavoured to suppress. The aged figure of Sybillia stands as a prophetic warning that Venus's appetites are doomed in a society where beauty, youth and erotic magnetism are synonymous. Sibylla remembers:

> Gentlemen that used to sigh from their hearts for my sweet love began to point with their fingers at my withered face and laughed to see the eyes out of which fires seemed to sparkle to be succoured, being old, with spectacles.
>
> (2.1.79–83)

Powerless to recover her youth, Sibylla resembles the queen of whom Monsieur de Maisse reported in 1597 'When anyone speaks of her beauty she says that she was never beautiful, although she had that reputation thirty years ago. Nevertheless, she speaks of her beauty as often as she can' (Strong and Oman 1972: 38). Sibylla can only maintain her status by remembering what is lost and by cultivating her wisdom (2.1.86–9), sharing her experiences of the ages of womanhood with the young Phao who comes to seek her advice on courtship (2.4.61–130). Sibylla presents the third phase of life to which female spectators, among them Queen Elizabeth herself, all looked forward.

Since women wrote from within the same language and culture, albeit from a different position, it is not surprising that connections between femininity, death and eroticism feature in their drama. However, as Elizabeth Bronfen has observed, their representations often 'cite conventional conceptions of feminine death so as to recode these radically in such a way that death emerges as an act of autonomous self-fashioning' (Bronfen 1992: 401). Lady Jane Lumley's translation of Euripides' *Iphigenia at Aulis* (*c*.1554), for example, rewrites virgin sacrifice as self-realization. Iphigenia subverts the patriarchal script in which she will be sacrificed to Diana by her father (or rescued by Achilles), by actively embracing her fate. She moves out of the family into the public arena, telling her mother 'I was not born for your sake only, but rather for the commodity of my country' (1.809). She claims subjectivity as a self-determining Greek citizen, rather than as a dutiful daughter or a commodity to be transferred between men. A miraculous rescue by Diana allows Iphigenia to transcend the text. 'This day your daughter hath been both alive and dead' (1.954–5), the messenger tells Clytemnestra, drawing parallels with the resurrection to transform the self-sacrificing woman into a powerful transcendent subject (Hodgson-Wright 1998).

Mary Sidney's later translation *The Tragedy of Antonie* (1592) offers a specifically gendered dramatization of Bataille's idea that 'consciousness of death is essentially self-consciousness' (Bataille 1997: 244). It explores suicide as a form of self-dissolution and self-realization in parallel plots tracing the fates of Antonie and Cleopatra. The two lovers are never brought together on stage, so the primary dramatic confrontation is with death itself. For Sidney this was a pertinent topic. The drama is one of several works on mortality she produced after the deaths of her brother Philip (*d*.1587), her father and mother (*d*.1586) and her daughter Katherine (*d*.1584). Her translation of *The Tragedie of Antonie* celebrates death as a maternal force.

At the beginning of the play, Antonie sees desire and death as bound together destructively. He believes Cleopatra has betrayed him to Caesar, and her 'heart-killing love shall burn me last' (1.140). Cleopatra becomes a fatally consuming power like death itself when Antonie imagines her 'evermore / Gaping for our great empire's government' (3.21–2). Her love dissolves his military and heroic masculinity, as is clear when Lucilius compares the fate of Antonie and his divine ancestor Hercules, whose subjection to Omphale took the form of shameful, infantile effeminization (3.347–68). The consuming nature of female desire, and its power to dissolve masculine selfhood, is linked closely to 'the analogy between earth and mother, and with it, that of death and birth, or death-conception and birth-resurrection. Death is here conceptualized as the return to symbiotic unity, to peace before the difference and tension of life, to the protective enclosure before individuation and culturation' (Bronfen 1992: 65). Once Antonie has resolved on suicide, death becomes a maternal embrace giving 'healthful succour' (3.393). The chorus at the end of act 3 points out:

> What goddess else more mild than she
> To bury all our pain can be,
> What remedy more pleasing?
> Our pained hearts when dolour stings,
> And nothing rest, or respite brings,
> What help have we more easing?
>
> (3.399–404)

From her first appearance, Cleopatra is indifferent to her fate, declaring she will follow Antonie both 'Dead and alive' (2.308). Dramatic conflict in the Egyptian scenes comes with Cleopatra's worldly duties rather than with death. Her attendants, citing her responsibilities to the kingdom, her dynasty and herself as an individual, claim that complete self-abandonment to Antonie is self-abuse. However, Cleopatra shows no qualms about dissolving herself into him:

CHARMION: Our first affection to ourself is due
CLEOPATRA: He is my self.

(2.350–1)

The strength of her passion outweighs arguments that it is 'Ill done to lose yourself' (2.313), especially since Diomede's description of Cleopatra's beauty and the reasons for preserving it are suspicious. His admiration for 'the alabaster covering of her face' and 'her fair hair the fiery and flaming gold' (2.477–480), objectifies Cleopatra, even though she can use these attributes, like Queen Elizabeth, to communicate with kings and 'Answer to each in his own language make' (2.488). Since Caesar hopes his glorious triumph in Rome 'by her presence beautified may be' (4.366), the idea of using her beauty to win his support seems futile. The play asks pertinent questions about the relationship between self-image and the exploitation of female beauty. Cleopatra's duties to her children present a more serious challenge to her deathwish, especially since they appear on stage in act 5. They become a focus for her betrayal of her kingdom, dynasty and the future, in order to gratify her own desires (5.11–14).

The plot's structure gives Cleopatra and her words final authority. Since her death follows that of Antonie, and takes place after he has been pulled up into her monument, the play reverses the conventional paradigm in which the male anatomist scrutinises the passive, beautiful female corpse. Cleopatra gives her final speeches over *his* dead body. From a dominant position, the male anatomist normally eroticizes the female body as a 'defensive reinscription of gender in the face of gender's destruction through death', since 'death exposes the cultural composition of gender itself' (Traub 1996: 50). In Sidney's play, however, it is the queen who triumphantly eroticizes the corpse of her dead lover:

> To die with thee and dying thee embrace;
> My body joined with thine, my mouth with thine,
> My mouth, whose moisture-burning sighs have dried
> To be in one self tomb, and one self chest,
> And wrapped with thee in one self sheet to rest.
>
> (5.172–6)

The still-living Cleopatra enacts the maternal embrace of death and pleasure, undoing the boundaries between male and female, active and passive, loss and self-fulfilment which have troubled the characters throughout the tragedy. Much more so than in Shakespeare's play, the ambiguity of the final lines brings together the two ends of the spectrum held within the mother / lover's arms:

> O neck, O arms, O hands, O breast where death
> (O mischief) comes to choke up vital breath.
> A thousand kisses, thousand, thousand more
> Let you my mouth for honour's farewell give,
> That in this office weak my limbs may grow,
> Fainting on you, and forth my soul may flow.
>
> (5.203–8)

It is unclear which kind of death is represented here. Ecstatic physical pleasure and mortality are beautifully combined to create, for the audience, a play of imagination which 'allows one to guess at the figure of death beneath that of love, and a desire, which allows one to misrecognise death because what is visibly figured is not death itself but its double, love.' (Bronfen 1992: 63). Sidney creates a sense of infinity that looks to future growth as well as to mortality, and these final lines carry an extra authority as Cleopatra's 'dying' words. The power of female creativity grows out of the weak limbs, so that woman's soul can flow forth from death, as Philip Sidney's death had been the catalyst for Mary's independent literary creativity. Her challenge to the conventional boundaries of life and death, male and female, has an important afterlife in her niece Lady Mary Wroth's play *Love's Victory*, which stages love's victory over death through an unlikely combination of Diana's chastity and Venus's maternal passion.

A striking difference in representations of the liminal point between life and death is seen by comparing *The Tragedie of Antonie* to Thomas Heywood's *A Woman Killed With Kindness* (1603), where a prolonged female death is central to the dramatic effect. While Sidney presents the dead Antonie as a spectacle, Heywood sets up the adulterous Anne Frankford for anatomic scrutiny by the audience. Anne is a sacrifice to her own desires and to the power of homosocial bonding which allows Wendoll to be welcomed to her husband's bed almost as easily as to his table (Findlay 1999: 157–9). When Frankford surprises the lovers in bed, Anne begins the process of self-erasure which will culminate in her physical death. 'I am no more your wife' (13.83) she tells Frankford, already looking forward to her role as a morbid spectacle in her plea that he will not injure her body or face:

> For womanhood – to which I am a shame,
> Though once an ornament – even for His sake
> That hath redeemed our souls, mark not my face
> Nor hack me with your sword but let me go
> Perfect and undeformed to my tomb . . .
>   as an abject this one suit I crave,
> This granted I am ready for my grave.
>
>   (13.96–105)

Having polluted the identity of living wife, Anne reconstructs herself as a perfect corpse, an ornament in death. An opposition between physical mutilation and spiritual purity continues bizarrely in her wish to pay for the sins of the flesh by having her hands cut off, her breasts seared, and her body whipped and tortured (13.134–8). She imagines a martyrdom of physical suffering to restore her soul's purity. However, at the hands of a husband determined to martyr her with kindness, she is given physical comfort and is psychologically tortured by being deprived of her identity as wife and mother. She appeals to women in the audience to 'make me your instance' and preserve their chastity since 'when you tread awry, / Your sins like mine will on your conscience lie' (13.143–4). The only escape from her suffering is physical self-abuse, in the form of suicide by starvation. Anne martyrs herself, slowly, and painfully.

Anne Frankford's death is a public event in which her neighbours and the audience off stage witness her physical self-erasure. Starvation atones for her past sins since, as her neighbours testify, her illness has not left enough blood in her face to let her blush. To Anne, sickness is 'a friend my fault would hide' (17.59–60). Only in this abject state can she win back the names of wife and mother and the love of her husband. Frankford tells her that her honour is fatally wounded, yet by her self-induced death she will become 'honest in heart' (17.120). The liminal point between life and death becomes a second marriage. Anne simultaneously asserts and annihilates herself, declaring 'Once more thy wife, dies thus embracing thee' (17.122). Bataille declares that 'of all the luxuries of life, human life is the most extravagantly expensive, that, finally, an increased apprehension of death, when life's security wears thin, is the highest level of ruinous refinement' (Bataille 1997: 246). Heywood's *A Woman Killed With Kindness* stages female death as a shamefully expensive form of ruinous refinement under rigid moral and social codes. Anne's life has literally been wasted by Frankford's strict adherence to conventional morality and Anne's inability to imagine herself outside the social roles of wife and mother prescribed by patriarchy. While in Mary Sidney's text, Cleopatra's soul 'flows forth' in a tide where desire and death blend into one another, Heywood's heroine dies as a moral spectacle, a wasted living corpse, subsumed into her husband.

In contrast to this slow murder by 'kindness', Elizabeth Cary's, *The Tragedy of Mariam* (1604–6) dramatizes the impetuous and violent execution of a wife, in a world

haunted by ghostly presences. Elisabeth Bronfen points out that 'death and femininity both involve the uncanny return of the repressed, the excess beyond the text which
the latter aims at stabilising by having signs and images represent' (1992: *xii*). In
Cary's play, the first original tragedy to be written by an Englishwoman, the repeated
images of death, resurrection, and disruptive feminine power, play out the return of
the repressed for male and female characters and beyond them, the readers or spectators for whom Cary wrote.[1]

At the beginning of the play Herod's supposed death offers an escape route from
destructive forms of patriarchal possession. Mariam feels a revival of the love she bore
him 'when virgin freedom left me unrestrained' (1.1.72). The sons of Baba, whom
Herod sentenced to death, are secretly preserved by Constabarus, and can now 'from
your living tomb depart' to reanimate their honour (2.2.31). Salome, who had
betrayed her first husband to execution, now plans to take a more humane way of dis-
posing of her second husband, by rewriting Mosaic law and divorcing him. She determines to become a proto-feminist 'custom breaker' who will 'show my sex the way
to freedom's door' (1.4.49–50). This is an exciting moment of possibility and ideas
of female autonomy return to haunt the men in the latter part of the play. There is,
however, little sense of unity between the female characters, even in the first two acts.
Mariam, Alexandra and Salome are depicted in aggressive competition, calling on
their respective forefathers to assert their rights of command in Judea, and adopting
patriarchal and racist attitudes to slander each other (1.3). The ghostly presence of
Herod's authority is still felt. His command to murder Mariam in the event of his
own death ominously predicts an extension of that husbandly authority from beyond
the grave.

Herod's return in act 4 is a most striking resurrection, an uncanny return of the
oppressive past. Salome can no longer divorce Constabarus and so plots his death by
revealing to Herod his preservation of Baba's sons, who have been reborn only to be
re-condemned to execution. Constabarus responds with a remarkable misogynistic
curse on the 'wavering crew' (4.6.33) of female spectators:

> You giddy creatures, sowers of debate,
> You'll love today, and for no other cause,
> But for yesterday you did deeply hate.
> You are the wreck of order, breach of laws,
> Your best are foolish, froward, wanton, vain;
> Your worst adulterous, murderous, cunning, proud . . .
> You are with nought but wickedness imbued.
>
> (4.6.51–6, 68)

This speech is totally uncharacteristic for Constabarus, a figure whose restrained
response to cuckoldry has won at least a degree of audience sympathy and respect. It
is easy to understand his anger against Salome, but why Elizabeth Cary should risk
giving him such a tirade against womankind, is intriguing. His disgust at the sex in

general is shared by Baba's sons, and seems to be a response to death itself, rather than betrayal. The second son declares:

> Come let us to our death. Are we not blest?
> Our death will freedom from these creatures give –
> The trouble-quiet sowers of unrest.
>
> (4.6.73–5)

The attempt to imagine an all-male paradise betrays an underlying fear of woman's power as the giver of life and death. Salome's betrayal is only the shadow of a much greater threat to masculine self-assertion: the uncertainty of life and certainty of death, iconically figured as feminine since woman is 'the site that generates the mortal inscription of the body at birth, the navel's mark' (Bronfen 1992: 66). Female sexual inconstancy, of which Salome is guilty and for which Mariam is killed, makes patrilineal identity uncertain from birth onwards, and Constabarus and the sons of Baba are heading back to a dissolution of selfhood in the womb / tomb from which they emerged. Their bonds of idealized male friendship are brittle as they move irrevocably towards the feminine embrace of death. Women are 'trouble-quiet sowers of unrest' whose presence constantly reminds the men of the mortal cycle which makes their dominance so fragile. By showing how misogyny erupts from the mouth of a condemned man, the play highlights and seeks to explain the traditional prejudice against which seventeenth-century women were obliged to construct themselves.

Even blame for Herod's murder of Mariam is displaced onto the female population. Constabarus defines women spectators or readers as a fatal presence: 'you your-selves will Mariam's life bereave' (4.6.35). The immediate cause of Mariam's death is Salome's plotting, and Herod says 'hadst thou not made Herod unsecure / I had not doubted Mariam's innocence' (4.7.158–9). In spite of Salome's proto-feminist decla-rations of autonomy (1.4.36), she is far more wedded to patriarchal authority than she admits. For Salome (and also for Alexandra), Herod's reappearance signals the return of a repressed dedication to patriarchy in which women compete for the attentions of the most powerful men in order to exercise their influence. Salome's villainous success offers a pessimistic message to female spectators about how to succeed. Mariam is the antithesis of Salome and Alexandra in refusing to perform Herod's script as a means to direct it covertly. She knows she could 'enchain him with a smile / And lead him captive with a gentle word' (3.3.45–6) but chooses to sacrifice herself for the cause of female self-integrity. By appearing in 'dusky habits' (4.3.4) before the reborn Herod, she dedicates herself to death as well as to the memories of her brother and grandfather.

The Tragedy of Mariam rewrites the aesthetic relationship between femininity and death as female complicity with death. Mariam is not represented on stage as a beau-tiful corpse, a spectacle which guarantees male ownership. Instead, the text reiterates Mariam's absence by the male reports of her death. Even these reports fail to fix her as the object of a male gaze. Herod describes her as 'heaven's model' (4.7.93), an 'inestimable jewel' (5.119), but the Nuntio reports 'her look did seem to keep the world in awe' (5.1.27). By returning the look of 'the curious gazing troop' (5.21), and picking out the Nuntio in particular (5.60–2), she fractures the framing technique which would contain her. Mariam's prison speech shows how she has abandoned faith in her beauty, recognizing that it has little power against Herod's misguided will or the indifferent hand of death:

> Now death will teach me: he can pale as well
> A cheek of roses, as a cheek less bright,
> And dim an eye whose shine doth most excel,
> As soon as one that casts a meaner light.
>
> (4.8.5–8)

Like her heroine, Elizabeth Cary, as author, appears to surrender to 'death' in terms of erasing a subversive female voice, in favour of more traditional inscriptions of female identity. The character who chose to tell her husband 'My lord I suit my garment to my mind' (4.3.5) is reduced to a silence characteriztic of female modesty. Mariam is given no dramatic scaffold speech with which to challenge Herod. Her words and actions are ventriloquized through the words of the male characters, who elevate her into the image of a silent saint. However, that silence is also a 'rhetoric of death' (Bronfen 1992: 406) beyond representation. Mariam's complete absence from the end of the text allows her to escape from the specular economy which would define her as the mirror image of her husband. Dod and Cleaver's very popular conduct book *A godly form of household government* (1598), pointed out that 'as the looking-glass, howsoever fair and beautifully adorned, is nothing worth if it show that countenance sad which is pleasant; or the same pleasant that is sad: so the woman deserveth no commendation that, as it were, contrarying her husband when he is merry, showeth herself sad, or in sadness uttereth her mirth' (Aughterson 1995: 81). Herod thinks of Mariam in these terms:

> A precious mirror made by wondrous art,
> I prized it ten times dearer than my crown,
> And laid it up fast folded in my heart,
> Yet I in sudden choler cast it down
> And pashed it all to pieces.
>
> (5.1.125–9)

It is not just Herod but Cary who has smashed the mirror of feminine representation by removing her heroine from the end of the play. Complicity with the *physical* realities of death provides another important escape from a possessive male framework. When Mariam's execution is reported by the Nuntio, Herod's response is bizarre:

I'st possible my Mariam should be dead?
   Is there no trick to make her breathe again?
NUNTIO: Her body is divided from her head.
HEROD: Why yet methinks there might be found, by art,
   Strange ways of cure. 'Tis sure rare things are done
   By an inventive head, and willing heart.

(5.88–93)

As well as indicating Herod's unbalanced mind, this potentially comic moment also speaks critically to the Scriptures and conduct books commanding wifely subjection. Citing Ephesians 5:22 and Corinthians 11 and 14:4, Dod and Cleaver claimed 'the husband is by God's ordinance the wife's head . . . so must the wife also submit and apply herself to the discretion and will of her husband, even as the government and conduct of everything resteth in the head, not in the body . . . she shall have no other direction or will, but what may depend upon her head' (Aughterson 1995: 80–1). Mariam's execution has literally and metaphorically divided her body from her head. By losing her head, she has won freedom from the discretion and will of her husband and is no longer subject to his government. Beyond death and representation, it is impossible to know what direction her 'body' and will may take. Herod's macabre idea of putting the two back together is a desperate attempt to re-create her as a 'willing heart' who will obey the schemes of his own invention. Cary's play conceals Mariam safely in the realm of death, beyond appropriation and misrepresentation. Like Lumley's *Iphigenia* and Sidney's *Tragedy of Antonie*, it demonstrates the skill of women dramatists in re-presenting death as a feminine form which exceeds the cultural models designed to reinforce a violent hierarchy of sexual difference.

NOTE

1 Although no records of a seventeenth century production have survived, it is obvious that the text was written with performance in mind. See Findlay, Hodgson-Wright and Williams (1999a and 1999b).

REFERENCES AND FURTHER READING

Aughterson, Kate (ed.) (1995). *Renaissance Woman, a Sourcebook: Constructions of Femininity in Renaissance England, A Sourcebook*. London: Routledge.

Bataille, Georges (1997). *The Bataille Reader*, eds Fred Botting and Scott Wilson. Oxford: Basil Blackwell.

Bronfen, Elisabeth (1992). *Over Her Dead Body: Death Femininity and the Aesthetic*. Manchester: Manchester University Press.

Cary, Elizabeth Tanfield (1996). *The Tragedy of Mariam*, ed. Stephanie J. Wright. Keele: Keele University Press.

Cotton, Nancy (1980). *Women Playwrights in England 1363–1750*. Lewisburg: Bucknell University Press.

Duncan-Jones, Katherine (1991). *Sir Philip Sidney, Courtier Poet*. London: Hamish Hamilton.

Findlay, Alison (1999). *A Feminist Perspective on Renaissance Drama*. Oxford: Basil Blackwell.

Findlay, Alison, Stephanie Hodgson-Wright and Gweno Williams (1999a). 'The Play is Ready to be Acted': Women and Dramatic Production 1570–1670', *Women's Writing*, 6 (1), 129–48.

——(1999b), *Women and Dramatic Production 1550–1670: Plays in Performance*. Lancaster: Lancaster University Television Unit (video).

Findlay, Alison and Hodgson-Wright, Stephanie with Gweno Williams (2000). *Women and Dramatic Production 1550–1700*. London: Longman.

Freud, Sigmund (1950). *Beyond the Pleasure Principle*, ed. James Strachey. London: Hogarth Press.

Hannay, Margaret P. (1990). *Philip's Phoenix: Mary Sidney: Countess of Pembroke*. Oxford and New York: Oxford University Press.

Heywood, Thomas (1961). *A Woman Killed With Kindness*, ed. R. W. Van Fossen, Revels Plays. London: Methuen and Co.

Hodgson-Wright, Stephanie (1998). 'Jane Lumley's *Iphigenia at Aulis*: Multum in parvo, or Less is More'. In S. P. Cerasano and M. Wynne-Davies (eds), *Readings in Renaissance Women's Drama: Criticism, History, and Performance 1594–1998* (pp. 129–41). London and New York: Routledge.

Howard, Jean E. (1992). 'Sex and Social Conflict: The Erotics of *The Roaring Girl*'. In S. Zimmerman (ed.), *Erotic Politics: Desire on the Renaissance Stage* (pp. 170–90). London: Routledge.

Hunter, G. K. (1962). *John Lyly: The Humanist as Courtier*. London: Routledge.

Irigaray, Luce (1981). 'Ce sexe qui n'est pas un'. In E. Marks and I. de Courtivron (eds), *New French Feminisms* (pp. 99–106). Brighton: Harvester.

Jones, Norman and Paul Whitefield White (1996). '*Gorboduc* and Royal Marriage Politics', *ELR*, 26, 3–16.

Lamb, Mary Ellen (1990). *Gender and Authorship in the Sidney Circle*. Madison, WI: University of Wisconsin Press.

Lumley, Jane (1998). *The Tragedie of Iphigenia* in *Three Tragedies by Renaissance Women*, ed. Diane Purkiss (pp. 1–35) Harmondsworth: Penguin.

Lyly, John (1967). *Gallathea*, in *The Complete Works of John Lyly*, Vol. 2, ed. R. Warwick Bond. Oxford: Clarendon Press.

——(1991). *Sappho and Phao*, in *Campaspe and Sappho and Phao*, eds George K. Hunter and David Bevington, Revels Plays (pp. 141–300) Manchester: Manchester University Press.

Perry, Maria (1990). *The Word of A Prince: A Life of Elizabeth I From Contemporary Documents*. Woodbridge: Boydell Press.

Pincombe, Michael (1996). *The Plays of John Lyly: Eros and Eliza*, Revels Plays Companion Library. Manchester: Manchester University Press.

Reese, Gertrude (1942). 'The Question of Succession in Elizabethan Drama', *University of Texas Studies in English*, 22, 75.

Sidney, Mary (1996), *The Tragedy of Antonie* (1595). In S. P. Cerasano and M. Wynne-Davies (eds), *Renaissance Drama by Women: Texts and Documents*. London: Routledge. All references are to this edition.

Strong, Roy and Julia Trevelyan Oman (1972). *Elizabeth R*. London: Book Club Associates.

Traub, Valerie (1996). 'Gendering Mortality in Early Modern Anatomies'. In V. Traub, M. Lindsay Kaplan and D. Callaghan (eds), *Feminist Readings of Early Modern Culture: Emerging Subjects* (pp. 42–92). Cambridge: Cambridge University Press.

Wolf, Naomi (1990). *The Beauty Myth*. London: Chatto and Windus.

Wroth, Lady Mary (c.1614–16). *Love's Victory*. In S. P. Cerasano and M. Wynne-Davies (eds), *Renaissance Drama by Women: Texts and Documents*. London: Routledge.

43
Tales of the City:
The Comedies of Ben Jonson
and Thomas Middleton

Peter J. Smith

In one way the period to which we refer as the English Renaissance might be thought of as the age of the new city and a case could be advanced for the fruition of one being inseparable from the rise of the other. Not that this attention to the formation of cities was an especially new phenomenon; literature had long dwelt on the importance of urban communities. Epic poetry celebrated the founding of cities and nation states that grew up around them. Virgil's *Aeneid* for instance, documented the exile of Aeneas, following the fall of Troy, and his founding a new capital, Rome, which was to become the centre of the Roman Empire and an exemplary city for the classically inspired humanists of the Italian (and later English) Renaissance. When Geoffrey of Monmouth composed his *Historia Regum Britanniae* in the twelfth century, he recounted the myth of the Trojan warrior Brut, the great-grandson of Aeneas, who conquered the race of giants that inhabited the ancient land of Albion. He too founded a city which he called Troynovant. It was this city which became London, the conspicuous seat of both royal and civic power consolidated during the Tudor and Stuart dynasties, a position which it continues to occupy to this day.

During the course of the later middle ages and throughout the sixteenth and seventeenth centuries, London's importance increased considerably. Standard English, as a result of civil service communications and other governmental and mercantile administrations, rippled out from London. The impact of this remains and, for example, accounts for the fact that Chaucer, writing in a London dialect for the court of Richard II, is so much easier to read than his west midlands contemporary, the Gawain poet. Chaucer's is the English which we have inherited, entirely because of the centrality, politically rather than geographically, of London. Of course, by modern standards, the capital was tiny. Tottenham Court and Hampstead were outlying villages and Westminster was still a separate town. But the city was beginning to expand at an alarming rate. In the reign of Henry VIII, the population was some fifty thousand. By the end of Elizabeth's reign it had more than tripled and was to increase further during the seventeenth century.[1]

Contemporary opinion relished this new metropolis and the consequent availability of consumer goods. John Lyly enthuses:

> London, a place both for the beauty of building, infinite riches, variety of all things, that excelleth all the cities in the world: insomuch that it may be called the store-house and Mart of all Europe. Close by this city runneth the famous river called the Thames . . . What can there be in any place under the heavens, that is not in this noble city either to be bought or borrowed?
>
> It hath divers hospitals for the relieving of the poor, six-score fair churches for divine service, a glorious burse which they call the Royal Exchange for the meeting of merchants of all countries where any traffic is to be had.[2]

But if Lyly's response anticipates the excitement of Dr Johnson derived from London life in the eighteenth century, Thomas Dekker regarded the place with pessimism:

> in every street, carts and coaches make such a thundering as if the world ran upon wheels: at every corner, men, women, and children meet in such shoals, that posts are set up of purpose to strengthen the houses, least with jostling one another they should shoulder them down. Besides, hammers are beating in one place, tubs hooping in another, pots clinking in a third, water-tankards running at tilt in a fourth.[3]

Dekker bemoans the ubiquitous urban scourges – pollution and traffic jams. His less than flattering portrayal of London recognizes that culture comes at a price. London may have contained palaces and hosted royal entertainments like the masques written by Ben Jonson or the pageants composed by Thomas Middleton, but it also played host to grinding poverty, dispossession and crime.

In the middle ages England had consisted of virtually self-sufficient, isolated communities producing foodstuffs and wool for their own consumption. From the fifteenth century, under the influence of exploration and foreign trade requirements, this wool began to be sold abroad. Sheep farmers were now transformed into commodity producers for an international market. The boom in the textile trade required large tracts of land for sheep grazing. Hitherto available for cultivation by villagers, areas of land were fenced off and the peasants evicted, losing their rights of common. Thomas More's *Utopia* captures the rapacity of the landowners as well as the pathos of the dispossessed. In this perverse world, sheep have

> become so great devourers and so wild, that they eat up and swallow down the very men them selves. They consume destroy and devour whole fields houses and cities . . . [Landowners] leave no ground for tillage: they enclose all in pastures: they throw down houses: they pluck down towns, and leave nothing standing but only the church to make of it a sheep-house . . . other by hook or crook they must needs depart away, poor silly, wretched souls men, women, husbands, wives, fatherless children, widows, woeful mothers with their young babes, and their hole household small in substance, and much in number, as husbandry requireth many hands. Away they trudge, I say . . . [and when

their savings are spent} what can they else do but steal, and then justly, God wote, be hanged, or else go about a begging? And yet then also they be cast in prison as vagabonds, because they go about and work not; whom no man will set a work, though they never so willingly offer them selves thereto.[4]

Many of these so-called 'masterless men' had nowhere to go but London where they attempted to eke out a living by all manner of activity – legal and, inevitably, illegal. The authorities responded with draconian measures. According to a piece of 1572 legislation vagrants were to be whipped and branded on the ear for the first crime and receive the death penalty for any subsequent offence, unless taken into service. In 1591 vagabonds were set to work in London cleaning ditches around the city. In his account of 'dicing houses . . . within the bowels of the famous City of London', George Whetstone laments the current degradation and the manner in which England's capital is inhabited by less savoury individuals who belong more properly in Italian cities:

> The daily guests of these privy houses, are masterless men, needy shifters, thieves, cutpurses, unthrifty servants, both serving men, and prentices. Here a man may pick out mates for all purposes, save such as are good. Here a man may find out bravoes of Rome and Naples, who for a pottle of wine, will make no more conscience to kill a man, than a butcher a beast . . . Here are they, that will not let to deceive their father, to rob their brother, and fire their neighbours house for an advantage . . . forsooth they have yet hands to filch, heads to deceive, and friends to receive: and by these helps, shift meetly badly well.[5]

It is this 'many headed hydra' which jostles at the edge of Renaissance drama – the fickle multitude in *Julius Caesar* manipulated by the cynical Mark Antony, or the hysterical rout in Ben Jonson's *Sejanus* who enter to tear the politician limb from limb. For the authorities, they constituted a dangerously volatile social force.

Seventeenth-century London then is the origin of two contradictory perspectives. It is the seat of government and the court, the centre of banking and commerce, the home of city professionals and the civil service. On the other hand, it is a concentration of vice, a den of iniquity, a cesspool of prostitution, alcoholism, pick-pocketing and confidence trickery documented in sensational accounts of the criminal underworld such as John Awdelay's *Fraternity of Vagabonds* (1603) or Thomas Harman's *Caveat for Common Cursetors* (1566). The popularity of these tracts indicates both a fascination with and an anxiety towards the (under)world that they document while the dramatization of their criminal fraternities yields such popular settings as the Eastcheap tavern of *Henry IV* or the brothels of *Measure for Measure*. The new metropolis, seat of a new vigorous English Protestantism, is also riddled with corruption and nowhere is this tension between virtue and vice as visible as in the theatre.

The purpose-built theatre, run by professional companies and staffed by professional actors was a comparatively recent invention and the pioneering of dramatic writing was experiencing a steep learning curve. The theatres themselves were micro-

cosmic versions of the city, riven in precisely the same way between virtue and vice
– places in which culture was disseminated, national identity celebrated (as in the
often jingoistic history plays) and moral exempla broadcast – but also, especially
according to their opponents, places of immorality which displayed lewd and subversive acts of cross-dressing, political insurgence and social discord. Moreover, their
iniquity was not only confined to the stage. More than once the theatres were shut
down because they were thought to provide excellent opportunities for the contagion
of plague while disease was seen to be a just retribution for the immoralities of the
players. Women's presence in theatre audiences was considered indelicate and the
siting of the theatres on the south bank, beyond the jurisdiction of the Lord Mayor,
placed them in close proximity to the brothels which also sought to elude the imposition of civic authority while pandering to the patronage of an immodest clientele.
The theatres existed, both geographically and ideologically, in a liminal zone, on the
margins of the city.

The varied careers of Jonson and Middleton are testament to the ambiguities inherent in this relationship between city and theatre. Both achieved celebrated establishment status. Jonson became the first Poet Laureate in receipt of a royal pension for
his authorship of court masques and entertainments. A volume of his work was presented to Prince Henry and he held the position from 1628 of the Chronologer of the
City of London. But more than once he found himself on the wrong side of the law.
Having been convicted of the murder in 1598 of Gabriel Spencer, a fellow actor, he
only escaped the death sentence by pleading benefit of clergy (he demonstrated that,
since he could read the Bible, he'd be more use alive than dead). But Jonson's dramatic career was no less controversial. After his involvement with *The Isle of Dogs* he
may well have been imprisoned. Jonson's truculence continued to upset the authorities. *Sejanus* (1603) dramatized the relationship between the corrupt Tiberius and his
eponymous favourite. Jonson was hauled up before the Privy Council who regarded
his attacks on tyranny and favouritism as a little too close to home. As Richard Dutton
puts it, 'There is every possibility . . . that Jonson had deliberately done in *Sejanus*
what Shakespeare found himself inadvertently having done in *Richard II*: constructed
an allegory of contemporary events'.[6] Jonson's conversion to Roman Catholicism made
his plays all the more suspicious in the first teetering months of the new regime and
the cutting and adaptation of the printed text of the play demonstrates (as also does
the difference between the stage and page versions of *Richard II*) that the playwright
was treading on some powerful and sensitive toes. In 1604 he was briefly imprisoned
following his involvement in *Eastward Ho!* – a play containing anti-Scottish satire
and attacks on the selling of knighthoods (the Scottish King James had been raising
money by selling honours). Yet, from 1605 to 1634 Jonson was to provide masques
for the very king he had been satirizing.

Middleton too had something of a chequered career in relation to the city fathers
and court authorities. He preceded Jonson in the job of Chronologer of the City of
London (1620–7) and composed pageants celebrating the place's virtues. Yet he was
also the author of the most infamous play of the English Renaissance. His *A Game at*

Chess, written right in the midst of his career as Chronologer in 1624, was both the most successful and 'the most controversial play of the Jacobean period'.[7] In a theatrical era in which the repertoire would change daily, the nine-day run of *A Game at Chess* was unprecedented. Before the authorities shut it down, it played at the Globe to packed houses. John Chamberlain wrote to Dudley Carleton that the play was 'frequented by all sorts of people old and young, rich and poor, masters and servants, papists and puritans, wise men etc., churchmen and statesmen'.[8] The reason for this popularity was the play's topical anti-Catholicism. Since the Reformation, Protestant England had been in a constant state of paranoia about the proximity and possible invasion of the Catholic superpowers of France, Spain and Italy to the south and east and the less powerful but a good deal more immediate Ireland to the west. The victory of the English navy over the Spanish Armada in 1588 (which animates plays like *Henry V* and gets a mention in *The Alchemist*) demonstrated both the iniquity of the continental enemy as well as the providential righteousness of embattled Protestantism. These anxieties were further fuelled by the possibilities of domestic insurgence from Catholics at home. In 1605 Robert Catesby and Guy Fawkes nearly succeeded in destroying both king and parliament in the spectacular Gunpowder Plot, a conspiracy which Jonson helped to expose and which forms the basis for the exaggerated suspicions of Sir Politic Would-be in *Volpone*. However, Elizabethan Protestant pride had declined at court since the accession of James VI and I. Son of the Catholic Mary Queen of Scots, James's foreign policy was motivated by a desire to form rapprochements with Catholic foes rather than to dare or challenge them. To this end, he sought to appease the Spanish ambassador, Gondomar, having the vehement Protestant, Sir Walter Ralegh, executed on a trumped-up charge. Ralegh had long been a thorn in the side of Spain having slaughtered Spanish troops in Ireland at Smerwick and having defeated Spanish forces at Cadiz in 1596 and the Azores in 1597. His execution typified the pacific policy of the Jacobean court and the shift from the belligerence of the Elizabethan state.

A Game at Chess satirizes James's own aspirations to weld the United Kingdom to Spain through their dynastic coupling. Early in the 1620s James had sent his son Charles, escorted by the Duke of Buckingham, to Madrid to woo the Spanish Infanta but the project failed and thy returned empty handed in 1623 much to the delight of the London populace and the fury of the Spanish ambassador. Thomas Scot, a Puritan satirist and preacher, capitalized on this popular feeling and, in 1620, published anonymously *Vox Populi or News from Spain* which pretended to be Gondomar's account of how he was toying with England diplomatically to advance the Catholic objective of world domination. At one point, the fictional Gondomar describes how he indulged in spying under the guise of securing the Spanish match:

First, it is well observed, by the wisdom of our state, that the King of England . . . extremely hunts after peace, and so affects the true name of a peacemaker, as that for it he will doe or suffer any thing . . . And for this purpose, whereas there was a marriage propounded betwixt them and us, (howsoever, I suppose our state too devout to deal with heretics in this kind, in good earnest, yet) I made that a cover for much intelligence, and a means to obtain whatsoever I desired, whilst the state of England longed after that marriage, hoping thereby, (though vainly) to settle peace, and fill the exchequer.[9]

Identified and pursued by the authorities, Scot fled to Holland from whence he continued with a stream of anti-Spanish pamphlets. Middleton drew upon these as he prepared his play for production in 1624. *A Game at Chess* opens with an induction comprising a conversation between Ignatius Loyola (founder of the Jesuit order and as such a Puritan *bête noire*) and Error in which the two discuss the Jesuit aspirations for world domination. Ignatius tells Error, 'I would rule myself, not observe rule . . . I would do any thing to rule alone: / 'Tis rare to have the world reigned in by one' (Induction, 71–4).[10] As well as this despotic urge, Ignatius is pilloried as a figure of lustful appetite as he remarks that he would happily cut the throat of one of his own bishops in order to get close to the Queen and whisper 'a love-tale in her ear / Would make her best pulse dance' (ll. 66–7). It is not difficult to imagine the Globe audience hissing at this pantomime villain as he rehearses his iniquitous aspirations.

A Game at Chess offers a series of characters as chess pieces in the manner of Lewis Carroll's *Through the Looking-Glass and what Alice Found There*. Obviously, the white pieces embody the virtue of Britain while the blackness of the opposite set symbolizes the depravity of the Spanish Court. The moral implications of the colours are illustrated when the White King's Pawn is unmasked by the Black Knight:

> B. KNIGHT: Pawn, thou art ours.
> [*Seizes* W. Kg.'s Pawn]
> W. KNIGHT: He's taken by default,
>   By wilful negligence. Guard the sacred persons;
>   Look well to the White Bishop, for that Pawn
>   Gave guard to the Queen and him in the third place.
> B. KNIGHT: See what sure piece you lock your confidence in!
>   I made this Pawn here by corruption ours,
>   As soon as honour by creation yours.
>   This whiteness upon him is but the leprosy
>   Of pure dissimulation: view him now,
>   His heart and his intents are of our colour.
> [*The upper garment of* W. Kg's Pawn *being taken off, he appears black underneath.*
>
>   (3.1.252–61)

In addition to the allegorical significance of colour some of the chess pieces stand in for real people. The identity of the White King and Queen are self-evident while the White Knight and the White Duke would have been fairly recognizable as Prince Charles and the Duke of Buckingham. Middleton's play actually steers clear of the controversy of the proposed marriage but at one point dramatizes the attempted seduction of the White Queen's Pawn by the Black Bishop's Pawn. This is clearly an allegory of the subversion of the Anglican church by Jesuits who were, it was feared, actively proselytizing and converting Protestants to Catholicism. But it is in the play's portrayal of the Spanish Ambassador, Gondomar, as the Black Knight that it succeeds in its most palpable hits. The players had obtained one of Gondomar's own suits as well as a special chair he habitually occupied, designed to ease his fistula. At one point, the Black Knight, in soliloquy like so many stage villains of the period, relishes his Machiavellian deviousness:

> But let me a little solace my designs
> With the remembrance of some brave ones past,
> To cherish the futurity of project,
> Whose motion must be restless till that great work,
> Called the possession of the earth, be ours.
> Was it not I procured a gallant fleet
> From the White Kingdom to secure our coasts
> Against the infidel pirate, under pretext
> Of more necessitous expedition?
> Who made the jails fly open, without miracle,
> And let the locusts out, those dangerous flies,
> Whose property is to burn corn without touching?
> (3.1.80–91)

The Black Knight refers here to the manner in which Gondomar had successfully persuaded the English to fight the Turks who had repeatedly attacked the Spanish fleet while during the negotiations over the marriage, Gondomar sought and achieved the release of imprisoned Jesuits. The Black Knight is a slyly effective diplomat — one without moral principle. Clearly it is not difficult to see why the play caused Gondomar and King James such offence. On the 18 August the players were called before the Privy Council but they pleaded since the play had been properly licensed that they were innocent. They were banned from playing till further notice and Middleton's son, Edward, was arrested (his father seems to have gone to ground). Since he was unable to offer any useful information, he was quickly released and within ten days, the players were allowed to recommence playing, provided they never again staged *A Game at Chess*.

Both Middleton and Jonson deliberately flirted with political controversy and these examples illustrate the manner in which satirical drama could profoundly inflect public opinion. In their city comedies, however, it is London itself, both as site of opportunity and vice which provides the vehicle for larger social satire. Brian Gibbons has identified the roots of city comedy in an amalgam of native and learned traditions. He argues that the genre is a blend of the medieval morality play with its allegorical characters and timeless ethical lessons, and the classical tradition of 'Roman intrigue comedy in Plautus and Terence, and its descendant in the *commedia dell'arte*'.[11] Both traditions are clearly visible. On the one hand characters with names like Richard Easy, Sir Bounteous Progress, Penitent Brothel, Frank Gullman, Savourwit, Master Overdone, Pecunius Lucre, Harry Dampit, Moneylove, Sir Walter Whorehound, Mr Allwit (all from

Middleton's plays) and Face, Subtle, Doll Common, Surly, Sir Epicure Mammon, Dame Pliant, Tribulation Wholesome, John Littlewit, Trouble-All, Morose, Sir Amorous La Foole, Truewit, Lady Tailbrush, Sir Paul Eitherside (all from Jonson's) stem from the morality tradition with its readily identifiable types who typify human virtues and flaws. As Anne Barton has noted, 'It was . . . in the nature of morality drama as a form that these authorial acts of naming should be absolutely essential, controlling plot as well as character to a degree unheard of in ancient comedy. . . . In morality drama, names sum up the true nature of their bearers . . . [T]he identity of name with nature [is] a cardinal rule of morality play nomenclature'.[12] It is in *Bartholomew Fair*, a play which contains perhaps the most ridiculous of all Jonson's characters, that the play-wright relishes the absurdity of this representative naming:

> WINWIFE: What call you the reverent elder, you told me of? Your Banbury man?
> LITTLEWIT: Rabbi Busy, sir, he is more than an elder, he is a prophet, sir.
> QUARLOUS: Oh, I know him! A baker, is he not?
> LITTLEWIT: He was a baker, sir, but he does dream now, and see visions, he has given over his trade.
> QUARLOUS: I remember that too: out of a scruple he took, that (in spiced conscience) those cakes he made were served to bridals, Maypoles, Morrises, and such profane feasts and meetings; his Christian-name is Zeal-of-the-land.
> LITTLEWIT: Yes, sir, Zeal-of-the-land Busy.
> WINWIFE: How, what a name's there!
> LITTLEWIT: Oh, they have all such names, sir; he was witness for Win, here (they will not be called Godfathers) and named her Win-the-fight, you thought her name had been Winifred, did you not?
> WINWIFE: I did indeed.
> LITTLEWIT: He would ha' thought himself a stark reprobate, if it had.
>
> (1.3.100–17)[13]

While the idiotic compound of the first name indicates the self-endowed gravitas of the Puritan's evangelical mission, the surname with its implications of 'busy-body' reveals the preacher's sanctimony. As if that were not enough, the fact that Win is an abbreviation of Win-the-fight rather than the expected Winifred, catches out the audience as well as Winwife because up until this point in the play, she has been identified only as Win. Jonson's technique is to offer the audience a sort of advance insight into his characters in the manner of a morality play. Again, in *The Alchemist*, Subtle tells the Anabaptists that, once they are in possession of the philosopher's stone, they will have no need to

> Rail against plays, to please the alderman,
> Whose daily custard you devour. Nor lie
> With zealous rage, till you are hoarse. Not one
> Of these so singular arts. Nor call yourselves,

> By names of Tribulation, Persecution,
> Restraint, Long-Patience, and such like, affected
> By the whole family, or wood of you,
> Only for glory, and to catch the ear
> Of the disciple.
>
> (3.2.89–97)

But Subtle's satire is entirely wasted on Tribulation who unwittingly admits that personal fame and profit are as important as the advance of Anabaptist cause:

> Truly, sir, they are
> Ways that the godly Brethren have invented
> For propagation of the glorious cause,
> As very notable means, and whereby also
> Themselves grow soon, and profitably famous.
>
> (3.2.97–101)

If naming is one of the devices which indicates that city comedy is derived in part from the native morality tradition, the emphasis on local colour and the use of intrigue plotting demonstrates that the genre is equally indebted to classical comedy. It is in 'L'Allegro' that John Milton contrasts the 'learned' Jonson with the 'natural' Shakespeare as though the former is more cultivated while the latter is somehow more empirical: 'Then to the well-trod stage anon, / If Jonson's learned sock be on, / Or sweetest Shakespeare fancy's child, / Warble his native wood-notes wild' (ll. 131–4).[14] Shakespeare espoused popular conventions of romance that informed so many comedies of the English Renaissance and infuse even a 'city comedy' like Dekker's *The Shoemaker's Holiday*. The 'sock' here is the low-heeled slipper worn conventionally by actors in classical comedy and it is 'learned' because Jonson's comedy shares with its classical models both form (in its use of intrigue plotting) and content (the acquisition of money or the satisfaction of lust – the two are frequently indistinguishable in the figure of the rich widow, for example). It employs a series of stock *commedia* characters such as witty servants, young lovers, old misers, cuckolded husbands. In particular, for the historical reasons explored above, contemporary London life is set before the audience in all its degradation.

Both Jonson and Middleton relish the immediacy of London. *A Trick to Catch the Old One* includes references to Fleet Street and Holborn (1.4.56), Cole Harbour (2.1.226) and Highgate (4.2.8) while *No Wit, No Help Like a Woman's* mentions Clerkenwell and Hound's Ditch (1.1.292), Townbull Street and the Red Lion on Tower Hill (2.1.233–6), New Fish Street (2.1.298) and Shoreditch (4.3.111). Occasionally the very titles of these city comedies locate the action in precise parts of London: *A Chaste Maid in Cheapside* or *Bartholomew Fair*, for instance.[15] The explanation for this geographical specificity can be most clearly found by reference to the Prologue of *The Alchemist*:

> Our scene is London, 'cause we would make known
> No country's mirth is better than our own.
> No clime breeds better matter, for your whore,
> Bawd, squire, impostor, many persons more,
> Whose manners, now called humours, feed the stage:
> And which have still been subject for the rage
> Or spleen of comic writers. Though this pen
> Did never aim to grieve, but better men;
> Howe'er the age he lives in doth endure
> The vices that she breeds, above their cure.
>
> (ll. 5–14)

Jonson's moral aim is targeted directly at his London audience. The purpose of his art is not to grieve his public but to improve them, to educate them: 'To mix profit with your pleasure' (*Volpone*, Prologue, 8). City comedy then, is fundamentally didactic, exposing the faults of human desire for financial or sexual fulfilment at the expense of other people. With characteristic precision, Jonson emphasizes the exact contemporaneousness of his drama. Dame Pliant in *The Alchemist* gives the date of her birth as 1591 (4.4.30) while Drugger mentions that she is now 'But nineteen, at the most' (2.6.31). This dates the action of the play to 1610. In the folio of Jonson's *Works* (1616) we are told that 'This comedy was first acted in the year 1610 by the King's Majesty's Servants.' This company had recently acquired the Blackfriars Theatre in which they played as well as the Globe. Constant reference within the play sets the action in Blackfriars. Both in terms of exact date and geography then, *The Alchemist* is a play for today. Face, the crafty servant figure, has succeeded in outwitting all the play's dupes and even his own co-conspirators. He has gone on to pacify his master (by giving him the rich widow and all the stolen property amassed over the course of the play) and steps forwards in the epilogue to address the audience directly: 'I put myself / On you, that are my country: and this pelf, / Which I have got, if your do quit me, rests / To feast you often, and invite new guests' (5.5.162–5). We are forced to acknowledge that in applauding Face's efforts we become complicit in his offences; we sanction his thieving and have no one to blame but ourselves if we are plucked by the sleeve as we leave the theatre by one of his real life peers. Face's master, the significantly named Lovewit, voices the delight we all share as we witness the adroit improvisations performed by the conspirators at the expense of the dupes, 'I love a teeming wit, as I love my nourishment' (5.1.16). Volpone seconds this, remarking that he actually enjoys the trickery more than the profits: 'I glory / More in the cunning purchase of my wealth / Than in the glad possession' (1.1.30–2).

But while Jonson succeeds in forcing us wryly to acknowledge our own avarice and culpability, Middleton's is a less jovial satire. For all his dexterity in multiple plotting, his detailed local colour and his masterful ear for cant (all qualities he shares with Jonson), the tone is much darker. Quomodo in *Michaelmas Term* for instance, has no charm such as that displayed by Volpone in the Mountebank scene (2.2). Rather his grim cupidity obscures all else; consider his perverse satisfaction at the demise of his dupe, Richard Easy:

> SHORTYARD: What is the mark you shoot at?
> QUOMODO: Why, the fairest to cleave the heir in twain,
>   I mean his title; to murder his estate,
>   Stifle his right in some detested prison:
>   There are means and ways enow to hook in gentry,
>   Besides our deadly enmity, which thus stands,
>   They're busy 'bout our wives, we 'bout their lands.

(1.1.103–9)

This is London at its lowest ebb and in Jonson's *The Devil is an Ass*, we hardly wonder, in a world so corrupt, that even a devil is out-devilled by the capital's iniquity. Pug who has spent a day away from Hell observing the vice of the city has proved an embarrassment to Satan who tells him that he is 'A scar upon our name! Whom hast thou dealt with, / Woman or man, this day, but have outgone thee / Some way, and most have proved the better fiends?' (5.6.60–2). The final lesson of city comedy, it seems, is that the only way to triumph over craft and iniquity is with an even more powerful cocktail of the same.

NOTES

1   Heinemann, p. 4.
2   Lyly, p. 434.
3   Dekker, p. 37.
4   More, Sig. Cvi^v–vii^v.
5   Whetstone, Sig. Ki^r–v.
6   Dutton (1983), p. 139.
7   White, p. 128.
8   Cited by J. W. Harper's edn, p. xii.
9   Scott, p. 512.
10   All refs to Middleton are to Bullen's edn.
11   Gibbons, p. 4.
12   Barton, pp. 44–5.
13   All refs to Jonson are to Wilkes's edn.
14   All refs to Milton are to Carey and Fowler's edn.
15   See Richard Perkins, 'Topographical Comedy in the Seventeenth Century', *ELH*, 3 (1936), 270–90.

REFERENCES AND FURTHER READING

Barton, Anne (1990). *The Names of Comedy*. Oxford: Clarendon Press.

Cave, Richard Allen (1991). *Ben Jonson*. London: Macmillan.

Cave, Richard, Elizabeth Schafer and Brian Woolland (eds) (1999). *Ben Jonson and Theatre: Performance, Practice and Theory*. London: Routledge.

Cox, John D. and David Scott Kastan (eds) (1997). *A New History of Early English Drama*. New York: Colombia University Press.

Dekker, Thomas (1922). *The Seven Deadly Sinnes of London*, ed. H. F. B. Brett-Smith. Oxford: Basil Blackwell.

Dutton, Richard (1983). *Ben Jonson: To the First Folio*. Cambridge: Cambridge University Press.

Friedenreich, Kenneth (ed.) (1983). '*Accompaninge the players*': *Essays Celebrating Thomas Middleton, 1580–1980*. New York: AMS Press.

Gibbons, Brian (1980). *Jacobean City Comedy: A Study of Satiric Plays by Jonson, Marston and Middleton*, 2nd edn. London: Methuen.

Greenblatt, Stephen (1980). *Renaissance Self-fashioning: From More to Shakespeare*. Chicago and London: University of Chicago Press.

Heinemann, Margot (1980). *Puritanism and Theatre: Thomas Middleton and Opposition Drama under the Early Stuarts*. Cambridge: Cambridge University Press.

Jonson, Ben (1970). *Selected Masques*, ed. Stephen Orgel. New Haven and London: Yale University Press.

——(1981–2). *Complete Plays*, ed. G. A. Wilkes. 4 vols. Oxford: Clarendon Press.

Limon, Jerzy (1986). *Dangerous Matter: English Drama and Politics 1623/4*. Cambridge: Cambridge University Press.

Lyly, John (1919). *Euphues The Anatomy of Wit and Euphues and his England*, ed. Edward Arber. London: Constable and Co.

Middleton, Thomas (1885–6). *Works*, ed. A. H. Bullen. 8 vols. London: John C. Nimmo.

——(1966). *A Game at Chess*, ed. J. W. Harper. London: Ernest Benn Limited.

Milton, John (1968). *The Poems*. ed. John Carey and Alastair Fowler. London: Longman.

More, Thomas (1551). *Utopia*, tr. Raphe Robynson. London: Abraham Vele.

Smith, David L., Richard Strier and David Bevington (eds) (1995). *The Theatrical City: Culture, Theatre and Politics in London, 1576–1649*. Cambridge: Cambridge University Press.

Scott, Walter (ed) (1809). *A Collection of Scarce and Valuable Tracts on the Most Interesting and Entertaining Subjects*. London: T. Cadell and W. Davies.

Whetstone, George (1584). *The Enemie of Vnthryftinesse*. London: Richard Jones.

White, Martin (1992). *Middleton and Tourneur*. London: Macmillan.

Womack, Peter (1986). *Ben Jonson*. Oxford: Basil Blackwell.

Yachnin, Paul (1997). *Stage-Wrights: Shakespeare, Jonson, Middleton, and the Making of Theatrical Value*. Philadelphia: University of Pennsylvania Press.

44
'Tied / To Rules of Flattery?':
Court Drama and the Masque
James Knowles

The Myth of Court and Coterie Theatre

To the special fountain of manners: the court. Thou art a beautiful and brave spring and waterest all the noble plants of this island. In thee the whole kingdom dresseth itself and is ambitious to use thee as her glass. Beware, then, thou render men's figures truly and teach them no less to hate their deformities than to love their forms – for to grace there should come reverence, and no man can call that lovely which is not also venerable. It is not powdering, perfuming and every each day smelling of the tailor that converteth to a beautiful object, but a mind shining through any suit which needs no false light either of riches or honours to help it.[1]

Jonson's dedication to *Cynthia's Revels* (1601) added to the text for his *Works* (1616) illustrates the centrality of the court within early modern culture: it is the 'special fountain' and 'glass' (mirror) of the nation. This dedication comes from a volume which opens with *Every Man In His Humour* (1599, revised 1608–9 and after 1611), a play that resolves the disorder of urban culture through the intervention of a royally appointed magistrate; includes poems and works dedicated to many members of the court; and closes with the quintessential royal form, the masque *The Golden Age Restored* (1616) which celebrates the Jacobean regime's legality and pacifism. It is unsurprising, then, that many critics have seen the court as the central institution in determining cultural policy, and especially theatrical taste.

Yet, the crucial incorporation in 1603 of the theatre companies under royal patronage, remains a controversial event.[2] For some critics the accession of James VI of Scotland as James I of England signals the start of a long-term decline in the drama. Thus, theatre companies, seeking to please the developing elite audience of London and the court, began to shift away from the broad, 'popular' and 'democratic' traditions of Elizabethan theatre into a more socially and culturally divisive repertoire, responsive to the cultural climate of the court. The strongest proponent of this view, Glynne Wickham, comments:

> The decadence in Jacobean and Caroline dramatic writing which has so frequently been remarked and debated by literary critics is thus, in my view, due in far greater measure to the censorship (in the widest sense of that word) as exercised by Stuart governments than to any particular failing in the writers themselves.[3]

This view of the 'decadence' of Jacobean and Caroline culture has been surprisingly persistent and the accompanying repressive assumption still surfaces in many critical texts.[4] This tacit assumption, that links stylistic features (perceived as 'decadence') to political structures is often supported by a plethora of economic and demographic arguments highlighting the opening of the Blackfriars and other, 'exclusive', 'private' theatres, or the impact of court commissions on the wealth of the playing companies.[5] In return for prosperity, it is argued, the players surrendered their liberty to increasing court control, not only through repertoire but, directly, through censorship mechanisms which were administered by a court official, the Master of the Revels. Other factors are cited, such as the growing use of masques and spectacular devices in plays, said to derive from the court masque, or the gradual emergence of a new generation of dramatists, notably Beaumont and Fletcher, whose tragedies and tragi-comedies are supposed to appeal to elite tastes.

In many ways this narrative looks forward to another key event, the 1642 closure of the theatres by parliament, and suggests that puritan hostility to drama stemmed from its close association with the court. In this version of history, the gradual separation of the two traditions, elite and popular, contributes to a far more pervasive divide in the nation between the court and the country, a fissure which eventually helped precipitate the English civil wars. Accordingly, as the theatre gained more from court performances it was drawn into the ideology of the court, seeking to appeal to courtly aesthetics (gradually losing touch with the popular and democratic tradition) and, thus, becoming the tool of the monarchy. Many of the individual elements of this narrative, however, have been questioned by historians and scholars, in particular the sense of an inevitable progression towards civil war and the corresponding divizion of culture into court / cavalier and (Anglo-) Catholic, and country / parliament and Protestant (or, even, Puritan).[6]

Scepticism needs to be exercised towards even the basic assumptions of this argument. First, to define the court or, indeed, a courtier is not straightforward as it consisted of a number of overlapping groups.[7] Many of the court were, merely, members of the royal household, the plethora of bodily and domestic servants, tradesfolk and artificers, who had little or no privileged access to the monarch or royal family. The important figures were members of the respective retinues, ranging from the main state officeholders, through the political classes and major aristocrats, and including some of the more intimate chamber offices and servants, such as those employed in the Privy Chamber and Bedchamber. Second, the interconnections between drama and the court are more attenuated, with little or no evidence that there was a royal 'policy' towards the arts. Masques, which are often regarded as the main theatrical vehicle for the royal image, can be shown to be more various than has been suggested (see below, pp. 531–4), while the connections between the court and theatre are even more circumscribed. Nothing in early modern English court culture suggests a programmatic use of theatre for propaganda and, indeed, drama was very much the poor relation of the masque in court entertainments, lacking even a permanent playing place until 1629–30 (the construction of the cockpit at court).[8] Beyond the patenting of companies, which offered a measure of legal protection (against vagabondage laws) and support in negotiating the administrative maze of Jacobean bureaucracy, drama represents an insignificant element within royal patronage. Indeed, looking more widely at the whole aristocratic culture, most nobles who might have sponsored theatre companies focused upon other patronage interests, notably art and architecture, using theatre companies only for irregular, normally seasonal, entertainment.[9] Thus, although court performances obviously benefited the London companies, there is very little evidence that such involvements resulted either in increased royal control or that companies responded to a 'court' taste. In this respect Dudley Carleton's description of royal attitudes to theatre is especially revealing as he reports how James took 'no extraordinary pleasure' in the players, while the queen and Prince Henry 'were more the players' friends' eventually bringing the players under 'their protection'.[10]

So what were the connections between the court and cultural production in the Jacobean period? Jonson's early Jacobean text, the *Panegyre*, published in 1604 as part of a composite volume of dramatic (and quasi-dramatic) texts, *Ben Jonson: His Part of King James His Royal and Magnificent Entertainment*, illustrates the complexity of court politics, the submerged artistic competition behind texts, and, the dominant ideal in Jonson's relations with the court, panegyric. Jonson's text responded to his rival Samuel Daniel's *Panegyric Congratulatory* (1603), part of James's entertainment during his progress south which, while praising James as a 'prototype' (stanza 23) of kings encourages him to 'seek only the corruptions to reform' (stanza 30, alternate version) of the court, making it a place of 'plain zeal and truth, free from base following' (stanza 23).[11] In contrast to Daniel's *Panegyric*, which participated in the reformist climate which greeted the new monarch's accession, Jonson's *Panegyre* celebrates London's acclamation of the monarch ('men's hearts had crowned him': line 143) and associates 'zeal' with the people and the nobles (lines 38 and 70) acceptance of is divinely ordained and sanctioned monarchy rather than in a religious vigilance for reform as in Daniel's poem.[12] Themis (supported by Dice, Eunomia and Irene) steers the monarch away from these acclamations towards the 'better pomp' (line 77) of the soul rather than the body, arguing rather

> That kings by their example more do sway,
> Than by their power, and men do more obey
> When they are led than when they are compelled.
>   (ll. 125–7)

Yet, although the poem offers images of tyranny and licence, the predominant image is of a king who already understands both his duties and the rule of law. Both poems, rooted in the classical idea of panegyric where praise was used not simply to flatter but to encourage the recipient to virtue ('*laudando praecipere*', teaching by praising), reveal distinct conceptions about the court and the nature and efficacy of critical praise.[13] Thus, Daniel clearly implies the need for reform, even if the suggestion is carefully moderated by the generous praise which softens any criticism, while in Jonson's text any doubts are almost entirely muted by the praise.

The context of *Ben Jonson: His Part of King James His Royal and Magnificent Entertainment* (1604) is also revealing. In addition to the *Panegyre*, the volume contained a partial text of the entertainment that marked the coronation (a royal triumphal entry), in which Jonson carefully excluded the sections by other rivals, Dekker and Middleton, and *A Particular Entertainment of the Queen and Prince to Althrop*. This text, which had been staged during Queen Anna and Prince Henry's progress to London, completes the volume, Jonson's first attempt to gain royal patronage, which appealed to the three most important figures at court, presenting himself, as it were, at their service, and showing his ability to provide the kinds of occasional texts (ceremonial entry, panegyric speech and entertainment or masque) which might attract court patronage. Just as the *Panegyre* responds directly to Daniel, so the *Royal and Magnificent Entertainment* advances Jonson's superior handling of the entry, while the *Particular Entertainment* promotes Jonson as a masque writer and alternative to Daniel who had been commissioned to produce Anna's first masque, *The Vision of the Twelve Goddesses*.[14]

As a text written at the outset of the reign much of the troubling balance between criticism and compliment is subsumed into the celebratory mood, but what Jonson is clearly offering to the new monarchy is a distinctive style rooted in Roman imperial imagery. Thus, all the texts borrow from classical sources and gesture towards Jonson's self-presentation as the Jacobean Horace, while also situating the monarchy in an imperial discourse. The *Royal and Magnificent Entertainment* describes a royal entry in the manner of a Roman triumph, the most famous of the arches, the Fenchurch arch, depicting London as 'Londinivm'. Here James was greeted by the 'Genivs Vrbis' and Thamesis (the spirit of the Thames) who welcomed James to his 'empire's seat'.[15] The occasion was also memorialized in Stephen Harrison's *Arches of Triumph* (1604) with engravings by William Kip which convey the scale of the entertainment and its classical and pan-European aspirations. Both Jonson's speeches and Harrison's engravings figure James as a new Augustus, ushering in an age of peace and renewal.

It is important to recognize that this volume embodies a bid to become poet laureate rather than a previously established Stuart style. Moreover, as a strenuously self-advertising text, it seeks to efface Jonson's competitors and associate his poetic style as the natural, royal style. The *Panegyre* concludes with the Latin tag '*Solus Rex et poeta non quotannis nascitur*' ('Only the poet and king are born not made') making the links between monarchy and poetry explicit. Yet, despite the 'classical' rhetoric and typography, Jonson's volume was only *Part of King James His Royal and Magnificent Entertainment* (containing only two arches and a pageant). In fact, the event was not a royal event: rather it was organized by the City of London and its institutions and sub-groups, such as the Dutch and Italian communities. The City, moreover, entrusted the overall organization to Jonson's rival playwright Thomas Dekker. Dekker's narrative of events, *The Magnificent Entertainment* (1604) yields a less serenely imperial picture of the occasion, showing how the triumph was less a product of royal propaganda than the accumulation of arches from different sections of the London community, each with different agendas, and each designed to persuade James to follow their views. Thus the Dutch Arch, built by a committee of the London Dutch Church, depicted the Low Countries, while the Latin speeches exhorted James to exercise 'heroic action' to support Religion and Justice, a thinly disguised plea to continue his predecessor's encouragement of the United Provinces against Spanish incursions.[16] This was a controversial issue in 1604 with negotiations for the Treaty of London (a peace treaty between England and Spain) about to commence: James simply rode past and ignored the arch and its Latin orations.

So, although the Jonsonian text may imply an unruffled Roman and imperial image for the opening years of the Stuart monarchy, the survival of multiple versions, each with different inflections, suggests a far greater contest as to who should counsel the monarch and in which direction policy might tend. Moreover, as James's reaction reveals, such propagandist or hortatory gestures were liable to the vagaries of royal mood. It may, thus, be no accident that Jonson's partial account of the *Entertainment* forms only part of a volume which appeals to all the main royal targets (the King, Queen Anna and Prince Henry), especially since, as Carleton's despatch reveals, the most likely source of court patronage in the immediate future was Anna rather than James I. Moreover, the appeal to multiple figures embodies the major difference between the Jacobean and Elizabethan courts. In contrast to Elizabeth's reign where one power centre dominated, the Jacobean court boasted three royal households or courts, each with its own structures and policies. To complicate the situation further, the major favourites (Carr, Hay, Villiers) each exercised a degree of political and cultural power; other factions such as the Pembrokes (Protestant) and the Howards (Catholic) were balanced against each other by the monarch; and James also imported a number of Scottish advisers and courtiers (such as the Duke of Lennox) along with a predominantly Scots bedchamber staff as his intimate servants.[17] The result was a far less homogenous and monolithic court with considerable factional competition structured into the political and cultural ethos. One historian, Malcolm Smuts, has argued that the Jacobean court should be seen as peculiarly 'poly-centric' in comparison to both the Elizabethan and Caroline courts, showing a much more dispersed power structure.[18]

These political structures had important cultural ramifications. Many of the features of the absolutist state, notably a centralized monarchy with a strong administration were simply not present, and thus any programmes of control or cultural propaganda, in so far as they existed, remain far more open to contradictory influences. The censorship practices illustrate this amply.[19] The term most commonly used at this time for censorship, licensing, suggests the possibility of protection afforded by the Master of the Revels to the players once their plays had been allowed and also the broad degree of licence that was allowed. Importantly, licence and licensing imply a system that is not proleptic but normally retrospective and *ad hoc*, in contrast to the kinds of censorship practice more commonly seen in the totalitarian states of the twentieth century. Although some critics still repeat the repressive assumption, seeing dramatic censorship functioning as an adjunct of the developing Stuart despotism, more recent studies have shown that censorship operated in very complex ways, involving not simply direct prohibition but the pressures of 'law, licensing and patronage' and even good, old-fashioned administrative confusion. Richard Dutton has argued that the relationship between the court official and the players was less 'adversarial than collegial', helping to steer players through the uncertain areas of what was permissible and what not.[20] Even where transgressions occurred, as apparently in the case of Massinger's *The King and No Subject* (1638: lost), the king, who was shown the play by the Master of the Revels, found it 'insolent' and insisted on changes but without any punishment inflicted upon writer or players.[21] Charles's direct involvement in censorship decisions occurred relatively infrequently, but it serves to illustrate in a system of personal monarchy how much depended upon the temper of the monarch and simply the vagaries of personal behaviour: James's impatience with the masque *Pleasure Reconciled to Virtue* (1618) is justly celebrated. Under a personal monarchy the boundaries of the licit and illicit are blurred or constantly shifting, so that the newsletter writer Howell reports one occasion when James was treated to a 'very abusive satire in verse' and still forgave the 'bitter, but witty knave' because he concluded with a protestation of loyalty.[22] In contrast to the repressive hypothesis offered by some commentators, contemporaries remarked instead: 'the players do not forbear to represent upon their stage the whole course of this present time, not sparing either King, state or religion, in so great an absurdity, and with such liberty, that any one would be afraid to hear them'.[23]

In most respects the conception of a monolithic court culture is outdated. Aristocratic culture shared certain values and preoccupations, but courtiers often brought with them important regional, confessional, political and intellectual differences which shaped their inflection of courtiership. Occasionally, culture might become a tool in the negotiations between different royal households and differing factions advancing divergent policies, as when the Francophile faction (those supporting a French rather than a Spanish match for Prince Charles) mounted a series of 'French' entertainments.[24] Given this dispersed structure, the fact that royal control was somewhat attenuated, there is little real evidence to suggest that James deliberately propagandised himself through theatricals. Indeed, even his son Charles, who was far more attuned to European political uses of culture, used other ceremonials, such as garter celebrations, and other media, such as art and architecture, as expressions of his more rigid absolutism. At the early Stuart court what cultural policy there was appears to have stemmed from the satellite royal households of the queen and Prince

Henry, so that the masque, often vaunted as the symbol of royal policy, was engineered more by Anna and her son than the monarch, especially during the first decade of the reign.[25]

'Her Majesty's Personal Presentations':
Masques and Cultural Politics

Court masques belong to the wider culture of aristocratic masquing, ceremonial and entertainment which punctuated early modern life, providing both amusement and a means of representation and self-presentation. Masques combined dramatic dialogue, music, dance and spectacle (especially scenery) both to embody an idealized vision of court life and, also, to provide a suitable social celebration of major calendrical festivals, notably Twelfth Night, or of significant dynastic or political events, such as marriages, installations or diplomatic missions. Court masques interact with theatre in several ways, in that their authors (predominantly, but not exclusively, Jonson) and many of their personnel were drawn from London's theatrical community, mainly to supply the technical expertise or take the speaking parts which formed the first part of the masque (known as the antimasque).

Masques in the Jacobean period were not, however, simply a direct expression of a royal policy. Writing in 1608 of *The Masque of Beauty* the Venetian ambassador stated, 'So well composed and ordered was it all that it is evident the mind of her Majesty, the authoress of the whole, is gifted no less highly than her person'.[26] This central role of Anna, as the inventor or authoress of the Jacobean masque has often not been recognized but it belongs to a wider pattern whereby masques were rarely, if ever, under James I, the direct demesne of the monarch. *The Vision of the Twelve Goddesses* (1604), *The Masque of Blackness*, (1605), *The Masque of Beauty* (1608), *The Masque of Queens* (1609) and *Love Freed* (1611) were organized at Queen Anna's behest, and the later *Tethys' Festival* may have been a collaborative project between her and Prince Henry.[27] Henry himself organized *Oberon* (1611) and his *Barriers* (1610), both expressions of his chivalric interests, perhaps to counter his father's attempts to moderate this image (at Henry's installation as prince of Wales, James had forbidden the prince to ride in procession through London). Like the censorship practice, royal intervention tends to be retrospective and ad hoc rather than constituting anything like a programme of royal image making.

Indeed, during the first decade of the Jacobean era any programme of court representation emerged from Anna's interests rather than from James's household. Anna's court, like that of her son Prince Henry slightly later, seems to have functioned as a court within a court, and it is notable that many of her courtiers were displaced associates of the Leicester–Essex faction with its interests in militant Protestantism, though the queen herself was a covert Catholic.[28] A good illustration of this Jonson's *Masque of Queens*. The central fiction of the masque concerns the banishment of 'hags or witches' representing 'Ignorance, Suspicion, Credulity, etc., the opposites to good

Fame' (lines 15–16) whose sabbat forms the antimasque for the main action or masque.[29] This consists of the magical banishment of the hags by Fame's trumpet and the appearance of Heroic Virtue (Perseus) who introduces images of true female virtue from the House of Fame, a sumptuous palace depicting classical heroes such as Achilles, Aeneas and Caesar supported by the poets, Homer, Virgil and Lucan, who have proclaimed their fame. The female virtues are, of course, represented by the Anna and her ladies who emerge dressed as classical queens (including Penthesilea, Queen of the Amazons, Camilla, Queen of the Volscians, Tomyris, Queen of the Scythians, even Boadicea, Queen of the Iceni), culminating in the vision of Anna dressed as Bel-Anna, Queen of the Ocean (lines 596–7). The spectacular sets and costumes for the occasion were designed to accentuate the magnificence of the Jacobean court but, in particular, the 'dignity and person' (line 597) of the queen who regarded such shows as her 'personal presentations' (line 2).

Yet *Queens* is highly ambiguous, and there is much debate as to whether Jonson's 'all-daring . . . poetry' (line 615), whose role he constantly stresses as the creator of fame, actually praises Anna or whether subtly Jonson suggests that female fame and virtue are subordinate to male virtue. Certainly, Perseus, a figure of male heroism, introduces and defines the women, while the image of the witches dancing 'full of preposterous change and gesticulation', 'dancing back to back, hip to hip' and 'contrary to the custom of men' (lines 319–21) insistently recalls the widespread derogation of women in early modern culture. Indeed, even the choice of roles for the women, such as Penthesilea, may suggest the dangers of female power, and it is interesting to note that in Jonson's contemporary play, *Epicene* (*c.*1609–10), 'Penthesilea' is used to describe a controlling woman and her 'Amazonian impudence' (3.4.57 and 3.5.41).[30] Moreover, it is equally uncertain what weight should be placed on the witch-lore of the masque some of which may derive from James I's own tracts on witchcraft as a substitute for the praise of him absent from the text: by implication it is the king who defines true female heroism by recognizing the falsity of witchcraft. The emphasis upon the role of the male poet (Jonson) in the creation of female fame continues this strategy of containment.

Jonson dedicated the quarto of *Queens* to Prince Henry situating the masque as an exhortation to virtue and positioning himself as a counsellor and chronicler of the Prince's coming reign 'whether in the camp or council chamber'.[31] Jonson wrote two major occasional texts for Henry, the *Barriers* and *Oberon*, both of which illustrate the divergences within Stuart iconography: where James was celebrated in Roman imagery, Prince Henry required Spenserian, neo-Arthurian chivalric romance. It has often been noted that *Oberon* sits awkwardly between praise for Henry 'the high-graced Oberon' (line 342) and his father 'the wonder . . . of tongues, or ears, of eyes' (line 226), and its style seems to recall the Elizabethan imagery which was already being used as a critique of James's rule. Indeed, the tensions in the text are so palpable that one recent study argues that Oberon embodies a 'legitimation crisis' for the Stuart monarch with the pacific, classical Jacobean imagery challenged by a rhetoric of a more active kingship.[32]

Henry's masques are striking in the use of chivalric material that puts the texts in tune with a socially widespread interest in romance, but also because they are far more accessible to a larger audience, eschewing the esoteric mythology which marked Anna's entertainments. In general, Jonson's masques stress the 'solid learnings' 'grounded in antiquity' (*Hymeneai*, line 14) which was designed to appeal to the soul rather than the body although, more accurately, it deliberately excluded 'porters and mechanics' (*Queens*, line 98) and those without the necessary learning to appreciate the symbolism. Ignorance was, in fact, one of the antimasque hags banished by learned Fame in *Queens*. This exclusivity fostered solidarity amongst the elite much as performance in the masque also signalled insider status. Even in the more visually oriented Caroline masque the symbolism was deliberately opaque in order to promote a sense of mystery and awe, while the complex pattern of intertextual relations between masquing texts meant that meanings were withheld from those who did not regularly attend and participate.

The striking feature of court masques, then, is their limited or reserved praise for the monarch and their use by the competing households and factions of the Jacobean establishment. Anna's court, in particular, seems to have sheltered some of the groups marginalized by the Jacobean settlement and, surprisingly, this dissent was even allowed to permeate beyond the court. Thus, Anna's dramatic patronage raises intriguing issues about the extent of *public* debate over politics and her dissent from her husband's views.[33] For instance, Queen Anna sponsored, to varying degrees, one of the most controversial companies of the Jacobean period: the Children of the Queen's Revels.[34] This company mounted a series of controversial plays (including *Philotas* (1604), *Eastward Ho* (1605), *The Fawn* (c.1604–6), *The Fleir* (1606), *The Isle of Gulls* (1606) and the *Conspiracy and Tragedy of Byron* (1608)) which often depicted the Jacobean court in a less than flattering light. Moreover, the licenser for this company was Samuel Daniel, Jonson's rival, and the author of *Philotas* (1604), widely suspected of glancing at the Essex rebellion and criticizing the role of Robert Cecil, Earl of Salisbury (*de facto* the first minister of the government).[35] Indeed, even after Daniel had been called before the Privy Council over this play, Anna continued to sponsor Daniel (albeit from a greater distance), and he produced *The Queen's Arcadia or Aracadia Reformed* for her in Oxford in 1605. As the title suggests, although Arcadia has long been ruled by liberty and peace, it has gradually declined and now wants reform, especially of the court vices, although these range from foreign over-dressing through to enclosure.[36] The French ambassador Beaumont famously observed 'what must be the state of and condition of a prince, whom the preachers publicly from the pulpit assail, whom the comedians of the metropolis bring on stage, whose wife attends these representations in order to enjoy the laugh against her husband'.[37]

Beaumont's image of the liberty of Jacobean England has its limits, but what can be suggested is that there was considerably more freedom of expression than under Elizabeth where matters such as the origin of royal authority were beyond question. Doubtless some of the debate derives from and depends upon James's image of himself as a Solomon and his training in the Scottish parliamentary system of argument, but some also develops from a more complex court, with several centres of influence (if not power) which act in competition. Moreover, especially in the dramatic field, whatever propagandist efforts there were on behalf of the court stemmed from Anna of Denmark rather than her husband. The repertoire of the companies associated with her and her masques, however, present far more debate than untroubled absolutist images.

'Fortune, Not Reason, Rules the State of Things': The Theatre of Counsel

> And for the authentical truth of either person or action, who (worth the respecting) will expect it in a poem, whose subject is not truth, but things like truth? Poor envious souls they are that cavil at truth's want in these natural fictions; material instruction, elegant and sententious excitation to virtue, and deflection from her contrary, being the soul, limbs, and limits of an authentical tragedy.
>
> (Chapman, *The Revenge of Bussy d'Ambois* (1613))[38]

This potential for political debate through drama was recognized as one of the functions of theatre, what Chapman terms 'material instruction'. Classical sources emphasized the potential of theatre to act as a form of oratory, an 'act of deliberation' through which moral and political issues could be debated, while contemporaries noted the potential for the 'excitation to heroical life' (*Revenge of Bussy*, epistle, line 11) or to correct faults.[39] Indeed, the companies protected by royal patent, notably the King's Men, and the boys' companies, notably the Children of the Queen's Revels, engaged in this political debate to a remarkable degree. This awareness of the deliberative function of drama was, indeed, shared across the supposed elite / popular binary as Thomas Heywood (a writer mainly associated with the popular amphitheatre, the Red Bull) argues:

> If we present a tragedy, we include the fatal and abortive ends of such as commit notorious murders, which is aggravated and acted with all art that may be, and terrify men from the like abhorred practices. If we present a foreign history, the subject is so intended, that in the lives of Romans, Grecians, or others, either the virtues of our countrymen are extolled or their vices reproved.
>
> (Heywood, *An Apology For Actors* (1611))[40]

Although Heywood and Chapman place slightly different emphases (Chapman highlighting the role of theatre in shaping individuals, Heywood stressing the social dimension), both articulate the role of theatre in fashioning the individual in social and political contexts. Indeed, these political and social dimensions are present in many of the writers who belonged to the new generation of playwrights (Beaumont and Fletcher, Chapman and Massinger) most associated with the supposed shift away from popular tastes. The problem for modern readers is that we have often failed to recognize this political dimension, or misrecognized the nature of early modern political discourse.

This is especially so in the case of the main genres which came to dominate the 1610s and 1620s: romance and tragi-comedy. Often, the growing interest in romance and tragi-comedy has been interpreted as signs of a degeneration of taste and an escape from politics (if not straightforward escapism). Yet romance, in fact, appealed across a wide spectrum of tastes and included, as in *Oberon*, styles which contrasted with the dominant representational modes of Jacobean and Jonsonian classicism. Romances, moreover, were performed at the whole range of early modern theatres, from the amphitheatres like the Red Bull (where *Mucedorus* was played) through to the hall playhouses. Texts such as *Eastward Ho!* (1605) and *The Knight of the Burning Pestle* (1607) testify to the wide dissemination of romance texts amongst the poorer and middling classes, and its emphatic openness allowed it appeal to a broad range of tastes and social classes, while its temporally and geographically vague settings provided a useful veil for political allusion.[41] In using romance forms, dramatists were not simply allying themselves to the court but negotiating the commercial realities of theatrical life whereby they had to appeal to the widest audience possible, creating plays suitable for a variety of different venues and audiences (of which the court was only one).

Plays written for companies outside the court (but sponsored to some degree from within) such as *Chapman's Bussy d'Ambois* (1604) and *The Revenge of Bussy d'Ambois* (1613) played at the Whitefriars (but also revised for amphitheatre performance) might use French settings to present parallels with current political issues.[42] Similarly, Beaumont and Fletcher's plays, such as *Philaster* (1610) use romance settings to pose political questions, though in both cases they are expressed through personal and ethical dilemmas accentuated by court settings. How to achieve a 'heroical life' and, more difficultly, how to maintain one at court, were key questions reflecting the interpenetration of personal and political values which accompany the diffuse sovereignties of early modern culture.[43]

Chapman's two *Bussy* plays, although written almost a decade apart use their French settings to cloak an insistent critique of court culture and its corruptions as well as exploring the dilemma of survival in such a world. From a position as an outsider as soon as Bussy is introduced into the court, he recognizes in his rhetoric ('I can sing pricksong, lady, at first sight': 1.2.81) the constituent duplicity that courtiership requires. The pervasive and crippling doubleness of the courtier's situation, where corruption is the means and method of the court and it seems impossible to avoid, like the 'dance' he offered on his arrival at court (1.2.214). The dance image neatly suggests the sociability required in courtiership while also insinuating the sexual implication contained within dance (dance was often a figure for sexual intercourse) as well as the more terrifying prospect that this dance mimics movement of fortune and even leads, eventually, to death. The play is filled with images which offer either transformations or escapes which are continually frustrated, so that metamorphosis becomes a matter of changing clothes (1.2.118) leading not to the enlightenment or godhead but becomes instead a 'transmigration' into the duchess's bed. Similarly, the pervasive animal images depict the substratum of bestiality which shadows courtlife, while even the images of flight are balked. Thus, Bussy, the 'brave falcon' (3.2.2) and 'eagle' (3.2.4) of the court is ultimately constrained by royal will: 'violence flies / the sanctuaries of princes' eyes' (3.2.81–2).

Throughout *Bussy* the corruption of the court is foregrounded, rationality appealed to, satire offered, but reform and change frustrated: fortune, not reason, rules the court. Significantly, the central satirist of the play is not Bussy but Henri III himself who recites the faults of his court:

> our French court
> Is a mere mirror of confusion to it:
> The king and subject, lord and every slave
> Dance a continual hay; our rooms of state
> Kept like our stables; no place more observed
> Than a rude market-place.
>
> (1.2.24–9)

Yet his central position as monarch also renders him incapable of achieving reform, bound by the ties of alliance and kinship to his family who are themselves the source of corruption and his own power. Thus his restriction of Bussy, and Bussy's appeals to the idea of the monarchical man ('let me be king myself, as man was made': 2.1.199) free from restraint, highlight the limitations of the role of satirist and reformer, bringing out the contradictions between criticism and compliment which Jonson's *Panegyre*.

Bussy both defines the ideal of the courtier and suggests the impossibility of its achievement. In particular, Bussy's own death, which gestures toward the classical and heroic end, only accentuates his failure:

> is my body, then,
> But penetrable flesh? And must my mind
> Follow my blood? Can my divine part add
> No aid to th'earthly in extremity?
> Then these divines are but for form, not fact:
> Man is of two, sweet courtly friends compact –
> A mistress and a servant. Let my death
> Define life nothing but a courtier's breath.
> Nothing is made of nought, of all things made
> Their abstract being a dream but of shade.
> I'll not complain to earth yet, but to heaven,
> And, like a man, look upwards even in death.
> [*Standing supported by his sword*] Prop me, true sword, as thou hast ever done:
> The equal thought I bear of life and death

Shall make me faint on no side. I am up
Here like a Roman statue. I will stand
Till death hath made me marble.

(5.3.125–41)

The speech moves from uncertainty ('is my?', 'And must my?', 'Can my?') through a sense of nullity ('nothing is made of nought') to the final heroic gesture of dying standing and the impossible dream of becoming 'like a Roman statue' made marble by death. This image, which contrasts greatly with the adulterous, murderous and satirical Bussy of the play, highlights the futility of heroism in a corrupted world, just as Bussy cannot become marble in any literal sense as he is made, as he himself recognizes, of 'but penetrable flesh'.

This concern with aspiration towards heroic virtue and its frustration recurs in Chapman's *Revenge* where the ethics of revenge form the central concern of the play, highlighting the dilemmas of the moral codes, such as honour and kinship, which constituted the early modern state. Revenge is constantly associated with haste (1.1.108) and 'wreak' (1.1.85) and 'vicious fury' rather than virtue (3.2.109). Indeed Clermont, when urged by Baligny's wife Charlotte to immediate and, thus, manly revenge, asks: 'Shall we revenge a villainy with a villainy?' (3.2.89–96). It is significant here that revenge is associated with women (it as after all a 'fury') and that Tamyra in particular becomes a 'votist of revenge' (3.2.164) her blood-lust echoing Renaissance views about the instability of women and their association with the fluid and the passionate. Thus revenge in the play becomes not only a political question – Clermont asks how revenge can be taken against the monarch when it is 'impious' (5.5.152) – but also a gendered issue, as Clermont wrestles to find a method of rational and male revenge rather than succumbing to the passionate, hasty vengeance urged by the women.

Although in some ways the issues of these plays are schematic they embody an important debate over the definition of proper behaviour, and especially the gendering of mores: what is it to be a proper man (or woman)? They give personal shape through ideas such as revenge and honour to issues which were urgent *political* concerns for individuals in this period.[44] Moreover, although Chapman, in particular, offers his plays in a difficult, tortive language, the emphasis upon the role of women and the use of revenge motifs and satire reached out beyond an elite audience. This process of debate which stretches beyond the court and beyond elite audiences is even more marked in the romances than 'historical' texts like Chapman's *Bussy* plays. Beaumont and Fletcher, in particular, use a clarified language and romance settings to render many of these debates accessible to a broader audience than might be imagined.

The best example of such romances remains Beaumont and Fletcher's *Philaster* (1610).[45] Like Chapman's *Bussy* plays it explores issues of honour, reputation and revenge in the context of a usurped monarchy (Philaster, the hero, has been usurped as King of Sicily by the King of Calabria). Much concerned with issues of female behaviour and honour, the play uses the attempts of the king to marry his daughter (notably named Arethusa) to a Spanish lord, Pharamond, when she desires Philaster, and the play concludes with the hero's marriage and his restoration. Significantly, the restoration is achieved through the intervention of the citizens who revolt against the king and hold Pharamond hostage. The issues of civility and politics are combined in this popular revolt as the citizens are seen as 'myrmidons' and 'roarers' (5.4.1 and 79) who threaten social order and who are controlled by Philaster who rescues Pharamond even though they are opponents. Philaster, called 'King of courtesy' (5.4.131) by the rebels, embodies the ability of true courtiership to civilize and to unite both commons and nobles. The key role of the plebeian revolt in the play illustrates how the text could appeal beyond the elite to a broader audience, perhaps catering to the wish-fulfilment fantasies that made romance so popular.

In its depiction of the court and courtiership *Philaster* suggests the complexity of these terms in early modern political culture.[46] On one hand the court and its courtiers are regarded as corrupt and debased (notably Galatea who can be 'courted in a shower of gold': 2.2.47) and *Philaster* offers an image of the country instead as the home of virtue, instructing Dion, 'Go get you home again, and make your country / A virtuous court' (1.1.301–2). The issue, however, is not the rejection of courtly values, but rather their reformation into virtue. Thus the country functions not as opposition outside the court but as part of the proper dialectic between court and country, maintaining the health and virtue of the political centre. It is important here that Philaster's management of the rebels is achieved through his 'courtesy' – a quality that they recognize in him. It is not simply courtesy that civilizes but the recognition of that civility in others, here giving the citizens a role in the balancing of the state between courtly vice and country virtue.

This political dialectic suggests a greater circulation between the court and non-court both in the idealized images of the theatre and, perhaps, in the culture within which that theatre actually operated. *Philaster* is not simply an elite play which criticizes the court from within, the involvement of the plebeians and the use of romance motifs deliberately opens the play to a wider audience. Indeed, King's Men plays had to move freely between the hall stage of the Blackfriars and the amphitheatre of the Globe, thus reaching the wider audience. Yet even within the more apparently exclusive theatres such as the Blackfriars the audience might be socially mixed, ranging (according to Jonson) from 'Gamester, captain, knight, knight's man / Lady or pucelle [whore].' to 'the shop's foreman' ('To the Worthy Author Mr John Fletcher', lines 3–6). The inclusion of women, an important segment of the early modern audience but also the knight's servant and the shopkeeper conveys something of the variety possible even in the more expensive hall theatres.

Whether it is audience demographics, staging styles, genre or even the legal framework of dramatic production in the Jacobean period, little conveys the kinds of political control which supports the absolutist arguments of Wickham or the new historicists. What is suggested is a vigorous theatre of debate in which political issues are considered, even if in veiled terms, by socially diverse audiences. Moreover, in the final analysis, theatre will always have the potential for radical impact because it rests between oral and literate cultures, disseminating ideas and concepts to an audience who cannot access them through written texts. The commercial basis of the London theatre industry meant that those audience and not the court were the main arbiters of taste, as John Cocke argued in 1615: 'howsoever he [the player] pretends to have a royal master or mistress, his wages and dependence prove him to be the servant of the people'.[47] Very often court forms borrow from, and depend upon, the commercial theatre rather than court forms dictating commercial priorities, while many of the features which have been associated with coterie theatre, such as spectacular stagings or the use of music, are as much a feature of amphitheatre performances as Blackfriars stagings. This is not to claim that the opening of smaller, intimate, indoor theatres did not impact upon staging and dramatic practice, merely to question the class-based assumptions about taste and the direction of influence.

Most striking of all is the complexity of the court in this period and the absence of anything which might be defined as a centrally administered programme to represent the royal image. The Jacobean court cannot be regarded as a forerunner of Versailles, and even Charles I who may have aspired in a more absolutist direction was thwarted in his most grandiose plans (such as the building of the massive new Whitehall Palace designed by Webb) by practicalities: the lack of money. Even within what limited artistic programmes of the court, it is striking how little theatre featured: it was simply not a vehicle for propaganda (perhaps because of its very interrogative nature). Above all, when examined closely the most quintessential of all royal forms, the masque, appears to have a far more mixed parentage and even bear more various messages than simply replicating a royal ideology. Once the complex factional politics of the court, and especially the still neglected role of Anna of Denmark (and, indeed, her successor as queen consort, Henrietta Maria) is weighed, then an entirely different picture starts to emerge. Rather than looking for 'decadence' and decline, perhaps it is time to consider the debate which early modern theatre fostered, and to move away from our monolithic conceptions of the court and culture, allowing the voices of women, other writers than Jonson, marginalized groups and the vibrant regional cultures of the period to sound. Perhaps it is time to stop looking at the reflection in Jonson's courtly glass and consider who is holding the mirror.

NOTES

1 Jonson, *Cynthia's Revels, or the Fountain of Self-Love*, dedicatory epistle (1616) cited in C. H. Herford, P. and E. Simpson eds, *Ben Jonson*, 11 vols (Oxford: Clarendon Press, 1925–52), vol. 4, p. 33.

2 The most authoritative account, A. Gurr's *The Shakespearian Playing Companies* (Oxford:

Clarendon Press, 1996). Ch. 6, surveys 'The Changes of 1603', typifying them as 'consolidation' rather than revolution.

3 G. Wickham, *Early English Stages, 1300–1660*, 3 vols in 4 (London: Routledge, Kegan and Paul, 1959–81), vol. 2, part 1, p. 94.

4 It explicitly underpins J. Dollimore, *Radical Tragedy: Religion, Ideology and Power in the Drama of Shakespeare and his Contemporaries* (Brighton: Harvester, 1983) and is implicit (in a far more sophisticated and intelligent form) in J. Goldberg, *James I and the Politics of Literature* (Baltimore: Johns Hopkins University Press, 1983). These are two of the best studies of the interface between politics and culture in this period.

5 For an authoritative study see A. Gurr, *Playgoing in Shakespeare's London* (Cambridge: Cambridge University Press, 1987) but see also his 'The General and the Caviar: Learned Audience in the Early Theatre', *Studies in English Literature*, 26 (1993), 7–20 and A. Cook's more sceptical views on the inclusiveness of early audiences in 'Audences: Investigation, Interpretation, Invention', in *A New History of Early English Drama*, eds J. D. Cox and D. S. Kastan (New York: Columbia University Press, 1997), pp. 305–20, esp. pp. 316–17.

6 For a useful summary, see S. Adams, 'Early Stuart Politics: Revizionism and After' in *Theatre and Government under the Early Stuarts*, eds J. R. Mulryne and M. Shewring (Cambridge: Cambridge University Press, 1993), pp. 29–56.

7 For the following discussion I use S. May, *The Elizabethan Courtier Poets: The Poems and Their Contexts* (Colombia: University of Missouri Press, 1991), pp. 11–21, and G. R. Elton, 'Tudor Government: The Points of Contact. III. The Court', *Transactions of the Royal Historical Society*, 5th ser, 26 (1976), 211–28, esp. pp. 215–17. May makes an important point about the status of poets, like Spenser, often loosely and erroneously seen as 'courtier poets' (*The Elizabethan Courtier Poets*, pp. 33–4).

8 G. E. Bentley, *The Jacobean and Caroline Stage*, 7 vols (Oxford: Clarendon Press, 1941–68), vol. 6, *Theatres* (1968), pp. 267–88. Bentley (pp. 268–9) notes earlier uses of the cockpit as a playing space while it continued as a cockfighting venue. For a full survey, see J. Astington, *English Court Theatre, 1558–1642* (Cambridge: Cambridge University Press, 1999) surveys court theatre in detail.

9 P. Finkelpearl, 'The Role of the Court in the Development of Jacobean Drama', *Criticism*, 24 (1982), 138–58.

10 *Dudley Carleton to John Chamberlain 1603–1624: Jacobean Letters*, ed. M. Lee Jr (New Brunswick: Rutgers University Press, 1972), p. 53.

11 *The Complete Works in Verse and Prose of Samuel Daniel*, ed. A. B. Grosart, 5 vols (London, 1885), vol. 1, pp. 150 and 153.

12 I. Donaldson ed., *Ben Jonson* (Oxford: Oxford University Press, 1985). All references to Jonson's poetry are taken from this edition.

13 The phrase is cited by Francis Bacon in his essay 'Of Praise': see *Essays, Civil and Moral*, ed. M. Kiernan (Oxford: Clarendon Press, 2000), p. 160.

14 J. Lowenstein, 'Printing and the "Multitudinous Press": the Contentious Texts of Jonson's Masques', in *Ben Jonson's 1616 Folio*, ed. J. Brady and W. Herendeen (Newark: University of Delaware Press, 1991), pp. 168–91.

15 Herford, Simpson and Simpson, *Ben Jonson*, vol. 8, *The Sad Shepherd, the Fall of Mortimer, Masques and Entertainments*, 'The King's Entertainment', line 335.

16 *The Magnificent Entertainment in the Works of Thomas Dekker*, ed. F. Bowers, vol. 2, pp. 231–309, line 686. See also G. Rosser, 'A Netherlandic Triumphal Arch for James I' in *Across the Narrow Seas: Studies in the History and Bibliography of Britain and the Low Countries*, ed. S. Roach (London: British Library, 1991), pp. 67–82, which discusses the Dutch sources, especially Conrad Jansen's *Beschryvinghe van de Herlycke Arcus Triumphal* (Middleburgh, 1604 or 1605).

17 N. Cuddy, 'The Revival of Entourage: the Bedchamber of James I' in *The English Court: From the Wars of the Roses to the Civil Wars*, ed. D. Starkey (London: Longman, 1987), pp. 173–225, and J. Wormald, 'James VI and I: Two Kings or One?', *History*, 68 (1983), 187–209, p. 202.

18 M. Smuts, 'Cultural Diversity and Cultural Change at the Court of James I' in *The Mental World of the Jacobean Court*, ed. L. Peck (Cambridge: Cambridge University Press, 1991), pp. 99–112.

19 R. Dutton, 'Censorship' in *A New History of Early English Drama*, pp. 287–304. For an even more sceptical view of censorship, see B. Worden, 'Literature and Political Censorship in Early Modern England' in *Too Mighty To Be Free: Censorship and the Press in Britain and the Netherlands*, eds A. C. Duke and C. A. Tamse (Zutphen: De Walberg Pers, 1987), pp. 45–62. The suggestion of administrative confusion is made in P. J. Finkelpearl, '"The Comedians' Liberty": Censorship of the Jacobean Stage Reconsidered' in *Renaissance Historicism*, ed. A. Kinney (Amherst: University of Massachusetts Press, 1987), pp. 191–206.

20 Dutton, 'Censorship', pp. 301 and 304.

21 Ibid., p. 300.

22 Finkelpearl, '"The Comedians' Liberty"', p. 201.

23 Samuel Calvert to Ralph Winwood, 28 March 1605, cited in E. K. Chambers, *The Elizabethan Stage*, 4 vols (Oxford: Clarendon Press), vol. 1, p. 325.

24 T. Raylor, *The Essex House Masque* of 1621, (Pittsburgh: Dusquesne University Press, 2000) and J. Knowles, 'The "Running Masque" Recovered?: A Masque for the Marquess of Buckingham (c.1619–20)', *English Manuscript Studies*, 8 (2000), 79–135.

25 L. Barroll, 'The Court of the First Stuart Queen' in *The Mental World of the Jacobean Court*, ed. Peck, pp. 191–208, provides a basic survey of Anna's court.

26 Cited in R. Dutton, *Ben Jonson, Authority, Criticism* (Basingstoke: Macmillan, 1991), p. 22.

27 The three masques which do embody the king's policy are the union masques, *Hymenaei* (1606), *Lord Hay's Masque* (1607) and the *Haddington Masque* (1608). As with *Lord Hay's Masque*, however, some of the cost and thus the responsibility was borne by the families: see D. Lindley, 'Who Paid For Campion's *Lord Hay's Masque?*' *Notes and Queries*, 224 (1979), 144–5.

28 Gurr, *The Shakespearian Playing Companies*, p. 352.

29 Jonson, *The Complete Masques*, ed. S. Orgel (New Haven: Yale University Press, 1969). All references are to this edition of Jonson's masques unless otherwise stated.

30 Herford, Simpson and Simpson, *Ben Jonson*, vol. 4, pp. 209–10. See S. Orgel, 'Jonson and the Amazons' in *Soliciting Interpretation*, eds E. D. Harvey and K. Maus (Chicago: University of Chicago Press, 1990), pp. 119–39.

31 Dedicatory epistle to *The Masque of Queens*, cited in *Court Masques*, ed. D. Lindley (Oxford: Oxford University Press, 1995), p. 226.

32 M. Butler, 'Courtly Negotiations' in *The Politics of the Stuart Court Masque*, eds D. Bevington and P. Holbrook (Cambridge: Cambridge University Press, 1998), pp. 20–40, p. 31.

33 K. McLuskie, 'Politics and Dramatic Form in Early Modern Tragedy' in *Theatre and Government under the Early Stuarts*, eds Mulryne and Shewring, pp. 217–36, esp. pp. 222–4 comments on Anne's patronage of adult dramatic companies.

34 Gurr, *The Shakespearian Playing Companies*, pp. 347–65 on this company and its shifting nomenclature.

35 Gurr, *The Shakespearian Playing Companies*, p. 350. On *Philotas*, see J. Pitcher, 'Samuel Daniel and the Authorities', *Medieval and Renaissance Drama in England*, 10 (1998), 113–48.

36 Daniel, *Complete Works in Verse and Prose*, vol. 3, esp. 1.1. *passim*.

37 Letter of 14 June 1604, cited in Chambers, *The Elizabethan Stage*, vol. 1, p. 325.

38 *Revenge of Bussy d'Ambois*, epistle, lines 22–9 in *The Plays of George Chapman: The Tragedies*, ed. A. Holaday (Cambridge: D. S. Brewer, 1987). All subsequent references are to this edition.

39 B. R. Smith observes that 'behind the dozens of theatrical instances and anecdotes in Cicero's treatises, speeches and letters is the assumption that plays are rhetorical events: occasions when speakers harangue an audience . . . In keeping with the notion of drama as a species of oratory, an act of deliberation, Cicero frequently mentions in his letters one particular kind of moral programme: it is the political side of plays in performance that inspires Cicero's most detailed observations. This too was a feature of drama that Renaissance readers readily

appreciated' (*Ancient Scripts and Modern Stage Experience* (New Jersey: Princeton University Press, 1998), p. 21).

40   T. Heywood, *An Apology for Actors* (1610), sig. F3v.

41   B. Gibbons, 'Romance and the Heroic Play' in *The Cambridge Companion to English Renaissance Drama*, eds A. R. Braunmuller and M. Hattaway (Cambridge: Cambridge University Press, 1990), pp. 207–236, esp. p. 213.

42   Gurr, *The Shakespearian Playing Companies*, p. 359.

43   See G. Chittolini, 'The "Private", the "Public" and the State', *Journal of Modern History*, 67 (1995), S34–61. Chittolini comments that ' [The] diffuse sovereignty [of pre-absolutist states operates through] a complex web of personal relations, both horizontal and vertical, which gave life to a plurality of social bodies (based on kinship, association, and subjugation), all bound up with one another and cemented by sworn pacts . . . the state was . . . a system of insti-

tutions, of powers and practices, that had as one of its defining features a sort of programmatic permeability to extraneous (or, if one prefers, "private") powers and purposes while retaining an overall unity of political organization' (S34).

44   R. Cust, 'Honour and Politics in Early Stuart England: The Case of Beaumont *v.* Hastings', *Past and Present*, 149 (1995), 57–94.

45   *Philaster, or Love Lies a-bleeding*, ed. A. Gurr (London: Methuen, 1969). All subsequent references are to this edition.

46   P. Finkelpearl, *Court and Country in the Plays of Beaumont and Fletcher* (New Jersey: Princeton University Press, 1990), esp. ch. 8 and 'Afterword' (pp. 246–7) makes a case for these playwrights as radicals rather than reactionaries.

47   Cocke, *Satirical Essays, Characters and Others* (1615) cited in K. E. McLuskie, 'The Poets' Royal Exchange: Patronage and Commerce in Early Modern Drama', *Yearbook of English Studies*, 21 (1991), 53–62, p. 54.

References and Further Reading

Adams, S. (1993). 'Early Stuart Politics: Revizionism and After'. In *Theatre and Government under the Early Stuarts*, eds J. R. Mulryne and M. Shewring. Cambridge: Cambridge University Press, pp. 29–56.

Astington, J. (1999). *English Court Theatre, 1558–1642*. Cambridge: Cambridge University Press.

Bacon, F. (2000). *Essays, Civil and Moral*. ed. M. Kiernan. Oxford: Clarendon Press.

Barroll, L. (1991). 'The Court of the First Stuart Queen'. In *The Mental World of the Jacobean Court*, ed. L. Peck. Cambridge: Cambridge University Press, pp. 191–208.

Bentley, G. E. (1941–68). *The Jacobean and Caroline Stage*. 7 vols. Oxford: Clarendon Press.

Butler, M. (1998). 'Courtly Negotiations'. In *The Politics of the Stuart Court Masque*, eds D. Bevington and P. Holbrook. Cambridge: Cambridge University Press, pp. 20–40.

Carleton, D. (1972). *Dudley Carleton to John Chamberlain 1603–1624: Jacobean Letters*, ed. M. Lee Jr. New Brunswick: Rutgers University Press.

Chambers, E. K., *The Elizabethan Stage*. 4 vols. Oxford: Clarendon Press.

Chapman, G. (1987). *The Plays of George Chapman: The Tragedies*, ed. A. Holaday. Cambridge: D. S. Brewer.

Chittolini, G. (1995). 'The "Private", the "Public" and the State', *Journal of Modern History*, 67, S34–64.

Cook, A. (1997). 'Audiences: Investigation, Interpretation, Invention'. In *A New History of Early English Drama*, eds J. D. Cox and D. S. Kastan. New York: Columbia University Press, pp. 305–20.

Cox J. D. and Kastan, D. S. (eds) (1997). *A New History of Early English Drama*. New York: Columbia University Press.

Cuddy, N. (1987). 'The Revival of Entourage: The Bedchamber of James I'. In *The English Court: from the Wars of the Roses to the Civil Wars*, ed. D. Starkey. London: Longman, pp. 173–225.

Cust, R. (1995). 'Honour and Politics in Early Stuart England: The Case of Beaumont *v.* Hastings', *Past and Present*, 149, 57–94.

Daniel, S. (1885). *The Complete Works in Verse and Prose of Samuel Daniel*, ed. A. B. Gros. 5 vols. London.

Dekker, T. (1951–). *The Magnificent Entertainment* in *The Works of Thomas Dekker*, ed. F. Bowers. 4 vols. Cambridge: Cambridge University Press.

Dollimore, J. (1983). *Radical Tragedy: Religion, Ideology and Power in the Drama of Shakespeare and His Contemporaries*. Brighton: Harvester.

Dutton, R. (1991). *Ben Jonson, Authority, Criticism*. Basingstoke: Macmillan.

——(1997). 'Censorship'. In *A New History of Early English Drama*, eds Cox and Kastan. New York: Columbia University Press, pp. 287–304.

Elton, G. R. (1976). 'Tudor Government: The Points of Contact. vol. 3. The Court', *Transactions of the Royal Historical Society*, 5th ser., 26, 211–28.

Finkelpearl, P. (1982). 'The Role of the Court in the Development of Jacobean Drama', *Criticism*, 24, 138–58.

——(1987). ' "The Comedians' Liberty": Censorship of the Jacobean Stage. Reconsidered'. In *Renaissance Historicism*, ed. A. Kinney. Amherst: University of Massachusetts Press, pp. 191–206.

——(1990). *Court and Country in the Plays of Beaumont and Fletcher*. New Jersey: Princeton University Press.

Fletcher, J. (1969). *Philaster, or Love Lies a-bleeding*, ed. A. Gurr. London: Methuen.

Gibbons, B. (1990). 'Romance and the Heroic Play'. In *The Cambridge Companion to English Renaissance Drama*, eds A. R. Braunmuller and M. Hattaway. Cambridge: Cambridge University Press, pp. 207–36.

Goldberg, J. (1983). *James I and the Politics of Literature*. Baltimore: Johns Hopkins University Press.

Gurr, A. (1987). *Playgoing in Shakespeare's London*. Cambridge: Cambridge University Press.

——(1993). 'The General and the Caviar: Learned Audience in the Early theatre', *Studies in English Literature*, 26, 7–20.

——(1996). *The Shakespearian Playing Companies*. Oxford: Clarendon Press.

Heywood, T. (1610). *An Apology for Actors*.

Jonson, B. (1925–52). *Ben Jonson*, eds C. H., P. Herford and E. Simpson. 11 vols. Oxford: Clarendon Press.

——(1969). *The Complete Masques*, ed. S. Orgel. New Haven: Yale University Press.

Knowles, J. (2000). 'The "Running Masque" Recovered?: A Masque for the Marquess of Buckingham' (*c.*1619–20), *English Manuscript Studies*, 8, 79–135.

Lindley, D. (1979). 'Who Paid for Campion's *Lord Hay's Masque*?', *Notes and Queries*, 224, 144–5.

——(1995). *Court Masques*. Oxford: Oxford University Press.

May, S. (1991). *The Elizabethan Courtier Poets: The Poems and Their Contexts*. Colombia: University of Missouri Press.

Lowenstein, J. (1991). 'Printing and the "Multitudinous Press": The Contentious Texts of Jonson's Masques'. In *Ben Jonson's 1616 Folio*, eds J. Brady and W. Herendeen. Newark: University of Delaware Press, pp. 168–91.

McLuskie, K. (1993). 'Politics and Dramatic Form in Early Modern Tragedy'. In *Theatre and Government under the Early Stuarts*, eds J. R. Mulryne and M. Shewring. Cambridge: Cambridge University Press, pp. 217–36.

McLuskie, K. E. (1991). 'The Poets' Royal Exchange: Patronage and Commerce in Early Modern Drama', *Yearbook of English Studies*, 21, 53–62.

Orgel, S. (1990). 'Jonson and the Amazons'. In *Soliciting Interpretation*, eds E. D. Harvey and K. Maus. Chicago: University of Chicago Press, pp. 119–39.

Pitcher, J. (1998). 'Samuel Daniel and the Authorities', *Medieval and Renaissance Drama in England*, 10, 113–48.

Raylor, T. (2000). *The Essex House Masque* of 1621. Pittsburgh: Dusquesne University Press.

Rosser, G. (1991). 'A Netherlandic Triumphal Arch for James I'. In *Across the Narrow Seas: Studies in the History and Bibliography of Britain and the Low Countries*, eds S. Roach. London: British Library, pp. 67–82.

Smith, B. R. (1998). *Ancient Scripts and Modern Stage Experience*. New Jersey: Princeton University Press.

Smuts, M. (1991). 'Cultural Diversity and Cultural Change at the Court of James I'. In *The Mental World of the Jacobean Court*, ed. L. Peck. Cambridge: Cambridge University Press, pp. 99–112.

Wickham, G. (1959–81). *Early English Stages,*

1300–1660, 3 vols in 4. London: Routledge and Kegan Paul.

Worden, B. (1987). 'Literature and Political Censorship in Early Modern England'. In *Too Mighty To Be Free: Censorship and the Press in Britain and the Netherlands*, eds A. C. Duke and C. A. Tamse. Zutphen: De Walberg Pers, pp. 45–62.

Wormald, J. (1983). 'James VI and I: Two Kings or One?', *History*, 68, 187–209.

45

Jacobean Tragedy

Rowland Wymer

Angelo, then, evil Duke of Squamuglia, has perhaps ten years before the play's opening murdered the good Duke of adjoining Faggio, by poisoning the feet on an image of Saint Narcissus, Bishop of Jerusalem, in the court chapel, which feet the Duke was in the habit of kissing every Sunday MA
(Thomas Pynchon, *The Crying of Lot 49*)

Thus Thomas Pynchon in *The Crying of Lot 49* begins his description of *The Courier's Tragedy*, his loving parody of some of the excesses of Jacobean tragic plotting. Pynchon's own excesses – the scene-by-scene synopsis of the fictitious play takes up eight pages of a short novel – only seem justifiable on the assumption that his readers already had a very strong mental image of what is a 'typical' Jacobean tragedy; as no doubt they did and still do. They, and we, expect a violent story of lust and revenge, set in an Italian dukedom riddled with Machiavellian intrigue and religious hypocrisy, in which great men and women meet bizarre and terrible deaths while disaffected cynics rail against court life and meditate gloomily on the frailty of the human condition. In fact, however, the strong brand image of the genre can only be maintained by concentrating on a very small group of plays (primarily *The Revenger's Tragedy*, *The White Devil*, and *The Duchess of Malfi*) and arbitrarily excluding many others.

'Jacobean' is a problematic label because it suggests that plays first performed between 1603 and 1625 share special characteristics which mark them off from Elizabethan and Caroline drama and that these characteristics are directly related to the nature of James I's rule. Literary periodization in terms of kings and queens is a dubious procedure and the adjective 'Jacobean' masks the fact that the characteristic preoccupations and tones of early seventeenth-century tragedy had already been anticipated in the work of Kyd and Marlowe and were definitively established by five plays first performed between 1599 and 1604, only one of which is certainly Jacobean. From *Hamlet* (*c*.1600) comes the revenge plot, the cynical quips, the disturbed sexuality, and death consciousness, all within a court where 'rank corruption, mining all within,

/ Infects unseen'.[1] From Marston's *Antonio's Revenge*, contemporaneous with Shake-speare's play and sharing its debt to the older *Hamlet* play of the 1580s, comes the Italian setting and the self-parodying excesses of rhetoric and plotting which Pynchon sought to reproduce ('Poison the father, butcher the son, and marry the mother – ha!').[2] Jonson's *Sejanus* (1603) provides later dramatists with an austere and historically authentic picture of a court filled with spies, sycophants, factional in-trigue, perverted desires and secret murders. In this unrelievedly grim play the restoration of 'freedom' and 'order' in the last Act ('And praise to Macro, that hath savèd Rome! / Liberty, liberty, liberty!')[3] is accompanied by the strangling of the fallen royal favourite's children, the girl first being raped by the public hangman because Roman law did not permit the execution of young virgins. In *Othello* (1602–4) we find the charismatic but fatally flawed soldier-hero who features in several early Jacobean tragedies, and also the obsessional eroticism ('Lie with her? lie on her? . . . Pish! Noses, ears, and lips? Is't possible?' (4.1.35–42)) which will gradually supplant political themes in importance and help to make *Othello* the most admired tragedy of the later seventeenth century. Chapman's *Bussy D'Ambois* (1604) gives us another heroic martial figure brought down by his own weaknesses and also includes eloquent outbursts against the emptiness of court life ('let my death / Define life nothing but a courtier's breath'),[4] despairing reflections on the random workings of the universe, passionate illicit sex, the onstage torture of a woman, the summoning of spirits from the underworld, and the appearance of a ghost. Not surprisingly, it was 'often acted with great applause'. Two of these plays (*Antonio's Revenge* and *Bussy D'Ambois*) were performed by the children's companies which had resumed commercial playing in 1599 after a ten-year hiatus. The cross-influence between these and the adult com-panies was crucial to the increased tonal range and sophistication which we see as characteristically Jacobean.

The poisonous court worlds 'embroiled with hate and faction' and the self-destructive martial protagonists we find in these plays are theatrical responses to the crisis of the last years of Elizabeth's reign when her ability to manage the vicious rival-ries at court deserted her and her refusal to name a successor greatly increased polit-ical anxieties, helping to provoke the failed rebellion of her former favourite and 'matchless general', the Earl of Essex. It matters little whether *Sejanus* happens to date from just before or just after the death of Elizabeth on 24 March 1603. 'What matters is the mental world which *Sejanus* evoked, and this was the mental world of the final years of Elizabeth I, because Jonson had been writing the play for two years before its first performance.'[5] All these five plays were immensely influential in forming the 'mental world' of Jacobean tragedy. Even *Sejanus*, which was a failure at the Globe when first performed, carried enough *literary* prestige to make a crucial impact on both Chapman and Webster. Once certain attitudes have been imaginatively and pow-erfully realized in art, they continue to be reproduced, whether or not they remain an appropriate response to new social and political circumstances. However, the lack of any necessary and direct relationship between the cynical mood of Jacobean tragedy and actual feelings about the new king and his court has been obscured by the long tradition of anti-Stuart historiography which dates back to the 1650s and which underpins both Whig and Marxist narratives of British history. Despite the efforts of modern historians to provide a more accurate picture, the story of a strong and popular monarch, 'good Queen Bess', being succeeded by an incompetent, corrupt and unpopular one in 1603 remains firmly lodged in many people's minds. The anti-court satire found in many Jacobean tragedies *may* have a direct and topical reference but it may also simply represent the continued exploitation of a tried and tested mode of dramatic writing which initially arose in a rather different political context. The dramatist whose plays are most obviously affected by the transition from Elizabeth to James is probably Shakespeare, but the changes in his work do not support the supposition of any new and sudden disillusion with the monarchy and the court, rather the reverse in fact.

If one begins to construct an outline map of Jacobean tragedy by setting aside plays not written for performance, such as those by Fulke Greville, William Alexander and Elizabeth Cary, and plays by dramatists such as Ford and Massinger whose major work was after 1625, then the most important figures will be Shakespeare, Chapman, Middleton and Webster, with interesting contributions – in addition to those plays already named – from Marston (*Sophonisba* and *The Insatiate Countess*),[6] Fletcher and his collaborators (*The Maid's Tragedy*, *Bonduca*, *Valentinian* and *Sir John van Olden Barnavelt*), Jonson (*Catiline*), Daniel (*Philotas*) and Tourneur (*The Atheist's Tragedy*). It is obviously not possible to address Shakespeare's work adequately within the scope of this chapter but it must be emphasized that generalizations about Jacobean tragedy which implicitly ignore Shakespeare are of little value. There was a continuous artistic dialogue between him and his fellow playwrights and we must not listen to only one side of the exchange. Moreover, Shakespeare's political and religious perspectives were quite different from those of, say, Middleton, and there are no very good grounds for claiming that *The Revenger's Tragedy* is more 'typical' of Jacobean tragedy than *Macbeth*.

Beginning with Chapman (and Shakespeare), as well as being chronologically appropriate, has the advantage of requiring an immediate consideration of a large number of major tragedies which do not fit the 'evil Duke of Squamuglia' stereotype. Both playwrights were, in their different ways, fascinated with martial heroes who are 'impossible mixtures' of vice and virtue, men 'broken loose from human limits'. Such are the protagonists of *Othello*, *Macbeth*, *Antony and Cleopatra*, *Coriolanus*, *Bussy D'Ambois* and the two Byron plays. In epic poetry men like these can be celebrated, but in tragedy their fiery souls come up against political and ethical limits which destroy them. The historical reasons why such figures appear particularly 'tragic' to Shakespeare and Chapman relate to the growing irrelevance of traditional heroic attributes in modern warfare and the erosion of aristocratic power by the centralizing monarchies which had emerged in Europe during the sixteenth century. The fall of Essex in 1601 epitomized both processes and was the single most important political event to have left its mark on Jacobean tragedy, partly because the traitor's death suffered by Essex did not put an end to his influence; the chivalric values which he championed were taken up by James's son Prince Henry and the 'Essex legacy' continued to divide the court. Elizabeth's glamorous but unstable general, aggressively placing his aristocratic honour above the law, conformed very well to the description by the great neo-classical critic Castelvetro of the type of character that is proper to tragedy:

> Tragic characters are regal and have exalted spirits and are haughty, and what they want, they want excessively, and if an injury is done to them, or if they are led to understand it might be done to them, they do not run off to the magistracy to complain of the aggressor, nor suffer the injury patiently, but take the law into their own hands according as their will dictates.[7]

This is a more Nietzschean view of the tragic hero than we are accustomed to finding in Aristotle or Sidney, and it helps explain why Essex was the model for a number of protagonists in Jacobean plays.

Daniel, in the 'Apology' he prefixed to *Philotas* (1605), was anxious to deny that he had Essex in mind when dramatizing the fall of one of Alexander's generals, while Shakespeare's allusions to Essex are, with one exception, a matter of inference rather than fact. Chapman, however, in his two-part play *The Conspiracy and Tragedy of Charles Duke of Byron* (1607–8) was happy to make explicit the resemblance between Henry of Navarre's great general who was executed for treason in 1602 and 'The matchless Earl of Essex who some make . . . A parallel with me in life and fortune' (*The Tragedy*, 4.1.133–5). Byron has an absolute conception of his own heroic virtues which puts him in conflict with the equally absolute claims of the king and the law, and 'It is the nature of things absolute, / One to destroy another' (*The Conspiracy*, 1.2.102–3). The two plays seem to mark Chapman's gradual rethinking of the place which self-consciously heroic figures might occupy in a modern state. In his earlier *Bussy D'Ambois*, the protagonist is accused by his enemies of being capable of every kind of villainy 'but killing of the King', yet the play leaves a strong impression that Bussy's disdain for laws and manners springs from a primal generosity of spirit. In emphasizing the very real danger to society which such heroic individualism represents, Chapman also moved towards a more austere dramatic style. The Byron plays are purged of the melodramatic excesses which made *Bussy* popular in the theatre, and their considerable intellectual and emotional excitements are of a more purely literary kind, conveyed in lengthy, highly wrought speeches, rather than in repartee or action.

Chapman wrote two further tragedies set in the recent French court, *The Revenge of Bussy D'Ambois* (1610–11) and *The Tragedy of Chabot, Admiral of France* (1611–21, rev. 1635), as well as a Roman play, *Caesar and Pompey* (*c*.1604–13) concerning the last days of the Republic, which culminates in the noble suicide of Cato following Caesar's victory in the civil wars. All three plays feature Stoic heroes whose commitment is to rational self-control rather than heroic self-assertion, and it is customary to draw a sharp distinction between Bussy and Byron on the one hand, and Clermont, Cato and Chabot on the other. Yet Chapman's Stoics are as much in pursuit of a dream of absolute selfhood as are his passionate aspirers. Although Stoicism encouraged an ideal of submission to a universal rational order, its psychological appeal both to Seneca and the Renaissance lay in its posture of total intransigence in the face of political and social pressures. As Gordon Braden points out, 'there is considerable justification for taking Stoicism as less a philosophy of its announced themes of reason or virtue than a philosophy of the will – even, as Arendt has it, of "the omnipotence of the will"'.[8] The Stoic emphasis on 'the Mind's inward, constant and unconquered Empire' is not just a retreat from the world but a claim to absolute power ('Empire') over it.[9] Much of the passionate Bussy's assertive individualism is expressed in a rhetoric which is at least partly Stoic: 'Who to himself is law, no law doth need, / Offends no king, and is a king indeed.' (2.1.203–4)). Clermont, Cato, and Chabot are also laws to themselves, and Bussy's Stoical brother is referred to as 'this absolute Clermont', a choice of adjective which reminds one that 'the plain and passive fortitude to suffer' can be as great a challenge to the power of princes as the ambitions of an unstable martial hero. When Chabot is unjustly convicted, his king tries to exercise his absolute prerogative of pardon (as James did in a carefully staged way with some of the 1603 plotters against him) but is told quietly, 'You cannot pardon me, sir' (4.1.234). As Chabot's wife says earlier, 'each soul has a prerogative, / And privilege royal that was signed by heaven' (3.1.144–5). Within a Stoic philosophical framework royal pretensions to absolutism are confounded.

If the Byron plays acknowledge the rights of the state as well as those of the individual, the Stoic tragedies revert to a Tacitean suspicion of the workings of power. The conventional dating of *Chabot* is around 1612, but it is possibly later, and it actually makes more sense to see it in relation to the fall of James's favourite Robert Carr, who was convicted in 1616, along with his wife Frances Howard, of involvement in the murder of Sir Thomas Overbury. Chapman, having sought patronage first from Essex and then from Prince Henry, was unlucky a third time when he dedicated his translation of the *Odyssey* to Carr shortly before his trial and conviction. Chapman, however, remained loyal to his new patron and saw him as an innocent victim of court intrigue and royal inconstancy. The reference in *Chabot* to the former favourite being supplanted by 'a newly entered minion' looks suspiciously like a glance at the sexual allure of Robert Villiers, the new apple of James's eye.

All Chapman's heroes are spiritual, if not literal, aristocrats, who see themselves as above and apart from the rules and practices which make up ordinary life. He is an unashamedly elitist writer, whose tragedies (with the exception of *Bussy D'Ambois*) make few concessions to popular taste and who has relatively little interest in female characters. Yet there is a highly distinctive intellectual and poetic energy and excitement in his work which is even more striking if one sees him, as Richard Ide has done, in constant dramatic dialogue with Shakespeare.[10] Shakespeare had already exposed some of the limitations of Stoic philosophy in *Julius Caesar*, and in *Coriolanus* he concluded his great sequence of tragedies with a devastatingly 'objective' representation of Chapman's favourite kind of hero, the man who stands alone, 'One against all the world'.

A much more famous tragedy than *Chabot*, Middleton's and Rowley's *The Changeling* (1622), also alludes to the Overbury murder case, but from a very different perspective. This story of an aristocratic young woman who hires a servant to carry out a murder and then finds that the social 'distance' between them now means nothing, that she is now his 'equal' and will be his partner forever 'in death and shame', powerfully but obliquely expresses moral disgust that Carr and Howard, the aristocratic instigators of Overbury's murder, should escape with a few years' confinement in the Tower whilst the servants who carried out the deed were executed. This drama of inexorable criminal and sexual entanglement is not a court tragedy but it is still 'political', and its topical edge resides in the fact that it was in early 1622 that Carr and Howard were released from imprisonment.

That this much admired and frequently revived play should be the outcome of collaboration is a reminder that the individual script-writer's role in Elizabethan and Jacobean drama was, as in modern cinema, only a part of the collective process which generated something pleasing and saleable. Paradoxically, however, the most important revision of the map of Jacobean tragedy in recent years has been the assigning of a number of previously anonymous plays to Middleton and the increased sense of his importance as a tragic dramatist which this has brought. Thirty years ago, an orthodox account of Middleton's career would have described the first two decades of his output as dominated by comedy and tragi-comedy. Apart from some lost plays and the quirky *Hengist, King of Kent*, there was little to suggest that he would crown his career with two major tragedies, *The Changeling* and *Women Beware Women* (1621), a complex study of insidious sexual corruption culminating in a spectacularly lethal masque. Thanks to the efforts of scholars like David J. Lake and MacDonald P. Jackson there is a new orthodoxy that Middleton was active in tragedy throughout his career.[11] He is now credited with *A Yorkshire Tragedy* (c.1606), a brief and brutal real-life story of domestic violence, in which hints of the husband's demonic possession are accompanied by the Calvinist insistence on inevitable sinfulness which we find everywhere in Middleton's work ('for 'tis our blood to love what we are forbidden');[12] *The Second Maiden's Tragedy* (1611), a powerful allegorical court tragedy in which a tyrant's lust outlives the death of its object, a grotesque plot-twist which was later repeated by Massinger in *The Duke of Milan* (1621); a substantial share in that oddity of the Shakespearean canon *Timon of Athens* (c.1607), one of the most unlikely collaborations in the history of Jacobean drama and one that may *not* have resulted in a successful performance; and, most famously, *The Revenger's Tragedy* (1606), previously often attributed to Cyril Tourneur.

Part of the difficulty in assigning an author to this play has been that it is filled with echoes of earlier plays. One of these, obviously, is *Hamlet*, and Vindice, clad in black and carrying a skull, tells us in the first scene that his life has become 'unnatural' to him, following his 'worthy father's funeral'.[13] This motif is not developed, however, and Vindice, disguised as the pander Piato, is not prevented by grief from carrying out his terrible revenge on the Duke who, nine years before, had murdered his mistress. In what has become perhaps the definitive popular image of Jacobean tragedy, he induces the old man to kiss her costumed and poisoned skull under the mistaken impression that she is a compliant 'country girl', albeit one who has 'somewhat / A grave look' about her. Within the confines of what is actually staged, Vindice appears to move swiftly enough towards this revenge, achieving his major objective as early as act 3, with the result that his ruthless celerity has often been contrasted with Hamlet's more protracted deliberations. So it remains a hitherto unexplained puzzle why he has waited as long as nine years to enact his vengeance.

The probable answer is to be found in *Hamlet* and takes us to the heart of Middleton's emblematic imagination. In the graveyard scene, Hamlet inquires 'How long will a man lie i'th'earth ere he rot?' (5.1.158) and is told by the gravedigger that the maximum period is eight or nine years. 'A tanner will last you nine year' (5.1.162). The emphasis here is on a *process* of decay, but the figure of nine years seems to have lodged in Middleton's mind as signifying the culmination of the process, a culmination crucial to the particular symbolism of *The Revenger's Tragedy*. After nine years the flesh will unquestionably have rotted away from Gloriana's skull, enabling it to function not just as a traditional *memento mori* but as a stark emblem of ultimate moral purity. The clothing of flesh must be stripped away to reveal the only true object in a world of false appearance. The play is obsessed with the sins of the flesh, which are seen as inevitable as long as there is any flesh to cover the bones. When asked what moved him to rape, the Duchess's youngest son replies, 'Why flesh and blood, my lord; / What should move men unto a woman else?' (1.2.47–8).

Free from its flesh, the skull is now free of sin. It can appear as something cold and white and chaste to set against the hot desires of the flesh. 'Thou mayst lie chaste now' Vindice tells it (3.5.89). After nine years in the ground it has reached a state of incorruptible purity which allows it to join forces with Castiza and the dead wife of Antonio as the main symbols of opposition to the life of the court. The nine years Vindice has waited have nothing to do with any doubts about the ethics of revenge but were the natural period of time necessary to produce the play's chief moral symbol. The skull, like truth itself, is *filia temporis*, the daughter of time. Ironically, of course, when Vindice turns from his role of moralist and preacher in the opening speech to become an active revenger, he perverts the elemental purity of the skull by dressing it up, masking it, and smearing it with poison. The natural process by which a compelling emblem of unadorned truth and purity was generated is put into rapid reverse, and the nine years of patient waiting are succeeded by a frenetic flurry of violence.

Middleton's tragedies are all very different from one another. There seems little to connect the nightmarish cartoon figures of *The Revenger's Tragedy* with the psychologically realistic characters of *The Changeling* and *Women Beware Women*. Yet there *is* an inner consistency derived from his strong Calvinist Protestantism and what Margot Heinemann in *Puritanism and Theatre* called his 'citizen' values. The idea, popularized by T. S. Eliot, that 'he has no point of view' is quite wrong.[14] All his plays, even the most 'realistic' of them, have tendencies towards the allegorical, the didactic, and the topical. His famous political allegory *A Game at Chess* (1624) is only the most striking example of his habit of seeing things in black and white. Since a number of pre-vious literary histories have expressed an unambiguous preference for Middleton and *The Revenger's Tragedy* over Webster, I feel it appropriate to record here a distinctly contrary view.[15] The 'moral coherence' for which Middleton is frequently praised at Webster's expense is grounded in a grim predestinarian theology which, while it might in some circumstances be politically progressive, has many repellent features, including strong tendencies towards misogyny ('That Heaven should say we must not sin and yet made women' (*A Yorkshire Tragedy*, scene 4.57–8)). Middleton was inca-pable of imagining a woman as both sexual and good, as Webster does so triumphantly in *The Duchess of Malfi*. Webster is the more 'romantic', ambiguous, and elusive writer and despite Middleton's much larger body of first-class work, to prefer him to Webster is like preferring Shaw and Brecht to Shakespeare on the grounds of their greater political 'coherence'.

Webster's reputation is based on only two plays, *The White Devil* (1612) and *The Duchess of Malfi* (1613–14), both intricately plotted Italianate revenge tragedies which take great artistic risks but are capable of overwhelming an audience's critical defences, compelling responses of horror and pity in certain scenes and shocked laughter in others. The language is rich and forever hinting at barely suppressed violence and dangerous desires. The characters frequently surprise us, with sudden glimpses of something previously unsuspected in them, whether heroism, brutality, lust or com-passion. The picture of court life combines an authentic Tacitean grimness with a certain melodramatic excess. To say that Webster fuses the different styles of Shake-speare, Marston, Chapman and Jonson is perfectly accurate but it does not entirely explain his distinctive appeal.

Although his tragedies are strongly influenced by Shakespeare, they represent an interesting revision of the Shakespearean norm. Rather than concentrating on the experience and sufferings of 'great men' he gives equal importance to the lesser men and the women who are dragged down with them. In many Elizabethan and Jacobean plays, ruthless princes 'use men like wedges, one strike out another', but Webster is special in the degree of attention and sympathy he gives to these 'wedges'. The depen-dence of Flamineo and Bosola on 'courtly reward and punishment' causes them to behave brutally, but they feel 'the maze of conscience' in their breasts and we can infer that, away from the 'rank pasture' of the court, their lives would have been less of a 'black charnel'.

Webster's major female characters, Vittoria and the Duchess of Malfi, have been constructed by redistributing and recombining the various antithetical qualities found in previous theatrical representations of women. In earlier tragedies, women tend to be either noble, brave and chaste like Marston's Sophonisba, or lustful and devious like his 'insatiate countess', Isabella. Webster's revisions of these well-established types to produce a brave and emotional 'bad' woman in Vittoria and a passionate and secre-tive 'good' one in the Duchess are fine examples, of how, for all his dependence on earlier plays, he represents something new in Jacobean theatre. And as his women and his discarded spies and go-betweens struggle to achieve and maintain a stable identity in the face of the 'hideous storm of terror' of their approaching death, Webster is like no other dramatist in the way he takes his characters beyond the comforting commonplaces of their culture (whether Christian or Stoic) and sends them on a lonely, personal voyage of discovery.

Both on the Jacobean and the modern stage, *The Duchess of Malfi* has been the more successful play in performance, and there are understandable reasons for this. Both plays are disturbing and violent, in language as well as action, but *The Duchess* has a greater emotional range, including scenes of romantic and domestic intimacy which give the play, from time to time, a deeply affecting elegiac tone. For modern audiences, *The Duchess* touches a particularly raw nerve because, at the centre of the play is the massacre of a family. In Daniel Goldhagen's controversial book about the participation of 'ordinary' Germans in the Holocaust, *Hitler's Willing Executioners*, there is a reproduction of a little-known photograph, which will surely become iconic, of a German soldier on the point of firing at a woman with a child in her arms. The death of innocents has not always been seen as a proper subject for tragedy, and a good deal of tragic theory, taking its cue from Greek religious thinking, has preferred to emphasize the mysterious logic which underpins the inevitable catastrophe. It is Webster's distinction to confront the moral and philosophical implications of such 'useless' suffering and to explore the psychology of the murderer acting under orders as well as that of his victim. In *Macbeth* we learn little about Lady Macduff and nothing about the men who murder her and her family. *King Lear*, of course, is Shakespeare's great tragedy of victims rather than heroes, standing interestingly apart from his line of plays with martial protagonists, and provoking his audience to reflect on the meaning of 'God's silence' at the murder of Cordelia. It is only since 1945 that *Lear* has been regarded as Shakespeare's most important play, and it is only since 1945 that Webster's tragedies have been revived with real conviction.

Fletcher and his collaborators concentrated on comedy and tragi-comedy, but it would be wrong not to make a brief mention here of the tragedies. In theme and tone, they are often virtually indistinguishable from the more numerous tragi-comedies, a single twist of the plot in the last act sometimes being sufficient to determine into which category the play falls. There is usually a strong sexual interest and some complicated variations on themes of male and female honour which serve to expose the tension between Christian and classical values present in all Renaissance formulations of noble conduct ('The thing that we call honour bears us all / Headlong unto sin and yet itself is nothing').[16] *The Maid's Tragedy*, written with Beaumont in 1611, is particularly successful in making these arguments about honour seem urgent and meaningful, rather than just a set of debating points. A much less typical Fletcher tragedy is *Sir John van Olden Barnavelt*, written with Massinger in 1619, and dealing with the trial and execution of one of the leaders of the Dutch republic, which had taken place only months before. This play survived in a single manuscript copy and did not appear in any of the folio editions of 'Beaumont and Fletcher'. In consequence it has been rather neglected until recently, but it is a fine piece of work, recalling Chapman's Byron plays in its ambivalent treatment of a great man's recent fall.

The range and variety of Jacobean tragedy is fully acknowledged in scholarly monographs and learned journals. In the classroom and in the theatre, however, the tendency is to stay conservatively with a 'canon' of little more than three or four non-Shakespearean plays. It is arguable that the most important method of critical investigation in drama is always through performance and many of these tragedies are still waiting for their first modern professional production. When good actors attempt a Jacobean play in an appropriate playing space such as the Swan at Stratford, the results are usually very exciting. Tourneur's *The Atheist's Tragedy* (1611) used to be seen as disappointingly flat and sententious compared with the sardonic wit of his supposed masterpiece, *The Revenger's Tragedy*. Yet two modern revivals – at the Belgrade Theatre, Coventry, in 1979, and the Birmingham Repertory Theatre in 1994 – revealed a wonderfully entertaining mixture of farce, horror, bawdry, intrigue and philosophizing. Beyond the corrupt court of Squamuglia, there is a rich theatrical world still waiting to be explored.

NOTES

1   3.4.149–50. Shakespeare's plays are quoted from *The Complete Pelican Shakespeare*, gen. ed. Alfred Harbage, rev. ed. (Baltimore: Penguin; London: Allen Lane, 1969).

2   *Antonio's Revenge*, ed. W. Reavley Gair, The Revels Plays (Manchester: Manchester University Press, 1978), 1.1.104.

3   *Sejanus His Fall*, ed. Philip Ayres, The Revels Plays (Manchester: Manchester University Press, 1990), 5.758–9.

4   *Bussy D'Ambois*, Quarto 1, 5.3.131–2. Chapman's plays are quoted (with modernization) from *The Plays of George Chapman: The Tragedies*, gen. ed. Allan Holaday (Cambridge: Brewer, 1987).

5   *The Reign of Elizabeth I: Court and Culture in the Last Decade*, ed. John Guy (Cambridge: Cambridge University Press, 1995), pp. 16–17.

6   The latter play was revised by William Barksted and Lewis Machin.

7   *Poetica d'Aristotele* (1570). Quoted (in his own translation) by David Farley-Hills in ''*Coriolanus* and the Tragic Use of History', in *Shakespeare and History*, eds Holger Klein and Rowland Wymer, vol. 6 of *Shakespeare Yearbook* (1996), p. 208.

8   *Renaissance Tragedy and the Senecan Tradition*, p. 30.

9   The phrase occurs in Chapman's dedicatory preface to his translation of *The Odyssey* as part of his characterization of Odysseus in Stoic terms.

10 This is the structuring principle of his book *Possessed with Greatness: The Heroic Tragedies of Shakespeare and Chapman*.

11 David J. Lake, *The Canon of Thomas Middleton's Plays: Internal Evidence for the Major Problems of Dramatic Authorship* (Cambridge: Cambridge University Press, 1975); MacDonald P. Jackson, *Studies in Attribution: Middleton and Shakespeare* (Salzburg: Salzburg University Press, 1979).

12 Sc.4.62, in *Three Elizabethan Domestic Tragedies*, ed. Keith Sturgess (Harmondsworth: Penguin, 1969).

13 1.2.119–20, in *Thomas Middleton: Five Plays*, eds Bryan Loughrey and Neil Taylor (Harmondsworth: Penguin, 1988).

14 T. S. Eliot, 'Thomas Middleton', in *Selected Essays*, 3rd edn (London: Faber, 1951), p. 162.

15 I am thinking in particular of the essay by L. G. Salingar, 'Tourneur and the Tragedy of Revenge', in volume 2 of *The Pelican Guide to English Literature* and the essay by Christopher Ricks, 'The Tragedies of Webster,

Tourneur, and Middleton', in *English Drama to 1710*, a volume in the Sphere History of Literature.

16 Beaumont and Fletcher, *The Maid's Tragedy*, ed. T. W. Craik (Manchester: Manchester University Press, 1988), 4.2.318–19.

REFERENCES AND FURTHER READING

Braden, G. (1985). *Renaissance Tragedy and the Senecan Tradition: Anger's Privilege*. New Haven, CT: Yale University Press.

Braunmuller, A. R. (1992). *Natural Fictions: George Chapman's Major Tragedies*. Newark: University of Delaware Press.

Brooke, N. (1979). *Horrid Laughter in Jacobean Tragedy*. London: Open Books.

Callaghan, D. (1989). *Woman and Gender in Renaissance Tragedy*. Hemel Hempstead: Harvester.

Clare, J. (1990). *'Art Made Tongue-tied by Authority': Elizabethan and Jacobean Dramatic Censorship*. Manchester: Manchester University Press.

Dollimore, J. (1984). *Radical Tragedy: Religion, Ideology and Power in the Drama of Shakespeare and His Contemporaries*. Brighton: Harvester.

Dutton, R. (1991). *Mastering the Revels: The Regulation and Censorship of English Renaissance Drama*. Basingstoke: Macmillan.

Ellis-Fermor, U. (1958). *The Jacobean Drama*. 4th edn, rev. London: Methuen.

Felperin, H. (1977). *Shakespearean Representation: Mimesis and Modernity in Elizabethan Tragedy*. Princeton, NJ: Princeton University Press.

Findlay, A. (1999). *A Feminist Perspective on Renaissance Drama*. Oxford: Blackwell.

Friedenreich, K. (ed.) (1983). *'Accompaninge the Players': Essays Celebrating Thomas Middleton, 1580–1980*. New York: AMS Press.

Heinemann, M. (1980). *Puritanism and Theatre: Thomas Middleton and Opposition Drama under the Early Stuarts*. Cambridge: Cambridge University Press.

Hogg, J. (ed.) (1995). *Jacobean Drama as Social Criticism*. Lewiston, NY and Salzburg: Edwin Mellen.

Holdsworth, R. V. (ed.) (1990). *Three Jacobean Revenge Tragedies*. Basingstoke: Macmillan.

Ide, R. (1980). *Possessed with Greatness: The Heroic Tragedies of Shakespeare and Chapman*. London: Scolar.

Kastan, D. S. and Stallybrass, P. (eds) (1991). *Staging the Renaissance: Reinterpretations of Elizabethan and Jacobean Drama*. London: Routledge.

Lever, J. W. (1971). *The Tragedy of State*. London: Methuen.

McAlindon, T. (1986). *English Renaissance Tragedy*. Basingstoke: Macmillan.

McLuskie, K. (1989). *Renaissance Dramatists*. Hemel Hempstead: Harvester.

Morris, B. (ed.) (1970). *John Webster*. London: Benn.

Neill, M. (1997). *Issues of Death: Mortality and Identity in the Drama of Shakespeare and His Contemporaries*. Oxford: Clarendon Press.

Ornstein, R. (1960). *The Moral Vision of Jacobean Tragedy*. Madison: University of Wisconsin Press.

Sturgess, K. (1986). *Jacobean Private Theatre*. London: Routledge.

Tricomi, A. H. (1989). *Anticourt Drama in England 1603–1642*. Charlottesville: University of Virginia Press.

Wymer, R. (1995). *Webster and Ford*. Basingstoke: Macmillan.

46

Caroline Theatre

Roy Booth

Caroline drama is crossed by long shadows. From the past, literary shades fall across the dramatists: Sir John Suckling, gambler, poet and court dramatist, chose to have himself painted by Van Dyck with a folio Shakespeare open at *Hamlet* in his hands.[1] The influence of earlier dramatists is everywhere apparent. Other, political, shadows are cast retrospectively by the English Civil War and the execution of Charles I. It is almost impossible to read the plays without applauding a dramatist for his perspicuity or slating a text for its obliviousness.

Despite the brilliant advocacy of Martin Butler, Caroline drama still suffers neglect – not critical so much as editorial and theatrical neglect. Butler makes a case for Brome as a seventeenth-century Brecht, 'a political dramatist of major significance'.[2] But the enthused reader may flag when confronted by the only available library text, the 1873 three-volume edition (reprinted in 1966), or, moving to other dramatists, the 'hopelessly dated'[3] Gifford–Dyce six-volume edition of Shirley (1833), or Davenant in five volumes from 1872–4, or Killigrew in a facsimile of the 1664 edition. Even Ford lacks a complete modern edition. Where edited single texts do exist, the theatre follows close behind, with notable RSC revivals of Shirley's *Hyde Park* and Jonson's *The New Inn* (both 1987), Ford's *The Broken Heart* (1994) and an adaptation of Brome's *The Jovial Crew* (1992).

One possible reason for the prior critical disregard of Caroline drama lies in the relative rarity of tragedy in the period: Ford is the major exception, but among the productive professionals, Massinger and Shirley wrote tragedies only intermittently: social comedy and romantic tragi-comedy were the preferred modes. Brome, on whom Butler bases his main case for attention, eschewed tragedy completely. Brome's prologues tell the story of his refusal to be considered a poet, and parade 'his wonted modesty'.[4] James Bulman suggests that Caroline drama gets measured to its detriment against the 'moral fervour' of Jacobean tragedy.[5] The transition from Webster to a Caroline tragedy like Massinger's *The Roman Actor* (1626), a self-subverting defence of the stage, with its actor protagonist failing to reform a miser when he performs a moral play, and exciting the sexual appetite of the empress when performing a lover, can indeed suggest a loss of artistic conviction.

There may be more to this: if Caroline theatre offered higher generic seriousness, it might seem adequate to our perception of the age. Perhaps there is a latter-day perception of the Caroline era as a great tragic age *manqué*, collectively engaged in a production of 'The Famous Tragedie of King Charles I'.[6] The type of gentlemen who attended the tragi-comedies of honour, who assimilated that ethos, became tragic figures in reality: the self-divided loyalists like Falkland, depressed beyond endurance, riding with slow deliberation to his death at Newbury, or Sir Edmund Verney, the King's standard bearer – a conspicuous target – at Edgehill, taking the field without any armour.

John Ford was the specialist in tragedy. His first surviving solo work, *The Lover's Melancholy* (1628), opens with an adaptation of Claudian's eclogue about the contest between a nightingale and a human performer. Shakespeare was Ford's inimitable nightingale. Ford revived *the* Shakespearean form, the English History play. Shakespeare had left out one reign from his long sequence of kings, that of Henry VII. Ford didn't fashion, however, a chronicle history centred on the king, but *Perkin Warbeck* (1625–34), the tragedy of a deluded pretender to the crown. In a sense, Ford *is* Perkin Warbeck, a pretender so possessed by his own rhetoric that he believes himself to be the real thing.

One curious effect in Ford is the impression we get of the immaturity of his tragic personages. They make us feel, as we do with Romeo and Juliet, that they wouldn't suffer such heartbreak if they weren't so inexperienced and bound up in the passions of their private worlds. The remarkable catastrophe of *The Broken Heart* (1630–3), in which Calantha dances on through multiplied tidings of personal disaster before expiring heartbroken, was possibly written by Ford with one eye on the demeanour of Charles when news of Buckingham's assassination reached him: regal self-control in public, followed by private heartbreak.[7] Ford's plays often cannot be precisely dated, so it is difficult to get a sense of his career's trajectory: particularly 'Caroline' in character was *The Queen, or the Excellency of her Sex* (staged somewhere between 1621 and 1642), with its bizarre royal marriage and happy outcome.[8]

The Two Royal Luminaries[9]

In the 1630s the nation was confronted by the disconcerting spectacle of an ostentatiously happy royal marriage. James I and Anne of Denmark had inhabited separate courts after 1606; his successor's emotional history seems to have been of dependence on Buckingham until the 1628 assassination, when Charles turned to his wife, and fell in love with her. The royal couple were recommended as models for a reformed drama: 'whose lives have brought / Virtue in fashion, and the world have taught, / That chaste innocuous sports become the stage'.[10] Celebration of '*Hymens Twin* the MARY-CHARLES' became material for court masques,[11] but, predictably, a more robust response to Charles's devotion to his wife appeared elsewhere. One remarkable commentary occurs in Killigrew's *The Parson's Wedding* (1641). Act 2, scene 7 is talk for its own sake, between libertine men and '*honnête*' women. Jolly protests that the king's example encourages women not to be 'kind'. The captain wishes that Charles would really make himself a father to his people by cuckolding husbands and siring bastards: 'These were the ways that made [Edward IV and Henry VIII] powerful at home.' The cavaliers create a fantasy Charles in their own image, a Charles leading the city by the horns. Jolly goes on to tell a tall story about Elizabeth I, mounted on the Lord Mayor of London on her way to give her rallying speech against the Spanish Armada at Tilbury.[12] This extraordinary critique of Charles, implying that if he were as masculine a monarch as Elizabeth, he might spare the nation all its troubles, involves a mental leap from the notion that the monarch's chastity encourages women to be intractable, to the political recalcitrance of the unsubmissive citizenry at large, which a more manly king would not suffer: 'all this mischief comes of love and constancy'.[13]

Massinger's *The Picture* (1629) exemplifies the Caroline marriage play, its double plot contrasting a slavishly devoted king with a husband who distrusts his highly moral wife simply because of her sex. An outspoken critic of the uxorious king features strongly, a counsellor who would rather see his king be a 'libidinous Caesar' than watch him 'slave [himself] to th'imperious humour / Of a proud beauty'.[14] The main plot has Mathias demonstrate mistrust of his wife Sophia by commissioning a magical portrait which will turn yellow if she is tempted in his absence, and black if she is unfaithful. The queen is piqued by Mathias's boasts, and she resolves to seduce him and corrupt his wife by means of two courtiers. Mathias is tempted, but avoids yielding: Sophia gets an elaborated account of her husband's adulteries at court. She briefly sees herself as a 'servant to voluptuousness' (III.vi.158), but is repelled by the courtiers' mutual denigration. Her wavering makes the magical portrait turn yellow with some black: Mathias weakens in his second scene with the queen (IV. i.), but is saved because a look of triumphant scorn escapes her. Learning fast, when they meet again (IV. iv.) Mathias rebukes the queen, forestalling her triumph, and making her genuinely repentant: their whole encounter is observed by the king, to whom she submits herself. Finally, the exonerated Sophia surprises Mathias by demanding a divorce. All the characters beg her to forgive him, and the king concludes the action with the admonition: 'to all married men be this a caution / Which they should duly tender as their life / Neither to dote too much nor doubt a wife'.

A feature which seems characteristic of Caroline drama is that the king's matrimonial behaviour, and new modes of thinking about sexual relationships, caused the personnel of domestic plays to change: the married lives of kings and dukes supplant the more obviously representative types of earlier marriage plays. Companionate marriage, mutually negotiated, was the emergent trend, but the dramatists couldn't reconcile in their stage kings the new ideal of partnership with a deep-rooted cultural insistence upon male dominance within marriage, and a preference for strong male monarchs. Butler's book highlights every form of overt or implied political dissent in

Caroline drama. Despite all his evidence, the Caroline actors believed themselves to be royalists, most of them enlisting for the king in 1642.[15] But they had also participated in a discourse which played a part in undermining Charles's stature, that corrective commentary upon infatuated husbands which Caroline theatre applied to royalty in particular.[16] After Naseby, parliament was able to publish Charles's captured letters in *The Kings Cabinet Opened* (July 1645): the final exposure of an 'effeminate and uxorious magistrate'.[17] Infatuated monarch plays, with their strands of political and social criticism, were topical, yet a more general fascination with dominant women could be imputed to Stuart dramatists. Shirley and Brome are prime examples.

James Shirley: 'The Beneficial and Cleanly Way of Poetry'[18]

At his most interesting, James Shirley allows female characters independence of action and sometimes unexpected freedom from moral condemnation. Celestina, the young widow of *The Lady of Pleasure* (1635), relishes her freedom; she is that rare thing in drama, a female misogamist who claims she will not 'Court myself new marriage fetters' (II.ii.47) and stays constant to her opinion. Equally striking is the career of Aretina, wife to Bornwell: she runs with a fast set, carefully arranges an untraceable liaison with another man, and is only made repentant by her chosen lover's account of earning his new finery through the nocturnal labour of pleasuring an old witch. 'My soul is miserable', the mortified Aretina concludes (V.ii.179). Her husband never learns about the adultery. Aphra Behn did a lively reworking of this plot for the Julia–Gayman intrigue in her play *The Lucky Chance* (1686) – the leading female dramatist of the Restoration stage finding in Shirley an anticipation of effects she needed.

The young widow Celestina is a prominent type in Caroline drama. Of the ninety 'widows' listed by the *Index of Characters in Early Modern English Drama* in plays published between 1576 and 1642, forty-one appear in Caroline plays (i.e., in seventeen of the sixty-six years). If marriage began as 'the supreme rule of the gift', as Levi-Strauss claims, marriage to a widow is very different negotiation: the widow is independent, and marries if and when she chooses to, rather than being given away by her father or brother in a male-to-male transaction. The ubiquitous Caroline widow is saying something about all women, in a new and alarming dispensation; on stage, the type would often have been performed as a Puritan citizen, the conduit of city wealth to 'decayed houses'.[19]

Shirley is interested in manipulators. Occasionally this appears at a political level, with hyper-scheming villains like Lorenzo in *The Traitor* (1631) or the title character in *The Cardinal* (1641). More often he offers social comedies, where moral characters manoeuvre into conformity with their ideas a member of the opposite sex. The moral education of a male character by a female is a classic Caroline pattern, and registers the impact of *précieux* or platonizing ideas. Fowler, a libertine, is straightened out by

Penelope, the main character in *The Witty Fair One* (1628). In *The Gamester* (1633), Mistress Wilding's plot to reform her husband is luckily augmented when, deeply involved in dice-play, he sends his friend Hazard in his place to fulfil a nocturnal tryst with his wife's relative. The two women have conspired 'to have made you blush, and chide you into honesty' (*Shirley* (1833) vol. 3, V. ii. p. 277), so the arrival of Hazard increases her power, by enabling her to represent the night's events as leading to her innocently cuckolding her husband. If men in Shirley are brought to virtue by female manipulators, his male manipulators are more concerned to bring women to heel. Fairfield conquers Mistress Carol's aversion to marriage in *Hyde Park* by a psychological masterstroke: 'I bind you never to desire my company / Hereafter; for no reason to affect me' (II. iv). Shirley's men are often being unscrupulous and are correspondingly unsuccessful. In a rare passage of Jonsonian satirical strength in *The Humorous Courtier* Contarino tries to persuade his wife that, as the Duchess loves him (as he believes), and he can therefore become Duke, she really ought to kill herself for her husband's benefit. He fails, of course.

Only a couple of Shirley's plays have been lost, while the surviving works of Massinger represent about half of his known solo output. It might be remarked that both dramatists might enjoy higher reputations if these proportions had been reversed.

'I'll Be Utopia': Brome's Antipodean Women

Reviewing the revival of *Hyde Park* at the Swan Theatre in 1987, Lois Potter asserted that 'for a genuinely critical view of Caroline social and dramaturgical conventions, you have to go to Brome. How about reviving *him* next year?'[20] The RSC took until 1992, when Stephen Jeffrey's adapted text of *A Jovial Crew* was performed.[21] Whether Brome is Donaldson's engaging but minor talent,[22] or Butler's 'political playwright of major significance' remains to be seen.

Brome's plays show his recurrent interest in inverted worlds. In Butler's view, 'Brome converts the festival notion of turning the world upside down from a gay but transient fantasy into a radical and enduring criticism of his society' (Butler, p. 228). While comic levelling and inversion have always allowed women characters freedom to voice opinions, Brome's plays, which so recurrently exploit comic inversion, have a remarkable array of activist females. Rachel and Muriel initiate the impersonation of beggars in *A Jovial Crew* (1641), and hold out against the rigours of sleeping rough rather better than the men they oblige to accompany them. Brome even allows some of his female characters to express physical desires. Dorcas in *Covent-Garden Weeded* (1632) seeks the sexual freedom of the courtesans of Italy: 'I fly out in brave rebellion; / And offer at the least to break these shackles / That holds our legs together' (I. i., *Brome* vol. 2 second pagination, p. 9). In *The English Moor* (1637), Millicent fights back sexually after being married off to the elderly usurer Quicksands, singing of how *'We'll make the new bed cry Jiggy Joggy'* (I. iii., *Brome* vol. 2 first pagination,

p. 13) and other immodesties, until he quails and agrees to postpone the consummation that she makes so intimidating. *The Asparagus Garden* offers another of Brome's remarkable portraits of male sexual evasiveness in Sir Arnold Cautious, who 'defies wedlock, because he thinks there is not a maiden-head in any marriageable beauty' (III. iv. *Brome* vol. 3, p. 159), but is reduced to voyeuristic drivelling whenever sees 'a delicate leg' emerging from a coach. The gratuitous elaboration of the only scene (II. i.) featuring Sir Raphael, who has 'vowed virginity' and is 'a lay-gospeller among the married sort and an especial pedant to the youth o' court' in *The Court Beggar* (1640), also reveals Brome's interest in the type.[23]

In *The Antipodes* (1638) Peregrine Joyless's fear of sex has left his wife Martha a virgin after three years of marriage. The play-within-a-play about the Antipodes, which their therapist Dr Hughball puts on, offers Martha a fantasy world of female sexual dominance – 'there the maids doe woo / The bachelors, and 'tis most probable / The wives lie uppermost' (ed. Haaker, I.vi.140–2) – where men beg to be made cuckolds. Act IV, scene ii, shows the Antipodean girl's brusque advances on the ludicrously coy gentleman. Less appealing is Brome's collaboration with Heywood, *The Late Lancashire Witches* (1634). The play was one of the rare commissions by an open-air amphitheatre, which, as Gurr points out, usually depended on revivals during these decades.[24] Here carnival inversion turns sour. The actual case was effectively still *sub judice*: the jury had convicted seventeen women, but the judges referred the case to the king in council. The play intervened, cheerfully dramatizing and improving upon the accusations made by young Edmund Robinson. King Charles, to his credit, finally pardoned those 'witches' who had survived imprisonment. Heywood handled the tragic action. Usually his good husbands discover that their wives have committed adultery, but the experience of Master Generous surpasses that horror – Mistress Generous turns out to be a witch, who has promised her soul to Satan, nor will she repent. Brome handled the bewitched household of Old Seely, where all relations – master and servant, husband and wife, parent and child – have been inverted.

A central scene dramatizes Robinson's wild story: Robin peeps through a cranny in a barn, and sees the 'Satanical sisterhood' (Heywood, 6 vols 1874, vol. 4, IV i, p. 219), who pull on ropes to make a wedding feast which has been spirited away descend to them. Such scenes of collective female depravity and appetite prepare for the caustically misogynistic masque in act IV, when the bastard Whetstone is empowered by his aunt to show each of the gentlemen present who his biological father really is: his father was at least a gallant, whereas the others were sired by a schoolteacher, a nimble tailor and a servant respectively: a form of witchcraft is present in all women, it seems. *The Late Lancashire Witches* is the sinister counterpart to the open-mindedness Brome shows elsewhere, and, as entertainment, a reminder that the popular theatre's rivals for public money were all the mindlessly exploitative shows that the Caroline state censor also licensed, featuring three-headed children, Siamese twins, hairy children and handless women.[25]

A link between *The Late Lancashire Witches* and Milton's *Comus* might seem unlikely, but it too was performed in the late summer / autumn of 1634, and both texts concern supernatural evil. Collocating the two makes it possible to draw together some of the typical concerns this chapter has suggested. The Lady in *Comus* resists magic and seduction; though reluctant to speak, she has much to say. Rescue delivers her back to the silence normal to her gender, age and breeding – after l.798, she says nothing. She only expresses her triumph over 'sensual folly' via the language of 'victorious dance'. *Comus* contains by far the best stage poetry of the period, and Alice Egerton also displayed her accomplishment in Lawes's exquisite and difficult setting of 'Sweet Echo'. Yet it does seem true to say that the focus of anxiety in the masque is really the lady, rather than the enchanter. Comus is a theatrical being, a libertine seducer performed by a male professional actor. The lady is an intruder upon performance; the dramatization of her resistance to seduction really involves our seduction by her, focussed through song, poetry and dance.

Much 'Caroline drama' might really be called 'Henriettan drama': the queen was the enthusiast, the royal actor. All the important innovations in theatre were made at court – women performers, scenery, lighting, elaboration of costume and make-up. The theatre's power of illusion was placed at the queen's disposal, and her much-resented hold over Charles, a king 'overpowered with the enchantments of a woman' was connected to theatre and performance.[26]

There were those in the ordinary theatre ready to see more, who knew that women abroad were 'the best actors, they play their own parts, a thing much desired in England by some ladies, inns o' court gentlemen, and others' (Shirley, *The Ball* V i, *Works* vol. 3, p. 79). But the nation, in what Comus would have called a 'pet of temperance', opted to 'feed on pulse' rather than be feasted. On Sept 2 1642 the theatres were closed; the second Globe was demolished in 1644, on Feb 11 1648 the 'Ordinance for the utter suppression and abolishing of all stage-plays and interludes' was passed, and the interiors of the surviving city playhouses demolished. July 1645 had also seen the Masquing House at Whitehall taken down: 'the queen's dancing barn', the Puritans called it, as if it had been the barn where Edmund Robinson peeped in on witchcraft.[27]

Notes

1 See Malcolm Rogers, 'The Meaning of Van Dyck's Portrait of Sir John Suckling', *The Burlington Magazine*, 120 (1978), 741–5.

2 Butler, p. 281.

3 Logan and Smith, p. 167.

4 Prologue, *The Sparagus Garden*.

5 Bulman, p. 354.

6 To borrow the title of the anonymous play of 1649.

7 See R. Booth, 'Royal Grief in Ford's *The Broken Heart*', *Notes and Queries*, vol. 232, no. 3 (Sept. 1987), p. 305.

8 The queen marries a misogynistic general who has rebelled against her rule. Groundless jealousy cures him by making him appreciate 'her perfections'.

9 Shirley, *The Lady of Pleasure* IV, iii, 180. In them, Celestina says, truth and love of innocence shine so brightly that 'At Court, you cannot lose your way to chastity'.

10 Epilogue to Joseph Rutter's *The Shepherd's Holiday* (1633–5), cited by Veevers, p. 55.

11 *Albion's Triumph* (1631), in *The Poems and Masques of Aurelian Townshend*, ed. Cedric C.

Brown (Reading: Whiteknights Press, 1983), p. 89.

12 Killigrew, *The Parson's Wedding* in A. S. Knowland (ed.), *Six Caroline Plays* (Oxford, World's Classics, 1962) 484.

13 Ibid. pp. 484–5.

14 *Massinger* eds Edwards / Gibson (Oxford, 1976) vol. 3, III, iv, 45; 49–50.

15 For details see *Randall* (1995) p. 43.

16 Other infatuated monarch plays include Davenant's *Albovine* (1628), Massinger's *The Emperor of the East* (*c.*1631), Brome's *The Queen and Concubine* (1635) and Heywood's *A Challenge for Beauty* (1635).

17 Milton, *Eikonoklastes* in *The Works of John Milton*, vol. 5 (Columbia, 1932) p. 139. The imputation was that Charles would deploy foreign (catholic) armies his wife helped him recruit. Lucy Hutchinson's *Memoirs* contain forthright criticism of Charles's uxoriousness, which she contrasts with her own husband's admirable freedom from such weakness.

18 Bawcutt item 259: Sir Henry Herbert's commendation of Shirley's *The Young Admiral* (1633).

19 Shackerley Marmion, quoted in *Wedgwood* p. 203. Sara Mendelson and Patricia Crawford in their *Women in Early Modern England 1550–1720* (Oxford, Clarendon Press, 1998) cite research (p. 182) which perhaps indi-

cates a growing reluctance among widows to remarry: while half the widows of late sixteenth century Abingdon remarried, only a quarter of later seventeenth-century widows did so.

20 *TLS* 1 May 1987, reviewing Barry Kyle's production at the Swan Theatre, Stratford.

21 Text published by Warner Chappell Plays Ltd, 1992. For discussion, see Martin White, *Renaissance Drama in Action* (Routledge, 1998).

22 Ian Donaldson, *The World Upside Down* (Oxford, 1974), p. 81.

23 Brome I pp. 201–2. There may be a lost element of personal caricature here. The play lampoons Suckling and Davenant.

24 'By the 1630s even the King's Men were not buying more than three or four new plays a year, compared with the twenty or more of the 1590s' Gurr (1996) p. 101.

25 Bawcutt (1996), items 175, 369, 250, 261.

26 Quotation from *The Life and Death of King Charles, or, the Pseudo Martyr discovered* (1650, p. 214), cited by Lois Potter, *Secret Rites and Secret Writing* (Cambridge: Cambridge University Press, 1989) p. 80. See also comments on Prynne's obsession with the Queen's erotic performances in *Sanders* (1999) p. 33.

27 Wedgwood, 'The Last Masque' in *Truth and Opinion*, p. 143.

References and Further Reading

Bawcutt, Nina (1996). *The Control and Censorship of Caroline Drama: The Records of Sir Henry Herbert, Master of the Revels 1623–73*. Oxford: Clarendon Press.

Berger, Thomas L, Bradford, William C. and Sondergard, Sidney L. (1998). *An Index of Characters in Early Modern English Drama, Printed Plays 1500–1660*. Cambridge: Cambridge University Press.

Bulman, James (1990). 'Caroline Theatre'. In A. R. Braunmuller and Michael Hattaway (eds), *The Cambridge Companion to English Renaissance Drama* (pp. 353–79). Cambridge: Cambridge University Press.

Butler, Martin (1984). *Theatre and Crisis 1632–1642*. Cambridge: Cambridge University Press.

Clark, Ira (1992). *Professional Playwrights: Massinger, Ford, Shirley, and Brome*. Lexington: University of Kentucky Press.

Edmond, Mary (1987). *Rare Sir William Davenant* (The Revels Plays Companion Library). Manchester: Manchester University Press.

Farr, Dorothy (1989). *John Ford and the Caroline Theatre*. London: Macmillan.

Gurr, Andrew (1996). *The Shakespearean Playing Companies*. Oxford: Clarendon Press.

Hopkins, Lisa (1994). *John Ford's Political Theatre* (The Revels Plays Companion Library). Manchester: Manchester University Press.

Kaufmann, R. J. (1961). *Richard Brome, Caroline Playwright*. New York: Columbia University Press.

Logan, Terence P. and Smith, Denzell S. (1978). *The Later Jacobean and Caroline Dramatists: A Survey and Bibliography of Recent Studies in English Renaissance Drama*. Nebraska: University of Nebraska Press.

McLuskie, Kathleen (1988). 'The Plays and Playwrights: 1613–42'. In Lois Potter et al. (eds), *The Revels History of Drama in English IV 1613–1660*. London: Methuen.

Parry, Graham (1981). *The Golden Age Restor'd: The Culture of the Stuart Court, 1603–42*. Manchester: Manchester University Press.

Randall, Dale B. J. (1995). *Winter Fruit English Drama 1642–1660*. Kentucky: University Press of Kentucky.

Sanders, Julie (1999). *Caroline Drama: The Plays of Massinger, Ford, Shirley and Brome* (British Council Writers and their Work). London: Northcote House.

Tricomi, Albert (1989). *Anticourt Drama, 1603–42*. Charlottesville: University of Virginia Press.

Veevers, Erica (1989). *Images of Love and Religion: Queen Henrietta Maria and Court Entertainments*. Cambridge: Cambridge University Press.

Wedgwood, C. V. (1960). *Social Comedy in the Reign of Charles I' in her 'Truth and Opinion'*. London: Collins.

Wiseman, Susan (1998). *Drama and Politics in the English Civil War*. Cambridge: Cambridge University Press.

47

Scientific Writing

David Colclough

It is perhaps best to begin with a warning. No one in the Renaissance would have recognized the term 'scientific writing'; and no one would have known what kind of strange creature a 'scientist' might be. The field of enquiry we now know as 'science' (with all the implications concerning the separation of 'cultures' that implies) was a branch of knowledge (Latin *scientia*) which investigated the phenomena of the natural world (Johns (1998), pp. 42–4; Rossi (1996)). Hence the term a Renaissance writer would have used to describe his or her pursuit in this field was 'natural philosophy'; and the distinction between its scope and aims and those of, say, moral philosophy, political philosophy or theology was (as we shall see) not as clear as it might seem to us.[1] Natural philosophy was, after all, the study of the created world, in which God (the great artificer) and the Christian message were held to be revealed. The Book of Nature was one of the texts (the other usually being identified as the Book of Scripture) through which the individual Christian could know God; in the Renaissance the metaphor shifted from one of clarity and intelligibility (everyone, even if they are illiterate, can read this book) to one of obscurity (this book is written in an especially difficult language or character) (Curtius (1953), pp. 319–26).

The ways in which the natural philosopher's claims were made, disseminated, verified or disputed, as well as his or her place in society, were also in many ways unrecognizably different. While many still tend to locate the birth of modern science in Renaissance England, it is also important to appreciate the gulf that separates us from the practice and the writing of natural philosophy in the sixteenth and seventeenth centuries. Only comparatively recently have historians of science begun to take seriously the varieties of natural-philosophical inquiry pursued by those we have been taught to regard as the fathers of science. Newton's lifelong interest in alchemy need no longer be dismissed as an embarrassing hobby, but may rather be recognized as a part of his understanding of the ends of knowledge. Similarly, the wider life of the natural philosopher has begun to be acknowledged as a crucial factor in understanding his or her work. Serious attention must be paid to Galileo's struggles for favour

from the Medici family or the pope when we know how far the desire for advancement may have influenced the presentation or the trajectory of his work (Johns (1998),
esp. pp. 20–8). Francis Bacon's relentless pursuit of high office is of as much relevance
to our understanding of his natural philosophy as to our reading of his *Essays* – even
if it simply serves to remind us that Bacon could only be a philosopher in his spare
time (Peltonen (1996), p. 10; Martin (1992); Jardine and Stewart (1998)).

This is to emphasize that the study of context has come to be a key component in
our understanding of the natural philosophy (and much else) of the Renaissance. The
Renaissance scientist is best seen not as an isolated thinker (or inventor) at work in
the privacy of his or her study or laboratory, but as a social and political animal whose
attempts to make sense are inescapably conditioned by social and historical circumstances. We need in turn, when trying to make sense of scientific writing of the time,
to take into account what kind of function the writer imagined for his or her text.
No less than other kinds of writing, scientific texts need to be read as interventions
in specific debates: far from being only building blocks in the history of ideas, they
were written for particular audiences with both local and wider concerns. Even when
they appear to be concerned with abstract concepts, these abstractions are themselves often used as a way of conceptualizing localized differences and as weapons for
assuming argumentative authority (Sherman (1995); Porter (1991), p. 4).

However much these caveats might undermine the notion of the 'scientific revolution' as a monolithic and sudden shift in thought, it is important that we do not
lose sight of the real innovations that occurred in natural philosophy during the
Renaissance. New cosmologies were indeed proposed (although it is important to
remember that Copernicus's theory was presented in the form of an hypothesis); 'new'
lands, and the human body, were mapped, in the earlier part of the period. The work
of Robert Boyle, Robert Hooke and Isaac Newton, published in the *Philosophical
Transactions* of the Royal Society and elsewhere from the early 1660s, was indeed
hugely significant in terms of experimental and mathematical practice and theory.
Copernicus's *De revolutionibus* (1543), Gilbert's *De magnete* (1600), Harvey's *De motu
cordis* (1628) and Galileo's *Dialogo . . . sopra i due Massimi Sistemi del Mondo* (1632) were
all immensely important works, sometimes (as in the case of Galileo) achieving an
effect well beyond that envisaged by their authors. In several of these cases innovation is strangely yoked to conservatism, which could be seen as a hallmark of most
scientific writing in the English Renaissance. Gilbert's work on the magnet is, for its
time, an impeccable example of experimental writing, but based on a traditionally
Aristotelian search for a necessary cause, while Harvey's treatise on the circulation of
the blood is, similarly, thoroughly Aristotelian and yet ground-breaking (Wallace
(1998), pp. 224–5).[2] This apparent contradiction might suggest that the transition
from medieval to Renaissance should best be envisaged as a continuum, rather than
a fissure: *pace* Foucault, it is hard to support the claim that an entirely new way of
knowing appears in this period (Foucault (1970)).

Continuity is especially evident in the canon of scientific writing.[3] Just as in the
middle ages, the basic framework of natural philosophy in the Renaissance was pro-

vided by Aristotle's scientific works, especially the *Physics*, *De caelo*, *De generatione et corruptione*, *Metereology*, *De anima* and *Parva naturalia*. The questions being asked by natural philosophers were also of the same kind: the object of enquiry was sensible matter and, ultimately, necessary causes. But the classification and valorization of different forms of knowledge was in transition. Here again, Aristotle – or a Christianized version of Aristotle – had been dominant in medieval thought from the thirteenth century on, the main texts being the *Posterior Analytics* and the *Metaphysics* (Kusukawa (1996), pp. 48–51). With the rise of the humanities in the fourteenth century and the new emphasis on the importance of grammar, rhetoric, history, poetics and moral philosophy, the scope of natural philosophy was re-examined. The concomitant return to classical sources, which resulted in increased knowledge of the Greek text of Aristotle and of commentaries on his works, meant that the central texts of scientific enquiry could be subjected to sceptical critical analysis; but it could also lead to a certain conservatism. The authority of Aristotle could be shored up by the attentions of the philologists, with critical attention concentrating on textual matters rather than scrutinizing basic claims and assumptions.[4]

Nonetheless, the boundaries of natural philosophy were expanding, with other schools of thought and areas of enquiry being incorporated. Mechanics, optics, astronomy and medicine (which are, to us, obviously parts of 'science') were newly accepted as part of natural philosophy. Similarly, Platonic, Hermetic, Neopythagorean, Stoic and Atomist ideas were making their presence felt. The alchemical theories of Cornelius Agrippa and the natural chemistry of Paracelsus spread to England, where the varieties of writing and activity were very extensive. This is evident in the productions of writers such as the natural magician Robert Fludd, John Dee, who cast horoscopes for major political figures as well as writing on navigation and conversing with angels, the mathematicians Leonard and Thomas Digges, the chemist Kenelm Digby, the astrologer and medic Simon Forman and, of course, Francis Bacon.[5] Along with changes in the methods of doing natural philosophy, the growing place given to mathematics (especially important to Copernicus, Kepler and Galileo), observation and mechanics (instrument makers are central to scientific work in this period), there were important changes in the way this work was presented. Turning from the medieval form of the disputation, where a proposition would be formally argued out in sequential sections *pro* and *contra* (a written form of an oral university exercise), natural-philosophical writing adopted more discursive, literary strategies. Much scientific writing in the Renaissance is itself concerned with the struggle to find a proper, truthful and persuasive means of communicating scientific argument. Can there be such a thing as a transparent discourse of natural philosophy, where presentation does not affect argument; and if so, would one want it? How far can rhetoric be used in the course of natural philosophy; and how far is it possible to avoid it? How does one's imagined readership affect the way in which one frames one's arguments? All of these questions are at the heart of the attempt by early modern natural philosophers to gain credit and legitimacy for their work, and, often, polemically to describe what the task of natural philosophy might be.

I want to turn for the remainder of this chapter to a figure who was perhaps above all preoccupied with these questions about the nature of scientific writing, and who also remains for many the incarnation of English science in the Renaissance: Francis Bacon. The latter picture is certainly one to which Bacon himself contributed the original outline; others have subsequently filled in the gaps, often somewhat colourfully. Writing around 1592 to William Cecil, Lord Burghley – Bacon's uncle and Elizabeth I's Lord Treasurer – he described the scale of his ambitions: 'I confess that I have as vast contemplative ends, as I have moderate civil ends: for I have taken all knowledge to be my province' (Bacon (1996), p. 20). The famous frontispiece to the 1620 *Novum Organum* shows a ship sailing through the pillars of Hercules, symbolizing the boundaries of the known world: Bacon is rejecting the limits set by the ancients, while associating his natural philosophy with the achievements of geographical discovery – and the ambitions of empire. This is emphasized by his use of the motto *'plus ultra'*: the Emperor Charles V's *'ne plus ultra'* given a positive gloss. Bacon had copies of this beautifully produced folio volume bound in purple velvet and embossed with his arms in order to donate them to the Bodleian Library in Oxford and Cambridge University Library, placing himself alongside (and perhaps hoping to supplant) the authorities already shelved there.[6] Always concerned to establish his textual legacy, he also asked in his will that 'books fair bound' of all his printed works should be

> placed in the Kings library, and in the library of the University of Cambridge, and in the library of Trinity College [where he was an undergraduate] . . . and in the library of Bennett College [now Corpus Christi] . . . and in the library of the University of Oxenford, and in the library of my Lord of Canterbury, and in the library of Eton.
>
> (Bacon (1857–74), vol. XIV, p. 539)

Many have taken Bacon at his word, and after his death he was invoked as a kind of scientific prophet by a startling variety of groups and individuals, ranging from the providentialist George Hakewill in the 1620s, through Samuel Hartlib and the Comenian reformers during the Republic, to the founders of the Royal Society: witness Bacon's presence on the engraved title-page of Sprat's *History of the Royal Society* (1667) and in Abraham Cowley's prefatory poem to the volume.[7] In the nineteenth century he was regarded by Whewell, among others, as the leader of a revolution in scientific thought that led to the modern perception of the world, while his status has been, if anything, reinforced by more recent debates over his legacy. Benjamin Farrington praised Bacon as a forward-looking 'philosopher of industrial science' (Farrington, 1951), while Karl Popper condemned him as the prophet of a misguided objectivity and Theodor W. Adorno and Max Horkheimer pictured him as the archrepresentative of instrumental science's attempt to dominate nature and mankind (Horkheimer and Adorno (1973), pp. 3–7).

In his vigorous engagement with, and polemical rejection of, the 'ancients', most of all Aristotle; in his attempts to redesign the scope and ends of learning; in his experiments with different forms of text; in his use of experiment; in his advocacy of collaborative research and his requests for state funding, Bacon appears a thoroughly modern scientist. Yet it is as easy to locate significant flaws in this depiction. Bacon relied heavily upon the ancients at the same time as he rejected them (Pliny is a major contributor to the supposedly observational *Sylva Sylvarum* (1627); his experimental life remains very obscure; his advocacy of collaboration seems only infrequently to have been translated into practice, and his requests for state funding were uniformly unsuccessful. Most of all, his grand plan for the transformation of natural philosophy, the *Instauratio magna*, was never completed: at his death he had treated the first part and contributed to the second: the last three, as Markku Peltonen writes, 'were left untouched' (Peltonen (1996), p. 17). Yet it is possible to argue that Bacon's projects were precisely dependent upon this anticipative or proleptic quality, and that it is his texts' attempts to provoke their readers into imagining and creating a future with a new form of knowledge that is their greatest quality. I shall try to demonstrate what I mean by looking at two of Bacon's most important works: *The Advancement of Learning* (1605) and *New Atlantis* (published posthumously with the *Sylva* in 1627).

Bacon presents *The Advancement of Learning* as a preparatory work, suggesting in the hyperbolic dedication to James I that it will 'excite your princely cogitations to visit the excellent treasury of your own mind' (Bacon (1996), p. 122). He is at pains to emphasize that the book is primarily intended to provoke thought (and action) in others, rather than to impose his own thoughts on his readers. Such a rhetorical side-stepping of personal, authorial authority is characteristic of this text, in which Bacon says he is clearing the way for others; and it becomes increasingly important to Bacon's natural philosophical writing more generally. Near the end of the *Advancement*, he reflects that

> looking back into that I have passed through, this writing seemeth to me . . . not much better than that noise or sound which musicians make while they are tuning their instruments; which is nothing pleasant to hear, but yet is a cause why the music is sweeter afterwards. So have I been content to tune the instruments of the muses, that they may play that have better hands.
>
> (Bacon (1996), p. 288)

As Kevin Dunn has noted, this topos of humility and prolepsis plays a crucial part in Bacon's attempt to shift the burden of authority and persuasion away from his words and his authorial persona and onto the tacit assent of a 'public' constituted by his readers (Dunn (1994)). Here the 'public' by which the claims of the text will be assessed remains undefined, but is nonetheless an important rhetorical function of the text. Refined and circumscribed to a particular set of 'gentlemanly' social and discursive markers, it would become increasingly significant throughout the century for the validation of natural-philosophical knowledge-claims (Johns (1998); Shapin (1994)).

The preparatory tasks Bacon sets himself in the *Advancement* are to defend learning from its detractors; describe its current state; define its aims, and urge their pursuit. He divides the text into two Books, corresponding to two rhetorical strategies; the first epideictic – designed to praise or blame – and the second deliberative – designed to persuade.[8] In both books Bacon is concerned with the establishment of a proper attitude to the past and to the authoritative canon of natural philosophical writings. The defence that he offers in the first Book has a place in a long tradition, as does his description of the field of learning in Book Two; and one of his main aims is to establish a proper relationship to such traditions (see Bacon (1996), pp. 577–8). In the letter to Burghley quoted above, Bacon had spoken of 'purging' the province of knowledge

> of two sorts of rovers, whereof the one with frivolous disputations, confutations, and verbosities, the other with blind experiments and auricular traditions and impostures, hath committed so many spoils, I hope I should bring in industrious observations, grounded conclusions, and profitable inventions and discoveries; the best state of that province.
>
> (Bacon (1996), p. 20)

The *Advancement* is, to a great extent, this programme writ large. His 'purging' in Book One corresponds to the 'destructive part' of the *Instauratio*, necessary before the 'constructive part' could begin (Bacon (1857–74), vol. X, pp. 364–5; vol. IV, p. 27). In order to praise learning as he defines it, Bacon requires an initial refutation of 'tacit objections', or 'discredits and disgraces'. All of these 'distempers' of learning arise from a particular, unsatisfactory way of reading; a misguided attitude towards textual authority. As he writes in book 1,

> as for the overmuch credit that hath been given unto authors in sciences, in making them dictators, that their words should stand, and not consuls to give advice; the damage is infinite that sciences have received thereby.
>
> (Bacon (1996), pp. 143–4)

It is the voluntary relinquishing of their own ability to go beyond the texts of the past, laments Bacon, that has led readers and philosophers to the state of degenerate learning where they now languish, producing ever more depraved versions of ancient notions rather than attempting to build upon them. In the sphere of philosophy 'disciples do owe unto masters only a temporary belief and a suspension of their own judgement till they be fully instructed, and not an absolute resignation or perpetual captivity' (Bacon (1996), p. 144). The only way that knowledge can accumulate and progress, Bacon declares, is if writers engage with their predecessors, since the belief that only the best has survived of past thought is entirely fallacious. He explains that even the wisest will choose superficiality over profundity for the sake of the multitude: 'for the truth is, that time seemeth to be of the nature of a river or stream, which carrieth down to us that which is light and blown up, and sinketh and drowneth that which is weighty and solid' (Bacon (1996), p. 145). However, the path of progress via such an engagement will be a difficult one 'while antiquity envieth there should be any new additions, and novelty cannot be content to add but it must deface' (Bacon (1996), p. 144). Reversing the traditional view of history and employing a topos common to Vives, Bruno, Gilbert and Galileo, Bacon declares that 'Antiquitas sæculi juventus mundi', ('what we call antiquity is the youth of the world': Bacon (1996), p. 145), transferring the authority of antiquity to the present, the world's true 'old age'. In order to move forward from the present state of learning, it is necessary to clamber above the confusion of disputation on the piled volumes of the textual archive; to find his way in the 'perambulation' of the book 2, Bacon needs to stand atop the accumulated trophies of learning and survey the landscape.

In order to revive learning, Bacon argues, both the manner of presenting knowledge and the intellectual and institutional means by which it is arrived at must be reformed. In book 1 he criticizes current ways of presenting knowledge as 'magistral and peremptory, and not ingenuous and faithful; in a sort as may be soonest believed, and not easiliest examined' (Bacon (1996), p. 147); in book 2 he praises aphorisms (used in the *Novum Organum*), which, 'representing a knowledge broken, do invite men to inquire further; whereas methods, carrying the show of a total, do secure men, as if they were at furthest' (Bacon (1996), p. 235). Also in book 2, he suggests institutional reforms that would be necessary to the reform of learning; he describes the necessary rectification as '*opera basilica*', works for a king (Bacon (1996), p. 174). They are concerned with 'the places of learning, the books of learning, and the persons of the learned', and include the foundation and endowment of seats of learning; the proper remuneration of scholars and lecturers; the dedication of colleges exclusively to the study of 'arts and sciences at large'; the 'allowance for expenses about experiments'; 'more intelligence mutual between the universities of Europe', and the 'public designation of writers and enquirers, concerning such parts of knowledge as may appear not to have been already sufficiently laboured or undertaken' (Bacon (1996), pp. 169–175). At the end of the *Advancement*, Bacon declares, 'I have made as it were a small Globe of the Intellectual World . . . with a note and description of those parts which seem to me not constantly occupate, or not well converted by the labour of man' (Bacon (1996), p. 299). Although his request for monarchical involvement in the reform of knowledge bore no fruit, in his writing Bacon continued to promote collaborative research and to experiment with ways of presenting knowledge for different groups of readers, especially after his prosecution for corruption and fall from public office in 1621. *De Sapientia Veterum* (1609) discovered messages of contemporary relevance in ancient fables; the Latin *Novum Organum* (1620) presented an inductive logic in the form of aphorisms; the *Advancement* was expanded and translated into Latin in 1623; the *History of the Reign of King Henry VII* was published in 1621, and all the while Bacon was writing works of speculative philosophy and scientific polemic to be distributed in manuscript among a select group of readers.

He also continued to work with geographical metaphors for the pursuit of natural philosophy; these are combined with his institutional ambitions for the new science in the quasi-utopian *New Atlantis*. The book is written in the form of a travel narrative; the narrator is one of nineteen sailors, whose nationality we never learn, and who arrive providentially at an unknown island called Bensalem after having been put off their course by bad weather (the island's name means 'son of peace'). Allowed by the generous and kindly inhabitants to remain and recover, they discover that the island is immensely technologically and philosophically advanced, and that it harbours an important research institution called Salomon's House. The description of this institution was later to prove immensely influential for both the republican Hartlib circle and the monarchist founders of the Royal Society. The utopian framework soon proves something of a red herring, however. The note attached to the work by Bacon's chaplain and posthumous editor, William Rawley, emphasizes its failure to fulfil its apparent promise, asserting (however unreliably) that

> his Lordship thought also in this present fable to have composed a frame of laws, or the best state or mould of a commonwealth; but foreseeing that it would be a long work, his desire of collecting the natural history diverted him.
>
> (Bacon (1996), p. 785)

Similarly, while More's *Utopia* offers a detailed description of the island and its constitution, readers of the *New Atlantis* remain ignorant of most of these aspects of Bensalem. Rather than being a political work about the 'best state of a commonwealth', the *New Atlantis* is instead a text which describes the ideal conditions for the reform of knowledge and offers a fable about the proper relationship of the present to the past. Its peacefulness is unrivalled; the island itself is Christian, but free of the confessional division that rent contemporary Europe, while freedom of worship is extended to the Jews, who were expelled from England in 1290. It is Salomon's House which above all demonstrates that the island of Bensalem is the ideal scientific state. This is exactly the sort of research institution whose establishment Bacon had pressed for in the *Advancement*. Established by a king and a central part of the state, it provides the results of the new philosophy and proceeds according to impeccably Baconian methods.

The *New Atlantis* is, as has been noted by Michèle Le Doeuff, markedly free of personal identity and the knowing subject (Le Doeuff (1995), p. 62). It is partly this feature that invites a reading of the text as a work about the nature of the Baconian mind in its relation to the past. Bensalem sends out spies (called 'Merchants of Light'), who visit other countries and study 'the sciences, arts, manufactures, and inventions of all the world', bringing back 'books, instruments, and patterns' (Bacon (1996), p. 471; see p. 486). These figures have often been interpreted as disturbing colonialists, but could better be seen as representing the kind of commerce (an exploitative one, to be sure) that the natural philosopher should have with the past: just as the texts, instruments or materials bought by Bensalem's merchants are valuable despite being under-used or not even recognized for what they are by its vendors, so the methods and even the conclusions of the ancients may be inadequate or inaccurate, but much can still be gleaned from their works through an eclectic approach such as that displayed by Bacon throughout his writings. The inhabitants of Bensalem thus show the reader how to negotiate between useful and useless knowledge, between the needs of the present and the materials of the past. The reader, on the other hand, is in the position of the sailors: able for the moment only to wonder at the proximity of this unknown land, and at their own position 'between death and life . . . beyond both the old world and the new' (Bacon (1996), p. 461), yet handed the ability to put what they have seen into practice in their own land. At the end of the work as we have it, the Father of Salomon's House tells the narrator 'I give thee leave to publish [this relation] for the good of other nations' (Bacon (1996), p. 488). Bacon felt that the time was ripe for his reform of knowledge, even if he was unable to complete it himself. He sought out a wide range of audiences for his message, and when imagining the likely success of his natural philosophy he combined almost millenarian hope with despairing cynicism – his will bequeathed his 'name and memory' to 'men's charitable speeches, and to foreign nations, and the next ages' (Bacon (1857–74), vol. XIV, p. 539). But his extraordinary range of interests; his continual search for the right textual form; his skilful deployment of persuasive prose; his vexed relationship with the ancients and his contemporaries, and the totemic status he achieved for such a motley group of followers all demonstrate his central place in any consideration of the scientific writing of the English Renaissance. I will end with a passage from the *Advancement of Learning* which could as well stand as a gloss on the *New Atlantis*, or a general comment on Bacon's idea of the nature of reason and the very purpose of scientific rhetoric:

> 'the affection beholdeth merely the present; reason beholdeth the future and sum of time'; and therefore the present filling the imagination more, reason is commonly vanquished; but after that force of eloquence and persuasion hath made things future and remote appear as present, then upon the revolt of the imagination reason prevaileth.
>
> (Bacon (1996), p. 239)

NOTES

1 I have chosen throughout this chapter to refer to the Renaissance scientist as 'he or she', since although very few natural-philosophical works were authored by women in the period, it is becoming clear that many more women were closely involved in the production of natural-philosophical knowledge than has hitherto been assumed. See Hunter and Hutton (1997); Jardine (1999), pp. 334–7; Johns (1998), pp. 613–14.

2 The search for necessary causes is described in Aristotle (1975).

3 This paragraph is indebted to Wallace (1988).

4 The legacy of Aristotle in the Renaissance is a highly complex one, and Aristotelianism was a continuing and strong influence on the 'new science'; it is important to avoid facile narratives of its outright rejection. See especially Schmitt (1983a); Schmitt (1983b) and Mercer (1993), p. 54.

5 On the traditions of natural magic, alchemy and astrology, see Thomas (1971).

6 The title is also a competitive gesture,

suggesting that the book will be a replacement for Aristotle's *Organon*.

7   On the contexts of Hartlib's works, see further the invaluable CD-ROM of the Hartlib papers, Greengrass and Leslie (1995).

8   On the complex printing history of the two Books of the *Advancement*, see Bacon (1996), p. 576.

REFERENCES AND FURTHER READING

Aristotle (1975). *Posterior Analytics*, ed. Jonathan Barnes. Oxford: Clarendon Press.

Bacon, Francis (1857–74). *Works*, eds James Spedding, Robert Leslie Ellis and Douglas Denon Heath. 14 vols London: Longman.

——(1996). *A Critical Edition of the Major Works*, ed. Brian Vickers. Oxford: Oxford University Press.

Curtius, Ernst Robert (1953). *European Literature and the Latin Middle Ages*, tr. Willard R. Trask. London: Routledge and Kegan Paul (original work published 1948).

Dunn, Kevin (1994). *Pretexts of Authority: The Rhetoric of Authorship in the Renaissance Preface*. Stanford: Stanford University Press.

Farrington, Benjamin (1951). *Francis Bacon: Philosopher of Industrial Science*. London: Lawrence and Wishart.

Foucault, Michel (1970). *The Order of Things*, tr. anon. London: Routledge (original work published 1966).

Greengrass, M. and Leslie, M. P. (eds) (1995). *Samuel Hartlib: The Complete Edition*. Ann Arbor: UMI.

Horkheimer, Max and Adorno, Theodor W. (1973). *Dialectic of Enlightenment*, tr. John Cumming. London: Allen Lane (original work published 1947).

Hunter, Sarah and Hunter, Lynette (eds) (1997). *Women, Science and Medicine 1500–1700: Mothers and Sisters of the Royal Society*. Stroud: Sutton.

Jardine, Lisa (1999). *Ingenious Pursuits: Building the Scientific Revolution*. London: Little, Brown.

Jardine, Lisa and Stewart, Alan (1998). *Hostage to Fortune: The Troubled Life of Francis Bacon 1561–1626*. London: Victor Gollancz.

Johns, Adrian (1998). *The Nature of the Book: Print and Knowledge in the Making*. Chicago: Chicago University Press.

Kusukawa, Sachiko (1996). 'Bacon's Classification of Knowledge'. In Markku Peltonen (ed.), *The Cambridge Companion to Bacon* (pp. 47–74). Cambridge: Cambridge University Press.

Le Doeuff, Michèle (1995). 'Introduction'. In Francis Bacon. *La Nouvelle Atlantide* (pp. 7–71), trs Michèle Le Doeuff and Margaret Llasera. Paris: G. F. Flammarion.

Martin, Julian (1992). *Francis Bacon, the State, and the Reform of Natural Philosophy*. Cambridge: Cambridge University Press.

Mercer, Christia (1993). 'The Vitality and Importance of Early Modern Aristotelianism'. In Tom Sorell (ed.), *The Rise of Modern Philosophy: The Tension between the New and Traditional Philosophies from Machiavelli to Leibniz* (pp. 33–67). Oxford: Clarendon Press.

Peltonen, Markku (1996). 'Introduction'. In Markku Peltonen (ed.), *The Cambridge Companion to Bacon* (pp. 1–24). Cambridge: Cambridge University Press.

Porter, Roy (1991). 'Introduction'. In Stephen Pumfrey, Paolo L. Rossi and Maurice Slawinski (eds), *Science, Culture and Popular Belief in Renaissance Europe*. Manchester: Manchester University Press.

Rossi, Paolo (1996). 'Bacon's idea of science'. In Markku Peltonen (ed.), *The Cambridge Companion to Bacon* (pp. 25–46). Cambridge: Cambridge University Press.

Schmitt, Charles B. (1983a). *Aristotle and the Renaissance*. Cambridge, MA: Harvard University Press.

——(1983b). *John Case and Aristotelianism in Renaissance England*. Kingston: McGill-Queen's University Press.

Shapin, Steven. *A Social History of Truth: Civility and Science in Seventeenth-Century England*. Chicago: University of Chicago Press.

Sherman, W. H. (1995). *John Dee: The Politics of Reading and Writing in the English Renaissance*. Amherst: University of Massachusetts Press.

Thomas, Keith (1971). *Religion and the Decline of Magic*. London: Weidenfeld and Nicolson.

Wallace, William A. (1988). 'Traditional Natural Philosophy'. In Charles B. Schmitt, Quentin Skinner, et al. (eds), *The Cambridge History of Renaissance Philosophy* (pp. 201–35). Cambridge: Cambridge University Press.

Webster, Charles (1975). *The Great Instauration: Science, Medicine and Reform 1626–1660*. London: Duckworth.

48

Prose Fiction

Andrew Hadfield

Prose fiction in English in the sixteenth and seventeenth centuries forms an amorphous and diverse category of writing. Like so many genres or kinds of literature produced in the Renaissance it is hard to underestimate the experimental nature of these works. Moreover, we do not really know that writers themselves realized what they were doing and were basing their efforts on tried and tested models that were commonly understood.[1] Prose fiction, like drama, did not generally occupy a high literary status – as various forms of poetry did – and was often produced by writers who followed different professions all of which may have been as important to them as their fiction.[2] Certainly this is the case with such major writers of prose as William Baldwin (*fl.* 1547–53) author of *Beware the Cat* (1553), often considered the first novel in English, who had an important political and later clerical career; Geoffrey Fenton (1539?–1608), translator of stories from the French and Italian collected in *Certain Tragical Discourses* (1567), who abandoned his literary endeavours for a career in the civil service in Ireland; George Gascoigne (1525?–77), author of *The Adventures of Master F. J.* (1573), who was at various times a soldier and MP; and Thomas Lodge (1557?–1628), author of *Rosalynde* and a host of other romances, who wrote little once he had graduated as a doctor of medicine in 1602. Writers who did not pursue other careers, such as Robert Greene (*c.*1558–92) and Thomas Nashe (1567–1601) were, notably, extremely prolific and very poor.[3]

It would be wrong, however, to suggest that prose fiction was a genre of *exclusively* low cultural status. After all, there were a large number of Greek and Roman writers of prose fiction studied by gentlemen as part of their humanist-inspired: Apuleius (*fl.* *c.*155 AD), Heliodorus (fourth or fifth century AD), Longus (late second century AD), Lucian (AD 115–200), and Xenophon (*c.*430–*c.*355 BC). Equally, there were contemporary Europeans such as Cinthio, Belleforest and Bandello.[4] Prose fiction, specifically romance, was closely associated with the court and courtly values through the efforts of John Lyly (1554?–1606), author of *Euphues, or the Anatomy of Wit* (1578) and *Euphues and His England* (1580), whose prose style of 'Euphuism' became the form of upper class English prose until supplanted by the sophisticated English of Sir Philip Sidney's *Arcadia*, first published in 1590, but circulating in an earlier form from 1580 onwards.[5] The literary and political careers of Lyly and Sidney serve to reinforce rather than undermine our sense of prose fiction's indeterminate nature and function; Lyly, whilst being a successful dramatist and writer, never achieved the preferment he hoped for and failed to secure the post of Master of the Revels.[6] Sidney's desire to influence contemporary political events and his vision of a Protestant literature as a major part of a contemporary public sphere provides some indication of the complex forces which informed his writing.[7]

In short, prose fiction undoubtedly performed a variety of roles in the English Renaissance, not all of which can easily be recovered. While some works may have been translated to help advance the careers of cynical authors, whether through providing their social superiors with useful advice in fictional form, or through simply telling diverting stories, others seek to mould and influence a whole way of writing and hence thinking, basing hopes for success on the marketplace of print rather than patronage.[8] If one work stands behind much prose fiction it is undoubtedly Thomas More's *Utopia* (1516), written in Latin but translated into English by Ralph Robinson (1551), just at the point when writers such as William Baldwin were becoming interested in experimenting with prose fiction. *Utopia*'s unsettling and stimulating blend of fiction and fact, sensible political advice and fantasy, helped to pave the way for later works that adopted the same mixture of aims, styles and forms.

Early Prose Experiments

William Baldwin's *A Mervelous Hystory Intitulede, Beware the Cat* (1553) is a hard work to classify and forms part of the vast range of literary experiments produced at the court of Edward VI.[9] Although it was written in 1553, it was not published until 1570, undoubtedly because it fell foul of the Marian authorities after Edward died on 6 July 1553. This multi-layered text combines a host of different types of writing – satire, beast fable, dream vision, proverb, hymn, chronicle – indicating the 'mixed' genesis of English prose fiction in the second half of the sixteenth century.[10] Baldwin's three sections cleverly play with the relationship between reader and narrator. The first part, narrated third hand via an English soldier or traveller to Ireland is set in Ireland in the aftermath of a successful cattle raid. The successful thieves rest in a churchyard roasting a sheep. A cat approaches and demands food, eating the cow as well as the sheep. The men flee and slay the cat after it chases them on a horse, at which point a host of cats appear. They kill and eat one of the two thieves. When the other returns home and tells his wife, their cat exclaims, 'Hast thou killed Grimalkin!' and strangles him.

The story is unsettling in a number of ways. First, it suggests that cats, as an allegorical representation of Catholics, function like the hydra. Grimalkin, the chief of cats, is destroyed but her death only leads to further destruction as more elusive but equally dangerous figures appear. The task of separating loyal and safe subjects from threatening and subversive ones is problematic enough, especially given the nature of the death of the second thief. As Robert Maslen has observed, many writers of early Elizabethan fiction were also either employed by the state as spies to catch Catholics, or were Catholics themselves, so there are extensive references to spying and espionage in many literary works.[11] Furthermore, as the above episode illustrates, the very nature of fiction served to complicate and challenge notions of straightforward 'truth', showing how close literature could come to subversion or even treason. The description does contain the names of Irish families and chieftains, the Kavanaghs and Butlers, and is set in real historical time after a feud between the two. However, the story of Grimalkin also bears an uncomfortably close resemblance to the sorts of superstitious tales that Protestants were so keen to discredit as remnants of the Catholic dark ages now superseded by Protestant light and truth.[12] In short, the very form of the story itself is double-edged, suggesting that what is the target of the satire is already contained in the writing itself.

The rest of the work confirms these suspicions. In the second part, the principal narrator, Streamer, applies a potion to his ears that enables him to understand what the beasts in England are saying. What he hears is an assault to his senses:

> Barking of dogs, grunting of hogs, wawling of cats, rumbling of rats, gaggling of geese, humming of bees, rousing of bucks, gaggling of ducks, singing of swans, ringing of pans, crowing of cocks, sewing of socks, cackling of hens, scrabbling of pens, peeping of mice, trulling of dice, curling of frogs, and toads in the bogs . . . with such a sort of commixed noises as would a-deaf anybody to have heard.
>
> (p. 46)

Streamer has to recognize that beneath the apparently calm surface of English life there is a distinct cacophony of voices showing that England is a divided land; much like Ireland, in fact, where the gulf between English Protestantism and Irish Catholicism was an open war.[13] The story of Grimalkin might look like an exaggerated traveller's tale from a remote land, but it is really a warning of what is happening much closer to home.

In part three, Streamer, using his special power to act as a spy, listens to the cats one night and overhears the trial of Mouse-Slayer, who has broken their laws. What he hears further reinforces the reader's sense of confusion, unease, and inability to control a threat from within as much as from without. Mouse-Slayer defends herself by narrating the story of her life to show that she has remained faithful to the principles of cat morality. Her story is a picaresque adventure through England of which we only hear a small part because most has been relayed on the previous four nights and Streamer's potion wears off before the trail is concluded; again, the uncertain and unstable relationship between fiction and truth is emphasized. Mouse-Slayer's experiences reveal the parlous and fractured state of contemporary English religion. She lives with a superstitious old lady who believes that her blindness has been cured by the priest's wafer-mass (the credulous cats have to be told that this is not a reliable cure) and then a pious hypocrite who prays before a statue of the Virgin but makes a good living out of receiving stolen goods and keeping a brothel. The brothel keeper feeds Mouse-Slayer mustard, making her weep, and then tricks a local beauty into sleeping with a young man when she claims that her daughter has turned into a cat for refusing his advances, constantly weeping as a result of her cruel misfortune. Mouse-Slayer is then mistaken for a devil and makes an old priest look ridiculous when he tries to exorcise her. Finally, she revenges herself on the old bawd and the young lecher by revealing him in compromising circumstances to the wife's husband.

Beware the Cat never allows readers to settle for easy answers and assume that the world can be neatly divided up into the sheep and the goats. The cats may be superstitious, greedy, tyrannical, spiteful and vindictive by turns, but they are significantly no worse than the humans encountered in the book, and their society bears an uncomfortable resemblance to that of their human counterparts. It is never easy to assume that the 'cats' can be equated with 'Catholics'; or, if they can, then rather a large number of Englishmen and women, whether they know it or not, are 'cats'.[14] In breaking down such binary oppositions, *Beware the Cat* struck a note of profound paranoia, arguably the definitive mood of the early English novel.

A similar sense of uncertainty and unease pervades the collections and translations of stories from Italian and French sources which had such an impact in the 1560s. Among the most significant of these are William Painter's *The Palace of Pleasure* (1566, 1567, and 1575), Geoffrey Fenton's *Certaine Tragical Discourses of Bandello* (1567) and William Pettie's *The Palace of Pleasure* (1566, 1576), all of which provided a fund of stories, many re-used by dramatists. It is clear that such collections were successfully aimed at a popular market.[15] They encountered the wrath of some observers, notably Roger Ascham, who railed against the Italianate Englishman and the malign influence of 'fond bookes, of late translated out of Italian into English, sold in every shop in London, commended by honest titles the soner to corrupt honest manners'.[16] Ascham's lament is that readers are neglecting sound humanist works of improving educational merit in favour of frivolous romances and scandalous tales.[17]

What needs to be pointed out is the miscellaneous and diverse character of the collections of prose fiction. Most did, as Ascham alleges, contain numerous Italianate tales many of which told stories of adultery – indirectly derived from Boccaccio and the medieval genre of the fabliau – and spectacular cruelty, not necessarily directed to any specifically educational end. However, it is worth noting that Painter's *Palace of Pleasure*, was originally entitled *The City of Civility* when it was entered into The Stationers' Register in 1562 and that the author's letter 'to the Reader' emphasizes the didactic 'profit' of reading stories which taught through positive and negative examples: 'they disclose what glory, honour, and preferment each man attaineth by good desert, what felicity by honest attempts . . . they do reveal the miseries of rapes and fleshy actions, the overthrow of noble men and princes by disordered government'.[18] Of course, such a defence could be made of virtually any collection of stories, but it is noticeable that the work contains a number of stories translated from the Livy's republican history of Rome, and is keen to place responsibility on the individual to behave well.

The collection contains a large number of stories of tyrants behaving badly towards their subjects, one reason why the nature of the project may have changed before it appeared in print (although commercial reasons might equally explain the title change).[19] The reader finds an interesting mixture of tales – as one does in Fenton and Pettie. The second story in the volume is that of Tarquin's rape of Lucrece, and her subsequent suicide, which results in his banishment and the transformation of the city from monarchy to republic. Tarquin's behaviour is a synecdoche for his tyrannical rule over Rome and shows how good government needs to be established with the consent of the people. The fourth story is that of Coriolanus, which concludes when the aristocratic rebel's mother persuades him to spare the city. Shakespeare's use of these two tales suggests that he either used Painter's work, or worked within a similar intellectual culture (tale twenty-eight is that of Timon of Athens). Intermingled with such stories are more obviously Italianate ones, some of which seem quite tame in comparison such as the story of Grimaldi, a mean Genoese gentleman, who is embarrassed into becoming more liberal with his wealth (tale thirty-one); the story of Giletta of Narbona, the source of *All's Well that Ends Well*, who wins the hand of Beltrano, count of Rossiglione, after she healed the French king, separating him from his wife and two children (tale thirty-eight); and the story of Sisterno, a Bolognian scholar, who is revenged on three ladies who ridicule his attempts to seduce them. More spectacular are the tales of dark deeds at Italian courts, the most significant of which is the story of the Duchess of Malfi, who is imprisoned and then murdered by her brothers after she has secretly married Antonio Bologna, her steward. Whereas John Webster's dramatization of the story is very sympathetic to the plight of the duchess, unable to have a private life because of the public pressures put upon her, Painter's version is a tale of excess passion leading a woman astray.[20] The Duchess is, in essence, a virtuous character, but, for Painter, her position is problematic because of the inherent weakness of her sex and the difficulty of women ruling. The story concludes with an exhortation to the reader: 'You see the miserable discourse of a princess' love, that was not very wise, and of a gentleman that had forgotten his estate, which ought to serve as a looking glass to them which be over-hardy in making enterprises, and do not measure their ability with the greatness of their attempts' [my emphasis] (iii, p. 43). Both Antonio and the Duchess have overstepped the mark and the story boils down to the simple message that one should know one's place in society. More specifically, it can be read as a misogynist tirade against the foolish wiles of female rulers who tend to make bad matches, neglect public duty and ruin the lives of their subjects. The target of this 'looking glasse' (mirror) may well be Elizabeth herself, who in the 1560s seemed very likely to get married, either to a foreign prince, or one of her subjects such as Robert Dudley, Earl of Leicester.[21]

Euphuistic and Arcadian Fiction

In many ways the most fascinating fictional experiment of the first half of Elizabeth's reign was George Gascoigne's *The Adventures of Master F. J.* (1573), a work that exploits literary and narratorial techniques established in works such as *Beware the Cat*.[22] The work tells the story of F. J. who tries to win the love of Elinor through the exchange of letters. The story is narrated by G. T., an unreliable presence who draws the reader's attention to 'the sexual opportunism and hypocrisy behind the poses' of courtly love and ideal passion.[23] F. J. has a female confidant in Frances, and there is the possibility of a genuine friendship developing between them, one independent of the exaggerated gender roles being played out between F. J. and Elinor. The story, which G. T. labels a 'thriftless history', challenging the reader to find a concluding moral, ends with F. J. a bitter, frustrated man, his desires doomed to failure.

The most influential work of the mid-Elizabethan period was John Lyly's *Euphues. The Anatomy of Wit* (1578), one of the best-selling works in Renaissance England. As G. K. Hunter has remarked, 'Every aspiring author in the period must have read *Euphues*' and Lyly's distinctive style of balanced shorter clauses and antitheses came to define a dominant form of literary English.[24] Lyly made the 'Petrarchan paradox into the capstone of a whole view of life'.[25] Lucilla, when infatuated with Euphues, for example, endures, 'terms and contraries', her heart caught 'betwixt faith and fancy . . . hope and fear . . . conscience and concupiscence' (I, p. 205).

Euphues tells the story of a witty but arrogant and morally suspect young Athenian. He travels to Naples where he betrays his friend, Philautus, when they are rivals for the affections of Lucilla, before she betrays him in turn. Lucilla dies in suitably miserable circumstances; Euphues and Philautus are reconciled; and Euphues, realizing the errors of his ways, returns to Athens to study moral philosophy, where he becomes a notable sage. The text ends with Euphues crossing the sea to England where he expects to 'see a court both braver in show and better in substance, more gallant courtiers, more godly consciences, as fair ladies and fairer conditions' (I, p. 323).

The sequel, *Euphues and his England*, casts Philautus as the principal actor, as Euphues slips into the background. Philautus again suffers in love until he woos and marries the chaste and beautiful Camilla. Euphues, one of a number of moral guides who the couple encounter on their travels, acts as a moral instructor, returning to Athens at the end of the book, where he writes 'Euphues' glass for Europe', a description of England for the edification of 'the ladies and gentlewomen of Italy'. The 'glass' ostensibly praises the pre-eminence of England, but the title is double-edged. On the one hand it indicates that England is the pre-eminent nation in Europe which other countries ought to observe and copy; on the other, the metaphor of the mirror implies that England represents an image in which all the good and bad of Europe is reflected back for the observer who has to decide what should be adopted and what rejected.

More pointed still is the fact that the arch moralist Euphues arrives in England armed only with Julius Caesar's *De Bello Gallico* and all the reader learns in the 'glass' is culled from William Harrison's *Description of England* (1577), a frequently reprinted and already well-known text.

Lyly's works have been taken at face value and interpreted as straightforward celebrations of England and Englishness.[26] But, like so much early modern English prose fiction, it proves to be elusive, duplicitous and sophisticated. Euphues is approached by an old Neapolitan gentleman near the start of the first work, who, respecting his abilities, warns him that his wit can either be used for good purposes or bad: 'he well knew that so rare a wit would in time either breed an intolerable trouble, or bring an incomparable treasure to the common weal' (I, p. 186). Euphues stands poised between future triumph and disaster. He chooses the first path in *Euphues* and pays dearly for it, but redeems himself somewhat in *Euphues and his England*. By implication, Lyly suggests, England stands at the same crossroads and future policies, such as the marriage of the queen to a suitable or unsuitable monarch, or the granting or withholding of political rights, will either lead to peace and prosperity or dearth and misery. From 1578 onwards Elizabeth had been considering the marriage proposal of François, Duke of Alençon, a diplomatic manoeuvre which might lead to a lasting alliance with Spain, or, as many Protestants feared, a loss of English sovereign integrity and the Catholic corruption of the reformed church.[27] There is extravagant praise of Elizabeth for her good government, justice and mercy, but the deliberate use of Julius Caesar and William Harrison to describe England may well indicate that a true description of the realm cannot be safely made. Perhaps the irony is that Naples and Athens are more accurate representations of England. However one interprets the slippery politics of the texts, it is clear that they belong as much to a humanist literary tradition of works of counsel or 'mirror for princes' as straightforward jingoistic propaganda.[28]

Euphues and *Euphues and his England* had an enormous influence on subsequent English fiction. Their influence has usually been attributed to a stylistic dominance but it is noticeable that writers of prose fiction such as Robert Greene and Thomas Lodge were also keen to address current political issues in works such as Greene's *Gwydonius. The Carde of Fancie* (1584) and *Pandosto* (1588) or Lodge's *Roasalynd* (1590), which was sub-titled 'Euphues Golden Legacy: found after his death in his cell at Silexedra. Bequeathed to Philautus's sons, nursed up with their father in England'. All these stories deal with the ways in which oppressed subjects and relations of kings have to escape from tyranny, their settings are ostensibly foreign but can clearly be seen as representations of England.

If Euphuism was one major strain of English fiction in the 1580s and 1590s, it was soon to lose its dominance to works inspired by Sir Philip Sidney's massive prose romance, *Arcadia*. Although Sidney referred to the *Arcadia* as 'this idle work of mine' and 'but a trifle', it is likely that he took his experimental prose fiction extremely seriously, given its length, the extensive revisions he undertook and the reflections of contemporary politics that it contains.

Sidney probably wrote the first version of the *Arcadia* (*The Old Arcadia*) after he was banished from the court to his sister's home at Wilton, after he had vehemently protested at the queen's projected marriage to the Duke of Alençon (see above, p. 582). This version of the prose romance was written in the mode of a tragi-comedy in five acts under the influence of theories of Latin dramatic composition. Eclogues and other poems were scattered throughout the narrative as commentaries on the action. It undoubtedly circulated widely in manuscript. The second version of the romance, *The New Arcadia*, was posthumously published in 1590. This version was some fifty thousand words longer than *The Old Arcadia*, having been meticulously revised, often sentence by sentence. In 1593, Mary Sidney, Countess of Pembroke, published a composite version of the work known as *The Countess of Pembroke's Arcadia*, probably revised by her. This reprinted the revised versions of the first three books of *The New Arcadia* together with the last two unrevised books of the *Old*.[29]

The romance revolves around the problems precipitated by Basilius, who rules Arcadia, without a proper constitution. He is warned of impending disasters and retires to the country with his wife, Gynecia, and daughters, Pamela and Philoclea, leaving government in the hands of Philanax, and elderly counsellor. Pyrocles and Musidorus, two young princes, arrive in Arcadia and fall in love with the daughters. Pyrocles decides to win Philoclea's heart by dressing up as an Amazon and wooing her; Musidorus, by disguising himself as a shepherd. Unfortunately Basilius and Gynecia fall in love with Pyrocles, leaving Philoclea confused. Musidorus elopes with Pamela and plans to force Basilius to allow Pyrocles to marry Philoclea. Pyrocles eventually wins the heart of Philoclea but he is unmasked by a loyal shepherd, Dametas, before they can elope, but not before he has fooled both parents into sleeping with each other in a cave believing that they are satisfying their desires with Pyrocles. Musidorus and Pamela are captured by rebels eager to win favour with Basilius. Gynecia accidentally poisons Basilius and she is put on trial with the two princes, accused of trying to overthrow the legitimate ruler. They are all found guilty and sentenced to death. Fortunately, Pyrocles turns out to be the long lost son of the Judge, Euachus, making Musidorus his nephew. Basilius revives, Gynecia is restored to her position and the princes and princesses get married.

The revised *Arcadia* is, in many ways, a distinct work of literature, albeit unfinished. Sidney added a great deal of new material, most significantly in book 3, where Cecropia, Basilius's sister-in-law, kidnaps the princesses, because she has ambitions that her son, Amphialus, will become the next king of Arcadia. He also included the story of the blind Paphlogonian king, which later formed the Gloucester sub-plot for *King Lear*. The text breaks off with Cecropia dying and Amphialus revealing what has happened to the princesses. Sidney appears to have been keen to highlight the political themes central to the romance and would probably have developed the text to foreground questions of rule, kingship, responsibility and rebellion, as these problems are emphasized in the revised text.

The *Arcadia* had a massive influence on the development of English prose fiction, especially in the early seventeenth century. For nearly two hundred years it was one of the most widely read works in English.[30] Sidney's characteristic style of periphrasis – providing the reader with a variety of ways of expressing the same idea – had replaced the literary vogue for 'Euphuism' by the turn of the century. Equally influential was the *Arcadia*'s overtly political allegory, particularly on the relatively neglected *Argenis* (1621) by John Barclay, first written in Latin but translated into English twice in the 1620s.[31]

Arcadian romance had a particular influence on women writers, as they became important producers of prose fiction in the seventeenth century.[32] The first and probably most important of these is *Urania* (1621, written *c*.1618), by Mary Wroth, Sidney's niece.[33] Wroth uses many of Sidney's characters, but also based much of the romance on events from her own life. This caused a considerable scandal, with one of the episodes particularly offending Sir Edward Denny. The heroine of the romance, Pamphilia, a writer, is in love with her cousin, Amphilanthus, a relationship that appears to mirror Wroth's affair with her cousin, William Herbert and there are instances of unhappy women, Bellamira and Lindamira, whose misery in love and disgrace at court also appear to allude to unfortunate events in Wroth's own life. The narrative places great emphasis on the sufferings of women and their lack of freedom. Whereas Amphilanthus is able to gallop around the countryside in the pursuit of his masculine heroic ideals, Pamphilia is doomed to withdraw into her gardens in solitary suffering. *Urania* is obviously an answer to sonnet sequences such as Sidney's *Astrophil and Stella*, which emphasizes male suffering, as well as a critique of the imbalance of gender roles that render women passive and men active.

Pamphilia is able to act in one sense. Her solitary musing leads her to write poetry and she uses a sonnet sequence she has written to woo Amphilanthus who is ignorant of her passion for him. The romance clearly endorses Pamphilia's view that the flashy poetry of court wits is less valuable than that produced from the heart. Pamphilia shows her poems to Amphilanthus at crucial points in the text, 'granting disclosure as a token of intimacy'.[34] In doing so, Wroth uses *Urania* to show how literature was becoming a means of finding a voice for women.

The Unfortunate Traveller and the Picaresque Novel

If much fiction in the late sixteenth century still remained within a humanist tradition of using the fictional text as an advice book, this relationship was consciously exploded by Thomas Nashe in his rhetorically pyrotechnic journalism and, most significantly, his picaresque novel, *The Unfortunate Traveller* (1594).[35] Picaresque novels developed in Spain in the early sixteenth century, the most significant being *Lazarillo de Tormes* (1554), which was translated into French, German, Latin, Italian, Dutch and English (1586) soon after its publication.[36] The genre takes its name from the central character, the *pícaro*, a rogue or dishonest delinquent, who has a series of adventures which help him to understand the wicked ways of the world. Picaresque novels tend to be episodic in style, as the hero moves from one location to another, and worldly-wise and cynical in their outlook.

The Unfortunate Traveller fits easily into this tradition, aiming a number of blows at the assumptions of contemporary fiction – notably the moralistic tone of *Euphues* and its imitators – as well as the belief that travel broadens the mind and teaches the traveller about the world.[37] The hero, Jack Wilton, is 'a certain kind of an appendix or page, belonging or appertaining in or unto the confines of the English Court' during Henry VIII's wars with the French.[38] Wilton is an involuntary traveller, a picaresque rogue *par excellence*, able to thrive in his environment by exploiting the possibilities which distance from the constraints of home provide for self-protection and, where possible, self-advancement. The pious discourse of humanist counsel counts for little in the harsh world of military conflict, as Wilton's first paragraph asserts: 'What strat-agemical acts and monuments do you think an ingenious infant of my years might enact? You will say it sufficient if he slur a die, pawn his master to the utmost penny, and minister the oath of the pantofle artificially. *These are signs of a good education*' [my emphasis] (p. 255).[39] Nashe's desire to subvert received wisdom and use the tools of rhetoric against those who would assume a monopoly on them is evident. As a writer who had to live by his wits, his world bore an uncomfortable resemblance to that of Jack Wilton (especially if one bears in mind that many writers served as soldiers).[40]

Wilton learns quickly in his first two 'jests', performed while serving in the English army. First, he dupes a cider-maker into believing that he is suspected of treachery, a ploy which refers to the paranoia rife in post-Armada England, where a large number of Catholics and 'extreme' Protestants were publicly persecuted.[41] Nothing significant comes of this affair, but Wilton is whipped, 'though they make themselves merry with it many a winter's evening after' (p. 261). Second, Wilton dupes a captain into believing that he has been chosen to assassinate the king of France by pretending to be an English traitor and bluffing his way into the French camp in order to gain the king's trust. The captain is exposed and only escapes torture because his story is too ridiculous to be believed. Wilton has learnt how to inflict suffering on others.

Images of torture and execution surround the rest of Wilton's adventures as he travels further afield to witness the slaughter of the Anabaptists in Münster, then Italy where the novel, after a series of satires of the absurdities of Italian tales, ends with horrific descriptions of the execution of the Jew, Zadoch, and the thief, Cutwolfe. The latter persuades Wilton to return home and lead a good life, the cynical moral being that coercion and fear influence people more than exhortations to be good. It is likely that *The Unfortunate Traveller* aided the rise of a more 'middle-class' prose fiction, notably Thomas Deloney's *Jack of Newberrie* (c.1597).[42] The picaresque novel contin-ued into the seventeenth century; Richard Head's *The English Rogue* (1665) was a notable bestseller.

Notes

1 See Andrew Hadfield, *Literature, Politics and National Identity: Reformation to Renaissance* (Cambridge: Cambridge University Press, 1994), introduction.
2 See Richard Rambuss, *Spenser's Secret Career* (Cambridge: Cambridge University Press, 1993).
3 For details see the respective *DNB* entries. For claims that *Beware the Cat* was the first novel in English, see William A. Ringler, Jr, '*Beware the Cat* and the Beginnings of English Fiction', *Novel* 12 (1979), 113–26.
4 See Andrew Hadfield, 'Renaissance Narrative', in Paul Schellinger, ed., *Encyclopedia of the Novel* (Chicago: Fitzroy-Dearborn, 1999), pp. 1087–91.
5 On Lyly and Sidney see Catherine Bates, *The Rhetoric of Courtship in Elizabethan Language and Literature* (Cambridge: Cambridge University Press, 1992), ch. 4.
6 See G. K. Hunter, *John Lyly: The Humanist as Courtier* (London: Routledge, 1962).
7 See Katherine Duncan-Jones, *Sir Philip Sidney: Courtier Poet* (New Haven: Yale University Press, 1991).
8 A sophisticated reading of late sixteenth-century fiction in the light of one such concern is Lorna Hutson, *The Usurer's Daughter: Male Friendship and Fictions of Women in Sixteenth-century England* (London: Routledge, 1994).
9 For details see John N. King, *English Reformation Literature: The Tudor Origins of the Protestant Tradition* (Princeton: Princeton University Press, 1982). All references in parentheses in the text to William Baldwin, *Beware the Cat/The Funerals of Edward VI*, ed. William P. Holden (N. London, CT: Connecticut College, 1963).
10 See King, *English Reformation Literature*, 387–406; Stephen Gresham, 'William Baldwin: Literary Voice of the Reign of Edward VI', *The Huntington Library Quarterly* 44 (1980–1), 101–16, pp. 113–15.
11 Robert W. Maslen, *Elizabethan Fictions: Espionage, Counter-espionage and the Duplicity of Fiction in Early Elizabethan Prose Narratives* (Oxford: Clarendon Press, 1997).
12 See, for example, Helen C. White, *Tudor Books of Saints and Martyrs* (Madison: Wisconsin University Press, 1963).
13 For details see Steven G. Ellis, *Tudor Ireland: Crown, Community and the Conflict of Cultures, 1470–1603* (Harlow: Longman, 1985).
14 Maslen, *Elizabethan Fictions*, pp. 79–80.
15 The classic study is Louis B. Wright, *Middle-Class Culture in Elizabethan England* (Chapel Hill: University of North Carolina Press, 1935), ch. 2; Constance C. Relihan, *Fashioning Authority: The Development of Elizabethan Novelistic Discourse* (Kent, OH: Kent State University Press, 1994), ch. 2.
16 Cited in Paul Salzman, *English Prose Fiction, 1558–1700: A Critical History* (Oxford: Clarendon Press, 1985), p. 7.
17 See Reid Barbour, *Deciphering Elizabethan Fiction* (Newark: University of Delaware Press, 1993), ch. 3; Lorna Hutson, *Thomas Nashe in Context* (Oxford: Clarendon Press, 1989).
18 William Painter, *The Palace of Pleasure*, ed. Joseph Jacobs, 3 vols (Hildesheim: Georg Olms Verlagsbuchhandlung, 1968, rpt of 1890), I, p. xxiv. All subsequent references to this edition in parentheses in the text.
19 For further details see Andrew Hadfield, *Literature, Travel, and Colonial Writing in the English Renaissance, 1545–1625* (Oxford: Clarendon Press, 1998), pp. 147–62.
20 See, for example, J. W. Lever, *The Tragedy of State* (London: Methuen, 1971), ch. 5.
21 See J. E. Neale, *Queen Elizabeth* (London: Cape, 1934), ch. 5.
22 Excellent discussions are contained in Maslen, *Elizabethan Fictions*, ch. 3; Richard Helgerson, *The Elizabethan Prodigals* (Berkeley: University of California Press, 1976), ch. 3.
23 Paul Salzman, ed., *An Anthology of Elizabethan Prose Fiction* (Oxford: Oxford University Press, 1987), p. xiv.
24 Hunter, *John Lyly*, p. 259; William Ringler, Jr, 'The Immediate Source of Euphuism', *PMLA* 53 (1938), 678–86.

25 *The Works of John Lyly*, ed. R. W. Bond, 3 vols (Oxford: Oxford University Press, 1902), iii, p. 3.

26 See, for example, E. D. Marcu, *Sixteenth-century Nationalism* (New York: Arabis, 1976), pp. 79–81; Salzman, *English Prose Fiction*, p. 42.

27 Geoffrey Elton, *England under the Tudors* (London: Methuen, 1965, rpt of 1955), pp. 324–5.

28 For further comments on this literary tradition, see Greg Walker, *Persuasive Fictions: Faction, Faith and Political Culture in the Reign of Henry VIII* (Aldershot: Scolar, 1996).

29 The two standard editions are *The Old Arcadia*, ed. Katherine Duncan-Jones (Oxford: Oxford University Press, 1985); *The New Arcadia*, ed. Victor Skretkowicz (Oxford: Clarendon Press, 1987). Useful analysis and commentary can be found in Richard McCoy, *Sir Philip Sidney: Rebellion in Arcadia* (Brighton: Harvester, 1979); Joan Rees, *Sir Philip Sidney and Arcadia* (Rutherford: Associated Universities Press, 1991).

30 Wright, *Middle-Class Culture*, p. 389.

31 See Salzman, *English Prose Fiction*, pp. 149–50. The work is the subject of an important PhD thesis by Ms Rebecca Moss at the University of Wales, Aberystwyth.

32 On women as readers of romance, see Caroline Lucas, *Writing for Woman: The Example of Woman as Reader in Elizabethan Romance* (Milton Keynes: Open University Press, 1989).

33 Comment here is indebted to Paul Salzman, ed., *An Anthology of Seventeenth-Century Fiction* (Oxford: Oxford University Press, 1991), pp. xii–xv; Helen Hackett, 'Courtly Writing by Women', in Helen Wilcox, ed., *Women and Literature in Britain, 1500–1700* (Cambridge: Cambridge University Press, 1996), pp. 169–89.

34 Hackett, 'Courtly Writing by Women', p. 184.

35 On Nashe, see Arthur F. Kinney, *Humanist Poetics: Thought, Rhetoric, and Fiction in Sixteenth-Century England* (Amherst, MA: Massachusetts University Press, 1986), ch. 9; Lorna Hutson, *Thomas Nashe in Context* (Oxford: Clarendon Press, 1989); Robert Weimann, *Authority and Representation in Early Modern Discourse* (Baltimore: Johns Hopkins University Press, 1996), ch. 12.

36 For details see *Two Spanish Picaresque Novels*, tr. Michael Alpert (Harmondsworth: Penguin, 1969).

37 For further discussion, see Hadfield, *Literature, Travel, and Colonial Writing*, pp. 192–6.

38 Thomas Nashe, *The Unfortunate Traveller and Other Works*, ed. J. B. Steane (Harmondsworth: Penguin, 1972), p. 254. All subsequent references to this work in parentheses in the text.

39 The oath of a pantofle (old shoe) was used to initiate a freshman at university and, possibly, at court.

40 For one study of this relationship, see Curtis C. Breight, *Surveillance, Militarism and Drama in the Elizabethan Era* (Basingstoke: Macmillan, 1996).

41 See R. B. Wernham, *After the Armada: Elizabethan England and the Struggle for Western Europe, 1588–95* (Oxford: Clarendon Press, 1984).

42 See Walter R. Davis, *Idea and Act in Elizabethan Fiction* (Princeton: Princeton University Press, 1969), ch. 7.

References and Further Reading

Barbour, Reid (1993). *Deciphering Elizabethan Fiction*. Newark: University of Delaware Press.

Bates, Catherine (1992). *The Rhetoric of Courtship in Elizabethan Language and Literature*. Cambridge: Cambridge University Press.

Davis, Walter R. (1969). *Idea and Act in Elizabethan Fiction*. Princeton: Princeton University Press.

Gresham, Stephen (1980–1). 'William Baldwin: Literary Voice of the Reign of Edward VI', *The Huntington Library Quarterly*, 44, 101–16.

Hackett, Helen (1996). 'Courtly Writing by Women'. In Helen Wilcox (ed), *Women and Literature in Britain, 1500–1700* (pp. 169–89). Cambridge: Cambridge University Press.

Hadfield, Andrew (1998). *Literature, Travel, and Colonial Writing in the English Renaissance, 1545–1625*. Oxford: Clarendon Press.

——(1999). 'Renaissance Narrative'. In Paul Schellinger (ed.), *Encyclopedia of the Novel*. Chicago: Fitzroy-Dearborn.

Helgerson, Richard (1976). *The Elizabethan Prodigals*. Berkeley: University of California Press.

Hunter, G. K. (1962). *John Lyly: The Humanist as Courtier*. London: Routledge.

Hutson, Lorna (1989). *Thomas Nashe in Context*. Oxford: Clarendon Press.

——(1994). *The Usurer's Daughter: Male Friendship and Fictions of Women in Sixteenth-century England*. London: Routledge.

Kinney, Arthur F. (1986). *Humanist Poetics: Thought, Rhetoric, and Fiction in Sixteenth-century England*. Amherst, MA: Massachusetts University Press.

Lucas, Caroline (1989). *Writing for Woman: The Example of Woman as Reader in Elizabethan Romance*. Milton Keynes: Open University Press.

McCoy, Richard (1979). *Sir Philip Sidney: Rebellion in Arcadia*. Brighton: Harvester.

Maslen, Robert W. (1997). *Elizabethan Fictions: Espionage, Counter-espionage and the Duplicity of Fiction in Early Elizabethan Prose Narratives*. Oxford: Clarendon Press.

Rees, Joan (1991). *Sir Philip Sidney and Arcadia*. Rutherford: Associated Universities Press.

Relihan, Constance C. (1994). *Fashioning Authority: The Development of Elizabethan Novelistic Discourse*. Kent, OH: Kent State University Press.

Ringler, William A. Jr (1979). '*Beware the Cat* and the Beginnings of English Fiction', *Novel*, 12, 113–26.

Salzman, Paul (1985). *English Prose Fiction, 1558–1700: A Critical History*. Oxford: Clarendon Press.

Weimann, Robert (1996). *Authority and Representation in Early Modern Discourse*. Baltimore: Johns Hopkins University Press.

Wright, Louis B. (1935). *Middle-class Culture in Elizabethan England*. Chapel Hill: University of North Carolina Press.

49

Theological Writings and Religious Polemic

Donna B. Hamilton

Challenges throughout the sixteenth century to the authority of the church from both Catholics and Protestants account in many respects for the pivotal nature of this period. Central to the pace and trajectory of these developing ecclesiastical issues was the body of polemical writing that defined and argued various positions. As ponderous and off-putting as many of the volumes seem, the commitments they articulated had comprehensive spiritual, political and economic implications. Many authors experienced exile, imprisonment or execution for the positions they took; others gained status and wealth. While consensus not conflict is more often the emphasis in history writing today, the value of that perspective does not alter the fact that the polemical writings were interventions in important controversies and that virtually every controversy presented itself in binaries. The issues, of course, were usually more complex, with disagreements existing also among Catholics, for example, and among the conformist leaders of the English church.

William Tyndale, Thomas More and Christopher St German

Influenced by Martin Luther and Huldreich Zwingli, the earliest English Protestant reformers – Robert Barnes, Thomas Bilney, William Tyndale, Hugh Latimer and John Frith – promoted a platform that privileged the authority of the Bible and preaching over papal authority, classified cults of saints and the veneration of images as idolatry, rejected the penitential system wherein deeds were efficacious for salvation, and replaced it with a theology of grace (Guy 119–20). Tyndale's special contribution lay in his translating the New Testament into English (1525) and, in *Obedience of a Christian Man* (1528), defending the role of the godly prince over the church. Thomas More's replies to Luther, Tyndale, Frith and Barnes, in response to which Tyndale defended both himself and Frith, established the key lines along which many future debates would be structured. More also engaged with other works which called for reform of the corrupt clergy, including those by two anticlerical common lawyers, Simon Fish, *A Supplication for the Beggars* (1529) and Christopher St German, *A Treatise Concerning the Division Between the Spirituality and Temporality* (1532). In *The Debellation of Salem and Bizance* (1533), More replied to St German's arguments for reform of heresy laws, common law jurisdiction over ecclesiastical matters involving issues of property, and secular control of the church. Faced with the Act of Supremacy, St German upheld the role of parliament in the making of law (Guy 122–3). More's defences of traditional policy remained significant to Catholics and became useful as well to Protestants such as Matthew Sutcliffe and Richard Cosin, who, during the 1590s, defended the authority of the episcopacy and the church courts against pressures for further reform.

John Bale

At first, Henry's Act of Supremacy provided opportunities for more reformist publications. Under the patronage of Thomas Cromwell, Richard Grafton and Edward Whitchurch printed the Great Bible (1539) with its bold title page representing Henry VIII as head of the church 'between God and man' (King 53). But when protests broke out, fuelling Henrician conservatism in religious policy, Cromwell was executed. Some Protestants displeased with this conservatism chose exile, including John Bale, who, fleeing to the Low Countries, developed in *The Image of Both Churches after the Revelation of Saint John* (1545) a history of the church based on the Book of Revelation and within that history the crystallizing and divisive definition of Protestants as the Christian elect and Catholics as among the reprobate, ideas that would make their way broadly into Protestant writing. While in exile, Bale wrote a polemical history of English literature, *Illustrium Majoris Britanniae Scriptorum Summarium*, that promoted John Wycliffe's importance as a forerunner of Tyndale, as well as accounts of the martyrdom of Sir John Oldcastle and Anne Askew, the latter of whom had been martyred by the conservatives in Henry's court and executed in 1546 for denying transubstantiation and the mass. Early in the reign of Edward VI, Stephen Gardiner's attempt to suppress copies of Bale's *Examinations* of Anne Askew registered the extent to which Bale had intended the account as an attack on Gardiner (King 72–5, 78–80).

The aggressive Protestant policies of Edward Seymour, duke of Somerset and Protector under Edward VI, included a renunciation of censorship and resulted in the publication of works by the early reformers – including previously banned works of Luther and Henry Bullinger, and works of Bale, Barnes, Frith, John Hooper, Tyndale and Wycliffe – and in significant opportunity for printers and publishers. There were 'thirty-one mass tracts published in 1548' supporting Cranmer's liturgical reforms (King 89). Seymour's openness backfired when rebellion erupted in 1549; the Act of Uniformity (1549) subsequently muffled debate. Put on trial, Seymour was executed in 1552.

Thomas Cranmer

In a career that would span the reigns of Henry VIII, Edward VI and Mary, Thomas Cranmer, Archbishop of Canterbury (1533–53), participated actively in writing the key documents that shaped religious policy under Henry VIII and Edward VI, beginning with 'The Necessary Doctrine and Erudition of a Christian Man' (1543), the product of a commission which met under the authority of Henry VIII. Upon the accession of Edward VI, the documents that were to define England's stake in Protestantism emanated largely from Cranmer. He had charge of producing the Book of Homilies – or *Certain Sermons, or Homilies, Appointed by the King's Majesty* (1547) – a set of official sermons to be preached in all churches; during the reign of Elizabeth, they would become sources of polemical debate for Presbyterians and other nonconforming Protestants. Of the twelve sermons issued in 1547, Cranmer probably wrote 'Exhortation to the Reading of Holy Scripture', and the homilies 'Of Salvation', 'Of Faith', and 'Of Good Works annexed to Faith', which together represent the core of beliefs along which Cranmer sought reform (MacCullough 372–3).

Cranmer also presided over the commission that wrote the first Book of Common Prayer, which, along with the Book of Homilies and Bible in English, represented the standard for Protestant conformity and, according to Maltby, served as a central tool of Protestant polemic and propaganda. At the heart of Catholic worship had been the *Primarium* or *Primer*, which, available in various forms, tended to contain the calendar of saints days and holy days, the hours of the Virgin Mary, the seven penitential psalms, the litany of the saints, the fifteen gradual psalms, the office for the dead, the commendations of souls. From 1530, the *Primer* was regularly revised according to Protestant reformulations. In 1545, Richard Grafton printed the first authorized *Primer* of Henry VIII, which included a shortened calendar of saints' days and holy days, prayers, the penitential psalms, a revised set of psalms of the passion, and, throughout, emendations reflecting Protestant theology and biblical translation. This *Primer* and the one issued during the reign of Edward VI condemned the use of any but the official versions (see Butterworth, Blom, Dickens, MacCullough and Duffy).

Incorporating sections from Henry's *Primer*, Cranmer supervised the writing of the Book of Common Prayer (printed in 1549), which, while doctrinally ambiguous, established English as the language of worship. Despite the popular protests in 1549, the revised second Prayer Book (1552) shifted the focus of the Holy Communion from an emphasis on the bread and wine to the changes being wrought on the communicant during the act of worship, and the language of the sacrament took the Zwinglian form of emphasizing not presence of the body of Christ but the remembrance of Christ. After the accession of Elizabeth, the Book of Common Prayer adopted the more conservative policy of conjoining the 1549 and 1552 language of administering the sacrament. A later but important Catholic response to Protestant inroads on popular worship was Richard Verstegan's *The Primer, or office of the blessed virgin Marie, in Latin and English* (1599), which used Gregory Martin's translations of both Old and New Testaments (Blom 16).

Cranmer also drafted, in 1552, the Forty-two Articles, which under Elizabeth would become the Thirty-nine Articles, and which iterate the doctrine of predestination, denounce purgatory, declare against the worship of images and saints, and, according to Dickens, place the English Church against both Rome and the Anabaptists (Dickens 252–3). Historians disagree in their assessment of Cranmer's changes in theological positioning and his declining to offer support to Protestants martyred under Henry VIII for positions he would later take himself. His execution in 1556 occurred as Mary continued to dismantle the forms of worship he had constructed.

Hugh Latimer

Another early supporter of Henry VIII's divorce and the supremacy, Hugh Latimer delivered a sermon to Convocation in 1536 calling for the clergy to lead a more aggressive reformation, an event that propelled Latimer to the centre of reform activity. In response, the clergy denounced him and then with his assistance drew up the Ten Articles; this first official doctrinal formulary of the Church of England reduced the sacraments from seven to three and endorsed justification by faith, but gave qualified approval to worship of images and saints and to the practice of praying for the dead. Duffy has detailed the reformers' next step, a scheme for diminishing the number and the observance of holy days and feast days (Duffy 394–5). When rebellion followed in the Pilgrimage of Grace, there also followed a series of reversals regarding policy. In June 1539, Henry VIII endorsed traditional Catholic theology by way of his Act of Six Articles; 'denial of transubstantiation became punishable by automatic burning' (Guy 185).

In 1539, amidst the see-saw of Henrician religious negotiations, Latimer was asked to resign, was ordered to stop preaching, and was later apprehended. Released from prison on Edward VI's accession, Latimer was enlisted to preach at Paul's Cross, in the Chapel Royal, and, to accommodate the court and city dignitaries who wanted to hear him, in the king's private garden at Westminster. From 1548 to 1549, his sermons were printed, in single and collected editions, including 'The Sermon on the Plough' and several sermons preached before Edward VI. Among his most political sermons were those supporting the execution of Seymour and attacking the conservative bishops (MacCullough 408). Following the fall of Seymour, Latimer became the guest of Katherine Willoughby, the Duchess of Suffolk, in Lincolnshire, where again he preached regularly. He was executed in 1555. In 1562, John Day printed an edition of twenty-seven of Latimer's sermons, including *Seven Sermons preached at Westminster* and *Certain Godly Sermons upon the Lord's Prayer*. While the earlier sermons focused on the king's role in relation to the church and the role of the clergy in the reformation, the sermons preached in Lincolnshire show Latimer more in his pastoral role denouncing abusive landlords, telling biblical stories, explaining doctrinal points, and urging the value of obedience, work, manners and virtuous living. Latimer exemplifies the social criticism, rhetorical power, and spiritual leadership available to Protestant preachers.

John Jewel

In exile during the reign of Mary, John Jewel returned at the accession of Elizabeth, and took his place alongside the leaders of the new English establishment. A significant polemical move was his 'Challenge' sermon, preached at Paul's Cross, 26 November 1559, in which he appealed to the primitive church and the scriptures as having authorized none of the Catholic practices, including their mass, prayers in a foreign tongue, papal authority and power, and image worship. Subsequent to this success, William Cecil commissioned him to write the official treatise defending the English Reformation. Drafted in the context of the Council of Trent and printed in 1562, Jewel explained in the introduction to *Apologia Ecclesiae Anglicanae* that England's break with Rome was founded on the premise that religious authority resided in scripture and the church fathers. Jewel summarized the doctrinal beliefs on which the English clergy agreed, rebutted charges that England was now overrun with division and sects, accused the papists of immorality, and cited the church fathers and councils to argue how far the Roman Church had departed from the primitive church. In a final section, Jewel argued for the authority and right of Christian princes to govern the church in their own realms, asserting again England's right not to submit to the pope or to the Council of Trent (Booty, *Apology*, xxxiii–xxxvii). Written in Latin, translated into several languages, *Apologia* prompted Catholic replies. Over the course of five years, 1564–8, the intellectual leaders of the English Catholics – Thomas Dorman, John Martiall, John Rastell, William Allen, Thomas Stapleton, Richard Shacklock, Nicholas Sander and Thomas Harding – all in exile, responded with one or more books, including Harding, *An Answer to Master Jewel's Challenge* (1564), Stapleton, *A Fortress of the Faith* (1565), Allen, *A Defence and Declaration of the Catholic Church's Doctrine touching Purgatory* (1565) and Sander, *The Rock of the Church* (1567) and *A Treatise of the Images of Christ* (1567) (Southern 60–118). Written in English, these replies made necessary an English translation of Jewel, which Anne Bacon, wife of Nicholas Bacon, provided in 1564; *The Apology for the Church of England* remains a storehouse of information regarding the doctrine and defence of early English Protestantism.

John Foxe

An equally authorizing but more affecting account of English Protestantism came in the form of John Foxe's *Acts and Monuments of These Latter and Perilous Days Touching Matters of the Church*, the major editions of which were printed in 1563, 1570 and

1583, each a revision of the preceding. The initial impetus to the work was the drive to record and report on Protestants martyred under Mary. After the succession of Elizabeth, Foxe's project took on larger historiographical goals. Seizing on methods current on the continent (Firth 74) and on interest in the apocalypse, Foxe developed a periodization scheme that synthesized themes from the Book of Revelation, English history and church history, patterns of persecution and martyrdom, and Protestant theology. Using the prophecies and images in the Book of Revelation as the grid on which to map English history, Foxe divided all history into periods, characterized by the degree to which the true church or Antichrist was in power. Assessing each segment of English history by the same criteria allowed him also to promote the British and Tudor agenda valued by Cecil, Nicholas Bacon and Matthew Parker. With these rhetorical strategies, Foxe developed a definition of English Protestantism that set it against Catholicism in a system of binaries that opposed the true church to the false church of Rome (similar to Bale's construction), and that set the godly prince defending true religion against the pope identified as Antichrist. Haller's view that hereby Foxe defined England as an elect nation has been challenged (Firth 106–9). During later decades of the sixteenth century and continuing through the seventeenth century, Foxe's rhetoric of difference became the defining discourse for Protestant polemics (Kemp 84–85). Catholic response included Stapleton's translation of Bede's *History of the Church of England*, Nicholas Harpsfield's *Dialogi Sex* (1566), and Richard Verstegan's *A Restitution of Decayed Intelligence* (1605).

The Jesuits and the Enterprise of England

During the 1570s and 1580s, new challenges appeared from both the Catholics and the Protestants. In the late 1570s, the Jesuits launched their Enterprise of England, by which they would return Jesuit priests to England to minister unto the Catholic community and prepare for returning England to Catholicism. In this context of resistance, Gregory Martin's *Treatise of Schism* (1578) and Robert Parsons's [or Persons's] *A Brief Discourse Containing Reasons Why Catholics Refuse to Go to Church* (1580) urged Catholics to choose recusancy rather than obedience to the government's orders for conformity. Edmund Campion's arrest and martyrdom, along with the execution of several other priests, called into being Burghley's *The Execution of Justice in England*, an attempt to justify the executions to European nations on the grounds that they had been for treason not religion. William Allen, replying with *A True, Sincere, and Modest Defence of English Catholics*, took the opposite position and also made the case against royal supremacy (see Kingdon). Parsons's *The Persecution of Catholics in England* provided a detailed account of the conditions of living under a persecutory government. And Gregory Martin completed an English translation of the Latin Vulgate that included marginal glosses and essays on doctrinal points; his Rheims New Testament was printed in 1582, the Douay Old Testament in 1610. In 1584, Persons's *A Christian Directory*, a devotional work aimed at Catholics and at conversion to Catholicism but framed rhetorically as non-polemical, prompted Edmund Bunny to reproduce the book in a slightly revised form and claim it for the Protestant side.

Presbyterians and Puritans

Protestants also tested and re-examined the results of anti-Catholic reform. With the principal polemical treatises emanating from Thomas Cartwright, Walter Travers, Dudley Fenner, John Penry, John Udall and Job Throckmorton, the opposition focused not on doctrine but on church ceremonies (in opposition to kneeling, using the sign of the cross in baptism, wearing elaborate clerical vestments, and enforced use of the *Book of Common Prayer*), on a preference for individualized preaching (not enforced use of the Homilies), and on reform of church government (to replace the episcopacy with parity among ministers). Defenders of the reformed English Protestant church were chiefly John Whitgift, soon to be Archbishop of Canterbury, who answered the books of Cartwright; John Bridges, Dean of Salisbury, who entered into debate with Fenner and Travers, and Matthew Sutcliffe, Dean of Exeter, who engaged Cartwright and Throckmorton (see Collinson 1967).

At a point in time when the Presbyterian movement was meeting its toughest opposition, suddenly the Martin Marprelate tracts, printed on secret presses, began to appear. During 1588–9, these anonymous tracts rearticulated the attack on the Protestant episcopacy with a satiric and comedic vigour that nearly outstripped the ability of the authorities to respond. In this print venture we find an illustrating moment of how censorship could function when the authorities were sufficiently provoked. Whether or not the tracts contributed to the demise of the Presbyterian movement, they represent a boldness in the use of print with which only Catholic polemicists publishing from the continent could compete. Hired to reply, John Lyly and Thomas Nashe wrote pamphlets in a similarly satiric tone; more traditional polemical replies by Bancroft, Bishop of London, Thomas Cooper, Bishop of Winchester and Sutcliffe confirm that the Marprelate event struck hard at the interest in muting dissension.

In the early 1590s, when Cartwright and eight ministers were being tried for disloyalty, the lawyers attacking and defending them became participants in these disputes. On the government's side were ecclesiastical lawyers Sutcliffe and Richard Cosin, on Cartwright's side were common lawyers Robert Beale and James Morice, the latter of whom was put under house arrest for his 1593 speech in parliament against the *ex officio* oath and so against practices that promoted self-incrimination. Morice's speech and writings challenged the totalizing conceptualizations of the Protestant episcopacy (Collinson 1967 403–31). In 1589, in the midst of Marprelate's satiric attacks, Bancroft had preached his famous Paul's Cross sermon declaring that the episcopacy was a divine institution with absolute power. That position was carried forward in his and Thomas Bilson's books in the early 1590s.

Richard Hooker

We may use the scholarly disagreement in evidence in the work of Lake (1988), White, and Maltby over how to describe Richard Hooker – his theology, politics and influence all being at issue – and to emphasize how Hooker's arguments call attention to the competing and mixed ideologies current in the 1580s and 1590s. In *Of the Laws of Ecclesiastical Polity*, which began to appear in 1590, Hooker's call for a more broadly constructed church in which worship and ceremonies displaced wrangling over theological distinction and his identifying Rome and Geneva as the two poles between which the church had to be constructed may be read as the oppressive voice of conformity or as the envisioning of a consensual alternative to an ever-splintering ecclesiological situation. For Hooker, 'since Christ died for all men, all men were actually or potentially part of Christ's body, the church' (Lake 1988 42). In imagining a Christian community in which Catholics were understood as part of the true church, he opposed other conformists, including Bancroft, and marked out an ideological space different from the more exclusive definition provided by William Perkins's Calvinist prescriptions (see William Perkins below).

The Policy of King James

Both Puritans and Catholics greeted the accession of King James with anxiety. The Puritan ministers, seeking reform of ceremonies, confronted James with the Millennary Petition. To give them a hearing, James called the Hampton Court Conference. Nevertheless, as is clear from William Barlow's *The Sum and Substance of the Conference* (1604), few concessions were granted: no changes in church government or church courts, and only minor changes in ceremonies. Meanwhile, the Catholics too pleaded their cause, as in *A Petition Apologetical, Presented to the King's most excellent Majesty, by the Lay Catholics of England* (1604), and in works by Parsons, including his attack on Foxe, *Treatise of Three Conversions of England* (1603), and his reply in *An Answer to the Fifth Part of Reports Lately Set Forth by Sir Edward Coke* (1606) to Edward Coke's defence of royal supremacy. In these years, Sutcliffe maintained a high profile responding to Catholic works.

The Gunpowder Plot and Oath of Allegiance

On 5 November 1605, a group of Jesuit conspirators discontent with English policies toward Catholicism, tried to blow up king and parliament by packing gunpowder into the cellar of a house that extended below the space where parliament was to meet. The subsequent trials and executions of Guy Fawkes and Henry Garnet stirred deeply both anti-Catholic feeling and Catholic fear of persecution. The Gunpowder

Plot and its aftermath also generated a large body of writing, including the report giving the government's view, *A True and Perfect Relation of the Proceedings against the Late Most Barbarous Traitors* (1606), written by Henry Howard, the earl of Northampton, with the assistance of Robert Cotton, and translated into Latin by William Camden. One result of the Plot was James's developing an Oath of Allegiance to him as temporal ruler, a move that triggered an enormous international paper war in which the English Archpriest George Blackwell, Cardinal Robert Bellarmine, and Parsons were chief representatives of the Catholic position, while King James, Lancelot Andrewes, John Donne and William Barlow took their places as the most prominent Protestant polemicists. These authors debated the authority of king and pope over matters temporal and spiritual and the implications of a Catholics' choosing obedience or martyrdom. Some Catholic polemicists, including Richard Sheldon and William Warmington, argued for taking the oath. And the Protestant William Barrett, who had converted to Catholicism in 1597, defended the king against the pope (see Patterson).

Calvin and Arminius

Late in James's reign dissension among Protestants became focused around the doctrine of predestination, the implications of which have been debated especially by Tyacke, Lake (1987) and White. In 1590, England's predominantly Calvinist theology had received a massive articulation in William Perkins's, *Armilla Aurea* (1590), translated in 1591 as *A Golden Chain . . . containing the Order of the Causes of Salvation and Damnation.* When William Barrett preached against it, the ensuing controversy led to the reaffirmation of the doctrine of predestination in the Lambeth Articles (1595), and subsequently to Barrett's leaving Cambridge with his mentor Peter Baro. A major challenge to predestination came in the form of Jacobus Arminius's reply to Perkins, *Examen Modestus* (1612), in which Arminius opposed the predestinarian belief that God had willed salvation to some and damnation to others and argued that God wills the salvation of all people who believe. While many defended Perkins, an important sign of change was William Laud's anti-Calvinist sermon in 1615, to which Robert Abbot replied. James responded to the Arminian challenge at an international level when, in 1619, he sent English representatives to the Synod at Dort, organized to condemn the doctrines of the Dutch Arminians. Later, during negotiations for an Anglo-Spanish marriage for Prince Charles, James softened his position on Arminianism, partly to moderate his stance on the pope. James continued to move in an Arminian direction, supporting publication of Richard Montagu's *A New Gag for an Old Goose* (1624). The central issues in the 1620s were 'the debate about the visibility and continuity of the church . . . the role and nature of 'worship' . . . and the relative importance of preaching compared to that of set prayer and the sacraments' (Lake 1987 43). Those who wished to advance in the church 'had to keep quiet about conformity and the polity of the church . . . had to defend the *iure divino* case for episcopacy and defend the king's status as a ruler by divine right' (Lake 1987 49–50).

While most English people did not engage in religious debate to the degree that polemicists did, we confront in polemical works a level of speaking out that is characteristic of the sixteenth century, and that resulted ultimately in an increased sectarianism within English religious society among both Catholics and Protestants. Nevertheless, efforts continued to construct the English religious community so that the values of uniformity and conformity could retain meaning as official policy and as normative practice.

References and Further Reading

Allison, A. F. and Rogers, D. M. (1989, 1994). *The Contemporary Printed Literature of the English Counter-Reformation between 1558 and 1640.* Vol. I: Works in Languages other than English. Vol. 2: Works in English. Aldershot: Scolar Press.

Blom, J. M. (1982). *The Post-Tridentine English Primer.* London: Catholic Record Society.

Booty, J. E. (ed.) (1963). *An Apology of the Church of England by John Jewel.* Charlottesville: University Press of Virginia.

Butterworth, Charles C. (1953). *The English Primers, 1529–1545.* Philadelphia: University of Pennsylvania Press.

Carrafiello, Michael L. (1998). *Robert Parsons and English Catholicism, 1580–1610.* Selinsgrove: Susquehanna University Press.

Collinson, Patrick (1967). *The Elizabethan Puritan Movement.* Berkeley: University of California Press.

——(1982). *The Religion of Protestants: The Church in English Society.* Oxford: Clarendon Press.

Dickens, A. G. (1964). *The English Reformation.* London: B. T. Batsford Ltd.

Duffy, Eamon (1992). *The Stripping of the Altars: Traditional Religion in England c.1400–c.1580.* New Haven: Yale University Press.

Firth, Katharine R. (1979). *The Apocalyptic Tradition in Reformation Britain, 1530–1645.* Oxford: Oxford University Press.

Greenslade, S. L. (1963). 'English Versions of the Bible, 1525–1611'. In S. L. Greenslade (ed.), *The Cambridge History of the Bible: The West from the Reformation to the Present Day* (pp. 141–73). Cambridge: Cambridge University Press.

Guy, J. A. (1988). *Tudor England.* Oxford: Oxford University Press.

Haller, William (1963). *Foxe's Book of Martyrs and the Elect Nation.* London: Jonathan Cape.

Kemp, Anthony (1991). *The Estrangement of the Past: A Study in the Origins of Modern Historical Consciousness.* Oxford: Oxford University Press.

King, John (1982). *English Reformation Literature: The Tudor Origins of the Protestant Tradition.* Princeton: Princeton University Press.

Kingdon, Robert (ed.) (1965). *Burghley's Execution of Justice and Allen's Defence of English Catholics.* Ithaca: Cornell University Press.

Lake, Peter (1987). 'Calvinism and the English Church, 1570–1635', *Past and Present*, 114, 32–76.

——(1988) *Anglicans and Puritans?: Presbyterianism and English Conformist Thought from Whitgift to Hooker.* London: Unwin Hyman.

MacCullough, Diarmaid (1996). *Thomas Cranmer: A Life.* New Haven: Yale University Press.

Maltby, Judith (1998). *Prayer Book and People in Elizabethan and Early Stuart England.* Cambridge: Cambridge University Press.

Milton, Anthony (1995). *Catholic and Reformed: The Roman and Protestant Churches in English Protestant Thought, 1600–1640.* Cambridge: Cambridge University Press.

Milward, Peter (1977, 1978). *Religious Controversies of the Elizabethan Age: A Survey of Printed Sources.* London: Scolar Press. *Religious Controversies of the Jacobean Age: A Survey of Printed Sources.* Lincoln: University of Nebraska Press.

Patterson, W. B. (1997). *King James VI and I and*

the Reunion of Christendom. Cambridge: Cambridge University Press.

Southern, S. V. (1953). *Elizabethan Recusant Prose, 1559–1582*. London: Sands and Co. Ltd.

Tyacke, Nicholas (1987). *Anti-Calvinists: The Rise of English Arminianism, c.1590–1640*. Oxford: Clarendon Press.

White, Peter (1992). *Predestination, Policy, and Polemic: Conflict and Consensus in the English Church from the Reformation to the Civil War*. Cambridge: Cambridge University Press.

50

The English Renaissance Essay: Churchyard, Cornwallis, Florio's Montaigne and Bacon

John Lee

Caveat Emptor: Or, Buyer Beware

'Essay' is a rather retrospective term, used originally more to identify a literary tradition than to define a new literary form. Francis Bacon (1561–1626), whose 1597 *Essays* were the first collection of short prose pieces to be published in English under that title, explained that 'the word is late [recent], but the thing is ancient', and cited Seneca's *Epistles to Lucilius* as previous examples. Michel de Montaigne (1533–92), who had published his *Essais* in France in 1580, pointed to a similar classical heritage which included, as well as Seneca, Cicero and Plutarch. What Bacon and Montaigne found interesting in these authors were the provisional qualities of their writings: Seneca's *Epistles* were essays, Bacon argued, because they were 'dispersed meditations', presented with more attention to the significance of their subject than to the elegance of their expression.[1] Such loose sallies of the mind, as Samuel Johnson would later call them in his *Dictionary*, assumed an intimacy in the relationship between reader and writer, which created a strong sense of personality; Montaigne, in particular, valued the sense of companionship with the dead that this allows the reader. 'Essay', as an English term, picks up on these provisional qualities well, deriving as it does from the French *essai*, a trial or attempt, and the older French-English 'assay', an examination or tasting.

The novelty of the 'essay', then, is that of discovery; the term uncovers a literary tradition, long practised but little noticed. In the vernacular, however, the position of the 'essay' is somewhat different. Writing secular and non-fictional literary works in English was a relatively recent occupation; when Roger Ascham, for example, explains his love for archery in *Toxophilus* in 1545, he feels the need to begin by defending his use of English in place of the more natural Latin. *Toxophilus* is a work aimed at showing that the vernacular might be as capable a literary medium as Latin or Greek. This was a point of controversy at the time and, though the arguments were effectively settled in English's favour by the end of the 1560s, they would continue to be raised well into the next century. Latin, meanwhile, would retain its prestige as the international language of learning and culture: Montaigne grew up speaking it (apparently before he spoke French) and Bacon wrote the majority of his work in it; later, John Milton would write his early poetry in Latin, and even at the end of the seventeenth century, Isaac Newton would publish his great theoretical work, the *Principia*, in Latin, reserving English for the more experiential *Optics*.[2]

It is difficult, however, to advance a claim for anything more than the relative novelty of the 'essay' in the vernacular. Ascham talks of *Toxophilus* as an 'assay', and in his introduction the sense is given of a particular voice examining itself in its likes and dislikes, in life and literature – though these 'assaying' qualities are lost in the body of the discussion of archery, which is set out as a dialogue. Thomas Churchyard has a far stronger claim to be writing essays before the name. Born in 1523, a professional soldier from the 1540s on, a famous poet by 1550, he began writing short pieces of prose alongside his poetry in the 1570s, only stopping, it sometimes seems, to die in 1604. Many of these 'little pieces' or 'discourses', as Churchyard calls them, have the qualities so far mentioned, and Churchyard gathered them together, along with his poetry, for publication. In *Churchyard's Challenge* (1593), for example, 'The Man is but his Mind' takes as its starting point the moment when Churchyard comes across his title, which is a quotation in Jerome Cardan's *De Consolatione*. 'Weighing the worth of that conclusion', Churchyard gives us his responses to it, 'plainly set down [. . .] doubting not but some one man or other shall see a piece of his own mind, in this my presumption of [suppositions about] the same'. The subject and method is essay-like: a mind thinking about how minds think, offering itself, unselfconsciously perhaps, as evidence of its subject. As the discourse moves on, however, it becomes, with its summary wit and classificatory habit, an early example of 'charactery', drawing a roll-call of types to demonstrate the mind's ability to shape men: 'A grave and modest minded man' is followed by 'The merry and pleasant companion' who in turn gives way to 'A greedy minded groper of this world', and so on. Another little piece, 'A Discourse of True Manhood', might be classified as more within the tradition of the courtesy manual or advice book than the essay; while 'A Discourse of Calamity', in its praise of sorrows as the route to happiness, is clearly related to the religious literatures of sermon and meditation.

Yet, even if one wanted to make such fine discriminations between the essay and what are, with the paradox and encomium, its related genres, it would be perverse to discount 'The Honour of a Soldier'. This *is* an essay, reaching for and ranging among sayings, speeches, customs and incidents drawn from classical literature, the Bible, and more recent European and Islamic history, all garnered as Churchyard tries to come to terms with his bewilderment before the facts of soldiering, which are also the facts of his life: 'Were not this a madness, and more than a mere folly [. . .] to watch and ward, fight, strive, and struggle with strangers for victory: and then to come home and be rewarded as common persons, and walk like a shadow in the Sun, without estimation or countenance?' Churchyard knew this madness well; twice he had returned from the wars to try to find employment at the court of Queen Eliza-beth, and twice he had failed. In the attempt, in the failure, and in the response, Churchyard could be said to be typical of his age. The dominant humanist education aimed to fashion fit servants to princes and their courts; and yet those courts and princes did not have enough posts and places to receive the aspirant courtiers. That Churchyard's literary response to his failure should be to seek to relate his own times, and his place in his times, to the past, as mediated through his reading of classical texts, is similarly typical. Humanist education began with the attempt to acquire pro-ficiency in Latin through the study and imitation of classical texts; central to that process, and the moral and personal benefits it was thought to bring, was the culling of choice quotations into commonplace books, arranged in sections and topics. These commonplace books could then be used to discover, develop and substantiate one's own arguments for the present and future. Out of such an education and out of such books grew the prose forms of the vernacular, sharing common features as they shared a common literary humanist culture.

Bacon and Montaigne's dismissal of the novelty of the essay form, as it owes more to honesty than modesty, deserves respect; and yet the desire to restrict the term's application – to see the essay as in some way beginning with and belonging to Bacon and Montaigne – remains strong. In large part, this desire is driven by the recogni-tion of Bacon's and Montaigne's literary qualities. More important, however, is the recognition that, in some ways, Bacon's and Montaigne's essays are different from those that come before and most of those that follow. This difference, though, does not lie in what the essay is, but rather in what is being done with the essay: Bacon and Montaigne discovered that writing sequences of essays, as opposed to single essays, allowed them to exploit the provisional nature of the essay in new ways.

In Strange Way / To Stand Inquiring Right, Is Not to Stray[3]

In their *Essays*, both Bacon and Montaigne are deeply concerned with the nature and status of human knowledge. Such epistemological questions are not immediately apparent, however, as both offer large amounts of practical and ethical counsel. This is most evident in the case of Bacon; he gave his final, 1625, edition the double-title of *Essays or Counsels, Civil and Moral*, and noted in his dedication that they were the most successful of his writings 'for that, as it seems, they come home to men's busi-ness and bosoms'. They came home in a wide variety of ways: some essays are the equivalent of guidebooks, advising the male and gentlemanly reader how to plant a garden, how to build a house and what to see on a tour of Europe; others are more like papers on topics of national interest, aimed more specifically at advising minis-ters and princes how to prevent rebellions, how to colonize countries, and in which ways to regulate the lending of money. Lists often feature in these essays, and regis-ter Bacon's delight in the details of the physical world: colonists should look first for natural foodstuffs, such as 'chestnuts, walnuts, pine-apples, olives, dates, plums, cherries, wild honey', and then they should think about what can be harvested in a year, such as 'parsnips, carrots, turnips, onions, radish, artichokes of Jerusalem, maize' ('Of Plantations'). Then there are the more directly moral essays, on death and how to die, on beauty and on friendship – which last, although strongly desired, seems almost impossible to find. Indeed, with the exception of the guidebook essays, in which man is not an actor, the world of the *Essays* is a rather grim and embattled place. 'Of Negotiating' never mentions the possibility of fair dealing: 'All practice is to discover, or to work.' Negotiation, in this world, can only be the art of discovering the opposing party's concealed intents and of manipulating him to your purpose, while, of course, resisting being so discovered or worked – by secrecy, concealment or dissimulation. And nothing helps deception more than the reputation for honesty ('Of Simulation and Dissimulation').

The *Essays* are a very concise user's guide to conduct and survival in the public world of the court, and they everywhere attempt to engage with life as it is, and not as it should be; Bacon's counsel is not morally didactic in any simple sense. Part of the interest of his dispassionate observation comes from the fact that Bacon is, or was, an insider. Through a career of some forty years he had risen, like his father, to hold the highest legal office of the land, the Lord Chancellorship, and he had also been a Member of Parliament and Privy Councillor to the king. Then, in 1621, he was charged by parliament with corruption, stripped of his Chancellorship, and banned from holding public office. Of more enduring interest than that observed world is the tolerant acceptance of humanity that comes out of Bacon's dispassionate stance. He is not surprised that every man should have his own ends: 'What would men have? Do they think those they employ and deal with are saints?' ('Of Suspicion'). He acknowledges the reality and necessity of emotion and finds perverse the Stoics attempt to deny, for example, anger. Occasionally, this strong sense of a human nature that must be understood, not denied, conjures up an elucidatory image: 'Suspicions amongst thoughts are like bats amongst birds, they ever fly by twilight' ('Of Suspicion'). The image is unusual in having a two-fold object of comparison: more typical might be, 'Suspicions are like bats, they ever fly [. . .]'. The presence of the birds allows, for a moment, a sense of the strange mix of the lovely and the ominous, the positive and negative aspects of the liberality of thought.

Montaigne's *Essais* exemplify the liberality of thought to an astonishing degree, though in a quite different, more discursive and conversational, register. He treats many of the same topics as Bacon (the title of the Italian edition of the *Essais* translates as *Moral, Political, and Military Discourses*), and he similarly refuses to be awed by place or finery – as he says at the end of his last essay, 'And sit we upon the highest throne of the World, yet sit we upon our own tail' ('Of Experience').[4] That mention of 'tail' marks the difference in register, though: Bacon is capable of a vigorous colloquialism in his counsel, but it is typically impersonal; Montaigne's counsel comes very much as part of Montaigne's personality. He wryly warns the reader in his preface, 'myself am the groundwork of my book: it is then no reason thou shouldest employ thy time about so frivolous and vain a subject'. As William Hazlitt rather breathlessly points out, however, '[Montaigne] did not set up for a philosopher, wit, orator, or moralist, but he became all these by merely daring to tell us whatever passed through his mind.'[5] Montaigne's essays have a vast historical and, especially, geographical range of example. Indeed, as he describes the lives of the natives of the new world of the Americas, it is tempting to see him as an early anthropologist: he argues, in response to other contemporary accounts, that the natives are neither natural savages nor barbarians, but rather people with different customs and culture ('Of the Cannibals'). Unlike an anthropologist, however, Montaigne then proceeds to judge the Native Americans by moral criteria; he argues that their fearlessness and devotion to honour has rendered them cultural savages. Here as elsewhere, Montaigne is using the new world to explore the old world, and in particular the French civil war, a type of national cannibalism, which had begun in 1562, when Montaigne was thirty, and would last until some three years after his death in 1592. He sees in the new world's cultural savagery a reflection of the savagery of his own culture; nobility in both, it seems, is intimately related to a violence born of inflexibility. Montaigne's sense of the innate savagery of nobility is a more sophisticated version of Bacon's sense of the inadequacy of stoicism; and Montaigne's humanity is similarly on a larger scale – if not deeper, then at least far more socially inclusive, dwelling on the troubles of women and the poor, and admiring of the ways in which they endure and alleviate adversity.

Yet, as counsels, both Bacon's and Montaigne's essays have one great drawback; when read closely, they tend not to make very good sense. To Ben Jonson, a very fine close-reader, inconsistency was the defining feature of the essay writer: 'what they have discredited, and impugned in one work, they have before, or after, extolled the same in another. Such are all the *Essayists*, even their Master Montaigne.' (*Timber: Or, Discoveries*) Jonson put these self-contradictions down to the immediacy of the form; essayists 'write out of what they presently find or meet, without choice'. Jonson's observations are accurate: there are contradictions, both explicit and implicit, between essays; within essays, time and again, when Bacon and Montaigne bring in an example, it cuts against the thrust of their argument; or, and sometimes as well, it leads the argument off in a completely new direction. Indeed, the more Bacon and Montaigne revise and expand their *Essays*, the more inconsistent and contradictory they become. In Bacon's case, what may have been a relatively clear argument in 1612, for instance, becomes troubled and contradictory at twice the length by 1625 – the most famous example being 'Of Friendship'; while Montaigne, by the time the three-volume edition of his essays comes out in 1588, sometimes seems to have trouble even in keeping sight of the titles of his chapters – as in 'Of Coaches'. This either represents carelessness on a truly grand scale or, what seems more likely, the ironies and inconsistencies are intended, and Bacon and Montaigne are intent on creating ambiguous and contradictory texts.[6]

Abrupt transitions lie at the heart of both their styles and reflect their epistemological concerns. In Bacon's case, this relationship between style and philosophy – which is the relationship between a form of address and a mode of perception – is clearest in the 1597 *Essays*. These ten very short pieces are dominated by aphorisms, often placed one after another, as consecutive paragraphs. In their terse abruptness a new direction in English prose can be seen, and the *Essays* have often been credited with inaugurating what is usually known as the plain style. Bacon avoids the long periodic sentences, built up of many subordinate clauses, and often elaborately figured, that were the hallmark of an English prose modelled upon the Latin of Cicero, and in their place uses short sentences related paratactically, taking Seneca and Tacitus as his models. Bacon does so not only for aesthetic, but also for philosophic reasons; he identifies the Ciceronian style as one of the defects of learning that hold back man's reason in the pursuit of truth. In *The Advancement of Learning* (1605), and later in the *Instauratio Magna* (1620), Bacon argues that humanist education trapped the present in the past, by privileging classical learning and, in particular, an Aristotelian dialectics which sought only to test the cogency of an argument without considering the correctness of its premises. The Ciceronian style, which Bacon rightly identified as one of the products of humanist education, buttressed this solipsistic attitude because, in its devotion to an ideal of copious eloquence, it both encouraged men 'to hunt after words more than matter' and, in its intricately fashioned nature, gave them the impression that the knowledge expressed was complete and fully understood. The delivering of knowledge or counsel 'in distinct and disjoined aphorism', by contrast, emphasized its incomplete nature, and encouraged readers to test it against their own experience of the world.[7] Bacon's use of the plain style, at the heart of which lies the aphorism, is not, then, aimed at achieving a complete and simple elucidation, but rather the contrary – at presenting the world in a particularly provisional, and so useful, a way to man's reason. What Jonson sees as Bacon's inconsistencies are Bacon's call to true knowledge. The *Essays'* counsels call attention to their status as first and incomplete formulations which are designed to be cast away; just as, in the mechanic arts, the first design for an object is soon discarded. As such they are a part of the great intellectual project of Bacon's life: the attempt to move his age away from a contemplative, Aristotelian philosophy, which assumed that the world was known and which was typically deductive in its methods, to an experimental and inductive natural philosophy which sought to discover and achieve increasing degrees of mastery over the world. Bacon's actual achievements in experimental science were limited; however, in his faith in the possibilities of collective progress and, relatedly, in his consciousness of the modernity of the present, Bacon has claims to be, if not the father of modern science (as was once asserted), then at least a founding figure in the philosophy of science.

A Book Consubstantial to His Author

Montaigne distrusts authority and tradition every bit as much as Bacon (though, again like Bacon, he also believes in the need for obedience to political and religious authority). Unlike Bacon, however, Montaigne is deeply sceptical of the power of human reason. In 'An Apology of Raymond Sebond' (an essay of some two hundred pages), Montaigne argues that man knows nothing with certainty, and takes as his conclusive proof the fact that man does not know himself. Montaigne's first step towards truth, therefore, is to try to gain a better understanding of himself; where Bacon looks outward at the world, Montaigne looks inward at the world of his mind. Ironically enough, as he points out in 'Of Vanity', the least vain subject for Montaigne is Montaigne. The man who looks outward with that 'trouble-feast' reason, as he calls it, is 'the magistrate without jurisdiction: and when all is done, the Vice of the play'. The last is a clever analogy: the Vice originated in medieval morality plays, where he was often instrumental in leading Everyman away from the true Christian path and into the clutches of the Devil. Making reasoning man the Vice is an ingenious move, a little like Christopher Marlowe's internalizing the figure of the Vice within his destructive and self-destructive Machiavel heroes, or William Shakespeare's more subtle suggestion of Falstaff's Vice-like qualities — all of which recognize in man's powers of reason great attractions and great dangers. That move, however, is not Montaigne's but rather the Montaigne's of John Florio (1553?–1625); a more literal translation of the French has man as 'the judge without jurisdiction and, when all is done, the jester of the farce'.[8] Florio's translation is less than accurate, but fundamentally sympathetic to Montaigne and more effectively Englished; Florio's Montaigne is a particularly rich English text, whose formulations often allow the reader that satisfying dual sense of a meaning understood and possibilities of meaning waiting to be found. What Florio is not sympathetic to is the relative plainness of Montaigne's style which, while far less terse than Bacon's, is similarly committed to moving away from a Ciceronian and towards a Senecan model of prose. Florio is above all the author of a *World of Words*, the first English–Italian dictionary. As his 74,000 definitions testify, Florio loved words as words; and he constantly expands Montaigne's sentences, doubling words, often yoking an unusual term (sometimes a neologism) with a more common English word for explanation, and adding clauses in parallel, particularly if it gives him a chance to indulge his encyclopaedic knowledge of English proverbs.

Sir William Cornwallis the Younger (1579–1614) was the first to capture Montaigne's conversational and discursive style in his own *Essays*, which appeared in two volumes, the first in 1600 and a second in 1601. Cornwallis probably drew on a manuscript version of Florio's translation, which was first published in 1603. Where Florio Englished the Montaignesque essay, Cornwallis could be said to have domesticated it. Cornwallis exchanges Montaigne's scepticism for a gentlemanly uncertainty, and his essays are perhaps the easiest to enjoy of any of these writers, because they never risk pushing a point too far. The world, for Cornwallis, is essentially given and ordered, and one must adjust to it. To do so, Cornwallis expounds a youthful stoicism: as a young man given to indulgence and indebtedness, he can appreciate the need for constancy. What Montaigne had found, by contrast, when he came to study himself, was the impossibility of such constancy, however desired. Each essay was, as he recognized, a painting of himself, and, by making many such pictures, he was able to catch sight of himself or, rather, the movement of his mind, in time. Self-study, particularly from the 1588 edition of the *Essais* onward, became a form of self-portrayal: what shocked Montaigne, however, was that the essays were not as repetitious as they should have been; instead of giving him an array of pictures which identified their subject with increasing precision, Montaigne found that, 'I cannot settle my object; it goeth so unquietly and staggering, with a natural drunkenness. I take it in this plight; as it is at the instant I amuse myself about it. I describe not the essence, but the passage [. . .] Were my mind settled, I would not essay, but resolve myself' ('Of Repenting'). The essays become the formal device by which Montaigne represents the truth, as he sees it, that life is not being – 'essence' – but becoming – 'passage'. For Montaigne, unlike Bacon, it is not our knowledge of the world or even of ourselves that is provisional, because in we err and lack information, but rather it is ourselves that are provisional, as we vary through time. The essays portray different Montaignes who are all Montaigne: or as he puts it, 'though the lines of my picture change and vary, yet lose they not themselves' ('Of Repenting'). There can be no science of man in this approach, nor any hope of self-mastery. In their places Montaigne inaugurates the notion of identity as self-discovery and self-creation. Where Bacon had used the essay as a mode of perception, then, Montaigne uses it as a mode of expression: 'I have no more made my book,' he realizes, 'than my book hath made me. A book consubstantial to his author' ('Of Giving the Lie').

NOTES

1 Dedication to the 1610–12 manuscript edition of the *Essays*. All quotations are from Vicker's edition.
2 See THE ENGLISH LANGUAGE OF THE EARLY MODERN PERIOD.
3 John Donne, *3rd Satire*.
4 All quotations are from *The Essays of Michael, Lord of Montaigne*, tr. John Florio.
5 'On the Periodical Essayists', published in *Lectures on the English Comic Writers* (1819).
6 See Stanley Fish on Bacon and Margaret McGowan (in McFarlane and Maclean) on Montaigne.
7 The quotation is from Bacon's Preface to *Maxims of the Law* (1597). A particularly interesting discussion of aphorism and method can be found in *The Advancement of Learning*, Book II, section heading '*De Methodo Sincera*'.
8 M. A. Screech's fine translation.

REFERENCES AND FURTHER READING

Bacon

Kiernan, Michael (ed.) (1985). *Sir Francis Bacon: The Essayes or Counsels, Civill and Morall*. Oxford: Clarendon Press.
Spedding, James, Ellis, Robert L. and Heath, Douglas D. (eds) (1857–74). *The Works of Francis Bacon*. London: Longman.
Vickers, Brian (ed.) (1996). *Francis Bacon: A Critical Edition of the Major Works*. Oxford: Oxford University Press.

Churchyard

Churchyard, Thomas (1593). *Churchyard's Challenge.*

Cornwallis

Allen, Don Cameron (ed.) (1946). *Essayes: By Sir William Cornwallis, the Younger.* Baltimore: Johns Hopkins University Press.

Montaigne

Screech, M. A. (tr.) (1991). *Michel de Montaigne: The Complete Essays.* London: Penguin.

Florio, John (tr.) (1603). *The Essays of Michael, Lord of Montaigne,* ed. A. R. Waller (1910). London: Dent.

Burke, Peter (1981). *Montaigne.* Oxford: Oxford University Press.

Bush, Douglas (1962). *English Literature in the Earlier Seventeenth Century: 1600–1660.* Oxford: Clarendon Press.

Fish, Stanley (1972). *Self-Consuming Artifacts.* Berkeley: University of California Press.

Frame, Donald M. (1965). *Montaigne: A Biography.* London: Hamish Hamilton.

Germer, Roger Anthony (1965). 'The Life and Works of Thomas Churchyard'. PhD, Northwestern University.

McFarlane, I. D. and Maclean, Ian (eds) (1982). *Montaigne: Essays in Memory of Richard Sayce.* Oxford: Clarendon Press.

Moss, Ann (1996). *Printed Commonplace Books and the Restructuring of Renaissance Thought.* Oxford: Clarendon Press.

Peltonen, Markku (ed.) (1996). *The Cambridge Companion to Bacon.* Cambridge. Cambridge University Press.

Quint, David (1998). *Montaigne and the Quality of Mercy: Ethical and Political Themes in the 'Essais'.* Princeton: Princeton University Press.

Regosin, Richard L. (1977). *The Matter of My Book: Montaigne's 'Essais' as the Book of the Self.* Berkeley: University of California Press.

Taylor, Charles Taylor (1989). *Sources of the Self: The Making of Modern Identity.* Cambridge: Cambridge University Press.

Vickers, Brian (1968). *Francis Bacon and Renaissance Prose.* Cambridge: Cambridge University Press.

Vickers, Brian (ed.) (1968). *Essential Articles for the Study of Francis Bacon.* Hamden, Conneticut: Archon.

Yates, Frances A. (1934). *John Florio: The Life of an Italian in Shakespeare's England.* Cambridge: Cambridge University Press.

Zagorin, Perez (1988). *Francis Bacon.* Princeton: Princeton University Press.

51

Diaries

Elizabeth Clarke

As Stuart Sherman complains in his intriguing study of diurnal form in literature, journals have hardly ever been given a literary treatment: they have been ransacked by historians for data, or classified into types. There are, however, two distinct categories of early modern journal. I am going to use the word 'diary' for the kind of document a modern reader would intuitively expect from the use of the word: a record of events, however brief or spasmodic, organized by date. The spiritual journal, which sometimes looks superficially like a diary, conforms to an entirely different set of rules. The link in this article with letters implies that diaries and journals are also 'private' documents. In fact, the truly 'private' diary, with its entrusting of intimate thoughts and experience to the printed page for the benefit of the writer, does not really occur until the nineteenth century (Bourcier, p. 7). In the early modern period, both types of document treated here are implicated in public discourse to a greater or lesser extent. No diary or journal was actually printed in the period under discussion, but in an age when manuscript culture was still strong, this does not rule out circulation, however limited. The place of diaries in manuscript culture, with its problems of survival and recovery, to some extent explains the lack of modern scholarship and the relative difficulty of conducting research.

The development of an individual self-consciousness during a 'Renaissance' has often been posited for the start and growth of diary culture, a theory confirmed in part by the early occurrence of journal-keeping in Italy, and the rather late emergence of the genre in England: it is not until 1660 that the practice is common. An alternative, or perhaps complementary origin may be found in the dissemination of a form of popular culture which emphasized the diurnal form, the almanac: this publication listed all kinds of events and information, including astrological changes, according to date, and was published yearly. There was a huge market for such pamphlets, and many were published with blank pages on which the owner could make his own notes (Bourcier, pp. 25–9). Many well-known diaries literally began in almanacs: Ralph Josselin, for example, and the famous John Evelyn, began separate diaries when they ran out of room on the blank pages in their almanacs. It is tempting to link the diary with the emergence of autobiographical writing in the later seventeenth century, but the impulse seems to be linked with a sense of history rather than autobiography, whatever 'history' meant to the individual. The subject often prefaces the diary proper with a brief account of his or her life to that date, as Elias Ashmole did. The word 'diary' as a title for a record of daily events seems to come into use in the 1640s, alongside the word 'diurnal'. It is thus deeply implicated in the recording and dissemination of public occurrences, and in fact many diary writers seem to be offering public news as well as or instead of personal event. In some cases of course, as in one of the earliest diaries by Edward VI, the two coincide to some extent. The chatty, informative diary of Samuel Pepys has shaped our idea of what a diary should be, although we tend to forget that it was entirely written in code, but of the diaries that survive, the tone and content vary enormously. Often a significant public event will prompt the commencement of a diary, as the execution of Sir Walter Ralegh did for William Whiteway in 1618. Sir Henry Slingsby's diary finishes with the execution of Charles I in 1649. There is certainly a sense that some writers feel that they are living in important times: Elizabeth Jekyll includes news of the battles of the Civil War, whilst John Ashton's short diary records his time as Privy Chamberman to Charles I during the first Bishops' War. Another common obsession is with the writer's own health: the recording of symptom and remedy, often rather explicit, is probably less due to hypochondria than a passionate interest in the emerging science of medicine.

The spiritual journal is more uniform in form and content, and it has a very specific origin, in the prescriptions of Puritan preachers. Again, England followed Europe, in this case Lutheran Germany, in the emergence of this discourse. Although the character of Protestant religion, with its practices of self-examination, clearly prompted the development of this form, there is a link with secular writing practices in that such daily examination is clearly a form of accounting. Richard Rogers in his *Seven Treatises* of 1603 suggests an evening reckoning-up of the blessings and sins of each day, but it is only to ministers that he suggests such an account should be written: he cannot count on the kind of widespread literacy that would make such a practice feasible.[1] Isaac Ambrose, writing in the mid-1650s, has no such scruple. His prescriptions for spiritual accounting are laid out as an account book, with columns: Elizabeth Mordaunt follows this practice.[2] He also offers sample entries from his own spiritual journal which he has been keeping from 1641 (Ambrose, I. *Media*. London, 1657, pp. 87–8, 163–8). In this example, the difference in conception from the secular diary is quite clear. The journal is not necessarily completed daily, but at any point considered spiritually significant by the writer: Elizabeth Turner chooses her wedding anniversary to make regular spiritual reckonings, whilst others use their birthday, and more commonly, Christmas and Easter (these last two Christian feasts entailed the taking of the Sacrament, for which there was a biblical injunction to self-examination). Isaac Ambrose does his spiritual accounting in the woods, as Mary Rich Countess of Warwick uses her 'wilderness', and writes down the results later. In fact, many spiritual journals have a retrospective character: the date at the top of the entry does not necessarily reflect the time of writing. To complicate the temporal scheme further, spiritual journals usually survive in transcripts, erasing what was clearly a feature of the original, the blank spaces left between entries to facilitate later addition, when, as Ambrose suggested for his final column, the 'Dispensation' of an event became clear. Eleanor Stockton's journal in Dr Williams's Library is one of the very few 'original' documents that survives (Dr Williams's Library MS 24. 8). This formal characteristic is linked to a providential theology in which God's purpose could only be ascertained from the outcome of an event, perhaps years later. Jane Ratcliffe was commended in her funeral sermon by John Ley in 1640, for keeping a journal in just this way. The emphasis in such documents is on God's actions in the world, rather than the subject's own, which is extremely frustrating for historians, who often find little detail of person, place or event within the spiritual journal. Isaac Ambrose's exemplary entries are entirely concerned with his spiritual state, as are the many volumes of Lady Mary Rich's journal: as Countess of Warwick she knew key figures in seventeenth century religion and politics, but alludes to events of the period indirectly and non-specifically (British Library MSS Add. 27351–8). Even more frustratingly, choice details such as names are often abbreviated, and sins committed are often written in incomprehensible code (Sir Humphrey Mildmay abbreviated the names of prostitutes, and John Winthrop registered his sins in code). It was only because Elizabeth Jekyll could see the hand of God so clearly in the conduct of 1640s battles that she recorded their outcomes in her own spiritual journal (Beinecke MS Osborn *b*.221). Katherine Austen described the progress of her lawsuits, convinced of similar Divine involvement (British Library Add MS 4454).

The survival of many of these manuscripts, several in scribal copies, indicates their value for the Protestant community, which had developed very little devotional literature in the early modern period, and often felt itself to be under siege. Ralph Josselin and Sarah Henry report the reading of other people's manuscript journals to be an encouragement.[3] The first printing of such a document was *A Narration of the Life of Mr. Henry Burton* in 1643, which was obviously politically motivated: he had suffered years of imprisonment under Archbishop Laud. In fact, several extracts from such 'closet-writing' appear in funeral sermons: such writing is assumed to be proof of one's spiritual virtue, as for Elizabeth Juxon, married to a wealthy London citizen, whose writing is embedded in her funeral sermon of 1619. It is also perceived as containing the trace of Holy Spirit, present in the closet as nowhere else except the deathbed. Richard Baxter produced, as conclusive proof of her elect condition, the spiritual diary of twenty-five-year-old Jane Baker, for whom he preached a funeral sermon in 1659. For more politically engaged personages such as the Earl of Warwick who died in 1658 and William Waller's wife Anne who died in 1663, such written proof of holiness turns the funeral sermon into political oratory. The spiritual journal acquired particular significance after the Restoration, when so many practices of personal holiness surviving from the devotion of the pre-Civil War Church of England became the property of the persecuted Dissenting community. The radical and astute

Lucy Hutchinson bequeathed her own journal to the Earl of Anglesey, whose influence was so important to Dissenters: he records reading it in the crucial year of 1682.[4] In the quest for truthful language which is the negative inheritance of earlier preoccupations with classical rhetoric, such 'closet-writing' is seen to escape the sin of insincerity inherent in any discourse which has an audience. Ironically, it could also be used against the writer, as Archbishop Laud's was by William Prynne, although his claim that sceptics could inspect the original, written in Laud's own hand, was somewhat disingenuous, as Prynne had altered it.[5] Two non-Puritan spiritual journals survive because their female authors clearly saw the potential of the form to achieve aims other than merely spiritual propaganda. Alice Thornton's first 'Book of Remembrances' is dated 1668, and was part of an attempt to refute accusations of unchastity: 'I sent my own Book of my Life, the collections of God's dealings and mercies to me and all mine . . . to satisfy all my friends of my life and conversation . . . that it was not such as my deadly enemies suggested.'[6] She offered a contents to help her readers interpret this document, and reported a successful outcome. Anne Halkett's well known autobiography, justifying her relationship with Colonel Bamfield, was composed in a break from writing her rather more extensive spiritual journal which was clearly perceived as a similar vindicatory project: her minister published extracts after her death (National Library of Scotland, MSS 6489-502).

It is tempting to see the lack of concern with external occurrence in spiritual writing in terms of class, as Margaret Spufford does (Spufford, p. 408): details of families and place could be seen as more important to aristocrats like Anne Clifford with genealogy and inheritance to consider, whilst the most important element in the Kent nonconformist Elizabeth Turner's life was her relationship with Christ (Kent Archives Office, MS F. 27). The gendered politics of the seventeenth century, which demanded higher levels of holiness from women, is probably one reason why fewer women's secular diaries survive. In any case, in this period, women's literacy rate was well below men's. Different communities will have found value in different kinds of document, which is why spiritual writings rather than secular diaries will have been preserved from a radical sectarian background. However, our perceptions are probably skewed by the low survival rate of manuscripts outside of an aristocratic context, where the stately home would have proved a safe repository for the family papers. Documents are still found in these private houses: Elizabeth Mordaunt's fascinating spiritual journal, with poems often linked to dates, was found in the mid-nineteenth century. The diary of Elizabeth, Countess of Burlington has just come to light at Chatsworth, uncatalogued in the Lismore Papers. One male artisan's diary does survive, however, and it challenges the priority of the spiritual journal in lower-class contexts. Roger Lowe was a passionate Presbyterian, but the interest driving his diary was clearly Romance: he records his courting of various women (sometimes simultaneously) and after his marriage the diary tails off rather quickly (Sachse, W. *The Diary of Roger Lowe of Ashton-in-Mansfield, Lancs., 1663–74*. London: Longman, 1938). His interest in diary-writing might stem from his acquaintance with the more famous diarist Adam Martindale, who offered to find him a wife.

Despite the categories posited in this chapter, it is probably a misrepresentation of early modern manuscript practice to assume that a writer consciously chose between the spiritual journal and the secular diary. Where substantial manuscripts survive, as with Grace Mildmay's papers, there is evidence of different kinds of documents being compiled simultaneously: sometimes a brief secular diary is later rewritten into a spiritual journal, as Samuel Sewall's was. It is difficult to make any generalizations about a manuscript form, simply because of eccentric patterns of survival. We have to thank the antiquarians of the eighteenth and nineteenth centuries for the diaries that were printed, despite their common practice of editing out material they did not consider 'interesting' — and to continue to search in record offices and stately homes for manuscripts that throw light on this common but elusive writing practice of the early modern period.

NOTES

The research for and writing of this chapter took place during a one-year Leverhulme Fellowship, 1999.

1 Rogers, R. *Seven Treatises, Containing such direction as is gathered out of the Holy Scriptures.* London: 1603, pp. 590, 586.
2 *The private diarie of Elizabeth, Viscountess Mordaunt.* E. Macrory (ed.) Duncairn: 1856, pp. 225–239.
3 Macfarlane, A. (ed). (1976). *The Diary of Ralph Josselin 1616–83.* Oxford: Oxford Uni-

versity Press, p. 296: Bodleian MS Eng. Misc. e. 331, p. 299.
4 Norbrook, D. (1997). 'Lucy Hutchinson's "Elegies" and the Situation of the Republican Woman Writer', *ELR* 27, p. 485.
5 Prynne, W. (ed.) (1644). *A Breviate of the Life of William Laud, Archbishop of Canterbury: Extracted (for the most part) Verbatim, out of his Own Diary, and other Writings, under His own Hand.*
6 *The Autobiography of Mrs Alice Thornton.* Surtees Society 62, Edinburgh, 1873, p. 259.

REFERENCES AND FURTHER READING

Bourcier, E. (1976). *Les journaux privés en Angleterre de 1600 à 1660. (Personal diaries in England from 1600–1660.)* Paris: Publications de la Sorbonne.

Crawford, P. (1988). 'Katherine and Philip Henry and Their Children: A Case Study in Family Ideology', *Transactions of the Historical Study of Lancashire and Cheshire*, 134, 39–74.

Halsey Thomas, M. (ed.), (1973). *The Diary of Samuel Sewall, 1674–1729.* New York: Farrar, Straus and Giroux.

Knappen, M. (ed.), (1933). *Two Elizabethan Puritan Diaries by Richard Rogers and Samuel Ward.* Chicago: American Society of Church History.

Mendelsson, S. H. (1987). *The Mental World of Stuart Women: Three Studies.* Brighton: Harvester.

Pollock, L. (1993). *With Faith and Physic: The Life of a Tudor Gentlewoman.* London: Collins and Brown.

Ponsonby, A. (1923). *English Diaries: A Review of English Diaries from the Sixteenth to the Twentieth Century.* London: Methuen.

——(1927). *More English Diaries: Further Reviews of Diaries from the Sixteenth to the Nineteenth Century.* London: Methuen.

Seaver, P. S. (1985). *Wallington's World: A Puritan Artisan in Seventeenth-Century London.* London: Methuen.

Sherman, S. (1986). *Telling Time: Clocks, Diaries*

and English Diurnal Form, 1660–1785. Chicago: University of Chicago Press.

Spufford, M. (1979). 'First Steps in Literacy: The Reading and Writing Experiences of the Humblest Spiritual Autobiographers', *Social History*, 4, 407–35.

Von Greyerz, K. (1990). *Vorsehungsglaube und Kosmologie: Studien zu englischen Selbstzeugnissen des 17. Jahrhunderts. (Providential Belief and Cosmology: Studies in English Spiritual Journals of the Seventeenth Century.)* Zurich: Vandenhoeck and Ruprecht.

52

Letters

Jonathan Gibson

Letters were central to early modern culture (Guillén; Thompson). They were important partly because the letter's notional restriction to two people (writer and addressee) mirrored the key part played by 'dyadic' (two-person) relationships in all aspects – 'public' and 'private' – of early modern life. The complexity and oddness of early modern letters is a reflection of the complexity of early modern social relations.

Throughout the early modern period, the composition of Latin letters, guided by handbooks by Erasmus and others, was at the heart of humanist grammar school education. Letter writing was introduced to pupils at the important transition between 'lower school' grammar lessons and 'upper school' lessons in rhetoric. The letter was thus the first extended rhetorical form most schoolboys were taught. For many it was also the last, as some schools chose not to make pupils compose orations.[1]

Early modern schoolboys were faced by a composite epistolary theory made up of three interrelated traditions: (1) the medieval *ars dictaminis*; (2) early modern rhetorical theory; (3) the revived theory of the 'familiar' letter. These approaches were also available in printed English epistolographies and formularies.[2] (*salutatio*) and a section currying favour with the addressee (*captatio benevolentiae*):

1 *narratio* (background narration)
2 *petitio* (request, a medieval innovation)
3 *peroratio* (conclusion).

The registering of hierarchical relationships was central both to the *ars dictaminis* and to renaissance epistolary theory and practice. Accordingly, in the early modern period dictaminal methods of demarcating the writer's and recipient's relative status were adapted and expanded (Magnusson; Hornbeak, pp. 1–29; Robertson, pp. 9–24). Pseudo-Ciceronian letter structure, meanwhile, continued to be important and can be found underpinning many early modern letters. More generally, Renaissance epistolography tended to follow the *ars dictaminis* in treating letters as orations, adding, however, many of elaborate prescriptions adapted from newly discovered classical texts such as Quintilian's *De institutione oratoria* (Henderson 1983). At the same time, early modern theorists brought to letter writing a stronger sense of the individual writer's potential for rhetorical power.

An added complication was the humanist revival of the classical idea that letters should be 'familiar': loosely structured, free of strict rhetorical rules and inspired by selfless *amicitia*.[3] The motivation of the 'familiar letter' was seen as twofold: to transmute into emotional presence the absence of writer and addressee and to strengthen the bonds of friendship. In pursuit of this ideal, letters by Cicero, Pliny the Younger and Seneca were read and imitated.

The early modern letter writer was pulled in three directions by these different approaches. The joker in the pack was the ideal of the familiar letter, opposed, in essence, both to the application of elaborate rhetorical rules to letter writing and, in its emphasis on friendship between equals, to the highlighting of social hierarchies. Much Renaissance epistolography – for example, Erasmus's key text, *De conscribendis epistolis*[4] – attempted, with varying degrees of success, to pull these traditions together, and the influence of all three can be detected in early modern letters written in English: throughout the period, English letter-writers struggled to find ways to balance epistolary 'familiarity', social deference and rhetorical power.

Over time, the ideal of the familiar letter became increasingly dominant, spurred on by the epistolographies of Juan Luis Vives and Justus Lipsius, both of which advocated the writing of flexible, non-rhetorical letters.[5] The middle of the seventeenth century saw a new influence on familiar letters: the witty, 'précieux' style pioneered in France by Jean Guez de Balzac and codified in the epistolographies of Jean Puget de la Serre (Hornbeak, pp. 50–76).

Many thousands of early modern letters are extant,[6] exemplifying most of the classes of letter catalogued in contemporary handbooks: petitionary letters written by clients seeking favour from their patrons; letters of command from superiors to those lower in the social scale; hortatory letters from parents to children; dutiful letters from children to parents; letters of recommendation, consolation and advice; love letters. Many letters can be classified rather vaguely as 'newsletters': 'news' of all kinds was retailed, *inter alia*, between friends and family, from servant to master (as a form of service) and from ambassadors to central government.[7] Many letters, of course, performed more than one function: theorists of the familiar letter often stressed its capacity to contain any and every sort of material. Letters written in the first half of the sixteenth century tend to use simpler rhetorical strategies than letters written later on, a stylistic shift particularly noticeable in *exordia*. Later still, in the seventeenth century, the influence of Balzac's preciosity produced extravagantly witty letters and unusual, fanciful imagery. In her famous love letters to William Temple (1652–4), unpublished until the nineteenth century, Dorothy Osborne cultivated a plain style in reaction against the French fashion.[8]

Letter-writing often involved the compilation (often in association with a scribe) of a manuscript 'letter-book'. Letter-books varied greatly, often bringing together several different types of letter: letters received; copies of letters sent; form letters; copies of interesting letters attributed to famous people.[9] The importance of the compilation of letter books for seventeenth-century women has recently been highlighted by Frances Harris.[10] Letter-writing was in itself particularly important for early modern women, as it offered a relatively rare opportunity for respectable 'literary' activity (Byrne, pp. 65–7; Steen).

Two categories of third party were often involved in the epistolary process: (1) Secretaries – sometimes they composed their employer's letters for them; sometimes they 'worked up' rough authorial drafts; sometimes they just took dictation;[11] (2) The messengers who, in the absence before 1680 of an assured public postal service, delivered the letters.

Recent scholarship has made much of complex homosocial relationships between renaissance secretaries and the employers to whose 'secrets' they were privy.[12] Messengers, though, were equally important: like secretaries, they were extensions (and sometimes traitors) of the will of the letter-writer. The ideal messenger was someone close to the writer – a friend or close personal servant whose presence could go some way towards compensating for the writer's absence and who could be trusted. Confiding one's text to the wrong messenger could have perilous repercussions. In such circumstances it is unsurprising that letter-delivery is discussed at length in many Renaissance letters. Uncertainty about the reliability of delivery meant that many early modern letter writers were very cagey about what they committed to paper. Many letters from the period in fact say very little: the important message was left to the messenger to give by word of mouth.

Behind early modern letters, then, are complicated secret histories – elaborately terraced negotiations, oral and written, often involving a surprisingly large number of people. Letters were often deliberately written to be passed on. Often they were, for example, written with the intention that they be read out and glossed by a 'primary addressee' to a 'secondary addressee'.[13] Many 'letters', such as Sidney's letter to Queen Elizabeth on the French match, were deliberately circulated more widely than this, functioning, in effect, as 'published' manuscript treatises. This practice had a long history, dating back to antiquity and persisting throughout the middle ages. Most medieval letters were, according to Giles Constable, 'self-conscious, quasi-public literary documents, often written with an eye to future collection and publication'.[14] 'Epistolary' circulation of this type was a central plank in early modern 'manuscript culture' and arguably underpinned the early modern literary system as a whole. For the Renaissance reading public, the letter, addressed from one individual to another, was the paradigmatic form of written communication. Accordingly, early modern printed books repeatedly (and often voyeuristically[15]) invoked the comforting ghosts of specific addressees. Letters – dedicatory epistles – prefaced most books printed in the early modern period, and printed books in many genres – reports on foreign wars; polemics; learned tracts; religious consolation – took an epistolary form. Letters abound in early modern prose fiction (a genre which overlaps significantly with the genre of the epistolary formulary (Robertson)) and drama. The verse epistle, meanwhile, enjoyed two periods of great popularity: in the first half of the sixteenth century (influenced by Chaucer's *Troilus and Criseyde* (Lerer)) and in the 1590s to 1630s.

Single-author collections of original letters in English were not much printed until after the period covered by this Companion. Pioneering examples of the genre include Joseph Hall's Senecan meditations (1608–10) and, in reaction against Balzacian preciosity, James Howell's newsy *Epistolae Ho-Elianae* (1645–55).[16] Sir John Suckling's witty, French-influenced, letters were published posthumously in 1646. Collections such as these had, since antiquity, fictionalized some of their contents to give the best possible impression of the author, a tradition reaching its apogee in the published letters of humanists such as Erasmus.[17] Howell's book follows in the same tradition, as, with a difference, do the collections of John Donne's letters made by his son in 1651 and 1660.[18] Donne the younger altered the names of the addressees of many of his father's letters to names of more important people primarily to gain favour for himself with his patron. Less obviously falsifying, the Spenser–Harvey correspondence (1580) is nevertheless a close and interesting Anglicization of self-puffing Latin humanist epistles.

Current critical interest in blurring the boundaries between literature and history suggests that early modern letters will increasingly be the object of research by 'literary' critics. Certainly, much more research is needed if the complexities and subtleties of the genre are to be adequately understood and appreciated.

NOTES

1   Baldwin, T. W. (1944). *William Shakespere's Small Latine and Lesse Greeke* (I, pp. 89–90 I, 99–101, 132–3, 155–63, 363, 402, 413). Urbana: University of Illinois Press.

2   For example, Fulwood, W. (1571). *The Enemie of Idlenesse*; Day, A. (1586). *The English Secretorie*. See Horbeak and Robertson. Manuscript formularies were also used.

3   Humanist interest in the 'familiar letter' was stimulated by Petrarch's discovery of Cicero's letters to Atticus. Even so, many elements of the classical theory of the familiar letter had persisted throughout the middle ages: see Constable, G. (1976). *Letters and Letter-Collections* (pp. 15–16, 40). Turnhout: Brepols.

4   Sowards, J. K. (ed.). (1985). *Collected Works of Erasmus: Literary and Educational Writings 3*. Toronto: University of Toronto Press.

5   Vives, J. L. (1989). *De conscribendis epistolis*. ed. and tr. C. Fantazzi. Leiden: Brill; Lipsius, J. (1996). *Principles of Letter-Writing: A Bilingual Text of Justi Lipsi Epistolica Institutio*, eds

R. V. Young and M. T. Hester. Carbondale: Southern Illinois University Press.

6   For a good list of printed sources see Watson, G. (1976). *The New Cambridge Bibliography of English Literature* (I). Cambridge: Cambridge University Press.

7   From the 1590s, professional writers of newsletters such as John Chamberlain started operating, producing personalized letters for several clients simultaneously.

8   Osborne, Dorothy (1987). *Letters*, ed. K. Parker, Harmondsworth: Penguin; Lerch-Davis, Genie S. (1978). 'Rebellion against Public Prose: The Letters of Dorothy Osborne to William Temple (1652–4)'. *Texas Studies in Literature and Language*, 20, pp. 386–415.

9   Braunmuller, A. R. (ed.). (1983). *A Seventeenth-century Letter-Book: A Facsimile of Folger MS. V.a. 321*. Newark: University of Delaware Press.

10 Harris, F. (1998). 'The Letterbooks of Mary

Evelyn', *English Manuscript Studies 1100–1700*, 7, pp. 202–15.

11 A letter written in one's own hand signified strong personal investment in the message. The use of a scribe conveyed respect and ceremony.

12 Rambuss, R. (1993). *Spenser's Secret Career* (Cambridge: Cambridge University Press); Stewart, A. (1997). *Close Readers: Humanism and Sodomy in Early Modern England*. Princeton, New Jersey: Princeton University Press.

13 A vivid window onto this world is provided by the letters written to Robert Sidney by Rowland Whyte, Sidney's agent at court during his absence in the low countries. See Collins, A. (ed.). (1746). *Letters and Memorials of State*, London, 3 vols.

14 Constable, p. 11.

15 For the complex relationship between voyeurism and letters see Lerer. Lerer's work usefully complements the post-structuralist analysis of early modern letters in Goldberg, Jonathan (1990). *Writing Matter: From the Hands of the English Renaissance*. Stanford: Stanford University Press.

16 For the political context of Howell's collection see Patterson, A. (1984). 'Letters to Friends: The Self in Familiar Form'. In *Censorship and Interpretation: The Conditions of Writing and Reading in Early Modern England* (pp. 203–32). Madison: University of Wisconsin Press.

17 Jardine, L. (1993). *Erasmus, Man of Letters: The Construction of Charisma in Print*. Princeton: Princeton University Press. For the medieval prehistory see Constable.

18 Donne, J. (1977). *Letters to Severall Persons of Honour (1651). A Facsimile Reproduction*. ed. M. Thomas Hester. Delmar: Scholars' Facsimiles and Reprints.

References and Further Reading

Braunmuller, A. R. (1981). 'Editing Elizabethan letters'. *Text*, 1, pp. 185–99.

Byrne, M. St C. (1981). 'Introduction'. In M. St C. Byrne (ed.), *The Lisle Letters* (Vol. 1, pp. 1–136). Chicago: University of Chicago Press.

Guillén, C. (1986). 'Notes toward the Study of the Renaissance Letter'. In B. K. Lewalski (ed.), *Renaissance Genres: Essays in Theory, History and Interpretation* (pp. 70–101). Cambridge, MA: Harvard University Press.

Henderson, J. R. (1983). 'Erasmus on the Art of Letter-writing'. In J. J. Murphy (ed.), *Renaissance Eloquence: Studies in the Theory and Practice of Renaissance Rhetoric* (pp. 331–55). Berkeley: University of California Press.

——(1993). 'On Reading the Rhetoric of the Renaissance Letter'. In H. F. Plett (ed.). *Renaissance-Rhetorik/Renaissance Rhetoric* (pp. 143–62). Berlin: De Gruyter.

Hornbeak, K. G. (1934). *The Complete Letter-Writer in English, 1568–1800*. Northampton, MA: Smith College.

Jardine, L. (1996). 'Reading and the Technology of Textual Affect: Erasmus's Familiar Letters and Shakespeare's *King Lear*'. In *Reading Shakespeare Historically* (pp. 78–97). London: Routledge.

Lerer, S. (1997). *Courtly Letters in the Age of Henry VIII: Literary Culture and the Arts of Deceit*. Cambridge: Cambridge University Press.

Magnusson, L. (1999). *Shakespeare and Social Dialogue: Dramatic Language and Elizabethan Letters*. Cambridge: Cambridge University Press.

Robertson, J. (1942). *The Art of Letter Writing: An Essay on the Handbooks Published in England during the Sixteenth and Seventeenth Centuries*. London: University Press of Liverpool.

Steen, S. J. (ed.), (1994). *The Letters of Lady Arabella Stuart*. New York: Oxford University Press.

Thompson, E. N. (1924). 'Familiar letters'. In Thompson, E. N. *Literary Bypaths of the Renaissance* (pp. 91–126). New Haven: Yale University Press.

Whigham, Frank (1981). 'The Rhetoric of Elizabethan Suitors' Letters', *PMLA*, 96, 864–82.

PART FIVE
Issues and Debates

53

Rhetoric

Marion Trousdale

'The duty and office of Rhetoric,' Francis Bacon wrote in *The Advancement of Learning*, 'is to apply Reason to Imagination for the better moving of the will'. To that end the art of rhetoric dominated Renaissance culture as it dominated the curricula of early modern schooling. The *reason* Bacon refers to is represented by Aristotelean dialectic, concerned with those things in life about which we cannot have certain knowledge. Aristotle's dialectic was based upon *topoi*, or places by means of which one could discover everything there was to say about any given subject. The imagination pertains to the power that bodies forth images and the language that shapes them. It meant using figures of speech to affect the emotions. It was by means of such language that the passions were engaged and the will was moved. Obviously classical in origin, rhetoric for the humanists was a means of attaining both a literature and a civilization comparable to that of Augustan Rome.

For the leading sophist in Greece and possibly the first rhetor, Isocrates, rhetoric was a means of teaching Greeks how to be politically and legally effective by means of their tongues. In Greece and again in the Renaissance persuasive speech was recognized as a civic responsibility and the ultimate accomplishment of any individual life.

The training itself in early modern schools and universities across Europe, drawing upon classical models, was obsessive in its taxonomy and in its exhaustive commitment to enumeration. Its faith in the ability of rules to create eloquent speaking or writing to those who have taught freshman composition can only seem naive. Yet both the belief in the practice and the craft by means of which it was mastered are a dominant aspect of Renaissance culture, one that shapes teaching practices, writing practices, political practices, social life. Roland Barthes, in one of the most useful discussions of this ancient practice, calls rhetoric a veritable empire, greater and more tenacious than any political empire in its dimensions and its duration (p. 6). And Brian Vickers observes rightly that no adequate account of human culture since the Greeks could be written without taking account of rhetoric (1988, p. 6).

Traditionally there are three kinds. Demonstrative also known as epidectic, the use of language to praise or blame, is the one most commonly associated with literary texts. Aristotle at the beginning of the *Poetics* writes that all poetic discourse is either praise or blame. The epidectic is very strongly linked to ethics, as praising or blaming were believed to be a means of controlling an individual's moral action. The other two are forensic, the rhetoric used in courts of law, and deliberative, the rhetoric of political discussions practised in town meetings, parliaments, deliberative governing bodies. But the rhetoric the Renaissance studied and that shaped common concerns was forensic in training and forensic in representation, though it sometimes went under other names (Sloane, p. 165). It was seen as a means of influencing those in power, of winning arguments, of controlling other minds. It was in essence a training for lawyers, and most importantly for our purposes here, one that enabled anyone so trained to argue both sides of a case.

When Socrates in Plato's dialogue *Phaedrus* argues first for love and then against love, as Brian Vickers points out in *In Defence of Rhetoric*, he presents the earliest example of *in utramque partem*, arguing both sides (pp. 15–16). Aristotle had said that one must be able to use rhetoric as one used logic on either side of an argument in order to determine where the truth lay. Cicero, in whose courtroom practices many of the technical aspects of argumentation were discovered, characterizes his own practice as that of first making his client explain his side of the case fully, then arguing the opponent's case to help the client make his own argument stronger. In the last stages of preparation for the courtroom, Cicero remarks, 'In my own person and with perfect impartiality I play three characters – myself, my opponent and the arbitrator. In this way I gain the advantage of reflecting first on what to say and saying it later' (*De Oratore*: Vickers, 1982, p. 13). But it was not only lawyers who were so trained. In the sixteenth and early seventeenth centuries at Oxford or Cambridge, university students in their first year were required to attend disputations, and in order to qualify for a degree they had to show themselves able to dispute. Disputations were performed at the universities to entertain important guests. It is a sensibility we can only partly understand. Disputations made up part of the entertainment for both Elizabeth and James. With Elizabeth as royal audience the students debated whether monarchy was the best form of government and whether frequent changes of law were dangerous.

One can see even in Cicero's remarks the extent to which the practices of rhetoric encouraged the playing of parts. It encouraged, as well, an acute awareness of verbal strategies and the recognition that whatever language might appear to represent, one could never simply accept verbal discourse at face value. All verbal structures were polysemous by nature and multi-faceted. But they were also strategic. Texts both oral and written had to be consciously constructed with full awareness of desired effect. The same texts had to be carefully listened to and read, with conscious awareness of the composer's craft. The significant statement here in Cicero's observations, one that becomes most important in Renaissance attitudes toward rhetoric, is his commitment to being able to do what Socrates had earlier done – argue both sides (*in utramque partem*). A man sufficiently skilled to argue persuasively two opposing points of view – and it is that that students had to master to be awarded a university degree – is a man capable not only of saving the just but of damning them as well. It is a highly skilled and highly trained technique of argument in which skill, which means effectiveness in use, is not dependent upon the truth of the argument being made.

That skill is what the Renaissance considered an art, that is to say a technique which today we would describe as a science. Once mastered, it imparts to the rhetor, potentially at least, enormous power, the power through speech to move others to action. And action very particularly is its aim. 'Although profoundness of wisdom will help a man to a name or admiration,' Francis Bacon noted, 'it is eloquence that prevaileth in an active life' (Vickers, 1982, p. 26).

How pervasive was this interest in personal power? I want to answer that question in part by looking briefly at the early texts and I start with what was to be the standard text for half a century in England. Thomas Wilson's *The Art of Rhetoric* was written during the summer of 1552 at the home of Edward Dymoke in Lincolnshire and first published in 1553. It was reissued in 1560 at the suggestion of the publisher but without the revision which Wilson had refused to undertake. It appeared in subsequent editions in 1562, 1563, 1567, 1580, 1584, and 1585. It was the third rhetoric text in English to be published in the sixteenth-century and the most complete. Wilson conceived of it as a companion to his logic, *The Rule of Reason*, first published in 1551. Earlier Leonard Cox, a grammar-school teacher, published *The Art or Craft of Rhetoric*, probably in 1530. Cox's book was a translation of Philip Melanchthon's *Institutiones Rhetoricae* addressed to Cox's students. The book was reissued in 1532. Richard Sherry published a *Treatise of Schemes and Tropes* in 1550. The first text principally concerned the topics (or 'places') by means of which students were meant to investigate any given subject to determine what material could be discovered before they determined how most effectively to arrange the material so as to make a persuasive argument. Sherry's treatise reflected the rhetoric devised by the French scholar known as Petrus Ramus (Pierre la Ramée) in which invention or the discovery of topics, was not deemed part of rhetoric. Sherry's treatise has only the verbal schemes and tropes which were seen as the ornaments added after the topics had been discovered and the structure of the argument determined. They constituted the embellishing of the argument that through pity and delight moved the hearer or reader to action. Later in 1570 Ramus was published in London in a translation under the title *The Logic of Pierre de la Ramée*. In 1588 Abraham Fraunce continued the emphasis upon figures of speech by publishing the *Arcadian Rhetoric* in which all of the examples were taken from Sir Philip Sidney's *Arcadia*. The tradition was continued by Henry Peacham the Elder in *The Garden of Eloquence* in 1593. Another very important text in English is George Puttenham's *The Art of English Poesie* written for courtiers which uses the principles of rhetoric for the writing of English verse.

Before any texts in English had appeared, Erasmus had written *De Utraque Verborum ac Rerum Copia* at the request of John Colet for the students at the new school of St Paul's. Erasmus's text was first published in 1512 and is particularly important both because of its widespread use in schools and because it shows us the ways in which both varying and copiousness were seen as a means of producing a national literature. It was felt that by tracing Virgil's use and transformation of figures in Homer and by learning to vary phrases of his own, a student would improve his knowledge of Greek and Latin and could learn as well how to write in English a verse as moving and incisive as Virgil's.

To judge by its publishing history it was Wilson's text that was the most popular of the texts in English. (Many scholars think it was the textbook Shakespeare used.) Wilson covered all parts of rhetoric, even demonstrative or epidectic. And in all instances the places of invention are the means of discovery of the matter from which an argument can be made. In recommending a particular course of action, for instance, he suggests the speaker consider whether it was honest, possible, easy to be done, hard to be done, possible to be done, impossible to be done. In an oration deliberative he advises the speaker to consider whether it was profitable, to whom, when, where, wherefrom. In analysing an action he suggests that one ask who did the deed, what was done, where it was done, what help did he to it, wherefore he did it, how he did it, at what time he did it. In illustrating the places of invention in order to discover the store of matter available he takes the example of a magistrate and he suggests one consider the definition, the general rule, the kind, words yoked, words necessarily joined, those casually joined, the thing containing, the efficient cause, the second efficient cause, the end. As an example of persuasive prose he includes Erasmus' 'Epistle to Persuade a Young Gentleman to Marriage'. Schemes and tropes he talks about only briefly at the end.

Erasmus's *De Copia* uses the places of invention in a slightly different way because he makes copiousness the most important skill in speaking or writing. The places of invention provide the means of creating such richness. Nothing, he says is more admirable or more splendid than a speech with a rich *copia* of thoughts and words overflowing in a golden stream. Speaking is not any different in its requirements from furnishing a house or in planning a meal. Erasmus wants the furnishings of a rich house to exhibit the greatest variety, but in good taste, and at a splendid banquet he wants various kinds of food, but all of it excellent. To illustrate variety, Erasmus takes the sentence 'Your letter has delighted me very much', and he varies it a hundred and forty-eight ways. 'Your letter has delighted me very much', he begins. 'In a wonderful way your letter has delighted me . . . I have been delighted in an unusually wonderful way by your letter . . . Your epistle has cheered me exceedingly. In truth by your epistle I have been exceedingly cheered. Your note has refreshed my spirit in no indifferent manner (Trousdale, 1982, pp. 44–5).' Erasmus's method of varying keeps the attention of its audience by engaging the mind and ear in systems of ordering that are at once continuous and continuously varied. Hamlet's 'To be or not to be' begins, for instance, by an explicit statement of its general idea, stated in both the affirmative and the negative. That semantic kernel is used in an unexpected way in the next four lines in which Shakespeare restates the general idea and unfolds it in Erasmian terms by dividing it into parts. *To be* Shakespeare associates not with action with which being has an affinity but with *inaction* – 'To suffer / The slings and sorrows of outrageous fortune'. To action, which he amplifies by drawing upon the place of circumstance, making the general question more specific, he gives as consequence, the ambiguous end of the sea of troubles – 'Or to take arms against a sea of troubles / And by opposing, end them'. In seeking copiousness Shakespeare does not fall into a kind of futile and amorphous loquacity that Erasmus warns against. Rather, he varies Hamlet's soliloquy in such a way that *end* by its use is attached syntactically to *die* and *sleep*, acquiring a semantic resonance that anticipates the use of *consummation* (Trousdale, 1982, pp. 58–60).

Handbooks of rhetoric not unlike those published in England proliferated throughout Europe in this period as part of the humanist agenda. James Murphy lists more than a thousand. Brian Vickers (1988, pp. 256–64) estimates that there were perhaps two thousand rhetoric books published between 1400 and 1700, each in an edition of between two hundred and fifty and a thousand copies. He also points out how intense the training was. 'The curriculum was not large, but the teaching was incredibly thorough. New facts were released sparely . . . and after the master's explanation the pupil would repeat it, memorise it, be asked to recite it, be tested again, repeat it, and be made to use it over and over' and he adds that the amount of repetition is frightening. In addition students started school at 6 a.m., and although there were breaks, and for lunch and dinner, remained in class until 7 in the evening. They did this for thirty-six weeks a year and for four to six years. They memorized the parts of an oration, the three styles, great quantities of sententiae from literary texts such as Virgil and Ovid, and more than a hundred figures of speech. They were to learn the figures, identify them in what they read, use them themselves in what they wrote. In addition they translated Latin passages into English and on another day put the English back into Latin. Obviously in school through the intense study of classical texts using the analytical tools furnished by rhetoric Elizabethan schoolboys learned to use what Vickers calls 'the full expressive resources of language'.

What were the effects of this training, of this preoccupation if not obsession with the fundamental importance of language in the structuring of society and in the enabling of civil life? Barthes argues that rhetoric was class-driven, a skill available only to an elite. But classical rhetoric was revived by the humanists who were committed to universal education. Erasmus had stated that he wanted the farmhand to be able to read the Bible while ploughing his fields, and the proliferation of manuals of rhetoric documented by James Murphy, many designed as how-to-do it books for those who could read, argues against any perceived restriction at the time to the entitled governing class. What it suggests instead is a belief, however naive, that anyone could master it, and a belief too that the skill was essential not only to lawyers but to the community as a whole. Because there is born in us the power to persuade each other and to show ourselves whatever we wish, Isocrates observed, we have become something different from brute beasts. It is speech that has made possible, laws about justice and injustice and honour and disgrace. Without such provisions we should not be able to live together.

Beyond that the ability to take a particular topic and to discover (*invenire*) in that topic an infinite number of other topics from which a speech could be constructed, a poem could be written, a play could be made, means that the discovery itself as an intellectual activity was indeed a means of invention as the etymology of the word ('coming upon') anticipates, and as such, a way of knowing. If what we know we know only by common words, then it is in the structures of discourse that the sources of such knowledge must lie. One of the most important texts in the period, Rudolph Agricola's *De Inventione Dialectica* published in the fifteenth century lists twenty-four places by means of which one can discover everything that is known about any given subject. Such investigation as a means of composition establishes a valid intellectual base for the human arts.

William J. Bouwsman in an important essay on 'Anxiety and the Formation of Early Modern Culture' argues that rhetoric was valued in the age for its plasticity, its ability to flow into and through every area of experience, for the ways in which it could cross inherited boundaries, infiltrate any discipline, structure any activity to create new and always malleable structures of its own. That fluidity came in part by the ways in which the practice was firmly situated both in place and occasion. No rhetorical argument was ever thought to be eternally valid or absolutely true. Rather, the discourse, as students were taught to perform it, was generated within the limited situations of the here and the now, and it was assumed that the situations would always be new. The verbal structures to be created, then, were finite and changeable and themselves constantly new. That is to say that the rhetorical activity was a means of discovery and hence not only of new literature but of new knowledge as well.

It is that sense of skilled improvisation, of the unexpected but seamless connectedness both to time and place that gives to so many of Shakespeare's plays their daunting energy and their verve. It is responsible as well for the ambiguity of argument and the covert possibilities of intent. Shakespeare's polysemous language and multifaceted characters reflect the double-edged skill of *utramque partem*. Shakespeare too, or at least his characters, knew how to argue on both sides. We see the practice of rhetoric in miniature, as it were, with its parts creaking in their mechanical, uncomprehending use as the Duke in *Love's Labour's Lost* reads out the letter that Costard has brought: 'as I am a gentleman, betook myself to walk: the time When? About the sixth hour, when beasts most graze, birds best peck, and men sit down to that nourishment which is called supper: so much for the time When. Now for the ground Which? Which, I mean, I walked upon: it is ycliped thy park. Then for the place Where? No where, I mean, I did encounter that obscene and most preposterous event that draweth from my snow-white pen the ebon-coloured ink which here thou viewest, beholdest, surveyest, or seest. But to the place Where? It standeth north-north-east and by east from the west corner of thy curious knotted garden' (1.1.234–46). Berowne's 'This is not so well as I looked for, but the best that ever I heard' brings the response from the king, 'Ay, the best for the worst' (1.1.279–82). The mental agility that rhetoric both encouraged and trained allows both Berowne and the king to play with figures of reversal while Costard in response to Armado's tendentious varying of a phrase 'that low-spirited swain . . . that base minnow of thy mirth . . . that unlettered small-knowing soul . . . that shallow vassal, which as I remember, hight Costard' to respond first with some doubt 'Me? . . . Still me?' And finally with relief as he hears his name 'O, me!' (1.1.247–57).

The humour created by this inept demonstration of the craft of persuasive speech might lend some credence to Barthes' observations about class. But it is the ineptness more than the class that is relevant here, for lack of skill in language is not only humorous but dangerous in the politics of the age. In *Coriolanus* Meninius quiets the hungry workers by the simple telling of a tale, but Coriolanus, unable to wrap his tongue around the words needed to win him the voices, and claiming his lack of strategical skill to be a self-defining virtue that allows him to betray Rome, is himself so moved by the words of Volumnia as she pleads for him to spare his city that the verbal agility that might have made him a senator instead, on the part of his mother, brings about his death. Such verbal agility is almost always seen as dangerous, but so is the lack of it, or at least the lack of awareness of it. Antony, allowed by Brutus to speak, draws from the topic of Caesar's death, Caesar's praise, even while professing that he has not come to praise Caesar but to bury him. Brutus, worried about Caesar's ambition, discovers a very different Caesar, one whom he imagines would become a tyrant if allowed to live. Shakespeare is here arguing both sides, *in utramque partem* with equal persuasiveness. But such verbal constructs, although they are seen as mimetic, are seen as well as constructs. It is the murder of Caesar, not his life, as used rhetorically by Antony, that brings an end to republican Rome.

This double-edged vision shows just how slippery the issues of rhetoric are in the period. Othello is brought down by one who is above all a superb rhetorician. Lacking knowledge of the skill, Othello lacks any defence against it. When Iago hesitates in his accusations of Desdemona (3.3) he is following the advice of Quintilian who points out that the technique of forcing the judge to beg for the needed information is an effective means of persuasion. Othello, who believes Iago to be honest, believes such reluctantly given testimony is evidence of his honesty and is hence convinced of the truth of his argument. Unaware of the techniques of persuasive verbal skills, he believes the feigning true. And Coriolanus, unwilling to be deceitful about the state of his true feelings, about what he professes to be his true self, for the sake of such honesty, betrays his country, not in order to save a friend, but in order not to violate his own sense of himself.

It cannot be stressed enough that these are in the period real-life situations. Advised by Francis Bacon in October 1596 to adopt a deceptive stance before the queen in order to keep her favour, Essex showed himself unable to do so. But Bacon's advice is the advice of a trained lawyer and a skilled rhetorician who knows that feigning is necessary in order to persuade, and that one must persuade to survive. Bacon tells Essex that the queen is under the impression that he is 'unrulable,' and she is particularly suspicious of his military ambitions. Bacon advises Essex to adopt several strategies in order to persuade the queen that he is ready to obey her every command. 'Your Lordship should never be without some particulars afoot which you should seem to pursue with earnestness and affection, and then let them fall, upon taking knowledge of her Majesty's opposition and dislike.' He advises Essex not to try for the Earl Marshal's place, a military position, but rather 'pretend to be as bookish and contemplative' as ever he was. He advises him as well to bring 'some martial man' into the Privy Council to deal directly with the queen on military affairs. He tells Essex that he (Essex) is accomplished in military matters and will eventually be given military command. But that in the meantime he should 'keep it in substance, but abolish it in shows to the Queen'. The queen is also concerned about his apparent popularity among the populace, and in this instance Bacon tells him again to abolish the impression of such popularity by talking against popularity with the queen, while continuing to do the things that have made him popular – keep it in substance but change it in words. He must, in other words, so order himself in the presence of the queen that he changes the opinion she has of him. Iago does this with Othello, while Coriolanus, like Essex, shows himself incapable of such deceit.

If we look again at *Coriolanus*, we can see other unexpected ways in which the practice of rhetoric changes the ways in which texts are read. Bouwsman (above) remarks on the plasticity that rhetoric created, the skill Erasmus thought the most important in the training of students. Machiavelli, in his *Discourses upon the first Decade of T. Livy* where his interest is in the preservation of commonwealths, looks at the story of Coriolanus in Livy and analyses what happened at Rome. He feels that without the tribunes, the citizens would have killed Coriolanus when he came out of the Senate. 'First you know Caius Martius is chief enemy to the people . . . We know't, we know't . . . Let us kill him' Shakespeare's play begins. 'How fit and useful it is, that the commonwealth with their laws give means to vent the choler which the universality hath conceived against any one citizen', Machiavelli observes, 'For if by an orderly course one citizen be suppressed, although it were wrongfully done, yet follows thereupon little or no disorder in the republic because the execution is done without any private man's power or assistance of foreign forces; which are those that take away the common liberty; but by the public and lawful power, which have particular bounds, nor any way pass so far as to damage the commonwealth'. The banishment of Coriolanus, then, to Machiavelli, far from being a tragedy, provided a legal means of preserving the republic. To Machiavelli it is not the commons but the nobility and what he describes as the poison that lurked in their breasts against the commons that is chiefly to blame. The great man who through military prowess and sheer bravery conquered Corioles was to Machiavelli not a great man at all. What he was, certainly, was a member of the nobility as he obviously was to Shakespeare. He was a skilled fighter capable of saving Rome. At the same time he was an irresponsible citizen who had no sense of civic duty. He had no skill in language. He was unable and unwilling to talk to the populace. He lacked that sense of civic duty that made skill at rhetoric a civic obligation.

What we see here is the fluidity of conceptual thinking that rhetoric enables. I once tried to describe this ingenuity as the separation between words and things. What I meant by that was that a particular narrative is not attached to a particular action. There are many ways of telling the story of Coriolanus just as there are many ways of praising the king. Such verbal dexterity is made possible within a culture only when language is seen as the most important gift given to man. Gombrich in *Art and Illusion* remarks that in classical writings on rhetoric we have perhaps the most careful analysis of any expressive medium ever undertaken (Rebhorn, p. 17) and certainly the importance given to rhetorical training meant a privileging of language over all other human traits. Nothing done with intelligence is done without speech, Isocrates had remarked (Vickers, 1988, p. 10) and in the period Coluccio Salutati pointed out that if men are distinguished from other living creatures by language, how much more excellent than other men is he who using his own reason stands forth with brilliant eloquence (Vickers, 1988, p. 270). One cannot separate such beliefs and the training by which they were implemented either from the events or from the literature created by the age. The historian Roger Lockyer points out how James I, trained when young in rhetoric and so adroit in his use of language, was so convinced of its primary importance to any human activity that he imagined that by letters alone he could prevent a European war.

'If there were perhaps two thousand rhetoric books published between 1400 and 1700, each in an edition of between two hundred and fifty and a thousand copies, and if each copy was read by anything from one reader to the dozens using a school text, then there must have been several million Europeans with a working knowledge of rhetoric', Brian Vickers writes in *In Defence of Rhetoric*. 'These included many of the Kings, princes and their counsellors, popes, bishops . . . all the professors, school-teachers, lawyers, historians, all the poets and dramatists, including the women' (p. 256), and he points out that 'credit for the ability of so many Renaissance writers to use the full expressive resources of language must be given to the humanist school-system'. He goes on to mention Christopher Marlowe at Canterbury, Edmund Spenser at Merchant Taylor's, Sir Philip Sidney and Fulke Greville at Shrewsbury, Shakespeare at Stratford Grammar School, Ben Jonson at Westminster, Hooker at Exeter Grammar School. The great works of the period are unimaginable without the intensive rhetorical training. But it was not only a way to write. It was also as we see in Machiavelli a way to read. And that reading had serious political implications. Classical texts like those of rhetoric were the means by which the humanists consciously undertook the creation of a new age. Fulke Greville, we know from a letter, went to Cambridge at one point to find a scholar to live with him and two others to remain at the university to collect passages from classical texts with which to inform political discussions. And Sir Thomas Arundel in writing to Sir Robert Cecil 18 February 1601 mentions that Henry Cuffe, once a professor of Greek at Oxford, was sent by Essex to read Aristotle's *Politics* to the Earl of Southampton in Paris, 'with such expositions', Arundel remarks, 'as I doubt did him but little good'. Lisa Jardine and Anthony Grafton call such readers facilitators and stress that the readings of the classical texts like the persuasive arguments that could be constructed from them were meant to move men to action. Thus rhetoric, the veritable empire as Barthes remarks, in both reading and writing as in the politics in which both were immersed definitively, structured the culture of the age.

REFERENCES AND FURTHER READING

Altman, Joel (1978). *The Tudor Play of Mind.* Berkeley: University of California Press.

Barthes, Roland (1994). 'The Old Rhetoric: An Aide-memoire'. In R. Howard (tr.), *Semiotic Challenge* (pp. 11–94). Oxford: Basil Blackwell.

Bouwsma, William J. (1980). 'Anxiety and the Formation of Early Modern Culture'. In Barbara C. Malament (ed.), *After the Reformation: Essays in Honour of J. H. Hexter* (pp. 215–46). Manchester: Manchester University Press.

Donawerth, Jane (1984). *Shakespeare and the 16th-century Study of Language.* Urbana, IL: University of Illinois Press.

Doran, Madeleine (1954). *Endeavors of Art.* Madison: University of Wisconsin Press.

Grafton, Anthony and Jardine, Lisa (1990). '"Studied for Action" How Gabriel Harvey Read His Livy', *Past and Present*, 129, 30–78.

Gray, Hanna H. (1963). 'Renaissance Humanism: The Pursuit of Eloquence', *Journal of the History of Ideas*, 24, 497–514.

Hoskins, John (1935). *Directions for Speech and Style*, ed. Hoyt H. Hudson. Princeton: Princeton University Press.

Howell, W. S. (1956). *Logic and Rhetoric in England, 1500–1700.* Princeton, NJ: Princeton University Press.

Joseph, Sister Miriam (1947). *Shakespeare's Use of the Arts of Language.* New York: Columbia University Press.

Kahn, Victoria (1985). *Rhetoric, Prudence and Skepticism in the Renaissance.* Ithaca, NY: Cornell University Press.

Lanham, Richard A. (1968). *A Handlist of Rhetorical Terms.* Berkeley: University of California Press.

——— (1976). *The Motives of Eloquence.* New Haven: Yale University Press.

McNally, Rudolph (1967). 'Rudolph Agricola's *De Inventione Dialectica Libri Tres*: A Translation of Selected Chapters'. Speech Monographs 34.

Machiavelli, N. (1636). *Discourses upon the first Decade of T. Livius translated out of the Italian*

with some marginal anidmaversions noting and taxing his errors. London: E.D.

Meerhoff, Kees (1994). 'The Significance of Philip Melanchthon's Rhetoric in the Renaissance'. In Peter Mack (ed.), *Renaissance Rhetoric* (pp. 46–62). New York: St Martin's Press.

Murphy, J. J. (1981). *Renaissance Rhetoric: A Short-title Catalogue of Works on Rhetorical Theory from the Beginning of Printing to A. D. 1700.* New York: Garland.

Norbrook, David (1994). 'Rhetoric, Ideology and the Elizabethan World Picture'. In Peter Mack (ed.), *Renaissance Rhetoric* (pp. 140–64). New York: St Martin's Press.

Ong, Walter J. (1958). *Ramus: Method and the Decay of Dialogue.* Cambridge: Harvard University Press.

Parker, Patricia (1987). *Literary Fat Ladies: Rhetoric, Gender, Property.* London: Methuen.

Pico Della Mirandola, G. (1952). 'On the Conflict of Philosophy and Rhetoric', tr. Q. Breem, *Journal of the History of Ideas*, 13, 384–412.

Pigman, G. W., the Third (1980). 'Versions of Imitation in the Renaissance', *Renaissance Quarterly*, 33, 1–32.

Plett, Heinrich F. (ed.) (1993). *Renaissance-Rhetorik / Renaissance Rhetoric.* Berlin: De Gruyter.

Puttenham, George (1936). *The Arte of English Poesie*, eds G. Willcock and A. Walker. Cambridge: Cambridge University Press.

Rebhorn, Wayne A. (1995). *The Emperor of Men's Minds: Literature and the Renaissance Discourse of Rhetoric.* Ithaca, NY: Cornell University Press.

Shuger, Debora (1988). *Sacred Rhetoric in the Renaissance.* Princeton, NJ: Princeton University Press.

Sloane, Thomas O. (1985). *Donne, Milton and the end of Humanist Rhetoric.* Berkeley: University of California Press.

Trimpi, W. (1983). *The Muses of One Mind: The Literary Analysis of Experience and Its Continuity.* Princeton, NJ: Princeton University Press.

Trousdale, Marion (1976). 'Recurrence and Renaissance', *English Literary Renaissance*, 6, 156–79.

——(1982). *Shakespeare and the Rhetoricians*. Chapel Hill: University of North Carolina Press.

Vickers, Brian (1982). *Rhetoric Revalued: Papers from the International Society for the History of Rhetoric*. Binghamton, NY: Center for Medieval and Early Renaissance Studies.

——(1988). *In Defence of Rhetoric*. Oxford: Clarendon.

54

Identity

A. J. Piesse

We are all framed of flaps and patches and of so shapeless and divers a contexture, that every piece and every moment playeth his part. And there is as much difference between us and ourselves, as there is between ourselves and others.

(Montaigne, Essays, tr. Florio, 1634 edn, p. 187)

Current Theory: Individuality and Subjectivity

It has been argued that humankind became conscious of its own innate diversity long before Montaigne articulated his assimilated, piecemeal sense of self. Before Sidney realized in *Astrophil and Stella* (published 1591) that study was a 'step-dame', an unnatural parent, and proposed instead to 'look in [his] heart and write', there are signs of different degrees of self-consciousness in English literature. The closing decades of the twentieth century have seen a proliferation of writing on the nature of identity in the early modern period. There are three or four recurrent themes: the notion of the individual, the construction of the subject, ideas of nationhood and the role of the ruler of the state.

As early as 1020, Colin Morris has pointed out, portraits differentiate between types and individual representation, and devotional writing in the first person exhorts the examination of an interior self (Morris 1972: 33, 65). But the critical trends of the late twentieth century saw the emergence of what Richard Hillman has called 'the self-speaking subject' in the later middle ages at the earliest, insisting further that the notion of self-interrogation in anything other than the religious sense flourishes across a range of disciplines only from the beginning of the sixteenth century (Hillman 1997: 2–3). Morris's investigations of individuality, and the works that corresponded to or furthered his thesis (Brandt 1966; Ullman 1967 and 1977; Hanning 1977), become sidelined by a continual redefinition of what constitutes the individual, with Belsey (1985), Greenblatt (1980) and Dollimore (1984) 'substantially displac[ing] earlier arguments (based on very different theoretical premises) that the Western European individual or self dates from around the twelfth century' (Hillman 3).

Late twentieth-century annexation of psychology and social history to the practice of literary criticism has led to fundamental re-readings of literary texts, and it is where these two disciplines meet that this newly defined history of individuality emerges. Since the huge impact created by Stephen Greenblatt's *Renaissance Self-Fashioning* (1980) and Catherine Belsey's *The Subject of Tragedy* (1985), the notion of the individual has come under pressure from a competing idea, that of the early modern subject. Belsey's formulation of the subject rests on a particular degree of self-consciousness:

> To be a subject is to have access to signifying practice, to identify with the 'I' of utterance and the 'I' who speaks. The subject is held in place in a specific discourse, a specific knowledge, by the meanings available there. In so far as signifying practice always precedes the individual, is always learned, the subject is a subjected being, an effect of the meanings it seems to possess. Subjectivity is discursively produced and is constrained by the range of subject positions defined by the discourses in which the concrete individual participates . . . existing discourses determine not only what can be said and understood, but the nature of subjectivity itself, what it is possible to be.
>
> (p. 5)

Belsey and Greenblatt have each argued that any formulation of individuality must be seen in the light of cultural context, that any exposition of self is a manifestation of a series of options, rather than something intrinsically different from anything else. Charles Taylor's *Sources of the Self* (1989) on the other hand, traces a fascinating development in western thought from the tensions between the Platonic and Aristotelian versions of the individual's relationship both to context and to interior self. Plato valorises *theoria*, contemplation of the unchanging order, a philosophical gaze focused on things exterior to the self. Aristotle, though, prefers *phronesis*, a practical wisdom, 'an understanding of the ever-changing, in which particular cases and predicaments are never exhaustively characterized in general rules' (Taylor: 125): in other words, a philosophical gaze that turns inward to the possibility of an individual account of Plato's *theoria*. Taylor goes on to explain how this distinction is refined through the work of Augustine, whom he credits with 'the proto-cogito' (p. 132), an early version of Descartes' famous *cogito ergo sum*, (I think, therefore I am), upon which dictum most accounts of modern individuality are based.

This is vital to an understanding of individuality in the early modern period, since it is to the classical philosophers that sixteenth-century scholars return with the arrival of Erasmian humanism in England. Erasmus' idea that proper investigation of any subject depended on going *ad fontes et ad res* – to the source and to the thing itself – urged a new way of seeing, relying simultaneously on knowledge – which we might equate loosely with Plato's *theoria* – and on experience.

Identifying the Issues

Whether we accept a self-conscious subject that is ready to construct itself and to be constructed by its context, or look instead for a subject whose image of self is the product of a more coherent connection between the inward and the outward gaze, it is easy to see that notions of the parameters of self are bound to change significantly if the context in which one lives undergoes a series of rapid changes. The sixteenth century is a period that sees a huge expansion of access to knowledge and experience. For example, it is recognized that the earth is not the centre of the known universe, which raises questions about humankind's place in relation to God (Copernicus, *De Revolutionibus*, 1530, published 1543). The establishment of the first printing presses in London (1476) begins a process by which texts are released to a wider audience; as the century progresses, the notion of the value of the printed text changes precisely because of its general availability (Eisenstein 1979; Davies 1976). Expansion in travel and trade routes reveals hitherto unthought-of cultures and races, which in turn forces western societies to reassess their own developments and practices, and their notions of nationhood (Hadfield 1998; Read 1992; Campbell 1992). The expansion of trade brings wealth to the mercantile classes and those classes begin to ponder their own role in society, especially with the foundation of grammar schools and the consequent rise of a formally educated class outside of the nobility (Gunn 1995: 18–21). Issues of nobility itself, especially the question of whether nobility is inborn or acquired, are investigated with a renewed enthusiasm and urgency. Reaction against the Catholic church in relation to the Reformation brings about a reassessment of the individual's relationship to both God and the church, in both spiritual and temporal terms, fanning the already fiercely glowing embers of the tensions between ecclesiastical and temporal authority (Tyndale 1528; Kantorowicz 1957; Axton 1977; Davies 1976). This debate brings with it questions about the appropriate language in which to pursue and express one's religious thoughts, especially in relation to the Bible, and the notion of an individuality in religion brings to the fore the need for a redefinition of the idea of conscience, especially in relation to the idea of self-consciousness.[1] Spiritual responsibility for self raises debate about the attainment of adulthood, and it is interesting that the end of the period sees the age of majority raised from fourteen to twenty-one (Stone 1977; Orgel 1999: 59). The investigation of appropriate hierarchical structures cannot leave unmoved the contingent question of the relative hierarchy of male and female, and debate around appropriate gender roles is continually aired, especially in the pamphlet war at the end of the sixteenth and beginning of the seventeenth century (Shepherd 1985; Aughterson 1995). And the ultimate tension between the interior and the exterior world must be to do with the working of the individual human frame, a more physical drive towards interior knowledge that culminates in experimental autopsy and a sophisticated relationship between the physical and metaphysical notions of interiority[2] (Barker 1984; Sawday1995; Aughterson 1995; Hanson 1998; Neill 1997).

Exterior pressures such as these, whether macrocosmic, to do with universal ideas or contexts, or microcosmic, to do with local or personal change, necessarily enforce a realignment of one's view of self, and sometimes conflicting views of self compete. As David Read has observed, new situations and perceptions require new expressions: 'the unconscious mind depends on a previous defined language, and definitions are not in every instance available. On the historical field the actors do not always know what they want because their desires have yet to find a form in language (Read 1992: 173).

The unconscious mind sometimes operates on more than just linguistic register, though. A text like Ralegh's *The Discovery of the Large, Rich and Beautiful Empire of Guyana* (1596) reveals the writer's sense of self as Elizabeth's conquistador at odds with the scholar-historian revelling in the newness of it all. Moments of wonder at the society encountered (Ralegh pp. 133–4, 157–8) and the sheer unspoiled beauty of the landscape (which he finds it hard to believe hasn't been landscaped, and represents as if it were a country park – Ralegh pp. 162–3) are continually being reined in, and the view realigned to focus on matters of political point-scoring against the Spanish (pp. 172, 174) or practical profit (pp. 198–9). There is also the issue of the truth trope in this kind of text, where the exact physical geography of the land is measured in detail to prove not only the possibility of profit, but to establish the basic fact of the writer's presence in the location.

This might seem odd, but the social and political issues dealt with in a text like *The Discovery* are not entirely alien to those constituted fictitiously by More's *Utopia* (1516, English translation 1551) where the detailed account of a newly discovered territory is fabulous – perhaps a kind of intellectual voyage of discovery – but carefully constructed, with its establishment of the narrator, its attendant letters and reference to genuine historical figures, as fact (Fox, 1983). Bacon will use the voyage of discovery as overt intellectual metaphor in *The New Atlantis* (published 1627). There is an intrinsic connection here between the expansion of physical and intellectual, even spiritual, limits.

While the texts of geographical discovery are looking outwards, other prose texts turn the gaze inwards. Tyndale's *Obedience of a Christian Man* (1528) operates in part as an apology for his work in translating the Bible into English not from the vulgate of Jerome, the version produced by and for the Catholic Church and interpreted through the Church Fathers throughout the history of the church, but from the Hebrew and Greek sources (Tyndale 1528; Daniell 1992, 1994; Hammond 1982). The *Obedience* is especially interesting in its urging of the importance of the availability of scripture in the vernacular, so that the individual might have direct access to the Word, and also in its voicing of the concern that the individual be conscious of differentiating between ways of knowing. At a broader level it also summarizes some early modern concerns about the ways in which certain methods of education can be obfuscatory as well as revelatory, because prescriptive systems of education bring with them a certain conformity of mind. Tyndale's writing is splendidly mimetic as he pours scorn on learning without real understanding:

Ye drive them from God's word and will let no man come there to until he have been two years Master of Art. First they nuzzle them in sophistry and in *benefundatii*, And there corrupt they their judgements with apparent arguments and with alleging unto them texts of logic of natural *philautia* of metaphysic and moral philosophy and of all manner books of Aristotle and of all manner doctors which they yet never saw. Moreover one holdeth this, another that. One is a real, another a nominal. What wonderful dreams have they of their predicaments universale, second intentions, quiddities, haeccaeities, and relatives. And whether *species fundata in chimera* be *vera species*. And whether this proposition be true: *non ens est aliquid*. Whether *ens* be *equivocum* or *univocii*. *Ens* is a voice only say some. *Ens* is *univocum* saith another and descendeth in to *ens creatum* and into *ens increatum per modos intrinsecos*, when they have this wise brawled eight, ten, or twelve or more years and after that their judgements are utterly corrupt: then they begin their divinity. Not at the scripture: but every man taketh a sundry doctor, which doctors are as sundry and as divers the one contrary unto the other as there are divers factions and monstrous shapes none like another among our sects of religion.

(fo. xviii verso.)

Richard Lanham's *Motives of Eloquence* (1976) draws attention to the restrictions that a rhetorical education of the type Tyndale criticizes might bring with it. He makes plain the constructedness of the resulting mindset, remarking how young scholars are taught 'a minute concentration on the word, how to write it, speak it, remember it . . . memory in a massive, almost brutalizing way . . . far in advance of conceptual understanding'. The Renaissance schoolmaster would 'require no original thought' but would 'demand instead an agile marshalling of the proverbial wisdom on any issue' (Lanham 1976: 2).

This sort of evaluation of the early modern scholar brings home clearly the tensions between Belsey's and Greenblatt's 'subject' and the competing notion of the self-searching individual. If the early modern subject is 'made of flaps and patches' to this degree, how is it possible for him or her to entertain an original thought? Is it possible for an assimilation of the classical and the English traditions of writing to bring about a newly directed gaze? What is the relationship between the process of assimilation and the process of creation? Even though the best examples of Renaissance practice in these areas produce 'something quite different from reproduction and translation . . . in no sense a copy of the old but rather a larger, denser . . . transformation of it' (Jones 1977: 20), it seems to me that these issues highlight the methodologies that identify the processes and the problems of both the public and the private struggle towards knowledge of self and an expression of that knowledge.

Constructed Selves, Representation and Self-Speaking

In Deloney's *Jack of Newbury* (1597), an episodic recital of the apprentice clothmaker's rise to high civic status, the overarching metaphor of the clothmaker as definer of identity[2] is paralleled by the explicit construction of a point of view. Unapologetic generic shifts draw attention to the literary figuring forth of a character, from narrative peppered with near dramatic episodes to allegorical representation, with notional art galleries inviting the gaze, balladic interludes insisting on aural attention, and episodes of fabliau suggesting that the early modern self-made subject is firmly rooted in the forms of its nation's earlier writings. Similarly, *Sidney's Old Arcadia* (?1577–80), a sustained narrative with a traceable linear plot, is dialectic in its representation, the five sections of the narrative, significantly labelled 'Acts' being interspersed with pastoral eclogues, suggesting that kinds of literature represent kinds of levels of society, and that a debate between the court and the pastoral life must be represented generically as well as in terms of its characters.

But if the tension between the socially constructed character and the self-conscious individual is ultimately to do with the tension between *theoria* and *phronesis*, then the critic in search of sixteenth-century identity inevitably returns to the idea of the interior voice, to the irresistible idea of the possibility of self-speaking, and therefore most obviously to the stage. It is quite possible to construct a more or less linear journey into the interior in the early modern drama, and along the way to observe both the shifting preoccupations among the contemporary issues sketched out above and the jostling between the traditional English forms and the alternatives offered by classical and continental forms. Medwall's *Fulgens and Lucres* (1497), a moral interlude played during a banquet for the household of Cardinal Morton, is the first secular play in English, deriving from an Italian prose debate on the subject of nobility. Throughout the play, notions of the true characters of the suitors, of the ability of language to communicate properly, and of the nature of drama itself, are examined, with reference to establishment of behaviour, representation of self through clothing, and the matter at the heart of the play, whether or not a person can be truly represented by the way he performs in a rhetorical debate. There is no attempt at interiority in this play; rather, character is revealed by an examination of the external signs that indicate the nature of the person within.

Bale's *King Johan* (1538–60) is also a moral play, but has utterly different concerns. There is an examination of the roles of kingship, Johan being concerned both 'to declare' how his power derives from God through Scripture and 'to show what I am' by insisting on his right to rule through lineal descent. At issue within Bale's play are the tensions between secular and ecclesiastical power, with Johan's fight against the malpractices of the Roman church, especially in regard to the suppression of vernacular scripture, being valorized by his consultation, in the proper order, with the secular powers within his realm, and by his insistence that he is obedient to God rather than to the church. Again, the debate is not represented as being *within* the character: rather, Johan is created as the historical 'real' site of a contradiction that is in the main fought out between allegorical figures. The most important of these is Sedition, who for part of the play inhabits the character of Stephen Langton, historically the archbishop who brings about Johan's downfall. The idea of a characteriztic inhabiting a 'real' character in this way, the rapprochement of allegory, history and mimetic representation, is a fundamental step towards the interrogation of particular traits of character determining behaviour.

Udall's *Jack Juggler* (1553–8) on the other hand examines explicitly the ways in which a person might know who he is, by the simple method of having Jake Juggler (a name with overtones of conjuring as well as simple sleight of hand) convince Jenkin Care away that he, Jake, is Jenkin, and that Jenkin is therefore nobody. Taking Plautus's *Amphitruo* as his source, Udall shows how reliance on exterior forms of knowledge of oneself – physical features, behaviour, dress, belonging to a particular household that one recognizes by dint of the fact the master beats one black and blue – can result very quickly in loss of one's own identity. Although the play is about the identity crisis of a specific character, undoubtedly 'the confusion of identity presented from the inside in wholly secular terms' (Axton 1982: 17), the language – ('But I marvel greatly, by our lord Jesus / How *he I* escaped, *I me* beat me thus. / And is not *he I* an unkind knave / That will no more pity on myself have?' 917–20) posits a logical rather than an emotional crisis.

In Pyckeryng's *Horestes* (?1567), we see how the methods of assimilation of classical drama into the English tradition might reveal a gradual process of interiorization. The chorus of classical drama is replaced by the self-proclaiming allegorical figure of Revenge, who fulfils the role of the Vice, and who also at one stage introduces himself as Master Patience. The alignment of the role of traditional classical truth-teller (the Chorus) with the traditionally subversive role in the English drama (the Vice) creates a dichotomy immediately. Is Horestes' allegorical adviser reliable or not? Revenge is doubly unstable as he exists in the play both as a character (affecting Horestes from the outside) and as a word, a notion, thus affecting his thoughts. The play is a hugely important moment of transition, explicitly addressing the relationship between competing external influences and the process of internalization.

The idea of competing versions of self being metaphorically externalized does not necessarily require utterly different characters. Shakespeare twice takes on the notion of self-questioning, competing selves through the motif of twinning, *in The Comedy of Errors* (1592) (which shares a source with *Jack Juggler*) and in *Twelfth Night* (1600). He also writes about the need for a strong sense of self to resist the constructions of identity imposed by others, especially in the case of women. In *Measure for Measure*, Isabella struggles against externalized competing male accounts of herself (Act II. ii), but her strength is demonstrated by her rhetorical manipulation of Angelo, whose own struggle between the public and private sense of self is voiced through a soliloquy riven with rhetorical questions, the medium that most clearly represents one side of self questioning another (2.3). Webster also uses issues of imposed external representation ('This is flesh and blood, sir, / 'Tis not the figure cut in alabaster / Kneels at my husband's tomb' (*The Duchess of Malfi* 1.2.72–4)) and the manipulation of public rhetoric (Vittoria's trial scene in *The White Devil*) to interrogate the struggle to determine the public self among his women characters.

As the canon progresses, Shakespeare works more and more towards this process of the internalization of dissenting voices. The insidious working of Iago on Othello, for example, is in part conveyed by the way in which Iago's mode of repetitive speech is increasingly assimilated by Othello. Lear is ultimately riven asunder by the competing roles he has played to satisfy the demands of the body natural and the body politic; his 'Who is it that can tell me who I am?' remains largely unanswered precisely the competing versions of self remain unreconciled.

But it is in *Hamlet*, with all its instability of language, its ultimate assimilation of the notion of revenge into complete consonance with the central protagonist, and the relentless self-questioning, that 'self-speaking' most clearly reveals the spiritual tangle created by the proximity of 'conscience' to 'consciousness', of *theoria* and *phronesis*. In the shift from the public to the private sense of 'conscience', the constructed subject and the self-speaking subject can clearly be seen to be simultaneously present and in opposition.

Summary

The investigation of early modern identity is a multi-disciplinary issue, and it is impossible even to begin to deal with it in so small a space as this. The philosophical limits of an appropriate investigation still need to be set, and although the important work of a handful of literary critics has until recently influenced the academy in a particular direction, a broader chronological sweep and a wider view of which issues are pertinent, especially in terms of kinds if language and kinds of texts, characterizes the most recent work cited here. This chapter might have taken a variety of forms, but by dividing it into theoretical, social-historical and literary-critical sections I have tried to represent the directions in which we might most usefully speak among ourselves.

NOTES

1   *OED* provides the following: 'Conscience 1. Privity of knowledge, knowledge within oneself, consciousness, conscience.' Citing '*Hamlet* (1602) 'Thus conscience doth make cowards of us all', the dictionary continues, 'The word is etymologically, as its form show, a noun of condition or function . . . and as such had no plural: a man or a people had more or less conscience. But in sense 4 [the internal acknowledgement or recognition of the quality of one's motives and actions] it came gradually to be thought of as an individual entity . . . was understood to mean no longer our respective shares or amounts of the common quality conscience, but to be two individual consciences, mine and yours.' It seems to me that this shift in meaning paral-

lels Taylor's account of the movement from *theoria* to *phronesis* as outlined above.

2   One area of the creation of identity that I haven't had space to discuss here is the issue of clothing. It is clear that Henrician and Elizabethan sumptuary laws, which dictated by law what materials might be worn, and in what degree, by different classes, go a long way towards controlling the public representation of the self. For a reproduction of one set of sumptuary laws, see Kinney (1999) 4–5; for one discussion of their significance, see Hunter (1980). A similar motif- that of the clothier-merchant as arbiter of identity can be seen in Dekker's *The Shoemaker's Holiday* (1599) which takes for its source Deloney's *The Gentle Craft* (1597).

REFERENCES AND FURTHER READING

Aughterson, K. (1995) *Renaissance Women: A Sourcebook. Constructions of Femininity in England.* London: Routledge.

Axton, M. (1977). *The Queen's Two Bodies: Drama and the Elizabethan Succession.* London: Royal Historical Society.

——(1982). *Three Tudor Classical Interludes.* Cambridge: D. S. Brewer.

Barker, F. (1984). *The Tremulous Private Body: Essays on Subjection.* London: Methuen.

Belsey, C. (1985). *The Subject of Tragedy.* London: Methuen.

Brandt, W. J. (1966). *The Shape of Medieval History: Studies in Modes of Perception.* New Haven: Yale University Press.

Campbell, M. B. (1992). 'The Illustrated Travel Book and the Birth of Ethnography: Part I of de Bry's America'. In D. G. Allen and R. A. White (eds), *The Work of Dissimilitude* (pp. 177–95). Newark, London and Toronto: University of Delaware Press / Associated University Presses.

Daniell, D. (1992). *Tyndale's Old Testament.* New Haven and London: Yale University Press.

——(1994). *William Tyndale: A Biography.* New Haven and London: Yale University Press.

Davies, C. S. L. (1976). *Peace, Print and Protestantism 1450–1558.* London: Hart-Davis MacGibbon.

Dollimore, J. (1984). *Radical Tragedy.* Brighton: Harvester.

Eisenstein, E. (1979). *The Printing Press as Agent of Change.* 2 vols. Cambridge: Cambridge University Press.

Fox, A. (1983). *Thomas More, History and Providence.* New Haven: Yale University Press. Relevant section repr. as 'An Intricate, Intimate Compromise'. In R. M. Adams (ed.), (1975, 2nd edn 1992) *Utopia. A Norton Critical Edition.* New York and London: W. W. Norton.

Greenblatt, S. (1980). *Renaissance Self-fashioning: from More to Shakespeare.* Chicago and London: University of Chicago Press.

Gunn, S. J. (1995). *Early Tudor Government, 1485–1558.* London: Macmillan.

Hadfield, A. (1998). *Literature, Travel, and Colonial Writing in the English Renaissance.* Oxford: Clarendon Press.

Hammond, G. (1982). *The Making of the English Bible.* Manchester: Carcanet.

Hanning, R. W. (1977). *The Individual in Twelfth-century Romance.* New Haven and London: Yale University Press.

Hanson, E. (1998). *Discovering the Subject in Renaissance England.* Cambridge: Cambridge University Press.

Hillman, R. (1997) *Self-speaking in Medieval and Early Modern English Drama.* Basingstoke: Macmillan.

Hunter, G. K. (1976). 'Flatcaps and Bluecoats: Visual Signals on the Elizabethan Stage'. *Essays and Studies.*

Jones, E. (1977). *The Origins of Shakespeare.* Oxford: Clarendon Press.

Kantorowicz, E. (1957). *The King's Two Bodies.* Princeton: Princeton University Press.

Kinney, A. (1999). *Renaissance Drama: An Anthology of Plays and Entertainments.* Oxford: Blackwell.

Lanham, R. (1976). *The Motives of Eloquence.* New Haven and London: Yale University Press.

Morris, C. (1972). *The Discovery of the Individual 1050–1200.* London: SPCK.

Neill, M. (1997). *Issues of Death: Mortality and Identity in English Renaissance Tragedy.* Oxford: Clarendon Press.

Orgel, S. (1999). *Impersonations: The Performance of Gender in Shakespeare's England.* Cambridge: Cambridge University Press.

Ralegh, W. (1997) *The Discoverie of the Large, Rich and Bewtiful Empyre of Guiana*, ed. N. L. Whitehead. Manchester: Manchester University Press.

Read, D. (1992). 'Ralegh's *Discoverie of Guiana* and the Elizabethan model of empire'. In D. G. Allen and R. A. White (eds), *The Work of Dissimilitude* (pp. 166–76). Newark, London and Toronto: University of Delaware Press/ Associated University Presses.

Sawday, J. (1995). *The Body Emblazoned: Dissection and the Human Body in Renaissance Culture.* London: Routledge.

Shepherd, S. (1985). *'The Women's Sharpe Revenge':*

Five Women Pamphlets from the Renaissance. London: Fourth Estate.

Stone, L. (1977). *The Family Sex and Marriage in England 1500–1800.* London: Weidenfeld and Nicholson.

Taylor, C. (1989). *Sources of the Self: The Making of Modern Identity.* Cambridge: Cambridge University Press.

Tyndale, W. (1528). *The Obedience of a Christian Man.* London: Scolar, 1970 (facsimile).

Ullman, W. (1967). *The Individual and Society in the Middle Ages.* London: Methuen.

——(1977). *Medieval Foundations of Renaissance Humanism.* London: Paul Elek.

55

Was There a Renaissance Feminism?

Jean E. Howard

Terminology matters in trying to make sense of a question like the one posed by the title of this essay. Several decades ago Joan Kelly asked a provocative question – 'Was there a Renaissance for women?' – that induced a new self-consciousness about the inclusiveness of the term 'Renaissance' (Kelly 1977). If there had been a 'rebirth' of classical culture in the fourteenth, fifteenth, and sixteenth centuries in many parts of Europe, and if for some this had included a sense of expanding horizons and opportunities, exactly who had gotten to participate in this process of revival and ebullient expansion? In particular, had women? Kelly, dealing primarily with elite women, felt that the answer was a qualified 'no'. Most importantly, she successfully called attention to the gender blindness that can surround the use of a word like 'Renaissance' so that the experience of the privileged sex comes to stand for the experience of everyone.

Of course, calling attention to the problematics of one term does not necessarily eradicate all difficulties with the alternative. When critics of English texts began to use the term 'early modern', which they borrowed from social historians, to describe the period stretching roughly from the reign of Henry VIII to the Restoration, they were critiqued for implying too sharp a break between the medieval and the early modern and for homogenizing a period in which older and emergent elements of culture coexisted. Nonetheless, the debate over these terms is important for the problem at hand. In attempting to discern an early modern feminism are we to focus on the large social transformations that the historians emphasize when they speak of the early modern? In other words, was there something in the inaugural moments of modernity that enabled a recognizable feminism to emerge? Or, conversely, are we looking in a more limited way at the domain of culture and asking whether the renewal of interest in classical literatures and the flourishing of vernacular ones were themselves the enablers of a feminism?

Before circling back to this question, however, I need to address the equally complicated issue of feminism itself. What would count as feminism in the early modern moment? Certainly no one called herself a feminist in this period, any more than people called themselves homosexuals, though in the latter case scholars have shown that that does not mean there were no varieties of same-sex affection and erotic practice in the sixteenth century (Goldberg 1992). While today definitions of feminism vary, most would agree that dominant versions of liberal feminism since at least the time of Mary Wollstonecraft have been committed to the goal of gender equality and have often used a post-Lockean language of 'rights' in which to make the case for such equality.[1] As a social movement, feminism has taken its actions in the name of a group, women, assumed to be subject to systematic oppression and exploitation on the basis of their sex. Moments of politicization have occurred around struggles over specific issues such as the right of women to vote, to divorce or to have legal abortions.

At first blush, not much of what I've just described maps easily or without acts of translation onto the social world of sixteenth- and early seventeenth-century England, a time prior to Locke and the emergence of a discourse of rights and in which there is little evidence of political action carried on specifically in the name of women for the alleviation of women's oppression. So how is it possible that we have books, and good ones, published with titles such as *Renaissance Feminism* (Jordan 1990)? What is being referenced?

Most often, when literary critics speak of Renaissance feminism they point first to the many texts that constitute explicit defences of women or play a role in the ongoing debate over the nature of woman, her proper role in marriage, and the education appropriate to her sex. In a groundbreaking book of 1984 Linda Woodbridge argued that what she calls the formal controversy over women had medieval origins, but that Renaissance humanism altered the tradition by adding classical materials to the exempla found in medieval treatises and by shaping the debates as often-elegant examples of humanist logic and rhetoric. She asserted, however, that this formal controversy had little relationship to 'real life'; that is, it neither expressed the actual views of its authors nor bore much relationship to existing social structures or beliefs. Instead, in her view the formal controversy was mostly a high-spirited game in which both male and female writers displayed their wit and their argumentative skills. Only in the more popular venue of the pamphlet wars involving cross-dressing in the decade before 1620 did aspects of the debate about women more closely approximate 'real' social concerns.

By contrast, Constance Jordan (1990) in a comprehensive account of English and continental texts on 'the woman question', argues that this literature was a place where serious philosophical and religious debate occurred, some of it laying the groundwork for the emergence, later in the seventeenth century, of a rights-based discourse premised on the equality of persons. She finds particularly important the emphasis in many of the texts of the controversy on the spiritual equality of men and women, since from an assertion of such equality could eventually follow a critique of men's presumptive dominance in other domains. Jordan is not bothered by the fact that she finds little evidence that actual women undertook collective political action to improve women's lot or that much of the period's pro-woman discourse focused on the merit of exceptional individuals. Rather, she sees the debates about women's nature preparing the way for later arguments about representative government and the limits that should be placed both on magisterial and on patriarchal authority (Jordan 1990: 27).

Jordan's work raises the discussion of this debate literature to a new level. I disagree with the elastic and unselfconscious way in which she uses the term 'feminist' to describe many writings that, while 'pro-woman' in the sense of refuting the worst attacks of misogynist writers, nonetheless often accept the subordinate status of women and do not argue for their equality, spiritual or otherwise. I think it is clearer to reserve the word feminist for Enlightenment and post-Enlightenment contexts and to speak, regarding earlier periods, of proto-feminisms. Nonetheless, Jordan's work makes clear that the flourishing of print publication in what we once unselfconsciously called 'the literary Renaissance' allowed the debate on women to develop exponentially and be widely disseminated. Moreover, literature developed certain arguments that in the long run helped to produce a feminism more recognizable to modern eyes. This was so, paradoxically, despite the regressive nature of some of the arguments put forward in this controversy and despite the fact that most of the writers, humanist or otherwise, who participated in this debate during the fifteenth and sixteenth centuries were men.

Besides their emphasis on female spiritual equality, the writings that comprise the debate on women are marked by productive contradictions that unsettle the idea of women's natural and inevitable subordination. The paradox of women's spiritual equality but social and political subservience to men is only the first of such contradictions, but one that could contribute both to the development of resistance theory (i.e., a wife should not obey her husband in cases where doing so would contravene her obedience to God) and also to the development of claims to the rights of all citizens as equal beings before the law. But contradictions also surround the woman's place as parent and manager of household servants and, sometimes, apprentices. Often these tracts acknowledge that woman's social place as wife and mother put her in a position of authority over subordinated men and made her the effective substitute for her husband in many daily matters. Hence the many pleas to respect the dignity of women and not, for example, to beat them as one would beat a slave (Fletcher 1995: 198–201). This ameliorist rhetoric about treating women better is not exactly revolutionary. Often it does not insist on an alternation of social relations, only greater kindness to subordinated subjects. However, the contradictions surrounding women's position in the household expose fault lines in patriarchal culture which could be exploited in subsequent political struggles. The Renaissance as a literary phenomenon thus indirectly contributed to a Renaissance proto-feminism – if by that we mean that the very process of proliferating printed texts on the woman question helped to materialize a body of discourse that not only voiced the contradictions of the existing gender system but could provide a stockpile of raw materials for subsequent moments of political struggle.

Moreover, certain of the writings about women, such as the cross-dressing tracts and debates about the conventional nature of men and women's gender roles, had powerful denaturalizing potential. In the *Haec Vir* tract of 1620, for example, the mannish woman, nattily dressed in the clothing of the opposite sex, holds forth at length about the way in which custom, rather than nature, determines not only what clothing should be worn by each sex, but also in what activities each should engage. Her argument culminates with the resounding assertion that 'Custom is an Idiot!' (Henderson and McManus 1985: 284). Such a sentiment has unpredictable consequences. Even though this tract backs down from its more radical implications by averring, ultimately, that women would be more womanly if men were only more manly, and hence reaffirming conventional gender roles, the ending of the narrative does not cancel the more subversive middle, whatever the intentions of the author.

A final point to be made about the 'feminist' implications of the debate about women has to do with the possibility that some key texts in this tradition were actually catalysts for the politicization of women as subjects whose gender could be a point of alliance with other women in the struggle against patriarchal oppression. Foucault pointed out that discourse can breed counter-discourse and resistance. For example, in the mid-sixteenth century John Knox's infamous attack on the legitimacy of Mary Tudor as Queen of England produced a spate of defences of women that rolled on for the ensuing fifty years. Perhaps of greater interest is the way in which the 1615 pamphlet, Joseph Swetnam's *Arraignment of Lewd, idle, froward, and unconstant women*, provoked a stinging rebuttal, a play entitled *Swetnam the Woman-hater Arraigned by Women*. In this case, a scurrilous attack on women led to the representation of women's imagined politicization. Though it is not known whether this play was written by a man or a woman, Valerie Wayne (in Frye and Robertson 1999: 221–40) interestingly argues that the gender of the writer is not as important as the way in which a violently anti-feminist polemical provoked a strong counter-discourse which imagined a collectivity of women bringing Swetnam into a court of law to indict him for crimes against women. The anonymity of the play ironically reveals the performativity of gender, in that the outraged 'feminist' point of view articulated in the drama is not secured by the biological identity of the writer but by the successful manipulation of rhetorical counters. At the same time the play reveals that gender – at least imaginatively – could be a recognized rallying point for political action. The women who dominate the play are depicted as a collectivity who use political and juridical institutions to defend their sex against slander. Whether 'real' women actually could and did act in this way is in part beside the point. What one sees in the Swetnam controversy is the possibility of the debate about women producing a discourse of collective female action in defence of themselves as an oppressed social class. And, as I have argued elsewhere, it is inconceivable that such a response could have taken shape as it did without both a flourishing popular print and theatrical culture in the city of London and also a pre-existing discursive tradition of debate on the woman question (Howard in Frye and Robertson 1999: 308–9). These provide the conditions of possibility for the emergence of a play that records the fantasy of women banding together to use a central cultural institution, a court of law, to indict a man for crimes against the female sex. This, I would argue, is a distinctly feminist fantasy, no matter what the intent of the person who was its author.

My first argument, then, is that what has been referred to as the debate about women, despite all its contradictions, is part of the prehistory of modern feminism, especially when it moves beyond the praise of exceptional women, or praise of women's virtue and modesty, to identify all women as a class of subjects unjustly subordinated because of their sex. The language in which 'feminist' arguments are cast, however, can sound quite unlike the secular terms in which claims for women's rights have been articulated from the eighteenth century on. Much discourse about equality and women's worthiness is couched in a religious register. It is the spiritual equality of women in the eyes of God, and to a lesser extent arguments about their actual power in the household and the family, that constituted the principal terms upon which discursive struggles against men's systematic privilege could be voiced.

In addition, the thirty years since Joan Kelly wrote her path-breaking essay have made it increasingly plain that at least some early modern women were themselves becoming authors, whether or not they were penning defences of women. Many of the best-known of these writers such as Mary Wroth, Amelia Lanyer or Katherine Philips were elite women, and certainly the content of what they wrote could not always be called 'feminist' or even pro-woman. Nonetheless, looked at another way, they were contributing to a tradition of writing by women that in the eighteenth century would so flourish that the race of 'scribbling women' would come under repeated attacks for the 'unchaste' nature of their public voice. By writing, and in some cases by publishing their texts, women authors were usurping a masculine subject position though they seldom did so for overtly subversive purposes. But separating effect from intentions, the increasing number of women writers created the potential for women's voices, including feminist ones, to be a part of the emerging public sphere of print.

At this point, however, I wish to turn from literary production to the social world of seventeenth-century England. While most literary discussions about Renaissance feminism start with the issue of the woman writer and with the formal debate about the nature of women, a debate which I would characterise as part of the efflorescence of vernacular literatures from the fourteenth to the sixteenth centuries, the relationship between this debate and actual social actions on behalf of women is more occluded and complex. It is somewhat naive, of course, to talk about discourse and 'real life' as if nothing has happened when 'mere' words and narratives are let loose upon the world. That, I think, is the fundamental flaw in Woodbridge's approach to the formal controversy about women. She assumes that mere texts, unaccompanied by documented evidence of organized political actions, are just sport without social consequence, rather than discursive events that can prepare for and indeed precipitate events in the political or economic realms.

And when we turn to those realms, much more evidence is now available than we possessed even two decades ago about women as social actors in the early modern period. And here I do self-consciously shift to the historians' term, early modern, to discuss the panoply of social, political and economic factors that affected women's situation and structured their possible 'feminism'. For me the benefit of the term early modern lies, first, in indicating that the genealogy of many of the institutions we associate with the modern era – the supposed separation of private from public spheres, the break-up of Catholic hegemony in Europe, the rise to cultural pre-eminence of the bourgeoisie, the emergence of capitalism – can be traced to the sixteenth and seventeenth centuries in much of northern Europe, though not all these events or phenomena came to fruition in these centuries. The adjective 'early' indicates that fact: namely, that we are dealing with a period of transition in which there has as yet been no sharp break with many aspects of medieval culture and in which emergent elements of modernity are hardly recognizable as such.

One major consequence of the intensive study of early modern women in the late twentieth century has been the recognition that they were much more active social agents than the prescriptive literature on the desirability of their chastity, silence and obedience would indicate. Whether one examines women's roles as active litigants defending themselves against charges of slander in the church courts (Gowing in Kermode and Walker 1994), their role in arranging marriages for their children (Ezell 1987), their role in enforcing community norms through charivaris and other forms of discipline (Underdown 1985) or their participation in radical religious sects (Hinds 1996), scholars have increasingly found evidence that early modern women exercised a sometimes surprising degree of power within the household and the community. They may not have been vested with formal *authority* within patriarchal structures, but they nonetheless found ways to exert influence and exercise agency in the interstices of those structures. The literature of the period often bears traces of their struggles to do so.

But the question at hand is whether, in real life as opposed to in literary representations, they expressed that agency in struggles for the amelioration of women's condition generally, rather than in individual efforts to make the situation of particular women more palatable? That is, was there a political or social form of 'feminism' in this period? The question is still difficult to answer, so little do we know about the actual participation of women in the vast political and social upheavals in the period. However, it is becoming clear that by the mid-seventeenth century, largely within the radical religious sects, women were in large numbers assuming public roles once reserved for men. Quaker women, women who were part of the Fifth Monarchist movement, women who were part of Digger communities – all of them were active participants in spiritual and political movements (and the two were inseparable in the period) that led to a general loosening of the strict bonds of social hierarchy that had only maintained a monarchy but a patriarchy as well (Weisner 1993: 203–10). As James Holstun has argued, while none of the radical sects actually preached the social equality of women, in practice, female members of these sects functioned as preachers, prophets and spiritual leaders, finding in the lived praxis of daily activity new and revolutionary possibilities for female agency and political efficacy (Holstun,

2000). In the Civil War period, women repeatedly petitioned parliament on issues such as the end of debt laws, the release of John Lilburne from prison, and the end of martial law. The 1649 petition on the latter subject contained the following language: 'Since we are assured of our Creation in the image of God, and of an interest in Christ, equal unto men, as also of a proportionable share in the Freedoms of this commonwealth' (Weisner 1993: 245). Asserting equality with men before God and as members of the commonwealth, these women asserted their political right to petition their parliament. A growing body of evidence suggests that through these and similar actions a large number of women participated in daily religious-political struggle of a sort that for a time effectively altered the terms of the gender system.

The case of Anna Trapnel is instructive. A member of the Fifth Monarchist movement, Trapnel gained a considerable notoriety in the 1650s as an opponent of Cromwell. The Fifth Monarchists were a millennarian sect that believed the kingdom of God was soon to be established on earth. They took their name from Daniel's vision of an everlasting kingdom that was to follow the four great monarchies of the world. After the collapse of the Barebone's parliament in 1653 and Cromwell's assumption of the protectorship, the Fifth Monarchists were steadfast in their opposition to his rule. Trapnel was a member of this movement, an unmarried woman whose economic independence as the sole child of a fairly wealthy widow provided the material basis for her remarkable independence even as the radical London churches with which she was associated in the 1640s prepared her for the role of public prophecy and spiritual leadership she was soon to assume. Supported by groups of Puritan women among whose households she was a frequent visitor, Trapnel undertook fasts and foretold, among other things, the collapse of the rump parliament. When, in fury, Cromwell imprisoned many male Fifth Monarchists at the beginning of his protectorate, Trapnel assumed a more public role. From an inn in Whitehall – at Cromwell's very doorstep – she fasted and uttered prayers and prophecies that were heard and discussed by many people (London preachers, Fifth Monarchists and others) who thronged to her chamber. Eventually two large books containing her prophecies were published, widely disseminating her plans for Christ's kingdom on earth and her subversive threats against Cromwell's authority.

The point is not that Trapnel was another 'exceptional woman' but rather that, though she is atypical in the notoriety which came to surround her, her practical role in the radical sects appears not to have been that anomalous. Radical women's participation in religious and political struggles of the mid-seventeenth century in effect eventuated in altered gender possibilities within the social communities where the sects flourished. This did not constitute a feminism that proclaimed itself in the terms of later middle-class languages of right and rationality. In fact, the irrational, visionary excesses of a Trapnel would probably have deeply offended an Enlightenment feminist such as Mary Wollstonecraft. Nonetheless, the praxis of such women, justified in religious terms, constituted a *de facto* proto-feminism of a fairly impressive order.

Ironically, however, it is not these radical women, but their middle-class sisters who came to dominate what has been perceived as the main strand of modern feminism. Affected by the enormous changes wrought by the transition to capitalism, middling sort women increasingly were pushed from roles in productive trades and became guardians of the domestic sphere, a story that has often been told. It was from that domestic field that women who were largely excluded from public life began to make claims to education and treatment as rational beings, often arguing that they would be better mothers, wives, and companions if granted the education befitting the dignity and importance of these roles. Later, demands for the right to divorce, to vote, to hold property while married, to have access to contraception and abortions, to gain entry to all-male institutions, and to achieve equal pay for equal work unfolded.

So was there a Renaissance feminism that inaugurated this later history? As I hope I have demonstrated, the answer to this question cannot be simple. The literary Renaissance produced what I have called particular proto-feminist effects. The debate about women, sometimes regressive in its politics, nonetheless widely circulated the idea of women as men's spiritual equals, denaturalised inherited notions of gender difference, and articulated the possibility of women uniting as an oppressed social class to demand redress from patriarchal oppression. In addition, a limited number of mostly elite women accrued cultural capital by participating in the efflorescence of writing that marked the Renaissance emergence of vernacular literatures. At the same time, social changes of an enormous sort were giving rise to two separate kinds of 'feminist' activity. On the one hand, the religious and political ferment of mid-century, itself very much part of an early modern transformation of society, spawned a radical religious politics in which women played a new and important role that for a time effectively, rather than theoretically, transformed gender practices within particular segments of English society. But the upheavals of mid-century also produced the eventual triumph of bourgeois forces, a triumph that has ironically occluded most of the vestiges of the radicalism of mid-century, including the radicalism of lower class women. It also produced, however, the conditions of possibility for a middle-class feminism to emerge, a feminism dependent on the supposed separation of private and public and on the elevation of domesticity as women's primary vocation. This kind of distinctly modern feminism hardly can be said to exist before the bourgeois era. But, as I have suggested, there were forms of early modern gender struggle, both discursive and material, through which resistance to gendered forms of subordination and oppression were articulated. If these struggles did not always look like Enlightenment versions of feminism, they were nonetheless there, and the inadequacies of our terminology should not erase them.

NOTE

1 For a complex discussion of the consequences, for women, of Locke's interventions into seventeenth-century political discourse and their attendant gender implications see C. Pateman (1988).

REFERENCES AND FURTHER READING

Charles, L. and Duffin, L. (eds) *Women and Work in Pre-Industrial England*. London: Croom Helm.

Clark, Alice (1919; rpt 1982) *The Working Life of Women in the Seventeenth Century*, eds M. Chaytor and J. Lewis. London: Routledge.

Erickson, A. L. (1993) *Women and Property in Early Modern England*. London: Routledge.

Ezell, M. J. M. (1987) *The Patriarch's Wife: Literary Evidence and the History of the Family*. Chapel Hill: University of North Carolina Press.

Ferguson, M., Quilligan, M. and Vickers, N. J. (eds) (1986) *Rewriting the Renaissance: The Discourses of Sexual Difference in Early Modern Europe*. Chicago and London: University of Chicago Press.

Fletcher, A. (1995) *Gender, Sex and Subordination in England 1500–1800*. New Haven and London: Yale University Press.

Frye, S. and Robertson, K. (eds) (1999) *Maids and Mistresses, Cousins and Queens: Women's Alliances in Early Modern England*. New York and Oxford: Oxford University Press.

Goldberg, J. (1992) *Sodometries: Renaissance Texts, Modern Sexualities*. Stanford: Stanford University Press.

Henderson, K. U. and McManus, B. F. (eds) (1985) *Half Humankind: Contexts and Texts of the Controversy about Women in England, 1540–1640*. Urbana and Chicago: University of Chicago Press.

Hinds, H. (1996) *God's Englishwomen: Seventeenth-century Radical Sectarian Writing and Feminist Criticism*. Manchester: Manchester University Press, 1996.

Holstun, J. (2000) *Ehud's Dagger: Class Struggle in the English Revolution*. London: Verso Books.

Hufton, Olwen (1998) *The Prospect before Her: A History of Women in Western Europe 1500–1800*. New York: Vintage.

Hull, S. (1982) *Chaste, Silent, and Obedient: English Books for Women 1475–1640*. San Marino: Huntington Library.

Jordan, C. (1990) *Renaissance Feminism: Literary Texts and Political Models*. Ithaca and London: Cornell University Press.

Kegl, R. (1994) *The Rhetoric of Concealment; Figuring Gender and Class in Renaissance Literature*. Ithaca: Cornell University Press.

Kelly, J. (1977) 'Did Women Have a Renaissance?'. In R. Bridenthal and C. Koonz (eds), *Becoming Visible: Women in European History* (pp. 139–64) Boston: Houghton Mifflin.

Kermode, J. and Walker, G. (eds) (1994) *Women, Crime, and the Courts in Early Modern England*. London: UCL Press.

Mendelson, S. and Crawford, P. (1998) *Women in Early Modern England, 1550–1720*. Oxford: Clarendon Press.

Pateman, C. (1988) *The Sexual Contract*. Stanford: Stanford University Press.

Prest, W. R. (1991) 'Law and Women's Rights in Early Modern England', *The Seventeenth Century*, 6 (2), 169–87.

Sanders, E. R. (1998) *Gender and Literacy on Stage in Early Modern England*. Cambridge: Cambridge University Press.

Traub, V., Kaplan, M. L. and Callaghan, D. (eds) (1996) *Feminist Readings of Early Modern Culture: Emerging Subjects*. Cambridge: Cambridge University Press.

Underdown, D. E. (1985) *Revel, Riot, and Rebellion*. Oxford: Oxford University Press.

Weisner, M. E. (1993) *Women and Gender in Early Modern Europe*. Cambridge: Cambridge University Press.

Woodbridge, L. (1984) *Women and the English Renaissance: Literature and the Nature of Womankind, 1540–1620*. Urbana and Chicago: University of Illinois Press.

56

The Debate on Witchcraft

James Sharpe

One of the more remarkable features of the early modern period was the European witch craze. Much written about and much misunderstood, the witch craze remains a fascinating subject which continually attracts the attention of both academic and popular writers. Briefly, between about 1450, when the witch stereotype really emerged, and about 1750, when Enlightenment thinkers derided witch-persecution and most states removed witchcraft as an offence from their law codes, large numbers of people, including many very intelligent and very educated people, believed in witchcraft, and in almost all European states witchcraft was regarded as a criminal offence. Gaps in the records make precision impossible, but current thinking suggests that, despite some much wilder estimates, in the three hundred years after 1450 some 100,000 persons were accused of witchcraft, of whom 40,000 were executed, women forming some 80 per cent of this total. Despite the attention devoted to the subject, its causes remain debatable: early modern witch-hunting has been variously attributed to the Reformation, the Counter Reformation, the intolerance of the Christian church more generally, the rise of the early modern state, the spread of rural capitalism and the break up of the village community, to patriarchy and misogyny, and, less certainly, to the use of hallucinogenic drugs or the shock which syphilis gave to Europe's moral system.

In England witchcraft became a legally defined offence punishable by death, witchcraft statutes being passed in 1542 (repealed in 1547), 1563 and 1604, these latter two Acts being repealed in 1736. Many of the relevant court records are missing, but a reasonable estimate would be that a maximum of 500 people were hanged for witchcraft in England.

The subject has inspired much good historical work. There were some excellent early pioneering studies, but for a generation or so thinking on the history of witchcraft in England was dominated by the approach enshrined by two books, those published by Alan Macfarlane in 1970 and Keith Thomas in 1971. This approach interprets English witchcraft from the perspective of neighbourly disputes and peasant beliefs and sets it in the context of the socio-economic changes of the Elizabethan and early Stuart periods. Witchcraft accusations, on this model, were characteristically launched by richer against poorer villagers, and could be interpreted as reactions to population pressure, worsening relations between comfortably off and poor villagers, and the erosion of communal solidarity.

Macfarlane and Thomas's work constituted a completely new approach to the history of witchcraft. No longer could popular thinking about witchcraft in the early modern period be written off as peasant superstition or ignorance. Their emphasis did, however, lead to a downgrading of what might be described as the intellectual history of witchcraft, of how the phenomenon looked to members of the educated elite. More recently, historians have returned to this issue, their interest in many ways paralleled by recent work on witchcraft by literary scholars. Thus this chapter hopes to examine some of the ideas expressed in print about witchcraft in England in the late sixteenth and early seventeenth centuries. My starting point will be 1566, when the first English witchcraft trial pamphlet was published. I shall end in 1634, with the publication of Heywood and Brome's *The Late Lancashire Witches*, a play based on an actual incident whose handling by central government symbolized an important shift in official thinking. One of the peculiarities of English witchcraft history is that the first full-scale text written on the subject, Reginald *Scot's Discovery of Witchcraft* of 1584, was unrelentingly sceptical. Scot was an obscure Kentish gentleman, his only other known publication being, as befits a native of Kent, on hop cultivation. His *Discovery* is a major achievement, pursuing a coherent and well structured argument over several hundred pages, and in the process citing over two hundred foreign and thirty-eight English works. Scot was clearly aware of local beliefs, and his book in fact opens with a classic exposition of the 'charity refused' model of a witchcraft accusation which was to become central to Macfarlane and Thomas's interpretation. But his main objective was to challenge the assumptions of learned authors. That famous witchcraft treatise, the *Malleus Maleficarum*, published by two Dominican friars in 1487 and noteworthy for both its virulence against witches and its misogyny, was ruthlessly attacked, as was Jean Bodin's *De la Démonomanie des Sorcières*, published in 1580 and the most respected work on demonology in the late sixteenth century. Scot's tract was obviously widely known. Playwrights used it, and it was frequently excoriated by demonologists, while there is an unsubstantiated but instructive tradition that James VI and I ordered it to be burnt by the common hangman.

Scot has attracted considerable praise from recent writers, who have tended to see him as an early rationalist, a thinker clearly ahead of his time. He was certainly guided by a rough common sense, which led him to regard much of what witches were meant to do as patently absurd. But his more philosophical objections are, in fact, founded on a clear and orthodox religious position (it should be noted, however, that Scot's personal religious beliefs have become a matter of some speculation). Scot was very hostile to Roman Catholicism: while not actually equating Catholicism with witchcraft, he frequently affirms (and this view was held by other English Protestant writers) that the type of superstitions which encouraged witch-hunting were very similar to what Scot regarded as the superstitious excrescences of the Catholic church. More importantly, Scot's writing demonstrates the major sceptical position of the period: uncritical belief in witchcraft gave too much agency to the devil and his human agents, and consequently downgraded the importance of God. Scot argued that the popular tendency to attribute misfortunes to witchcraft demonstrated an imperfect grasp of God's purposes: the problems attributed to witchcraft were, in fact, the outcome of divine providence, not of demonic agency combined with human malice. Scot also opened a theme which was to become common among sceptics when he claimed that the scriptural references so often adduced by demonological writers were mistranslations or misinterpretations of the Hebrew of the original texts.

Scot, therefore, was not a precocious proto-rationalist, but somebody firmly located in the intellectual world of his time. His *Discovery* demonstrates clearly that, despite the modern predisposition to regard witch-hunting as a metaphor for the unthinking bigotry of past ages, there was a number of intellectual positions which could be held on witchcraft, and the subject was one which was a matter for debate rather than something on which opinion was hegemonic. Much the same is true of the writings of another author who has been claimed as an early rationalist by some modern commentators, George Gifford. Gifford (*c.* 1548–1620) was a Church of England clergyman, educated at Cambridge, and minister of the small Essex port of Maldon. A man of advanced Protestant views, he was deprived of his living in 1584, but was so highly regarded by the townsfolk of Maldon that they retained his services as a lecturer. Gifford was obviously a dedicated spreader of God's word, and wrote a number of tracts on how to bring right religion to the populace. His books on witchcraft, published in 1587 and 1593, are unusual in demonstrating a keen interest in and informed knowledge of the popular beliefs and folklore of the locality. This has led to Gifford being described as a Tudor anthropologist.

Once again, however, a contextualized reading of Gifford's works demonstrates that he was not some proto-rationalist or early ethnographer, but rather that his writings too reflected the religious concerns of his period. Gifford describes popular thinking on witchcraft in southern Essex with sensitivity, but uses this description to demonstrate the popular superstition and ignorance which had to be combatted and overcome if a godly commonwealth were to be erected in England. It was not the abstract possibility of witchcraft, but rather the widely held beliefs which obscured correct thinking on the subject, which Gifford attacked. And, like Scot, Gifford was insistent that these beliefs, by attributing too much agency to the devil and his human minions, detracted from divine providence and God's glory. When men ascribed 'so much to the power and to the anger of witches', wrote Gifford, they neglected 'the high sovereignty and providence of God over all things'.[1]

The attention focused on Scot and Gifford by those looking for early symptoms of modernity has clouded our understanding of these two authors. It has also obscured the development, from the late sixteenth century, of a distinctive body of English demonological writing. This began with Henry Holland's *A Treatise against Witchcraft*, published in 1590. Holland (*d.* 1604) was another Cambridge-educated clergyman and was author of several other religious works. His Treatise was entirely conventional, informed by the writings of Jean Bodin, the important French Protestant theologian Lambert Daneau, and the Danish demonologist Neils Hemmingsen, and also contained what was to become a standard feature of English demonological writing, a refutation of Reginald Scot. Holland was a respected clergyman and controversist, but the next major work on witchcraft came from the most celebrated English theologian of the period, William Perkins (1558–1602). Perkins's *A Discourse of the Damned Art of Witchcraft*, published posthumously in 1608, apparently originated as a series of sermons. The work is again very conventional, but was lengthy, and remarkable for the solidity of its scriptural foundations. Its major significance was that it was written by somebody of Perkins's standing: that fact that such a major figure supported witch-hunting was still thought to be worth bringing forward in 1692 when New England clergymen were justifying the Salem witch trials. And, of course, English witchcraft writers could also derive considerable comfort from the *Daemonologie* written by James VI and I, first published at Edinburgh in 1597.

Other works followed that of Perkins. James Mason, an obscure figure, published his *Anatomy of Sorcery* in 1612. In 1616 John Cotta, a Cambridge-trained physician, published *The Trial of Witchcraft* (a second edition with a different title came in 1625), a work which, as was appropriate, concentrated on the medical aspects of witchcraft cases. Also in 1616, Alexander Roberts, an obscure clergyman living at Kings Lynn in Norfolk, published *A Treatise of Witchcraft*, in which a short exposition of demonological thinking was followed by an account of an actual incident of witchcraft in that town. The year 1617 witnessed the publication of *The Mystery of Witchcraft*, written by another clergyman, in this instance Oxford-educated, Thomas Cooper. And, finally, there appeared in 1627 a treatise which summed up this period of English demonological writing, Richard Bernard's *A Guide to Grand-Jury Men with respect to Witches*. Bernard was another of those clerical writers and controversists who enjoyed considerable respect in their own time, and who managed to maintain a formidable publication rate while ministering very effectively to his flock in the Somerset village of Batcombe. The *Guide*, which was republished in 1629, demonstrates the range of materials from which an English demonology could be constructed by the time of its writing. Bernard was working within the established Protestant demonological framework, but he referred to continental Catholic works, notably Bodin's *Démonomanie* and another treatise of major importance, Martin Del Rio's *Disquisitionum Magicarum Libri Sex* of 1599. He was fully conversant with the relevant English writers, and was, moreover, happy to illustrate or buttress arguments with evidence from pamphlet descriptions of English trials. These demonological tracts varied slightly in their emphasis, length and profundity of scholarship, but there were a number of areas in which they broadly agreed. Despite their use of continental, and more specifically continental Catholic, authors, there was little by way of sexual prurience, concern over sexual intercourse between human beings and animals, and the absurd obscenities of the sabbat (it is noteworthy that the *Malleus Maleficarum*, despite the extravagant claims which have been made for its importance, was very rarely cited by these English

Protestant writers). There was a strong emphasis on the demonic pact, and witches were clearly identified as agents of Satan, locked into a cosmic struggle between good and evil. The wickedness of malefic (evil doing) witches, and the need to extirpate them, were therefore clearly set out. There was, despite the attention which modern scholars have devoted to the theme, little discussion of the connection between women and witchcraft, which was obviously regarded as a marginal and unproblematic issue. These treatises were written by clerical authors who were accustomed to see the planting of right religion and the eradication of superstitious errors as key objectives of the reformed church. Accordingly, they sometimes devoted many pages to decrying folkloric countermeasures against witches, and the widespread recourse to 'good' witches, or cunning folk. Good Christians who thought themselves bewitched should have recourse to fasting, prayer, or going to the magistrate: using charms against witchcraft, scratching suspected witches, burning supposedly bewitched animals, or going to the cunning man or woman were prohibited. These practices were seen as unjustified by scripture, as contrary to true religion, and coming from a pact with the devil as surely as did the powers of the malefic witch. Cunning folk, the 'good' witches whose services were so frequently sought by the ill-informed populace came in for special opprobrium: they derived their powers from the devil as much as did malefic witches, while the fact that they pretended to do good made them even more reprehensible. 'Death therefore', declared William Perkins, 'is the just and deserved portion of the good witch.'[2]

In England major works of demonology started late, in 1590. But by that date there was another printed genre where the literate could learn about witchcraft, the pamphlet literature devoted to describing, contextualizing, and sensationalizing witch trials. From the early Elizabethan period there had developed what might be described as 'wonder literature', short and accessible works at once sensationalist and moralistic, sometimes clearly aimed at a wide audience, and usually concerned with describing an unusual event and employing it to demonstrate God's providence on earth. Thus cases of witchcraft were recorded and their significance pondered along with monstrous births, earthquakes, floods, whales washed up on beaches, cities destroyed by fire, and frogs rained down on the earth from the heavens. The first such tract to survive which describes a witchcraft trial, dating from 1566, is concerned with the trial of three witches at Essex. Court documents also survive for this case.

A steady trickle of such publications followed, of which we shall note only the most important. In 1582 a lengthy tract was published describing the trial of a number of witches at St Osyths in Essex. This is a detailed work which contains much information on broader popular beliefs about witches, and was possibly written by Brian D'Arcy, the justice of the peace who carried out the initial interrogations. Another tract came in 1593, a very full narrative of the events which led to the execution in that year of three witches from Warboys in Huntingdonshire. In 1613 one of the most celebrated local witch-hunts in English history, the 1612 trials of the Pendle witches, was commemorated in a tract written by Thomas Potts, who had been clerk of the court which had tried the witches, and sentenced a dozen of them to death. And, the last in this particular series, *The Wonderful Discovery of Elizabeth Sawyer*, published in 1621. This was written by Henry Goodcole, a London clergyman who ministered to prisoners in Newgate, and who wrote a number of crime pamphlets based on the offences of some of those he had prepared spiritually for execution. This tract formed the basis for the dramatization of Sawyer's case by the team which put together *The Witch of Edmonton*, one of the very few English plays which took a quasi-documentary approach to witchcraft.[3]

The witchcraft tracts varied in length, depth of scholarship and tone, and many of them, like other items of 'wonder literature', were clearly sensationalist. Yet most of them were anxious to set witchcraft in the context of the cosmic struggle between good and evil, between God and the devil. The tone was set by the epistle to the reader of a tract dealing with a witchcraft trial at Windsor in 1579 which had resulted in the execution of four alleged witches. The 'swarms of witches and enchanters' to be found in England were interpreted as one of 'the punishments which the Lord God hath laid upon us, for the manifest impiety and careless contempt of His word abounding in these our desperate days'. 'The old serpent Satan' was at work, and in matters of witchcraft it was he 'that doeth all, that plagueth with sickness, that maimeth, murdereth, and robbeth, and at his lust restoreth. The witch beareth the name, but the devil dispatcheth the deeds'. The epistle declared that witches should be done death, according to both 'the law of the Lord of life' and 'the law of this land', and in a brief flourish of classical learning noted Cicero's opinion that witches 'are to be rather shut up in prison and tied with fetters, than moved to amend with counsel and persuasions, only afterwards suffered to escape'. Moreover, readers were warned, in the spirit of the major works of demonology, against going to cunning folk.[4]

There was, therefore, a noteworthy body of works published on witchcraft in late sixteenth- and early seventeenth-century England. Yet despite these works, witch-hunting was, in the years around 1600, being challenged from the very top of the Church of England. The basic issue was the related problem of demonic possession and exorcism. The Church of England, like other Protestant churches, rejected exorcism as a meaningless peace of popish superstition, which left the way open for Catholic priests to demonstrate that theirs was the true church by exorcizing those thought to be demonically possessed (Protestants recommended prayer and fasting as the correct remedies). In 1585–6 a group of Catholic priests, headed by a Jesuit named Weston, carried out a series of exorcisms in a propaganda exercise which were thought to have brought in four or five thousand converts. As if this were not bad enough, the Church authorities became worried by worried about over-enthusiastic dispossessions, in effect Protestant exorcisms, notably those performed in the north and the midlands by a young Puritan preacher named John Darrell. In 1600 Darrell was hauled before Richard Bancroft, bishop of London, and severely censured. The affair provoked a literary war, with Darrell and his associates defending their actions, Bancroft's chaplain, Samuel Harsnett, attacking them. (A book by Harsnett, *A Declaration of Egregious Popish Impostures* (London, 1603) was one of Shakespeare's sources for *King Lear*.)

In 1602, just as the dust from the Darrell affair had settled, Bancroft found himself involved in another case, this time involving a fourteen-year-old girl called Mary Glover. Bancroft was heavily involved in mobilizing support for the woman accused of bewitching Glover, and in particular presented medical evidence which attempted to prove that the girl's afflictions were the result of natural causes, and not of witch-craft. A number of clergymen who took the rival position were subsequently disci-plined. In 1605 a similar case occurred, this time involving a girl aged about twenty named Anne Gunter. Anne's afflictions had led to two women being accused of witch-craft at Abingdon in March of that year. The two women were acquitted, but Anne's father Brian Gunter, who had strong connections with Oxford University, attempted to reopen the case with James I when the monarch visited Oxford later that year. James was sceptical, and asked Bancroft, now Archbishop of Canterbury, to investi-gate the case. Bancroft in turn entrusted the girl to Samuel Harsnett, who soon had her confessing that she had simulated being possessed and bewitched at her father's direction, with the result that Brian and Anne Gunter were tried at Star Chamber for false accusation. In the meantime Harsnett had, in 1603, published his *Declaration of Egregious Popish Impostures*, a work which, although focusing on the Catholic exorcisms of 1585–6, also took a few swipes at Protestant dispossessions, and came very near to denying the reality of witchcraft, at least as it was understood by most of Harsnett's compatriots.

Obviously witch-trials, notably those in Lancaster in 1612, continued after this flurry of incidents, but both the frequency of trials and the probability of conviction declined. The reasons for this are still obscure, but two major elements must have been the development of scepticism among the judiciary and the arrival of that new religious tendency which historians describe as Arminianism. At the very least, central authority during the reign of Charles I seems to have been very cautious about witch-craft. This caution was demonstrated in 1633–4, when another body of witchcraft accusations arose from the Pendle area of Lancashire. At the centre of the accusations lay an eleven-year-old boy, Edmund Robinson, who claimed that he had been taken to the sabbat by a witch, and gave a vivid description of what he had witnessed there which implicated a number of local women. The judge trying the initial batch of witches sensed that a major witch panic was brewing, and informed Westminster. The bishop of Chester was instructed to investigate the accusations, and subsequently young Robinson, his father, and several of the supposed witches were brought down to London.

The accusations were exploded. Young Robinson confessed that he made up the story about witchcraft and being taken to the sabbat because he was late getting the cattle home, and was fearful of chastisement from his mother, while the suspected witches were examined by a medical team headed by William Harvey, and it was declared that the supposed witches' marks they carried were in fact of natural origins. The incident thus provoked an actively sceptical response from officialdom. It also, intriguingly, served as the basis for a witchcraft play, Heywood and Brome's *The Late Lancashire Witches*. Plays incorporating witchcraft themes had flourished in the years around 1600, although they had been in abeyance since *The Witch of Edmonton* of 1621. Heywood and Brome's play was, therefore, the last of a series, and it is a curious work deserving detailed analysis. Yet, even on an initial reading, the work demonstrates a duality about witchcraft which was well established in educated circles by the 1630s. Although the play ends with a confirmation of the existence of witchcraft, contrary to the authorities' decisions in 1634, the reality of the phenomenon is contested throughout the play. There are numerous references to contemporary folklore about witchcraft, as well as to *Macbeth* and Ovid's *Metamorphoses* but there is also a humorous tone, while the playwrights' decision to write much of the dialogue in an excruciating pastiche of a Lancashire accent must have helped distance the play's theme from London audiences. Both the government's treatment of the 1633–4 Lancashire witch scare and the play the affair spawned demonstrate how complex attitudes to witch accusations had become.

By the 1630s it therefore seemed that England was one of those European states where witchcraft, although still a crime, and although still a phenomenon whose reality few would have been able to deny absolutely, had been to a large extent marginalized among the educated. Prosecutions at the court were few, executions almost unknown, no demonological tracts or trial pamphlets were published in that decade, the upper reaches of the Church of England were sceptical and, as the handling of the Lancashire affair demonstrated, central government was willing to intervene to suppress witch-hunts. But in 1642 the Civil Wars began, and as a byproduct of the religious fervour and dilution of authority which those wars produced, witch-hunting began again, most infamously through the mass trials associated with Matthew Hopkins; trial pamphlets revived popular interest in the issue, and witchcraft again became a matter of intellectual speculation.[5] Although large-scale witch-hunts never occurred after the Restoration, the trials continued, as did the publication of learned tracts denying or supporting the reality of witchcraft: the last known execution came in 1685, the last conviction (overturned by the judge) in 1712, the last learned debate a few years later. But all this is another story, one that few could have foreseen in 1634.

NOTES

1   George Gifford, *A Dialogue concerning Witches and Witchcrafts. In which is laid open how craftily the Devil deceiveth not only the Witches but many other and so leadeth them awry into many great Errors* (London, 1593), sig. M2v.

2   William Perkins, *A Discourse of the damned Art of Witchcraft. So far forth as it is revealed in the Scriptures, and manifest by true Experience* (Cambridge, 1608), p. 257.

3   The relevant tracts are: *A true and just Recorde, of the Information, Examination, and Confession*

of all the Witches taken at S.Osies in the Countie of Essex, whereof some were executed, and some entreated according to the Determination of the Lawe* (London, 1582); Thomas Potts, *The Wonderfull Discoverie of Witches in the Countie of Lancaster. With the Arraignment and Triall of nineteene notorious Witches, at the Assizes and generall Gaole Deliverie, holden at the Castle of Lancaster, upon Munday the seventeenth of August last, 1612* (London, 1612); and Henry Goodcole, *The wonderfull Discoverie of Elizabeth Sawyer a*

Witch, late of Edmonton, her Conviction and Condemnation and Death (London, 1621). The best edition of the play based on this last case is Thomas Dekker, John Ford and William Rowley, *The Witch of Edmonton: A Critical Edition*, ed. Etta Soirey Onat (New York, 1980).

4 Cited in Barbara Rosen, *Witchcraft*, p. 84.
5 For a recent reassessment of the Hopkins episode, see James Sharpe, (1996), ch. 5, 'England's MA Witch-Hunt: East Anglia, 1645–7.

REFERENCES AND FURTHER READING

Ewen, Cecil l'Estrange (1929). *Witch Hunting and Witch Trials: The Indictments for Witchcraft from the Records of 1373 Assizes held for the Home Circuit A.D. 1559–1736*. London: Kegan, Paul, Trench, Trubner and Co; repr. London: Frederick Muller, 1971.

——(1933). *Witchcraft and Demonianism: A Concise Account Derived from Sworn Depositions and Confessions Obtained in the Courts of England and Wales*. London, Heath Cranton.

Gibson, Marion (1999). *Reading Witchcraft: Stories of Early English Witches*. London, Routledge.

Harris, Anthony (1980). *Night's Black Agents: Witchcraft and Magic in Seventeenth-century English Drama*. Manchester: Manchester University Press.

Kittredge, G. L. (1929). *Witchcraft in Old and New England*. Cambridge MA: Harvard University Press; repr. New York: Russell and Russell, 1956.

MacDonald, Michael (1990). *Witchcraft and Hysteria in Elizabethan London: Edward Jorden and the Mary Glover Case*. London: Routledge.

Macfarlane, Alan (1970). *Witchcraft in Tudor and Stuart England: A Regional and Comparative Study*. London: Routledge and Kegan Paul; reissued with introduction by James Sharpe, London: Routledge, 1999.

——(1977). 'A Tudor Anthropologist: George Gifford's *Discourse* and Dialogue'. In Sidney Anglo (ed.), *The Damned Art: Essays in the Literature of Witchcraft*. London: Routledge and Kegan Paul.

Notestein, Wallace (1911). *A History of Witchcraft in England from 1558 to 1718*. Washington, DC, repr. New York, Thomas Y. Crowell, 1968.

Purkiss, Diane (1996). *The Witch in History: Early Modern and Twentieth-century Representations*. London, Routledge.

Rosen, Barbara. (1969). *Witchcraft*. London: Edward Arnold.

Sharpe, James (1996). *Instruments of Darkness: Witchcraft in England 1550–1750*. London, Hamish Hamilton.

——(1999). *The Bewitching of Anne Gunter: A Horrible and True Story of Football, Witchcraft, Murder, and the King of England*. London: Profile Books.

Thomas, Keith (1971). *Religion and the Decline of Magic: Studies in Popular Beliefs in Sixteenth and Seventeenth-century England*. London, Weidenfeld and Nicolson.

Willis, Deborah (1995). *Malevolent Nurture: Witchhunting and Maternal Power in Early Modern England*. Ithaca, NY: Cornell University Press.

57
Reconstructing the Past: History, Historicism, Histories
James R. Siemon

All history is only half-made because it is always being made.
(Homi K. Bhabha, *Nation and Narration*)

In an exchange rich with implications for Renaissance historiography as well as for current debates about historicizing approaches to Renaissance texts, Shakespeare's Prince Edward responds to the claim that Julius Caesar constructed the Tower of London. First, he boldly proclaims that 'the truth' will survive independently of its discursive embodiment whether in written 'record' or oral 'report':

> But say, my lord, it were not registered,
> Methinks the truth should live from age to age,
> As 'twere retailed to all posterity,
> Even to the general all-ending day.
> (*Richard III* 3.3.75–8)[1]

This proclamation of the enduring power of *the* truth prompts Richard of Gloucester's notoriously equivocal assent – 'I say, without characters fame lives long' – which in turn, inexplicably, causes the Prince to reverse himself and acclaim language, and, even more specifically, writing as the guarantor of immortality:

> That Julius Caesar was a famous man;
> With what his valour did enrich his wit,
> His wit set down to make his valour live.
> Death makes no conquest of this conqueror,
> For now he lives in fame, though not in life.
> (3.1.84–8)

As Paul Werstine has noted, these passages convey the variety of what could count as 'history' in the Renaissance (Werstine, 71). History could be found embodied in monument, institutional record, oral report, and memoir, as well as, of course, in the historical poem (e.g. *The Mirror for Magistrates*) or drama. They also suggest apparent contradictions between a faith in *the* truth and an investment in the power of verbal self-fashioning, suggesting early modern interest in the longstanding problem of the relationship between history and language, a relation that continues to appear problematic in recent discussions of new historicism.

By now, the once new historicism has been around long enough to accrete a substantial following, arouse serious antagonists, and to experience internal divisions and revisions (see Howard; Kamps 1995; R. Wilson; Veeser; Tricomi). While critical movements such as cultural materialism or materialist feminism may be usefully differentiated from new historicism proper, the broad historicist imperative in Renaissance, and especially Renaissance *literary* studies continues to make itself felt almost universally through two interrelated effects: unhistoricized accounts of early modern works of art have become virtually inconceivable, while *the* history of cultural production and reproduction has been decisively reconstituted as plural, as histories (Belsey, 29–31; Werstine).

Even if new historicism itself is, in H. Aram Veeser's account, 'a phrase without an adequate referent' (Veeser, x), it is nevertheless true that what Louis A. Montrose calls the movement's 'historical *orientation*' (Montrose, 'New Historicisms', 406) has communicated itself very broadly indeed. However, despite this compelling interest in materials that might have seemed recently to belong to the province of the historian – in diaries, genealogies, institutional records, artefacts, and monuments, etc. – historicist literary theory and practice continue to be attacked for associations with poststructuralism. While these connections have never been secret (see Montrose's declaration of interest in 'the history of texts' and the 'textuality of history' [Veeser, 20]), it is striking that scholars who write about the English Renaissance period from very different disciplinary and ideological perspectives offer remarkably similar warnings about them. Francis Barker denounces new historicists, and especially Stephen Greenblatt, for 'turning society more or less wholly into discourse' and thus reducing the 'coercive pressures of actual social power' to de-realized figuration (Barker 157, 162; cf. 162, 200; cf. Porter, 781). More generally, D. R. Woolf warns that 'deconstruction and post-modernism threaten to undermine the "reality" of the past by turning everything into discourse, reducing all "fact" to rhetorical and social construction' (Woolf 1999, 193). Whatever the merits of such attempts to preserve the realities of 'actual social power' and 'fact', their stress on the importance of the discursive and the rhetorical to current forms of historicism is not at all out of place, especially in light of certain aspects of early modern historiography. However, attention to discursive elements may be seen as a source of positive opportunity rather than as a threat to the real, however defined by historian or materialist. Whether one agrees with any given form or practice of 'new' historicism, the general historicist impetus to recover the disparate, the anecdotal, the ancillary site, the marginal, silenced or resistant group, should be taken as a virtue. Thus, what Hayden White has called the 'distinctively poetic' nature of new historicism – i.e., the yoking together of the (seemingly) unrelated instance and event to enable the recovery of relations and codes (Veeser, 300) – certainly need imply neither quietism nor cognitive nihilism. Instead of 'aestheticis[ing] history' (R. Wilson, 18), new historicist practices may form the basis for distinctly politicized recoveries of the conflictual reality that M. M. Bakhtin described under the term social heteroglossia.

In offering to 'get historicisation right', Barker cites Foucault to propose a conflictual model of historical understanding in place of the linguistic model that Barker finds informing historicist enterprises. Foucault writes:

> I believe that it is not to the great model of signs and language [*la langue*] that reference should be made, but to war and battle. The history which bears and determines us is war-like, not language-like. Relations of power, not relations of sense. History has no 'sense', which is not to say that it is absurd or incoherent. On the contrary, it is intelligible and should be able to be analysed down to the slightest detail: but according to the intelligibility of struggles, of strategies and tactics.
>
> (Barker, 233n)

One may agree with Foucault's priorities, but modelling historical inquiry on struggle hardly diminishes the importance of discursive phenomena, as Foucault himself insisted (Foucault).

Furthermore, Foucault's resistance to the structuralist model of *langue* with its attendant senses of system, order and stasis, sounds precisely the note of the Bakhtin circle's translinguistics. M. M. Bakhtin, P. Medvedev and V. N. Voloshinov understand language as a site of constant struggle and contention among *languages* – rather than as an order defined by stable polarities of *la langue* – and make that understanding central to their social analyses. Voloshinov insists that it is expression that organizes experience, rather than the other way around, and every word, every signifying practice, indeed every aspect of human reality, from complex cultural productions such as works of art or historiography down to apparently simple physical sensations (Voloshinov, 86–9), is riven by historical relations of contention and agreement among social groups, their values, and the orientations of their behavioural ideologies. In heteroglot utterance, the Bakhtin circle found the great model and first instance of this pervasive dialogical struggle and contention:

> The internal stratification of any single national language into social dialects, characteristic group behaviour, professional jargons, generic languages, languages of generations and age groups, tendentious languages, languages of the authorities, of various circles, and of passing fashions, languages that serve the specific socio-political purposes of the day, even of the hour (each day has its own slogan, its own vocabulary, its own emphases) – this internal stratification [is] present in every language at any given moment of its historical existence.
>
> (Bakhtin, 262–3)

Such a dialogical model of society may result in analyses that are less orderly than those provided by classical materialist dialectics, but it is no less conflictual, no less material, and no less historical for its stress on language(s).

Given this dialogical sense of the constitutive role of socio-linguistic discord, division and conflict, the great enemies of historical consciousness for Bakhtin and Voloshinov are the centripetal tendencies manifested in monological forms of signifying practice: official pronouncements, orthodox creeds, sanctioned histories, ritualised forms of ideological domination by one class or group that assume the aspect of universality and thus may go – almost – without saying. Writing largely under the monological imperatives of Stalinism's drive to rewrite the past, present, and future according to one all-determining, unified 'history', they championed voices that did not fit the plan. Famously, Bakhtin found those voices aloud in popular carnival, but he also detected their presence in the carnivalesque aspects of written works of art – in Menippean satire, in Rabelais, in Dostoevsky, and in Shakespeare. For Bakhtin the early modern period was a time when the centrifugal tendencies of language exerted a particularly powerful shaping presence, but ultimately Bakhtin found traces of heteroglot orientation in *all* utterance, not just in the laughter, sorrow and anger of the oppressed, but also in the signifying practices of the dominant – even if only in the harsh accents, the strained hyperboles, the complacent indifferences, the evident formal distortions and strategic silences that repressive monologism adopts in exercising its hegemony (cf. Voloshinov, 72).

For a brief but significant moment, the historical enterprise in sixteenth-century England exhibited a particularly centripetal form and content that both literary critics (e.g. Rackin) and historians (Woolf) have characterized in terms that would be monological in Bakhtin's sense. Of course, the chronicle histories that loom so large in their effects on early modern literature and historiography took some of their unifying impetus from the demands of Tudor national and religious consolidation (Woolf, *Idea*). This meant that 'the truth' supposedly derived from, and certainly applied to, history often amounted to the same repeated clichés. D. R. Woolf maintains that 'All Tudor and early Stuart historical writing . . . reflects a conservative ideology of obedience, duty, and deference to social and political hierarchy. Historians used the past to sanction certain types of behaviour and to deplore others; they also used it to justify the authority structures of their present, structures which in turn shaped and coloured what they said about the past' (Woolf, *Idea* xiii). Under such pressure, the various histories of past reigns tended to turn into one history; and since E. M. W. Tillyard scholarship has often identified that totalized history with the ideology of early modern history plays (Kamps 1996, 52). One reaction has been a scholarly counter-tradition which opposes Shakespeare to his chronicle sources. Eloquently epitomizing this view, Phyllis Rackin employs Bakhtin's vocabulary to contrast the 'polyphonic form' of Shakespeare's theatrically enacted history to the 'univocal form of history writing' found in the chronicles, wherein 'a single authorial voice' often obscures the 'plurality' of sources and contributors (Rackin, 24–5).

This stress on the polyphony of early modern history plays may be accurate, but unfair to the historical sources. There are some significant reservations to the centripetal, monological trend in sixteenth-century history writing. If few scholars credit F. Smith Fussner's account of a 'historical revolution' any more, recent studies suggest what Bakhtin would have predicted: the chronicles themselves betray traces of centrifugal, counter- or hetero-orientations (Patterson, 7). In Holinshed, for example, many have pointed out the discrepancies between the appended morals and the evidence provided by the inclusion of diverse pamphlets and manuscript sources. In such cases, it is precisely the discursive and social construction of history that is revealed, not as instancing post-modern drift or slippage *avant la lettre* but as registering – even when the compilers are attempting to resist it – the heteroglot contentions of groups, classes and interests (and here one might remember the group and class significance of micro-narratives in Jean-François Lyotard's accounts of post-modernity). Although Holinshed's inclusion of primary documents and anecdotes has been characterized negatively by F. J. Levy as history 'by agglomeration' (Levy 1967, 183–4), it constitutes a source of obvious usefulness for historicizing studies. But even single-author histories devoted to the most ideologically unified of subject matters display revealing traces of socially heteroglot struggle and contention. Accounts of Richard III offer particularly telling examples, for in portraying the most 'persistently vilified of all English kings' (Ross, 227), the chronicles might be expected to display an untroubled Tudor unanimity, yet the discourse(s) that embody that history reveal different histories.

The basics were established early and handed along sometimes verbatim from Bernard André and Polydore Vergil to Sir Thomas More to Grafton, Halle, Hardyng, Stow and Holinshed. Yet, the articulation of Richard's history betrays remarkable fissures. Relating what might appear to qualify precisely as an opportunity for Tudor panegyric, the first official Tudor historian, Henry VII's poet laureate and family tutor, Bernard André (Hanham, 21) provides a strange non-account of the battle of Bosworth that ended Richard's life and reign in 1485. Since military victories constitute a generic staple of 'King and Battle' history and of the panegyric rhetoric often preferred by official historiography, André's reticence is indeed striking as both history and rhetoric. Writing in 1502 ostensibly for Bosworth's victor, André breaks off his account with a dramatically blank page and a strangely worded explanation:

> I have heard something of the battle by oral report, but the eye is a safer judge than the ear in such a matter. Therefore I pass over the date, the place, and the order of battle, rather than assert anything rashly; for as I have said before, I lack clear sight. And so until I obtain more knowledge of this debatable field, I leave both it and this page a blank.
>
> (Hanham, 53)

In the context of a discussion of discursive elements in historiography, André's pun on the term 'field' is revealing: '*Et pro tam bellico campo, donec plenius instructus fuero, campum quoque latum hoc in albo relinquo*' (André, 32). As Hanham points out, *campus* here punningly equates 'field of battle', 'subject of debate' and 'blank space in a manuscript' (Hanham, 54). For reasons that are not now immediately apparent, and that were not apparent to André's successors among early modern writers of history, basic factual matters – dates, places and events – occasion a reticence which signals, according to André's trope, their charged nature as contentious fields of utterance, as sites of battle. What sort of battle this might be is suggested by further – specifically discursive – dimensions to this passage.

André himself was physically blind, so nothing that he reported could ever answer the demand that the historian report only what had been experienced with 'clear sight'. Yet the joke is not aimed simply at himself, for his witty rejection of hearsay in favour of that which is known with clear sight mocks that sixteenth-century demand for a direct relation between history and truth that is famously formulated in Sidney's denigration of historians in his *Defence of Poesy* for constructing their so-called 'truth' upon other histories which are based ultimately on a 'notable foundation of hearsay'. Perhaps not surprisingly, one of the earliest historians to respond explicitly to André's gaps seems to miss these ironies at the expense of his own discipline. In 1611 John Speed takes the blank spaces to signify simple lapses of knowledge occasioned by André's physical blindness, while condescending to praise his work as noteworthy for its discursive aspirations:

> having as well the title of poet laureate as of the king's historiographer (how hardlysoever those two faculties meet with honour in the same person), [André] meant to have historified and poetised the acts of this king, but (for want of competent and attended instructions in many places of chief importance) left his labour full of wilde [*sic*] breaches and unfinished, yet in such points as he hath professed to know not unworthy to be vouched, for there is in him a great deal of clear elocution and defecated [purified] conceit above the ordinary of that age.
>
> (Speed, 728)

Speed also seems not to notice that this collapse of André's otherwise 'clear elocution and defecated conceit', occurs at a point of considerable historical conflict.

In fact, a 'historified and poetised' account of Bosworth remained problematic seventeen years after the event because the battle was at once a dynastic watershed and also a potential source of reproach for the survivors (and their families). Noteworthy among those whose role at Bosworth remained controversial well into the Tudor period was the Earl of Northumberland, about whose activities completely contradictory claims were made (Hanham). Even after his death in 1489, a statement of 'fact' in such a context could be highly inflammatory, given the implications for heirs and allies as well as Henry's own tenuous grip on the crown. Thus, André's witty refusal registers the unsettled nature of the royal hegemony in the earliest Tudor years. In the climate of continuing royal insecurity that lasted throughout Henry's reign (Chrimes, 68–94), even opportunities for panegyric might be passed up, since it meant taking the risk of saying the wrong things about noble families and factions. Besides, by the time André writes, those noble families had their own insecurities dramatically compounded by the extraordinary financial demands that Henry made upon them as testimony of their loyalty (Chrimes, 215).

Informed by histories such as André's and probably Polydore Vergil's manuscript for the *Anglica Historica*, Sir Thomas More constructed his own highly influential history of Richard III. More's biographical account does not extend to Bosworth, but odd suggestions of conflict and struggle are evident enough. Despite its original and resolutely polemical reduction of Richard to a premeditative, hunchbacked murderer, More's text often creates a bizarre sense of tentativeness about its assertions. Much is attributed to what 'wise men say' or is 'for truth reported' by others, but such discursive self-qualification takes much more extreme form in More's account Richard's role in the murder of his brother, Clarence:

> Some wise men also ween, that his drift covertly conveyed, lacked not in helping forth his brother of Clarence to his death, which he resisted openly, howbeit somewhat (as men deemed) more faintly than he that were heartily minded to his wealth. And they that thus deem, think that he long time in king Edward's life forethought to be king in case that the king his brother (whose life he looked that evil diet should shorten) should happen to decease (as indeed he did) while his children were young. And they deem that for this intent he was glad of his brother's death, the Duke of Clarence, whose life must needs have hindered him so intending, whether the same Duke of Clarence had kept him true to his nephew the young king, or enterprised to be king himself. But of all this point is there no certainty, and who so divineth upon conjectures may as well shoot too far as too short.
>
> (More *CW* 2: 8–9)

In phrasing that mocks the diction of other historians (Hanham, 15; cf. Ross, xxxix), More reports what he proceeds to take back, or seems to. He hedges to the edge of self-cancellation, dragging in reporters and wise men to attest to claims which eventually he drops as conjectural anyway. Furthermore, immediately after this passage More betrays all its cautions:

> Howbeit this have I by credible information learned, that the self night in which King Edward died, one Mystelbrooke long ere morning, came in great haste to the house of one Pottyer dwelling in Redcross street without Cripplegate; and when he was with hasty rapping quickly let in, he showed unto Pottyer that king Edward was departed. 'By my troth', man, quoth Pottyer, 'then will my master the Duke of Gloucester be king.' What cause he had so to think, hard it is to say, whether he being toward him, any thing knew that he such thing purposed, or otherwise had any inkling thereof, for he was not likely to speak it of nought.
>
> (More *CW* 2: 9)

What is one to make of this? How credit the merely 'likely' so soon after stern cautions against conjecture? In light of the self-cancelling nature of such passages, it may seem ironic that More furnished the principal backbone of later historiography, and that these very passages, so larded with cancellations and self-contradictions, first offer the subsequently repeated notion that Richard for a 'long time . . . forethought to be king' (*CW* 2: lxxix).

As in the case of his *Utopia* which More says 'includes nothing false and omits nothing true' (*CW* 4: 43), the *History of Richard III* performs handsprings of irony around its assertions, giving with one hand, taking back with the other. Although such formal features might recall the witty self-mockery characteristic of the Lucianic discourse that More appreciated and elsewhere imitated, there is reason to resist the judgement dating back to the eighteenth century that More offers, in Horace Walpole's words, 'a fabric of fiction' rather than a history written in a highly contested socio-historical context (Ross, xxvi). After all, as Hanham notes, such passages are not random but appear to target the language of the chroniclers, mocking their characteristic locutions, while also making fun of their frequently unacknowledged self-contradictions by making More's own so laughably obvious. With what intention is not clear, but to what effect is perhaps less mysterious: the discursive form in fact parallels More's content. Again and again, More recounts the ironies produced by the limited knowledge and self-knowledge of human agents; Shakespeare, like Halle and Holinshed before him, remains true to More's moral for Hastings: 'O good God, the blindness of our mortal nature, when [Hastings] most feared he was in good surety: when he reckoned himself surest, he lost his life, and that within two hours after' (*CW* 2: 52). Orthodox enough in matter, such a Christian truism is yet in its form, in its mode of discourse, suggestive of a less orthodox purpose: registering that this account is written by an author who violates expectations and rules – of logical and tonal self-consistency, of clarity, of genre – but does so boldly and knowingly, wittily rather than from limitation or ignorance.

When seen in a Renaissance context, such a gesture against decorum repays consideration for its social construction. Whatever its positive emulation of classical models like Sallust and Tacitus from whom More's work takes features such as its emphasis on constructed speeches, it also conveys a negative message of authorial distinction and difference from the dull-witted and earnest among More's contemporaries. More reproduces, in other words, a humanist, academic version of a key prejudice of the courtly milieu, which, according to Castiglione, valued apparently effortless achievements of *sprezzatura* and wit over accomplishments that manifested dull application. More's prefatory letter to Peter Giles suggests the discursive equivalence of this social opposition by contrasting those who are 'dull-minded' or 'who approve only of what is old' to the 'careless simplicity' of Raphael, the ostensible narrator of *Utopia* (*CW* 4: 45, 39). These terms may reintroduce the social dimensions of the discussion between Shakespeare's Richard and his nephew concerning the Tower and the role of 'wit' in the survival of 'truth'.

Meditating on history and discourse, Shakespeare's little prince first proclaims the conviction that 'truth' is more substantial and enduring than any discursive vehicle that might chance to convey it. Subsequently, he significantly modifies this claim and in fact appears to reverse himself. The terms of this early modern discussion bear directly on the concerns about the reduction of history to language and social construction raised by Woolf and Barker.

As if in unwitting recognition of the fact that the opaque witticisms of his uncle will outlive the clichés of his own reverent optimism, Shakespeare's little victim recurs to Caesar's immortality in a very different – and more characteristically Shakespearean

– light. In response to his uncle's assertion that fame survives without written 'characters', the prince appears to contradict his earlier denigration of writing by maintaining that it is precisely Caesar's 'wit' as 'set down' in his writings that insures eternal survival:

> That Julius Caesar was a famous man;
> With what his valour did enrich his wit,
> His wit set down to make his valour live.
> Death makes no conquest of this conqueror,
> For now he lives in fame, though not in life.
>   (3.1.84–8)

There is a 'witty' double meaning here that is seldom noted.

The claim that his 'wit' in writing about his exploits enabled the valour of those exploits to outlive Caesar's material body makes sense, but, as the puzzlement of generations of editors recorded in the *Variorum* edition suggests, it is less clear how his valour could be said to 'enrich' Caesar's wit. This discursive crux is complicated by the fact that the term in the earliest quarto texts (Q1, Q2) is not 'valour' but 'valure', a term with at least three possible historical senses: battlefield valour, value in a clearly material sense, or value in a more general abstract sense of worth (*OED*). Thus, the prince's remark invokes the worth of Caesar, his *value* in some vague undefined sense, without tying that value to any definition according to a specific quality such as bravery. The one certainty here is that 'valure' is manifested in 'wit' and that wit is itself dependent on its mode of articulation, on being 'set down' in writing. Far from being merely amusing, such a conceited witticism sits uneasily astride a historical conflict of social groups and values that registered itself discursively in polemic exchanges that were exactly contemporary with Shakespeare's play: the social conflict between pen and sword, between the bureaucratic practices and values of the so-called new men and the values of a traditional military, honour culture (see James). Caesar was an interesting figure for both sides of the contention, for if he was known as a martial conqueror, he was also, as Thomas Wilson notes, famous among 'wits' for his discursive capacities: 'Julius Caesar is reported that he could read, hear, and tell one what he should write, so fast as his pen could run, and indite letters himself altogether at one time' (T. Wilson, 237).

Another, less-elevated version of such an interrelation among value, wit, and discursive capacity occurs in a later passage of the play in which Richard himself perversely recurs to the Prince's terms. Attempting to woo the murdered Prince's own grieving mother to surrender her daughter to him, Richard echoes his previous little victim in defining how the queen should speak the unspeakable by rhetorically characterising his own incestuous and thoroughly politic desire for his niece:

> And when this arm of mine hath chastisèd
> The petty rebel, dull-brained Buckingham,
> Bound with triumphant garlands will I come

> And lead thy daughter to a conqueror's bed;
> To whom I will retail my conquest won,
> And she shall be sole victoress, Caesar's Caesar.
> (4.4.331–6)

Here again, as earlier, the value of wit is presumed: the 'petty rebel' Buckingham mocked for the contrast between his puny 'dull-brained' efforts and the grandiose rebelliousness embodied in Richard's own ongoing crimes against law, order, family and religion. Also, it is again predicted that a conqueror's fame will be 'retailed', but this time not so grandly, not everlastingly and to everyone unto 'the general all-ending day'. Rather, Richard recycles the prince's sweeping language to describe a conjugal scenario which both mocks the grandeur of the prince's inflated sense of truth's substantiality and, more subtly, mocks the petty demands such a minor domestic situation will put upon Richard's own prodigious rhetorical capabilities. Richard speaks as if seducing his niece would require what would be for him no more than a little small-scale verbal retailing. Here discursive facility is portrayed with a mercenary pettiness of scale that belittles the value of great Caesar's martial fame, by reducing it to serve as a figure for a little Caesar's marital foreplay.

The specific social dimensions of the ironies suggested by the use of 'retail' here are clearer in the overt mockery aimed at small-scale wit in *Love's Labour's Lost*. Berowne mocks 'honey-tongued Boyet' as 'the ape of form', comparing him to a retailer who elaborately over-packages a very little wit:

> He is wit's peddler, and retails his wares
> At wakes and wassails, meetings, markets, fairs;
> And we that sell by gross, the Lord doth know,
> Have not the grace to grace it with such show.
> This gallant pins the wenches on his sleeve.
> Had he been Adam, he had tempted Eve.
> 'A can carve too, and lisp. Why, this is he
> That kissed his hand away in courtesy.
> This is the ape of form, Monsieur the Nice.
> (*LLL* 5.2.318–26)

Show, form, courtesy, grace – the standard qualities of courtliness here appear depicted as commodified and improperly appropriated by a smallholder who retails them for what appear to be from the perspective of the courtly observers distinctly minor-league amatory profits.

The point of these examples is twofold. On the one hand, early modern 'history' is as riddled with discursive traces of socially defined conflicts about what matters and what is to be taken for real as early modern literature; on the other, histories of courtly or professional distinction, with their oppositions of pen to sword or of wholesale to retail, have things to reveal about early modern literary discourses. One might usefully quarrel with currently existing forms of new historicism on many grounds – for focusing on canonical works (Holstun); stressing recuperation and stasis rather than change and agency (Howard, *Stage* 11–12); recurring to a limited number of opponents to stand for diverse intellectual traditions (Tricomi, 157n); totalizing despite its claims (Porter) – the dangers of turning the real into discourse and social construction pale beside the potential benefits of the historical orientation in generating multiple *histories* that offer opportunity for fuller encounters with the pastness as well as the presentness of the past. In this vein, excellent recent historicized scholarship of the early modern period – e.g. Emily Bartels on Marlowe and imperialism, William Carroll on Shakespeare and poverty and vagrancy, Theodore Leinwand on theatre and finance, Kim Hall on early modern literature, race and gender – sets a high standard for the future.

NOTE

1 Shakespeare quotations from David M. Bevington, *The Complete Works of Shakespeare*, 4th edn (Chicago: Addison, Wesley, Longman, 1997).

REFERENCES AND FURTHER READING

André, Bernard (1858). *Historia Regis Henrici Septimi*, ed. James Gairdner. Rolls Series 10. London: Longman.

Bakhtin, M. M. (1981). *The Dialogic Imagination*, ed. Michael Holquist, trs Holquist and Caryl Emerson. Austin: University of Texas Press.

Barker, Francis (1993). *The Culture of Violence: Essays on Tragedy and History*. Manchester: University of Manchester Press.

Bartels, Emily C. (1993). *Spectacles of Strangeness: Imperialism, Alienation, and Marlowe*. Philadelphia: University of Philadelphia Press.

Belsey, Catherine (1991). 'Making Histories Then and Now: Shakespeare from *Richard II* to *Henry V*'. In Francis Barker, Peter Hulme and Margaret Iverson (eds), *Uses of History: Marxism, Postmodernism and the Renaissance* (pp. 24–46). Manchester: Manchester University Press.

Carroll, William C. (1996). *Fat King, Lean Beggar: Representations of Poverty in the Age of Shakespeare*. Ithaca: Cornell University Press.

Chrimes, S. B. (1972). *Henry VII*. Berkeley: University of California Press.

Foucault, Michel (1981) 'The Order of Discourse'. In Robert Young (ed.), *Untying the Text: A Post-Structuralist Reader* (pp. 48–78). London: Routledge and Kegan Paul.

Greenblatt, Stephen (1988). *Shakespearean Negotiations: The Circulation of Social Energy in Renaissance England*. Berkeley: University of California Press.

Hall, Kim F. (1995). *Things of Darkness: Economies of Race and Gender in Early Modern England*. Ithaca: Cornell University Press.

Hanham, Alison (1975). *Richard III and His Early Historians 1483–1535*. Oxford: Clarendon Press.

Holstun, James (1989). 'Ranting at the New Historicism', *English Literary Renaissance*, 19, 189–225.

Howard, Jean E. (1987). 'The New Historicism in Renaissance Studies'. In Dan S. Collins and Arthur F. Kinney (eds), *Renaissance Historicism* (pp. 3–31). Amherst: University of Massachusetts Press.

——(1994). *The Stage and Social Struggle in Early Modern England*. London: Routledge.

James, Mervyn (1986). *Society, Politics, Culture: Studies in Early Modern England*. Cambridge: Cambridge University Press.

Kamps, Ivo (ed.) (1995). *Materialist Shakespeare: A History*. New York: Verso.

——(1996). *Historiography and Ideology in Stuart Drama*. Cambridge: Cambridge University Press.

Leinwand, Theodore B. (1999). *Theatre, Finance, and Society in Early Modern England*. Cambridge: Cambridge University Press.

Levy, F. J. (1967). *Tudor Historical Thought*. San Marino: Huntington Library.

Montrose, Louis A. (1989). 'Professing the Renaissance: The Poetics and Politics of Culture'. In Veeser (1989) (pp. 15–36).

——(1992). 'New Historicisms'. In Stephen Greenblatt and Giles Gunn (eds), *Redrawing the Boundaries: The Transformation of English and American Literary Studies* (pp. 392–418). New York: Modern Language Association.

More, Thomas (1964). *The Complete Works of St Thomas More*, Vol. 2, ed. Richard S. Sylvester. New Haven: Yale University Press.

——(1965). *The Complete Works of St Thomas More*, vol. 4, ed. Edward Surtz and J. H. Hexter. New Haven: Yale University Press.

Patterson, Annabel (1994). *Reading Holinshed's 'Chronicles'*. Chicago: University of Chicago Press.

Porter, Carolyn (1988). 'Are We Being Historical Yet?', *South Atlantic Quarterly*, 87, 743–86.

Rackin, Phyllis (1990). *Stages of History: Shakespeare's English Chronicles*. Ithaca: Cornell University Press.

Ross, Charles (1981). *Richard III*. Berkeley: University of California Press.

Speed, John (1611). *The History of Great Britain*. London: STC 23045.

Tricomi, Albert H. (1996). *Reading Tudor–Stuart Texts through Cultural Historicism*. Gainesville, FL: University Press of Florida.

Veeser, H. Aram (ed.) (1989). *The New Historicism*. London: Routledge.

Voloshinov, V. N. (1986). *Marxism and the Philosophy of Language*, trs Ladislav Matejka and I. R. Titunik. Cambridge, MA: Harvard University Press.

Werstine, Paul (1998). '"Is It upon Record?": The Reduction of the History Play to History'. In W. Speed Hill (ed.), *New Ways with Old Texts II: Papers of the Renaissance English Text Society, 1992–1996* (pp. 71–82). Binghamton, NY: Medieval and Renaissance Texts and Studies.

Wilson, Richard (1993). *Will Power: Essays on Shakespearean Authority*. Detroit: Wayne State University Press.

Wilson, Richard and Dutton, Richard (eds) (1992). *New Historicism and Renaissance Drama*. London: Longman.

Wilson, Thomas (1553; 1962). *The Arte of Rhetorique*, intro. Robert Hood Bowers. Gainesville, FL: Scholars' Facsimiles.

Woolf, D. R. (1990). *The Idea of History in Early Stuart England*. Toronto: University of Toronto Press.

——(1999). 'The Shapes of History'. In David Scott Kastan (ed.), *A Companion to Shakespeare* (pp. 186–205). London: Blackwell.

58

Sexuality: A Renaissance Category?

James Knowles

Come live with me, and be my love,
And we will all the pleasures prove
That valleys, groves, hills and fields,
Woods, or steepy mountain yields.

And we will sit upon the rocks,
Seeing the shepherds feed their flocks
By shallow rivers, to whose falls
Melodious birds sing madrigals.

And I will make thee beds of roses,
And a thousand fragrant poesies,
A cap of flowers, and a kirtle,
Embroidered all with leaves of myrtle.

A gown made of the finest wool
Which from our pretty lambs we pull,
Fair linèd slippers for the cold:
With buckles of the purest gold.

A belt of straw, and ivy-buds,
With coral clasps and amber studs,
And if these pleasures may thee move,
Come live with me, and be my love.

The shepherd swains shall dance and sing,
For thy delight each May morning.
If these delights thy mind may move;
Then live with me, and be my love.[1]

Marlowe's 'Come Live With Me and Be My Love' is one of the most evocative and notorious lyrics of the late sixteenth century. First published in 1599 (six years after

Marlowe's death) snatches of the text appear in *The Merry Wives of Windsor* and *The Jew of Malta*, and the poem occasioned many responses, including Ralegh's 'The Nymph's Reply' and Donne's 'The Bait'.[2] It is suffused with teasing sexual allure, made even more explicit in Ralegh's reply where the nymph rejects 'folly ripe' and 'reason rotten', and in Donne's images of lovers like fishes caught by 'curious traitors' (nets).[3] Clearly contemporary readers understood the poem's 'delights' as moving far more than the mind.

So, Marlowe's poem supposes sex, but does it, therefore, require 'sexuality'? This is more problematic as the term 'sexuality' only appears in the language in the nineteenth century as an accompaniment to the developing science of sexology and the classificatory desires that instituted terms such as homosexuality and heterosexuality.[4] As part of the broader project to discipline and control individuals through their identity, nineteenth-century medical discourses catalogued and named identities, describing some as perversions and others as acceptable and 'normal'. Michel Foucault argues that the process of the 'incorporation of perversions' and the 'specification of individuals' created a new kind of identity (based on sexual object choice) and installed sexuality at the centre of modern senses of the self and as the primary targets of modern modes of social discipline. Foucault outlines an important distinction between acts and identities, using the creation of first, the 'homosexual', then homosexuality, as his model:

> As defined by the ancient civil or canonical codes, sodomy was a category of forbidden acts; their perpetrator was nothing more than the juridical subject of them. The nineteenth-century homosexual became a personage, a past, a case history, and a childhood, in addition to being a type of life, a life form, and a morphology, with an indiscreet anatomy and possibly a mysterious physiology . . . The sodomite had been a temporary aberration; the homosexual was now a species.[5]

This important distinction between acts (the temporary aberration of sodomy) and identity (the homosexual as a separate, defined species) has shaped recent histories of sexuality. Some critics argue that the institution of sexual differences as 'identities' creates the modern subject. Indeed, Eve Sedgwick extends the argument, regarding the prior creation of the homosexual as a foundational moment in the constitution of the modern western, *heterosexual* subject and the sexual binaries which have oppressed both men and women.[6]

Foucault's reading of sexual history has several important ramifications. First, Foucault disrupts any sense of continuity with the past: we cannot look for gay or homosexual histories because none exist. It also powerfully challenges and simple notions of identity, directing research towards historically specific categories and discourse, based on particular societies and eras, rather than broad generalizations and transhistorical ideas (universals). Perhaps, most importantly, Foucault places same-sex relations and their description and interpretation at the heart of any attempt to understand any sexuality. Taking a lead from Foucault in this respect, the rest of this chapter will explore the issue of same-sex relations as a tool to expose how a wider sexuality might, or might not, have existed and operated in the early modern period.

Acts, Identity and Sodomy

For early modern historians Foucault's interest in acts has focused attention on the most prominent and strident concepts associated with inter-male relations: sodomy and the sodomite. Foucault described sodomy as an 'utterly confused category' partly because, despite the constant reiteration of its horrors, the term evades precise definition. Yet, alongside this repressive rhetoric of absolute prohibition stands the extensive and highly contradictory evidence of tolerance of male societies and relations (sometimes referred to as 'homosocial' bonds) in the central institutions of society.[7] Alan Bray has filled out the details of this account showing how sodomy was mobilized as a catch-all crime against those who threatened social order, including heretics (especially Catholics and Jesuits), witches, demons and werewolves. It was an idea more akin to modern debauchery and was thus less a sexual than a political and religious crime.[8] Yet (or, perhaps, because) the rhetoric surrounding sodomy was so paradoxically extreme and harsh – yet also vague – that the basic male bonds which held this society together, and which demanded a male intimacy which might easily fall within the purlieu of this crime, seem rarely to have been considered in those terms. Except, of course, in times of political and social crisis, when the potency of sodomy as a catch-all came into force.

If Foucault's powerful and compelling arguments are followed, does this necessarily mean that we must imagine a society *entirely* without sexuality, that there can be 'no gay history' and that we are stuck with a hetero-normative past and a queer modernity?[9] Marlowe's 'Come Live with me' troubles this argument in a number of ways. We might accept that the poem is about 'sex' but that is itself an equivocal term: does it refer to the sexual act (to have sex) or to gender difference (to have *a* sex)? In fact, only the second of these senses was current in the 1590s, yet even that is not unambiguous within the poem (see below).[10] Moreover, the teasing opacity of the poem and our unwillingness to speak sex plainly hides but also (potentially) reveals, a much wider range of sexual possibilities than those proposed by modern historians of sexuality, who primarily study official discourses (medicine and science) rather than the more subversive discourses of literary texts. Linguistic utterances, especially complex texts, may act as imaginative, temporary, spaces beyond the control of the sex police.[11]

'Come Live With Me and Be my Love' problematizes sex in another sense which bears out the subversive potential of texts. The responses from Ralegh and Donne onwards all assume that the addressee is female.[12] One anonymous version praises the shepherd's 'summer queen', another gives the nymph a name ('Clarinda'), and Isaac Walton translates the poem into 'The Milkmaid's Song'. These responses illustrate how quickly the apparently neutral term 'sex' shades into areas which we would place under the headings of gender and sexuality. Thus, the seductive attitude and the proffered gifts are as much about gender roles and the power relations they embody as they are about the sex of the speaker and addressee. Men seduce women with gifts, demonstrating their manliness through their wealth obtained through activity (work), women their femininity through their passive acceptance and the adoration offered by men.

Yet the responses are revealing in another way, in that they suggest a certain anxiety about the teasing, alluring eroticism of the poem, writing about and re-writing it in a resolutely sexed fashion. All the revisions assume that Marlowe writes about sex between different sexes, when the text is more equivocal. At no point is the sex/gender of the addressee actually given, nor, indeed, of the speaker (which facilitates Walton's female ventriloquism). Ralegh may *assume* the addressee to be a nymph, and the other anonymous response in *England's Helicon* may *believe* the object is 'summer's queen' but the poem offers us only ambiguity. The key term is 'kirtle', which may (as in *Hero and Leander*) be a woman's gown (sometimes outer coat) or, as here, also a man's tunic, especially a shepherd's smock.[13]

Genre may offer us another approach. 'Come Live With Me' belongs to the pastoral, and as such draws on a range of ideas and models important in Renaissance culture. Pastoral might be used for a range of purposes, including political commentary, often amatory or sexual dalliance, and at least one inflection allows that it might speak those desires between men. One of the best-known pastoral poems in the Renaissance, Virgil's *Eclogues*, included the famous story of Corydon's love for Alexis, the beautiful shepherd boy: *'Formosum pastor Corydon ardebat Alexin / delicias domini'*.[14] The classically educated Marlowe certainly knew this poem and, indeed, *Hero and Leander* associates pastoral with the homoerotic in the tale of the 'shepherd sitting in a vale / Played with a boy so fair and kind' told by Neptune to seduce a reluctant Leander.[15] The sexual associations of pastoral were widely recognized in the period. In *The Shepheardes Calender* Spenser uses Virgil's shepherd as the model for Hobbinol, who is enamoured of Colin, while in *The Affectionate Shepherd* (1594) Barnfield describes the love of Daphnis for Ganymede. In the commentary to *The Shepheardes Calender* written by 'E.K.' (opinions are divided whether this persona conceals Spenser or Gabriel Harvey) Hobbinol's desire for Colin is glossed as 'pæderastice' which is carefully differentiated from sodomy ('disorderly love') and also from 'gynerastice', the love of women, which is also defined as degenerate.[16]

This choice of 'learned' terms may in itself be revealing as it suggests that at least some sixteenth-century readers saw male–male relations in terms of the sexual (pederastic) patterns of classical society. This would fit another aspect of the poem's genre as pastoral, classed as a lower and simpler genre, was regarded as a suitable adolescent or apprentice piece for the poet who would then aspire to higher forms, such as epic. Both genre and intertext might then point towards a pattern of neo-classical sexual behaviour used to explore and explain ideas and feelings for which there were no readily available categories or vocabularies, beyond the condemnatory discourses of the church.

Indeed, although we cannot be certain how they understood themselves, the historical record provides ample evidence of same-sex sexual activity, especially in continental cities such as Florence and Venice.[17] In Florence, recent research suggests that up to 17,000 individuals (of whom 3,000 were convicted) were incriminated for sodomy during a seventy-year period, in a city of roughly 40,000 inhabitants.[18] Italy's sexual reputation was so notorious that it erupted in commonplace sayings and proverbs, such as 'back-door'd Italian', or the German synonym for buggery, 'Florenzen'.[19] The continental evidence may provide the faint traces of sexual sub-cultures, while texts like Marlowe's suggest that it was possible to imagine eroticism between men, and even that texts provided an imaginary space where those relations could be depicted in relative safety. Barnfield certainly suggests this in his dedicatory epistle to *Cynthia* (1595):

> Some there were that did interpret *The Affectionate Shepherd* otherwise than, in truth, I meant, touching the subject thereof, to wit, the love of a shepherd to a boy – a fault, the which I will not excuse, because I never made. Only this: I will unshadow my conceit, being nothing else but an imitation of Virgil, in the second eclogue of Alexis.[20]

Barnfield stages a most offensive defence. On one hand, the dangerous and sodomitical implications are rejected and turned back on the reader (*their* interpretation sees sodomy where there is none, or perhaps only E.K.'s pederasty). Indeed, Barnfield claims merely to imitating pious and highly respectable Virgil. Yet, in drawing attention to the potential sexual subtext, Barnfield also gives another kind of reader a handy signpost' the love of a shepherd to a boy' which some might see (and have seen) as sexual. Far from 'unshadow[ing] his conceit' Barnfield deftly cloaks it while alerting readers to the possible sexual subtexts.

A careful reading of Marlowe's poem leaves us, then, with several, sometimes contradictory, notions. On one hand, there is a sense of the distance between our conceptions of sex and, especially, gender (which must impact upon our understanding of the sexual and sexuality in the period). This is perhaps compounded by our unfamiliarity with the subtexts of the poem, especially the literary intertext and how to interpret its potential sexual meanings. Montaigne's 'On Some Verses of Virgil' comments how 'we beat it [sex] by circumlocution and picture', and this opacity is only compounded in a world where we have lost the ability to read what might be complex, sub-cultural symbols and signs which allow the text's 'conceit' to be unshadowed to a knowing reader.[21] But, even if we accept that the poem shows an awareness of sex, sexual roles, and a certain sexual consciousness that lies akin to sexuality, if we accept the post-Foucaultian argument (there are only sexual acts and concept of identity, such as the homosexual) how can we read the relations between men in the poem? Indeed, more broadly, how do we understand the sexuality of an era that lacks that category of thought and where the evidence is so partial and contradictory? What sexual topography *can* we discern for the early modern period?

The first, clearest, difference lies in the conceptions of sex and gender, the boundaries of the former being more fluid, the latter more rigid. Sexual knowledge in the period revolved round two overlapping medical traditions, the Galenic and the Aristotelian.[22] The two traditions focused their discussion of sex around two key issues: the nature of the male and female sexes and the process of generation (reproduction).[23] Although there were considerable variations and contradictions within the explanations offered for the aetiology of gender, many subscribed to the idea of homology between the sexes, that is, that male and female were not so much different sexes, but rather variations of a unitary species.[24] In this explanation female genitals were regarded merely as simple inversions of the male genitals, internal rather than external:

> Axiomatic to medical theory was that women were weaker. Man was the measure of all things, so woman's body was explained by the male model . . . her ovaries were termed 'the female testes' or testicles, and her reproductive organs were described as 'no other than those of a man reversed, or turned inward'. Belief in the primacy of the male over the female informed explanations of reproduction: the male foetus was perfect earlier than the female, received a soul sooner, and was born sooner.[25]

Here the process of generation assumes its main significance in early modern sexual theories. Aristotelian tradition treated women as primarily incubators, while men produced the material necessary for the seed (almost an echo of the female body / male soul binary), arguing that conception did not require either female seed or orgasm. However, another powerful tradition countered that sexual generation required both male and female seed and male and female orgasm.[26] Jane Sharp, the seventeenth-century midwife, argued that 'man in the act of procreation is the agent and tiller and sower of the ground, woman is the patient or ground to be tilled', an interestingly metaphorical passage which bestows on the uterus (the ground) an almost autonomous status.[27] Most importantly, the boundaries between the sexes were regarded as more fragile, and often examples were cited of women who became men through the generation of excessive heat (men were seen as hot, women as moist in a humoural economy).

If sex boundaries were more fluid, gender ones were more heavily demarcated, although they too, seem to have been more easily permeated. The ultimate authority for this demarcation was taken from biblical texts, such as Ephesians:

> Wives, submit yourselves unto your husbands, as unto the Lord. For the husband is the head of the wife, even as Christ is the head of the church: and he is the saviour of the body. Therefore as the church is subject unto Christ, so let the wives be in every thing.[28]

Biology even informed the division of labour, with medical 'science', arguing:

> Women were made to stay at home and look after household employments . . . accompanied without any vehement stirring of the body . . . therefore hath provident Nature assigned them their monthly courses, that by the benefit of these evacuations, the fecu-

lent [fetid] and corrupt blood might be purified, which otherwise, being that purest part of blood, would turn to rank poison.[29]

As one contemporary proverb expressed it 'men are deeds, women they are words'. Yet although such views insisted upon clear differences between genders, determined by biology, a counter-discourse stressed the fragility of manliness so that, as Orgel suggests, 'manhood was not a natural condition but a quality that had to be striven for and maintained only through constant vigilance'.[30] The main male deed, indeed, was performing manliness. This effort included the careful shaping of the manly body and behaviour towards suitable and through physical exercise and the cultivation of qualities such as grace and civility. This was the subject of numerous manuals, from the courtesy books of Elyot (*The Book of the Governor*) and Castiglione (*The Book of the Courtier*), through to the more practical manuals such as Cleland's *Hero-Paidea* (1607) and Peacham's *The Complete Gentleman* (1622). The aim of these texts was to fashion a civilized manliness whilst avoiding the possible fall into effeminacy.

In the cases of both sex and gender the ability of man to transform himself or be transformed was both a danger and a goal. On one hand, Pico della Mirandola argued that it was precisely man's transformative abilities which defined his place between the divine and animal:

> Whatever seed each man cultivates will grow to maturity and bear in him their own fruit. If they be vegetative, he will be like a plant. If sensitive, he will become brutish. If rational, he will grow into a heavenly being. If intellectual, he will be an angel and the son of God. And if, happy in the lot of no created thing, he withdraw into the centre of his won unity, his spirit, made one with God, in the solitary darkness of God, who is set above all things, shall surpass them all. Who would not admire this our chameleon? . . . It is a man who Asclepius of Athens, arguing from his mutability of character and from his self-transforming nature, on just grounds says was symbolised by Proteus in the mysteries.[31]

On the other hand, these transformative abilities also endangered man, as the boundaries of his gender, although strongly marked, could easily be dissolved. As Thomas Wright commented: 'a personable body is so linked with a penitent soul; a valiant Captain in the field for the most part is infected with an effeminate affection at home'.[32]

Despite the implication of much early modern generative theory that all foetuses start as female, and despite the constant concern focused upon the regulation of female sexuality, the central sex and gender was male. Relations between males dominated social ordering, and everyone was defined in relation with other males, either fathers and brothers (for men) and fathers and husbands (for women). All the major institutions were entirely male, the social structure was built round systems of patronage and clientage between men, and many institutions, such as schools and universities, required men to share domestic space, and especially beds. The relations of master/

servant, master / secretary, patron / client, tutor / pupil were all central to society and were often couched in terms of an idealized friendship.[33] These relations were, then, sites of most intense affective bonds, which may gloss E.K.'s preference for 'pederastice' to 'gynerastice'.

The dual emphasis upon the importance of manliness as a performed role and the centrality of inter-male relations as the basis of social order places the men and the male body at the centre of society in a way totally alien to modern thinking (which certainly for most of the twentieth century has erased the male body). Take, for example, William Laud (later Archbishop of Canterbury) recording a dream in his diary:

21 August 1625

Sunday. I preached at Brecknock; where I stayed two days, very busy in performing some business.

That night, in my sleep, it seemed to me that the Duke of Buckingham came into bed to me; where he behaved himself with great kindness towards me, after that rest, wherewith wearied persons are wont to solace themselves. Many also seemed to me to enter the chamber who saw this.[34]

The dream recounts a fantasy of power for Laud, as the Duke shows him favour by sharing his bed (it is important that this is seen by those who entered the chamber), but it also raises the issue of whether such bed-sharing and the opaque 'great kindness' also contained sexual elements. The lack of concern in the rest of the diary (contrast this with how an early twentieth-century writer might have responded to an earlier dream of bed-sharing) suggests that Laud regarded the situation as non-erotic, or that he was unwilling to commit any troubling erotic potentials to paper. Yet might not the situation be erotic, and this was so commonplace that the absence of commentary marks its normativity? We are faced here with a situation parallel to that raised by the viewing of male portraits in Renaissance art. Having discussed a number of male portraits which seem to us highly erotic (such as Bronzino's depiction of a young, nude Lorenzo de Medici as Orpheus) Patricia Simons articulates the difficulties we face in describing this world of male affectivity:

The social circumstances, sexual practices, written languages and visual discourses of male bonding suggest that charged, erotic elements often informed the formation and performance of Renaissance masculinity. Whether or not bodily contact occurred, or would satisfy criteria of the 'sexual' kind for twentieth-century observers, Renaissance men addressed each other in affective ways which were so often tinged with the arousal of desire, that they were erotic. Male sexuality was performed across a wider spectrum of sensualities than modern standards usually allow, collapsing any clear boundaries between essential 'gayness' and a straightforward 'heterosexuality'.[35]

This 'wider spectrum of sensualities' complicates the ways in which we might frame our understanding of sexuality in this period since modern binarizations of the sexual and erotic occlude some of the complex modes of male affectivity and contain the desire we associate with the sexual, even if it might seem impossible to label them sexual in a post-Freudian sense.

Simons raises indirectly one of the most difficult issues in understanding earlier sexualities, not simply the boundaries of the sexual, but whether this consciousness created the kind of consciousness necessary for sexuality to exist, even if not articulated through the exact term. Her description of the complex and multiple viewing positions of Renaissance male portraits implies the necessary sexual consciousness but also a complex pattern of sexual responses, differently defined from ours and, largely, operating outside the heterosexual–homosexual dichotomy.[36] Indeed, historians of sexuality argue that the period was filled with all kinds of advice, usually couched either within religious or medical discourses, which recognized the importance of sex, sexual satisfaction (for both men and women) and a striking ease with the idea of the erotic.[37] Yet, these are very limited categories, and there seems no corresponding discourse for male sexuality (outside of the condemnatory rhetoric of the church), even if we can detect the beginnings of the sexual consciousness necessary for 'sexuality'.

Beyond Acts and Identities:
The Possibility of Early Modern Sexuality

Given this context, some recent scholarship has started to question the rigid Foucaultian division of acts and identity. For instance, identities can be said to be made by acts, so how did people who repeated these interdicted acts understand themselves and their motivations?[38] Moreover, must we insist only upon an understanding of sexuality and identity as concepts created by ideology rather than other, more diffuse kinds of experience? Might not there be kinds of identity which are not our modern, autonomous and self-contained senses of selfhood? Foucault's own language is revealing here in that when he described the nineteenth-century discovery of the homosexual as a 'species' he implies a whole raft of biological and medical ideas as defining identity, concepts which simply have no place in this period.[39] Whereas the Foucaultian critics have been keen to insist upon (homo)sexuality as a 'cultural construct' and the arbitrary and contingent nature of the hetero / homo binary, they seem less keen to recognize that other forms of identity, which we have not yet learned to recognize, may have existed. In contrast to early modern scholars, many medievalists dispute the Foucaultian depiction of sexuality as an 'exclusively modern concept'.[40] Simon Gaunt, writing of medieval romance, insists both upon the pluralities of gay identities, arguing that a 'similar though not identical' homo / hetero dialectic operates in those texts.[41]

An example which illustrates the difficulties in discerning and understanding early modern sexuality is the case of Sir Francis Bacon, who was impeached for corruption whilst Lord Chancellor. The diarist Simonds D'Ewes commented at length on his fall, but also on the sexual mores of the Bacon household:

His most abominable and darling sin I should rather bury in silence then mention it; were it not a most admirable instance how men are enflamed by wickedness and held captive by the devil . . .

[Bacon] would not relinquish the practice of his most horrible and secret sin of sodomy, keeping still one Godrick, a very effeminate-faced youth, to be his catamite and bedfellow – although he had discharged the most of his other household servants – which was the more to be admired because men generally, after his fall, began to discourse of that unnatural crime which he had practised many years, deserting the bed of his lady (which he accounted as the Italians and Turks do, a poor and mean pleasure in respect of the other). And it was thought by some that he should have been tried at the bar of justice for it, and have satisfied the law most severe against that horrible villainy with the price of his blood.[42]

Superficially, the D'Ewes account fulfils all the elements of the sodomy discourse (political motivation, foreign vice, other crimes in which sex is only a minor component), and Bacon's 'secret sin of sodomy' fits what Alan Stewart has called the 'crisis model' whereby sodomy, or more properly the accusation of sodomy, only emerges after Bacon's fall as part of his political disgrace.[43] Thus far the D'Ewes account follows the pattern whereby sodomy accusations were levelled as adjuncts to other charges and symbolized how far individuals had transgressed the law.[44] Yet, the second part of the diary continues:

[Bacon] never came to any public trial for his crime; nor did ever, that I could hear, forbear his old custom of making his servants his bedfellows, so to avoid the scandal was raised of him.[45]

The striking elements in this account is Bacon's continuation of his 'old custom' and the reported insistence not only on its 'pleasure' but its superiority to sex with his wife. In some ways, the diary seems to suggest a model which is close to E.K's image of pederasty and, interestingly, John Aubrey in *Brief Lives* described Bacon as '*paiderastos*' claiming his 'Ganymedes and favourites took bribes'.[46] The emphasis in the account upon the serving boys ('one Godrick, a very effeminate-faced youth . . . his catamite and bedfellow') also meshes with the patterns of sexual behaviour charted in many accusations, where the sexual relations shadow the power relations of master and servant. Indeed, to this extent, the Bacon case seems to echo the kinds of classical pattern outlined by critics like Foucault and David Halperin, whereby relationships depended upon a 'structured inequality' and a clear hierarchy.[47] Halperin, describing Athenian sexuality, argues that the essence of this lies in 'a single, undifferentiated phallic "sexuality" of penetration and domination, a socio-sexual discourse whose basic terms are phallus and non-phallus'.[48] In terms which could equally be applied to early modern society he further comments:

Sexual penetration, and sexual activity in general, are . . . thematized as domination: the relation between the 'active' and the 'passive' sexual partner is thought of as the same kind of relation between that obtaining between social superior and inferior, between master and servant.[49]

Although it is tempting to argue that the use of classical terms, images and myths which pervaded early modern society may suggest that similar patterns of sexual mores operated, in fact a careful examination of the Bacon passage suggests that slightly different issues are raised within the hierarchy of the relationship. The insistence upon both pleasure and continuation, despite the threat of discovery, suggests a lack of control which, in fact, threads throughout the narrative. D'Ewes, for instance, tells how a libel was thrown into Bacon's home, York House, an act of symbolic penetration which furthers the impression of lack of control, while the poem, which he reproduces claims:

> Within this sty a hog doth lie,
> That must bee hanged for sodomy.[50]

Although the pig image clearly draws upon the association of sodomy and bestiality, it also insinuates ideas of prodigality. Indeed, one of the many accusations levelled at Bacon and his followers was their extravagance and immoderation, and interestingly some versions of the poem substitute 'bribery', the symbol of his immoderate desire for money, for sodomy. Like the 'continuance' of his catamitic connection and the description of Bacon 'enflamed' with lust and pursuing 'pleasure' irrespective of its moral rectitude, the juxtaposition of bribery and sodomy seems to suggest that lack of self-control is the issue.

Interestingly, it is precisely this point that has been used to articulate a critique of the Foucault/Halperin reading of ancient sexuality. In *Courtesans and Fishcakes*, James Davidson has argued, forcibly, that penetration is not the issue in Greek culture (he associates this obsession much more with Christian and modern cultures) but rather insatiability and incontinenece, which in a man makes him effeminate, that is, like the 'leaky vessels' that are women.[51] Failure in self-control is the problem (as in the Baconian exemplar), suggesting an 'economic rather than absolute' system of morals, which required moderation and restraint as central qualities.[52] These, too, are issues stressed in early modern tracts on manliness.

The similarities of this model to Bacon's incontinence are very suggestive, although it might also be said that the diary seems to combine elements of both the concern over penetration and the lack of self-control. Importantly, for our main interest in sexuality, Davidson's reading undermines the simpler versions of the acts / identities dichotomy because it suggests a reciprocity and a pleasure in sexual acts which the Foucault/Halperin model denies (or downplays), and which, in turn, implies a different type of sexual consciousness and, therefore, sexuality. Moreover, as we study early modern sexual behaviour we can see a combination of both the penetration/power model and the imperative towards self-control, along with more obviously Christian concerns about bodily integrity and, of course, an entirely different moral and juridical system built on ideas of sin and vice.

If this reading is correct and early modern sexuality consists of an overlaying of several differing systems, often not entirely consistent with each other, this might explain the strange texture of early modern sexual discourses to modern perceptions. In particular, the incontinence model might explain how such a large range of sexual and other crimes become linked together under one label (sodomy), and also how men-loving-men and women's behaviours are connected. The supposed 'effeminacy' of men may have nothing to do with penetration or passivity, but rather with a lack of self-control. They, literally, become like women in gender discourse:

> This discourse inscribes women as leaky vessels by isolating one element of the female body's material expressiveness – its production of fluids – as excessive, hence, either disturbing or shameful. It also characteristically links this liquid expressiveness to excessive verbal fluency. In both formations, the issue is women's bodily self-control or, more precisely, the representation of a particular kind of uncontrol as a function of gender.[53]

This returns us to the interconnections between sexualities and a much more modern perception of the interconnection between oppressions rooted in gender and sexual identity.

Sex is, ultimately, one of the things we cannot recover about the past. What happened in intimate moments between men, between men and women is inaccessible. Sexuality, or the sense of sexual selfhood, is less unknowable. In a period where gender identity is so crucial, where being a man (or woman) has such profound meanings, and where those roles were heavily discussed, its seems improbable that there was not a sense of sexual consciousness. Within that, modern ideas of sexuality (especially the ways in which we insist on the hetero/homo binarism) may not have existed, or, rather different patters operated, some of which we have not yet learned how to read. What is important, however, is that we have begun to discuss the possibility of sexual histories, sexual categories and even sexualities, so that new interpretations are constantly revealed to us as new case histories are uncovered and new questions thus posed about our categories and ideas.

NOTES

1 Marlowe, *The Complete Poems and Translations*, ed. S. Orgel (Harmondsworth: Penguin, 1971), p. 211. This is the five-stanza version first printed in *England's Helicon* (1600). A four-stanza version, which may be an earlier draft, appeared in *The Passionate Pilgrim* (1599): see *The Complete Works of Christopher Marlowe*, ed. R. Gill, *Volume 1: Translations* (Oxford: Clarendon Press, 1987).

2 R. S. Forsythe, '*The Passionate Shepherd* and

English Poetry', *PMLA*, 40 (1925), 692–742, esp. p. 701 on dating.

3 Marlowe, *Complete Poems and Translations* handily reprints these responses.

4 D. Halperin, 'Sex Before Sexuality' in *Hidden From History: Reclaiming the Gay and Lesbian Past*, eds M. Duberman, M. Vicinus and G. Chauncey (Harmondsworth: Penguin Books, 1991), pp. 37–53, n. 2 (p. 482) discusses the origins of these terms which he traces to a pamphlet published in Leipzig in 1869.

The terms became current through Kraft-Ebbing's *Psychopathia Sexualis* (1887) which was translated into English in 1892.

5   M. Foucault, *The History of Sexuality, Volume One: An Introduction*, tr. R. Hurley (Harmondsworth: Penguin, 1981), p. 43.

6   E. Sedgwick, *The Epistemology of the Closet* (Harmondsworth: Penguin, 1990), pp. 8–11 and 67–90.

7   Foucault, *The History of Sexuality, Volume One*, p. 101. The utility of sodomy for political oppression is discussed in J. Goldberg, Sodometries: *Renaissance Texts, Modern Sexualities* (Stanford: Stanford University Press, 1985), pp. 1–26.

8   A. Bray, 'Homosexuality and the Signs of Male Friendship in Elizabethan England', *History Workshop Journal*, 29 (1990), reprinted in *Queering the Renaissance*, ed. J. Goldberg (Durham, NC: Duke University Press), pp. 40–61. For an interesting application of these ideas to *Timon of Athens*, see J. Greene, '"You must eat men": The Sodomitic Economy of Renaissance Patronage', *Gay and Lesbian Quarterly*, 1 (1994), 163–97.

9   J. Boswell, 'Revolutions, Universals and Sexual Categories', in *Hidden From History*, pp. 17–36, p. 20, and L. Fradenburg and C. Freccero, 'Caxton, Foucault and the Pleasures of History', in *Premodern Sexualities*, eds L. Fradenberg and C. Freccero, (London: Routledge, 1996), xii–xxiv.

10 *OED* attributes the first usage of 'to have sex' to D. H. Lawrence in 1929.

11 Both B. R. Smith, *Homosexual Desire in Shakespeare's England: A Cultural Poetics* (Chicago: University of Chicago Press, 1991) and P. Hammond, *Love Between Men in English Literature* (Basingstoke: Macmillan, 1996) pursue this argument exploring the cultural and literary roles available in the early modern period.

12 Forsythe '*The Passionate Shepherd* and English Poetry', p. 695, argues that the poem cannot owe anything to Virgil's *Eclogues*, 2, because, he assumes and implies, it must be addressed to a woman.

13 *OED*, 'kirtle', 1, 2 and 2b.

14 Virgil, *The Eclogues and Georgics*, ed. R. D. Williams (Bristol: Bristol Classical Press, 1979). Williams comments (p. 96) that Alexis is the *puer delicatus* (favourite slave) of his master and hence Corydon's frustration. '*Delicias domini*' may have more overt sexual senses: on '*deliciae*' as a synonym for sexual pleasure, see J. N. Adams, *The Latin Sexual Vocabulary* (London; Duckworth, 1982), pp. 196–7.

15 *Hero and Leander*, lines 678–9 in *The Complete Works of Christopher Marlowe*, ed. R. Gill, *Volume 1: Translations*.

16 Spenser, *Eclogues*, 'January', gloss to line 59, cited from *The Complete Shorter Poems of Edmund Spenser* (New Haven: Yale University Press, 1990), pp. 33–4.

17 See G. Ruggiero, *The Boundaries of Eros: Sex Crime and Sexuality in Renaissance Venice* (New York: Oxford University Press, 1985), pp. 109–45.

18 M. Rocke, *Forbidden Friendships: Homosexuality and Male Culture in Renaissance Florence* (New York: Oxford University Press, 1996), p. 4.

19 The phrase is from Dekker's *The Honest Whore* (1604), 2.1.353, cited *sub* 'back door' (anus) in G. Williams, *A Dictionary of Sexual Language and Imagery in Shakespearean and Stuart Literature*, 3 vols (London: Athlone Press, 1994), but see also 'Italian'. For *florenzen* and *Florenzer* (sodomite), see Rocke, *Forbidden Friendships*, p. 3.

20 R. Barnfield, *The Complete Poems*, ed. G. Klawitter (London and Toronto: Associated University Press, 1990), pp. 115–16.

21 Smith, *Homosexual Desire*, pp. 4–5 explores Montaigne's views on sexuality and language.

22 K. Park and R. A. Nye, 'Destiny is Anatomy', *The New Republic* (18 February 1991), 53–7.

23 The best account of reproductive and sex biology in this period is T. Laqueur's *Making Sex: Body and Gender from the Greeks to Freud* (Cambridge, MA: Harvard University Press, 1990). Laqueur argues that the 'one sex model' dominated early modern sexual discourse, associating the two sex model with the Enlightenment. Park and Nye criticize this view, as does J. Sawday, *The Body Embla-*

zoned: Dissection and the Human Body in Renaissance Culture (London: Routledge, 1995), pp. 213–15.

24 S. Orgel, *Impersonations: The Performance of Gender in Shakespeare's England* (Cambridge: Cambridge University Press, 1996), pp. 19–30 has an important discussion which illustrates the variations and contradictions in early modern medical models.

25 P. Crawford, 'Sexual Knowledge in England, 1500–1750', in *Sexual Knowledge, Sexual Science*, eds R. Porter and M. Teich (Cambridge: Cambridge University Press, 1994), pp. 82–106, p. 91.

26 Children were supposedly formed from the active principle in male sperm shaping the female matter of menstrual blood according to some versions: see Crawford, 'Sexual Knowledge in England, 1500–1750', p. 92.

27 *The Midwives Book* (1671) cited in Sawday, *The Body Emblazoned*, p. 214.

28 *The Bible: Authorized King James Version*, eds R. Carroll and S. Prickett (Oxford: Oxford University Press, 1997), Ephesians, 5.22–5.

29 Anon, *The Compleat Doctress*, cited by R. Martenson, 'The Transformation of Eve: Women's Bodies, Medicine and Culture in Early Modern England', *Sexual Knowledge, Sexual science*, pp. 107–33.

30 Orgel, *Impersonations*, p. 19.

31 Pico della Mirandola, 'The Oration on the Dignity of Man', in *The Renaissance Philosophy of Man*, eds E. Cassirer et al. (Chicago: University of Chicago Press, 1948), pp. 223, 225–6.

32 T. Wright, *The Passions of the Mind in General*, cited in Orgel, *Impersonations*, p. 25.

33 A. Bray and M. Rey, 'The Body of the Friend' in *English Masculinities, 1660–1800*, eds T. Hitchcock and M. Cohen (Harlow: Longman, 1999), pp. 65–84 covers this topic superbly.

34 *The Works of Archbishop Laud*, eds W. Scott and P. Bliss, 7 vols (Oxford: Clarendon Press, 1847–60), vol. 3, *Devotions, Diary and History* (1853), p. 170.

35 P. Simons, 'Homosociality and Erotics in Italian Renaissance Portraiture' in *Portraiture: Facing the Subject*, ed. J. Woodall (Manchester: Manchester University Press, 1997), pp. 29–51, p. 29.

36 Simons, 'Homosociality and Erotics', p. 40.

37 Crawford, 'Sexual Knowledge in England, 1500–1750', pp. 84–90.

38 Fradenburg and Freccero, 'Caxton, Foucault and the Pleasures of History', in *Premodern Sexualities*, p. xx.

39 The French of the passage reads '*Le sodomite était un relaps, l'homosexuel est maintenant une espèce*', see *La volonté de savoir* (Paris: Gallimard, 1976), p. 59. The English translation as 'species' emphasizes the zoological sense, while '*une espèce*' can also simply mean a type, sort or kind. 'Type', 'sort', and 'kind' lack the biological implications of 'species'.

40 Ann Matter, 'Introduction', *Medieval Feminist Newsletter*, 13 (1992), 2.

41 S. Gaunt, 'Straight Minds / "Queer" Wishes in Old French Hagiography' in *Premodern Sexualities*, pp. 155–73, p. 157.

42 Simond's D'Ewes, 'Life' in BL, MS Harl. 646, fo. 59v.

43 We might note there are strong implications that this information has previously circulated with no official response or sanction.

44 A. Bray, 'Homosexuality and the Signs of Male Friendship', p. 41.

45 BL, MS Harl. 646, fo. 59v.

46 J. Aubrey, *Brief Lives*, ed. A. Clark, 2 vols (Oxford: Oxford University Press, 1898), vol. 1, p. 71.

47 D. Halperin, ' "Homosexuality: A Cultural Construct" ' in *One Hundred Years of Homosexuality* (London: Routledge, 1990), pp. 41–53, p. 47.

48 D. Halperin, 'Sex Before Sexuality', p. 51.

49 Ibid., p. 49.

50 A marginal note adds: 'Alluding both to his surname of Bacon and to that swinish abominable sin'.

51 James Davidson, *Courtesans and Fishcakes: the Consuming Passions of Classical Athens* (London: Fontana Press, 1998), pp. 167–82, esp. pp. 175–7.

52 *Courtesans and Fishcakes*, p. 314.

53 G. K. Paster, *The Body Embarrassed: Drama and the Disciplines of Shames in Early modern England* (Ithaca: Cornell University Press, 1993), p. 25.

REFERENCES AND FURTHER READING

Boswell, J. (1980). *Christianity, Social Tolerance and Christianity: Gay People in Western Europe from the Beginning of the Christian Era*. Chicago: Chicago University Press.

——(1989). 'Revolution, Universals and Sexual Categories'. In M. Duberman, M. Vicinus and G. Chauncey (eds), *Hidden from History: Reclaiming the Gay and Lesbian Past* (pp. 17–36). Harmondsworth: Penguin.

Bray, A. (1982; 1988). *Homosexuality in Renaissance England*. London: Gay Men's Press.

——(1994). 'Homosexuality and the Signs of Male Friendship in Elizabethan England'. In J. Goldbery (ed.), *Queering the Renaissance* (pp. 40–61). Durham, NC: Duke University Press.

Bray, A. and Rey, M. (1999). 'The Body of the Friend'. In T. Hitchcock and M. Cohen (eds), *English Masculinities, 1660–1800* (pp. 65–84). Harlow: Longman.

Brown, J. (1986). *Immodest Acts: The Life of a Lesbian Nun in Renaissance Italy*. New York: Oxford University Press.

——'Lesbian Sexuality in Medieval and Early Modern Europe'. In Duberman, Vicinus, and Chauncey (eds), *Hidden From History: Reclaiming the Gay and Lesbian Past* (pp. 67–75).

Crawford, P. (1994). 'Sexual Knowledge in England, 1500–1750'. In R. Porter and M. Teich (eds), *Sexual Knowledge, Sexual Science* (pp. 82–106). Cambridge: Cambridge University Press.

Davidson, J. (1998). *Courtesans and Fishcakes: The Consuming Passions of Classical Athens*. London: Fontana.

Foucault, M. (1976; 1987). *The History of Sexuality*, esp. *Vol. 1: An Introduction* (1976); and *Vol. 2: The Use of Pleasure* (1987). Harmondsworth: Penguin.

Fradenberg, L. and Freccero, C. (eds) (1996). *Premodern Sexualities*. London: Routledge.

Gaunt, S. (1996). 'Straight Minds "Queer" Wishes in Old French Hagiography'. In Fradenburg and Freccero (eds), pp. 155–73.

Gerard K. and Hekma, G. (eds) (1989). *The Pursuit of Sodomy: Male Homosexuality in Renaissance and Enlightenment Europe*. New York: Harrington Books.

Goldberg, J. (1985). *Sodometries: Renaissance Texts, Modern Sexualities*. Stanford: Stanford University Press.

Greene, J. (1994). '"You must eat men": The Sodomitic Economy of Renaissance Patronage', *Gay and Lesbian Quarterly*, 1, 163–97.

Halperin, D. (1989). 'Sex Before Sexuality: Pederasty, Politics and Power in Classical Athens'. In Duberman, Vicinus and Chauncey (eds), *Hidden from History: Reclaiming the Gay and Lesbian Past* (pp. 37–53). Harmondsworth: Penguin.

Halperin, D. (1990). '"Homosexuality: A Cultural Construct"'. In *One Hundred Years of Homosexuality* (pp. 41–53). London: Routledge.

Hammond, P. (1996). *Love Between Men in English Literature*. Basingstoke: Macmillan.

Hekma, G. (1994). 'The Homosexual, the Queen and Models of Gay History', *Perversions*, 3, 119–38.

Laqueur, T. (1990). *Making Sex: The Body and Gender from the Greeks to Freud*. Cambridge, MA: Harvard University Press.

Martenson, R. (1994). 'The Transformation of Eve: Women's bodies, Medicine and Culture in Early Modern England'. In R. Porter and M. Teich (eds), *Sexual Knowledge, Sexual Science* (pp. 82–106). Cambridge: Cambridge University Press.

Orgel, S. (1988). 'Nobody's Perfect: Or Why Did the English State Take Boys for Women?' In R. Butters et al. (eds), *Displacing Homophobia: Gay Male Perspectives in Literature and Culture*. Durham, NC: Duke University Press.

——(1996). *Impersonations: The Performance of Gender in Shakespeare's England*. Cambridge: Cambridge University Press.

Park, K. and Nye, R. A. (1991). 'Destiny is Anatomy', *The New Republic*, 18 February, 53–7.

Paster, G. K. (1993). *The Body Embarrassed: Drama and the Disciplines of Shames in Early Modern England*. Ithaca: Cornell University Press.

Rocke, M. (1996). *Forbidden Friendships: Homosexuality and Male Culture in Renaissance Florence*. New York: Oxford University Press.

Ruggiero, G. (1985). *The Boundaries of Eros: Sex*

Crime and Sexuality in Renaissance Venice. New York: Oxford University Press.

Sawday, J. (1995). *The Body Emblazoned: Dissection and the Human Body in Renaissance Culture.* London: Routledge.

Sedgwick, E. K. (1985). *Between Men: English Literature and Male Homosocial Desire.* New York: Columbia University Press.

——(1990). *Epistemology of the Closet.* Harmondsworth: Penguin.

Shepherd, S. (1992). 'What's So Funny about Ladies' Tailors? A Survey of Some Male (Homo) Sexual Types in the Renaissance', *Textual Practice,* 6, 17–30.

Simons, P. (1997). 'Homosociality and Erotics in Italian Renaissance Portraiture'. In J. Woodall (ed.), *Portraiture: Facing the Subject* (pp. 29–51). Manchester: Manchester University Press.

Sinfield, A. (1994). *Cultural Politics: Queer Reading.* London: Routledge.

Smith, B. R. (1991). *Homosexual Desire in Shakespeare's England: A Cultural Poetics.* Chicago: Chicago University Press.

Stewart, A. (1995). 'The Early Modern Closet Discovered', *Representations,* 50, 76–100.

Summers, C. (ed.) (1992). *Homosexuality in Renaissance and Enlightenment England.* New York: Harrington Books.

Traub, V. 'The (In)significance of "Lesbian" Desire in Early Modern England'. In Goldberg (ed.), *Queering the Renaissance* (pp. 62–83).

59

Race: A Renaissance Category?

Margo Hendricks

In the beginning was the word, and the word was race.

For a four-letter word that has preoccupied and defined Anglo-American societies for nearly four hundred years, the term 'race' remains a somewhat under-theorized epistemological category within Renaissance English studies. Despite the in-roads made by historians, literary scholars, cultural studies, sociologists and philosophers, our knowledge of the complex and often problematic ways Renaissance England defined and understood the concept of race remains somewhat tenuous. On the one hand, this tenuous hold can be explained in part by the extraordinary semiotic malleability of the word race: it can mean whatever a social formation wants it to mean. In its literature, philosophy, art, theological debates and politics, Renaissance England made use of the word 'race' to both define and differentiate itself from the rest of the world. A borrowed term, 'race' provided English writers a certain flexibility of meaning as they classified and ordered English society.[1]

The *OED* cites John Foxe's *Acts and Monuments* as an example of one of the earliest usages of race and, as the dictionary notes, the meaning of the term, for Foxe, principally denoted genealogy or lineage: 'Thus was the outward race and stock of Abraham after flesh refused.' Race also was used to differentiate the sexes; that is, men and women frequently were described as being different races. In the works of William Shakespeare, for example, the word race was used seventeen times in the whole of his canon. With two exceptions, Shakespeare uses the word to refer to person's genealogy or lineage in terms of social status. Shakespeare's exceptions occur in in *The Tempest* (when Miranda refers to Caliban's 'vile race'); and in *Macbeth* ('Duncan's horses – a thing most strange certain – / Beauteous and swift, the minions of their race' 2.4.14–15).

Over the course of the latter half of the sixteenth century and the first half of the seventeenth, however, the idea of race and the word's usage underwent a semiotic sea-change. As we shall see, this alteration in meaning occurs in large measure because of the ease with which the governing precepts behind a concept of race can be linguistically corrupted, disestablished or rendered ambiguous. Moreover, it is obvious that the word was understood to be malleable as a signifier of classificatory hierarchy, particularly within human societies. And, I will argue, it is this malleability that generated increasing anxiety about the nature and meaning of race.

This chapter does not aim to provide a comprehensive historical study of the complex origins of race in early modern cultures, but rather it seeks to offer a brief overview of race through the two conceptual threads that contributed to the formation of the Renaissance concept / category of race: the philological history of the word race from its entry into the English language and the Renaissance theory of 'generation', which attempts to explain away the problematics that surface in relation to the use of 'race' as a category of social identity. I have chosen this trajectory rather than colour for my discussion for a number of reasons. First, an abundant body of scholarship tracing the significance of race as colour in Renaissance English literature and culture already exists.[2] Second, shifts in semantics, semiotics, and usage often are shaped by the specific socio-economic and cultural needs of a given society, and the lexical history of the word of race appears to reflect just such a process. Finally, the Renaissance concept of race is based on an elaborate system of metaphors and synonyms whose rhetorical and interpretive strength lies in its fluidity and, as I hope to illustrate, Renaissance medicine and Renaissance philology are inextricably linked to the conceptualisation of race in Renaissance English culture.

Genealogy

The origins of the word race are as ambiguous as the term itself. Race appears to have enter written English sometime *circa* 1500, though it is likely that its oral history can be traced to the 'Crusades'. Even the word's etymological genesis is open to debate; some argue for a Latin etymology (*radix*), others contend that the word is Germanic, and still others argue for a Spanish / Moorish heritage. Whatever the source, race quickly became instantiated in the English tongue and culture by the end of the sixteenth century. Notably, the word apparently was culturally significant enough to warrant inclusion in a number of Renaissance English dictionaries, both monolingual and bilingual. For example, John Florio, in his *World of Words* (1590) offers the following entry for the Italian term for race: *Razza, Raza*, as *Raggia*, a kind, a race, a brood, a blood, a stock, a name, a pedigree' (p. 309).

Richard Percyvale's *Biblioteca Hispanica* (1591), on the other hand, does not provide a separate entry for the Spanish term '*raza*' and the English equivalent 'race'.[3] Percyvale does, however, incorporate the term in other Spanish word entries – *casta, abolengo* and *abolorio* – as a synonym. When he turns to English, however, not only does Percyvale include the English term 'race', he also provides a list of synonyms: 'a race, a lineage, a breed, genus'. The absence of an entry for '*raza*' may be explained by looking to the word's problematic semantics in Spain. As a number of critics have shown, *'raza'* was already signifying a complex (and often contradictory) classification system, which included ethnicity and phenotype, in Renaissance Spain.[4] For some unknown reason Percyvale deems a separate entry for the word *raza* unnecessary. After Percyvale's death, John Minsheu revised and expanded the *Biblioteca Hispanica*. Though Minsheu's 'augmentation' was not quantitatively substantial, a careful scrutiny reveals that Minsheu's additions are nonetheless far more significant entries to the *Biblioteca Hispanica* than his title page suggests.[5]

In his dictionary, Minsheu includes not only an entry for *'raza'* but another term which will have major ideological consequences in the long run, *'mestizo'*. Minsheu's handling of the Spanish *'raza'* and English 'race' does indeed 'enlarge' on what is missing in Percyvale. For example, in the Spanish-to-English section, the entry for *'raza'* (or *'raca'*) is defined as 'a ray or beam shining through a hole. Also a race, stock, kind or breed'. Additionally, in the English to Spanish, Minsheu writes, 'line or race – *vide Casta, Raca'*; and under the entry titled 'race or stock' he directs the reader to *'vide Raca, caste, Abolorio, Abolengo'*. In doing so, Minsheu creates a dictionary which offers its users as much information as they will need to comprehend all the vagaries of the Spanish language and its racial lexicon, even going so far as to provide definitions for subsets within entries. Yet every entry seems to reiterate a prevailing semantics; whatever Spanish word one uses, caste, *'raza'*, abolorio, abolengo, it will inevitably signify in English 'a race, a lineage, a breed, issue of one's body, a progeny, a stock an offspring' or 'pedigree, stock, or descent of kindred'.

The sudden florescence of dictionaries offering similar or exact English versions of this meaning of race – John Baret's *An Alvearie or Triple Dictionarie* (1573, 1580); Claudius Holyband's *A Dictionarie French and English* (1570–1); and Thomas Wilson's *A Christian Dictionary* (1612) – suggests how pervasive the link between the word race and the idea of nobility was in Renaissance English culture. These attempts carefully to delineate (and limit) the meaning of race are not a coincidence. On the contrary, such dictionaries contribute to a major recalibration of the semantic possibilities of the word 'race' in the face of expanding internationalism within and without England, as well as of the growing social and economic power of a mercantile class. Between 1560 and 1660, England's political economy and social institutions underwent a radical realignment. Works such as William Harrison's *A Description of England* and John Stow's *A Geographical History* testify to the gradual alteration of the English social hierarchy. Merchants, lawyers, and other professionals (especially as civil servants) were an important defining presence in Renaissance English culture. Though a portion of the merchants and financiers came from the nobility or the gentry (younger sons), the majority of this class were 'commoners'. The increased wealth of this emergent class produced fundamental changes in a social fabric once thought immutable. Money enabled these 'commoners' to live in a manner once thought solely the privilege of the nobility, to acquire the trappings of 'civility' (land, education, luxury goods), and, more importantly, to procure titles (either through service, purchase, or marriage).

In other words, economic changes effectively forced the redrawing of the taxonomic boundaries of one form of racial classification. It is, perhaps, this social and cultural reformation which may have prompted sixteenth- and seventeenth-century English lexicographers such as Percyvale, Minsheu and John Florio (among others) to undertake the onerous task of constructing a taxonomic system for the word 'race' that would be, paradoxically, exclusive and, when necessary, inclusive. In this way early modern writers could deploy the word in a variety of ways without once having to evince concern for the ideological contradictions that may surface. Race, it seems was a semiotic category, best dealt with in ambiguities.

Familial Ties

For most individuals in Renaissance England, use of the word race was tied to both ancestry and social status. For example, in an anonymous elegy on the death of Sir Philip Sidney, the poet describes Sidney in the following way: 'Drawn was thy race aright from princely line / Nor less than such (by gifts that Nature gave / The common mother that all creatures have) / Doth virtue show, and princely lineage shine.' In his 'Verse in Praise of Lord Henry Howard, Earl of Surrey', George Tuberville similarly deploys the term: 'Though want of skill to silence me procures / I write of him whose fame for aye endures / A worthy wight, a noble for his race / A learned lord that had an earl's place.'[6] Strikingly, the rhetoric of race become localized in key words: worth, learning, honour, valour and courtesy. As James Casey notes, 'the cornerstone of nobility is religion, honour, talent and valour'[7] (*The History of the Family*, 9) – to which we might also add loyalty, magnanimity and courtesy. In addition, these attributes were considered transmittable from father to child (or, in those problematic situations, from mother to child) and would make themselves known at every instance.

What is readily apparent in the usage of the word 'race' is that both word and concept become a crucial category of identity in Renaissance England because English patriarchy 'depends on the principle of inheritance in which the father's identity – his property, name, his authority is transmitted from father to son ... But this transmission from father to son can take place only insofar as both father and son pass through the body of a woman'.[8] Furthermore, 'the insistence on chastity and virtue for wives as a condition for the economic strength of the ... family was also closely connected with the concern about lineage. Since noble birth was crucial feature of knighthood, only true-born sons would be brave and worthy of their families ... Confusion of blood produced unreliable men'.[9] It is especially significant that, 'in a political culture where the notions of inheritance, name, title, and lineage [i.e., race] were reinforced by multiple rights (birthrights, rights to inheritance, entails, and so forth), the question of paternity had considerable urgency. The uncertainty of legitimacy also explains the success of a theory that attributed a lack of resemblance to the power of the mother's imagination',[10] and this theory was called 'generation'.

Since Aristotle's *De Generatione Animalium*, physicians and natural philosophers have debated one of the central paradoxes in Aristotle's theory of generation: why it is that occasionally children do not resemble their fathers. Within Renaissance medical and scientific discourses, explanations were as varied as the persons providing them (we find historians, poets, philosophers and physicians all contributing to the discourse of generation). Without question the most influential Renaissance voice in this on-going debate was the sixteenth-century French physician Ambroise Paré. Paré's *De la chirurgie* (1585) quickly became an encyclopaedic reference for English physicians and medical practitioners,[11] such as Helkiah Crooke. Like Paré's *Des monstre et prodiges* (1573), portions of Crooke's *Microcosmographia* (1613) are intended to provide an explanation for one of the more troubling anomalies in generation, the problem of resemblance. Aristotelian tradition held that, by virtue of the male seed's 'natural' superiority, a man's offspring should resemble him. Not surprisingly, all types of difficulties arose when a child bore little or no resemblance to the father – questions of legitimacy in particular. If the male seed is dominant (as Aristotelian theory held), then how is it possible for a man's offspring to resemble him neither in appearance or sex? Either his wife has committed adultery or, if she is virtuous, then the answer lies elsewhere. Not surprisingly, theorists looked to Aristotle's concept of the malleability of 'seed' after conception to explain this problematic.

In his discussion of the matter of resemblance, Helkiah Crooke implicitly seeks to assure the anxious father that the causes for the absence of paternal resemblance are both explicable and natural:

> The infant sometimes is altogether like the mother, sometimes altogether like the father, other sometimes like them both, that is, in some parts resembling the mother, in others the father. Oftentimes he resembleth neither the father nor the mother, but the grandfather or the great grandfather, sometimes he will be like an unknown friend, as for example, an Ethiopian or such like who never had hand in his generation. Of all these similitudes we have many examples in authors of approved credit.
>
> (*Microcosmographia*, Book V, 26).

While Crooke alludes to classical authors such Herodotus, Pliny, Aristotle and others as sources for his commentary, it is clear that he is deeply indebted to Ambroise Paré's *Des monstre et prodiges*.

Paré's text similarly draws upon 'many examples in authors of approved credit' in its efforts to address the problematics of resemblance.[12] However, there is a marked difference between Paré's and Crooke's handling of the matter. Paré begins by adumbrating the difference between 'monsters' and 'marvels': 'Monsters are things that appear outside the course of nature (and are usually signs of some forthcoming misfortune), such as a child who is born with one arm, another who will have two heads, and additional members over and above the ordinary' (p. 3). Prodigies, or 'marvels,' on the other hand, are 'things which happened that are complete against Nature as when a woman will give birth to a serpent, or a dog, or some other thing that is totally against Nature' (p. 3). In perhaps an unconscious parody of the ten commandments, Paré provides his readers a list of the 'several things that cause monsters': the 'glory' or the 'wrath' of God; too much or too little 'seed', 'imagination', 'posture', 'hereditary or accidental illnesses'; 'rotten or corrupt seed'; or 'through mixture or mingling of seed' (p. 4).

For Paré, as for Crooke, the principal causes of monsters and marvels is the human imagination, which Paré identifies as the 'fifth cause of monstrosity'. As part of his explanation, Paré first turns to Heliodorus' *Aethiopica* and an explanation that we would immediately recognize as racial in its semiotic register. According to Paré, Heliodorus 'writes that Persina, the Queen of Ethiopia, conceived by King Hidustes – both of them being Ethiopian – a daughter who was white and this [occurred] because of the appearance of the beautiful Andromeda that she [Persina] summoned up in her imagination, for she had a painting of her before her eyes during the embraces from which she became pregnant' (Paré, 38). Paré then tells the story of Hippocrates saving the life of 'a princess accused of adultery, because she had given birth to a child as black as a Moor, her husband and she both having white skin; which woman was absolved upon Hippocrates' persuasion that it was [caused by] the portrait of a Moor, similar to the child, which was customarily attached to her bed' (p. 38).

Paré cites these examples as 'true accounts' of the extraordinary power of the female imagination, and he advises that, 'it is necessary that women – at the hour of conception and when the child is not yet formed (which takes thirty to thirty-five days for males and forty or forty-two, as Hippocrates says, for females) – not be forced to look at or to image monstrous things' (pp. 39–40). Paré's examples, of course, illuminate more than just an ancient belief. In reiterating Herodotus's tales of imaginative miscegenation, Paré highlights the impossibility of completely alleviating male anxiety about the legitimacy of his offspring. Race as lineage proved too permeable, too malleable a term for a society undergoing social and cultural change.

Race: A Renaissance Category?

I want to conclude by returning to John Minsheu's 'augmentation' of Percyvale's *Bibliotheca Hispanica*. As I noted earlier, Percyvale's *Bibliotheca Hispanica* does not provide entries for most of the Spanish racializing lexicon (*raza*, *mestizo* and *mulatto*). Minsheu adds two of the three; interestingly enough, he includes *mestizo* but not *mulatto*. Moreover, in his definition of *mestizo* Minsheu does not cross-reference other Spanish terms or offer English equivalents. Instead, he writes, '*mestizo*, m. that which is come or sprung of a mixture of two kinds, as a black-Moor and a Christian, a mongrel dog or beast'. What Minsheu's definition elides, or more accurately what it misrepresents, is that the word was coined to describe offspring of Spanish and American Indian unions and was rarely applied to anyone born of the sexual relations between African (or

Moor) and Christian. Moreover, mestizo was not used to describe non-human animals. What Minsheu does to create his definition is to combine a number of different terms in the Spanish racial lexicons (mestizo, mestico, mulatto and morisco) and offer his English readers a hybrid explanation. As Minsheu constitutes it, mestizo functions as a less than desirable term of reference. To categorize a person as a mestizo, then, is not only to point to a problematic genealogy but to deny that individual a 'racial' history.

Ultimately, it was England's pursuit of power in the Americas that triggered the kind of redefinition reflected in Minsheu's translation of the Spanish racial lexicon.[13] Engendered by a combination of political unrest, economic dearth and political oppression, the migration of Englishmen to the emerging colonies in the Americas wrought unexpected changes in the Englishman's social consciousness. In this 'brave new world', the aristocratic ideology that had given rise to the word 'race', and its social legitimacy, proved inadequate as a method for categorizing in the colonial space. Sexual and marital unions across ethnic, social and geographical lines created a group of individuals whose identities threatened to undermine the conceptualization of race as solely based on patrilineal descent tied to social status. Moreover, those persons born in the colonies and could claim an English father posed a singular difficulty for the prevailing discourse of race: what exactly was the race of the mulatto or mestizo if the father was 'nobly born'?

Certainly, the most significant factor in the changing definition of race as a category of identity during the sixteenth and early seventeenth centuries was the impact of colonialism and the African slave trade. The shift in race's meaning can be mapped in those Renaissance texts whose methodological impulses we would now classify as constitutive of cultural anthropology and physical anthropology: travel narratives, ethnographic writings, and writings that included specific references to Africa, America and Asia. Texts such as Ralegh's *The Discovery of Guiana*, Leo Africanus's *The Geographical History of Africa*, Richard Hakluyt's *Voyages and Discoveries*, and the myriad plays, ballads, official reports, personal letters associated with the mercantile and colonising project signalled a radical change in the English consciousness. No longer looking inward, Renaissance England cast its gaze to the world and discovered that the world was decidedly not English.

In the end, the Renaissance usage of the word 'race' reveals a multiplicity of loci, of axes of determinism, as well as metaphorical systems to aid and abet its deployment across a variety of boundaries in the making.[14] As an expression of fundamental distinctions, race's meaning varied depending upon whether a writer wanted to specify difference born of a class-based concept of genealogy, a psychological (and essentialised) nature, or group typology. Nonetheless, in all these variations, race is envisioned as something fundamental, something immutable, knowable and recognizable, yet it can only be 'seen' when its boundaries are violated, and thus race is also, paradoxically, mysterious, illusory and mutable. As a classificatory category the Renaissance concept of race, it turns out, was rift with fault-lines, which human beings proved quite adept at exploiting.

Over the course of the sixteenth century, race proved itself a useful social category. In its linguistic and ideological permutations, race allowed for the classification of all humankind but with distinct variants according to political and cultural needs. A Renaissance category that once defined a person's ability to claim a noble heritage, race quickly proved useful as a generic typological term. Depending on context, audience and gender, Renaissance writers moved freely between phrases such as 'the English race', 'the Irish race', 'race of women', 'black race' and 'white race'. Race became divorced from its strict genealogical semiotics and became increasingly associated with a colour-based taxonomy ('black race' or 'white race'). Furthermore, nation-states and continents became tied to this taxonomy and lineage took on a different importance. Racial descent was no longer defined solely through the father, and 'seed' no longer determined the contours of racial identity. Although it would take two centuries for the word race to be defined solely in terms of colour, it is in Renaissance English culture that the first steps were taken towards establishing race as an unquestioned detail of cultural identity. Race, indeed, is a Renaissance category.

NOTES

1 As a term to define a category of social identity, 'race' is a word borrowed from the French language. Despite the *OED*'s assertion that the word 'race' appears in the English language *circa*1500, I suspect that its appearance in England occurred much earlier, perhaps even as early as the conquest of 1066 when French-speaking Normans invaded and conquered England. Because the language of the court and nobility prior to the sixteenth century was French, it is quite likely that 'race' was already part of the vernacular tongue and the social consciousness of English culture by the sixteenth century.

2 For recent general studies dealing with the matter of colour as a racializing feature see Kim Hall, *Things of Darkness: Economies of Race and Gender in Early Modern England* (Ithaca and London: Cornell University Press, 1996); John Gillis, *Shakespeare and the Geography of Difference* (Cambridge: Cambridge University Press, 1995); and Joyce Greene Macdonald, ed., *Race, Ethnicity, and Power in the Renaissance* (Delaware: University of Delaware Press, 1998).

3 Richard Percyvale, *Bibliotheca Hispanica. Containing a Grammar, with a Dictionarie in Spanish, English and Latine, gathered out of divers good Authors: very profitable for the studious of the Spanish toong. By Richard Percyvall Gent. The Dictionarie being inlarged with the latine, by the advise and conference of Master Thomas Doyley Doctor in Physicke. Imprinted at London, by Iohn Iackson, for Richard Watkins* (1591).

4 See Verena Stolcke, 'Invade Women: Gender, Race, and Class in the Formation of Colonial Society', *Women, 'Race' and Writing in the Early Modern Period*, eds Margo Hendricks and Patricia Parker (London and New York: Routledge, 1994), 272–86, and Paul Julian Smith, *Representing the Other: 'Race', Text, and Gender in Spanish and Spanish American Narrative* (Oxford: Clarendon Press, 1992).

5 John Minsheu (1613). *A dictionarie in Spanish and English: first published into the English tongue by Ric. Percivale gent. Now enlarged and amplified with many thousand words . . . for all such as shall be desirous to attaine the perfection of the Spanish tongve. All done by John Minsheu* (London, 1619).

6 These citations are taken from Hyder Rollins, *The Renaissance in England: Non-dramatic Prose and Verse of the Sixteenth*

Century, ed. (Lexington, MA: DC Heath and Company, 1954).

7   James Casey, *The History of the Family* (Oxford: Basil Blackwell, 1989), 19.

8   Janet Adelman, *Suffocating Mothers: Fantasies of Maternal Origin in Shakespeare's Plays, 'Hamlet' to 'The Tempest'* (New York: Routledge 1992), 106.

9   Nicholas Abercrombie, Stephen Hill and Bryan S. Turner, *Dominant Ideology Thesis* (1980), 80.

10 Marie-Hélène Huet, *Monstrous Imagination* (Cambridge, MA and London: Harvard University Press, 1993), 34.

11 Finally, translated into English in 1634 as *The Works of that Famous Chirugeon Ambrose Parey*, the writings of Ambroise Paré were quite influential in the medical community in England throughout the late sixteenth century and all of the seventeenth century, most late sixteenth- and early seventeenth-

century readers read either the French or Latin versions. The edition of Paré's work cited in this chapter was translated by Thomas Johnson and published in London in 1634.

12 Ambroise Paré, *On Monsters and Marvels*, tr. Janis L. Pallister (Chicago: University of Chicago Press, 1982), xv.

13 See Theodore W. Allen, *The Invention of The White Race: The Origin of Racial Oppression in Anglo-America* (London and New York: Verso, 1997), 2 volumes, for an excellent discussion of the links between early modern England's political economy, colonialism, and the emergence of whiteness as a definition notion of race.

14 Margo Hendricks, 'Obscured by Dreams: Race, Empire, and Shakespeare's *A Midsummer Night's Dream*,' *Shakespeare Quarterly*, 2 (1) (1996), 37–60.

REFERENCES AND FURTHER READING

Abercrombie, Nicholas, Hill, Stephen and Turner, Bryan S. (1980). *Dominant Ideology Thesis*. London: George Allen and Unwin.

Adelman, Janet (1992). *Suffocating Mothers: Fantasies of Maternal Origin in Shakespeare's Plays, Hamlet to The Tempest*. New York: Routledge.

Allen, Theodore W. (1997). *The Invention of The White Race: The Origin of Racial Oppression in Anglo-America*. London and New York: Verso.

Casey, James (1989). *The History of the Family*. Oxford: Basil Blackwell.

Gillis, John (1995). *Shakespeare and the Geography of Difference*. Cambridge: Cambridge University Press.

Goldberg, David (1993). *Racist Culture: Philosophy and the Politics of Meaning*. Oxford and Cambridge, USA: Basil Blackwell.

Hall, Kim (1996). *Things of Darkness: Economies of Race and Gender in Early Modern England*. Ithaca and London: Cornell University Press.

Hendricks, Margo (1996). 'Obscured by Dreams: Race, Empire, and Shakespeare's *A Midsummer*

Night's Dream', *Shakespeare Quarterly*, 2 (1), 37–60.

Hendricks, Margo and Parker, Patricia (eds) (1994). *Women. 'Race' and Writing in the Early Modern Period*. London and New York: Routledge.

Huet, Marie-Hélène (1993). *Monstrous Imagination*. Cambridge, MA and London: Harvard University Press.

Macdonald, Joyce Greene (ed.) (1998). *Race, Ethnicity, and Power in the Renaissance*. Delaware: University of Delaware Press.

Paré, Ambroise (1982). *On Monsters and Marvels*, tr. Janis L. Pallister. Chicago: University of Chicago Press.

Smith, Paul Julian (1992). *Representing the Other: 'Race', Text and Gender in Spanish and Spanish American Narrative*. Oxford: Clarendon Press.

Sollors, Werner (1997). *Neither Black Nor White Yet Both: Thematic Explorations of Interracial Literature*. New York and Oxford: Oxford University Press.

60

Writing the Nation

Nicola Royan

In 1469, the Scottish parliament declared that the Scottish king had 'full jurisdiction and free empire within his realm'. In practice this meant that he could appoint bishops and other church dignitaries without reference to Rome; it also marked a new point in Scottish self-conceptions. To reach the same stage, some sixty years later, the English required a change of dynasty and a divorce, but the Scots had always been precocious in matters of national identity. Despite the discrepancy in timing of this particular gesture, however, the years between 1469 and 1625 saw huge changes in the ways both the Scots and the English presented themselves, whether in response to external political pressures or to more scholarly and intellectual concerns. The aim of this chapter is to highlight some of the elements underpinning the national identities of the independent realms of Scotland and England, and how these were refigured during the sixteenth century. It will also consider the relationship between the two traditions, which were parallel, but responsive to the other, and how this relationship was affected by the Union of the Crowns in 1603.

Modernist critics of nationalism sometimes question whether the terms 'nationhood' and 'national identity' are appropriate to the early modern period.[1] In strictly sociological terms, it is correct to question whether the sixteenth-century inhabitants of Scotland and England viewed their government and their community in a manner comparable to that of their twentieth-century successors. Equally, it cannot be denied that notions of ethnic identity – what it is to be Scots or to be English – were discussed in a variety of texts, but also that these same notions of ethnic identity correspond to features of modern national identity. With that proviso, the discussion here relates only to early modern Scotland and England, I propose to use the terms 'nation' and 'national identity', rather than struggle for unfamiliar alternatives.

Many different circumstances made the early modern transformations of national identity particularly dynamic and particularly long-lasting. Firstly, the political circumstances of each realm demanded attention. The Tudors, as a new dynasty, required justification and support, found in both chronicle and poem. The Scots retained the

Stewarts as their royal dynasty: despite a succession of minorities and James III's violent death after Sauchieburn and Mary's deposition, the Stewart hold on the crown was never really challenged. However, the frequent lack of an adult male ruler made the realm peculiarly vulnerable to outside influences, and much ink was spent on asserting independence either from France or from England.

The absorption of Humanist ideas at the beginning of the sixteenth century brought many changes. In the first place, a realm was not a realm without its humanist history, which was written in an elegant Latin style, and demonstrated cause and effect, copious speeches and an interest in character.[2] Later, history and story began to diverge, as the influence of humanism became a matter of scholarship more than a matter of style, as interests turned to the study of manuscripts and artefacts.

The reformation of the church also affected the presentation of national identity: in brief, not only was the Apocalypse approaching, it was approaching in English. Vernacular Bibles were essential to Protestantism; so were vernacular descriptions, histories and definitions of the saved.[3] Aided by the printing press, chronicles and other writings were disseminated through a wider population than before.[4] Religion, patriotism and the printing press had come together before the Reformation, in such efforts as the production of the Aberdeen Breviary, designed to replace the Sarum Use in Scotland with a calendar of Scottish saints, but its influence was slight compared to the rhetoric of salvation and dissent introduced by the reformers.

The basic criteria for ethnic, and hence on the terms of this chapter, national, identity had been well established for some time amongst the Scots and the English at the beginning of the early modern period.[5] Regular outbreaks of war between their sovereigns meant that there was a common name for each people, and although the border between them was not entirely fixed, there was a clear understanding of native territory. Most of Europe had also grasped the difference between the Scots and the English, doubtless aided by the opposing alliances undertaken by each realm. So much is established by political circumstances. However, a substantial part of national identity remained open to reworking, namely the images and narratives which displayed it, such as the myths of origin and ancestry, myths of national heroes, and myths of regeneration and government, which look towards the future. These are where the figuring of nationhood takes place.[6]

Myths of Origin and Ancestry

The most memorable myth of antiquity from this period is to be found in Hector Boece's *Scotorum Historia a prima gentis origine* (1527). His introduction retells the story of the Greek Gathelos and his Egyptian wife Scota, whose wanderings in exile lead them to Portugal, and their descendants first to Ireland and then to Scotland. This story challenges the British myth of Brutus, the Trojan refugee, and places the Scots in possession of their territory before the arrival of the British. However, Boece confines his narrative of origins to his introduction; his primary concern is the unbroken line of kings from Fergus mac Ferquhard, inaugurated in 330 BC, to his own day and James V. Although both the origin myth and the date of the first royal inauguration are part of a long tradition in Scottish historiography, no one prior to Boece had named all forty kings before Fergus mac Ferquhard and Fergus mac Erc.[7] The historicity of Boece's account is a complicated matter, but not of primary importance to this chapter, since for Boece's audience, his line of kings is mesmerizing because of its statement about the Scots, rather than its revelation about his historical methods.[8] The line of kings asserts Scottish independence and civilization from the earliest times: the Scots were a people with established government and clear sovereignty over themselves, who were at no time subject to the Britons, Romans, Saxons or the English. At the one point at which the Scots are nearly subjugated, they and their king choose exile over surrender, and two generations later, the new king leads them to reconquer their lands.[9]

The emphasis in this view of identity is on the people, not on the territory, and on the king as a representative of the people. As well as asserting the independence of the realm, the foregrounding of the king also helped to distract attention from the continuing division between the Gaelic-speaking and Scots-speaking peoples. To admit such troublesome diversity within a nation was problematic, since it challenged several assumptions of nationhood, such as shared language and shared history. Other Scottish historiographers are blunt in their attitude towards the Gaels: in his *Historia Maioris Britanniae*, John Mair refers to them as *Scoti montani*, 'wild Scots', a traditional designation that denies them participation in his own civilized culture and its conceptions of national identity;[10] George Buchanan, a Gaelic-speaker himself, chooses to favour Latin over all the Celtic languages, and thus to undermine claims to rival civilizations.[11] Boece tries to integrate the Gael into Scottish history, and thus to offer an inclusive identity; through his emphasis on the kingship, he is by and large successful, for both peoples could share a symbol, if not a language.

Boece's view of national identity became authoritative, whether challenged, by proponents of the British history, or accepted by his fellow-Scots and by other English chroniclers, notably Holinshed. The propagation of his view was helped tremendously by the translations commissioned from John Bellenden by James V, since the vernacular version found an even broader audience within Britain. As well as suggesting unassailable independence and courage, in the context of contemporary as well as past English aggression, the line of kings also offered excellent opportunities for political precedent. Thus were the benefits reaped by two later writers, John Lesley and George Buchanan. Lesley, Bishop of Ross, was a supporter of Mary Queen of Scots, accompanying her into exile in England. *De origine, moribus et gestis Scotorum* (1578) was his second attempt at historiography. His first, vernacular, account merely supplemented the *Scotorum Historia* from 1437 until his own day, and it was designed to provide an explanation of Mary's deposition, and to allocate blame to her rebellious subjects. When it became apparent that Mary's restoration would require international support, he rewrote his history in Latin, summarizing Boece's narrative with his own gloss, highlighting the Scots' long support for kingship, and their movement towards inheritance and away from deposition. Only four years later, George Buchanan offered a diametrically opposed view of Scottish kingship, finding instead in Boece's early narrative proof for his arguments in *De iure regni apud Scotos*, that the Scots not only had a tradition of electing their monarchs, but also of deposing them when they were unsatisfactory. For Buchanan, then, part of Scottish national identity was a non-sacramental view of kingship and government, and a figuring of the monarch as a (dispensable) servant of the realm. While Buchanan's interpretation is probably nearer to Boece's austere vision of successful monarchy, however, that two radically different readings of political identity should emerge from the *Scotorum Historia* is striking. Neither Buchanan nor Lesley reject the core of Boece's presentation, that the Scots were forever independent and valiant; they are instead able to attribute the maintenance of that independence to entirely different political causes.

The English also had their myth of antiquity, the British myth. Like the Scottish myth, it was medieval in origin, and also pervasive in earlier accounts of the realm. Whereas the Scottish origin myth asserted only independence, the British myth claimed supremacy of the descendants of Locrinus, kings of Loegria, over all the realms of Britain, and championed a pre-Saxon identity, later reaffirmed in the person of Arthur. For the Scots, such assertions were alarming: despite the origin of this as a British myth, the English read it as giving them authority over the Scots, hence the Scottish insistence on their prior claims to Scotland and their perpetual independence. The myths are entirely incompatible: either one or the other must be accepted, or else neither. Clearly, Boece and his followers took the Scottish line, and some of the English writers took the British line, but at least two writers in the early years of the century chose to accept neither. As part of his argument that the Scots and the English should unite as equals, John Mair was forced to deny both narratives, since either one would have offered supremacy.[12] Polydore Vergil found both ridiculous on scholarly grounds, and says as much in the *Historia Anglica*. Of the two, he does give primacy to the British myth, as might be expected in a history of England. The Scottish version only appears, according to Vergil, as the result of pressure brought to bear on him by Gavin Douglas, who was perturbed by the printing of Mair's view of national origins. This incident neatly dissociated Vergil from any credence in the tale; it also demonstrates the importance of these myths to national identity. Douglas was a friend of Mair's and no fool, but to him, to weaken the Scottish case for independence was foolhardy. As it happens, Vergil maintains the argument derived from the British myth, namely that of English supremacy over the Scots, but he finds his evidence for it in later, more verifiable, narratives. His interpretation lacks only the sense of permanence granted by the myths of origin.

Myths of National Heroes

In discounting the British myth, Polydore Vergil stood on some ardently British toes. While it was possible to survive without Brutus, as it was possible to survive without

Gathelos, to lose Arthur was to take too much damage to the myth of identity. Arthur was crucial to the British myth, as a devoted Christian, a noble warrior and the 'once and future king'. As one of the Nine Worthies, as the king who had repelled the Saxon invasions, and also as the reputed conqueror of most of western Europe, Arthur was an essential part of English identity. His British origins make his appeal all the more certain, for in returning to Arthur as a focus, it was possible to ignore the three intervening invasions, of the Saxons, of the Danes and finally of the Normans. In holding Arthur as a hero, it was possible to ignore the mongrel nature of the English people, and perhaps to be less perturbed by the Scots' claims to independence.

Polydore Vergil has a similar attitude to Arthur as he has to the rest of the British myth. For him, certainty in the English realm begins really with the Normans, for at that point he is able to structure his work on the reigns of single, certain kings, rather than the heptarchies and confusions of the Saxon period. Vergil places English identity in statutes and formal arrangements rather than in heroes, a representation that displaced the older myths only gradually. His reduction of Arthur to a warrior-king limited to the boundaries of his kingdom was part of his humanist scholarship in checking other sources, for there is simply no reference to Arthur's continental conquests in any of the European chronicles. Boece happily points this out as well, although for the Scots, like the challenge of the king-lists, Arthur's diminution is also political: if he was indeed acknowledged as the conqueror of Europe, then they too had been subject to his dominion, and they were one of the most obvious targets for future English imperialism. To deny Arthur was one means of attempting to keep such desires in check.

Arthur's political importance is best shown by Henry VII's naming of his eldest son after the king, an action repeated in Scotland by James IV, whose son was then briefly heir presumptive to the English throne. Henry had allowed himself through his Welsh origins to be associated with Arthur, as a bringer of peace, if not quite the return of the 'once and future king'. It is perhaps not surprising therefore that the reaction against Vergil's descriptions was so vocal. John Leland went so far as to pen a defence of Arthur, *Assertio inclytissimi Arthurii Regis Britanniae*, published in 1544. As the century progressed, however, although he continued to be defended as a genuine historical figure, Arthur gradually slipped from his previous status into the realm of symbol and legend.[13] That he was effective there is most easily demonstrated by his use by Spenser in *The Faerie Queene*; his power as a model of good kingship and a symbol of a happy reign were unaffected by the change.

However, a historical champion was still required. Fortunately, the English did not have to search too far. In place of Arthur appeared his fellow-Welshman Henry VII. Henry brought an end to the Plantagenet dynasty and to a long civil war, and cemented his victory by marriage with Elizabeth of York. In accounts of his reign, the marriage takes equal precedence with the battle, not least because it legitimated his claim to the throne, since after the death of her brothers, Elizabeth was the heir. Edward Halle, for instance, foregrounds the marriage in the title of *The Union of the Two Noble and Illustre Families of Lancastre and Yorke* (1548) and also in his introduction.[14] Since Henry was technically a usurper from the Lancastrian house of usurpers, such legitimation was essential. Hence the aggressive vilification of his enemy. Thomas More's *Richard III* is probably the most sophisticated account of the king, and other writers concur with his opinion: Richard is unnatural, inadequate, evil. On Bosworth Field in Hall's account, Richard demonstrates all these in his speech before battle. His main means of encouragement is to emphasize Henry's obscurity and his Welshness, while asking forgiveness for his crimes. His defeat is assured, and the triumph of the Tudor dynasty guaranteed.[15]

While the English favoured initially a liberator from violence as their most recent hero, the Scots continued to favour a liberator by violence. Of their succession of national heroes, Robert Bruce and William Wallace stand out.[16] Like Arthur, they liberated their people from a foreign aggressor; unlike Arthur, they were undoubtedly real, and also were without the stain of illegitimacy or association with wizardry. Bruce is the acknowledged hero of the humanist histories, for he is both part of the legitimate kingship and also the choice of the people, nicely combining election and inheritance.[17] In that way, it is possible to compare his portrayal with that of Henry Tudor, although Bruce has the advantage in that his enemies can be figured as foreigners. He is also, however, an ambiguous figure, for he had taken fealty to Edward I in his early years, and he changes allegiance several times before leading the Scots to victory. While this can be presented as demonstration of his true conversion to the Scottish cause, it can also leave the suspicion of a self-seeking hunger for power. Wallace, on the other hand, is an unchallenged hero. Mair especially goes to some lengths to refute what he describes as Caxton's lies about the Scottish hero.[18] However, he also appeared in his own narrative, since Hary's *Wallace*, composed around 1475, was printed three times during the next century, and another twice in the one following.[19]

It is possible to read the *Wallace* as a racist text, for it dehumanizes the English as 'Sotheron' and also revels in the hero's violence. At the same time, it offers acute perspectives on Scottish nationhood, sharper than those of the more diffuse historiographers. Firstly, the *Wallace* removes national identity from the person of the king: the realm and the people still recognize themselves as Scottish, even under English domination and without an active monarch. Furthermore the privilege to determine skittishness is attributed, not to the aristocracy, but to the barony – Wallace is not a peasant, but in the conventions of romance and even historiography, he might as well be. Secondly, however unpleasant the implications of dehumanizing the English, there is no denying the unmistakable difference drawn between the English and the Scots, in both language and in character. These differences are reinforced by various other witnesses: William Harrison, for example, talks of having to translate John Bellenden's preface to the *Chronicles of Scotland* into English, while Robert Wedderburn, in *The Complaynt of Scotland* insists that the Scots and the English are as like as 'scheip and voluis'.[20] Finally, it is a narrative of loss: the victor is Bruce, who succeeds in returning Scotland to independence, yet is also the one who gains personal advantage for his endeavours. Wallace fought only for the realm, and died for his loyalty. The poem may therefore be read as a critique of royal government, and as an assertion that true national piety lies with the people and not with the king or his aristocracy. At the time of the poem's composition, there were specific political circumstances to which it seems to draw attention, but its concentrated printing around the Union of the Crowns suggests that it also spoke to another Scottish anxiety of identity. Despite the benefits held out by Mair, it would seem that some Scots at least were not entirely sure about the merits of Union.

Myths of Regeneration

The most striking myth of regeneration of this period is the return to a golden age of Christendom. The reformers began as small groups whom others joined, and their vision was of conversion rather than conquest, a return to simple practices and true faith. The relationship between government and reformers was frequently uneasy in both realms, so Protestant identity often focuses on the righteous people, rather than the corrupt monarch. This can be clearly seen in John Knox's rejection of accusations of 'tumult and rebellion', for he and his confederates seek only to preach the gospel and secondly to defend Scotland from the 'bondage and tyranny of strangers', by which he means France.[21]

Later, once Protestant religious settlements had been achieved, a different historiographic model appeared. In Foxe's view, for example, Elizabeth could be figured as Constantine and himself as Eusebius, in celebration of a righteous settlement.[22] The choice of models is revealing, for Constantine is a British emperor, and so the figuring here is very close to a reassertion of the British myth, even without Arthur. Against such rhetoric, Buchanan's line of kings, and Knox's search for Scottish proto-Protestants and martyrs seem to have had no strength to insist on a Scottish perspective. What began as apocalyptic visions in which the union of all Protestants is to be welcomed, becomes a movement towards political absorption; even the militant Presbyterianism of the Scots becomes viewed as something only to be corrected by proper English control.[23]

Myths of Union

That there could have been an identity equally reflective of Scotland and England in 1603 seems to have been impossible. The sheer strength of each tradition made it so, and even those who tried were defeated.[24] The myths of origin were incompatible; the heroes likewise, for the English could not have accepted either Wallace or Bruce any more than the Scots could accept Arthur. The myth of supremacy was too engrained in English tradition to be eradicated easily. So when a combined history of Scotland, England and Ireland is offered in 'Holinshed's' *Chronicles*, the histories are not integrated, but rather presented serially. In his preface to the reader attached to the *History of Scotland*, Holinshed says 'I meant rather to deliver what I found in their own histories extant, than correct them by others . . . so that whatsoever ye read in the same, consider that a Scotishman writ it'.[25] While this shows an understanding of the Scots' position, it nonetheless does not give the Scots' view any authority, for as it is welcomed by a Scot, it may be despised by an Englishman. While Holinshed refers to Edward I's presence in Scotland as bondage in *The History of Scotland*, following Bellenden's lead, William Harrison in his *Description of Britain*, which leads seamlessly into his *Description of England*, is asserting English dominance over the Scots.[26] *Henry V* bears this out: men of all four nations of Britain and Ireland happily join to fight for a king of England on a project of conquering an ally of one of the other nations.[27] Mair's vision of a union of equals had come to nought, and the English had won the parallel race.

NOTES

1 For a summary of these discussion, see Smith, *Myths and Memories* pp. 110–18, and for other negotiations of this criticism, see Mason, 'Chivalry and Citizenship: Aspects of National Identity in Renaissance Scotland', in *Kingship and Commonweal*, pp. 78–103, esp. pp. 78–80, and Hadfield, *Literature, Politics and National Identity*, pp. 1–22.

2 For the place of humanist historiography in western Europe, see Cochrane, *Historians and Historiographers in the Italian Renaissance*; for the growth of antiquarianism and a document-based historiography, see Levy, *Tudor Historical Thought*, pp. 124–66, and Kelley, *Foundations of Modern Historical Scholarship*.

3 See Patterson, *Reading Holinshed's Chronicles*, pp. ix–x.

4 This change is surely akin to the print-capitalism discussed by Benedict Anderson, although not on the same scale. See Anderson, *Imagined Communities*, pp. 20–5.

5 Smith, 'Ethno-symbolism and the Study of Nationalism', in *Myths and Memories*, pp. 3–27, esp. p. 13.

6 See Smith, *Myths and Memories*, pp. 62–70.

7 The myth is Irish in origin, and had been the main feature of the arguments presented to the Pope against Edward I during the first War of Independence. See Dauvit Broun, *The Irish Identity of the Kingdom of the Scots*, pp. 195–200.

8 Mason, 'Aspects of National Identity in Renaissance Scotland', pp. 95–7.

9 Hector Boece, *Scotorum Historia*, fos 114–22 (books 6 and 7). The Scots are exiled in AD 379 and return in AD 424.

10 John Mair, *History of Greater Britain*, book 1, ch. 8, pp. 47–50.

11 Buchanan, *The History of Scotland*, book 1, chs 15–16, vol. 1: pp. 87–90.

12 Mair, *History of Greater Britain*, book 1, chs 1 and 9, pp. 1–3 and 51–3.

13 See Kendrick, *British Antiquity* pp. 78–133 for an account of Arthur's transformation.

14 Edward Halle, *The Union of the Two Noble and Illustre Famelies of Lancastre and Yorke* (Hall's *Chronicle*) pp. 1–2. When the event is described in its proper place, it is noticeable that the bride herself gets less attention than the sweating sickness which follows the marriage.

15 Halle, pp. 415–16.

16 In the preface to the *Scotorum Historia*, Boece mentions four others, Caratacus and Galdus (books 3 and 4, fos 37–52 and 59–75), who repelled the Romans, Fergus mac Erc (books 7; fos 118–26) and Gregor who resists the Danes (book 10, fos 215–21).

17 See, for example, Boece, *Scotorum Historia*,

book 14, fos 314–6; Mair, *History of Greater Britain*, 4: 17–19, pp. 209–24; Buchanan, *History*, vol. 2, pp. 400–14. On Buchanan, see also Williamson, *Scottish National Consciousness*, pp. 112–13.

18 See Mair, *History of Greater Britain*, 4: 13–15, pp. 191–206.

19 McDiarmid, *Hary's Wallace*, vol. 1, pp. ix–xi. Its dates of printing were *c.*1509, 1570, 1594, 1601 and 1611.

20 William Harrison, *Description of Scotland*, in Holinshed, *Chronicles*, vol. 5, preface; *The Complaynt of Scotland*, p. 84.

21 *John Knox's Historie*, vol. 1, p. 146.

22 See History for more discussion of John Foxe. The figuring occurs in Foxe's 1563 Preface to *The Acts and Monuments*. See also

Mason, 'George Buchanan, James VI and the Presbyterians' in *Kingship and Commonweal* pp. 202–5, and 'The Origins of Anglo-British Imperialism' in *Kingship and Commonweal*, 261–6.

23 Williamson, *Scottish National Consciousness*, pp. 85–96.

24 Michael Drayton, for example, whose *Poly-Olbion* never reached Scotland, despite urgings from William Drummond and William Alexander. See Hardin, *Michael Drayton and the Passing of Elizabethan England*, pp. 65–7.

25 Holinshed, *Chronicles* (1808), vol. 5, p. vi.

26 Ibid., vol. 1, pp. 195–214.

27 *Henry V*, 3.2.54–142, and see Maley, ' "This Sceptred Isle" ', pp. 96–101.

References and Further Reading

Anderson, Benedict (1991). *Imagined Communities: Reflections on the Origins and Spread of Nationalism*, 2nd edn. London: Verso.

Bellenden, John (1821). *The History and Chronicles of Scotland*. Edinburgh: W and C Tait.

Boece, Hector (1527). *Scotorum Historia a prima gentis origine*. Paris: Badius Ascensius.

Broun, Dauvit (1999). *The Irish Identity of the Kingdom of the Scots in the Twelfth and Thirteenth Centuries*, Studies in Celtic History 18. Woodbridge: Boydell and Brewer.

Buchanan, George (1582). *Historia Rerum Scoticarum*. Edinburgh: Alexander Arbuthnet.

——(1827). *The History of Scotland*, tr. James Aikman. 4 vols. Glasgow: Blackie.

Cochrane, Eric (1981). *Historians and Historiography in the Italian Renaissance*. Chicago and London: University of Chicago Press.

Hadfield, Andrew (1994). *Literature, Politics and National Identity: Reformation to Renaissance*. Cambridge: Cambridge University Press.

Hall, Edward (1809). *Hall's Chronicle*, ed. Henry Ellis. London: n.p.

Hardin, Richard F. (1973). *Michael Drayton and the Passing of Elizabethan England*. Lawrence: University of Kansas Press.

Hary's Wallace (1968–9). Ed. M. P. McDiarmid. 2 vols. Edinburgh: Scottish Text Society.

Holinshed, Raphael (1808). *Chronicles of England, Scotland and Ireland*. 6 vols. London: J. Johnson.

Kelley, Donald R. (1970). *Foundations of Modern Historical Scholarship: Language, Law and History in the French Renaissance*. New York: Columbia University Press.

John Knox's Historie of the Reformation (1949). Ed. W. C. Dickinson. 2 vols. Edinburgh: Nelson.

Levy, F. J. (1967). *Tudor Historical Thought*. San Marino: Huntington Library.

McEachern, Claire (1996). *The Poetics of English Nationhood, 1590–1612*. Cambridge: Cambridge University Press.

Mair, John (1521). *Historia Maioris Britanniae, tam Angliae quan Scotiae*. Paris: Badius Ascensius.

——(1892). *A History of Greater Britain, England as well as Scotland*, tr. A. Constable. Edinburgh: Scottish History Society.

Maley, Willy (1997). ' "This Sceptr'd Isle": Shakespeare and the British Problem.' In J. Joughlin (ed.), *Shakespeare and National Culture* (pp. 83–108). Manchester: Manchester University Press.

Mason, Roger A. (1998). *Kingship and the Commonweal: Political Thought in Renaissance and*

Reformation Scotland. East Linton: Tuckwell Press.

Patterson, Annabel (1994). *Reading Holinshed's Chronicles*, Chicago and London: University of Chicago Press.

Smith, Anthony D. (1999). *Myths and Memories of the Nation.* Oxford: Oxford University Press.

Wedderburn, Robert (1979). *The Complaynt of Scotland*, ed. A. M. Stewart. Edinburgh: Scottish Text Society.

Williamson, Arthur H. (1979). *Scottish National Consciousness in the Age of James VI: The Apocalypse, the Union and the Shaping of Scotland's Popular Culture.* Edinburgh: John Donald.

Index